LIST OF APPLICATIONS

PLANNING FOR OBJECTS

SPECIAL FEATURES CROSS REFERENCE TABLE

Topic	Type	Page
Accessor Functions	Point of Information	408
Al-Khowarizmi	Bit of Background	30
Anagrams and Palindromes	Bit of Background	646
Atanasoff, John	Bit of Background	44
Atomic Data	Point of Information	72
Braces, in Compound Statements	Programming Note	193
Braces, in for loops	Programming Note	263
Byron, Ada	Bit of Background	11
Character and String Variables	Point of Information	530
Classification of Languages	Point of Information	389
Comptometer Arithmetic	Bit of Background	236
Constructors	Point of Information	407
cout Formatting	Point of Information	134
DeMorgan's laws	Bit of Background	184
Deques	Bit of Background	793
Encapsulation	Point of Information	421
Fibonacci	Bit of Background	266
File Location	Programming Note	544
Flags	Point of Information	135
for versus while loops	Programming Note	262
Formatting File Stream Data	Point of Information	535
fstream Objects	Point of Information	532
Function Definitions and Prototypes	Point of Information	304
Gauss, Carl	Bit of Background	31
Homogeneous & Heterogeneous Data Structures	Point of Information	733
Hopper, Grace	Bit of Background	685
Input and Output Streams	Point of Information	525
Interfaces and Implementations	Point of Information	399
Isolation Testing	Programming Note	308
istream get and putback Methods	Programming Note	540
LISP	Bit of Background	578
Lukasiewicz, Jan	Bit of Background	778
lvalues and rvalues	Point of Information	121
Monte Carlo Simulation	Bit of Background	359
Napier's Bones	Bit of Background	117
Numerosophy	Bit of Background	697
Object-Based and Object-Oriented Languages	Point of Information	483
ostream put Method	Programming Note	538
Pascal, Blaise	Bit of Background	21
Pointers vs. References	Point of Information	502
Pre and Post Conditions	Point of Information	307
Precision	Point of Information	71
Preprocessor Directives	Programming Note	668
Privacy, Security, and Files	Bit of Background	523
Procedural Abstraction	Bit of Background	306
Program and Class Libraries	Point of Information	471
Statistics	Bit of Background	600
Storage Classes	Point of Information	335
String Initializations	Programming Note	650
Strings, Allocating Space	Programming Note	720
Structured Data Type	Point of Information	575
Subprograms	Bit of Background	298
Successful Stream Opens	Point of Information	528
Syntax	Point of Information	19
True and False	Programming Note	188
Turing Machine	Bit of Background	6
typedef Statement	Programming Note	501
Universal Algorithm Machine	Bit of Background	345
Values and Identities	Point of Information	435
Wirth, Niklaus	Bit of Background	29

PROGRAM DEVELOPMENT and DESIGN USING C++

PROGRAM DEVELOPMENT and DESIGN USING C++

Gary J. Bronson
Fairleigh Dickinson University

Contributing Editor: R. Kenneth Walter
Weber State University

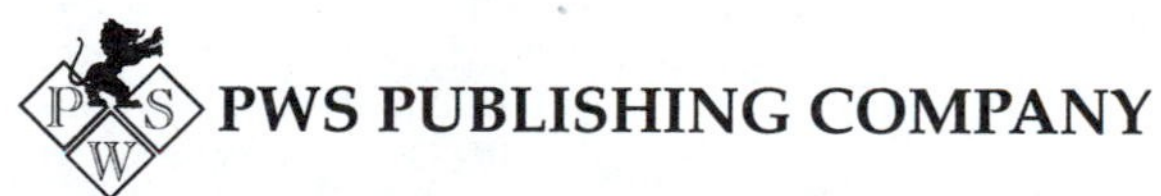

I(T)P An International Thomson Publishing Company

Boston • Albany • Bonn • Cincinnati • Detroit • London • Madrid
Melbourne • Mexico City • New York • Pacific Grove • Paris
San Francisco • Singapore • Tokyo • Toronto • Washington

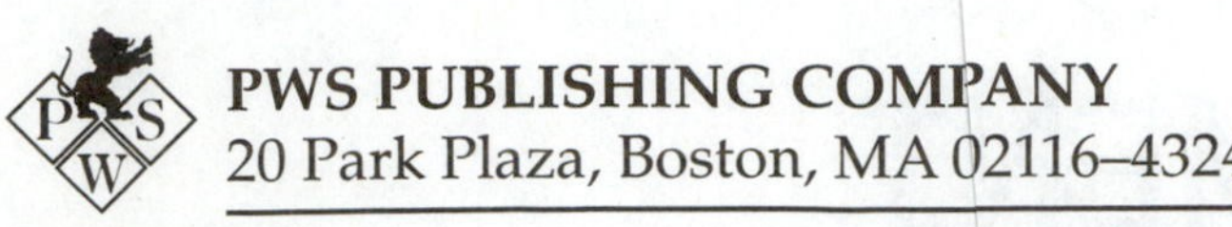

PWS PUBLISHING COMPANY
20 Park Plaza, Boston, MA 02116–4324

Sponsoring Editor: *David Dietz*
Developmental Editor: *Dean DeChambeau*
Marketing Manager: *Nathan Wilbur*
Production Coordinator: *Jayne Lindesmith*
Interior Designer: *Linda Robertson*
Copyeditor: *Lorretta Palagi*
Compositor: *Carlisle Communications, Ltd.*
Interior Illustration: *Tom Richardson*
Cover Image: *Doug Armand/Tony Stone Images*
Cover Designer: *Tom Richardson*

Production, Prepress, Printing, and Binding by West Publishing Company.

Photo credits are included on pages containing photos.

British Library Cataloguing-in-Publication Data. A catalogue record for this book is available from the British Library.

 TEXT IS PRINTED ON 10% POST CONSUMER RECYCLED PAPER 

Library of Congress Cataloguing-in-Publication Data

Bronson, Gary J.
Program development and design using C++ / Gary J. Bronson.
p. cm.
Includes index.
ISBN 0-314-20338-9(pbk. :alk. paper)
1. C++ (Computer program language) 2. Electronic digital computers—Programming. I. Title.
QA76.73.C153B77 1997
005.13'3—DC21 96-47078
CIP

Printed in the United States of America

04 03 02 01 00 99 98 — 10 9 8 7 6 5 4 3

Student Edition ISBN 0-314-20338-9

For more information contact:

PWS Publishing Company
20 Park Plaza
Boston, MA 02116–4324

Nelson Canada
1120 Birchmount Road
Scarborough, Ontario
Canada M1K 5G4

International Thomson Publishing Asia
221 Henderson Road
#05-10 Henderson Building
Singapore 0315

International Thomson Publishing Europe
Berkshire House 168-173
High Holborn
London, England SCIV 7AA

International Thomson Editores
Campos Eliseos 385, Piso 7
Col. Polanco
11560 Mexico D.F., Mexico

International Thomson Publishing Japan
Hirakawacho Kyowa Building, 31
2-2-1 Hirakawacho
Chiyoda-ku, Tokyo IO2
Japan

Thomas Nelson Australia
102 Dodds Street
South Melbourne, 3205
Australia

International Thomson Publishing GmbH
Königswinterer Strasse 418
53227 Bonn, Germany

Dedicated to

Rochelle,
Matthew,
Jeremy,
David,
and
Sparky

Contents

Preface

"In my experience, the safest bet is to learn C++ from the bottom up, that is, first learn the features C++ provides for traditional procedural programming, the better-C subset, then learn to use and appreciate the data abstraction features, and then learn to use class hierarchies to organize sets of related classes."[1]

Bjarne Stroustrup

For most people, employing the full potential of a hybrid language such as C++, which contains both procedural and object-oriented features, requires a gradual refinement of programming skills from a procedural to an object orientation. This is the approach taken by this text. It was written with the intention of making the adjustment to a complete object-oriented approach as rapidly as possible within the confines of a pedagogically sound and achievable progression.

Even as the progression from a procedural to full object-oriented implementation is now the preferred approach, there is still a widely varying opinion within the C++ community as to how much procedural programming should be learned before serious object-oriented programming is attempted. As a practical matter this question is phrased as "Should object-oriented programming be presented towards the middle or towards the end of an introductory course?"

My personal answer to this question, which is a unique feature of this text book, is based on my fundamental belief that ultimately college-level textbooks do not teach students—professors teach students. As such, all of my textbooks have been written with the intent of making them a "supporting actor" to the "leading role" belonging to the professor. In practical terms this means that the textbook must be sufficiently flexible so that those professors who subscribe to my basic approach can still mold the text to their individual preference of topic presentation. This is achieved in the following way.

Excluding Chapter One, which presents computer literacy material for those who require this background, Part I of the text presents the basic procedural syntax, flow control, and modularity topics that are needed for an effective presentation of C++'s object features. Included within each procedural chapter are optional *Planning for Objects* sections, which can be used to help students begin the mental shift to object-oriented development and design techniques.

Once Part I is completed, Parts II and III on object-oriented programming and data structures, respectively, *are interchangeable.* Thus, if you want to present object-oriented programming early, you would follow a Part I–Part II–Part III progression. On the other hand, if you want to continue with additional procedural

[1] The Design and Evolution of C++, copyright 1994 by AT&T Bell Labs, published by Addison-Wesley Pub. Co.

programming reinforcement and present object-oriented programming toward the end of the course, you would use the sequence Part I–Part III–Part II. In either case, the material on files presented in Chapter 10 can be introduced at any time after Part I. On the other hand, the object-oriented string class (Section 12.4) and stack and queue data structures can be introduced only after Part II.

The flexibility of introducing topics, within the overall context of procedural programming, abstract data types, and inheritance, is illustrated by the following topic dependency chart:

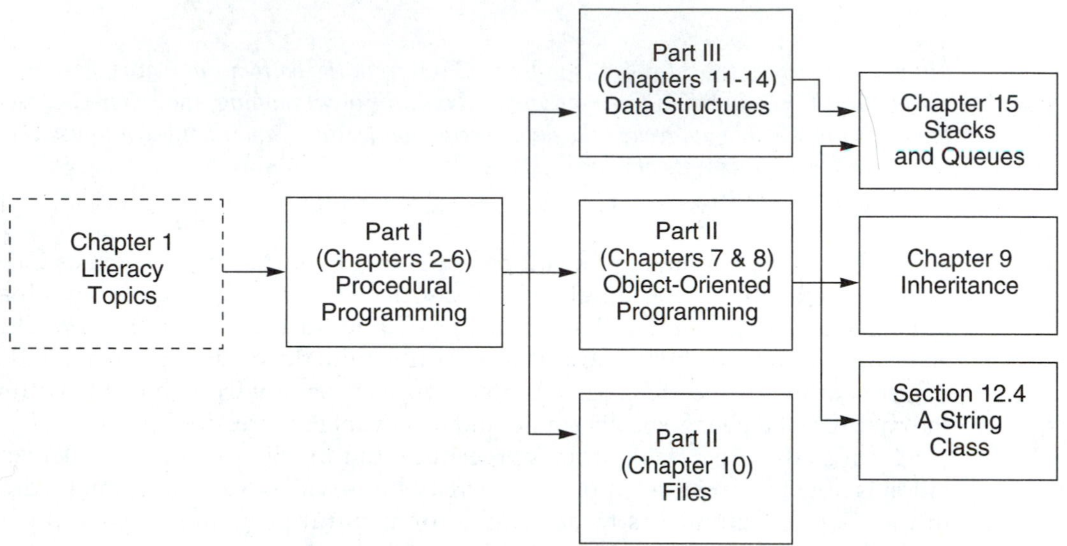

Finally, as the topics shown in the dependency chart indicate, this text is designed for a CS1 course, with an introduction to CS2, and follows the guideline of the Association of Computing Machinery (ACM-IEEE-CS) Joint Curriculum Task Force for this first course. The topics recommended by the ACM for a CS1 course form the central content of the text.

In using this text students should be familiar with fundamental algebra but no other prerequisites are assumed. Chapter 1 presents the computer literacy material for students who need this background. Large numbers of examples are drawn from everyday experience, business, and technical fields. As such, the instructor may choose applications that match students' experience or for a particular course emphasis.

DISTINCTIVE FEATURES OF THIS BOOK

Writing Style. The one thing that I have found most important in my own teaching is that *regardless of what is written about, it must be written so that students can read it.* Once the professor sets the stage, the selected textbook must encourage, nurture, and assist the student in acquiring and "owning" the material presented in class. My primary concern, and one of the distinctive features of this book is that it has been written for the student. Thus, first and foremost, I feel the writing style used to convey the concepts presented is an important and distinctive aspect of the text.

Modularity. To produce readable and maintainable code, modularity is essential. C++ by its nature, is a modular language. Thus, the connection between C++ functions and modules is made early in the text, in Section 2.1, and sustained throughout the book. The idea of parameter passing into modules is also made early using C++'s function library in Section 3.3. In this manner students are introduced to functions and argument passing as a natural technique of programming. This modular emphasis is both continued and strengthened by the object-oriented programming techniques introduced in Chapter 7.

Software Engineering. Rather than simply introduce students to programming in C++, this text introduces students to the fundamentals of software engineering, from both a procedural and object-oriented viewpoint. This introduction begins in Section 1.3 with the introduction of the software development cycle. This is immediately followed by an introduction to algorithms and the first Planning for Objects section. The main theme of the text, which is a more formal emphasis on problem solving techniques, is presented in Chapter 2. Here the importance of understanding a problem and selecting and refining the solution is highlighted and the relationship between analysis, design, coding, and testing is introduced. Additionally, the Planning for Objects sections both introduce and reinforce the concepts and techniques needed for an object-oriented design solution.

Focus on Problem Solving. Starting with Chapter 2, each chapter contains a Focus on Problem Solving section with an average of 2 complete problems per chapter. Each application is used to demonstrate effective problem solving, within the context of a compete program solution. This is done for both procedural and object-oriented designs.

Program Testing. Every single C++ program in this text has been successfully compiled and run under Borland's Turbo C++ Compiler. A source diskette of all programs is included with the text. This will permit students to both experiment and extend the existing programs and more easily modify them as required by a number of end-of-section exercises.

PEDAGOGICAL FEATURES

To facilitate the goal of making C++ accessible as a first level course, the following pedagogical features have been incorporated into the text:

Planning for Objects. A set of 6 sections that provides a self-contained and brief "mini-course" introduction to object-oriented concepts and design techniques. These sections can be included within the initial phase of a course or used as enrichment material during the object-oriented phase of your course.

End of Section Exercises. Almost every section in the book contains numerous and diverse skill builder and programming exercises. Additionally, solutions to selected odd-numbered exercises are provided in an appendix.

Pseudocode Descriptions. Pseudocode is stressed throughout the text. Flowchart symbols are presented, but are only used in visually presenting flow-of-control constructs.

Common Programming Errors and Chapter Review. Each chapter ends with a section on common programming errors and a review of the main topics covered in the chapter.

Focus on Problem Solving. These sections contain two thorough exercises that walk students through problem definition, analysis, solution development, coding, testing, and debugging. A broad mix of applications, both procedural and object-oriented, have been selected to both heighten student interest and reinforce program development concepts.

Enrichment and Closer Look Sections. Given the many different emphases that can be applied in teaching C++, a number of enrichment sections have been included. These allow you to provide different emphases with different students or different C++ classes.

Point of Information Boxes. A set of shaded boxes that provide additional brief clarification of commonly used and/or difficult concepts, such as abstraction, lvalues and rvalues, values versus identities, flags, dequeues, and stream formatting.

Programming Notes. A set of shaded boxes that highlight alternative and advanced programming techniques.

Bit of Background Boxes. To make the study of computer science even more rewarding and to provide breadth material, these notes are carefully placed throughout the book. These notes supplement the technical material with historical, biographical, and other interesting factual asides.

APPENDICES AND SUPPLEMENTS

An expanded set of appendices is provided. This set includes appendices on operator precedence, ASCII codes, program entry and compilation, I/O redirection, floating point number storage, and additional C++ features.

Additionally, a solutions manual to selected odd- and even-numbered exercises on a 3 1/2″ IBM-PC compatible diskette (containing both ASCII and WordPerfect formats) is available to adopters.

A NOTE TO PASCAL PROGRAMMERS

The emerging trend towards C++ from both the C and Pascal user community is now clearly discernable. As it is my experience that there is sometimes a slight initial confusion with three basic C features that are also fundamental to C++, I have briefly summarized these features below:

The first concept that is unique to both C and C++ is that they do not have a built-in boolean data type. Since this data type is not built-in, a tested expression cannot evaluate to a boolean value. Thus, the syntax

```
if(boolean expression)
  execute this statement;
```

is also not built-in to either C or C++. Rather, both C and C++ use the more encompassing syntax:

```
if(expression)
  execute this statement;
```

where expression is any expression that evaluates to a numeric value. If the result of the tested expression is a non-zero value it is treated as if it were true, and only a zero value is treated as false. Conversely, the result of a relational expression that is true evaluates to a numeric value of 1, while a relational expression that is false evaluates to a 0.

The second feature that is unique to both C and C++ is their construction and use of pointers. In C++ a pointer is a variable that is used to store a memory address. Although pointer variables are primarily used with the indirection operator, *, to explicitly dereference the pointer and obtain the desired "pointed to" target, C++'s pointers are much richer than Pascal's. This is because the contents of a pointer variable can be displayed or manipulated much like any other variable and arithmetic on pointers is supported.

Finally, C++ does not impose rigid rules on the placement of statements. In this regard, the only really relevant rule in C++ is that an identifier must be declared before it is used. Although a sensible placement of statements is always a good programming practice, C++ does not impose a placement order to the extent that Pascal does.

Acknowledgements

This book began as an idea. It became a reality only due to the encouragement, skills, and efforts supplied by many people. I would like to acknowledge their contribution.

First, I would like to thank Jerry Westby, my editor at West Publishing Company. In addition to his continuous faith and encouragement, his ideas and partnership were instrumental in creating this text. I would also like to thank Dean DeChambeau for his handling of numerous scheduling and review details that permitted me to concentrate on the actual writing of the text. Additionally, I would like to express my gratitude to the individual reviewers.

Stephen Allan
Utah State University

Clark B. Archer
Winthrop University

Tom Cheatham
Middle Tennessee State University

Blase B. Cindric
Westminster College

William Clark
University of Alaska, Anchorage

Herbert Dunsmore
Purdue University

Peter J. Gingo
University of Akron

Jeff Guan
University of Louisville

R. James Guild
California Lutheran University

Jack Hodges
San Francisco State University

Mike Holland
North Virginia Community College

Joseph Hurley
Texas A & M University

Peter Isaacson
University of Northern Colorado

Stephen P. Leach
Florida State University

Merry McDonald
Northwest Missouri State University

Randall J. Molmen
Baldwin-Wallace College

Robert Norton
San Diego Mesa Community College

Joan Ramuta
College of Saint Francis

David A. Retterer
Ohio Northern University

Larry Ruzzo
University of Washington

Ali Salehnia
South Dakota State University

Bob Signorile
Boston College

Winie Yu
Southern Connecticut State University

Each of these individuals supplied extremely detailed and constructive reviews of both the original manuscript and a number of revisions. Their suggestions, attention to detail, and comments were extraordinarily helpful to me as the manuscript evolved and matured through the editorial process.

Once the review process was completed, the task of turning the final manuscript into a textbook depended on many people other than myself. For this I especially want to thank the production editor, Jayne Lindesmith, the copy editor, Lorretta Palagi, and the compositor, Carlisle Communications, Ltd. The dedication of this team of people was incredible and very important to me. Almost from the moment the book moved to the production stage this team seemed to take personal ownership of the text and I am very grateful to them. I am also very appreciative of the suggestions and work of the assistant promotion manager at West, Debra Pickett.

Special acknowledgement goes to two of my colleagues who provided material for this text. In addition to numerous contributions made by R. Kenneth Walter of Weber State University, I am especially grateful for his graciously providing the Bit of Background notes as well as numerous end-of-chapter exercises. I also wish to acknowledge John Lyon of The University of Arizona who originally provided the analogy used in the introduction to Chapter 6, the material on stub functions, as well as exercises in Chapter 6 for my FORTRAN text with Scott/Jones Publishers. This material is used in this text by permission of the publisher. As always, any errors in the text rest solely on my shoulders.

Finally, the direct encouragement and support of Fairleigh Dickinson University is also gratefully acknowledged. Specifically, this includes the constant encouragement, support, and positive academic climate provided by Dr. Geoffrey Weinman, the Vice President of Academic Affairs, my Dean, Dr. Paul Lerman, and my Chairperson, Professor Ron Heim. Without their support, this text could not have been written.

Finally, I deeply appreciate the patience, understanding, and love provided by my friend, wife, and partner, Rochelle.

Gary Bronson

CHAPTER

1 Introduction to Computers and Programming

1.1 HARDWARE AND SOFTWARE

The process of using a machine to add and subtract is almost as old as recorded history. The earliest machine was the abacus (Figure 1.1)—a device as common in China as hand–held calculators are in the United States. Both of these machines, however, require direct human involvement as they are being used. To add two numbers with an abacus requires the movement of beads on the device, while adding two numbers with a calculator requires that the operator push both the number and the addition operator keys.

It is worth distinguishing between these two distinct types of input—the operations to be performed, such as addition and subtraction, and the actual data that is being operated on—because the distinction forms the basis for programming a computer. As we will see shortly, the operations to be performed constitute the basis for a computer program, while the data becomes the input on which the program works. The construction of a computing machine that separated these two types of input (operations and data) and permitted the loading and prestoring of operations separately from the data was attempted in England in the early 1800s. Figure 1.2 illustrates the conceptual design of such a machine.

As illustrated by this hypothetical machine, space is allocated for a set of instructions that can be loaded into the machine separately from the data. The instructions might be as simple as:

Instruction 1: Accept a number from the input device and store it in location A.
Instruction 2: Add the next number entered to the stored number in location A and store it in location B.
Instruction 3: Multiply the number stored in location B by the next number entered and store it in location C.

FIGURE 1.1 An Abacus

FIGURE 1.2 Conceptual Design of a Self-Operating Calculating Machine

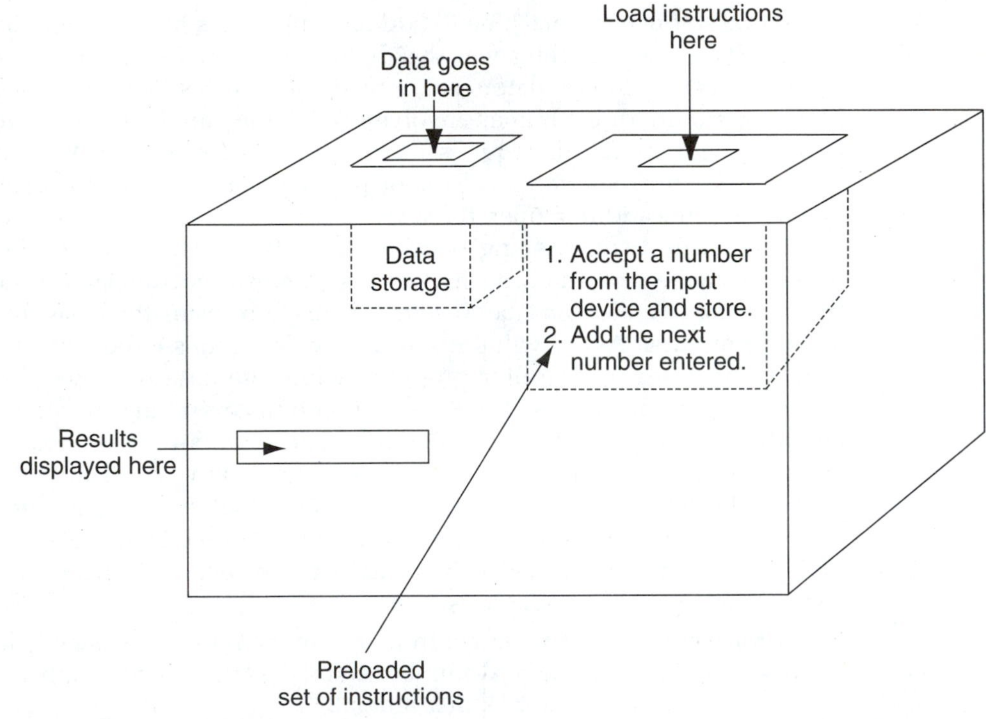

Instruction 4: Subtract the next number entered from the number stored in location C and store the result in location D.
Instruction 5: Display the number stored in location D.

The advantage of the hypothetical machine illustrated in Figure 1.2 has over a simple calculator is that it permits a set of instructions to be preloaded into the machine before any data is entered. Once the preceding instructions have been loaded, the machine will operate when it is given any four numbers. For example, if the numbers 2, 3, 6, and 8 are entered, the machine would display the number 22.

The first recorded attempt at creating such a machine was made by Charles Babbage, in England, in 1835. The set of instructions to be input to this machine, which Babbage called an analytical engine (Figure 1.3), was developed by Ada Byron, the daughter of the poet Lord Byron. Although Babbage's machine was not successfully built in his lifetime, the concept developed by him was partly

FIGURE 1.3 Charles Babbage's Analytical Engine (Crown Copyright)

realized in 1937 at Iowa State University by Dr. John V. Atanasoff and a graduate student named Clifford Berry. The machine was known as the ABC, which stood for Atanasoff-Berry computer. This computer manipulated binary numbers, but required external wiring of the machine to perform the desired operations. Thus, the goal of internally storing a replaceable set of instructions had still not been achieved.

The impending outbreak of World War II provided the impetus for a more concentrated effort, which began in late 1939, to develop the computer. One of the pioneers of this work was Dr. John W. Mauchly at the Moore School of Engineering of the University of Pennsylvania. Dr. Mauchly, who had visited Dr. Atanasoff, began working with J. Presper Eckert in 1939 on a computer called ENIAC (for Electrical Numerical Integrator and Computer). Funding for this project was provided by the U.S. government, and one of the early functions performed by this machine was the calculation of trajectories for ammunition fired from large guns. When completed in 1946 ENIAC contained 18,000 vacuum tubes, weighed approximately 30 tons, and could perform 5000 additions or 360 multiplications in one second (Figure 1.4).

FIGURE 1.4 ENIAC (Courtesy IBM Archives)

While work was progressing on ENIAC with vacuum tubes, work on a computer named the Mark I, which used mechanical relay switches, was being done at Harvard University. The Mark I (Figure 1.5) was completed in 1944, but could only perform six multiplications in one second. Both of these machines, however, like the Atanasoff-Berry computer required external wiring to perform the desired operations.

The final goal of a stored program computer was achieved at Cambridge University in England, with the design of EDSAC (Electronic Delayed Storage Automatic Computer). In addition to performing calculations, EDSAC permitted storage of instructions that directed the computer's operation. The means of using the computer's memory to store both instructions and data, and the design to accomplish this so that the computer first retrieved an instruction and then the data needed by the instruction, was developed by John Von Neumann. This same design and operating principle is still used by the majority of computers manufactured today. The only things that have significantly changed are the size and speeds of the components used to make a computer and the types of programs that are stored internal to it. Collectively, the components used to make a computer are referred to as *hardware*, while the programs are known as *software*.

FIGURE 1.5 The MARK I (Courtesy IBM Archives)

A BIT OF BACKGROUND

The "Turing Machine"

In the 1930s and 1940s, Alan Mathison Turing (1912–1954) and others developed the theory of what a computing machine should be able to do. Turing invented a theoretical, pencil-and-paper machine, which is referred to as the Turing machine, that contains the minimum set of operations for solving programming problems. Turing had hoped to prove that all problems could be solved by a set of instructions to such a hypothetical computer. What he succeeded in proving was that some problems cannot be solved by *any* machine, just as some problems cannot be solved by any person.

Alan Turing's work formed the foundation of computer theory before the first electronic computer was built. His contributions to the team that developed the critical code-breaking computers during World War II led directly to the practical implementation of his theories.

Computer Hardware

All computers, from large supercomputers costing millions of dollars to smaller desktop personal computers, must perform a minimum set of functions and provide the capability to:

1. Accept input
2. Display output
3. Store information in a logically consistent format (traditionally binary)
4. Perform arithmetic and logic operations on either the input or stored data
5. Monitor, control, and direct the overall operation and sequencing of the system.

Figure 1.6 illustrates the computer components that support these capabilities. These physical components are collectively referred to as **hardware.**

Memory Unit The **memory unit** stores information in a logically consistent format. Typically, both instructions and data are stored in memory, usually in separate and distinct areas. Each computer contains memory of two fundamental types: RAM and ROM. **RAM,** which is an acronym for *random-access memory,* is usually volatile, which means that whatever is stored there is lost when the computer's power is turned off. Your programs and data are stored in RAM while you are using the computer. The size of a computer's RAM is usually specified in terms of how many bytes of RAM are available to the user. Personal computer (PC) memories currently consist of from 1 to 32 million bytes (denoted as megabytes or MB).

ROM, which is an acronym for *read-only memory,* contains fundamental instructions that cannot be lost or changed by the casual computer user. These instructions include those necessary for initially loading software into the machine when it is first turned on and any other instructions the manufacturer requires to be permanently accessible while the computer is operating. ROM is nonvolatile; its contents are not lost when the power goes off.

FIGURE 1.6 Basic Hardware Units of a Computer

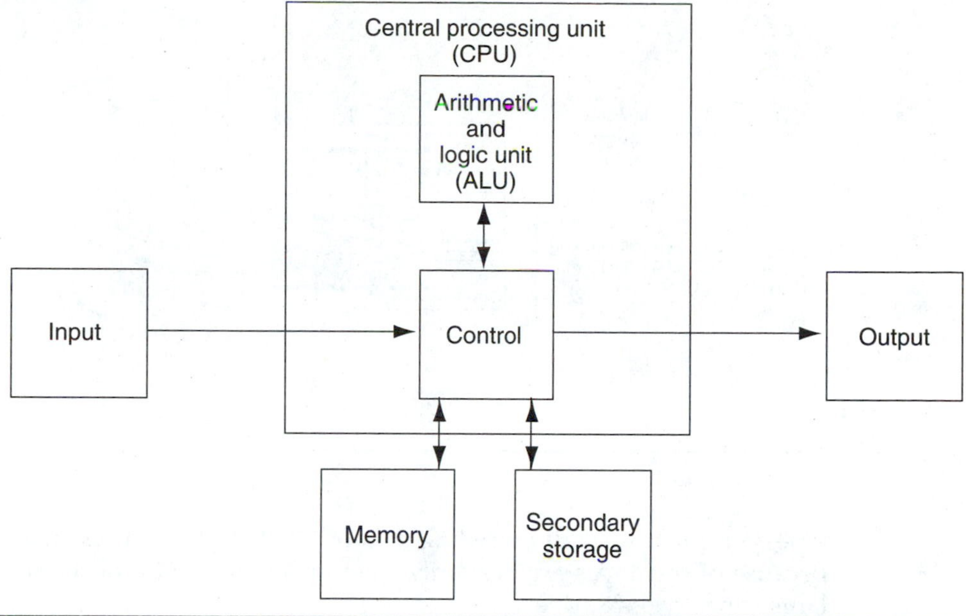

Control Unit The **control unit** directs and monitors the overall operation of the computer. It keeps track of where in memory the next instruction resides, issues the signals needed to both read data from and write data to other units in the system, and executes all instructions.

Arithmetic and Logic Unit (ALU) The **ALU** performs all the arithmetic and logic functions, such as addition, subtraction, comparison, etc., provided by the system.

Input/Output (I/O) Unit This unit provides access to and from the computer. The **Input/Output (I/O) Unit** is the interface to which peripheral devices such as keyboards, monitors, and printers are attached.

Secondary Storage Because RAM memory is volatile, it cannot be used as a permanent storage area for programs and data. Secondary or auxiliary storage devices are used for this purpose. Although data have been stored on punched cards, paper tape, and other media in the past, virtually all **secondary storage** is now done on magnetic tape, magnetic disks, and optical storage media.

The surfaces of magnetic tapes and disks are coated with a material that can be magnetized by a mechanism called a *write head,* and the stored magnetic field can be detected by a mechanism called a *read head.* Current tapes are capable of storing thousands of characters per inch of tape, and a single tape may store up to hundreds of megabytes. Tapes, by nature, are sequential storage media, which means that they allow data to be written or read in one sequential stream from beginning to end. Should you desire access to a block of data in the middle of the

FIGURE 1.7 Internal Structure of a Hard Disk Drive

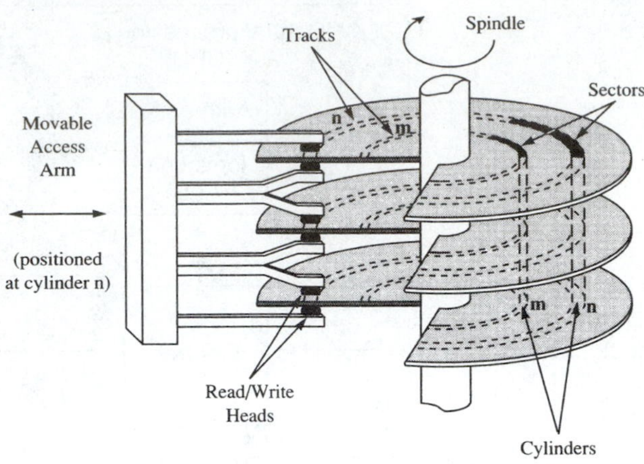

tape, you must scan all preceding data on the tape to find the block of interest. Because of this tapes are primarily used for mass backup of the data stored on large-capacity disk drives.

A more convenient method of rapidly accessing stored data is provided by a *direct access storage device* (DASD), in which any one file or program can be written or read independent of its position on the storage medium. The most popular DASD in recent years has been the magnetic disk. A magnetic **hard disk** consists of either a single rigid platter or several platters that spin together on a common spindle. A movable access arm positions the read/write heads over, but not quite touching, the recordable surfaces. Such a configuration is shown in Figure 1.7.

Another common magnetic disk storage device is the removable **floppy diskette.** Currently, the most popular size for these are 3 1/2 inches in diameter, with a capacity of 1.44 megabytes. Earlier versions of these diskettes were 5 1/4 inches in size with a capacity of 1.2 megabytes. Figure 1.8 illustrates the construction of a typical 3 1/2-inch floppy diskette.

In optical media, data is stored by using laser light to change the reflective surface properties of a single removable diskette similar or identical to a video compact disk. The disk is called a **CD-ROM** and is capable of storing several thousand megabytes.[1] Although the majority of CD-ROMS are currently read-only devices, erasable methods are available that permit the user to record, erase, and reuse optical disks in the same manner as a very high capacity magnetic disk.

Hardware Evolution

In the first commercially available computers of the 1940s and 1950s, all hardware units except the secondary storage, which consisted of punched cards and paper tape, were built using relays and vacuum tubes (Figure 1.9). The resulting computers were extremely large pieces of equipment, capable of thousands of calculations per second, and costing millions of dollars.

---

[1] A thousand megabytes is referred to as a *gigabyte*.

FIGURE 1.8 Construction of a 3 1/2 inch Floppy Diskette

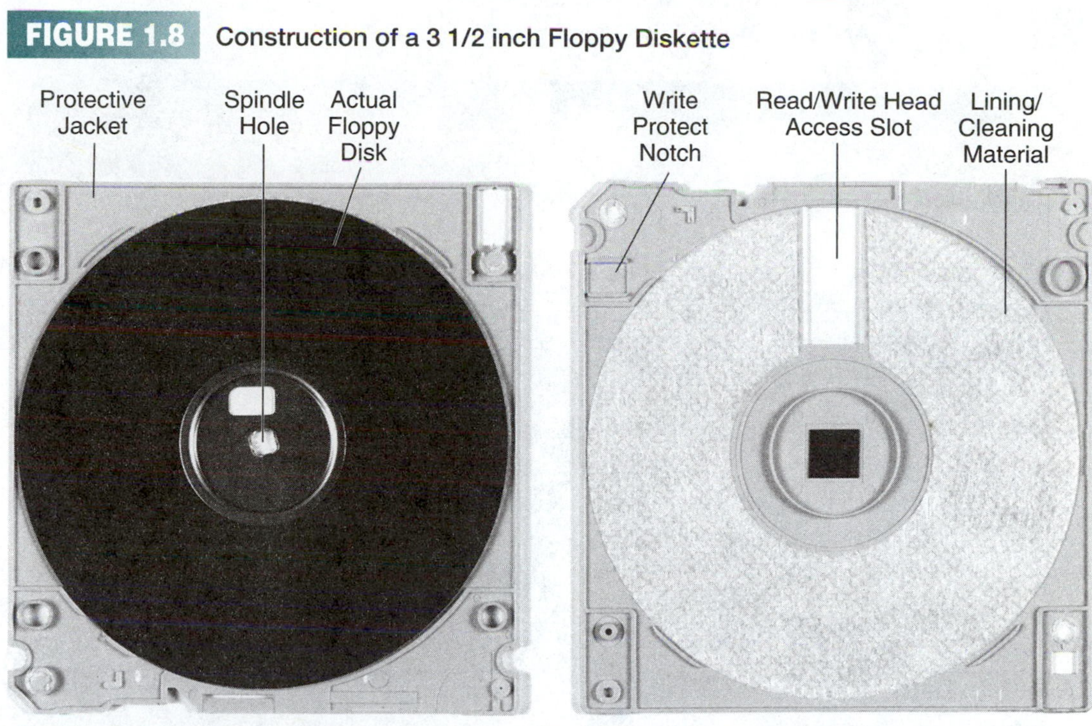

With the commercial introduction of transistors in the 1960s, both the size and cost of computer hardware were reduced. The transistor was approximately one-twentieth the size of its vacuum tube counterpart, which allowed manufacturers to combine the arithmetic and logic unit with the control unit into a single new unit. This combined unit was called the **central processing unit (CPU)**. The combination of the ALU and control units into one CPU made sense because the majority of control signals generated by a program are directed to the ALU in response to arithmetic and logic instructions within the program. Combining the ALU with the control unit simplified the interface between these two units and provided improved processing speed.

The mid-1960s saw the introduction of integrated circuits (ICs), which resulted in still another significant reduction in the space required to produce a CPU. Initially, integrated circuits were manufactured with up to 100 transistors on a single 1-cm^2 chip of silicon. Such devices are referred to as small-scale integrated (SSI) circuits. Current versions of these chips contain hundreds of thousands to over a million transistors and are referred to as **very large scale integrated (VLSI)** chips.

VLSI chip technology has provided the means of transforming the giant computers of the 1950s into today's desktop personal computers. Each individual unit required to form a computer (CPU, memory, and I/O) is now manufactured on its own individual VLSI chip, and the single-chip CPU is referred to as a **microprocessor.** Figure 1.10 illustrates the size and internal structure of a

[2]The term *software* is sometimes also used to denote both the programs and the data on which the programs will operate.

FIGURE 1.9 An IBM 701 in 1952 (Courtesy IBM Archives)

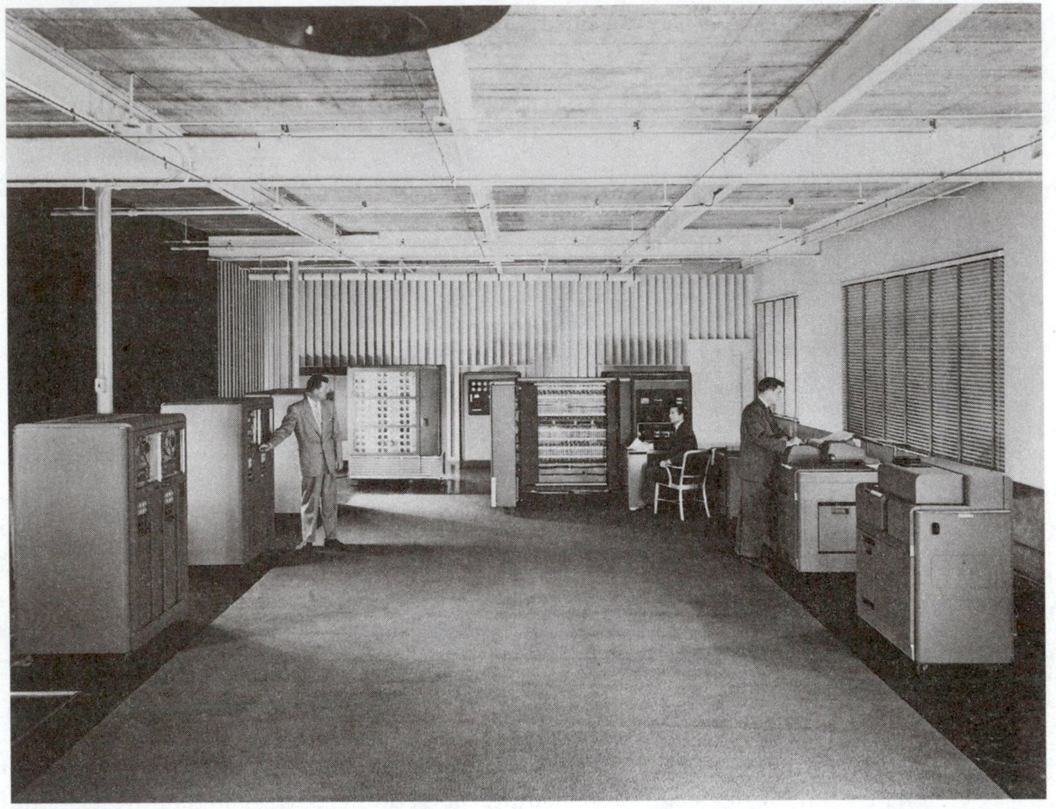

FIGURE 1.10 Internal Picture of a Pentium Microprocessor Chip

A BIT OF BACKGROUND

Ada Augusta Byron, Countess of Lovelace

Ada Byron, the daughter of Lord Byron, was a colleague of Charles Babbage in his attempt throughout the mid 1800s to build an analytical engine. It was Ada's task to develop the algorithms—solutions to problems in the form of step-by-step instructions—that would allow the engine to compute the values of mathematical functions. Babbage's machine was not successfully built in his lifetime, primarily because the technology of the time did not allow mechanical parts to be constructed with necessary tolerances. Nonetheless, Ada is recognized as the first computer programmer. She published a collection of notes that established the basis for computer programming; and the modern Ada programming language is named in her honor.

state-of-the art VLSI microprocessor chip. The chip itself is in the center of the square on the right and the cover for the package is on the left. Internally the chip is connected with wires to the pins on the outside of the package. The insides of these pins appear as a series of silver dots in the square on the right side of the figure.

Figure 1.11 illustrates how the complete set of chips needed for a computer is put on boards and connected internally to create a computer, such as the early IBM PCs of the 1980s (Figure 1.12) and more current notebook computers (Figure 1.13).

Concurrent with the remarkable reduction in computer hardware size has been an equally dramatic decrease in cost and increase in processing speeds. The equivalent computer hardware that cost more than a million dollars in 1950 can now be purchased for less than 500 dollars. If the same reductions occurred in the automobile industry, for example, a Rolls-Royce could now be purchased for 10 dollars! The processing speeds of current computers have also increased by a factor of a thousand over their 1950s predecessors, with the computational speeds of current machines being measured in both millions of instructions per second (MIPS) and billions of instructions per second (BIPS).

FIGURE 1.11 VLSI Chip Connections for a Desktop Computer

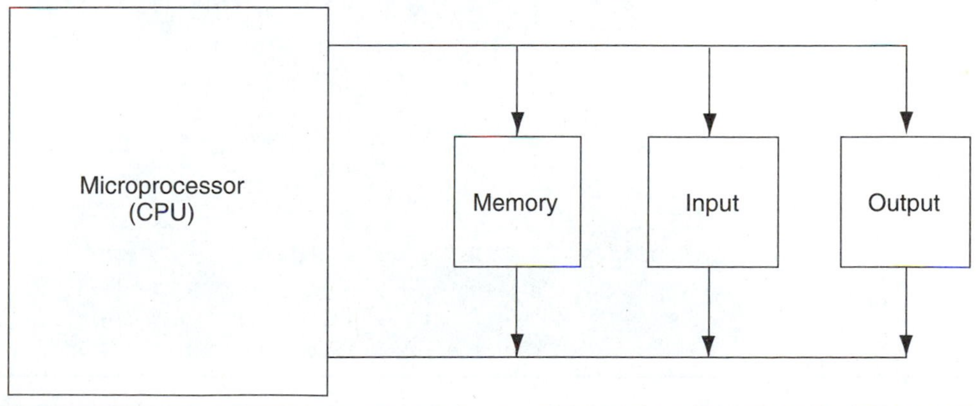

FIGURE 1.12 An Original (1980s) IBM Personal Computer (Courtesy IBM Corporation)

FIGURE 1.13 A 1997 Texas Instruments Notebook Computer (Courtesy Texas Instruments)

Computer Software

As we have seen, a computer is a machine made of physical components. In this regard it is the same as any other machine, such as an automobile or lawn mower. Like these other machines, it must be turned on and then driven, or controlled, before it can do the task it was meant to do. How this gets done is what distinguishes a computer from other types of machinery.

In an automobile, for example, control is provided by the driver, who sits inside of and directs the car. In a computer, the driver is a set of instructions, called a program. More formally, a **computer program** is a self-contained set of instructions used to operate a computer to produce a specific result. Another term for a program or set of programs is **software,** and we will use both terms interchangeably throughout the text.[2]

The process of writing a program, or software, is called **programming,** and the set of instructions that can be used to construct a program is called a **programming language.** Programming languages are available in a variety of forms and types.

Machine Language At its most fundamental level the only programs that can actually be used to operate a computer are **machine language** programs. Such programs, which are also referred to as *executable programs,* or *executables* for short, consist of a sequence of instructions composed of binary numbers such as[3]:

```
11000000 000000000001 000000000010
11110000 000000000010 000000000011
```

Such machine language instructions consist of two parts: an instruction part and an address part. The instruction part, which is referred to as the **opcode** (short for operation code), is usually the leftmost set of bits in the instruction and tells the computer the operation to be performed, such as add, subtract, multiply, etc., while the rightmost bits specify the memory addresses of the data to be used. For example, assuming that the 8 leftmost bits of the first instruction listed previously is the operation code to add, and the next two groups of 12 bits are the addresses of the two operands to be added, this instruction would be a command to "add the data in memory location 1 to the data in memory location 2."[4] Similarly, assuming that the opcode 111100000 means multiply, the next instruction is a command to "multiply the data in memory location 2 by the data in location 3."

Assembly Languages Although each class of computer, such as IBM PCs, Apple Macintoshes, and DEC VAX computers, has its own particular machine language, it is very tedious and time consuming to write such machine language programs. One of the first advances in programming was the substitution of word-like symbols, such as ADD, SUB, MUL, for the binary opcodes, and both decimal numbers and labels for memory addresses. For example, using the following symbols and decimal values for memory addresses, the previous two machine language instructions can be written:

```
ADD 1, 2
MUL 2, 3
```

---

[3] Review Section 1.6 if you are unfamiliar with binary numbers.

[4] To obtain the address values as decimal numbers, convert the binary values to decimal using the method presented in Section 1.6.

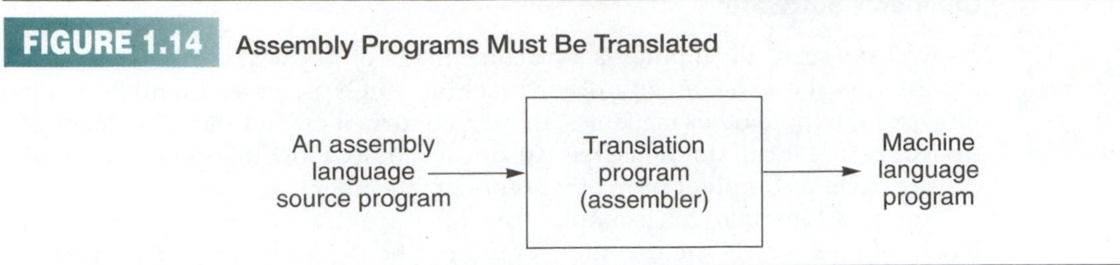

FIGURE 1.14 Assembly Programs Must Be Translated

Programming languages that use this type of symbolic notation are referred to as **assembly languages.** Since computers can only execute machine language programs, the set of instructions contained within an assembly language program must be translated into a machine language program before it can be executed on a computer (Figure 1.14). Translation programs that perform this function for assembly language programs are known as **assemblers.**

Low-Level and High-Level Languages Both machine level and assembly languages are classified as **low-level languages.** This is because both of these language types use instructions that are directly tied to one type of computer. As such, an assembly language program is limited in that it can only be used with the specific computer type for which the program is written. Such programs do, however, permit the use of special features of a particular computer and generally execute at the fastest speed possible.

In contrast to low-level languages are languages that are classified as high level. A **high-level language** uses instructions that resemble written languages, such as English, and can be run on a variety of computer types. FORTRAN, BASIC, Pascal, and C++ are all examples of high-level languages. Using C++, an instruction to add two numbers and multiply by a third number can be written:

```
result = (first + second) * third;
```

Programs written in a computer language (high or low level) are referred to interchangeably as both **source programs** and **source code.** Once a program is written in a high-level language it must also, like a low-level assembly program, be translated into the machine language of the computer on which it will be run. This translation can be accomplished in two ways.

When each statement in a high-level source program is translated individually and executed immediately upon translation, the programming language used is called an **interpreted language,** and the program doing the translation is called an **interpreter.**

When all of the statements in a high-level source program are translated as a complete unit before any one statement is executed, the programming language used is called a **compiled language.** In this case, the program doing the translation is called a **compiler.** Both compiled and interpreted versions of a language can exist, although typically one dominates. For example, although compiled versions of BASIC do exist, BASIC is predominantly an interpreted language. Similarly, although interpreted versions of C++ exist, C++ is predominantly a compiled language.

Procedure and Object Orientations In addition to classifying programming languages as high or low level, they are also classified as either procedure or object oriented. In a **procedure-oriented language** the available instructions are used to create self-contained units, referred to as *procedures*. The purpose of a procedure is to accept data as input and transform the data in some manner to produce a specific result as an output. For the last 25 years most high-level programming languages have been procedure oriented.

Within the past few years a second orientation, referred to as object oriented, has taken center stage. One of the motivations for **object-oriented languages** was the development of graphical screens and support for graphical user interfaces (GUIs) capable of displaying multiple windows. In such an environment each window on the screen can conveniently be considered an object, with associated characteristics, such as color, position, and size. Using an object approach, a program must first define the characteristics of the objects it will be manipulating and then be constructed of units that pass information to each object to produce the desired results. C++, which is classified as an object-oriented language, contains features found in both procedural and object-oriented languages.

Application and System Software Two logical categories of computer programs are application software and system software. **Application software** consists of those programs written to perform particular tasks required by the users. Most of the examples in this book would be called application software.

System software is the collection of programs that must be readily available to any computer system in order for it to operate at all. In the early computer environments of the 1950s and 1960s, the user initially had to load the system software by hand to prepare the computer to do anything at all. This was done by using rows of switches on a front panel. Those initial, hand-entered commands were said to **boot** the computer, an expression derived from "pulling oneself up by the bootstraps." Today the so-called "bootstrap loader" is internally contained in ROM and is a permanent, automatically executed component of the computer's system software.

Additionally, before the 1960s, it was not uncommon for the user to have to load a separate set of programs necessary for reading from and writing to the input and output devices that were being used. Similarly, it was the user's responsibility to find the code that would translate an application program to the computer's internal machine language so that it could be executed. Typically, most of these *utilities* are now kept on either a hard disk or floppy diskette and are booted into the computer either automatically when the system is powered up or on command by the user.

Various terms are used by different manufacturers for the collection of system utilities called the **operating system.** Often, the system software name ends with *OS* or *DOS* (for Disk Operating System). Additional tasks handled by modern operating systems include memory, input and output, and secondary storage management. Many systems handle very large programs, as well as multiple users concurrently, by dividing programs into segments or pages that are moved between the disk and memory as needed. Such operating systems create a *virtual memory,* which appears to be as large as necessary to handle any job; and a multiuser environment is produced that gives each user the impression that the computer and peripherals are his or hers alone. Additionally, many operating systems, including most windowed environments, permit each user to run multiple programs. Such operating systems are referred to as *multitasking* systems.

Most system operations are *transparent* to the user; that is, they take place internally without user intervention. However, some operating system commands are provided intentionally for you to interact directly with the system. The most common of these commands are those that allow the handling of data files on disk. Some of these are listed in Table 1.1 by the names with which they are implemented in both MS-DOS and UNIX operating systems.

TABLE 1.1 Common Operating System Commands

Task	DOS Command	UNIX Command
Display the directory of all files available.	`DIR`	`ls`
Delete a specified file or group of files.	`ERASE or DELETE filename(s)`	`rm filename(s)`
List the contents of a program to the monitor.	`TYPE filename`	`cat filename`
Print the contents of a program to the printer.	`PRINT filename`	`lp or lpr filename`
Copy a file.	`COPY source destination`	`cp source destination`
Rename a file.	`RENAME oldname newname`	`mv oldname newname`
Force a permanent halt to a running program.	`CTRL Break or CTRL Z or CTRL C`	`Del key, CTRL Break, or \`
Force a temporary suspension of the current operation.	`CTRL S or Pause`	`CTRL S`
Resume the current operation (recover from a CTRL S).	`CTRL S`	`CTRL S`

Exercises 1.1

1. Define the following terms:
   a. computer program
   b. programming
   c. programming language
   d. high-level language
   e. low-level language
   f. machine language
   g. assembly language
   h. procedure-oriented language
   i. object-oriented language
   j. source program
   k. compiler
   l. interpreter
2. Describe the accomplishments of the following people:
   a. Charles Babbage
   b. Ada Byron

c. John Atanasoff

d. Clifford Berry

e. John W. Mauchly

f. J. Presper Eckert

g. John Von Neumann

3. Describe where the following machines were designed and the advancement in computer technology provided by them:

   a. analytic engine

   b. ABC

   c. ENIAC

   d. Mark I

   e. EDSAC

4. Describe the hardware units of a computer and the purpose of each unit.

5. a. Describe the difference between high- and low-level languages.

   b. Describe the difference between procedure- and object-oriented languages.

6. Describe the similarities and differences between assemblers, interpreters, and compilers.

7. a. Assume the following operation codes:

   11000000 means add the 1st operand to the 2nd operand
   10100000 means subtract the 1st operand from the 2nd operand
   11110000 means multiply the 2nd operand by the 1st operand
   11010000 means divide the 2nd operation by the 1st operand

Translate the following instructions into English:

Opcode	Address of 1st Operand	Address of 2nd Operand
11000000	000000000001	0000000000010
11110000	000000000010	0000000000011
10100000	000000000100	0000000000011
11010000	000000000101	0000000000011

   b. Assuming the following locations contain the following data, determine the result produced by the instructions listed in Exercise 7a.

Address	Initial Value (in decimal) Stored at This Address
00000000001	5
00000000010	3
00000000011	6
00000000100	14
00000000101	4

8. Rewrite the machine-level instructions listed in Exercise 7a using assembly language notation. Use the symbolic names ADD, SUB, MUL, and DIV for addition, subtraction, multiplication, and division operations, respectively. In writing the instructions use decimal values for the addresses.

1.2 PROGRAMMING LANGUAGES

On a fundamental level, all computer programs do the same thing (Figure 1.15); they direct a computer to accept data (input), to manipulate the data (process), and to produce reports (output). This implies that all computer programming languages that support a procedure orientation must provide essentially the same capabilities for performing these operations. These capabilities are provided either as specific instruction types, or "prepackaged" groups of instructions that can be called to do specific tasks. In C++, the "prepackaged" groups of instructions are contained in *function libraries*. Table 1.2 lists the fundamental set of instructions provided by FORTRAN, COBOL, Pascal, C, and C++ for performing input, processing, and output tasks.

TABLE 1.2 Fundamental Programming Language Instruction Summary

Operation	FORTRAN	BASIC	COBOL	Pascal	C	C++
Input	READ	INPUT	READ	READ	scanf()	cin
(get the data)		READ/DATA	ACCEPT	READLN	gets()	cin.get
					getchar()	cin.getline
Processing	=	LET	COMPUTE	:=	=	=
(use the data)	IF/ELSE	IF/ELSE	IF/ELSE	IF/ELSE	if/else	if/else
	DO	FOR	PERFORM	FOR	for	for
		WHILE		WHILE	while	while
		UNTIL		REPEAT	do	do
	+	+	ADD	+	+, =+, ++	+, =+, ++
	-	-	SUBTRACT	-	-, =-, --	-, =-, --
	*	*	MULTIPLY	*	*, =*	*, =*
	/	/	DIVIDE	/	/, =/	/, =/
	**	^		**	pow()	pow()
Output	WRITE	PRINT	WRITE	WRITE	printf()	cout
(display	PRINT	PRINT/	DISPLAY	WRITELN	puts()	
the data)		USING			putchar()	

If all programming languages provide essentially the same features, why are there so many of them? The answer is that there are vast differences in the types of input data, calculations needed, and output reports required by various appli-

FIGURE 1.15 All Programs Perform the Same Operations

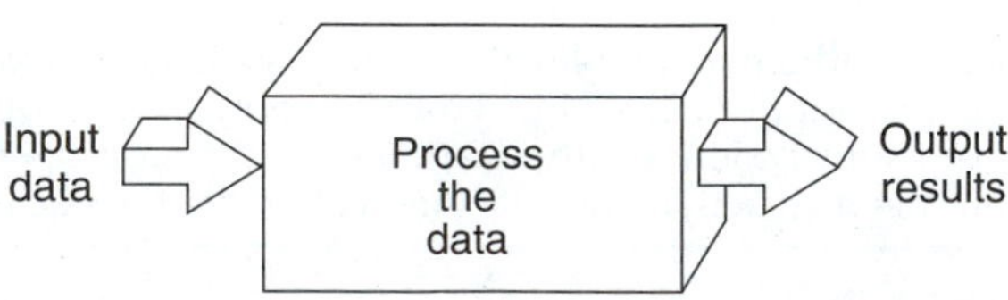

▲ POINT OF INFORMATION ▲

What Is Syntax?

A programming language's **syntax** is the set of rules for formulating grammatically correct language statements. In practice this means that a C++ statement with correct syntax has the proper form specified for the compiler. As such, the compiler will accept the statement and not generate an error message.

It should be noted that an individual statement or program can be syntactically correct and still be logically incorrect. Such a statement or program would be correctly structured but produce an incorrect result. This is similar to an English statement that is grammatically correct but makes no sense. For example, although the sentence "The tree is a ragged cat" is grammatically correct, it makes no sense.

cations. For example, scientific and engineering applications require high-precision numerical outputs, accurate to many decimal places. In addition, these applications typically use many algebraic or trigonometric formulas to produce their results. For example, calculating the bacterial concentration level in a polluted pond, as illustrated in Figure 1.16, requires evaluation of an exponential equation to a high degree of numerical accuracy. The FORTRAN programming language, with its algebra-like instructions, was initially developed for such applications. FORTRAN, whose name is an acronym derived from FORmula TRANslation, was introduced in 1957. It was the first commercially available high-level language and is the oldest high-level language still in use.

Business applications usually deal in whole numbers, representing inventory quantities, for example, or dollar-and-cents data accurate to only two decimal places. These applications require simpler mathematical calculations than those

FIGURE 1.16 FORTRAN Was Developed for Scientific and Engineering Applications

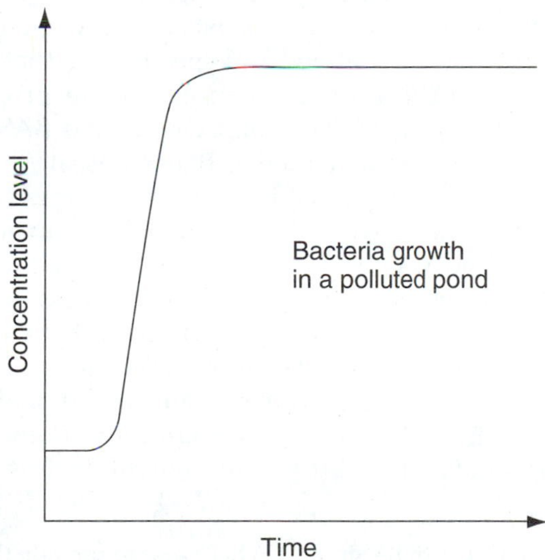

needed for scientific applications. The outputs required from business programs frequently consist of reports containing extensive columns of neatly formatted dollar-and-cents numbers and totals (Figure 1.17). For these applications the COBOL programming language, with its picture output formats, is an ideal language. COBOL, which was commercially introduced in the 1960s, stands for COmmon Business Oriented Language.

FIGURE 1.17 COBOL Is Ideal for Many Business Applications

```
                    INVENTORY REPORT

 Item                                  In      On      Unit
 No.        Description              Stock   Order     Cost

10365     360KB -Diskette             20       0       5.95
10382     720KB -Diskette             10      50      10.70
10420     1.2MB -Diskette              2      60       8.40
10436    1.44MB -Diskette              6
10449      20MB -Cartridge
10486      40MB -Cartrid
```

Teaching programming to students has its own set of requirements. Here, a relatively straightforward, easy-to- understand language is needed that does not require detailed knowledge of a specific application. Both the BASIC and Pascal programming languages were developed for this purpose. BASIC stands for Beginners All-purpose Symbolic Instruction Code, and was developed in the 1960s at Dartmouth College. BASIC is ideal for creating small, easily developed, interactive programs.

Pascal was developed in 1971 to provide students with a firmer foundation in modular and structured programming than was provided by early versions of BASIC.[5] Modular programs consist of many small subprograms, each of which performs a clearly defined and specific task that can be tested and modified without disturbing other sections of the program. Pascal is not an acronym, like the words FORTRAN, COBOL, and BASIC; it is named after the seventeenth century mathematician, Blaise Pascal. The Pascal language is so rigidly structured, however, that there are no escapes from the structured modules when such escapes would be useful. This is unacceptable for many real-world projects, and is one of the reasons why Pascal did not become widely accepted in the scientific, engineering, and business fields. The design philosophy, called *structured programming,* that led to the development of Pascal is, however, very relevant to C++ programmers. A structured programming approach results in readable, reliable, and maintainable programs. We introduce the elements of this program design philosophy in the next section, and continue to expand on it and use it throughout the text.

[5] Current versions of both BASIC and FORTRAN do provide the same structures found in Pascal.

A BIT OF BACKGROUND

Blaise Pascal

The Pascal language is named after Blaise Pascal, a French mathematician and philosopher who lived from 1623 to 1662. He is credited with having invented the first mechanical calculating machine in 1642 at the age of 19.

"All our dignity consists then in thought. By it we must elevate ourselves, and not by space and time, which we cannot fill. Let us endeavor then to think well; this is the principle of morality." (Pascal's *Penses*, Number 347)

C++ began as an extension to C, which is a procedure-oriented language developed in the 1970s at AT&T Bell Laboratories by Ken Thompson, Dennis Ritchie, and Brian Kernighan. In the early 1980s, Bjarne Stroustrup (also at AT&T) used his simulation language background to develop C++. A central feature of simulation languages is that they model real-life situations as objects. This object orientation, which was ideal for graphical screen objects such as rectangles and circles, was combined with existing C features to form the C++ language. Thus, C++ retained the extensive set of capabilities provided by C and is itself a true general-purpose programming language. As such, it can be used for everything from simple, interactive programs to highly sophisticated and complex engineering and scientific programs, within the context of a truly structured language.

1.3 PROBLEM SOLUTION AND SOFTWARE DEVELOPMENT

No matter what field of work you choose or what your lifestyle may be, you will have to solve problems. Many of these, such as adding up the change in your pocket, can be solved quickly and easily. Others, such as riding a bicycle, require some practice but soon become automatic. Still others require considerable planning and forethought if the solution is to be appropriate and efficient. For example, constructing a cellular telephone network or creating an inventory management system for a department store are problems for which trial-and-error solutions could prove expensive and disastrous.

Creating a program is no different, because a program is a solution developed to solve a particular problem. As such, writing a program is almost the last step in a process of first determining what the problem is and the method that will be used to solve the problem. Each field of study has its own name for the systematic method used to solve problems by designing suitable solutions. In science and engineering the approach is referred to as the *scientific method,* while in quantitative analysis the approach is referred to as the *systems approach.*

One technique used by professional software developers for understanding the problem that is being solved and for creating an effective and appropriate software solution is called the **software development procedure.** This procedure, as illustrated in Figure 1.18 consists of three overlapping phases:

- Development and design
- Documentation
- Maintenance.

FIGURE 1.18 The Three Phases of Program Development

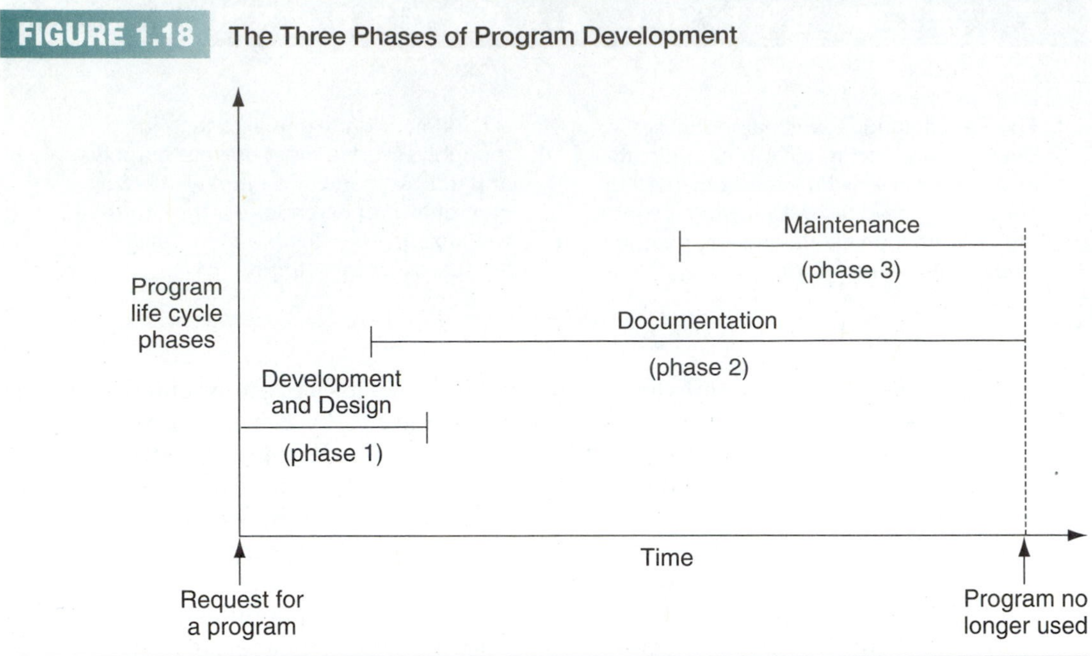

As a discipline, **software engineering** is concerned with creating readable, efficient, reliable, and maintainable programs and systems and uses the software development procedure to achieve this goal.

Phase I: Development and Design

Phase I begins with either a statement of a problem or a specific request for a program, which is referred to as a *program requirement*. Once a problem has been stated or a specific request for a program solution has been made, the development and design phase begins. This phase consists of the four well-defined steps illustrated in Figure 1.19 and summarized next:

1. Analyze the Problem This step is required to ensure that the problem is clearly defined and understood. The determination that the problem is clearly defined is made only after the person doing the analysis understands what outputs are required and what inputs will be needed. To accomplish this, the analyst must have an understanding of how the inputs can be used to produce the desired output. For example, assume that you receive the following assignment:

> Write a program that gives the information we need about circles. Complete by tomorrow.
>
> —Management

A simple analysis of this program requirement reveals that it is not a well-defined problem at all because we do not know exactly what output information is required. As such, it would be a major mistake to begin immediately writing a program to solve it. To clarify and define the problem statement your first step should be to contact "Management" to define exactly what the program is to produce (its outputs).

FIGURE 1.19 The Development and Design Steps

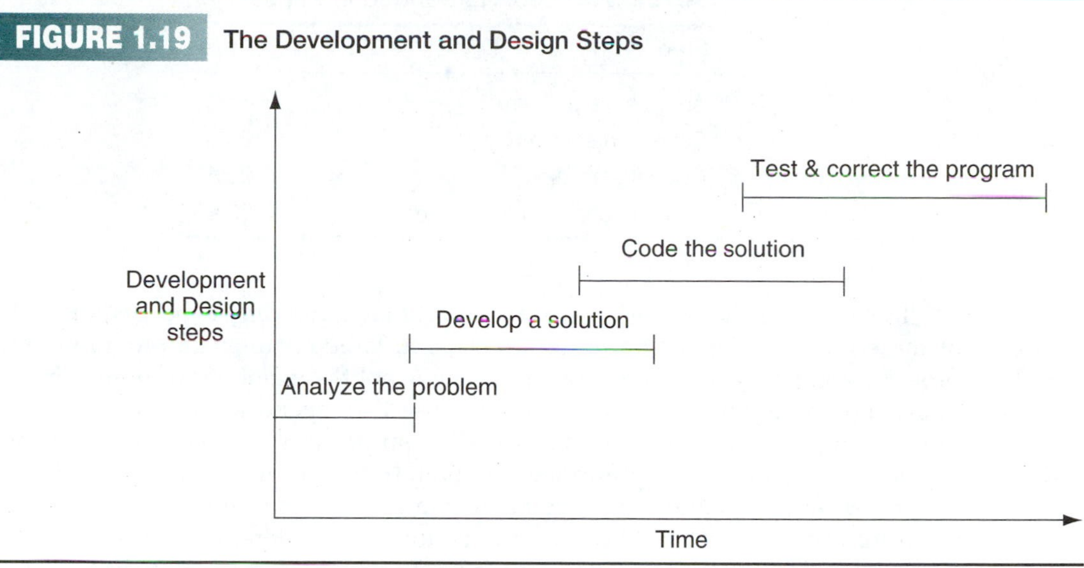

Suppose you do this and you learn that what is really desired is a program to calculate and display the circumference of a circle when given the radius. Because a formula exists for converting the input to the output, you may proceed to the next step. If we are not sure of how to obtain the required output or exactly what inputs are needed, a more in-depth background analysis may be called for. This typically means obtaining more background information about the problem or application. It also frequently entails doing one or more hand calculations to ensure that we understand what inputs are needed and how they must be combined to achieve the desired output.

2. Develop a Solution In this step we select the exact set of steps, called an **algorithm,** that we will use to solve the problem. The solution is typically obtained by a series of refinements, starting with the initial algorithm found in the analysis step, until an acceptable and complete algorithm is obtained. This algorithm must be checked, if this was not already done in the analysis step, to ensure that it correctly produces the desired outputs. The check is typically done by doing one or more hand calculations not already done.

Sometimes the selected solution is quite easy, and sometimes it is quite complex. For example, the solution to determine the dollar value of the change in one's pocket or to determine the circumference of a circle is quite simple and consists of a simple calculation. The construction of an inventory tracking and control system for a computer store, however, is more complex. Techniques for solving these more complex problems are presented in Chapter 2.

3. Code the Solution This step, which is also referred to as writing the program and implementing the solution, consists of translating the solution into a computer program.

4. Test and Correct the Program As its name suggests, this step requires testing of the completed computer program to ensure that it does, in fact, provide a solution to the problem. Any errors that are found during the tests must be corrected.

TABLE 1.3 Effort Expended in Phase I

Step	Effort
Analyze the problem	10%
Develop a solution	20%
Code the solution	20%
Test and correct the program	50%

Table 1.3 lists the relative amount of effort that is typically expended on each of these four development and design steps in large commercial programming projects. As this listing demonstrated, coding is not the major effort in this phase. Many new programmers have trouble because they spend the majority of their time writing the program, without spending sufficient time understanding the problem or designing an appropriate solution. In this regard, it is worthwhile to remember this programming proverb: "It is impossible to write a successful program for a problem or application that is not fully understood." A somewhat equivalent and equally valuable proverb is "The sooner you start coding a program the longer it usually takes to complete."

Phase II: Documentation

So much work becomes useless or lost, and so many tasks must be repeated because of inadequate documentation that it could be argued that documenting your work is the most important step in problem solving. Actually, many of the critical documents are created during the analysis, design, coding, and testing steps. Completing the documentation requires collecting these documents, adding additional material, and presenting it in a form that is most useful to you and your organization.

Although not everybody classifies them in the same way, there are essentially five documents for every problem solution:

1. Program description
2. Algorithm development and changes
3. Well-commented program listing
4. Sample test runs
5. Users' manual.

"Putting yourself in the shoes" of a member of a large organization's team that might use your work—anyone from the secretary to the programmer/analysts and management—should help you to make the content and design of the important documentation clear. The documentation phase formally begins in the development and design phase and continues into the maintenance phase.

Phase III: Maintenance

The **software maintenance** phase is concerned with ongoing correction of problems, revisions to meet changing needs, and addition of new features. Maintenance is often the major effort, the primary source of revenue, and the longest lasting of the engineering phases. While development may take days or months, maintenance may continue for years or decades. The better the documentation is, the more efficiently this phase can be performed and the happier the customer and user will be.

A Closer Look at Phase I

Because the majority of this text is concerned with phase I of the software development procedure, we elaborate further on the four steps required for this phase. The use of these steps forms the central focus of our work in creating useful programming solutions.

Step 1: Analyze the Problem Countless hours have been spent writing computer programs that either have never been used or have caused considerable animosity between programmer and user because the programmer did not produce what the user needed or expected. Successful programmers understand and avoid this by ensuring that the problem's requirements are understood. This is the first step in creating a program and the most important, because in it the specifications for the final program solution are determined. If the requirements are not fully and completely understood before programming begins, the results are almost always disastrous.

Imagine designing and building a house without fully understanding the architect's specifications. After the house is completed, the architect tells you that a bathroom is required on the first floor, where you have built a wall between the kitchen and the dining room. In addition, that particular wall is one of the main support walls for the house and contains numerous pipes and electrical cables. In this case, adding one bathroom requires a rather major modification to the basic structure of the house.

Experienced programmers understand the importance of analyzing and understanding a program's requirements before coding, if for no other reason than that they too have constructed programs that later had to be entirely dismantled and redone. The following exercise should give you a sense of this experience.

Figure 1.20 illustrates the outlines of six individual shapes from a classic children's puzzle. Assume that as one or more shapes are given, starting with shapes A and B, an easy-to-describe figure must be constructed. Typically, shapes A and B are initially arranged to obtain a square, as illustrated in Figure 1.21. Next, when shape C is considered, it is usually combined with the existing square to form a rectangle, as illustrated in Figure 1.22. Then when pieces D and E are added, they are usually arranged to form another rectangle, which is placed alongside the existing rectangle to form a square, as shown in Figure 1.23.

FIGURE 1.20 Six Individual Shapes

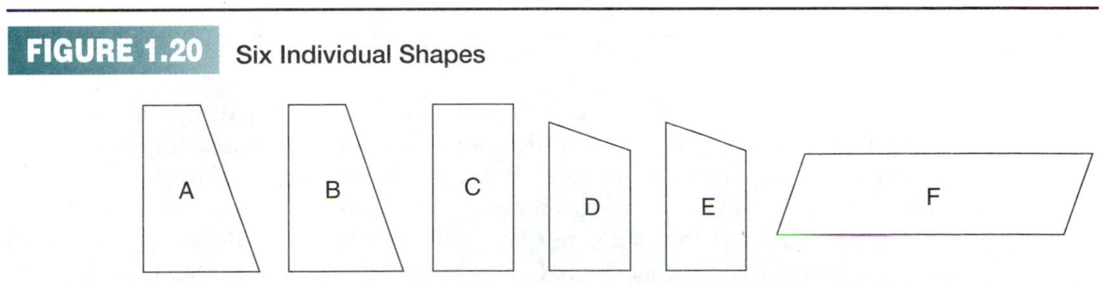

FIGURE 1.21 Typical First Figure

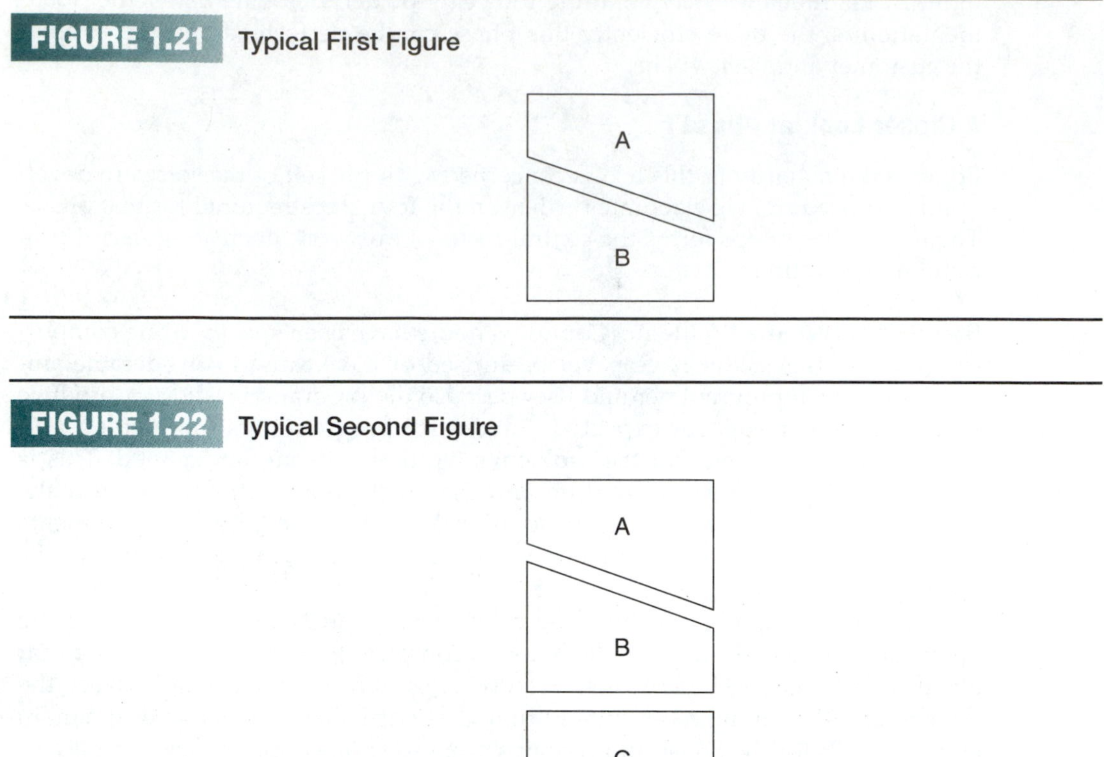

FIGURE 1.22 Typical Second Figure

FIGURE 1.23 Typical Third Figure

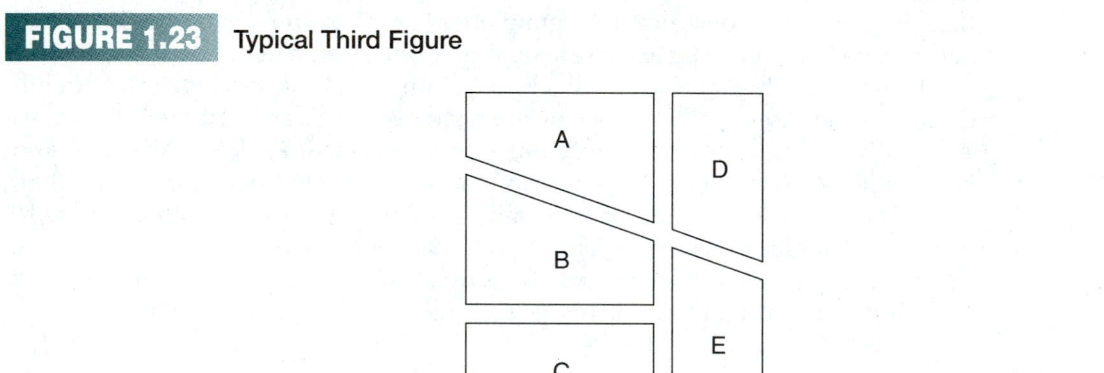

The process of adding new pieces onto the existing structure is identical to constructing a program and then adding to it as each subsequent requirement is understood, rather than completely analyzing the problem before a solution is undertaken. The problem arises when the program is almost finished and a requirement is added that does not fit easily into the established pattern. For example, assume that the last shape (shape F; see Figure 1.24) is now to be added.

FIGURE 1.24 The Last Piece

This last piece does not fit into the existing pattern that has been constructed. To include this piece with the others, the pattern must be completely dismantled and restructured.

Unfortunately, many programmers structure their programs in the same sequential manner used to construct Figure 1.23. Rather than taking the time to understand the complete set of requirements, new programmers frequently start coding based on the understanding of only a small subset of the total requirements. Then, when a subsequent requirement does not fit the existing program structure, the programmer is forced to dismantle and restructure either parts or all of the program.

Now, let's approach the problem of creating a figure from another view. If we started by arranging the first set of pieces as a parallelogram, all the pieces could be included in the final figure, as illustrated in Figure 1.25. It is worthwhile observing that the piece that caused us to dismantle the first figure (Figure 1.23) actually sets the pattern for the final figure illustrated in Figure 1.25. This is often the case with programming requirements. The requirement that seems to be the least clear is frequently the one that determines the main interrelationships of the program. It is worthwhile to include and understand all known requirements before beginning coding. Thus, before any solution is attempted the analysis step must be completed.

The person performing the analysis must initially take a broad perspective, see all of the pieces, and understand the main purpose of what the program or system is meant to achieve. The key to success here, which ultimately determines the success of the final program, is to determine the main purpose of the system as seen by the person making the request. For large systems, the analysis is usually conducted by a systems analyst. For smaller systems or individual programs, the analysis is typically performed directly by the programmer.

Regardless of how the analysis is done, or by whom, at its conclusion you should have a clear understanding of:

- What the system or program must do
- What outputs must be produced
- What inputs are required to create the desired outputs.

Step 2: Develop (Design) a Solution Once the problem is clearly understood a solution can be developed. In this regard the programmer is in a similar position to that of an architect who must draw up the plans for a house: The house must conform to certain specifications and meet the needs of its owner, but it can be designed and built in many possible ways. The same is true of a program.

For small programs the selected algorithm may be extremely simple and consist of only one or more calculations that must be performed. More typically, the initial solution must be refined and organized into smaller subsystems, with

FIGURE 1.25 Including All the Pieces

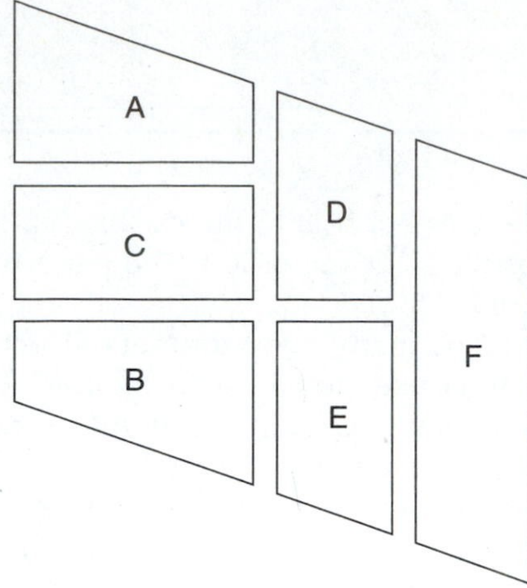

specifications for how the subsystems will interface with each other. To achieve this goal, the description of the solution starts from the highest level (topmost) requirement and proceeds downward to the parts that must be constructed to achieve this requirement. To make this more meaningful, consider a computer program that is required to track the number of parts in inventory. The required output for this program is a description of all parts carried in inventory and the number of units of each item in stock; the given inputs are the initial inventory quantity of each part, the number of items sold, the number of items returned, and the number of items purchased.

For these specifications, a designer could initially organize the requirements for the program into the three sections illustrated in Figure 1.26. This is called a *top-level structure diagram* because it represents the first overall structure of the program selected by the designer.

Once an initial structure is developed, it is refined until the tasks indicated in the boxes are completely defined. For example, both the data entry and report subsections shown in Figure 1.26 would be further refined as follows: The data

FIGURE 1.26 First-Level Structure Diagram

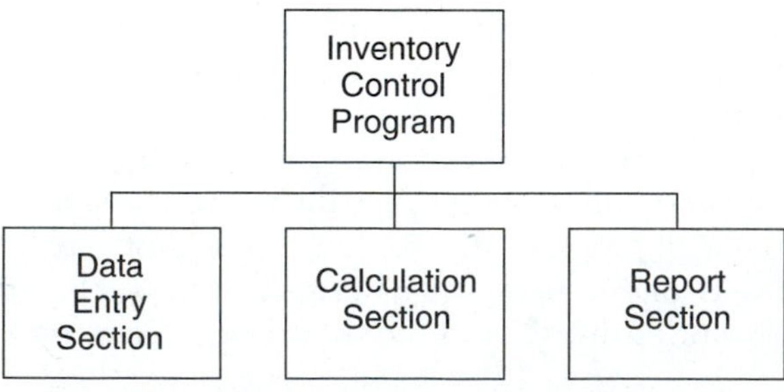

A BIT OF BACKGROUND

Niklaus Wirth

Niklaus Wirth received an M.S. degree from the University of Quebec in 1962 and the Ph.D. from the University of California at Berkeley in 1963. He then returned to his undergraduate alma mater, the Swiss Federal Institute of Technology, to teach. While serving there in 1971, he announced a new language he had designed and named *Pascal.* Pascal became very popular in the 1970s and early 1980s because of its emphasis on the sequence, selection, iteration, and invocation control structures.

entry section certainly must include provisions for entering the data. Since it is the system designer's responsibility to plan for contingencies and human error, provisions must also be made for changing incorrect data after an entry has been made and for deleting a previously entered value altogether. Similar subdivisions for the report section can also be constructed. Figure 1.27 illustrates a second-level structure diagram for an inventory tracking system that includes these further refinements.

The process of refining a solution continues until the smallest requirement is included within the solution. Notice that the design produces a tree-like structure where the levels branch out as we move from the top of the structure to the bottom. When the design is complete, each task designated in a box is typically coded with separate sets of instructions that are executed as they are called on by tasks higher up in the structure.

Step 3: Code the Solution **Coding** involves translating the chosen design solution into a computer program. If the analysis and solution steps have been correctly performed, the coding step becomes rather mechanical in nature. In a well-designed program, the statements making up the program will, however,

FIGURE 1.27 Second-Level Refinement Structure Diagram

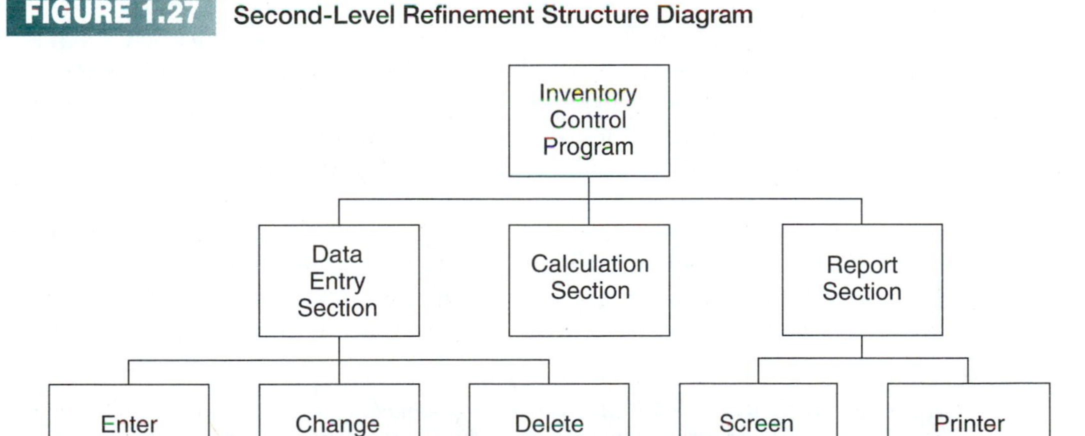

A BIT OF BACKGROUND

Al-Khowarizmi

One of the first great mathematicians was Mohammed ibn Musa al-Khowarizmi, who wrote a treatise in about 825 A.D. called *Ilm al-jabr wa'l muqabalah* ("the science of reduction and calculation").

The word *algorism* or *algorithm* is derived from al-Khowarizmi's name, and our word *algebra* is derived from the word *al-jabr* in the title of his work.

conform to certain well-defined patterns, or structures, that have been defined in the solution step. These structures control how the program executes and consist of the following types:

1. Sequence
2. Selection
3. Iteration
4. Invocation.

Sequence defines the order in which instructions are executed by the program. The specification of which instruction comes first, which comes second, and so on, is essential if the program is to achieve a well-defined purpose.

Selection provides the capability to make a choice between different operations, depending on the result of some condition. For example, the value of a number can be checked before a division is performed. If the number is not zero, it can be used as the denominator of a division operation; otherwise, the division will not be performed and the user will be issued a warning message.

Iteration, which is also referred to as looping and **repetition,** provides the ability for the same operation to be repeated based on the value of a condition. For example, grades might be repeatedly entered and added until a negative grade is entered. In this case the entry of a negative grade is the condition that signifies the end of the repetitive input and addition of grades. At that point a calculation of an average for all the grades entered could be performed.

Invocation involves invoking, or summoning, a set of statements as needed. For example, the computation of a person's net pay involves the tasks of obtaining pay rates and hours worked, calculating the net pay, and providing a report or check for the required amount. Each of these individual tasks would typically be coded as separate units that are called into execution, or invoked, as they are needed.

Step 4: Test and Correct the Solution The purpose of testing is to verify that a program works correctly and actually fulfills its requirements. In theory, testing would reveal all existing program errors (in computer terminology, a program error is called a *bug*[6]). In practice, this would require checking all possible combi-

[6] The derivation of this term is rather interesting. When a program stopped running on the Mark I at Harvard University in September 1945, Grace Hopper traced the malfunction to a dead insect that had gotten into the electrical circuits. She recorded the incident in her logbook at 15:45 hours as "Relay #70. . . . (moth) in relay. First actual case of bug being found."

A BIT OF BACKGROUND

The Young Gauss

German mathematical genius Johann Carl Fredrich Gauss (1777–1855) professed that he could "reckon" before he could talk. When only two years old he discovered an error in his father's business records.

One day in school, young Johann's teacher asked his class to add up the numbers between 1 and 100. To the chagrin of the teacher, who had thought the task would keep the class busy for a while, Gauss almost instantly wrote the number on his slate and exclaimed, "There it is!" He had reasoned that the series of numbers could be written forward and backward and added term-by-term to get 101 one hundred times. Thus, the sum was 100(101)/2; and Gauss, at the age of 10, had discovered that

$$1 + 2 + \ldots + n = n\,(n + 1)\,/\,2.$$

nations of statement execution. Because of the time and effort required, this is usually an impossible goal except for extremely simple programs. (We illustrate why this is generally an impossible goal in Section 4.7.)

Because exhaustive testing is not feasible for most programs, different philosophies and methods of testing have evolved. At its most basic level, however, testing requires a conscious effort to ensure that a program works correctly and produces meaningful results. This means that careful thought must be given to what the test is meant to achieve and the data that will be used in the test. If testing reveals an error (bug), the process of debugging, which includes locating, correcting, and verifying the correction, can be initiated. It is important to realize that although testing may reveal the presence of an error, it does not necessarily indicate the absence of one. Thus, the fact that a test revealed one bug does not indicate that another one is not lurking somewhere else in the program.

To catch and correct errors in a program, it is important to develop a set of test data that can be used to determine whether the program gives correct answers. In fact, an accepted step in formal software development many times is to plan the test procedures and create meaningful test data before writing the code. This tends to help the person be more objective about what the program must do, because it essentially circumvents any subconscious temptation after coding to choose test data that will not work. The procedures for testing a program should examine every possible situation under which the program will be used. The program should be tested with data in a reasonable range as well as at the limits and in areas where the program should tell the user that the data are invalid. Developing good test procedures and data for sophisticated problems can be more difficult than writing the program code itself.

Backup

Although not part of the formal design process, it is critical to make and keep **backup copies** of the program at each step of the programming and debugging process. It is easy to delete or change beyond recognition the current working version of a program. Backup copies allow the recovery of the last stage of work with a minimum of effort. The final working version of a useful program should be backed up at least twice. In this regard, another useful programming proverb is "Backup is unimportant if you don't mind starting all over again." The three most fundamental rules of maintaining program and data integrity are:

1. backup!
2. Backup!
3. BACKUP!

Many organizations keep at least one backup on site, where it can be easily retrieved, and another backup copy either in a fireproof safe or at a remote location.

Exercises 1.3

1. a. List and describe the four steps required in the design and development stage of a program.

   b. In addition to the design and development phase, what are the other two phases required in producing a program and why are they required?

2. A note from your supervisor, Ms. J. Williams, says:

   Solve our payroll deduction problems.

   —J. Williams

   a. What should be your first task?

   b. How would you accomplish this task?

   c. How long would you expect this to take, assuming everyone cooperates?

3. Program development is only one phase in the overall software development procedure. Assuming that documentation and maintenance require 60% of the total software effort in designing a system, use Table 1.3 to determine the amount of effort required for initial program coding as a percentage of total software effort.

4. Many people requesting a program or system for the first time consider coding to be the most important aspect of program development. They feel that they know what they need and think that the programmer can begin coding with minimal time spent in analysis. As a programmer, what pitfalls can you envision in working with such people?

5. Many first-time computer users try to contract with programmers to provide programming for a fixed fee (total amount to be paid is fixed in advance). What is the advantage to the user in having this arrangement? What is the advantage to the programmer in having this arrangement? What are some disadvantages to both user and programmer in this arrangement?

6. Many programmers prefer to work on an hourly rate basis. Why do you think this is so? Under what conditions would it be advantageous for a programmer to give a client a fixed price for the programming effort?

7. Experienced users generally want a clearly written statement of programming work to be done, including a complete description of what the program will do, delivery dates, payment schedules, and testing requirements. What is the advantage to the user in requiring this? What is the advantage to a programmer in working under this arrangement? What disadvantages does this arrangement have for both user and programmer?

1.4 ALGORITHMS

Before a program is written, the programmer must clearly understand what data are to be used, the desired result, and the procedure to be used to produce this result. The procedure, or solution, selected is referred to as an algorithm. More precisely, an **algorithm** is defined as a step-by-step sequence of instructions that must terminate and describes how the data is to be processed to produce the desired outputs. In essence, an algorithm answers the question "What method will you use to solve this problem?"

Only after we clearly understand the data that we will be using and select an algorithm (the specific steps required to produce the desired result) can we code the program. Seen in this light, **programming** is the translation of a selected algorithm into a language that the computer can use.

To illustrate an algorithm, we will consider a simple problem. Assume that a program must calculate the sum of all whole numbers from 1 through 100. Figure 1.28 illustrates three methods we could use to find the required sum. Each method constitutes an algorithm.

Clearly, most people would not bother to list the possible alternatives in a detailed step-by-step manner, as we have done here, and then select one of the algorithms to solve the problem. But then, most people do not think algorithmically; they tend to think intuitively. For example, if you had to change a flat tire on your car, you would not think of all the steps required—you would simply change the tire or call someone else to do the job. This is an example of intuitive thinking.

Unfortunately, computers do not respond to intuitive commands. A general statement such as "add the numbers from 1 to 100" means nothing to a computer, because the computer can only respond to algorithmic commands written in an acceptable language such as C++. To program a computer successfully, you must clearly understand this difference between algorithmic and intuitive commands. A computer is an "algorithm-responding" machine; it is not an "intuitive-responding" machine. You cannot tell a computer to change a tire or to add the numbers from 1 through 100. Instead, you must give the computer a detailed step-by-step set of instructions that, collectively, forms an algorithm. For example, the following set of instructions forms a detailed method, or algorithm, for determining the sum of the numbers from 1 through 100:

Set n equal to 100.
Set a = 1.
Set b equal to 100.

Calculate $sum = \frac{n(a + b)}{2}$.

Print the sum.

Notice that these instructions are not a computer program. Unlike a program, which must be written in a language the computer can respond to, an algorithm can be written or described in various ways. When English-like phrases are used to describe the algorithm (the processing steps), as in this example, the description is called **pseudocode.** When mathematical equations are used, the descrip-

FIGURE 1.28 Summing the Numbers 1 Through 100

Method 1 — Columns: Arrange the numbers from 1 to 100 in a column and add them

$$\begin{array}{r} 1 \\ 2 \\ 3 \\ 4 \\ \bullet \\ \bullet \\ \bullet \\ 98 \\ 99 \\ +\ 100 \\ \hline 5050 \end{array}$$

Method 2 — Groups: Arrange the numbers in groups that sum to 100. Multiply the number of groups by 100 and add in any unused numbers.

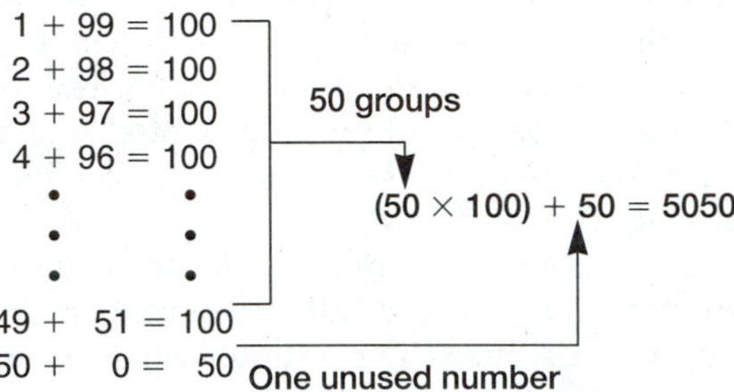

Method 3 — Formula: Use the formula

$$\text{Sum} = \frac{n(a+b)}{2}$$

where

n = number of terms to be added (100)
a = first number to be added (1)
b = last number to be added (100)

$$\text{Sum} = \frac{100(1+100)}{2} = 5050$$

tion is called a *formula*. When diagrams that employ the symbols shown in Figure 1.29 are used, the description is referred to as a **flowchart.** Figure 1.30 on p. 36 illustrates the use of these symbols in depicting an algorithm for determining the average of three numbers.

Because flowcharts are cumbersome to revise and can easily support unstructured programming practices, they have fallen out of favor by professional programmers, whereas the use of pseudocode to express the logic of

FIGURE 1.29 Flowchart Symbols

SYMBOL	NAME	DESCRIPTION
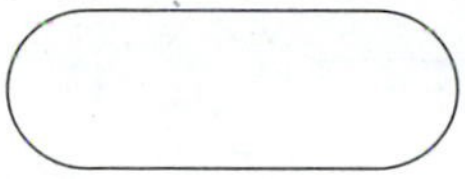	Terminal	Indicates the beginning or end of an algorithm
	Input/Output	Indicates an input or output operation
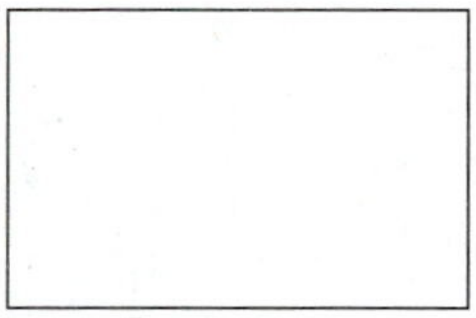	Process	Indicates computation or data manipulation
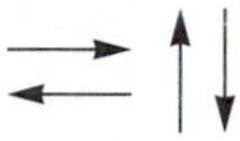	Flow Lines	Connects the flowchart symbols and indicates the logic flow
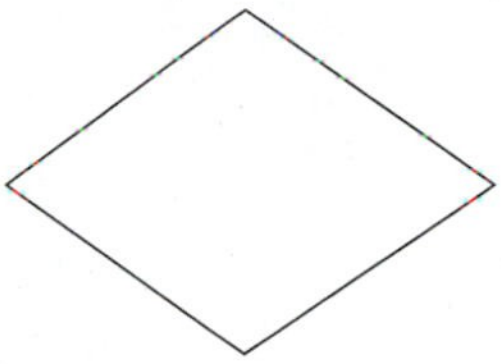	Decision	Indicates a program branch point
	Loop	Indicates the initial, limit, and increment values of a loop
	Predefined Process	Indicates a predefined process, as in calling a function
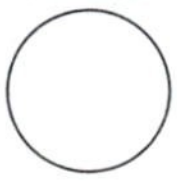	Connector	Indicates an entry to, or exit from, another part of the flowchart or a connection point
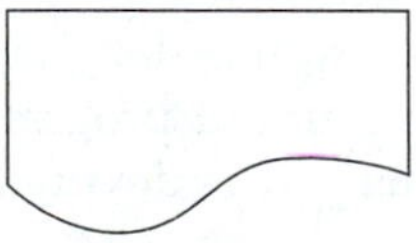	Report	Indicates a written output report

FIGURE 1.30 Flowchart for Calculating the Average of Three Numbers

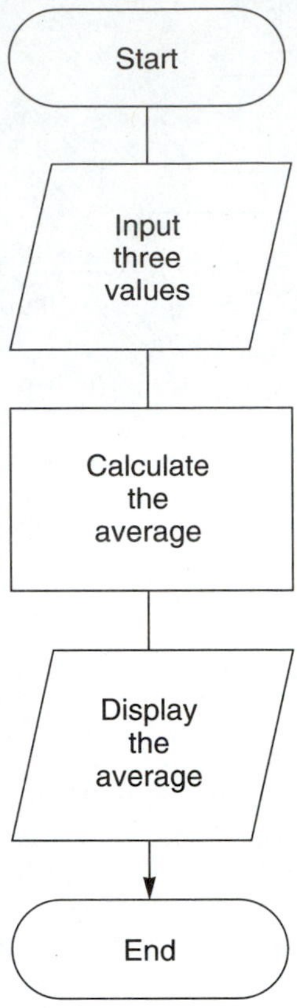

algorithms has gained increasing acceptance. In describing an algorithm using pseudocode, short English phrases are used. For example, acceptable pseudocode for describing the steps needed to compute the average of three numbers is:

Input the three numbers into the computer's memory.
Calculate the average by adding the numbers and dividing the sum by three.
Display the average.

Only after an algorithm has been selected and the programmer understands the steps required can the algorithm be written using computer-language statements. The writing of an algorithm using computer-language statements is called coding the algorithm, which is the third step in our program development procedure (see Figure 1.31). Most of Part I of this text is devoted to showing you how to develop and code algorithms into C++.

FIGURE 1.31 Coding an Algorithm

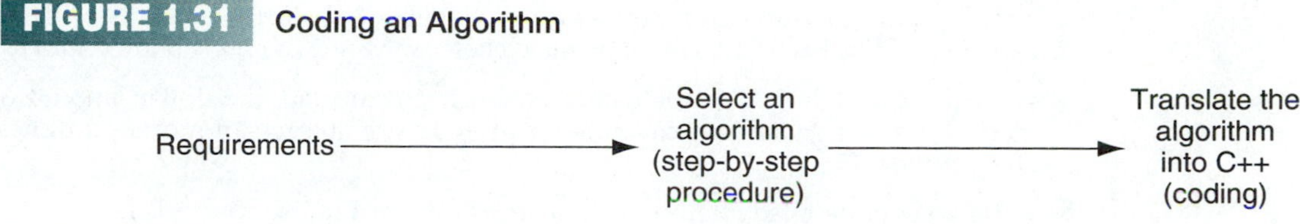

Exercises 1.4

1. Determine a step-by-step procedure (list the steps) to do the following tasks (*Note:* There is no one single correct answer for each of these tasks. The exercise is designed to give you practice in converting intuitive-type commands into equivalent algorithms and making the shift between the thought processes involved in the two types of thinking.)
   a. Fix a flat tire.
   b. Make a telephone call.
   c. Go to the store and purchase a loaf of bread.
   d. Roast a turkey.
2. a. Determine the six possible step-by-step procedures (list the steps) to paint the flower shown in Figure 1.32, with the restriction that each color must be completed before a new color can be started. (*Hint:* One of the algorithms is "Use yellow first, green second, black last.)
   b. Which of the six painting algorithms (series of steps) is best if we are limited to using one paintbrush and there is no turpentine to clean the brush?

FIGURE 1.32 A Simple Paint-by-Number Figure

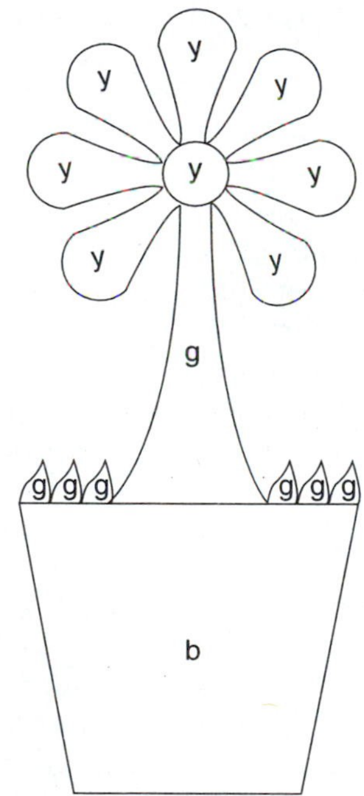

Code:
y=yellow
g=green
b=black

3. Determine and write an algorithm (list the steps) to interchange the contents of two cups of liquid. Assume that a third cup is available to hold the contents of either cup temporarily. Each cup should be rinsed before any new liquid is poured into it.
4. Write a detailed set of instructions, in English, to calculate the dollar amount of money in a piggybank that contains *h* half-dollars, *q* quarters, *n* nickels, *d* dimes, and *p* pennies.
5. Write a set of detailed, step-by-step instructions, in English, to find the smallest number in a group of three integer numbers.
6. a. Write a set of detailed, step-by-step instructions, in English, to calculate the change remaining from a dollar after a purchase is made. Assume that the cost of the goods purchased is less than a dollar. The change received should consist of the smallest number of coins possible.
   b. Repeat Exercise 6a, but assume the change is to be given only in pennies.
7. a. Write an algorithm to locate the first occurrence of the name WESTBY in a list of names arranged in random order.
   b. Discuss how you could improve your algorithm for Exercise 7a if the list of names were arranged in alphabetical order.
8. Write an algorithm to determine the total occurrences of the letter *e* in any sentence.
9. Determine and write an algorithm to sort four numbers into ascending (from lowest to highest) order.

1.5 PLANNING FOR OBJECTS: OBJECT-ORIENTED PROGRAMMING

We live in a world full of objects—planes, trains, cars, telephones, books, computers, etc. Until quite recently, however, programming techniques have not reflected this at all. The primary programming paradigm[7] has been procedural, where a program is defined as an algorithm written in a machine-readable language. The reasons for this emphasis on procedural programming are primarily historical.

When computers were developed in the 1940s they were initially used by mathematicians for military purposes, such as computing bomb trajectories and decoding enemy orders and diplomatic transmissions. After World War II computers were still used primarily by mathematicians for mathematical computations. This reality was reflected in the name of the first commercially available high-level language introduced in 1957. The language's name was FORTRAN, an acronym for FORmula TRANslation. Further reflecting this predominant mathematical/engineering use was the fact that in the 1960s almost all computer courses were taught in either engineering or mathematics departments. The term *computer science* was not yet in common use and computer science departments were just being formed.

This situation has changed dramatically, primarily for two reasons. One of the reasons for disenchantment with strictly procedural-oriented programs has been their failure in containing software costs. Software costs include all costs associated with initial program development and subsequent program maintenance. As illustrated in Figure 1.33, the major cost of most computer projects today, whether technical or commercial, is for software.

[7] A *paradigm* is a standard way of thinking about or doing something.

FIGURE 1.33 Software Is the Major Cost of Most Computer Projects

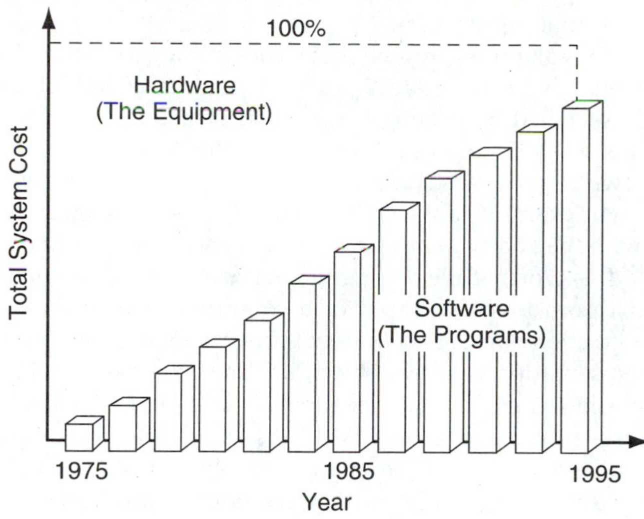

Software costs contribute so heavily to total project costs because they are directly related to human productivity, which is labor intensive, while the equipment associated with hardware costs is related to manufacturing technologies. For example, microchips that cost over $500 ten years ago can now be purchased for less than $1.

It is far easier, however, to dramatically increase manufacturing productivity a thousand-fold, with the consequent decrease in hardware costs, than it is for programmers to double either the quantity or quality of the code they produce. So as hardware costs have plummeted, software productivity and its associated costs have remained relatively constant. Thus, the ratio of software costs to total system costs (hardware plus software) has increased dramatically.

One way to significantly increase programmer productivity is to create code that can be reused without extensive revision, retesting, and revalidation. The inability of procedurally structured code to provide this type of reusability has led to the search for other software approaches.

The second reason for disenchantment with strictly procedural-based programming has been the emergence of graphical screens and the subsequent interest in window applications. Programming multiple windows on the same graphical screen is virtually impossible using standard procedural programming techniques.

The solution to producing programs that efficiently manipulate graphical screens and provide reusable windowing code was found in artificial intelligence-based and simulation programming techniques. The former area, artificial intelligence, contained extensive research on geometrical object specification and recognition. The latter area, simulation, contained considerable background on simulating items as objects with well-defined interactions between them. This object-based paradigm fitted well in a graphical windows environment, in which each window can be specified as a self-contained object.

An object is also well suited to a programming representation because it can be specified by two basic characteristics: a current *state*, which defines how the object appears at the moment, and a *behavior*, which defines how the object reacts to external inputs.

To make this more tangible, consider a geometric object, such as a rectangle. A rectangle's current state is defined by its shape and location. The shape is traditionally specified by its length and width, while its location can be specified in a number of ways. One simple way is to list the values of two corner positions. The behavior we provide a rectangle depends on what we are willing to have our rectangle do. For example, if we intend to display the rectangle on a screen we might provide it with the ability to move its position and change either its length or width.

It is worthwhile distinguishing here between an actual rectangle, which might exist on a piece of paper or a computer screen, and our description of it. Our description is more accurately termed a model. By definition, a **model** is merely a representation of a real object, it is not the object itself. Very few models are ever complete; that is, a model typically does not reveal every aspect of the object it represents. Each model is defined for a particular purpose that usually only requires representing the part of an object's state or behavior that is of interest to us. To clarify this point further, consider another common object, an elevator.

Like all objects, an elevator can be modeled in terms of a state and a behavior. Its state might be given in terms of its size, location, interior decoration, or any number of attributes. Likewise, its behavior might be specified in terms of its reaction when one of its buttons is pushed. Constructing a model of an elevator, however, requires that we select those attributes and behavior that are of interest to us. For purposes of a simulation, for example, we may only be concerned with the current floor position of the elevator and how to make it move to another floor location. Other attributes and behavior of the elevator may be left out of the model because they do not affect the aspects of the elevator that we want to study.

It is also important to distinguish between the attributes we choose to include in our model and the values that these attributes can have. The attributes and behavior together define a category or type of object out of which many individual objects can be designated. In object-oriented programming the category of objects defined by a given set of attributes and behavior is called a **class**. Only when specific values have been assigned to the attributes is a particular object defined.

For example, the attributes of length and width can be used to define a general type of shape called a rectangle. Only when specific values have been assigned to these attributes have we represented a particular rectangle. This distinction carries over into C++: The attributes and behavior we select are said to define a general class, or type, of object. The object itself only comes into existence when we assign specific values to the attributes.

Before we can become fluent with C++'s object-oriented capabilities, however, we will first need to understand C++'s procedure-oriented side. The procedural aspects of C++ are the focus of Part I. The object-oriented aspects of C++ are then presented in Part II.

Exercises 1.5

1. Define the following terms:

   a. attribute

   b. behavior

c. state

d. model

e. class

f. object

g. interface

2. Define an appropriate class for each of the following specific objects:

   a. the number 5

   b. a square that is 4″ by 4″

   c. this textbook

   d. a 1955 Ford Thunderbird car

   e. the last ballpoint pen that you used

3. a. For each of the following, determine what attributes might be of interest to someone considering buying the item.

   a book
   a can of soda
   a pen
   a cassette tape
   a cassette tape player
   an elevator
   a car

   b. Do the attributes you used in Exercise 3a model an object or a class of objects?

4. a. What operations should the following objects be capable of doing?:

   a Ford Thunderbird car
   the last ballpoint pen that you used

   b. Do the operations determined for Exercise 4a apply only to the particular object listed or are they more general and thus applicable to all objects of the type listed?

5. a. Besides the attributes of length and width that are necessary to describe a rectangle, what other characteristics of a rectangle would be useful if the rectangle is to be drawn on a color monitor?

   b. Determine how a rectangle's position on a screen might be specified.

6. a. What characteristics are necessary to specify the position and size of a circle that is to be placed on a monitor's screen?

   b. What additional characteristics could be specified for a circle if it is to be drawn on a color monitor?

7. All of the examples of classes considered in this section have consisted of inanimate objects. Do you think classes of animate objects could be constructed? Why or why not?

8. a. Consider a class of dates, in which each date is of the form month/day/year. For such a class, is it appropriate to consider the date 12/25/98 as an object?

   b. Determine what operations might be appropriate for a date class.

   c. Determine what operations would not be appropriate for a date class.

9. Consider a class of strings, where each string consists of a sequence of alphanumeric characters (letters, digits, and special characters, such as $,?,!,.,*).

   a. Determine what operations would be appropriate for this class.

   b. Determine what operations would not be appropriate for this class.

10. a. The attributes of a class represent how objects of the class appear to the outside world. The behavior represents how an object of a class reacts to an external

stimulus. Given this information, what do you think is the mechanism by which one object "triggers" the designated behavior in another object? (*Hint:* Consider how one person typically gets another person to do something.)

b. If behavior in C++ is constructed by defining an appropriate function, how do you think the behavior is activated in C++?

Improving Communication

11. Respond to the following request:

    MEMORANDUM

    To: U. R. Aprogramer

    From: Head of Programming Dept.

    Subject: Preliminary Analysis Phase

    Per our prior discussion, you will be interviewing a number of people in the company. Your goal, as we discussed, is to determine how many projects they have been involved in that have been completely specified at the start of the project. Please give me a list of questions you intend to ask and how you intend to approach the interviewees for their permission to conduct the interview.

12. Respond to the following request:

    MEMORANDUM

    To: U. R. It

    From: Head of Programming Dept.

    Subject: Sampling Project

    We spent a large part of the last meeting with the marketing department discussing how the input screen should look for the new Sampling Project. Jan Programmer complained to me after the meeting that she had no interest in the input screen; that it was a boring and professionally unexciting topic, and that we should just give her the required specifications for the screen and let her do her job. Later in the day, Joan Muchsuccess, head of marketing, contacted me and said she was not impressed with Jan, did not think Jan really understood or cared about the project, and would like another programmer assigned to the task. I know Jan is one of our cracker-jack programmers and that the analysis of the data is extremely complicated and requires someone as capable as Jan. How should we handle this?

Working in Teams

13. One of the major phases of any programming project is determining what must be accomplished. Most students never get a real understanding of this phase because assignments, both programming and nonprogramming, are usually well defined, either by the professor or as written exercises in a textbook.

    a. Discuss with each of your team members how homework has been assigned throughout their educational careers. See if there is some consensus on the percentage of problems assigned for which there was sufficient information to solve the problem.

b. How might you quantify the results of your discussions with your team members?

c. Take a moment and review how you typically react when an assignment is not totally specified; that is, when some piece of information is missing from the problem. Do you get annoyed or angry? Do you feel relieved? Determine with your team members what their reactions have been. Can you determine a pattern in reactions? Which reactions do you think are most likely to yield negative results in the working world?

d. Take a moment and review what you typically do when an assignment is not totally specified; that is, when some piece of information is missing from the problem. For example, do you:

Use it as an excuse not to do the assignment at all?
Attempt to solve the problem and stop when you reach the point where the missing information is needed?
Make assumptions about what the missing information is, and solve the problem using your assumed data?
Use it as a means of making the instructor wrong for not giving you all the information required?

e. Determine what your team members typically do when an assignment is not totally specified and see if the team can determine a pattern.

f. Summarize the findings of your team in a memorandum to your professor.

14. a. Decide with your team members what might be some useful questions to ask people in the working world to find out their experience with assigned projects. Specifically, you want to determine the percentage of projects that are completely specified at the start of a project. Include in your discussions ways you can approach people to encourage them to speak with you, both for this project and for future projects.

b. Use the results of Exercise 12a to question as many people in the working world as you can. Compare your results with those obtained by your team members and see if there is a pattern to your results.

c. Summarize the finding of your team members in a memorandum to your professor.

15. Computer science professionals work in a number of different environments that include academia, scientific research labs, new-venture computer companies, and commercial corporations. To be successful in each environment, a different mixture of skills is frequently needed.

a. Decide with your team members what might be some useful questions to ask people in these working environments to determine what skills they think are required for success. Include in your discussions ways you might approach people to encourage them to speak with you, both for this project and for future projects.

b. Use the results of Exercise 13a to question as many computer professionals as you can.

c. Use the results of Exercise 13a to question supervisors of computer professionals. If possible, contact the supervisors of the people you interviewed in Exercise 13b. (*Hint:* Use both the academic departments in your college as well as the nonacademic departments.)

d. Compare your results with those of your team members and prepare a summary of your findings in a memorandum to your professor.

16. Two interesting statements are the following: "If you think something is true, it is true" and "Just because you think something is true does not make it so." Discuss these statements with your team members and see if you can come to some consensus as to their validity. Are these statements necessarily contradictory? How might these statements be of value to you in interviewing people and determining the requirements for a new computer system?

A BIT OF BACKGROUND

Binary ABC

Dr. John V. Atanasoff agonized several years over the design of a computing machine to help his Iowa State University graduate students solve complex equations. He considered building a machine based on binary numbers—the most natural system to use with electromechanical equipment that had one of two easily recognizable states, on and off—but feared people would not use a machine that was not based on the familiar and comfortable decimal system.

Finally, on a cold evening at a roadhouse in Illinois in 1937, he determined that it had to be done the simplest and least expensive way, with binary digits (bits). During the next two years he and graduate student Clifford Berry built the first electronic digital computer, called the *ABC* (for Atanasoff-Berry computer). Since that time the vast majority of computers have been binary machines.

17. Suppose you interview 10 people in an organization and all of them agree on exactly what is needed and what you must do to produce a desired computer system. As a programmer, can you proceed with complete confidence to the design phase? Discuss this with your team members and come up with a few examples that confirm your position. Determine if there are any situations in which your conclusions might not be 100% correct.
18. Some programmers take the position that whatever their client or supervisor requests they, as programmers, should do without question. Discuss the pros and cons of taking this approach with your team members assuming you are all programmers. Then discuss the pros and cons of this approach assuming you are all supervisors of programmers.

1.6 A CLOSER LOOK AT DIGITAL STORAGE CONCEPTS

The physical components used in manufacturing a computer require that the numbers and letters stored by a computer are not stored using the same symbols that people use. The number that we know as 126, for example, is not stored using the symbols 126. Nor is the letter that we recognize as A stored using this symbol. In this section, we will see why this is so, and how most computers store numbers. In Chapter 2 we will see how letters are stored.

The smallest and most basic data item in a computer is called a **bit**. Physically, a bit is really a switch that can be either open or closed. By convention, the open and closed positions of each switch are represented as a 0 and a 1, respectively.

A single bit that can represent the value 0 or 1, by itself, has limited usefulness. All computers, therefore, group a set number of bits together, both for storage and transmission. The grouping of eight bits to form a larger unit is an almost universal computer standard. Such groups are commonly referred to as **bytes**. A single byte consisting of eight bits, where each bit can be set to either a 0 or 1, can represent any one of 256 distinct patterns. These consist of the pattern 00000000 (all eight switches open) to the pattern 11111111 (all eight switches closed), and all possible combinations of 0's and 1's between. Each of these patterns can be used to represent either a letter of the alphabet, other single charac-

FIGURE 1.34 An Eight-Bit Value Box

−128	64	32	16	8	4	2	1

ters, such as a dollar sign, comma, etc., a single digit, or numbers containing more than one digit. The collection of patterns consisting of 0's and 1's used to represent letters, single digits, and other single characters are called *character codes* (two such codes, the ASCII and EBCDIC codes, are presented in Section 2.3). The patterns used to store numbers are called *number codes,* one of which is presented next.

Two's Complement Numbers

The most common number code for storing integer values inside a computer is called the **two's complement** representation. Using this code, the integer equivalent of any bit pattern, such as 10001101, is easy to determine and can be found for either positive or negative integers with no change in the conversion method. For convenience we will assume byte-sized bit patterns consisting of a set of eight bits each, although the procedure carries directly over to larger size bit patterns.

The easiest way to determine the integer represented by each bit pattern is to first construct a simple device called a *value box.* Figure 1.34 illustrates such a box for a single byte. Mathematically, each value in the box illustrated in Figure 1.34 represents an increasing power of two. Since two's complement numbers must be capable of representing both positive and negative integers, the leftmost position, in addition to having the largest absolute magnitude, also has a negative sign.

Conversion of any binary number, for example, 10001101, simply requires inserting the bit pattern in the value box and adding the values having ones under them. Thus, as illustrated in Figure 1.35, the bit pattern 10001101 represents the integer number −115.

The value box can also be used in reverse, to convert a base 10 integer number into its equivalent binary bit pattern. Some conversions, in fact, can be made by inspection. For example, the base 10 number −125 is obtained by adding 3 to −128. Thus, the binary representation of −125 is 10000011, which equals −128 + 2 + 1. Similarly, the two's complement representation of the number 40 is 00101000, which is 32 plus 8.

FIGURE 1.35 Converting 10001101 to a Base 10 Number

−128		64		32		16		8		4		2		1	
1		0		0		0		1		1		0		1	
−128	+	0	+	0	+	0	+	8	+	4	+	0	+	1	= −115

Although the value box conversion method is deceptively simple, the method is directly related to the underlying mathematical basis of two's complement binary numbers. The original name of the two's complement code was the weighted-sign code, which correlates directly to the value box. As the name *weighted sign* implies, each bit position has a weight, or value, of two raised to a power and a sign. The signs of all bits except the leftmost bit are positive and the sign of the leftmost bit is negative.

In reviewing the value box, it is evident that any two's complement binary number with a leading 1 represents a negative number, and any bit pattern with a leading 0 represents a positive number. Using the value box it is easy to determine the most positive and negative values capable of being stored. The most negative value that can be stored in a single byte is the decimal number −128, which has the bit pattern 10000000. Any other nonzero bit will simply add a positive amount to the number. Additionally, it is clear that a positive number must have a 0 as its leftmost bit. From this you can see that the largest positive eight-bit two's complement number is 01111111 or 127.

Words and Addresses

One or more bytes may themselves be grouped into larger units, called *words*, which facilitate faster and more extensive data access. For example, retrieving a word consisting of four bytes from a computer's memory results in more information than that obtained by retrieving a word consisting of a single byte. Such a retrieval is also considerably faster than four individual byte retrievals. This increase in speed and capacity, however, is achieved by an increase in the computer's cost and complexity.

Early personal computers, such as the Apple IIe and Commodore machines, internally stored and transmitted words consisting of single bytes. AT&T 6300 and IBM PC/XTs use word sizes consisting of two bytes, whereas Digital Equipment computers and Intel 486 and pentium computers process words consisting of four bytes each. Super computers, such as the CRAY-1 and Control Data 7000, have six- and eight-byte words, respectively.

The arrangement of words in a computer's memory can be compared to the arrangement of suites in a very large hotel, where each suite is made up of rooms of the same size. Just as each suite has a unique room number to locate and identify it, each word has a unique numeric address. In computers that allow each byte to be individually accessed, each byte has its own address. Like room numbers, word and byte addresses are always non-negative, whole numbers that are used for location and identification purposes. Also, like hotel rooms with connecting doors for forming larger suites, words can be combined to form larger units for the accommodation of different size data types.

1.7 COMMON PROGRAMMING ERRORS

The most common errors associated with the material presented in this chapter are as follows:

1. A major programming error made by most beginning programmers is the rush to write and run a program before fully understanding what is required, including the algorithms that will be used to produce the desired result. A symptom of this haste to get a program entered into the computer is the lack of any documentation or even a program outline or a written program itself. Many problems can be caught just by checking a copy of the program or even a description of the algorithm written in pseudocode.

2. A second major error is not backing up a program. Almost all new programmers make this mistake until they lose a program that has taken considerable time to code.

3. The third error made by many new programmers is the lack of understanding that computers respond only to explicitly defined algorithms. Telling a computer to add a group of numbers is quite different than telling a friend to add the numbers. The computer must be given the precise instructions for doing the addition in a programming language.

1.8 CHAPTER REVIEW

Key Terms

algorithm
ALU
analysis
application software
assembler
assembly language
backup copies
bit
boot
bytes
CD-ROM
central processing unit (CPU)
class
coding
compiled language
compiler
computer program
control unit
documentation
floppy diskette
flowchart
hard disk
hardware
high-level language
input/output (I/O) unit
invocation
iteration
interpreted language
interpreter
low-level language
machine language
memory unit
microprocessor
model
object-oriented language
opcode
operating system
procedure-oriented language
programming
programming language
pseudocode
RAM
refinement
repetition
ROM
secondary storage
selection
sequence
software
software development procedure
software engineering
software maintenance
source code
source program
syntax
system software
testing
two's complement
very large scale integrated (VLSI)

Summary

1. The first attempt at creating a self-operating computational machine was attempted by Charles Babbage in 1822. The concept became a reality with the Atanasoff-Berry computer built in 1937 at Iowa State University, which was

the first computer to use a binary numbering scheme to store and manipulate data. Two of the earliest large-scale digital computers were the ENIAC, built in 1946 at the Moore School of Engineering of the University of Pennsylvania, and the Mark I, built at Harvard University in 1944. All of these machines, however, required external wiring to perform the desired operations. The first computer to employ the concept of a stored program was the EDSAC, built at Cambridge University in England. The design and operating principles used in the design of this machine, developed by the mathematician John Von Neumann, are still used by most of the computers manufactured today.

2. The physical components used in constructing a computer are called its hardware. These components include input, processing, output, memory, and storage units.
3. The programs used to operate a computer are referred to as software.
4. Programming languages come in a variety of forms and types. Machine language programs, also known as executable programs, contain the binary codes that can be executed by a computer. Assembly languages permit the use of symbolic names for mathematical operations and memory addresses. Programs written in assembly languages must be converted to machine language, using translator programs called assemblers, before the programs can be executed. Assembly and machine languages are referred to as low-level languages.

   Compiler and interpreter languages are referred to as high-level languages. This means that they are written using instructions that resemble a written language, such as English, and can be run on a variety of computer types. Compiler languages require a compiler to translate the program into a binary language form, whereas interpreter languages require an interpreter to do the translation.
5. As a discipline, software engineering is concerned with creating readable, efficient, reliable, and maintainable programs and systems.
6. The software development procedure consists of three phases:
   - Program development and design
   - Documentation
   - Maintenance.
7. The program development and design phase consists of four well-defined steps:
   - Analyze the problem
   - Develop a solution
   - Code the solution
   - Test and correct the solution.
8. An algorithm is a step-by-step procedure that must terminate and describes how a computation or task is to be performed.
9. A computer program is a self-contained unit of instructions used to operate a computer to produce a specific result. More formally, a computer program is a description of an algorithm written in a language that can be processed by a computer.

10. The four fundamental control structures are:

    - Sequence
    - Selection
    - Iteration
    - Invocation.

Exercises

1. List the type of programming languages used with each generation.
2. a. What are the phases required in the software development procedure?

   b. List the steps required in the first phase of the software development procedure.
3. Define the term *algorithm.*
4. Define the term *syntax.*
5. Determine the input(s) and output(s) for the following:

   a. Given the radius of a circle find the circumference

   b. Given two real numbers, A and B, calculate a sum (A + B), a difference (A − B), a product (A * B) and the quotients A / B and B / A.

   c. The final grades for your four courses last semester were B+ (3.3), A (4.0), B (3.0), and A− (3.6). What was your average grade point (on a 4.0 scale) for the term, assuming each course was worth three credits.
6. Assume that a computer store makes, on average, 15 sales per day. Assuming that the store is open six days a week and that each sale requires an average of 100 characters, determine the minimum storage that the system must have to keep all sales records for a two-year period.
7. Assume that you are creating a sales recording system for a client. Each sale input to the system requires that the operator type in a description of the item sold, the name and address of the firm buying the item, the value of the item, and a code for the person making the trade. This information consists of a maximum of 300 characters. Estimate the time it would take for an average typist to input 200 sales. (*Hint:* To solve this problem, you must make an assumption about the number of words per minute that an average typist can type and the average number of characters per word.)
8. Many dot matrix printers can print at a speed of 165 characters per second. Using such a printer, determine the time it would take to print a complete list of 10,000 records. Assume that each record consists of 300 characters.

PART

I

Procedure–Oriented Programming in C++

Although C++ is an object-oriented language, it was developed as an extension to C, which is a procedural-oriented language. As such, C++ is a hybrid language having both procedural and object features. Because of this hybrid nature it is not only possible to write a complete C++ program using only procedural code but it is impossible to write an object-oriented program in C++ that does not include procedural elements. Thus, a proper start to learning C++ requires familiarity with its procedural aspects.

In addition to presenting the procedural basics of C++, Part I also introduces C++'s object side. This is done by presenting the `cin` and `cout` objects, which have immediate use in providing interactive input and output capabilities, respectively, and by the Planning for Objects sections included within each chapter. These Planning sections provide an understanding of the thought processes needed for developing and creating object-based programs. They can either be read along with the material in their respective chapters or postponed and read concurrently with the material in Part II.

CHAPTER

2 Problem Solving Using C++

2.1 INTRODUCTION TO C++

A well-designed program is constructed using a design philosophy similar to that used in constructing a well-designed building: It doesn't just happen; it depends on careful planning and execution if the final design is to accomplish its intended purpose. Just as an integral part of the design of a building is its structure, the same is true for a program.

Programs whose structure consists of interrelated segments, arranged in a logical and easily understandable order to form an integrated and complete unit, are referred to as *modular programs* (Figure 2.1). Modular programs are noticeably easier to develop, correct, and modify than programs constructed in some other manner. In programming terminology, the smaller segments used to construct a modular program are referred to as **modules.**

Each module is designed and developed to perform a specific task, and is really a small subprogram all by itself. A complete C++ program is constructed by combining as many modules as necessary to produce the desired result. The

FIGURE 2.1 A Well-Designed Program Is Built Using Modules

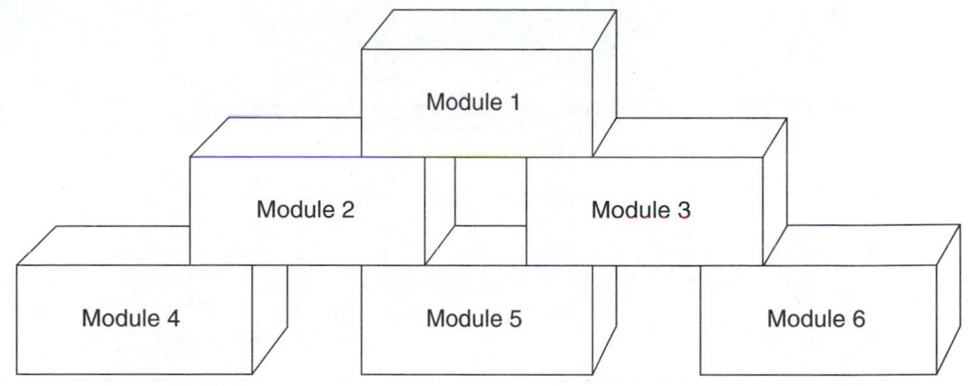

advantage of modular construction is that the overall design of the program can be developed before any single module is written. Once the requirements for each module are finalized, the modules can be programmed and integrated within the overall program as they are completed.

In C++, modules can be either classes or functions. It helps to think of a **function** as a small machine that transforms the data it receives into a finished product. For example, Figure 2.2 illustrates a function that accepts two numbers as inputs and multiplies the two numbers to produce one output. As shown, the interface to the function is its inputs and results. The process of converting the inputs to results is both encapsulated and hidden within the function. In this regard the function can be thought of as a single unit providing a special-purpose operation. A similar analogy is appropriate for a class.

A **class** is a more complicated unit than a function because it contains both data and specific functions appropriate for manipulating the data. Thus, unlike a function, which is used to encapsulate a set of operations, a class encapsulates both data and one or more sets of operations. As such, each class contains all of the elements required for the input, output, and processing of its objects and can be thought of as a small dedicated computer. Initially, we will be predominantly concerned with the more basic function module.

One important requirement for designing a good function or class is to give it a name that conveys to the reader some idea about what the function or class does. The names permissible for functions and classes are also used to name other elements of the C++ language, and are collectively referred to as **identifiers.** Identifiers can be made up of any combination of letters, digits, or underscores (_) selected according to the following rules:

1. The first character of the name must be a letter or underscore (_).
2. Only letters, digits, or underscores may follow the initial letter. Blank spaces are not allowed; use the underscore to separate words in a name consisting of multiple words.

FIGURE 2.2 A Multiplying Function

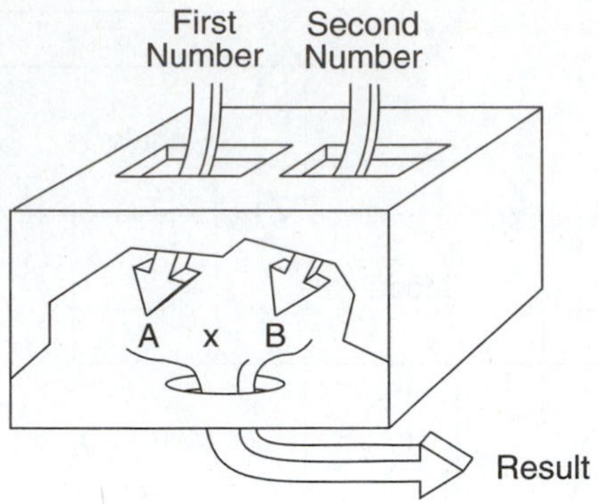
First Number
Second Number
A x B
Result

3. A function name cannot be one of the keywords listed in Table 2.1. (A **keyword** is a word that is set aside by the language for a special purpose and can only be used in a specified manner.[1])
4. The number of characters in a function name is limited to 31 characters.

Examples of valid C++ identifiers are:

```
DegToRad     intersect     addNums     slope
bessel1      mult_two      FindMax     density
```

Examples of invalid identifiers are:

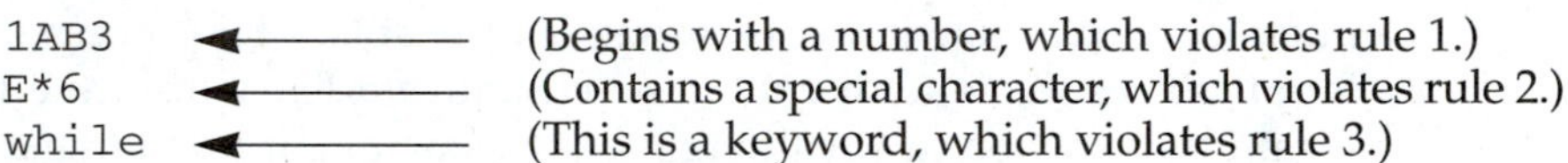
1AB3
E*6
while
(Begins with a number, which violates rule 1.)
(Contains a special character, which violates rule 2.)
(This is a keyword, which violates rule 3.)

TABLE 2.1 Keywords

auto	delete	goto	public	template
break	do	if	register	this
case	double	inline	return	typedef
catch	else	int	short	union
char	enum	long	signed	unsigned
class	extern	new	sizeof	virtual
const	float	overload	static	void
continue	for	private	struct	volatile
default	friend	protected	switch	while

[1] Keywords in C++ are also reserved words, which means they must be used only for their specified purpose. If you attempt to use them for any other purpose, C++ will generate an error message.

In addition to conforming to C++'s identifier rules, a C++ function name must always be followed by parentheses (the reason for this is explained shortly). Also, a good function name should be a mnemonic. A **mnemonic** is a word or name designed as a memory aid. For example, the function name `DegToRad()` (note that we have included the required parentheses after the identifier, which clearly marks this as a function name) is a mnemonic if it is the name of a function that converts degrees to radians. Here, the name itself helps to identify what the function does.

Examples of valid function names that are not mnemonics are:

```
easy()    c3po()    r2d2()    TheForce()    mike()
```

Function names that are not mnemonic should not be used because they convey no information about what the function does.

Notice that function names can be typed in mixed uppercase and lowercase letters. This is becoming increasingly common in C++, although it is not absolutely necessary. All uppercase identifiers are usually reserved for symbolic constants, a topic covered in Section 3.5.

Note that C++ is a *case-sensitive* language. This means that the compiler distinguishes between uppercase and lowercase letters. Thus, in C++, the names TOTAL, total, and TotaL represent three distinct and different names.

The `main()` Function

A distinct advantage of using functions and classes in C++ is that the overall structure of the program, in general, and individual modules, in particular, can be planned in advance, including provisions for testing and verifying each module's operation. Each function and class can then be written to meet its intended objective.

To provide for the orderly placement and execution of modules, each C++ program must have one and only one function named `main()`. The `main()` function is referred to as a *driver function,* because it drives, or tells the other modules the sequence in which they are to execute (Figure 2.3).[2]

Figure 2.4 illustrates a structure for the `main()` function. The first line of the function, in this case `int main()` is referred to as a *function header line.* A function header line, which is always the first line of a function, contains three pieces of information[3]:

1. What type of data, if any, is returned from the function
2. The name of the function
3. What type of data, if any, is sent into the function.

The keyword before the function name defines the type of value the function returns when it has completed operating. When placed before the function's name the keyword `int` (see Table 2.1) designates that the function will return an integer value. Similarly, when the parentheses following the function name are empty, `it` signifies that no data will be transmitted into the function when it is run. (Data transmitted into a function at run time are referred to as **arguments** of the function.) The braces, `{` and `}`, determine the beginning and end of the function body and enclose the statements making up the function. The statements inside the braces determine what the function does. Each statement inside the function must end with a semicolon (`;`).

[2] Modules executed from `main()` may, in turn, execute other modules. Each module, however, always returns to the module that initiated its execution. This is true even for `main()`, which returns control to the operating system.

[3] A class method must also begin with a header line that adheres to these same rules.

FIGURE 2.3 The `main()` Function Directs All Other Functions

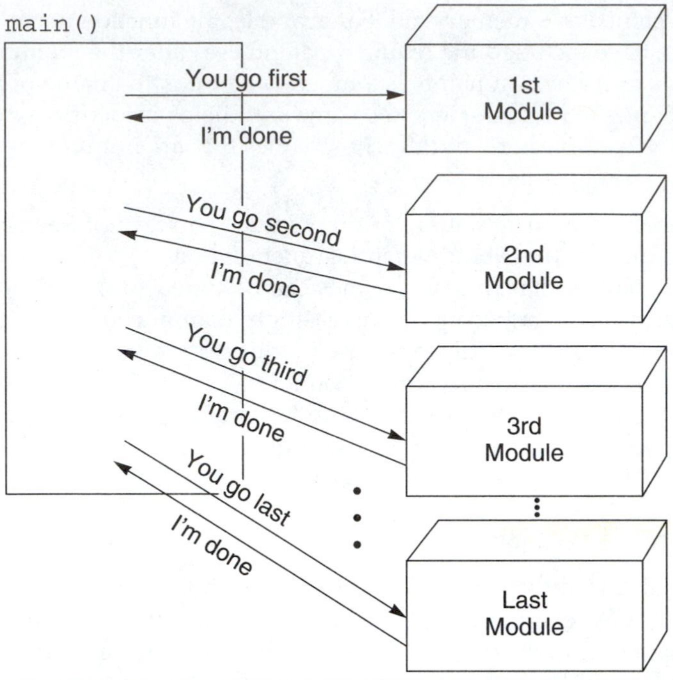

You will be naming and writing many of your own C++ functions. In fact, the rest of this book is primarily about the statements required to construct useful functions and how to combine functions and data into useful classes and programs. Each program, however, must have one and only one `main()` function. Until we learn how to pass data into a function and return data from a function (the topics of Chapter 6), the header line illustrated in Figure 2.4 will serve us for all the programs we need to write. For simple programs the first two lines

```
int main()
{
```

designate that "the program begins here," while the last two lines

```
  return 0;
}
```

designate the end of the program. Fortunately, many useful functions and classes have already been written for us. We will now see how to use an object created from one of these classes to create our first working C++ program.

The `cout` Object

One of the most versatile and commonly used objects provided in C++ is named `cout` (pronounced "see out"). This object, whose name is derived from Console OUTput, is an output object that sends data given to it to the standard output

FIGURE 2.4 The Structure of a `main()` Function

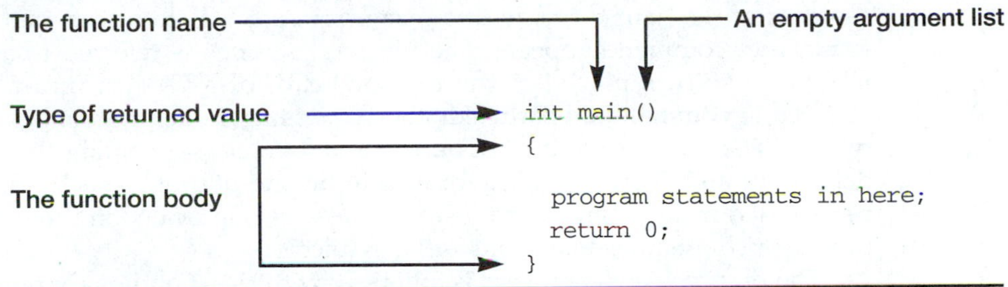

display device.[4] For most systems this display device is a video screen. The `cout` object displays on the monitor whatever is passed to it. For example, if the data `Hello there world!` is passed to `cout`, this data is printed (or displayed) on your terminal screen. The data `Hello there world!` is passed to the `cout` object by simply putting the insertion ("put to") symbol, <<, before the message and after the object's name, as shown in Figure 2.5.

FIGURE 2.5 Passing a Message to `cout`

```
cout << "Hello there world!";
```

Now let's put all this together into a working C++ program that can be run on your computer. Consider Program 2.1.

PROGRAM 2.1

```
#include <iostream.h>

int main()
{
  cout << "Hello there world!";

  return 0;
}
```

The first line of the program:

```
#include <iostream.h>
```

[4] The `cout` object is formally created from the `ostream` class, which is described in detail in Chapter 10.

is a preprocessor command. Preprocessor commands begin with a pound sign, (#), and perform some action before the compiler translates the source program into machine code. Specifically, the `#include` preprocessor command causes the contents of the named file, in this case `iostream.h`, to be inserted where the `#include` command appears. The file `iostream.h` is referred to as a **header file** because it is placed at the top, or head, of a C++ program using the `#include` command. In particular, the `iostream.h` file provide descriptions of two classes, `istream` and `ostream`. These two classes contain the actual data definitions and operations used for data input and output.[5] This header file must be included in all programs that use `cout`. As also indicated in Program 2.1, preprocessor commands do not end with a semicolon.

The preprocessor command is followed by the start of the program's `main()` function. The `main()` function begins with the header line developed in the previous section, and the body of the function, enclosed in braces, consists of only one statement. Remember that all statements end with a semicolon (`;`). The statement in `main()` passes one message to the `cout` object. The message is the string `"Hello there world!"`.

Since `cout` is an object of a prewritten class, we do not have to write it; it is available for use just by activating it correctly. Like all C++ objects, `cout` can only perform certain well-defined actions. For `cout` the action is to assemble data for output display. When a string of characters is passed to `cout`, the object sees to it that the string is correctly displayed on your monitor, as shown in Figure 2.6.

Strings in C++ are any combination of letters, numbers, and special characters enclosed in double quotes `"string in here"`. The double quotes are used to delimit (mark) the beginning and ending of the string and are not considered part of the string. Thus, the string of characters making up the message sent to `cout` must be enclosed in double quotes, as we have done in Program 2. 1.

Let us write another program to illustrate `cout`'s versatility. Read Program 2.2 to determine what it does.

PROGRAM 2.2

```
#include <iostream.h>

int main()
{
  cout << "Computers, computers everywhere";
  cout << "\n as far as I can C";

  return 0;
}
```

When Program 2.2 is run, the following is displayed:

```
Computers, computers everywhere
       as far as I can C
```

[5] Formally, `cout` is an object of the class `ostream`.

FIGURE 2.6 The Output from Program 2.1

```
Hello there world!
```

You might be wondering why the `\n` did not appear in the output. The two characters `\` and `n`, when used together, are called a newline escape sequence. They tell `cout` to send instructions to the display device to move to a new line. In C++, the backslash (\) character provides an "escape" from the normal interpretation of the character following it by altering the meaning of the next character. If the backslash were omitted from the second `cout` statement in Program 2.2, the `n` would be printed as the letter `n` and the program would print:

```
Computers, computers everywheren as far as I can C
```

Newline escape sequences can be placed anywhere within the message passed to `cout`. See if you can determine the display produced by Program 2.3.

PROGRAM 2.3

```
#include <iostream.h>

int main()
{
  cout << "Computers everywhere\n as far as\n\nI can see";

  return 0;
}
```

The output for Program 2.3 is:

```
Computers everywhere
 as far as

I can see
```

Exercises 2.1

1. State whether the following are valid function names. If they are valid, state whether they are mnemonic names. (Recall that a mnemonic function name conveys some idea about the function's purpose.) If they are invalid names, state why.

`m1234()`	`newBal()`	`abcd()`	`A12345()`	`1A2345()`
`power()`	`absVal()`	`mass()`	`do()`	`while()`
`add_5()`	`taxes()`	`netPay()`	`12345()`	`int()`
`cosine()`	`a2b3c4d5()`	`netPay()`	`amount()`	`$sine()`
`oldBalance()`	`nevValue()`	`salestax()`	`1stApprox()`	`float()`

2. Assume that the following functions have been written:

   `getLength(),` `getWidth(),` `calcArea(),` `displayArea()`

   a. From the functions' names, what do you think each function might do?

   b. In what order do you think a `main()` function might execute these functions (based on their names)?

3. Assume that the following functions have been written:

   `input_price(),` `calc_salestax(),` `calc_total()`

   a. From the functions' names, what do you think each function might do?

   b. In what order do you think a `main()` function might execute these functions (based on their names)?

4. Determine names for functions that do the following:

   a. Find the average of a set of numbers.

   b. Find the area of a rectangle.

   c. Find the minimum value in a set of numbers.

   d. Convert a lowercase letter to an uppercase letter.

   e. Convert an uppercase letter to a lowercase letter.

   f. Sort a set of numbers from lowest to highest.

   g. Alphabetize a set of names.

5. Just as the keyword `int` can be used to signify that a function will return an integer, the keywords `void`, `char`, `float`, and `double` can be used to signify that a function will return no value, a character, a floating-point number, and a double-precision number, respectively. Using this information, write header lines for a `main()` function that will receive no arguments but will return:

   a. no value

   b. a character

   c. a floating-point number

   d. a double-precision number

6. a. Using `cout`, write a C++ program that displays your name on one line, your street address on a second line, and your city, state, and zip code on the third line.

   b. Run the program you have written for Exercise 6a on a computer. (*Note:* You must understand the procedures for entering and running a C++ program on the particular computer installation you are using.)

7. a. Write a C++ program to display the following verse:

```
Computers, computers everywhere
   as far as I can see
I really, really like these things,
   Oh joy, Oh joy for me!
```

   b. Run the program you have written for Exercise 7a on a computer.

8. a. How many `cout` statements would you use to display the following output?

```
PART NO.      PRICE
T1267         $6.34
T1300         $8.92
T2401         $65.40
T4482         $36.99
```

   b. What is the minimum number of `cout` statements that could be used to print the table in Exercise 8a?

   c. Write a complete C++ program to produce the output illustrated in Exercise 8a.

d. Run the program you have written for Exercise 8c on a computer.

9. In response to a newline escape sequence, `cout` positions the next displayed character at the beginning of a new line. This positioning of the next character actually represents two distinct operations. What are they?

10. a. Many computer operating systems can redirect the output produced by `cout` either to a printer or directly to a floppy or hard disk file. Read the first part of Appendix D for a description of this redirection capability.

    b. If your computer supports output redirection, run the program written for Exercise 7a using this feature. Have your program's display redirected to a file named `poem`.

    c. If your computer supports output redirection to a printer, run the program written for Exercise 7a using this feature.

Note for Exercises 11 through 16: Most projects, both programming and nonprogramming, can be structured into smaller subtasks or units of activity. These smaller subtasks can often be delegated to different people so that when all the tasks are finished and integrated, the project or program is completed. For Exercises 11 through 16, determine a set of subtasks that, taken together, complete the required task. (The purpose of these exercises is to have you consider the different ways that complex tasks can be structured. Although there is no one correct solution to these exercises, there are incorrect solutions and solutions that are better than others. An incorrect solution is one that does not complete the task correctly. One solution is better than another if it more clearly or easily identifies what must be done or does it more efficiently.)

11. You are given the task of wiring and installing lights in the attic of your house. Determine a set of subtasks that, taken together, will accomplish this. (*Hint:* The first subtask would be to determine the placement of the light fixtures.)

12. You are given the job of preparing a complete meal for five people next weekend. Determine a set of subtasks that, taken together, accomplish this. (*Hint:* One subtask, not necessarily the first one, would be to buy the food.)

13. You are a sophomore in college and are planning to go to law school after graduation. List a set of major objectives that you must fulfill to meet this goal. (*Hint:* One objective is "Take the right courses.")

14. You are given the job of planting a vegetable garden. Determine a set of subtasks that will accomplish this. (*Hint:* One such subtask would be to plan the layout of the garden.)

15. You are responsible for planning and arranging the family camping trip this summer. List a set of subtasks that, taken together, will accomplish this objective successfully. (*Hint:* One subtask would be to select the camp site.)

16. a. A national electrical supply distribution company wants a computer system that can prepare its customer invoices. The system must, of course, be capable of creating each day's invoices. Additionally, the company wants to be able to retrieve and output a printed report of all invoices that meet certain criteria; for example, all invoices sent in a particular month with a net value of more than a given dollar amount, all invoices sent in a year to a particular client, or all invoices sent to firms in a particular state. For this system determine three or four major program units into which the system could be separated. (*Hint:* One program unit is "Prepare Invoices" to create each day's invoices.)

    b. Suppose someone enters incorrect data for a particular invoice. This error is discovered after the data has been entered and stored by the system. What program unit is needed to take care of correcting this problem? Discuss why such a program unit might or might not be required by most business systems.

    c. Assume a program unit exists that allows a user to alter or change data that has been incorrectly entered and stored. Discuss the need for including an "audit trail" that would allow for reconstruction of the changes made, when they were made, and who made them.

2.2 PROGRAMMING STYLE

C++ programs start execution at the beginning of the `main()` function. Since a program can have only one starting point, every C++ language program must contain one and only one `main()` function. As we have seen, all of the statements that make up the `main()` function are then included within the braces `{ }` following the function name. Although the `main()` function must be present in every C++ program, C++ does not require that the word `main`, the parentheses `( )`, or the braces `{ }` be placed in any particular form. The form used in the last section

```
int main()
{
  program statements in here;

  return 0;
}
```

was chosen strictly for clarity and ease in reading the program.[6] For example, the following general form of a `main()` function would also work:

```
int main
(
) { first statement;second statement;
        third statement;fourth
statement;

return 0;
}
```

Notice that more than one statement can be put on a line, or one statement can be written across lines. Except for strings, double quotes, identifiers, and keywords, C++ ignores all white space (white space refers to any combination of one or more blank spaces, tabs, or new lines). For example, changing the white space in Program 2.1 and making sure not to split the string `Hello there world!` across two lines results in the following valid program:

```
#include <iostream.h>
int main
(
){
cout <<
"Hello there world!";

return 0;
}
```

Although this version of `main()` does work, it is an example of extremely poor programming style. It is difficult to read and understand. For readability, the `main()` function should always be written in standard form as:

```
int main()
{
  program statements in here;

  return 0;
}
```

---

[6] If one of the program statements uses `cout`, the `#include <iostream.h>` preprocessor command would have to be used.

In this standard form the function name starts in column 1 and is placed with the required parentheses on a line by itself. The opening brace of the function body follows on the next line and is placed under the first letter of the line containing the function name. Similarly, the closing function brace is placed by itself in column 1 as the last line of the function. This structure serves to highlight the function as a single unit.

Within the function itself, all program statements are indented at least two spaces. Indentation is another sign of good programming practice, especially if the same indentation is used for similar groups of statements. Review Program 2.2 to see that the same indentation was used for both `cout` object calls.

As you progress in your understanding and mastery of C++, you will develop your own indentation standards. Just keep in mind that the final form of your programs should be consistent and should always serve as an aid to the reading and understanding of your programs.

Comments

Comments are explanatory remarks made within a program. When used carefully, comments can be very helpful in clarifying what the complete program is about, what a specific group of statements is meant to accomplish, or what one line is intended to do. C++ supports two types of comments: line and block. Both types of comments can be placed anywhere within a program and have no effect on program execution. The computer ignores all comments; they are there strictly for the convenience of anyone reading the program.

A line comment begins with two slashes (`//`) and continues to the end of the line. For example, the following lines are all line comments:

```
// this is a comment
// this program prints out a message
// this program calculates a square root
```

The symbols `//`, with no white space between them, designate the start of the line comment. The end of the line on which the comment is written designates the end of the comment.

A line comment can be written either on a line by itself or at the end of the same line containing a program statement. Program 2.4 illustrates the use of line comments within a program.

PROGRAM 2.4

```
// this program displays a message
#include <iostream.h>

int main()
{
  cout << "Hello there world"; // a call to cout

  return 0;
}
```

The first comment appears on a line by itself at the top of the program and describes what the program does. This is generally a good location to include a short comment describing the program's purpose. If more comments are required, they can be placed, one per line. Thus, when a comment is too long to be contained on one line, it can be separated into two or more line comments, with each separate comment preceded by the double slash symbol set, //. The comment

```
// this comment is invalid because it
   extends over two lines
```

will result in a C++ error message on your computer. This comment is correct when written as:

```
// this comment is used to illustrate a
// comment that extends across two lines
```

Comments that span across two or more lines are, however, more conveniently written as C-type block comments rather than as multiple-line comments. Such comments begin with the symbols /* and end with the symbols */. For example,

```
/* This is a block comment that
   spans
   across three lines */
```

In C++, a program's structure is intended to make the program readable and understandable, making the use of extensive comments unnecessary. This is reinforced if function, class, and variable names, described in the next chapter, are carefully selected to convey their meaning to anyone reading the program. However, if the purpose of a function, class, or statement is still not clear from its structure, name, or context, include comments where clarification is needed. Obscure code with no comments is a sure sign of bad programming when the program must be maintained or read by others. Similarly, excessive comments are also a sign of bad programming, because they imply that insufficient thought was given to making the code self- explanatory.

Exercises 2.2

1. a. Will the following program work?

```
#include <iostream.h>
int main(){cout << "Hello there world!"; return 0;}
```

   b. Why is the program given in Exercise 1a not a good program?

2. Rewrite the following programs to conform to good programming practice:

   a.
```
#include <iostream.h>
int main(
){
cout          <<
"The time has come"
; return 0;}
```

   b.
```
#include <iostream.h>
int main
(){cout << "Newark is a city\n"cout <<
"In New Jersey\n"; cout <<
"It is also a city\n"
; cout << "In Delaware\n"
; return 0;}
```

c.
```
#include <iostream.h>
int main(){cout << Reading a program\n"cout <<
"is much easier\n"
;cout << "if a standard form for main is used\n")
;cout
<<"and each statement is written\n"cout
<<          "on a line by itself\n")
; return 0;}
```

d.
```
#include <iostream.h>
int main
(){cout << "Every C++ program"
;cout
<<"\nmust have one and only one"
;
cout << "main function"
;
cout <<
"\n the escape sequence of characters")
;cout <<
 "\nfor a newline can be placed anywhere"
;cout
<<"\n within the data placed on the cout stream"
; return 0;}
```

3. a. When used in a message, the backslash character alters the meaning of the character immediately following it. If we wanted to print the backslash character, we would have to tell cout to escape from the way it normally interprets the backslash. What character do you think is used to alter the way a single backslash character is interpreted?

   b. Using your answer to Exercise 3a, write the escape sequence for printing a backslash.

4. a. A token of a computer language is any sequence of characters that, as a unit, with no intervening characters or white space, has a unique meaning. Using this definition of a token, determine whether escape sequences, function names, and the keywords listed in Table 2.1 are tokens of the C++ language.

   b. Discuss whether adding white space to a message alters the message. Discuss whether messages can be considered tokens of C++.

   c. Using the definition of a token given in Exercise 4a, determine whether the following statement is true: "Except for tokens of the language, C++ ignores all white space."

2.3 DATA VALUES AND ARITHMETIC OPERATIONS

C++ programs can process different types of data in different ways. For example, calculating the bacteria growth in a polluted pond requires mathematical operations on numerical data, while sorting a list of names requires comparison operations using alphabetical data. In this section we introduce C++'s elementary data types and the operations that can be performed on them. Additionally, we show how to use the `cout` object function to display the results of these operations.

The three basic data values used in C++ are integers, floating-point numbers, and character values. Each of these data values is described in the following subsections.

TABLE 2.2 Integer Values and Word Size[7]

Word Size (bytes)	Maximum Integer Value	Minimum Integer Value
1	127	−128
2	32,767	−32,768
4	2,147,483,647	−2,147,483,648

Integer Values

An **integer value** is zero or any positive or negative number without a decimal point. Examples of valid integer values are:

```
0  5  -10  +25  1000  253  -26351  +36
```

As these examples illustrate, integers may be signed (have a leading + or − sign) or unsigned (no leading + or − sign). No commas, decimal points, or special symbols, such as the dollar sign, are allowed. Examples of invalid integer values are:

```
$255.62  2,523  3.  6,243,892  1,492.89  +6.0
```

Different computer types have their own internal limit on the largest (most positive) and smallest (most negative) integer values that can be used in a program. These limits depend on the amount of storage each computer sets aside for an integer; as such, they are said to be implementation dependent. The more commonly used storage allocations are listed in Table 2.2.[7] (Review Section 1.6 if you are unfamiliar with the concept of a byte.) By referring to your computer's reference manual or using the `sizeof` operator introduced in Section 2.5 you can determine the actual number of bytes allocated by your computer for each integer value. To store integer values greater than those supported by the memory allocation shown in Table 2.2, you must use integer qualifiers. These qualifiers are described in Section 2.5.

Floating-Point Numbers

A **floating point number,** which is also called a *real number,* is any signed or unsigned number having a decimal point. Examples of floating point numbers are:

```
+10.625  5.  -6.2  3251.92  0.0  0.33  -6.67  +2.
```

Notice that the numbers 5., 0.0, and +2. are classified as floating-point numbers, while the same numbers written without a decimal point (5, 0, +2) would be integer values. As with integer values, special symbols, such as the dollar sign and the comma, are not permitted in real numbers. Examples of invalid real numbers are:

```
5,326.25  24  123  6,459  $10.29
```

---

[7] It is interesting to note that in all cases the magnitude of the most negative integer allowed is always one more than the magnitude of the most positive integer. This is due to the method most commonly used to represent integers, called two's complement representation. For an explanation of two's complement representation, see Section 1.6.

C++ supports three different categories of floating-point numbers: float, double, and long double. The difference between these numbers is the amount of storage that a computer uses for each type. Most computers use twice the amount of storage for doubles than for floats, which allows a double to have approximately twice the precision of a float (for this reason floats are sometimes referred to as *single-precision numbers* and doubles as **double-precision numbers**). Similarly, long double numbers typically use twice the storage used for doubles, with a consequent increase in precision. The actual storage allocation for each data type, however, depends on the particular computer. In computers that use the same amount of storage for double- and single-precision numbers, these two data types become identical. The same is true for long doubles, and the `sizeof` operator introduced in Section 2.5 will allow you to determine the amount of storage reserved by your computer for each of these data types. A float number is indicated to the computer by appending either an `F` or `f` after the number and a double is created by appending either an `L` or `l` to the number. In the absence of these suffixes, a floating-point number is considered to be a double. For example:

`9.234` indicates a double.
`9.234f` indicates a float.
`9.234L` indicates a long double.

The only difference in these numbers is the amount of storage the computer may use to store them. For numbers having more than six significant digits to the right of the decimal point, this storage becomes important. Appendix E describes the binary storage format typically used for real values and its impact on number precision. The exact difference, if any, in allocated storage is compiler dependent. The only requirement made by C++ is that a long double must provide at least the same precision as a double and that a double must provide at least the same precision as a float.

Exponential Notation Floating-point numbers can be written in exponential notation, which is similar to scientific notation and is commonly used to express both very large and very small numbers in a compact form. The following examples illustrate how numbers with decimals can be expressed in exponential and scientific notation:

Decimal Notation	Exponential Notation	Scientific Notation
1625.	1.625e3	1.625×10^3
63421.	6.3421e4	6.3421×10^4
.00731	7.31e−3	7.31×10^{-3}
.000625	6.25e−4	6.25×10^{-4}

In exponential notation the letter `e` stands for exponent. The number following the `e` represents a power of 10 and indicates the number of places the decimal point should be moved to obtain the standard decimal value. The decimal point is moved to the right if the number after the `e` is positive, or to the left if the number after the `e` is negative. For example, the e3 in the number 1.625e3 means move the decimal place three places to the right, so that the number becomes 1625. The e−3 in the number 7.31e−3 means move the decimal point three places to the left, so that 7.31e−3 becomes .00731.

TABLE 2.3 The ASCII and EBCDIC Uppercase Letter Codes

Letter	ASCII Code	EBCDIC Code	Letter	ASCII Code	EBCDIC Code
A	01000001	11000001	N	01001110	11010101
B	01000010	11000010	O	01001111	11010110
C	01000011	11000011	P	01010000	11010111
D	01000100	11000100	Q	01010001	11011000
E	01000101	11000101	R	01010010	11011001
F	01000110	11000110	S	01010011	11100010
G	01000111	11000111	T	01010100	11100011
H	01001000	11001000	U	01010101	11100100
I	01001001	11001001	V	01010110	11100101
J	01001010	11010001	W	01010111	11100110
K	01001011	11010010	X	01011000	11100111
L	01001100	11010011	Y	01011001	11101000
M	01001101	11010100	Z	01011010	11101001

Character Values

The third basic type of data recognized by C++ are characters. Characters include the letters of the alphabet (both uppercase and lowercase), the 10 digits 0 through 9, and special symbols such as + $. , − !. A single **character value** is any one letter, digit, or special symbol enclosed by single quotes. Examples of valid character values are:

```
'A'   '$'   'b'   '7'   'y'   '!'   'M'   'q'
```

Character values are typically stored in a computer using either the ASCII or EBCDIC codes. **ASCII,** pronounced "as-key," is an acronym for American Standard Code for Information Interchange. **EBCDIC,** pronounced either as "ebb-sah-dick" or "ebb-see-dick," is an acronym for Extended Binary Coded Decimal Interchange Code. Each of these codes assigns individual characters to a specific pattern of 0's and 1's.

Table 2.3 lists the correspondence between bit patterns and the uppercase letters of the alphabet used by the ASCII and EBCDIC codes. Using Table 2.3, we can determine how the characters 'W', 'E', 'S', 'T', 'B', and 'Y', for example, are stored inside a computer that uses the ASCII character code. Using the ASCII code, this sequence of characters requires six bytes of storage (one byte for each letter) and would be stored as illustrated in Figure 2.7.

FIGURE 2.7 The Letters WESTBY Stored Inside a Computer

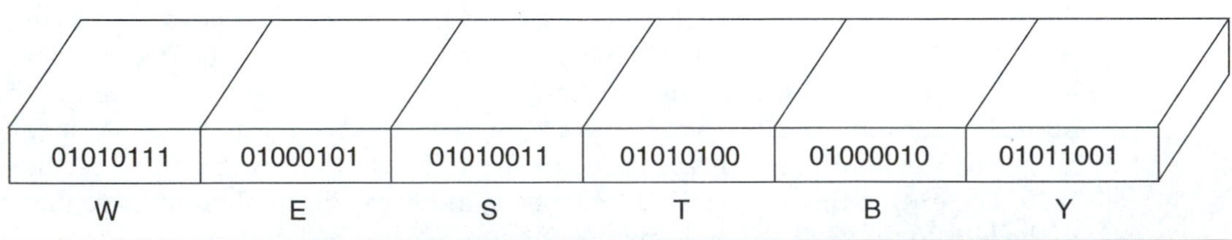

Escape Sequences

When a backslash (\) is used directly in front of a select group of characters, the backslash tells the computer to escape from the way these characters would normally be interpreted. For this reason, the combination of a backslash and these specific characters are called **escape sequences.** We have already encountered an example of this in the newline escape sequence, \n.

TABLE 2.4 Escape Sequences

Escape Sequence	Meaning
\b	Move back one space
\f	Move to next page
\n	Move to next line
\r	Carriage return
\t	Move to next tab setting
\\	Backslash character
\'	Single quote
\nnn	Treat nnn as an octal number

Table 2.4 lists C++'s most commonly used escape sequences. Although each escape sequence listed in Table 2.4 is made up of two distinct characters, the combination of the two characters with no intervening white space causes the computer to store one character code. Table 2.5 lists the ASCII code byte patterns for the escape sequences listed in Table 2.4.

Arithmetic Operations

Integers and real numbers can be added, subtracted, multiplied, and divided. Although it is usually better not to mix integers and real numbers when performing arithmetic operations, predictable results are obtained when different data types are used in the same arithmetic expression. Somewhat surprising is the fact

TABLE 2.5 The ASCII Escape Sequence Codes

C++ Escape Sequence	Meaning	Computer Code
\b	Backspace	00001000
\f	Form feed	00001100
\n	Newline	00001010
\r	Carriage return	00001101
\\	Backslash	01011100
\'	Single quote	00100111
\"	Double quote	00100010

that character data can also be added and subtracted with both character and integer data to produce useful results.

The operators used for arithmetic operations are called **arithmetic operators,** and are listed next:

Operation	Operator
Addition	+
Subtraction	−
Multiplication	*
Division	/
Modulus division	%

A *simple arithmetic expression* consists of an arithmetic operator connecting two operands in the form:

operand *operator* operand

Examples of arithmetic expressions are:

```
3 + 7
18 - 3
12.62 + 9.8
.08 * 12.2
12.6 / 2.
```

The spaces around the arithmetic operators in these examples are inserted strictly for clarity and can be omitted without affecting the value of the expression.

The value of any arithmetic expression can be displayed on the standard output device using `cout`. To do this we must pass the desired value to this object. For example, the statement

```
cout << (6 + 15);
```

yields the display `21`. Strictly speaking, the parentheses surrounding the expression `6 + 15` are required to indicate that it is the value of the expression, which is `21`, that is being placed on the output stream. In practice, most compilers will accept and correctly process this statement without the parentheses.

In addition to displaying a numerical value, a string identifying the output can also be displayed by passing the string to `cout` as we did in Section 2.1. For example, the statement:

```
cout << "The sum of 6 and 15 is " << (6 + 15);
```

causes two pieces of data to be sent to `cout`, a string and a value. Individually, each set of data is sent to the cout preceded by its own insertion operator symbol (<<). Here, the first data sent to the stream is the string `"The sum of 6 and 15 is"`, and the second item sent to the stream is the value of the expression `6 + 15`. The display produced by this statement is:

```
The sum of 6 and 15 is 21
```

▲ POINT OF INFORMATION ▲

What is Precision?

In numerical theory the term precision typically refers to numerical accuracy. In this context a statement such as, this computation is accurate, or precise, to the 5th decimal place, is used. What this means is that the 5th digit after the decimal point has been rounded and that the number is accurate to within $\pm 1/2\ 10^{-5}$.

In computer programming precision can either refer to the accuracy of a number *or* the number of significant digits in the number, where significant digits is defined as the number of clearly correct digits plus one. For example, if the number 12.6874 has been rounded to the 4th decimal place, it is correct to say that this number is precise (that is accurate) to the 4th decimal place. This statement means that all of the digits in the number are accurate except for the fourth digit, which has been rounded. Similarly, it can be said that the number has a precision of 6 digits, which means that the first five digits are correct and the 6th digit has been rounded. Another way of saying this is that the number 12.6874 has 6 significant digits.

Notice that the significant digits in a number need not have any relation to the number of displayed digits. For example, if the number 687.45678921 has five significant digits, it is only accurate to the value 687.46, where the last digit is assumed to be rounded. In a similar manner, dollar values in many very large financial applications are frequently rounded to the nearest hundred thousand dollars. In such applications a displayed dollar value of $12,400,000. for example, is not accurate to the closest dollar. Since this value only has three significant digits it is only accurate to the hundred thousandths digit. In C++ the number of displayed digits to the left of the decimal point are assumed to be significant.

Notice that the space between the word `is` and the number `21` is caused by the space placed within the string passed to `cout`. As far as `cout` is concerned, its input is simply a set of characters that is sent on to be displayed in the order in which they are received. Characters from the input are queued, one behind the other, and sent to an output stream for display. Placing a space in the input causes this space to be part of the output stream that is ultimately displayed. For example, the statement

```
cout << "The sum of 12.2 and 15.754 is " << (12.2 + 15.754);
```

yields the display

```
The sum of 12.2 and 15.754 is 27.954
```

We should mention that insertion of data into the output stream can be made over multiple lines and is only terminated by a semicolon. Thus, the prior display is also produced by this statement

```
cout << "The sum of 12.2 and 15.754 is "
     << (12.2 + 15.754);
```

The requirements for using multiple lines are that a string contained within double quotes cannot be split across lines and that the terminating semicolon can appear only on the last line. Within a line multiple insertion symbols can be used.

As the last display indicates, floating-point numbers are displayed with sufficient decimal places to the right of the decimal place to accommodate the frac-

POINT OF INFORMATION

Atomic Data

The variables we have declared have all been used to store atomic data values. An **atomic data value** is a value that is considered a complete entity by itself and is not decomposable into a smaller data type supported by the language. For example, although an integer can be decomposed into individual digits, C++ does not have a numerical digit type. Rather, each integer is regarded as a complete value by itself and, as such, is considered atomic data. Similarly, since the integer data type only supports atomic data values, it is said to be an **atomic data type.** As you might expect, floats and chars are atomic data types also.

tional part of the number. This is true if the number has six or fewer decimal digits. If the number has more than six decimal digits, the fractional part is rounded to six decimal digits, and if the number has no decimal digits, neither a decimal point nor any decimal digits are displayed.[8]

Character data can also be displayed using `cout`. For example, the statement

```
cout << "The first letter of the alphabet is an " << 'a';
```

causes the display

```
The first letter of the alphabet is an a
```

Program 2.5 illustrates the use of `cout` to display the results of an expression within the statements of a complete program.

PROGRAM 2.5

```
#include <iostream.h>

int main()
{
  cout << "15.0 plus 2.0 equals "        << (15.0 + 2.0) << '\n'
       << "15.0 minus 2.0 equals "       << (15.0 - 2.0) << '\n'
       << "15.0 times 2.0 equals "       << (15.0 * 2.0) << '\n'
       << "15.0 divided by 2.0 equals " << (15.0 / 2.0) << '\n';

  return 0;
}
```

The output of Program 2.5 is:

```
15.0 plus 2.0 equals 17
15.0 minus 2.0 equals 13
15.0 times 2.0 equals 30
15.0 divided by 2.0 equals 7.5
```

[8] Note that none of this output is defined as part of the C++ language. Rather, it is defined by a set of classes and routines provided with each C++ compiler.

Expression Types An **expression** that contains only integer operands is called an *integer expression*, and the result of the expression is an integer value. Similarly, an expression containing only floating-point operands (single and double precision) is called a *floating-point expression*, and the result of such an expression is a floating-point value. An expression containing both integer and floating-point operands is called a **mixed-mode expression.** Although it is usually better not to mix integer and floating-point operands in an arithmetic operation, the data type of each operation is determined by the following rules:

1. If both operands are integers, the result of the operation is an integer.
2. If one operand is a floating-point value, the result of the operation is a double-precision value.

Note that the result of an arithmetic expression is never a single-precision (float) number. This is because the computer temporarily converts all floats to double-precision numbers when arithmetic is being done.

Integer Division

The division of two integers can produce rather strange results for the unwary. For example, dividing the integer 15 by the integer 2 yields an integer result. Since integers cannot contain a fractional part, the expected result, 7.5, is not obtained. In C++, the fractional part of the result obtained when dividing two integers is dropped (truncated). Thus, the value of 15/2 is 7, the value of 9/4 is 2, and the value of 19/5 is 3.

Often, however, we would like to retain the remainder of an integer division. To do this C++ provides an arithmetic operator that captures the remainder when two integers are divided. This operator, called the **modulus operator,** uses the symbol `%`. The modulus operator can be used only with integers. For example,

` 9 % 4` is 1
`17 % 3` is 2
`14 % 2` is 0

A Unary Operator (Negation)

Besides the binary operators for addition, subtraction, multiplication, and division, C++ also provides unary operators. One of these unary operators uses the same symbol that is used for binary subtraction (−). The minus sign used in front of a single numerical operand negates (reverses the sign of) the number.

Table 2.6 summarizes the six arithmetic operations we have described so far and lists the data type of the result produced by each operator based on the data type of operand involved.

Operator Precedence and Associativity

Besides such simple expressions as `5 + 12` and `.08 * 26.2`, we frequently need to create more complex arithmetic expressions. C++, like most other programming languages, requires that certain rules be followed when writing expressions containing more than one arithmetic operator. These rules are:

1. Two binary arithmetic operator symbols must never be placed side by side. For example, `5 * %6` is invalid because the two operators `*` and `%` are placed next to each other.

TABLE 2.6 Summary of Arithmetic Operators

Operation	Operator	Type	Operand	Result
Addition	+	Binary	Both integers One operand not an integer	Integer Double precision
Subtraction	–	Binary	Both integers One operand not an integer	Integer Double precision
Multiplication	*	Binary	Both integers One operand not an integer	Integer Double precision
Division	/	Binary	Both integers One operand not an integer	Integer Double precision
Modulus negation	%	Binary	Both integers One integer	Integer Integer
Negation	–	Unary	One floating-point or double-precision operand	Double precision

2. Parentheses should be used to form groupings, and all expressions enclosed within parentheses are evaluated first. For example, in the expression `(6 + 4) / (2 + 3)`, the `6 + 4` and `2 + 3` are evaluated first to yield `10 / 5`. The `10 / 5` is then evaluated to yield `2`.
3. Sets of parentheses may also be enclosed by other parentheses. For example, the expression `(2 * (3 + 7) ) / 5` is valid. When parentheses are used within parentheses, the expressions in the innermost parentheses are always evaluated first. The evaluation continues from innermost to outermost parentheses until the expressions of all parentheses have been evaluated. The number of right-facing parentheses, `(`, must always equal the number of left-facing parentheses, `)`, so that there are no unpaired sets.
4. Parentheses cannot be used to indicate multiplication. The multiplication operator, *, must be used. For example, the expression `(3 + 4) (5 + 1)` is invalid. The correct expression is `(3 + 4) * (5 + 1)`.

Parentheses should be used to specify logical groupings of operands and to indicate clearly to both the computer and programmers the intended order of arithmetic operations. In the absence of parentheses, expressions containing multiple operators are evaluated by the priority, or **precedence,** of the operators. Table 2.7 lists both the precedence and associativity of the operators considered in this section.

TABLE 2.7 Operator Precedence and Associativity

Operator	Associativity
unary –	Right to left
* / %	Left to right
+ –	Left to right

The precedence of an operator establishes its priority relative to all other operators. Operators at the top of Table 2.7 have a higher priority than operators at the bottom of the table. In expressions with multiple operators, the operator with the higher precedence is used before an operator with a lower precedence. For example, in the expression `6 + 4 / 2 + 3`, the division is done before the addition, yielding an intermediate result of `6 + 2 + 3`. The additions are then performed to yield a final result of `11`.

Expressions containing operators with the same precedence are evaluated according to their **associativity.** This means that evaluation is either from left to right or from right to left as each operator is encountered. For example, in the expression `8 + 5 * 7 % 2 * 4`, the multiplication and modulus operator are of higher precedence than the addition operator and are evaluated first. Both of these operators, however, are of equal precedence. Therefore, these operators are evaluated according to their left-to-right associativity, yielding

```
8 + 5 * 7 % 2 * 4 =
    8 + 35 % 2 * 4 =
         8 + 1 * 4 =
              8 + 4 = 12
```

Exercises 2.3

1. Determine data types appropriate for the following data:
   a. the average of four grades
   b. the number of days in a month
   c. the length of the Golden Gate Bridge
   d. the numbers in a state lottery
   e. the distance from Brooklyn, New York, to Newark, New Jersey
   f. the names in a mailing list
2. Convert the following numbers into standard decimal form:

   `6.34e5   1.95162e2   8.395e1   2.95e−3   4.623e−4`
3. Write the following decimal numbers using exponential notation:

   `126.   656.23   3426.95   4893.2   .321   .0123   .006789`
4. The following list shows algebraic expressions and incorrect C++ expressions corresponding to them. Find the errors and write corrected C++ expressions.

	Algebra	*C++ Expression*
a.	$(2)(3) + (4)(5)$	`(2) (3) + (4) (5)`
b.	$\frac{6 + 18}{2}$	`6 + 18 / 2`
c.	$\frac{4.5}{12.2 - 3.1}$	`4.5 / 12.2 - 3.1`
d.	$4.6(3.0 + 14.9)$	`4.6(3.0 + 14.9)`
e.	$(12.1 + 18.9)(15.3 - 3.8)$	`(12.1 + 18.9)(15.3 - 3.8)`

5. Determine the value of the following integer expressions:

   a. 3 + 4 * 6
   b. 3 * 4 / 6 + 6
   c. 2 * 3 / 12 * 8 / 4
   d. 10 * (1 + 7 * 3)
   e. 20 - 2 / 6 + 3
   f. 20 - 2 / (6 + 3)
   g. (20 - 2) / 6 + 3
   h. (20 - 2) / (6 + 3)
   i. 50 % 20
   j. (10 + 3) % 4

6. Determine the value of the following floating-point expressions:

   a. 3.0 + 4.0 * 6.0
   b. 3.0 * 4.0 / 6.0 + 6.0
   c. 2.0 * 3.0 / 12.0 * 8.0 / 4.0
   d. 10.0 * (1.0 + 7.0 * 3.0)
   e. 20.0 - 2.0 / 6.0 + 3.0
   f. 20.0 - 2.0 / (6.0 + 3.0)
   g. (20.0 - 2.0) / 6.0 + 3.0
   h. (20.0 - 2.0) / (6.0 + 3.0)

7. Assume that amount has the integer value 1, m has the integer value 50, n has the integer value 10, and p has the integer value 5. Evaluate the following expressions:

   a. n / p + 3
   b. m / p + n - 10 * amount
   c. m - 3 * n + 4 * amount
   d. amount / 5
   e. 18 / p
   f. -p * n
   g. -m / 20
   h. (m + n) / (p + amount)
   i. m + n / p + amount

8. Using the system reference manuals for your computer, determine the character code used by your computer.

9. Determine the output of the following program:

```
#include <iostream.h>
int main()   // a program illustrating integer truncation
{
  cout << "answer1 is the integer " << 9 / 4;
  cout << "\nanswer2 is the integer " << 17 / 3;
}
```

10. Determine the output of the following program:

```
#include <iostream.h>
int main() // a program illustrating the % operator
{
  cout << "The remainder of 9 divided by 4 is " << 9 % 4;
  cout << "\nThe remainder of 17 divided by 3 is " << 17 % 3;
}
```

11. Write a C++ program that displays the results of the expressions 3.0 * 5.0, 7.1 * 8.3 - 2.2, and 3.2 / (6.1 * 5). Calculate the value of these expressions manually to verify that the displayed values are correct.

12. Write a C++ program that displays the results of the expressions `15 / 4, 15 % 4`, and `5 * 3 - (6 * 4)`. Calculate the value of these expressions manually to verify that the displayed values are correct.

13. a. Show how the name KINGSLEY would be stored inside a computer that uses the ASCII code. That is, draw a figure similar to Figure 2.7 for the letters KINGSLEY.

    b. Show how the name KINGSLEY would be stored inside a computer that uses the EBCDIC code.

14. a. Repeat Exercise 13a using the letters of your own last name.

    b. Repeat Exercise 13b using the letters of your own last name.

15. Enter, compile, and run Program 2.5 on your computer system.

16. Since computers use different representations for storing integer, floating-point, double-precision, and character values, discuss how a program might alert the computer to the data types of the various values it will be using.

17. Although we have concentrated on operations involving integer and floating-point numbers, C++ allows characters and integers to be added or subtracted. This can be done because C++ always converts a character to an equivalent integer value whenever a character is used in an arithmetic expression. Thus, characters and integers can be freely mixed in such expressions. For example, if your computer uses the ASCII code, the expression `'a' + 1` equals `'b'`, and `'z' - 1` equals `'y'`. Similarly, `'A' + 1` is `'B'`, and `'Z' - 1` is `'Y'`. With this as background, determine the character results of the following expressions (assume that all characters are stored using the ASCII code):

    a. `'m' - 5`

    b. `'m' + 5`

    c. `'G' + 6`

    d. `'G' - 6`

    e. `'b' - 'a'`

    f. `'g' - 'a' + 1`

    g. `'G' - 'A' + 1`

    Note: For the following exercise the reader should have an understanding of basic computer storage concepts. Specifically, if you are unfamiliar with the concept of a byte, refer to Section 1.6 before doing the next exercise.

18. Although the total number of bytes varies from computer to computer, memory sizes of 65,536 to more than several million bytes are not uncommon. In computer language, the letter K is used to represent the number 1024, which is 2 raised to the 10th power and M is used to represent the number 1,048,576, which is 2 raised to the 20th power. Thus, a memory size of 640K is really 640 times 1024, or 655,360 bytes, and a memory size of 4M is really 4 times 1,048,576, which is 4,194,304 bytes. Using this information, calculate the actual number of bytes in:

    a. a memory containing 512K bytes

    b. a memory containing 2M bytes

    c. a memory containing 8M bytes

    d. a memory containing 16M bytes

    e. a memory consisting of 4M words, where each word consists of 2 bytes

    f. a memory consisting of 4M words, where each word consists of 4 bytes

    g. a floppy diskette that can store 1.44M bytes.

2.4 VARIABLES AND DECLARATION STATEMENTS

All integer, floating-point, and other values used in a computer program are stored and retrieved from the computer's memory unit. Conceptually, individual memory locations in the memory unit are arranged like the rooms in a large hotel. Like hotel rooms, each memory location has a unique address ("room number"). Before high-level languages such as C++ existed, memory locations were referenced by their addresses. For example, the storage of integer values 45 and 12 in the memory locations 1652 and 2548 (see Figure 2.8), respectively, required instructions equivalent to

Put a 45 in location 1652.
Put a 12 in location 2548.

To add the two numbers just stored and save the result in another memory location, for example, at location 3000, we need a statement comparable to

Add the contents of location 1652
to the contents of location 2548
and store the result into location 3000.

Clearly this method of storage and retrieval is a cumbersome process. In high-level languages like C++, symbolic names are used in place of actual memory addresses. These symbolic names are called **variables.** A variable is simply a name chosen by the programmer that is used to refer to computer storage locations. The term *variable* is used because the value stored in the variable can change, or vary. For each name the programmer uses, the computer keeps track of the actual memory address corresponding to that name. In our hotel room analogy, this is equivalent to putting a name on the door of a room and referring to the room by this name, such as the BLUE room, rather than using the actual room number.

In C++ the selection of variable names is left to the programmer, as long as the following rules are observed.

1. The variable name must begin with a letter or underscore (_), and may contain only letters, underscores, or digits. It cannot contain any blanks, commas, or special symbols, such as ( ) & , $ # . ! \ ?.
2. A variable name cannot be a keyword (see Table 2.1).
3. The variable name cannot consist of more than 31 characters.

FIGURE 2.8 Enough Storage for Two Integers

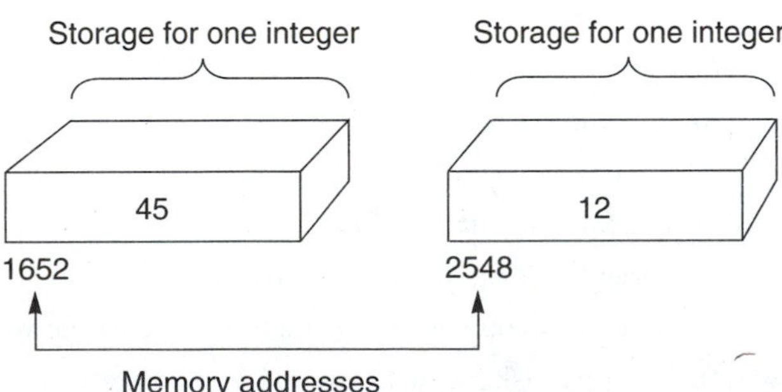

FIGURE 2.9 Naming Storage Locations

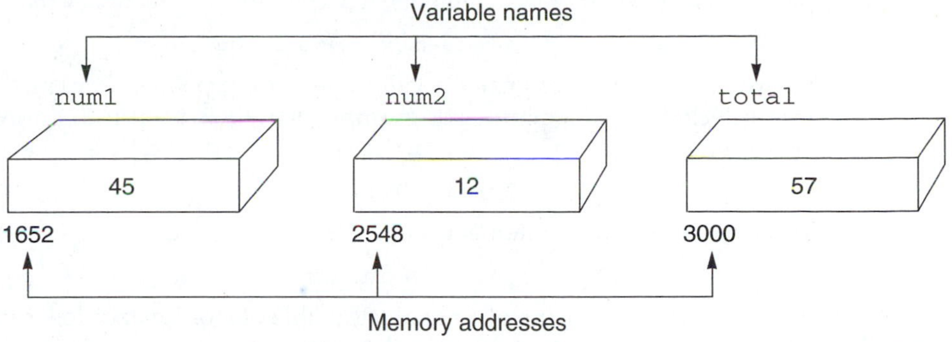

These rules are similar to those used for selecting function names. As with function names, variable names should be mnemonics that give some indication of the variable's use. For example, a good name for a variable used to store a value that is the total of some other values would be `sum` or `total`. Variable names that give no indication of the value stored, such as `r2d2`, `linda`, `bill`, and `getum` should not be selected. As with function names, variable names can be typed in uppercase and lowercase letters.

Now assume that the first memory location illustrated in Figure 2.9, which has address 1652, is given the name `num1`. Also assume that memory location 2548 is given the variable name `num2`, and memory location 3000 is given the variable name `total`, as illustrated in Figure 2.9.

Using these variable names, the operation of storing 45 in location 1652, storing 12 in location 2548, and adding the contents of these two locations is accomplished by the C++ statements

```
num1 = 45;
num2 = 12;
total = num1 + num2;
```

Each of these three statements is called an **assignment statement** because it tells the computer to assign (store) a value into a variable. Assignment statements always have an equal (=) sign and one variable name immediately to the left of this sign. The value on the right of the equal sign is determined first and this value is assigned to the variable on the left of the equal sign. The blank spaces in the assignment statements are inserted for readability. We will have much more to say about assignment statements in the next chapter, but for now we can use them to store values in variables.

A variable name is useful because it frees the programmer from concern over where data is physically stored inside the computer. We simply use the variable name and let the compiler worry about where in memory the data is actually stored. Before storing a value into a variable, however, C++ requires that we clearly declare the type of data that is to be stored in it. We must tell the compiler, in advance, the names of the variables that will be used for characters, the names that will be used for integers, and the names that will be used to store the other C++ data types.

Declaration Statements

Naming a variable and specifying the data type that can be stored in it are accomplished using **declaration statements.** A declaration statement has the general form:

```
data-type variable name;
```

where `data-type` designates a valid C++ data type and `variable name` is a user-selected variable name. For example, variables used to hold integer values are declared using the keyword **`int`** to specify the data type and have the form:

```
int variable-name;
```

Thus, the declaration statement

```
int sum;
```

declares `sum` as the name of a variable capable of storing an integer value.

In addition to the reserved word `int`, which is used to specify an integer, the reserved word **`long,`** which is considered a data type qualifier, is used to specify a long integer.[9] For example, the statement

```
long int datenum;
```

declares `datenum` as a variable that will be used to store a long integer. When using the `long qualifier the keyword int` can be omitted. Thus, the previous declaration can be written as:

```
long datenum;
```

Variables used to hold single-precision floating point values are declared using the keyword **`float,`** whereas variables that will be used to hold double-precision values are declared using the keyword **`double.`** For example, the statement

```
float firstnum;
```

declares `firstnum` as a variable that will be used to store a floating-point number. Similarly, the statement

```
double secnum;
```

declares that the variable `secnum` will be used to store a double-precision number.

Although declaration statements may be placed anywhere within a function, most declarations are typically grouped together and placed immediately after the function's opening brace. In all cases, however, a variable must be declared before it can be used, and like all C++ statements, declaration statements must end with a semicolon. If the declaration statements are placed after the opening function brace, a simple `main()` function containing declaration statements would have the following general form:

```
#include <iostream.h>

int main()
{
  declaration statements;

  other statements;
}
```

---

[9] Additionally, the reserved words unsigned int are used to specify an integer that can only store nonnegative numbers and the reserved words short int are used to specify a short integer.

Program 2.6 illustrates this form in declaring and using four floating-point variables, with the cout object used to display the contents of one of the variables.

PROGRAM 2.6

```
#include <iostream.h>

int main()
{
  float grade1;  // declare grade1 as a float variable
  float grade2;  // declare grade2 as a float variable
  float total;   // declare total as a float variable
  float average; // declare average as a float variable

  grade1 = 85.5;
  grade2 = 97.0;
  total = grade1 + grade2;
  average = total/2.0; // divide the total by 2.0
  cout << "The average grade is " << average << endl;

  return 0;
}
```

The placement of the declaration statements in Program 2.6 is straightforward, although we will see shortly that the four individual declarations can be combined into a single declaration. When Program 2.6 is run, the following output is displayed:

```
The average grade is 91.25
```

Notice that when a variable name is sent to cout, the value stored in the variable is placed on the output stream and displayed. Also notice the use of the term endl as the last item to be inserted into the output stream. endl is an example of a C++ **manipulator,** which is an item used to manipulate how the output stream of characters is displayed. In particular, the endl manipulator first causes a newline character ('\n') to be added to the output stream and then forces an immediate flushing of the output stream. When used with the cout object, this has the effect of ensuring an immediate display of the stream on the terminal. (Section 3.2 contains a list of the more commonly used manipulators.)

Just as integer and real (floating-point, double-precision, and long double) variables must be declared before they can be used, a variable used to store a single character must also be declared. Character variables are declared using the reserved word char. For example, the declaration

```
char ch;
```

declares ch to be a character variable. Program 2.7 illustrates this declaration and the use of cout to display the value stored in a character variable.

PROGRAM 2.7

```
#include <iostream.h>

int main()
{
  char ch;      // this declares a character variable

  ch = 'a';     // store the letter a into ch
  cout << "The character stored in ch is " << ch << endl;
  ch = 'm';     // now store the letter m into ch
  cout << "The character now stored in ch is "<< ch << endl;

  return 0;
}
```

When Program 2.7 is run, the output produced is:

```
The character stored in ch is a
The character now stored in ch is m
```

Notice in Program 2.7 that the first letter stored in the variable `ch` is `a` and the second letter stored is `m`. Since a variable can only be used to store one value at a time, the assignment of `m` to the variable automatically causes `a` to be overwritten.

Multiple Declarations

Variables having the same data type can always be grouped together and declared using a single declaration statement. The common form of such a declaration is:

```
data-type variable list;
```

For example, the four separate declarations used in Program 2.6,

```
float grade1;
float grade2;
float total;
float average;
```

can be replaced by the single declaration statement

```
float grade1, grade2, total, average;
```

Similarly, the two character declarations,

```
char ch;
char key;
```

can be replaced with the single declaration statement

```
char ch, key;
```

Note that declaring multiple variables in a single declaration requires that the data type of the variables be given only once, that all the variables names be separated by commas, and that only one semicolon be used to terminate the declaration. (The space after each comma is inserted for readability, and is not required.)

Declaration statements can also be used to store an initial value into declared variables. For example, the declaration statement

```
int num1 = 15;
```

both declares the variable `num1` as an integer variable and sets the value of the variable to 15. When a declaration statement is used to store a value into a variable, the variable is said to be *initialized*. Thus, in this example it is correct to say that the variable `num1` has been initialized to 15. Similarly, the declaration statements

```
float grade1 = 87.0;
float grade2 = 93.5;
float total;
```

declare three floating-point variables and initialize two of them. When initializations are used, good programming practice dictates that each initialized variable be declared on a line by itself. Constants, expressions using only constants (such as 87.0 + 12 − 2), and expressions using constants and previously initialized variables can all be used as initializers within a function. For example, Program 2.6 rewritten with a declaration initialization becomes Program 2.6a.

PROGRAM 2.6a

```
#include <iostream.h>

int main()
{
  float grade1 = 85.5;
  float grade2 = 97.0;
  float total, average;

  total = grade1 + grade2;
  average = total/2.0; // divide the total by 2.0
  cout << "The average grade is " << average << endl;

  return 0;
}
```

Notice the blank line after the last declaration statement. Inserting a blank line after the variable declarations placed at the top of a function body is a good programming practice. It improves both a program's appearance and its readability.

An interesting feature of C++ is that variable declarations may be freely intermixed and even contained with other statements; the only requirement is that a variable must be declared prior to its use. For example, the variable `float` in Program 2.6a could have been declared when it is first used using the statement `float total = grade1 + grade2`. In very restricted situations (such as debugging as described in Section 4.7, or in a for loop, described in Section 5.4), declaring a variable at its point of use can be helpful. In general, it is preferable not to disperse declarations but rather to group them, in as concise and clear manner as possible, at the top of each function.

Memory Allocation

The declaration statements we have introduced have performed both software and hardware tasks. From a software perspective, declaration statements always provide a list of all variables and their data types. In this software role, variable declarations also help to control an otherwise common and troublesome error caused by the misspelling of a variable's name within a program. For example, assume that a variable named `distance` is declared and initialized using the statement

```
int distance = 26;
```

Now assume that this variable is inadvertently misspelled in the statement

```
mpg = distnce / gallons;
```

In languages that do not require variable declarations, the program would treat `distnce` as a new variable and either assign an initial value of zero to the variable or use whatever value happened to be in the variable's storage area. In either case a value would be calculated and assigned to `mpg`, and finding the error or even knowing that an error occurred could be extremely troublesome. Such errors are impossible in C++, because the compiler will flag `distnce` as an undeclared variable. The compiler cannot, of course, detect when one declared variable is typed in place of another declared variable.

In addition to their software role, declaration statements can also perform a distinct hardware task. Since each data type has its own storage requirements, the computer can allocate sufficient storage for a variable only after knowing the variable's data type. Because variable declarations provide this information, they can be used to force the compiler to reserve sufficient physical memory storage for each variable. Declaration statements used for this hardware purpose are also called **definition statements,** because they define or tell the compiler how much memory is needed for data storage.

All the declaration statements we have encountered so far have also been definition statements. Later, we will see cases of declaration statements that do not cause any new storage to be allocated and are used simply to declare or alert the program to the data types of variables that are created elsewhere in the program.

Figure 2.10 (parts a–d) illustrates the series of operations set in motion by declaration statements that also perform a definition role. The figure shows that definition statements (or, if you prefer, declaration statements that also cause memory to be allocated) "tag" the first byte of each set of reserved bytes with a name. This name is, of course, the variable's name and is used by the computer to correctly locate the starting point of each variable's reserved memory area.

Within a program, after a variable has been declared, it is typically used by a programmer to refer to the contents of the variable (that is, the variable's value). Where in memory this value is stored is generally of little concern to the programmer. The compiler, however, must be concerned with where each value is stored and with correctly locating each variable. In this task the computer uses the variable name to locate the first byte of storage previously allocated to the variable. Knowing the variable's data type then allows the compiler to store or retrieve the correct number of bytes.

FIGURE 2.10a Defining the Integer Variable Named `total`

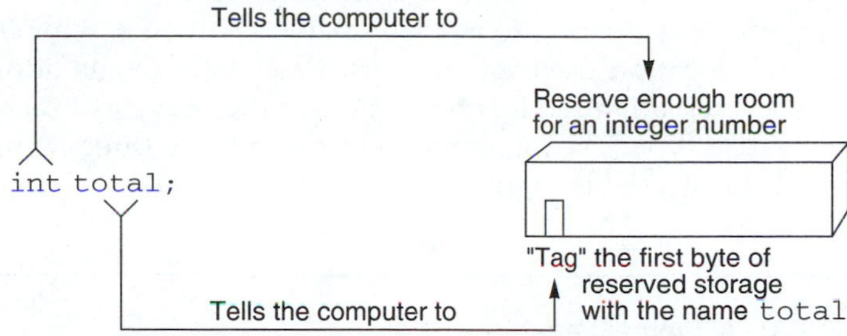

FIGURE 2.10b Defining the Floating Point Variable Named `firstnum`

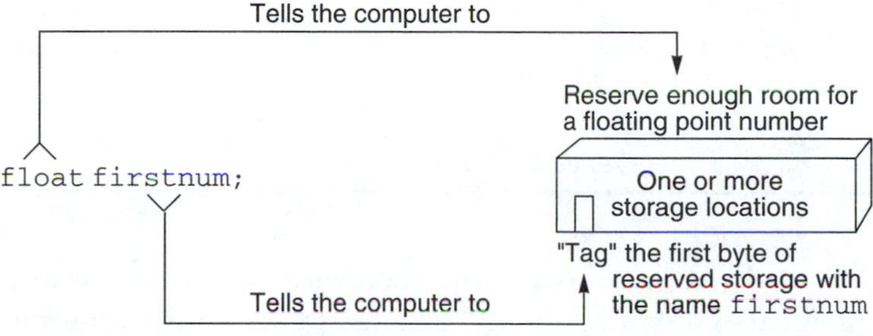

FIGURE 2.10c Defining the Double-Precision Variable Named `secnum`

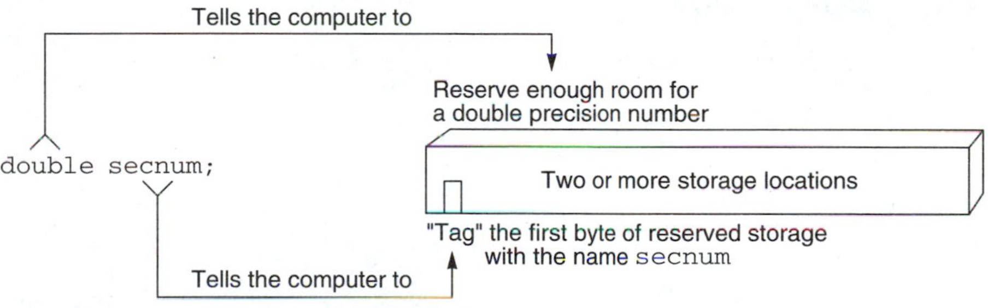

FIGURE 2.10d Defining the Character Variable Named `ch`

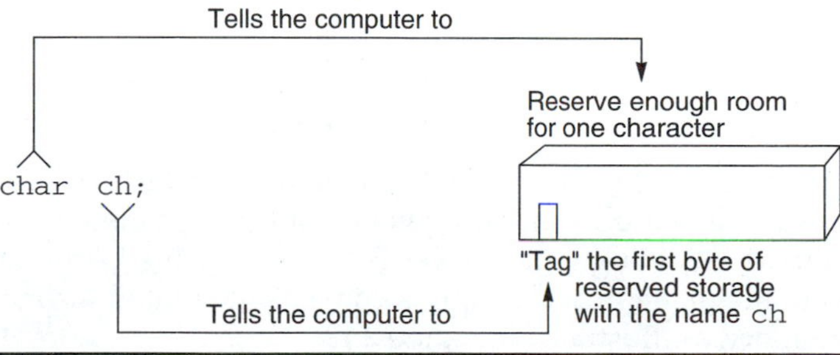

Displaying a Variable's Address

Every variable has three major items associated with it: its data type, the actual value stored in the variable, and the address of the variable. The value stored in the variable is referred to as the variable's contents, while the address of the first memory location used for the variable constitutes its address. How many locations are actually used for the variable, as we have just seen, depends on the variable's data type. The relationship between these three items (type, contents, location) is illustrated in Figure 2.11.

FIGURE 2.11 A Typical Variable

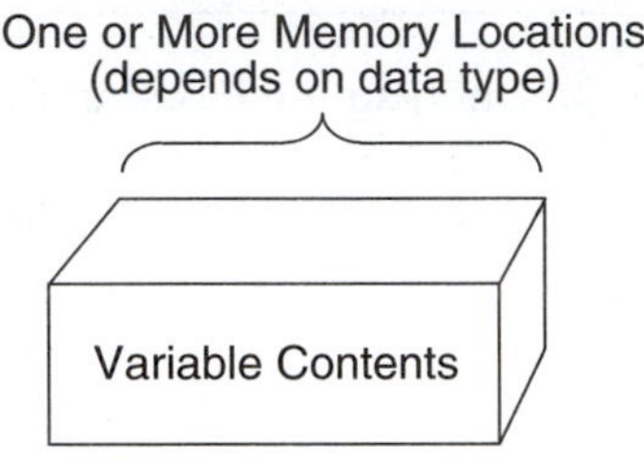

Programmers are usually concerned only with the value assigned to a variable (its contents) and give little attention to where the value is stored (its address). For example, consider Program 2.8.

PROGRAM 2.8

```
#include <iostream.h>

int main()
{
  int num;

  num = 22;
  cout << "The value stored in num is " << num << endl;

  return 0;
}
```

The output displayed when Program 2.8 is run is:

```
The value stored in num is 22
```

Program 2.8 merely prints the value 22, which is the contents of the variable num. We can go further, however, and ask "where is the number 22 actually stored?" Although the answer is "in num," this is only half of the answer. The variable name `num` is simply a convenient symbol for real, physical locations in memory, as illustrated in Figure 2.12.

FIGURE 2.12 Somewhere in Memory

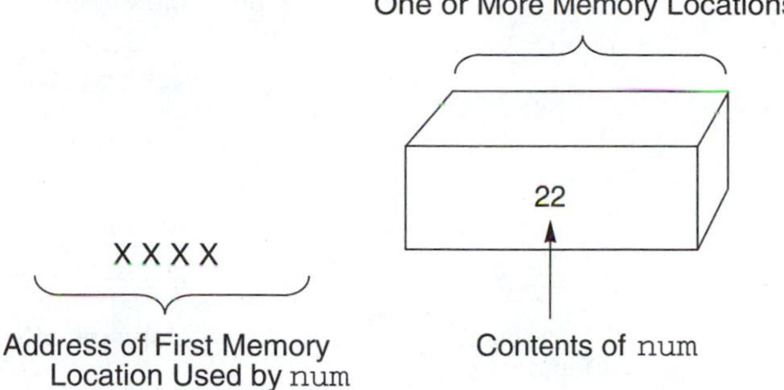

To determine the address of num, we can use C++'s address operator, &, which means "the address of." Except when used in a declaration statement, the address operator placed in front of a variable's name refers to the address of the variable.[10] For example, `&num` means *the address of* `num`, `&total` means *the address of* `total`, and `&price` means *the address of* `price`. Program 2.9 uses the address operator to display the address of the variable num.

PROGRAM 2.9

```
#include <iostream.h>

int main()
{
  int num;

  num = 22;
  cout << "The value stored in num is " << num << endl;
  cout << "The address of num = " << &num << endl;

  return 0;
}
```

The output of Program 2.9 is:

```
The value stored in num is 22
The address of num = 0x8f5afff4
```

Figure 2.13 on p. 88 illustrates the additional address information provided by the output of Program 2.9.

[10] When used in declaring reference variables and parameters, which is presented in Chapter 6, the ampersand refers to the data type *preceding* it. Thus, the declaration `float& num` is read as "num is the address of a float", or more commonly as "num is a reference to a float".

FIGURE 2.13 A More Complete Picture of the Variable `num`

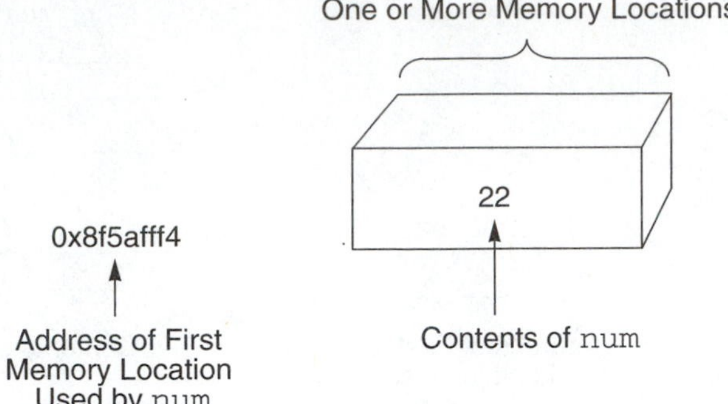

Clearly, the address output by Program 2.9 depends on the computer used to run the program. Every time Program 2.9 is executed, however, it displays the address of the first memory location used to store the variable `num`. As illustrated by the output of Program 2.9, the display of addresses is in hexadecimal notation. This display has no effect on how addresses are used internal to the program; it merely provides us with a means of displaying addresses that is helpful in understanding them. As we shall see in Chapters 6 and 13, using addresses as opposed to only displaying them is an extremely important and powerful programming tool.

Exercises 2.4

1. State whether the following variable names are valid or not. If they are invalid, state the reason why.

```
prod_a     c1234      abcd       _c3        12345
newbal     while      $total     new bal    a1b2c3d4
9ab6       sum.of     average    grade1     fin_grad
```

2. State whether the following variable names are valid or not. If they are invalid, state the reason why. Also indicate which of the valid variable names should not be used because they convey no information about the variable.

```
salestax   a243       r2d2       first_num  cc_a1
harry      sue        c3p0       average    sum
maximum    okay       a          awesome    goforit
3sum       for        tot.a1     c$five     netpay
```

3. a. Write a declaration statement to declare that the variable `count` will be used to store an integer.

   b. Write a declaration statement to declare that the variable `grade` will be used to store a floating-point number.

   c. Write a declaration statement to declare that the variable `yield` will be used to store a double-precision number.

   d. Write a declaration statement to declare that the variable `initial` will be used to store a character.

4. Write declaration statements for the following variables:

   a. `num1, num2`, and `num3` used to store integer numbers

   b. `grade1, grade2, grade3`, and `grade4` used to store floating-point numbers

   c. `tempa, tempb`, and `tempc` used to store double-precision numbers

   d. `ch, let1, let2, let3`, and `let4` used to store character types

5. Write declaration statements for the following variables:

   a. `firstnum` and `secnum` used to store integers

   b. `price, yield`, and `coupon` used to store floating-point numbers

   c. `maturity` used to store a double-precision number

6. Rewrite each of the following declaration statements as three individual declarations:

   a. `int month, day = 30, year;`

   b. `double hours, rate, otime = 15.62;`

   c. `float price, amount, taxes;`

   d. `char in_key, ch, choice = 'f';`

7. a. Determine what each statement causes to happen in the following program:

```
#include <iostream.h>
int main()
{
  int num1, num2, total;

  num1 = 25;
  num2 = 30;
  total = num1 + num2;
  cout << "The total of" << num1 << " and "
        << num2 << " is " << total;
  return 0;
}
```

   b. What output will be printed when the program listed in Exercise 7a is run?

8. Write a C++ program that stores the sum of the integer numbers 12 and 33 in a variable named `sum`. Have your program display the value stored in `sum`.

9. Write a C++ program that stores the integer value 16 in the variable `length` and the integer value 18 in the variable `width`. Have your program calculate the value assigned to the variable `perimeter`, using the assignment statement

```
perimeter = 2 * length + 2 * width;
```

   and print the value stored in the variable `perimeter`. Make sure you declare all the variables as integers at the beginning of the `main()` function.

10. Write a C++ program that stores the integer value 16 in the variable `num1` and the integer value 18 in the variable `num2`. (Make sure you declare the variables as integers.) Have your program calculate the total of these numbers and their average. The total should be stored in an integer named `total` and the average in an integer named `average`. (Use the statement `average = total/2.0;` to calculate the average.) Use the `cout` object to display `total` and `average`.

11. Repeat Exercise 10, but store the number 15 in `num1` instead of 16. With a pencil, write down the average of `num1` and `num2`. What do you think your program will store in the integer variable that you used for the average of these two numbers? How can you ensure that the correct answer will be printed for the average?

12. Write a C++ program that stores the number 105.62 in the variable `firstnum`, 89.352 in the variable `secnum`, and 98.67 in the variable `thirdnum`. (Make sure to declare the variables first as either float or double.) Have your program calculate the total of the three numbers and their average. The total should be stored in the variable total and the average in the variable average. (Use the statement `average = total /3.0;` to calculate the average.) Use the `cout` object to display the total and average.

13. Every variable has at least two items associated with it. What are these two items?

14. a. A statement used to clarify the relationship between squares and rectangles is "All squares are rectangles but not all rectangles are squares." Write a similar statement that describes the relationship between definition and declaration statements.

    b. Why must a variable be defined before any other C++ statement that uses the variable?

Note for Exercises 15 through 17: Assume that a character requires one byte of storage, an integer two bytes, a floating-point number four bytes, a double-precision number eight bytes, and that variables are assigned storage in the order in which they are declared. (Review Section 1.6 if you are unfamiliar with the concept of a byte).

15. a. Using Figure 2.14 and assuming that the variable name `rate` is assigned to the byte having memory address 159, determine the addresses corresponding to each variable declared in the following statements. Also fill in the appropriate bytes with the initialization data included in the declaration statements (use letters for the characters, not the computer codes that would actually be stored).

```
float rate;
char ch1 = 'w', ch2 = 'o', ch3 = 'w', ch4 = '!';
double taxes;
int num, count = 0;
```

    b. Repeat Exercise 15a, but substitute the actual byte patterns that an ASCII code computer would use to store the characters in the variables `ch1, ch2, ch3,` and `ch4`. (*Hint:* Use Table 2.3.)

16. a. Using Figure 2.14 and assuming that the variable named `cn1` is assigned to the byte at memory address 159, determine the addresses corresponding to each variable declared in the following statements. Also fill in the appropriate bytes with the initialization data included in the declaration statements (use letters for the characters and not the computer codes that would actually be stored).

```
char cn1 = 'a', cn2 = ' ', cn3 = 'b', cn4 = 'u', cn5 = 'n';
char cn6 = 'c', cn7 = 'h', key = '\\', sch = '\'', inc = 'o';
char inc1 = 'f';
```

    b. Repeat Exercise 16a, but substitute the actual byte patterns that an ASCII code computer would use to store the characters in each of the declared variables. (*Hint:* Use Table 2.3.)

17. Using Figure 2.14 and assuming that the variable name `miles` is assigned to the byte at memory address 159, determine the addresses corresponding to each variable declared in the following statements:

```
float miles;
int count, num;
double dist, temp;
```

FIGURE 2.14 Memory Bytes for Exercises 15, 16, and 17

Address:	159	160	161	162	163	164	165	166

Address:	167	168	169	170	171	172	173	174

Address:	175	176	177	178	179	180	181	182

Address:	183	184	185	186	187	188	189	190

2.5 INTEGER QUALIFIERS

Integer numbers are generally used in programs as counters to keep track of the number of times that something has occurred. For most applications, the counts needed are less than 32,767, which is the maximum signed integer value that can be stored in two bytes. Since most computers allocate at least two bytes for integers, there is usually no problem.

Cases do arise, however, where larger integer numbers are needed. In financial applications, for example, dates such as 7/12/89 are typically converted to the number of days from the turn of the century. This conversion makes it possible to store and sort dates using a single number for each date. Unfortunately, for dates after 1987, the number of days from the turn of the century is larger than the maximum value of 32,767 allowed when only two bytes are allocated for each integer variable. For financial programs dealing with mortgages and bonds maturing after 1987 that are run on computers allocating only two bytes per integer (PCs, for example), the limitation on the maximum integer value must be overcome.

To accommodate real application requirements such as this, C++ provides long integer, short integer, and unsigned integer data types. These three additional integer data types are obtained by adding the qualifiers `long`, `short`, or `unsigned`, respectively, to the normal integer declaration statements. For example, the declaration statement

```
long int days;
```

declares the variable `days` to be a long integer. The word `int` in a long integer declaration statement is optional, so the previous declaration statement can also be written as `long days;`. The amount of storage allocated for a long integer depends on the computer being used. Although you would expect that a long integer variable would be allocated more space than a standard integer, this may not be the case. About all that can be said is that long integers will provide no less space than regular integers. The actual amount of storage allocated by your computer should be checked using the `sizeof` operator described at the end of this section.
Once a variable is declared as a long integer, integer values can be assigned in the same way they are assigned for standard integers, or an optional letter `L` (either uppercase or lowercase, with no space between the number and letter) can be appended to the integer. For example, the declaration statement

```
long days = 38276L;
```

declares days to be of type long integer and assigns the long integer constant `38276` to the variable `days`.

In addition to the long qualifier, C++ also provides for a short qualifier. Although you would expect a short integer to conserve computer storage by reserving fewer bytes than are used for an integer, this is not always the case. Some computers use the same amount of storage for both integers and short integers. Again, the amount of memory space allocated for a short integer data type depends on your computer, and can be checked using the `sizeof` operator (described at the end of this section). As with long integers, short integers may be declared using the terms `short` or `short int` in a declaration statement. Once a variable is declared as a short integer, values are assigned in the same way they are assigned for integers.

The final integer data type is the unsigned integer. This data type is obtained by prefixing the reserved word `int` with the qualifier `unsigned`. For example, the declaration statement

```
unsigned int days;
```

declares the variable `days` to be of type `unsigned`. Unsigned integers are generally only used for positive integers and they effectively double the positive value that can be stored without increasing the number of bytes allocated to an integer. This is accomplished by effectively treating all unsigned integers as positive numbers, as illustrated in Figure 2.15.

FIGURE 2.15 Unsigned Integer Storage Using Two Bytes

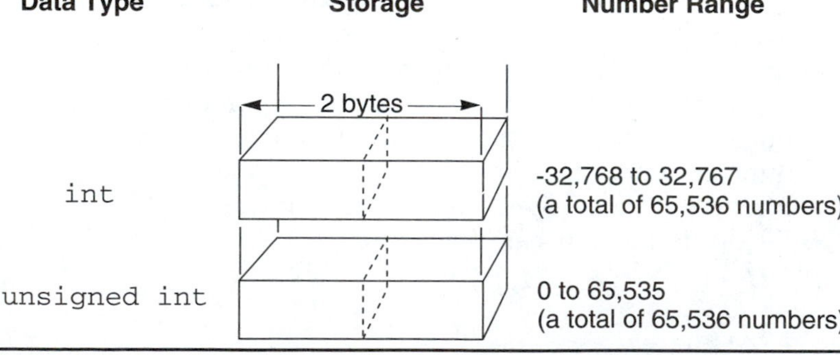

FIGURE 2.16 C++'s Fundamental Data Types

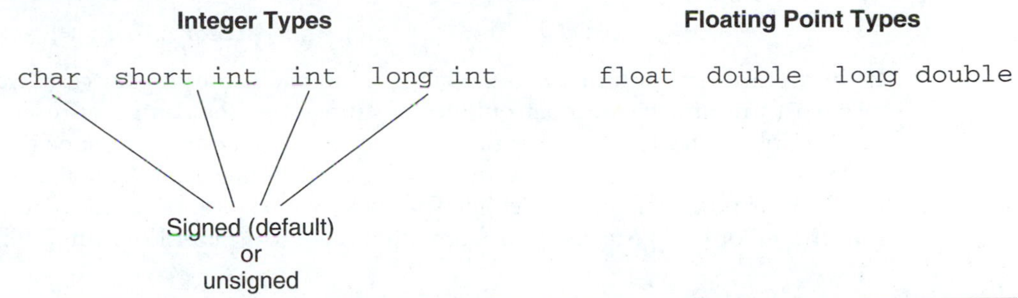

Figure 2.16 illustrates all of C++'s fundamental data types and their relationship to each other.

Data Type Conversions

The general rules for converting integer and floating point operands in mixed-mode arithmetic expressions were presented in Section 2.3. A more complete set of conversion rules for arithmetic operators, which includes character, short, and long integer operands, is provided in Table 2.8, where the rules are applied in order, starting with rule 1. Note that these rules apply to each individual arithmetic operation in their correct order of evaluation. For example, in the expression `14.78F - 4 * 3L`, multiplication, which has a higher precedence than subtraction, is performed first. For this multiplication of two integer operands, the integer `4` is converted to a long integer value, and the result of the expression is `12L` (rule 1b). The result of the next operation, `14.78F - 12L`, is the single-precision (float) value `2.78` (rule 2a).

TABLE 2.8 Conversion Rules for Arithmetic Operators

1. If both operands are either character or integer operands then:
   a. when both operands are character, short, or integer data types the result of the expression is an integer value.
   b. when one of operands is a long integer the result is a long integer, unless one of the operands is an unsigned integer. In this latter case the other operand is converted to an unsigned integer value and the resulting value of the expression is an unsigned value.
2. If any one operand is a floating-point value then:
   a. when one or both operands are floats the result of the operation is a float value.
   b. when one or both operands are doubles the result of the operation is a double value.
   c. when one or both operands are long doubles the result is a long double value.

Determining Storage Size[11]

C++ provides an operator for determining the amount of storage your compiler allocates for each data type. This operator, called the `sizeof()` operator, returns the number of bytes of the variable or data type included in the paren-

[11] This section assumes a basic understanding of computer storage concepts and terms. If you are unfamiliar with these concepts, please review Section 1.6.

theses. Unlike a function, which itself is made of C++ statements, the `sizeof()` operator is an integral part of the C++ language itself. Examples using the `sizeof` operator are:

```
sizeof(num1)      sizeof(int)      sizeof(float)
```

If the item in parentheses is a variable, as in the example `sizeof(num1)`, `sizeof()` returns the number of bytes of storage that the computer reserved for the variable. If the item following the word `sizeof` is a data type, such as `int` or `char`, `sizeof` will return the number of bytes of storage that the computer uses for the given data type. Using either approach, we can use `sizeof` to determine the amount of storage used by different data types. Consider Program 2.10:

PROGRAM 2.10

```
#include <iostream.h>

int main()
{
  char ch;
  int num1;
  cout << "Bytes of storage used by a character: "
       << sizeof(ch) << endl;
  cout << "Bytes of storage used by an integer: "
       << sizeof(num1) << endl;

  return 0;
}
```

Program 2.10 declares that the variable `ch` is used to store a character and that the variable `num1` is used to store an integer. From our discussion in the last section, we know that each of these declaration statements is also a definition statement. As such, the first declaration statement instructs the compiler to reserve enough storage for a character, and the second declaration statement instructs the compiler to reserve enough storage for an integer. The `sizeof()` operator is then used to tell us how much room the computer really set aside for these two variables. The `sizeof()` operator itself is used as an argument to the `cout` object. When Program 2.10 is run on an IBM personal computer the following output is obtained:

```
Bytes of storage used by a character: 1
Bytes of storage used by an integer: 2
```

Exercises 2.5

1. a. Run Program 2.10 to determine how many bytes your computer uses to store character and integer data types.

   b. Expand Program 2.10 to determine how many bytes your computer uses for short integers, long integers, and unsigned integers.

2. After running the program written for Exercise 1b, use Table 2.2 to determine the maximum and minimum numbers that can be stored in integer, short integer, and long integer variables for your computer.
3. Program 2.10 did not actually store any values into the variables `ch` and `num1`. Why was this not necessary?
4. a. Expand Program 2.10 to determine how many bytes your computer uses to store floating-point and double-precision numbers.

   b. Although there is no long float data class, double-precision numbers are sometimes considered as the equivalent long form for floating-point numbers. Why is this so? Does the output of the program written for Exercise 4a support this statement?

2.6 APPLYING THE SOFTWARE DEVELOPMENT PROCEDURE

Recall from Section 1.3 that writing a C++ program is the third step in the programming process. The first two steps in the process are determining what is required and selecting the algorithm to be coded into C++. In this section we show how the steps presented in Section 1.3 are applied in practice when converting programming problems into working C++ programs. To review, once a program requirement or problem is stated, the software development procedure consists of the following steps.

Step 1: Analyze the Problem

The analysis can consist of up to two parts. The first is a *basic analysis* that must be performed on all problems and consists of extracting the complete input and output information supplied by the problem. That is, you must (1) determine and understand the desired output items that the program must produce and (2) determine the required input items.

Together these two items are referred to as the problem's input/output, or I/O for short. Only after a problem's I/O has been determined is it possible to select an initial algorithm for transforming the inputs into the desired outputs. At this point it is sometimes necessary and/or useful to perform a hand calculation to verify that the output can indeed be obtained from the inputs. Clearly, if a formula is given that relates the inputs to the output, this step can be omitted at this stage. If the required inputs are available and the desired output(s) can be produced, the problem is said to be clearly defined and can be solved.

For a variety of reasons it may not be possible to complete a basic analysis. If this is the case, an extended analysis may be necessary. An *extended analysis* simply means that you must obtain additional information about the problem so that you thoroughly understand what is being asked for and how to achieve the result. In this text any additional information required for an understanding of the problem will be supplied along with the problem statement.

Step 2: Develop a Solution

This step is frequently referred to as the design step, and we will use the terms *development* and *design* interchangeably. In this step you must settle on an algorithm for transforming the input items into the desired outputs and refine it as necessary so that it adequately defines all of the features that you want your program to have. If you have not performed a hand calculation using the algorithm in the analysis step, you should do so here, using specific input values.

In designing a solution, the specific approach we will take is often referred to as the *top-down approach.* This approach consists of starting with the most general solution and refining it in a manner such that the final program solution consists of clearly defined tasks that can be accomplished by individual program functions.

Step 3: Code the Solution

At this point you actually write the C++ program that corresponds to the solution developed in step 2.

Step 4: Test and Correct the Program

This is done by means of selected test data and is used to make corrections to the program when errors are found. One set of test data that should always be used is the data used in your previous hand calculation.

To see how each of these steps can be implemented in practice, we now apply it to a simple programming problem.

> The circumference, C, of a circle is given by the formula $C = 2\pi r$, where π is the constant 3.1416 (accurate to four decimal places), and r is the radius of the circle. Using information, write a C program to calculate the circumference of a circle that has a 2-inch radius.

Step 1: Analyze the Problem The first step in developing a program for this problem statement is to perform a basic analysis. We begin by determining the required outputs. Frequently, the statement of the problem will use such words as *calculate, print, determine, find,* or *compare,* which can be used to determine the desired outputs.

For our sample problem statement, the key phrase is "to calculate the circumference of a circle." This clearly identifies an output item. Since there are no other such phrases in the problem, only one output item is required.

After we have clearly identified the desired output, the basic analysis step continues with the identification of all input items. It is essential at this stage to distinguish between input items and input values. An *input item* is the name of an input quantity, whereas an *input value* is a specific number or quantity for the input item. For example, in our sample problem statement, the input item is the radius of the circle (the known quantity). Although this input item has a specific numerical value in this problem (the value 2), actual input item values are generally not of importance at this stage because the initial selection of an algorithm is typically independent of specific input values. The algorithm depends on knowing what the output and input items are and if there are any special limits. Let us see why this is so.

From the problem statement it is clear that the algorithm for transforming the input items to the desired output is given by the formula $C = 2\pi r$. Notice that this formula can be used regardless of the specific values assigned to r. Although we cannot produce an actual numerical value for the output item (circumference) unless we have an actual numerical value for the input item, the correct relationship between inputs and outputs is expressed by the formula. Recall that this is precisely what an algorithm provides: a description of how the inputs are to be transformed into outputs that work for all inputs.

Step 2: Develop a Solution The basic algorithm for transforming the inputs into the desired output is provided by the given formula. We must now refine it by listing, in detail, how the inputs, outputs, and algorithm are to be combined to produce a solution. This listing indicates the steps that will be taken by the program to solve the problem. As such it constitutes an outline of the final form that will be followed by the program code. Using pseudocode, the complete algorithm for solving this problem is:

Assign a value to r.
Calculate the circumference using the formula C = 2πr.
Display the result.

Notice that the structure of this algorithm conforms to the sequential control structure presented in Section 1.3.

Having selected and refined the algorithm, the next step in the design (if it was not already done in the analysis step) is to check the algorithm by hand using specific data. Performing a manual calculation, either by hand or using a calculator, helps to ensure that you really do understand the problem. An added feature of doing a manual calculation is that the results can be used later in the testing phase to verify program operation. Then, when the final program is used with other data, you will have established a degree of confidence that a correct result is being calculated.

Doing a manual calculation requires that we have specific input values that can be assigned and used by the algorithm to produce the desired output. For this problem one input value is given: a radius of 2 inches. Substituting this value into the formula, we obtain a circumference = 2 (3.1416)(2) = 12.5664 inches.

Step 3: Code the Solution Since we have carefully developed a program solution, all that remains is to code the solution algorithm in C++. This means declaring appropriate input and output variables, initializing the input variables appropriately, computing the circumference, and printing the calculated circumference value. Program 2.11 performs these steps.

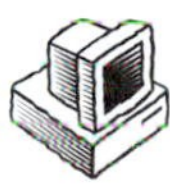

PROGRAM 2.11

```
#include <iostream.h>

int main()
{
  float radius, circumference;

  radius = 2.0;
  circumference = 2.0 * 3.1416 * radius;
  cout << "The circumference of the circle is "
       << circumference << endl;

  return 0;
}
```

When program 2.11 is executed, the following output is produced:

```
The circumference of the circle is 12.5664
```

Now that we have a working program that produces a result, the final step in the development process, testing the program, can begin.

Step 4: Test and Correct the Program The purpose of testing is to verify that a program works correctly and actually fulfills its requirements. Once testing has been completed the program can be used to calculate outputs for differing input data without the need to retest. This is, of course, one of the real values in writing a program; the same program can be used over and over with new input data.

The simplest test method is to verify the program's operation for carefully selected sets of input data. One set of input data that should always be used is the data that was selected for the hand calculation made previously in step 2 of the development procedure. In this case the program is relatively simple and performs only one calculation. Because the output produced by the test run agrees with our hand calculation we have a good degree of confidence that it can be used to correctly calculate the circumference for any input radius.

Exercises 2.6

Note: In each of these exercises a programming problem is given. Read the problem statement first and then answer the questions pertaining to the problem.

1. Consider the following programming problem: A C++ program is required that calculates the amount, in dollars, contained in a piggybank. The bank contains half dollars, quarters, dimes, nickels, and pennies.
   a. For this programming problem, how many outputs are required?
   b. How many inputs does this problem have?
   c. Write an algorithm for converting the input items into output items.
   d. Test the algorithm written for Exercise 1c using the following sample data: half dollars = 0, quarters = 17, dimes = 24, nickels = 16, pennies = 12.
2. Consider the following programming problem: A C++ program is required to calculate the value of distance, in miles, given the relationship

   ```
   distance = rate * elapsed time
   ```

   a. For this programming problem, how many outputs are required?
   b. How many inputs does this problem have?
   c. Write an algorithm for converting the input items into output items.
   d. Test the algorithm written for Exercise 2c using the following sample data: rate is 55 miles per hour and elapsed time is 2.5 hours.
   e. How must the algorithm you wrote in Exercise 2c be modified if the elapsed time is given in minutes instead of hours?
3. Consider the following programming problem: A C++ program is required to determine the value of Ergies, given the relationships

   $$\texttt{Ergies = Fergies * }\sqrt{\texttt{Lergies}}$$

   a. For this programming problem how many outputs are required?
   b. How many inputs does this problem have?
   c. Determine an algorithm for converting the input items into output items.
   d. Test the algorithm written for Exercise 3c using the following sample data: Fergies = 14.65, and Lergies = 4.

4. Consider the following programming problem: A C++ program is required to display the following name and address:

```
Mr. S. Hazlet
63 Seminole Way
Dumont, NJ 07030
```

   a. For this programming problem, how many lines of output are required?
   b. How many inputs does this problem have?
   c. Write an algorithm for converting the input items into output items.

5. Consider the following program problem: A C++ program is required to determine how far a car has traveled after 10 seconds assuming the car is initially traveling at 60 miles per hour and the driver applies the brakes to decelerate uniformly at a rate of 12 miles/sec^2. Use the fact that distance = s − (1/2)dt^2, where *s* is the initial speed of the car, *d* is the deceleration, and *t* is the elapsed time.
   a. For this programming problem how many outputs are required?
   b. How many inputs does this problem have?
   c. Write an algorithm for converting the input items into output items.
   d. Test the algorithm written for Exercise 5c using the data given in the problem.

6. Consider the following programming problem: In 1627, Manhattan Island was sold to the Dutch settlers for approximately $24. If the proceeds of that sale had been deposited in a Dutch bank paying 5% interest, compounded annually, what would the principal balance be at the end of 1995? A display is required as follows:

```
Balance as of December 31, 1995 is: xxxxxx
where xxxxxx is the amount calculated by the program.
```

   a. For this programming problem, how many outputs are required?
   b. How many inputs does this problem have?
   c. Write an algorithm for converting the input items into output items.
   d. Test the algorithm written for Exercise 6c using the data given in the problem statement.

7. Consider the following programming problem: A C++ program is required that calculates and displays the weekly gross pay and net pay of two individuals. The first individual is paid an hourly rate of $8.43 and the second individual is paid an hourly rate of $5.67. Both individuals have 20% of their gross pay withheld for income tax purposes and both pay 2% of their gross pay, before taxes, for medical benefits.
   a. For this programming problem, how many outputs are required?
   b. How many inputs does this problem have?
   c. Write an algorithm for converting the input items into output items.
   d. Test the algorithm written for Exercise 7c using the following sample data: The first person works 40 hours during the week and the second person works 35 hours.

8. Consider the following programming problem: The formula for the standard normal deviate, *z*, used in statistical applications is

$$z = \frac{x - \mu}{\sigma}$$

   where μ refers to a mean value and σ to a standard deviation. Using this formula, write a program that calculates and displays the value of the standard normal deviate when $X = 85.3$, $\mu = 80$, and $\sigma = 4$.
   a. For this programming problem, how many outputs are required?
   b. How many inputs does this problem have?

c. Write an algorithm for converting the input items into output items.

d. Test the algorithm written for Exercise 8c using the data given in the problem.

9. Consider the following programming problem: The equation describing exponential growth is:

$$y = e^x$$

Using this equation, a C++ program is required to calculate the value of y.

a. For this programming problem, how many outputs are required?

b. How many inputs does this problem have?

c. Write an algorithm for converting the input items into output items.

d. Test the algorithm written for Exercise 9c assuming $e = 2.718$ and $x = 10$.

2.7 FOCUS ON PROBLEM SOLVING

In this section the software development procedure presented in the previous section is applied to two specific programming problems. Although each problem is different, the top-down development procedure works for both situations. This procedure can be applied to any programming problem to produce a completed program and forms the foundation for all programs developed in this text.

Problem 1: Pendulum Clocks

Pendulums used in clocks, such as grandmother and grandfather clocks, keep fairly accurate time for the following reason: When the length of a pendulum is relatively large compared to the maximum arc of its swing the time to complete one swing is independent of both the pendulum's weight and the maximum displacement of the swing. When this condition is satisfied the relationship between the time to complete one swing and the length of the pendulum is given by the formula

$$length = g[time/(2\pi)]^2$$

where π, being accurate to four decimal places, is equal to 3.1416 and g is the gravitational constant equal to 32.2 ft/sec^2. When the time of a complete swing is given in seconds, the length of the pendulum is in feet. Using the given formula, write a C++ program to calculate and display the length of a pendulum needed to produce a swing that will be completed in one second. The length should be displayed in inches.

We now apply the top-down software development procedure to this problem.

Step 1: Analyze the Problem For this problem a single output is required by the program: the length of the pendulum. Additionally, the problem specifies that the actual value be displayed be in units of inches. The input items required to solve for the length are the time to complete one swing, the gravitational constant, g, and π.

Step 2: Develop a Solution The algorithm given for transforming the three input items into the desired output item is given by the formula $length = g[time/(2\pi)]^2$. Since this formula calculates the length in feet and the problem specifies that the result should be displayed in inches, we will have to multiply the result of the formula by 12. Thus, the complete algorithm for our program solution is:

Assign values to g, π, and time.
Calculate the length (in inches) using the formula
length = 12g [time/(2π)]².
Display the result.

A hand calculation, using the data that g = 32.2, time = 1, and π = 3.1416, yields a length of 9.79 inches for the pendulum.

Step 3: Code the Solution Program 2.12 provides the necessary code.

PROGRAM 2.12

```
#include <iostream.h>

int main()
{
  float time, length, pi;

  pi = 3.1416;
  time = 1.0;
  length = 12.0 * 32.2 * time/(2.0*pi) * time/(2.0*pi);
  cout << "The length is " << length << " inches\n";

  return 0;
}
```

Program 2.12 begins with an `#include` preprocessor command followed by a `main()` function. This function starts with the keyword `main` and ends with the closing brace, }. Additionally, Program 2.12 contains one declaration statement, three assignment statements, and one output statement. The assignment statements `pi = 3.1416` and `time = 1.0` are used to initialize the `pi` and `time` variables, respectively. The assignment statement

```
length = 12.0 * 32.2 * time/(2.0*pi) * time/(2.0*pi);
```

calculates a value for the variable `length`. Notice that the `12.0` is used to convert the calculated value from feet into inches. Also notice the placement of parentheses in the expression `time/(2.0*pi)`. The parentheses ensures that the value of pi is multiplied by `2.0` before the division is performed. If these parentheses were not included, the value of time would first be divided by `2.0`, and then the quantity `time/2.0` would be multiplied by pi. Finally, this same quantity is multiplied by itself to obtain the necessary squared value. (In the next chapter we will see how to use C++'s power function to obtain the same result.) When Program 2.12 is compiled and executed the following output is produced:

```
The length is 9.79 inches
```

Step 4: Test and Correct the Program The last step in the development procedure is to test the output. Because the displayed value agrees with the previous hand calculation, we have established a degree of confidence in the program. This permits us to use the program for different values of time. Note that if the parentheses were not correctly placed in the assignment statement that calculated a value for `length`, the displayed value would not agree with our previous hand calculation. This would have alerted us to the fact that the program had an error.

Problem 2: Telephone Switching Networks

A directly connected telephone network is one in which all telephones in the network are connected directly and do not require a central switching station to establish calls between two telephones. For example, financial institutions on Wall Street use such a network to maintain direct and continuously open phone lines between firms.

The number of direct lines needed to maintain a directly connected network for n telephones is given by the formula

$$lines = n(n - 1)/2$$

For example, directly connecting four telephones requires six individual lines (see Figure 2.17). Adding a fifth telephone to the network illustrated in Figure 2.17 would require an additional 4 lines for a total of 10 lines.

Using the given formula, write a C++ program that determines the number of direct lines required for 100 telephones, and the additional lines required if 10 new telephones were added to the network. Use our top-down software development procedure.

Step 1: Analyze the Problem For this program two outputs are required: the number of direct lines for 100 telephones and the additional number of lines needed when 10 new telephones are added to the existing network. The input item required for this problem is the number of telephones, which is denoted as `n` in the formula.

FIGURE 2.17 Directly Connecting Four Telephones

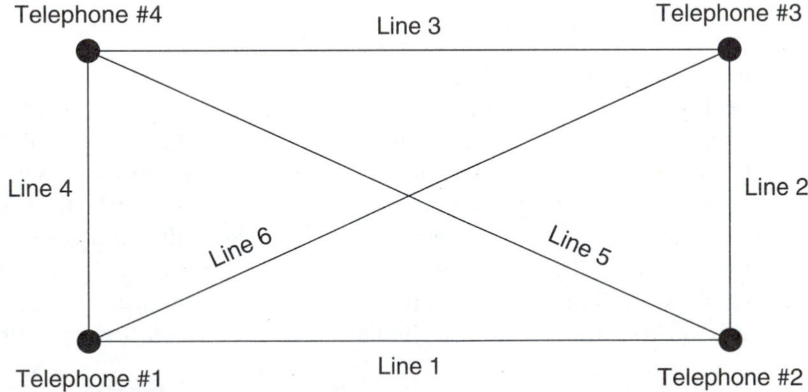

Step 2: Develop a Solution The first output is easily obtained using the formula lines = $n(n-1)/2$. Although there is no formula given for additional lines, we can use the given formula to determine the total number of lines needed for 110 subscribers. Subtracting the number of lines for 100 subscribers from the number of lines needed for 110 subscribers will then yield the number of additional lines required. Thus, the complete algorithm for our program, in pseudocode, is

Calculate the number of direct lines for 100 subscribers.
Calculate the number of direct lines for 110 subscribers.
Calculate the additional lines needed, which is the
difference between the second and first calculation.
Display the number of lines for 100 subscribers.
Display the additional lines needed.

Checking our algorithm by hand, using the data given, yields this answer: lines = $100(100 - 1)/2 = 100(99)/2 = 4950$ for 100 telephones and lines = 5995 for 110 telephones. Thus, an additional 1045 lines would be needed to directly connect the 10 additional telephones into the existing network.

Step 3: Code the Solution Program 2.13 provides the necessary code.

PROGRAM 2.13

```
#include <iostream.h>

int main()
{
  int numin1, numin2, lines1, lines2;

  numin1 = 100;
  numin2 = 110;
  lines1 = numin1 * (numin1 - 1)/2;
  lines2 = numin2 * (numin2 - 1)/2;
  cout << "The number of initial lines is " << lines1 << ".\n";
  cout << "There are " << lines2-lines1
       << " additional lines needed.\n";

  return 0;
}
```

As before, the C++ program includes the `iostream.h` header file and consists of one `main()` function. The body of this function begins with the opening brace, {, and ends with the closing brace, }. Since the number of lines between subscribers must be an integer (a fractional line is not possible) the variables `lines1` and `lines2` are specified as integer variables. The first two assignment statements initialize the variables `numin1` and `numin2`. The next assignment statement calculates the number of lines needed for 100 subscribers and the last assignment statement calculates the number of lines for 110 subscribers. The first `cout` statement is used to display a message and the result of the first calculation. The next `cout` statement is used to display the difference between the two calculations. The following output is produced when Program 2.13 is compiled and executed:

```
The number of initial lines is 4950.
There are 1045 additional lines needed.
```

Step 4: Test and Correct the Program Because the displayed value agrees with the previous hand calculation, we have established a degree of confidence in the program.

Exercises 2.7

1. a. Modify Program 2.12 to calculate the length of a pendulum that produces an arc that takes two seconds to complete.

   b. Compile and execute the program written for Exercise 1a on a computer.

2. a. Modify Program 2.12 to determine the time it takes a three-foot pendulum to complete one swing. Your program should produce the following display:

   ```
   The time to complete one swing (in seconds) is: ______
   ```

   where the underscores are replaced by the actual value calculated by your program.

   b. Compile and execute the program written for Exercise 2a on a computer. Make sure you do a hand calculation so that you can verify the results produced by your program.

   c. After you have verified the results of the program written in Exercise 2a, modify the program to calculate the time it takes a four-foot pendulum to complete one swing.

3. a. Modify Program 2.13 to calculate and display the total number of lines needed to connect 1000 individual phones directly to each other.

   b. Compile and execute the program written for Exercise 3a on a computer.

4. a. Modify Program 2.13 so that the variable `numfin` is initialized to 10, which is the additional number of subscribers to be connected to the existing network. Make any other changes in the program so that the program produces the same display as Program 2.13.

   b. Compile and execute the program written for Exercise 4a on a computer. Check that the display produced by your program matches the display shown in the text.

5. a. Design, write, compile, and execute a C++ program to convert temperature in degrees Fahrenheit to degrees Celsius. The equation for this conversion is

   $Celsius = 5.0/9.0\ (Fahrenheit - 32.0)$

   Have your program convert and display the Celsius temperature corresponding to 98.6 degrees Fahrenheit. Your program should produce the display:

   ```
   For a fahrenheit temperature of _____ degrees, the equivalent
   celsius temperature is _____ degrees
   ```

   where appropriate values are inserted by your program in place of the underscores.

   b. Check the values computed by your program by hand. After you have verified that your program is working correctly, modify it to convert 86.5 degrees Fahrenheit into its equivalent Celsius value.

6. a. Design, write, compile, and execute a C++ program to calculate the dollar amount contained in a piggy bank. The bank currently contains 12 half dollars, 20 quarters, 32 dimes, 45 nickels, and 27 pennies.

   b. Check the values computed by your program by hand. After you have verified that your program is working correctly, modify it to determine the dollar value of a bank containing no half dollars, 17 quarters, 19 dimes, 10 nickels, and 42 pennies.

7. a. Design, write, compile, and execute a C++ program to calculate the elapsed time it took to make a 183.67-mile trip. The equation for computing elapsed time is

   elapsed time = total distance/average speed

   Assume that the average speed during the trip was 58 miles per hour.

   b. Check the values computed by your program by hand. After you have verified that your program is working correctly, modify it to determine the elapsed time it takes to make a 372-mile trip at an average speed of 67 miles per hour.

8. a. Design, write, compile, and execute a C++ program to calculate the sum of the numbers from 1 to 100. The formula for calculating this sum is

   $$sum = (n/2)[2 * a + (n - 1)d]$$

   where n = number of terms to be added, a = the first number, and d = the difference between each number.

   b. Check the values computed by your program by hand. After you have verified that your program is working correctly, modify it to determine the sum of the integers from 100 to 1000.

Note: Exercises 9, 10, and 11 require raising a number to a power. This can be accomplished using C++'s power function `pow()`. For example, the statement `pow(2.0,5.0);` raises the number 2.0 to the fifth power, and the statement `pow(num1,num2);` raises the variable `num1` to the `num2` power. To use the power function, either place an `#include math.h` preprocessor command on a line by itself after the `#include iostream.h` command or include the declaration statement `double pow();` with the variable declaration statements used in your program. The power function is explained in more detail in Section 3.3.

9. a. Newton's law of cooling states that when an object with an initial temperature T is placed in a surrounding substance of temperature A, it will reach a temperature $TFIN$ in t minutes according to the formula

   $$TFIN = (T - A)e^{-kt} + A$$

   In this formula e is the irrational number 2.71828 rounded to five decimal places, commonly known as Euler's number, and k is a thermal coefficient, which depends on the material being cooled. Using this formula write, compile, and execute a C++ program that determines the temperature reached by an object after 20 minutes when it is placed in a glass of water whose temperature is 60 degrees. Assume that the object initially has a temperature of 150 degrees and a thermal constant of 0.0367.

   b. Check the value computed by your program by hand. After you have verified that your program is working correctly, modify it to determine the temperature reached after 10 minutes when it is placed in a glass of water whose temperature is 50 degrees.

10. a. Given an initial deposit of money, denoted as A, in a bank that pays interest annually, the amount of money at a time N years later is given by the formula

    $$Amount = A\ a\ (1 + I)^N$$

    where I is the interest rate as a decimal number (e.g., 9.5% is .095). Using this formula, design, write, compile, and execute a C++ program that determines the amount of money that will be available in four years if $10,000 is deposited in a bank that pays 10% interest annually.

b. Check the value computed by your program by hand. After you have verified that your program is working correctly, modify it to determine the amount of money available if $24 dollars is invested at 4% for 300 years.

11. a. If an initial deposit of A dollars is made in a bank and the interest, I, is compounded M times a year, the amount of money available after N years is given by the expression

$$A * (1 + I/M)^{M*N}$$

Using this expression, design, write, compile, and run a C++ program to determine the amount of money available after 10 years if $5000 is invested in a bank paying 6% interest compounded quarterly ($M = 4$).

b. Check the value computed by your program by hand. After you have verified that your program is working correctly, modify it to determine the amount of money available if $1000 dollars is invested at 8%, compounded quarterly, for 10 years.

2.8 PLANNING FOR OBJECTS: INTRODUCTION TO ABSTRACTION

A very important programming concept, and one that is central to object-oriented programming, is the idea of abstraction. In its most general usage, an **abstraction** is simply an idea or term that identifies the general qualities or characteristics of a group of objects, independent of any one specific object in the group. For example, consider the term "car." As a term, this is an abstraction: It refers to a group of objects that individually contain the characteristics associated with a car, such as a motor, passenger compartment, wheels, steering capabilities, brakes, etc. A particular instance of a car, such as my car or your car are not abstractions; they are real objects that are classified as "type car" because they have the attributes associated with a car.

Although we use abstract concepts all the time, we tend not to think of them as such. For example, the words *tree, dog, cat, table,* and *chair* are all abstractions, just as *car* is. Each of these terms refers to a set of qualities that are met by a group of particular things. For each of these abstractions there are many individual trees, dogs, and cats, each instance of which conforms to the general characteristics associated with the abstract term. As such, a type—such as dog or cat,— is considered an abstraction that defines a general type of which specific instances can be realized. Such types, then, simply identify common qualities of each group.

Having defined what we mean by a type, we can now create the definition of a data type. In programming terminology a **data type** consists of *both* an acceptable range of values for a particular type and a set of operations that can be applied to those values. Thus, the integer data type not only defines a range of acceptable integer values, but also defines what operations can be applied to those values.

Although users of programming languages such as C++ ordinarily assume that mathematical operations such as addition, subtraction, multiplication, and division will be supplied for integers, the designers of C++ had to consider carefully what operations would be provided as part of the integer data type. For example, the designers of C++ did not include an exponentiation operator as part of the integer data type, whereas it is included in FORTRAN's data abstraction of integers (in C++, exponentiation is supplied as a library function).

TABLE 2.9 C++'s Data Types

Data Type	Minimum Acceptable Domain	Operations
Integer (includes long, short, and unsigned)	−32,768 to +32,767	+, −, *, /, %, =, ==, !=, <=, >=, < and bit operations
Floating point (includes double and long double)	−1E−37 to +1E+37	+, −, *, /, =, ==, !=, <=, and >=
Character	All characters with an ASCII value between 0 and 127	+, −, *, /, =, ==, !=, <= and >=

To summarize then, a data type is an abstraction that consists of

A set of values of a particular type

and

A set of operations that can be applied to those values.

The set of allowed values is more formally referred to as the data type's *domain*. Table 2.9 lists the domain and the most common operations defined for the data types `int`, `float`, and `char`.[12]

Built-In and Abstract Data Types (ADTs)

All of the data types listed in Table 2.9 are provided as part of the C++ language. As such, they are formally referred to as *built-in* or *primitive* data types (the two terms are synonyms). In contrast to built-in data types, some programming languages permit programmers to create their own data types; that is, define a type of value with an associated domain and operations that can be performed on the acceptable values. Such user-defined data types are formally referred to as *abstract data types*.

In C++ abstract data types are called *classes*, and the ability to create classes is the major enhancement provided to C by C++. (In fact, the original name for C++ was *C with Classes*.) After we obtain a basic understanding of C++'s syntax and how to use its built-in data types, we will be ready to use C++'s class capabilities.

Improving Communication

1. Respond to the following request:

MEMORANDUM

To: U. R. It

From: Head of Programming Dept.

Subject: Moving to an Object Orientation

[12] The actual domain for integers can be found in the <limits.h> header file supplied by your compiler. Similarly, the domain for floating-point numbers can be found in the header file <float.h>.

The term *abstraction* keeps popping up in our discussions of object-oriented programming (OOP). I understand that abstraction is somewhat of an important concept that is central to OOP. Could you please explain what abstraction is and how it relates to OOP.

Working in Teams

2. Every object has a set of attributes and a set of behaviors. For example, a radio's attributes consist of its size, its color, its type (AM or FM), whether it has a tape player or not, etc. Similarly, its behaviors should include being able to respond to an on–off switch, being able to respond to a volume control, and so on. Consider the following objects:
   - A car
   - A computer
   - A house
   - A computer programming class
   - An elevator

   a. Have the team select one object.

   b. For the selected object have the team determine a list of attributes and behaviors.

3. Establish a criteria for names of variables and functions that will be consistently used by each member of the group in all of their programs. Some choices are
   - Always use lowercase letters.
   - Always start with a lowercase or uppercase letter.
   - Use uppercase letters to separate words.
   - Use the underscore character, (_), to separate words.

   For example, using your rules, should a variable's name be maxnumber, max_number, maxNumber, MaxNumber, or Max_number? Make a determination for both variable and function names. Make sure your criteria are acceptable to your professor.

   b. After your group has come up with its recommendation, designate a representative to list your selections on the board. Then, either have all of the groups choose one of the criteria that will be common to the class, or have your professor choose one and tell you why, based on experience, he or she prefers the chosen style.

4. Now that you have had at least one team meeting, discuss among your team members the following issues:

   a. How did each team member feel about your last meeting? That is, did each one participate in discussions or did one person tend to dominate? Was input solicited from each person and did each person feel that their input was really listened to and heard? Was it an open discussion or was the discussion more of a "I'm right, you're wrong" type?

   b. Was a leader appointed or did a leader emerge? If not, first find out which members might have an interest in leading the group, because effective groups always have one or two people who organize and focus the discussion. Select a leader. If more than one person wants to lead, alternate leaders on different team projects. If no one wants to lead, take time to select a leader anyway.

   c. Was someone keeping track of the time spent on each issue? Effective groups allocate time before discussing an issue and someone is designated as the timekeeper. Find out who in the group is good at keeping time and is willing to be the timekeeper.

d. Discuss whether team members tend to ignore or even sabotage group decisions if the decision is not the one they want. Discuss the difference between agreeing on a course of action and aligning on a course of action. Aligning on a course of action refers to the willingness to support a course of action and make it successful even if it is not the one you personally wanted. Make sure each member is comfortable with aligning on a course of action before closing an issue.

e. Do you think alignment or agreement is necessary for a group of people to accomplish a given task successfully?

2.9 COMMON PROGRAMMING ERRORS

Part of learning any programming language is making the elementary mistakes commonly encountered as you begin to use the language. These mistakes tend to be quite frustrating, because each language has its own set of common programming errors waiting for the unwary. The more common errors made when initially programming in C++ are:

1. Omitting the parentheses after `main`.
2. Omitting or incorrectly typing the opening brace, `{`, that signifies the start of a function body.
3. Omitting or incorrectly typing the closing brace, `}`, that signifies the end of a function.
4. Misspelling the name of an object or function; for example, typing `cot` instead of `cout`.
5. Forgetting to close a string sent to `cout` with a double quote symbol.
6. Forgetting to separate individual data streams passed to `cout` with an insertion ("put to") symbol, <<.
7. Omitting the semicolon at the end of each C++ statement.
8. Adding a semicolon at the end of the `#include` preprocessor command.
9. Forgetting the `\n` to indicate a new line.
10. Incorrectly typing the letter O for the number zero (0), or vice versa. Incorrectly typing the letter l for the number 1, or vice versa.
11. Forgetting to declare all the variables used in a program. This error is detected by the compiler and an error message is generated for all undeclared variables.
12. Storing an inappropriate data type in a declared variable. This error is detected by the compiler and the assigned value is converted to the data type of the variable to which it is assigned.
13. Using a variable in an expression before a value has been assigned to the variable. Here, whatever value happens to be in the variable will be used when the expression is evaluated, and the result will be meaningless.
14. Dividing integer values incorrectly. This error is usually disguised within a larger expression and can be a very troublesome error to detect. For example, the expression

```
3.425 + 2/3 + 7.9
```

yields the same result as the expression

```
3.425 + 7.9
```

because the integer division of 2/3 is 0.

15. Mixing data types in the same expression without clearly understanding the effect produced. Since C++ allows expressions with "mixed" data types, it is important to understand the order of evaluation and the data type of all intermediate calculations. As a general rule, you should never mix data types in an expression unless a specific effect is desired.

The third, fifth, seventh, eighth, and ninth errors in this list are initially the most common, while even experienced programmers occasionally make the tenth error. It is worthwhile for you to write a program and specifically introduce each of these errors, one at a time, to see what error messages are produced by your compiler. Then, when these error messages appear due to inadvertent errors, you will have experience with the messages and understand how to correct the errors.

On a more fundamental level, a major programming error made by all beginning programmers is the rush to code and run a program before the programmer fully understands what is required and the algorithms and procedures that will be used to produce the desired result. A symptom of this haste to get a program entered into the computer is the lack of either an outline of the proposed program or a written program itself. Many problems can be caught just by checking a copy of the program, either handwritten or listed from the computer, before it is ever compiled.

2.10 CHAPTER REVIEW

Key Terms

abstraction
argument
ASCII
arithmetic operators
assignment statement
atomic data type
atomic data value
associativity
`char`
character values
class
comments
cout
data type
declaration statement
definition statement
double
double-precision number
EBCDIC
escape sequence
expression
float
floating-point number
function
header file
identifier
`int`
integer value
keyword
`long`
manipulator
mixed-mode expression
mnemonic
module
modulus operator
precedence
reference declaration
`sizeof()`
variable

Summary

1. A C++ program consists of one or more modules called functions. One of these functions must be named main(). The main() function identifies the starting point of a C++ program.
2. The simplest C++ program consists of the single function main().
3. Following the function name, the body of a function has the general form:

```
{
    All C++ statements in here;
}
```

4. All C++ statements must be terminated by a semicolon.
5. Three types of data were introduced in this chapter: integer, floating-point, and character data. Each of these types of data is typically stored in a computer using different amounts of memory. C++ recognizes each of these data types, in addition to other types yet to be presented.
6. The cout object can be used to display all of C++'s data types.
7. When the cout object is used within a program, the preprocessor command #include <iostream.h> must be placed at the top of the program. Preprocessor commands do not end with a semicolon.
8. Every variable in a C++ program must be declared as to the type of value it can store. Declarations within a function may be placed anywhere within a function, although a variable can only be used after it is declared. Variables may also be initialized when they are declared. Additionally, variables of the same type may be declared using a single declaration statement. Variable declaration statements have the general form:

```
data-type variable-name(s);
```

9. A simple C++ program containing declaration statements has the typical form:

```
#include <iostream.h>

int main()
{
    declaration statements;

    other statements;

    return 0;
}
```

   Although declaration statements may be placed anywhere within the function's body, a variable may only be used after it is declared.

10. Declaration statements always play a software role of informing the compiler of a function's valid variable names. When a variable declaration also causes the computer to set aside memory locations for the variable, the declaration statement is also called a definition statement. (All the declarations we have used in this chapter have also been definition statements.)
11. The sizeof() operator can be used to determine the amount of storage reserved for variables.

Exercises

1. Given the following variable declarations, determine which statements and commands are valid and which are invalid. If illegal, explain why.

```
int numOfApples, numOfOranges;
int vector, digitialTemp;
float average, distance;
char letter, symbol;
```

   a. `average = 89.4;`

   b. `distyance= 130;`

   c. `numOfOranges = (54 * numOfApples) % 3;P  92    92`

   d. `vector = numOfApples;`

   e. `digitalTemp = float (average);`

   f. `numOfApples = numOfOranges + letter;`

   g. `symbol = letter;`

   h. `distance = distance % average;`

   i. `vector = distance / average;`

   j. `numOfApples = float(average);`

   k. `numOfOranges = int (distance);`

   l. `average = float (vector);`

   m. `distance = float(numOfApples);`

   n. `numOfApples = numOfOranges - distance;`

   o. `numOfOragnes = -17;`

2. Evaluate the following mixed-mode expressions and list the data type of the result. In evaluating the expressions be aware of the data types of all intermediate calculations.

   a. `10.0 + 15 / 2 + 4.3`

   b. `10.0 + 15.0 / 2 + 4.3`

   c. `3.0 * 4 / 6 + 6`

   d. `3 * 4.0 / 6 + 6`

   e. `20.0 - 2 / 6 + 3`

   f. `10 + 17 * 3 + 4`

   g. `10 + 17 / 3. + 4`

   h. `3.0 * 4 % 6 + 6`

   i. `10 + 17 % 3 + 4.`

3. Repeat Exercise 7 in Section 2.3 assuming that `amount` has the value 1.0, `m` has the value 50.0, `n` has the value 10.0, and `p` has the value 5.0.

4. Analyze the following problem statements and determine if each problems statement is well defined. If the problem is not well defined, explain why.

   a. In a list consisting of 50 test grades, find the grade that appears most frequently.

   b. If a person can only pay $600 to $750 for house payments, what range of houses should be considered.

c. Determine the smallest number such that the difference of its digits is 31.

d. Find the first 10 sets of integer numbers *a*, *b*, and *c* such that $a^2 + b^2 = c^2$.

5. Determine if the given algorithm solves the following problem:

Problem: Determine the largest value for any two given numbers.
Algorithm: Compute the difference, *D*, between the two numbers *A* and *B* as $D = A - B$.

If *D* is greater than 1, the first number is larger; otherwise, the second number is larger.

6. Design and write a C++ program that determines which letter lies halfway between any two letters of the alphabet. Test your program using the following letters:

A and C
A and Z
M and Q
M and P
Z and Z

7. a. The table in Appendix B lists the integer values corresponding to each letter stored using the ASCII code. Using this table, notice that the uppercase letters consist of contiguous codes starting with an integer value of 65 for A and ending with 90 for the letter Z. Similarly, the lowercase letters begin with the integer value of 97 for the letter a and end with 122 for the letter z. With this as background, determine the character value of the expressions 'A' + 32 and 'Z' + 32.

b. Using Appendix B, determine the integer value of the expression 'a' − 'A'.

c. Determine the character value of the following expression, where uppercase letter can be any uppercase letter from A to Z:

```
uppercase letter + 'a' - 'A'
```

8. You decide to make your company's logo—a red circle surrounded by a concentric blue ring—a well-recognized symbol. To do this you intend to pay farmers throughout the country to paint the logo on their barns. The problem is to determine, for a given-size barn, how much red paint and how much blue paint will be required. From experience, the number of quarts of paint is equal to the area to be painted (in square feet) divided by 125. Using this information, construct a structure chart for determining the quarts of red and blue paint that will be needed. (*Hint:* You will have to determine the area of the inner circle and outer ring. Assume that the outer circle has a radius of *b*, and the inner circle has a radius of *a*.)

9. Design, write, test, and run a C++ program to do the following: Given the current time (hours and minutes) on a 24-hour clock, add a whole number of hours and determine what the new clock reading is and how many days later it will be. (*Hint:* Use / 24 and % 24, and designate midnight as 0:00 hours instead of 24:00 hours. Example: 17:30 + 37 hours is 6:30, two days later.

10. In a game of Woodenbleevit, three players make up a team. At the end of each round, the teams core is the total points accumulated by the team divided by 3 and truncated to the net smaller whole number. For example, if your team received 76 points in a round, the team score for that round would be 25 (76/3 = 25.333 = 25 truncated). A game consists of five rounds.

Design, write, test, and run a C++ program that uses the following team scores:

Round 1: 14 points (still learning)
Round 2: 292 points (beginners luck)
Round 3: 77 points
Round 4: 82 points
Round 5: 45 points

Your program should divide each round's score by 3 and truncate to get the team score for the round. Add the team scores for the five rounds to get the team score for the game. Determine how many points the team lost because of the truncation process. (*Hint:* Use both the division and modular operations.)

11. Hap's Hazard County Phone Company, Inc., charges for phone calls by distance (miles) and length of time (minutes). The cost of a call (in dollars) is computed as 0.30 * (time + 0.05 * distance). Design, write, test, and run a C++ program that calculates the cost for each of three phone calls and the total cost of all three calls using the following data:

    Call 1: 3 miles, 20 minutes
    Call 2: 2 miles, 15 minutes
    Call 3: 6 miles, 4 minutes

    The output of your program should include the time, distance, and cost of each call.

Note: Exercises 12 and 13 require raising a number to a power. This can be accomplished using C++'s power function `pow()`. For example, the statement `pow(2.0,5.0);` raises the number 2.0 to the fifth power, and the statement `pow(num1,num2);` raises the variable `num1` to the `num2` power. To use the power function, either place an `#include math.h` preprocessor command on a line by itself after the `#include iostream.h` command or include the declaration statement `double pow();` with the variable declaration statements used in your program. The power function is explained in more detail in Section 3.3.

12. a. Effective annual interest is the rate that must be compounded annually to generate the same interest as a stated rate compounded over a stipulated conversion period. For example, a stated rate of 8% compounded quarterly is equivalent to an effective annual rate of 8.24%. The relationship between the effective annual rate, E, and the stated rate, I, compounded M times a year is $E = (1 + I/M)M - 1$. Using this formula, design, write, compile, and execute a C++ program to determine the effective annual rate for a stated rate of 6% compounded four times a year (quarterly).

    b. Check the value computed by your program by hand. After you have verified that your program is working correctly, modify it to determine the effective annual rate for a stated rate of 8% compounded monthly.

13. a. The present value of a dollar amount is the amount of money that must be deposited in a bank account today to yield a specified dollar amount in the future. For example, if a bank is currently paying 8% interest annually, you would have to deposit \$6,947.90 in the bank today to have \$15,000 in 10 years. Thus, the present value of the \$15,000 is \$6,947.90. Using this

information, design, write, compile, and execute a C++ program that calculates how much must be deposited in a bank today to provide exactly $8,000 in 9 years at an annual interest rate of 8%. Use the formula

$$\text{present value} = \text{future amount}/(1.0 + \text{annual interest rate})^{\text{years}}$$

b. Check the value computed by your program by hand. After you have verified that your program is working correctly, modify it to determine the amount of money that must be invested in a bank today to yield $15,000 in 18 years at an annual rate of 6%.

14. a. The set of linear equations

$$a_{11}X_1 + a_{12}X_2 = c_1$$

$$a_{21}X_1 + a_{22}X_2 = c_2$$

can be solved using Cramer's rule as

$$X_1 = \frac{c_1 a_{22} - a_{12} c_2}{a_{11} a_{22} - a_{12} a_{21}}$$

$$X_2 = \frac{a_{11} c_2 - c_1 a_{21}}{a_{11} a_{22} - a_{12} a_{21}}$$

Using these equations, design, write, compile, and execute a C++ program to solve for the X_1 and X_2 values that satisfy the following equations:

$$3X_1 + 4X_2 = 40$$
$$5X_1 + 2X_2 = 34$$

b. Check the values computed by your program by hand. After you have verified that your program is working correctly, modify it to solve the following set of equations:

$$3X_1 + 12.5X_2 = 22.5$$
$$4.2X_1 - 6.3X_2 = 30$$

CHAPTER

3 Completing the Basics

In the last chapter we explored how results are displayed using C++'s `cout` object and how numerical data is stored and processed using variables and assignment statements. In this chapter we complete our introduction to C++ by presenting additional processing and input capabilities.

3.1 ASSIGNMENT OPERATIONS

We have already encountered simple assignment statements in Chapter 2. Assignment statements are the most basic C++ statements for both assigning values to variables and performing computations. This statement has the syntax:

```
variable = expression;
```

The simplest expression in C++ is a single constant. In each of the following assignment statements, the operand to the right of the equal sign is a constant:

```
length = 25;
width = 17.5;
```

In each of these assignment statements, the value of the constant to the right of the equal sign is assigned to the variable on the left of the equal sign. It is important to note that the equal sign in C++ does not have the same meaning as an equal sign

A BIT OF BACKGROUND

Napier's Bones

Scottish mathematician John Napier, born near Edinburgh, England, in 1550, spent most of his life creating methods and devices to make mathematical calculations easier. One of his early inventions was a set of square rods, made of bone, that were used for multiplying whole numbers.

Napier is also credited with the discovery that the weight of any object can be found by balancing the object on a scale against weights of relative size 1, 2, 4, 8,.... His most valuable invention, however, was the natural logarithm, which replaced multiplication and division problems with the addition and subtraction of logarithms. For 25 years beginning in 1590, Napier devoted himself almost entirely to generating tables of logarithms.

The contribution of the logarithmic technique to science and technology is immeasurable. Until the advent of electronic calculators and computers, logarithms were *the* approach to lengthy calculations. The logarithmic slide rule, invented by William Oughtred early in the seventeenth century, was the only reasonably affordable computing tool for engineers, scientists, and students until the mid-1970s.

In most modern high-level languages, including C++, you will find a function, such as `log(x)`, for calculating logarithms.

in algebra. The equal sign in an assignment statement tells the computer first to determine the value of the operand to the right of the equal sign and then to store (or assign) that value in the locations associated with the variable to the left of the equal sign. In this regard, the C++ statement `length = 25;` is read "`length` is assigned the value `25`." The blank spaces in the assignment statement are inserted for readability only.

Recall that a variable can be initialized when it is declared. If an initialization is not done within the declaration statement, the variable should be assigned a value with an assignment statement or input operation before it is used in any computation. Subsequent assignment statements can, of course, be used to change the value assigned to a variable. For example, assume the following statements are executed one after another and that `total` was not initialized when it was declared:

```
total = 3.7;
total = 6.28;
```

The first assignment statement assigns the value of 3.7 to the variable named `total`.[1] The next assignment statement causes the computer to assign a value of 6.28 to `total`. The 3.7 that was in `total` is overwritten with the new value of 6.28, because a variable can store only one value at a time. It is sometimes useful to think

---

[1] Since this is the first time a value is explicitly assigned to this variable it is frequently referred to as an *initialization*. This stems from historical usage that said a variable was initialized the first time a value was assigned to it. Under this usage it is correct to say that "`total` is initialized to `3.7`." From an implementation viewpoint, however, this later statement is incorrect. This is because the assignment operation is handled differently by the C++ compiler than an initialization performed when a variable is created by a declaration statement. This difference is only important when using C++'s class features and is explained in detail in Section 8.1.

of the variable to the left of the equal sign as a temporary parking spot in a huge parking lot. Just as an individual parking spot can be used only by one car at a time, each variable can store only one value at a time. The "parking" of a new value in a variable automatically causes the program to remove any value previously parked there.

In addition to being a constant, the operand to the right of the equal sign in an assignment statement can be a variable or any other valid C++ expression. An *expression* is any combination of constants, variables, and function calls that can be evaluated to yield a result. Thus, the expression in an assignment statement can be used to perform calculations using the arithmetic operators introduced in Section 2.3. Some assignment statements that use expressions containing these operators follow:

```
sum = 3 + 7;
diff = 15 - 6;
product = .05 * 14.6;
tally = count + 1;
newtotal = 18.3 + total;
taxes = .06 * amount;
totalWeight = factor * weight;
average = sum / items;
slope = (y2 - y1) / (x2 - x1);
```

As always in an assignment statement, the computer first calculates the value of the expression to the right of the equal sign and then stores this value in the variable to the left of the equal sign. For example, in the assignment statement `totalWeight = factor * weight;` the arithmetic expression `factor * weight` is first evaluated to yield a result. This result, which is a number, is then stored in the variable `totalWeight`.

In writing assignment expressions, you must be aware of two important considerations. Since the expression to the right of the equal sign is evaluated first, all variables used in the expression must previously have been given valid values if the result is to make sense. For example, the assignment statement `totalWeight = factor * weight;` causes a valid number to be stored in `totalWeight` only if the programmer first takes care to assign valid numbers to `factor` and `weight`. Thus the sequence of statements

```
factor = 1.06;
weight = 155.0;
totalWeight = factor * weight;
```

tells us what values are being used to obtain the result that will be stored in `totalWeight`. Figure 3.1 illustrates the values stored in the variables `factor`, `weight`, and `totalWeight`.

FIGURE 3.1 Values Stored in the Variables

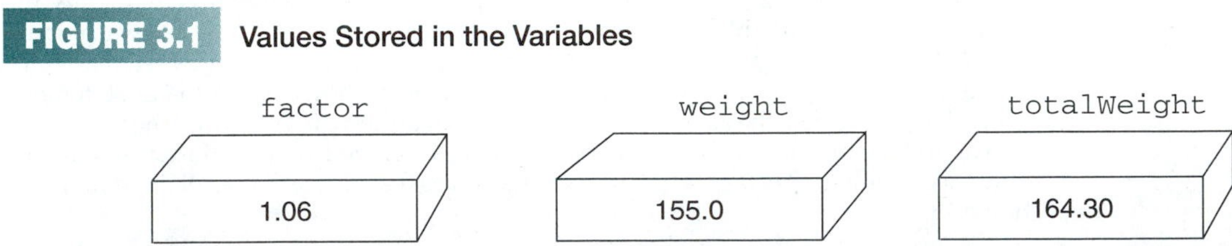

The second consideration to keep in mind is that since the value of an expression is stored in the variable to the left of the equal sign, only one variable can be listed in this position. For example, the assignment statement

```
amount + 1892 = 1000 + 10 * 5;
```

is invalid. The right side of the expression evaluates to the integer 1050, which can only be stored in a variable. Since `amount + 1892` is not a valid variable name, the computer does not know where to store the calculated value. Program 3.1 illustrates the use of assignment statements to calculate the volume of a cylinder. As illustrated in Figure 3.2, the volume of a cylinder is determined by the formula volume $= \pi r^2 h$, where r is the radius of the cylinder, h is the height, and π is the constant 3.1416 (accurate to four decimal places).

PROGRAM 3.1

```
//    this program calculates the volume of a cylinder,
//      given its radius and height
#include <iostream.h>

int main()
{
  float radius, height, volume;

  radius = 2.5;
  height = 16.0;
  volume = 3.1416 * radius * radius * height;
  cout << "The volume of the cylinder is " << volume << endl;

  return 0;
}
```

When Program 3.1 is compiled and executed, the output is

```
The volume of the cylinder is 314.16
```

FIGURE 3.2 Determining the Volume of a Cylinder

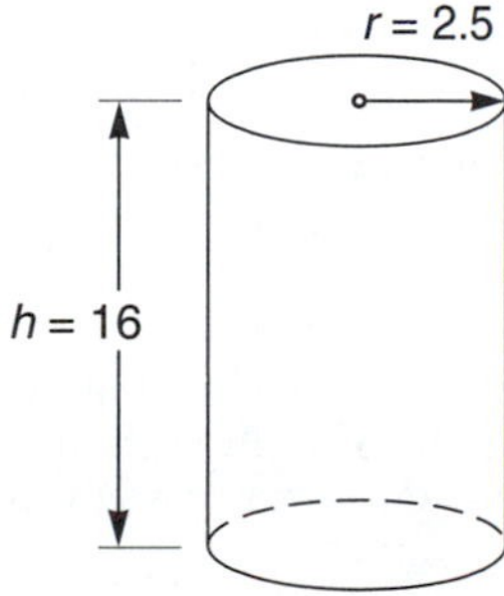

Consider the flow of control that the computer uses in executing Program 3.1. Program execution begins with the first statement within the body of the main() function and continues sequentially, statement by statement, until the closing brace of main is encountered. This flow of control is true for all programs. The computer works on one statement at a time, executing that statement with no knowledge of what the next statement will be. This explains why all operands used in an expression must have values assigned to them before the expression is evaluated. When the computer executes the statement

```
volume = 3.1416 * radius * radius * height;
```

in Program 3.1, it uses whatever value is stored in the variables radius and height at the time the assignment statement is executed.[2] If no values have been specifically assigned to these variables before they are used in the assignment statement, the computer uses whatever values happen to occupy these variables when they are referenced (on some systems all variables are automatically initialized to zero). The computer does not "look ahead" to see if you assign values to these variables later in the program.

It is important to realize that in C++, the equal sign, =, used in assignment statements is itself an operator, *which differs from the way most other high-level languages process this symbol.* In C++ (as in C), the = symbol is called the **assignment operator,** and an expression using this operator, such as a = b * c, is an assignment expression. Since the assignment operator has a lower precedence than any other arithmetic operator, the value of any expression to the right of the equal sign will be evaluated first, prior to assignment.

Like all expressions, assignment expressions themselves have a value. The value of the complete assignment expression is the value assigned to the variable to the left of the assignment operator. For example, the expression a = 5 assigns a value of 5 to the variable a and also results in the expression itself having a value of 5. The value of the expression can always be verified using a statement such as

```
cout << "The value of the expression is " << (a = 5);
```

Here, the value of the expression itself is displayed and not the contents of the variable a. Although both the contents of the variable and the expression have the same value, you should realize that we are dealing with two distinct entities.

From a programming perspective, it is the actual assignment of a value to a variable that is significant in an assignment expression; the final value of the assignment expression itself is of little consequence. However, the fact that assignment expressions have a value has implications that must be considered when C++'s relational operators are used.

Any expression that is terminated by a semicolon becomes a C++ statement. The most common example of this is the assignment statement, which is simply an assignment expression terminated with a semicolon. For example, terminating the assignment expression a = 33 with a semicolon results in the assignment statement a = 33;, which can be used in a program on a line by itself.

---

[2] Since C++ does not have an exponentiation operator, the square of the radius is obtained by the term radius * radius. In Section 3.3 we introduce C++'s power function pow(), which allows us to raise a number to a power.

POINT OF INFORMATION

lvalues and rvalues

The terms lvalue and rvalue are frequently used terms in programming technology. Both of these terms are language independent and mean the following: An **lvalue** can have a value assigned to it while an **rvalue** cannot.

In both C and C++ this means that an lvalue can appear on the left side of an assignment operator while an rvalue can appear on the right side of an assignment operator. For example, each variable we have encountered can be either an lvalue or rvalue, while a number can only be an rvalue. Not all variables, however, can be lvalues and rvalues. For example, an array type, which is introduced in Chapter 11, cannot be an lvalue or an rvalue, while individual array elements can be both.

Since the equal sign is an operator in C++, multiple assignments are possible in the same expression or its equivalent statement. For example, in the statement `a = b = c = 25;` all the assignment operators have the same precedence. Because the assignment operator has a right-to-left associativity, the final evaluation proceeds in the sequence

```
c = 25;
b = c;
a = b;
```

In this case, this has the effect of assigning the number 25 to each of the variables individually, and can be represented as

```
a = (b = (c = 25));
```

Note that data type conversions can take place across assignment operators; that is, the value of the expression on the right side of the assignment operator is converted to the data type of the variable to the left of the assignment operator. Thus, assigning an integer value to a real variable causes the integer to be converted to a real value. Similarly, assigning a real value to an integer variable forces conversion of the real value to an integer, which always results in the loss of the fractional part of the number due to truncation. For example, if `temp` is an integer variable, the assignment `temp = 25.89` causes the integer value `25` to be stored in the integer variable `temp`.[3]

A more complete example of data type conversions, which includes both mixed-mode and assignment conversion is the evaluation of the statement

```
a = b * d;
```

where `a` and `b` are integer variables and `d` is a floating-point variable. When the mixed-mode expression `b * d` is evaluated,[4] the value of `d` used in the expression is converted to a double-precision number for purposes of computation. (It is important

[3] The correct integer portion, clearly, is retained only when it is within the range of integers allowed by the compiler.

[4] Review the rules in Table 2.8 in Section 2.5 for the evaluation of mixed-mode expressions, if necessary.

to note that the value stored in d remains a floating-point number). Since one of the operands is a double-precision variable, the value of the integer variable b is converted to a double-precision number for the computation (again, the value stored in b remains an integer) and the resulting value of the expression b * d is a double-precision number. Finally, data type conversion across the assignment operator comes into play. Since the left side of the assignment operator is an integer variable, the double precision value of the expression (b * d) is truncated to an integer value and stored in the variable a.

Assignment Variations

Although only one variable is allowed immediately to the left of the equal sign in an assignment expression, the variable to the left of the equal sign can also be used on the right side of the equal sign. For example, the assignment expression sum = sum + 10 is valid. Clearly, as an algebra equation sum could never be equal to itself plus 10. But in C++, the expression sum = sum + 10 is not an equation—it is an expression that is evaluated in two major steps. The first step is to calculate the value of sum + 10. The second step is to store the computed value in sum. See if you can determine the output of Program 3.2.

PROGRAM 3.2

```
#include <iostream.h>

int main()
{
  int sum;

  sum = 25;
  cout << "The number stored in sum is " << sum << endl;
  sum = sum + 10;
  cout << "The number now stored in sum is " << sum << endl;

  return 0;
}
```

The assignment statement sum = 25; tells the computer to store the number 25 in sum, as shown in Figure 3.3. The first activation of cout causes the value stored in sum to be displayed by the message The number stored in sum

FIGURE 3.3 The Integer 25 Is Stored in sum

sum
25

FIGURE 3.4 `sum = sum + 10;` **Causes a New Value to be Stored in** `sum`

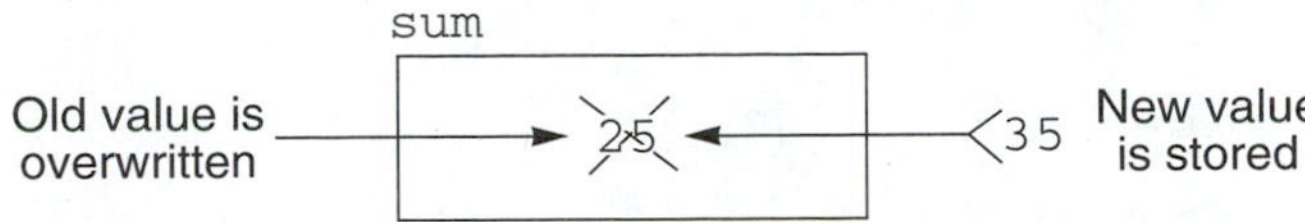

is 25. The second assignment statement in Program 3.2, `sum = sum + 10;` causes the computer to retrieve the 25 stored in `sum` and add 10 to this number, yielding the number 35. The number 35 is then stored in the variable on the left side of the equal sign, which is the variable `sum`. The 25 that was in `sum` is simply overwritten with the new value of 35, as shown in Figure 3.4.

Assignment expressions such as `sum = sum + 25`, which use the same variable on both sides of the assignment operator, can be written using the following shortcut **assignment operators:**

```
+=   -=   *=   /=   %=
```

For example, the expression `sum = sum + 10` can be written as `sum += 10`. Similarly, the expression `price *= rate` is equivalent to the expression `price = price * rate`.

When you use these new assignment operators it is important to note that the variable to the left of the assignment operator is applied to the *complete* expression on the right. For example, the expression `price *= rate + 1` is equivalent to the expression `price = price * (rate + 1)`, not `price = price * rate + 1`.

Accumulating

Assignment expressions such as `sum += 10` or its equivalent, `sum = sum + 10`, are very common in programming. These expressions are used for **accumulating** subtotals when data is entered one number at a time. For example, if we want to add the numbers 96, 70, 85, and 60 in calculator fashion, the following statements could be used:

Statement	Value in sum
`sum = 0;`	0
`sum = sum + 96;`	96
`sum = sum + 70;`	166
`sum = sum + 85;`	251
`sum = sum + 60;`	311

The first statement initializes `sum` to 0. This removes any number ("garbage value") stored in `sum` that would invalidate the final total. As each number is added, the value stored in `sum` is increased accordingly. After completion of the last statement, `sum` contains the total of all the added numbers. Program 3.3 illustrates the effect of these statements by displaying `sum`'s contents after each addition is made.

PROGRAM 3.3

```
#include <iostream.h>

int main()
{
  int sum;

  sum = 0;
  cout << "The value of sum is initially set to " << sum << endl;
  sum = sum + 96;
  cout << "  sum is now " << sum << endl;
  sum = sum + 70;
  cout << "  sum is now " << sum << endl;
  sum = sum + 85;
  cout << "  sum is now " << sum << endl;
  sum = sum + 60;
  cout << "  The final sum is " << sum << endl;

  return 0;
}
```

The output displayed by Program 3.3 is:

```
The value of sum is initially set to 0
  sum is now 96
  sum is now 166
  sum is now 251
  The final sum is 311
```

Although Program 3.3 is not a practical program (it is easier to add the numbers by hand), it does illustrate the subtotaling effect of repeated use of statements having the form

```
variable = variable + new_value;
```

We will find many uses for this type of statement when we become more familiar with the repetition statements introduced in Chapter 5.

Counting

An assignment statement that is very similar to the accumulating statement is the **counting** statement. Counting statements have the form:

```
variable = variable + fixed_number;
```

Examples of counting statements are:

```
i = i + 1;
n = n + 1;
count = count + 1;
j = j + 2;
m = m + 2;
kk = kk + 3;
```

In each of these examples the same variable is used on both sides of the equal sign. After the statement is executed the value of the respective variable is increased by a fixed amount. In the first three examples the variables `i`, `n`, and `count` have all been increased by one. In the next two examples the respective variables have been increased by two, and in the final example the variable `kk` has been increased by three.

For the special case in which a variable is either increased or decreased by one, C++ provides two unary operators. Using the *increment operator*,[5] ++, the expression `variable = variable + 1` can be replaced by either the expression `variable++` or `++variable`. Examples of the increment operator are:

Expression	**Alternative**
`i = i + 1`	`i++ or ++i`
`n = n + 1`	`n++ or ++n`
`count = count + 1`	`count++ or ++count`

Program 3.4 illustrates the use of the increment operator.

PROGRAM 3.4

```
#include <iostream.h>

int main()
{
  int count;

  count = 0;
  cout << "The initial value of count is " << count << endl;
  count++;
  cout << "   count is now " << count << endl;
  count++;
  cout << "   count is now " << count << endl;
  count++;
  cout << "   count is now " << count << endl;
  count++;
  cout << "   count is now " << count << endl;

  return 0;
}
```

The output displayed by Program 3.4 is:

```
The initial value of count is 0
   count is now 1
   count is now 2
   count is now 3
   count is now 4
```

[5] As an historical note, the ++ in C++ was inspired from the increment operator symbol. It was used to indicate that C++ was the next increment to the C language.

When the ++ operator appears before a variable it is called a *prefix increment operator;* when it appears after a variable it is called a *postfix increment operator.* The distinction between a prefix and postfix increment operator is important when the variable being incremented is used in an assignment expression. For example, the expression `kk = ++n` does two things in one expression. Initially the value of `n` is incremented by one and then the new value of `n` is assigned to the variable `k`. Thus, the statement `k = ++n;` is equivalent to the following two statements:

```
n = n + 1;        // increment n first
k = n;            // assign n's value to k
```

The assignment expression `k = n++`, which uses a postfix increment operator, reverses this procedure. A postfix increment operates after the assignment is completed. Thus, the statement `k = n++;` first assigns the current value of `n` to `k` and then increments the value of `n` by one. This is equivalent to the two statements

```
k = n;            // assign n's value to k
n = n + 1;        // and then increment n
```

In addition to the increment operator, C++ also provides a **decrement operator**, `--`. As you might expect, the expressions `variable--` and `--variable` are both equivalent to the expression `variable = variable - 1`. Examples of the decrement operator are:

Expression	Alternative
`i = i - 1`	`i-- or --i`
`n = n - 1`	`n-- or --n`
`count = count - 1`	`count-- or --count`

When the – operator appears before a variable it is called a *prefix decrement operator.* When the decrement appears after a variable it is called a *postfix decrement operator.* For example, both of the expressions `n--` and `--n` reduce the value of `n` by one. These expressions are equivalent to the longer expression `n = n - 1`. As with the increment operator, however, the prefix and postfix decrement operators produce different results when used in assignment expressions. For example, the expression `k = --n` first decrements the value of `n` by one before assigning the value of `n` to `k`, while the expression `k = n--` first assigns the current value of `n` to `k` and then reduces the value of `n` by one.

The increment and decrement operators can often be used advantageously to reduce program storage requirements significantly and increase execution speed. For example, consider the following three statements:

```
count = count + 1;
count += 1;
count++;
```

All perform the same function; however, when these instructions are compiled for execution on an IBM personal computer the storage requirements for the instructions are 9, 4, and 3 bytes, respectively.[6] If we use the assignment operator, =, instead of the increment operator, we use three times the storage space for the instruction, with an accompanying decrease in execution speed.

[6] This is clearly a compiler-dependent result.

Exercises 3.1

1. Write an assignment statement to calculate the circumference of a circle having a radius of 3.3 inches. The equation for determining the circumference, c, of a circle is $c = 2\pi r$, where r is the radius and π equals 3.1416.

2. Write an assignment statement to calculate the area of a circle. The equation for determining the area, a, of a circle is $a = \pi r^2$, where r is the radius and $\pi = 3.1416$.

3. Write an assignment statement to convert temperature in degrees Fahrenheit to degrees Celsius. The equation for this conversion is *Celsius* = *5/9 (Fahrenheit* − *32)*.

4. Write an assignment statement to calculate the round-trip distance, *d*, in feet, of a trip that is *s* miles long, one way.

5. Write an assignment statement to calculate the elapsed time, in minutes, that it takes to make a trip. The equation for computing elapsed time is *elapsed time* = *total distance/average speed*. Assume that the distance is in miles and the average speed is in miles/hour.

6. Write an assignment statement to calculate the n'th term in an arithmetic sequence. The formula for calculating the value, v, of the n'th term is $v = a + (n - 1)d$, where a = the first number in the sequence and d = the difference between any two numbers in the sequence.

7. Determine the output the following program:

```
#include <iostream.h>

int main() // a program illustrating integer truncation
{
  int num1, num2;

  num1 = 9/2;
  num2 = 17/4;
  cout << "the first integer displayed is " << num1 << endl;
  cout << "the second integer displayed is " << num2 << endl;
  return 0;
}
```

8. Determine the output produced by the following program:

```
#include <iostream.h>

int main()
{
  float average = 26.27;

  cout << "the average is " << average << endl;
  average = 682.3;
  cout << "the average is " << average << endl;
  average = 1.968;
  cout << "the average is " << average << endl;
  return 0;
}
```

9. Determine the output produced by the following program:

```
#include <iostream.h>

int main()
```

(continued on next page)

```
{
  float sum;

  sum = 0.0;
  cout << "the sum is " << sum << endl;
  sum = sum + 26.27;
  cout << "the sum is " << sum << endl;
  sum = sum + 1.968;
  cout << "the final sum is "<< sum << endl;
  return 0;
}
```

10. a. Determine what each statement causes to happen in the following program:

```
#include <iostream.h>

int main()
{
  int num1, num2, num3, total;

  num1 = 25;
  num2 = 30;
  total = num1 + num2;
  cout << num1 << " + " << num2 << " = " << total;
  return 0;
}
```

b. What output will be produced when the program listed in Exercise 10a is compiled and executed?

11. Determine and correct the errors in the following programs:

a.
```
#include <iostream.h>

int main()
{
  width = 15
  area = length * width;
  cout << "The area is " << area
}
```

b.
```
#include <iostream.h>

int main()
{
  int length, width, area;
  area = length * width;
  length = 20;
  width = 15;
  cout << "The area is " << area;
}
```

c.
```
#include <iostream.h>

int main()
{
  int length = 20; width = 15, area;
  length * width = area;
  cout << "The area is " , area;
}
```

12. By mistake a programmer reordered the statements in Program 3.3 as follows:

```
#include <iostream.h>

int main()
{
  int sum;
  sum = 0;
  sum = sum + 96;
  sum = sum + 70;
  sum = sum + 85;
  sum = sum + 60;
  cout << "The value of sum is initially set to " << sum << endl;
  cout << " sum is now " << sum << endl;
  cout << " sum is now " << sum << endl;
  cout << " sum is now " << sum << endl;
  cout << " The final sum is " << sum << endl;
  return 0;
}
```

Determine the output that this program produces.

13. Using Program 3.1, determine the volume of cylinders having the following radii and heights:

Radius (in.)	Height (in.)
1.62	6.23
2.86	7.52
4.26	8.95
8.52	10.86
12.29	15.35

14. The area of an ellipse (see Figure 3.5) is given by the formula

$$\text{area} = \pi ab$$

Using this formula, write a C++ program to calculate the area of an ellipse having a minor axis of 2.5 inches and a major axis of 6.4 inches.

FIGURE 3.5 The Minor Axis *a* and the Major Axis *b* of an Ellipse

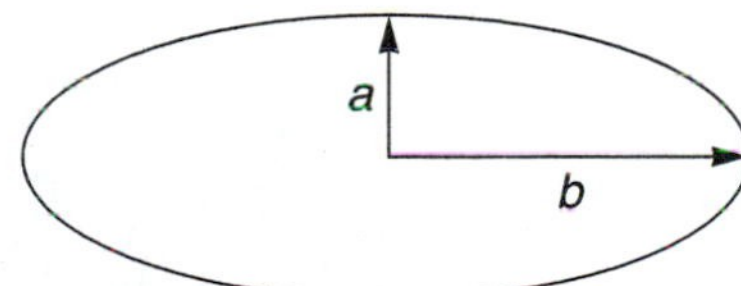

3.2 FORMATTING NUMBERS FOR PROGRAM OUTPUT

Besides displaying correct results, a program should present its results attractively. Most programs are judged, in fact, on the perceived ease of data entry and the style and presentation of their output. For example, displaying a monetary result as 1.897000 is not in keeping with accepted reporting conventions. The display should be either $1.90 or $1.89, depending on whether rounding or truncation is used.

TABLE 3.1 Commonly Used Stream Manipulators

Manipulator	Action
`setw(n)`	Set the field width to `n`
`setprecision(n)`	Set the floating-point precision to `n` places
`setiosflags(flags)`	Set the format flags (see Table 3.3 for flag settings)
dec	Set output for decimal display
hex	Set output for hexadecimal display
`oct`	Set output for octal display

The format of numbers displayed by `cout` can be controlled by **field width manipulators** included in each output stream. Table 3.1 lists the most commonly used manipulators available for this purpose.[7]
For example, the statement

```
cout << "The sum of 6 and 5 is" << setw(3) << 21;
```

causes the printout

```
The sum of 6 and 15 is 21
```

The `setw(3)` field width manipulator included in the stream of data passed to `cout` is used to set the displayed field width. The `3` in this manipulator sets the default field width for the next number in the stream to three spaces. This field width setting causes the `21` to be printed in a field of three spaces, which includes one blank and the number `21`. As illustrated, integers are right-justified within the specified field.

Field width manipulators are useful in printing columns of numbers that are correctly aligned. For example, Program 3.5 illustrates how a column of integers would align in the absence of field width manipulators.

PROGRAM 3.5

```
#include <iostream.h>

int main()
{
  cout << 6 << endl
       << 18 << endl
       << 124 << endl
       << "---\n"
       << (6+18+124) << endl;

  return 0;
}
```

[7] As was noted in Chapter 2, the `endl` manipulator inserts a newline and then flushes the stream.

The output of Program 3.5 is

```
6
18
124
---
148
```

Since no field width manipulators are given, the cout object allocates enough space for each number as it is received. To force the numbers to align on the units digit, we need to set a field width wide enough for the largest displayed number. For Program 3.5, a width of three suffices. The use of this field width is illustrated in Program 3.6.

PROGRAM 3.6

```
#include <iostream.h>
#include <iomanip.h>

int main()
{
  cout << setw(3) << 6 << endl
       << setw(3) << 18 << endl
       << setw(3) << 124 << endl
       << "---\n"
       << (6+18+124) << endl;

  return 0;
}
```

The output of Program 3.6 is

```
  6
 18
124
---
148
```

Notice that the field width manipulator must be included for each occurrence of a number inserted onto the data stream sent to cout, and that the manipulator only applies to the next insertion of data immediately following it. Also notice that if manipulators are to be included within an output display, the iomanip.h header file must be included as part of the program. This is accomplished by the preprocessor command #include <iomanip.h>.[8]

Formatted floating-point numbers require the use of two field width manipulators. The first manipulator sets the total width of the display, including the decimal point; the second manipulator determines how many digits can be printed to the right of the decimal point. For example, the statement

[8] Since the iomanip.h header file will include the iostream.h header file if it has not already been included, the #include statement for iostream.h can be omitted.

```
cout << "|" << setw(10) << setprecision(3) << 25.67 << "|";
```

causes the printout *

```
|     25.67|
```

The bar symbol, |, in the example is used to delimit (mark) the beginning and end of the display field. The `setw` manipulator tells `cout` to display the number in a total field of 10, while the `setprecision` manipulator tells `cout` to display a maximum of three digits to the right of the decimal point. Since the number contains only two digits to the right of the decimal point, only two decimal digits are displayed.

For all numbers (integers, floating point, and double precision), `cout` ignores the `setw` manipulator specification if the total specified field width is too small; instead, it allocates enough space for the integer part of the number to be printed. The fractional part of both floating-point and double-precision numbers is displayed up to the precision set with the `setprecision` manipulator (in the absence of a `setprecision` manipulator, the default precision is set to six decimal places). If the fractional part of the number to be displayed contains more digits than called for in the `setprecision` manipulator, the number is rounded to the indicated number of decimal places; if the fractional part contains fewer digits than specified, the number is displayed with the fewer digits. Table 3.2 illustrates the effect of various format manipulator combinations. Again, for clarity, the bar symbol, |, is used to delineate clearly the beginning and end of the output fields.

In addition to the `setw` and `setprecision` manipulators, a field justification manipulator is also available. As we have seen, numbers sent to `cout` are normally displayed right-justified in the display field, and strings are displayed left-justified.

TABLE 3.2 Effect of Format Manipulators

Manipulators	Number	Display	Comments
`setw(2)`	3	`¦ 3¦`	Number fits in field
`setw(2)`	43	`¦43¦`	Number fits in field
`setw(2)`	143	`¦143¦`	Field width ignored
`setw(2)`	2.3	`¦2.3¦`	Field width ignored
`setw(5)` `setprecision(2)`	2.366	`¦ 2.37¦`	Field width of five with two decimal digits
`setw(5)` `setprecision(2)`	42.3	`¦ 42.3¦`	Number fits in field
`setw(5)` `setprecision(2)`	142.364	`¦142.36¦`	Field width ignored but precision specification used
`setw(5)` `setprecision(2)`	142.366	`¦142.37¦`	Field width ignored but precision specification used
`setw(5)` `setprecision(2)`	142	`¦  142¦`	Field width used precision irrelevant

* Unless the `ios::fixed` format flag is set in both Borland and Microsoft's C++ Version 4.0, `setprecision()` will set the total number of significant digits.

To alter the default **justification** for a stream of data, the `setiosflags` manipulator can be used. For example, the statement

```
cout << "|" << setw(10) << setiosflags(ios::left) << 142 << "|";
```

causes the following left-justified display

```
|142       |
```

As we have previously seen, because data passed to `cout` may be continued across multiple lines, the previous display would also be produced by this statement:

```
cout << "|" << setw(10)
     << setiosflags(ios::left)
     << 142 << "|";
```

As always, the field width manipulator is only in effect for the next single set of data passed to `cout`. Right-justification for strings in a stream is obtained by the manipulator `setiosflags(ios::right)`. The symbols `ios` in both the function name and the `ios::right` argument come from the first letters of the words input output stream.

In addition to the use of left and right flags with the setiosflags( ) manipulator, other flags can also be used to affect the output. The most commonly used flags for this manipulator are listed in Table 3.3.

Notice that all of the flags in Table 3.3 are used as arguments to the `setiosflags()` manipulator function. Since the terms argument and parameter are synonymous, another name for a manipulator function that uses arguments is a **parametized manipulator**. As an example of using parameterized manipulator functions, consider the statement:

```
cout << setiosflags(ios::fixed) << setprecision(4)
```

This forces all subsequent floating-point numbers sent to the output stream to be displayed with a decimal point and four decimal digits. If the number has fewer than four decimal digits it will be padded with trailing zeros.

In addition to outputting integers in decimal notation, the `ios::oct` and `ios::hex` flags premit conversions to **octal** and **hexadecimal**, respectively. Programs 3.7 illustrates the use of these flags. Since decimal is the default display, the `dec` manipulator is not required in the first output stream.

TABLE 3.3 Format Flags for Use with `setiosflags()`

Flag	Meaning
`ios::showpoint`	Always show the decimal point with a default of six decimal digits
`ios::showpos`	Display a leading + sign when the number is positive
`ios::fixed`	Display up to three integer digits and two digits after the decimal point; for larger integer values revert to exponential notation
`ios::scientific`	Use exponential display on output
`ios::dec`	Display in decimal format
`ios::oct`	Display in octal format
`ios::hex`	Display in hexadecimal format
`ios::left`	Left-justify output
`ios::right`	Right-justify output

POINT OF INFORMATION

Formatting `cout` Stream Data

The data in a `cout` output stream can be formatted in precise ways. One of the most common format requirements is to display numbers in a monetary format by always displaying two digits after the decimal point, such as 123.45. This can be done with the following statement:

```
cout << setiosflags(ios::fixed)
     << setiosflags(ios::showpoint)
     << setprecision(2);
```

The first manipulator flag, `ios::fixed`, forces all numbers placed on the `cout` stream to be placed as if they were floating point values. The next flag, `ios::showpoint`, tells the stream to always display a decimal point. Thus, a value such as 1.0 will appear as 1.0, and not as a 1 with no displayed decimal value. Finally, the `setprecision` manipulator tells the stream to always display 2 decimal values after the decimal point. Thus, the number 1.0 for example, will appear as 1.00. Instead of using manipulators, you can also use the `cout` stream functions `setf()` and `precision()`. For example, the previous formatting can also be accomplished using the code:

```
cout.setf(ios::fixed);
cout.setf(ios::showpoint);
cout.precision(2);
```

Note the syntax here: the name of the object, `cout`, is separated from the function with a period. As we shall see in Chapter 7 this is the standard way of specifying a function and connecting it to a specific object.

Which style you select is a matter of preference. In both cases the formats need only be specified once and remain in effect for every number subsequently inserted into the `cout` stream.

PROGRAM 3.7

```
// a program to illustrate output conversions
#include <iostream.h>
#include <iomanip.h>

int main()
{
  cout << "The decimal (base 10) value of 15 is " << 15 << endl
       << "The octal (base 8) value of 15 is "
       << setiosflags(ios::oct) << 15 << endl
       << "The hexadecimal (base 16) value of 15 is "
       << setiosflags(ios::hex) << 15 << endl;

  return 0;
}
```

▲ POINT OF INFORMATION ▲

What is a Flag?

In current programming usage the term **flag** refers to an item, such as a variable or argument, that sets a condition usually considered as either active or nonactive. Although the exact origin of this term in programming is not known it probably originates from the use of real flags to signal a condition, such as the Stop, Go, Caution, and Winner flags commonly used at car races.

In a similar manner each flag argument to the `setiosflags()` manipulator function activates a specific condition. For example, the `ios::dec` flag sets the display format to decimal, while the flag `ios::oct` activates the octal display format. Since these conditions are mutually exclusive, which means that only one condition can be active at a time, activating one such flag automatically deactivates the other flags.

Flags that are not mutually exclusive, such as `ios::dec`, `ios::showpoint`, and `ios::fixed` can all be set on at the same time. This can be done using three individual `setiosflag()` calls or combining all arguments into one call as follows:

```
cout << setiosflags(ios::dec || ios::showpoint || ios::fixed);
```

The output produced by Program 3.7 is:

```
The decimal (base 10) value of 15 is 15
The octal (base 8) value of 15 is 17
The hexadecimal (base 16) value of 15 is f
```

In place of the conversion flags `ios::dec`, `ios::oct`, and `ios::hex`, three simpler manipulators, `dec`, `oct`, and `hex` are provided in `<iostream.h>`. These simpler manipulators, unlike their longer counterparts, leave the conversion base set for all subsequent output streams. Using these simpler manipulators, Program 3.7 can be rewritten as:

```
#include <iostream.h>
int main() // a program to illustrate output conversions
{
  cout << "The decimal (base 10) value of 15 is " << 15 << endl
       << "The octal (base 8) value of 15 is " << oct << 15 << endl
       << "The hexadecimal (base 16) value of 15 is " << hex << 15 << endl;
  return 0;

}
```

The display of integer values in one of the three possible number systems (decimal, octal, and hexadecimal) does not affect how the number is actually stored inside a computer. All numbers are stored using the computer's own internal codes. The manipulators sent to `cout` simply tell the object how to convert the internal code for output display purposes.

Besides displaying integers in octal or hexadecimal form, integer constants can also be written in a program in these forms. To designate an octal integer constant, the number must have a leading zero. The number 023, for example, is an octal number in C++. Hexadecimal numbers are denoted using a leading 0x. The use of octal and hexadecimal integer constants is illustrated in Program 3.8.

PROGRAM 3.8

```
#include <iostream.h>

int main()
{
  cout << "The decimal value of 025 is " << 025 << endl
       << "The decimal value of 0x37 is "<< 0x37 << endl;

  return 0;
}
```

When Program 3.8 is run, we get the following output:

```
The decimal value of 025 is 21
The decimal value of 0x37 is 55
```

The relationship between the input, storage, and display of integers is illustrated in Figure 3.6.

Exercises 3.2

1. Determine the output of the following program:

```
#include <iostream.h>
int main() // a program illustrating integer truncation
{
  cout << "answer1 is the integer " << 9/4
       << "\nanswer2 is the integer " << 17/3;
  return 0;

}
```

2. Determine the output of the following program:

```
#include <iostream.h>
int main() // a program illustrating the % operator
{
  cout << "The remainder of 9 divided by 4 is " << 9 % 4
       << "\nThe remainder of 17 divided by 3 is " << 17 % 3;
  return 0;

}
```

3. Write a C++ program that displays the results of the expressions `3.0 * 5.0`, `7.1 * 8.3 - 2.2`, and `3.2 / (6.1 * 5)`. Calculate the value of these expressions manually to verify that the displayed values are correct.

4. Write a C++ program that displays the results of the expressions `15 / 4`, `15 % 4`, and `5 * 3 - (6 * 4)`. Calculate the value of these expressions manually to verify that the display produced by your program is correct.

5. Determine the errors in each of the following statements:

   a. `cout << "\n << " 15)`

   b. `cout << "setw(4)" << 33;`

   c. `cout << "setprecision(5)" << 526.768;`

FIGURE 3.6 Input, Storage, and Display of Integers

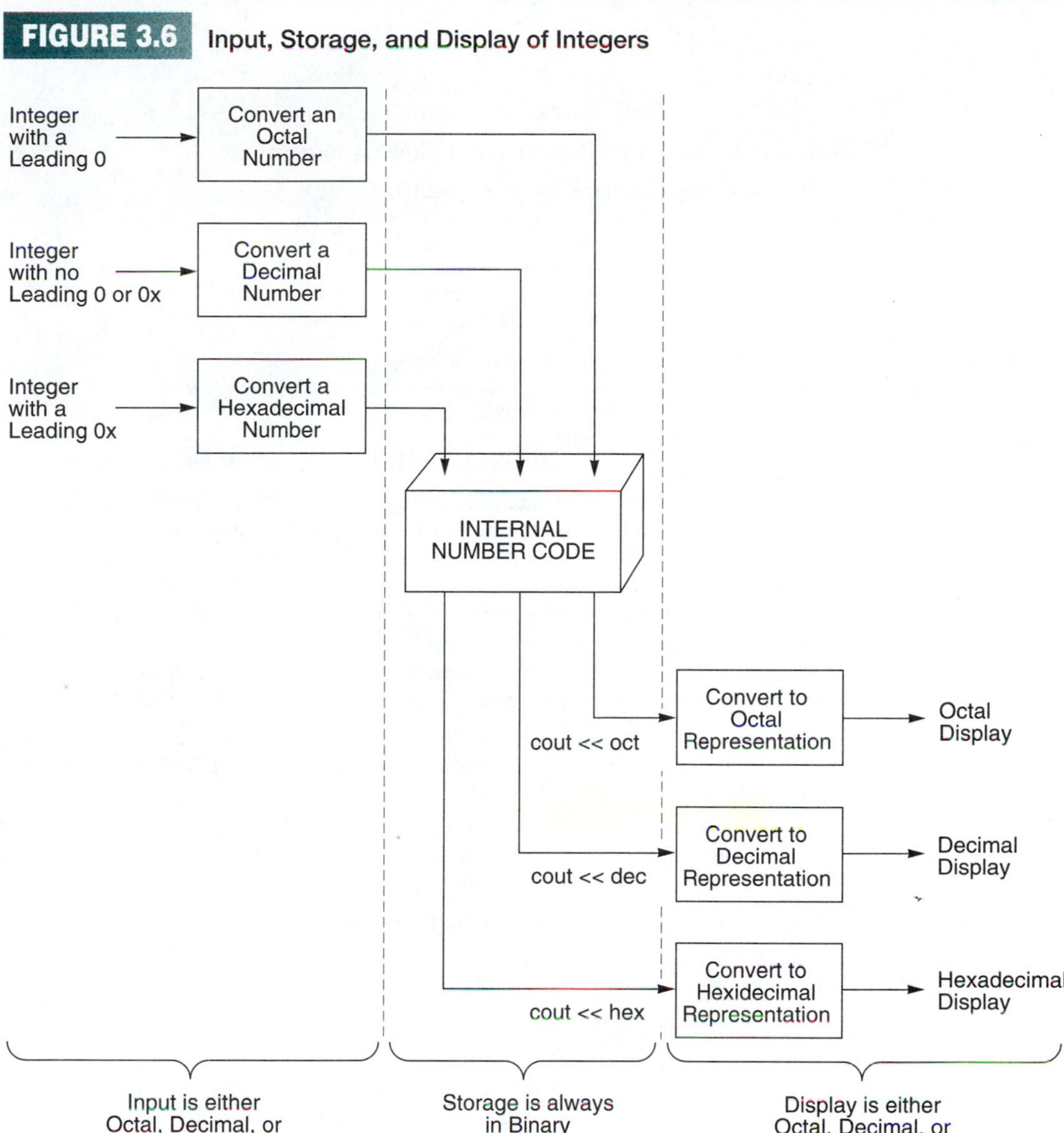

d. `"Hello World!" >> cout;`

e. `cout << 47 << setw(6);`

f. `cout << set(10) <.768 << setprecision(2);`

6. Determine and write out the display produced by the following statements:

a. `cout << "|" << 5 <<"|";`

b. `cout << "|" << setw(4) << 5 << "|";`

c. `cout << "|" << setw(4) << 56829 << "|";`

d. `cout << "|" << setw(5) << setprecision(2) << 5.26 << "|";`

e. `cout << "|" << setw(5) << setprecision(2) << 5.267 << "|";`

f. `cout << "|" << setw(5) << setprecision(2) << 53.264 << "|";`

g. `cout << "|" << setw(5) << setprecision(2) << 534.264 << "|";`

h. `cout << "|" << setw(5) << setprecision(2) << 534. << "|";`

7. Write out the display produced by the following statements.

a.
```
cout << "The number is " << setw(6)
     << setprecision(2) << 26.27 << endl;
cout << "The number is " << setw(6)
     << setprecision(2) << 682.3 << endl;
cout << "The number is " << setw(6)
     << setprecision(2) << 1.968 << endl;
```

b.
```
cout << setw(6) << setprecision(2) << 26.27 << endl;
cout << setw(6) << setprecision(2) << 682.3 << endl;
cout << setw(6) << setprecision(2) << 1.968 << endl;
cout << "--------\n";
cout << setw(6) << setprecision(2) << 27.27 + 682.3 + 1.968 << endl;
```

c.
```
cout << setw(5) << setprecision(2) << 26.27 << endl;
cout << setw(5) << setprecision(2) << 682.3 << endl;
cout << setw(5) << setprecision(2) << 1.968 << endl;
cout << "--------\n";
cout << setw(5) << setprecision(2)
     << 27.27 + 682.3 + 1.968 << endl;
```

d.
```
cout << setw(5) << setprecision(2) << 36.164 << endl;
cout << setw(5) << setprecision(2) << 10.003 << endl;
cout << "-----" << endl;
```

8. The following table lists the correspondence between the decimal numbers 1 through 15 and their octal and hexadecimal representations:

Decimal:	1	2	3	4	5	6	7	8	9	10	11	12	13	14	15
Octal:	1	2	3	4	5	6	7	10	11	12	13	14	15	16	17
Hexadecimal:	1	2	3	4	5	6	7	8	9	a	b	c	d	e	f

Using this table, determine the output of the following program.

```
#include <iostream.h>
#include <iomanip.h>

int main()
{
  cout << "\nThe value of 14 in octal is " << oct << 14
       << "\nThe value of 14 in hexadecimal is " << hex << 14
       << "\nThe value of 0xA in decimal is " << dec << 0xA
       << "\nThe value of 0xA in octal is " << oct << 0xA
       << endl;
  return 0;
}
```

3.3 USING MATHEMATICAL LIBRARY FUNCTIONS

As we have seen, assignment statements can be used to perform arithmetic computations. For example, the assignment statement

```
total_price = unit_price * amount;
```

multiplies the value in `unit_price` times the value in `amount` and assigns the resulting value to `total_price`. Although addition, subtraction, multiplication, and division are easily accomplished using C++'s arithmetic operators, no such operators exist for raising a number to a power, finding the square root of a number, or determining trigonometric values. To facilitate such calculations, C++ provides standard preprogrammed functions that can be included in a program.

Before using one of C++'s mathematical functions, you need to know:

- the name of the desired mathematical function
- what the mathematical function does
- the type of data required by the mathematical function
- the data type of the result returned by the mathematical function
- how to include the library.

To illustrate the use of C++'s mathematical functions, consider the mathematical function named `sqrt`, which calculates the square root of a number. The square root of a number is computed using the expression

```
sqrt(number)
```

where the function's name, in this case `sqrt`, is followed by parentheses containing the number for which the square root is desired. The purpose of the parentheses following the function name is to provide a funnel through which data can be passed to the function (see Figure 3.7). The items that are passed to the function through the parentheses are called **arguments** of the function and constitute its input data. For example, the following expressions are used to compute the square root of the arguments 4, 17.0, 25, 1043.29, and 6.4516, respectively:

```
sqrt(4)
sqrt(17.0)
sqrt(25)
sqrt(1043.29)
sqrt(6.4516)
```

FIGURE 3.7 Passing Data to the `sqrt()` Function

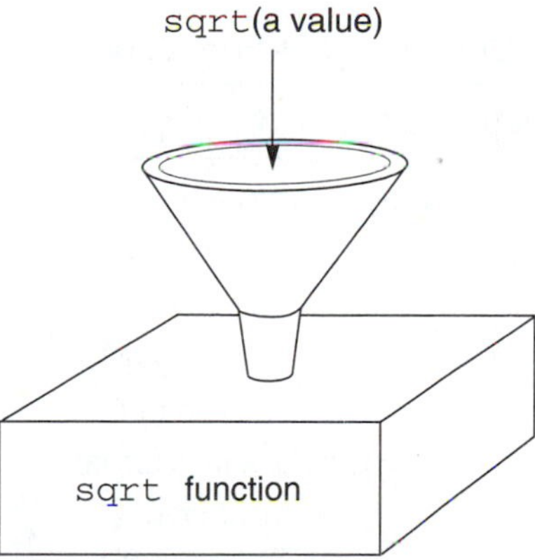

Notice that the argument to the `sqrt` function can be either an integer or real value. This is an example of C++'s function overloading capabilities. Function overloading permits the same function name to be defined for different argument data types. In this case there are really five square root functions named `sqrt()`—one defined for integer, long integer, float, double, and long double arguments. The correct `sqrt` function is called depending on the type of value given it. The `sqrt()` function determines the square root of its argument and returns the result as a double. The values returned by the previous expressions are:

Expression	Value Returned
`sqrt(4)`	2.0
`sqrt(17.0)`	4.123106
`sqrt(25)`	5.0
`sqrt(1043.29)`	32.3
`sqrt(6.4516)`	2.54

In addition to the `sqrt` function, Table 3.4 lists the more commonly used mathematical functions provided in C++. To access these functions in a program requires that the **mathematical header** file named `math.h`, which contains appropriate declarations for the mathematical function, be included with the function. This is done by placing the following preprocessor statement at the top of any program using a mathematical function:

```
#include <math.h>   ←———— no semicolon
```

Although some of the mathematical functions listed require more than one argument, all functions, by definition, can directly return at most one value. Additionally, all of the functions listed are overloaded; this means the same function name can be used with integer and real arguments. Table 3.5 illustrates the value returned by selected functions using example arguments.

When a mathematical function is used, it is called into action by giving the name of the function and passing any data to it within the parentheses following the function's name (see Figure 3.8).

The arguments that are passed to a function need not be single constants. Expressions can also be arguments provided that the expression can be computed to yield a value of the required data type. For example, the following arguments are valid for the given functions:

TABLE 3.4 Common C++ Functions

Function Name	Description	Returned Value
`abs(a)`	Absolute value	Same data type as argument
`pow(a1,a2)`	a1 raised to the a2 power	Data type of argument a1
`sqrt(a)`	Square root of a	Same data type as argument
`sin(a)`	Sine of a (a in radians)	Double
`cos(a)`	Cosine of a (a in radians)	Double
`tan(a)`	Tangent of a (a in radians)	Double
`log(a)`	Natural logarithm of a	Double
`log10(a)`	Common log (base 10) of a	Double
`exp(a)`	e raised to the a power	Double

TABLE 3.5 Selected Function Examples

Example	Returned Value
`abs(-7.362)`	7.362000
`abs(-3)`	3
`pow(2.0,5.0)`	32.00000
`pow(10,3)`	1000
`log(18.697)`	2.928363
`log10(18.697)`	1.271772
`exp(-3.2)`	0.040762

```
sqrt(4.0 + 5.3 * 4.0)       abs(2.3 * 4.6)
sqrt(16.0 * 2.0 - 6.7)      sin(theta - phi)
sqrt(x * y - z/3.2)         cos(2.0 * omega)
```

The expressions in parentheses are first evaluated to yield a specific value. Thus, values would have to be assigned to the variables `theta`, `phi`, `x`, `y`, `z`, and `omega` before their use in the preceeding expressions. After the value of the argument is calculated, it is passed to the function.

Functions may be included as part of larger expressions. For example,

```
  4 * sqrt(4.5 * 10.0 - 9.0) - 2.0
= 4 * sqrt(36.0) - 2.0
= 4 * 6.0 - 2.0
= 24.0 - 2.0
= 22.0
```

The step-by-step evaluation of an expression such as

```
3.0 * sqrt(5 * 33 - 13.71) / 5
```

is:

Step	Result
1. Perform multiplication in argument.	`3.0 * sqrt(165 - 13.71) / 5`
2. Complete argument calculation.	`3.0 * sqrt(151.29) / 5`
3. Return a function value.	`3.0 * 12.3 / 5`
4. Perform the multiplication.	`36.9 / 5`
5. Perform the division.	`7.38`

Program 3.9 illustrates the use of the `sqrt` function to determine the time it takes a ball to hit the ground after it has been dropped from an 800-foot tower. The

FIGURE 3.8 Using and Passing Data to a Function

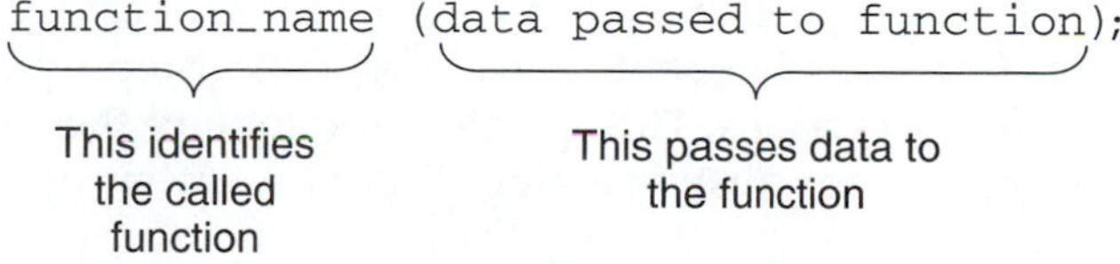
function_name (data passed to function);
This identifies the called function
This passes data to the function

mathematical formula used to calculate the time, in seconds, that it takes to fall a given distance, in feet, is:

$$time = sqrt(2 * distance/g)$$

where g is the gravitational constant equal to 32.2 ft/sec^2.

PROGRAM 3.9

```
#include <iostream.h>  // this line may be placed second instead of first
#include <math.h>      // this line may be placed first instead of second

int main()
{
  int height;
  double time;

  height = 800;
  time = sqrt(2 * height / 32.2);
  cout << "It will take " << time << " seconds to fall "
       << height << " feet.\n";

  return 0;
}
```

The output produced by Program 3.9 is:

```
It will take 7.049074 seconds to fall 800 feet.
```

As used in Program 3.9, the value returned by the `sqrt` function is assigned to the variable `time`. In addition to assigning a function's returned value to a variable, the returned value may be included within a larger expression, or even used as an argument to another function. For example, the expression

```
sqrt( pow( abs(num1),num2 ) )
```

is valid. Because parentheses are present the computation proceeds from the inner to the outer pairs of parentheses. Thus, the absolute value of `num1` is computed first and used as an argument to the `pow()` function. The value returned by the `pow()` function is then used as an argument to the `sqrt` function.

Casts

We have already seen the conversion of an operand's data type within mixed-mode arithmetic expressions and across assignment operators. In addition to these implicit data type conversions that are automatically made within mixed-mode arithmetic and assignment expressions, C++ also provides for explicit user-specified **type conversions.** The operator used to force the conversion of a value to another type is the cast operator. This is a unary operator having the syntax:

`data_type (expression)`, where `data_type` is the desired data type of the expression following the **cast**. For example, the expression

```
int (a * b)
```

ensures that the value of the expression `a * b` is converted to an integer value.[9]

Exercises 3.3

1. Write function calls to determine the following:
   a. the square root of 6.37
   b. the square root of $x - y$
   c. the sine of 30 degrees
   d. the sine of 60 degrees
   e. the absolute value of $a^2 - b^2$
   f. the value of e raised to the third power
2. For a = 10.6, b = 13.9, and c = −3.42, determine the following values:
   a. `int (a)`
   b. `int (b)`
   c. `int (c)`
   d. `int (a + b)`
   e. `int (a) + b + c`
   f. `int (a + b) + c`
   g. `int (a + b + c)`
   h. `float (int (a)) + b`
   i. `float (int (a + b))`
   j. `abs(a) + abs(b)`
   k. `sqrt(abs(a - b))`
3. Write C++ statements for the following:
   a. $b = \sin x - \cos x$
   b. $b = \sin^2 x - \cos^2 x$
   c. $\text{area} = (c * b * \sin \text{a})/2$
   d. $c = \sqrt{\text{a}^2 + b^2}$
   e. $p = \sqrt{|m - n|}$
   f. $\text{sum} = \dfrac{a\,(r^n - 1)}{r - 1}$
4. Write, compile, and execute a C++ program that calculates and returns the fourth root of the number 81.0, which is 3. When you have verified that your program works correctly, use it to determine the fourth root of 1,728.8964. Your program should make use of the `sqrt` function.

[9] The C type cast syntax, in this case, `(int)(a * b)`, also works in C++.

5. Write, compile, and execute a C++ program that calculates the distance between two points whose coordinates are (7,12) and (3,9). Use the fact that the distance between two points having coordinates (*x*1,*y*1) and (*x*2,*y*2) is *distance* = *sqrt([x1 – x2]2* + [y1 – y2]^2). When you have verified that your program works correctly, by calculating the distance between the two points manually, use your program to determine the distance between the points (–12,–15) and (22,5).
6. If a 20-foot ladder is placed on the side of a building at an 85-degree angle, as illustrated on Figure 3.9, the height at which the ladder touches the building can be calculated as *height = 20 * sin 85°*. Calculate this height by hand and then write, compile, and execute a C++ program that determines and displays the value of the height. When you have verified that your program works correctly, use it to determine the height of a 25-foot ladder placed at an angle of 85 degrees.

FIGURE 3.9 Illustration for Exercise 6

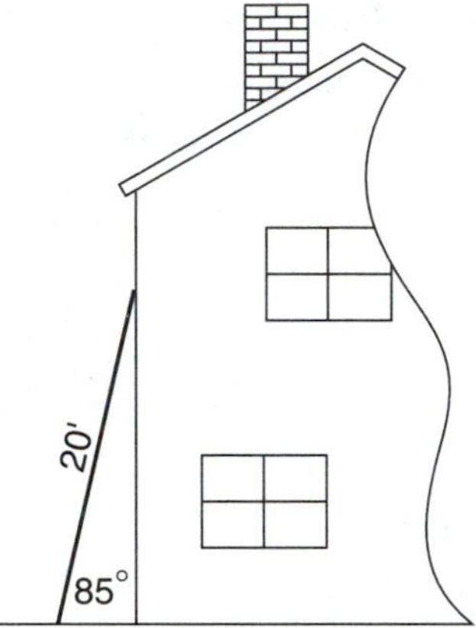

7. A model of worldwide population, in billions of people, after 1990 is given by the equation

$$\text{population} = 5.5(1 + e^{.02[year - 1990]})$$

Using this formula, write, compile, and execute a C++ program to estimate the worldwide population in the year 1995. Verify the result displayed by your program by calculating the answer manually. After you have verified your program is working correctly, use it to estimate the world's population in the year 2012.

3.4 PROGRAM INPUT USING THE `cin` OBJECT

Data for programs that are only going to be executed once may be included directly in the program. For example, if we wanted to multiply the numbers 30.0 and 0.05, we could use Program 3.10.

The output displayed by Program 3.10 is:

```
30.0 times 0.05 is 1.5
```

Program 3.10 can be shortened, as illustrated in Program 3.11. Both programs, however, suffer from the same basic problem in that they must be rewritten in order to multiply different numbers. Both programs lack the facility for entering different numbers on which to operate.

PROGRAM 3.10

```
#include <iostream.h>

int main()
{
  float num1, num2, product;

  num1 = 30.0;
  num2 = 0.05;
  product = num1 * num2;
  cout << "30.0 times 0.05 is " << product << endl;

  return 0;
}
```

Except for the practice provided to the programmer of writing, entering, and running the program, programs that do the same calculation only once, on the same set of numbers, are clearly not very useful. After all, it is simpler to use a calculator to multiply two numbers than to enter and run either Program 3.10 or 3.11.

PROGRAM 3.11

```
#include <iostream.h>

int main()
{
  cout << "30.0 times 0.05 is " << 30.0 * 0.05 << endl;

  return 0;
}
```

This section presents the **`cin`** object, which is used to enter data into a program while it is executing. Just as the `cout` object displays a copy of the value stored inside a variable, the `cin` object allows the user to enter a value at the terminal (see Figure 3.10), which is then stored directly in a variable. When a statement such as `cin >> num1;` is encountered, the computer stops program execution and accepts data from the keyboard. When a data item is typed, the `cin` object stores the item into the variable listed after the extraction ("get from") operator, >>. The program then continues execution with the next statement after the call to `cin`. Consider Program 3.12.

FIGURE 3.10 `cin` **Is Used to Enter Data;** `cout` **Is Used to Display Data**

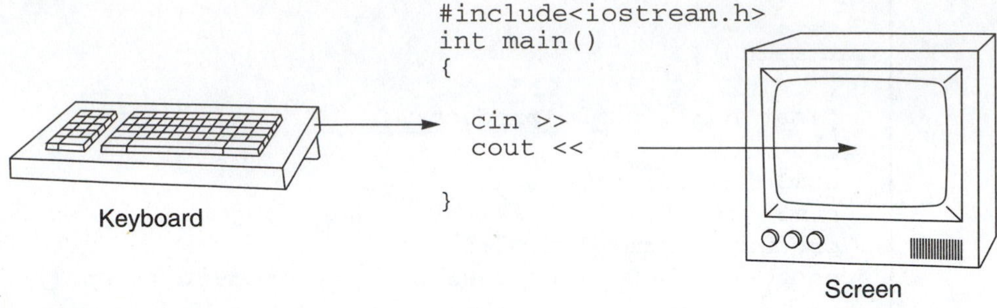

The first `cout` statement in Program 3.12 prints a string that tells the person at the terminal what should be typed. When an output string is used in this manner it is called a **prompt.** In this case the prompt tells the used to type a number. The computer then executes the next statement, which is a call to `cin`. The `cin` object puts the computer into a temporary pause (or wait) state for as long as it takes the user to type a value. Then the user signals the `cin` object that the data entry is finished by pressing the return key after the value has been typed. The entered value is stored in the variable to the right of the extraction symbol, and the computer leaves the paused state. Program execution then proceeds with the next statement, which in Program 3.12 is another call to `cout`. This call causes the next message to be displayed. The second call to `cin` again puts the computer into a temporary wait state while the user types a second value. This second number is stored in the variable `num2`.

The following sample run was made using Program 3.12:

```
Please type in a number: 30
Please type in another number: 0.05
30 times 0.05 is 1.5
```

PROGRAM 3.12

```
#include <iostream.h>

int main()
{
  float num1, num2, product;

  cout << "Please type in a number: ";
  cin >> num1;
  cout << "Please type in another number: ";
  cin >> num2;
  product = num1 * num2;
  cout << num1 << " times " << num2 << " is " << product << endl;

  return 0;
}
```

In Program 3.12, each time cin is invoked it is used to store one value into a variable. The cin object, however, can be used to enter and store as many values as there are extraction symbols, >>, and variables to hold the entered data. For example, the statement

```
cin >> num1 >> num2;
```

results in two values being read from the terminal and assigned to the variables num1 and num2. If the following data were entered at the terminal

```
0.052 245.79
```

the variables num1 and num2 would contain the values 0.052 and 245.79, respectively. Notice that when actually entering numbers such as 0.052 and 245.79, there must be at least one space between the numbers. The space between the entered numbers clearly indicates where one number ends and the next begins. Inserting more than one space between numbers has no effect on cin.

The same spacing is also applicable to entering character data; that is, the extraction operator, >>, will skip blank spaces and store the next nonblank character in a character variable. For example, in response to the statements

```
char ch1, ch2, ch3; // declare three character variables
cin >> ch1 >> ch2 >> ch3; // accept three characters
```

the input

```
a    b c
```

causes the letter a to be stored in the variable ch1, the letter b to be stored in the variable ch2, and the variable c to be stored in the variable ch3. Since a character variable can only be used to store one character, the input

```
abc
```

can also be used.

Any number of statements using the cin object can be made in a program, and any number of values can be input using a single cin statement. Program 3.13 illustrates use of the cin object to input three numbers from the keyboard. The program then calculates and displays the average of the numbers entered.

PROGRAM 3.13

```
#include <iostream.h>

int main()
{
  int num1, num2, num3;
  float average;

  cout << "Enter three integer numbers: ";
  cin >> num1 >> num2 >> num3;
  average = (num1 + num2 + num3) / 3.0;
  cout << "The average of the numbers is " << average << endl;

  return 0;
}
```

FIGURE 3.11 Inputting Data into the Variables num1, num2, and num3

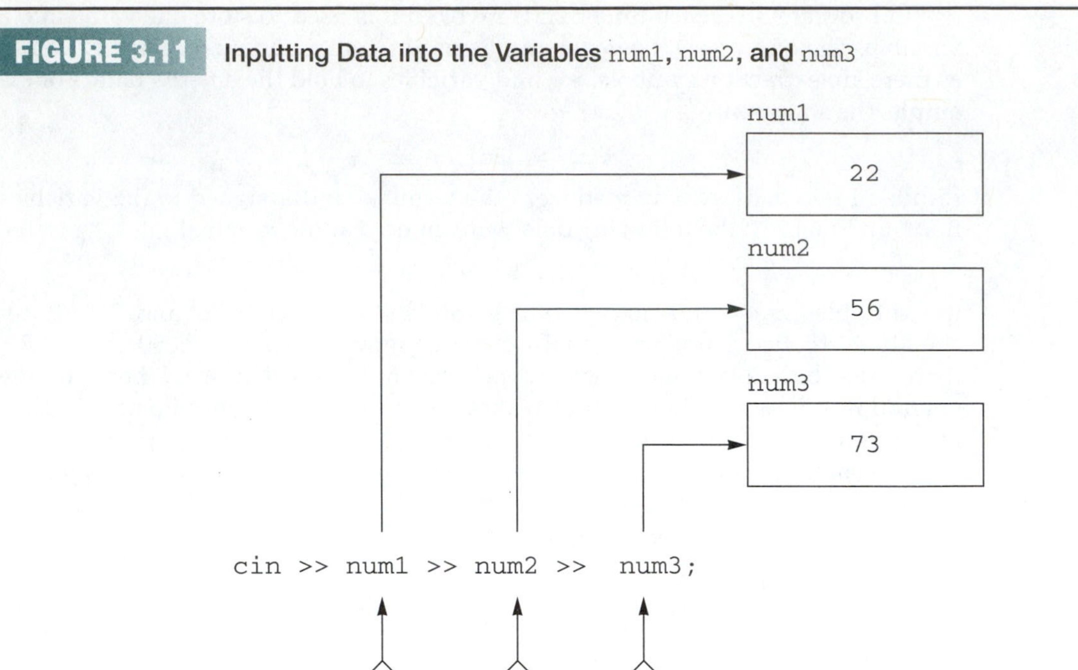

The following sample run was made using Program 3.13:

```
Enter three integer numbers: 22 56 73
The average of the numbers is 50.333333
```

Note that the data typed at the keyboard for this sample run consists of the input:

```
22 56 73
```

In response to this stream of input, Program 3.13 stores the value 22 in the variable `num1`, the value 56 in the variable `num2`, and the value 73 in the variable `num3` (see Figure 3.11). Since the average of three integer numbers can be a floating-point number, the variable `average`, which is used to store the average, is declared as a floating-point variable. Note also that the parentheses are needed in the assignment statement `average = (num1 + num2 + num3) / 3.0;`. Without these parentheses, the only value that would be divided by three would be the integer in `num3` (because division has a higher precedence than addition).

The `cin` extraction operation, like the `cout` insertion operation, is "clever" enough to make a few data type conversions. For example, if an integer is entered in place of a floating-point or double-precision number, the integer will be converted to the correct data type.[10] Similarly, if a floating-point or double-precision number is entered when an integer is expected, only the integer part of the num-

[10] Strictly speaking, what comes in from the keyboard is not any data type, such as an `int` or `float`; instead it is simply a sequence of characters. The extraction operation handles the conversion from the character sequence to a defined data type.

ber will be used. For example, assume the following numbers are typed in response to the statement `cin >> num1 >> num2 >> num3;`, where `num1` and `num3` have been declared as floating-point variables and `num2` is an integer variable:

```
56 22.879 33.923
```

The `56` will be converted to `56.0` and stored in the variable `num1`. The extraction operation continues extracting data from the input stream sent to it, expecting an integer value. As far as `cin` is concerned, the decimal point after the `22` in the number `22.879` indicates the end of an integer and the start of a decimal number. Thus, the number `22` is assigned to `num2`. Continuing to process its input stream, `cin` takes the `.879` as the next floating-point number and assigns it to `num3`. As far as `cin` is concerned, `33.923` is extra input and is ignored. If, though, you do not initially type enough data, the `cin` object will continue to make the computer pause until sufficient data has been entered.

Exercises 3.4

1. For the following declaration statements, write a statement using the `cin` object that will cause the computer to pause while the appropriate data is typed by the user.

   a. `int firstnum;`

   b. `float grade;`

   c. `double secnum;`

   d. `char keyval;`

   e.
   ```
   int month years;
   float average;
   ```

   f.
   ```
   char ch;
   int num1,num2;
   double grade1,grade2;
   ```

   g.
   ```
   float interest, principal, capital;
   double price,yield;
   ```

   h.
   ```
   char ch,letter1,letter2;
   int num1,num2,num3;
   ```

   i.
   ```
   float temp1,temp2,temp3;
   double volts1,volts2;
   ```

2. a. Write a C++ program that first displays the following prompt:

   ```
   Enter the temperature in degrees Celsius:
   ```

   Have your program accept a value entered from the keyboard and convert the temperature entered to degrees Fahrenheit, using the equation *Fahrenheit = (9.0 / 5.0) * Celsius + 32.0*. Your program should then display the temperature in degrees Celsius, using an appropriate output message.

   b. Compile and execute the program written for Exercise 2a.

   Verify your program by calculating by hand, and then by using your program, the Fahrenheit equivalent of the following test data:

   Test data set 1: 0 degrees Celsius.
   Test data set 2: 50 degrees Celsius
   Test data set 3: 100 degrees Celsius

When you are sure your program is working correctly, use it to complete the following table:

Celsius	Fahrenheit
45	
50	
55	
60	
65	
70	

3. Write, compile, and execute a C++ program that displays the following prompt:

```
Enter the radius of a circle:
```

After accepting a value for the radius, your program should calculate and display the area of the circle. (*Hint: area = 3.1416 * radius*^{2}.) For testing purposes, verify your program using a test input radius of 3 inches. After manually determining that the result produced by your program is correct, use your program to complete the following table:

Radius (in.)	Area (sq. in.)
1.0	
1.5	
2.0	
2.5	
3.0	
3.5	

4. a. Write, compile, and execute a C++ program that displays the following prompts:

```
Enter the miles driven:
Enter the gallons of gas used:
```

After each prompt is displayed, your program should use a `cin` statement to accept data from the keyboard for the displayed prompt. After the gallons of gas used number has been entered, your program should calculate and display miles per gallon obtained. This value should be included in an appropriate message and calculated using the equation *miles per gallon = miles/gallons used.* Verify your program using the following test data:

Test data set 1: miles = 276, gas = 10 gallons
Test data set 2: miles = 200, gas = 15.5 gallons

When you have completed your verification, use your program to complete the following table:

Miles Driven	Gallons Used	MPG
250	16.00	
275	18.00	
312	19.54	
296	17.39	

b. For the program written for Exercise 4a, determine how many verification runs are required to ensure the program is working correctly and give a reason supporting your answer.

5. a. Write, compile, and execute a C++ program that displays the following prompts:

```
Enter a number:
Enter a second number:
Enter a third number:
Enter a fourth number:
```

After each prompt is displayed, your program should use a `cin` statement to accept a number from the keyboard for the displayed prompt. After the fourth number has been entered, your program should calculate and display the average of the numbers. The average should be included in an appropriate message. Check the average displayed by your program using the following test data:

```
Test data set 1: 100, 100, 100, 100
Test data set 2: 100, 0, 100, 0
```

When you have completed your verification, use your program to complete the following table:

Numbers	Average
92, 98, 79, 85	
86, 84, 75, 86	
63, 85, 74, 82	

b. Repeat Exercise 5a, making sure that you use the same variable name, `number`, for each number input. Also use the variable `sum` for the sum of the numbers. (*Hint:* To do this, you may use the statement `sum = sum + number` after each number is accepted. Review the material on accumulating presented in Section 3.1.)

6. a. Write, compile, and execute a C++ program that computes and displays the value of the second-order polynomial $ax^2 = + bx + c$ for any user input values of the coefficients a, b, c, and the variable x. Have your program first display a message informing the user as to what the program will do, and then display suitable prompts to alert the user to enter the desired data. (*Hint:* Use a prompt such as *Enter the coefficient of the x squared term:*)

b. Check the result produced by your program written for Exercise 6a using the following test data:

Test data set 1: $a = 0, b = 0, c = 22, x = 56$
Test data set 2: $a = 0, b = 22, c = 0, x = 2$
Test data set 3: $a = 22, b = 0, c = 0, x = 2$
Test data set 4: $a = 2, b = 4, c = 5, x = 2$
Test data set 5: $a = 5, b = -3, c = 2, x = 1$

When you have completed your verification, use your program to complete the following table:

a	*b*	*c*	*x*	polynomial value
2.0	17.0	–12.0	1.3	
3.2	2.0	15.0	2.5	
3.2	2.0	15.0	–2.5	
–2.0	10.0	0.0	2.0	
–2.0	10.0	0.0	4.0	
–2.0	10.0	0.0	5.0	
–2.0	10.0	0.0	6.0	
5.0	22.0	18.0	8.3	
4.2	–16	–20	–5.2	

7. The number of bacteria, B, in a certain culture that is subject to refrigeration can be approximated by the equation $B = 300000\, e^{-.032t}$, where e is the irrational number 2.71828 rounded to five decimal places, known as Euler's number, and t is the amount of time, in hours, the culture has been refrigerated. Using this equation, write, compile, and execute a single C++ program that prompts the user for a value of time, calculates the number of bacteria in the culture, and displays the result. For testing purposes, check your program using a test input of 10 hours. When you have verified the operation of your program, use it to determine the number of bacteria in the culture after 12, 18, 24, 36, 48, and 72 hours.

8. Write, compile, and execute a program that calculates and displays the square root value of a user-entered real number. Verify your program by calculating the square roots of the following data: 25, 16, 0, and 2. When you have completed your verification, use your program to determine the square root of 32.25, 42, 48, 55, 63, and 79.

9. Program 3.12 prompts the user to input two numbers, where the first value entered is stored in `num1` and the second value is stored in `num2`. Using this program as a starting point, write a program that swaps the values stored in the two variables.

10. a. Write a C++ program that displays the following prompts:

    ```
    Enter a number:
    Enter a second number:
    Enter a third number:
    Enter a fourth number:
    ```

    After each prompt is displayed, your program should use a `cin` object call to accept a number from the keyboard for the displayed prompt. After the fourth number has been entered, your program should calculate and display the average of the numbers. The average should be included in an appropriate message.

    b. Check the average displayed for the program written in Exercise 10a by calculating the result manually.

    c. Repeat Exercise 10a, making sure that you use the same variable name, `number`, for each number input. Also use the variable `sum` for the sum of the numbers. (*Hint:* To do this, you must use the statement `sum = sum + number;` after each number is accepted. Review the material on accumulating presented in Section 3.1.)

11. Write a C++ program that prompts the user to type in a number. Have your program accept the number as an integer and immediately display the integer using a `cout` object call. Run your program three times. The first time you run the program enter a valid integer number, the second time enter a floating-point number, and the third time enter a character. Using the output display, see what number your program actually accepted from the data you entered.

12. Repeat Exercise 11 but have your program declare the variable used to store the number as a floating-point variable. Run the program four times. The first time enter an integer, the second time enter a decimal number with fewer than six decimal places, the third time enter a number having more than six decimal places, and the fourth time enter a character. Using the output display, keep track of what number your program actually accepted from the data you typed. What happened, if anything, and why?

13. Repeat Exercise 11 but have your program declare the variable used to store the number as a double-precision variable. Run the program four times. The first time enter an integer, the second time enter a decimal number with fewer than six decimal places, the third time enter a number having more than six decimal places, and the fourth time enter a character. Using the output display, keep track of what number your program actually accepted from the data you typed. What happened, if anything, and why?

14. a. Why do you think that successful applications programs contain extensive data input validity checks? (*Hint:* Review Exercises 11, 12, and 13.)
    b. What do you think is the difference between a data type check and a data reasonableness check?
    c. Assume that a program requests that a month, day, and year be entered by the user. What are some checks that could be made on the data entered?

3.5 THE `const` QUALIFIER

Literal data is any data within a program that explicitly identifies itself. For example, the constants `2` and `3.1416` in the assignment statement

```
circum = 2 * 3.1416 * radius;
```

are also called literals because they are literally included directly in the statement. Additional examples of literals are contained in the following C++ assignment statements. See if you can identify them.

```
perimeter = 2 * length * width;
        y = (5 * p) / 7.2;
 salestax = 0.05 * purchase;
```

The literals are the numbers 2, 5 and 7.2, and 0.05 in the first, second, and third statements, respectively.

Quite frequently, literal data used within a program have a more general meaning that is recognized outside the context of the program. Examples of these types of constants include the number 3.1416, which is π accurate to four decimal places; 32.2 ft/sec^2, which is the gravitational constant; and the number 2.71828, which is Euler's number accurate to five decimal places. The meaning of certain other constants appearing in a program are defined strictly within the context of the application being programmed. For example, in a program used to determine bank interest charges, the interest rate would typically appear in a number of different places throughout the program. Similarly, in a program used to calculate taxes, the tax rate might appear in many individual instructions. Numbers such as these are referred to by programmers as **magic numbers.** By themselves the numbers are quite ordinary, but in the context of a particular application they have a special ("magical") meaning.

Frequently, the same magic number appears repeatedly within the same program. This recurrence of the same constant throughout a program is a potential source of error should the constant have to be changed. For example, if either the interest rate or sales tax rate change, as rates are prone to do, the programmer would have the cumbersome task of changing the value everywhere it appears in the program. Multiple changes, however, are subject to error—if just one rate value is overlooked and not changed, the result obtained when the program is run will be incorrect and the source of the error difficult to locate.

To avoid the problem of having a magic number spread throughout a program in many places and to permit clear identification of more universal constants, such as π, C++ allows the programmer to give these constants their own symbolic name. Then, instead of using the number throughout the program, the symbolic name is used instead. If the number ever has to be changed, the change need only be made once at the point where the symbolic name is equated to the actual number value. Equating numbers to symbolic names is accomplished using a const variable declaration qualifier. The const qualifier specifies that the declared variable can only be read after it is initialized; it cannot be changed. Three examples using this qualifier are:

```
const float PI = 3.1416;
const double SALESTAX = 0.05;
const int MAXNUM = 100;
```

The first declaration statement creates a floating-point variable named PI and initializes it with the value 3.1416; the second declaration statement creates the double-precision variable named SALESTAX and initializes it to 0.05. Finally, the third declaration creates an integer variable named MAXNUM and initializes it with the value 100.

Once a const variable is created and initialized, the value stored in the variable cannot be changed. Thus, for all practical purposes the name of the variable and its value are linked together for the duration of the program that declares them.

Although we have typed the const variables in uppercase letters, lowercase letters could have been used. It is common in C++, however, to use uppercase letters for const variables to easily identify them as such. Then, whenever a programmer sees uppercase letters in a program, he or she will know the value of the variable cannot be changed within the program.

Once declared, a const variable can be used in any C++ statement in place of the number it represents. For example, the assignment statements

```
circum = 2 * PI * radius;
amount = SALESTAX * purchase;
```

are both valid. These statements must, of course, appear after the declarations for all their variables. Since a const declaration effectively equates a constant value to a variable, and the variable name can be used as a direct replacement for its initializing constant, such variables are commonly referred to as **symbolic constants** or **named constants.** We use these terms interchangeably.

Placement of Statements

At this stage we have introduced a variety of statement types. The general rule in C++ for statement placement is simply that a variable or named constant must be declared before it can be used. Although this rule permits both preprocessor directives and declaration statements to be placed throughout a program, doing so results in a very poor program structure. As a matter of good programming form, the following statement ordering should be used:

```
Preprocessor directives

Named constants

int main()
{
  main function declarations

  other executable statements

  return value
}
```

As new statement types are introduced we will expand this placement structure to accommodate them. Notice that comment statements can be freely intermixed anywhere within this basic structure.

Program 3.14 illustrates the use of a named constant using this placement order.

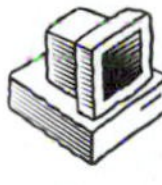

PROGRAM 3.14

```
#include <iostream.h>
#include <iomanip.h>

const float SALESTAX = 0.05;

int main()
{
  float amount, taxes, total;

  cout << "\nEnter the amount purchased: ";
  cin  >> amount;
  taxes = SALESTAX * amount;
  total = amount + taxes;

    // set output formats
  cout << setiosflags(ios::fixed)
       << setiosflags(ios::showpoint)
       << setprecision(2);

  cout << "The sales tax is " << setw(4) << taxes << endl;
  cout << "The total bill is " << setw(5) << total << endl;

  return 0;
}
```

The following sample run was made using Program 3.14.

```
Enter the amount purchased: 36.00
The sales tax is 1.80
The total bill is 37.80
```

Although we have used the `const` qualifier to construct symbolic constants, we will encounter this data type once again in Chapter 6, where we will show that they are useful as function arguments in ensuring that the argument is not modified within the function.

Exercises 3.5

Determine the purpose of the programs given in Exercises 1, 2, and 3. Then rewrite each program using a symbolic constant for the appropriate literals.

1.
```
#include <iostream.h>

int main()
{
  float radius, circum;
  cout << <"Enter a radius: ";
  cin >> radius;
  circum = 2.0 * 3.1416 * radius;
  cout << "\nThe circumference of the circle is " << circum << endl;

  return 0;
}
```

2.
```
#include <iostream.h>

int main()
{
  float prime, amount, interest;
  prime = .08; // prime interest rate
  cout << <Enter the amount: ";
  cin >> amount;
  interest = prime * amount;
  cout << "\nThe interest earned is" << interest << endl;

  return 0;
}
```

3.
```
#include <iostream.h>

int main()
{
  float fahren, celsius;
  cout << "Enter a temperature in degrees Fahrenheit: ";
  cin >> fahren;
  celsius = (5.0/9.0) * (fahren - 32.0);
  cout << "\nThe equivalent Celsius temperature is "
       << celsius << endl;

  return 0;
}
```

3.6 FOCUS ON PROBLEM SOLVING

In this section we present two programming problems to further illustrate both the use of `cin` statements to accept user input data and the use of library functions for performing calculations.

Problem 1: Acid Rain

The use of coal as the major source of steam power began with the Industrial Revolution. Currently coal is one of the principal sources of electrical power generation in many industrialized countries.

Since the middle of the nineteenth century we have known that the oxygen used in the burning process combines with the carbon and sulfur in the coal to produce both carbon dioxide and sulfur dioxide. When these gases are released into the atmosphere the sulfur dioxide combines with the water and oxygen in the air to form sulfuric acid, which itself is transformed into separate hydronium ions and

FIGURE 3.12 The Formation of Acid Rain

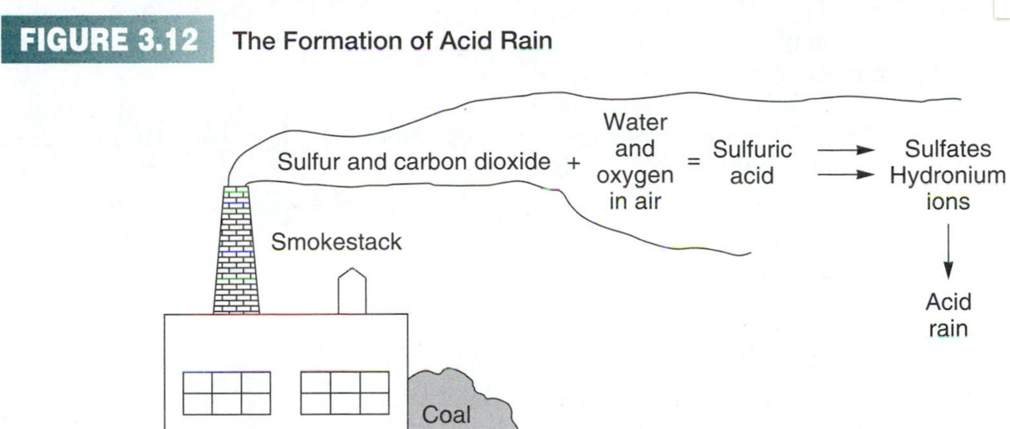

sulfates (see Figure 3.12). It is the hydronium ions in the atmosphere that fall to earth, either as components of rain or as a dry deposition, that change the acidity level of lakes and forests.

The acid level of rain and lakes is measured on a pH scale using the formula

$$\text{pH} = -\log_{10} (\text{concentration of hydronium ions})$$

where the concentration of hydronium ions is measured in units of moles/liter. A pH value of 7 indicates a neutral value (neither acid nor alkaline), whereas levels below 7 indicate the presence of an acid, and levels above 7 indicate the presence of an alkaline substance. For example, sulfuric acid has a pH value of approximately 1, lye has a pH value of approximately 13, and water typically has a pH value of 7. Marine life usually cannot survive in water with a pH level below 4.

Using the formula for pH, we will write a C++ program that calculates the pH level of a substance based on a user input value for the concentration of hydronium ions. In the following subsections, we use the top-down development procedure described in Section 2.6.

Step 1: Analyze the Problem Although the statement of the problem provides technical information on the composition of acid rain, from a programming viewpoint this is a rather simple problem. Here there is only one required output (a pH level) and one input (the concentration of hydronium ions).

Step 2: Develop a Solution The algorithm required to transform the input to the required output is a rather straightforward use of the pH formula that is provided. The pseudocode representation of the complete algorithm for entering the input data, processing the data to produce the desired output, and displaying the output is:

Display a prompt to enter an ion concentration level.
Read a value for the concentration level.
Calculate a pH level using the given formula.
Display the calculated value.

To ensure that we understand the formula used in the algorithm, we will do a hand calculation. The result of this calculation can then be used to verify the result produced by the program. Assuming an hydronium concentration of 0.0001 (any value would do), the pH level is calculated as $-\log_{10} 10^{-4}$. Either by knowing that the logarithm of 10 raised to a power is the power itself, or by using a log table, the value of this expression is $-(-4) = 4$.

Step 3: Code the Solution Program 3.15 describes the selected algorithm in C++. The choice of variable names is arbitrary.

PROGRAM 3.15

```
#include <iostream.h>
#include <math.h>

int main()
{
  float hydron, pHlevel;

  cout << "Enter the hydronium ion concentration: ";
   cin >> hydron;
  pHlevel = -log10(hydron);
  cout << "The pH level is " << pHlevel << endl;

  return 0;
}
```

Program 3.15 begins with two `#include` preprocessor statements, followed by the function `main()`. Within `main()`, a declaration statement declares two floating-point variables, `hydron` and `pHlevel`. The program then displays a prompt requesting input data from the user. After the prompt is displayed, a `cin` statement is used to store the entered data in the variable `hydron`. Finally, a value for `pHlevel` is calculated, using the logarithmic library function, and displayed. As always, the program is terminated with a closing brace.

Step 4: Test and Correct the Program A test run using Program 3.15 produced the following:

```
Enter the hydronium ion concentration: 0.0001
The pH level is 4
```

Because the program performs a single calculation, and the result of this test run agrees with our previous hand calculation, the program has been completely tested. It can now be used to calculate the pH level of other hydronium concentrations with confidence that the results being produced are accurate.

Problem 2: Approximating the Exponential Function

The exponential function e^x, where e is known as Euler's number (and has the value 2.718281828459045...) appears many times in descriptions of natural phenomena. For example, radioactive decay, population growth, and the normal (bell-shaped) curve used in statistical applications all can be described using this function.

The value of e^x can be approximated using the following series:[11]

$$1 + \frac{x^1}{1} + \frac{x^2}{2} + \frac{x^3}{6} + \frac{x^4}{24} + \frac{x^5}{120} + \frac{x^6}{720}\cdots$$

Using this polynomial as a base, write a program that approximates e raised to a user input value of x using the first four terms of this series. For each approximation display the value calculated by C++'s exponential function, `exp()`, the approximate value, and the absolute difference between the two. Make sure to verify your program using a hand calculation. Once the verification is complete, use the program to approximate e^4. Using the top-down development procedure described in Section 2.6 we perform the following steps.

Step 1: Analyze the Problem The statement of the problem specifies that four approximations are to be made, using one, two, three, and four terms of the approximating polynomial, respectively. For each approximation three output values are required: the value of the ex produced by the exponential function, the approximate value, and the absolute difference between the two values. Figure 3.13 illustrates, in symbolic form, the structure of the required output display. The output indicated in Figure 3.13 can be used to get a "feel" for what the program must look like. Realizing that each line in the display can only be produced by executing a `cout` statement, it should be clear that four such statements must be executed. Additionally, since each output line contains three computed values, each `cout` statement will have three items in its expression list.

The only input to the program consists of the value of x. This will, of course, require a single prompt and a `cin` statement to input the necessary value.

Step 2: Develop a Solution Before any output items can be calculated, the program will need to prompt the user for a value of x and then have the program accept the entered value. The actual output display consists of two title lines followed by four lines of calculated data. The title lines can be produced using two `cout` statements. Now let's see how the actual data being displayed is produced.

The first item on the first data output line illustrated in Figure 3.13 can be obtained using the `exp()` function. The second item on this line, the approximation to ex, can be obtained by using the first term in the polynomial that was given in the program specification. Finally, the third item on the line can be calculated by using the `fabs()` function on the difference between the first two items. When all of these items are calculated, a single `cout` statement can be used to display the three results on the same line.

The second output line illustrated in Figure 3.13 displays the same type of items as the first line, except that the approximation to e^x requires the use of two terms of the approximating polynomial. Notice also that the first item on the second line, the value obtained by the `exp()` function, is the same as the first item on the first line. This means that this item does not have to be recalculated and the value calculated for the first line can simply be displayed a second time. Once the data for the second line has been calculated, a single `cout` statement can be used to display the required values.

[11] The formula from which this is derived is $e^x = \frac{x^0}{0!} + \frac{x^1}{1!} + \frac{x^2}{2!} + \frac{x^3}{3!} + \ldots + \frac{x^n}{n!}$

PROGRAM 3.16

```
// this program approximates the function e raised to the x power
// using one, two, three, and four terms of an approximating polynomial
#include <iostream.h>
#include <iomanip.h>
#include <math.h>

int main()
{
  float x, func_val, approx, difference;

  cout << "\nEnter a value of x: ";
  cin >> x;

    // print two title lines
  cout << " e to the x      Approximation      Difference\n";
  cout << "-------------    -------------    -------------\n";

  func_val = exp(x);      // use the library function

    // calculate the first approximation
  approx = 1;
  difference = fabs(func_val - approx);
  cout << setw(10) << setiosflags(ios::showpoint) << func_val
       << setw(18) << approx
       << setw(18) << difference << endl;

    // calculate the second approximation
  approx = approx + x;
  difference = fabs(func_val - approx);
  cout << setw(10) << setiosflags(ios::showpoint) << func_val
       << setw(18) << approx
       << setw(18) << difference << endl;

    // calculate the third approximation
  approx = approx + pow(x,2)/2.0;
  difference = fabs(func_val - approx);
  cout << setw(10) << setiosflags(ios::showpoint) << func_val
       << setw(18) << approx
       << setw(18) << difference << endl;

    // calculate the fourth approximation
  approx = approx + pow(x,3)/6.0;
  difference = fabs(func_val - approx);
  cout << setw(10) << setiosflags(ios::showpoint) << func_val
       << setw(18) << approx
       << setw(18) << difference << endl;

  return 0;
}
```

FIGURE 3.13 Values Stored in the Variables

e^x	Approximation	Difference
library function value	1st approximate value	1st difference
library function value	2nd approximate value	2nd difference
library function value	3rd approximate value	3rd difference
library function value	4th approximate value	4th difference

Finally, only the second and third items on the last two output lines shown in Figure 3.13 need to be recalculated, since the first item on these lines is the same as previously calculated for the first line. Thus, for this problem, the complete algorithm described in pseudocode is:

Display a prompt for the input value of x.
Read the input value.
Display the heading lines.
Calculate the exponential value of x using the `exp()` *function.*
Calculate the first approximation.
Calculate the first difference.
Print the first output line.
Calculate the second approximation.
Calculate the second difference.
Print the second output line.
Calculate the third approximation.
Calculate the third difference.
Print the third output line.
Calculate the fourth approximation.
Calculate the fourth difference.
Print the fourth output line.

To ensure that we understand the processing used in the algorithm, we will do a hand calculation. The result of this calculation can then be used to verify the result produced by the program that we write. For test purposes we will use a value of 2 for x, which causes the following approximations:

Using the first term of the polynomial the approximation is

$$e^2 = 1$$

Using the first two terms of the polynomial the approximation is

$$e^2 = 1 + 2/1 = 3$$

Using the first three terms of the polynomial the approximation is

$$e^2 = 3 + 2^2/2 = 5$$

Using the first four terms of the polynomial the approximation is

$$e^2 = 5 + 2^3/6 = 6.3333$$

Notice that in using four terms of the polynomial that it was not necessary to recalculate the value of the first three terms; instead, we used the previously calculated value.

Step 3: Code the Solution Program 3.16 represents a description of the selected algorithm in C++.

In reviewing Program 3.16 notice that the input value of x is obtained first. The two title lines are then printed prior to any calculations being made. The value of the e^x is then computed using the `exp()` library function and assigned to the variable `func_val`. This assignment will permit this value to be used in the four `difference` calculations and displayed four times without the need for recalculation.

Since the approximation to the e^x is "built up" using more and more terms of the approximating polynomial, only the new term for each approximation is calculated and added to the previous approximation. Finally, to permit the same variables to be used over, the values in them are immediately printed before the next approximation is made. The following is a sample run produced by Program 3.16.

```
Enter a value of x: 2
          e to the x        Approximation       Difference
        -------------       -------------     -------------
          7.389056          1.000000            6.389056
          7.389056          3.000000            4.389056
          7.389056          5.000000            2.389056
          7.389056          6.333333            1.055723
```

Step 4: Test and Correct the Program The first two columns of output data produced by the sample run agree with our hand calculation. A hand check of the last column verifies that it also correctly contains the difference in values between the first two columns.

Because the program only performs nine calculations, and the result of the test run agrees with our hand calculations, it appears that the program has been completely tested. However, it is important to understand that this is because of our choice of test data. Selecting a value of 2 for x forced us to verify that the program was, in fact, calculating 2 raised to the required powers. A choice of 0 or 1 for our hand calculation would not have given us the verification that we need. Do you see why this is so?

Using 0 or 1 would not adequately test whether the program used the `pow()` function correctly, or even if it used it at all! That is, an incorrect program that did not use the `pow()` function could have been constructed to produce correct values for $x = 0$ and $x = 1$, but for no other values of x. Because the test data we used does adequately verify the program, however, we can use it with confidence in the results produced. Clearly, however, the output demonstrates that to achieve any level of accuracy with the program, more terms than four would be required.

Exercises 3.6

1. Enter, compile, and run Program 3.15 on your computer system.
2. a. Enter, compile, and run Program 3.16 on your computer system.
   b. Determine how many terms of the approximating polynomial should be used to achieve an error of less than 0.0001 between the approximation and the value of e^2 as determined by the `exp()` function.
3. By mistake a student wrote Program 3.16 as follows:

```
// this program approximates the function e raised to the x power
// using one, two, three, and four terms of an approximating polynomial
#include <iostream.h>
#include <iomanip.h>
#include <math.h>

int main()
{
  float x, func_val, approx, difference;

    // print two title lines
  cout << " e to the x          Approximation      Difference\n";
  cout << "-------------        -------------      -------------\n";

  cout << "\nEnter a value of x: ";
  cin >> x;
  func_val = exp(x);        // use the library function

    // calculate the first approximation
  approx = 1;
  difference = fabs(func_val - approx);
  cout << setw(10) << setiosflags(ios::showpoint) << func_val
       << setw(18) << approx
       << setw(18) << difference << endl;
    // calculate the second approximation
  approx = approx + x;
  difference = fabs(func_val - approx);
  cout << setw(10) << setiosflags(ios::showpoint) << func_val
       << setw(18) << approx
       << setw(18) << difference << endl;
    // calculate the third approximation
  approx = approx + pow(x,2)/2.0;
  difference = fabs(func_val - approx);
  cout << setw(10) << setiosflags(ios::showpoint) << func_val
       << setw(18) << approx
       << setw(18) << difference << endl;
    // calculate the fourth approximation
  approx = approx + pow(x,3)/6.0;
  difference = fabs(func_val - approx);
  cout << setw(10) << setiosflags(ios::showpoint) << func_val
       << setw(18) << approx
       << setw(18) << difference << endl;

  return 0;
}
```

Determine the output that will be produced by this program.

4. The value of π can be approximated by the series

$$4(1 - \frac{1}{3} + \frac{1}{5} - \frac{1}{7} + \ldots)$$

Using this formula, write a program that calculates and displays the value of π using the first four terms of the series.

5. a. The formula for the standard normal deviate, z, used in statistical applications is

$$z = \frac{x - m}{\sigma}$$

where μ refers to a mean value and σ to a standard deviation. Using this formula, write a program that calculates and displays the value of the standard normal deviate when $x = 85.3$, $\mu = 80$, and $\sigma = 4$.

b. Rewrite the program written in Exercise 5a to accept the values of x, μ, and σ as user inputs while the program is executing.

6. a. The equation of the normal (bell-shaped) curve used in statistical applications is:

$$y = \frac{1}{\sigma\sqrt{2\pi}} e^{-(1/2)[(x-\mu)/\sigma^2}$$

Using this equation, the asuming $\mu = 90$ and $\sigma = 4$, write a program that determines and displays the value of y when $x = 80$.

b. Rewrite the program written in Exercise 6a to accept the values of x, μ, and σ as user inputs while the program is executing.

7. a. Write, compile, and execute a program that calculates and displays the gross pay and net pay of two individuals. The first individual works 40 hours and is paid an hourly rate of $8.43. The second individual works 35 hours and is paid an hourly rate of $5.67. Both individuals have 20% of their pay withheld for income tax purposes and both pay 2% of their net pay, before taxes, for medical benefits.

b. Redo Exercise 7a assuming that the individuals' hours and rate are entered when the program is run.

8. The volume of oil stored in an underground 200-foot-deep cylindrical tank is determined by measuring the distance from the top of the tank to the surface of the oil. Knowing this distance and the radius of the tank, the volume of oil in the tank can be determined using the formula *volume* = π *radius2* (200 − distance). Using this information, write, compile, and execute a C++ program that accepts the radius and distance measurements, calculates the volume of oil in the tank, and displays the two input values and the calculated volume. Verify the results of your program by doing a hand calculation using the following test data: Radius equals 10 feet and distance equals 12 feet.

9. The perimeter, approximate surface area, and approximate volume of an in-ground pool are given by the following formulas:

perimeter = 2(length + width)
volume = length * width * average depth
underground surface area = 2(length + width)average depth + length * width

Using these formulas as a basis, write a C++ program that accepts the length, width, and average depth measurements, and then calculates the perimeter, volume, and underground surface area of the pool. In writing your program make the following two calculations immediately after the input data has been entered: *length * width* and *length + width*. The results of these two calculations should then be used, as appropriate, in the assignment statements for determining the perimeter, volume, and underground surface area. Verify the results of your program by doing a hand calculation using the following test data: Length equals 25 feet, width equals 15 feet, and average depth equals 5.5 feet. When you have verified that your program is working, use it to complete the following table:

Length	Width	Depth	Perimeter	Volume	Underground Surface Area
25	10	5.0			
25	10	5.5			
25	10	6.0			
25	10	6.5			
30	12	5.0			
30	12	5.5			
30	12	6.0			
30	12	6.5			

3.7 PLANNING FOR OBJECTS: PROGRAM PERFORMANCE MEASURES AND OBJECT-ORIENTED TECHNOLOGY

Assume that you have a choice to become either an amateur, semiprofessional, or professional programmer—which do you choose? "Ah," you might say, of course I want to be a professional programmer." But before you make your selection, let's take a moment to see what this decision implies.

Just as programmers can be categorized as amateur or professional, programs can also be categorized, using common terms, from slapped-together to bullet-proof, industrial-strength programs.

Now you might make the assumption that amateurs produce slapped-together programs and that professionals produce bullet-proof, industrial-strength programs. Your assumption, however, would be only half correct. In general, amateurs almost always do produce amateur programs, because that is all they can produce. Professionals, on the other hand, can produce both types of software because, in addition to programming language skills, they have mastered a necessary set of analysis and design skills. This background permits professionals to not only understand and be able to spot the difference, but more importantly, to know when it is appropriate to produce industrial-strength software and when it is not appropriate. Knowing how much effort is appropriate to expend on a program is what truly distinguishes the professional from the amateur.

Each application is different. Professional programmers know the appropriate level of effort, care, and complexity to apply to each situation. Spending too much time and applying too much sophistication to a program *is just as much an error* as spending too little time and being too simplistic. But professional programmers can make this distinction because they have gained an understanding of the appropriate measures of program performance that they are trying to achieve.

Measures of Program Performance

The actual writing of a program is always an implementation process, where the word **implement** means *to put into effect according to a definite plan.* In practice, the plan being implemented is developed during the design phase. In this sense, programming is the last step the programming process illustrated in Figure 3.14.

Because writing a program produces something immediate and tangible, which is a working program that can be run and tested, how to write a program is almost always one of the first courses presented in a computer science curriculum. Thus the sequence of learning all of the tools in the complete programming process is generally that shown in Figure 3.15.

The sequence illustrated in Figure 3.15 is typical of that used in learning almost all skills. For example, you learned to read and write English words before you learned how to write sentences, paragraphs, and structure complete written compositions. Later, some people go on to analyze and design more intricate

FIGURE 3.14 The Programming Process

Requirements Specification → Analysis → Design → Programming

FIGURE 3.15 The Programming Learning Sequence

Programming → Analysis → Design → Requirement Specification

compositions, such as essays and novels. Similarly, you always learn how to use tools, such as a hammer and screwdriver, before actually building something. Later, some people go on to analyze people's requirements and actually design more complicated structures such as houses. This learning sequence, however, does have its downside, especially in programming.

To enable a student to learn basic programming techniques simple program requirements are initially used in almost all programming texts, including this one. This permits the analysis and design steps to be reduced to a minimum. Thus a new programmer becomes somewhat like a new carpenter building a house who knows how to build it without necessarily knowing how to design it. The positive side of the traditional learning sequence, however, is that being an implementor does provide a framework for understanding what is actually possible, which is indispensable for a designer. Therefore, before we attempt to understand the design process, we should understand what constitutes a good implementation.

Clearly, at a minimum, a program should be correct. Obviously any program that works is better than a program that does not work. But this criterion provides little help in determining what is a good program. Besides just working, a good program should provide:

- clarity
- robustness
- extensibility
- reusability
- efficiency
- programming-in-the-large.

Clarity has two meanings. From a programming viewpoint it means both that another programmer can read and understand your code and that you can read and understand your own code months after you have written it. From a user's viewpoint it means that the program clearly identifies what inputs are required and what outputs are being produced.

Robustness means that a program or function will not fail even if it receives improper data. For example, if your program is expecting an integer and the user types a letter, the program should not crash. Robust programs are sometimes referred to as bullet-proof programs.

Extensibility means that a program can easily be modified and extended to handle cases and situations that the original designers did not expect. Being able to accommodate bigger tasks than originally designed for makes a program industrial strength.

Reusability means that existing code can be reused, both within an existing project and for new projects.

Efficiency means that a program or function produces its results in the most time efficient manner. This includes both computer run time as well as human time spent in preparing to run the program and analyzing and understanding the results of a program or function.

Programming-in-the-large means that large, complex programs can be written using teams of programmers.

Procedure-oriented programming has always had the capability to produce clear, efficient, robust programs that could be programmed in the large. Where procedural techniques have not produced the desired result is in reusability and extensibility. Once written, procedure-oriented programs have generally proven to be very cumbersome and extremely time consuming and costly to extend or reuse for new applications.

Object-oriented technology provides a framework for rectifying this situation by producing both extendable and reusable code. The guidelines for producing object-oriented programs include traditional procedural programming techniques with the addition of new principles that are unique to the object-oriented methodology.

Moving to Object-Oriented Technology

True object-oriented technology (OOT) works with objects from the problem definition stage through the programming stage. It encompasses all of the following object-oriented methods:

- OOR, object-oriented requirements
- OOA, object-oriented analysis
- OOD, object-oriented design
- OOP, object-oriented programming.

Thus, from an OOT viewpoint, the programming process previously shown in Figure 3.14 appears as illustrated in Figure 3.16. As you might expect, the actual learning of OOT proceeds in the sequence illustrated in Figure 3.17. This, of course, simply implements the standard learning sequence previously shown in Figure 3.15 as it applies to OOT.

FIGURE 3.16 The Object-Oriented Technology Programming Process

Object-Oriented Requirements Specifications →	Object-Oriented Analysis →	Object-Oriented Design →	Object-Oriented Programming
OOR ——→	OOA ——→	OOD ——→	OOP

As a practical application of the learning sequence shown in Figure 3.17, consider Figure 3.18. This figure represents how OOT was introduced by one development group within AT&T over a four-year period. In reviewing Figure 3.18, notice that OOT began with C++ as the implementation language of choice (remember that C++ was developed at AT&T) and progressed, in an incremental and systematic way, to object-oriented analysis, object-oriented design, and finally to object-oriented requirements specification.

FIGURE 3.17 The Object-Oriented Technology Learning Sequence

Object-Oriented Programming →	Object-Oriented Analysis →	Object-Oriented Design →	Object-Oriented Requirements Specifications
OOP ——→	OOA ——→	OOD ——→	OOR

FIGURE 3.18 Introduction of OOT by One Development Group at AT&T

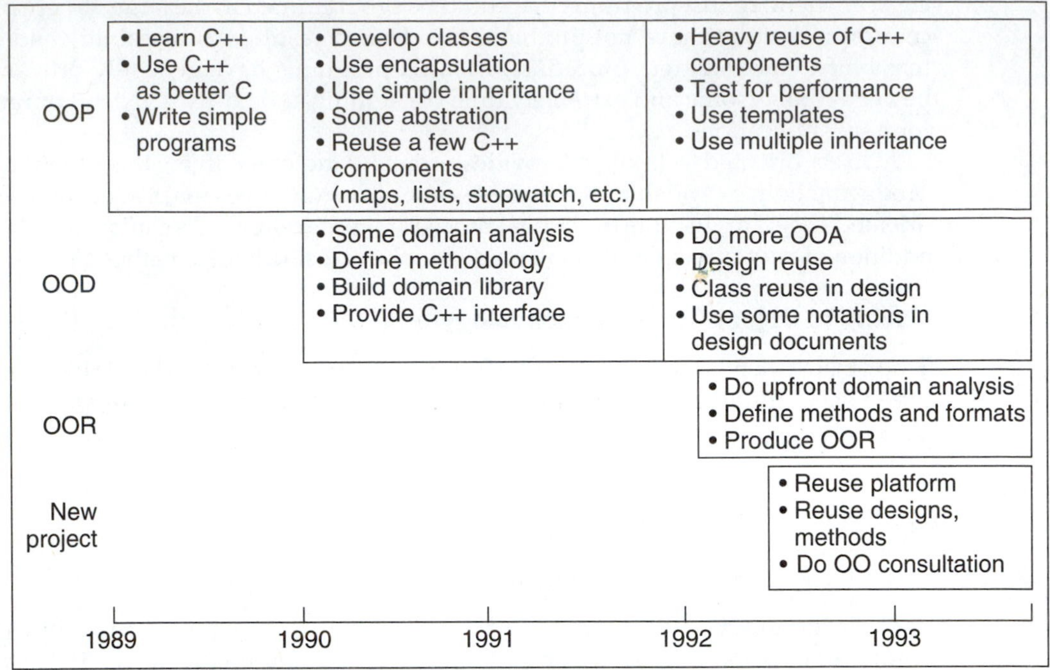
OOP
• Learn C++
• Use C++ as better C
• Write simple programs
• Develop classes
• Use encapsulation
• Use simple inheritance
• Some abstration
• Reuse a few C++ components (maps, lists, stopwatch, etc.)
• Heavy reuse of C++ components
• Test for performance
• Use templates
• Use multiple inheritance
OOD
• Some domain analysis
• Define methodology
• Build domain library
• Provide C++ interface
• Do more OOA
• Design reuse
• Class reuse in design
• Use some notations in design documents
OOR
• Do upfront domain analysis
• Define methods and formats
• Produce OOR
New project
• Reuse platform
• Reuse designs, methods
• Do OO consultation
1989
1990
1991
1992
1993

(*Source:* Reaping Benefits with Object-Oriented Technology, AT&T Technical Journal, Vol. 72, No. 5, p. 17.)

Exercises 3.7

1. Define the terms:
   a. clarity
   b. efficiency
   c. robustness
   d. extensibility
   e. reusability
   f. programming-in-the-large.
2. a. For a simple one-user amateur program, which measures of program performance do you think are *least* important?
   b. From a user's viewpoint, which two measures of programming performance do you think are *most* important in a program written by someone else?
3. a. In reviewing how you respond to assignments, have you ever done an assignment just to hand it in on time rather than doing the assignment right?
   b. In general, do you complete assignments to just get them in on time or do you spend the time on them to do them right? What does right mean?
   c. Have you ever been so concerned with doing an assignment perfectly that you either fail to start it or fail to complete it?

d. Do you think your answer to Exercise 3b is the answer that an amateur or professional would give? Do you think your answer to Exercise 3c is the answer that an amateur or professional would give?

4. a. Review how you have approached programming assignments made in this and other programming courses you have taken. Have you tended to approach these assignments as an amateur or as a professional? Has your approach been reasonable based on the time pressures of other commitments?

   b. Based on your responses to Exercise 4a, what sacrifices or adjustments do you think professionals made in their lives, regardless of their chosen fields, to become professionals?

3.8 A CLOSER LOOK AT ERRORS

The ideal in programming is to produce readable, error-free programs that work correctly and efficiently and can be modified or changed with a minimum of testing required for reverification. In this regard it is useful to know the different types of errors that can occur, when they are detected, and how to correct them.

Compile-Time and Run-Time Errors

A program error can be detected at a variety of times:

1. before a program is compiled
2. while the program is being compiled
3. while the program is being run
4. after the program has been executed and the output is being examined

or not at all. Errors detected by the compiler are formally referred to as **compile-time errors,** and errors that occur while the program is being run are formally referred to as **run-time errors.**

Methods are available for detecting errors before a program is compiled and after it has been executed. The method for detecting errors after a program has been executed is called **program verification and testing.** The method for detecting errors before a program is compiled is called **desk checking**. Desk checking refers to the procedure of checking a program, by hand, at a desk or table for syntax and logic errors, which are described next.

Syntax and Logic Errors

Computer literature distinguishes between two primary types of errors, called syntax and logic errors. A **syntax error** is an error in the structure or spelling of a statement. For example, the statements

```
cout << "There are four syntax errors here\n
cot " Can you find tem";
```

contain four syntax errors:

1. A closing quote is missing in line 1.
2. A terminating semicolon (;) is missing in line 1.
3. The keyword `cout` is misspelled in line 2.
4. The insertion symbol is missing in line 2.

All of these errors will be detected by the compiler when the program is compiled. This is true of all syntax errors: Because they violate the basic rules of C++, if they are not discovered by desk checking, the compiler will detect them and display an error message indicating that a syntax error exists.[12] In some cases the error message is extremely clear and the error is obvious; in other cases it takes a little detective work to understand the error message displayed by the compiler. Since all syntax errors are detected at compile time, the terms *compile-time error* and *syntax error* are frequently used interchangeably. Strictly speaking, however, *compile time* refers to when the error was detected and *syntax* refers to the type of error detected. Note that the misspelling of the word `tem` in the second `cout` statement is not a syntax error. Although this spelling error will be displayed, it is not a violation of C++'s syntactical rules. It is a simple case of a typographical error, commonly referred to as a "typo."

Logic errors are characterized by erroneous, unexpected, or unintentional errors that are a direct result of some flaw in the program's logic. These errors, which are never caught by the compiler, may either be detected by desk checking, by program testing, by accident when a user obtains an obviously erroneous output, while the program is executing, or not at all. If the error is detected while the program is executing a run-time error occurs that results in an error message being generated and/or abnormal and premature program termination.

Since logic errors may not be detected by the computer, they are always more difficult to detect than syntax errors. If not detected by desk checking, a logic error will reveal itself in two predominant ways. In one instance the program executes to completion but produces incorrect results. Logic errors of this type include:

No output: This is either caused by an omission of a `cout` statement or a sequence of statements that inadvertently bypasses a `cout` statement.

Unappealing or misaligned output: This is caused by an error in a `cout` statement.

Incorrect numerical results: This is caused by either incorrect values assigned to the variables used in an expression, the use of an incorrect arithmetic expression, an omission of a statement, round-off error, or the use of an improper sequence of statements.

See if you can detect the logic error in Program 3.17.

A sample run of Program 3.17 follows:

```
This program calculates the amount of money
in a bank account for an initial deposit
invested for n years at an interest rate r.

Enter the initial amount in the account: 1000.
Enter the number of years: 5

The final amount of money is $ 1000.00
```

As indicated in the output, the final amount of money is identical to the initial amount input. Did you spot the error in Program 3.17 that produced this apparently erroneous output? Unlike a misspelled output message, the error in Program 3.17 causes a mistake in a computation. Here the error is that the program does not initialize the vari-

[12] They may not, however, all be detected at the same time. Frequently, one syntax error "masks" another error and the second error is only detected after the first error is corrected.

PROGRAM 3.17

```
#include <iostream.h>
#include <iomanip.h>
#include <math.h>

int main() // a compound interest program
{
  float capital, amount, rate, nyrs;

  cout << "This program calculates the amount of money\n";
  cout << "in a bank account for an initial deposit\n";
  cout << "invested for n years at an interest rate r.\n\n";
  cout << "Enter the initial amount in the account: ";
  cin >> amount;
  cout << "Enter the number of years: ";
  cin >> nyrs;
  capital = amount * pow((1 + rate/100.0), nyrs);

    // set output formats
  cout << setiosflags(ios::fixed)
       << setiosflags(ios::showpoint)
       << setprecision(2);

  cout << "\nThe final amount of money is "
       << setw(8) << '$' << capital << endl;

  return 0;
}
```

able rate before this variable is used in the calculation of `capital`. When the assignment statement that calculates `capital` is executed, the program uses whatever value is stored in `rate`. On those systems that initialize all variables to zero, the value zero will be used for `rate`. However, on those systems that do not initialize all variables to zero, the program will use whatever "garbage" value happens to occupy the storage locations corresponding to the variable `rate`. (The manuals supplied with your compiler will indicate which of these two actions your compiler takes.) In either case an error is produced.

Although the logic error in this example program did not cause premature program termination, faulty or incomplete program logic can cause run-time errors. Examples of this type of logic error are attempts to divide by zero or to take the square root of a negative number.

Any program testing that is done should be well thought out to maximize the possibility of locating errors. An important programming realization is that although a single test can reveal the presence of an error, it does not verify the absence of one. The fact that one error is revealed by a particular verification run does not indicate that another error is not lurking somewhere else in the program; the fact that one test revealed no errors does not indicate that there are no errors.

Although there are no hard and fast rules for isolating the cause of an error, some useful techniques can be applied. The first of these is a preventive technique. Frequently, many errors are simply introduced by the programmer in the rush to code and run a program before fully understanding what is required and how the result is to be achieved. A symptom of this haste to get a program entered into the computer is the lack of an outline of the proposed program (pseudocode or flowcharts) or a handwritten program itself. Many errors can be eliminated simply by checking a copy of the program before it is ever entered or compiled by desk checking the program.

A second useful technique is to mimic the computer and execute each statement, by hand, as the computer would. This means writing down each variable as it is encountered in the program and listing the value that should be stored in the variable as each input and assignment statement is encountered. Doing this also sharpens your programming skills, because it requires that you fully understand what each statement in your program causes to happen. Such a check is called program **tracing.**

A third and very powerful debugging technique is to use one or more diagnostic `cout` statements to display the values of selected variables. For example, consider Program 3.17 again. Since this program produced an incorrect value for `capital`, it is worthwhile to place a `cout` statement immediately before the assignment statement for `capital` to display the value of all variables used in the computation. If the displayed values are correct, then the problem is in the assignment statement; if the values are incorrect, we must determine where the incorrect values were actually obtained.

In this same manner, another use of `cout` statements in debugging is to display immediately the values of all input data. This technique is referred to as **echo printing,** and is useful in establishing that the computer is correctly receiving and interpreting the input data.

Finally, no discussion of program verification is complete without mentioning the primary ingredient needed for successful isolation and correction of errors. This is the attitude and spirit you bring to the task. Since you wrote the program, your natural assumption is that it is correct or you would have changed it before it was compiled. It is extremely difficult to back away and honestly test and find errors in your own software. As a programmer you must constantly remind yourself that just because you *think* your program is correct does not make it so. Finding errors in your own programs is a sobering experience, but one that will help you become a master programmer. It can also be exciting and fun if approached as a detection problem with you as the master detective.

3.9 COMMON PROGRAMMING ERRORS

In using the material presented in this chapter, be aware of the following possible errors:

1. Forgetting to assign or initialize values for all variables before the variables are used in an expression. Such values can be assigned by assignment statements, initialized within a declaration statement, or assigned interactively by entering values using the `cin` object.

2. Using a mathematical library function without including the preprocessor statement `#include <math.h>` (and on a UNIX-based system forgetting to include the `-lm` argument to the `cc` command).

3. Using a library function without providing the correct number or arguments having the proper data type.

4. Applying either the increment or decrement operator to an expression. For example, the expression

```
(count + n)++
```

is incorrect. The increment and decrement operators can only be applied to individual variables.

5. Forgetting to separate all variables passed to `cin` with an extraction symbol, >>.

6. A more exotic and less common error occurs when the increment and decrement operators are used with variables that appear more than once in the same expression. This error basically occurs because C++ does not specify the order in which operands are accessed within an expression. For example, the value assigned to result in the statement

```
result = i + i++;
```

is compiler dependent. If your compiler accesses the first operand, `i`, first, the preceding statement is equivalent to

```
result = 2 * i;
i++;
```

However, if your compiler accesses the second operand, `i++`, first, the value of the first operand will be altered before it is used the second time and the value `2i + 1` is assigned as the result. As a general rule, therefore, do not use either the increment or decrement operator in an expression when the variable it operates on appears more than once in the expression.

7. Being unwilling to test a program in depth. After all, since you wrote the program you assume it is correct or you would have changed it before it was compiled. It is extremely difficult to back away and honestly test your own software. As a programmer you must constantly remind yourself that just because you *think* your program is correct does not make it so. Finding errors in your own program is a sobering experience, but one that will help you become a master programmer.

3.10 CHAPTER REVIEW

Key Terms

accumulating
arguments
assignment operators
cast
`cin`
compile-time errors
counting
decrement operator
desk checking
echo printing
field width manipulators
hexadecimal
increment operator
implement
justification
logic errors
lvalues
magic numbers
mathematical header
mathematical library
named constants
octal

program verification and testing
prompt
run-time errors
rvalues
symbolic constants
syntax errors
tracing
type conversions

Summary

1. An *expression* is a sequence of one or more operands separated by operators. An operand is a constant, a variable, or another expression. A value is associated with an expression.
2. Expressions are evaluated according to the precedence and associativity of the operators used in the expression.
3. The assignment symbol, =, is an operator. Expressions using this operator assign a value to a variable; additionally, the expression itself takes on a value. Since assignment is an operation in C++, multiple uses of the assignment operator are possible in the same expression.
4. The increment operator, ++, adds one to a variable; the decrement operator, --, subtracts one from a variable. Both of these operators can be used as prefixes or postfixes. In prefix operation the variable is incremented (or decremented) before its value is used. In postfix operation the variable is incremented (or decremented) after its value is used.
5. C++ provides library functions for calculating square root, logarithmic, and other mathematical computations. Each program using one of these mathematical functions must either include the statement `#include <math.h>` or have a function declaration for the mathematical function before it is called.
6. Every mathematical library function operates on its arguments to calculate a single value. To use a library function effectively, you must know what the function does, the name of the function, the number and data types of the arguments expected by the function, and the data type of the returned value.
7. Data passed to a function is called an argument of the function. Arguments are passed to a library function by including each argument, separated by commas, within the parentheses following the function's name. Each function has its own requirements for the number and data types of the arguments that must be provided.
8. Functions may be included within larger expressions.
9. The `cin` object is used for data input. This object accepts a stream of data from the keyboard and assigns the data to variables. The general form of a statement using `cin` is:

   ```
   cin >> var1 >> var2 . . . >> varn;
   ```

   The extraction symbol, >>, must be used to separate the variable names.
10. When a `cin` statement is encountered, the computer temporarily suspends statement execution until sufficient data has been entered for the number of variables contained in the `cin` function.
11. It is good programming practice to display a message, prior to a `cin` statement, that alerts the user as to the type and number of data items to be entered. Such a message is called a prompt.

12. A value can be equated to a single variable, using the `const` variable qualifier when the variable is declared. This makes the variable a read-only variable after it is initialized within the declaration statement. This declaration has the syntax

```
const data-type variable-name = initial value;
```

and permits the variable to be used instead of the initial value anywhere in the program after the command. Generally, such declarations are placed at the top of a C++ program.

Exercises

1. a. Write a C++ program to calculate and display the value of the slope of the line connecting the two points whose coordinates are (3,7) and (8,12). Use the fact that the slope between two points having coordinates ($x1$,$y1$) and ($x2$,$y2$) is ($y2 - y1$) / ($x2 - x1$).
   b. How do you know that the result produced by your program is correct?
   c. Once you have verified the output produced by your program, modify it to determine the slope of the line connecting the points (2,10) and (12,6).
   d. What do you think will happen if you use the points (2,3) and (2,4), which results in a division by zero? How do you think this situation can be handled?
2. a. Write a C++ program to calculate and display the coordinates of the midpoint of the line segment connecting the two end points given in Exercise 1a. Use the fact that the coordinates of the midpoint between two points having coordinates ($x1$,$y1$) and ($x2$,$y2$) are (($X1 + X2$)/2, ($Y1 + Y2$)/2). Your program should produce the following display:

```
The x midpoint coordinate is _____
The y midpoint coordinate is _____
```

   where the blank spaces are replaced with the values calculated by your program.
   b. How do you know that the midpoint values calculated by your program are correct?
   c. Once you have verified the output produced by your program, modify it to determine the midpoint coordinates of the line connecting the points (2,10) and (12,6).
3. Redo Exercise 1 but change the output produced by your program to be:

```
The value of the slope is xxx.xx
```

   where `xxx.xx` denotes that the calculated value should be placed in a field wide enough to fit three places to the left of the decimal point, and two places to the right of it.
4. Redo Exercise 2 but change the output produced by your program to be:

```
The x coordinate of the midpoint is xxx.xx
The y coordinate of the midpoint is xxx.xx
```

   where `xxx.xx` denotes that the calculated value should be placed in a field wide enough to fit three places to the left of the decimal point, and two places to the right of it.

5. The dollar change remaining after an amount paid is used to pay a restaurant check of amount check can be calculated using the following C++ statements:

```
// determine the amount of pennies in the change
   change = (paid - check) * 100;
// determine the number of dollars in the change
   dollars = (int) (change/100);
```

   a. Using the previous statements as a starting point, write a C++ program that calculates the number of dollar bills, quarters, dimes, nickels, and pennies in the change when $10 is used to pay a bill of $6.06.
   b. Without compiling or executing your program check the effect, by hand, of each statement in the program and determine what is stored in each variable as each statement is encountered.
   c. When you have verified that your algorithm works correctly, compile and execute your program. Verify that the result produced by your program is correct. After you have verified your program is working correctly, use it to determine the change when a check of $12.36 is paid using a $20 bill.

6. a. For display purposes the setprecision manipulator allows the programmer to round all outputs to the desired number of decimal places. This can, however, yield seemingly incorrect results when used in financial programs that require all monetary values to be displayed to the nearest penny. For example, the display produced by the program:

```
#include <iostream.h>
#include <iomanip.h>
void main(void)
{
  float a, b, c;

  a = 1.674;
  b = 1.322;
  cout << setprecision(2) << a << endl;
  cout << setprecision(2) << b << endl;
  cout << "----\n";
  c = a + b;
  cout << setiosflags(ios::showpoint)
       << setprecision(2) << c << endl;
}
```

is:

```
1.67
1.32
----
3.00
```

Clearly, the sum of the displayed numbers should be 2.99 and not 3.00. The problem is that although the values in a and b have been displayed with two decimal digits, they were added internal to the program as three-digit numbers. The solution is to round the values in a and b before they are added by the statement c = a + b;. Using the int cast, devise a method to round the values in variables a and b to the nearest hundredth (penny value) before they are added.

b. Include the method you have devised for Exercise 6a into a working program that produces the following display:

```
1.67
1.32
----
2.99
```

7. Design, write, compile, and execute a program that calculates and displays the fourth root of a user-entered number. Recall from elementary algebra that the fourth root of a number can be found by raising the number to the 1/4 power. (*Hint:* Do not use integer division—do you know why?) Verify your program by calculating the fourth root of the following data: 81, 16, 1, and 0. When you have completed your verification, use your program to determine the fourth root of 42, 121, 256, 587, 1240, and 16256.

8. Using `cin` statements, write, compile, and execute a C++ program that accepts the `x` and `y` coordinates of two points. Have your program determine and display the midpoints of the two points (use the formula given in Exercise 2). Verify your program using the following test data:

   Test data set 1: Point 1 = (0,0) and Point 2 = (16,0).
   Test data set 2: Point 1 = (0,0) and Point 2 = (0,16)
   Test data set 3: Point 1 = (0,0) and Point 2 = (–16,0)
   Test data set 4: Point 1 = (0,0) and Point 2 = (0,–16)
   Test data set 5: Point 1 = (–5,–5) and Point 2 = (5,5)

   When you have completed your verification, use your program to complete the following table:

Point 1	Point 2	Midpoint
(4,6)	(16,18)	
(22,3)	(8,12)	
(–10,8)	(14,4)	
(–12,2)	(14,3.1)	
(3.1,–6)	(20,16)	
(3.1,–6)	(–16,–18)	

9. Design, write, compile, and execute a C++ program that calculates and displays the amount of money, A, available in N years when an initial deposit of X dollars is deposited in a bank account paying an annual interest rate of R percent. Use the relationship that $A = X(1.0 + R/100)^N$. The program should prompt the user to enter appropriate values and use `cin` statements to accept the data. In constructing your prompts use statements such as `Enter the amount of the initial deposit`. Verify the operation of your program by calculating, by hand and with your program, the amount of money available for the following test cases:

```
Test data set 1: $1000 invested for 10 years at 0% interest
Test data set 2: $1000 invested for 10 years at 6% interest
```

   When you have completed your verification, use your program to determine the amount of money available for the following cases:

   a. $1000 invested for 10 years at 8% interest

   b. $1000 invested for 10 years at 10% interest

c. \$1000 invested for 10 years at 12% interest

d. \$5000 invested for 15 years at 8% interest

e. \$5000 invested for 15 years at 10% interest

f. \$5000 invested for 15 years at 12% interest

g. \$24 invested for 300 years at 4% interest

10. Write a C++ program that prompts the user for a cost per item, number of items purchased, and a discount rate. The program should then calculate and print the total cost, tax due, and amount due. Use the formulas:

```
total cost = number of items * cost-per-item
total cost (discounted) = total cost - (discount rate * total cost)
tax due = total cost * TAXRATE
amount due = total cost + tax due
```

For this problem assume that the `TAXRATE` is 6%.

11. The roads of Kansas are laid out in a rectangular grid at exactly one-mile intervals, as shown in Figure 3.19. Pete drives his pickup *x* miles east and *y* miles north to get to Sally's farm. Both *x* and *y* are integer numbers. Using this information, write, test, and run a C++ program that prompts the user for the values of *x* and *y* and then uses the formula

```
distance = sqrt(x * x + y * y);
```

to find the shortest driving distance across the fields to Sally's farm. Round the answer to the nearest integer value before it is displayed.

FIGURE 3.19 Illustration for Exercise 11

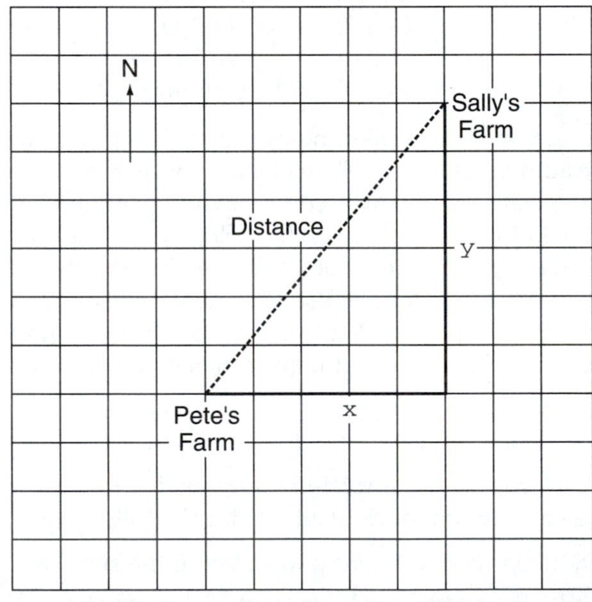

12. When a particular rubber ball is dropped from a given height (in meters) its impact speed (in meters/second) when it hits the ground is given by the formula *speed = sqrt(2 * g * height)*. The ball then rebounds to two-thirds the height from which it last fell. Using this information write, test, and run a C++ program that calculates and displays the impact speed of the first three bounces and the rebound height of each bounce. Test your program using an initial height of 2.0 meters. Run the program twice and compare the results for dropping the ball on earth (g = 9.81 meters/sec^2) and on the moon (g = 1.67 meters/sec^2).

Improving Communication

13. MEMORANDUM

    To: Chief Programmer

    From: Head of Programming Dept.

    Subject: OOP

    The Executive Committee is considering moving to an object-oriented programming environment and has asked for my recommendation. Please provide me with your thoughts and understanding as to the advantages of OOP.

14. MEMORANDUM

    To: Chief Programmer

    From: Head of Programming Dept.

    Subject: Moving to an OOP Environment

    Thank you for your last memorandum to me on the advantages of OOP. At our last Executive Committee meeting the directors asked for a timetable and brief explanation on how we should proceed to a fully implemented OOP environment. Please provide me with a schedule and backup documentation on how you see us moving to such an environment.

Working in Teams

15. a. Have each team member make a list of their objectives in taking this course.
    b. Have each team member make a list of five attributes of the courses that they have enjoyed taking.
16. a. Have each team member list and rank three technical traits that they feel are most important for a successful programmer.
    b. Have each team member list and rank three personality traits that they feel are most important for a successful programmer.
    c. Using each member's lists as a starting point, come up with three technical and three personality traits that the group, as a whole, considers most important.
    d. Put the list constructed in Exercise 16c on the board and compare lists with the other groups in the class.
    e. How could you verify that the traits you have identified are indeed valid?

17. a. Have each team member list three technical traits that they feel would be detrimental to success as a programmer.
    b. Have each team member list three personality traits that they feel would be detrimental for success as a programmer.
    c. Using each member's lists as a starting point, come up with three technical and three personality traits that the group, as a whole, agrees would be detrimental.
    d. Put the list constructed in Exercise 17c on the board and compare lists with the other groups in the class.
    e. How could you verify that the traits you have identified are indeed detrimental?

CHAPTER

4 Selection Structures

Many advances have occurred in the theoretical foundations of programming since the inception of high-level languages in the late 1950s. One of the most important of these advances was the recognition in the late 1960s that any algorithm, no matter how complex, could be constructed using combinations of four standardized *flow of control* structures: sequential, selection, repetition, and invocation.

The term *flow of control* refers to the order in which a program's statements are executed. Unless directed otherwise, the normal flow of control for all programs is *sequential*. This means that statements are executed in sequence, one after another, in the order in which they are placed within the program.

Selection, repetition, and invocation structures permit the sequential flow of control to be altered in precisely defined ways. As you might have guessed, the selection structure is used to select which statements are to be performed next and the repetition structure is used to repeat a set of statements. In this chapter we present C++'s selection statements. Repetition and invocation techniques are presented in Chapters 5 and 6.

4.1 SELECTION CRITERIA

In the solution of many problems, different actions must be taken depending on the value of the data. Examples of simple situations include calculating an area *only if* the measurements are positive, performing a division *only if* the divisor is not zero, printing different messages *depending on* the value of a grade received, and so on.

FIGURE 4.1 Anatomy of a Simple Relational Expression

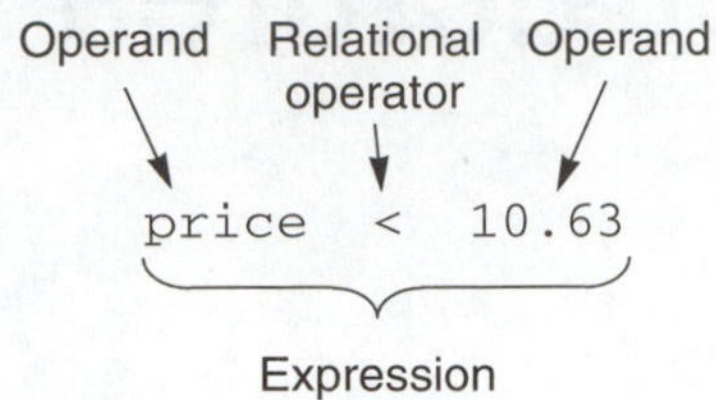

The `if-else` statement in C++ is used to implement such a decision structure in its simplest form—that of choosing between two alternatives. The most commonly used pseudocode syntax of this statement is:

```
if (condition)
  statement executed if condition is "true";
else
  statement executed if condition is "false";
```

When an executing program encounters the `if` statement, the condition is evaluated to determine its numerical value, which is then interpreted as either true or false. If the condition evaluates to any positive or negative nonzero numerical value, the condition is considered to be a **"true" condition** and the statement following the `if` is executed. If the condition evaluates to a zero numerical value, the condition is considered to be a **"false" condition** and the statement following the `else` is executed. The `else` part of the statement is optional and may be omitted.

The condition used in an `if` statement can be any valid C++ expression (even including, as we will see, an assignment expression). The most commonly used expressions, however, are called *relational expressions.* A **simple relational expression** consists of a relational operator that compares two operands as shown in Figure 4.1.

While each operand in a relational expression can be either a variable or a constant, the relational operators must be one of those listed in Table 4.1. These relational operators may be used with integer, float, double, or character operands, but must be typed exactly as given in Table 4.1. Thus, while the following examples are all valid:

```
age > 40     length <= 50    temp > 98.6
  3 < 4      flag == done   id_num == 682
day != 5      2.0 > 3.3       hours > 40
```

the following are invalid:

```
length =< 50        // operator out of order
2.0 >> 3.3          // invalid operator
flag = = done       // spaces are not allowed
```

Relational expressions are sometimes called **conditionals** or **conditions,** for short, and we will use both terms to refer to these expressions. Like all C++ expressions, relational expressions are evaluated to yield a numerical result.[1] In the case of a relational expression, the value of the expression can only be the

[1]In this regard C++ differs from other high-level languages that yield a Boolean (true, false) result.

Table 4.1 Relational Operators

Operator	Meaning	Example
<	Less than	`age < 30`
>	Greater than	`height > 6.2`
<=	Less than or equal to	`taxable <= 20000`
>=	Greater than or equal to	`temp >= 98.6`
==	Equal to	`grade == 100`
!=	Not equal to	`number != 250`

integer value of 1 or 0, which is interpreted as true or false, respectively. *A relational expression that we would interpret as true evaluates to an integer value of 1, and a false relational expression results in an integer value of 0.* For example, because the relationship 3 < 4 is always true, this expression has a value of 1, and because the relationship 2.0 > 3.3 is always false, the value of the expression itself is 0. This can be verified using these statements:

```
cout << "The value of 3 < 4 is " << (3 < 4) << endl;
cout << "The value of 2.0 > 3.0 is " << (2.0 > 3.3) << endl;
```

which results in the display

```
The value of 3 < 4 is 1
The value of 2.0 > 3.0 is 0
```

The value of a relational expression such as `hours > 40` depends on the value stored in the variable `hours`. In a C++ program, a relational expression's value is not as important as the interpretation C++ places on the value when the expression is used as part of a selection statement. In these statements, which are presented in the next section, we will see that *a zero value is used by C++ to represent a false condition and any nonzero value is used to represent a true condition.* The selection of which statement to execute next is then based on the value obtained.

In addition to numerical operands, character data can also be compared using relational operators. For example, in ASCII code the letter `'A'` is stored using a code having a lower numerical value than the letter `'B'`, the code for a 'B' is lower in value than the code for a `'C'`, and so on. For character sets coded in this manner, the following conditions are evaluated as shown:

Expression	Value	Interpretation
`'A' > 'C'`	0	False
`'D' <= 'Z'`	1	True
`'E' == 'F'`	0	False
`'G' >= 'M'`	0	False
`'B' != 'C'`	1	True

Comparing letters is essential in alphabetizing names or using characters to select a particular choice in decision-making situations.

Logical Operators

In addition to using simple relational expressions as conditions, more complex conditions can be created using the logical operators `AND`, `OR`, and `NOT`. These operators are represented by the symbols `&&`, `||`, and `!`, respectively.

A BIT OF BACKGROUND

De Morgan's Laws

Augustus De Morgan was born at Madura, India, in 1806 and died in London in 1871. He became a professor of mathematics in London in 1828 and spent many years performing investigations into a variety of mathematical topics. He was a revered teacher and wrote numerous textbooks that contained a wealth of information on mathematics and its history, but which generally were very difficult for his students to understand.

De Morgan's contributions to modern computing include two laws by which AND statements can be converted to OR statements and vice versa. They are:

1. `NOT(A AND B) = (NOT A) OR (NOT B)`
2. `NOT(A OR B) = (NOT A) AND (NOT B)`

Thus, from De Morgan's first law, the statement "Either it is not raining or I am not getting wet" says the same thing as "It is not true that it is raining and I am getting wet." Similarly, from the second law; "It is not true that politicians always lie or that teachers always know the facts" becomes "Politicians do not always lie and teachers do not always know the facts."

In computer usage, De Morgan's laws are typically more useful in the following form:

1. `A AND B = NOT( (NOT A) OR (NOT B) )`
2. `A OR B = NOT( (NOT A) AND (NOT B) )`

The ability to convert from an OR statement to an AND statement and vice versa is extremely useful in many programming situations.

When the AND operator, `&&`, is used with two simple expressions, the condition is true only if both individual expressions are true by themselves. Thus, the compound condition

```
(age > 40) && (term < 10)
```

is true (has a value of 1) only if `age` is greater than `40` and `term` is less than `10`. Since relational operators have a higher precedence that logical operators, the parentheses in this logical expression could have been omitted.

The logical OR operator, `||`, is also applied between two expressions. When using the OR operator, the condition is satisfied if either one or both of the two expressions is true. Thus, the compound condition

```
(age > 40) || (term < 10)
```

will be true if either `age` is greater than `40`, `term` is less than `10`, or both conditions are true. Again, the parentheses surrounding the relational expressions are included to make the expression easier to read. Because of the higher precedence of relational operators with respect to logical operators the same evaluation would be made even if the parentheses were omitted.

For the declarations

```
int i, j;
float a, b, complete;
```

the following represent valid conditions:

```
a > b
(i == j) || (a < b) || complete
(a/b > 5) && (i <= 20)
```

Before these conditions can be evaluated, the values of `a, b, i, j,` [illegible] `plete` must be known. Assuming `a` = 12.0, `b` = 2.0, `i` = 15, `j` = 30, and [illegible] = 0.0, the previous expressions yield the following results:

Expression	Value	Interpretation
`a > b`	1	True
`(i == j) || (a < b) || complete`	0	False
`(a/b > 5) && (i <= 20)`	1	True

The NOT operator is used to change an expression to its opposite state; that is, if the expression has any nonzero value (true), `!expression` produces a zero value (false). If an expression is false to begin with (has a zero value), `!expression` is true and evaluates to 1. For example, assuming the number `26` is stored in the variable `age`, the expression `age > 40` has a value of zero (it is false), while the expression `!(age > 40)` has a value of 1. Since the NOT operator is used with only one expression, it is a unary operator.

The relational and logical operators have a hierarchy of execution similar to the arithmetic operators. Table 4.2 lists the precedence of these operators in relation to the other operators we have used.

Table 4.2 Operator Precedence

Operator	Associativity
`! unary - ++ --`	Right to left
`* / %`	Left to right
`+ -`	Left to right
`< <= > >=`	Left to right
`== !=`	Left to right
`&&`	Left to right
`||`	Left to right
`= += -= *= /=`	Right to left

The following example illustrates the use of an operator's precedence and associativity to evaluate relational expressions, assuming the following declarations:

```
char key = 'm';
int i = 5, j = 7, k = 12;
double x = 22.5;
```

Expression	Equivalent Expression	Value	Interpretation
`i + 2 == k - 1`	`(i + 2) == (k - 1)`	0	False
`3 * i - j < 22`	`(3 * i) - j < 22`	1	True
`i + 2 * j > k`	`(i + (2 * j)) > k`	1	True
`k + 3 <= -j + 3 * i`	`(k + 3) <= ((-j) + (3*i))`	0	False
`'a' + 1 == 'b'`	`('a' + 1) == 'b'`	1	True
`key - 1 > 'p'`	`(key - 1) > 'p'`	0	False
`key + 1 == 'n'`	`(key + 1) == 'n'`	1	True
`25 >= x + 1.0`	`25 >= (x + 1.0)`	0	True

As with all expressions, parentheses can be used to alter the assigned operator priority and improve the readability of relational expressions. By evaluating the expressions within parentheses first, the following compound condition is evaluated as:

```
(6 * 3 == 36 / 2) || (13 < 3 * 3 + 4) && !(6 - 2 < 5)
        (18 == 18) ||   (13 < 9 + 4)    && !(4 < 5)
                 1 ||   (13 < 13)       && !1
                 1 ||        0          &&  0
                 1 ||        0
                     1
```

A Numerical Accuracy Problem

A problem that can occur with C++'s relational expressions is a subtle numerical accuracy problem related to floating-point and double-precision numbers. Due to the way computers store these numbers, tests for equality of floating-point and double-precision values and variables using the relational operator == should be avoided because many decimal numbers, such as 0.1, for example, cannot be represented exactly in binary using a finite number of bits. Thus, testing for exact equality for such numbers can fail. When equality of noninteger values is desired, it is better to require that the absolute value of the difference between operands be less than some extremely small value. Thus, for floating-point and double-precision operands the general expression

```
operand_1 == operand_2
```

should be replaced by the condition

```
fabs(operand_1 - operand_2) <. 0.000001
```

where the value 0.000001 can be altered to any other acceptably small value. Thus, if the difference between the two operands is less than 0.000001 (or any other user selected amount), the two operands are considered essentially equal. For example if x and y are floating-point variables, a condition such as

```
x/y == 0.35
```

should be programmed as

```
fabs(x/y - 0.35) < epsilon
```

where epsilon can be a const set to any acceptably small value, such as 0.000001.[2] This latter condition ensures that slight inaccuracies in representing noninteger numbers in binary do not affect evaluation of the tested condition. Since all computers have an exact binary representation of zero, comparisons for exact equality to zero do not encounter this numerical accuracy problem.

---

[2] Using the fabs() function requires inclusion of the math.h header file. This is done by placing the preprocessor statement #include <math.h> either immediately before or after the #include <iostream.h> preprocessor statement. It may also require specific inclusion of the math library at compile time with a -lm command line argument.

Exercises 4.1

1. Determine the value of the following expressions. Assume `a = 5, b = 2, c = 4, d = 6, and e = 3.`
   a. `a > b`
   b. `a != b`
   c. `d % b == c % b`
   d. `a * c != d * b`
   e. `d * b == c * e`
   f. `!(a * b)`
   g. `!(a % b * c)`
   h. `!(c % b * a)`
   i. `b % c * a`
2. Using parentheses, rewrite the following expressions to correctly indicate their order of evaluation. Then evaluate each expression assuming `a = 5, b = 2,` and `c = 4.`
   a. `a % b * c && c % b * a`
   b. `a % b * c || c % b * a`
   c. `b % c * a && a % c * b`
   d. `b % c * a || a % c * b`
3. Write relational expressions to express the following conditions (use variable names of your own choosing):
   a. a person's age is equal to 30
   b. a person's temperature is greater than 98.6
   c. a person's height is less than 6 feet
   d. the current month is 12 (December)
   e. the letter input is m
   f. a person's age is equal to 30 and the person is taller than 6 feet
   g. the current day is the 15th day of the 1st month
   h. a person is older than 50 or has been employed at the company for at least 5 years
   i. a person's identification number is less than 500 and the person is older than 55
   j. a length is greater than 2 feet and less than 3 feet
4. Determine the value of the following expressions, assuming `a = 5, b = 2, c = 4,` and `d = 5.`
   a. `a == 5`
   b. `b * d == c * c`
   c. `d % b * c > 5 || c % b * d < 7`

4.2 THE `if-else` STATEMENT

The **`if-else` statement** directs the computer to select a sequence of one or more instructions based on the result of a comparison. For example, the state of New Jersey has a two-level state income tax structure. If a person's taxable income is

PROGRAMMING NOTE

True and False

Many computer languages provide a Logical or Boolean data type that consists of two values only, True and False, for evaluating relational expressions. In these languages relational and logical expressions are restricted to yielding one of these values, and selection statements are restricted to evaluating only relational and logical expressions. This is not the case in C++.

In C++ any expression can be tested within a selection statement, be it a relational, arithmetic, or assignment expression, or even a function call. Within a selection statement, an expression that evaluates to zero or a function that returns a 0 is considered as false, while any nonzero value (negative or positive) is considered as true. If a relational or logical expression is tested, however, the expression itself will yield only a 1 or a 0; 1 if the relational or logical expression is true and 0 if it is false.

Sometimes it is convenient to create the following two symbolic constants:

```
const int TRUE = 1;
const int FALSE = 0;
```

These constants are convenient as values to clearly identify a True or False condition. For example, consider the algorithm

```
if (it is a leap year)
  set yearType to true
else
  set yearType to false
```

Although a C++ programmer will automatically understand this to mean "set year type to 1" and "set year type to 0", respectively, the actual code could use the named constants TRUE and FALSE in the assignment to yearType.

less than $20,000, the applicable state tax rate is 2%. For incomes exceeding $20,000, a different rate is applied. The `if-else` statement can be used in this situation to determine the actual tax based on whether the gross income is less than or equal to $20,000. The general form of the `if-else` statement is:

```
if (expression) statement1;
else statement2;
```

The expression is evaluated first. If the value of the expression is nonzero, *`statement1`* is executed. If the value is zero the statement after the keyword `else` is executed. Thus, one of the two statements (either *`statement1`* or *`statement2`*, but not both) is always executed depending on the value of the expression. Notice that the tested expression must be put in parentheses and a semicolon is placed after each statement.

For clarity, the `if-else` statement should be written on four lines using the form:

```
if (expression)   <------ No semicolon here
  statement1;
else   <-------------- No semicolon here
  statement2;
```

The form of the `if-else` statement that is selected generally depends on the length of statements 1 and 2. However, when using the second form, do not put a

FIGURE 4.2 The `if-else` Flowchart

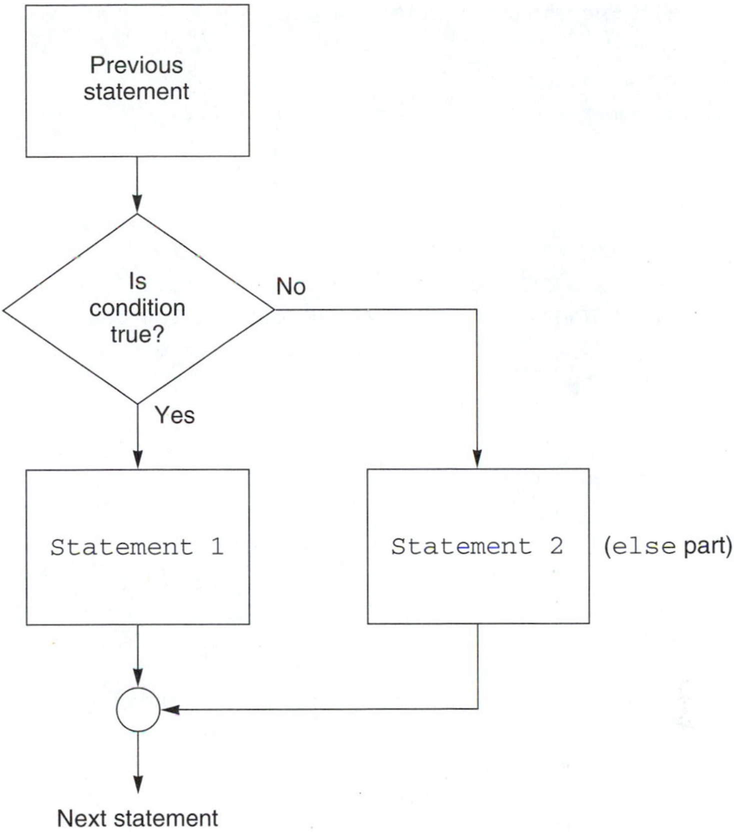

semicolon after the parentheses or the keyword `else`. The semicolons go only after the ends of the statements.

The flowchart for the `if-else` statement is shown in Figure 4.2.

As a specific example of an `if-else` statement, we construct a C++ program for determining New Jersey income taxes. As previously described, these taxes are assessed at 2% of taxable income for incomes less than or equal to $20,000. For taxable income greater than $20,000, state taxes are 2.5% of the income that exceeds $20,000 plus a fixed amount of $400. The expression to be tested is whether taxable income is less than or equal to $20,000. An appropriate `if-else` statement for this situation is[3]:

```
if (taxable <= 20000.0)
  taxes = 0.02 * taxable;
else
  taxes = 0.025 * (taxable - 20000.0) + 400.0;
```

Here we have used the relational operator <= to represent the relation "less than or equal to." If the value of `taxable` is less than or equal to 20000, the condition

[3] Note that in actual practice the numerical values in this statement would be defined as constants.

is true (has a value of 1) and the statement `taxes = .02 * taxable;` is executed. If the condition is not true, the value of the expression is zero, and the statement after the keyword `else` is executed. Program 4.1 illustrates the use of this statement in a complete program.

PROGRAM 4.1

```
#include <iostream.h>
#include <iomanip.h>

const float LOWRATE = 0.02;     // lower tax rate
const float HIGHRATE = 0.025;   // higher tax rate
const float CUTOFF = 20000.0;   // cut off for low rate
const float FIXEDAMT = 400;     // fixed dollar amount for higher rate amounts

int main()
{
  float taxable, taxes;

  cout << "Please type in the taxable income: ";
  cin >> taxable;
  if (taxable <= CUTOFF)
    taxes = LOWRATE * taxable;
  else
    taxes = HIGHRATE * (taxable - CUTOFF) + FIXEDAMT;

    // set output format
  cout << setiosflags(ios::fixed)
       << setiosflags(ios::showpoint)
       << setprecision(2);

  cout << "Taxes are $ " << taxes << endl;

  return 0;
}
```

A blank line was inserted before and after the `if-else` statement to highlight it in the complete program. We will continue to do this throughout the text to emphasize the statement being presented.

To illustrate selection in action, Program 4.1 was run twice with different input data. The results are:

```
Please type in the taxable income: 10000
Taxes are $ 200.00
```

and

```
Please type in the taxable income: 30000
Taxes are $ 650.00
```

Observe that the taxable income input in the first run of the program was less than $20,000, and the tax was correctly calculated as 2% of the number entered.

In the second run, the taxable income was more than $20,000, and the else part of the if-else statement was used to yield a correct tax computation of

```
0.025 * ($30,000. - $20,000.) + $400. = $650.
```

Although any expression can be tested by an if-else statement, relational expressions are predominantly used. However, statements such as

```
if (num)
  cout << "Bingo!";
else
  cout << "You lose!";
```

are valid. Since num, by itself, is a valid expression, the message Bingo! is displayed if num has any nonzero value and the message You lose! is displayed if num has a value of zero.

Compound Statements

Although only a single statement is permitted in both the if and else parts of the if-else statement, this statement can be a single compound statement. A **compound statement** is a sequence of single statements contained between braces, as shown in Figure 4.3. The use of braces to enclose a set of individual statements creates a single block of statements, which may be used anywhere in a C++ program in place of a single statement. The next example illustrates the use of a compound statement within the general form of an if-else statement.

```
if (expression)
{
  statement1;     // as many statements as necessary
  statement2;     // can be put within the braces
  statement3;     // each statement must end with a ;
}
else
{
  statement4;
  statement5;
        .
        .
  statementn;
}
```

FIGURE 4.3 A Compound Statement Consists of Individual Statements Enclosed Within Braces

```
{
  statement1;
  statement2;
  statement3;
        .
        .
        .
  last statement;
}
```

Program 4.2 illustrates the use of a compound statement in an actual program.

PROGRAM 4.2

```
#include <iostream.h>
#include <iomanip.h>

// a temperature conversion program
int main()
{
  char temp_type;
  float temp, fahren, celsius;

  cout << "Enter the temperature to be converted: ";
  cin  >> temp;
  cout << "Enter an f if the temperature is in Fahrenheit";
  cout << "\n or a c if the temperature is in Celsius: ";
  cin  >> temp_type;

    // set output formats
  cout << setiosflags(ios::fixed)
       << setiosflags(ios::showpoint)
       << setprecision(2);

  if (temp_type == 'f')
  {
     celsius = (5.0 / 9.0) * (temp - 32.0);
     cout << "\nThe equivalent Celsius temperature is "
          << celsius << endl;
  }
  else
  {
    fahren = (9.0 / 5.0) * temp + 32.0;
    cout << "\nThe equivalent Fahrenheit temperature is "
         << fahren << endl;
  }

  return 0;
}
```

Program 4.2 checks whether the value in `temp_type` is `f`. If the value is `f`, the compound statement corresponding to the `if` part of the `if-else` statement is executed. Any other letter results in execution of the compound statement corresponding to the `else` part. A sample run of Program 4.2 follows:

```
Enter the temperature to be converted: 212
Enter an f if the temperature is in Fahrenheit
 or a c if the temperature is in Celsius: f
The equivalent Celsius temperature is 100.00
```

PROGRAMMING NOTE

Placement of Braces in a Compound Statement

A common practice for some C++ programmers is to place the opening brace of a compound statement on the same line as the if and else statements. Using this convention, the if statement in Program 4.2 would appear as shown. (This placement is a matter of style only—both styles are used and both are acceptable.):

```
if (temp_type == 'f') {
  celsius = (5.0 / 9.0) * (temp - 32.0);
  cout << setiosflags(ios::showpoint)
       << setprecision(2)
       << "\nThe equivalent Celsius temperature is "
    << celsius << endl;
  }
  else {
    fahren = (9.0 / 5.0) * temp + 32.0;
    cout << "\nThe equivalent Fahrenheit temperature is "
         << fahren << endl;
  }
```

Block Scope

All statements contained within a compound statement constitute a single block of code and any variable declared within such a block only has meaning between its declaration and the closing braces defining the block. For example, consider the following section of code, which consists of two blocks of code:

```
{ // start of outer block
  int a = 25;
  int b = 17;

  cout << "The value of a is " << a
       <<" and b is " << b << endl;

  {    // start of inner block
    float a = 46.25;
    int c = 10;

    cout << "a is now " << a
         << " b is now " << b
         << " and c is " << c << endl;
  }    // end of inner block

    cout << "a is now " << a
         << " and b is " << b << endl;
}   // end of outer block
```

The output that is produced by this section of code is:

```
The value of a is 25 and b is 17
a is now 46.25 b is now 17 and c is 10
a is now 25 and b is 17
```

FIGURE 4.4 Flowchart for the One-Way `if` Statement

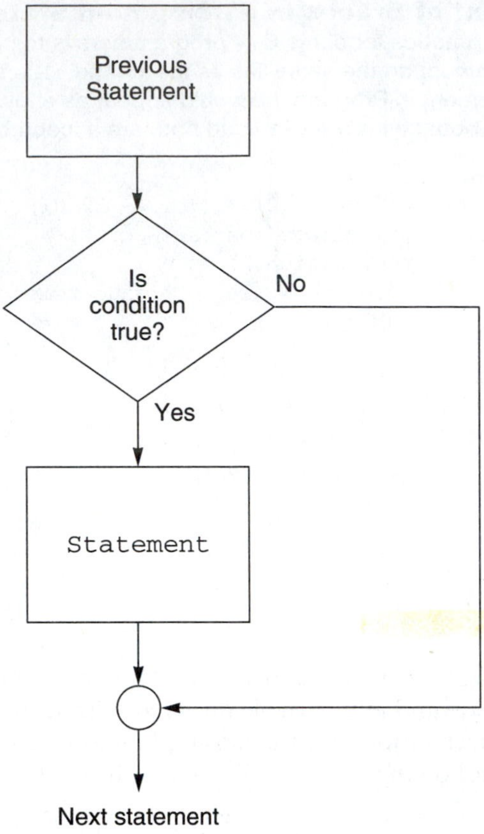

This output is produced as follows: The first block of code defines two variables named a and b, which may be used anywhere within this block after their declaration, including any block contained inside of it. Within the inner block, two new variables have been declared, named a and c. At this stage then, we have created four different variables, two of which have the same name. Any referenced variable first results in an attempt to access a variable correctly declared within the block containing the reference. If no variable is defined within the block, an attempt is made to access a variable in the next immediate outside block until a valid access results.

Thus, the values of the variables a and c referenced within the inner block use the values of the variables a and c declared in that block. Since no variable named b was declared inside the inner block, the value of b displayed from within the inner block is obtained from the outer block. Finally, the last `cout` object, which is outside of the inner block, displays the value of the variable a declared in the outer block. If an attempt is made to display the value of c anywhere in the outer block, the compiler would issue an error message stating that c is an undefined symbol.

The location within a program where a variable can be used is formally referred to as the **scope** of the variable, and we will have much more to say on this subject in Chapter 6.

One-Way Selection

A useful modification of the `if-else` statement involves omitting the `else` part of the statement altogether. In this case, the `if` statement takes the shortened and frequently useful form:

```
if (expression)
  statement;
```

The statement following `if (expression)` is only executed if the expression has a nonzero value (a true condition). As before, the statement may be a compound statement. The flowchart for this statement is shown in Figure 4.4 on p. 194.

This modified form of the `if` statement is called a **one-way `if` statement.** Program 4.3 uses this statement to selectively display a message for cars that have been driven more than 3000.0 miles.

PROGRAM 4.3

```
#include <iostream.h>
const float LIMIT = 3000.0;
int main()
{
  int id_num;
  float miles;

  cout << "Please type in car number and mileage: ";
  cin  >> id_num >> miles;

  if(miles > LIMIT)
    cout << " Car " << id_num << " is over the limit.\n";

  cout << "End of program output.\n";

  return 0;
}
```

As an illustration of its one-way selection criteria in action, Program 4.3 was run twice, each time with different input data. Only the input data for the first run causes the message `Car 256 is over the limit.` to be displayed.

```
Please type in car number and mileage: 256 3562.8
  Car 256 is over the limit.
End of program output.
```

and

```
Please type in car number and mileage: 23 2562.3
End of program output.
```

Problems Associated with the `if-else` Statement

Two of the most common problems encountered in initially using C++'s `if-else` statement are:

1. misunderstanding the full implications of what an expression is
2. using the assignment operator = in place of the relational operator ==.

Recall that an expression is any combination of operands and operators that yields a result. This definition is extremely broad and more encompassing than is initially apparent. For example, all of the following are valid C++ expressions:

```
age + 5
age = 30
age == 40
```

Assuming that the variables are suitably declared, each of the preceding expressions yields a result. Program 4.4 uses the `cout` object to display the value of these expressions when `age` = 18.

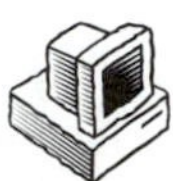

PROGRAM 4.4

```
#include <iostream.h>
int main()
{
  int age = 18;

  cout << "The value of the first expression is " << (age + 5) << endl;
  cout << "The value of the second expression is " << (age = 30) << endl;
  cout << "The value of the third expression is " << (age == 40) << endl;

  return 0;
}
```

The display produced by Program 4.4 is:

```
The value of the first expression is 23
The value of the second expression is 30
The value of the third expression is 0
```

As the output of Program 4.4 illustrates, each expression, by itself, has a value associated with it. The value of the first expression is the sum of the variable `age` plus `5`, which is `23`. The value of the second expression is `30`, which is also assigned to the variable `age`. The value of the third expression is zero, since `age` is not equal to `40`, and a false condition is represented in C++ with a value of zero. If the value in `age` had been `40`, the relational expression `a == 40` would be true and would have a value of 1.

Now assume that the relational expression `age == 40` was intended to be used in the following `if` statement

```
if (age == 40)
  cout << "Happy Birthday!";
```

but was mistyped as `age = 40`, resulting in

```
if (age = 40)
  cout << "Happy Birthday!";
```

Since the mistake results in a valid C++ expression, and any C++ expression can be tested by an `if` statement, the resulting `if` statement is valid and will cause the message `Happy Birthday!` to be printed regardless of what value was previously assigned to age. Can you see why?

The condition tested by the `if` statement does not compare the value in `age` to the number `40`, but assigns the number `40` to `age`. That is, the expression `age = 40` is not a relational expression at all, but an assignment expression. At the completion of the assignment the expression itself has a value of `40`. Since C++ treats any nonzero value as true, the call to `cout` is made. Another way of looking at this is to realize that the `if` statement is equivalent to the following two statements:

```
age = 40;       // assign 40 to age
if (age)        // test the value of age
cout << "Happy Birthday!";
```

Since a C++ compiler has no means of knowing that the expression being tested is not the desired one, you must be especially careful when writing conditions.

Exercises 4.2

1. Write appropriate `if` statements for each of the following conditions:

   a. If an angle is equal to 90 degrees, print the message "The angle is a right angle," else print the message that "The angle is not a right angle."

   b. If the temperature is above 100 degrees, display the message "above the boiling point of water," else display the message "below the boiling point of water."

   c. If the number is positive, add the number to `possum`, else add the number to `negsum`.

   d. If the slope is less than .5, set the variable `flag` to zero, else set `flag` to one.

   e. If the difference between `num1` and `num2` is less than .001, set the variable `approx` to zero, else calculate `approx` as the quantity `(num1 - num2) / 2.0`.

   f. If the difference between `temp1` and `temp2` exceeds 2.3 degrees, calculate error as `(temp1 - temp2) * factor`.

   g. If `x` is greater than `y` and `z` is less than 20, read in a value for `p`.

   h. If `distance` is greater than 20 and it is less than 35, read in a value for `time`.

2. Write `if` statements corresponding to the conditions illustrated by each of the following flowcharts:

a.

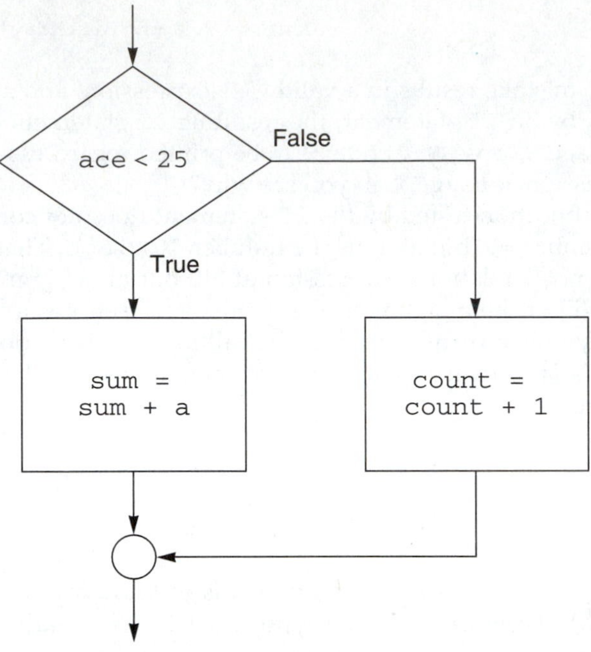

b.

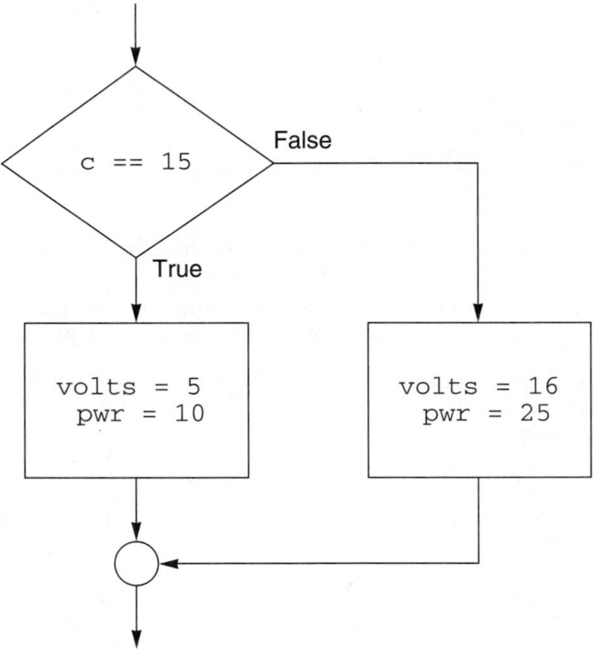

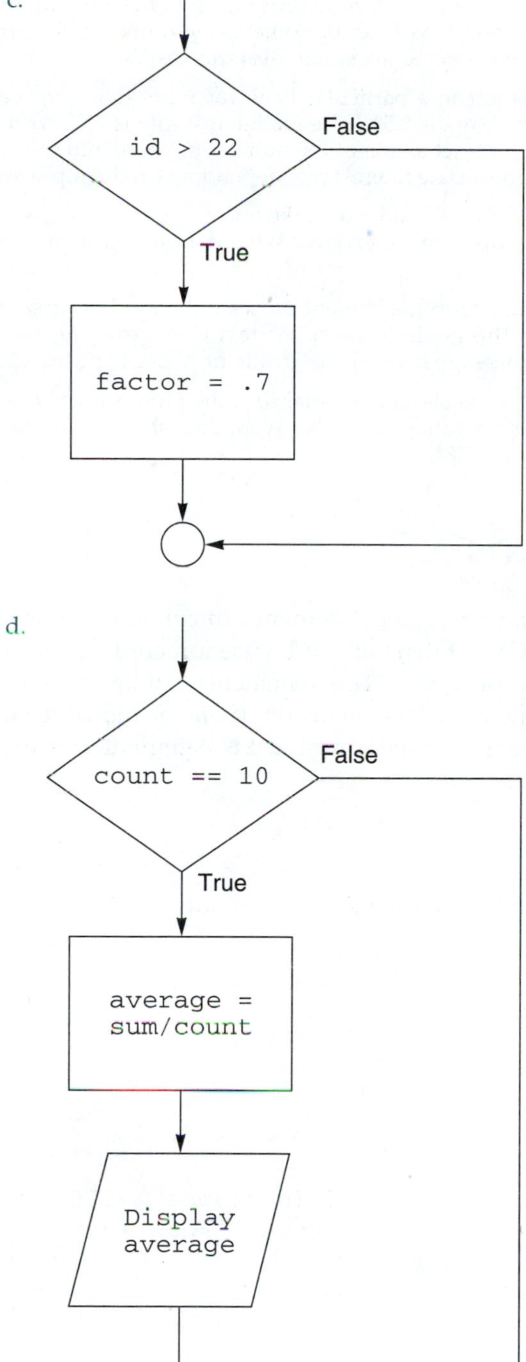

3. Write a C++ program that asks the user to input two numbers. If the first number entered is greater than the second number, the program should print the message `The first number is greater`, else it should print the message `The first`

number is smaller. Test your program by entering the numbers 5 and 8 and then using the numbers 11 and 2. What do you think your program will display if the two numbers entered are equal? Test this case.

4. a. If money is left in a particular bank for more than two years, the interest rate given by the bank is 8.5%, else the interest rate is 7%. Write a C++ program that uses the cin object to accept the number of years into the variable nyrs and display the appropriate interest rate depending on the input value.

   b. How many runs should you make for the program written in Exercise 5a to verify that it is operating correctly? What data should you input in each of the program runs?

5. a. In a pass/fail course, a student passes if the grade is greater than or equal to 70 and fails if the grade is lower. Write a C++ program that accepts a grade and prints the message A passing grade or A failing grade, as appropriate.

   b. How many runs should you make for the program written in Exercise 6a to verify that it is operating correctly? What data should you input in each of the program runs?

4.3 NESTED if STATEMENTS

As we have seen, an if-else statement can contain simple or compound statements. Any valid C++ statement can be used, including another if-else statement. Thus, one or more if-else statements can be included within either part of an if-else statement. The inclusion of one or more if statements within an existing if statement is called a **nested if** statement. For example, substituting the one-way if statement

```
if (distance > 500)
  cout << "snap";
```

for statement1 in the following if statement

```
if (hours < 9)
  statement1;
else
  cout << "pop";
```

results in the nested if statement

```
if (hours < 9)
{
  if (distance > 500)
  cout << "snap";
}
else
  cout << "pop";
```

The braces around the inner one-way if are essential, because in their absence C++ associates an else with the closest unpaired if. Thus, without the braces, the previous statement is equivalent to

```
if (hours < 9)
  if (distance > 500)
    cout << "snap";
  else
    cout << "pop";
```

Here the `else` is paired with the inner `if`, which destroys the meaning of the original `if-else` statement. Notice also that the indentation is irrelevant as far as the compiler is concerned. Whether the indentation exists or not, *the statement is compiled by associating the last* `else` *with the closest unpaired* `if`*, unless braces are used to alter the default pairing.*

The process of nesting `if` statements can be extended indefinitely, so that the `cout << "snap";` statement could itself be replaced by either a complete `if-else` statement or another one-way `if` statement.

Figure 4.5 illustrates the general form of a nested `if-else` statement when an `if-else` statement is nested (a) within the `if` part of an `if-else` statement and (b) within the `else` part of an `if-else` statement.

The `if-else` Chain

In general, the nesting illustrated in Figure 4.5a tends to be confusing and is best avoided in practice. However, an extremely useful construction occurs for the nesting illustrated in Figure 4.5b, which has the form:

```
if (expression_1)
  statement1;
else
  if (expression_2)
    statement2;
  else
    statement3;
```

FIGURE 4.5a The `if-else` Nested within the `if` Part

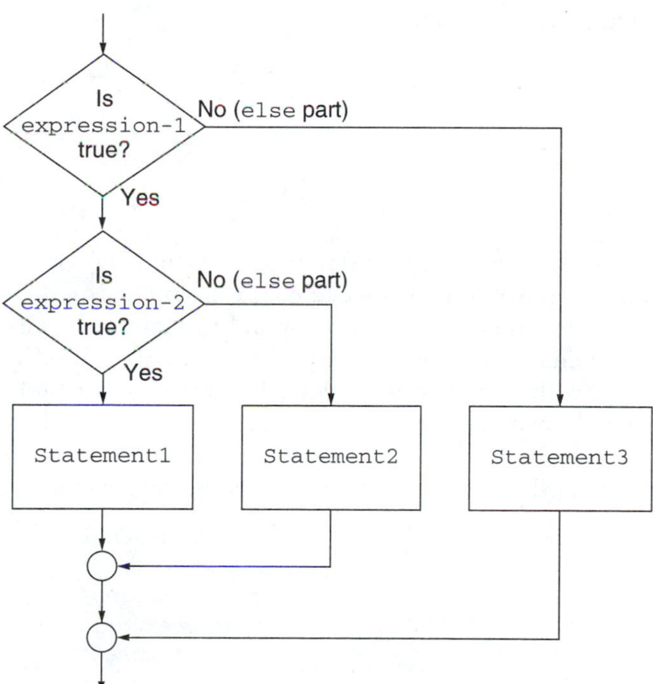

FIGURE 4.5b The `if-else` Nested within the `else` Part

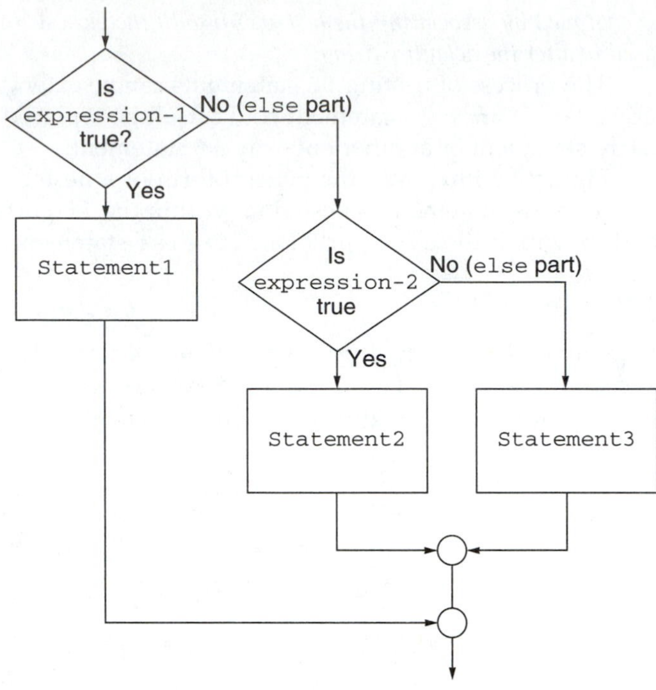

As with all C++ programs, since white space is ignored, the indentation shown is not required. More typically, the preceding construction is written using the following arrangement:

```
if (expression_1)
  statement1;
else if (expression_2)
  statement2;
else
  statement3;
```

This form of a nested `if` statement is extremely useful in practice, and is formally referred to as an **`if-else` chain.** Each condition is evaluated in order, and if any condition is true the corresponding statement is executed and the remainder of the chain is terminated. The statement associated with the final `else` is only executed if none of the previous conditions is satisfied. This serves as a default or catchall case that is useful for detecting an impossible or error condition.

The chain can be continued indefinitely by repeatedly making the last statement another `if-else` statement. Thus, the general form of an `if-else` chain is:

```
if (expression_1)
  statement1;
else if (expression_2)
  statement2;
else if (expression_3)
```

```
      statement3;
         .
         .
         .
    else if (expression_n)
      statement_n;
    else
      last_statement;
```

Each condition is evaluated in the order in which it appears in the statement. For the first condition that is true, the corresponding statement is executed, and the remainder of the statements in the chain are not executed. Thus, if `expression_1` is true, only `statement1` is executed; otherwise `expression_2` is tested. If `expression_2` is then true, only `statement2` is executed; otherwise `expression_3` is tested, and so on. The final `else` in the chain is optional, and `last_statement` is only executed if none of the previous expressions were true. As a specific example, consider the following `if-else` chain:

```
if (marcode == 'M')
  cout << "Individual is married.\n";
else if (marcode == 'S')
  cout << "Individual is single.\n";
else if (marcode == 'D')
  cout << "Individual is divorced.\n";
else if (marcode == 'W')
  cout << "Individual is widowed.\n")
else
  cout << "An invalid code was entered.\n";
```

Execution through this chain begins with a test of the expression `marcode == 'M'`. If the value in `marcode` is an `M`, the message `Individual is married.` is displayed, no further expressions in the chain are evaluated, and execution resumes with the next statement immediately following the chain. If the value in `marcode` was not an `M`, the expression `marcode == 'S'` is tested, and so on, until a true condition is found. If none of the conditions in the chain is true, the message `An invalid code was entered` would be displayed. In all cases, execution resumes with whatever statement immediately follows the chain. Program 4.5 uses this `if-else` chain within a complete program.

In reviewing Program 4.5 note that the message `Thanks for participating in the survey.` is always printed. This is the statement immediately after the `if-else` chain to which execution is transferred once the chain completes its execution. Which message is printed within the `if-else` chain depends on the value entered into `marcode`.

As a final example illustrating the `if-else` chain, let us calculate the monthly income of a computer salesperson using the following commission schedule:

Monthly Sales	**Income**
Greater than or equal to $50,000	$375 plus 16% of sales
Less than $50,000 but greater than or equal to $40,000	$350 plus 14% of sales
Less than $40,000 but greater than or equal to $30,000	$325 plus 12% of sales
Less than $30,000 but greater than or equal to $20,000	$300 plus 9% of sales
Less than $20,000 but greater than or equal to $10,000	$250 plus 5% of sales
Less than $10,000	$200 plus 3% of sales

PROGRAM 4.5

```
#include <iostream.h>

int main()
{
  char marcode;

  cout << "Enter a marital code: ";
  cin  >> marcode;

  if (marcode == 'M')
    cout << "Individual is married.\n";
  else if (marcode == 'S')
    cout << "Individual is single.\n";
  else if (marcode == 'D')
    cout << "Individual is divorced.\n";
  else if (marcode == 'W')
    cout << "Individual is widowed.\n";
  else
    cout << "An invalid code was entered.\n";

  cout << "Thanks for participating in the survey.\n";

  return 0;
}
```

The following `if-else` chain can be used to determine the correct monthly income, where the variable `mon_sales` is used to store the salesperson's current monthly sales:

```
if (mon_sales >= 50000.00)
  income = 375.00 + 0.16 * mon_sales;
else if (mon_sales >= 40000.00)
  income = 350.00 + 0.14 * mon_sales;
else if (mon_sales >= 30000.00)
  income = 325.00 + 0.12 * mon_sales;
else if (mon_sales >= 20000.00)
  income = 300.00 + 0.09 * mon_sales;
else if (mon_sales >= 10000.00)
  income = 250.00 + 0.05 * mon_sales;
else
  income = 200.000 + 0.03 * mon_sales;
```

Notice that this example makes use of the fact that the chain is stopped once a true condition is found. This is accomplished by checking for the highest monthly sales first. If the salesperson's monthly sales is less than $50,000, the `if-else` chain continues checking for the next highest sales amount until the correct category is obtained.

Program 4.6 uses this `if-else` chain to calculate and display the income corresponding to the value of monthly sales input in the `cin` object.

PROGRAM 4.6

```
#include <iostream.h>
#include <iomanip.h>

int main()
{
  float mon_sales, income;

  cout << "Enter the value of monthly sales: ";
  cin  >> mon_sales;

  if (mon_sales >= 50000.00)
    income = 375.00 + 0.16 * mon_sales;
  else if (mon_sales >= 40000.00)
    income = 350.00 + 0.14 * mon_sales;
  else if (mon_sales >= 30000.00)
    income = 325.00 + 0.12 * mon_sales;
  else if (mon_sales >= 20000.00)
    income = 300.00 + 0.09 * mon_sales;
  else if (mon_sales >= 10000.00)
    income = 250.00 + 0.05 * mon_sales;
  else
    income = 200.00 + 0.03 * mon_sales;

    // set output format
  cout << setiosflags(ios::fixed)
       << setiosflags(ios::showpoint)
       << setprecision(2);

  cout << "The income is $" << income << endl;

  return 0;
}
```

A sample run of Program 4.6 is illustrated here:

```
Enter the value of monthly sales: 36243.89
The income is $4674.27
```

As with all C++ statements, each individual statement within an if-else chain can be replaced by a compound statement bounded by the braces { and }.

Exercises 4.3

1. Modify Program 4.5 to accept both lowercase and uppercase letters as marriage codes. For example, if a user enters either an m or an M, the program should display the message Individual is married.

2. Write nested `if` statements corresponding to the conditions illustrated in each of the following flowcharts:

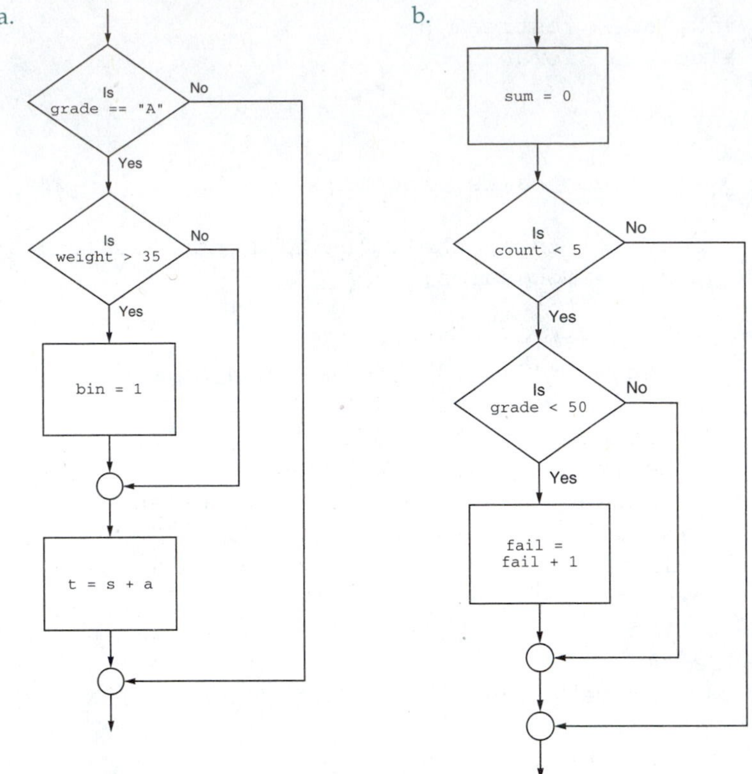

3. An angle is considered acute if it is less than 90 degrees, obtuse if it is greater than 90 degrees, and a right angle if it is equal to 90 degrees. Using this information, write a C++ program that accepts an angle, in degrees, and displays the type of angle corresponding to the degrees entered.

4. The grade level of undergraduate college students is typically determined according to the following schedule:

Number of Credits Completed	Grade Level
Less than 32	Freshman
32 to 63	Sophomore
64 to 95	Junior
96 or more	Senior

Using this information, write a C++ program that accepts the number of credits a student has completed, determines the student's grade level, and displays the grade level.

5. A student's letter grade is calculated according to the following schedule:

Numerical Grade	Letter Grade
Greater than or equal to 90	A
Less than 90 but greater than or equal to 80	B
Less than 80 but greater than or equal to 70	C
Less than 70 but greater than or equal to 60	D
Less than 60	F

Using this information, write a C++ program that accepts a student's numerical grade, converts the numerical grade to an equivalent letter grade, and displays the letter grade.

6. The interest rate used on funds deposited in a bank is determined by the amount of time the money is left on deposit. For a particular bank, the following schedule is used:

Time on Deposit	Interest Rate
Greater than or equal to 5 years	0.095
Less than 5 years but greater than or equal to 4 years	0.090
Less than 4 years but greater than or equal to 3 years	0.085
Less than 3 years but greater than or equal to 2 years	0.075
Less than 2 years but greater than or equal to 1 year	0.065
Less than 1 year	0.058

Using this information, write a C++ program that accepts the time that funds are left on deposit and displays the interest rate corresponding to the time entered.

7. Write a C++ program that accepts a number followed by one space and then a letter. If the letter following the number is `f`, the program is to treat the number entered as a temperature in degrees Fahrenheit, convert the number to the equivalent degrees Celsius, and print a suitable display message. If the letter following the number is `c`, the program is to treat the number entered as a temperature in Celsius, convert the number to the equivalent degrees Fahrenheit, and print a suitable display message. If the letter is neither an `f` or `c`, the program is to print a message that the data entered is incorrect and terminate. Use an `if-else` chain in your program and make use of the conversion formulas:

```
Celsius = (5.0 / 9.0) * (Fahrenheit - 32.0)
Fahrenheit = (9.0 / 5.0) * Celsius + 32.0
```

8. Using the commission schedule from Program 4.6, the following program calculates monthly income:

```
#include <iostream.h>
#include <iomanip.h>
int main()
{
  float mon_sales, income;

  cout << "Enter the value of monthly sales: ";
  cin  >> mon_sales;

  if (mon_sales >= 50000.00)
    income = 375.00 + .16 * mon_sales;
  if (mon_sales >= 40000.00 && mon_sales < 50000.00)
    income = 350.00 + .14 * mon_sales;
  if (mon_sales >= 30000.00 && mon_sales < 40000.00)
    income = 325.00 + .12 * mon_sales;
  if (mon_sales >= 20000.00 && mon_sales < 30000.00)
    income = 300.00 + .09 * mon_sales;
  if (mon_sales >= 10000.00 && mon_sales < 20000.00)
    income = 250.00 + .05 * mon_sales;
  if (mon_sales < 10000.00)
    income = 200.00 + .03 * mon_sales;

  cout << setiosflags(ios::showpoint)
       << setiosflags(ios:: fixed)
       << setprecision(2)
       << "\n\nThe income is $" << income << endl;

return 0;
}
```

a. Will this program produce the same output as Program 4.6?

b. Which program is better and why?

9. The following program was written to produce the same result as Program 4.6:

```
#include <iostream.h>
#include <iomanip.h>
int main()
{
  float mon_sales, income;

  cout << "Enter the value of monthly sales: ";
  cin >> mon_sales;

  if (mon_sales < 10000.00)
    income = 200.00 + .03 * mon_sales;
  else if (mon_sales >= 10000.00)
    income = 250.00 + .05 * mon_sales;
  else if (mon_sales >= 20000.00)
    income = 300.00 + .09 * mon_sales;
  else if (mon_sales >= 30000.00)
    income = 325.00 + .12 * mon_sales;
  else if (mon_sales >= 40000.00)
    income = 350.00 + .14 * mon_sales;
  else if (mon_sales >= 50000.00)
    income = 375.00 + .16 * mon_sales;

  cout << setiosflags(ios::showpoint)
       << setiosflags(ios:: fixed)
       << setprecision(2)
       << "\n\nThe income is $" << income << endl;

return 0;
}
```

a. Will this program run?

b. What does this program do?

c. For what values of monthly sales does this program calculate the correct income?

4.4 THE `switch` STATEMENT

The `if-else` chain is used in programming applications where one set of instructions must be selected from many possible alternatives. The **`switch` statement** provides an alternative to the `if-else` chain for cases that compare the value of an integer expression to a specific value. The switch statement syntax is:

```
switch (expression)
{    // start of compound statement
  case value_1:  <-------------------  Terminated with a colon
    statement1;
    statement2;
        .
        .
    break;
  case value_2:  <-------------------  Terminated with a colon
```

```
      statementm;
      statementn;
          .
          .
      break;
          .
          .
    case value_n:    <------------------ Terminated with a colon
      statementw;
      statementx;
          .
          .
      break;
    default:         <------------------ Terminated with a colon
      statementaa;
      statementbb;
          .
          .
}      // end of switch and compound statement
```

The `switch` statement uses four new keywords: `switch`, `case`, `default`, and `break`. Let's see what each of these words does.

The keyword `switch` identifies the start of the `switch` statement. The expression in parentheses following this word is evaluated and the result of the expression compared to various alternative values contained within the compound statement. The expression in the `switch` statement must evaluate to an integer result or a compilation error results.

Internal to the `switch` statement, the keyword `case` is used to identify or label individual values that are compared to the value of the `switch` expression. The `switch` expression's value is compared to each of these case values in the order in which these values are listed until a match is found. When a match occurs, execution begins with the statement immediately following the match. Thus, as illustrated in Figure 4.6, the value of the expression determines where in the `switch` statement execution actually begins.

Any number of `case` labels may be contained within a `switch` statement, in any order. If the value of the expression does not match any of the case values, however, no statement is executed unless the keyword `default` is encountered. The word `default` is optional and operates just like the last `else` operates in an `if-else` chain. If the value of the expression does not match any of the case values, program execution begins with the statement following the word `default`.

Once an entry point has been located by the `switch` statement, all further case evaluations are ignored and execution continues through the end of the compound statement unless a `break` statement is encountered. This is the reason for the `break` statement, which identifies the end of a particular `case` and causes an immediate exit from the `switch` statement. Thus, just as the word `case` identifies possible starting points in the compound statement, the `break` statement determines terminating points. If the `break` statements are omitted, all cases following the matching case value, including the `default` case, are executed.

When writing a `switch` statement, you can use multiple case values to refer to the same set of statements; the default label is optional. For example, consider the following:

```
switch (number)
{
  case 1:
    cout << "Have a Good Morning\n";
    break;
  case 2:
    cout << "Have a Happy Day\n";
    break;
  case 3:
  case 4:
  case 5:
    cout << "Have a Nice Evening\n";
}
```

FIGURE 4.6 The Expression Determines an Entry Point

```
                                  switch (expression) // evaluate expression
                                  {
Start here if             ------>  case value_1:
expression equals value_1               .
                                        .
                                        .
                                      break;
Start here if             ------>  case value_2:
expression equals value_2               .
                                        .
                                        .
                                      break;
Start here if             ------>  case value_3:
expression equals value_3               .
                                        .
                                        .
                                      break;
                                  •
                                  •
                                  •
Start here if             ------>  case value_n:
expression equals value_n               .
                                        .
                                        .
                                      break;
Start here if no          ------>  default:
previous match                          .
                                        .
                                        .
                                  }    // end of switch statement
```

If the value stored in the variable `number` is 1, the message `Have a Good Morning` is displayed. Similarly, if the value of `number` is 2, the second message is displayed. Finally, if the value of `number` is 3 or 4 or 5, the last message is displayed. Since the statement to be executed for these last three cases is the same, the cases for these values can be "stacked together" as shown in the example. Also, since there is no default, no message is printed if the value of `number` is not one of the listed case values. Although it is good programming practice to list case values in increasing order, this is not required by the `switch` statement. A `switch` statement may have any number of case values, in any order; only the values being tested for need be listed.

Program 4.7 uses a `switch` statement to select the arithmetic operation (addition, multiplication, or division) to be performed on two numbers depending on the value of the variable opselect.

PROGRAM 4.7

```
#include <iostream.h>

int main()
{
  int opselect;
  double fnum, snum;

  cout << "Please type in two numbers: ";
  cin  >> fnum >> snum;
  cout << "Enter a select code: ";
  cout << "\n        1 for addition";
  cout << "\n        2 for multiplication";
  cout << "\n        3 for division : ";
  cin  >> opselect;

  switch (opselect)
  {
    case 1:
      cout << "The sum of the numbers entered is " << fnum+snum;
      break;
    case 2:
      cout << "The product of the numbers entered is " << fnum*snum;
      break;
    case 3:
      cout << "The first number divided by the second is " << fnum/snum;
      break;
  }    // end of switch

  cout << endl;

  return 0;
}
```

Program 4.7 was run twice. The resulting display clearly identifies the case selected. The results are:

```
Please type in two numbers: 12 3
Enter a select code:
          1 for addition
          2 for multiplication
          3 for division : 2
```

```
The product of the numbers entered is 36
```

and

```
Please type in two numbers: 12 3
Enter a select code:
          1 for addition
          2 for multiplication
          3 for division : 3
The first number divided by the second is 4
```

In reviewing Program 4.7 notice the `break` statement in the last case. Although this break is not necessary, it is a good practice to terminate the last case in a `switch` statement with a break. This prevents a possible program error later, if an additional case is subsequently added to the `switch` statement. With the addition of a new case, the break between cases becomes necessary; having the break in place ensures you will not forget to include it at the time of the modification.

Because character data types are always converted to integers in an expression, a `switch` statement can also be used to "switch" based on the value of a character expression. For example, assuming that `choice` is a character variable, the following `switch` statement is valid:

```
switch(choice)
{
  case 'a':
  case 'e':
  case 'i':
  case 'o':
  case 'u':
    cout << "The character in choice is a vowel\n";
    break;
  default:
  cout << "The character in choice is not a vowel\n";
  break;    // this break is optional
} // end of switch statement
```

Exercises 4.4

1. Rewrite the following `if-else` chain using a `switch` statement:

```
if (let_grad == 'A')
  cout << "The numerical grade is between 90 and 100\n";
else if (let_grad == 'B')
  cout << "The numerical grade is between 80 and 89.9\n";
else if (let_grad == 'C')
  cout << "The numerical grade is between 70 and 79.9\n";
else if (let_grad == 'D';
  cout << "How are you going to explain this one?\n";
else
{
  cout << "Of course I had nothing to do with my grade.\n";
  cout << "It must have been the professor's fault.\n";
}
```

2. Rewrite the following `if-else` chain using a `switch` statement:

```
if (res_typ == 1)
  {
    in_data();
    check();
  }
else if (res_typ == 2)
{
  capacity();
  devtype();
}
else if (res_typ == 3)
{
  volume();
  mass();
}
else if (res_typ == 4)
{
  area();
  weight();
}
else if (res_typ == 5)
{
  files();
  save();
}
else if (res_typ == 6)
{
  retrieve();
  screen();
}
```

3. Each disk drive in a shipment of these devices is stamped with a code from 1 through 4, which indicates a drive of the following type:

Code	Disk Drive Type
1	360-kilobyte drive (5 1/2 inch)
2	1.2-megabyte drive (5 1/2 inch)
3	720-kilobyte drive (3 1/4 inch)
4	1.4-megabyte drive (3 1/4 inch)

Write a C++ program that accepts the code number as an input, and based on the value entered, displays the correct disk drive type.

4. Rewrite Program 4.5 using a `switch` statement.
5. Determine why the `if-else` chain in Program 4.6 cannot be replaced with a `switch` statement.
6. Rewrite Program 4.7 using a character variable for the select code.

4.5 FOCUS ON PROBLEM SOLVING

Two major uses of C++'s `if` statements are to select appropriate processing paths and to prevent undesirable data from being processed at all. In this section examples of both uses are provided.

Problem 1: Data Validation

An important use of C++'s `if` statements is to validate data by checking for clearly invalid cases. For example, a date such as 5/33/86 contains an obviously invalid day. Similarly, the division of any number by zero within a program, such as 14/0, should not be allowed. Both of these examples illustrate the need for a technique called *defensive programming,* in which the program includes code to check for improper data before an attempt is made to process it further. The defensive programming technique of checking user input data for erroneous or unreasonable data is referred to as *input data validation.*

Consider the case where we are to write a C++ program to calculate the square root and the reciprocal of a user-entered number. Before calculating the square root, validate that the number is not negative, and before calculating the reciprocal, check that the number is not zero.

Step 1: Analyze the Problem The statement of the problem requires that we accept a single number as an input, validate the entered number, and based on the validation produce two possible outputs: If the number is non-negative we are to determine its square root, and if the input number is not zero we are to determine its reciprocal.

Step 2: Develop a Solution Since the square root of a negative number does not exist as a real number and the reciprocal of zero cannot be taken, our program must contain input data validation statements to screen the user input data and avoid these two cases. The pseudocode describing the processing required is:

Display a program purpose message.
Accept a user input number.
If the number is negative
  print a message that the square root cannot be taken.
Else
  calculate and display the square root.
Endif.
If the number is zero then
  print a message that the reciprocal cannot be taken.
Else
  calculate and display the reciprocal.
Endif.

Step 3: Code the Solution The C++ code corresponding to our pseudocode solution is listed in Program 4.8.

Program 4.8 is a rather straightforward program containing two separate (non-nested) `if` statements. The first `if` statement checks for a negative input number; if the number is negative, a message indicating that the square root of a negative number cannot be taken is displayed, else the square root is taken. The second `if` statement checks whether the entered number is zero; if it is a zero, a message indicating that the reciprocal of zero cannot be taken is displayed, else the reciprocal is taken.

PROGRAM 4.8

```
#include <iostream.h>
#include <math.h>

int main()
{
  double usenum;

  cout << "This program calculates the square root and\n"
       << "reciprocal (1/number) of a number\n"
       << "\nPlease enter a number: ";
  cin  >> usenum;
  if (usenum < 0.0)
    cout << "The square root of a negative number does not exist.\n";
  else
    cout << "The square root of " << usenum
         << " is " << sqrt(usenum) << endl;
  if (usenum == 0.0)
    cout << "The reciprocal of zero does not exist.\n";
  else
    cout << "The reciprocal of " << usenum
         << " is " << (1.0/usenum) << endl;

  return 0;
}
```

Step 4: Test and Correct the Program Test values should include an appropriate value for the input, such as 5, and values for the limiting cases, such as a negative and zero input value. Test runs follow for two of these cases:

```
This program calculates the square root and
reciprocal (1/number) of a number

Please enter a number: 5

The square root of 5 is 2.236068
The reciprocal of 5 is 0.2
```

and

```
This program calculates the square root and
reciprocal (1/number) of a number

Please enter a number: -6

The square root of a negative number does not exist
The reciprocal of -6 is -0.166667
```

Problem 2: Solving Quadratic Equations

A *quadratic equation* is an equation that has the form $ax^2 + bx + c = 0$ or that can be algebraically manipulated into this form. In this equation x is the unknown variable, and a, b, and c are known constants. Although the constants b and c can be any numbers, including zero, the value of the constant a cannot be zero (if a is zero, the equation would become a *linear equation* in x). Examples of quadratic equations are:

$$5x^2 + 6x + 2 = 0$$

$$x^2 - 7x + 20 = 0$$

$$34x^2 + 16 = 0$$

In the first equation $a = 5$, $b = 6$, and $c = 2$; in the second equation $a = 1$, $b = -7$, and $c = 20$; and in the third equation $a = 34$, $b = 0$, and $c = 16$.

The real roots of a quadratic equation can be calculated using the quadratic formula as:

$$\text{root } 1 = \frac{-b + \sqrt{b^2 - 4ac}}{2a}$$

and

$$\text{root } 2 = \frac{-b - \sqrt{b^2 - 4ac}}{2a}$$

Using these equations we will write a C++ program to solve for the roots of a quadratic equation.

Step 1: Analyze the Problem The problem requires that we accept three inputs—the coefficients a, b, and c of a quadratic equation—and compute the roots of the equation using the given formulas.

Step 2: Develop a Solution A first attempt at a solution would be to use the user-entered values of a, b, and c to calculate directly a value for each of the roots. Thus, our first solution would be:

Display a program purpose message.
Accept user-input values for a, b, and c.
Calculate the two roots.
Display the values of the calculated roots.

However, this solution must be refined further to account for a number of possible input conditions. For example, if a user entered a value of 0 for both a and b, the equation is neither quadratic or linear and has no solution (this is referred to as a *degenerate case*). Another possibility is that the user supplies a nonzero value for b but makes a zero. In this case the equation becomes a linear one with a single solution of $-c/b$. A third possibility is that the value of the term b^2-4ac, which is called the *discriminant*, is negative. Since the square root of a negative number cannot be taken, this case will have no real roots. Finally, when the discriminant is zero, both roots are the same (this is referred to as the *repeated roots case*).

Taking into account all four of these limiting cases, a refined solution for correctly determining the roots of a quadratic equation is expressed by the following pseudocode:

Display a program purpose message.
Accept user-input values for a, b, *and* c.
If a = *0 and* b = *0 then*
display a message saying that the equation has no solution.
Else if a = zero then
calculate the single root equal to –c/b.
Display the single root.
Else
calculate the discriminant.
If the discriminant > 0 then
solve for both roots using the given formulas.
Display the two roots.
Else if the discriminant < 0 then
display a message that there are no real roots.
Else
calculate the repeated root equal to –b/(2a).
Display the repeated root.
Endif.
Endif.

Notice in the pseudocode that we have used nested `if-else` structures. The outer `if-else` structure is used to validate the entered coefficients and determine that we have a valid quadratic equation. The inner `if-else` structure is then used to determine if the equation has two real roots (discriminant > 0) two imaginary roots (discriminant < 0) or repeated roots (discriminant = 0).

Step 3: Code the Solution The equivalent C++ code corresponding to our pseudocode solution is listed in Program 4.9.

Step 4: Test and Correct the Program Test values should include values for a, b, and c that result in two real roots, plus limiting values for a and b that result in either a linear equation ($a = 0, b \neq 0$), a degenerate equation ($a = 0, b = 0$), and a negative and zero discriminant. Two such test runs of Program 4.9 follow:

```
This program calculates the roots of a
   quadratic equation of the form

              ax^2 + bx + c = 0

Please enter values for a, b, and c: 1 2 -35

The two real roots are 5 and -7
```

and

```
This program calculates the roots of a
   quadratic equation of the form

              ax^2 + bx + c = 0

Please enter values for a, b, and c: 0 0 16

The equation is degenerate and has no roots.
```

PROGRAM 4.9

```
##include <iostream.h>
#include <math.h>

// this program solves for the roots of a quadratic equation
int main()
{
  double a, b, c, disc, root1, root2;

  cout << "This program calculates the roots of a\n";
  cout << "   quadratic equation of the form\n";
  cout << "              2\n";
  cout << "           ax + bx + c = 0\n\n";
  cout << "Please enter values for a, b, and c: ";
  cin  >> a >> b >> c;
  if ( a == 0.0 && b == 0.0)
    cout << "The equation is degenerate and has no roots.\n";
  else if (a == 0.0)
    cout << "The equation has the single root x = "
         << -c/b << endl;
  else
  {
    disc = pow(b,2.0) - 4 * a * c; // calculate discriminant
    if (disc > 0.0)
    {
      disc = sqrt(disc);
      root1 = (-b + disc) / (2 * a);
      root2 = (-b - disc) / (2 * a);
      cout << "The two real roots are "
           << root1 << " and " << root2 << endl;
    }
    else if (disc < 0.0)
      cout << "Both roots are imaginary.\n";
    else
      cout << "Both roots are equal to " << -b / (2 * a) << endl;
  }

  return 0;
}
```

The first run solves the quadratic equation $x^2 + 2x - 35 = 0$, which has the real roots $x = 5$ and $x = -7$. The input data for the second run results in the equation $0x^2 + 0x + 16 = 0$. Because this degenerates into the mathematical impossibility of $16 = 0$, the program correctly identifies this as a degenerate equation. We leave it as an exercise to create test data for the other limiting cases checked for by the program.

Exercises 4.5

1. a. Write a program that accepts two real numbers from a user and a select code. If the entered select code is 1, have the program add the two previously entered numbers and display the result; if the select code is 2, the numbers should be multiplied, and if the select code is 3, the first number should be divided by the second number.

   b. Determine what the program written in Exercise 1a does when the entered numbers are 3 and 0, and the select code is 3.

   c. Modify the program written in Exercise 1a so that division by 0 is not allowed and an appropriate message is displayed when such a division is attempted.

2. a. Write a program to display the following two prompts:

```
Enter a month (use a 1 for Jan, etc.):
Enter a day of the month:
```

   Have your program accept and store a number in the variable `month` in response to the first prompt, and accept and store a number in the variable `day` in response to the second prompt. If the month entered is not between 1 and 12 inclusive, print a message informing the user that an invalid month has been entered. If the day entered is not between 1 and 31, print a message informing the user that an invalid day has been entered.

   b. What will your program do if the user types a number with a decimal point for the month? How can you ensure that your `if` statements check for an integer number?

   c. In a non-leap year February has 28 days, the months January, March, May, July, August, October, and December have 31 days, and all other months have 30 days. Using this information, modify the program written in Exercise 2a to display a message when an invalid day is entered for a user-entered month. For this program ignore leap years.

3. a. The quadrant in which a line drawn from the origin resides is determined by the angle that the line makes with the positive *X* axis as follows:

Angle from the Positive X Axis	Quadrant
Between 0 and 90 degrees	I
Between 90 and 180 degrees	II
Between 180 and 270 degrees	III
Between 270 and 360 degrees	IV

   Using this information, write a C++ program that accepts the angle of the line as user input and determines and displays the quadrant appropriate to the input data. (*Note:* If the angle is exactly 0, 90, 180, or 270 degrees the corresponding line does not reside in any quadrant but lies on an axis.)

   b. Modify the program written for Exercise 3a so that a message is displayed that identifies an angle of zero degrees as the positive *X* axis, an angle of 90 degrees as the positive *Y* axis, an angle of 180 degrees as the negative *X* axis, and an angle of 270 degrees as the negative *Y* axis.

4. a. All years that are evenly divisible by 400 or are evenly divisible by four and not evenly divisible by 100 are leap years. For example, since 1600 is evenly divisible by 400, the year 1600 was a leap year. Similarly, since 1988 is evenly divisible by four but not by 100, the year 1988 was also a leap year. Using this information, write a C++ program that accepts the year as user input, determines if the year is a leap year, and displays an appropriate message that tells the user if the entered year is or is not a leap year.

b. Using the code written in Exercise 4a redo Exercise 2c such that leap years are taken into account.

5. Based on an automobile's model year and weight, the state of New Jersey determines the car's weight class and registration fee using the following schedule:

Model Year	Weight	Weight Class	Registration Fee
1970 or earlier	Less than 2700 lbs	1	$16.50
	2700 to 3800 lbs	2	25.50
	More than 3800 lbs	3	46.50
1971 to 1979	Less than 2700 lbs	4	27.00
	2700 to 3800 lbs	5	30.50
	More than 3800 lbs	6	52.50
1980 or later	Less than 3500 lbs	7	19.50
	3500 or more lbs	8	52.50

Using this information, write a C++ program that accepts the year and weight of an automobile and determines and displays the weight class and registration fee for the car.

6. Modify Program 4.9 so that the imaginary roots are calculated and displayed when the discriminant is negative. For this case the two roots of the equation are:

$$x_1 = \frac{-b}{2a} + \frac{sqrt[-(b^2 - 4ac)]}{2a} i$$

and

$$x_2 = \frac{-b}{2a} - \frac{sqrt[-(b^2 - 4ac)]}{2a} i$$

where i is the imaginary number symbol for the square root of –1. (*Hint:* Calculate the real and imaginary parts of each root separately.)

7. In the game of Blackjack the cards 2 through 10 are counted at their face values, regardless of suit, all face cards (jack, queen, and king) are counted as 10, and an ace is counted as either a 1 or an 11, depending on the total count of all the cards in a player's hand. The ace counts as 11 only if the resulting total value of all cards in a player's hand does not exceed 21, else it is counted as a 1. Using this information write a C++ program that accepts three card values as inputs (a 1 corresponding to an ace, a 2 corresponding to a two, and so on), calculates the total value of the hand appropriately, and displays the value of the three cards with a printed message.

4.6 PLANNING FOR OBJECTS: INSIDES AND OUTSIDES

The primary distinction between procedural and object-oriented programming is their treatment of data and processing. In contrast to procedural programming, where software is organized by what it does (its function) to the data, object-oriented programming organizes software as a collection of discrete objects that include both data and functional behavior.

As such, procedural programs are constructed as a sequence of processing transformations that convert input data into output data. In a well-constructed procedural program each transformation is captured within a procedure, which in C++ is coded as a function. In this context the overall effect of a procedural program can be illustrated as shown in Figure 4.7.

FIGURE 4.7 Processing Inputs to Produce Outputs

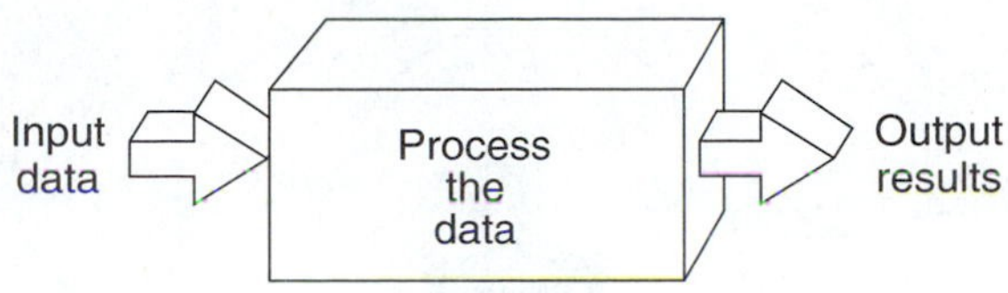

The method for converting inputs to outputs is described by an algorithm, which explains the importance of algorithms to procedure-oriented code. Seen in this light, procedural code is nothing more than an algorithm written in a programming language.

In object-oriented programming, the packaging of data and processing is handled in a much different manner. Both the data and the processing that can be applied to it are combined and packaged in a new unit called an *object*. Once suitable objects are defined, object-oriented programming is concerned with the interactions between objects. Notice that this way of thinking about code does not remove the necessity to understand data and the algorithms applied to them. It simply binds the data and procedures in a new package, called an object, and then concerns itself with the interactions between objects. One advantage to this approach is that once objects are defined for one application they can be used—as is and without reprogramming—in other applications. They can also be easily enhanced by adding additional code to the existing code, rather than completely rewriting all of the code.

Just as the concept of an algorithm is central to procedures, the concept of encapsulation is central to objects. In this section we present this encapsulation concept using an inside–outside analogy, which should help your understanding of what object-oriented programming is all about.

Recall from our discussion in Section 1.5 that an object is defined by two distinct aspects, its attributes and behavior.

In programming terms, an object's attributes are described by data, such as the length and width of a rectangle, and the operations that can be applied to the attributes are described by functions.

As a practical example of this, assume that we will be writing a program that can deal a hand of cards. From an object-oriented approach, one of the objects that we must model is clearly a deck of cards. For our purposes, the attributes of interest for the card deck is that it contains 52 cards, consisting of four suits (hearts, diamonds, spades, and clubs), with each suit consisting of 13 pip values (ace to ten, jack, queen, and king).

Now consider the behavior of our deck of cards, which consists of the operations that can be applied to the deck. At a minimum we will want the ability to shuffle the deck and be able to deal single cards. Let's now see how this simple example relates to encapsulation using an inside–outside concept.

A useful visualization of the inside–outside concept is to consider an object as a boiled egg, such as that shown in Figure 4.8. Notice that the egg consists of three parts: a very inside yolk, a less inside white surrounding the yolk, and an outside shell, which is the only part of the egg visible to outside world.

In terms of our boiled egg model, the attributes and behavior of an object correspond to the yolk and white, respectively, which are inside of the egg. That

FIGURE 4.8 The Boiled Egg Object Model

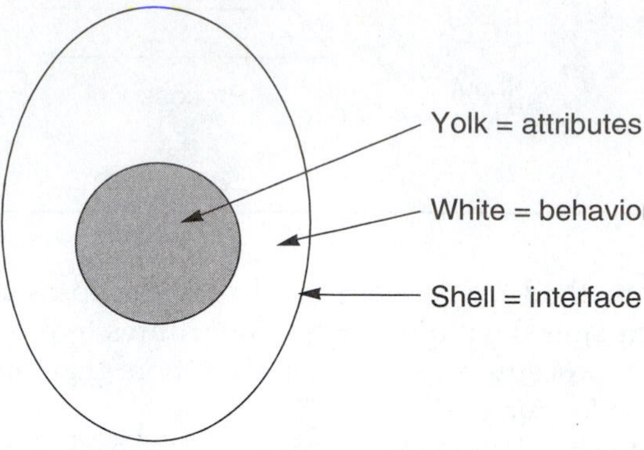

is, the innermost protected area of an object, its data attributes, can be compared to the egg yolk.

Surrounding the data attributes, in a manner similar to the way an egg's white surrounds its yolk, are the operations that we choose to incorporate within an object. Finally, in this analogy, the interface to the outside world, which is represented by the shell, represents how a user gets to invoke the object's internal procedures.

The egg model, with its eggshell interface separating the inside of the egg from the outside, is useful precisely because it so clearly depicts the separation between what should be contained inside an object and what should be seen from the outside. This separation forms an essential element in object-oriented programming. Let's see why this is so.

From an inside–outside perspective, an object's data attributes, the selected algorithms for the object's operations, and how these algorithms are actually implemented are always inside issues that are hidden from the view of an object user. What remains—how a user or another object can actually activate an inside procedure—is an outside issue.

Now let's apply this concept to our card deck example. First, consider how we might represent cards in the deck. Any of the following attributes (and there are others) could be used to represent a card:

1. Two integer variables, one representing a suit (a number from 1 to 4) and one representing a value (a number from 1 to 13).
2. One character value and one integer value. The character represents a card's suit, and the integer represents a card's value.
3. One integer variable having a value from 0 to 51. The expression `int (number / 13 + 1)` provides a number from 1 to 4, which represents the suit, and the expression `(number % 13 + 1)` represents a card value from 1 to 13.

Whichever representation we decide on, however, is not relevant to the outside. The specific way we choose to represent a card is an inside issue to be decided on by the designer of the deck object. From the outside, all that is of concern is that we have access to a deck consisting of 52 cards having the necessary suits and pip values.

The same is true for the operations we decide to provide as part of our card deck object. Consider just the shuffling for now.

A number of algorithms are available for producing a shuffled deck. For example, we could use C++'s `rand()` library function or create our own random number generator using a power residue algorithm (see Section 6.7). Again, the selected algorithm is an inside issue to be determined by the designer of the deck. The specifics of which algorithm is selected and how it is applied to the attributes we have chosen for each card in the deck are not relevant from the object's outside. For purposes of illustration, assume that we decide to use C++'s `rand()` function to produce a randomly shuffled deck.

If we use the first attribute set previously given, each card in a shuffled deck is produced using `rand()` at least twice; once to create a random number from 1 to 4 for the suit and then to create a random number from 1 to 13 for the card's pip value. This sequence must be done to construct 52 different attribute sets, with no duplicates allowed.

If, on the other hand, we use the second attribute set previously given, a shuffled deck can be produced in exactly the same fashion as earlier, with one modification: The first random number (from 1 to 4) must be changed into a character to represent the suit.

Finally, if we use the third representation for a card, we need to use `rand()` once for each card, to produce 52 random numbers from 0 to 51, with no duplicates allowed.

The important point here is that the selection of an algorithm and how it will be applied to an object's attributes are implementation issues and *implementation issues are always inside issues.* A user of the card deck, who is outside, does not need to know how the shuffling is done. All the user of the deck must know is how to produce a shuffled deck. In practice, this means that the user is supplied with sufficient information to correctly invoke a shuffle function. This corresponds to the interface, or outer shell of the egg.

Abstraction and Encapsulation

The distinction between insides and outsides relates directly to the concepts of abstraction and encapsulation. *Abstraction* means concentrating on what an object is and does, before making any decisions about how the object will be implemented. Thus, abstractly, we define a deck and the operations we want to provide. (Clearly, if our abstraction is to be useful, it had better capture the attributes and operations of a real-world deck.) Once we have decided on the attributes and operations, we can actually implement them.

Encapsulation, which is also referred to as information hiding, means separating and hiding the implementation details of the chosen abstract attributes and behavior from outside users of the object. The external side of an object should provide only the necessary interface to users of the object for activating internal procedures. Imposing a strict inside–outside discipline when creating objects is really another way of saying that the object successfully encapsulates all implementation details. In our deck-of-cards example, encapsulation means that the user need never know how we have internally modeled the deck or how an operation, such as shuffling, is performed; the user need only know how to activate the given operations. (How the implementation is actually done is provided in Chapter 7.)

Code Reuse and Extensibility

A direct advantage of an inside–outside object approach is that it encourages both code reuse and extensibility. This is a direct result of having all interactions between objects centered on the outside interface and hiding all implementation details within the object's inside.

For example consider the object shown in Figure 4.9. Here, any of the two object's operations can be activated by correctly stimulating either the circle or square on the outside. In practice, the stimulation is simply a function call. We have used a circle and square to emphasize that two different functions are provided for outside use. In our card deck example, activation of one function might produce a shuffled deck, while activation of the other function results in a card suit and pip value being returned from the object.

Now assume that we want to alter the implementation of an existing operation or add more functionality to our object. *As long as the existing outside interface is maintained, the internal implementation of any and all operations can be changed without the user ever being aware that a change took place.* This is a direct result of encapsulating the attribute data and operations within an object.

Additionally, as long as the interface to existing operations is not changed, new operations can be added as they are needed. Essentially, from the outside world, all that is being added is another function call that accesses the inside attributes and modifies them in a new way.

FIGURE 4.9 Using an Object's Interface

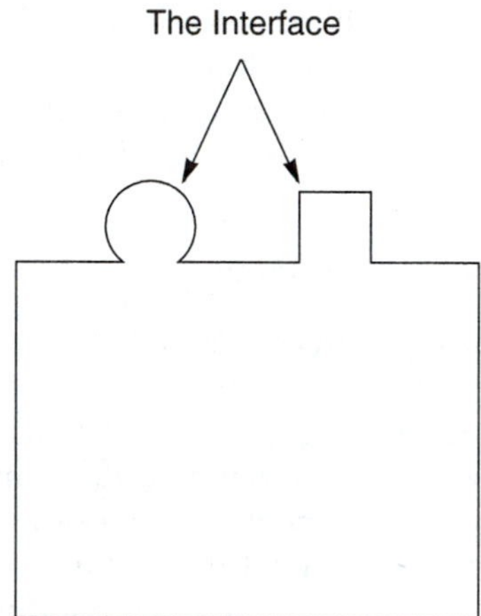

Exercises 4.6

1. Define the terms:
   a. abstraction
   b. encapsulation
   c. extensibility
   d. implementation
   e. information hiding

2. a. An automobile provides a gas pedal, a brake pedal, and a gear shift. Using the boiled egg analogy presented in this section, do these correspond to the yolk, white, or egg shell?

   b. Give two different implementations for the engine, brakes, and gear shifting methods used in automobiles.

3. Defining suitable attributes for distinguishing individual objects typically depends on the universe of objects being considered. For the following set of telephone objects, list attributes that can be used to identify individual telephones within each group:

   a. all telephones within a single office

   b. all telephones within a state

   c. all telephones in the world

4. a. Describe a computer program that you developed in the past that required a user to know something about its internal operation in order for it to be used.

   b. Would you classify a program that required a user to know something about its internal operation as a "good" program. Why or why not?

5. For the following objects, list a set of attributes and behavior that appropriately model the object:

   a. a bicycle

   b. a book

   c. a pencil

   d. a person

   e. a date

   f. an employee

   g. a printer

6. For a typical programming assignment estimate what percentage of the time you spent in analysis, design, and coding, respectively.

7. In terms of the programming assignments you have had in the past, answer these questions:

   a. How much time do you spend selecting the algorithm you will use to solve the problem?

   b. What criteria do you generally use when selecting an algorithm?

4.7 A CLOSER LOOK AT PROGRAM TESTING

In theory, a comprehensive set of test runs would reveal all possible program errors and ensure that a program will work correctly for any and all combinations of input and computed data. In practice, this requires checking all possible combinations of statement execution. Due to the time and effort required, this is an impossible goal except for extremely simple programs. Let us see why this is so. Consider Program 4.10.

PROGRAM 4.10

```
#include <iostream.h>

int main()
{
  int num;

  cout << "Enter a number: ";
  cin  >> num;
  if (num == 5)
    cout << "Bingo!\n";
  else
    cout << "Bongo!\n";

  return 0;
}
```

Program 4.10 has two paths that can be traversed from when the program is run to when the program reaches its closing brace. The first path, which is executed when the input number is 5, is in the sequence:

```
cout << "Enter a number";
cin >> num;
cout << "Bingo!\n";
```

The second path, which is executed whenever any number except 5 is input, includes the sequence of instructions:

```
cout << "Enter a number";
cin >> num;
cout << "Bongo!\n";
```

To test each possible path through Program 4.10, we must conduct two runs, with a judicious selection of test input data to ensure that both paths of the `if` statement are exercised. The addition of one more `if` statement in the program increases the number of possible execution paths by a factor of two and requires four (2^2) runs of the program for complete testing. Similarly, two additional `if` statements increase the number of paths by a factor of four and requires eight (2^3) runs for complete testing, and three additional `if` statements would produce a program that required sixteen (2^4) test runs.

Now consider a modestly sized application program consisting of only ten modules, each module containing five `if` statements. If we assume the modules are always called in the same sequence, then there are 32 possible paths through each module (2 raised to the fifth power) and more than 1,000,000,000,000,000 (2 raised to the fiftieth power) possible paths through the complete program (all modules executed in sequence). The time needed to create individual test data to exercise each path and the actual computer run time required to check each path make the complete testing of such a program impossible.

The inability to fully test all combinations of statement execution sequences has led to the programming saying that "there is no error-free program." It has also led to the realization that any testing that is done should be well thought out to maximize the possibility of locating errors. At a minimum, test data should include appropriate values for input values, illegal input values that the program should reject, and limiting values that are checked by selection statements within the program.

4.8 COMMON PROGRAMMING ERRORS

Three programming errors are common to C++'s selection statements:

1. Using the assignment operator = in place of the relational operator ==. This can cause an enormous amount of frustration because any expression can be tested by an `if-else` statement. For example, the statement:

```
if (opselect = 2)
   cout << "Happy Birthday\n";
else
   cout << "Good Day\n";
```

always results in the message `Happy Birthday` being printed, regardless of the initial value in the variable `opselect`. The reason for this is that the assignment expression `opselect = 2` has a value of 2, which is considered a true value in C++. The correct expression to determine the value in opselect is `opselect == 2`.

2. Letting the `if-else` statement appear to select an incorrect choice. In this typical debugging problem, the programmer mistakenly concentrates on the tested condition as the source of the problem. For example, assume that the following `if-else` statement is part of your program:

```
if (key == 'F')
{
  contemp = (5.0/9.0) * (intemp - 32.0);
  cout << "Conversion to Celsius was done";
}
else
{
  contemp = (9.0/5.0) * intemp + 32.0;
  cout << "Conversion to Fahrenheit was done";
}
```

This statement will always display `Conversion to Celsius was done` when the variable key contains an F. Therefore, if this message is displayed when you believe `key` does not contain F, investigation of `key`'s value is called for. As a general rule, whenever a selection statement does not act as you think it should, test your assumptions about the values assigned to the tested variables by displaying their values. If an unanticipated value is displayed, you have at least isolated the source of the problem to the variables themselves, rather than the structure of the `if-else` statement. From there you will have to determine where and how the incorrect value was obtained.

3. Using nested `if` statements without including braces to indicate the desired structure. Without braces the compiler defaults to pairing elses with the closest unpaired ifs, which sometimes destroys the original intent of the selection statement. To avoid this problem and to create code that is readily adaptable to change, it is useful to write all `if-else` statements as compound statements in the form:

```
if (expression)
{
   one or more statements in here
}
else
{
  one or more statements in here
}
```

By using this form, no matter how many statements are added later, the original integrity and intent of the `if` statement are maintained.

4.9 CHAPTER REVIEW

Key Terms

compound statement
conditional (condition)
encapsulation
false condition
`if-else` chain
`if-else` statement
nested `if`
one-way `if` statement
scope
simple relational expression
`switch` statement
true condition

Summary

1. Relational expressions, which are also called *simple conditions*, are used to compare operands. If a relational expression is true, the value of the expression is the integer 1. If the relational expression is false, it has an integer value of 0. Relational expressions are created using the following relational operators:

Relational Operator	Meaning	Example
`<`	Less than	`age < 30`
`>`	Greater than	`height > 6.2`
`<=`	Less than or equal to	`taxable <= 20000`
`>=`	Greater than or equal to	`temp >= 98.6`
`==`	Equal to	`grade == 100`
`!=`	Not equal to	`number != 250`

2. More complex conditions can be constructed from relational expressions using C++'s logical operators, `&& (AND)`, `|| (OR)`, and `! (NOT)`.
3. An `if-else` statement is used to select between two alternative statements based on the value of an expression. Although relational expressions are usually used for the tested expression, any valid expression can be used. In testing an expression, `if-else` statements interpret a nonzero value as true and a zero value as false. The general form of an `if-else` statement is:

```
if (expression)
  statement1;
else
  statement2;
```

This is a two-way selection statement. If the expression has a nonzero value, it is considered as true, and `statement1` is executed; otherwise `statement2` is executed.

4. An `if-else` statement can contain other `if-else` statements. In the absence of braces, each `else` is associated with the closest preceding unpaired `if`.

5. The `if-else` chain is a multiway selection statement having the general form:

```
if (expression_1)
  statement_1;
else if (expression_2)
  statement_2;
else if (expression_3)
  statement_3;
     .
     .
     .
else if (expression_m)
   statement_m;
else
    statement_n;
```

Each expression is evaluated in the order in which it appears in the chain. Once an expression is true (has a nonzero value), only the statement between that expression and the next `else if` or `else` is executed, and no further expressions are tested. The final `else` is optional, and the statement corresponding to the final `else` is only executed if none of the previous expressions is true.

6. A compound statement consists of any number of individual statements enclosed within the brace pair, `{` and `}`. Compound statements are treated as a single unit and can be used anywhere a single statement is used.
7. The `switch` statement is a multiway selection statement. The general form of a switch statement is:

```
switch (expression)
{     // start of compound statement
  case value_1:  <-------- Terminated with a colon
    statement1;
    statement2;
        .
        .
    break;
  case value_2:  <-------- Terminated with a colon
    statementm;
    statementn;
        .
        .
    break;
        .
        .
  case value_n:  <-------- Terminated with a colon
    statementw;
    statementx;
        .
        .
    break;
  default:       <-------- Terminated with a colon
    statementaa;
    statementbb;
        .
        .
}    // end of switch and compound statement
```

For this statement the value of an integer expression is compared to a number of integer or character constants or constant expressions. Program execution is transferred to the first matching case and continues through the end of the `switch` statement unless an optional `break` statement is encountered. The cases in a `switch` statement can appear in any order and an optional default case can be included. The default case is executed if none of the other cases is matched.

Exercises

1. Write C++ code sections to make the following decisions:
   a. Ask for two integer temperatures. If their values are equal, display the temperature; otherwise do nothing.
   b. Ask for character values `letter1` and `letter2`, representing capital letters of the alphabet, and display them in alphabetical order.
   c. Ask for three integer values, `num1`, `num2`, and `num3`, and display them in decreasing order.
2. a. Write a C++ program to compute and display a person's weekly salary as determined by the following conditions:

   If the hours worked are less than or equal to 40, the person receives $8.00 per hour; else the person receives $320.00 plus $12.00 for each hour worked over 40 hours.

   The program should request the hours worked as input and should display the salary as output.

   b. How many runs should you make for the program written in Exercise 2a to verify that it is operating correctly? What data should you input in each of the program runs?
3. a. Write a program that displays either the message `I FEEL GREAT TODAY!` or `I FEEL DOWN TODAY #$*!` depending on the input. If the character `u` is entered in the variable code, the first message should be displayed; else the second message should be displayed.

   b. How many runs should you make for the program written in Exercise 3a to verify that it is operating correctly? What data should you input in each of the program runs?
4. a. A senior engineer is paid $1000 a week and a junior engineer $600 a week. Write a C++ program that accepts as input an engineer's status in the character variable `status`. If `status` equals `'S'`, the senior person's salary should be displayed, else the junior person's salary should be output.

   b. How many runs should you make for the program written in Exercise 4a to verify that it is operating correctly? What data should you input in each of the program runs?
5. Write a C++ program that accepts a character as input data and determines if the character is an uppercase letter. An uppercase letter is any character that is greater than or equal to `'A'` and less than or equal to `'Z'`. If the entered character is an uppercase letter, display the message `The character just entered is an uppercase letter.` If the entered letter is not uppercase, display the message: `The character just entered is not an uppercase letter.`

6. Repeat Exercise 5 to determine if the character entered is a lowercase letter. A lowercase letter is any character greater than or equal to `'a'` and less than or equal to `'z'`.
7. The following program displays the message `Hello there!` regardless of the letter input. Determine where the error is.

```
#include <iostream.h>

int main()
{
  char letter;
  cout << "Enter a letter: ";
  cin  >> letter;
  if (letter = 'm')
    cout << "Hello there!\n";

  return 0;
}
```

8. a. Write, run, and test a C++ program that accepts a user input integer number and determines whether it is even or odd. Display the entered number and the message `Even` or `Odd`.
   b. Modify the program written for Exercise 8a to determine if the entered number is exactly divisible by a value specified by the user. That is, is it divisible by 3, 7, 13, or any other user-specified value?
9. As a part-time student, you took two courses last term. Write, run, and test a C++ program that calculates and displays your grade-point average (GPA) for the term. Your program should prompt the user to enter the grade and credit hours for each course. These should then be displayed with the lower grade first. The grade-point average for the term should be calculated and displayed. A warning message should be printed if the GPA is less than 2.0 and a congratulatory message if the GPA is 3.5 or above.
10. Write a program that will give the user only three choices: Convert from Fahrenheit to Celsius, convert from Celsius to Fahrenheit, or quit. If the third choice is chosen, the program stops. If one of the first two choices is selected, the program should prompt the user for either a Fahrenheit or Celsius temperature, as appropriate, and then calculate and display the corresponding temperature. Use the conversion equations

$$F = (9/5)\,C + 32$$
$$C = (5/9)\,(F - 32)$$

Improving Communication

11. MEMORANDUM

    To: Chief Programmer

    From: Head of Programming Dept.

    Subject: OOP Course

    Now that you have returned from a course in OOP, could you please explain what encapsulation means and why it is important in OOP.

12. MEMORANDUM

    To: U. R. It

    From: Chief Programmer

    Subject: OOP Approach

    Please provide me with a brief summary of the difference between procedural and object-oriented programming. Specifically, our latest project will require us to use dates extensively by comparing a beginning date to an ending date and determining the actual number of days between the two dates. What do you see as the main differences in the implementation if this is programmed procedurally as opposed to using object-oriented methods?

Working in Teams

13. Your team is responsible for analyzing a gas station pumping system. The pump itself consists of a gun, holster, pump display, and meter. Connected to the pump is the main gas tank. The tank supplies gas to the pump. The attributes of the tank are its capacity, current level, and grade of gas. The pump's attributes are the amount it dispenses and its cost. It is enabled when the gun is removed from the holster and is disabled when the gun is replaced.

    For this description have the team, as a group, identify potential objects in the problem. Typically, objects are identified by locating the nouns, such as pump, tank, etc., in the problem statement.

    Once you have identified potential objects, have each team member select one object and write a paragraph describing what the object does, and how it interacts with other objects.

14. Your team is responsible for developing a software simulation program to model the operation of a single elevator. The elevator is capable of moving from the basement of the building it is housed in to the sixth floor, which is at the top of the building. The elevator responds to the external up and down buttons as follows:

    If the elevator is moving down and a down button is activated on a lower floor, the elevator will stop at the designated floor.

    If the elevator is moving up and an up button is activated on a higher floor the elevator will stop at the designated floor.

    The external buttons are pushed by people, who arrive randomly at any floor.

    Internally, the elevator responds to an activated floor button by turning on the button's light and then stopping at the next floor in the direction it is moving. When it reaches the designated floor it opens the doors and turns off the internal floor button.

    For this description have the team, as a group, identify potential objects in the problem. Typically, objects are identified by locating the nouns, such as people, button, etc., in the problem statement.

    Once you have identified potential objects, have each team member select one object and write a paragraph describing what the object does, and how it interacts with other objects.

CHAPTER

5 Repetition Structures

The programs examined so far have illustrated the programming concepts involved in input, output, assignment, and selection capabilities. By this time you should have gained enough experience to be comfortable with these concepts and the mechanics of implementing them using C++. Many problems, however, require a repetition capability, in which the same calculation or sequence of instructions is repeated, over and over, using different sets of data. Examples of such repetition include continual checking of user data entries until an acceptable entry, such as a valid password, is entered, counting and accumulating running totals, and constant acceptance of input data and recalculation of output values that only stops on entry of a sentinel value.

This chapter explores the different methods programmers use to construct repeating sections of code and how that code can be implemented in C++. More commonly, a section of code that is repeated is referred to as a *loop,* because after the last statement in the code is executed the program branches, or loops, back to the first statement and starts another repetition through the code. Each repetition is also referred to as an iteration or pass through the loop.

5.1 INTRODUCTION

The real power of a program is realized when the same type of operation must be made over and over. For example, consider Program 3.16 in Section 3.6, where the same set of instructions is repeated three times. Retyping this same set of instructions is tedious, time consuming, and subject to error. It would certainly be more convenient to type such repeating instructions only once and then inform the program to repeat execution of the instructions three times, which we can do using repetitive sections of code.

Constructing a repetitive section of code requires that four elements be present. The first necessary element is a repetition statement. This **repetition statement** defines the boundaries containing the repeating section of code and also controls whether the code will be executed or not. In general, there are three different forms of repetition structures, all of which are provided in C++:

1. `while` structure
2. `for` structure
3. `do-while` structure.

Each of these structures requires a condition that must be evaluated, which is the second required element for constructing repeating sections of code. Valid conditions are identical to those used in selection statements. If the condition is true, the code is executed; otherwise, it is not.

The third required element is a statement that initially sets the condition. This statement must always be placed before the condition is first evaluated to ensure correct loop execution the first time the condition is evaluated.

Finally, there must be a statement within the repeating section of code that allows the condition to become false. This is necessary to ensure that, at some point, the repetitions stop.

FIGURE 5.1 A Pretest Loop

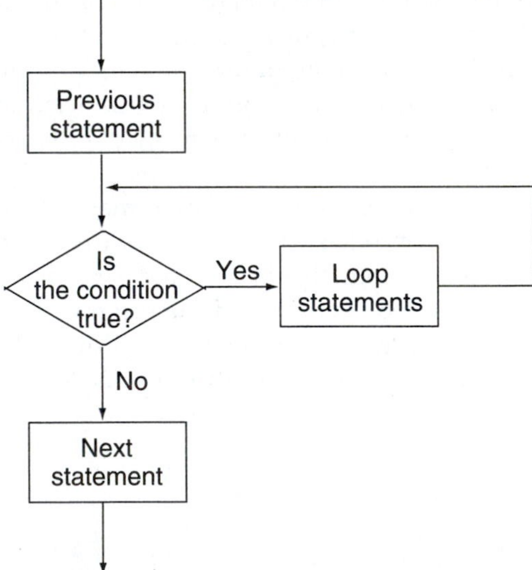

Pretest and Post-Test Loops

The condition being tested can be evaluated at either the beginning or the end of the repeating section of code. Figure 5.1 illustrates the case where the test occurs at the beginning of the loop. This type of loop is referred to as a **pretest loop** because the condition is tested before any statements within the loop are executed. If the condition is true, the executable statements within the loop are executed. If the initial value of the condition is false, the executable statements within the loop are never executed at all and control transfers to the first statement after the loop. To avoid infinite repetitions, the condition must be updated within the loop. Pretest loops are also referred to as *entrance-controlled loops*. Both the `while` and `for` loop structures are examples of such loops.

A loop that evaluates a condition at the end of the repeating section of code, as illustrated in Figure 5.2, is referred to as **post-test loop** or *exit-controlled loop*. Such loops always execute the loop statements at least once before the condition is tested. Since the executable statements within the loop are continually executed until the condition becomes false, there always must be a statement within the loop that updates the condition and permits it to become false. The `do-while` construct is an example of a post-test loop.

Fixed Count Versus Variable Condition Loops

In addition to where the condition is tested (pretest or post-test), repeating sections of code are also classified as to the type of condition being tested. In a **fixed count loop,** the condition is used to keep track of how many repetitions have occurred.

FIGURE 5.2 A Post-Test Loop

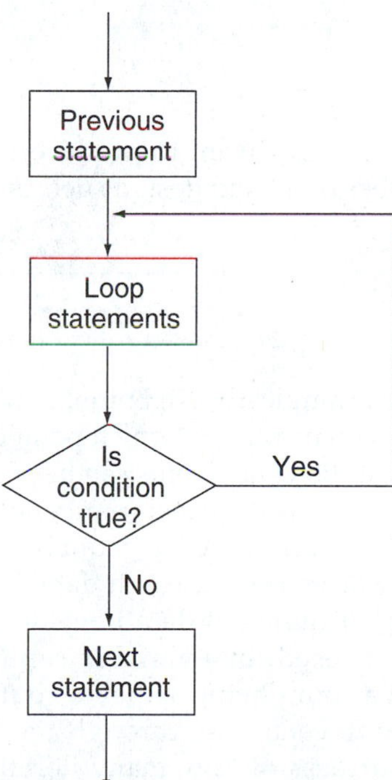

A BIT OF BACKGROUND

Comptometer Arithmetic

In the early 1900s, mechanical calculators, called *comptometers,* performed only addition. Since multiplication is only a quick method of addition (for example, 5 times 4 is really 5 added 4 times), producing multiplication results presented no problems—the results were obtained using repeated additions. Subtraction and division, however, initially did present a problem. Clever accountants soon discovered that subtraction and division were possible. Subtraction was accomplished by writing the nine's complement on each numeric key. That is, 9 was written on the 0 key, 8 on the 1 key, 7 on the 2 key, and so on. Subtraction was then performed by adding the nine's complement numbers, then adding 1 to the result. For example, consider the subtraction problem

637 - 481 = 156

The nine's complement of 481 is 518, and

637 + 518 + 1 = 1,156

which gives the answer (156) to the problem when the leftmost carry digit is ignored.

It did not take accountants long to solve division problems using repeated subtractions—all on a machine designed to handle only additions.

Early computers, which had only the facilities for doing addition, used similar algorithms for performing subtraction, multiplication, and division. They used, however, two's complement numbers rather than nine's complement. (See Section 1.6 for an introduction to two's complement numbers.)

Although many computers now come with special-purpose hardware, called floating-point processors, to perform multiplication and division directly, they still use two's complement number representation internally and perform subtraction using two's complement addition. And when a floating-point processor is not used, sophisticated software algorithms are employed that perform multiplications and divisions based on repeated additions and subtractions.

For example, we might want to produce a table of 10 numbers, including their squares and cubes or a fixed design such as

```
*************************
*************************
*************************
*************************
```

In each of these examples, a fixed number of calculations are performed or a fixed number of lines are printed, at which point the repeating section of code is exited. All of C++'s repetition statements can be used to produce fixed count loops.

In many situations the exact number of repetitions is not known in advance or the items are too numerous to count beforehand. For example, when entering a large amount of market research data we might not want to take the time to count the number of actual data items to be entered. In such cases, a variable condition loop is used. In a **variable condition loop** the tested condition does not depend on a count being achieved, but rather on a variable that can change interactively with each pass through the loop. When a specified value is encountered, regardless of how many iterations have occurred, repetitions stop.

All of C++'s repetition statements can be used to create variable condition loops.[1] In this chapter we will encounter examples of both fixed count and variable condition loops.

5.2 while LOOPS

In C++, a **while loop** is constructed using a while statement. The syntax of this statement is:

```
while (expression)
  statement;
```

The expression contained within parentheses is the condition tested to determine if the statement following the parentheses is executed. The expression is evaluated in exactly the same manner as that of an if-else statement; the difference is in how the expression is used. As we have seen, when the expression is true (has a nonzero value) in an if-else statement, the statement following the expression is executed once. In a while statement, the statement following the expression is executed repeatedly as long as the expression evaluates to a nonzero value. Considering just the expression and the statement following the parentheses, the process used by the computer in evaluating a while statement is:

1. Test the expression.
2. If the expression has a nonzero (true) value
   a. execute the statement following the parentheses.
   b. go back to step 1.
 else
   exit the while statement and execute the next
   executable statement following the while statement.

Notice that step 2b forces program control to be transferred back to step 1. This transfer of control back to the start of a while statement in order to reevaluate the expression is what forms the program loop. The while statement literally loops back on itself to recheck the expression until it evaluates to zero (becomes false). This naturally means that somewhere in the loop provision must be made to permit the value of the tested expression to be altered. As we will see, this is indeed the case.

This looping process produced by a while statement is illustrated in Figure 5.3. A diamond shape is used to show the two entry and two exit points required in the decision part of the while statement.

To make this a little more tangible, consider the relational expression count <= 10 and the statement cout << count;. Using these, we can write the following valid while statement:

```
while (count <= 10)
  cout << count;
```

---

[1] In this respect, C++ differs from most other languages such as BASIC, FORTRAN, and Pascal. In those languages, the for structure (which is implemented using a DO statement in FORTRAN) can only be used to produce fixed count loops. C++'s for structure, as we will see shortly, is virtually interchangeable with its while structure.

FIGURE 5.3 Structure of a `while` Loop

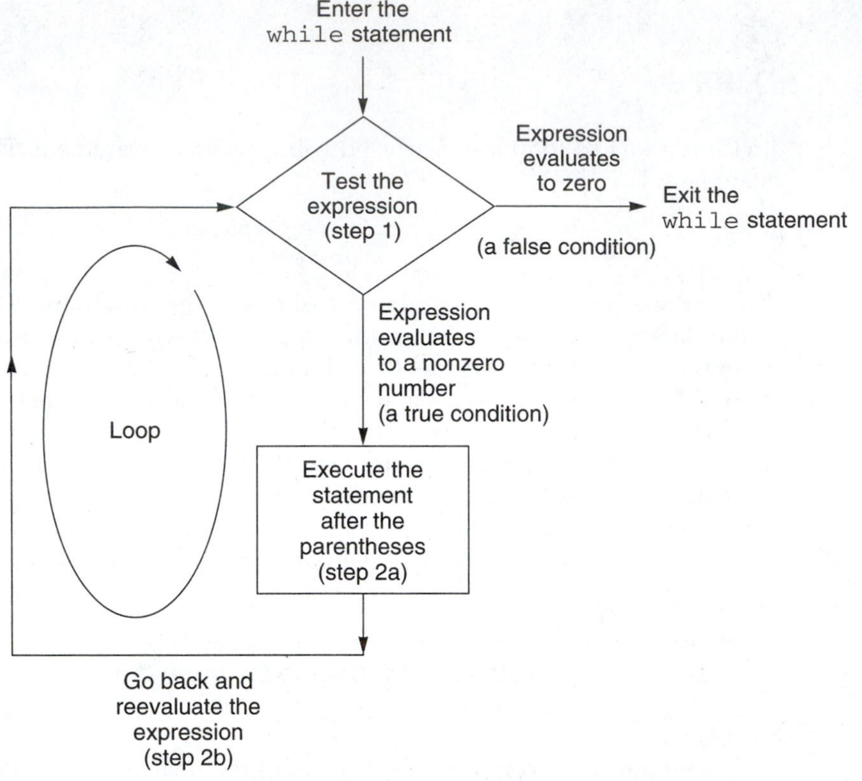

Although this statement is valid, the alert reader will realize that we have created a situation in which the `cout` object either is called forever (or until we stop the program) or is not called at all. Let us see why this happens.

If `count` has a value less than or equal to 10 when the expression is first evaluated, a call to `cout` is made. The `while` statement then automatically loops back on itself and retests the expression. Because we have not changed the value stored in `count`, the expression is still true and another call to `cout` is made. This process continues forever, or until the program containing this statement is prematurely stopped by the user. However, if `count` starts with a value greater than 10, the expression is false to begin with and the `cout` object call is never made.

How do we set an initial value in `count` to control what the `while` statement does the first time the expression is evaluated? The answer, of course, is to assign values to each variable in the tested expression before the `while` statement is encountered. For example, the following sequence of instructions is valid:

```
count = 1;
while (count <= 10)
  cout << count;
```

Using this sequence of instructions, we have ensured that `count` starts with a value of 1. We could assign any value to `count` in the assignment statement—the important thing is to assign some value. In practice, the assigned value depends on the application.

We must still change the value of count so that we can finally exit the while statement. To do this, we need an expression such as count = count + 1 to increment the value of count each time the while statement is executed. The fact that a while statement provides for the repetition of a single statement does not prevent us from including an additional statement to change the value of count. All we have to do is replace the single statement with a compound statement. For example:

```
count = 1;              // initialize count
while (count <= 10)
{
  cout << count;
  count++;              // increment count
}
```

Note that, for clarity, we have placed each statement in the compound statement on a different line. This is consistent with the convention adopted for compound statements in the last chapter. Let us now analyze the preceding sequence of instructions.

The first assignment statement sets count equal to 1. The while statement is then entered and the expression is evaluated for the first time. Since the value of count is less than or equal to 10, the expression is true and the compound statement is executed. The first statement in the compound statement is a call to the cout object to display the value of count. The next statement adds 1 to the value currently stored in count, making this value equal to 2. The while statement now loops back to retest the expression. Since count is still less than or equal to 10, the compound statement is again executed. This process continues until the value of count reaches 11. Program 5.1 illustrates these statements in an actual program.

PROGRAM 5.1

```
#include <iostream.h>

int main()
{
  int count;

  count = 1;              // initialize count
  while (count <= 10)
  {
    cout << count << " ";
    count++;              // increment count
  }

  return 0;
}
```

The output for Program 5.1 is:

```
1 2 3 4 5 6 7 8 9 10
```

There is nothing special about the name count used in Program 5.1. Any valid integer variable could have been used.

Before we consider other examples of the while statement, two comments concerning Program 5.1 are in order. First, the statement count++ can be replaced with any statement that changes the value of count. A statement such as count = count + 2, for example, would cause every second integer to be displayed. Second, it is the programmer's responsibility to ensure that count is changed in a way that ultimately leads to a normal exit from the while loop. For example, if we replace the expression count++ with the expression count--, the value of count will never exceed 10 and an infinite loop will be created. An **infinite loop** is a loop that never ends. The computer will not reach out, touch you, and say, "Excuse me, you have created an infinite loop." It just keeps displaying numbers until you realize that the program is not working as you expected.

Now that you have some familiarity with the while statement, see if you can read and determine the output of Program 5.2.

PROGRAM 5.2

```
#include <iostream.h>

int main()
{
  int i;

  i = 10;
  while (i >= 1)
  {
    cout << i << "  ";
    i--;               // subtract 1 from i
  }

  return 0;
}
```

The assignment statement in Program 5.2 initially sets the int variable i to 10. The while statement then checks to see if the value of i is greater than or equal to 1. While the expression is true, the value of i is displayed by the cout object and the value of i is decremented by 1. When i finally reaches zero, the expression is false and the program exits the while statement. Thus, the following display is obtained when Program 5.2 is run:

```
10 9 8 7 6 5 4 3 2 1
```

To illustrate the power of the while statement, consider the task of printing a table of numbers from 1 to 10 with their squares and cubes. This can be done with a simple while statement as illustrated by Program 5.3.

PROGRAM 5.3

```
#include <iostream.h>
#include <iomanip.h>

int main()
{
  int num;

  cout << "NUMBER     SQUARE     CUBE\n"
       << "------     ------     ----\n";

  num = 1;
  while (num < 11)
  {
    cout << setw(3) << num << "        "
         << setw(3) << num * num      << "        "
         << setw(4) << num * num * num <<"\n";
    num++;         // increment num
  }

  return 0;
}
```

When Program 5.3 is run, the following display is produced:

```
NUMBER    SQUARE    CUBE
------    ------    ----
   1         1         1
   2         4         8
   3         9        27
   4        16        64
   5        25       125
   6        36       216
   7        49       343
   8        64       512
   9        81       729
  10       100      1000
```

Note that the expression used in Program 5.3 is `num < 11`. For the integer variable `num`, this expression is exactly equivalent to the expression `num <= 10`. The choice of which to use is entirely up to you.

If we want to use Program 5.3 to produce a table of 1000 numbers, all we do is change the expression in the `while` statement from `num < 11` to `num < 1001`. Changing the `11` to `1001` produces a table of 1000 lines—not bad for a simple five-line `while` statement.

All the program examples illustrating the `while` statement are examples of fixed count loops, because the tested condition is a counter that checks for a fixed number of repetitions. A variation on the fixed count loop can be made where the counter is not incremented by one each time through the loop, but by some other value. For example, consider the task of producing a Celsius to Fahrenheit temperature conversion table. Assume that Fahrenheit temperatures corresponding to Celsius temperatures ranging from 5 to 50 degrees are to be displayed in increments of 5 degrees. The desired display can be obtained with this series of statements:

```
celsius = 5;      // starting Celsius value
while (celsius <= 50)
{
  fahren = (9.0/5.0) * celsius + 32.0;
  cout << celsius
       << fahren;
  celsius = celsius + 5;
}
```

PROGRAM 5.4

```
#include <iostream.h>
#include <iomanip.h>

const int MAX_CELSIUS = 50;
const int START_VAL = 5;
const int STEP_SIZE = 5;

// a program to convert Celsius to Fahrenheit
int main()
{

  int celsius;
  float fahren;

  cout << "DEGREES   DEGREES\n"
       << "CELSIUS   FAHRENHEIT\n"
       << "-------   ----------\n";

  celsius = START_VAL;

    // set output formats for floating point numbers only
  cout << setiosflags(ios::showpoint)
       << setprecision(2);

  while (celsius <= MAX_CELSIUS)
  {
    fahren = (9.0/5.0) * celsius + 32.0;
    cout << setw(4) << celsius
         << setw(13) << fahren << endl;
    celsius = celsius + STEP_SIZE;
  }

  return 0;
}
```

As before, the `while` statement consists of everything from the word `while` through the closing brace of the compound statement. Prior to entering the `while` loop we have made sure we assigned a value to the counter being evaluated, and there is a statement to alter the value of the counter within the loop (in increments of 5) to ensure an exit from the `while` loop. Program 5.4 illustrates the use of this code in a complete program. The display obtained when Program 5.4 is executed is:

```
DEGREES   DEGREES
CELSIUS  FAHRENHEIT
-------  ----------
   5        41.00
  10        50.00
  15        59.00
  20        68.00
  25        77.00
  30        86.00
  35        95.00
  40       104.00
  45       113.00
  50       122.00
```

Exercises 5.2

1. Rewrite Program 5.1 to print the numbers 2 to 10 in increments of two. The output of your program should be:

   ```
   2  4  6  8  10
   ```

2. Rewrite Program 5.4 to produce a table that starts at a Celsius value of −10 and ends with a Celsius value of 60, in increments of 10 degrees.

3. a. For the following code, determine the total number of items displayed. Also determine the first and last numbers printed.

   ```
   int num = 0;
   while (num <= 20)
   {
     num++;
     cout << num << " ";
   }
   ```

   b. Enter and run the code from Exercise 3a within the context of a complete program to verify your answers to the exercise.

   c. How would the output be affected if the two statements within the compound statement were reversed (that is, if the `cout` call were made before the `n++` statement)?

4. Write a C++ program that converts gallons to liters. The program should display gallons from 10 to 20 in 1-gallon increments and the corresponding liter equivalents. Use the relationship that 1 *gallon* contains 3.785 *liters*.

5. Write a C++ program to produce the following display:

   ```
   0
    1
     2
      3
       4
        5
         6
          7
           8
            9
   ```

6. Write a C++ program to produce the following displays:

a.
```
****
 ****
  ****
   ****
```

b.
```
   ****
  ****
  ****
 ****
```

7. Write a C++ program that converts feet to meters. The program should display feet from 3 to 30 in 3-foot increments and the corresponding meter equivalents. Use the relationship there are 3.28 feet to a meter.

8. A machine purchased for $28,000 is depreciated at a rate of $4000 a year for seven years. Write and run a C++ program that computes and displays a depreciation table for seven years. The table should have the form:

Year	Depreciation	End-of-Year Value	Accumulated Depreciation
1	4000	24000	4000
2	4000	20000	8000
3	4000	16000	12000
4	4000	12000	16000
5	4000	8000	20000
6	4000	4000	24000
7	4000	0	28000

9. An automobile travels at an average speed of 55 miles per hour for four hours. Write a C++ program that displays the distance driven, in miles, that the car has traveled after 1, 2, etc., hours until the end of the trip.

10. a. An approximate conversion formula for converting Fahrenheit to Celsius temperatures is

$$\text{Celsius} = (\text{Fahrenheit} - 30)\ /\ 2$$

Using this formula, and starting with a Fahrenheit temperature of zero degrees, write a C++ program that determines when the approximate equivalent Celsius temperature differs from the exact equivalent value by more than four degrees. (*Hint:* Use a `while` loop that terminates when the difference between approximate and exact Celsius equivalents exceeds four degrees.)

b. Using the approximate Celsius conversion formula given in Exercise 10a, write a C++ program that produces a table of Fahrenheit temperatures, exact Celsius equivalent temperatures, approximate Celsius equivalent temperatures, and the difference between the correct and approximate equivalent Celsius values. The table should begin at zero degrees Fahrenheit, use two-degree Fahrenheit increments, and terminate when the difference between exact and approximate values differs by more than four degrees.

11. Write a C++ program to find the sum, sum of squares, and the sum of cubes of the first n integers, beginning with 1 and ending with $n = 100$. Verify that in each case

$$1 + 2 + 3 + \ldots + n = n(n + 1)/2$$

$$1^2 + 2^2 + 3^2 + \ldots + n^2 = n(n + 1)(2n + 1)/6$$

$$1^3 + 2^3 + 3^3 + \ldots + n^3 = n^2(n + 1)^2/4$$

12. Write a C++ program to find the sum of the first 100 terms in the series

$$1/(1 * 2) + 1/(2 * 3) + 1/(3 * 4) + \ldots + 1/[n*(n + 1)]$$

Verify that the sum equals n/(n + 1). Determine the value that the sum approaches as n gets infinitely large.

5.3 INTERACTIVE while LOOPS

Combining interactive data entry with the repetition capabilities of the while statement produces very adaptable and powerful programs. To understand the concept involved, consider Program 5.5, where a while statement is used to accept and then display four user-entered numbers, one at a time. Although it uses a very simple idea, the program highlights the flow of control concepts needed to produce more useful programs.

PROGRAM 5.5

```
#include <iostream.h>
#include <iomanip.h>

const int MAXNUMS = 4;

int main()
{
  int count;
  float num;

  cout << "\nThis program will ask you to enter "
       << MAXNUMS << " numbers.\n";
  count = 1;

  while (count <= MAXNUMS)
  {
    cout << "\nEnter a number: ";
    cin  >> num;
    cout << "The number entered is " << num;
    count++;
  }
  cout << endl;

  return 0;
}
```

The following is a sample run of Program 5.5. The italicized items were input in response to the appropriate prompts.

```
This program will ask you to enter some numbers.

Enter a number: 26.2
The number entered is 26.2
Enter a number: 5
The number entered is 5
Enter a number: 103.456
The number entered is 103.456
Enter a number: 1267.89
The number entered is 1267.89
```

Let us review the program so we clearly understand how the output was produced. The first message displayed is caused by execution of the first `cout` object call. This call is outside and before the `while` statement, so it is executed once before any statement in the `while` loop.

Once the `while` loop is entered, the statements within the compound statement are executed while the tested condition is true. The first time through the compound statement, the message `Enter a number:` is displayed. The program then calls `cin`, which forces the computer to wait for a number to be entered at the keyboard. Once a number is typed and the return or enter key is pressed, the `cout` object displays the number and the loop is executed. The variable `count` is then incremented by one. This process continues until four passes through the loop have been made and the value of `count` is 5. Each pass causes the message `Enter a number:` to be displayed, causes one call to `cin` to be made, and causes the message `The number entered is` to be displayed. Figure 5.4 on p. 248 illustrates this flow of control.

Rather than simply displaying the entered numbers, Program 5.5 can be made to use the entered data. For example, let us add the numbers entered and display the total. To do this, we must be very careful about how we add the numbers, since the same variable, `num`, is used for each number entered. Because of this, the entry of a new number in Program 5.5 automatically causes the previous number stored in `num` to be lost. Thus, each number entered must be added to the total before another number is entered. The required sequence is:

Enter a number.
Add the number to the total.

How do we add a single number to a total? A statement such as `total = total + num` does the job perfectly. This is the accumulating statement introduced in Section 3.1. After each number is entered, the accumulating statement adds the number into the total, as illustrated in Figure 5.5 on p. 249. The complete flow of control required for adding the numbers is illustrated in Figure 5.6. In reviewing Figure 5.6, note that we have made a provision for initially setting the total to zero before the `while` loop is entered. If we were to clear the total inside the `while` loop, it would be set to zero each time the loop was executed and any value previously stored would be erased.

Program 5.6 incorporates the necessary modifications to Program 5.5 to total the numbers entered. As indicated in the flow diagram shown in Figure 5.6 on p. 250, the statement `total = total + num;` is placed immediately after the `cin` object call. Putting the accumulating statement at this point in the program ensures that the entered number is immediately "captured" by the total.

Let us review Program 5.6. The variable `total` was created to store the total of the numbers entered. Prior to entering the `while` statement, the value of `total` is set to zero. This ensures that any previous value present in the storage location(s) assigned to the variable `total` is erased. Within the `while` loop the statement `total = total + num;` is used to add the value of the entered number into `total`. As each value is entered, it is added into the existing total to create a new total. Thus, `total` becomes a running subtotal of all the values entered. Only when all numbers are entered does `total` contain the final sum of all the numbers. After the `while` loop is finished, the last `cout` statement is used to display this sum.

PROGRAM 5.6

```
#include <iostream.h>
#include <iomanip.h>

const int MAXNUMS = 4;

int main()
{
  int count;
  float num, total;

  cout << "\nThis program will ask you to enter "
       << MAXNUMS << " numbers.\n";
  count = 1;
  total = 0;

  while (count <= MAXNUMS)
  {
    cout << "Enter a number: ";
    cin  >> num;
    total = total + num;
    cout << "The total is now " << total;
    count++;
  }

  cout << "\nThe final total is " << total << endl;

  return 0;
}
```

Using the same data we entered in the sample run for Program 5.5, the following sample run of Program 5.6 was made:

```
This program will ask you to enter some numbers.

Enter a number: 26.2
The total is now 26.2
Enter a number: 5
The total is now 31.2
Enter a number: 103.456
The total is now 134.656
Enter a number: 1267.89
The total is now 1402.546

The final total is 1402.546
```

Having used an accumulating assignment statement to add the numbers entered, we can now go further and calculate the average of the numbers. Where do we calculate the average: within the `while` loop or outside of it?

FIGURE 5.4 Flow of Control Diagram for Program 5.5

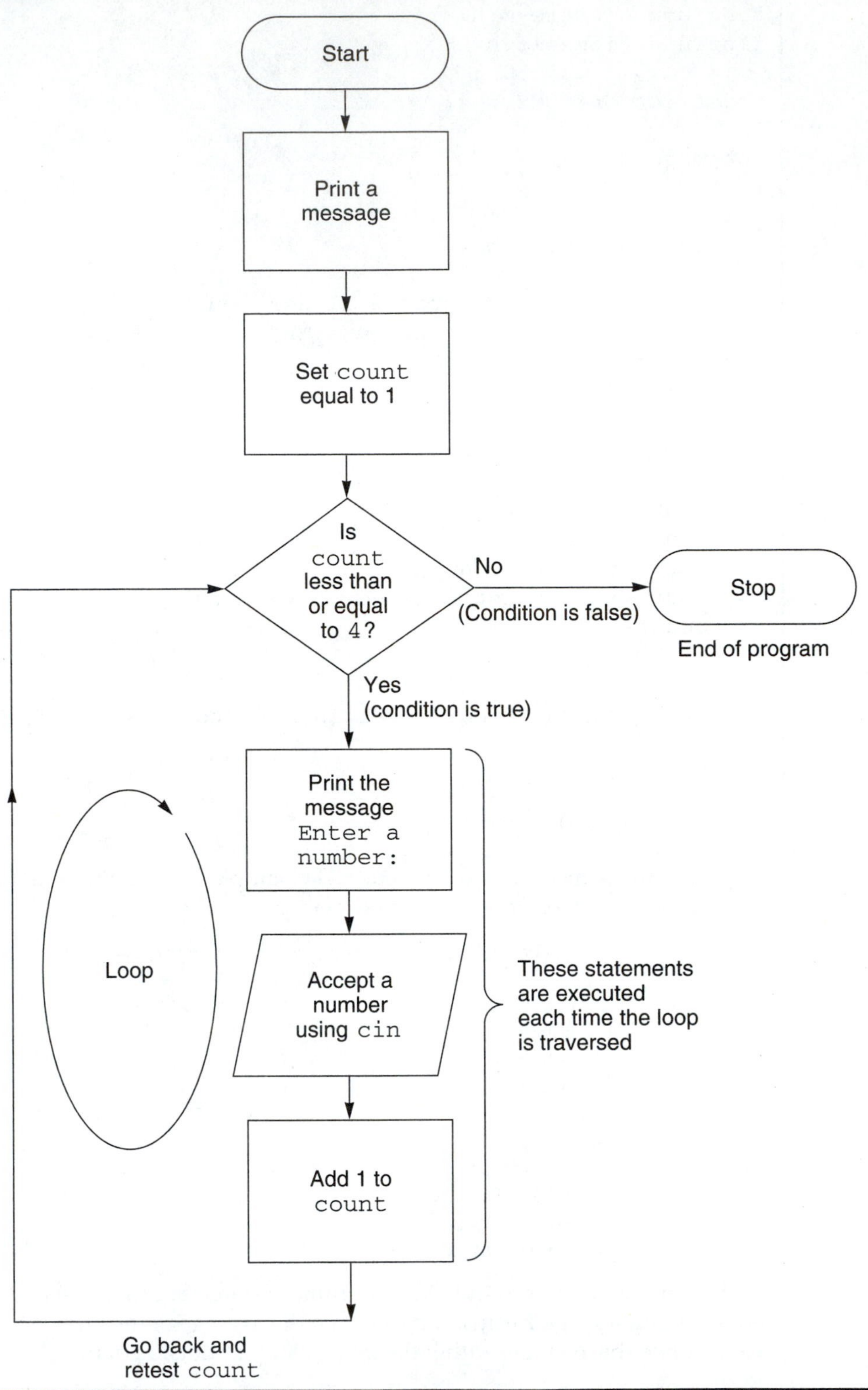

FIGURE 5.5 Accepting and Adding a Number to a Total

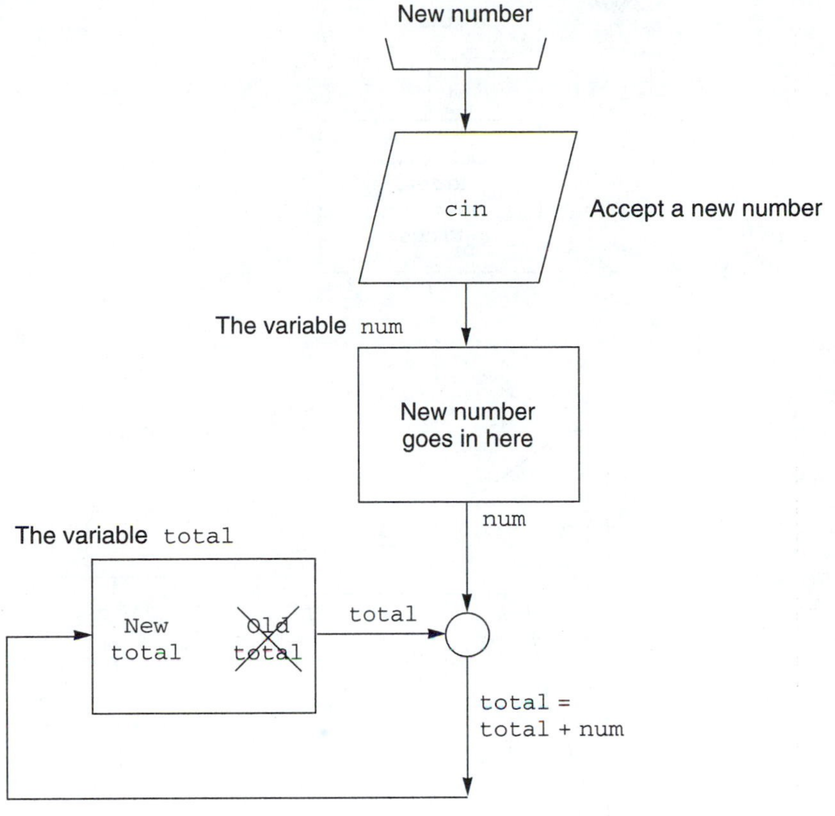

In the case at hand, calculating an average requires that both a final sum and the number of items in that sum be available. The average is then computed by dividing the final sum by the number of items. At this point, we must ask, "At what point in the program is the correct sum available, and at what point is the number of items available?" In reviewing Program 5. 6 we see that the correct sum needed for calculating the average is available after the `while` loop is finished. In fact, the whole purpose of the `while` loop is to ensure that the numbers are entered and added correctly to produce a correct sum. After the loop is finished, we also have a count of the number of items used in the sum. However, due to the way the `while` loop was constructed, the number in `count` (5) when the loop is finished is one more than the number of items (4) used to obtain the total. Knowing this, we simply subtract one from `count` before using it to determine the average. With this as background, see if you can read and understand Program 5.7 on p. 251.

FIGURE 5.6 Accumulation Flow of Control

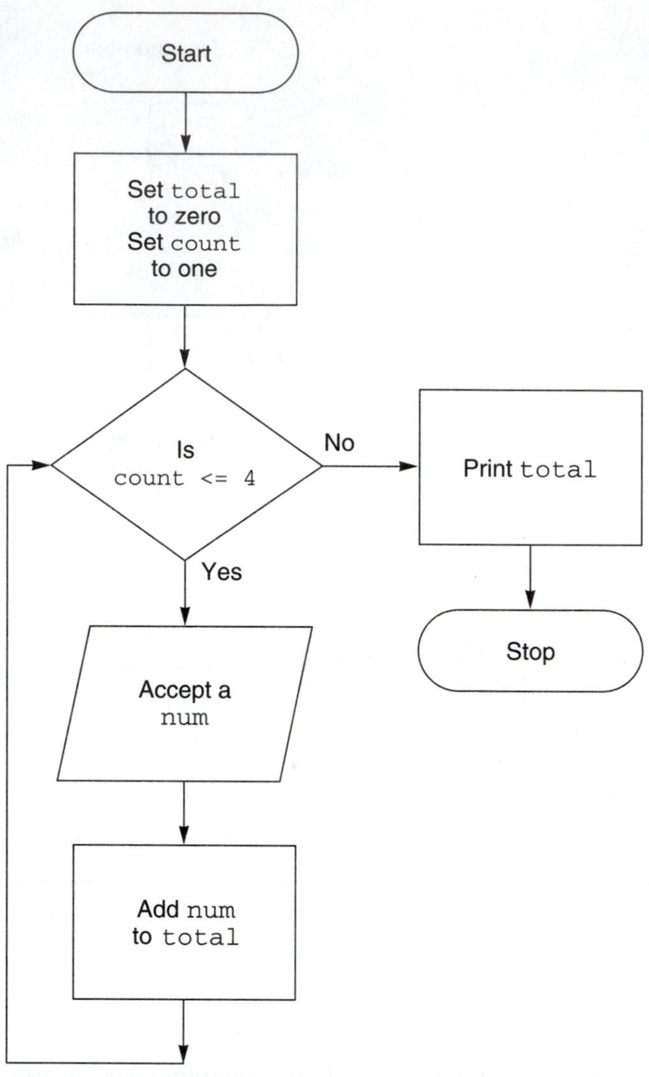

Program 5.7 is almost identical to Program 5.6, except for the calculation of the average. We have also removed the constant display of the total within and after the `while` loop. The loop in Program 5.7 is used to enter and add four numbers. Immediately after the loop is exited, the average is computed and displayed. A sample run of Program 5.7 follows:

```
This program will ask you to enter some numbers.

Enter a number: 26.2
Enter a number: 5
Enter a number: 103.456
Enter a number: 1267.89

The average of the numbers is 350.6365
```

PROGRAM 5.7

```
#include <iostream.h>
#include <iomanip.h>

const int MAXNUMS = 4;

int main()
{
  int count;
  float num, total, average;

  cout << "\nThis program will ask you to enter "
       << MAXNUMS << " numbers.\n";
  count = 1;
  total = 0;

  while (count <= MAXNUMS)
  {
    cout << "Enter a number: ";
    cin  >> num;
    total = total + num;
    count++;
  }

  count--;
  average = total / count;
  cout << "The average of the numbers is " << average << endl;

  return 0;
}
```

Sentinels

All of the loops we have created thus far have been examples of fixed count loops, where a counter has been used to control the number of loop iterations. By means of a `while` statement, variable condition loops may also be constructed. For example, when entering grades we may not want to count the number of grades that will be entered, but would prefer to enter the grades continuously and, at the end, type in a special data value to signal the end of data input.

In computer programming, data values used to signal either the start or end of a data series are called **sentinels.** The sentinel values must, of course, be selected so as not to conflict with legitimate data values. For example, if we were constructing a program to process a student's grades (assume that no extra credit is given that could produce a grade higher than 100), we could use any grade higher than 100 as a sentinel value. Program 5.8 illustrates this concept. In Program 5.8 data is continuously requested and accepted until a number larger than 100 is entered. Entry of a number higher than 100 alerts the program to exit the `while` loop and display the sum of the numbers entered.

We show a sample run using Program 5.8 next. As long as grades less than or equal to 100 are entered, the program continues to request and accept additional data. When a number less than or equal to 100 is entered, the program adds this number to the total. When a number greater than 100 is entered the `while` loop is exited and the sum of the grades that were entered is displayed.

```
To stop entering grades, type in any number greater than 100.

Enter a grade: 95
Enter a grade: 100
Enter a grade: 82
Enter a grade: 101

The total of the grades is 277
```

PROGRAM 5.8

```
#include <iostream.h>

const int HIGHGRADE = 100;

int main()
{
  float grade, total;

  grade = 0;
  total = 0;
  cout << "\nTo stop entering grades, type in any number";
  cout << "\n greater than 100.\n\n";

  while (grade <= HIGHGRADE)
  {
    total = total + grade;
    cout << "Enter a grade: ";
    cin >> grade;
  }

  cout << "\nThe total of the grades is " << total << endl;

  return 0;
}
```

`break` and `continue` Statements

Two useful statements in connection with repetition statements are the **`break`** and **`continue` statements**. We encountered the `break` statement when we studied the `switch` statement. The general form of this statement is:

```
break;
```

A `break` statement, as its name implies, forces an immediate break, or exit, from the `switch`, `while`, `for` and `do-while` statements presented in the next sections.

For example, execution of the following while loop is immediately terminated if a number greater than 76 is entered.

```
while(count <= 10)
{
  cout << "Enter a number: ";
  cin  >> num;
  if (num > 76)
  {
    cout << "You lose!\n";
    break;        // break out of the loop
  }
  else
    cout << "Keep on trucking!\n";
  count++;
}
// break jumps to here
```

The break statement violates pure structured programming principles because it provides a second, nonstandard exit from a loop. Nevertheless, the break statement is extremely useful and valuable for breaking out of loops when an unusual condition is detected. The break statement is also used to exit from a switch statement, but this is because the desired case has been detected and processed.

The continue statement is similar to the break statement but applies only to loops created with while, do-while, and for statements. The general format of a continue statement is:

```
continue;
```

When a continue statement is encountered in a loop, the next iteration of the loop is immediately begun. For while loops this means that execution is automatically transferred to the top of the loop and reevaluation of the tested expression is initiated. Although the continue statement has no direct effect on a switch statement, it can be included within a switch statement that itself is contained in a loop. Here the effect of continue is the same: The next loop iteration is begun.

As a general rule the continue statement is less useful than the break statement, but it is convenient for skipping over data that should not be processed while remaining in a loop. For example, invalid grades are simply ignored in the following section of code and only valid grades are added to the total[2]:

```
while (count < 30)
{
  cout << "Enter a grade: ";
  cin  >> grade;
  if(grade < 0 || grade > 100)
    continue;
  total = total + grade;
  count++;
}
```

---

[2] The continue is not essential, however, and the selection could have been written as:

```
If (grade >= 0 && grade <= 100)
{
  total = total + grade;
  count++;
}
```

The Null Statement

All statements must be terminated by a semicolon. A semicolon with nothing preceding it is also a valid statement, called the **null statement.** Thus, the statement

```
;
```

is a null statement. This is a do-nothing statement that is used where a statement is syntactically required, but no action is called for. Null statements typically are used with either `while` or `for` statements. An example of a `for` statement that uses a null statement is found in Program 5.10c in the next section.

Exercises 5.3

1. Rewrite Program 5.6 to compute the total of eight numbers.
2. Rewrite Program 5.6 to display the prompt:

   `Please type in the total number of data values to be added:`

   In response to this prompt, the program should accept a userentered number and then use this number to control the number of times the `while` loop is executed. Thus, if the user enters 5 in response to the prompt, the program should request the input of five numbers and display the total after five numbers have been entered.
3. a. Write a C++ program to convert Celsius degrees to Fahrenheit. The program should request the starting Celsius value, the number of conversions to be made, and the increment between Celsius values. The display should have appropriate headings and list the Celsius value and the corresponding Fahrenheit value. Use the relationship *Fahrenheit = (9.0 / 5.0) * Celsius + 32.0.*

   b. Run the program written in Exercise 3a on a computer. Verify that your program starts at the correct starting Celsius value and contains the exact number of conversions specified in your input data.
4. a. Modify the program written in Exercise 3 to request the starting Celsius value, the ending Celsius value, and the increment. Thus, instead of the condition checking for a fixed count, the condition will check for the ending Celsius value.

   b. Run the program written in Exercise 4a on a computer. Verify that your output starts at the correct beginning value and ends at the correct ending value.
5. Rewrite Program 5.7 to compute the average of ten numbers.
6. Rewrite Program 5.7 to display the prompt:

   `Please type in the total number of data values to be averaged:`

   In response to this prompt, the program should accept a user-entered number and then use this number to control the number of times the `while` loop is executed. Thus, if the user enters 6 in response to the prompt, the program should request the input of six numbers and display the average of the next six numbers entered.
7. By mistake, a programmer put the statement `average = total / count;` within the `while` loop immediately after the statement `total = total + num;` in Program 5.7. Thus, the `while` loop becomes:

```
while (count <= MAXNUMS)
{
  cout << "Enter a number: ";
  cin  >> num;
  total = total + num;
  average = total / count;
  count++;
}
```

Will the program yield the correct result with this `while` loop? From a programming perspective, which `while` loop is better to use, and why?

8. An arithmetic series is defined by

$$a + (a + d) + (a + 2d) + (a + 3d) + \ldots + (a + (n - 1)d)$$

where a is the first term, d is the "common difference," and n is the number of terms to be added. Using this information write a C++ program that uses a `while` loop to display each term and determine the sum of the arithmetic series having $a = 1$, $d = 3$, and $n = 15$. Make sure that your program displays the value it has calculated.

9. A geometric series is defined by

$$a + ar + ar^2 + ar^3 + \ldots + ar^{n-1}$$

where a is the first term, r is the "common ratio," and n is the number of terms in the series. Using this information write a C++ program that uses a `while` loop to display each term and determine the sum of a geometric having $a = 1$, $r =$, and $n = 10$. Make sure that your program displays the value it has calculated.

10. In addition to the arithmetic average of a set of numbers, both a geometric and a harmonic mean can be calculated. The geometric mean of a set of n numbers x_1, x_2, . . . xn is defined as

$$\sqrt[n]{x_1 \cdot x_2 \cdot \ldots \cdot x_n}$$

and the harmonic mean as

$$\frac{n}{\frac{1}{x_1} + \frac{1}{x_2} + \ldots + \frac{1}{x_n}}$$

Using these formulas, write a C++ program that continues to accept numbers until the number 999 is entered, and then calculates and displays both the geometric and harmonic means of the entered numbers. (*Hint:* It will be necessary for your program to correctly count the number of values entered.)

11. a. The following data were collected on a recent automobile trip:

	Mileage	Gallons
Start of trip:	22495	Full tank
	22841	12.2
	23185	11.3
	23400	10.5
	23772	11.0
	24055	12.2
	24434	14.7
	24804	14.3
	25276	15.2

Write a C++ program that accepts mileage and gallons values and calculates the miles per gallon (mpg) achieved for that segment of the trip. The mpg is the difference in mileage between fill-ups divided by the number of gallons of gasoline used in the fill-up.

b. Modify the program written for Exercise 11a to additionally compute and display the cumulative mpg achieved after each fill-up. The cumulative mpg is the difference between each fill-up mileage and the mileage at the start of the trip divided by the sum of the gallons used to that point in the trip.

12. a. A bookstore summarizes its monthly transactions by keeping the following information for each book in stock:

    Book identification number
    Inventory balance at the beginning of the month
    Number of copies received during the month
    Number of copies sold during the month

    Write a C++ program that accepts these data for each book and then displays the book identification number and an updated book inventory balance using the relationship:

    new balance = inventory balance at the beginning of the month
    + number of copies received during the month
    − number of copies sold during the month

    Your program should use a `while` loop with a fixed count condition so that information on only three books is requested.

    b. Run the program written in Exercise 12a on a computer. Review the display produced by your program and verify that the output produced is correct.

13. Modify the program you wrote for Exercise 12a to keep requesting and displaying results until a sentinel identification value of 999 is entered. Run the program on a computer.

5.4 `for` LOOPS

In C++, a **`for` loop** is constructed using a `for` statement. This statement performs the same functions as the `while` statement, but it uses a different form. In many situations, especially those that use a fixed count condition, the `for` statement format is easier to use than its `while` statement equivalent.

The general form of the `for` statement is:

```
for (initializing list; expression; altering list) statement;
```

Although the `for` statement looks a little complicated, it is really quite simple if we consider each of its parts separately.

Within the parentheses of the `for` statement are three items, separated by semicolons. Each of these items is optional and can be described individually, but the semicolons must be present.

In its most common form, the initializing list consists of a single statement used to set the starting (initial) value of a counter, the expression contains the maximum or minimum value the counter can have and determines when the loop is finished, and the altering list provides the increment value that is added to or subtracted from the counter each time the loop is executed. Examples of simple `for` statements having this form are:

```
for (count = 1; count < 10; count = count + 1)
  cout << count;
```

and

```
for (i = 5; i <= 15; i = i + 2)
  cout << i;
```

In the first for statement, the counter variable is named count, the initial value assigned to count is 1, the loop continues as long as the value in count is less than 10, and the value of count is incremented by one each time through the loop. In the next for statement, the counter variable is named i, the initial value assigned to i is 5, the loop continues as long as i's value is less than or equal to 15, and the value of i is incremented by two each time through the loop. In both cases a cout statement is used to display the value of the counter. Another example of a for loop is given in Program 5.9.

PROGRAM 5.9

```
#include <iostream.h>
#include <iomanip.h>
#include <math.h>

const int MAXCOUNT = 5;

int main()
{
  int count;

  cout << "NUMBER     SQUARE ROOT\n";
  cout << "------     -----------\n";

  cout << setiosflags(ios::showpoint);
  for (count = 1; count <= MAXCOUNT; count++)
    cout << setw(4) << count
         << setw(15) << sqrt(count) << endl;

  return 0;
}
```

When Program 5.9 is executed, the following display is produced:

```
NUMBER   SQUARE ROOT
------   -----------
   1       1.000000
   2       1.414214
   3       1.732051
   4       2.000000
   5       2.236068
```

The first two lines displayed by the program are produced by the two cout statements placed before the for statement. The remaining output is produced by the for loop. This loop begins with the for statement and is executed as follows:

The initial value assigned to the counter variable count is 1. Since the value in count does not exceed the final value of 5, the execution of the cout statement within the loop produces the display

```
   1       1.000000
```

Control is then transferred back to the `for` statement, which then increments the value in count to 2, and the loop is repeated, producing the display

```
2      1.414214
```

This process continues until the value in `count` exceeds the final value of 5, producing the complete output table. For comparison purposes, a `while` loop equivalent to the `for` loop contained in Program 5.9 is:

```
count = 1
while (count <= MAXCOUNT)
{
  cout << setw(4) << count
       << setw(15) << setiosflags(ios::showpoint)
       << sqrt(count) << endl;
  count++;
}
```

As seen in this example, the difference between the `for` and `while` loops is the placement of the initialization, condition test, and incrementing items. The grouping of these items in the `for` statement is very convenient when fixed count loops must be constructed. See if you can determine the output produced by Program 5.10.

PROGRAM 5.10

```
#include <iostream.h>

int main()
{
  int count;

  for (count = 2; count <= 20; count = count + 2)
    cout << count << "  ";

  return 0;
}
```

Did you figure it out? The loop starts with a count initialized to 2, stops when count exceeds 20, and increments count in steps of 2. The output of Program 5.10 is

```
2 4 6 8 10 12 14 16 18 20
```

The `for` statement does not require that any of the items in parentheses be present or that they be used for initializing or altering the values in the expression statements. However, the two semicolons must be present within the `for`'s parentheses. For example, the construction for (; count <= 20 ;) is valid.

If the initializing list is missing, the initialization step is omitted when the `for` statement is executed. This, of course, means that the programmer must provide the required initializations before the `for` statement is encountered. Similarly, if the altering list is missing, any expressions needed to alter the evaluation of the tested expression must be included directly within the statement part of the loop.

The for statement only ensures that all expressions in the initializing list are executed once, before evaluation of the tested expression, and that all expressions in the altering list are executed at the end of the loop before the tested expression is rechecked. Thus, Program 5.10 can be rewritten in any of the three ways shown in Programs 5.10a, 5.10b, and 5.10c.

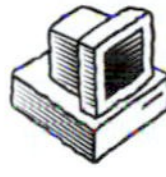

PROGRAM 5.10a

```
#include <iostream.h>

int main()
{
  int count;

  count = 2;     // initializer outside for statement
  for ( ; count <= 20; count = count + 2)
    cout << count << " ";

  return 0;
}
```

PROGRAM 5.10b

```
#include <iostream.h>

int main()
{
  int count;

  count = 2;     // initializer outside for loop
  for( ; count <= 20; )
  {
    cout << count << " ";
    count = count + 2;      // alteration statement
  }

  return 0;
}
```

In Program 5.10a, count is initialized outside the for statement and the first list inside the parentheses is left blank. In Program 5.10b, both the initializing list and the altering list are removed from within the parentheses. Program 5.10b also uses a compound statement within the for loop, with the expression-altering statement included in the compound statement. Finally, Program 5.10c has included all items within the parentheses, so there is no need for any useful statement following the parentheses. Here the null statement satisfies the syntactical requirement of one statement to follow the for's parentheses.

PROGRAM 5.10c

```
#include <iostream.h>

int main()    // all expressions within the for's parentheses
{
  int count;

  for (count = 2; count <= 20; cout << count << "  ", count = count + 2);

  return 0;
}
```

Observe also in Program 5.10c that the altering list (last set of items in parentheses) consists of two items, and that a comma has been used to separate these items. The use of commas to separate items in both the initializing and altering lists is required if either of these two lists contains more than one item. Last, note the fact that Programs 5.10a, 5.10b, and 5.10c are all inferior to Program 5.10 and although you may encounter them in your programming career, you should not use them. Adding items other than loop control variables and their updating conditions within the `for` statement tends to confuse its readability and can introduce unwanted effects. Keeping the loop control structure "clean," as is done in Program 5.10, is important and a good programming practice.

Although the initializing and altering lists can be omitted from a `for` statement, omitting the tested expression results in an infinite loop. For example, such a loop is created by the statement

```
for (count = 2; ; count = count + 1)
  cout << count;
```

As with the `while` statement, both `break` and `continue` statements can be used within a `for` loop. The `break` forces an immediate exit from the `for` loop, as it does in the `while` loop. The `continue`, however, forces control to be passed to the altering list in a `for` statement, after which the tested expression is reevaluated. This differs from the action of `continue` in a `while` statement, where control is passed directly to the reevaluation of the tested expression.

Figure 5.7 illustrates the internal workings of a `for` loop. As shown, when the `for` loop is completed, control is transferred to the first executable statement following the loop. To avoid the necessity of always illustrating these steps, a simplified set of flowchart symbols is available for describing `for` loops. Using the fact that a `for` statement can be represented by the flowchart symbol

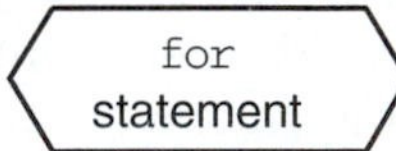

complete `for` loops can be alternatively illustrated as shown in Figure 5.8.

To understand the enormous power of `for` loops, consider the task of printing a table of numbers from 1 to 10, including their squares and cubes, using this statement. Such a table was previously produced using a `while` loop in Program 5.3. You may wish to review Program 5.3 and compare it to Program 5.11 to get a further sense of the equivalence between `for` and `while` loops.

FIGURE 5.7 `for` Loop Flowchart

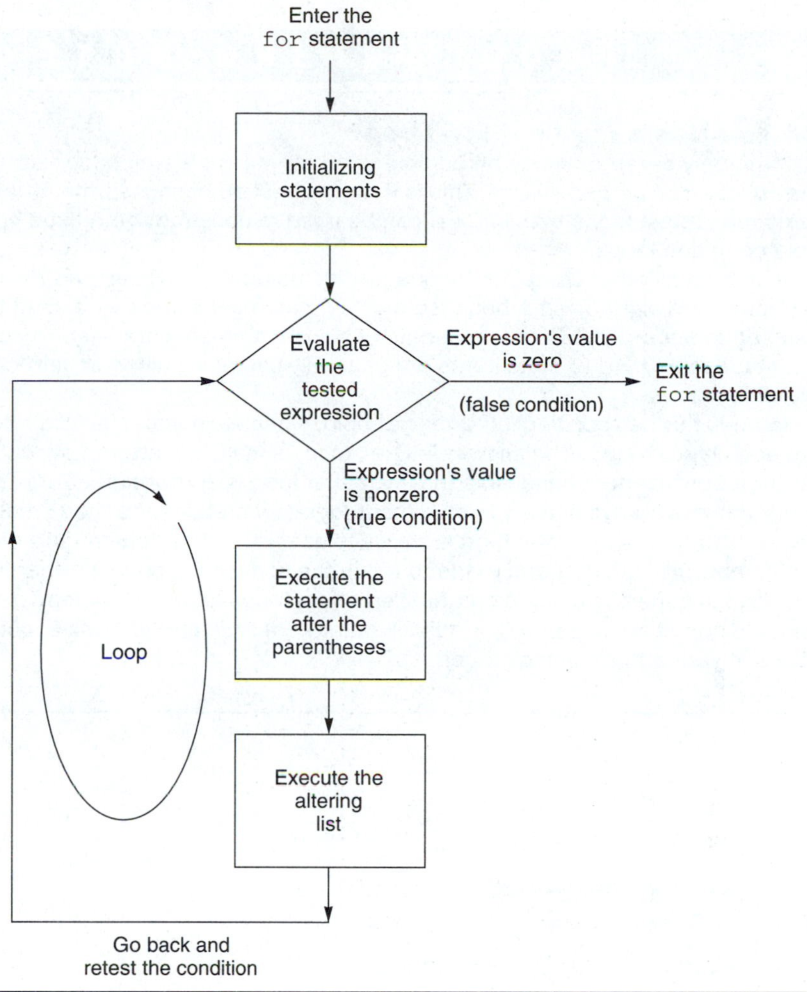

FIGURE 5.8 Simplified `for` Loop Flowchart

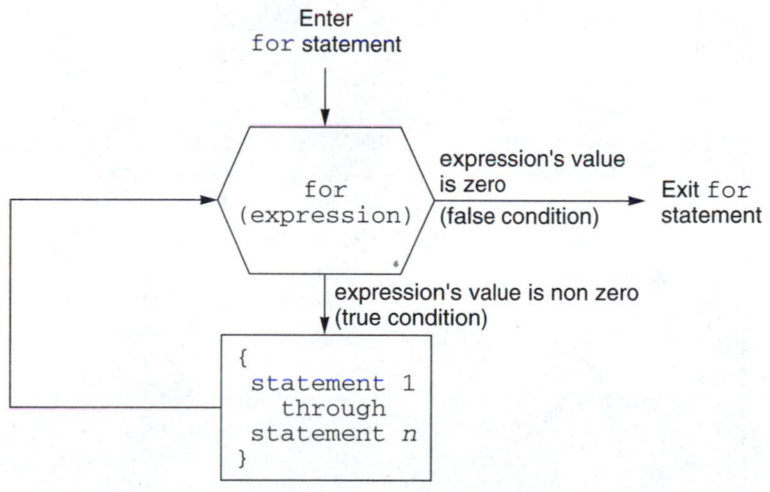

PROGRAMMING NOTE

Do You Use a `for` or `while` Loop?

A commonly asked question by beginning programmers is which loop structure should they use: a `for` or `while` loop? This is a good question because both of these loop structures are pretest loops that, in C++, can be used to construct both fixed count and variable condition loops.

In almost all other computer languages, including Visual Basic and Pascal, the answer is relatively straightforward, because the `for` statement can only be used to construct fixed count loops. Thus, in these languages `for` statements are used to construct fixed count loops and `while` statements are generally used only when constructing variable condition loops.

In C++, this easy distinction does not hold, since each statement can be used to create each type of loop. The answer in C++, then, is really a matter of style. Since `for` and `while` loops are interchangeable in C++, either loop is appropriate. Some professional programmers always use a `for` statement for every pretest loop they create and almost never use a `while` statement; others always use a `while` statement and rarely use a `for` statement. Still a third group tends to retain the convention used in other languages: A `for` loop is generally used to create fixed count loops and a `while` loop is used to create variable condition loops. In C++ it is all a matter of style and you will encounter all three styles in your programming career.

PROGRAM 5.11

```
#include <iostream.h>
#include <iomanip.h>

const int MAXNUMS = 10;

int main()
{

  int num;

  cout << "NUMBER     SQUARE     CUBE\n"
       << "------     ------     ----\n";

  for (num = 1; num <= MAXNUMS; num++)
    cout << setw(3) << num << "         "
         << setw(3) << num * num << "       "
         << setw(4) << num * num * num << endl;

  return 0;
}
```

PROGRAMMING NOTE

Where to Place the Opening Braces

There are two styles of writing for loops that are used by professional C++ programmers. These styles only come into play when the for loop contains a compound statement. The style illustrated and used in the text takes the form:

```
for (expression)
{
  compound statement in here
}
```

An equally acceptable style that is used by many programmers places the initial brace of the compound statement on the first line. Using this style, a for loop appears as:

```
for (expression) {
  compound statement in here
}
```

The advantage of the first style is that the braces line up under one another, making it easier to locate brace pairs. The advantage of the second style is that it makes the code more compact and saves a display line, permitting more code to be viewed in the same display area. Both styles are used but are almost never intermixed. Select whichever style appeals to you and be consistent in its use. As always, the indentation you use within the compound statement (two or four spaces, or a tab) should also be consistent throughout all of your programs. The combination of styles that you select becomes a "signature" for your programming work.

When Program 5.11 is run, the display produced is:

```
NUMBER    SQUARE    CUBE
------    ------    ----
   1         1         1
   2         4         8
   3         9        27
   4        16        64
   5        25       125
   6        36       216
   7        49       343
   8        64       512
   9        81       729
  10       100      1000
```

Simply changing the number 10 in the for statement of Program 5.11 to a 1000 creates a loop that is executed 1000 times and produces a table of numbers from 1 to 1000. As with the while statement this small change produces an immense increase in the processing and output provided by the program. Notice also that the expression ++num was used in the altering list in place of the usual num = num + 1.

Exercises 5.4

1. Write individual `for` statements for the following cases:

   a. Use a counter named `i` that has an initial value of 1, a final value of 20, and an increment of 1.

   b. Use a counter named `icount` that has an initial value of 1, a final value of 20, and an increment of 2.

   c. Use a counter named `j` that has an initial value of 1, a final value of 100, and an increment of 5.

   d. Use a counter named `icount` that has an initial value of 20, a final value of 1, and an increment of −1.

   e. Use a counter named `icount` that has an initial value of 20, a final value of 1, and an increment of −2.

   f. Use a counter named `count` that has an initial value of 1.0, a final value of 16.2, and an increment of 0.2.

   g. Use a counter named `xcnt` that has an initial value of 20.0, a final value of 10.0, and an increment of −0.5.

2. Determine the number of times each `for` loop is executed for the `for` statements written for Exercise 1.

3. Determine the value in `total` after each of the following loops is executed:

   a.
   ```
   total = 0;
   for (i = 1; i <= 10; i = i + 1)
     total = total + 1;
   ```

   b.
   ```
   total = 1;
   for (count = 1; count <= 10; count = count + 1)
     total = total * 2;
   ```

   c.
   ```
   total = 0;
   for ( i = 10; i <= 15; i = i + 1)
     total = total + i;
   ```

   d.
   ```
   total = 50;
   for (i = 1; i <= 10; i = i + 1)
     total = total - i;
   ```

   e.
   ```
   total = 1;
   for (icnt = 1; icnt <= 8; ++icnt)
     total = total * icnt;
   ```

   f.
   ```
   total = 1.0;
   for (j = 1; j <= 5; j++)
     total = total / 2.0;
   ```

4. Determine the output of the following program:

   ```
   #include <iostream.h>
   int main()
   {
     int i;

     for (i = 20; i >= 0; i = i - 4)
        cout << i << " ";

     return 0;
   }
   ```

5. Modify Program 5.11 to produce a table of the numbers 0 through 20 in increments of two, with their squares and cubes.

6. Modify Program 5.11 to produce a table of numbers from 10 to 1, instead of 1 to 10 as it currently does.

7. Write and run a C++ program that displays a table of 20 temperature conversions from Fahrenheit to Celsius. The table should start with a Fahrenheit value of 20 degrees and be incremented in values of 4 degrees. Recall that *Celsius* = *(5 .0/9.0)* * *(Fahrenheit* − *32)*.

8. Modify the program written for Exercise 7 to initially request the number of conversions to be made.

9. A programmer starts with a salary of $25,000 and expects to receive a $1500 raise each year.

   a. Write a C++ program to compute and print the programmer's salary for each of the first 10 years and the total amount of money the programmer would receive over the 10-year period.

   b. Write a C++ program to compute and print the programmer's salary for 10 years if the programmer begins at $25,000 and receives a 5% raise each year.

10. The probability that an individual telephone call will last less than t minutes can be approximated by the exponential probability function

$$\text{probability that a call lasts less than } t \text{ minutes} = 1 - e^{-t/a}$$

where a is the average call length and e is Euler's number (2.71828). For example, assuming that the average call length is 2 minutes, the probability that a call will last less than 1 minute is calculated as $1 - e^{-1/2} = 0.3297$.

Using this probability function, write a C++ program that calculates and displays a list of probabilities of a call lasting less than 1 to less than 10 minutes, in 1-minute increments.

11. a. The arrival rate of customers in a busy New York bank can be estimated using the Poisson probability function:

$$P(x) = \frac{\lambda^x e^{-2}}{x!}$$

where x = the number of customer arrivals per minute; λ = the average number of arrivals per minute; and e = Euler's number (2.71828). For example, if the average number of customers entering the bank is three customers per minute, then λ is equal to three. Thus,

$$\text{probability of one customer arriving in any one minute} =$$

$$P(x = 1) = \frac{3^1 e^{-3}}{1!} = 0.149361$$

and

$$\text{probability of two customers arriving in any one minute} =$$

$$P(x = 2) = \frac{3^2 e^{-3}}{2!} = 0.224042$$

Using the Poisson probability function, write a C++ program that calculates and displays the probability of 1 to 10 customer arrivals in any one minute when the average arrival rate is 3 customers per minute.

   b. The formula given in Exercise 11a is also applicable for estimating the arrival rate of planes at a busy airport (here, an arriving "customer" is an incoming airplane). Using this same formula, modify the program written in Exercise 11a to accept the average arrival rate as an input data item. Then run the modified program to determine the probability of 0 to 10 planes attempting to land in any one-minute period at an airport during peak arrival times. Assume that the average arrival rate for peak arrival times is 2 planes per minute.

A BIT OF BACKGROUND

The Blockhead

One mathematician of the Middle Ages who has had a profound influence on modern science is Leonardo of Pisa (1170–1250). In his youth he was called *Filus Bonacci,* which means "son of (Guglielmo) Bonacci," and the name "stuck." Hence, he is commonly known today as Fibonacci. He traveled widely, met with scholars throughout the Mediterranean area, and produced four very significant works on arithmetic and geometry. One of his discoveries is the sequence of numbers that bears his name: 0,1,1,2,3,5,8,13, ... After the first two values, 0 and 1, each number of the Fibonacci sequence is obtained from the sum of the preceding two numbers.

Fibonacci often referred to himself as Leonardo Bigollo, probably because *bigollo* is Italian for "traveler." However, another meaning of *bigollo* in Italian is "blockhead." Some people suspect he may have adopted this name to show the professors of his time what a blockhead—a person who had not been educated in their schools—could accomplish.

Some blockhead! The Fibonacci sequence alone describes such natural phenomena as the spiraling pattern of nautilus shells, elephant tusks, sheep horns, bird's claws, pineapples, branching patterns of plants, *and* the proliferation of rabbits. The ratio of successively higher adjacent terms in the sequence also approaches the "golden section," a ratio that describes an aesthetically pleasing proportion used in the visual arts.

12. Write and run a program that calculates and displays the amount of money available in a bank account that initially has $1000 deposited in it and that earns 8% interest a year. Your program should display the amount available at the end of each year for a period of 10 years. Use the relationship that the money available at the end of each year equals the amount of money in the account at the start of the year plus 0.08 times the amount available at the start of the year.

13. The Fibonacci sequence is 0, 1, 1, 2, 3, 5, 8, 13, . . . where the first two terms are 0 and 1, and each term thereafter is the sum of the two preceding terms; that is $Fib[n] = Fib[n-1] + Fib[n-2]$. Using this information, write a C++ program that calculates the n'th number in a Fibonacci sequence, where n is interactively entered into the program by the user. For example, if $n = 6$, the program should display the value 5.

14. A machine purchased for $28,000 is depreciated at a rate of $4000 a year for seven years. Write and run a C++ program that computes and displays a depreciation table for seven years. The table should have the form:

Depreciation Schedule

Year	Depreciation	End-of-Year Value	Accumulated Depreciation
1	4000	24000	4000
2	4000	20000	8000
3	4000	16000	12000
4	4000	12000	16000
5	4000	8000	20000
6	4000	4000	24000
7	4000	0	28000

15. A well-regarded manufacturer of widgets has been losing 4% of its sales each year. The annual profit for the firm is 10% of sales. This year the firm had $10 million in sales and a profit of $1 million. Determine the expected sales and profit for the next 10 years. Your program should complete and produce a display as follows:

Year	Sales and Profit Projection Expected Sales	Projected Profit
1	$10000000	$1000000
2	$ 9600000	$ 960000
3	.	.
.	.	.
.	.	.
.	.	.
10	.	.
Totals:	$.	$.

5.5 LOOP PROGRAMMING TECHNIQUES

In this section we present four common programming techniques associated with pretest (`for` and `while`) loops. All of these techniques are commonly used by experienced programmers.

Technique 1: Interactive Input Within a Loop

In Section 5.3 we presented the effect of including a `cin` statement within a `while` loop. Interactively entering data within a loop is a general technique that is equally applicable to `for` loops. For example, in Program 5.12 a `cin` statement is used to allow a user to input interactively a set of numbers. As each number is input, it is added to a total. When the `for` loop is exited, the average is calculated and displayed.

PROGRAM 5.12

```
#include <iostream.h>

const int MAXCOUNT = 5;

// This program calculates the average of MAXCOUNT
// user-entered numbers
int main()
{
  int count;
  float num, total, average;

  total = 0.0;

  for (count = 0; count < MAXCOUNT; count++)
  {
    cout << "Enter a number: ";
    cin  >> num;
    total = total + num;
  }

  average = total / MAXCOUNT;
  cout << "The average of the data entered is "
       << average << endl;

  return 0;
}
```

The `for` statement in Program 5.12 creates a loop that is executed five times. The user is prompted to enter a number each time through the loop. After each number is entered, it is immediately added to the total. Notice that `total` is initialized to zero as part of the `for` statement's initializing list is executed. The loop in Program 5.12 executes as long as the value in `count` is less than or equal to five, and is terminated when `count` becomes six (the increment to six, in fact, is what causes the loop to end).

Technique 2: Selection Within a Loop

Another common programming technique is to use either a `for` or `while` loop to cycle through a set of numbers and select those numbers that meet one or more criteria. For example, assume that we want to find both the positive and negative sum of a set of numbers. The criterion here is whether the number is positive or negative, and the logic for implementing this program is given by the following pseudocode:

While the loop condition is true
    Enter a number.
    If the number is greater than zero
        add the number to the positive sum.
    Else
        add the number to the negative sum.
EndWhile.

Program 5.13 describes this algorithm in C++ for a fixed count loop where five numbers are to be entered.

The following is a sample run of Program 5.13:

```
Enter a number (positive or negative) : 10
Enter a number (positive or negative) : -10
Enter a number (positive or negative) : 5
Enter a number (positive or negative) : -7
Enter a number (positive or negative) : 11
The positive total is 26.000000
The negative total is -17.000000
```

Technique 3: Evaluating Functions of One Variable

Loops can be conveniently constructed to determine and display the values of a single-variable mathematical function for a set of values over any specified interval. For example, assume that we want to know the values of the function

$$y = 10x^2 + 3x - 2$$

for x between 2 and 6. Assuming that x has been declared as an integer variable, the following `for` loop can be used to calculate the required values:

```
for (x = 2; x <= 6; ++x)
{
   y = 10 * pow(x,2) + 3 * x - 2;
   cout << setw(4) << x
      << setw(11) << y << endl;
}
```

PROGRAM 5.13

```
#include <iostream.h>

const int MAXNUMS = 5;

// this program computes the positive and negative sums of a set
// of MAXNUMS user entered numbers
int main()
{
  int i;
  float usenum, postot, negtot;

  postot = 0; // this initialization can be done in the declaration

  negtot = 0; // this initialization can be done in the declaration

  for (i = 1; i <= MAXNUMS; i++)
  {
    cout << "Enter a number (positive or negative) : ";
    cin  >> usenum;
    if (usenum > 0)
      postot = postot + usenum;
    else
      negtot = negtot + usenum;
  }
  cout << "The positive total is " << postot << endl;
  cout << "The negative total is " << negtot << endl;

  return 0;
}
```

For this loop we have used the variable x as both the counter variable and the unknown (independent variable) in the function. For each value of x from two to five a new value of y is calculated and displayed. This `for` loop is contained within Program 5.14, which also displays appropriate headings for the values printed.

The following is displayed when Program 5.14 is executed:

```
x value   y value
-------   -------
   2         44
   3         97
   4        170
   5        263
   6        376
```

Two items are of importance here. The first is that any equation with one unknown can be evaluated using a single `for` or an equivalent `while` loop. The method requires substituting the desired equation into the loop in place of the equation used in Program 5.14, and adjusting the counter values to match the desired solution range.

PROGRAM 5.14

```
#include <iostream.h>
#include <iomanip.h>
#include <math.h>

int main()
{
  int x, y;

  cout << "x value   y value\n";
  cout << "-------   -------\n";
  for (x = 2; x <= 6; x++)
  {
    y = 10 * pow(x,2) + 3 * x - 2;
    cout << setw(4) << x
         << setw(11) << y << endl;
  }

  return 0;
}
```

The second item of note is that we are not constrained to the use of integer values for the counter variable. For example, by specifying a noninteger increment, solutions for fractional values can be obtained. This is shown in Program 5.15, where the equation $y = 10x^2 + 3x - 2$ is evaluated in the range $x = 2$ to $x = 6$ in increments of 0.

PROGRAM 5.15

```
#include <iostream.h>
#include <iomanip.h>
#include <math.h>

int main()
{
  float x, y;

  cout << "x value      y value\n";
  cout << "-------      -------\n";
  cout << setiosflags(ios::showpoint);
  for (x = 2.0; x <= 6.0; x = x + 0.5)
  {
    y = 10.0 * pow(x,2.0) + 3.0 * x - 2.0;
    cout << setw(8) << x
         << setw(14) << y << endl;
  }

  return 0;
}
```

Notice that `x` and `y` have been declared as floating-point variables in Program 5.15 to allow these variables to take on fractional values. The following output is produced by this program:

```
x value        y value
--------      ---------
2.000000       44.000000
2.500000       68.000000
3.000000       97.000000
3.500000      131.000000
4.000000      170.000000
4.500000      214.000000
5.000000      263.000000
5.500000      317.000000
6.000000      376.000000
```

Technique 4: Interactive Loop Control

Values used to control a loop may be set using variables rather than constant values. For example, the four statements

```
i = 5;
j = 10;
k = 1;
for (count = i; count <= j; count = count + k)
```

produce the same effect as the single statement

```
for (count = 5; count <= 10; count = count + 1)
```

Similarly, the statements

```
i = 5;
j = 10;
k = 1;
count = i;
while (count <= j)
  count = count + k;
```

produce the same effect as the following `while` loop:

```
count = 5;
while (count <= 10)
  count = count + 1;
```

The advantage of using variables in the initialization, condition, and altering expressions is that it allows us to assign values for these expressions external to either the `for` or `while` statement. This is especially useful when a `cin` statement is used to set the actual values. To make this a little more tangible, consider Program 5.16.

PROGRAM 5.16

```
#include <iostream.h>
#include <iomanip.h>

// this program displays a table of numbers, their squares and cubes
// starting from the number 1. The final number in the table is
// input by the user

int main()
{
  int num, final;

  cout << "Enter the final number for the table: ";
  cin  >> final;

  cout << "NUMBER SQUARE CUBE\n";
  cout << "------ ------ ----\n";

  for (num = 1; num <= final; ++num)
    cout << setw(3) << num
         << setw(8) << num*num
         << setw(7) << num*num*num << endl;

  return 0;
}
```

In Program 5.16, we have used a variable to control both the condition (middle) and altering expressions. Here a `cin` statement has been placed before the loop to allow the user to decide what the final value should be. Notice that this arrangement permits the user to set the size of the table at run time, rather than having the programmer set the table size at compile time. This also makes the program more general, since it now can be used to create a variety of tables without being reprogrammed or recompiled.

Exercises 5.5

1. *cin within a loop:* Write and run a C++ program that accepts six Fahrenheit temperatures, one at a time, and converts each value entered to its Celsius equivalent before the next value is requested. Use a `for` loop in your program. The conversion required is *Celsius = (5.0 / 9.0) * (Fahrenheit − 32).*
2. *cin within a loop:* Write and run a C++ program that accepts 10 individual values of gallons, one at a time, and converts each value entered to its liter equivalent before the next value is requested. Use a `for` loop in your program. Use the fact that there are 3.785 liters in one gallon.
3. *Interactive loop control:* Modify the program written for Exercise 2 to initially request the number of data items that will be entered and converted.
4. *Interactive loop control:* Modify Program 5.13 so that the number of entries to be input is specified by the user when the program is executed.

5. *Selection:* Modify Program 5.13 so that it displays the average of the positive and negative numbers. (*Hint:* Be careful not to count the number zero as a negative number.) Test your program by entering the numbers 17, −10, 19, 0, and −4. The positive average displayed by your program should be 18 and the negative average, −7.

6. a. *Selection:* Write a C++ program that selects and displays the maximum value of five numbers that are to be entered when the program is executed. (*Hint*: Use a `for` loop with both a `cin` and an `if` statement internal to the loop.)

   b. Modify the program written for Exercise 6a so that it displays both the maximum value and the position in the input set of numbers where the maximum occurs.

7. *Selection:* Write a C++ program that selects and displays the first 20 integer numbers that are evenly divisible by 3.

8. *Selection:* A child's parents promised to give the child $10 on her twelfth birthday and double the gift on every subsequent birthday until the gift exceeded $1000. Write a C++ program to determine how old the girl will be when the last amount is given, and the total amount she received including the last gift.

9. *Mathematical functions:* Modify Program 5.15 to produce a table of Y values for the following:

   a. $y = 3x^5 - 2x^3 + x$
   for x between 5 and 10 in increments of .2

   b. $y = 1 + x + \frac{x^2}{2} + \frac{x^3}{6} + \frac{x^4}{24}$

   for x between 1 and 3 in increments of .1

   c. $y = 2e^{.8t}$

   for t between 4 and 10 in increments of .2

10. *Mathematical functions:* A model of worldwide population, in billions of people, is given by the equation

$$\text{population} = 4.88(1 + e^{0.02*t})$$

where t is the time in years (t = 0 represents January 1985 and t = 1 represents January 1986). Using this formula, write a C++ program that displays a yearly population table for the years January 1994 though January 2005.

11. *Mathematical functions:* The height, as a function of time t, of a projectile fired with an initial velocity v straight into the air is given by

$$\text{height} = vt - \tfrac{1}{2}gt^2$$

where g is the gravitational constant equal to 32.2 ft/sec^2. Using these formulas, write a C++ program that displays a table of heights for a projectile fired with an initial velocity of 500 ft/sec. The table should contain values corresponding to the time interval 0 to 10 seconds in increments of one-half seconds.

12. *Interactive loop control:* Modify Program 5.16 to accept the starting and increment values of the table produced by the program.

13. *Interactive loop control:* Write a C++ program that converts Fahrenheit to Celsius temperature in increments of 5 degrees. The initial value of the Fahrenheit temperature and the total conversions to be made are to be requested as user input during program execution. Recall that *Celsius = (5.0/9.0) * (Fahrenheit − 32.0).*

14. a. *Interactive loop control:* Modify the program written for Exercise 12 of Section 5.4 to initially prompt the user for the amount of money deposited in the account.

    b. Modify the program written for Exercise 14a to additionally prompt the user for the number of years that should be used.

    c. Modify the program written for Exercise 14a to additionally prompt the user for both the interest rate and the number of years to be used.

5.6 NESTED LOOPS

In many situations it is convenient to use a loop contained within another loop. Such loops are called **nested loops.** A simple example of a nested loop is:

```
for(i = 1; i <= 5; i++)            // start of outer loop
{                                           //
  cout << "\ni is now " << i << '\n'; //
                                     //
  for(j = 1; j <= 4; j++)          // start of inner loop
    cout << "  j = " << j;         // end of inner loop
}                                  // end of outer loop
```

The first loop, controlled by the value of `i`, is called the *outer loop*. The second loop, controlled by the value of `j`, is called the *inner loop*. Notice that all statements in the inner loop are contained within the boundaries of the outer loop and that we have used a different variable to control each loop. For each single trip through the outer loop, the inner loop runs through its entire sequence. Thus, each time the `i` counter increases by 1, the inner `for` loop executes completely. This situation is illustrated in Figure 5.9. Program 5.17 includes the preceding code in a working program.

PROGRAM 5.17

```
#include <iostream.h>

const int MAXI = 5;
const int MAXJ = 4;

int main()
{
  int i, j;

  for(i = 1; i <= MAXI; i++)      // start of outer loop
 {                                        //
    cout << "\ni is now " << i <<  endl; //
                                          //
    for(j = 1; j <= MAXJ; j++)    // start of inner loop
      cout << "  j = " << j;      // end of inner loop
  }                               // end of outer loop

  cout << endl;

  return 0;
}
```

The output of a sample run of Program 5.17 is:

```
i is now 1
  j = 1  j = 2  j = 3  j = 4
i is now 2
  j = 1  j = 2  j = 3  j = 4
```

FIGURE 5.9 For Each `i`, `j` Loops

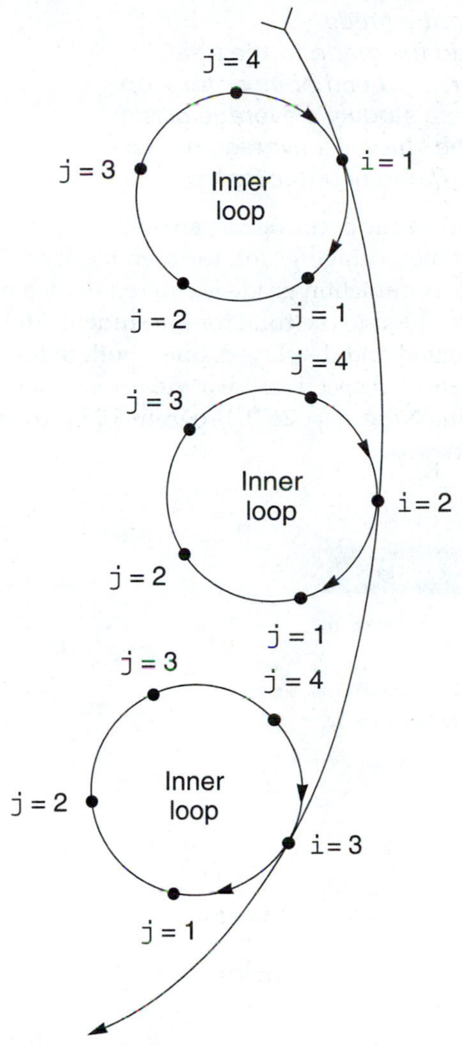


```
i is now 3
  j = 1  j = 2  j = 3  j = 4
i is now 4
  j = 1  j = 2  j = 3  j = 4
i is now 5
  j = 1  j = 2  j = 3  j = 4
```

To illustrate the usefulness of a nested loop, we will use one to compute the average grade for each student in a class of 20 students. Each student has taken four exams during the course of the semester. The final grade is calculated as the average of these examination grades. The following pseudocode describes how this computation can be done:

For 20 times
Set the student grade total to zero.
For 4 times
Input a grade.
Add the grade to the total.
EndFor // end of inner for loop
Calculate student's average grade.
Print the student's average grade.
EndFor // end of outer for loop

As described by the pseudocode, an outer loop consisting of 20 passes will be used to compute the average grade for each student. The inner loop will consist of 4 passes. One examination grade is entered in each inner loop pass. As each grade is entered it is added to the total for the student, and at the end of the loop the average is calculated and displayed. Since both outer and inner loops are fixed count loops of 20 and 4, respectively, we will use `for` statements to create these loops (see Programming Note on p. 262). Program 5.18 provides the C++ code corresponding to the pseudocode.

PROGRAM 5.18

```
#include <iostream.h>

const int NUMGRADES = 4;
const int NUMSTUDENTS = 2;

int main()
{

  int i,j;
  float grade, total, average;

  for (i = 1; i <= NUMSTUDENTS; i++) // start of outer loop
  {
    total = 0;                       // clear the total for this student
    for (j = 1; j <= NUMGRADES; j++) // start of inner loop
    {
      cout << "Enter an examination grade for this student: ";
      cin  >> grade;
      total = total + grade;         // add the grade into the total
    }                                // end of the inner for loop
    average = total / NUMGRADES;     // calculate the average
    cout << "\nThe average for student " << i
         << " is " << average << "\n\n";
  }                                  // end of the outer for loop

  return 0;
}
```

In reviewing Program 5.18, pay particular attention to the initialization of `total` within the outer loop, before the inner loop is entered. `total` is initialized 20 times, once for each student. Also notice that the average is calculated and displayed immediately after the inner loop is finished. Since the statements that compute and print the average are also contained within the outer loop, 20 averages are calculated and displayed. The entry and addition of each grade within the inner loop use techniques we have seen before, which should now be familiar to you.

Exercises 5.6

1. Four experiments are performed, each experiment consisting of six test results. The results for each experiment are given in the following list. Write a program using a nested loop to compute and display the average of the test results for each experiment.

1st experiment results:	23.2	31	16.9	27	25.4	28.6
2nd experiment results:	34.8	45.2	27.9	36.8	33.4	39.4
3rd experiment results:	19.4	16.8	10.2	20.8	18.9	13.4
4th experiment results:	36.9	39	49.2	45.1	42.7	50.6

2. Modify the program written for Exercise 1 so that the number of test results for each experiment is entered by the user. Write your program so that a different number of test results can be entered for each experiment.

3. a. A bowling team consists of five players. Each player bowls three games. Write a C++ program that uses a nested loop to enter each player's individual scores and then computes and displays the average score for each bowler. Assume that each bowler has the following scores:

1st bowler:	286	252	265
2nd bowler:	212	186	215
3rd bowler:	252	232	216
4th bowler:	192	201	235
5th bowler:	186	236	272

   b. Modify the program written for Exercise 3a to calculate and display the average team score. (*Hint:* Use a second variable to store the total of all the players' scores.)

4. Rewrite the program written for Exercise 3a to eliminate the inner loop. To do this, you will have to input three scores for each bowler rather than one at a time.

5. Write a program that calculates and displays values for Y when

$$Y = XZ/(X - Z)$$

Your program should calculate Y for values of X ranging between 1 and 5 and values of Z ranging between 2 and 6. X should control the outer loop and be incremented in steps of 1 and Z should also be incremented in steps of 1. Your program should also display the message `"FUNCTION UNDEFINED"` when the X and Z values are equal.

6. Write a program that calculates and displays the yearly amount available if $1000 is invested in a bank account for 10 years. Your program should display the amounts available for interest rates from 6% to 12% inclusively, in 1% increments. Use a nested loop, with the outer loop controlling the interest rate and the inner loop controlling the years. Use the relationship that the money available at the end of each year equals the amount of money in the account at the start of the year, plus the interest rate times the amount available at the start of the year.

7. In the Duchy of Upenchuck, the fundamental unit of currency is the Upenchuck dragon (UD). Income tax deductions are based on salary in units of 10,000 UD and on the number of dependents the employee has. The formula, designed to favor low-income families, is

$$\text{deduction (UD)} = \text{dependents} \times 500 + 0.05 \times (50{,}000 - \text{salary})$$

Beyond five dependents and beyond 50,000 UD, the deduction does not change. There is no tax, hence no deduction, on incomes of less than 10,000 UD. Based on this information, create a table of Upenchuck income tax deductions, with dependents 0 to 5 as the column headings and salary 10000, 20000, 30000, 40000, and 50000 as the rows.

5.7 do-while LOOPS

Both the `while` and `for` statements evaluate an expression at the start of the repetition loop; as such they are always used to create pretest loops. Post-test loops, which are also referred to as exit-controlled loops can also be constructed in C++. The basic structure of such a loop, which is referred to as a **do-while loop,** is illustrated in Figure 5.10. Notice that a `do-while` loop continues to iterate through the loop while the condition is true and exits the loop when the condition is false.

FIGURE 5.10 `do-while` **Loop Structure**

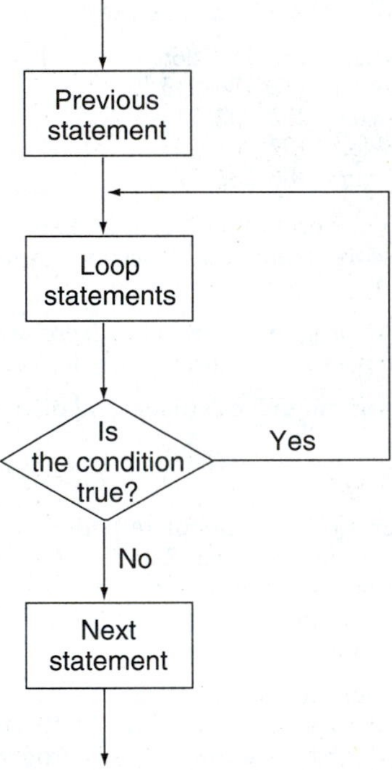

In C++, a post-test loop is created using a `do` statement. As its name implies, this statement allows us to do some statements before an expression is evaluated at the end of the loop. The general form of C++'s `do` statement is:

```
do
   statement;
while (expression);  <---------- do not forget the final ;
```

As with all C++ programs, the single statement in the do may be replaced with a compound statement. A flow control diagram illustrating the operation of the do statement is shown in Figure 5.11.

As illustrated, all statements within the do statement are executed at least once before the expression is evaluated. Then, if the expression has a nonzero value, the statements are executed again. This process continues until the expression evaluates to zero (becomes false). For example, consider the following do statement:

```
do
{
  cout << "\nEnter a price: ";
  cin >> price;
  if (abs(price - SENTINEL) < 0.0001)
    break;
  salestax = RATE * price;
  cout << setiosflags(ios::showpoint)
       << setprecision(2)
        << "The sales tax is $ " << salestax;
}
while (price != SENTINEL);
```

FIGURE 5.11 The do Statement's Flow of Control

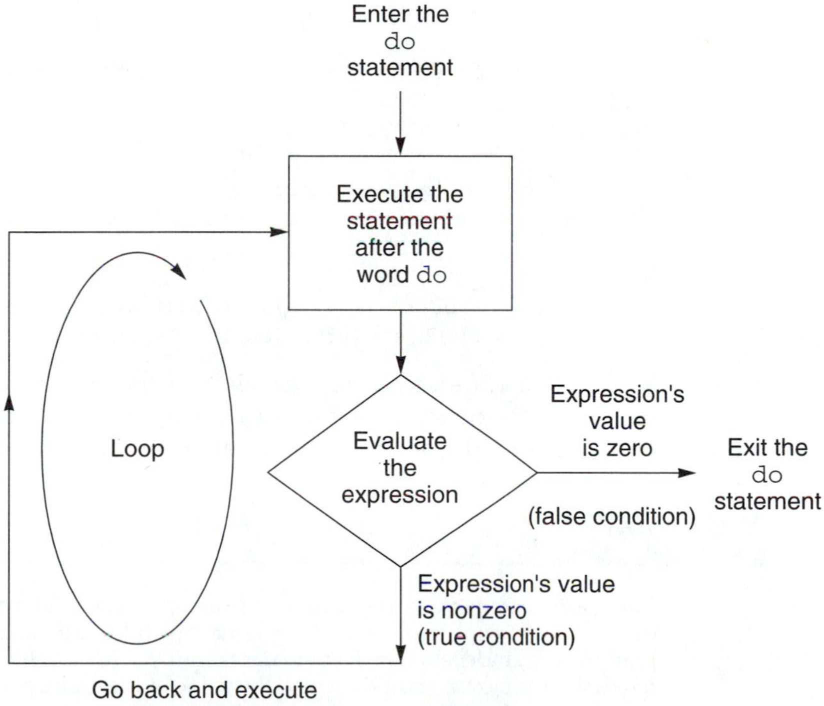

Observe that only one prompt and one cin statement are used here because the tested expression is evaluated at the end of the loop.

As with all repetition statements, the do statement can always replace or be replaced by an equivalent while or for statement. The choice of which statement to use depends on the application and the style preferred by the programmer. In general, the while and for statements are preferred because they clearly let anyone reading the program know what is being tested "right up front" at the top of the program loop.

Validity Checks

The do statement is particularly useful in filtering user-entered input and providing data validation checks. For example, assume that an operator is required to enter a valid customer identification number between the numbers 1000 and 1999. A number outside this range is to be rejected and a new request for a valid number made. The following section of code provides the necessary data filter to verify the entry of a valid identification number:

```
do
{
  cout << "\nEnter an identification number: ";
  cin >> id_num;
}
while (id_num < 1000 || id_num > 1999);
```

Here, a request for an identification number is repeated until a valid number is entered. This section of code is "bare bones" in that it neither alerts the operator to the cause of the new request for data nor allows premature exit from the loop if a valid identification number cannot be found. An alternative removing the first drawback is:

```
do
{
  cout << "\nEnter an identification number: ";
  cin >> id_num;
  if (id_num < 1000 || id_num > 1999)
  {
    cout << "An invalid number was just entered\n";
    cout << "Please check the ID number and re-enter\n";
  }
  else
    break;  // break if a valid id num was entered
} while(1); // this expression is always true
```

Here we have used a break statement to exit from the loop. Since the expression being evaluated by the do statement is always 1 (true), an infinite loop has been created that is only exited when the break statement is encountered.

Exercises 5.7

1. a. Using a do statement, write a program to accept a grade. The program should request a grade continuously as long as an invalid grade is entered. An invalid grade is any grade less than 0 or greater than 100. After a valid grade has been entered, your program should display the value of the grade entered.

b. Modify the program written for Exercise 1a so that the user is alerted when an invalid grade has been entered.

c. Modify the program written for Exercise 1b so that it allows the user to exit the program by entering the number 999.

d. Modify the program written for Exercise 1b so that it automatically terminates after five invalid grades have been entered.

2. a. Write a program that continuously requests a grade to be entered. If the grade is less than 0 or greater than 100, your program should print an appropriate message informing the user that an invalid grade has been entered, else the grade should be added to a total. When a grade of 999 is entered the program should exit the repetition loop and compute and display the average of the valid grades entered.

b. Run the program written in Exercise 2a on a computer and verify the program using appropriate test data.

3. a. Write a program to reverse the digits of a positive integer number. For example, if the number 8735 is entered, the number displayed should be 5378. [*Hint:* Use a `do` statement and continuously strip off and display the units digit of the number. If the variable `num` initially contains the number entered, the units digit is obtained as `(num % 10)`. After a units digit is displayed, dividing the number by 10 sets up the number for the next iteration. Thus, `(8735 % 10)` is 5 and `(8735 / 10)` is 873. The `do` statement should continue as long as the remaining number is not zero.]

b. Run the program written in Exercise 3a on a computer and verify the program using appropriate test data.

4. Repeat Exercise 5 in Section 5.4 using a `do` statement rather than a `for` statement.

5. Given a number n, and an approximation for its square root, a closer approximation to its actual square root can be obtained using the formula:

$$\text{new approximation} = \frac{(n/\text{previous approximation}) + \text{previous approximation}}{2}$$

Using this information, write a C++ program that prompts the user for a number and an initial guess at its square root. Using this input data your program should calculate an approximation to the square root that is accurate to 0.00001. (*Hint:* Stop the loop when the difference between the two approximations is less than 0.00001.)

6. Here is a challenging problem for those who know a little calculus. The Newton-Raphson method can be used to find the roots of any equation $y(x) = 0$. In this method the $(i + 1)$st approximation, x_{i+1}, to a root of $y(x) = 0$ is given in terms of the ith approximation, x_i, by the formula

$$x_{i+1} = x_i - y(x_i) \;/\; y'(x_i)$$

For example, if $y(x) = 3x^2 + 2x - 2$, then $y'(x) = 6x + 2$, and the roots are found by making a reasonable guess for a first approximation x_1, and iterating using the equation

$$x_{i+1} = x_i - (3x_i^2 + 2x_i - 2) \;/\; (6x_i + 2)$$

a. Using the Newton-Raphson method, find the two roots of the equation $3x^2 + 2x - 2 = 0$. (*Hint:* There is one positive root and one negative root.)

b. Extend the program written for Exercise 6a so that it will find the roots of any function $y(x) = 0$, when the function for $y(x)$ and the derivative of $y(x)$ are placed in the code.

5.8 PLANNING FOR OBJECTS: THE OBJECT MODELING TECHNIQUE

In terms of programming technologies, the object-oriented approach is a relative newcomer. As such, it is not surprising that a number of object-oriented analysis and design methods are currently being used.

Whichever analysis and design method is used, its primary purpose is to provide a coherent approach to describing the system being modeled. In our case an equally important purpose is to introduce the important aspects involved in performing an object-oriented analysis and design in an understandable way.

To meet these two objectives, we will use the object modeling technique (OMT).[3] This technique is reasonably easy to understand, supports all of the features required for a full object-oriented technology, and is becoming one of the dominant methods in actual use.

In essence an object-oriented analysis and design is always somewhat more complicated than a procedure-oriented analysis. This is because a strictly procedure-oriented approach is limited to specifying the sequence of transformations required in producing outputs from inputs. In an object orientation this focus is shifted and enlarged. Although the analysis becomes more complicated, the resulting program design should yield less complicated code that can be more easily reused and extended. Specifically, an object-oriented analysis requires you to understand and specify:

- the objects in the system
- what can happen to these objects
- when it happens.

In an OMT analysis, each of these three items is addressed by its own model. An *object model* is used to describe the objects in the system. This includes the attributes and operations for each type of objects and the relationship between different object types. A *functional model* is used to describe what can happen to an object. This model is procedural in nature and defines the algorithms applicable to each object. Finally a *dynamic model* is used to describe when things happen to the objects. Although each of these models contains information present in the other two models, each model emphasizes a different aspect of the system. As such, each model simply views the same system from a different angle and highlights a particular aspect of the system (see Figure 5.12).

Of the three models, object, functional, and dynamic, the most important and useful is the object model, which is described in this section (the other two models are essentially adjuncts to the object model that are required for more complicated systems.) The object model highlights both the objects in a system and what can happen to them. For many systems, this description is more than sufficient for design and implementation purposes.

Object Diagrams

In the OMT method the object model is described by an object diagram. An *object diagram* graphically illustrates objects, classes, and the relationships between them. Object diagrams can be of two types: class or instance diagrams. Class diagrams

[3] Rumbaugh, J., M. Blaha, W. Premerlani, *et al.*, *Object-Oriented Modeling and Design*, Prentice Hall, Englewood Cliffs, NJ, 1991.

FIGURE 5.12 Three Views of the Same System

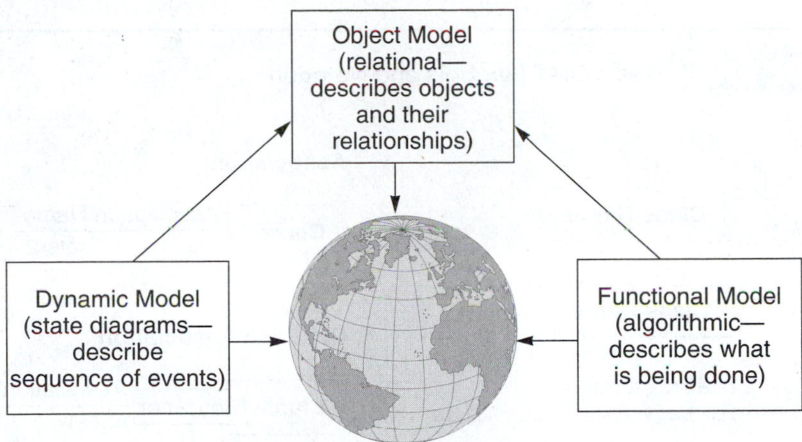

are used to describe classes, and instance diagrams are used to describe the relationship between specific objects. Before we proceed, let's make sure we are clear about the difference between objects and classes. (Review Section 1.5 for a more complete description.)

Formally, an object refers to a specific, single item. For example, this book is a specific object. A class refers to a type of object, of which many specific objects can exist. For example, a class of books might be described by its type (fiction or nonfiction), of which many specific instances, or objects, exist. Thus, it is always the class that is the abstraction. A *class* describes the properties (attributes) and operations (behavior) that each object must have to be a member of the class.

An *attribute* is simply a data value that each object in the class must have. For example, title and author are attributes of Book objects, while name, age, sex, weight, and height are attributes of Person objects. Once data values are assigned to attributes, a unique object is created. Note that objects have *identities,* in that one object can be distinguished from another object of the same class. This is not true of a pure data value, such as the number 5, where all occurrences of this number are indistinguishable from one another.

In OMT a class is represented by a box and a specific instance of the class, which is an object, by a rounded box. The class name is always listed at the top of a class box and within parentheses at the top of an object box. For example, Figure 5.13 illustrates the representation of a Person class, along with one Person object. The basic symbols and notations used in construction object diagrams, including the class symbol shown in Figure 5.13, are presented in Figure 5.14.

FIGURE 5.13 A Class and Object Representation

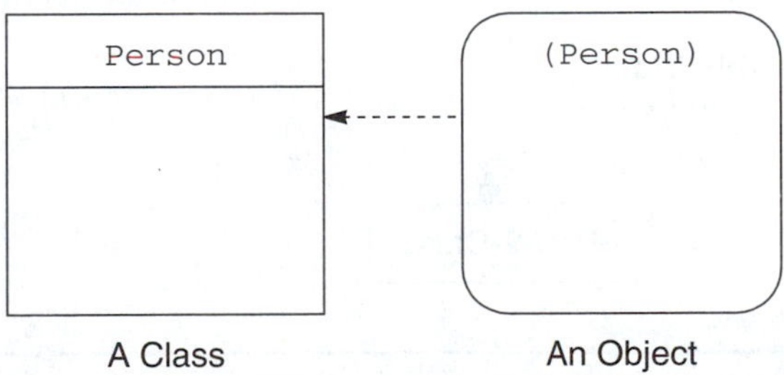

FIGURE 5.14 Basic OMT Symbols and Notation

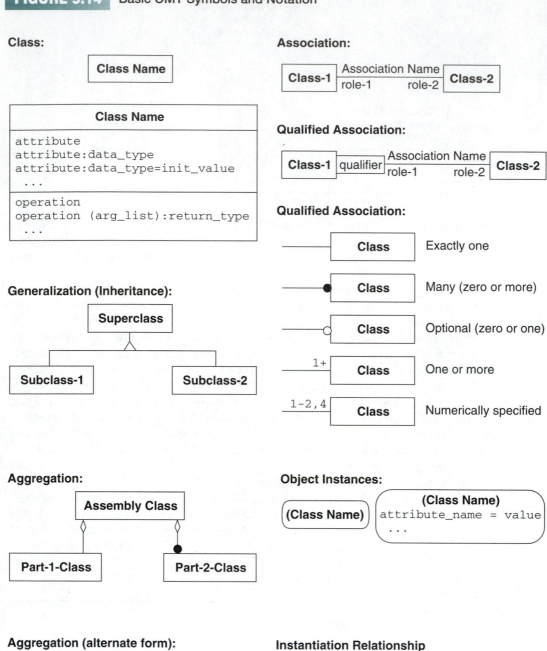

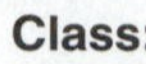

Class:

Class Name

Class Name

```
attribute
attribute:data_type
attribute:data_type=init_value
 ...
operation
operation (arg_list):return_type
 ...
```

Generalization (Inheritance):

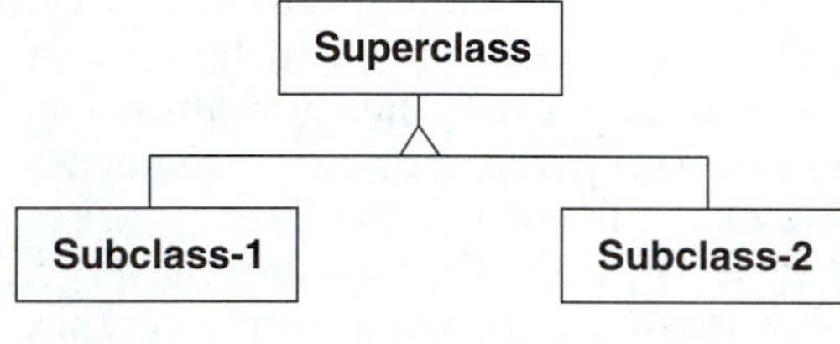

Aggregation:

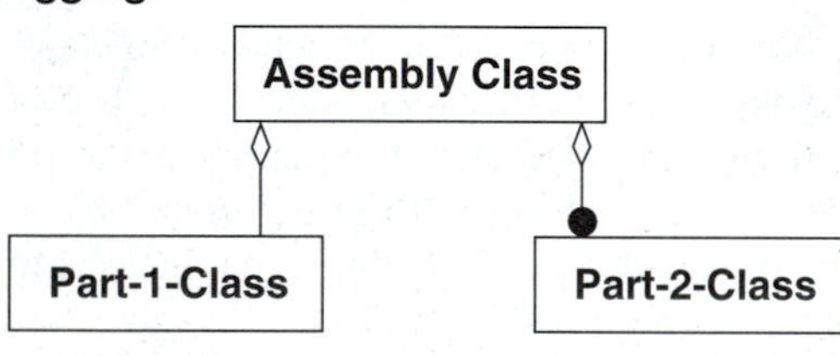

Aggregation (alternate form):

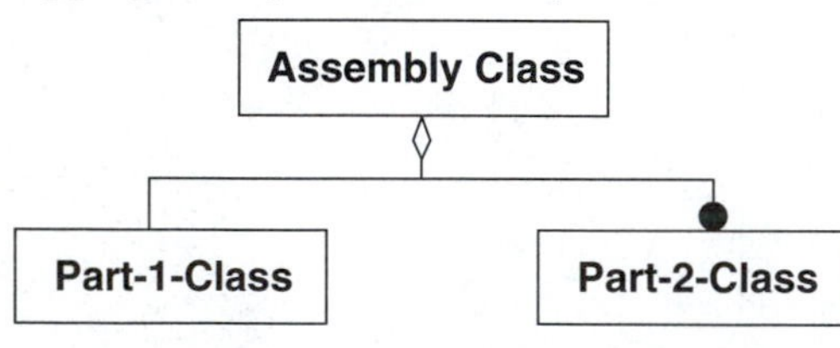

Association:

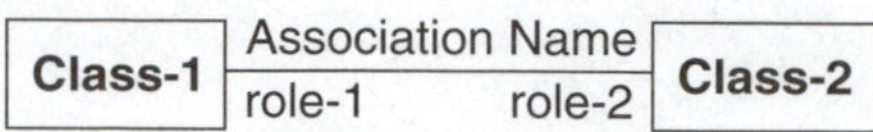

Qualified Association:

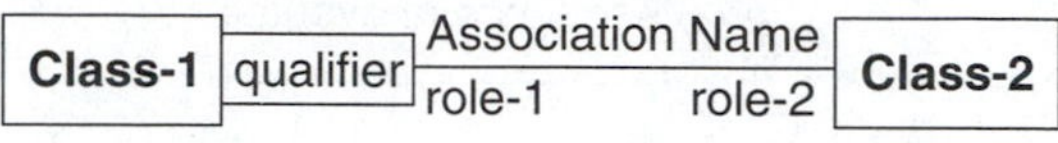

Qualified Association:

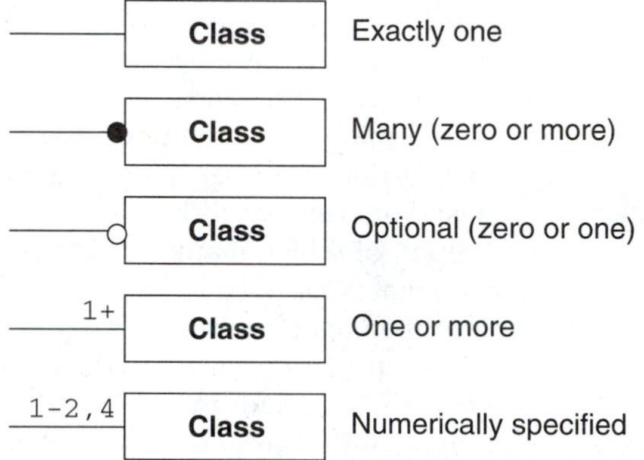

Object Instances:

Instantiation Relationship

Once the attributes of a class have been identified, they are listed in a class box below the class name, separated by a line. Specific objects are shown in a similar manner, with data values listed instead of attribute names. For example, Figure 5.15 shows the attributes and values associated with the class Country and two Country objects.

FIGURE 5.15 Including Attributes in the Object Diagram

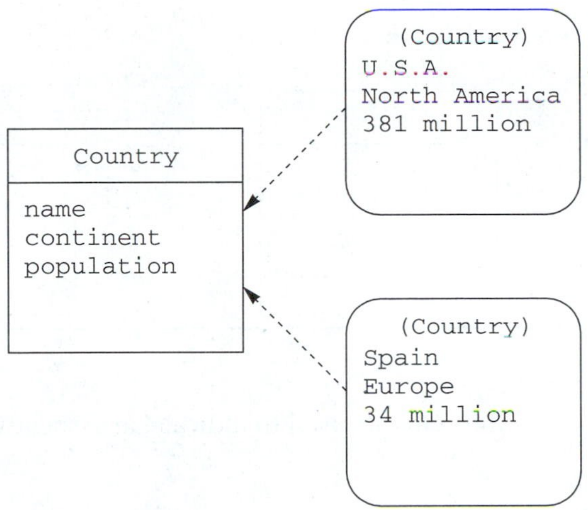

Just as attributes can be designated on an object diagram, so can operations. *Operations* are transformations that can be applied to attributes. Operation names are listed in a class box below the attributes and separated from them by a line. Figure 5.16 illustrates two object diagrams that include operations.

FIGURE 5.16 Including Operations in the Object Diagram

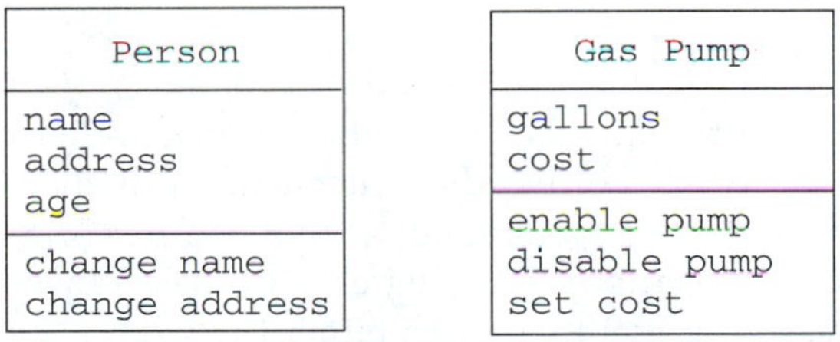

Person
name address age
change name change address

Gas Pump
gallons cost
enable pump disable pump set cost

Relationships

Besides graphically describing classes and objects, OMT object diagrams describe the relationships existing between classes and objects. The three basic relationships are association, aggregation, and generalization.

Associations between classes are typically signified by phrases such as "is related to," "is associated with," "has a," "is employed by," "works for," etc. This type of association between classes or objects is indicated by a straight line connecting the two classes or object, where the type of association is listed above and/or below the line. For example, Figure 5.17 shows an association between a Person and a Company. As indicated, a Person is "employed by" a Company, and a Company "employs" zero or more Persons. The designation of "zero or more," which is referred to as the multiplicity of the relationship, is indicated by the filled in circle at the end of the line.

FIGURE 5.17 An Association

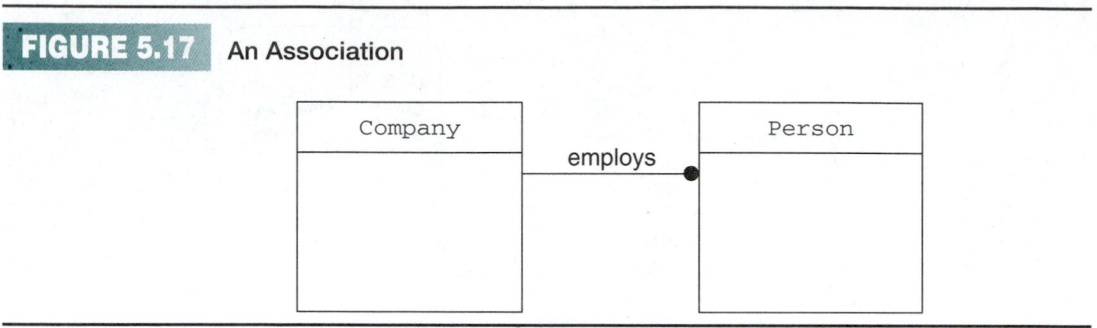

Table 5.1 lists the symbols used to indicate an association's multiplicity.

TABLE 5.1 Multiplicity Relationships

Symbol	Relationship
——	Exactly one
——●	Zero or more
——○	Zero or one
——1+	One or more
——1,2,4	Numerically specified

An *aggregation* is a particular type of an association where one object "consists of" or, alternatively, "is composed of" another type of object. For example, a sentence consists of words, which consist of characters. This type of association is indicated by a diamond symbol. Figures 5.18 and 5.19 illustrates two aggregation associations. Reading each of these object diagrams is much easier if you replace the diamond with either the words "consists of" or "is composed of."

The last type of relationship we consider is the generalization, which is more commonly referred to as an inheritance. *Generalization* is a relationship between a class and a derived version of the class. The initial class that is used as the basis for the derived class is referred to as either the *base, parent,* or *superclass.* The derived class is referred to as either *derived,* the *child,* or *subclass.*

For example, a derived class of a Vehicle base class can be either a Land, Space, or Water version. In this case, Vehicle would be the base class, and Land, Space, and Water are the derived classes. Figure 5.20 shows how this generalization relationship is illustrated using an object diagram.

FIGURE 5.18 Single-Level Aggregation

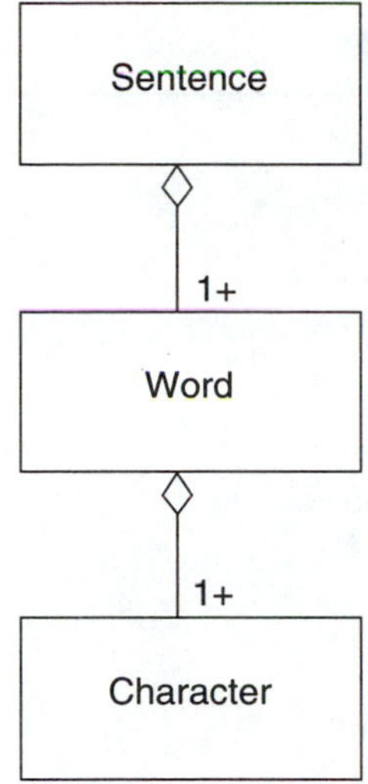

FIGURE 5.19 Multilevel Aggregation

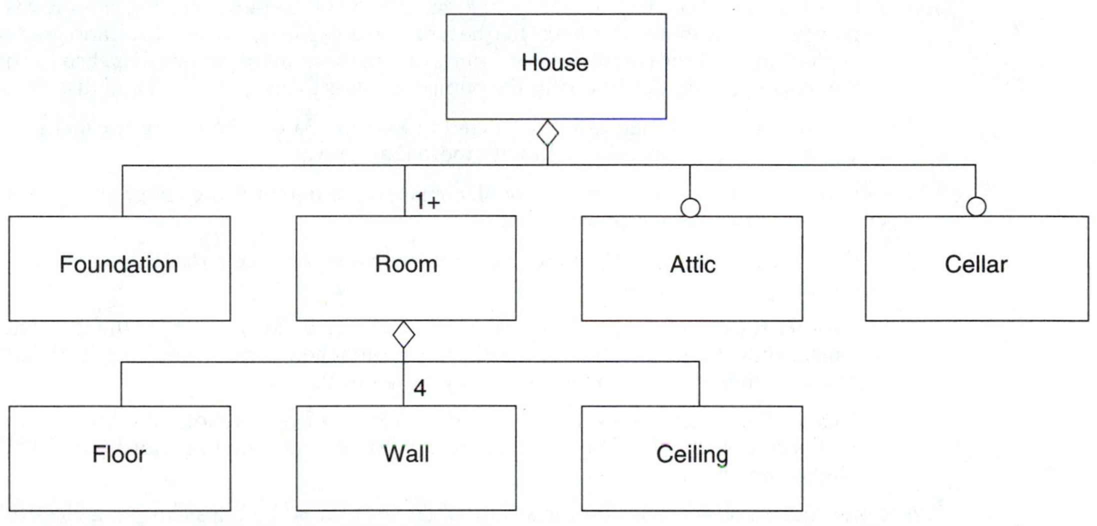

FIGURE 5.20 A Generalization Relationship

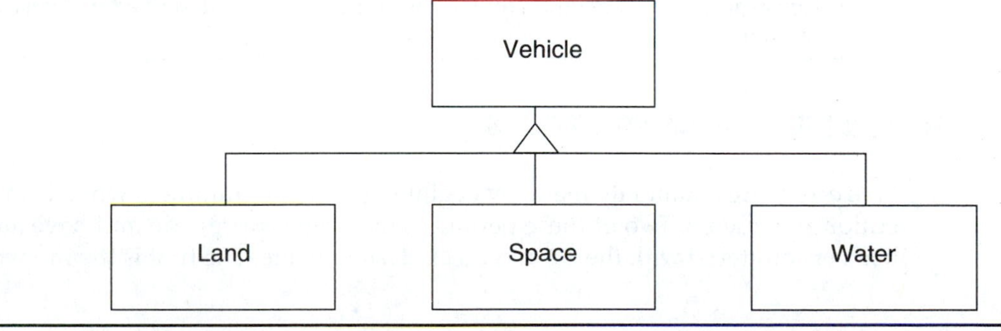

Exercises 5.8

1. Define the terms:
   a. aggregation
   b. association
   c. class
   d. dynamic model
   e. functional model
   f. generalization
   g. inheritance
   h. multiplicity
   i. object
   j. object diagram
   k. object model
2. Construct an object diagram for a Country class. Each Country has a capital city. The attributes of interest for each Country are its population, size, main agricultural product, and main manufactured product.
3. a. Construct an object diagram for a single gas tank that is connected to one or more gas pumps. The attributes of interest for the tank are its capacity, current level, and grade of gas. The attributes of interest for a pump are the amount of gallons dispensed and the cost per gallon. Additionally, the pump responds to being enabled and disabled.
   b. Modify the object diagram constructed in Exercise 3a to account for the fact that a gas pump may be associated with more than one gas tank.
4. Construct an object diagram for a book consisting of one or more chapters, each of which consists of one or more sections.
5. a. Construct an object diagram for a computer that consists of a monitor, keyboard, mouse, printer, and system box.
   b. Modify the object diagram constructed in Exercise 5a to account for the fact that one or more monitors and keyboards may be attached to the system box and that the system may have no mouse or may have multiple mice.
   c. Extend the object diagram constructed for Exercise 5b to denote that the system box is composed of a CPU chip, a memory board containing zero or more RAM chips, and one case.
6. Construct an object diagram for a class of circles that is the base class to a class of spheres and a class of cylinders.
7. Construct an object diagram for a collection of cards that consists of zero or more individual cards. The collection of cards forms a base class for both a deck of cards and an individual hand of cards.
8. Construct an object diagram for the gas pumping system described in Exercise 13 in Section 4.9.

5.9 COMMON PROGRAMMING ERRORS

Five errors are commonly made by beginning C++ programmers when using repetition statements. Two of these pertain to the tested expression and have already been encountered with the `if` and `switch` statements. The first is the inadvertent use of the assignment operator = for the equality operator == in the tested expression. An example of this error is typing the assignment expression `a = 5` instead of the desired relational expression `a == 5`. Since the tested expression can be any valid C++ expression, including arithmetic and assignment expressions, this error is not detected by the compiler.

As with the `if` statement, repetition statements should not use the equality operator == when testing floating-point or double-precision operands. For example, the expression `fnum == 0.01` should be replaced by a test requiring that the absolute value of `fnum - 0.01` be less than an acceptable amount. The reason for this is that all numbers are stored in binary form. Using a finite number of bits, decimal numbers such as .01 have no exact binary equivalent, so that tests requiring equality with such numbers can fail.

The next two errors are particular to the `for` statement. The most common is to place a semicolon at the end of the `for`'s parentheses, which frequently produces a do-nothing loop. For example, consider these statements:

```
for(count = 0; count < 10; count++);
  total = total + num;
```

Here the semicolon at the end of the first line of code is a null statement. This has the effect of creating a loop that is executed 10 times with nothing done except the incrementing and testing of `count`. This error tends to occur because C++ programmers are used to ending most lines with a semicolon.

The next error occurs when commas are used to separate the items in a `for` statement instead of the required semicolons. An example of this is the statement

```
for (count = 1, count < 10, count++)
```

Commas are used to separate items within the initializing and altering lists, but semicolons must be used to separate these lists from the tested expression.

The last error occurs when the final semicolon is omitted from the `do` statement. This error is usually made by programmers who have learned to omit the semicolon after the parentheses of a `while` statement and carry over this habit when the reserved word `while` is encountered at the end of a `do` statement.

5.10 CHAPTER REVIEW

Key Terms

`break` statement
`continue` statement
counter
data validation
`do-while` loop
fixed count loop
`for` loop
infinite loop
nested loop
null statement
post-test loop
pretest loop
repetition statement
sentinel
variable condition loop
`while` loop

Summary

1. A section of repeating code is referred to as a loop. The loop is controlled by a repetition statement that tests a condition to determine whether the code will be executed. Each pass through the loop is referred to as a repetition or iteration. The tested condition must always be explicitly set prior to its first evaluation by the repetition statement. Within the loop there must always be a statement that permits altering of the condition so that the loop, once entered, can be exited.

2. There are three basic type of loops: `while`, `for`, and `do-while`.

   The `while` and `for` loops are *pretest* or *entrance-controlled loops*. In this type of loop the tested condition is evaluated at the beginning of the loop, which requires that the tested condition be explicitly set prior to loop entry. If the condition is true, loop repetitions begin; otherwise the loop is not entered. Iterations continue as long as the condition remains true. In C++, `while` and `for` loops are constructed using `while`, and `for` statements, respectively.

   The `do-while` loop is a *post-test* or *exit-controlled loop*, where the tested condition is evaluated at the end of the loop. This type of loop is always executed at least once. `do-while` loops continue to execute as long as the tested condition remains true.

3. Loops are also classified as to the type of tested condition. In a *fixed count loop*, the condition is used to keep track of how many repetitions have occurred. In a *variable condition loop* the tested condition is based on a variable that can change interactively with each pass through the loop.

4. In C++, a `while` loop is constructed using a `while` statement. The most commonly used form of this statement is:

```
while (expression)
{
  statements;
}
```

   The expression contained within parentheses is the condition tested to determine if the statement following the parentheses, which is generally a compound statement, is executed. The expression is evaluated in exactly the same manner as that contained in an `if-else` statement; the difference is how the expression is used. In a `while` statement the statement following the expression is executed repeatedly as long as the expression retains a nonzero value, rather than just once, as in an `if-else` statement. An example of a `while` loop is:

```
count = 1;                  // initialize count
while (count <= 10)
{
  cout << count << "  ";
  count++;                    // increment count
}
```

The first assignment statement sets count equal to 1. The while statement is then entered and the expression is evaluated for the first time. Since the value of count is less than or equal to 10, the expression is true and the compound statement is executed. The first statement in the compound statement uses the cout object to display the value of count. The next statement adds 1 to the value currently stored in count, making this value equal to 2. The while statement now loops back to retest the expression. Because count is still less than or equal to 10, the compound statement is again executed. This process continues until the value of count reaches 11.

The while statement always checks its expression at the top of the loop. This requires that any variables in the tested expression must have values assigned before the while is encountered. Within the while loop there must be a statement that alters the tested expression's value.

5. In C++, a for loop is constructed using a for statement. This statement performs the same functions as the while statement, but uses a different form. In many situations, especially those that use a fixed count condition, the for statement format is easier to use than its while statement equivalent. The most commonly used form of the for statement is:

```
for (initializing list; expression; altering list)
{
  statements;
}
```

Within the parentheses of the for statement are three items, separated by semicolons. Each of these items is optional but the semicolons must be present.

The initializing list is used to set any initial values before the loop is entered; generally it is used to initialize a counter. Statements within the initializing list are only executed once. The expression in the for statement is the condition being tested: It is tested at the start of the loop and prior to each iteration. The altering list contains loop statements that are not contained within the compound statement; generally it is used to increment or decrement a counter each time the loop is executed. Multiple statements within a list are separated by commas. An example of a for loop is:

```
for (total = 0, count = 1; count < 10; count++)
{
  cout << "Enter a grade: ";
  cin  << grade;
  total = total + grade;
}
```

In this for statement, the initializing list is used to initialize both total and count. The expression determines that the loop will execute as long as the value in count is less than 10, and the value of count is incremented by one each time through the loop.

6. The for statement is extremely useful in creating fixed count loops. This is because the initializing statements, the tested expression, and statements affecting the tested expression can all be included in parentheses at the top of a for loop for easy inspection and modification.

7. The do statement is used to create post-test loops because it checks its expression at the end of the loop. This ensures that the body of a do loop is executed at least once. Within a do loop there must be at least one statement that alters the tested expression's value.

Exercises

1. Write sections of C++ code to do the following:
   a. Display the multiples of 3 backward from 33 to 3, inclusive.
   b. Display the capital letters of the alphabet backward from Z to A.
2. Write, run, and test a C++ program to find the value of $2n$ using a `for` loop where n is an integer value entered by the user at the keyboard. (*Hint:* Initialize result = 1 and then let result = 2 * result.)
3. The value of Euler's number e, can be approximated using the formula

$$e = 1 + 1/1! + 1/2! + 1/3! + 1/4! + 1/5! + \ldots.$$

   Using this formula, write a C++ program that approximates the value of e using a `while` loop that terminates when the difference between two successive approximations differs by less than 1.0E−6.
4. Using the formula provided in Exercise 3, determine how many terms are needed to approximate the value returned by the intrinsic `exp()` function with an error less than 1.0E−6. [*Hint:* Use a `while` loop that terminates when the difference between the value returned by the `exp()` function and the approximation is less than 1.0E−6.]
5. a. The outstanding balance on Rhona Karp's car loan is $5000. Each month Rhona is required to make a payment of $300, which includes both interest and principal repayment of the car loan. The monthly interest is calculated as 0.09/12 of the outstanding balance of the loan. After the interest is deducted, the remaining part of the payment is used to pay off the loan. Using this information, write a C++ program that produces a table indicating the beginning monthly balance, the interest payment, the principal payment, and the remaining loan balance after each payment is made. Your output should resemble and complete the entries in the following table until the outstanding loan balance is zero.

Beginning Balance	Interest Payment	Principal Payment	Ending Loan Balance
5000.00	37.50	121.50	4878.50
4874.50	36.59	122.41	4756.09
4756.09	.	.	.
.	.	.	.
.	.	.	.
.	.	.	0.000000

   b. Modify the program written in Exercise 5a to display the total of the interest and principal paid at the end of the table produced by your program.

6. The monthly payment due on an outstanding car loan is typically calculated using the formula:

$$\text{Monthly payment} = \frac{(\text{loan amount})\ (\text{monthly interest rate})}{1.0 - (1.0 + \text{Monthly interest rate})^{-(\text{number of months})}}$$

where

Monthly interest rate = Annual percentage rate/(12.0 * 100)

Using these formulas write, run, and test a C++ program that prompts the user for the amount of the loan, the annual percentage rate, and the number of years of the loan. From this input data produce a loan amortization table similar to the one shown below:

What is the amount of the loan? $ 1500.00
What is the annual percentage rate? 14.0
How many years will you take to pay back the loan? 1.0

Amount	Annual % Interest	Years	Monthly Payment
1500.00	14.00	1	134.68

Payment Number	Interest Paid	Principal Paid	Cumulative Interest	Total Paid to Date	New Balance Due
1	17.50	117.18	17.50	134.68	1382.82
2	16.13	118.55	33.63	269.36	1264.27
3	14.75	119.93	48.38	404.04	1144.34
4	13.35	121.33	61.73	538.72	1023.01
5	11.94	122.75	73.67	673.40	900.27
6	10.50	124.18	84.17	808.08	776.09
7	9.05	125.63	93.23	942.76	650.46
8	7.59	127.09	100.81	1077.45	523.37
9	6.11	128.57	106.92	1212.13	394.79
10	4.61	130.07	111.53	1346.81	264.72
11	3.09	131.59	114.61	1481.49	133.13
12	1.55	133.13	116.17	1616.17	0.00

In constructing the loop necessary to produce the body of the table, the following initializations must be made:

New balance due = original loan amount
Cumulative interest = 0.0
Paid to date = 0.0
Payment number = 0

Within the loop the following calculations and accumulations should be used:

Payment number = payment number + 1
Interest paid = new balance due * monthly interest rate
Principal paid = monthly payment − interest paid
Cumulative interest = cumulative interest + interest paid
Paid to date = paid to date + monthly payment
New balance due = new balance due − principal paid

7. Modify the program written for Exercise 6 to prevent the user from entering an illegal value for the interest rate. That is, write a loop that asks the user repeatedly for the annual interest rate until a value between 1.0 and 20.0 is entered.

8. In the hypothetical Republic of Dwump, the basic unit of currency is the dwork, and the exchange rate at present is 27 dworks per U.S. dollar. Develop, run, and test a C++ program to create a table of dollars versus dworks in steps of $0.25 from `MinDollars` to `MaxDollars`, where values for these two variables will be entered by the user at the keyboard. The exchange rate (27 dworks per dollar) and the step value (0.25) should be declared as named constants, so that they can be found and changed easily. The exchange rate should be displayed at the head of the output table, and the columns `Dollars` and `Dworks` should be labeled.
9. Develop, test, and execute a C++ program that uses a `while` loop to determine the smallest integer power of 3 that exceeds 30,000. That is, find the smallest value of n such that $3^n > 30{,}000$. (*Hint*: Initialize PowerOfThree = 1 and then let PowerOfThree = 3 * PowerOfThree.)
10. A prime integer number is one that has exactly two different divisors, namely, 1 and the number itself. Write, run, and test a C++ program that finds and prints all the prime numbers less than 100. [*Hint:* 1 is a prime number. For each number from 2 to 100, find `Remainder = Number % n`, where `n` ranges from 2 to sqrt(number). If `n` is greater than `sqrt(number)`, then the number is not equally divisible by `n`. (Why?) If any Remainder equals 0, then the number is not a prime number.]
11. Print the decimal, octal, and hexadecimal values of all characters between the start and stop characters entered by a user. For example, if the user enters an `'a'` and a `'z'` the program should print all the characters between `a` and `z` and their respective values. Make sure that the second character entered by the user occurs later in the alphabet than the first character. If it does not, write a loop that asks the user repeatedly for a valid second character.
12. Create a table of selling price versus purchase price. Have the user enter the range of purchase prices (from lowest to highest), the percent markup, and the increment between purchase prices. Display the table of purchase prices and selling prices on the screen, with appropriate headings. The formula for calculating the selling price from the purchase price are:

```
Markup fraction = Percent markup / 100.0
Selling price = (1.0 + Markup fraction) * Purchase price
```

13. The quotient in long division is the number of times the divisor can be subtracted from the dividend. The remainder is what is left over after the last subtraction. Write a C++ program that performs division using this method.
14. Write a C++ program that uses iteration to accumulate the sum $1 + 2 + 3 + \ldots + N$, where N is a user-entered integer number. Then evaluate the expression $N(N + 1)/2$ to verify that this expression yields the same result as the iteration.
15. a. An old Arabian legend has it that a fabulously wealthy but unthinking king agreed to give a beggar one cent and double the amount for 64 days. Using this information write, run, and test a C++ program that displays how much the king must pay the beggar on each day. The output of your program should appear as follows:

```
Day     Amount Owed
---     -----------
 1         0.01
 2         0.02
 3         0.04
 .          .
 .          .
 .          .
64          .
```

b. Modify the program you wrote for Exercise 15b to determine on which day the king will have paid a total of one million dollars to the beggar.

16. According to legend the island of Manhattan was purchased from the Native American population in 1626 for $24. Assuming that this money was invested in a Dutch bank paying 5 percent simple interest per year, construct a table showing how much money the Native Americans would have at the end of each 20-year period starting in 1626 and ending in 2006.

Improving Communication

17. MEMORANDUM

To: Chief Programmer
From: Head of Programming Dept.

Subject: Object-Oriented Analysis

Please explain to me why the structured top-down analysis and design approach that we have been using cannot be used after we switch to an OOP environment.

18. MEMORANDUM

To: Chief Programmer
From: Head of Programming Dept.

Subject: Objects and Values

Please explain to me the difference between the values we have been using in our programs and objects. For example, is the string "England" an object or a value?

Working in Teams

19. Have the team as a group determine a car's major subsystems, such as brakes, steering, etc. Then, considering these subsystems as classes, construct an object diagram for a Car class that simply shows the associations between classes (no attributes or operations). Assign each subsystem to individual team members. Have them determine a set of attributes and oper-

ations appropriate to the assigned subsystem. When each member has completed the task, modify the original object diagram to include the additional information.

20. Have the team as a group determine a cellular telephone's major subsystems, such as keypad, antenna, etc. Then, considering these subsystems as classes, construct an object diagram for a Cellular class that simply shows the associations between classes (no attributes or operations). Assign each subsystem to individual team members. Have them determine a set of attributes and operations appropriate to the assigned subsystem. When each member has completed the task, modify the original object diagram to include the additional information.

CHAPTER

6 Modularity Using Functions

Professional programs are designed, coded, and tested very much like hardware, as a set of modules that are integrated to perform a completed whole. A good analogy of this is an automobile in which one major module is the engine, another is the transmission, a third the braking system, a fourth the body, and so on. Each of these modules is linked and ultimately placed under the control of the driver, which can be compared to a supervisor or main program module. The whole now operates as a complete unit that is able to do useful work, such as driving to the store. During the assembly process, each module is individually constructed, tested, and found to be free of defects (bugs) before it is installed in the final product.

Now think of what you might do if you wanted to improve your car's performance. You might alter the existing engine or remove it altogether and bolt in a new engine. Similarly, you might change the transmission or tires or shock absorbers, making each modification individually as your time and budget allowed. In each case the majority of the other modules can stay the same, but the car now operates differently.

A BIT OF BACKGROUND

Subprograms

Although the concepts are similar, user-defined program units are generically referred to as *subprograms*, but are called by different names in different programming languages. C++ language subprograms are all referred to as *functions.* In Pascal they are named *procedures* and *functions.* Modula-2 names them *PROCEDURES* (even though some of them are actual functions). COBOL refers to them as *paragraphs*, and FORTRAN and BASIC refer to them as *subroutines* and *functions.*

In this analogy, each of the major components of a car can be compared to a function. For example, the driver calls on the engine when the gas pedal is pressed. The engine accepts inputs of fuel, air, and electricity to turn the driver's request into a useful product—power—and then sends this output to the transmission for further processing. The transmission receives the output of the engine and converts it to a form that can be used by the drive axle. An additional input to the transmission is the driver's selection of gears (drive, reverse, neutral, etc.).

In each case, the engine, transmission, and other modules only "know" the universe bounded by their inputs and outputs. The driver need know nothing of the internal operation of the engine, transmission, air conditioning, or other modules that are being controlled. All that is required is an understanding of *what* each unit does and *how* to use it. The driver simply "calls" on a module, such as the engine, brakes, air conditioning, or steering, when that module's output is required. Communication between modules is restricted to passing needed inputs to each module as it is called on to perform its task, and each module operates internally in a relatively independent manner. This same modular approach is used by engineers to create and maintain reliable C++ programs using functions.

As we have seen, each C++ program must contain a `main()` function. In addition to this required function, C++ programs can also contain any number of additional functions. In this chapter we learn how to write these functions, pass data to them, process the passed data, and return a result.

6.1 FUNCTION AND ARGUMENT DECLARATIONS

In creating C++ functions we must be concerned with both the function itself and how it interacts with other functions, such as `main()`. These concerns include correctly passing data into a function when it is called and returning values from a function. In this section we describe the first part of the interface, passing data to a function and having the function correctly receive, store, and process the transmitted data.

As we have already seen with mathematical functions, a function is called, or used, by giving the function's name and passing any data to it, as arguments, in the parentheses following the function name (see Figure 6.1).

FIGURE 6.1 Calling and Passing Data to a Function

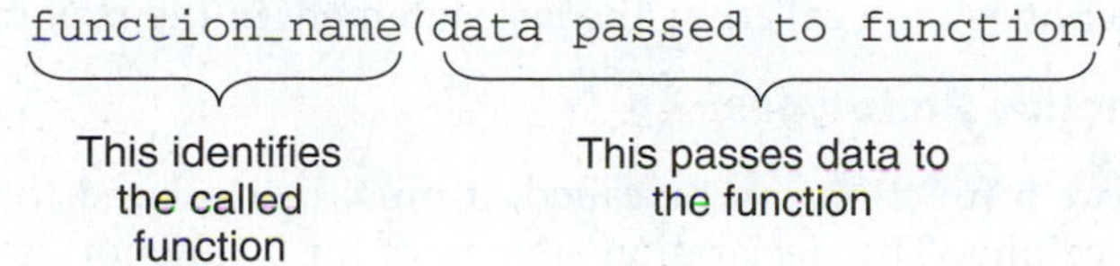
function_name(data passed to function);
This identifies the called function
This passes data to the function

The called function must be able to accept the data passed to it by the function doing the calling. Only after the called function successfully receives the data can the data be manipulated to produce a useful result.

To clarify the process of sending and receiving data, consider Program 6.1, which calls a function named `FindMax()`. The program, as shown, is not yet complete. Once the function `FindMax()` is written and included in Program 6.1, the completed program, consisting of the functions `main()` and `FindMax()`, can be compiled and executed.

PROGRAM 6.1

```
#include <iostream.h>

void FindMax(int, int);  // the function declaration (prototype)

int main()
{
  int firstnum, secnum;

  cout << "\nEnter a number: ";
  cin  >> firstnum;
  cout << "Great! Please enter a second number: ";
  cin  >> secnum;

  FindMax(firstnum, secnum); // the function is called here

  return 0;
}
```

Let us examine the declaration and calling of the function `FindMax()` from `main()`. We will then write `FindMax()` to accept the data passed to it and determine the largest or maximum value of the two passed values.

The function `FindMax()` is referred to as the **called function,** since it is called or summoned into action by its reference in `main()`. The function that does the calling, in this case `main()`, is referred to as the **calling function.** The terms called and calling come from standard telephone usage, where one party calls the other on a telephone.

The called function, `FindMax()` in this case, is declared as a function that expects to receive two integer numbers and to return no value (a void) to `main()`. This declaration is formally referred to as a function prototype. The function is then called by the last statement in the program.

Function Prototypes

Before a function can be called, it must be declared to the function that will do the calling. The declaration statement for a function is referred to as a **function prototype.** The function prototype tells the calling function the type of value that will be formally returned, if any, and the data type and order of the values that the calling function should transmit to the called function. For example, the function prototype previously used in Program 6.1

```
void FindMax(int, int);
```

declares that the function `FindMax()` expects two integer values to be sent to it, and that this particular function formally returns no value (void). Function prototypes may be placed with the variable declaration statements of the calling function, above the calling function name, as in Program 6.1, or in a separate header file that will be included using an `#include` preprocessor statement. Thus, the function prototype for `FindMax()` could have been placed either before or after the statement `#include <iostream.h>`, prior to `main()`, or within `main()`. (The reasons for the choice of placement are presented in Section 6.3.) The syntax of function prototype statements is:

```
return-data-type function-name(list of argument data types);
```

where `data-type` refers to the data type of the value that will be formally returned by the function.

Examples of function prototypes are:

```
int fmax(int, int);
float swap(int, char, char, double);
void display(double, double);
```

The function prototype for `fmax()` declares that this function expects to receive two integer arguments and will formally return an integer value. The function prototype for `swap()` declares that this function requires four arguments consisting of an integer, two characters, and a double-precision argument, in that order, and will formally return a floating-point number. Finally, the function prototype for `display()` declares that this function requires two double-precision arguments and does not return any value. Such a function might be used to display the results of a computation directly, without returning any value to the called function.

The use of function prototypes permits error checking of data types by the compiler. If the function prototype does not agree with data types defined when the function is written, an error message (typically `Undefined symbol`) will occur. The prototype also serves another task; it ensures conversion of all arguments passed to the function to the declared argument data type when the function is called.

Calling a Function

Calling a function is a rather easy operation. The only requirements are that the name of the function be used and that any data passed to the function be enclosed within the parentheses following the function name using the same order and type as declared in the function prototype. The items enclosed within the parentheses are called **actual arguments** of the called function (see Figure 6.2).

FIGURE 6.2 Calling and Passing Two Values to `FindMax()`

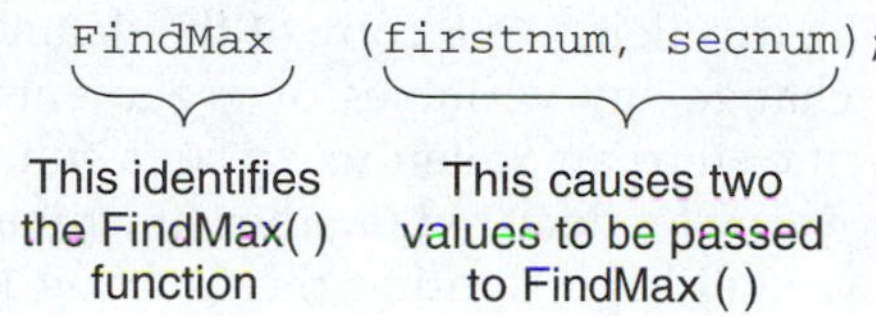

If a variable is one of the actual arguments in a function call, the called function receives a copy of the value stored in the variable. For example, the statement `FindMax(firstnum,secnum);` calls the function `FindMax()` and causes the values currently residing in the variables `firstnum` and `secnum` to be passed to `FindMax()`. The variable names in parentheses are actual arguments that provide values to the called function. After the values are passed, control is transferred to the called function.

As illustrated in Figure 6.3, *the function* `FindMax()` *does not receive the variable names* `firstnum` *and* `secnum` *and has no knowledge of these variable names.*[1] The function simply receives the values in these variables and must itself determine

FIGURE 6.3 `FindMax()` Receives Actual Values

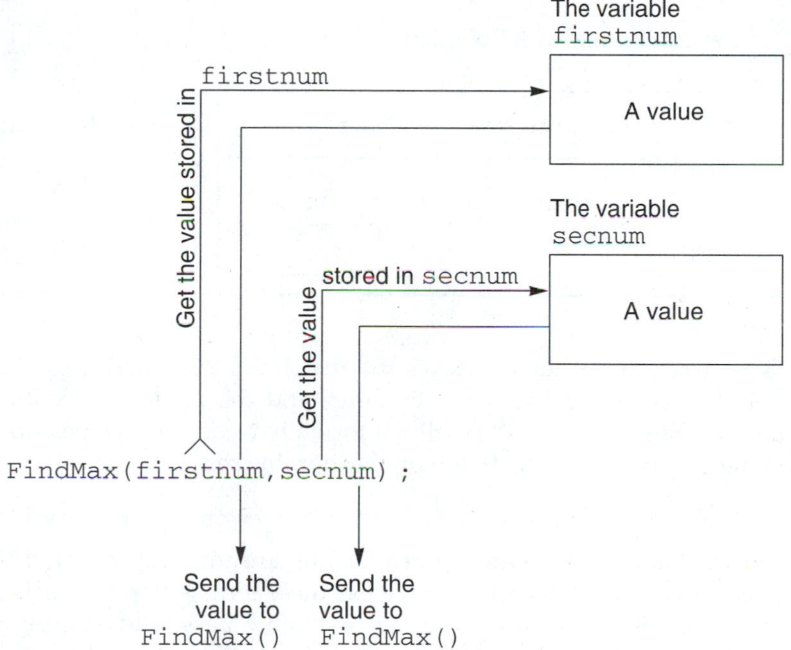

[1] This is significantly different from computer languages such as FORTRAN, where functions and subroutines receive access to the variable and can pass data back through them. In Section 6.5 we will see how, using reference variables, C++ can also permit direct access to the calling function's variables.

where to store these values before it does anything else. Although this procedure for passing data to a function may seem surprising, it is really a safety procedure for ensuring that a called function does not inadvertently change data stored in a variable. The function gets a copy of the data to use. It may change its copy and, of course, change any variables or arguments declared inside itself. However, unless specific steps are taken to do so, a function is not allowed to change the contents of variables declared in other functions.

Now we will begin writing the function `FindMax()` to process the values passed to it.

Defining a Function

A function is defined when it is written. Each function is defined once (that is, written once) in a program and can then be used by any other function in the program that suitably declares it.

Like the `main()` function, every C++ function consists of two parts, a **function header** and a **function body,** as illustrated in Figure 6.4. The purpose of the function header is to identify the data type of the value returned by the function, provide the function with a name, and specify the number, order, and type of arguments expected by the function. The purpose of the function body is to operate on the passed data and directly return, at most, one value to the calling function. (We will see, in Section 6.5, how a function can be made to return multiple values through the parameter list.)

FIGURE 6.4 General Format of a Function

```
function header line                    } Function header
{
  variable declarations;                } Function body
  any other C++ statements;
}
```

The function header is always the first line of a function and contains the function's returned value type, its name, and the names and data types of its arguments. Since `FindMax()` will not formally return any value and is to receive two integer arguments, the following header line can be used:

```
void FindMax(int x, int y)   <----------  No semicolon
```

The argument names in the header line are formally referred to as **formal parameters** or **formal arguments;** we use these terms interchangeably.[2] Thus, the argument `x` will be used to store the first value passed to `FindMax()` and the argument `y` will be used to store the second value passed at the time of the function call. The function does not know where the values come from when the call is made from `main()`. The first part of the call procedure executed by the com-

[2] The portion of the function header that contains the function name and parameters is formally referred to as a *function declarator.*

puter involves going to the variables `firstnum` and `secnum` and retrieving the stored values. These values are then passed to `FindMax()` and ultimately stored in the formal arguments `x` and `y` (see Figure 6.5).

FIGURE 6.5 Storing Values into Parameters

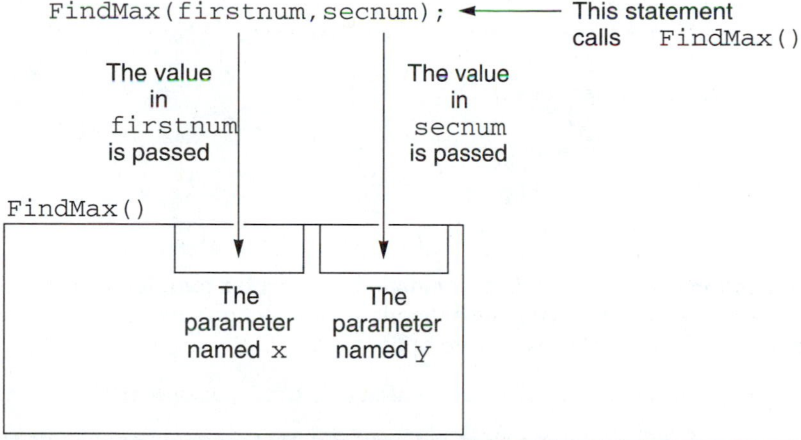

The function name and all parameter names in the header line, in this case `FindMax`, `x`, and `y`, are chosen by the programmer. Any names selected according to the rules used to choose variable names can be used. All parameters listed in the function header line must be separated by commas and must have their individual data types declared separately.

Now that we have written the function header for the `FindMax()` function, we can construct its body. Let us assume that the `FindMax()` function selects and displays the larger of the two numbers passed to it.

As illustrated in Figure 6.6, a function body begins with an opening brace, `{`, contains any necessary variable declarations and other C++ statements, and ends with a closing brace, `}`. This should be familiar to you because it is the same structure used in all the `main()` functions we have written. This should not be a surprise, because `main()` is itself a function and must adhere to the rules required for constructing all legitimate functions.

In the body of the function `FindMax()`, we will declare one variable to store the maximum of the two numbers passed to it. We will then use an `if-else`

FIGURE 6.6 Structure of a Function Body

```
{
    Variable declarations and
    other C++ statements
}
```

POINT OF INFORMATION

Function Definitions and Function Prototypes

A **function definition** defines a function. Thus, when you write a function, you are really writing a function definition. Each definition begins with a header line that includes a formal parameter list, if any, enclosed in parentheses and ends with the closing brace that terminates the function's body. The parentheses are required whether or not the function uses any parameters. The syntax for a function definition is:

```
return-data-type function-name(parameter list)
{
  variable declarations

  other C++ statements

  return value
}
```

A **function prototype** declares a function. The syntax for a function prototype, which provides the return data type of the function, the function's name, and a list of parameter data types (parameter names are optional) is:

```
return-data-type function-name(list of parameter data types);
```

As such, the prototype along with pre and postcondition comments (see Point of Information box on p. 307) should provide a user with all the programming information needed to successfully call the function.

Generally, all functions prototypes are placed at the top of the program, and all definitions are placed after the main( ) function. However, this placement can be changed. The only requirement in C++ is that a function cannot be called before it has been either declared or defined.

statement to find the maximum of the two numbers. Finally, a `cout` object stream will be used to display the maximum. The complete function definition for the `FindMax()` function is:

```
void FindMax(int x, int y)
{                      // start of function body
  int maxnum;          // variable declaration

  if (x >= y)          // find the maximum number
     maxnum = x;
  else
     maxnum = y;

  cout << "\nThe maximum of the two numbers is "
       << maxnum << endl;

  return;

} // end of function body and end of function
```

Notice that the parameter declarations are made within the header line and the variable declaration is made immediately after the opening brace of the function's body. This is in keeping with the concept that parameter values are passed to a function from outside the function, and that variables are declared and assigned values from within the function body.

Program 6.2 includes the `FindMax()` function within the program code previously listed in Program 6.1.

PROGRAM 6.2

```
#include <iostream.h>

void FindMax(int, int);    // the function prototype

int main()
{
  int firstnum, secnum;

  cout << "\nEnter a number: ";
  cin  >> firstnum;
  cout << "Great! Please enter a second number: ";
  cin  >> secnum;

  FindMax(firstnum, secnum);  // the function is called here

  return 0;
}

// following is the function FindMax()

void FindMax(int x, int y)
{                     // start of function body
  int maxnum;         // variable declaration

  if (x >= y)         // find the maximum number
     maxnum = x;
  else
     maxnum = y;

  cout << "\nThe maximum of the two numbers is "
       << maxnum << endl;

  return;
}  // end of function body and end of function
```

Program 6.2 can be used to select and print the maximum of any two integer numbers entered by the user. A sample run of Program 6.2 follows:

```
Enter a number: 25
Great! Please enter a second number: 5

The maximum of the two numbers is 25
```

A BIT OF BACKGROUND

Procedural Abstraction

The assigning of a name to a data type, as we have seen (see Section 2.8), refers to *data abstraction.* The assigning of a name to a function or procedure in such a way that the function is invoked by simply using a name with appropriate arguments is formally referred to as *procedural abstraction.* In writing your own user-named functions you are actually creating procedural abstractions.

Notice that procedural abstraction effectively hides the implementation details of how a function actually performs its task. This hiding of the details is one of the hallmarks and strengths of abstraction. By thinking of tasks on an abstract procedural level, programmers can solve problems at a higher level without immediately being concerned with the nitty-gritty details of the actual solution implementation.

The placement of the `FindMax()` function after the `main()` function in Program 6.2 is a matter of choice. Some programmers prefer to put all called functions at the top of a program and make `main()` the last function listed. We prefer to list `main()` first because it is the driver function that should give anyone reading the program an idea of what the complete program is about before encountering the details of each function. Either placement approach is acceptable and you will encounter both styles in your programming work. In no case, however, can the definition of `FindMax()` be placed inside `main()`. This is true for all C++ functions: *Each function must be defined by itself outside any other function.* Each C++ function is a separate and independent entity with its own parameters and variables; nesting of functions is never permitted.

Placement of Statements

C++ does not impose a rigid statement ordering structure on the programmer. The general rule for placing statements in a C++ program is simply that all preprocessor directives, variables, named constants, and function calls must be either declared or defined *before* they can be used. As we have noted previously, although this rule permits both preprocessor directives and declaration statements to be placed throughout a program, doing so results in a very poor program structure.

As a matter of good programming form, the following statement ordering should form the basic structure around which all of your C++ programs are constructed.

```
Preprocessor directives
Named constants
Global variable declarations
Function prototypes
int main()
{
  variable declarations
  other executable statements
  return value
}
Function definitions
```

POINT OF INFORMATION

Preconditions and Postconditions

Preconditions are any set of conditions required by a function to be true if it is to operate correctly. For example, if a function uses the named constant MAXCHARS, which must have a positive value, a precondition is that MAXCHARS be declared with a positive value before the function is called.

Similarly, a postcondition is a condition that will be true after the function is executed, assuming that the preconditions are met.

Pre and postconditions are typically documented by user comments. For example, consider the following function definition and comments:

```
int leapyr(int year)
// Preconditions: the parameter year must represent a year in a four
//              : digit form, such as 1999
// Postcondition: a 1 is returned if the year is a leap year;
//              : otherwise a 0 will be returned
```

Pre and postcondition comments should be included with both function prototypes and function definitions whenever clarification is needed.

As always, comment statements can be freely intermixed anywhere within this basic structure.

Function Stubs

An alternative to completing each function required in a complete program is to write the `main()` function first and then add the functions later, as they are developed. The problem that arises with this approach, however, is the same problem that occurred with Program 6.1, that is, the program cannot be run until all of the functions are included. For convenience we have reproduced the code for Program 6.1:

```
#include <iostream.h>

void FindMax(int, int);  // the function declaration (prototype)

int main()
{
  int firstnum, secnum;

  cout << "\nEnter a number: ";
  cin  >> firstnum;
  cout << "Great! Please enter a second number: ";
  cin  >> secnum;

  FindMax(firstnum, secnum); // the function is called here

  return 0;
}
```

PROGRAMMING NOTE

Isolation Testing

One of the most successful software testing method known is to always embed the code being tested within an environment of working code. For example, assume you have two untested functions that are called in the order shown below, and the result returned by the second function is incorrect.

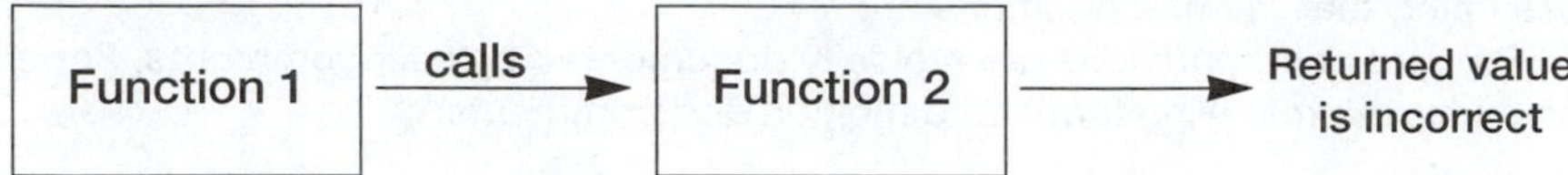

From the information shown on this figure, one or possibly both of the functions could be operating incorrectly. The first order of business is to isolate the problem to a specific function.

One of the most powerful methods of performing this code isolation is to decouple the functions. This is done by either testing each function individually or by testing one function first, and only when you know it is operating correctly, reconnecting it to the second function. Then, if an error occurs you have isolated the error to either the transfer of data between functions or the internal operation of the second function.

This specific procedure is an example of the **Basic rule of testing,** which states that each function should only be tested in a program in which all other functions are known to be correct. This means that one function must first be tested by itself, using stubs if necessary for any called functions, that a second tested function should be tested either by itself or with a previously tested function, and so on. This ensures that each new function is isolated within a test bed of correct functions, with the final program effectively built-up of tested function code.

This program would be complete if there were a function definition for `FindMax`. But we really don't need a *correct* `FindMax` function to test and run what has been written, we just need a function that *acts* like it is: A "fake" `FindMax` that accepts the proper number and types of arguments and returns values of the proper form for the function call is all we need to allow initial testing. This fake function is called a stub. A **stub** is the beginning of a final function that serves as a placeholder until the function is completed. A stub for `FindMax` follows:

```
void FindMax(int x, int y)
{
  cout << "In FindMax()\n";
  cout << "The value of x is " << x << endl;
  cout << "The value of y is " << y << endl;

  return;

}
```

This stub function can now be compiled and linked with the previously completed code to obtain an executable program. The code for the function can then be further developed and when it is completed, it replaces the stub portion. As illustrated, a stub should always display the name of the function that it represents.

The minimum requirement of a stub function is that it compile and link with its calling module. In practice, it is a good idea to have a stub display a message that it has been entered successfully along with the value(s) of its received arguments, as in the stub for `FindMax`.

As the function is refined, you let it do more and more, perhaps allowing it to return intermediate or incomplete results. This incremental, or stepwise, refinement is an important concept in efficient program development that provides you with the means to run a program that does not yet meet all of its final requirements.

Functions with Empty Parameter Lists

Although useful functions having an empty parameter list are extremely limited (one such function is provided in Exercise 9 for Section 6.1), they can occur. The function prototype for such a function requires either the keyword `void` or nothing at all between the parentheses following the function name. For example, both prototypes

```
int display();
```

and

```
int display(void);
```

indicate that the `display()` function takes no arguments and returns an integer value. A function with an empty parameter list is called by its name with nothing written inside the required parentheses following the function's name. For example, the statement `display();` correctly calls the `display()` function whose prototype was just given.

Default Arguments[3]

A convenient feature of C++ is its flexibility for providing default arguments in a function call. The primary use of default arguments is to extend the parameter list of existing functions without requiring any change in the calling argument lists already in place within a program.

Default argument values are listed in the function prototype and are automatically transmitted to the called function when the corresponding arguments are omitted from the function call. For example, the function prototype

```
void example(int, int = 5, float = 6.78);
```

provides default values for the last two arguments. If any of these arguments is omitted when the function is actually called, the C++ compiler will supply these default values. Thus, all of the following function calls are valid:

```
example(7, 2, 9.3);    // no defaults used
example(7, 2);         // same as example(7, 2, 6.78);
example(7);            // same as example(7, 5, 6.78);
```

Four rules must be followed when using default parameters. The first is that default values can only be assigned in the function prototype. The second is that if any parameter is given a default value in the function prototype, all parameters following it must also be supplied with default values. The third rule is that if one argument is omitted in the actual function call, then all

[3] This topic may be omitted on first reading with no loss of subject continuity.

arguments to its right must also be omitted. These latter two rules make it clear to the C++ compiler which arguments are being omitted and permits the compiler to supply correct default values for the missing arguments, starting with the rightmost argument and working toward the left. The last rule specifies that the default value used in the function prototype may be an expression consisting of both constants and previously declared variables. If such an expression is used, it must pass the compiler's check for validly declared variables, even though the actual value of the expression is evaluated and assigned at run time.

Default arguments are extremely useful when extending an existing function to include more features that require additional arguments. Adding the new arguments to the right of the existing arguments and providing each new argument with a default value permit all existing function calls to remain as they are. Thus, the effect of the new changes is conveniently isolated from existing code in the program.

Reusing Function Names (Overloading)[4]

In most high-level languages, including C++'s immediate predecessor, C, each function requires its own unique name. In theory this makes sense, but in practice it can lead to a profusion of function names, even for functions that perform essentially the same operations. For example, consider determining and displaying the absolute value of a number. If the number passed into the function can be either an integer, a long integer, or a double-precision value, three distinct functions must be written to handle each case correctly. As was done in C, we could give each of these functions a unique name, such as `abs()`, `labs()`, and `fabs()`, respectively, having the function prototypes:

```
void abs(int);
void labs(long);
void fabs(double);
```

Clearly, each of these three functions performs essentially the same operation, but on different argument data types. In C++, as long as the compiler can determine which function to use based on the data types of the arguments (not the data type of the return value, if any), the same function name can be used for more than one function. Using the same function name for more than one function is referred to as **function overloading.**

Applying function overloading to our absolute value functions permits us to write three C++ functions that all have the same name. Using the function name `showabs()` for our functions, they can be written as follows:

```
void showabs(int x)  // display the absolute value of an integer
{
  if ( x < 0 )
    x = -x;
  cout << "The absolute value of the integer is  " << x << endl;
}

void showabs(long x)  // display the absolute value of a long integer
```

[4] This topic may be omitted on first reading with no loss of subject continuity.

```
{
  if ( x < 0 )
    x = -x;
  cout << "The absolute value of the long integer is  " << x << endl;
}

void showabs(double x)  // display the absolute value of a double
{
  if ( x < 0 )
    x = -x;
  cout << "The absolute value of the double is  " << x << endl;
}
```

Which of the three functions named `abs()` is actually called depends on the argument types supplied at the time of the call. Thus, the function call `showabs(10);` would cause the compiler to use the function named `abs` that expects an integer argument, and the function call `abs(6.28);` would cause the compiler to use the function named `abs` that expects a double-valued argument.[5]

Notice that overloading a function's name simply means using the same name for more than one function. Each function that uses the name must still be written and exists as a separate entity. The use of the same function name does not require that the code within the functions be similar, although good programming practice dictates that functions with the same name should perform essentially the same operations. The only formal requirement when using the same function name is that the compiler must be able to distinguish which function to select based on the data types of the arguments when the function is called.

Exercises 6.1

1. For the following function headers, determine the number, type, and order (sequence) of the values that must be passed to the function:
   a. `void factorial(int n)`
   b. `void price(int type, double yield, double maturity)`
   c. `void yield(int type, double price, double maturity)`
   d. `void interest(char flag, float price, float time)`
   e. `void total(float amount, float rate)`
   f. `void roi(int a, int b, char c, char d, float e, float f)`
   g. `void get_val(int item, int iter, char decflag, char delim)`
2. a. Write a function named `check()` that has three parameters. The first parameter should accept an integer number, the second argument a floating-point number, and the third parameter a double-precision number. The body of the function should just display the values of the data passed to the function when it is called. (*Note:* When tracing errors in functions, it is very helpful to have the function display the values it has been passed. Quite frequently, the error is not in the function, but in the data received and stored.)

[5] This is accomplished by a process referred to as *name mangling*. Using this process the function name actually generated by the C++ compiler differs from the function name used in the source code. The compiler appends information to the source code function name depending on the type of data being passed, and the resulting name is said to be a mangled version of the source code name.

b. Include the function written in Exercise 2a in a working program. Make sure your function is called from `main()`. Test the function by passing various data to it.

3. a. Write a function named `FindAbs()` that accepts a double-precision number passed to it, computes its absolute value, and displays the absolute value. The absolute value of a number is the number itself if the number is positive, and the negative of the number if the number is negative.

   b. Include the function written in Exercise 3a in a working program. Make sure your function is called from `main()`. Test the function by passing various data to it.

4. a. Write a function called `Mult()` that accepts two floating-point numbers as parameters, multiplies these two numbers, and displays the result.

   b. Include the function written in Exercise 4a in a working program. Make sure your function is called from `main()`. Test the function by passing various data to it.

5. a. Write a function named `SqrIt()` that computes the square of the value passed to it and displays the result. The function should be capable of squaring numbers with decimal points.

   b. Include the function written in Exercise 5a in a working program. Make sure your function is called from `main()`. Test the function by passing various data to it.

6. a. Write a function named `PowFun()` that raises an integer number passed to it to a positive integer power and displays the result. The positive integer should be the second value passed to the function. Declare the variable used to store the result as a long integer data type to ensure sufficient storage for the result.

   b. Include the function written in Exercise 6a in a working program. Make sure your function is called from `main()`. Test the function by passing various data to it.

7. a. Write a function that produces a table of the numbers from 1 to 10, their squares, and cubes. The function should produce the same display as that produced by Program 5.11.

   b. Include the function written in Exercise 7a in a working program. Make sure your function is called from `main()`. Test the function by passing various data to it.

8. a. Modify the function written for Exercise 7 to accept the starting value of the table, the number of values to be displayed, and the increment between values. If the increment is not explicitly sent, the function should use a default value of 1. Name your function `SelTab()`. A call to `SelTab(6,5,2);` should produce a table of five lines, the first line starting with the number 6 and each succeeding number increasing by 2.

   b. Include the function written in Exercise 8a in a working program. Make sure your function is called from `main()`. Test the function by passing various data to it.

9. A useful function with an empty parameter can be constructed to return a value for π that is accurate to the maximum number of decimal places allowed by your computer. This value is obtained by taking the arcsine of 1.0, which is $\pi/2$, and multiplying the result by 2. In C++, the required expression is `2.0 * asin(1.0)`, where the `asin()` function is provided in the standard C++ mathematics library (remember to include `math.h`). Using this expression, write a C++ function named `Pi()` that calculates and displays the value of π.

6.2 RETURNING VALUES

Using the method of passing data into a function presented in the previous section, the called function only receives copies of the values contained in the arguments at the time of the call (review Figure 6.3 if this is unclear to you). This method of calling a function and passing values to it is referred to as a function **call by value,** and is a distinct advantage of C++. Since the called function does not have direct access to any of the calling function's variables, it cannot inadvertently alter the value stored in one of these variables.

When a function is called by value it may process the data sent to it in any fashion desired and directly return at most one, and only one, "legitimate" value to the calling function (see Figure 6.7). In this section we see how such a value is returned to the calling function. As you might expect, given C++'s flexibility, there is a way of returning more than a single value, but that is the topic of the next section.

As with the calling of a function, directly returning a single value requires that the interface between the called and calling functions be handled correctly. From its side of the return transaction, the called function must provide the following items:

- the data type of the returned value
- the actual value being returned.

A function returning a value must specify, in its header line, the data type of the value that will be returned. Recall that the function header line is the first line of the function, which includes both the function's name and a list of parameter names. As an example, consider the `FindMax()` function written in the last section. It determined the maximum value of two numbers passed to the function. For convenience, the `FindMax()` code is listed again:

```
void FindMax(int x, int y)
{                         // start of function body
  int maxnum;             // variable declaration

  if (x >= y)             // find the maximum number
    maxnum = x;
  else
    maxnum = y;

  cout << "\nThe maximum of the two numbers is "
       << maxnum << endl;

  return;

} // end of function body and end of function
```

FIGURE 6.7 A Function Directly Returns at Most One Value When It Is Called by Value

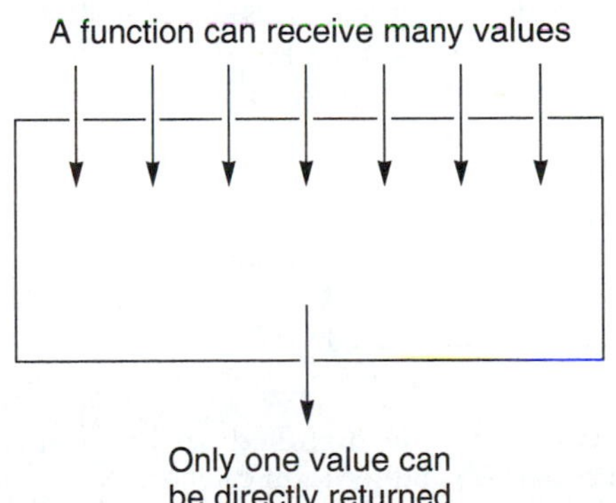
A function can receive many values
Only one value can
be directly returned

As written, the function's header line is

```
void FindMax(int x, int y)
```

where x and y are the names chosen for the function's formal parameters.

If FindMax() is now to return a value, the function's header line must be amended to include the data type of the value being returned. For example, if an integer value is to be returned, the proper function header line is

```
int FindMax(int x, int y)
```

Similarly, if the function is to return a floating-point value the correct function header line is

```
float FindMax(float x, float y)
```

and if the function is to return a double-precision value the header line would be

```
double FindMax(double x, double y)
```

Let us now modify the function FindMax() to return the maximum value of the two numbers passed to it. To do this, we must first determine the data type of the value that is to be returned and include this data type in the function's header line.

Since the maximum value determined by FindMax() is stored in the integer variable maxnum, it is the value of this variable that the function should return. Returning an integer value from FindMax() requires that the function header line be

```
int FindMax(int x, int y)
```

Observe that this is the same as the original function header line for FindMax() with the substitution of the keyword int for the keyword void.

Having declared the data type that FindMax() will return, all that remains is to include a statement within the function to cause the return of the correct value. To return a value, a function must use a return statement, which has the form[6]:

return expression;

When the **return statement** is encountered, the expression is evaluated first. The value of the expression is then automatically converted to the data type declared in the function header before being sent back to the calling function. After the value is returned, program control reverts to the calling function. Thus, to return the value stored in maxnum, all we need to do is add the statement return maxnum; before the closing brace of the FindMax() function. The complete function code is:

These should be the same data type.

```
int FindMax(int x, int y)   // function header line
{                           // start of function body
  int maxnum;               // variable declaration

  if (x >= y)
    maxnum = x;
  else
    maxnum = y;

  return maxnum;            // return statement
}
```

[6] The expression can be enclosed within parentheses, yielding the statement return(expression);. Either form can be used.

In this new code for the function FindMax(), note that the data type of the expression contained within the parentheses of the return statement correctly matches the data type in the function's header line. It is up to the programmer to ensure that this is true for every function returning a value. Failure to exactly match the return value with the function's declared data type may not result in an error when your program is compiled, but it may lead to undesired results since the return value is always converted to the data type declared in the function declaration. Usually this is a problem only when the fractional part of a returned floating-point or double-precision number is truncated because the function was declared to return an integer value.

Having taken care of the sending side of the return transaction, we must now prepare the calling function to receive the value sent by the called function. On the calling (receiving) side, the calling function must:

- be alerted to the type of value to expect
- properly use the returned value.

Alerting the calling function as to the type of return value to expect is properly taken care of by the function prototype. For example, including the function prototype

```
int FindMax(int, int);
```

before main() is sufficient to alert main() that FindMax() is a function that will return an integer value.

To actually use a returned value we must either provide a variable in which to store the value or use the value directly in an expression. Storing the returned value in a variable is accomplished using a standard assignment statement. For example, the assignment statement

```
max = FindMax(firstnum,secnum);
```

can be used to store the value returned by FindMax() in the variable named max. This assignment statement does two things. First the right-hand side of the assignment statement calls FindMax(); then the result returned by FindMax is stored in the variable max. Since the value returned by FindMax() is an integer, the variable max must also be declared as an integer variable within the calling function's variable declarations.

The value returned by a function need not be stored directly in a variable, but can be used wherever an expression is valid. For example, the expression 2 * FindMax(firstnum,secnum) multiplies the value returned by two, and the statement

```
cout << FindMax(firstnum,secnum);
```

displays the returned value.

Program 6.3 illustrates the inclusion of both prototype and assignment statements for main() to correctly declare, call, and store a returned value from FindMax(). As before, and in keeping with our convention of placing the main() function first, we have placed the FindMax() function after main().

PROGRAM 6.3

```
#include <iostream.h>

int FindMax(int, int); // the function prototype

int main()
{
  int firstnum, secnum, max;

  cout << "\nEnter a number: ";
  cin  >> firstnum;
  cout << "Great! Please enter a second number: ";
  cin  >> secnum;

  max = FindMax(firstnum, secnum); // the function is called here

  cout << "\nThe maximum of the two numbers is " << max << endl;

  return 0;
}

int FindMax(int x, int y)
{                        // start of function body
  int maxnum;            // variable declaration

  if (x >= y)            // find the maximum number
    maxnum = x;
  else
    maxnum = y;

  return maxnum;         // return statement
}
```

In reviewing Program 6.3 it is important to note the four items we have introduced in this section. The first item is the prototype for `FindMax()`. This statement, which ends with a semicolon as all declaration statements do, alerts `main()` and any subsequent function definitions to the data type that `FindMax()` will be returning. The second item to notice in `main()` is the use of an assignment statement to store the returned value from the `FindMax()` call into the variable `maxnum`. We have also made sure to correctly declare `maxnum` as an integer within `main()`'s variable declarations so that it matches the data type of the returned value.

The last two items of note concern the coding of the `FindMax()` function. The first line of `FindMax()` declares that the function will return an integer value, and the expression in the return statement evaluates to a matching data type. Thus, `FindMax()` is internally consistent in sending an integer value back to `main()`, and `main()` has been correctly alerted to receive and use the returned integer.

In writing your own functions you must always keep these four items in mind. For another example, see if you can identify these four items in Program 6.4.

PROGRAM 6.4

```
#include <iostream.h>

const CONVERTS = 4;   // number of conversions to be made

double tempvert(double);   // function prototype

int main()
{
  int count;                  // start of declarations
  double fahren;

  for(count = 1; count <= CONVERTS; count++)
  {
    cout << "\nEnter a Fahrenheit temperature: ";
    cin  >> fahren;
    cout << "The Celsius equivalent is "
         << tempvert(fahren) << endl;
  }

  return 0;
}

// convert fahrenheit to celsius
double tempvert(double in_temp)
{
  return (5.0/9.0) * (in_temp - 32.0);
}
```

In reviewing Program 6.4 let us first analyze the function `tempvert()`. The complete definition of the function begins with the function's header line and ends with the closing brace after the return statement. The function is declared as a double; this means the expression in the function's return statement must evaluate to a double-precision number, which it does. Since a function header line is not a statement but the start of the code defining the function, the function header line does not end with a semicolon.

On the receiving side, the prototype for the function `tempvert()` agrees with `tempvert()`'s function definition and alerts `main()` as to the type of value reutrned by `tempvert()`. As with all declaration statements, multiple declarations of the same type may be made within the same statement. No additional variable is declared in `main()` to store the returned value from `tempvert()` because the returned value is immediately passed to `cout` for display.

One further point is worth mentioning here. One of the purposes of declarations, as we learned in Chapter 2, is to alert the compiler to the amount of internal storage reserved for the data. The prototype within `main()` for `tempvert()`

performs this task and tells the computer how much storage area must be accessed by `main()` when the returned value is retrieved. Had we placed the `tempvert()` function before `main()`, however, the function header line for `tempvert()` would suffice to alert the computer to the type of storage needed for the returned value. In this case, the function prototype for `tempvert()`, within `main()`, could be eliminated. Since we have chosen always to list `main()` as the first function in a file, we must include function prototypes for all functions called by `main()`. This style also serves to document what functions `main()` will access.

Inline Functions[7]

Calling a function places a certain amount of overhead on a computer: This consists of placing argument values in a reserved memory region that the function has access to (this memory region as referred to as the *stack*), passing control to the function, providing a reserved memory location for any returned value (again, the stack region of memory is used for this purpose), and finally returning to the proper point in the calling program. Use of this overhead is well justified when a function is called many times, because it can significantly reduce the size of a program. Rather than repeating the same code within a function each time it is needed, the code is written once, as a function, and called whenever it is needed.

For small functions that are not called many times, however, paying the overhead for passing and returning values may not be warranted. It still would be convenient, though, to group repeating lines of code together under a common function name and have the compiler place this code directly into the program wherever the function is called. This capability is provided by inline functions.

Telling the C+ compiler that a function is *inline* causes a copy of the function code to be placed in the program at the point the function is called. For example, consider the function `tempvert()` defined in Program 6.4. Since this is a relatively short function it is an ideal candidate to be an inline function. To make this, or any other function, an inline one, we simply place the reserved word `inline` before the function name, and defining the function before any calls are made to it. This is done for the `tempvert()` function in Program 6.5.

Observe in Program 6.5 that the inline function is placed ahead of any calls to it. This is a requirement of all inline functions and obviates the need for a function prototype before any subsequent calling function. Since the function is now an inline one, its code will be expanded directly into the program wherever it is called.

The advantage of using an inline function is increased execution speed. Since the inline function is directly expanded and included in every expression or statement calling it, there is no execution time loss due to the call and return overhead required by a non-inline function. The disadvantage is the increase in program size when an inline function is called repeatedly. Each time an inline function is referenced the complete function code is reproduced and stored as an integral part of the program. A non-inline function, however, is stored in memory only once. No matter how many times the function is called, the same code is used. Therefore, inline functions should only be used for small functions that are not extensively called in the program.

---

[7] This section is optional and may be omitted on first reading without loss of subject continuity.

PROGRAM 6.5

```
#include <iostream.h>

const CONVERTS = 4;    // number of conversions to be made

inline double tempvert(double in_temp)  // an in-line function
{
  return (5.0/9.0) * (in_temp - 32.0);
}

int main()
{
  int count;                     // start of declarations
  double fahren;

  for(count = 1; count <= CONVERTS; count++)
  {
    cout << "\nEnter a Fahrenheit temperature: ";
    cin >> fahren;
    cout << "The Celsius equivalent is "
         << tempvert(fahren) << endl;
  }

  return 0;
}
```

Exercises 6.2

1. Rewrite Program 6.3 so that the function `FindMax()` accepts two floating-point arguments and returns a floating-point value to `main()`. Make sure you modify `main()` to pass two floating-point values to `FindMax()` and accept and store the floating-point value returned by `FindMax()`.
2. For the following function headers, determine the number, type, and order (sequence) of values that should be passed to the function when it is called and the data type of the value returned by the function.
   a. `int factorial(int n)`
   b. `double price(int type, double yield, double maturity)`
   c. `double yield(int type, double price, maturity)`
   d. `char interest(char flag, float price, float time)`
   e. `int total(float amount, float rate)`
   f. `float roi(int a, int b, char c, char d, float e, float f)`
   g. `void get_val(int item, int iter, char decflag)`
3. Write function headers for the following:
   a. A function named `check` that has three parameters. The first parameter should accept an integer number, the second parameter a floating-point number, and the third parameter a double-precision number. The function returns no value.

b. A function named `FindAbs()` that accepts a double-precision number and returns its absolute value.

c. A function named `Mult()` that accepts two floating-point numbers as parameters, multiplies these two numbers, and returns the result.

d. A function named `SqrIt()` that computes and returns the square of the integer value passed to it.

e. A function named `PowFun()` that raises an integer number passed to it to a positive integer power and returns the result.

f. A function that produces a table of the numbers from 1 to 10, their squares, and cubes. No parameters are to be passed to the function and the function returns no value.

4. a. Write a C++ function named `FindAbs()` that accepts a double-precision number passed to it, computes its absolute value, and returns the absolute value to the calling function. The absolute value of a number is the number itself if the number is positive, and the negative of the number if the number is negative.

   b. Include the function written in Exercise 4a in a working program. Make sure your function is called from `main()` and correctly returns a value to `main()`. Have `main()` use a `cout` statement to display the value returned. Test the function by passing various data to it.

5. a. Write a C++ function called `Mult()` that accepts two double-precision numbers as arguments, multiplies these two numbers, and returns the result to the calling function.

   b. Include the function written in Exercise 5a in a working program. Make sure your function is called from `main()` and correctly returns a value to `main()`. Have `main()` use a `cout` statement to display the value returned. Test the function by passing various data to it.

6. a. Write a C++ function named `PowFun()` that raises an integer number passed to it to a positive integer power and returns the result to the calling function. Declare the variable used to return the result as a long integer data type to ensure sufficient storage for the result.

   b. Include the function written in Exercise 6a in a working program. Make sure your function is called from `main()` and correctly returns a value to `main()`. Have `main()` use a `cout` statement to display the value returned. Test the function by passing various data to it.

7. A second-degree polynomial in x is given by the expression $ax2 + bx + c$, where a, b, and c are known numbers and a is not equal to zero. Write a C++ function named `PolyTwo(a,b,c,x)` that computes and returns the value of a second-degree polynomial for any passed values of `a`, `b`, `c`, and `x`.

8. a. Rewrite the function `tempvert()` in Program 6.4 to accept a temperature and a character as arguments. If the character passed to the function is the letter `f`, the function should convert the passed temperature from Fahrenheit to Celsius, else the function should convert the passed temperature from Celsius to Fahrenheit.

   b. Modify the `main()` function in Program 6.4 to call the function written for Exercise 8a. Your `main()` function should ask the user for the type of temperature being entered and pass the type (`f` or `c`) into `tempvert()`.

9. a. An extremely useful programming algorithm for rounding a real number to n decimal places is:

   Step 1: Multiply the number by 10^n.
   Step 2: Add .5.
   Step 3: Delete the fractional part of the result.
   Step 4. Divide by $10n$.

For example, using this algorithm to round the number 78.374625 to three decimal places yields:

Step 1: 78.374625 $\times$ 10^3 = 78374.625
Step 2: 78374.625 + .5 = 78375.125
Step 3: Retaining the integer part = 78375
Step 4: 78375 divided by 10^3 = 78.375

Using this algorithm, write a C++ program that accepts a user-entered value of money, multiplies the entered amount by an 8.675% interest rate, and displays the result rounded to two decimal places.

b. Enter, compile, and execute the program written for Exercise 9a.

10. a. Write a C++ function named `whole()` that returns the integer part of any number passed to the function. (*Hint:* Assign the passed argument to an integer variable.)

    b. Include the function written in Exercise 10a in a working program. Make sure your function is called from `main()` and correctly returns a value to `main()`. Have `main()` use a `cout` statement to display the value returned. Test the function by passing various data to it.

11. a. Write a C++ function named `fracpart()` that returns the fractional part of any number passed to the function. For example, if the number 256.879 is passed to `fracpart()`, the number .879 should be returned. Have the function `fracpart()` call the function `whole()` that you wrote in Exercise 10. The number returned can then be determined as the number passed to `fracpart()` less the returned value when the same argument is passed to `whole()`. The completed program should consist of `main()` followed by `fracpart()` followed by `whole()`.

    b. Include the function written in Exercise 11a in a working program. Make sure your function is called from `main()` and correctly returns a value to `main()`. Have `main()` use a `cout` statement to display the value returned. Test the function by passing various data to it.

12. a. Write a function named `totamt()` that accepts four actual integer arguments named `quarters`, `dimes`, `nickels`, and `pennies`, which represent the number of quarters, dimes, nickels, and pennies in a piggybank. The function should determine the dollar value of the number of quarters, dimes, nickels, and pennies passed to it and display the calculated value.

    b. Include the `totamt()` function written for Exercise 12a in a working program. The `main()` function should correctly call and pass the values of 26 quarters, 80 dimes, 100 nickels, and 216 pennies to `totamt()`. Make sure you do a hand calculation to verify the result displayed by your program.

6.3 VARIABLE SCOPE

Now that we have begun to write programs containing more than one function, we can look more closely at the variables declared within each function and their relationship to variables in other functions.

By their very nature, C++ functions are independent modules. As we have seen, values are passed to a function using the function's argument list and a value is returned from a function using a return statement. Seen in this light, a function can be thought of as a closed box, with slots at the top to receive values and a single slot at the bottom of the box to return a value (see Figure 6.8). The metaphor of a closed box is useful because it emphasizes the fact that what goes on inside the function, including all variable declarations within the function's body, are hidden from the view of all other functions.

FIGURE 6.8 A Function Can Be Thought of As a Closed Box

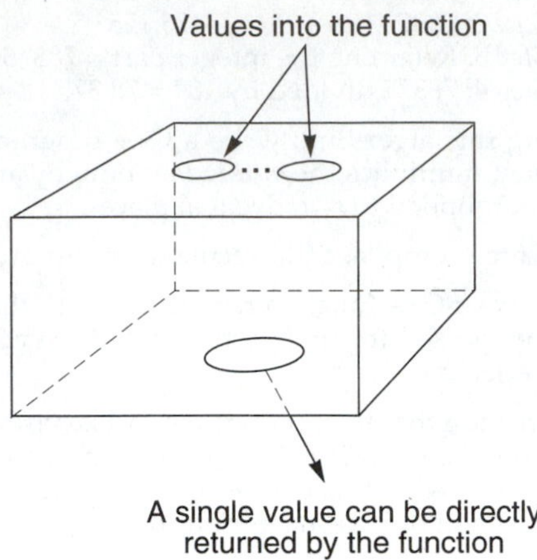
Values into the function
A single value can be directly returned by the function

Since the variables created inside a function are conventionally available only to the function itself, they are said to be local to the function, or *local variables*. This term refers to the *scope* of a variable, where scope is defined as the section of the program where the variable is valid or "known." This section of the program is also referred to as the part in which the variable is visible. A variable can have either a local scope or a global scope. A variable with a *local scope* is simply one that has had storage locations set aside for it by a declaration statement made within a function body. Local variables are only meaningful when used in expressions or statements inside the function that declared them. This means that the same variable name can be declared and used in more than one function. For each function that declares the variable, a separate and distinct variable is created.

All the variables we have used until now have been local variables. This is a direct result of placing our declaration statements inside functions and using them as definition statements that cause the computer to reserve storage for the declared variable. As we shall see, declaration statements can be placed outside functions and need not act as definitions that cause new storage areas to be reserved for the declared variable.

A variable with *global scope,* more commonly termed a *global variable,* is one whose storage has been created for it by a declaration statement located outside any function. These variables can be used by all functions that are physically placed after the global variable declaration. This is shown in Program 6.6, where we have purposely used the same variable name inside both functions contained in the program.

The variable `firstnum` in Program 6.6 is a global variable because its storage is created by a definition statement located outside a function. Because both functions, `main()` and `valfun()`, follow the definition of `firstnum`, both of these functions can use this global variable with no further declaration needed.

Program 6.6 also contains two separate local variables, both named `secnum`. Storage for the `secnum` variable named in `main()` is created by the definition statement located in `main()`. A different storage area for the `secnum` variable in

PROGRAM 6.6

```
#include <iostream.h>

int firstnum;         // create a global variable named firstnum

void valfun(void);   // function prototype (declaration)

int main()
{
  int secnum;        // create a local variable named secnum

  firstnum = 10;   // store a value into the global variable
  secnum = 20;     // store a value into the local variable

  cout << "From main(): firstnum = " << firstnum << endl;
  cout << "From main(): secnum = " << secnum << endl;

  valfun();  // call the function valfun

  cout << "\nFrom main() again: firstnum = " << firstnum << endl;
  cout << "From main() again: secnum = " << secnum << endl;

  return 0;
}

void valfun(void) // no values are passed to this function
{
  int secnum;    // create a second local variable named secnum

  secnum = 30;  // this only affects this local variable's value

  cout << "\nFrom valfun(): firstnum = " << firstnum << endl;
  cout << "From valfun(): secnum = " << secnum << endl;

  firstnum = 40; // this changes firstnum for both functions

  return;
}
```

`valfun()` is created by the definition statement located in the `valfun()` function. Figure 6.9 illustrates the three distinct storage areas reserved by the three definition statements found in Program 6.6.

Each of the variables named `secnum` is local to the function in which their storage is created, and each of these variables can only be used from within the appropriate function. Thus, when `secnum` is used in `main()`, the storage area reserved by `main()` for its `secnum` variable is accessed, and when `secnum` is

FIGURE 6.9 The Three Storage Areas Created by Program 6.6

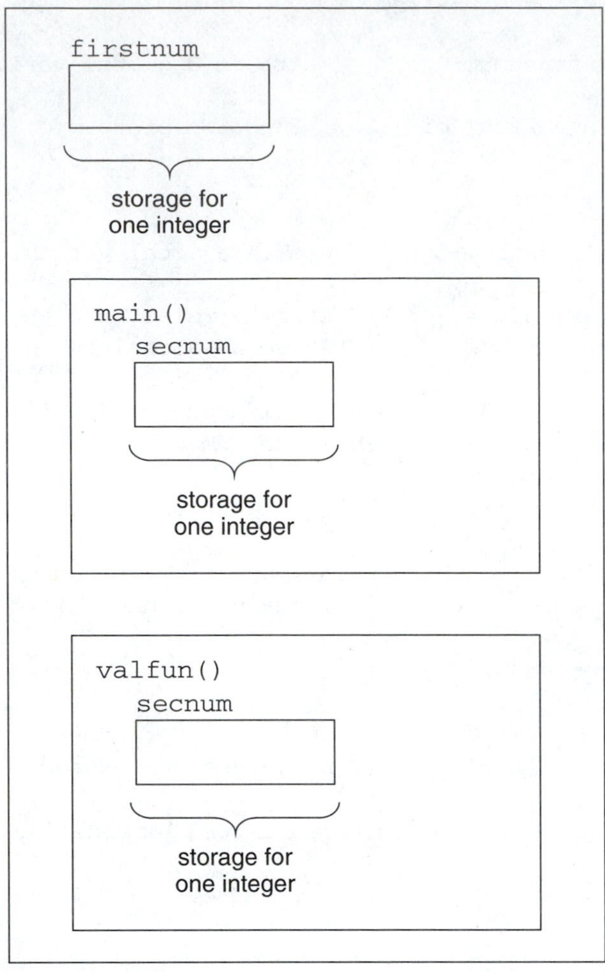

used in `valfun()`, the storage area reserved by `valfun()` for its `secnum` variable is accessed. The following output is produced when Program 6.6 is run:

```
From main(): firstnum = 10
From main(): secnum = 20

From valfun(): firstnum = 10
From valfun(): secnum = 30

From main() again: firstnum = 40
From main() again: secnum = 20
```

Let's analyze this output. Since `firstnum` is a global variable, both the `main()` and `valfun()` functions can use and change its value. Initially, both functions print the value of 10 that `main()` stored in `firstnum`. Before returning, `valfun()` changes the value of `firstnum` to 40, which is the value displayed when the variable `firstnum` is next displayed from within `main()`.

Because each function only "knows" its own local variables, `main()` can only send the value of its `secnum` to the `cout` object, and `valfun()` can only send the value of its `secnum` to the `cout` object. Thus, whenever `secnum` is obtained from `main()`, the value of 20 is displayed, and whenever `secnum` is obtained from `valfun()` the value 30 is displayed.

C++ does not confuse the two `secnum` variables because only one function can execute at a given moment. While a function is executing, only those variables and parameters that are "in scope" for that function (global and local) can be accessed.

The scope of a variable in no way influences or restricts the data type of the variable. Just as a local variable can be a character, integer, float, double, or any of the other data types (long/short) we have introduced, so can global variables be of these data types, as illustrated in Figure 6.10. The scope of a variable is determined by the placement of the definition statement that reserves storage for it and optionally by a declaration statement that makes it visible, whereas the data type of the variable is determined by using the appropriate keyword (`char`, `int`, `float`, `double`, etc.) before the variable's name in a declaration statement.

Scope Resolution Operator

When a local variable has the same name as a global variable, all references to the variable name made within the scope of the local variable refer to the local variable. This situation is illustrated in Program 6.7, where the variable name `number` is defined as both a global and local variable.

PROGRAM 6.7

```
#include <iostream.h>

float number = 42.8;        // a global variable named number

int main()
{
  float number = 26.4;      // a local variable named number

  cout << "The value of number is " << number << endl;

  return 0;
}
```

When Program 6.7 is executed, the following output is displayed:

```
The value of number is 26.4
```

As shown by this output, the local variable name takes precedence over the global variable. In such cases, we can still access the global variable by using C++'s scope resolution operator. This operator, which is the symbol `::`, must be placed immediately before the variable name, as in `::number`. When used in this manner the `::` tells the compiler to use the global variable. As an example, the scope resolution operator is used in Program 6.7a.

FIGURE 6.10 Relating the Scope and Type of a Variable

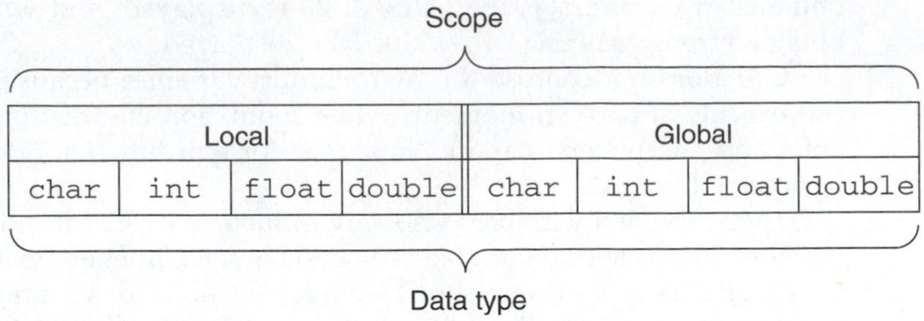

PROGRAM 6.7a

```
#include <iostream.h>

float number = 42.5;          // a global variable named number

int main()
{
  float number = 26.4;        // a local variable named number

  cout << "The value of number is " << ::number << endl;

  return 0;
}
```

The output produced by Program 6.7a is:

```
The value of number is 42.5
```

As indicated by this output, the scope resolution operator causes the global, rather than the local, variable to be accessed.

Misuse of Globals

Global variables allow the programmer to "jump around" the normal safeguards provided by functions. Rather than passing variables to a function, it is possible to make all variables global ones. **Do not do this.** By indiscriminately making all variables global, you instantly destroy the safeguards C++ provides to make functions independent and insulated from each other, including the necessity of carefully designating the type of arguments needed by a function, the variables used in the function, and the value returned.

Using only global variables can be especially disastrous in larger programs that have many user-created functions. Since all variables in a function must be declared, creating functions that use global variables requires that you remember to write the appropriate global declarations at the top of each program using the function—they no longer come along with the function. More devastating than this, however, is the horror of trying to track down an error in a large program that uses global variables. Since a global variable can be accessed and changed by any function following the global declaration, it is a time-consuming and frustrating task to locate the origin of an erroneous value.

Global variables, however, are sometimes useful in creating variables that must be shared between many functions. Rather than passing the same variable to each function, it is easier to define the variable once as a global. Doing so also alerts anyone reading the program that many functions use the variable. Most large programs almost always make use of a few global variables. Smaller programs containing a few functions, however, should almost never contain globals.

Exercises 6.3

1. a. For the following section of code, determine the data type and scope of all declared variables. To do this, use a separate sheet of paper and list the three column headings that follow (we have filled in the entries for the first variable):

Variable Name	Data Type	Scope
`price`	`int`	Global to `main`, `roi`, and `step`

```
#include <iostream.h>
int price;
long int years;
double yield;

int main()
{
  int bondtype;
  double interest, coupon;
      .
      .
      .
  return 0;
}

double roi(int mat1, int mat2)
{
  int count;
  double eff_int;
      .
      .
  return eff_int;
}
int step(float first, float last)
{
  int numofyrs;
  float fracpart;
      .
      .
  return (10*numofyrs);
}
```

   b. Draw boxes around the appropriate section of the Exercise 1a code to enclose the scope of each variable.

   c. Determine the data type of the parameters that the functions `roi` and `step` expect, and the data type of the value returned by these functions.

2 a. For the following section of code, determine the data type and scope of all declared variables. To do this, use a separate sheet of paper and list the three column headings that follow (we have filled in the entries for the first variable):

Variable Name	Data Type	Scope
key	char	Global to main, func1, and func2

```
#include <iostream.h>
char key;
long int number;

int main()
{
  int a,b,c;
  double x,y;
     .
     .
  return 0;
}

double secnum;

int func1(int num1, int num2)
{
  int o,p;
  float q;
     .
     .
  return p;
}

double func2(float first, float last)
{
  int a,b,c,o,p;
  float r;
  double s,t,x;
     .
     .
  return (s * t);
}
```

b. Draw a box around the appropriate section of the Exercise 2a code to enclose the scope of the variables key, secnum, y, and r.

c. Determine the data type of the arguments that functions func1 and func2 expect, and the data type of the value returned by these functions.

3. Besides speaking about the scope of a variable, we can also apply the term to a function's parameters. What do you think is the scope of all function parameters?

4. Consider the following program structure:

```
#include <iostream.h>
int a, b;
float One(float);
void Two(void);

int main()
{
  int c, d;
  float e, f;
     .
     .
```

```
return 0;
}
float One(float p2)
{
  char m, n;
    .
    .
}
void Two(void)
{
  int p, d;
  float q, r;
    .
    .
}
```

Define the scope of the parameter p2 and the variables a, b, c, d, m, n, p, d, q, and r.

5. Determine the values displayed by each `cout` statement in the following program:

```
#include <iostream.h>
int firstnum = 10;  // declare and initialize a global variable
void display(void);  // function prototype

int main()
{
  int firstnum = 20;    // declare and initialize a local variable

  cout << "\nThe value of firstnum is " << firstnum << endl;
  display();
  return 0;
}
void display(void)
{
  cout << "The value of firstnum is now " << firstnum << endl;
  return;
}
```

6.4 VARIABLE STORAGE CLASS

The scope of a variable defines the location within a program where that variable can be used. Given a program, you could take a pencil and draw a box around the section of the program where each variable is valid. The space inside the box would represent the scope of a variable. From this viewpoint, the scope of a variable can be thought of as the space within the program where the variable is valid.

In addition to the space dimension represented by its scope, variables also have a time dimension. The time dimension refers to the length of time that storage locations are reserved for a variable. This time dimension is referred to as the variable's "lifetime." For example, all variable storage locations are released back to the computer when a program is finished running. However, while a program is still executing, interim variable storage areas are reserved and subsequently released back to the computer. Where and how long a variable's storage locations are kept before they are released can be determined by the **storage class** of the variable.

Besides having a data type and scope, every variable also has a storage class. The four available storage classes are called `auto`, `static`, `extern`, and `register`. If one of these class names is used, it must be placed before the variable's data type in a declaration statement. Examples of declaration statements that include a storage class designation are:

```
auto int num;      // auto storage class and int data type
static int miles;  // static storage class and int data type
register int dist; // register storage class and int data type
extern int price;  // extern storage class and int data type
auto float coupon; // auto storage class and float data type
static double yrs; // static storage class and double data type
extern float yld;  // extern storage class and float data type
auto char in_key;  // auto storage class and char variable
```

To understand what the storage class of a variable means, we first consider local variables (those variables created inside a function) and then global variables (those variables created outside a function).

Local Variable Storage Classes

Local variables can only be members of the auto, static, or register storage classes. If no class description is included in the declaration statement, the variable is automatically assigned to the `auto` class. Thus, `auto` is the default class used by C++. All the local variables we have used, since the storage class designation was omitted, have been `auto` variables.

The term `auto` is short for *automatic.* Storage for automatic local variables is automatically reserved or created each time a function declaring automatic variables is called. As long as the function has not returned control to its calling function, all automatic variables local to the function are "alive"—that is, storage for the variables is available. When the function returns control to its calling function, its local automatic variables "die"—that is, the storage for the variables is released back to the computer. This process repeats itself each time a function is called. For example, consider Program 6.8, where the function `testauto()` is called three times from `main()`.

The output produced by Program 6.8 is:

```
The value of the automatic variable num is 0
The value of the automatic variable num is 0
The value of the automatic variable num is 0
```

Each time `testauto()` is called, the automatic variable `num` is created and initialized to zero. When the function returns control to `main()`, the variable `num` is destroyed along with any value stored in `num`. Thus, the effect of incrementing `num` in `testauto()`, before the function's return statement, is lost when control is returned to `main()`.

For most applications, the use of automatic variables works just fine. Sometimes, however, we would like a function to remember values between function calls. This is the purpose of the static storage class. A local variable that is declared as `static` causes the program to keep the variable and its latest value even when the function that declared it is through executing. Examples of static variable declarations are:

```
static int rate;
static float taxes;
static double amount;
static char in_key;
static long years;
```

PROGRAM 6.8

```
#include <iostream.h>

void testauto(void);          // function prototype

int main()
{
  int count;                  // count is a local auto variable

  for(count = 1; count <= 3; count++)
    testauto();

   return 0;
}

void testauto(void)
{
  int num = 0;   // num is a local auto variable
                 // that is initialized to zero
  cout << "The value of the automatic variable num is "
       << num << endl;
  num++;

  return;
}
```

A local static variable is not created and destroyed each time the function declaring the static variable is called. Once created, local static variables remain in existence for the life of the program. This means that the last value stored in the variable when the function is finished executing is available to the function the next time it is called.

Because local static variables retain their values, they are not initialized within a declaration statement in the same way as automatic variables. To understand why, consider the automatic declaration `int num = 0;`, which causes the automatic variable `num` to be created and set to zero each time the declaration is encountered. This is called a *run-time initialization* because initialization occurs each time the declaration statement is encountered. This type of initialization would be disastrous for a static variable, because resetting the variable's value to zero each time the function is called would destroy the very value we are trying to save.

The initialization of static variables (both local and global) is done only once, when the program is first compiled. At compilation time the variable is created and any initialization value is placed in it.[8] Thereafter, the value in the variable is kept without further initialization each time the function is called. To see how this works, consider Program 6.9.

---

[8] Some compilers initialize static local variables the first time the definition statement is executed rather than when the program is compiled.

PROGRAM 6.9

```
#include <iostream.h>

void teststat(void);        // function prototype

int main()
{
  int count;                // count is a local auto variable

  for(count = 1; count <= 3; count++)
      teststat();

  return 0;
}

void teststat(void)
{
  static int num = 0;       // num is a local static variable
  cout << "The value of the static variable num is now "
       << num << endl;
  num++;

  return;
}
```

The output produced by Program 6.9 is:

```
The value of the static variable num is now 0
The value of the static variable num is now 1
The value of the static variable num is now 2
```

As illustrated by this output, the static variable `num` is set to zero only once. The function `teststat()` then increments this variable just before returning control to `main()`. The value that `num` has when leaving the function `teststat()` is retained and displayed when the function is next called.

Unlike automatic variables that can be initialized by either constants or expressions using both constants and previously initialized variables, static variables can only be initialized using constants or constant expressions, such as 3.2 + 8.0. Also, unlike automatic variables, all static variables are set to zero when no explicit initialization is given. Thus, the specific initialization of `num` to zero in Program 6.9 is not required.

The remaining storage class available to local variables, the register class, is not used as extensively as either automatic or static variables. Examples of register variable declarations are:

```
register int time;
register double diffren;
register float coupon;
```

Register variables have the same time duration as automatic variables; that is, a local register variable is created when the function declaring it is entered, and is destroyed when the function completes execution. The only difference between register and automatic variables is where the storage for the variable is located.

Storage for all variables (local and global), except register variables, is reserved in the computer's memory area. Most computers have a few additional high-speed storage areas located directly in the computer's processing unit that can also be used for variable storage. These special high-speed storage areas are called registers. Since registers are physically located in the computer's processing unit, they can be accessed faster than the normal memory storage areas located in the computer's memory unit. Also, computer instructions that reference registers typically require less space than instructions that reference memory locations because there are fewer registers than there are memory locations.

For example, although the AT&T WE 32100 central processing unit has nine registers that can be used for local C++ program variables, it can be connected to memories that have more than four billion bytes. Most other computers have a similar set of user-accessible registers but millions of memory locations. When the compiler substitutes the location of a register for a variable during program compilation, less space in the instruction is needed than is required to address a memory having millions of locations.

Besides decreasing the size of a compiled C++ program, using register variables can also increase the execution speed of a C++ program if the computer you are using supports this data type. Variables declared with the register storage class are automatically switched to the auto storage class if your computer does not support register variables or if the declared register variables exceed the computer's register capacity.

The only restriction in using the register storage class is that the address of a register variable, using the address operator `&`, cannot be taken. This is easily understood when you realize that registers do not have standard memory addresses.

Global Variable Storage Classes

Global variables are created by definition statements external to a function. By their nature, these externally defined variables do not come and go with the calling of any function. Once a global variable is created, it exists until the program in which it is declared is finished executing. Thus, external variables cannot be declared as either auto or register variables that are created and destroyed as the program is executing. Global variables may additionally be declared as members of the static or extern storage classes (but not both). Examples of declaration statements including these two class descriptions are:

```
extern int sum;
extern double price;
static double yield;
```

The static and extern classes affect only the scope, not the time duration, of global variables. As with static local variables, all global variables are initialized to zero at compile time.

FIGURE 6.11 A Program May Extend Beyond One File

```
file1                                file2

int price;                           double interest;
float yield;                         int func3( )
static double coupon;                {
      .                                    .
      .                                    .
      .                                    .
int main( )                          }
{                                    int func4( )
    func1( );                              .
    func2( );                              .
    func3( );                              .
    func4( );                        }
}
int func1( )
{
      .
      .
      .
}
int func2( )
{
      .
      .
      .
}
```

The purpose of the extern storage class is to extend the scope of a global variable beyond its normal boundaries. To understand this, we must first note that all of the programs we have written so far have always been contained together in one file. Thus, when you have saved or retrieved programs you have only needed to give the computer a single name for your program. This is not required by C++.

Larger programs typically consist of many functions stored in multiple files. An example of this is shown in Figure 6.11, where the three functions `main()`, `func1()`, and `func2()` are stored in one file and the two functions `func3()` and `func4()` are stored in a second file. For the files illustrated in Figure 6.11, the global variables `price`, `yield`, and `coupon` declared in `file1` can only be used by the functions `main()`, `func1()`, and `func2()` in this file. The single global variable, `interest`, declared in `file2` can only be used by the functions `func3()` and `func4()` in `file2`.

Although the variable `price` has been created in `file1`, we may want to use it in `file2`. Placing the declaration statement `extern int price;` in `file2`, as shown in Figure 6.12, allows us to do this. Putting this statement at the top of `file2` extends the scope of the variable price into `file2` so that it may be used by both `func3()` and `func4()`. Thus, the extern designation simply declares a global variable that is defined in another file. So placing the statement `extern float yield;` in `func4()` extends the scope of this global variable, created in `file1`, into `func4()`, and the scope of the global variable interest, created in `file2`, is extended into `func1()` and `func2()` by the declaration

POINT OF INFORMATION

Storage Classes

Variables of the type auto and register are always local variables.

Only nonstatic global variables may be externed, which extends the variable's scope into another file or function.

Making a global variable static makes the variable private to the file in which it is declared. Thus, static variables cannot be externed. Except for static variables, all variables are initialized each time they come into scope.

statement `extern double interest;` placed before `func1()`. Notice that interest is not available to `main()`.

A declaration statement that specifically contains the word extern is different from every other declaration statement in that it does not cause the creation of a new variable by reserving new storage for the variable. An extern declaration statement simply informs the computer that a global variable already exists and can now be used. The actual storage for the variable must be created somewhere else in the program using one, and only one, global declaration statement in which the word extern has not been used. Initialization of the global variable

FIGURE 6.12 Extending the Scope of a Global Variable

file1

```
int price;
float yield;
static double coupon;
      .
      .
      .
int main( )
{
    func1( );
    func2( );
    func3( );
    func4( );
}
extern double interest;
int func1( )
{
      .
      .
      .
}
int func2( )
{
      .
      .
      .
}
```

file2

```
double interest;
extern int price;
int func3( )
{
      .
      .
      .
}
int func4( )
{
    extern float yield;
      .
      .
      .
}
```

can, of course, be made with the original declaration of the global variable. Initialization within an `extern` declaration statement is not allowed and will cause a compilation error.

The existence of the extern storage class is the reason we have been so careful to distinguish between the creation and declaration of a variable. Declaration statements containing the word `extern` do not create new storage areas; they only extend the scope of existing global variables.

The last global class, static global variables, is used to prevent the extension of a global variable into a second file. Global static variables are declared in the same way as local static variables, except that the declaration statement is placed outside any function.

The scope of a global static variable cannot be extended beyond the file in which it is declared. This provides a degree of privacy for static global variables. Since they are only "known" and can only be used in the file in which they are declared, other files cannot access or change their values. Static global variables cannot be subsequently extended to a second file using an `extern` declaration statement. Trying to do so will result in a compilation error.

Exercises 6.4

1. a. List the storage classes available to local variables.

   b. List the storage classes available to global variables.

2. Describe the difference between a local auto variable and a local static variable.

3. What is the difference between the following functions?:

```
void init1(void)
{
  static int yrs = 1;
  cout << "The value of yrs is " << yrs << endl;
  yrs = yrs + 2;
}

void init2(void)
{
  static int yrs;
  yrs = 1;
  cout << "The value of yrs is " << yrs << endl;
  yrs = yrs + 2;
}
```

4. a. Describe the difference between a static global variable and an extern global variable.

   b. If a variable is declared with an extern storage class, what other declaration statement must be present somewhere in the program?

5. The declaration statement `static double years;` can be used to create either a local or global static variable. What determines the scope of the variable years?

6. For the function and variable declarations illustrated in Figure 6.13, place an extern declaration to individually accomplish the following:

   a. Extend the scope of the global variable choice into all of `file2`.

   b. Extend the scope of the global variable flag into function `pduction()` only.

   c. Extend the scope of the global variable date into `pduction()` and `bid()`.

FIGURE 6.13 Files for Exercise 6.

file1

```
char choice;
int flag;
long date, time;
int main( )
{
     .
     .
     .
}
double coupon;
double price( )
{
     .
     .
     .
}
double yield( )
{
     .
     .
     .
}
```

file2

```
char b_type;
double maturity;
double roi( )
{
     .
     .
     .
}
double pduction( )
{
     .
     .
     .
}
double bid( )
{
     .
     .
     .
}
```

d. Extend the scope of the global variable `date` into `roi()` only.

e. Extend the scope of the global variable `coupon` into `roi()` only.

f. Extend the scope of the global variable `b_type` into all of `file1`.

g. Extend the scope of the global variable `maturity` into both `price()` and `yield()`.

6.5 CALL BY REFERENCE USING REFERENCE ARGUMENTS

In a typical function invocation the called function receives values from its calling function, stores and manipulates the passed values, and directly returns at most one single value. As we have seen, this method of calling a function and passing values to it is referred to as a function *call by value.*

Calling a function by value is a distinct advantage of C++. It allows functions to be written as independent entities that can use any variable name without concern that other functions may also be using the same name. It also alleviates any concern that altering a parameter or local variable in one function may inadvertently alter the value of a variable in another function. Under this approach, formal (receiving) arguments or parameters (these terms are synonymous) can be considered as either initialized variables or variables that will be assigned values when the function is executed. At no time, however, does the called function have direct access to any local variable contained in the calling function.

There are times, however, when it is necessary to alter this approach by giving a called function direct access to the local variables of its calling function. This allows one function, which is the called function, to use and change the value of another function's local variable. To do this, the address of the variable must be passed to the called function. Once the called function has the variable's address, it "knows where the variable lives," so to speak, and can access and change the value stored there directly.

Passing addresses is referred to as a function **call by reference,** since the called function can reference, or access, the variable using the passed address. C++ provides two types of address arguments, references and pointers. In this section we describe reference arguments.

Passing and Using Reference Arguments

As always, in exchanging data between two functions we must be concerned with both the sending and receiving sides of the data exchange. From the sending side, however, calling a function and passing an address as an actual argument that will be accepted as a reference parameter on the receiving side is exactly the same as calling a function and passing a value: The called function is summoned into action by giving its name and a list of arguments. For example, the statement `newval(firstnum, secnum);` calls the function named `newval()` and passes two arguments to it. Whether a value or and address is actually passed depends on the function prototype declared for `newval()`. Let us now write the `newval` function and prototype so that the function receives the addresses of the variables `firstnum` and `secnum`, which we will assume to be floating-point variables, rather than their values.

One of the first requirements for writing `newval()` is to declare two reference parameters for accepting passed addresses. In C++ a reference parameter is declared using the following syntax:

```
data-type& reference-name
```

For example, the reference declaration

```
float& num1
```

declares that `num1` is a reference parameter that will be used to store the address of a float. Similarly, `int& secnum` declares that `secnum` is a reference to an integer and `char& key` declares that `key` is a reference to a character.

Recall from Section 2.3 that the ampersand, `&`, symbol in C++ means "the address of." Additionally, when an `&` symbol is used within a declaration it refers to "the address of" the preceding data type. Using this information, declarations such as `float& num1` and `int& secnum` are sometimes more clearly understood if they are read backwards. Reading the declaration `float& num1` in this manner yields the information that "`num1` is the address of a floating-point value."

Since we need to accept two addresses in the parameter list for `newval()`, the declarations `float& num1, float& num2` can be used. Including these declarations within the parameter list for `newval()`, and assuming that the function returns no value (void), the function header for `newval()` becomes:

```
void newval(float& num1, float& num2)
```

For this function header line, an appropriate function prototype is:

```
void newval(float&, float&);
```

This prototype and header line are included in Program 6.10, which i completed `newval()` function body that both displays and directly alters the values stored in these reference parameters from within the called function.

PROGRAM 6.10

```
#include <iostream.h>

void newval(float&, float&);  // prototype with two reference
                              // parameters

int main()
{
  float firstnum, secnum;


  cout << "Enter two numbers: ";
  cin  >> firstnum >> secnum;
  cout << "\nThe value in firstnum is: " << firstnum << endl;
  cout << "The value in secnum is: " << secnum << "\n\n";

  newval(firstnum, secnum);   // call the function

  cout << "The value in firstnum is now: " << firstnum << endl;
  cout << "The value in secnum is now: " << secnum << endl;

  return 0;
}

void newval(float& xnum, float& ynum)
{
  cout << "The value in xnum is: " << xnum << endl;
  cout << "The value in ynum is: " << ynum << "\n\n";
  xnum = 89.5;
  ynum = 99.5;

return;
}
```

In calling the `newval()` function within Program 6.10 it is important to understand the connection between the actual arguments, `firstnum` and `secnum`, used in the function call and the formal parameters, `xnum` and `ynum`, used in the function header. *Both reference the same data items.* The significance of this is that the values in the actual arguments (`firstnum` and `secnum`) can now be altered from within `newval()` by using the formal parameter names (`xnum` and `ynum`). Thus, the formal parameters `xnum` and `ynum` do not store copies of the values in `firstnum` and `secnum`, but directly access the locations in memory set aside for these two arguments. The equivalence of argument names in Program 6.10, which is the essence of a call by reference, is illustrated in Figure 6.14, where

FIGURE 6.14 The Equivalence of Arguments and Parameters in Program 6.10

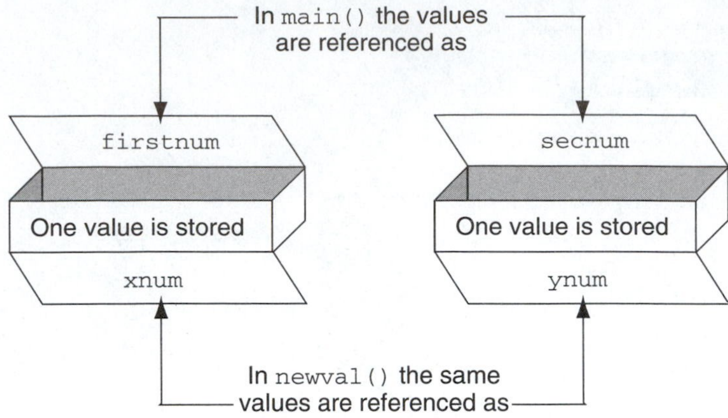

both actual argument names and their matching formal parameter names are simply different names referring to the same memory storage areas. In `main()` these memory locations are referenced by the names `firstnum` and `secnum`, respectively, while in `newval()` the same locations are referenced by the formal parameter names `xnum` and `ynum`, respectively.

The following sample run was obtained from Program 6.10:

```
Enter two numbers: 22.5 33.0

The value in firstnum is: 22.5
The value in secnum is: 33

The value in xnum is: 22.5
The value in ynum is: 33

The value in firstnum is now: 89.5
The value in secnum is now: 99.5
```

In reviewing this output notice that the values initially displayed for the formal parameters `xnum` and `ynum` are the same as those displayed for the actual arguments `firstnum` and `secnum`. Since `xnum` and `ynum` are reference variables, however, `newval()` now has direct access to the arguments `firstnum` and `secnum`. Thus, any change to `xnum` within `newval()` directly alters the value of `firstnum` in `main()` and any change to `ynum` directly changes `secnum`'s value. As illustrated by the final displayed values, the assignment of values to `xnum` and `ynum` within `newval()` is reflected in `main()` as the altering of `firstnum`'s and `secnum`'s values.

The equivalence between actual calling arguments and formal function parameters illustrated in Program 6.10 provides the basis for returning multiple values from within a function. For example, assume that a function is required to accept three values, compute these values' sum and product, and return these computed results to the calling routine. Naming the function `calc()` and providing five formal parameters (three for the input data and two references for the returned values), the following function can be used:

```
void calc(float num1, float num2, float num3, float& total, float& product)
{
  total = num1 + num2 + num3;
  product = num1 * num2 * num3;
  return;
}
```

This function has five formal parameters, named `num1`, `num2`, `num3`, `total`, and `product`, of which only the last two are declared as references. Within the function only the last two parameters are altered. The value of the fourth parameter, `total`, is calculated as the sum of the first three parameters and the last parameter, `product`, is computed as the product of the parameters `num1`, `num2`, and `num3`. Program 6.11 includes this function in a complete program.

Within `main()`, the function `calc()` is called using the five actual arguments `firstnum`, `secnum`, `thirdnum`, `sum`, and `product`. As required, these arguments agree in number and data type with the formal parameters declared by `calc()`. Of the five actual arguments passed, only `firstnum`, `secnum`, and `thirdnum` have been assigned values when the call to `calc()` is made. The remaining two arguments have not been initialized and will be used to receive values back from `calc()`. Depending on the compiler used in compiling the program, these arguments will initially contain either zeros or "garbage" values. Figure 6.15 illustrates the relationship between actual argument and formal parameter names and the values they contain after the return from `calc()`.

PROGRAM 6.11

```
#include <iostream.h>

void calc(float, float, float, float&, float&);  // function prototype

int main()
{
  float firstnum, secnum, thirdnum, sum, product;

  cout << "Enter three numbers: ";
  cin  >> firstnum >> secnum >> thirdnum;

  calc(firstnum, secnum, thirdnum, sum, product);  // function call

  cout << "\nThe sum of the numbers is: " << sum << endl;
  cout << "The product of the numbers is: " << product << endl;

  return 0;
}

void calc(float num1, float num2, float num3, float& total, float& product)
{
  total = num1 + num2 + num3;
  product = num1 * num2 * num3;
  return;
}
```

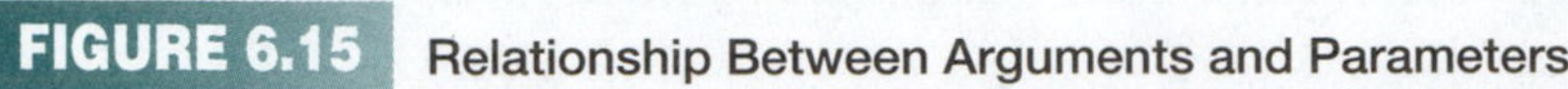

FIGURE 6.15 Relationship Between Arguments and Parameters

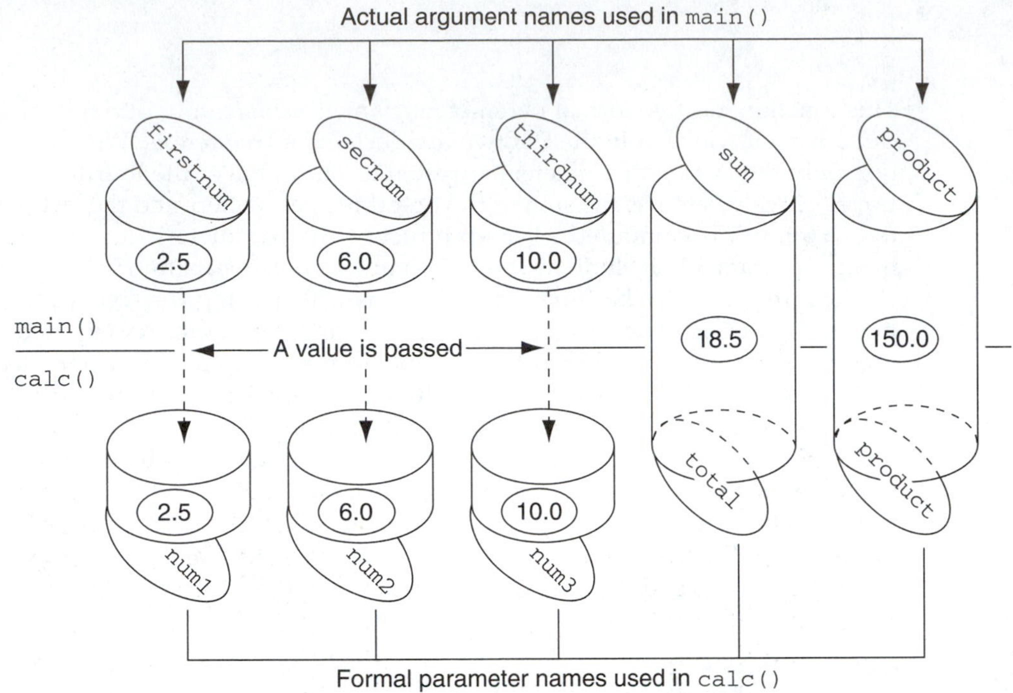

Once `calc()` is called, it uses its first three parameters to calculate values for `total` and `product` and then returns control to `main()`. Because of the order of its actual calling arguments, `main()` knows the values calculated by `calc()` as `sum` and `product`, which are then displayed. A sample run of Program 6.11 follows:

```
Enter three numbers: 2.5 6.0 10.0
The sum of the numbers is: 18.5
The product of the numbers is: 150
```

As a final example illustrating the usefulness of passing references to a called function, we will construct a function named `swap()` that exchanges the values of two of `main()`'s floating-point variables. Such a function is useful when sorting a list of numbers and will be used again in Chapter 11 for just such an application.

Since the value of more than a single variable is affected, `swap()` cannot be written as a call by value function that returns a single value. The desired exchange of `main()`'s variables by `swap()` can only be obtained by giving `swap()` access to `main()`'s variables. One way to do this is to use reference variables.

We have already seen how to pass two references in Program 6.11. We will now construct a function to exchange the values in the passed reference arguments. Exchanging values in two parameters is accomplished using the three-step exchange algorithm:

1. Store the first parameter's value in a temporary location (see Figure 6.16a).
2. Store the second parameter's value in the first variable (see Figure 6.16b).
3. Store the temporary value in the second parameter (see Figure 6.16c).

FIGURE 6.16a Save the First Value

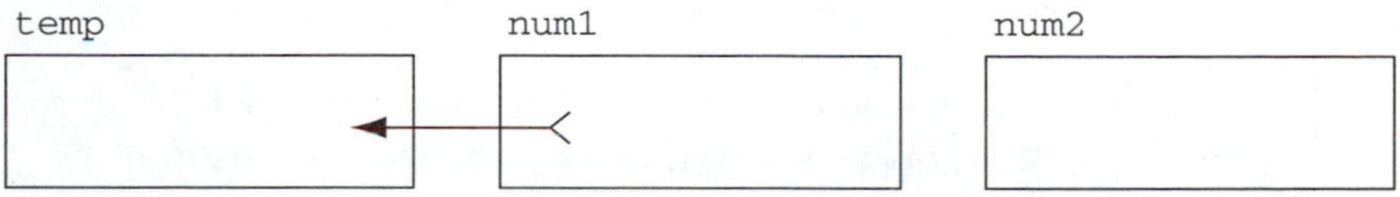

temp num1 num2

FIGURE 6.16b Replace the First Value with the Second Value

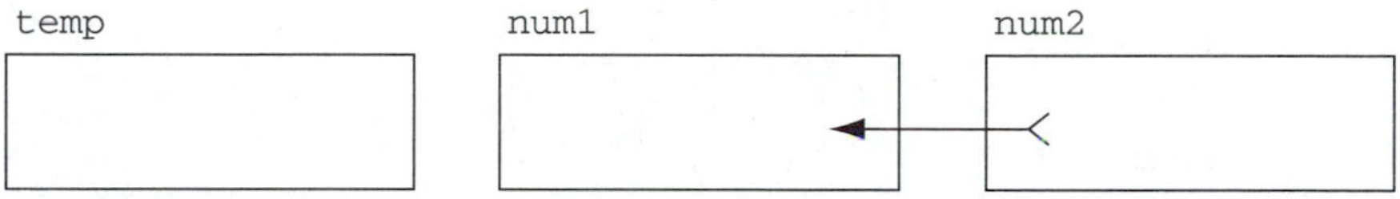

temp num1 num2

FIGURE 6.16c Change the Second Value

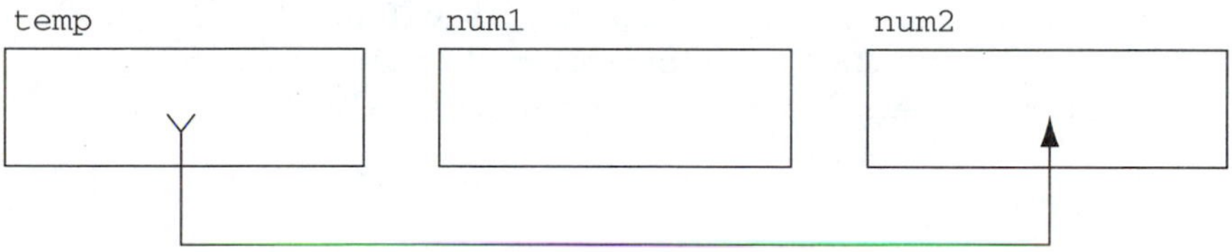

temp num1 num2

The function swap(), written according to these specifications follows:

```
void swap(float& num1, float& num2)
{
  float temp;

  temp = num1;          // save num1's value
  num1 = num2;          // store num2's value in num1
  num2 = temp;          // change num2's value

  return;
}
```

Notice that the use of references in swap()'s header line gives swap() access to the equivalent arguments in the calling function. Thus, any changes to the two reference parameters in swap() automatically change the values in the calling function's arguments. Program 6.12 contains swap() in a complete program.

PROGRAM 6.12

```
#include <iostream.h>

void swap(float&, float&);     // function receives 2 references

int main()
{
  float firstnum = 20.5, secnum = 6.25;

  cout << "The value stored in firstnum is: " << firstnum << endl;
  cout << "The value stored in secnum is: "<< secnum << "\n\n";

  swap(firstnum, secnum);   // call the function with references

  cout << "The value stored in firstnum is now: "
       << firstnum << endl;
  cout << "The value stored in secnum is now: "
       << secnum << endl;

  return 0;
}

void swap(float& num1, float& num2)
{
  float temp;

  temp = num1;      // save num1's value
  num1 = num2;      // store num2's value in num1
  num2 = temp;      // change num2's value

  return;
}
```

The following sample run was obtained using Program 6.12:

```
The value stored in firstnum is: 20.5
The value stored in secnum is: 6.25

The value stored in firstnum is now: 6.25
The value stored in secnum is now: 20.5
```

As illustrated by this output, the values stored in `main()`'s variables have been modified from within `swap()`, which was made possible by the use of reference parameters. If a call by value had been used instead, the exchange within `swap()` would affect only `swap()`'s parameters and would accomplish nothing with respect to `main()`'s variables. Thus, a function such as `swap()` can only be written using references or some other means that provide access to `main()`'s variables. (This other means is by the use of pointers, the topic of Chapter 13.)

A BIT OF BACKGROUND

The "Universal Algorithm Machine"

In the 1930s and 1940s, Alan Mathison Turing (1912–1954) and others studied in considerable depth the theory of what a computing machine should be able to do. Turing invented a theoretical, pencil-and-paper computer—now appropriately called a Turing machine—that he hoped would be a "universal algorithm machine." That is, he hoped to prove theoretically that all problems could be solved by a set of instructions to a hypothetical computer. What he succeeded in proving was that some problems cannot be solved by *any* machine, just as some problems cannot be solved by any person. However, he did show that algorithms that can be defined recursively can indeed be solved by machine, though it may not be possible to predict how long it will take the machine to find the solution.

Alan Turing's work formed the foundation of computer theory before the first electronic computer was built. His contribution to the team that developed the critical code-breaking computers during World War II led directly to the practical implementation of his theories.

In using reference arguments two cautions need to be mentioned. The first is that reference arguments *cannot* be used to change constants. For example, calling `swap()` with two constants, such as in the call `swap(20.5, 6.5)` passes two constants to the function. Although `swap()` may execute, it will not change the values of these constants.[9]

The second caution to note is that a function call itself gives no indication that the called function will be using reference arguments. The default in C++ is to make calls by value rather than calls by reference, precisely to limit a called function's ability to alter variables in the calling function. This calling procedure should be adhered to whenever possible, which means that reference parameters should only be used in very restricted situations that actually require multiple return values, such as in the `swap()` function illustrated in Program 6.12. The `calc()` function, included in Program 6.11, while useful for illustrative purposes, could also be written as two separate functions, each returning a single value.

Exercises 6.5

1. Write parameter declarations for the following:
   a. A formal parameter named `amount` that will be a reference to a floating-point value.
   b. A formal parameter named `price` that will be a reference to a double-precision number.
   c. A formal parameter named `minutes` that will be a reference to an integer number.

[9] Most compilers will catch this error.

d. A formal parameter named key that will be a reference to a character.

e. A formal parameter named yield that will be a reference to a double-precision number.

2. Three integer arguments are to be used in a call to a function named time(). Write a suitable function header for time(), assuming that time() accepts sec, min, and hours as reference parameters and returns no value to its calling function.

3. Rewrite the FindMax() function in Program 6.3 so that the variable max, declared in main(), is used to store the maximum value of the two passed numbers. The value of max should be set directly from within FindMax() [*Hint:* A reference to max will have to be accepted by FindMax().]

4. Write a function named change() that has a floating-point parameter and four integer reference parameters named quarters, dimes, nickels, and pennies. The function is to consider the floating-point passed value as a dollar amount and convert the value into an equivalent number quarters, dimes, nickels, and pennies. Using the references the function should directly alter the respective actual arguments in the calling function.

5. Write a function named time() that has an integer parameter named seconds and three integer reference parameters named hours, min, and sec. The function is to convert the passed number of seconds into an equivalent number of hours, minutes, and seconds. Using the references the function should directly alter the respective actual arguments in the calling function.

6. Write a function named yr_calc() that has a long integer parameter representing the total number of days from the turn of the century and reference parameters named year, month, and day. The function is to calculate the current year, month, and day for the given number of days passed to it. Using the references the function should directly alter the respective actual arguments in the calling function. For this problem assume that each year has 365 days and each month has 30 days.

7. Write a function named liquid() that has an integer number parameter and reference parameters named gallons, quarts, pints, and cups. The passed integer represents the total number of cups and the function is to determine the number of gallons, quarts, pints, and cups in the passed value. Using the references the function should directly alter the respective actual arguments in the calling function. Use the relationships of 2 cups to a pint, 4 cups to a quart, and 16 cups to a gallon.

8. The following program uses the same parameter names in both the calling and called function. Determine if this causes any problem for the computer.

```
#include <iostream.h>
void time(int&, int&);     // function prototype
int main()
{
  int min, hour;

  cout << "Enter two numbers :";
  cin >> min >> hour;
  time(min, hour);
  return 0;
}

void time(int& min, int& hour) // accept two references
{
  int sec;

  sec = (hour * 60 + min) * 60;
  cout << "The total number of seconds is " << sec << endl;
}
```

6.6 RECURSION[10]

Because C++ allocates new memory locations for parameters and local variables each time a function is called, it is possible for a function to call itself. Functions that do so are referred to as *self-referential* or **recursive functions.** When a function invokes itself, the process is called *direct recursion*. Similarly, a function can invoke a second function, which in turn invokes the first function. This type of recursion is referred to as *indirect* or *mutual recursion*.

In 1936 Alan Turing showed that, although not every possible problem can be solved by computer, those problems that have recursive solutions also have computer solutions, at least in theory.

Mathematical Recursion

The recursive concept is that the solution to a problem can be stated in terms of "simple" versions of itself. Some problems can be solved using an algebraic formula that shows recursion explicitly. For example, consider finding the factorial of a number n, denoted as $n!$, where n is a positive integer. This is defined as:

$$1! = 1$$
$$2! = 2 * 1 = 2 * 1!$$
$$3! = 3 * 2 * 1 = 3 * 2!$$
$$4! = 4 * 3 * 2 * 1 = 4 * 3!$$

and, so on. The definition for $n!$ can be summarized by the following statements:

$$1! = 1$$
$$n! = n * (n - 1)! \qquad \text{for } n > 1$$

This definition illustrates the general considerations that must be specified in construction of a recursive algorithm:

1. What is the first case?
2. How is the nth case related to the $(n - 1)$th case?

Although the definition seems to define a factorial in terms of a factorial, the definition is valid, because it can always be computed. For example, using the definition, 3! is first computed as:

$$3! = 3 * 2!$$

The value of 3! is determined from the definition as:

$$2! = 2 * 1!$$

Substituting this expression for 2! in the determination of 3! yields:

$$3! = 3 * 2 * 1!$$

1! is not defined in terms of the recursive formula, but is simply defined as being equal to 1. Substituting this value into the expression for 3! gives us

$$3! = 3 * 2 * 1 = 6$$

[10] This topic may be omitted on first reading with no loss of subject continuity.

To see how a recursive function is defined in C++, we construct the function factorial( ). In pseudocode, the processing required of this function is:

If n = 1
  factorial = n.
Else
  *factorial = n * factorial(n − 1).*

Notice that this algorithm is simply a restatement of the recursive definition previously given. In C++, this can be written as:

```
int factorial(int n)
{
  if (n == 1)
    return 1;
  else
  return n * factorial(n);
}
```

Program 6.13 illustrates this code in a complete program.

PROGRAM 6.13

```
#include <iostream.h>

long factorial(int);    // function prototype

int main ()
{
  int n;
  long result;

  cout << "Enter a number: ";
  cin  >> n;
  result = factorial(n);
  cout << "\nThe factorial of " << n << " is " << result << endl;

  return 0;
}

long factorial(int n)
{
  if (n == 1)
    return n;
  else
    return n * factorial(n-1);
}
```

Following is a sample run of Program 6.13:

```
Enter a number: 3

The factorial of 3 is 6
```

How the Computation Is Performed

The sample run of Program 6.13 invoked factorial from `main()` with a value of 3 using the call

```
result = factorial(n);
```

Let's see how the program actually performs the computation. The mechanism that makes it possible for a C++ function to call itself is that C++ allocates new memory locations for all function parameters and local variables as each function is called. This allocation is made dynamically, as a program is executed, in a memory area referred to as the stack.

A **memory stack** is simply an area of memory used for rapidly storing and retrieving data. It is conceptually similar to a stack of trays in a cafeteria, where the last tray placed on top of the stack is the first tray removed. This last-in/first-out mechanism provides the means for storing information in order of occurrence. Each function call simply reserves memory locations on the stack for its parameters, its local variables, a return value, and the address where execution is to resume in the calling program when the function has completed execution. Thus, when the function call `factorial(n)` is made, the stack is initially used to store the address of the instruction being executed (`result = factorial(n);`), the argument value for `n`, which is 3, and a space for the value to be returned by the factorial function. At this stage the stack can be envisioned as shown in Figure 6.17. From a program execution standpoint the function that made the call to `factorial`, in this case `main()`, is suspended and the compiled code for the `factorial` function starts executing.

Within the `factorial` function itself, another function call is made. That this call is to `factorial` is irrelevant as far as C++ is concerned. The call simply is another request for stack space. In this case the stack stores the address of the instruction being executed in `factorial`, the number 2, and a space for the value to be returned by the function. The stack can now be envisioned as shown in Figure 6.18. At this point a second version of the compiled code for `factorial` begins execution, while the first version is temporarily suspended.

Once again, the currently executing code, which is the second invocation of `factorial`, makes a function call. That this call is to itself is irrelevant in C++. The call is once again handled in the same manner as any function call and begins with allocation of the stack's memory space. Here the stack stores the address of the instruction being executed in the calling function, which happens to be `factorial`, the number 1, and a space for the value to be returned by the function. The stack can now be envisioned as shown in Figure 6.19. At this point

FIGURE 6.17 The Stack for the First Call to `factorial`

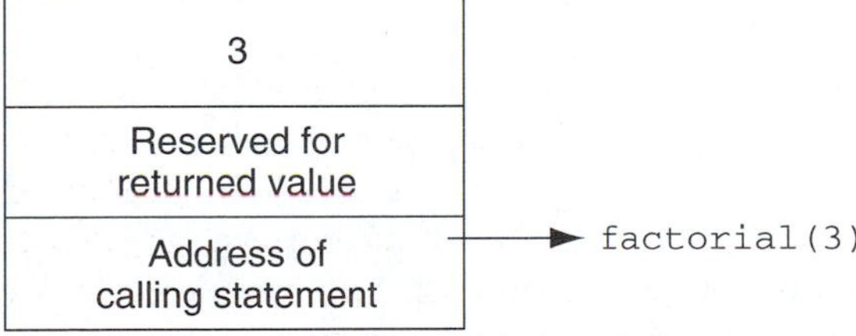

FIGURE 6.18 The Stack for the Second Call to `factorial`

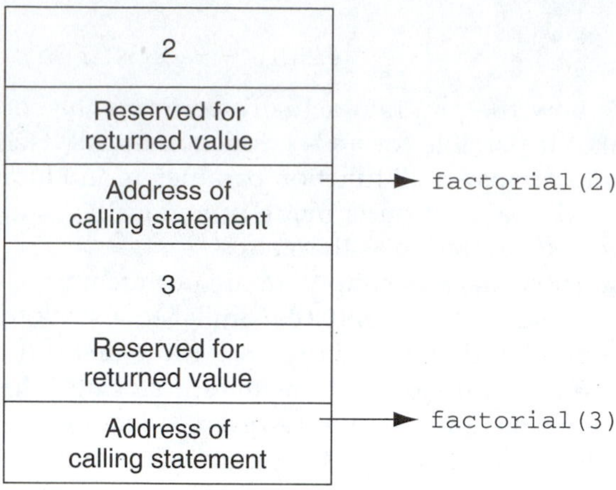

FIGURE 6.19 The Stack for the Third Call to `factorial`

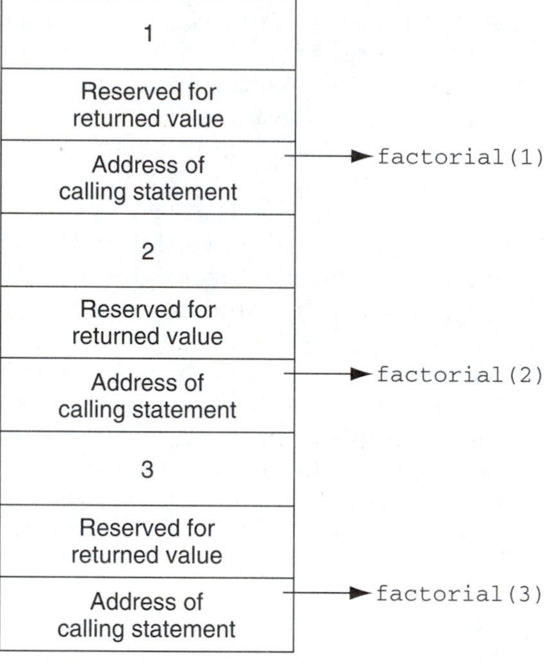

the third and final version of the compiled code for `factorial` begins execution, while the second version is temporarily suspended.

This third call to `factorial` results in a returned value of 1 being placed on the stack. This completes the set of recursive calls and permits the suspended calling functions to resume execution and be completed in reverse order. The value of 1 is used by the second invocation of `factorial` to complete its operation and place a return value of 2 on the stack. This value is then used by the first invocation of `factorial` to complete its operation and place a return value of 6 on the stack, with execution now returning to `main()`. The original calling statement within `main()` stores the return value of its invocation of `factorial` into the variable result.

Recursion Versus Iteration

The recursive method can be applied to any problem in which the solution is represented in terms of solutions to simpler versions of the same problem.

The most difficult tasks when implementing recursion are deciding how to create the process and visualizing what happens at each successive invocation.

Any recursive function can always be written in a nonrecursive manner using an iterative solution. For example, the `factorial` function can be written using an iteration algorithm as:

```
int factorial(int n)
{
  int fact;

  for(fact = 1; n > 0; n--)
    fact = fact * n;
  return fact;
}
```

Since recursion is usually a difficult concept for beginning programmers, under what conditions would you use it in preference to a repetitive solution? The answer is rather simple.

If a problem solution can be expressed iteratively or recursively with equal ease, the iterative solution is preferable because it executes faster (there are no additional function calls, which consumes processing time) and uses less memory (the stack is not used for the multiple function calls needed in recursion). There are times, however, when recursive solutions are preferable.

First, some problems are simply easier to visualize using a recursive algorithm than a repetitive one. The Towers of Hanoi problem, which is a classic recursion problem, is an example of this (see Exercise 28 at the end of this chapter).

A second reason for using recursion is that it sometimes provides a much simpler solution. In these situations obtaining the same result using repetition requires extremely complicated coding that can be avoided by using recursion. An example of this is the quick sort sorting algorithm presented in Section 11.6.

Related to both of these reasons is a third. In many advanced applications recursion is both simpler to visualize and the only practical means of implementing a solution. Examples of these applications are the implementation of a quick sort algorithm (see Section 11.6) and in creating dynamically allocated data structures (see Section 14.5).

Exercises 6.6

1. The Fibonacci sequence is 0, 1, 1, 2, 3, 5, 8, 13, . . ., such that the first two terms are 0 and 1, and each term thereafter is defined recursively as the sum of the two preceding terms; that is,

$$\text{Fib}(n) = \text{Fib}(n-1) + \text{Fib}(n-2)$$

Write a recursive function that returns the nth number in a Fibonacci sequence when n is passed to the function as an argument. For example, when $n = 8$, the function returns the 8th number in the sequence, which is 13.

2. The sum of a series of consecutive numbers from 1 to n can be defined recursively as:

```
sum(1) = 1;
sum(n) = n + sum(n - 1)
```

Write a recursive C++ function that accepts n as an argument and calculates the sum of the numbers from 1 to n.

3. a. The value of x^n can be defined recursively as:

$$x^0 = 1$$
$$x^n = x * x^{n-1}$$

Write a recursive function that computes and returns the value of x^n.

b. Rewrite the function written for Exercise 3a so that it uses a repetitive algorithm for calculating the value of x^n.

4. a. Write a function that recursively determines the value of the nth term of a geometric sequence defined by the terms

$$a, ar, ar^2, ar^3, \ldots, ar^{n-1}$$

The argument to the function should be the first term, a, the common ratio, r, and the value of n.

b. Modify the function written for Exercise 4a so that the sum of the first n terms of the sequence is returned.

5. a. Write a function that recursively determines the value of the nth term of an arithmetic sequence defined by the terms

$$a, a + d, a + 2d, a + 3d, \ldots, a + (n-1)d$$

The argument to the function should be the first term, a, the common difference, d, and the value of n.

b. Modify the function written for Exercise 5a so that the sum of the first n terms of the sequence is returned. (*Note:* This is a more general form of Exercise 2.)

6.7 FOCUS ON PROBLEM SOLVING

There are many mathematical and simulation problems in which probability must be considered or statistical sampling techniques must be used. For example, in simulating automobile traffic flow or telephone usage patterns, statistical models are required. Additionally, applications such as simple computer games and more involved "strategy games" in business and science can only be described statistically. All of these statistical models require the generation of *random numbers;* that is, a series of numbers whose order cannot be predicted.

In practice, there are no truly random numbers. Dice never are perfect; cards are never shuffled completely randomly; the supposedly random motions of molecules are influenced by the environment; and digital computers can handle numbers only within a finite range and with limited precision. The best one can do is generate *pseudorandom numbers,* which are sufficiently random for the task at hand.

Some computer languages contain a library function that produces random numbers; others do not. The functions provided by C++ are named `rand()` for generating random numbers and `srand()` for setting initial random "seed" values. We present these two functions and then use them in three applications: The first simulates the tossing of a coin to determine the number of resulting heads and tails; the second creates a game of HiLo; and the third finds an approximation to the area under a curve using Monte Carlo simulation.

Generating Pseudorandom Numbers

Two functions are provided by C++ compilers for creating random numbers: `rand()` and `srand()`. The `rand()` function produces a series of random numbers in the range $0 \leq$ `rand()` $\leq$ `RAND_MAX`, where the constant `RAND_MAX` is defined in the `stdlib.h` header file. The `srand()` function provides a starting "seed" value for `rand()`. If `srand()` or some other equivalent "seeding" technique is not used, `rand()` will always produce the same series of random numbers.

The general procedure for creating a series of *N* random numbers using C++'s library functions is illustrated by the following code:

```
srand(time(NULL));   // this generates the first "seed" value

for (int i = 1; i <= N; ++i)   // this generates N random numbers
{
  rvalue = rand();
  cout << rvalue << endl;
}
```

Here, the argument to the `srand()` function is a call to the `time()` function with a `NULL` argument. With this argument the `time()` function reads the computer's internal clock time, in seconds. The `srand()` function then uses this time, converted to an unsigned int, to initialize the random number generator function `rand()`.[11] Program 6.14 uses this code to generate a series of 10 random numbers:

The following is the output produced by one run of Program 6.14:

```
20203
21400
15265
26935
 8369
10907
31299
15400
 5074
20663
```

Because the `srand()` function was used in Program 6.14 the series of 10 random numbers will differ each time the program is executed. Without the randomizing "seeding" effect of this function, the same series of random numbers always would be produced. Note also the inclusion of the `stdlib.h` and `time.h` header files. The `stdlib.h` file contains the function prototypes for the `srand()` and `rand()` functions, while the `time.h` header file contains the function prototype for the `time()` function.

---

[11] Alternatively, many C++ compilers have a `randomize()` routine that is defined using the `srand()` function. If this routine is available, the call `randomize()` can be used in place of the call `srand(time(NULL))`.

PROGRAM 6.14

```
#include <iostream.h>
#include <iomanip.h>
#include <stdlib.h>
#include <time.h>

const int NUMBERS = 10;

// this program generates ten pseudorandom numbers
// using C++'s rand() function

int main()
{

  float randvalue;
  int i;

  srand(time(NULL));
  for (i = 1; i <= NUMBERS; i++)
  {
    randvalue = rand();
    cout << setw(20) << randvalue << endl;
  }

  return 0;
}
```

Scaling One modification to the random number produced by the `rand()` function typically must be made in practice. In most applications either the random numbers are required as floating-point values within the range 0.0 to 1.0 or as integers within a specified range, such as 1 to 100. The method for adjusting the random numbers produced by a random number generator to reside within such ranges is called *scaling*.

Scaling random numbers to reside within the range 0.0 to 1.0 is easily accomplished by dividing the returned value of `rand()` by `RAND_MAX`. Thus, the expression `float(rand())/RAND_MAX` produces a floating-point random number between 0.0 and 1.0.

Scaling a random number as an integer value between 0 and *N* is accomplished using either of the expressions `rand() % (N + 1)` or `int(rand()/RAND_MAX * N)`. For example, the expression `int(rand()/RAND_MAX * 100)` produces a random integer between 0 and 100.[12]

---

[12] Many C++ compilers have a routine named `random()` that can be used to produce the same result. For example, if your compiler has the `random()` function, the call `random(100)` will produce a random integer between 0 and 100.

To produce an integer random number between 1 and N the expression `1 + rand() % N` can be used. For example, in simulating the roll of a die, the expression `1 + rand() % 6` produces a random integer between 1 and 6. The more general scaling expression `a + rand() % (b + 1 - a)` can be used to produce a random integer between the numbers `a` and `b`.

Having presented the basics of C++'s random number functions, we will now use them to solve three different problems.

Problem 1: Create a Coin Toss Simulation

A common use of random numbers is to simulate events using a program, rather than going through the time and expense of constructing a real-life experiment. For example, statistical theory tells us that the probability of having a single tossed coin turn up heads is one-half. Similarly, there is a 50 percent probability of having a single tossed coin turn up tails.

Using these probabilities we would expect a single coin that is tossed 1000 times to turn up heads 500 times and tails 500 times. In practice, however, this is never exactly realized for a single experiment consisting of 1000 tosses. Instead of actually tossing a coin 1000 times we can use a random number generator to simulate these tosses. In particular, we will use the random number function developed in the previous application.

Analyze the Problem for Input/Output Requirements For this problem two outputs are required: the percentage of heads and the percentage of tails that result when a simulated coin is tossed 1000 times. No input item will be required for the random number generator function.

Develop a Solution The percentage of heads and tails is determined as:

$$\text{percentage of heads} = \frac{\text{number of heads}}{1000} \times 100\%$$

$$\text{percentage of tails} = \frac{\text{number of tails}}{1000} \times 100\%$$

To determine the number of heads and tails, we will have to simulate 1000 random numbers in such a manner that we can define a result of "heads" or "tails" from each generated number. There are a number of ways to do this.

One way is to use the `rand()` function to generate integers between 0 and `RAND_MAX`. Knowing that any single toss has a 50% chance of being either a head or a tail, we could designate a "head" as an even random number and a "tail" as an odd random number. A second method would be to scale the return value from `rand()` to reside between 0.0 and 1.0 as described earlier. Then we could define a "head" as any number greater than 0.5 and any other result as a "tail." This is the algorithm we will adopt.

Having defined how we will create a single toss that has a 50% chance of turning up heads or tails, the generation of 1000 tosses is rather simple: we use a fixed count loop that generates 1000 random numbers. For each generation we identify the result as either a head or tail, and accumulate the results in a heads and tails counter. Thus, the complete simulation algorithm is given by the pseudocode:

Initialize a heads count to zero.
Initialize a tails count to zero.
For 1000 times
generate a random number between 0 and 1.
If the random number is greater than .5
consider this as a head and
add one to the heads count.
Else
consider this as a tail and
add one to the tails count.
Endif.
Endfor.
Calculate the percentage of heads as
the number of heads divided by 1000 × 100%.
Calculate the percentage of tails as
the number of tails divided by 1000 × 100%.
Print the percentage of heads and tails obtained.

Code the Solution Program 6.15 shows the C++ algorithm.
Two sample runs of Program 6.15 follow:

```
Heads came up 51.599998 percent of the time
Tails came up 48.400002 percent of the time
```

and

```
Heads came up 47.299999 percent of the time
Tails came up 52.700001 percent of the time
```

Writing and executing Program 6.15 is certainly easier than manually tossing a coin 1000 times. Note, however, that the validity of the results produced by the program depends on how random the numbers produced by `rand()` actually are.

Test and Correct the Program Program 6.15 must pass two tests. The more important test concerns the randomness of each generated number. This, of course, is really a test of the random number function. For our purposes, we have used a previously written function supplied by the compiler. So at this point we accept the "randomness" of the generator. (See Exercise 4 for Section 6.7 for a method of verifying the function's randomness.)

Once the question of the random number generator has been settled, the second test requires that we correctly generate 1000 numbers and accumulate a head and tail count. That this is correctly accomplished is adequately verified by a simple desk check of the `for` loop within Program 6.15. Also, we do know that the result of the simulation must be close to 50% heads and 50% tails. The results of the simulation verify this to be the case.

Problem 2: Write a HiLo Computer Game

For this problem a computer game named HiLo is required. In this game the computer chooses an integer number between 0 and 100 and asks the user/player to guess its value. Guesses are counted and the player is told after each incorrect guess whether the guess was too high or too low, and is asked for another guess. When the player has found the number, he or she is told how many guesses it took.

PROGRAM 6.15

```
#include <iostream.h>
#include <iomanip.h>
#include <stdlib.h>
#include <time.h>

const int NUMTOSSES = 1000;

// a program to simulate the tossing of a coin NUMTOSSES times
int main()
{

  int heads = 0;  // initialize heads count
  int tails = 0;  // initialize tails count
  int i;
  float flip, perheads, pertails;

    // simulate NUMTOSSES tosses of a coin
  srand(time(NULL));
  for (i = 1; i <= NUMTOSSES; i++)
  {
    flip = float(rand())/RAND_MAX;   // scale the number between 0 and 1
    if (flip > 0.5)
      heads = heads + 1;
    else
      tails = tails + 1;
  }
  perheads = (heads / float (NUMTOSSES)) * 100.0;  // calculate heads percentage
  pertails = (tails / float (NUMTOSSES)) * 100.0;  // calculate tails percentage
  cout << "\nHeads came up " << perheads << " percent of the time";
  cout << "\nTails came up " << pertails << " percent of the time" << endl;

  return 0;
}
```

Analyze the Problem for Input/Output Requirements The generation of a random number will require using the `srand()` and `rand()` functions. Additionally, the user will repeatedly be asked to input a guess until the randomly generated number is found. When the correct guess is made, the program is required to display the number of guesses.

Develop a Solution On entry of the program, a random number between 0 and 100 must be generated. This is easily accomplished using the scaling algorithm.

number = int (rand ( )/RAND_MAX * 100)

A loop, beginning with a `count` of 0, can then be used to ask for the `guess`, increment `count`, compare the `guess` with the `number`, and repeat until the `guess` equals the number. A `repeat-until` structure ensures that the player gets to guess at least once. The pseudocode describing this procedure is:

Generate a random number.
Initialize `count` *= 0.*
REPEAT
  Ask for guess.
  Increment count.
  If guess < random number
    Print "Too Low."
  Else if guess > random number
    Print "Too High."
UNTIL guess equals random number.
Write count.

Code the Solution Program 6.16 presents the algorithm written as C++ code:

PROGRAM 6.16

```
#include <iostream.h>
#include <stdlib.h>
#include <time.h>

const int DEBUG = 0;

int main()
{

  int guess, count, val;
  float rnum;

  srand(time(NULL));

  rnum = rand();
    // scale the number to be between 0 and 100
  val = int(rnum/RAND_MAX * 100);
  if (DEBUG)
    cout << "rnum = " << rnum << " val = " << val;
  count = 0;

  do
  {
  cout << "\nEnter your guess: ";
  cin >> guess;
  count++;
  if (guess < val)
    cout << "\nYour guess was too low - guess again!";
  else if (guess > val)
    cout << "\nYour guess was too high - guess again!";
  } while (guess != val);

cout << "\nCongratulations!  You did it in " << count << " guesses\n";

  return 0;
}
```

A BIT OF BACKGROUND

Monte Carlo

Monte Carlo is a community within the principality of Monaco on the Mediterranean coast of France. Monte Carlo's fame as a gambling resort is responsible for its name being adopted for mathematical methods involving random numbers.

Monte Carlo techniques involve creating random numbers within given limits and determining what percentage of those numbers meet certain criteria. They can be used to calculate the area between curves (as in this section), to estimate the arrival of airplanes at an airport, to predict the percentage of manufactured parts that will be defective, to project the growth and decline of populations with fixed resources, to specify the needed thickness of nuclear reactor shielding, and so forth.

Monte Carlo calculations were hardly feasible before the development of high-speed computers. In many cases, billions of random numbers must be generated in order to achieve statistically accurate results. If, on a superfast computer, one random number selection and test calculation required a microsecond, then a billion calculations would take about 1000 seconds (roughly 17 minutes). On a typical 486-style personal computer, where the same calculation could take a millisecond, a billion such calculations would require a million seconds (or 11.5 days).

Clearly the speed and capacity of a computer are critical for effective application of Monte Carlo techniques. It has not been unusual for a single highly accurate computation of this nature to monopolize a $10 million computer for hours. However, new parallel-processing machines, which can handle many operations concurrently, are reducing the time required for Monte Carlo calculations using large data samples.

Test and Correct the Program Included within Program 6.16 is the named constant DEBUG. When this constant is set to 1, the program will display its randomly generated number. Using this display, we can run the program and select guesses that are known to be too high and too low to see that the program reacts correctly. Once this testing is done, the debug constant should be set to 0. Here is a sample run:

```
Enter your guess: 50

Your guess was too high - guess again!
Enter your guess: 25

Your guess was too low - guess again!
Enter your guess: 37

Your guess was too low - guess again!
Enter your guess: 41

Congratulations! You did it in 4 guesses
```

Problem 3: Use Monte Carlo Simulation to Estimate the Area Under a Curve

Here is a more serious application of random numbers. It uses a technique called a *Monte Carlo* method, by which large numbers of experiments involving random outcomes are performed to find an approximate solution to a problem.

FIGURE 6.20 A General Curve $y = f(x)$

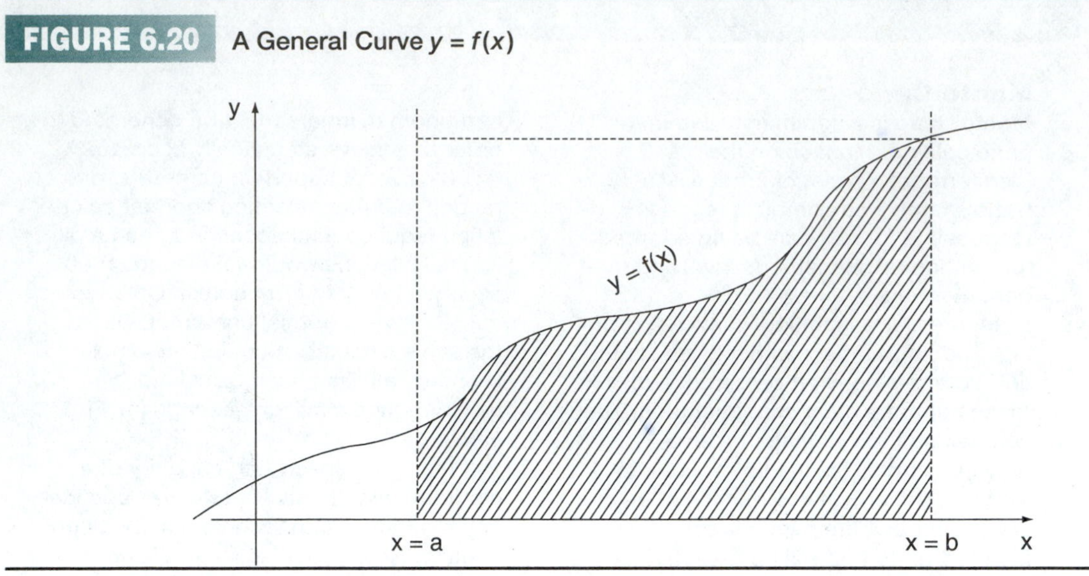

The area under a curve can be approximated by using Monte Carlo simulation. To understand how this simulation works, consider that we wish to determine the area under the curve $y = f(x)$ shown in Figure 6.20, between the limits $x = a$ and $x = b$. On top of this curve we build a rectangular box bounded by the *x axis*, the lines $x = a$, $x = b$, and the line defined by the curve at its highest y value.

Now assume that we toss N darts at random into the rectangular box and that M of these darts land between the curve and the *x axis*. Calculate the ratio M/N as

$$\frac{M}{N} \approx \frac{\text{number of darts between the curve and the } x \text{ axis}}{\text{total number of darts in the box}}$$

The ratio M/N will be approximately equal to the ratio of the shaded area under the curve to the total area of the box; that is:

$$\frac{M}{N} \approx \frac{\text{area under the curve (shaded area)}}{\text{total area of the box}}$$

From this, we can calculate the area under the curve as:

$$\text{Area under the curve (shaded area)} \approx \text{total area of the box } \frac{M}{N}$$

where the total area of the box is found by multiplying the length by the width. The problem is to write a computer program that effectively tosses darts and determines the area under any curve $y = f(x)$ between the limits $x = a$ and $x = b$.

Analyze the Problem for Input/Output Requirements The inputs required for this problem will be

1. the equation of the curve we want the area for
2. the lower x limit, a, between which the area is to be calculated
3. the upper x limit, b, between which the area is to be calculated

The output will be the approximate area under the curve.

Develop a Solution We will restrict ourselves to functions and ranges in which the curve is generally increasing or decreasing within the desired range, and in which the curve lies entirely above the *x axis*. These restrictions are not necessary to find the area, but help to simplify the solution. The increasing/decreasing restriction makes it easy to locate the maximum y value, because for increasing curves the maximum y value occurs at $x = b$ and has the value $f(b)$. For decreasing curves the maximum y value occurs at $x = a$ and has the value $f(a)$. Requiring that the curve lie above the *x axis* removes the problem of assessing which parts of the curve are above and below the *x axis*.

The equation $y = f(x)$ for the curve will be written in a function that finds y for a given argument value of x. For example, if the function is $y = 3x^2 + 2x + 1$, the function is simply:

```
float fcn(float x)
{
  return (3.0 * pow(x,2) + 2.0 * x + 1.0);
}
```

For any other function $y = f(x)$, just replace the content of the return statement with the expression defining $f(x)$.

The formula for determining the total area of the box is

$$width * length = (b-a) * \text{ymax}$$

where *ymax* = f(b) for an increasing curve and $f(a)$ for a decreasing curve.

Now choose a pair of random numbers `xrnd`, and `yrnd` such that $a \leq$ *xrnd* $< b$ and $0 \leq$ *yrnd* $\leq$ `ymax` to simulate the coordinates where a dart would land in the box. A random number between a and b can be found using the equation $(b-a)$ * *random number* + a, where *random number* is between 0.0 and 1.0. Using `xrnd`, determine ycalc = f(xrnd), and then determine if yrnd lies under the curve; that is, whether `yrnd` $\leq$ `ycalc`. If so, increment the count of numbers under the curve. Increment the count of total number of points selected. Repeat this process for a large number of randomly selected points. Then calculate and display the area under the curve.

A structure chart for the solution is shown in Figure 6.21 on p. 362. The pseudocode for this solution is:

```
Define the function fcn(x).
Define whether the function is increasing or decreasing.
Define the number of iterations as MAXREPS.
Ask for the limits a and b.
If the function is increasing
   ymax = f(b).
Else
   ymax = f(a).
Calculate the total area as (b-a)(ymax).
Initialize undercount and totalcount to zero.
While totalcount # MAXREPS
  Generate an xrnd and yrnd random number.
  Calculate ycalc = f(xrnd)
    If yrnd # ycalc
      increment undercount
  increment totalcount.
End While.
Calculate area = (total area)(undercount / totalcount).
Print the area.
```

FIGURE 6.21 Structure Chart for Monte Carlo Simulation

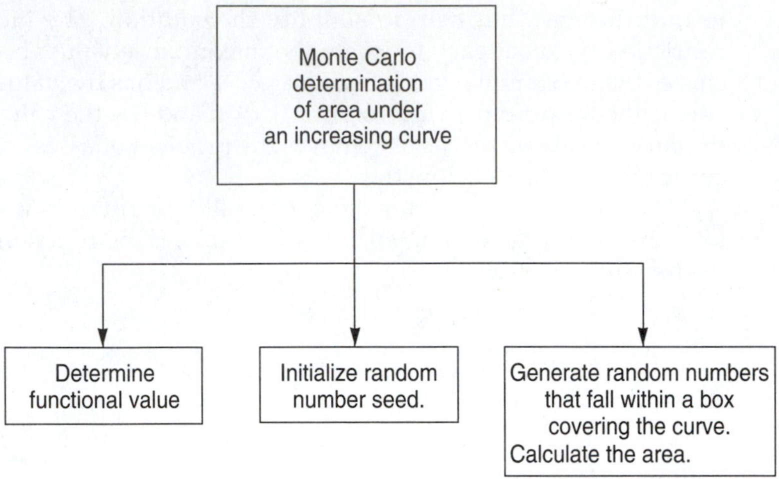

Code the Solution Program 6.17 presents the algorithm written as C++ code:

PROGRAM 6.17

```
#include <iostream.h>
#include <stdlib.h>
#include <math.h>

const int MAXCOUNT  = 1000;
const int INCREASE = 1;    // this is an increasing curve

float fcn(float x)
{
  return (3.0*pow(x,2) + 2.0*x + 1.0);
}

int main()
{
  int undercount = 0;
  int totalcount = 0;
  float rnumx, rnumy;
  float x, val, xrnd, yrnd, ymax, ycalc, a, b, boxarea, area;
  float fcn(float);

  srand(time(NULL));
  cout << "What is the lower limit on x? ";
  cin  >> a;
  cout << "What is the upper limit on x? ";
  cin  >> b;
```

(continued on next page)

(continued from previous page)

```
  if (INCREASE)
    ymax = fcn(b);
  else
    ymax = fcn(a);

  boxarea = (b - a) * ymax;

  while (totalcount < MAXCOUNT)
  {
    rnumx = rand(); // get a random x value
    val = rnumx / RAND_MAX; // creates a number between 0 and 1
    xrnd = (b - a) * val + a;
    rnumy = rand(); // get a random y value
    val = rnumy / RAND_MAX;
    yrnd = ymax * val;
    if (yrnd <= fcn(xrnd))
      undercount++;
    totalcount++;
  }

  area = boxarea * (float)undercount/(float)totalcount;

  cout << "\nFor the curve defined in the function fcn(x),\n";
  cout << "between x = " << a << " and x = " << b << endl;
  cout << "The area is approximately " << area << endl;

  return 0;
}
```

Notice that we have placed the `fcn()` function, which defines the curve, at the top of the program. This is to alert us that this function must be changed for each curve $y = f(x)$.

Test and Correct the Program During the testing phase, statements could be inserted into the code to display the values of `xrnd`, `yrnd`, `ycalc`, `undercount`, and `totalcount` during each iteration. If you assign a very large value to `MAXREPS`, you may want to print a message during each iteration that tells the user that the program is executing. Test the program for various values of a and b. Increase `MAXREPS` for greater accuracy. Alter the function *`fcn(x)`* to find the area under a different curve. If you are comfortable with calculus, compare your answers with the integral of the function; otherwise, sketch the curve on graph paper and estimate the area to see if you are getting reasonable results. A sample run looks like:

```
What is the lower limit on x? 2.0
What is the upper limit on x? 4.0

For the curve defined in the function fcn(x),
between x = 2.00 and x = 4.00
The area is approximately 69.084
```

For this curve, using calculus, the true area under the curve between x = 2.0 and x = 4.0 is 70.0.

Exercises 6.7

1. Modify Program 6.15 so that it requests the number of tosses from the user. (*Hint:* Make sure the program correctly determines the percentages of heads and tails obtained.)
2. *Central Limit Theorem Simulation:* Modify Program 6.15 so that it automatically generates 20 simulations, with each simulation having 1000 tosses. Print out the percentage for each run and the percentages for the 20 runs combined.
3. Modify Program 6.16 to allow the user to run the game again after a game has been completed. The program should display the message `"WOULD YOU LIKE TO PLAY AGAIN - 'Y'/'N'?: "` and restart if the user enters either `Y` or `y`.
4. Write a program that tests the effectiveness of the `rand()` library function. Start by initializing 10 counters such as `zerocount`, `onecount`, `twocount`, `...`, `ninecount` to 0. Then generate a large number of pseudorandom integers between 0 and 9. Each time a 0 occurs increment `zerocount`, when a 1 occurs increment `onecount`, etc. Finally, print out the number of 0's, 1's, 2's, etc., that occurred and the percentage of the time they occurred.
5. Many algorithms have been developed for generating pseudorandom numbers. Some of these algorithms utilize a counting scheme, such as counting bits beginning at some arbitrary location in a changing memory. Another scheme, which creates pseudorandom numbers by performing a calculation, is the *power residue method*. The power residue method begins with an odd n-digit integer, which is referred to as the "seed" number. The seed is multiplied by the value $(10^{n/2}-3)$. Use of the lowest n digits of the result (the "residue") produces a new seed. Continuing this procedure produces a series of random numbers, with each new number used as the seed for the next number. If the original seed has four or more digits (n equal to or greater than 4) and is not divisible by either 2 or 5, this procedure will yield $5 \times 10^{(n-2)}$ random numbers before a sequence of numbers repeats itself. For example, starting with a six-digit seed (n = 6), such as 654321, a series of 5×10^4 = 50,000 random numbers can be generated.

   As an algorithm, the specific steps in generating pseudorandom numbers using a power residue procedure consists of the following steps:

   Step 1: Have a user enter a six-digit integer seed that is not divisible by 2 or 5; this means the number should be an odd number not ending in 5.
   Step 2: Multiply the seed number by 997, which is 10^3-3.
   Step 3: Extract the lower six digits of the result produced by step 2. Use this random number as the next seed.
   Step 4: Repeat steps 2 and 3 for as many random numbers as needed.

   Thus, if the user-entered seed number is 654321 (step 1), the first random number generated is calculated as follows:

   Step 2: 654321 * 997 = 652358037
   Step 3: Extract the lower six digits of the number obtained in step 2. This is accomplished using a standard programming "trick."

   The trick involves:

   Step 3a: Dividing the number by 10^6 = 1000000. For example, 652358037 / 1000000 = 652.358037.
   Step 3b: Taking the integer part of the result of step 3a. For example, the integer part of 652.358037 = 652.
   Step 3c: Multiplying the previous result by 10^6. For example, 652×10^6 = 652000000.
   Step 3d: Subtracting this result from the original number. For example, 652358037 − 652000000 = 358037.

The integer part of a floating-point number can either be taken by assigning the floating-point number to an integer variable, or by a C++ cast (see Section 3.3). In our procedure we will use the cast mechanism. Thus, the algorithm for producing a random number can be accomplished using the following code:

```
i = int(997.0 * x / 1.e6);    // take the integer part
x = 997.0 * x - i * 1.e6;
```

Using this information:

a. Create a function named `randnum()` that accepts a floating-point "seed" as a parameter and returns a floating-point random number between 0 and 1.e6.

b. Incorporate the `randnum()` function created in Exercise 5a into a working C++ program that produces 10 random numbers between 0 and 1.e6.

c. Test the randomness of the `randnum()` function created in Exercise 5a using the method described in Exercise 4. Try some even seed values and some odd seed values that end in 5 to determine whether these affect the randomness of the numbers.

6. In the game of Blackjack the cards 2 through 10 are counted at their face values, regardless of suit, all picture cards (jack, queen, and king) are counted as 10, and an ace is counted as either a 1 or an 11, depending on the total count of all the cards in a player's hand. The ace is counted as 11 only if the total value of all cards in a player's hand does not exceed 21, else it is counted as a 1. Using this information write a C++ program that uses a random number generator to select three cards (a 1 initially corresponding to an ace, a 2 corresponding to a face card of two, and so on), calculate the total value of the hand appropriately, and display the value of the three cards with a printed message.

7. Write a C++ function that determines the quadrant in which a line drawn from the origin resides. The determination of the quadrant is made using the angle that the line makes with the positive X as follows:

Angle from the positive *X* axis	Quadrant
Between 0 and 90 degrees	1
Between 90 and 180 degrees	2
Between 180 and 270 degrees	3
Between 270 and 360 degrees	4

Note: If the angle is exactly 0, 90, 180, or 270 degrees the corresponding line does not reside in any quadrant but lies on an axis. For this case, your function should return a zero.

8. All years that are evenly divisible by 400 or are evenly divisible by four and not evenly divisible by 100 are leap years. For example, since 1600 is evenly divisible by 400, the year 1600 was a leap year. Similarly, since 1988 is evenly divisible by four but not by 100, the year 1988 was also a leap year. Using this information, write a C++ function that accepts the year as a user input, and returns a one if the passed year is a leap year or a zero if it is not.

9. Based on an automobile's model year and weight the state of New Jersey determines the car's weight class and registration fee using the following schedule:

Model Year	Weight	Registration Fee
1970 or earlier	Less than 2,700 lbs	$16.50
	2,700 to 3,800 lbs	25.50
	More than 3,800 lbs	46.50
1971 to 1979	Less than 2,700 lbs	27.00
	2,700 to 3,800 lbs	30.50
	More than 3,800 lbs	52.50
1980 or later	Less than 3,500 lbs	19.50
	3,500 or more lbs	52.50

Using this information, write a C++ function that accepts the year and weight of an automobile and returns the registration fee for the car.

10. Deal and display a hand of four different cards that can come from four different suits (hearts, clubs, diamonds, spades) of 13 cards each named ace = 1, 2, 3, 4, 5, 6, 7, 8, 9, 10, jack = 11, queen = 12, king = 13. [*Hint:* use the expressions `suit = (int)(4.0 * random number + 1.0)` and `card = (int)(13.0 * random number + 1)`, where the random number is between 0 and 1.]

11. It has been said that a monkey pushing keys at random on a typewriter could produce the works of Shakespeare, given sufficient time. Simulate this by having a program select and display letters at random. Count the number of letters typed until the program produces one of these two-letter words: *at, is, he, we, up,* or *on.* When one of these words is produced, stop the program and display the total number of letters typed. (*Hint:* Choose a letter by selecting a random integer number between 1 and 26.)

12. Write a program to simulate the rolling of two dice. If the total of the two dice is 7 or 11 you win; otherwise, you lose. Embellish this program as much as you like, with betting, different odds, different combinations for win or lose, stopping play when you have no money left or reach the house limit, displaying the dice, etc. [*Hint:* Calculate the dots showing on each die by the expression `dots = (int)(6.0 * random number + 1)`, where the random number is between 0 and 1.]

13. Modify the value of the named constant `MAXCOUNT` to 10, 100, and 10000, respectively, and rerun Program 6.17 to see how these values affect the accuracy of the result. Fill in the following table with the area reported by each run of the program. Comment on what did occur and what you think should have occurred. If there were any differences between what did occur and what you expected, comment on what you think the differences were caused by.

	MAXCOUNT		
10	**100**	**1000**	**10000**

14. Use the Monte Carlo algorithm developed in Program 6.17 to find an approximate value for π, which is 3.14159 accurate to five decimal places. In Figure 6.22, the shaded area represents one-quarter of a circle having a radius r of 1 unit. The area of the box bounded by the axes and the lines $x = 1$ and $y = 1$ is 1 square unit. The area of the quarter-circle is $1/4\pi r^2$, but since $r = 1$ this area equals $\pi/4$ square units. Therefore,

$$\frac{\pi}{4} = \frac{\text{area of quarter circle}}{\text{area of the box}} \approx \frac{M}{N}$$

where M is the number of random numbers that fall under the curve and N is the total number of random numbers selected within the box. Generate random points inside the box (`xrnd`, `yrnd`) such that 0 ≤ `xrnd` ≤ 1 and 0 ≤ `yrnd` ≤ 1, and test to see if `yrnd` ≤ `ycalc`, where `ycalc = f(xrnd)`, and f(x) is the curve defined by the circle

$$y = f(x) = sqrt(1-x^2)$$

15. Here is a version of a problem called "the random walk." It can be extended to two or three dimensions and used to simulate molecular motion, to determine the effectiveness of reactor shielding, or to calculate a variety of other probabilities.

FIGURE 6.22 Calculation of π

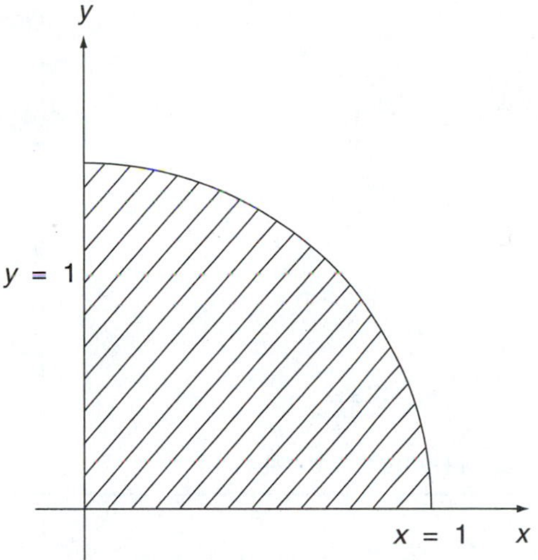

Assume that your very tired and sleepy pet dog leaves his favorite lamppost on warm summer evenings and staggers randomly either 2 steps in the direction toward home or 1 step in the opposite direction. After the first step the dog again staggers randomly 2 steps toward home or 1 step backward, and does this again, and again. If the pet reaches a total distance of 10 steps from the lamppost in the direction toward home, you find him and take him home. If the dog arrives back at the lamppost before reaching 10 steps in the direction toward home, he lies down and spends the night at the foot of the lamppost.

Write a C++ program that simulates 500 summer evenings, and calculate and print the percentage of the time your pet sleeps at home for these evenings. [*Hint*: In a loop, determine forward or backward based on the value of a random number. Accumulate the distance the dog has reached toward your home. If the distance reaches 10, stop the loop and increment the home count. If the distance reaches 0 before it reaches 10, stop the loop but do not increment the home count. Repeat this loop 500 times and find the ratio of (home count)/500.]

6.8 PLANNING FOR OBJECTS: THE DYNAMIC OMT MODEL

The object modeling technique (OMT) analysis and design method introduced in Section 5.8 consists of three different graphical models: object, dynamic, and functional. Of these three models the object model is the most important and becomes the basis for designing a program. The dynamic model is next in importance. Although it is auxiliary to the object model, it can be very helpful in describing the operations that need to be incorporated into the object model. The **dynamic model** is considered a behavioral model because it describes the behavior of the system. As such, it defines *what* operations are required. The last one, the **functional model** describes *how* each operation is performed by defining the algorithms used in each operation. In practice the functional model is little used. In its place pseudocode, which is currently unrivaled for describing a single operational algorithm, is used.

FIGURE 6.23 The Dynamic Model Identifies Operations to Be Included in the Object Model

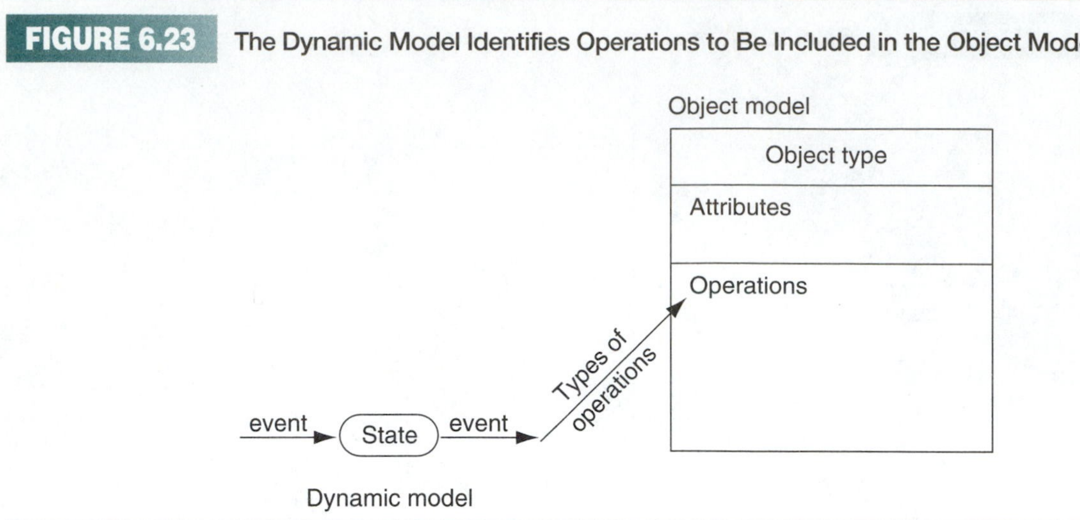

The Dynamic Model

Each object's operations are described by the dynamic model. This is accomplished by describing how a typical object's attributes change over time. The most important part of describing these changes is the identification of the events causing the changes. Each event becomes associated with an operation that is then included in the object model. Figure 6.23 illustrates the relationship between the object and dynamic models. The dynamic model consists of one or more state diagrams that use events and states in their construction. An *event* is defined as an individual signal (stimulus) from one object to another. For example, turning the key in a car's ignition is a signal to the electrical system to turn on or off. As such, in object terms, turning the key is an event. Similarly, pushing the button on an elevator is considered an event. The press of the button is a signal to the elevator to move to another floor.

In contrast to events are states. An object's *state*, in its simplest form, is defined by the values of an object's attributes. For example, a switch that can be either on or off has two states: on and off. Similarly, if a rectangle is described by three attributes, its length, width, and position, giving values to these attributes defines a single state for a rectangle object.

A dynamic model is composed of state diagrams, where each object in the system has its own state diagram. For example, if the system being programmed has three objects, the dynamic model will consist of three state diagrams, one for each object. Each state diagram is a structured network of events and states. Figure 6.24 illustrates the basic symbols and notation used in a state diagram. As shown, the two primary symbols are a flow line, which denotes an event, and a rectangle with rounded corners, which denotes a state. Each event shown in a state diagram can be augmented by a guard, attribute, or action, all of which are explained later in this section. Similarly, each state can have an optional state name listed in the state rectangle plus activity information.

Notice in Figure 6.24 that events separate states. A state has duration in that it exists over an interval of time and only changes in response to an event, which is assumed to occur in zero time. For example, turning a car's ignition key to

FIGURE 6.24 State Diagram Symbols

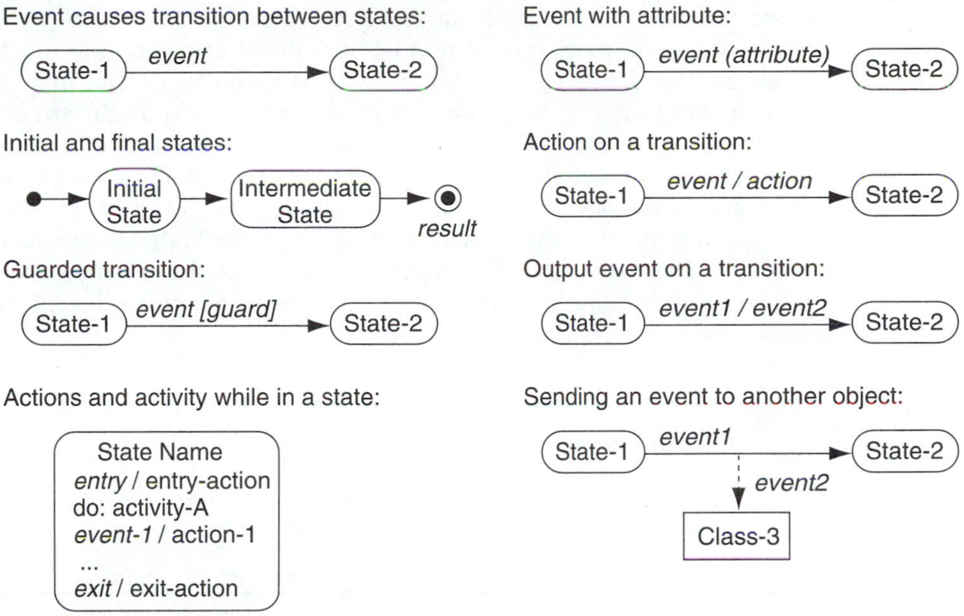

Event causes transition between states:

State-1 —*event*→ State-2

Initial and final states:

● → Initial State → Intermediate State → ◉ *result*

Guarded transition:

State-1 —*event [guard]*→ State-2

Actions and activity while in a state:

State Name
entry / entry-action
do: activity-A
event-1 / action-1
...
exit / exit-action

Event with attribute:

State-1 —*event (attribute)*→ State-2

Action on a transition:

State-1 —*event / action*→ State-2

Output event on a transition:

State-1 —*event1 / event2*→ State-2

Sending an event to another object:

State-1 —*event1*→ State-2
event2 → Class-3

start the engine is an event. Once the car's engine is started the state of the engine, which is running, is assumed to continue until an event occurs that turns the engine off. Figure 6.25 illustrates a state diagram for a car's ignition system. As shown, the ignition system consists of three states: On, Off, and Starting. The events associated with these states are "Turn key to on," "Turn key to start," "Release key," and "Turn key to off." Notice that the event "Turn key to start" has the precondition "[transmission in park]." Preconditions, which are also referred to as *guards*, are listed within square brackets after the event's name. A precondition specifies that the event cannot take place unless the precondition is satisfied. In this case, "Turn key to start" will not force a change in state unless the transmission is in park.

Events are always one-way signals from one object to another. If the signal also provides data values to an object, the data values are listed in parentheses following the event name. These data values are referred to as an event's

FIGURE 6.25 A Car's Ignition System State Diagram

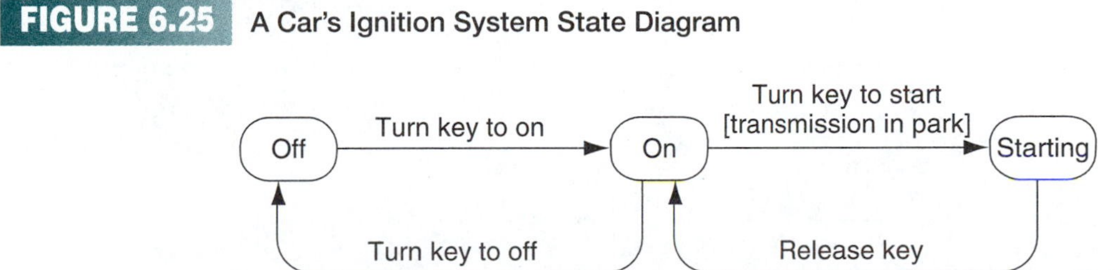

attributes. Since each event eventually defines an operation, which in C++ is coded as a function, an event's attributes become the function's arguments. As one-way signals, however, events never receive a return value from the implemented function. Any reply from the receiving object is considered a separate event to the sending object, which must be realized using another function.

Just as events may have actions associated with them, states may have activities. The difference between an action and an activity is the time needed to accomplish them. Actions, as we have noted, are assumed to be accomplished in zero time (instantaneously), whereas activities take time to complete. As such, activities are associated with states. The notation `do: activity` within a state rectangle denotes that the activity begins when the state is entered and terminates when the state is left. For example, as illustrated in Figure 6.26, if the state of a house bell-chime system is ringing in response to the event "Push bell-button," the action is "ring the chimes."

FIGURE 6.26 A State with an Activity

A state diagram can either represent a continuously operating system or a finite, one-shot life cycle. For example, making one phone call, or filling a car with a tank of gas is a finite, one-shot activity. The operation of the phone itself or the gas pump, however, where the system goes from idle to active is a continuous operation. One-shot activities can be modeled by one-shot state diagrams where the initial state, which represents the creation of an object, is shown by a solid circle. The final state, which represents the end of the cycle and the destruction of an object, is shown by a bull's-eye circle, as illustrated in Figure 6.27.

FIGURE 6.27 A One-Shot Diagram of a Water Sprinkler

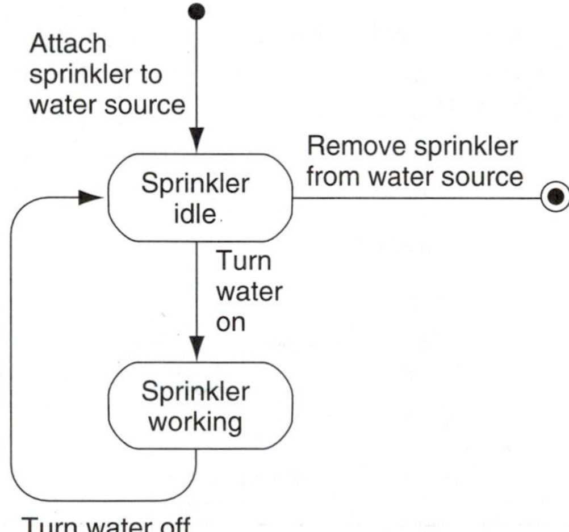

FIGURE 6.28 The Initial `Pump` Class Object Model

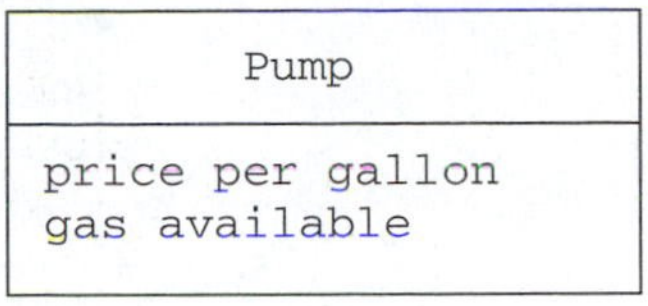

Pump
price per gallon gas available

An Example

Consider the operation of a single gas pump. Pumping from the gas tank begins when a request for gas is made, which in reality is the activation of the pump nozzle, and stops when a specified number of gallons of gas have been pumped. Assume that the attributes of interest are the price per gallon of gas and the amount of gas in the supply tank.

Calling the object type `Pump`, having attributes `price per gallon` and `gallons available`, results in the initial object model shown in Figure 6.28. Notice that the `Pump` class has no operations listed. To determine what operations we need to provide, we construct a dynamic model. The purpose of such a model is to provide the behavior of a typical object, which in programming terms corresponds to the operations that the class must possess. An operation represents what an object does in response to an event. The response can be either to change its own state or to send another event to another object. This new event can be sent either to the originator of the first event or to some other object. Figure 6.29 shows a possible one-shot diagram for a typical transaction using a `Pump` object. Such one-shot transactions are frequently beneficial in identifying an object's behavior.

Since a gas pump is in continuous operation, the one-shot dynamic diagram shown in Figure 6.29 is only useful in beginning the process of thinking in object terms. A dynamic diagram of the continuous operation of the pump is shown by

FIGURE 6.29 A One-Shot `Pump` Class Dynamic Model

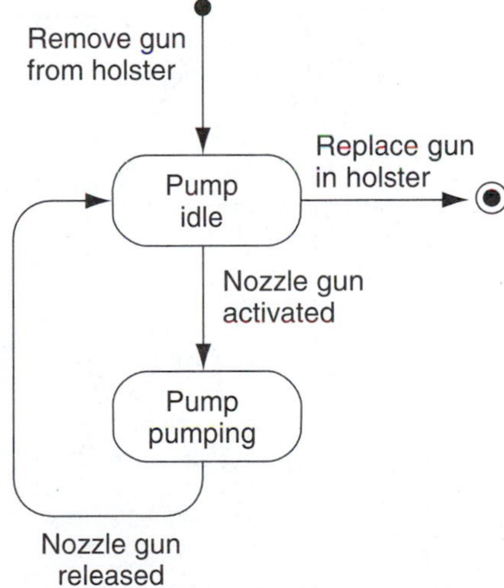

FIGURE 6.30 A Continuous `Pump` Class Dynamic Model

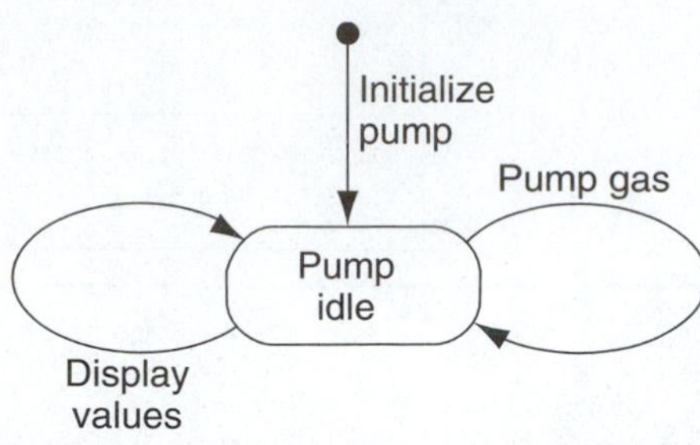

Figure 6.30. In keeping with the concept of a dynamic model, events are assumed to be zero-time activities. In our model this implies that the event "Pump gas" is done in zero time, which means that the pump is effectively always in an idle state and the pump gas event performs as per the following algorithm:

If sufficient gas is in the supply tank to meet the request
  Set amount pumped to amount requested.
Else
  Set amount pumped equal to the amount remaining in the tank.
EndIf.
Deduct the amount pumped from the amount in the tank.
Calculate the total price as price per gallon * amount pumped.

Using Figure 6.30 to identify the important pump events, we can incorporate the three events shown into operations within our initial object model. The completed object model is shown in Figure 6.31. The implementation of this object is completed in Section 7.4.

We should again mention that the dynamic model serves as an adjunct to the object model. Thus, if you can determine what operations are required for a class without the need to focus explicitly on them using a dynamic model, you can dispense with the dynamic model altogether.

FIGURE 6.31 The Final `Pump` Class Object Model

```
Pump
-----------------------------
price per gallon
gallons available
-----------------------------
Initialize pump
Display price per
  gallon and gallons
  available
Pump gas by deducting
  amount requested
  and calculate
  total price
```

Exercises 6.8

1. Describe the differences between the object, dynamic, and functional models.
2. Describe the relationship between a dynamic model and state diagrams.
3. Construct a one-shot state diagram for a game of checkers.
4. Construct a state diagram for using the brakes on a car.
5. Construct a state diagram for shifting a car's transmission. Assume that there are six gears: Park, Reverse, Neutral, Drive, Drive-1, and Drive-2.
6. The control switch on a thermostat has three positions: Cool, Off, and Heat. Construct a state diagram for the switch.
7. Draw a state diagram for a traffic light that can be in one of three states: Green, Yellow, or Red.

6.9 COMMON PROGRAMMING ERRORS

An extremely common programming error related to functions is passing incorrect data types. The values passed to a function must correspond to the data types of the parameters declared for the function. One way to verify that correct values have been received is to display all passed values within a function's body before any calculations are made. Once this verification has taken place, you can dispense with the display.[13]

Another common error can occur when the same variable is declared locally within both the calling and called functions. Even though the variable name is the same, a change to one local variable does *not* alter the value in the other local variable.

Related to this error is the error that can occur when a local variable has the same name as a global variable. Within the function declaring it, the use of the variable's name only affects the local variable's contents unless the global scope resolution operator, `::`, is used.

Another common error is omitting the called function's prototype either within or before the calling function. The called function must be alerted to the type of value that will be returned, and this information is provided by the function prototype. The prototype can be omitted if the called function is physically placed in a program before its calling function. The actual value returned by a function can be verified by displaying it both before and after it is returned.

The last two common errors are those of terminating a function's header line with a semicolon and forgetting to include the data type of a function's parameters within the header line.

[13] In practice, a good debugger program should be used.

6.10 CHAPTER REVIEW

Key Terms

actual arguments
`auto`
call by reference
call by value
called function
calling function
dynamic model
`extern`
formal arguments
formal parameters
function body
function header
function overloading
function prototype
functional model
global scope
global variable
local scope
local variable
memory stack
recursive functions
`register`
return statement
scaling
scope
`static`
storage class
stub
variable scope

Summary

1. A function is called by giving its name and passing any data to it in the parentheses following the name. If a variable is one of the arguments in a function call, the called function receives a copy of the variable's value.
2. The common form of a user-written function is:

```
return-type function-name(formal parameter list)
{
   declarations and other C++ statements;
   return expression;
}
```

   The first line of the function is called the function header. The opening and closing braces of the function and all statements in between these braces constitute the function's body. The returned data type is, by default, an integer when no returned data type is specified. The formal parameter list is a comma-separated list of parameter declarations.
3. A function's return type is the data type of the value returned by the function. If no type is declared, the function is assumed to return an integer value. If the function does not return a value it should be declared as a `void` type.
4. Functions can directly return at most a single data type value to their calling functions. This value is the value of the expression in the return statement.
5. Using reference arguments, a function can be passed the address of a variable. If a called function is passed an address, it has the ability to access directly the respective calling function's variable. Using passed addresses permits a called function effectively to return multiple values.
6. Functions can be declared to all calling functions by means of a function prototype. The prototype provides a declaration for a function that specifies the data type returned by the function, its name, and the data types of the arguments expected by the function. As with all declarations, a function proto-

type is terminated with a semicolon and may be included within local variable declarations or as a global declaration. The most common form of a function prototype is:

data-type function-name(parameter data type list);

If the called function is placed physically above the calling function, no further declaration is required, since the function's definition serves as a global declaration to all following functions.

7. Every variable used in a program has a scope, which determines where in the program the variable can be used. The scope of a variable is either local or global and is determined by where the variable's definition statement is placed. A local variable is defined within a function and can only be used within its defining function or block. A global variable is defined outside a function and can be used in any function following the variable's definition. All global variables that are not specifically initialized by the user are initialized to zero by the compiler and can be shared between files using the keyword `extern`.
8. Every variable has a class. The class of a variable determines how long the value in the variable will be retained: `auto` variables are local variables that exist only while their defining function is executing; `register` variables are similar to automatic variables but are stored in a computer's internal registers rather than in memory; `static` variables can be either global or local and retain their values for the duration of a program's execution. The `static` variables are also set to zero when they are defined if they are not explicitly initialized by the user.
9. A recursive solution is one in which the solution can be expressed in terms of a "simpler" version of itself. A recursive algorithm must always specify the first case or cases and how the nth case is related to the $(n-1)$ case.
10. If a problem solution can be expressed repetitively or recursively with equal ease, the repetitive solution is preferable because it executes faster and uses less memory. In many advanced applications, recursion is simpler to visualize and the only practical means of implementing a solution.

Exercises

1. A function is defined by the following code:

```
float FractionToDecimal(real numerator, real denominator)
{
  return (numerator/denominator);
}
```

Write the shortest driver program module you can to test this function and check the passing of parameters.

2. A formula to raise a real number a to the real power b is given by the formula

$$a^b = e^{[b * \ln(a)]}$$

where a must be positive and b must be positive or zero. Using this formula write a function named `power()` that accepts a and b as real values and returns a^b.

3. A fraction handling program contains this menu:

```
A. Add two fractions
B. Convert a fraction to decimal
C. Multiply two fractions
Q. Quit
```

   a. Write C++ code for the program with stub functions for the choices.

   b. Insert the function `FractionToDecimal()` from Exercise 1 into the code with appropriate commands to pass and display the parameters.

   c. Complete the program by replacing the stub functions with functions that perform appropriate operations.

4. a. The time in hours, minutes, and seconds is to be passed to a function named `totsec()`. Write `totsec()` to accept these values, determine the total number of seconds in the passed data, and display the calculated value.

   b. Include the `totsec()` function written for Exercise 4a in a working program. The `main()` function should correctly call `totsec` and display the value returned by the function. Use the following test data to verify your program's operation: hours = 10, minutes = 36, and seconds = 54. Make sure you do a hand calculation to verify the result displayed by your program.

5. A value that is sometimes useful is the greatest common divisor of two integers $n1$ and $n2$. A famous mathematician, Euclid, discovered an efficient method to do this more than 2000 years ago. Right now, however, we'll settle for a stub. Write the integer function stub `gcd(n1, n2)`. Simply have it return a value that suggests it received its arguments correctly. (*Hint:* `N1 + N2` is a good choice of return values. Why isn't `N1 / N2` a good choice?)

6. Euclid's method for finding the greatest common divisor (GCD) of two positive integers consists of the following steps:

   Step 1: Divide the larger number by the smaller and retain the remainder.
   Step 2: Divide the smaller number by the remainder, again retaining the remainder.
   Step 3: Continue dividing the prior remainder by the current remainder until the remainder is zero, at which point the last nonzero remainder is the greatest common divisor.

   For example, assume the two positive integers are 84 and 49, we have:

   Step 1: 84/49 yields a remainder of 35.
   Step 2: 49/35 yields a remainder of 14.
   Step 3: 35/14 yields a remainder of 7.
   14/7 yields a remainder of 0.

   Thus, the last nonzero remainder, which is 7, is the greatest common divisor of 84 and 49.

   Using Euclid's algorithm, replace the stub function written for Exercise 5 with an actual function that determines and returns the GCD of its two integer arguments.

7. a. Write a function named `tax()` that accepts a dollar amount and a tax rate as formal arguments, and returns the tax due on the dollar amount. For example, if the numbers 100.00 and .06 are passed to the function, the value returned should be 6.00, which is 100.00 times .06.

b. Include the `tax()` function written for Exercise 7a in a working program. The `main()` function should correctly call `tax()` and display the value returned by the function.

8. a. Write a function named `daycount()` that accepts a month, day, and year as its input parameters, calculates an integer representing the total number of days from the turn of the century corresponding to the passed date, and returns the calculated integer to the calling function. For this problem assume that each year has 365 days and each month has 30 days. Test your function by verifying that the date 1/1/00 returns a day count of one.

   b. Include the `daycount()` function written for Exercise 8a in a working program. The main() function should correctly call `daycount()` and display the integer returned by the function.

9. a. A clever and simple method of preparing to sort dates into either ascending (increasing) or descending (decreasing) order is to first convert a date having the form month/day/year into an integer number using the formula $date = year * 10000 + month * 100 + day$. For example, using this formula the date 12/6/88 converts to the integer 881206 and the date 2/28/90 converts to the integer 900228. Sorting the resulting integer numbers automatically puts the dates into the correct order. Using this formula, write a function named `convertdays()` that accepts a month, day, and year, converts the passed data into a single date integer, and returns the integer to the calling function.

   b. Include the `convertdays()` function written for Exercise 9a in a working program. The `main()` function should correctly call `convertdays()` and display the integer returned by the function.

10. The following program uses the same variable names in both the calling and called function. Determine if this causes any problem for the compiler.

```
#include <iostream.h>
void main(void)
{
  int min, hour, sec;
  int time(int, int); // function prototype

  cout << "Enter two numbers: ";
  cin >> min, hour;
  sec = time(min, hour);
  cout << "The total number of seconds is " << sec << endl;
}

int time(int min, int hour)
{
  int sec;

  sec = (hour * 60 + min) * 60;
  return (sec);
}
```

11. Write a program that reads a key pressed on the keyboard and displays its code on the screen. Use the program to determine the code for the enter key. Then write a function named `ReadOneChar()` that reads a character and ignores any succeeding characters until the enter key is pressed. The entered character should be returned by the function.

12. Write a function named `pass()` that returns a reject or accept code depending on whether the mean tolerance of a group of parts is less than or greater than 1%. If the average is less than 1.0%, the function should return an `A` for accept, else it should return an `R` for reject.

13. a. Write and test a C++ function MakeMilesKmTable( ) to display a table of miles converted to kilometers. The arguments to the function should be the starting and stopping values of miles and the increment. The output should be a table of miles and their equivalent kilometer values. Use the relationship that 1 mile equals 1.61 kilometers.

    b. Modify the function written for Exercise 13a so that two columns are printed. For example, if the starting value is 1 mile, the ending value 20 miles, and the increment is 1, the display should look like:

```
Miles  =  Kilometer     Miles  =  Kilometers
 1           1.61        11          17.70
 2           3.22        12          19.31
 .            .           .            .
 .            .           .            .
10          16.09        20          32.18
```

    [*Hint:* Find `split = (start + stop)/2`. Let a loop execute from miles = start to split, and calculate and print across one line the values of miles and kilometers for both miles and `(miles - start + split + 1)`.]

14. Heron's formula for the area A of a triangle with sides of length a, b, and c is $A = sqrt([s(s - a)(s - b)(s - c)]$, where $s = (a + b + c)/2$. Write, test, and execute a function that accepts the values of a, b, and c as parameters from a calling function, and then calculates the values of s and $s(s - a)(s - b)(s - c)$. If this quantity is positive, the function calculates A. If the quantity is negative, a, b, and c do not form a triangle, and the function should set $A = -1$. The value of A should be returned by the function.

15. Write and test two functions EnterData( ) and PrintCheck( ) to produce the sample paycheck illustrated in Figure 6.32 on the screen. The items in parentheses should be accepted by EnterData( ) and passed to PrintCheck( ) for display.

FIGURE 6.32

Zzyz Corp.
1164 Sunrise Avenue
Kalispell, Montana

Date: (today's date)

Pay to the order of: (first and last name)

$ (amount)

UnderSecurity Bank
Missoula, MT

Authorized Signature

16. Your company will soon open a new office in France. So that they can do business there, they have asked you to prepare a comprehensive package that will perform the following conversions on demand:

Measure	American	to	Metric	by	Formula
Distance	Inch		Centimeter		2.54 cm/in
	Foot		Meter		0.305 m/ft
	Yard		Meter		0.9144 m/yd
	Mile		Kilometer		1.6909 km/mi
Temperature	Fahrenheit		Celsius		C = (5/9)(F – 32)
Weight	Pound		Kilogram		0.454 kg/lb
	Ounce		Gram		28.35 gm/oz
Currency	Dollar		Franc		Entered by the user About 5 Franc/$
Capacity	Quart		Liter		0.946 liter/qt
	Teaspoon		Milliliter		4.9 ml/tsp
Math	Degree		Radian		rad = (π/180)(degree)
	Degree		Grad		Grad = (200/180)(degree)

17. Write a function named `time()` that has an integer argument named `seconds` and three integer reference arguments named `hours`, `min`, and `sec`. The function is to convert the passed number of seconds into an equivalent number of hours, minutes, and seconds. Using the references, the function should directly alter the respective actual arguments in the calling function.

18. a. Write a function named `date()` that accepts a long integer of the form yymmdd, such as 980412, determines the corresponding month, day, and year, and returns these three values to the calling function. For example, if `date()` is called using the statement:

```
date(980412, &month, &day, &year)
```

the number 4 should be returned in `month`, the number 12 in `day`, and the number 98 in `year`.

    b. Include the `date()` subroutine written for Exercise 18a in a working program. The `main()` function should correctly call `date()` and display the three values returned by the function.

19. Write a function named `payment()` that has three arguments: `principal`, which is the amount financed; `int`, which is the monthly interest rate; and `months`, which is length of the loan in the number of months. The function should return the monthly payment according to the following formula:

$$payment = \frac{principal}{\left[\dfrac{1 - (1 + interest)^{-months}}{interest}\right]}$$

Note that the interest value used in this formula is a monthly rate, as a decimal. Thus if the yearly rate were 10%, the monthly rate would be (.10/12). Test your function. What argument values cause it to malfunction (and should not be input)?

20. The volume of a right circular cylinder is given by its radius squared times its height times π. Write a function that accepts two floating-point arguments, the radius of a cylinder and the cylinder's height, and returns the cylinder's volume.

21. Write a function named `distance()` that accepts the rectangular coordinates of two points (x_1, y_1) and (x_2, y_2), and calculates and returns the distance between the two points. The distance, d, between two points is given by the formula

$$d = \sqrt{(x_2 - x_1)^2 + (y_2 - y_1)^2}$$

Include your function in a complete working C++ program.

22. a. Write a function that calculates the area a of a circle when its circumference c is given. This function should call a second function that returns the radius r of the circle, given c. The relevant formulas are $r = c/2\pi$ and $a = \pi r^2$.

    b. Write a structure chart for a program that accepts the value of the circumference from the user, calculates the radius and area, and displays the calculated values.

    c. Write and run a C++ program for the structure chart developed in Exercise 22b.

23. a. A recipe for making enough acorn squash for four people requires the following ingredients:

    2 acorn squashes
    2 teaspoons of lemon juice
    1/4 cup of raisins
    1 1/2 cups of applesauce
    1/4 cup of brown sugar
    3 tablespoons of chopped walnuts.

    Using this information, write and test six functions that each accepts the number of people that must be served and returns the amount of each ingredient, respectively, that is required.

    b. Write a structure chart for a program that accepts the number of people to be served, calculates the quantity of each ingredient needed, and displays the calculated values.

    c. Write and run a C++ program for the structure chart developed in Exercise 23b.

24. The owner of a strawberry farm has made the following arrangement with a group of students: They may pick all the strawberries they want. When they are through picking the strawberries will be weighed. The farm will retain 50% of the strawberries and the students will divide the remainder evenly between them. Using this information, write and test a C++ function named `straw()` that accepts the number of students and the total pounds picked as input arguments, and returns the approximate number of strawberries each receives. Assume that a strawberry weighs approximately one ounce. There are 16 ounces to a pound. Include the `straw()` function in a working C++ program.

25. a. The determinant of a 2 × 2 matrix

$$\begin{vmatrix} a_{11} & a_{12} \\ a_{21} & a_{22} \end{vmatrix}$$

is $a_{11}a_{22} - a_{21}a_{12}$. Similarly, the determinant of a 3 × 3 matrix

$$\begin{vmatrix} a_{11} & a_{12} & a_{13} \\ a_{21} & a_{22} & a_{23} \\ a_{31} & a_{32} & a_{33} \end{vmatrix} =$$

$$a_{11} \begin{vmatrix} a_{22} & a_{23} \\ a_{32} & a_{33} \end{vmatrix} - a_{21} \begin{vmatrix} a_{12} & a_{13} \\ a_{32} & a_{33} \end{vmatrix} + a_{31} \begin{vmatrix} a_{12} & a_{13} \\ a_{22} & a_{23} \end{vmatrix}$$

Using this information write and test two functions, named `det2()` and `det3()`. The `det2()` function should accept the four coefficients of a 2 × 2 matrix and return its determinant. The `det3()` function should accept the nine coefficients of a 3 × 3 matrix and return its determinant by calling `det2()` to calculate the required 2 × 2 determinants.

b. Write a structure chart for a program that accepts the nine coefficients of a 3 × 3 matrix in one function, passes these coefficients to `det3()`, and uses a third function to display the calculated determinant.

c. Write and run a C++ program for the structure chart developed in Exercise 25b.

FIGURE 6.33 Correspondence Between Polar (Distance and Angle) and Cartesian (*x,y*) Coordinates

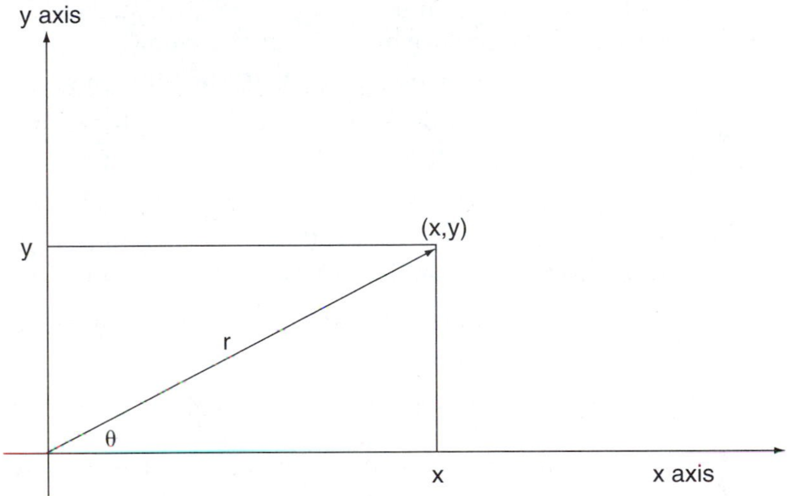

26. Assume that we must write a C++ program to convert the rectangular (x,y) coordinates of a point into polar form. That is, given an x and y position on a Cartesian coordinate system, as illustrated in Figure 6.33, we must calculate the distance from the origin, r, and the angle from the *x axis*, θ, specified by the point. The values of r and θ are referred to as the point's *polar coordinates.*

    When the x and y coordinates of a point are known, the equivalent r and θ coordinates can be calculated using the following formulas:

$$r = \sqrt{x^2 + y^2}$$

$$\theta = \text{atan}(y/x) \quad \text{for} \quad x \neq 0$$

Using these formulas, write a function named `polar()` that returns the r and θ values, respectively, for a point having rectangular coordinates x and y.

27. In the Fibonacci series 1, 1, 2, 3, 5 each element, after the first two elements, is simply the sum of the prior two values. In Exercise 1 of Section 6.6, you were asked to write a function that recursively computed the nth term of this series. For this exercise write a function that uses repetition to calculate the nth term.

28. A classic recursion problem is represented by the Towers of Hanoi puzzle, which consists of three pegs and a set of disks initially set up as shown in Figure 6.34. The object of the puzzle is to move all the disks from peg A to peg C, using peg B as needed, with the following constraints:

    1. Only one disk may be moved at a time.
    2. A larger disk can never be placed on a smaller disk. The legend associated with this problem is that it was initially given, with 64 disks, to ancient monks in a monastery with the understanding that when the task was completed and all 64 disks reached peg C in the correct order, the world would end.

    The solution to this puzzle is easily expressed as a recursive procedure where each n disk solution is defined in terms of an $n-1$ disk solution. To see how this works, first consider a one-disk puzzle. Clearly this has a simple solution, where we move the disk from peg A to peg C.

    Now consider the two-disk problem. The solution to this puzzle is:

    1. Use a one-disk solution to move the first disk to peg B.
    2. Move the second disk to peg C.
    3. Use a one-disk solution to move the disk on peg B to peg C.

    The three-disk problem is slightly more complicated, but can be solved in terms of the two- and one-disk puzzles. The solution is:

    1. Use a two-disk solution to get the first two disks in the right order on peg B.
    2. Move the third disk to peg C.
    3. Use a two-disk solution to correctly move the two disks from peg B to peg C.

    Notice how the three disk solution uses the two-disk solution and the two-disk solution uses the one-disk solution. Let's see if this same recursive reference holds for a four-disk puzzle.

FIGURE 6.34 The Towers of Hanoi Puzzle

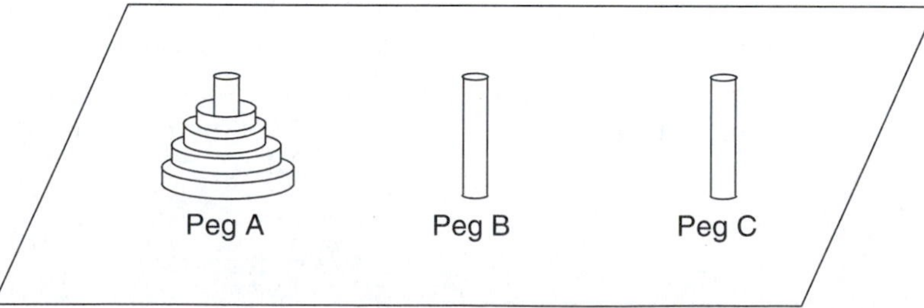

The solution to the four-disk puzzle is:

1. Use a three-disk solution to get the first three disks in the right order on peg B.
2. Move the fourth disk to peg C.
3. Use a three-disk solution to move the three disks from peg B to peg C.

At this stage we are ready to generalize the solution to n disks, which is:

1. Use an $n-1$ disk solution to get the first $n-1$ disks in the right order on peg B.
2. Move the nth disk to peg C.
3. Use the $n-1$ solution to move the $n-1$ disks from peg B to peg C.

Using this information, write a C++ program that asks the user how many disks to use and then prints the individual moves that must be made to solve the puzzle. For example, if the user responded with 3 for the number of disks the program should display the following:

```
Move a disk from Peg A to Peg C
Move a disk from Peg A to Peg B
Move a disk form Peg C to Peg B
Move a disk from Peg A to Peg C
Move a disk from Peg B to Peg A
Move a disk from Peg B to Peg C
Move a disk from Peg A to Peg C
```

Improving Communication

29. **MEMORANDUM**
To: Chief Programmer
From: Head of Programming Dept.

Subject: Object Models

Please explain to me why we need three models to do an object-oriented analysis when a single functional model was sufficient in our procedure-oriented projects.

Working in Teams

30. Have your team list the sequence of events that occurs when selecting an item from a soda vending machine. The sequence should start when a customer puts money in the machine and end when the customer removes a can of soda. From this list complete the event trace diagram shown in Figure 6.35.

Each vertical line on the event trace diagram corresponds to an object, while the horizontal lines correspond to events. The arrowhead on the event line corresponds to the event receiver while the line's tail corresponds to the event sender. Although time is assumed to increase from the top of the diagram to the bottom, the spacing between events is not drawn to time scale. The sequence of events, from first to last, however, is indicated on the diagram starting with the first event shown and ending with the last event.

FIGURE 6.35

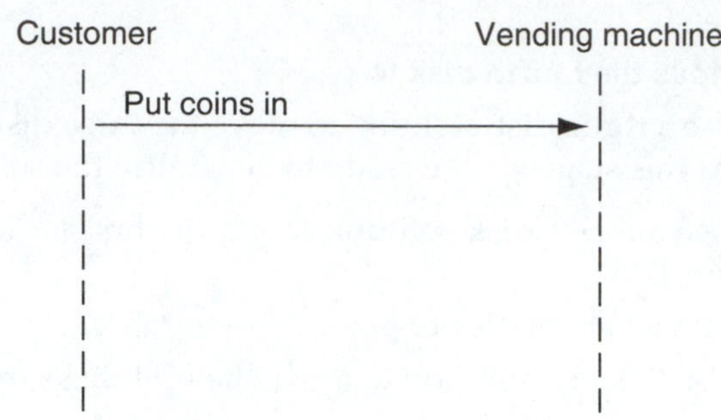

Once your team has completed the event trace diagram, use it to create a state diagram for the vending machine.

31. Have your team list the sequence of events that occurs when using an ATM machine. The sequence should start when the customer inserts his or her card and end when the card is returned. From this list complete the event trace diagram shown in Figure 6.36.

FIGURE 6.36

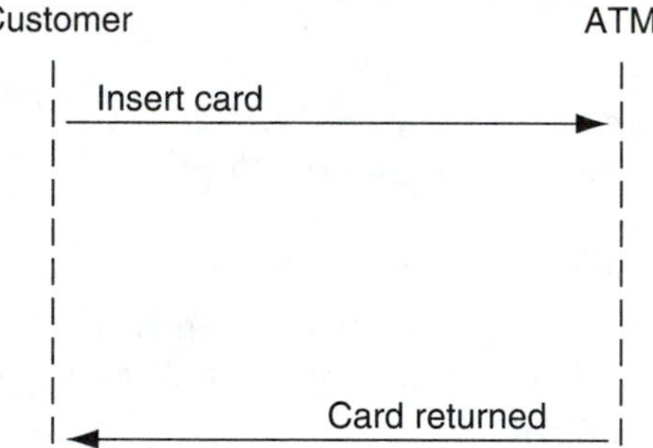

Each vertical line on the event trace diagram corresponds to an object, while the horizontal lines correspond to events. The arrowhead on the event line corresponds to the event receiver while the line's tail corresponds to the event sender. Although time is assumed to increase from the top of the diagram to the bottom, the spacing between events is not drawn to time scale. The sequence of events, from first to last, however, is indicated on the diagram starting with the first event shown and ending with the last event.

Once your team has completed the event trace diagram, use it to create a state diagram for the ATM machine.

32. Have your team list the sequence of events that occurs when making a phone call. The sequence should start when the caller picks up the phone and end when the caller hangs up. From this list complete the event trace diagram shown in Figure 6.37.

FIGURE 6.37

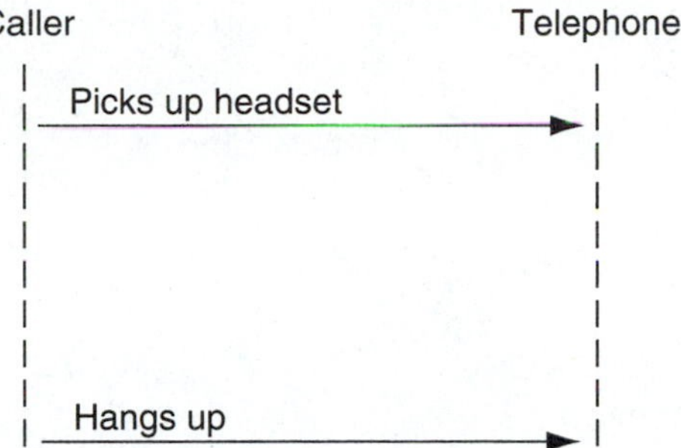

Each vertical line on the event trace diagram corresponds to an object, while the horizontal lines correspond to events. The arrowhead on the event line corresponds to the event receiver while the line's tail corresponds to the event sender. Although time is assumed to increase from the top of the diagram to the bottom, the spacing between events is not drawn to time scale. The sequence of events, from first to last, however, is indicated on the diagram starting with the first event shown and ending with the last event.

Once your team has completed the event trace diagram, use it to create a state diagram for the phone system.

Object-Oriented Programming in C++

For a programming language to be classified as object-oriented it most provide three features: user-definable data types, inheritance, and polymorphism. The description of each of these features and their implementation in C++ is provided in this part of the text. Specifically, the fundamentals of constructing data types, which in C++ are referred to as classes, are presented in Chapters 7 and 8. Inheritance and polymorphism are then described in Chapter 9.*

In addition to providing the fundamentals of object-oriented programming, the fundamentals of using I/O streams as they apply to creating, reading, and writing data files is presented in Chapter 10. The material in Chapter 10 can be read independently of the material in Chapters 7 through 9.

* The material in both Parts II and III, with the notable exception of the advanced dynamically linked lists covered in Chapter 15 and other minor exceptions noted in the text, are essentially independent of each other. Both Parts II and III do, however, depend on the procedural aspects of C++ presented in Part I. Thus, Parts II and III need not be covered in sequence and Part I can be followed equally well by either Parts II or III.

CHAPTER

7 Introduction to Classes

Besides being an improved version of C, the distinguishing characteristic of C++ is its support of object-oriented programming. Central to this object orientation is the concept of an abstract data type, which is a programmer-defined data type.

In this chapter we explore the implications of permitting programmers to define their own data types and then present C++'s mechanism for constructing abstract data types. As we will see, the construction of a data type is based on both variables and functions; variables provide the means for creating new data configurations, and functions provide the means for performing operations on these configurations. What C++ provides is a unique way of combining variables and functions together in a self-contained, cohesive unit from which objects can be created.

7.1 ABSTRACT DATA TYPES IN C++ (CLASSES)

The programming environment has changed dramatically during the last few years with the emergence of graphical screens and the subsequent interest in window applications. Providing a graphical user interface (GUI) where a user can easily move around in even a single window is a challenge when using procedural code. Programming multiple and possibly overlapping windows on the same graphical screen increases the complexity enormously when procedural code is used.

Unlike a procedural approach, however, an object-oriented approach works well on a graphical windowed environment, where each window can be specified as a self-contained rectangular object that can be moved and resized in relation to

POINT OF INFORMATION

Procedural, Hybrid, and Pure Object-Oriented Languages

Most high-level programming languages can be categorized into one of three main categories: procedural, hybrid, or object-oriented. FORTRAN, which was the first commercially available high-level programming language, is procedural. This makes sense because FORTRAN was designed to perform mathematical calculations that used standard algebraic formulas. Formally, these formulas were described as algorithms and then the algorithms were coded using function and subroutine procedures. Other procedural languages that followed FORTRAN included BASIC, COBOL, and Pascal.

Currently there are only two pure object-oriented languages: Smalltalk and Eiffel. The first requirement of a pure object-oriented language is that it contain three specific features: classes, inheritance, and polymorphism (each of these features is described in the next three chapters). In addition to providing these features, however, a "pure" object-oriented language must, as a minimum, always use classes. In a pure object-oriented language all data types are constructed as classes, all data values are objects, all operators can be overloaded, and every data operation can only be executed using a class member function. *It is impossible in a pure language not to use object-oriented features throughout a program.* This is not the case in a hybrid language.

In a hybrid language, such as C++, *it is impossible not to use elements of a procedural program.* This is because the use of any built-in data type or operation effectively violates the pure object-oriented paradigm. Although a hybrid language must have the ability to define classes, the distinguishing feature of a hybrid language is that it is possible to write a complete program using only procedural code. Additionally, hybrid languages need not even provide inheritance and polymorphic features—but they must provide classes. Languages that use classes but do not provide inheritance and polymorphic features are referred to as *object-based* languages rather than *object-oriented* languages. All versions of Visual Basic prior to Version 4, are examples of object-based hybrid languages.

other objects on the screen. Additionally, within each window other graphical objects, such as check boxes, option buttons, labels, and text boxes, can easily be placed and moved.

To provide this object creation capability, extensions to the procedural language C were developed. This extension became the new language named C++, which permits a programmer both to use and create new objects.

Central to the creation of objects is the concept of an abstract data type, which is simply a user-defined data type, as opposed to the built-in data types provided by all languages (such as integer and floating-point types). Permitting a programmer to define new data types, such as a rectangular type, out of which specific rectangular objects can be created and displayed on a screen, forms the basis of C++'s object orientation.

Abstract Data Types

To gain a clear understanding of what an abstract data type is, consider the following three built-in data types supplied in C++: integers, floats, and characters. In using these data types we typically declare one or more variables of the desired type, use them in their accepted ways, and avoid using them in ways that are not specified. Thus, for example, we would not use the modulus operator on two floating-point numbers. Because this operation makes no sense for floating-point numbers it is never defined, in any programming language, for such numbers. Thus, although we typically do not consider it, each data type consists of *both* a type of data, such as integer or float, *and* specific operational capabilities provided for each type.

In computer terminology, the combination of data and their associated operations is defined as a **data type**. That is, a data type defines both the types of data and the types of operations that can be performed on the data. Seen in this light the integer data type, the floating-point data type, and the character data type provided in C++ are all examples of *built-in* data types that are defined by a type of data and specific operational capabilities provided for initializing and manipulating the type. In a simplified form this relationship can be described as

data type = allowable data + operational capabilities

Thus, the operations that we have been using in C++ are an inherent part of each data type we have been using. For each of these data types the designers of C++ had to consider carefully, and then implement, specific operations.

To understand the importance of the operational capabilities provided by a programming language, let's take a moment to list some of those supplied with C++'s built-in data types (`ints`, `floats`, and `chars`). The minimum set of the capabilities provided by C++'s built- in data types is listed in Table 7.1.[1]

TABLE 7.1 C++ Built-In Data Type Capabilities

Capability	Example
Define one or more variables of the data type.	`int a, b;`
Initialize a variable at definition.	`int a = 5;`
Assign a value to a variable.	`a = 10;`
Assign one variable's value to another variable.	`a = b;`
Perform mathematical operations.	`a + b`
Perform relational operations.	`a > b`
Convert from one data type to another.	`a = (int) 7.2;`

After examining Table 7.1, let's look at how all of this relates to abstract data types (ADTs). By definition an **abstract data type** is simply a user-defined type that defines both a type of data and the operations that can be performed on them. Such user-defined data types are required when we wish to create objects that are more complex than simple integers and characters. If we are to create our own data types, we must be aware of both the type of data we are creating and the capabilities that we will provide to initialize and manipulate the data.

As a specific example, assume that we are programming an application that uses dates extensively. Clearly, from a data standpoint a date must be capable of accessing and storing a month, day, and year designation. Although from an

[1] You might notice the absence of reading and writing operations. In both C and C++, except for very primitive operations, input and output is provided by standard library routines and class functions.

implementation standpoint there are a number of means of storing a date, from a user viewpoint the actual implementation is not relevant. For example, a date can be stored as three integers, one for the month, day, and year, respectively. Alternatively, a single long integer in the form `yyyymmdd` can also be used. Using the long integer implementation, the date 5/16/98 would be stored as the integer `19980516`. For sorting dates the long integer format is very attractive, because the numerical sequence of the dates corresponds to their calendar sequence.

The method of internally structuring the date, unfortunately, supplies only a partial answer to our programming effort. We must still supply a set of operations that can be used with dates. Clearly, such operations could include assigning values to a date, subtracting two dates to determine the number of days between them, comparing two dates to determine which is earlier and which is later, and displaying a date in a form such as 6/3/96.

Notice that the details of how each operation works is dependent on how we choose to store a date (formally referred to as its data structure) and is only of interest to us as we develop each operation. For example, the implementation of comparing two dates will differ if we store a date using a single long integer as opposed to using separate integers for the month, day, and year, respectively.

The combination of the storage structure used for dates with a set of available operations appropriate to dates would then define an abstract date data type. Once this date type is developed, programmers that want to use it need never be concerned with *how* dates are stored or *how* the operations are performed. All that they need to know is *what* each operation does and *how* to invoke it, much as they use C++'s built-in operations. For example, we do not really care how the addition of two integers is performed but only that it is done correctly.

In C++ an abstract data type is referred to as a **class.** Construction of a class is inherently easy and we already have all the necessary tools in variables and functions. What C++ provides is a mechanism for packaging these two items into a self-contained unit. Let's see how this is done.

Class Construction

A class defines both data and functions. This is usually accomplished by constructing a class in two parts, consisting of a declaration section and an implementation section. As illustrated in Figure 7.1, the declaration section declares

FIGURE 7.1 Format of a Class Definition

```
// class declaration section
class class_name
{
 data members
  (instance and variables)
 function members
  (inline or prototypes)
};
// class implementation section
function definitions
```

both the data types and functions of the class. The implementation section is then used to define the functions whose prototypes have been declared in the declaration section.[2]

Both the variables and functions listed in the class declaration section are collectively referred to as **class members.** Individually, the variables are referred to as both **data members** and as **instance variables** (the terms are synonymous), whereas the functions are referred to as **member functions.** A member function name may not be the same as a data member name.

As a specific example of a class, consider the following definition of a class named `Date`:

```
//--- class declaration section

class Date
{
  private:          // notice the colon after the word private
    int month;      // a data member
    int day;        // a data member
    int year;       // a data member
  public:           // again, notice the colon here
    Date(int = 7, int = 4, int = 96);          // a member function - the constructor
    void setdate(int, int, int);  // a member function
    void showdate(void);          // a member function
};

//--- class implementation section

Date::Date(int mm, int dd, int yy)
{
  month = mm;
  day = dd;
  year = yy;
}

void Date::setdate(int mm, int dd, int yy)
{
  month = mm;
  day = dd;
  year = yy;

  return;
}

void Date::showdate(void)
{
  cout << "The date is " << month << "/" << day << "/" << year << endl;

  return;
}
```

[2] This separation into two parts is not mandatory, because the implementation can be included within the declaration section if inline functions are used, as described in the next section.

This definition may initially look overwhelming, but start simply by noticing that it does consist of two sections—a declaration section and an implementation section. Now consider each of these sections individually.

A class **declaration section** begins with the keyword `class` followed by a class name. Following the class name are the class's variable declarations and function prototypes, enclosed in a brace pair that is terminated with a semicolon. Thus, the general structure of the form that we have used is[3]

```
class Name
{
  private:
    a list of variable declarations
  public:
    a list of function prototypes
};
```

Notice that this format is followed by our Date class, which for convenience we have listed below with no internal comments:

```
//--- class declaration section

class Date
{
  private:
     int month;
     int day;
     int year;
  public:
      Date(int = 7, int = 4, int = 96);
      void setdate(int, int, int);
      void showdate(void);
};    // this is a declaration - don't forget the semi-colon
```

The name of this class is `Date`. Although the initial capital letter is not required, it is conventionally used to designate a class. The body of the declaration section, which is enclosed within braces, consists of variable and function declarations. In this case the data members `month`, `day`, and `year` are declared as integers and three functions named `Date()`, `setdate()`, and `showdate()` are declared via prototypes. The keywords `private` and `public` are access specifiers that define access rights. The `private` keyword specifies that the class members following, in this case the data members `month`, `day`, and `year`, may only be accessed by using the class functions (or friend functions, as will be discussed in Section 8.2).[4] The purpose of the `private` designation is specifically meant to enforce data security by requiring all access to private data members through the provided member functions. This type of access, which restricts a user from seeing how the data is actually stored, is referred to as **data hiding**. Once a class category such as `private` is designated it remains in force until a new category is listed.

---

[3] Other forms are possible. Because this form is one of the most commonly used and easily understood, it will serve as our standard model throughout the text.

[4] Note that the default membership category in a class is `private`, which means that this keyword can be omitted. In this text we will explicitly use the `private` designation to reinforce the idea of access restrictions inherent in class membership.

Following the `private` class data members, the function prototypes listed in the `Date` class have been declared as `public`. This means that these class functions *can* be called by any objects and functions not in the class. In general, all class functions should be public; as such they furnish the capabilities to manipulate the class variables from outside of the class. For our `Date` class we have initially provided three functions named `Date()`, `setdate()`, and `showdate()`. Notice that one of these member functions has the same name, `Date`, as the class name. This particular function is referred to as a **constructor** function, and it has a specially defined purpose: It can be used to initialize class data members with values. Also notice that the constructor function has no return type, which is a requirement for this special function. The two remaining functions declared in our declaration example are `setdate()` and `showdate()`, both of which have been declared as returning no value (void). In the implementation section of the class, these three member functions will be written to permit initialization, assignment, and display capabilities, respectively.

The **implementation section** of a class is where the member functions declared in the declaration section are written.[5] Figure 7.2 illustrates the general form of functions included in the implementation section. This format is correct for all functions except the constructor, which, as we have stated, has no return type.

As shown in Figure 7.2 member functions defined in the implementation section have the same format as all user-written C++ functions with the addition of the class name and scope resolution operator, `::`, which identifies the function as a member of a particular class. Let us now reconsider the implementation section of our `Date` class, which is repeated below for convenience:

```
//--- class implementation section

Date::Date(int mm, int dd, int yy)
{
  month = mm;
  day = dd;
  year = yy;
}

void Date::setdate(int mm, int dd, int yy)
{
  month = mm;
  day = dd;
  year = yy;

  return;
}

void Date::showdate(void)
{
  cout << "The date is " << month << '/' << day << '/' << year << endl;

  return;
}
```

[5] It is also possible to define these functions within the declaration section by declaring and writing them as inline functions. Examples of inline member functions are presented in Section 7.2.

FIGURE 7.2 Format of a Member Function

```
return_type class_name::function_name(argument list)
{
 function body
}
```

Notice that the first function in this implementation section has the same name as the class, which makes it a constructor function. As such, it has no return type. The `Date::` included at the beginning of the function header line identifies this function as a member of the `Date` class. The rest of the header line,

```
Date(int mm, int dd, int yy)
```

defines the function as having three integer parameters. The body of this function simply assigns the data members `month`, `day`, and `year` with the values of the arguments `mm`, `dd`, and `yy`, respectively.

The next function header line

```
void Date::setdate(int mm, int dd, int yy)
```

defines this as the `setdate()` function belonging to the `Date` class (`Date::`). This function returns no value (void) and expects three integer parameters, `mm`, `dd`, and `yy`. In a manner similar to the `Date()` function, the body of this function assigns the data members `month`, `day`, and `year` with the values of its arguments. In a moment we will look at the difference between `Date()` and `setdate()`.

Finally, the last function header line in the implementation section defines a function named `showdate()`. This function has no parameters, returns no value, and is a member of the `Date` class. The body of this function outputs the values stored in `month`, `day`, and `year`.

To see how our `Date` class can be used within the context of a complete program, consider Program 7.1. To make the program easier to read it has been shaded in light and darker areas. The lighter area contains the class declaration and implementation sections that we have already considered. The darker area contains the header and `main()` function. For convenience we will retain this shading convention for all programs using classes.[6]

[6] This shading is not accidental. In practice the lighter shaded region containing the class definition would be placed in a separate file. A single `#include` statement would then be used to include this class declaration in the program. Thus, the final program would consist of the two darker shaded regions illustrated in Program 7.1 with the addition of one more `#include` statement in the first region.

PROGRAM 7.1

```
#include <iostream.h>

// class declaration

class Date
{
  private:
    int month;
    int day;
    int year;
  public:
    Date(int = 7, int = 4, int = 96);          // constructor
    void setdate(int, int, int); // member function to copy a date
    void showdate(void);         // member function to display a date
};

// implementation section

Date::Date(int mm, int dd, int yy)
{
  month = mm;
  day = dd;
  year = yy;
}

void Date::setdate(int mm, int dd, int yy)
{
  month = mm;
  day = dd;
  year = yy;

  return;
}

void Date::showdate(void)
{
  cout << "The date is " << month << '/' << day << '/' << year << endl;

  return;
}

int main()
{
  Date a, b, c(4,1,98);  // declare 3 objects - initializes 1 of them

  b.setdate(12,25,97);  // assign values to b's data members
  a.showdate();         // display object a's values
  b.showdate();         // display object b's values
  c.showdate();         // display object c's values

  return 0;
}
```

The declaration and implementation sections contained in the lighter shaded region of Program 7.1 should look familiar to you, because they contain the class declaration and implementation sections that we have already discussed. Notice, however, that this region only declares the class, it does not create any variables of this class type. This is true of all C++ types, including the built-in types such as integers and floats. Just as a variable of an integer type must be defined, variables of a user-declared class must also be defined. Variables defined to be of a user-declared class are referred to as **objects.**

Using this new terminology, the first statement in Program 7.1's `main()` function, contained in the darker area, defines three objects, named `a`, `b`, and `c`, to be of class type `Date`. In C++ whenever a new object is defined, memory is allocated for the object and its data members are automatically initialized. This is done by an automatic call to the class constructor function. For example, consider the definition `Date a, b, c(4,1,96);` contained in `main()`. When the object named a is defined the constructor function `Date` is automatically called. Since no arguments have been assigned to a, the default values of the constructor function are used, resulting in the initialization:

```
a.month = 7
a.day = 4
a.year = 96
```

Notice the notation that we have used here. It consists of an object name and an attribute name separated by a period. This is the standard syntax for referring to an object's attribute, namely,

```
object-name.attribute-name
```

where `object-name` is the name of a specific object and `attribute-name` is the name of a data member defined for the object's class. Thus, the notation `a.month = 7` refers to the fact that object `a`'s `month` data member has been set to the value 7. Similarly, the notation `a.day = 4` and `a.year = 96` refers to the fact that `a`'s `day` and `year` data members have been set to the values 4 and 96, respectively. In the same manner, when the object named `b` is defined the same default arguments are used, resulting in the initialization of `b`'s data members as:

```
b.month = 7
b.day = 4
b.year = 96
```

The object named `c`, however, is defined with the arguments 4, 1, and 96. These three arguments are passed into the constructor function when the object is defined, resulting in the initialization of `c`'s data members as:

```
c.month = 4
c.day = 1
c.year = 98
```

The next statement in `main()`, `b.setdate(12,25,97)`, calls `b`'s `setdate` function, which assigns the argument values 12, 25, and 97 to `b`'s data members, resulting in the assignment:

```
b.month = 12
b.day = 25
b.year = 97
```

Notice the syntax for referring to an object's function. This syntax is

```
object-name.function-name(parameters)
```

where `object-name` is the name of a specific object and `function-name` is the name of one of the functions defined for the object's class. Since we have defined all class functions as public, a statement such as `b.setdate(12,25,95)` is valid inside the `main()` function and is a call to the class's `setdate()` function. This statement tells the `setdate()` function to operate on the `b` object with the arguments 12, 25, and 95. It is important to understand that because all class data members were specified as private, a statement such as `b.month = 12` would be invalid from within `main()`. We are, therefore, forced to rely on member functions to access data member values.

The last three statements in `main()` call the `showdate()` function to operate on the `a`, `b`, and `c` objects. The first call results in the display of `a`'s data values, the second call in the display of `b`'s data values, and the third call in the display of `c`'s data values. Thus, the output of Program 7.1 is:

```
The date is 7/4/96
The date is 12/25/98
The date is 4/1/97
```

Notice that a statement such as `cout << a;` is invalid within `main()` because `cout` does not know how to handle an object of class `Date`. Thus, we have supplied our class with a function that can be used to access and display an object's internal values.

Terminology

Because confusion sometimes arises about the terms *classes, objects,* and other terminology associated with object-oriented programming, we will take a moment to clarify and review the terminology.

A **class** is a programmer-defined data type out of which objects can be created. **Objects** are created from classes; they have the same relationship to classes as variables do to C++'s built-in data types. For example, in the declaration

```
int a;
```

a is said to be a variable, whereas in Program 7.1's declaration

```
Date a;
```

a is said to be an object. If it initially helps you to think of an object as a variable, do so.

Objects are also referred to as *instances* of a class and the process of creating a new object is frequently referred to as an *instantiation* of the object. Each time a new object is instantiated (created), a new set of data members belonging to the object is created.[7] The particular values contained in these data members determine the object's *state.*

---

[7] Note that only one set of class functions is created. These functions are shared between objects. The mechanism for using the same function on different objects' data members is presented in Section 9.3.

▲ POINT OF INFORMATION ▲

Interfaces, Implementations, and Information Hiding

The terms *interface* and *implementation* are used extensively in object-oriented programming literature. Each of these terms can be equated to specific parts of a class's declaration and implementation sections.

An *interface* consists of a class's public member function declarations and any supporting comments. As such, the interface should be all that is required to tell a programmer how to use the class.

The *implementation* consists of both the class's implementation section, which consists of both private and public member definitions *and* the class's private data members, which is contained in a class's declaration section.

The implementation is the essential means of providing information hiding. In its most general context *information hiding* refers to the principle that *how* a class is internally constructed is not relevant to any programmer who wishes to use the class. That is, the implementation can and should be hidden from all class users precisely to ensure that the class is not altered or compromised in any way. All that a programmer need know to use the class correctly should be provided by the interface.

Seen in this way, a class can be thought of as a blueprint out of which particular instances (objects) can be created. Each instance (object) of a class will have its own set of particular values for the set of data members specified in the class declaration section.

In addition to the data types allowed for an object, a class also defines behavior—that is, the operations that are permitted to be performed on an object's data members. Users of the object need to know *what* these functions can do and how to activate them through function calls, but unless run-time or space implications are relevant, they do not need to know *how* the operation is done. The actual implementation details of an object's operations are contained in the class implementation, which can be hidden from the user. Other names for the operations defined in a class implementation section are procedures, functions, services, and methods. We will use these terms interchangeably throughout the remainder of the text.

Exercises 7.1

1. Define the following terms:

a. class	g. data member
b. object	h. constructor
c. declaration section	i. class instance
d. implementation section	j. services
e. instance variable	k. methods
f. member function	l. interface

2. Write a class declaration section for each of the following specifications. In each case include a prototype for a constructor and a member function named `showdata()` that can be used to display member values.

   a. A class named `Time` that has integer data members named `secs`, `mins`, and `hours`.

   b. A class named `Complex` that has floating-point data members named `real` and `imaginary`.

   c. A class named `Circle` that has integer data members named `xcenter` and `ycenter` and a floating-point data member named `radius`.

   d. A class named `System` that has character data members named `computer`, `printer`, and `screen`, each capable of holding 30 characters (including the end-of-string `NULL`), and floating-point data members named `comp_price`, `print_price`, and `scrn_price`.

3. a. Construct a class implementation section for the constructor and `showdate()` function members corresponding to the class declaration created for Exercise 2a.

   b. Construct a class implementation section for the constructor and `showdate()` function members corresponding to the class declaration created for Exercise 2b.

   c. Construct a class implementation section for the constructor and `showdate()` function members corresponding to the class declaration created for Exercise 2c.

   d. Construct a class implementation section for the constructor and `showdate()` function members corresponding to the class declaration created for Exercise 2d.

4. a. Include the class declaration and implementation sections prepared for Exercises 2a and 3a in a complete working program.

   b. Include the class declaration and implementation sections prepared for Exercises 2b and 3b in a complete working program.

   c. Include the class declaration and implementation sections prepared for Exercises 2c and 3c in a complete working program.

   d. Include the class declaration and implementation sections prepared for Exercises 2d and 3d in a complete working program.

5. Determine the errors in the following class declaration section:

```
class employee
{
public:
  int empnum;
  char code;
private:
  class(int = 0);
  void showemp(int, char);
};
```

6. a. Add another member function named convrt( ) to the `Date` class in Program 7.1 that does the following: The function should access the `month, year,` and `day` data members and display and then return a long integer that is the calculated as *year * 10000 + month * 100 + day*. For example, if the date is 4/1/98, the returned value is 980401. (Dates in this form are useful when performing sorts, because placing the numbers in numerical order automatically places the corresponding dates in chronological order.)

   b. Include the modified `Date` class constructed for Exercise 6a in a complete C++ program.

7. a. Add an additional member function to Program 7.1's class definition named `leapyr()` that returns a 1 when the year is a leap year and a 0 if it is not a leap year. A leap year is any year that is evenly divisible by 4 but not evenly divisible by 100, with the exception that all years evenly divisible by 400 are leap years.

For example, the year 1996 is a leap year because it is evenly divisible by 4 and not evenly divisible by 100. The year 2000 will be a leap year because it is evenly divisible by 400.

b. Include the class definition constructed for Exercise 7a in a complete C++ program. The `main()` function should display the message `The year is a leap year` or `The year is not a leap year` depending on the date object's year value.

8. Modify the `Date` class in Program 7.1 to contain a function that compares two `Date` objects and returns the larger of the two. The function should be written according to the following algorithm:

   Comparison function
   Accept two `Date` *values as arguments.*
   Determine the later date using the following procedure:
   Convert each date into an integer value having the form yymmdd. This can be accomplished by using the algorithm described in Exercise 6a. Compare the corresponding integers for each date. The larger integer corresponds to the later date.
   Return the later date.

9. a. Add a member function to Program 7.1's class definition named `da_of_wk()` that determines the day of the week for any date object. An algorithm for determining the day of the week, known as Zeller's algorithm, is the following:

   If the month is greater than 2
   Set the variable mp = 0 and yp = year − 1.
   Else
   *set mp = int(0.4 * month + 2.3) and yp = year.*
   Endif.
   Set the variable t = int(yp/4) − int(yp/100) + int(yp/400).
   *Day-of-week = (365L * year + 31L * (month − 1) + day + t − mp) % 7.*

   Using this algorithm the variable da_of_wk( ) will have a value of 0 if the date is a Sunday, 1 if a Monday, etc.

   b. Include the class definition constructed for Exercise 9a in a complete C++ program. The `main()` function should display the name of the day (Sun, Mon, Tue, etc.) for the `Date` object being tested.

7.2 CONSTRUCTORS

A **constructor** function is any function that has the same name as its class. Multiple constructors can be defined for each class as long as they are distinguishable by the number and types of their parameters.

The intended purpose of a constructor is to initialize a new object's data members. As such, depending on the number and types of supplied arguments, one constructor function is automatically called each time an object is created. If no constructor function is written, the compiler supplies a default constructor. In addition to its initialization role, a constructor function may also perform other tasks when it is called and can be written in a variety of ways. In this section we present the possible variations of constructor functions and introduce another function, the destructor, which is automatically called whenever an object goes out of existence.

FIGURE 7.3 Constructor Format

```
class_name::class_name(parameter list)
{
 function body
}
```

Figure 7.3 illustrates the general format of a constructor. As shown in this figure, a constructor:

- must have the same name as the class to which it belongs
- must have no return type (not even void).

If you do not include a constructor in your class definition, the compiler supplies a do-nothing default one for you. For example, consider the following class declaration:

```
class Date
{
  private:
    int month, day, year;
  public
    void setdate(int, int, int);
    void showdate(void)
};
```

Because no user-defined constructor has been declared here, the compiler creates a default constructor. For our `Date` class this default constructor is equivalent to the implementation `Date::Date(void){}`— that is, the compiler-supplied default constructor expects no parameters and has an empty body. Clearly this default constructor is not very useful, but it does exist if no other constructor is declared.

The term **default constructor** is used quite frequently in C++. It refers to any constructor that does not require any parameters when it is called. This can be because no parameters are declared, which is the case for the compiler-supplied default, or because all parameters have been given default values. For example the constructor `Date::Date(int = 7, int = 4, int = 96)` is a valid prototype for a default constructor. Here, each parameter has been given a default value, and an object can be declared as type `Date` without supplying any further parameters. Using such a constructor, the declaration `Date a;` initializes the `a` object with the default values 7, 4, and 96.

To verify that a constructor function is automatically called whenever a new object is created, consider Program 7.2. Notice that in the implementation section the constructor function uses `cout` to display the message `Created a new data object with data values`. Thus, whenever the constructor is called this message is displayed. Since the `main()` function creates three objects, the constructor is called three times and the message is displayed three times.

PROGRAM 7.2

```
#include <iostream.h>

// class declaration section

class Date
{
  private:
    int month;
    int day;
    int year;
  public:
    Date (int = 7, int = 4, int = 96);       // constructor
};

// implementation section

Date::Date(int mm, int dd, int yy)
{
  month = mm;
  day = dd;
  year = yy;
  cout << "Created a new data object with data values "
       << month << ", " << day << ", " << year << endl;
}

int main()
{
  Date a;            // declare an object
  Date b;            // declare an object
  Date c(4,1,96);    // declare an object

  return 0;
}
```

The following output is produced when Program 7.2 is executed:

```
Created a new data object with data values 7, 4, 96
Created a new data object with data values 7, 4, 96
Created a new data object with data values 4, 1, 96
```

Although any legitimate C++ statement can be used within a constructor function, such as the `cout` call made in Program 7.2, it is best to keep constructors simple and use them only for initialization purposes. One further point needs to be made with respect to the constructor function contained in Program 7.2. According to the rules of C++, object members are initialized in the order in which they are declared in the class declaration section and *not* in the order in which they may appear in the function's definition within the implementation section. Usually this will not be an issue, unless one member is initialized using another data member's value.

Calling Constructors

As we have seen, constructors are called whenever an object is created. The actual declaration, however, can be made in a variety of ways. For example, the declaration

```
Date c(4,1,96);
```

used in Program 7.2 could also have been written as

```
Date c = Date(4,1,96);
```

This second form declares `c` as being of type `Date` and then makes a direct call to the constructor function with the arguments 4, 1, and 96. This second form can be simplified when only one argument is passed to the constructor. For example, if only the `month` data member of the `c` object needed to be initialized with the value 8 and the `day` and `year` members can use the default values, the object can be created using the declaration

```
Date c = 8;
```

Since this resembles declarations in C, it and its more complete form using the equal sign are referred to as the C *style of initialization.* The form of declaration used in Program 7.2 is referred to as the C++ *style of initialization,* and is the form we will use predominantly throughout the remainder of the text.

Regardless of which initialization form you use, in no case should an object be declared with empty parentheses. For example, the declaration `Date a();` is not the same as the declaration `Date a;`. The latter declaration uses the default constructor values, while the former declaration results in no object being created.

Overloaded and Inline Constructors

The primary difference between a constructor and other user-written functions is how the constructor is called: Constructors are called automatically each time an object is created, while other functions must be explicitly called by name.[8] As a function, however, a constructor must still follow all of the rules applicable to user-written functions that were presented in Chapter 6. This means that constructors may have default arguments, as illustrated in Program 7.1, may be overloaded, and may be written as inline functions.

Recall from Section 6.1 that function overloading permits the same function name to be used with different argument lists. Based on the supplied argument types the compiler determines which function to use when the call is encountered. Let's see how this can be applied to our `Date` class. For convenience the appropriate class declaration is repeated below:

```
// class declaration section
class Date
{
  private:
    int month;
    int day;
    int year;
  public:
    Date(int = 7, int = 4, int = 96);          // constructor
};
```

[8] This is true for all functions except destructors, which are described later in this section. A destructor function is automatically called each time an object is destroyed.

Here, the constructor prototype specifies three integer parameters, which are used to initialize the `month`, `day`, and `year` data members.

An alternate method of specifying a date is to use a long integer in the form *year * 10000 + month * 100 + day*. For example, the date 12/24/88 using this form is 881224 and the date 2/5/91 is 910205.[9] A suitable prototype for a constructor that uses dates of this form is:

```
Date(long); // an overloaded constructor
```

Here, the constructor is declared as receiving one long integer argument. The code for this new `Date` function must, of course, correctly convert its single argument into a month, day, and year, and would be included within the class implementation section. The actual code for such a constructor is:

```
Date::Date(long yymmdd) // a second constructor
{
  year = int(yymmdd/10000.0);     // extract the year
  month = int( (yymmdd - year * 10000.0) / 100.00 ); // extract the month
  day = int(yymmdd - year * 10000.0 - month * 100.0); // extract the day
}
```

Do not be overly concerned with the actual conversion code used within the function's body. The important point here is the concept of overloading the `Date()` function to provide two constructors. Program 7.3 contains a complete class definition that uses this new constructor function within the context of a working program.

The output provided by Program 7.3 is:

```
The date is 7/4/95
The date is 4/1/96
The date is 5/15/97
```

Three objects are created in Program 7.3's `main()` function. The first object, `a`, is initialized with the default constructor using its default arguments. Object `b` is also initialized with the default constructor, but it uses the arguments 4, 1, and 96. Finally, object `c`, which is initialized with a long integer, uses the second constructor in the class implementation section. The compiler knows that it should use this second constructor because the argument specified, 970515, is a long integer. It is worthwhile pointing out that a compiler error would occur if both `Date` constructors had default values. In such a case a declaration such as `Date d;` would be considered ambiguous by the compiler, because it would not be able to determine which constructor to use. Thus, in each implementation section only one constructor can be written as the default.

Just as constructors may be overloaded, they may also be written as **inline member functions.** Doing so simply means defining the function in the class declaration section. For example, making both of the constructors contained in Program 7.3 inline is accomplished by the declaration section:

---

[9] The reason for specifying dates in this manner is that only one number needs to be used per date, and that sorting the numbers automatically puts the corresponding dates into chronological order. For dates after the turn of the century, 100 is added to the year. Thus 7/15/03 is represented as the long integer 1030715.

PROGRAM 7.3

```
#include <iostream.h>

// class declaration

class Date
{
  private:
    int month;
    int day;
    int year;
  public:
    Date(int = 7, int = 4, int = 96);      // constructor
    Date(long);                  // another constructor
    void showdate(void);         // member function to display a date
};

// implementation section

Date::Date(int mm, int dd, int yy)
{
  month = mm;
  day = dd;
  year = yy;
}

Date::Date(long yymmdd)
{
  year = int(yymmdd/10000.0);     // extract the year
  month = int( (yymmdd - year * 10000.0)/100.00 ); // extract the month
  day = int(yymmdd - year * 10000.0 - month * 100.0); // extract the day
}

void Date::showdate(void)
{
  cout << "The date is " << month << '/' << day << '/' << year << endl;

  return;
}

int main()
{
  Date a, b(4,1,96), c(970515); // declare three objects

  a.showdate();          // display object a's values
  b.showdate();          // display object b's values
  c.showdate();          // display object c's values

  return 0;
}
```

▲ POINT OF INFORMATION ▲

Constructors

A *constructor* is any function that has the same name as its class. The primary purpose of a constructor is to initialize an object's member variables when an object is created. As such, a constructor is automatically called when an object is declared.

A class can have multiple constructors provided that each constructor is distinguishable by having a different formal parameter list. A compiler error results when unique identification of a constructor is not possible. If no constructor is provided, the compiler will supply a do-nothing default constructor.

Every constructor function must be declared with *no return type* (not even void). Since they are functions, constructors may also be explicitly called in nondeclarative statements. When used in this manner the function call requires parentheses following the constructor name, even if no parameters are used. However, when used in a declaration, parentheses *must not* be included for a zero parameter constructor. For example, the declaration `Date a();` is incorrect. The correct declaration is `Date a;`. When parameters are used, however, they must be enclosed within parentheses in both declarative and nondeclarative statements. Default parameter values should be included within the constructor's prototype.

```
// class declaration

class Date
{
  private:
    int month;
    int day;
    int year;
  public:
    Date(int mm = 7, int dd = 4, int yy = 96)
    {
      month = mm;
      day = dd;
      year = yy;
    }
    Date(long yymmdd)    // here is the overloaded constructor
    {
      year = int(yymmdd/10000.0);      // extract the year
      month = int( (yymmdd - year * 10000.0)/100.00 );  // extract the month
      day = int(yymmdd - year * 10000.0 - month * 100.0); // extract the day
    }
};
```

The keyword `inline` is not required in this declaration because member functions defined inside the class declaration are inline by default.

Generally, only functions that can be coded on a single line are good candidates for inline functions. This reinforces the convention that inline functions should be small. Thus, the first constructor is more conventionally written as

```
Date(int mm = 7, int dd = 4, int yy = 96)
  { month = mm; day = dd; year = yy; }
```

The second constructor, which extends over three lines, should not be written as an inline function.

POINT OF INFORMATION

Accessor Functions

An *accessor function* is any nonconstructor member function that accesses a class's private data members. For example, the function `showdate()` in the `Date` class is an accessor function. Such functions are extremely important because they provide a means of displaying private data members' stored values.

When you construct a class make sure to provide a complete set of accessor functions. Each accessor function does not have to return a data member's exact value, but it should return a useful representation of the value. For example, assume that a date such as 12/25/98 is stored as a long integer member variable in the form 982512. Although an accessor function could display this value, a more useful representation would typically be either 12/25/98, or December 25, 1998.

Besides being used for output, accessor functions can also provide a means of data input. For example, the `setdate()` function in the `Date` class is an example of an input accessor function. As we will see in Section 8.6, both the extraction and insertion operators can be overloaded to provide another means of object data input and output. Constructor functions, whose primary purpose is to initialize an object's member variables, are not considered as accessor functions.

Destructors

The counterpart to constructor functions are destructor functions. **Destructors** are functions that have the same class name as constructors, but are preceded by a tilde (`~`). Thus, for our `Date` class, the destructor name is `~Date()`. Like constructors, a default do-nothing destructor is provided by the C++ compiler in the absence of an explicit destructor. Unlike constructors, however, there can only be one destructor function per class. This is because destructors take no parameters and they return no values.

Destructors are automatically called whenever an object goes out of existence, and are meant to "clean up" any undesirable effects that might be left by the object. Generally such effects only occur when an object contains a pointer member, which is the topic of Section 9.5.

Exercises 7.2

1. Determine whether the following statements are true or false:
   a. A constructor function must have the same name as its class.
   b. A class can only have one constructor function.
   c. A class can only have one default constructor function.
   d. A default constructor can only be supplied by the compiler.
   e. A default constructor can have no parameters or all parameters must have default values.
   f. A constructor must be declared for each class.
   g. A constructor must be declared with a return type.
   h. A constructor is automatically called each time an object is created.

i. A class can have only one destructor function.

j. A destructor must have the same name as its class, preceded by a tilde (~).

k. A destructor can have default arguments.

l. A destructor must be declared for each class.

m. A destructor must be declared with a return type.

n. A destructor is automatically called each time an object goes out of existence.

o. Destructors are not useful when the class contains a pointer data member.

2. For Program 7.3, what date would be initialized for object `c` if the declaration `Date c(9);` were used in place of the declaration `Date c(970515);`?

3. Modify Program 7.3 so that the only data member of the class is a long integer named `yymmdd`. Do this by substituting the declaration

```
long yymmdd;
```

for the existing declarations

```
int month;
int day;
int year;
```

Then, using the same constructor function prototypes currently declared in the class declaration section, rewrite them so that the `Date(long)` function becomes the default constructor and the `Date(int, int, int)` function converts a month, day, and year into the proper form for the class data member.

4. a. Construct a `Time` class containing integer data members `seconds`, `minutes`, and `hours`. The class should contain two constructors: The first should be a default constructor having the prototype `Time(int, int, int)`, which uses default values of 0 for each data member. The second constructor should accept a long integer representing a total number of seconds and disassemble the long integer into hours, minutes, and seconds. The final function member should display the class data members.

   b. Include the class written for Exercise 4a within the context of a complete program.

5. a. Construct a class named `Student` consisting of an integer student identification number, an array of five floating-point grades, and an integer representing the total number of grades entered. The constructor for this class should initialize all `Student` data members to zero. Included in the class should be member functions to (1) enter a student ID number, (2) enter a single test grade and update the total number of grades entered, and (3) compute an average grade and display the student ID followed by the average grade.

   b. Include the class constructed in Exercise 5a within the context of a complete program. Your program should declare two objects of type `Student` and accept and display data for the two objects to verify operation of the member functions.

7.3 FOCUS ON PROBLEM SOLVING

Now that you have an understanding of how classes are constructed and the terminology used to describe them, let us apply this knowledge to two new applications. In the first application we construct a single elevator object. We assume that the elevator can travel between the first and fifteenth floors of a building and that the location of the elevator must be known at all times. In the second application we simulate the operation of a gas pump.

Problem 1: Constructing an Elevator Object

In this application you are required to simulate the operation of an elevator. Output is required that describes the current floor on which the elevator is either stationed at or is passing by. Additionally, an internal elevator request button that is pushed as a request to move to another floor should be provided. The elevator can travel between the first and fifteenth floors of the building in which it is situated.

Analyze the Problem For this application we have one object, an elevator. The only attribute of interest is the location of the elevator. The single requested service is the ability to request a change in the elevator's position (state). Additionally, we must be able to establish the initial floor position when a new elevator is put in service. Figure 7.4 illustrates an object diagram that includes both the required attributes and operations.

FIGURE 7.4 An Elevator Object Diagram

Elevator
Floor location
Initialize the floor position Request a new floor

Develop a Solution For this application the location of the elevator, which corresponds to its current floor position, can be represented by an integer member variable whose value ranges between 1 and 15. The value of this variable, which we will name `cur_floor`, for current floor, effectively represents the current state of the elevator. The services that we will provide for changing the state of the elevator will be an initialization function to set the initial floor position when a new elevator is put in service, and a request function to change the elevator's position (state) to a new floor. Putting an elevator in service is accomplished by declaring a single class instance (declaring an object of type `Elevator`), and requesting a new floor position is equivalent to pushing an elevator button.

The response to the elevator button should be as follows:

```
If a request is made for either a non-existent floor or the current floor
    Do nothing
Else if the request is for a floor above the current floor
    Display the current floor number
    While not at the designated floor
        Increment the floor number
        Display the new floor number
    End While
    Display the ending floor number
Else     // the request must be for a floor below the current floor
    Display the current floor number
```

(continued on next page)

While not at the designated floor
Decrement the floor number
Display the new floor number
End While
Display the ending floor number
EndIf

Code the Solution From the design, a suitable class declaration is:

```
// class declaration section
class Elevator
{
  private:
    int cur_floor;
  public:
     Elevator(int = 1);       // constructor
     void request(int);
};
```

Notice that we have declared one data member, `cur_floor`, and two class functions. The data member `cur_floor` is used to store the current floor position of the elevator. As a private member it can only be accessed through member functions. The two declared public member functions, `Elevator()` and `request()`, will be used to define the external services provided by each `Elevator` object. The `Elevator()` function, which has the same name as its class, becomes a constructor function that is automatically called when an object of type `Elevator` is created. We will use this function to initialize the starting floor position of each elevator. The `request()` function is used to alter the position of the elevator. To accomplish these services a suitable class implementation section is:

```
// class implementation section

Elevator::Elevator(int cfloor)    // constructor
{
  cur_floor = cfloor;
}

void Elevator::request(int newfloor)  // access function
{
  if (newfloor < 1 || newfloor > MAXFLOOR || newfloor == cur_floor)
    ;  // do nothing
  else if ( newfloor > cur_floor)   // move elevator up
  {
    cout << "\nStarting at floor " << cur_floor << endl;
    while (newfloor > cur_floor)
    {
      cur_floor++;     // add one to current floor
      cout << "   Going Up - now at floor " << cur_floor << endl;
    }
    cout << "Stopping at floor " << cur_floor << endl;
  }
  else  // move elevator down
  {
    cout << "\nStarting at floor " << cur_floor << endl;
```

```
      while (newfloor < cur_floor)
      {
        cur_floor--;    // subtract one from current floor
        cout << "   Going Down - now at floor " << cur_floor << endl;
      }
      cout << "Stopping at floor " << cur_floor << endl;
    }

    return;
  }
```

The constructor function is straightforward. When an `Elevator` object is declared it is initialized to the floor specified; if no floor is explicitly given, the default value of 1 will be used. For example, the declaration

```
Elevator a(7);
```

initializes the variable `a.cur_floor` to 7, whereas the declaration

```
Elevator a;
```

uses the default argument value and initializes the variable `a.cur_floor to 1.`

The `request()` function defined in the implementation section is more complicated and provides the class's primary service. Essentially this function consists of an `if-else` statement having three parts: If an incorrect service is requested, no action is taken; if a floor above the current position is selected, the elevator is moved up; and if a floor below the current position is selected, the elevator is moved down. For movement up or down the function uses a `while` loop to increment the position one floor at a time, and reports the elevator's movement using a `cout` object call. Program 7.4 includes this class in a working program.

Test and Correct the Program Testing the `Elevator` class entails testing each class operation. To do this we first include the `Elevator` class within the context of a working program, as given in Program 7.4.

PROGRAM 7.4

```
#include <iostream.h>

const int MAXFLOOR = 15;
// class declaration

class Elevator
{
  private:
    int cur_floor;
  public:
    Elevator(int = 1);        // constructor
    void request(int);
};

// implementation section
```

(continued on next page)

(continued from previous page)

```
Elevator::Elevator(int cfloor)
{
  cur_floor = cfloor;
}

void Elevator::request(int newfloor)
{
  if (newfloor < 1 || newfloor > MAXFLOOR || newfloor == cur_floor)
    ;  // do nothing
  else if ( newfloor > cur_floor)  // move elevator up
  {
    cout << "\nStarting at floor " << cur_floor << endl;
    while (newfloor > cur_floor)
    {
      cur_floor++;     // add one to current floor
      cout << "   Going Up - now at floor " << cur_floor << endl;
    }
    cout << "Stopping at floor " << cur_floor << endl;
  }
  else  // move elevator down
  {
    cout << "\nStarting at floor " << cur_floor << endl;
    while (newfloor < cur_floor)
    {
      cur_floor--;    // subtract one from current floor
      cout << "   Going Down - now at floor " << cur_floor << endl;
    }
    cout << "Stopping at floor " << cur_floor << endl;
  }

  return;
}

int main()
{
  Elevator a;   // declare 1 object of type Elevator
  a.request(6);
  a.request(3);

  return 0;
}
```

The lightly shaded portion of Program 7.4 contains the class construction that we have already described. To see how this class is used, concentrate on the darker shaded section of the program. At the top of the program we have included the `iostream.h` header file and declared a named constant `MAXFLOOR`, which corresponds to the highest floor that can be requested.

Within the `main()` function three statements are included. The first statement creates an object named `a` of type `Elevator`. Since no explicit floor has been given, this elevator will begin at floor 1, which is the default constructor argument.

A request is then made to move the elevator to floor 6, which is followed by a request to move to floor 3. The output produced by Program 7.4 is:

```
Starting at floor 1
   Going Up - now at floor 2
   Going Up - now at floor 3
   Going Up - now at floor 4
   Going Up - now at floor 5
   Going Up - now at floor 6
Stopping at floor 6

Starting at floor 6
   Going Down - now at floor 5
   Going Down - now at floor 4
   Going Down - now at floor 3
Stopping at floor 3
```

The basic requirements of object-oriented programming are evident in even as simple a program as Program 7.4. Before the `main()` function can be written, a useful class must be constructed. This is typical of programs that use objects. For such programs the design process is front-loaded with the requirement that careful consideration of the class—its declaration and implementation—be given. Code contained in the implementation section effectively removes code that would otherwise be part of `main()`'s responsibility. Thus, any program that uses the object does not have to repeat the implementation details within its `main()` function. Rather, the `main()` function [and any function called by `main()`] is only concerned with sending messages to its objects to activate them appropriately. How the object responds to the messages and how the state of the object is retained is not `main()`'s concern; these details are hidden within the class construction.

One further point should be made concerning Program 7.4. Note that control is provided by the `main()` function. This control is sequential, with two calls made to the same object operation using different argument values. This control is perfectly correct for testing purposes. However, by incorporating calls to `request()` within a `while` loop and using the random number function `rand()` to generate random floor requests, a continuous simulation of the elevator's operation is possible (see Exercise 3 at the end of this section).

Problem 2: A Single Object Gas Pump Simulation

We have been requested to write a program that simulates the operation of a gas pump. At any time during the simulation we should be able to determine, from the pump, the price per gallon of gas and the amount remaining in the supply tank from which the gas is being pumped. If a request for gas, in gallons, is less than the amount of gas in the tank, the request should be filled; otherwise only the available amount in the supply tank should be used. Once the gas is pumped, the total price of the gallons pumped should be displayed and the amount of gas, in gallons, that was pumped should be subtracted from the amount in the supply tank.

For the simulation, assume that the pump is randomly idle between 1 to 15 minutes between customer arrivals and that a customer randomly requests between 3 and 20 gallons of gas. Although the tank capacity is 500 gallons, assume that the initial amount of gas in the tank is only 300 gallons. Initially, the program should simulate a one-half hour time frame.

Additionally, for each arrival and request for gas we want to know the idle time before the customer arrived, how many gallons of gas were pumped, and the total price of the transaction. The pump itself must keep track of the price per gallon of gas and the amount of gas remaining in the tank. Typically, the price per gallon is $1.00, but the price per gallon to use for this simulation should be $1.25.

For this part of the simulation, construct a gas pump class that can be used in the final simulation, which is completed in Section 8.6.

Analyze the Problem This problem involves two distinct object types. The first is a person who can arrive randomly between 1 and 15 minutes and can randomly request between 3 and 20 gallons of gas. The second object type is the gas pump. For this part of the problem our goal is to create a suitable gas pump class.

The model for constructing a gas pump class that meets the requirements of the simulation is the same one that we previously constructed in Section 6.8. For convenience the object and dynamic models for this class are reproduced as Figures 7.5 and 7.6, respectively.

FIGURE 7.5 The Object Model

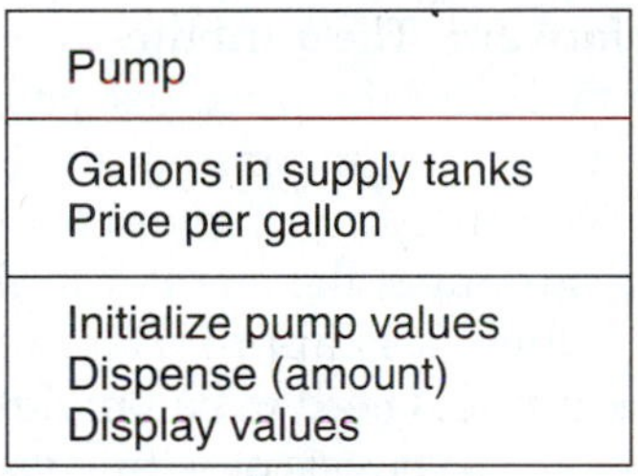

Pump
Gallons in supply tanks Price per gallon
Initialize pump values Dispense (amount) Display values

FIGURE 7.6 The Dynamic Model

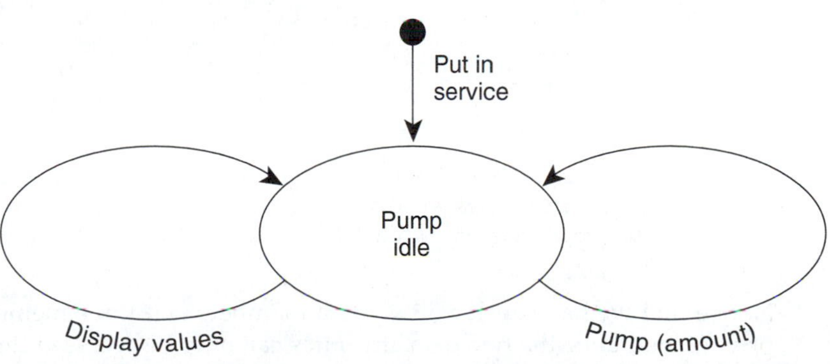

The functional requirements for the operations listed in Figures 7.5 and 7.6 are easily described in pseudocode as:

Put in service
  Initialize the amount of gas in the tank.
  Initialize the price per gallon of gas.

Display values function
  Display the amount of gas in the tank.
  Display the price per gallon.

Pump(amount) function
  If the amount in the tank is greater than or equal to the amount to be pumped
    Set pumped amount equal to the amount to be pumped.
  Else
    Set pumped amount equal to the amount in the tank.
  EndIf.
  Subtract the pumped amount from the amount in the tank.
  Calculate the total price as (price per gallon * pumped amount).
  Display the pumped amount.
  Display the amount remaining in the tank.
  Display the total price.

Develop a Solution From the object model the implementation of a `Pump` class is rather straightforward. The attributes of interest for the pump are the amount of gallons in the tank and the price per gallon. The required operations include supplying initial values for the pump attributes, interrogating the pump for its attribute values, and satisfying a request for gas.

Since the two attributes, the amount in the tank and the price per gallon, can have fractional values, it is appropriate to make them floating-point values. Additionally, three services need to be provided. The first consists of initializing the pump's attributes, which consists of setting values for the amount in the supply tank and the price per gallon. The second consists of satisfying a request for gas, while the third service simply provides a reading of the pump's current attribute values.

Code the Solution From the design, a suitable class declaration is:

```
// class declaration
class Pump
{
  private:
    float amtInTank;
    float price;
  public:
    Pump(float = 500.0, float = 1.00);        // constructor
    void values(void);
    void request(float);
};
```

Notice that we have declared two data members and three member functions. As private members, the two data attributes can only be accessed through the class's declared member functions, `Pump()`, `values()`, and `request()`. It is these functions that provide the external services available to each Pump object.

The `Pump()` function, which has the same name as its class, is the constructor function that is automatically called when an object of type `Pump` is created. The `values()` function simply provides a readout of the current attribute values, and the `request()` function handles the logic for fulfilling a customer's request for gas. To accomplish these services, a suitable class implementation section follows:

```
// class implementation

Pump::Pump(float start, float todaysPrice)
{
  amtInTank = start;
  price = todaysPrice;
}

void Pump::values(void)
{
  cout << "The gas tank has " << amtInTank << " gallons of gas." << endl;
  cout << "The price per gallon of gas is $" << setiosflags(ios::showpoint)
       << setprecision(2) << price << endl;

  return;
}

void Pump::request(float pumpAmt)
{
  float pumped;

  if (amtInTank >= pumpAmt)
     pumped = pumpAmt;
  else
     pumped = amtInTank;

  amtInTank -= pumped;
  cout << pumpAmt << " gallons were requested " << endl;
  cout << pumped << " gallons were pumped" << endl;
  cout << amtInTank << " gallons remain in the tank" << endl;
  cout << "The total price is $" << setiosflags(ios::showpoint)
       << setprecision(2) << (pumped * price) << endl;

  return;
}
```

The constructor function is straightforward. When a `Pump` object is declared, it will be initialized to a given amount of gas in the supply tank and a given price per gallon. If no values are given, the defaults of 500 gallons and $1 per gallon will be used.

The `values()` function defined in the implementation section simply provides a readout of the current attribute values. It is the `request()` function that is the most complicated because it provides the primary `Pump` service. The code follows the requirements of the pump as previously described in pseudocode; that is, it provides all of the gas required unless the amount remaining in the supply tank is less than the requested amount. Finally, it subtracts the amount pumped from the amount in the tank and calculates the total dollar value of the transaction.

Test and Correct the Solution Testing the `Pump` class entails testing each class operation. To do this we first include the `Pump` class within the context of a working program, which is listed as Program 7.5.

PROGRAM 7.5

```
#include <iostream.h>
#include <iomanip.h>
const float AMT_IN_TANK = 300;  // initial gallons in the tank
const float TODAYS_PRICE = 1.25;  // price-per-gallon

// class declaration

class Pump
{
  private:
    float amtInTank;
    float price;
  public:
    Pump(float = 500.0, float = 1.00);        // constructor
    void values(void);
    void request(float);
};

// implementation section

Pump::Pump(float start, float todaysPrice)
{
  amtInTank = start;
  price = todaysPrice;
}

void Pump::values(void)
{
  cout << "The gas tank has " << amtInTank << " gallons of gas." << endl;
  cout << "The price per gallon of gas is $" << setiosflags(ios::showpoint)
       << setprecision(2) << price << endl;

  return;
}

void Pump::request(float pumpAmt)
{
  float pumped;

  if (amtInTank >= pumpAmt)
     pumped = pumpAmt;
  else
     pumped = amtInTank;
```

(continued on next page)

(continued from previous page)

```
    amtInTank -= pumped;
    cout << pumpAmt << " gallons were requested " << endl;
    cout << pumped << " gallons were pumped" << endl;
    cout << amtInTank << " gallons remain in the tank" << endl;
    cout << "The total price is $" << setiosflags(ios::showpoint)
         << setprecision(2) << (pumped * price) << endl;

    return;
}

int main()
{
    Pump a(AMT_IN_TANK, TODAYS_PRICE);    // declare 1 object of type Pump

    a.values();
    cout << endl;
    a.request(30.0);
    cout << endl;
    a.request(280.0);

    return 0;
}
```

The lightly shaded portion of Program 7.5 contains the class construction that we have already described. To see how this class is used, concentrate on the darker shaded section of the program. At the top of the program we have included the required `include` files and two constants, `AMT_IN_TANK` and `TODAYS_PRICE`, which correspond to the data that is to be used in the simulation.

Seven statements are included within the `main()` function. The first statement creates an object named `a` of type `Pump`. The supply tank for this pump contains `AMT_IN_TANK` gallons and the price per gallon is set to `TODAYS_PRICE`.

A request is then made to `values()` to display the pump's attribute values, which are correctly set at 300 gallons and $1.25 per gallon. The next `cout` statement simply provides a blank line.

The first request for gas is for 30 gallons, followed by a `cout` statement to again provide a blank line. Finally, the last statement is a request for 280 gallons, which should exceed the available gas in the supply tank. The output produced by Program 7.5 is:

```
Starting a new simulation—simulation time is 30 minutes
The gas tank has 300 gallons of gas.
The price per gallon of gas is $1.25

30.00 gallons were requested
30.00 gallons were pumped
270.00 gallons remain in the tank
The total price is $37.50

280.00 gallons were requested
270.00 gallons were pumped
0.00 gallons remain in the tank
The total price is $337.50
```

Exercises 7.3

1. Enter Program 7.4 in your computer and execute it.
2. a. Modify the Elevator class in Program 7.4 to account for a second elevator. Put this elevator in service starting at the fifth floor. Have this second elevator move to the first floor and then move to the twelfth floor.

   b. Verify that the constructor function is called by adding a message within the constructor that is displayed each time a new object is created. Run your program to ensure its operation.
3. Modify Program 7.4 to use a `while` loop that calls the elevator's request function with a random number between 1 and 15. If the random number is the same as the elevator's current floor, generate another request. The `while` loop should terminate after five valid requests have been made and satisfied by movement of the elevator. (Hint: Add a movement return code to the `request()` function.)
4. a. Modify the `main()` function in Program 7.5 to use a `while` loop that calls the pump's request function with a random number between 3 and 20. The `while` loop should terminate after five requests have been made.

   b. Modify the `main()` function written for Exercise 4a to provide a 30-minute simulation of the gas pump's operation. To do this you will have to modify the `while` loop to select a random number between 1 and 15 that represents the idle time between customer requests. Have the simulation stop once the idle time exceeds 30 minutes.
5. a. Construct a class definition of a Person object type. The class is to have three member functions and no attributes as shown in Figure 7.7. The constructor function should simply call `srand()` with the argument `time(NULL)` to initialize the `rand()` function. The `arrive()` function should provide a random number between 1 and 15 as a return value, and the `gallons()` function should provide a random number between 3 and 20.

   b. Test the `Person` class functions written for Exercise 5a in a complete working program.

   c. Use the `Person` class function of Exercise 5a to simulate a random arrival of a person and a random request for gallons of gas within the program written for Exercise 4b.
6. Modify Program 7.5 so that the `Pump` class definition resides in a file named `PUMP.H`. Then have Program 7.5 use an `#include` statement to include the class definition within the program. Make sure you use a full path name in the `include` statement. For example, if `PUMP.H` resides in the directory named `FOO` on the `C:` drive, the include statement should be `#include <C:\FOO\PUMP.C>`.

FIGURE 7.7 A Person Object with No Attributes

Person

`Initialize rand()`
`arrive()`
`gallons()`

POINT OF INFORMATION

Encapsulation

The term *encapsulation* refers to the packaging of a number of items into a single unit. For example, a function is used to encapsulate the details of an algorithm. Similarly, a class encapsulates both variables and functions together in a single package.

Although the term *encapsulation* is sometimes used to refer to the process of information hiding, this usage is not technically accurate. The correct relationship between terms is that information hiding refers to the encapsulation *and* hiding of all implementation details.

7. Construct a class named `Light` that simulates a traffic light. The color attribute of the class should change from `Green` to `Yellow` to `Red` and then back to green by the class's `change()` function. When a new `Light` object is created its initial color should be `Red`.

8. a. Construct a class definition that can be used to represent an employee of a company. Each employee is defined by an integer ID number, a floating-point pay rate, and the maximum number of hours the employee should work each week. The services provided by the class should be the ability to enter data for a new employee, the ability to change data for a new employee, and the ability to display the existing data for a new employee.

   b. Include the class definition created for Exercise 8a in a working C+ program that asks the user to enter data for three employees and displays the entered data.

   c. Modify the program written for Exercise 8b to include a menu that offers the user the following choices:

```
1. Add an employee
2. Modify employee data
3. Delete an employee
4. Exit this menu
```

   In response to a choice, the program should initiate appropriate action to implement the choice.

9. a. Construct a class definition that can be used to represent types of food. A type of food is classified as basic or prepared. Basic foods are further classified as either `Dairy`, `Meat`, `Fruit`, `Vegetable`, or `Grain`. The services provided by the class should be the ability to enter data for a new food, the ability to change data for a new food, and the ability to display the existing data for a new food.

   b. Include the class definition created for Exercise 9a in a working C+ program that asks the user to enter data for four food items and displays the entered data.

   c. Modify the program written for Exercise 9b to include a menu that offers the user the following choices:

```
1. Add a food item
2. Modify a food item
3. Delete a food item
4. Exit this menu
```

   In response to a choice, the program should initiate appropriate action to implement the choice.

7.4 COMMON PROGRAMMING ERRORS

The more common programming errors initially associated with the construction of classes are as follows:

1. Failing to terminate the class declaration section with a semicolon.
2. Including a return type with the constructor's prototype or failing to include a return type with the other functions' prototypes.
3. Using the same name for a data member as for a member function.
4. Defining more than one default constructor for a class.
5. Forgetting to include the class name and scope operator, `::`, in the header line of all member functions defined in the class implementation section.

All of these errors will result in a compiler error message.

7.5 CHAPTER REVIEW

Key Terms

abstract data type
class
class members
constructor
data hiding
data members
data type
declaration section
default constructor
destructor
implementation section
inline member function
instance variables
member functions
object
`private`
`public`

Summary

1. A *class* is a programmer-defined data type. *Objects* of a class may be defined and have the same relationship to their class as variables do to C++'s built-in data types.
2. A class definition consists of a declaration and implementation section. The most common form of a class definition is:

```
// class declaration section
class name
{
  private:
   a list of variable declarations;
  public:
    a list of function prototypes;
};

// class implementation section
class function definitions
```

The variables and functions declared in the class declaration section are collectively referred to as *class members*. The variables are individually referred to as class data members and the functions as class member functions. The terms `private` and `public` are access specifiers. Once an access specifier is listed it remains in force until another access specifier is given. The `private` keyword specifies that the class members following it are private to the class and can only be accessed by the class's member functions. The `public` keyword specifies that the class members following may be accessed from functions outside the class. Generally all data members should be specified as `private` and all member functions as `public`.

3. Class functions listed in the declaration section may be either written inline or their definitions included in the class implementation section. Except for constructor and destructor functions, all class functions defined in the class implementation section have the header line syntax:

```
return-type class-name::function-name(parameter list);
```

   Except for the addition of the class name and scope operator, `::`, which are required to identify the function name with the class, this header line is identical to the header line used for any user-written function.

4. A *constructor function* is a special function that is automatically called each time an object is declared. It must have the same name as its class and cannot have any return type. Its purpose is to initialize each declared object.
5. If no constructor is declared for a class the compiler will supply a *default constructor*. This is a do-nothing function having the definition `class-name::class-name(void){}`.
6. The term *default constructor* refers to any constructor that does not require any arguments when it is called. This can be because no parameters are declared (as is the case for the compiler-supplied default constructor) or because all parameters have been given default values.
7. Each class may only have one default constructor. If any constructor is user defined, the compiler will not create its default constructor.
8. Objects are created using either a C++ or C style of declaration. The C++ style of declaration has the form:

```
class-name list of object names(list of initializers);
```

   where the list of initializers is optional. An example of this style of declaration, including initializers, for a class named `Date` is:

```
Date a, b, c(12,25,98);
```

   Here the objects `a` and `b` are declared to be of type `Date` and are initialized using the default constructor, whereas the object `c` is initialized with the values 12, 25, and 98.

   The equivalent C style of declaration, including the optional list of initializers, has the form:

```
class-name object-name = class-name(list of initializers);
```

   An example of this style of declaration for a class named `Date` is:

```
Date c = Date(12,25,98)
```

   Here the object `c` is created and initialized with the values 12, 25, and 98.

9. Constructors may be overloaded in the same manner as any other user-written C++ function.

10. If a constructor is defined for a class, a user-defined default constructor also should be written, because the compiler will not supply it.
11. A *destructor function* is called each time an object goes out of scope. Destructors must have the same name as their class, but are preceded by a tilde (~). There can only be one destructor per class.
12. A *destructor function* takes no arguments and returns no value. If a user-defined destructor is not included in a class the compiler will provide a do-nothing destructor.

Exercises

1. Define the following terms:
   a. attribute
   b. behavior
   c. state
   d. model
   e. class
   f. object
   g. interface
2. a. In place of specifying a rectangle's location by listing the position of two corner points, what other attributes could be used?
   b. What other attributes, besides length and width, might be used to describe a rectangle if the rectangle is to be drawn on a color monitor?
   c. Describe a set of attributes that could be used to define circles that are to be drawn on a black-and-white monitor.
   d. What additional attributes would you add to those selected in response to Exercise 2c if the circles were to be drawn on a color monitor?
3. a. For each of the following, determine what attributes might be of interest to someone considering buying the item.
      - a book
      - a can of soda
      - a pen
      - a cassette tape
      - a cassette tape player
      - an elevator
      - a car
   b. Do the attributes you used in Exercise 3a model an object or a class of objects?
4. For each of the following items, what behavior might be of interest to someone considering buying the item?
   a. a car
   b. a cassette tape player
5. All of the examples of classes considered in this chapter have consisted of inanimate objects. Do you think that animate objects such as pets and even human beings could be modeled in terms of attributes and behavior? Why or why not?

6. a. The attributes of a class represent how objects of the class appear to the outside world. The behavior represents how an object of a class reacts to an external stimulus. Given this information, what do you think is the mechanism by which one object "triggers" the designated behavior in another object? (*Hint:* Consider how one person typically gets another person to do something.)

   b. If behavior in C++ is constructed by defining an appropriate function, how do you think the behavior is activated in C++?

7. a. Construct a class named `Rectangle` that has floating-point data members named `length` and `width`. The class should have a constructor that sets each data member to 0, member functions named `perimeter()` and `area()` to calculate the perimeter and area of a rectangle, respectively, and a member function named `getdata()` to set a rectangle's length and width, and a member function named `showdata()` that displays a rectangle's length, width, perimeter, and area.

   b. Include the `Rectangle` class constructed in Exercise 7a within a working C++ program.

8. a. Modify the `Date` class constructor defined in Program 7.1 to include a check that all day values reside between 1 and 31, and all month values reside between 1 and 12.

   b. Modify the day validation written for Exercise 8a to account for the month. Thus, for January (month 1) a day value between 1 and 31 is valid, whereas for February (month 2) a day value between 1 and 28 is valid, and so on.

   c. Modify the day validation written for Exercise 8b to account for leap years. (*Hint:* See Section 7.1, Exercise 7a.)

9. a. Modify the `Date` class defined in Program 7.1 to include a `nextDay()` function that increments a date by one day. Test your function to ensure that it correctly increments days into a new month and into a new year.

   b. Modify the `Date` class defined in Program 7.1 to include a `priorDay()` function that decrements a date by one day. Test your function to ensure that it correctly decrements days into a prior month and into a prior year.

10. a. In Exercise 4 of Section 7.2 you were asked to construct a `Time` class. For such a class include a `tick()` function that increments the time by one second. Test your function to ensure that it correctly increments into a new minute and a new hour.

    b. Modify the `Time` class written for Exercise 10a to include a `detick()` function that decrements the time by one second. Test your function to ensure that it correctly decrements time into a prior hour and into a prior minute.

CHAPTER

8 Class Functions and Conversions

The creation of a class requires that we provide the capability to declare, initialize, assign, manipulate, and display data members. In the previous chapter the declaration, initialization, and display of objects was presented. In this chapter we continue our construction of classes by providing the ability to create operator and conversion capabilities similar to those inherent in C++'s built-in types. With these additions our user-defined types will have all of the functionality of built-in types.

8.1 ASSIGNMENT

In Chapter 3 we saw how C++'s assignment operator, =, performs assignment between variables. In this section we see how assignment works when it is applied to objects and how to define our own assignment operator to override the default provided for user-defined classes.

For a specific assignment example, consider the `main()` function of Program 8.1. Notice that the implementation section of the `Date` class in Program 8.1 contains no assignment function. Nevertheless, we would expect the assignment statement `a = b;` in `main()` to assign b's data member values to their counterparts in a. This is, in fact, the case and is verified by the output produced when Program 8.1 is executed:

```
The date stored in a is originally 4/1/97
After assignment the date stored in a is 12/18/98
```

PROGRAM 8.1

```
#include <iostream.h>

// class declaration

class Date
{
  private:
     int month;
     int day;
     int year;
   public:
     Date(int = 7, int = 4, int = 96);      // constructor
     void showdate(void);      // member function to display a Date
};

// implementation section

Date::Date(int mm, int dd, int yy)
{
  month = mm;
  day = dd;
  year = yy;
}

void Date::showdate(void)
{
  cout << month << '/' << day << '/' << year << endl;

  return;
}

int main()
{
  Date a(4,1,97), b(12,18,98); // declare two objects

  cout << "The date stored in a is originally ";
  a.showdate();  // display the original date
  a = b;         // assign b's value to a
  cout << "After assignment the date stored in a is ";
  a.showdate();  // display a's values

  return 0;
}
```

The type of assignment illustrated in Program 8.1 is referred to as **memberwise assignment.** In the absence of any specific instructions to the contrary, the C++ compiler builds this type of default assignment operator for each class. If the class does *not* contain any pointer data members, this default assignment operator is adequate and can be used without further consideration. Before considering the problems that can occur with pointer data members, let's see how to construct our own explicit assignment operators. The information gained is then applicable to constructing all other user-defined operators.

Assignment operators, like all class members, are declared in the class declaration section and defined in the class implementation section. For the declaration of operators, however, the keyword `operator` must be included in the declaration. Using this keyword, a simple assignment operator declaration has the form:

```
void operator=(class-name&);
```

Here the keyword `void` indicates that the assignment returns no value, `operator=` indicates that we are overloading the assignment operator with our own version, and the class name and ampersand within the parentheses indicate that the argument to the operator is a class reference. For example, to declare a simple assignment operator for our `Date` class, the declaration

```
void operator=(Date&);
```

can be used.

The actual implementation of the assignment operator is defined in the implementation section. For our declaration, a suitable implementation is:

```
void Date::operator=(Date& newdate)
{
  day = newdate.day;        // assign the day
  month = newdate.month;    // assign the month
  year = newdate.year;      // assign the year
}
```

The use of the reference argument in the definition of this operation is not accidental. In fact, one of the primary reasons for reference variables in C++ is to facilitate the construction of overloaded operators and make the notation more natural.[1] In this definition `newdate` is defined as a reference to a `Date` class. Within the body of the definition, the day member of the object referenced by `newdate` is assigned to the day member of the current object, which is then repeated for the month and year members. Assignments such as `a.operator=(b);` can then be used to call the overloaded assignment operator and assign `b`'s member values to `a`. For convenience, the expression `a.operator=(b)` can be replaced with `a = b`;. Program 8.2 contains our new assignment operator within the context of a complete program.

Except for the addition of the overloaded assignment operator declaration and definition, Program 8.2 is identical to Program 8.1 and produces the same output. Its usefulness to us is that it illustrates how we can explicitly construct our own assignment definitions. In Section 9.5, when we introduce pointer data members, we will see how C++'s default assignment can cause troublesome errors that are circumvented by constructing our own assignment operators. Before moving on, however, two simple modifications to our assignment operator need to be made.

---

[1] Passing a reference is preferable to passing an object by value because it reduces the overhead required in making a copy of each object's data members.

PROGRAM 8.2

```
#include <iostream.h>

// class declaration

class Date
{
  private:
     int month;
     int day;
     int year;
   public:
     Date(int = 7, int = 4, int = 96);      // constructor
     void operator=(Date&);    // define assignment of a date
     void showdate(void);      // member function to display a
date
};

// implementation section

Date::Date(int mm, int dd, int yy)
{
  month = mm;
  day = dd;
  year = yy;
}

void Date::operator=(Date& newdate)
{

  day = newdate.day;          // assign the day
  month = newdate.month;      // assign the month
  year = newdate.year;        // assign the year

  return;
}

void Date::showdate(void)
{
  cout << month << '/' << day << '/' << year << endl;

  return;
}

int main()
{
  Date a(4,1,97), b(12,18,98); // declare two objects
```

(continued on next page)

(continued from previous page)

```
  cout << "The date stored in a is originally ";
  a.showdate();   // display the original date
  a = b;          // assign b's value to a
  cout << "After assignment the date stored in a is ";
  a.showdate();   // display a's values

  return 0;
}
```

First, to preclude any inadvertent alteration to the object used on the right-hand side of the assignment, a constant reference argument should be used. For our `Date` class, this takes the form:

```
void Date::operator=(const Date& newdate);
```

The final modification concerns the operation's return value. As constructed, our simple assignment operator returns no value, which precludes us from using it in multiple assignments such as `a = b = c`. The reason for this is that overloaded operators retain the same precedence and associativity as their equivalent built-in versions. Thus, an expression such as `a = b = c` is evaluated in the order `a = (b = c)`. As we have defined assignment, unfortunately, the expression `b = c` returns no value, making subsequent assignment to `a` an error. To provide for multiple assignments, a more complete assignment operation would return a reference to its class type. Because the implementation of such an assignment requires a special class pointer, the presentation of this more complete assignment operator is deferred until the material presented in the next chapter is introduced. Until then, our simple assignment operator will be more than adequate for our needs.

Copy Constructors

Although assignment looks similar to initialization, it is worthwhile noting that they are two entirely different operations. In C++ an initialization occurs every time a new object is created. In an assignment no new object is created—the value of an existing object is simply changed. Figure 8.1 illustrates this difference.

One type of initialization that closely resembles assignment occurs in C++ when one object is initialized using another object of the same class. For example, in the declaration

```
Date b = a;
```

or its entirely equivalent form

```
Date b(a);
```

FIGURE 8.1 Initialization and Assignment

```
                   c = a;  <------ Assignment
Type definition --> Date c = a;  <------ Initialization
```

the b object is initialized to a previously declared a object. The constructor that performs this type of initialization is called a **copy constructor,** and if you do not declare one the compiler will construct one for you. The compiler's **default copy constructor** performs in a similar manner to the default assignment operator by doing a memberwise copy between objects. Thus, for the declaration `Date b = a;` the default copy constructor sets b's month, day, and year values to their respective counterparts in a. As with default assignment operators, default copy constructors work just fine unless the class contains pointer data members. Before considering the complications that can occur with pointer data members and how to handle them, it is helpful to look at how we can construct our own copy constructors.

Copy constructors, like all class functions, are declared in the class declaration section and defined in the class implementation section. The declaration of a copy constructor has the general form:

```
class-name(const class-name&);
```

As with all constructors, the function name must be the class name. As further illustrated by the declaration, the argument is a reference to the class, which is a characteristic of all copy constructors.[2] To ensure that the argument is not inadvertently altered, it is always specified as a `const`. Applying this general form to our `Date` class, a copy constructor can be explicitly declared as:

```
Date(const Date&);
```

The actual implementation of this constructor, if it were to perform the same memberwise initialization as the default copy constructor, would take the form:

```
Date:: Date(const Date& olddate)
{
   month = olddate.month;
   day = olddate.day;
   year = olddate.year;
}
```

As with the assignment operator, the use of a reference argument for the copy constructor is no accident: The reference argument again facilitates a simple notation within the body of the function. Program 8.3 contains this copy constructor within the context of a complete program.

PROGRAM 8.3

```
#include <iostream.h>

// class declaration

class Date
{
  private:
    int month;
    int day;
    int year;
```

(continued on next page)

[2] A copy constructor is frequently defined as a constructor whose first argument is a reference to its class type, with any additional arguments being defaults.

(continued from previous page)

```
  public:
    Date(int = 7, int = 4, int = 96);      // constructor
    Date(const Date&);        // copy constructor
    void showdate(void);      // member function to display a date
};

// implementation section

Date::Date(int mm, int dd, int yy)
{
  month = mm;
  day = dd;
  year = yy;
}

Date::Date(const Date& olddate)
{
  month = olddate.month;
  day = olddate.day;
  year = olddate.year;
}

void Date::showdate(void)
{
  cout << month << '/' << day << '/' << year << endl;

  return;
}
```

```
int main()
{
  Date a(4,1,97), b(12,18,98); // use the constructor
  Date c(a);   // use the copy constructor
  Date d = b;  // use the copy constructor

  cout << "The date stored in a is ";
  a.showdate();
  cout << "The date stored in b is ";
  b.showdate();
  cout << "The date stored in c is ";
  c.showdate();
  cout << "The date stored in d is ";
  d.showdate();

  return 0;
}
```

The output produced by Program 8.3 is:

```
The date stored in a is 4/1/97
The date stored in b is 12/18/98
The date stored in c is 4/1/97
The date stored in d is 12/18/98
```

As illustrated by this output, c's and d's data members have been initialized by the copy constructor to a's and b's values, respectively. Although the copy constructor defined in Program 8. 3 adds nothing to the functionality provided by the compiler's default copy constructor, it does provide us with the fundamentals of defining copy constructors. In Section 9.5 we will see how to modify this basic copy constructor to handle cases that are not adequately taken care of by the compiler's default.

Base/Member Initialization[3]

Except for the reference names olddate and secdate, a comparison of Program 8.3's copy constructor to Program 8.2's assignment operator shows them to be essentially the same function. The difference in these functions is that the copy constructor first creates an object's data members before the body of the constructor uses assignment to specify member values. Thus, the copy constructor does not perform a true initialization, but rather a creation followed by assignment.

A true initialization would have no reliance on assignment whatsoever and is possible in C++ using a *base/member initialization list*. Such a list can only be applied to constructor functions and may be written in two ways.

The first way to construct a base/member initialization list is within a class's declaration section using the form:

```
class-name(argument list) : list of data members(initializing values) {}
```

For example, using this form a default constructor that performs a true initialization is:

```
// class declaration section

public:
  Date(int mo = 4, int da = 1, int yr = 96) : month(mo), day(da), year(yr) {}
```

The second way is to declare a prototype in the class's declaration section followed by the initialization list in the implementation section. For our Date constructor this takes the form:

```
// class declaration section

public:
  Date(int = 4, int = 1, int = 96);  // prototype with defaults

// class implementation section

Date::Date(int mo, int da, int yr) : month(mo), day(da), year(yr) {}
```

[3] The material in this section is presented for completeness only, and may be omitted without loss of subject continuity.

Notice that in both forms the body of the constructor function is empty. This is not a requirement, and the body can include any subsequent operations that you would like the constructor to perform. The interesting feature of this type of constructor is that it clearly differentiates between the initialization tasks performed in the member initialization list contained between the colon and the braces, and any subsequent assignments that might be contained within the function's body. Although we will not be using this type of initialization subsequently, it is required whenever there is a `const` class instance variable.

Exercises 8.1

1. Describe the difference between assignment and initialization.
2. a. Construct a class named `Time` that contains three integer data members named `hrs`, `mins`, and `secs`, which will be used to store hours, minutes, and seconds. The function members should include a constructor that provides default values of 0 for each data member, a display function that prints an object's data values, and an assignment operator that performs a memberwise assignment between two time objects.

   b. Include the `Time` class developed in Exercise 2a in a working C++ program that creates and displays two time objects, the second of which is assigned the values of the first object.
3. a. Construct a class named `Complex` that contains two floating-point data members named `real` and `imag`, which will be used to store the real and imaginary parts of a complex number. The function members should include a constructor that provides default values of 0 for each member function, a display function that prints an object's data values, and an assignment operator that performs a memberwise assignment between two complex number objects.

   b. Include the class written for Exercise 3a in a working C++ program that creates and displays the values of two complex objects, the second of which is assigned the values of the first object.
4. a. Construct a class named `Car` that contains the following four data members: a floating-point variable named `engine_size`, a character variable named `body_style`, and an integer variable named `color_code`. The function members should include a constructor that provides default values of 0 for each numeric data member and an `'X'` for each character variable; a display function that prints the engine size, body style, and color code; and an assignment operator that performs a memberwise assignment between two car objects for each instance variable.

   b. Include the class written for Exercise 4a in a working C++ program that creates and displays two car objects, the second of which is assigned the values of the first object, except for the pointer data member.

8.2 ADDITIONAL CLASS FEATURES

This section presents additional features pertaining to classes. These features include the scope of a class, creating static class members, and granting access privileges to nonmember functions. Each of these topics may be read independently of the others.

Class Scope

We have already encountered local and global scope in Chapter 6. As we saw there, the scope of a variable defines the portion of a program in which the variable can be accessed.

POINT OF INFORMATION

Values and Identities

Apart from any behavior that an object is supplied with, a characteristic feature that objects share with variables is that they always have a unique identity. It is an object's identity that permits one object to be distinguished from another. This is not true of a value, such as the number 5, because all occurrences of 5 are indistinguishable from one another. As such, values are not considered to be objects in object-oriented programming languages such as C++.

Another distinguishing feature between an object and a value is that a value can never be a container whose value can change, while an object clearly can. A value is simply an entity that stands for itself.

Now consider a string such as `"Chicago"`. As a string this is a value. However, since `Chicago` could also be a specific and identifiable object of type `City`, the context in which the name is used is important. Notice that if the string `"Chicago"` were assigned to an object's name attribute, it reverts to being a value.

For local variables this scope is defined by any block contained within a brace pair, `{ }`. This includes both the complete function body and any internal subblocks. Additionally, all parameters of a function are considered to be local function variables.

Global variables are accessible from their point of declaration throughout the remaining portion of the file containing them, with three exceptions:

1. If a local variable has the same name as a global variable, the global variable can only be accessed within the scope of the local variable by using the scope resolution operator, `::`.
2. The scope of a non static global variable can be extended into another file by using the keyword `extern`.
3. The same global name can be reused in another file to define a separate and distinct variable by using the keyword `static`. Static global variables are unknown outside of their immediate file.

In addition to local and global scopes, each class also defines an associated **class scope.** That is, the names of the data and function members are local to the scope of their class. Thus, if a global variable name is reused within a class, the global variable is hidden by the class data member in the same manner as a local function variable hides a global variable of the same name. Similarly, member function names are local to the class in which they are declared, and can only be used by objects declared for the class. Additionally, local function variables also hide the names of class data members having the same name. Figure 8.2 illustrates the scope of the variables and functions for the following declarations:

```
float rate;     // global
// class declaration
class Test
{
  private:
    float amount, price, total;  // class scope
  public:
    float extend(float, float);  // class scope
};
```

FIGURE 8.2 Example of Scopes

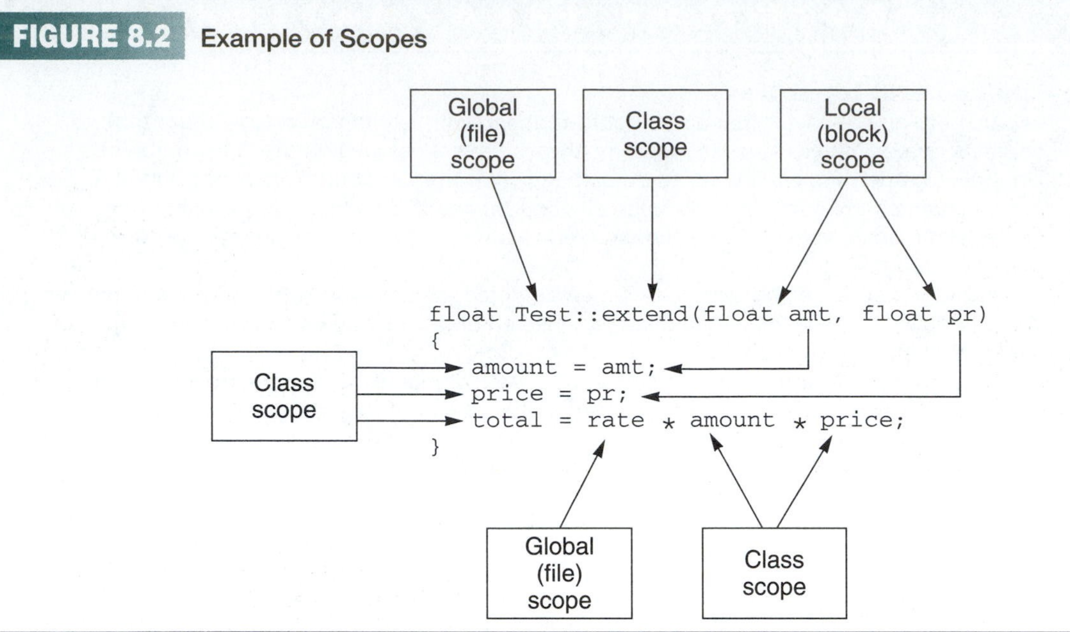

Static Class Members

As each class object is created, it gets its own block of memory for its data members. In some cases, however, it is convenient for every instantiation of a class to share the *same* memory location for a specific variable. For example, consider a class consisting of employee records, where each employee is subject to the same state sales tax. Clearly we could make the sales tax a global variable, but this is not very safe. Such data could be modified anywhere in the program, could conflict with an identical variable name within a function, and certainly violates C++'s principle of data hiding.

This type of situation is handled in C++ by declaring a class variable to be `static`. **Static class data members** share the same storage space for all objects of the class; as such, they act as global variables for the class and provide a means of communication between objects.

C++ requires that static variables be declared as such within the class declaration section. Since a static data member requires only a single storage area, regardless of the number of class instantiations, it is defined in a single place outside of the class definition. This is typically done in the global part of the program where the class implementation section is provided. For example, assuming the class declaration

```
//class declaration

class Employee
{
  private:
    static float tax_rate;
    int id_num;
  public:
    Employee(int);    //constructor
    void display();
};
```

the definition and initialization of the static variable `tax_rate` is accomplished using a statement such as

```
float Employee::tax_rate = 0.0025;
```

Here the scope resolution operator `::` is used to identify `tax_rate` as a member of the class `Employee` and the keyword `static` is not included. Program 8.4 uses this definition within the context of a complete program.

PROGRAM 8.4

```
#include <iostream.h>

// class declaration

class Employee
{
  private:
    static float tax_rate;
    int id_num;
  public:
    Employee(int = 0); // constructor
    void display();    // access function
};

// static member definition
float Employee::tax_rate = 0.0025;

// implementation section

Employee::Employee(int num)
{
  id_num = num;
}

void Employee::display()
{
  cout << "Employee number " << id_num
       << " has a tax rate of " << tax_rate << endl;

  return;
}

int main()
{
  Employee emp1(11122), emp2(11133);

  emp1.display();
  emp2.display();

  return 0;
}
```

The output produced by Program 8.4 is

```
Employee number 11122 has a tax rate of 0.0025
Employee number 11133 has a tax rate of 0.0025
```

Although it might appear that the initialization of tax_rate is global, it is not. Once the definition is made, any other definition will result in an error. Thus, the actual definition of a static member remains the responsibility of the class creator. The storage sharing produced by the static data member and the objects created in Program 8.4 is illustrated in Figure 8.3.

FIGURE 8.3 **Sharing the** static **Data Member** tax_rate

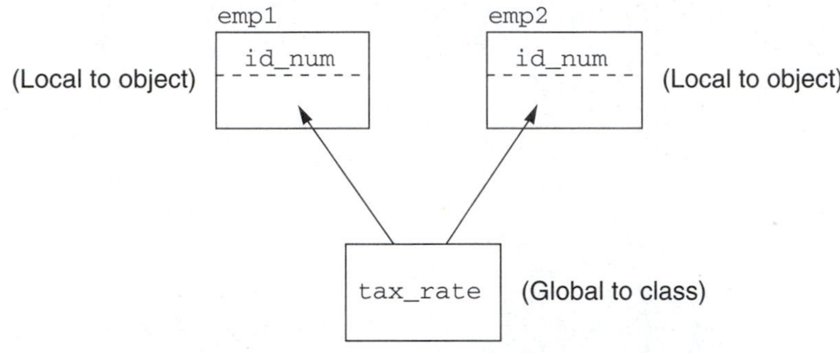

In addition to static data members, **static member functions** can also be created. Such functions apply to a class as a whole rather than to individual class objects and can only access static data members and other static member functions of the class.[4] An example of such a function is provided by Program 8.5.

The output produced by Program 8.5 is:

```
The static tax rate is 0.0025
Employee number 11122 has a tax rate of 0.0025
Employee number 11133 has a tax rate of 0.0025
```

In reviewing Program 8.5 notice that the keyword static is used only when static data and function members are declared; it is not included in the definition of these members. Also notice that the static member function is called using the scope resolution operator with the function's class name. Finally, since static functions access only static variables that are not contained within a specific object, static functions may be called before any instantiations are declared.

Friend Functions

The only method we currently have for accessing and manipulating private class data members is through the class's member functions. Conceptually, this arrangement can be viewed as illustrated in Figure 8.4a. There are times, however,

[4] The reason for this is that the this pointer, discussed in Section 9.3, is not passed to static member functions.

PROGRAM 8.5

```
#include <iostream.h>

// class declaration

class Employee
{
  private:
    static float tax_rate;
    int id_num;
  public:
    Employee(int = 0);    // constructor
    void display();       // access function
    static void disp();   // static function
};

// static member definition
float Employee::tax_rate = 0.0025;

// implementation section

Employee::Employee(int num)
{
  id_num = num;
}

void Employee::display()
{
  cout << "Employee number " << id_num
       << " has a tax rate of " << tax_rate << endl;

  return;
}

void Employee::disp()
{
  cout << "The static tax rate is " << tax_rate << endl;

  return;
}

int main()
{
  Employee::disp();   // call the static functions
  Employee emp1(11122), emp2(11133);

  emp1.display();
  emp2.display();

  return 0;
}
```

FIGURE 8.4a Direct Access Is Provided to Member Functions

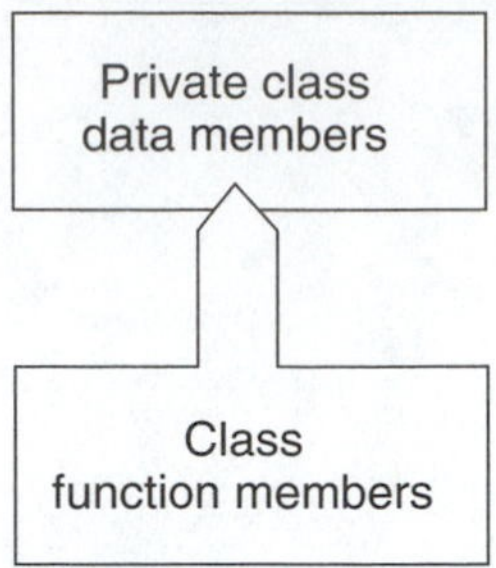

when it is useful to provide such access to selected nonmember functions. The procedure for providing this external access is rather simple—the class maintains its own approved list of nonmember functions that are granted the same privileges as member functions. The nonmember functions on the list are called **friend functions**, and the list is referred to as a friends list.

Figure 8.4b conceptually illustrates the use of such a list for nonmember access. Any nonmember function attempting access to an object's private data members is first checked against the friends list: If the function is on the list, access is approved; otherwise access is denied.

From a coding standpoint the friends list is simply a series of function prototype declarations that is preceded with the word `friend` and included in the class's declaration section. For example, if the functions named `addreal()` and `addimag()` are to be allowed access to the private members of a class named `Complex`, the following prototypes would be included within `Complex`'s declaration section:

```
friend float addreal(Complex&, Complex&);
friend float addimag(Complex&, Complex&);
```

Here the friends list consists of two declarations. The prototypes indicate that each function returns a floating-point number and expects two references to objects of type `Complex` as arguments. Program 8.6 includes these two friend declarations in a complete program.

FIGURE 8.4b Access Provided to Nonmember Functions

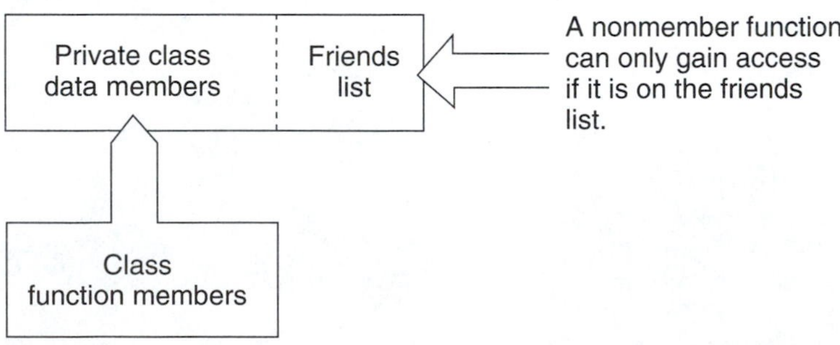

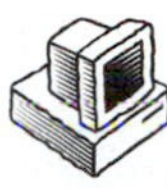

PROGRAM 8.6

```
#include <iostream.h>
#include <math.h>

// class declaration

class Complex
{
  // friends list
  friend float addreal(Complex&, Complex&);
  friend float addimag(Complex&, Complex&);
  private:
    float real;
    float imag;
  public:
    Complex(float = 0, float = 0);  // constructor
    void display();

};

// implementation section

Complex::Complex(float rl, float im)
{
  real = rl;
  imag = im;
}

void Complex::display()
{
  char sign = '+';

  if(imag < 0) sign = '-';
  cout << real << sign << fabs(imag) << 'i';

  return;
}

// friend implementations

float addreal(Complex &a, Complex &b)
{
  return(a.real + b.real);
}

float addimag(Complex &a, Complex &b)
{
  return(a.imag + b.imag);
}
```

(continued on next page)

(continued from previous page)

```
int main()
{
  Complex a(3.2, 5.6), b(1.1, -8.4);
  float re, im;

  cout << "\nThe first complex number is ";
  a.display();
  cout << "\nThe second complex number is ";
  b.display();


  re = addreal(a,b);
  im = addimag(a,b);
  Complex c(re,im);  // create a new Complex object
  cout << "\n\nThe sum of these two complex numbers is ";
  c.display();

  return 0;
}
```

The output produced by Program 8.6 is:

```
The first complex number is 3.2+5.6i
The second complex number is 1.1-8.4i

The sum of these two complex numbers is 4.3-2.8i
```

In reviewing Program 8.6 notice four items. The first is that since friends are not class members, they are unaffected by the access section in which they are declared—*they may be declared anywhere within the declaration section.* The convention we have followed is to include all friend declarations immediately following the class header. The second item to notice is that the keyword `friend` (like the keyword `static`) is used only within the class declaration and not in the actual function definition. Third, since a friend function is intended to have access to an object's private data members, at least one of the friend's arguments should be a reference to an object of the class that has made it a friend. Finally, as illustrated by Program 8.6, it is the class that grants friend status to a function and not the other way around. The function can never confer friend status on itself, because to do so would violate the concepts of data hiding and access provided by a class.

Exercises 8.2

1. a. Rewrite Program 8.5 to include an integer static data member named `numemps`. This variable should act as a counter that is initialized to zero and is incremented by the class constructor each time a new object is declared. Rewrite the static function `disp()` to display the value of this counter.

   b. Test the program written for Exercise 1a. Have the `main()` function call `disp()` after each `Employee` object is created.

2. a. Construct a class named Circle that contains two integer data members named `x_cent` and `y_cent`, and a floating-point data member named `radius`. Additionally, the class should contain static data member named `scal_factor`. Here the `x_cent` and `y_cent` values represent the center point of a circle, `radius` represents the circle's actual radius, and `scal_factor` represents a scale factor that will be used to scale the circle to fit on a variety of display devices.

   b. Include the program written for Exercise 2a in a working C++ program.

3. a. Could the following three statements from Program 8.6

```
re = addreal(a,b);
im = addimag(a,b);
complex c(re,im);  // create a new complex object
be replaced by the single statement
complex(addread(a,b), addimag(a,b));
```

   b. Verify your answer to Exercise 3a by running Program 8.6 with the suggested replacement statement.

4. a. Rewrite the program written for Exercise 2a, but include a friend function that multiplies an object's `radius` by the static scale factor and then displays the actual radius value and the scaled value.

   b. Include the program written for Exercise 4a in a working C++ program.

5. Rewrite Program 8.6 so that it has only one friend function named `addcomplex()`. This function should accept two complex objects and return a complex object. The real and imaginary parts of the returned object should be the sum of the real and imaginary parts, respectively, of the two objects passed to `complex()`.

8.3 OPERATOR FUNCTIONS

A simple assignment operator was constructed in Section 8.1. In this section we extend this capability and show how to broaden C++'s built-in operators to work with class objects. We will discover that class operators are themselves either member or friend functions.

The only symbols permitted for user-defined purposes are the subset of C++'s built-in symbols listed in Table 8.1. Each of these symbols can be adopted for class use with no limitation as to its meaning.[5] This is done by making each operation a function that can be overloaded like any other function.

The operation of the symbols listed in Table 8.1 can be redefined as we see fit for our classes, subject to the following restrictions:

- Symbols not in Table 8.1 cannot be redefined. For example, the `.`, `::`, and `?:` symbols cannot be redefined.
- New operator symbols cannot be created. For example, since `%%` is not an operator in C++ it cannot be defined as a class operator.

---

[5] The only limitation is that the syntax of the operator cannot be changed. Thus, a binary operator must remain binary and a unary operator must remain unary. Within this syntax restriction an operator symbol can be used to produce any operation, whether or not the operation is consistent with the symbol's accepted usage. For example, we could redefine the addition symbol to provide multiplication. Clearly this violates the intent and spirit of making these symbols available to us. We shall be very careful to redefine each symbol in a manner consistent with its accepted usage.

TABLE 8.1 Operators Available for Class Use

<table>
<tr><th>Operator</th><th>Description</th></tr>
<tr><td>()</td><td>Function call</td></tr>
<tr><td>[]</td><td>Array element</td></tr>
<tr><td>-></td><td>Structure member pointer reference</td></tr>
<tr><td>new</td><td>Dynamically allocate memory</td></tr>
<tr><td>delete</td><td>Dynamically deallocate memory</td></tr>
<tr><td>++</td><td>Increment</td></tr>
<tr><td>--</td><td>Decrement</td></tr>
<tr><td>-</td><td>Unary minus</td></tr>
<tr><td>!</td><td>Logical negation</td></tr>
<tr><td>~</td><td>One's complement</td></tr>
<tr><td>*</td><td>Indirection</td></tr>
<tr><td>*</td><td>Multiplication</td></tr>
<tr><td>/</td><td>Division</td></tr>
<tr><td>%</td><td>Modulus (remainder)</td></tr>
<tr><td>+</td><td>Addition</td></tr>
<tr><td>-</td><td>Subtraction</td></tr>
<tr><td><<</td><td>Left shift</td></tr>
<tr><td>>></td><td>Right shift</td></tr>
<tr><td><</td><td>Less than</td></tr>
<tr><td><=</td><td>Less than or equal to</td></tr>
<tr><td>></td><td>Greater than</td></tr>
<tr><td>>=</td><td>Greater than or equal to</td></tr>
<tr><td>==</td><td>Equal to</td></tr>
<tr><td>!=</td><td>Not equal to</td></tr>
<tr><td>&&</td><td>Logical AND</td></tr>
<tr><td>||</td><td>Logical OR</td></tr>
<tr><td>&</td><td>Bitwise AND</td></tr>
<tr><td>^</td><td>Bitwise exclusive OR</td></tr>
<tr><td>|</td><td>Bitwise inclusive OR</td></tr>
<tr><td>=</td><td>Assignment</td></tr>
<tr><td>+= -= *=</td><td>Assignment</td></tr>
<tr><td>/= %= &=</td><td>Assignment</td></tr>
<tr><td>^= |=</td><td>Assignment</td></tr>
<tr><td><<= >>=</td><td>Assignment</td></tr>
<tr><td>,</td><td>Comma</td></tr>
</table>

- Neither the precedence nor the associativity of C++'s operators can be modified. Thus, you cannot give the addition operator a higher precedence than the multiplication operator.
- Operators cannot be redefined for C++'s built-in types.
- A C++ operator that is unary cannot be changed to a binary operator and a binary operator cannot be changed to a unary operator.
- The operator must either be a member of a class or be defined to take at least one class member as an operand.

The first step in providing a class with operators from Table 8.1 is to decide which operations make sense for the class and how they should be defined. As a specific example, we continue to build on the `Date` class introduced previously. For this class a small, meaningful set of class operations is defined.

Clearly the addition of two dates is not meaningful. The addition of a date with an integer, however, does make sense if the integer is taken as the number of days to be added to the date. Likewise, the subtraction of an integer from a date makes sense. Also, the subtraction of two dates is meaningful if we define the difference to mean the number of days between the two dates. Similarly, it makes sense to compare two dates and determine if the dates are equal or if one date occurs before or after another date. Let's see how these operations can be implemented using C++'s operator symbols.

A user-defined operation is created as a function that redefines C++'s built-in operator symbols for class use. Functions that define operations on class objects and use C++'s built-in operator symbols are referred to as **operator functions.**

Operator functions are declared and implemented in the same manner as all member functions, with one exception: It is the function's name that connects the appropriate operator symbol to the operation defined by the function. An operator function's name is always of the form `operator<symbol>` where `<symbol>` is one of the operators listed in Table 8.1. For example, the function name `operator+` is the name of the addition function, while the function name `operator==` is the name of the equal to comparison function.

Once the appropriate function name is selected, the process of writing the function simply amounts to having it accept the desired inputs and produce the correct returned value.[6] For example, in comparing two `Date` objects for equality we would select C++'s equality operator. Thus, the name of our function becomes `operator==`. We would want our comparison operation to accept two `Date` objects, internally compare them, and return an integer value indicating the result of the comparison: 1 for equality and 0 for inequality. As a member function, a suitable prototype that could be included in the class declaration section is:

```
int operator==(Date&);
```

This prototype indicates that the function is named `operator==`, that it returns an integer, and that it accepts a reference to a `Date` object.[7] Only one `Date` object is required here because the second `Date` object will be the object

[6] As previously noted, this implies that the specified operator can be redefined to perform any operation. Good programming practice, however, dictates against such redefinitions.

[7] The prototype `int operator==(Date)` also works. Passing a reference, however, is preferable to passing an object because it reduces the function call's overhead. This is because passing an object means that a copy of the object must be made for the called function, whereas passing a reference gives the function direct access to the object whose address is passed.

that calls the function. Let's now write the function definition to be included in the class implementation section. Assuming our class is named `Date`, a suitable definition is:

```
int Date::operator==(Date& Date2)
{
  if( day == Date2.day && month == Date2.month && year == Date2.year)
    return 1;
  else
    return 0;
}
```

Once this function has been defined, it may be called using the same syntax that is used for C++'s built-in types. For example, if `a` and `b` are objects of type `Date`, the expression if `(a == b)` is valid. Program 8.7 includes the call as well as the declaration and definition of this operator function within the context of a complete program.

The output produced by Program 8.7 is:

```
Dates a and b are not the same.
Dates a and c are the same.
```

The first new feature to be illustrated in Program 8.7 is the declaration and implementation of the function named `operator==`. Except for its name, this operator function is constructed in the same manner as any other member function: It is declared in the declaration section and defined in the implementation section. The second new feature is how the function is called. Operator functions may be called using their associated symbols rather than in the way other functions are called. Since operator functions are true functions, however, the traditional method of calling them can also be used—by specifying their name and including appropriate arguments. Thus, in addition to being called by the expression `a == b` in Program 8.7, the call `a.operator==(b)` could also have been used.

Let's now create another operator for our `Date` class—an addition operator. As before, creating this operator requires that we specify three items:

1. the name of the operator function
2. the processing that the function is to perform
3. the data type, if any, that the function is to return.

Clearly, for addition we will use the operator function named `operator+`. Having selected the function's name we must now determine what we want this function to do, as it specifically relates to `Date` objects. As we noted previously, the sum of two dates is without meaning. Adding an integer to a date is meaningful, however, when the integer represents the number of days either before or after the given date. Here the sum of an integer to a `Date` object is simply another `Date` object, which should be returned by the addition operation. Thus, a suitable prototype for our addition function is:

```
Date operator+(int);
```

This prototype would be included in the class declaration section. It specifies that an integer is to be added to a class object and the operation returns a `Date` object. Thus, if `a` is a `Date` object, the function call `a.operator+(284)`, or its more commonly used alternative, `a + 284`, should cause the number 284 to be correctly added to `a`'s date value. We must now construct the function to accomplish this.

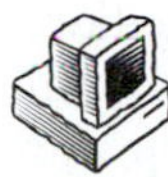

PROGRAM 8.7

```
#include <iostream.h>

// class declaration

class Date
{
  private:
    int month;
    int day;
    int year;
  public:
    Date(int = 7, int = 4, int = 96);      // constructor
    int operator==(Date &);  // declare the operator== function
    void showdate(void);     // member function to display a date
};

// implementation section

Date::Date(int mm, int dd, int yy)
{
  month = mm;
  day = dd;
  year = yy;
}

int Date::operator==(Date &date2)
{
  if(day == date2.day && month == date2.month && year == date2.year)
    return 1;
  else
    return 0;
}

int main()
{
  Date a(4,1,97), b(12,18,98), c(4,1,97); // declare 3 objects

  if (a == b)
    cout << "Dates a and b are the same." << endl;
  else
    cout << "Dates a and b are not the same." << endl;

  if (a == c)
    cout << "Dates a and c are the same." << endl;
  else
    cout << "Dates a and c are not the same." << endl;

  return 0;
}
```

Constructing the function requires that we first select a specific date convention. For simplicity we will adopt the financial date convention that considers each month to consist of 30 days and each year to consist of 360 days. Using this convention, our function will first add the integer number of days to the Date object's day value and then adjust the resulting day value to lie within the range 1 to 30 and the month value to lie within the range 1 to 12. A function that accomplishes this follows:

```
Date Date::operator+(int days)
{
  Date temp;  // a temporary Date to store the result

  temp.day = day + days;  // add the days
  temp.month = month;
  temp.year = year;
  while (temp.day > 30)    // now adjust the months
  {
    temp.month++;
    temp.day -= 30;
  }
  while (temp.month > 12)  // adjust the years
  {
    temp.year++;
    temp.month -= 12;
  }
  return temp;     // the values in temp are returned
}
```

The important feature to notice here is the use of the `temp` object. The purpose of this object is to ensure that none of the function's arguments, which become the operator's operands, is altered. To understand this, consider a statement such as `b = a + 284;` that uses this operator function, where `a` and `b` are `Date` objects. This statement should never modify `a`'s value. Rather, the expression `a + 284` should yield a `Date` value that is then assigned to `b`. The result of the expression is, of course, the `temp Date` object returned by the `operator+()` function. Program 8.8 uses this function within the context of a complete program.

PROGRAM 8.8

```
#include <iostream.h>

// class declaration

class Date
{
  private:
    int month;
    int day;
    int year;
  public:
    Date(int = 0, int = 0, int = 0);      // constructor
    Date operator+(int);      // overload the + operator
    void showdate(void);      // member function to display a date
};
```

(continued on next page)

(continued from previous page)

```
// implementation section

Date::Date(int mm, int dd, int yy)
{
  month = mm;
  day = dd;
  year = yy;
}

Date Date::operator+(int days)
{
  Date temp;  // a temporary date to store the result

  temp.day = day + days;  // add the days
  temp.month = month;
  temp.year = year;
  while (temp.day > 30)     // now adjust the months
  {
    temp.month++;
    temp.day -= 30;
  }
  while (temp.month > 12)  // adjust the years
  {
    temp.year++;
    temp.month -= 12;
  }
  return temp;       // the values in temp are returned
}

void Date::showdate(void)
{
  cout << month << '/' << day << '/' << year << endl;

  return;
}
```

```
int main()
{
  Date a(4,1,97), b; // declare two objects

  cout << "The initial date is ";
  a.showdate();
  b = a + 284;   // add in 284 days = 9 months and 14 days
  cout << "The new date is ";
  b.showdate();

  return 0;
}
```

The output produced by Program 8.8 is:

```
The initial date is 4/1/97
The new date is 1/15/98
```

Operator Functions as Friends

The operator functions in both Programs 8.7 and 8.8 have been constructed as class members. An interesting feature of operator functions is that, except for the operator functions `=`, `()`, `[]`, and `->`, they may also be written as friend functions. For example, if the `operator+()` function used in Program 8.8 were written as a friend, a suitable declaration section prototype would be:

```
friend Date operator+(Date&, int);
```

Notice that the friend version contains a reference to a `Date` object that is not contained in the member function version. In all cases the equivalent friend version of a member operator function *must* contain an additional class reference that is not required by the member function.[8] This equivalence is listed in Table 8.2 for both unary and binary operators.

Table 8.2 Operator Function Argument Requirements

	Member Function	Friend Function
Unary operator	1 implicit	1 explicit
Binary operator	1 implicit and 1 explicit	2 explicit

We now write Program 8.8's `operator+()` function as a friend function:

```
Date Date::operator+(Date& op1, int days)
{
  Date temp;  // a temporary Date to store the result

  temp.day = op1.day + days;  // add the days
  temp.month = op1.month;
  temp.year = op1.year;
  while (temp.day > 30)     // now adjust the months
  {
    temp.month++;
    temp.day -= 30;
  }
  while (temp.month > 12)   // adjust the years
  {
    temp.year++;
    temp.month -= 12;
  }
  return temp;      // the values in temp are returned
}
```

[8] This extra argument is necessary to identify the correct object. This argument is not needed when using a member function because the member function"knows" on which object it is operating. The mechanism of this "knowing" is supplied by an implied member function argument named `this`, which is explained in detail in Section 9.3.

The only difference between this version and the member version is the explicit use of a `Date` argument named `op1` (the choice of this name is entirely arbitrary) in the friend version. This means that within the body of the friend function the first three assignment statements explicitly reference `op1`'s data members as `op1.day`, `op1.month`, and `op1.year`, whereas the member function simply refers to its arguments as `day`, `month`, and `year`.

In making the determination to overload a binary operator as either a friend or member operator function, the following convention can be applied: *Friend functions are more appropriate for binary functions that modify neither of their operands, such as ==, +, –, etc., while member functions are more appropriate for binary functions, such as =, +=, –= and etc., which are used to modify one of their operands.*

Exercises 8.3

1. a. Define a greater than relational operator function named `operator>` that can be used with the `Date` class declared in Program 8.7.

   b. Define a less than operator function named `operator<()` that can be used with the `Date` class declared in Program 8.7.

   c. Include the operator functions written for Exercises 1a and 1b in a working C++ program.

2. a. Define a subtraction operator function named `operator-()` that can be used with the `Date` class defined in Program 8.7. The subtraction, should accept a long integer argument that represents the number of days to be subtracted from an object's date and return a `Date`. In doing the subtraction use the financial assumption that all months consist of 30 days and all years of 360 days. Additionally, an end-of-month adjustment should be made, if necessary, that converts any resulting day of 31 to a day of 30, except if the month is February. If the resulting month is February and the day is either 29, 30, or 31, it should be changed to 28.

   b. Define another subtraction operator function named `operator-()` that can be used with the `Date` class defined in Program 8.7. The subtraction should yield a long integer that represents the difference in days between two dates. In calculating the day difference, use the financial day count basis that assumes that all months have 30 days and all years have 360 days.

   c. Include the overloaded operators written for Exercises 2a and 2b in a working C++ program.

3. a. Determine if the following addition operator function provides the same result as the function used in Program 8.8:

```
Date Date::operator+(int days)     // return a Date object
{
  Date temp;

  temp.day = day + days;     // add the days in
  temp.month = month + int(day/30);  // determine total months
  temp.day = temp.day % 30;          // determine actual day
  temp.year = year + int(temp.month/12);  // determine total years
  temp.month = temp.month % 12;      // determine actual month

  return temp;
}
```

   b. Verify your answer to Exercise 3a by including the function in a working C++ program.

4. a. Rewrite the equality relational operator function in Program 8.7 as a friend function.

b. Verify the operation of the friend operator function written for Exercise 4a by including it within a working C++ program.

5. a. Rewrite the addition operator function in Program 8.8 to account for the actual days in a month, neglecting leap years.

   b. Verify the operation of the operator function written for Exercise 5a by including it within a working C++ program.

6. a. Construct an addition operator for the Complex class declared in Program 8.6. This should be a member function that adds two complex numbers and returns a complex number.

   b. Add a member multiplication operator function in the program written for Exercise 6a that multiplies two complex numbers and returns a complex number.

   c. Verify the operation of the operator functions written for Exercises 6a and 6b by including them within a working C++ program.

8.4 TWO USEFUL ALTERNATIVES: `operator()` AND `operator[]`

There are times when it is convenient to define an operation having more than two arguments, which is the limit imposed on all binary operator functions. For example, each of our `Date` objects contains three integer data members: `month`, `day`, and `year`. For such an object we might want to add an integer value to any of these three members, instead of just the day member as was done in Program 8.8. C++ provides for this possibility by supplying the parentheses operator function, `operator()`, which has no limits on the number of arguments that may be passed to it.

On the other end of the spectrum, the case illustrated by Program 8.8, in which only a single nonobject argument is required, occurs so frequently that C++ also provides an alternative means of achieving it. For this special case, C++ supplies the subscript operator function, `operator[]`, which permits a maximum of one argument. The only restriction imposed by C++ on the `operator()` and `operator[]` functions is that they must be defined as member (not friend) functions. For simplicity, we consider the `operator[]` function first.

The subscript operator function, `operator[]`, is declared and defined in the same manner as any other operator function, but is called differently from the normal function and operator call. For example, if we wanted to use this operator function to accept an integer argument and return a `Date` object, the following prototype is valid:

```
Date operator[](int);  // declare the subscript operator
```

Except for the operator function's name, this is similar in construction to any other operator function prototype. Assuming we want this function to add its integer argument to a `Date` object, a suitable function implementation is:

```
Date Date::operator[](int days)
{
  Date temp;  // a temporary Date to store the result

  temp.day = day + days;   // add the days
  temp.month = month;
  temp.year = year;
  while (temp.day > 30)    // now adjust the months
```

```
  {
    temp.month++;
    temp.day -= 30;
  }
  while (temp.month > 12)  // adjust the years
  {
    temp.year++;
    temp.month -= 12;
  }
  return temp;      // the values in temp are returned
}
```

Again, except for the initial header line, this is similar in construction to other operator function definitions. Once the function is created, however, it can only be called by passing the required argument through the subscript brackets. For example, if a is a Date object, the function call a[284] calls the subscript operator function and causes the function to operate on the a object using the integer value 284. This call is illustrated in Program 8.9.

PROGRAM 8.9

```
#include <iostream.h>

// class declaration

class Date
{
  private:
    int month;
    int day;
    int year;
  public:
    Date(int = 0, int = 0, int = 0);    // constructor
    Date operator[](int);  // overload the subscript operator
     void showdate(void);  // member function to display a date
};

// implementation section

Date::Date(int mm, int dd, int yy)
{
  month = mm;
  day = dd;
  year = yy;
}

Date Date::operator[](int days)
{
  Date temp;  // a temporary date to store the result
```

(continued on next page)

(continued from previous page)

```
  temp.day = day + days;   // add the days
  temp.month = month;
  temp.year = year;
  while (temp.day > 30)     // now adjust the months
  {
    temp.month++;
    temp.day -= 30;
  }
  while (temp.month > 12)   // adjust the years
  {
    temp.year++;
    temp.month -= 12;
  }
  return temp;       // the values in temp are returned
}

void Date::showdate(void)
{
  cout << month << '/' << day << '/' << year << endl;

  return;
}
```

```
int main()
{
  Date a(4,1,96), b; // declare two objects

  cout << "The initial date is ";
  a.showdate();
  b = a[284];   // add in 284 days = 9 months and 14 days
  cout << "The new date is ";
  b.showdate();

  return 0;
}
```

Program 8.9 is identical in every way to Program 8.8, except that we have used an overloaded subscript operator function in place of an overloaded addition operator function. Programs 8.9 and 8.8 produce identical output.[9]

The parentheses operator function, `operator()`, is almost identical in construction and calling to the subscript function, `operator[]`, with the substitution of the parentheses, `()`, for the brackets, `[]`. The difference between these two operator functions is in the number of allowable arguments. Whereas the sub-

[9] If you are familiar with arrays, notice that the expression a[284] used in Program 8.9 *appears* to indicate that a is an array, but it is not. It is simply the notation that is required to call an overloaded subscript function.

script operator permits zero or one argument to be passed, the parentheses operator has no limit on the number of its arguments. For example, a suitable operator prototype to add an integer number of months, days, or years to a `Date` object is:

```
Date operator()(int, int, int);
```

Once such a function is implemented (which is left as an exercise), a call such as `a(2,4,3)` can be used to add 2 months, 4 days, and 3 years to the `Date` object named `a`.

These two extra functions provide a great deal of programming flexibility. In the case where only one argument is needed, they permit two different overloaded functions to be written, both of which have the same argument type. For example, we could use the `operator[]` to add an integer number of days to a `Date` object and the `operator()` to add an integer number of months. Since both functions have the same argument type, one function name could not be overloaded for both of these cases. These two functions also permit us the flexibility to restrict the other operator functions to class member arguments and use these two functions for any other argument types or operations, such as adding an integer to a `Date` object.

Exercises 8.4

1. Replace the subscript `operator[]` function in Program 8.9 with the parentheses `operator()` function.

2. a. Replace the subscript `operator[]` `function` in Program 8.9 with a member `operator()` function that accepts an integer month, day, and year count. Have the function add the input days, months, and years to the object's date and return the resulting date. For example, if the input is 3,2,1 and the object's date is 7/16/98, the function should return the date 10/18/98. Make sure that your function correctly handles an input such as 37 days and 15 months and adjusts the calculated day to be within the range 1 to 30 and the month within the range 1 to 12.

   b. Include the operator function written for Exercise 2a in a working C++ program and verify its operation.

3. a. Construct a class named `Student` consisting of the following private data members: an integer ID number, an integer count, and four floating-point grades. The constructor for this class should set all data member values to zero. The class should also include a member function that displays all valid member grades, as determined by the grade count, and calculates and displays the average of the grades. Include the class in a working C++ program that declares three class objects named `a`, `b`, and `c`.

   b. Include a member `operator[]` function in the class constructed for Exercise 3a that has a floating-point grade argument. The function should check the count data member, and if fewer than four grades have been entered the function should store its argument into the next grade slot available. If four grades have already been entered, the function should return an error message indicating that the new grade cannot be accepted. Additionally, a new grade should force an increment to the count data member.

   c. Include a member `operator()` function in the class constructed for Exercise 3a that has a grade identification number and grade value as arguments. The function should force a change to the grade corresponding to the identification number and update the count if necessary. For example, an argument list of 4,98.5 should change the fourth test grade value to 98.5.

4. a. Add a member `operator[]` function to Program 8.6 that multiplies an object's complex number (both the real and imaginary parts) by a real number and returns a complex number. For example, if the real number is 2 and the complex number is `3+4i`, the result is `6+8i`.

   b. Verify the operation of the operator function written for Exercise 4a by including it within a working C++ program.

8.5 DATA TYPE CONVERSIONS

The conversion from one built-in data type to another was previously described in Chapter 3. With the introduction of user-defined data types the possibilities for **data type conversions** expand to the following cases:

- conversion from built-in type to built-in type
- conversion from built-in type to user-defined type
- conversion from user-defined type to built-in type
- conversion from user-defined type to user-defined type

The first conversion is handled either by C++'s built-in implicit conversion rules or its explicit cast operator. The second conversion type is made using a *type conversion constructor*. The third and fourth conversion types are made using a *conversion operator function*. In this section the specific means of performing each of these conversions is presented.

Built-In to Built-In Conversion

The conversion from one built-in data type to another has already been presented in Sections 3.1 and 3.3. To review this case briefly, this type of conversion is either implicit or explicit.

An implicit conversion occurs in the context of one of C++'s operations. For example, when a floating-point value is assigned to an integer variable, only the integer portion of the value is stored. The conversion is implied by the operation and is performed automatically by the compiler.

An explicit conversion occurs whenever a cast is used. In C++ two cast notations exist. Using the older C notation, a cast has the form *`(data-type) expression`* while the newer C++ notation has the function-like form *`data-type(expression)`*. For example, both of the expressions `(int)24.32` and `int(24.32)` cause the floating-point value 24.32 to be truncated to the integer value 24.

Built-In to Class Conversion

User-defined casts for converting a built-in to a user-defined data type are created using constructor functions. A constructor whose first parameter is not a member of its class and whose remaining parameters, if any, have default values is a **type conversion constructor.** If the first argument of a type conversion constructor is a built-in data type, the constructor can be used to cast the built-in data type to a class object. Clearly, one restriction of such functions is that, as constructors, they must be member functions.

Although this type of cast occurs when the constructor is invoked to initialize an object, it is actually a more general cast than might be evident at first glance. This is because a constructor function can be explicitly invoked after all objects have been declared regardless of whether it was invoked previously as part of an object's declaration. Before exploring this further, let's first construct a type conversion constructor. We will then see how to use it as a cast independent of its initialization purpose.

The cast we will construct converts a long integer into a `Date` object. Our `Date` object will consist of dates in the form month/day/year and use our by now familiar `Date` class. The long integer will be used to represent dates in the form year * 10000 + month * 100 + day. For example, using this representation the date 12/31/98 becomes the long integer `981231`. Dates represented in this fashion are very useful for two reasons: First, a date can be stored as a single integer and, second, such dates are in numerically increasing date order, making sorting extremely easy. For example, the date 1/1/99, which occurs after 12/31/98 becomes the integer 990101, which is larger than 981231.[10] Since the integers representing dates can exceed the size of a normal integer, the integers are always declared as longs.

A suitable constructor function for converting from a long integer date to a date stored as a month, day, and year is:

```
// type conversion constructor from long to Date

Date::Date(long findate)
{
  year = int(findate/10000.0);
  month = int((findate - year * 10000.0)/100.0);
  day = int(findate - year * 10000.0 - month * 100.0);
}
```

Program 8.10 uses this type conversion constructor both as an initialization function at declaration time and as an explicit cast later in the program.

PROGRAM 8.10

```
#include <iostream.h>

// class declaration

class Date
{
  private:
    int month, day, year;
  public:
    Date(int = 7, int = 4, int = 96);  // constructor
    Date(long);            // type conversion constructor
    void showdate(void);
};
```

(continued on next page)

[10] For dates after the turn of the century, 100 must be added to the year value. Thus, the date 6/15/00 is considered to be 6/15/100 and the date 2/12/01 is considered to be 2/12/101.

(continued from previous page)

```
// implementation section

// constructor
Date::Date(int mm, int dd, int yy)
{
  month = mm;
  day = dd;
  year = yy;
}

// type conversion constructor from long to date
Date::Date(long findate)
{
  year = int(findate/10000.0);
  month = int((findate - year * 10000.0)/100.0);
  day = int(findate - year * 10000.0 - month * 100.0);
}

// member function to display a date
void Date::showdate(void)
{
  cout << month << '/' << day << '/' << year;

  return;
}
```

```
int main()
{
  Date a, b(961225), c(4,1,97);  // declare 3 objects - initialize 2 of them

  cout << "Dates a, b, and c are ";
  a.showdate();
  cout << ", ";
  b.showdate();
  cout << ", and ";
  c.showdate();
  cout << ".\n";

  a = Date(980101);  // cast a long to a date

  cout << "Date a is now ";
  a.showdate();
  cout << ".\n";

  return 0;
}
```

The output produced by Program 8.10 is:

```
Dates a, b, and c are 7/4/96, 12/25/96, and 4/1/97.
Date a is now 1/1/98.
```

The change in a's date value illustrated by this output is produced by the assignment expression `a = Date(980101)`, which uses a type conversion constructor to perform the cast from `long` to `Date`.

Class to Built-In Conversion

Conversion from a user-defined data type to a built-in data type is accomplished using a conversion operator function. A **conversion operator function** is a member operator function having the name of a built-in data type or class. When the operator function has a built-in data type name, it is used to convert from a class to a built-in data type. For example, a conversion operator function for casting a class object to a long integer would have the name `operator long()`. Here the name of the operator function indicates that a conversion to a `long` will take place. If this function were part of a `Date` class it would be used to cast a `Date` object into a long integer. This usage is illustrated by Program 8.11.

PROGRAM 8.11

```
#include <iostream.h>

// class declaration

class Date
{
  private:
    int month, day, year;
  public:
    Date(int = 7, int = 4, int = 96);    // constructor
    operator long();          // conversion operator function
    void showdate(void);
};

// implementation section

// constructor
Date::Date(int mm, int dd, int yy)
{
  month = mm;
  day = dd;
  year = yy;
}
```

(continued on next page)

(continued from previous page)

```
// conversion operator function converting from Date to long
Date::operator long()    // must return a long
{
  long yymmdd;

  yymmdd = year * 10000.0 + month * 100.0 + day;

  return(yymmdd);
}

// member function to display a date
void Date::showdate(void)
{
  cout << month << '/' << day << '/' << year;

  return;
}
```

```
int main()
{
  Date a(4,1,97);   // declare and initialize one object of type date
  long b;           // declare an object of type long

  b = a;            // a conversion takes place here

  cout << "a's date is ";
  a.showdate();
  cout << "\nThis date, as a long integer, is " << b << endl;

  return 0;
}
```

The output produced by Program 8.11 is:

```
a's date is 4/1/97
This date, as a long integer, is 970401
```

The change in a's date value to a long integer illustrated by this output is produced by the assignment expression `b = a`. This assignment, which also could have been written explicitly as `b = long(a)`, calls the conversion operator function `long()` to perform the cast from `Date` to `long`. In general, since explicit conversion more clearly documents what is happening, its use is preferred to implicit conversion.

Notice that the conversion operator has no explicit argument and has no explicit return type. This is true of all conversion operators: Its implicit argument will always be an object of the class being cast from, and the return type is implied by the name of the function. Additionally, as previously indicated, a conversion operator function *must* be a member function.

Class to Class Conversion

Converting from a user-defined data type to a user-defined data type is performed in the same manner as a cast from a user-defined to a built-in data type—it is done using a member *conversion operator function*. In this case, however, the operator function uses the class name being converted to rather than a built-in data name. For example, if two classes named `Date` and `Intdate` exist, the operator function named `operator Intdate()` could be placed in the `Date` class to convert from a `Date` object to an `Intdate` object. Similarly, the operator function named `Date()` could be placed in the `Intdate` class to convert from an `Intdate` to a `Date`.

Notice that as before, in converting from a user-defined data type to a built-in data type, *the operator function's name determines the result of the conversion;* the class containing the operator function determines which type of data type are being converted.

Before providing a specific example of a class to class conversion, one additional point must be noted. Converting between classes clearly implies that we have two classes, one of which is always defined first and one of which is defined second. Having, within the second class, a conversion operator function with the name of the first class poses no problem because the compiler knows of the first class's existence. However, including a conversion operator function with the second class's name in the first class does pose a problem because the second class has not yet been defined. This is remedied by including a declaration for the second class prior to the first class's definition. This declaration, which is formally referred to as a *forward declaration,* is illustrated in Program 8.12, which also includes conversion operators between the two defined classes.

PROGRAM 8.12

```
#include <iostream.h>

// forward declaration of class Intdate
class Intdate;

// class declaration for Date

class Date
{
  private:
    int month, day, year;
  public:
    Date(int = 7, int = 4, int = 96);     // constructor
    operator Intdate();      // conversion operator Date to Intdate
    void showdate(void);
};

// class declaration for Intdate
```

(continued on next page)

(continued from previous page)

```
class Intdate
{
  private:
    long yymmdd;
  public:
    Intdate(long);     // constructor
    operator Date();   // conversion operator intdate to date
    void showint(void);
};

// implementation section for Date

Date::Date(int mm, int dd, int yy)  // constructor
{
  month = mm;
  day = dd;
  year = yy;
}

// conversion operator function converting from Date to Intdate class
Date::operator Intdate()    // must return an Intdate object
{
  long temp;

  temp = year * 10000.0 + month * 100.0 + day;

  return(Intdate(temp));
}

// member function to display a Date
void Date::showdate(void)
{
  cout << month << '/' << day << '/' << year;

  return;
}

// implementation section for Intdate

Intdate::Intdate(long ymd = 0)  // constructor
{
  yymmdd = ymd;
}

// conversion operator function converting from Intdate to Date class
Intdate::operator Date()    // must return a Date object
{
```

(continued on next page)

(continued from previous page)

```
  int mo, da, yr;

  yr = int(yymmdd/10000.0);
  mo = int((yymmdd - yr * 10000.0)/100.0);
  da = int(yymmdd - yr * 10000.0 - mo * 100.0);

  return(Date(mo,da,yr));
}

// member function to display an Intdate
void Intdate::showint(void)
{
  cout << yymmdd;

  return;
}
```

```
int main()
{
  Date a(4,1,97), b;      // declare two Date objects
  Intdate c(981215), d;  // declare two Intdate objects

  b = Date(c);          // cast c into a Date object
  d = Intdate(a);       // cast a into an Intdate object

  cout << " a's date is ";
  a.showdate();
  cout << "\n   as an Intdate object this date is ";
  d.showint();

  cout << "\n c's date is ";
  c.showint();
  cout << "\n   as a Date object this date is ";
  b.showdate();
  cout << endl;

  return 0;
}
```

The output produced by Program 8.12 is:

```
a's date is 4/1/97
  as an Intdate object this date is 970401
c's date is 981215
  as a Date object this date is 12/15/98
```

As illustrated by Program 8.12, the cast from `Date` to `Intdate` is produced by the assignment `b = Date(c)` and the cast from `Intdate` to `Date` is produced by the assignment `d = Intdate(a)`. Alternatively, the assignments `b = c` and `d = a` would produce the same results. Notice also the forward declaration of the `Intdate` class prior to the `Date` class's declaration. This is required so that the `Date` class can reference `Intdate` in its operator conversion function.

Exercises 8.5

1. a. Define the four data type conversions available in C++ and the method of accomplishing each conversion.

   b. Define the terms *type conversion constructor* and *conversion operator function* and describe how they are used in user-defined conversions.

2. Write a C++ program that declares a class named `Time` having integer data members named `hours`, `minutes`, and `seconds`. Include in the program a type conversion constructor that converts a long integer, representing the elapsed seconds from midnight into an equivalent representation as hours:minutes:seconds. For example, the long integer `30336` should convert to the time 8:25:36. Use a military representation of time so that 2:30 P.M. is represented as 14:30:00. The relationship between time representations is

$$\text{elapsed seconds} = \text{hours} * 3600 + \text{minutes} * 60 + \text{seconds}$$

3. A Julian date is a date represented as the number of days from a known base date. One algorithm for converting from a Gregorian date, in the form month/day/year, to a Julian date with a base date of 0/0/0 is given. All of the calculations in this algorithm use integer arithmetic, which means that the fractional part of all divisions must be discarded. In this algorithm M = month, D = day, and Y = year.

   If M is less than or equal to 2
   set the variable MP = 0 and YP = Y−1.
   Else
   set MP = int(0.4 * M + 2.3) and YP = Y.

   T = int(YP/4) − int(YP/100) + int(YP/400).
   Julian date = 365 * Y + 31 * (M − 1) + D + T − MP.

   Using this algorithm, modify Program 8.11 to cast from a Gregorian `date` object to its corresponding Julian representation as a long integer. Test your program using the Gregorian dates 1/31/85 and 3/16/86, which correspond to the Julian dates 31077 and 31486, respectively.

4. Modify the program written for Exercise 2 to include a member conversion operator function that converts an object of type `Time` into a long integer representing the number of seconds from midnight.

5. Write a C++ program that has a `Date` class and a `Julian` class. Use the `Date` class from Program 8.12. The Julian class should represent a date as a long integer. For this program include a member conversion operator function within the `Date` class that converts a `Date` object to a `Julian` object, using the algorithm presented in Exercise 3. Test your program by converting the dates 1/31/95 and 3/16/96, which correspond to the Julian dates 34729 and 35139, respectively.

6. Write a C++ program that has a `Time` class and an `Ltime` class. The `Time` class should have integer data members named `hours`, `minutes`, and `seconds`, while the `Ltime` class should have a long data member named `elsecs`, which represents the number of elapsed seconds since midnight. For the `Time` class include a member conversion operator function named `Ltime()` that converts a `Time` object to an `Ltime` object. For the `Ltime` class include a member conversion operator function named `Time()` that converts an `Ltime` object to a `Time` object.

8.6 FOCUS ON PROBLEM SOLVING

The problem presented in this section completes the gas pump simulation begun in Section 7.3. In place of a second design problem an application is presented that shows how to overload both the extraction, >>, and the insertion, <<, operators for `Date` objects. Doing so permits us to input and output `Date` types as complete entities using `cout` and `cin` in the same manner as built-in data types use these two objects. Once you understand how the overloading is done, you will be able to provide standard input and output using the `cin` and `cout` stream objects for any class that you construct.

Problem 1: A Multi-object Gas Pump Simulation

In Problem 2 of Section 7.3, we presented a requirement to construct a C++ program that simulated a gas pump's operation over the course of one-half hour. For convenience we repeat this requirement here:

> We have been requested to write a program that simulates the operation of a gas pump. At any time during the simulation we should be able to determine, from the pump, the price per gallon of gas and the amount remaining in the supply tank from which the gas is being pumped. If a request for gas, in gallons, is less than the amount of gas in the tank, the request should be filled; otherwise only the available amount in the supply tank should be used. Once the gas is pumped, the total price of the gallons pumped should be displayed and the amount of gas, in gallons, that was pumped should be subtracted from the amount in the supply tank.
>
> For the simulation, assume that the pump is randomly idle between 1 to 15 minutes between customer arrivals and that a customer randomly requests between 3 and 20 gallons of gas. Although the tank capacity is 500 gallons, assume that the initial amount of gas in the tank is only 300 gallons. Initially, the program should simulate a one-half hour time frame.
>
> Additionally, for each arrival and request for gas we want to know the idle time before the customer arrived, how many gallons of gas were pumped, and the total price of the transaction. The pump itself must keep track of the price per gallon of gas and the amount of gas remaining in the tank. Typically, the price per gallon is $1.00, but the price per gallon to use for the simulation should be $1.25.

In Section 7.3 we constructed a `Pump` object type that can be used for this simulation. In this problem we complete the simulation by providing a `Customer` object type and the controlling code within a `main()` function to create an actual multi-object simulation program.

Analyze the Problem As specified, the problem entails two types of objects: a gas pump and a customer. Let's consider these object types separately.

The Pump A `Pump` class was designed and implemented in Section 7.3 and is repeated here for convenience:

```
// class declaration

class Pump
{
  private:
    float amtInTank;
    float price;
```

```
  public:
    Pump(float = 500.0, float = 1.00);     // constructor
    void values(void);
    void request(float);
};
// implementation section

Pump::Pump(float start, float todaysPrice)
{
  amtInTank = start;
  price = todaysPrice;
}

void Pump::values(void)
{
  cout << "The gas tank has " << amtInTank
       << " gallons of gas." << endl;
  cout << "The price per gallon of gas is $"
       << setiosflags(ios::showpoint)
       << setprecision(2) << price << endl;

  return;
}

void Pump::request(float pumpAmt)
{
  float pumped;

  if (amtInTank >= pumpAmt)
     pumped = pumpAmt;
  else
     pumped = amtInTank;

  amtInTank -= pumped;
  cout << pumpAmt << " gallons were requested " << endl;
  cout << pumped << " gallons were pumped" << endl;
  cout << amtInTank << " gallons remain in the tank" << endl;
  cout << "The total price is $" << setiosflags(ios::showpoint)
       << setprecision(2) << (pumped * price) << endl;

  return;
}
```

You should review Problem 2 in Section 7.3 if either the data or function members of this Pump class are not clear. For later convenience in writing the required simulation program, assume that the code for the Pump class has been stored in a file named PUMP.H within a directory named CLASSES on the C: drive. Once this is done, you can include the Pump class definition within a program simply by using the single line preprocessor directive #include <C:\CLASSES\PUMP.H>.[11]

---

[11] The reason for using a full path name in the #include statement is to ensure that the preprocessor accesses the PUMP.H class that we have placed in the named directory. We do not want the preprocessor to either search its default directory and possibly locate some other PUMP.H that we do not know about or be unable to locate the PUMP.H file at all.

The Customer For this problem, there are multiple instances of customers arriving randomly between 1 and 15 minutes and requesting gas in amounts that vary randomly between 3 and 20 gallons. From an object viewpoint, however, we are not interested in storing the arrival and number of gallons requested by each customer. We simply need a customer object to present us with an arrival time and a request for gas, in gallons. The object diagram for a customer is shown in Figure 8.5. Notice that the `Customer` object type consists of no attributes, which is indicated by the double line in the object diagram, and three operations. The initialize operation will be used to randomize the random number generator. The operation, named `arrival()`, will be used to provide a random arrival time between 1 and 15 minutes. The next operation, named `gallons()`, will be used to provide a random request of between 3 and 20 gallons of gas. This class is relatively simple and its design and implementation as coded here follows the structure of the object diagram:

```
#include <stdlib.h>
#include <time.h>

//class declaration and implementation
class Customer
{
  public:
    Customer(void) {srand(time(NULL));};
    int arrive(void) {return(1 + rand() % 16);};
    int gallons(void) {return(3 + rand() % 21);};
};
```

In reviewing this code notice that the class constructor is used to randomize the `rand()` function. [Review Section 6.7 if you are unfamiliar with either the `srand()` or `rand()` functions.] The `arrive()` function simply returns a random integer between 1 and 15, while the `gallons()` function returns a random integer between 3 and 20. [We leave it as an exercise for you to rewrite the `gallons()` function to return a floating-point value.] Since all of the functions are single line, we have included their definitions within the declaration section as inline functions.

Again, for later convenience in writing the complete simulation program, assume that the code for the `Customer` class is placed in a file named `CUSTOMER.H` within a directory named `CLASSES` on the `C:` drive. Once this is done, you can include the `Customer` class definition within a program simply by using the single line preprocessor directive `#include <C:\CLASSES\CUSTOMER.H>`.

Program Logic Having analyzed and defined the two classes that we will be using, we still need to analyze and define the logic to correctly control the interaction between these two objects for a valid simulation.

In this particular case, the only interaction between a `Customer` object and the single `Pump` object is that a customer's arrival, followed by a request, determines when the pump is activated and how much gas it delivers. Thus, each interaction between a `Customer` and the `Pump` can be expressed by the following pseudocode:

Obtain a Customer arrival time.
Obtain a Customer request for gas.
Activate the Pump with the request.

FIGURE 8.5 The Customer Object Diagram

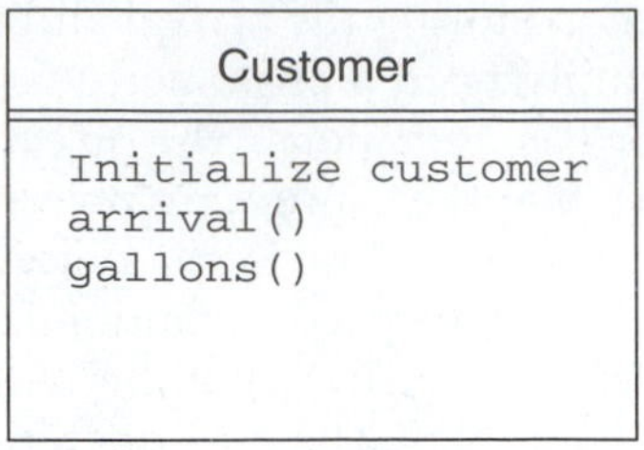

Customer
Initialize customer arrival() gallons()

Although this repetition of events takes place continuously over the course of a day, we are only interested in a one-half hour period. Therefore, we can place these three events in a loop that is executed until the required simulation time has elapsed.

Develop a Solution We have already developed and coded the two required classes, `Pump` and `Customer`, for the simulation. What remains to be developed is the control logic within the `main()` function for correctly activating class events. From the analysis we know that a loop controlled by the total arrival time for all customers is required. A suitable control structure for `main()` is described by the following algorithm:

Create a Pump object with the required initial gallons of gas and price-per-gallon.
Display the values in the initialized Pump.
Set the total time to 0.
Obtain a Customer arrival time // first arrival.
Add the arrival time to the total time.
While the total time does not exceed the simulation time
  Display the total time.
  Obtain a Customer request for gas.
  Activate the Pump with the request.
  Obtain a Customer arrival time // next arrival.
  Add the arrival time to the total time.
EndWhile.
Display a message that the simulation is over.

Code the Solution The C++ code corresponding to our design is illustrated in Program 8.13.

Test and Correct the Program Assuming that the `Pump` and Customer classes have been thoroughly tested and debugged, testing and correcting Program 8.13 is really restricted to testing and debugging the `main()` function. This specificity of testing is precisely one of the advantages of using an object-oriented approach.

Typically, all prewritten and tested classes are included in a *class library* (see box p. 471), just as library functions are included in a function library. By using previously written and tested class definitions in a program we can focus our

PROGRAM 8.13

```
#include <iostream.h>
#include <iomanip.h>

#include <C:\CLASSES\PUMP.H>       // note use of full path name here
#include <C:\CLASSES\CUSTOMER.H>   // again - a full path name is used

const float SIMTIME = .5;          // simulation time in hours
const int MINUTES = 60;            // number of minutes in an hour
const float AMT_IN_TANK = 300;     // initial gallons in the tank
const float TODAYS_PRICE = 1.25;   // price-per-gallon

int main()
{
  Pump a(AMT_IN_TANK, TODAYS_PRICE);    // declare 1 object of type Pump
  Customer b;                          // declare 1 object of type Customer
  int totalTime = 0;
  int idleTime;
  int amtRequest;
  int SimMinutes;  // simulation time in minutes

  SimMinutes = SIMTIME * MINUTES;
  cout << "\nStarting a new simulation - simulation time is "
     << SimMinutes << " minutes" << endl;
  a.values();

  // get the first arrival
  idleTime = b.arrive();
  totalTime += idleTime;

  while (totalTime <= SimMinutes)
  {
    cout << "\nThe idle time is " << idleTime << " minutes" << endl
         << "   and we are " << totalTime
         << " minutes into the simulation." << endl;
    amtRequest = b.gallons();
    a.request(float(amtRequest));

    // get the next arrival
    idleTime = b.arrive();
    totalTime += idleTime;
  }
  cout << "\nThe idle time is " << idleTime << " minutes." << endl
       << "As the total time now exceeds the simulation time, " << endl
       << "   this simulation run is over." << endl;

  return 0;
}
```

attention on the remaining code that controls the flow of events between objects. In this case then, assuming that the Pump and Customer classes correctly meet their respective specifications, testing and correcting of Program 8.13 centers on the `main()` function.

By itself, the `main()` function in Program 8.13 uses a straightforward `while` loop where the `Pump` idle time corresponds to the time between customer arrivals. The output of a sample run verifies that the loop is operating correctly:

```
Starting a new simulation - simulation time is 30 minutes
The gas tank has 300 gallons of gas.
The price per gallon of gas is $1.25

The idle time is 12 minutes
   and we are 12 minutes into the simulation.
15.00 gallons were requested
15.00 gallons were pumped
285.00 gallons remain in the tank
The total price is $18.75

The idle time is 15 minutes
   and we are 27 minutes into the simulation.
7.00 gallons were requested
7.00 gallons were pumped
278.00 gallons remain in the tank
The total price is $8.75

The idle time is 10 minutes.
As the total time now exceeds the simulation time,
   this simulation run is over.
```

In reviewing the operation of Program 8.13, note that we have used the same `Customer` object for each arrival and request. In Section 9.4 we will see how to dynamically create a new `Customer` object for each arrival and destroy the created object when it has completed its designated task.

Application 1: Overloading the Insertion, <<, and Extraction, >>, Operators

For all of the class examples seen so far a display function has been used to output an object's attribute values. Since a user-defined type should provide all of the functionality of a built-in type, we should be able to input and output object values using `cin` and `cout`, respectively. This is, in fact, the case.

Every C++ compiler provides a class library that includes a number of predefined classes. Three of these classes are named `ostream`, `istream`, and `iostream`, respectively. The relationship between these classes is shown in Figure 8.6 and explained in detail in Section 10.6. As you might have guessed, the `istream` name is derived from *in*stream, the `ostream` name from *out*stream,

FIGURE 8.6 The Relationship Between Classes

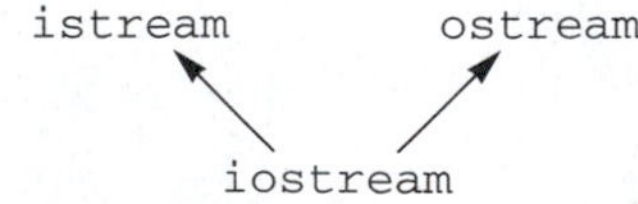

POINT OF INFORMATION

Program and Class Libraries

The concept of a program library began with FORTRAN, which was the first commercial high-level language, introduced in 1954. The FORTRAN library consisted of a group of completely tested and debugged mathematical routines that were provided with the compiler. Since that time every programming language has provided its own library of functions. In both C and C++, this library is referred to as the standard program library, and includes more than 100 functions declared in 15 different header files. Examples of standard library functions include `sqrt()`, `pow()`, `abs()`, `rand()`, `srand()`, and `time()`. The advantage of library functions is that they significantly enhance program development and design by providing code that is known to work correctly without the need for additional testing and debugging.

With the introduction of object-oriented languages, the concept of a program library has been extended to include class libraries. A *class library* is a library of tested and debugged classes that includes both interfaces and implementations. Generally, the interface portion is placed in a header file and the implementation in a separate implementation file.

One of the key practical features of class libraries is that they help realize the goal of code reuse in a significant way. By providing tested and debugged code consisting of both data and function members, class libraries furnish large sections of prewritten and reusable code ready for incorporation within new applications. This shifts the focus of writing application programs from the creation of new code to understanding how to use predefined objects and stitch them together in a cohesive and useful way. A prime example of this is the visual object classes consisting of check boxes, list boxes, dialogs, command buttons, and option buttons provided in both Visual C++ and Visual Basic.

and the `iostream` name from *input/output* stream. In this context a *stream* is simply a one-way path between a source and a destination down which a sequence of bytes can be sent. A good analogy to a stream of bytes is a stream of water that provides a one-way path for the water from a source to a destination. Specifically, `cin` is the name of an input stream object of the class `istream` that connects data sent from the standard input device, which is the keyboard, to a program. Similarly, `cout` is an output stream object of class `ostream` that connects output from the program to the standard output device, which is the screen.[12]

For our current purposes all we need know is that the insertion, or "put to," operator << is both defined and overloaded in the `ostream` class to handle the output of built-in types, while the extraction, or "get from," operator >> is both defined and overloaded in the `istream` class to handle input of built-in types. The capabilities of both the `ostream` and `istream` classes are available to the `iostream` class (through the process of inheritance, explained in the next chapter). Thus, we have access to the `cin` and `cout` streams and to the insertion and extraction operators through the `iostream` class that we have been including in all of our programs. This access permits us to create our own overloaded versions of the << and >> operator functions to handle user-defined object types.

[12] A third object, `cerr`, is an output stream object of class `ostream` from the program to the standard output device, which is usually the screen. The major difference between `cerr` and `cout` is that the `cout` stream object is buffered while the `cerr` stream object is not.

Specifically, the process of making `cin` extractions and `cout` insertions available to a user-defined class consists of these steps:

1. Make each overloaded operator function a friend of the user-defined class (this ensures that these overloaded functions will have access to a class's private data members).
2. Construct an overloaded version for each operator function that is appropriate to the user-defined class.

What makes overloading the insertion and extraction operators so easy is that the function prototypes and header lines for each overloaded function are essentially "cookbook" steps. To understand how this is accomplished in practice, consider Program 8.14, which overloads the insertion and extraction operators to handle objects of type `Date`.

PROGRAM 8.14

```
#include <iostream.h>

// class declaration

class Date
{
  friend ostream& operator<<(ostream&, const Date&);  // overload inserter operator
  friend istream& operator>>(istream&, Date&);         // overload extractor operator
  private:
    int month;
    int day;
    int year;
  public:
    Date(int = 7, int = 4, int = 96);     // constructor
};

// implementation section

// overloaded insertion operator function
ostream& operator<<(ostream& out, const Date& adate)
{
  out << adate.month << '/' << adate.day << '/' << adate.year;

  return out;
}

// overloaded extraction operator function
istream& operator>>(istream& in, Date& somedate)
{
  in >> somedate.month;    // accept the month part
  in.ignore(1);            // ignore 1 character, the / character
  in >> somedate.day;      // get the day part
```

(continued on next page)

(continued from previous page)

```
  in.ignore(1);             // ignore 1 character, the / character
  in >> somedate.year;      // get the year part

  return in;
}

Date::Date(int mm, int dd, int yy)    // constructor
{
  month = mm;
  day = dd;
  year = yy;
}
```

```
int main()
{
  Date a;

  cout << "Enter a date: ";
  cin  >> a;          // accept the date using cin
  cout << "The date just entered is " << a << endl;

  return 0;
}
```

A sample run of Program 8.14 follows:

```
Enter a date: 1/15/98
The date just entered is 1/15/98
```

In reviewing Program 8.14 first notice that within the `main()` function a `Date` object is entered using `cin` and is output using `cout`. Now take a look at the class declaration for `Date` and notice that two friend functions have been included in the friend's list using these function prototype declarations:

```
friend ostream& operator<<(ostream&, const Date&);
friend istream& operator>>(istream&, Date&);
```

The first declaration makes the overloaded insertion operator function << a friend of the `Date` class, while the second statement does the same for the overloaded extraction operator function >>. In the first declaration the << operator has been declared to return a reference to an `ostream` object and to have two formal parameters, a reference to an `ostream` and a reference to a `Date` class, which is a constant. Similarly, in the second declaration the >> operator has been declared to return a reference to an `istream` object and to have two formal parameters, a reference to an `istream` object and a reference to a `Date` object. By simply changing the class name `Date` to the name of any other class and including these declarations within the class's declaration section, these two prototypes can be used in any user-defined class. Thus, the general syntax of these declarations, applicable to any class, is:

```
friend ostream& operator<<(ostream&, const class-name&);
friend istream& operator>>(istream&, class-name&);
```

Now consider the implementations of these overloaded functions. Consider first the overloaded insertion operator function, which for convenience we repeat here:

```
ostream& operator<<(ostream& out, const Date& adate)
{
  out << adate.month << '/' << adate.day << '/' << adate.year;

  return out;
}
```

Although the name of the reference to a `Date` object has been named `adate`, any user-selected name would do. Similarly, the argument named `out`, which is a reference to an `ostream` object, can be any user-selected name. Within the body of the function we insert the `month`, `day`, and `year` members of the `Date` object to the `out` object, which is then returned from the function. Also notice the notation used in inserting the `month`, `day`, and `year` to `out`, namely:

```
adate.month
adate.day
adate.year
```

This notation follows the dot notation introduced in Section 7.1 that includes both the object name and attribute name with the names separated by a period. This was the reason for making the overloaded operator function a friend of the `Date` class. By doing so, the overloaded insertion operator has direct access to a `Date` object's `month`, `day`, and `year` data members.

Now consider the implementations of the overloaded extraction operator function, which for convenience is repeated here:

```
// overloaded extraction operator function
istream& operator>>(istream& in, Date& somedate)
{
  in >> somedate.month;    // accept the month part
  in.ignore(1);            // ignore 1 character, the / character
  in >> somedate.day;      // get the day part
  in.ignore(1);            // ignore 1 character, the / character
  in >> somedate.year;     // get the year part

  return in;
}
```

The header line for this function declares that it will return a reference to an `istream` object and has two reference parameters: a reference to an `istream` object and a reference to a `Date` object. The parameter names, `in` and `somedate`, can be replaced by any other user-selected names.

The body of the function first extracts a value for the `month` member of the `Date`, then it uses the `ignore()` member function of `istream` to ignore the next input character, which is usually a slash, `/`. The value for the `day` member is then extracted, the next character is ignored, and finally the value of the `year` member is extracted. Thus, if the user typed in the date 1/15/98 or the date 1-15-98, the overloaded extractor function would extract 1, 15, and 98 as the `month`, `day`, and `year` values, respectively. Although, this same effect is produced by the single line

```
in >> somedate.month >> '/' >> somedate.day >> '/' >> somedate.year;
```

the coding used in Program 8.14 makes it clear that we are ignoring the delimiting character, whatever it might be.

Exercises 8.6

1. Enter Program 8.13 on your computer and execute it.
2. a. Remove the inline functions in the `Customer` class declaration and implementation section used in Program 8.13 by constructing individual declaration and implementation sections. Discuss which form of the `Customer` class you prefer and why.

   b. Rewrite the `gallons()` function in the Customer class so that it returns a floating-point number between 3.0 and 20.0 gallons.
3. Using the `Elevator` class defined in Section 7.3 and defining a new class named `Person`, construct a simulation whereby a person randomly arrives on any floor and calls the elevator. If the elevator is not on the same floor as the person, it must move to the floor the person is on. Once inside the elevator, the person can select any floor except the current one. Run the simulation for three randomly arriving people and have the simulation display the movement of the elevator.
4. In place of the `main()` function used in Program 8.13, a student proposed the following:

```
int main()
{
  Pump a(AMT_IN_TANK, TODAYS_PRICE);    // declare 1 object of type Pump
  Customer b;                          // declare 1 object of type Customer
  int totalTime = 0;
  int idleTime;
  int amtRequest;
  int SimMinutes;  // simulation time in minutes

  SimMinutes = SIMTIME * MINUTES;
  cout << "\nStarting a new simulation - simulation time is "
       << SimMinutes << " minutes" << endl;
  a.values();

  do
  {
    idleTime = b.arrive();
    totalTime += idleTime;
    if (totalTime > (SimMinutes))
    {
      cout << "\nThe idle time is " << idleTime << " minutes." << endl
           << "As the total time now exceeds the simulation time, " << endl
           << "   this simulation run is over." << endl;
      break;
    }
    else
    {
      cout << "\nThe idle time is " << idleTime << " minutes" << endl
           << "   and we are " << totalTime
           << " minutes into the simulation." << endl;
      amtRequest = b.gallons();
      a.request(float(amtRequest));
    }
  } while (1);  // always true

  return 0;
}
```

Determine if this `main()` function produces a valid simulation. If it does not, discuss why not. If it does, discuss which version you prefer and why.

5. Enter Program 8.14 on your computer and execute it.
6. a. Modify the overloaded insertion operator function in Program 8.14 so that it displays dates in the form day-month-year, which is the European standard.
   b. Modify the overloaded insertion operator function in Program 8.14 to accept a third character argument. If the actual argument is an E, the displayed date should be in European format of day-month-year; otherwise it should be in the American standard form of month/day/year.
7. For the `Time` class constructed in Exercise 2 of Section 8.1, remove the display function and include overloaded extraction and insertion extraction operator functions for the input and output of `Time` objects using `cin` and `cout`, respectively. Times should be displayed in the form hrs:min:sec.
8. For the Complex class constructed in Exercise 3 of Section 8.1, remove the display function and include overloaded extraction and insertion extraction operator functions for the input and output of `Complex` objects using `cin` and cout, respectively.

8.7 COMMON PROGRAMMING ERRORS

1. Using a user-defined assignment operator in a multiple assignment expression when the operator has not been defined to return an object.
2. Using the keyword `static` when defining either a static data or function member. Here, the `static` keyword should be used only within the class declaration section.
3. Using the keyword `friend` when defining a friend function. The `friend` keyword should be used only within the class declaration section.
4. Failing to instantiate `static` data members before creating class objects that must access these data members.
5. Attempting to redefine an operator's meaning as it applies to C++'s built-in data types.
6. Redefining an overloaded operator to perform a function not indicated by its conventional meaning. Although this will work, it is an example of extremely bad programming practice.
7. Attempting to make a conversion operator function a friend, rather than a member function.
8. Attempting to specify a return type for a member conversion operator function.

8.8 CHAPTER REVIEW

Key Terms

assignment operator	memberwise assignment
class scope	operator functions
conversion operator function	`operator()`
copy constructor	`operator[]`
data type conversions	static class data member
default copy constructor	static member function
friend functions	type conversion constructor

Summary

1. An assignment operator may be declared for a class with the function prototype:

   ```
   void operator=(class-name&);
   ```

   Here, the argument is a reference to the class name. The return type of `void` precludes the use of this operator in multiple assignment expressions such as `a = b = c`.

2. A type of initialization that closely resembles assignment occurs in C++ when one object is initialized using another object of the same class. The constructor that performs this type of initialization is called a copy constructor and has the function prototype:

   ```
   class-name(const class-name&);
   ```

   This is frequently represented using the notation X(X&).

3. Each class has an associated class scope, which is defined by the brace pair, `{}`, containing the class declaration. Data and function members are local to the scope of their class and can only be used by objects declared for the class. If a global variable name is reused within a class, the global variable is hidden by the class variable. Within the scope of the class variable the global variable may be accessed using the scope resolution operator `::`.

4. For each class object, a separate set of memory locations is reserved for all data members, except those declared as `static`. A `static` data member is shared by all class objects and provides a means of communication between objects. `Static` data members must be declared as such within the class declaration section and are defined outside of the declaration section.

5. `Static` function members apply to the class as a whole, rather than individual objects. As such, a `static` function member can access only `static` data members and other `static` function members. `Static` function members must be declared as such within the class declaration section and are defined outside of the declaration section.

6. A nonmember function may access a class's private data members if it is granted `friend` status by the class. This is accomplished by declaring the function as a `friend` within the class's declaration section. Thus, it is always the class that determines which nonmember functions are friends; a function can never confer `friend` status on itself.

7. User-defined operators can be constructed for classes using member operator functions. An operator function has the form `operator<symbol>`, where `<symbol>` is one of the following:

   ```
   ()  []  ->  new  delete  ++  --  !~  ~  *  /  %  +  -
   <<  >>  <  <=  >  >=  ++  !=  &&  ||  &  ^  |  =  +=
   -=  *=  /=  %=  &=  ^=  |=  <<=  >>=  ,
   ```

   For example, the function prototype `Date operator+(int);` declares that the addition operator will be defined to accept an integer and return a `Date` object.

8. User-defined operators may be called in either of two ways—as a conventional function with arguments or as an operator expression. For example, for an operator having the header line

   ```
   Date Date::operator+(int)
   ```

if dte is an object of type Date, the following two calls produce the same effect:

```
dte.operator+(284)
dte + 284
```

9. Operator functions may also be written as friend functions. The equivalent friend version of a member operator function will always contain an additional class reference that is not required by the member function.
10. The subscript operator function, operator[], permits a maximum of one nonclass argument. This function can only be defined as a member function.
11. The parentheses operator function, operator(), has no limits on the number of arguments. This function can only be defined as a member function.
12. There are four categories of data type conversions. They are conversions from

    - built-in types to built-in types
    - built-in types to user-defined (class) types
    - user-defined (class) types to built-in types
    - user-defined (class) types to user-defined (class) types.

    Built-in to built-in type conversions are performed using C++'s implicit conversion rules or explicitly using casts. Built-in to user-defined type conversions are performed using type conversion constructors. Conversions from user-defined types to either built-in or other user-defined types are performed using conversion operator functions.
13. A type conversion constructor is a constructor whose first argument is not a member of its class and whose remaining parameters, if any, have default values.
14. A conversion operator function must be a member function. It has no explicit parameters or return type; rather, the return type is the name of the function.
15. The cout insertion operator, <<, and the cin extraction operator, >>, can be overloaded to work with any class objects using this process:

    - Make each overloaded operator function a friend of the user-defined class (this ensures that these overloaded functions will have access to a class's private data members).
    - Construct an overloaded version for each operator function that is appropriate to the user-defined class.

    The general function prototype syntax for providing these operator functions with friend status is:

    ```
    friend ostream& operator<<(ostream&, const class-name&);
    friend istream& operator>>(istream&, class-name&);
    ```

    These prototypes should be placed in the declaration section of the desired class and the class-name entry in each declaration changed to the actual class name.

Exercises

1. a. Construct a class named Cartesian that contains two floating-point data members named x and y, which will be used to store the *x* and *y* values of a point in rectangular coordinates. The function members should include a

constructor that initializes the x and y values of an object to 0, and functions to input and display an object's x an y values. Additionally, there should be an assignment function that performs a memberwise assignment between two Cartesian objects.

b. Include the class written for Exercise 1a in a working C++ program that creates and displays the values of two Cartesian objects, the second of which is assigned the values of the first object.

2. a. Construct a class named Savings that contains three floating-point data members named balance, rate, and interest, and a constructor that initializes each of these members to 0. Additionally, there should be a member function that inputs a balance and rate and then calculates an interest. The rate should be stored as a percent, such as 6.5 for 6.5%, and the interest computed as $interest = balance \times rate/100$. Additionally, there should be a member function to display all member values.

   b. Include the class written for Exercise 2a in a working C++ program that tests each member function.

3. a. Redo Exercise 2 except make rate a static data member and include a static member function to input and alter rate's value.

   b. Include the class written for Exercise 3a in a working C++ program that tests each member function.

4. a. Construct a class named Coord that contains two floating-point data members named xval and yval, which will be used to store the x and y values of a point in rectangular coordinates. The function members should include appropriate constructor and display functions and a friend function named conv_pol(). The conv_pol() function should accept two floating-point numbers that represent a point in polar coordinates and convert them into rectangular coordinates. For conversion from polar to rectangular coordinates use the formulas:

$$x = r \cos \theta$$
$$y = r \sin \theta$$

   b. Include the program written for Exercise 4a in a working C++ program.

5. a. Construct two classes named Rec_coord and Pol_coord. The class named Rec_coord should contain two floating-point data members named xval and yval, which will be used to store the x and y values of a point in rectangular coordinates. The function members should include appropriate constructor and display functions and a friend function named conv_pol().

   The class named Pol_coord should contain two floating-point data members named dist and theta, which will be used to store the distance and angle values of a point represented in polar coordinates. The function members should include appropriate constructor and display functions and a friend function named conv_pol().

   The friend function should accept an integer parameter named dir; two floating-point parameters named val1 and val2; and two reference parameters named recref and polref, the first of which should be a reference to an object of type rec_coord, and the second to an object of type pol_coord. If the value of dir is 1, val1 and val2 are to be considered as x and y rectangular coordinates that are to be converted to polar coordinates; if the value of dir is any other value, val1 and val2 are to be considered as distance and angle values that are to be converted to rectangular coordinates. For conversion from rectangular to polar coordinates use these formulas:

$$r = \sqrt{x^2 + y^2}$$
$$\theta = \text{atan}(y/x), x \neq 0$$

For conversion from polar to rectangular coordinates, use these formulas:

$$x = r \cos \theta$$
$$y = r \sin \theta$$

b. Include the program written for Exercise 5a in a working C++ program.

6. List three C++ operators that cannot be overloaded.

7. a. Create a class named `Fractions` having two integer data members named for a fraction's numerator and denominator. The class's default constructor should provide both data members with default values of 1 if no explicit user initialization is provided. The constructor must also prohibit a 0 denominator value. Additionally provide member functions for displaying an object's data values. Also provide the class with overloaded operators that are capable of adding, subtracting, multiplying, and dividing two `Fraction` objects according to the following formulas:

Sum of two fractions: $\frac{a}{b} + \frac{c}{d} = \frac{ad + cb}{bd}$

Difference of two fractions: $\frac{a}{b} + \frac{c}{d} = \frac{ad - cb}{bd}$

Product of two fractions: $\frac{a}{b} \times \frac{c}{d} = \frac{ab}{bd}$

Division of two fractions: $\frac{a}{b} \div \frac{c}{d} = \frac{ad}{cb}$

b. Include the class written for Exercise 7a within a working C++ program that tests each of the class's member functions.

8. a. Include a member function named `gcd()` in the `Fraction` class constructed in Exercise 7 that reduces a fraction to its lowest common terms. Thus, a fraction such as 2/4 would be reduced to 1/2. The means of doing this is to divide both the numerator and denominator values by their greatest common divisor. (See Exercise 6 in Section 6.10 for a description of how to obtain the greatest common divisor of two numbers.)

b. Modify the constructor written for Exercise 7a to include a call to `gcd()` so that every initialized fraction is in lowest common terms. Also make sure that each overloaded operator function also uses `gcd()` to return a fraction in lowest common terms.

c. Replace the display function with an overloaded insertion operator so that a `Fraction` object can be inserted directly into the `cout` stream. Also include an overloaded extraction operator that will use the `cin` stream with a `Fraction` object.

CHAPTER

9 Inheritance and Dynamic Memory Allocation

This chapter shows how a class designed by one programmer can be altered by another in a way that retains the integrity and design of the original class. This is accomplished using inheritance, a new feature that is central to object-oriented programming. Inheritance permits the reuse and extension of existing code in a way that ensures the new code does not adversely affect what has already been written.

In addition to class construction and inheritance, the third required feature of all object-oriented languages is the ability to produce polymorphic behavior. This feature permits the same method name to invoke different responses in inherited class objects. Polymorphism is presented in Section 9.2.

Finally, the topic of dynamic creation and allocation of objects, as a program is executing, is presented.

9.1 CLASS INHERITANCE

The ability to create new classes from existing ones is the underlying motivation and power behind class and object-oriented programming techniques. This ability facilitates the reuse of existing code in new ways without the need for retesting and validation. It permits the designers of a class to make it available to others for additions and extensions, without relinquishing control over the existing class features.

Constructing one class from another is accomplished using a capability called inheritance. Related to this capability is an equally important feature named polymorphism. Polymorphism provides the ability to redefine how

POINT OF INFORMATION

Object-Based Versus Object-Oriented Languages

An *object-based language* is one in which data and operations can be incorporated in such a way that data values can be isolated and accessed through the specified class functions. The ability to bind the data members with operations in a single unit is referred to as *encapsulation.* In C++ encapsulation is provided by its class capability.

For a language to be classified as object-oriented it must also provide inheritance and polymorphism. *Inheritance* is the capability to derive one class from another. A derived class is a completely new data type that incorporates all of the data members and member functions of the original class with any new data and function members unique to itself. The class used as the basis for the derived type is referred to as the *base* or *parent class* and the derived data type is referred to as the *derived* or *child class*.

Polymorphism permits the same method name to invoke one operation in objects of a parent class and a different operation in objects of a derived class.

C++, which provides encapsulation, inheritance, and polymorphism, is a true object-oriented language. Because C, which is C++'s predecessor, does not provide these features, it is neither an object-based nor object-oriented language.

member functions of related classes operate based on the class object being referenced. In fact, for a programming language to be classified as a true object-oriented language it must provide the features of classes, inheritance, and polymorphism. In this section we describe the inheritance features provided in C++. Polymorphism is presented in Section 9.2.

Inheritance is the ability to derive one class from another class. The initial class used as the basis for the derived class is referred to as either the **base class,** parent class, or superclass. The derived class is referred to as either the **derived class,** child class, or subclass.

A derived class is a completely new class that incorporates all of the data and member functions of its base class. It can, and usually does, however, add its own additional new data and function members, and it can override any base class function.

As an example of inheritance, consider three geometric shapes consisting of a circle, cylinder, and sphere. All of these shapes share a common characteristic, a radius. Thus, for these shapes we can make the circle a base type for the other two shapes, as illustrated in Figure 9.1.[1] Reformulating these shapes as class types we would make the circle the base class and derive the cylinder and sphere classes from it.

The relationships illustrated in Figure 9.1 are examples of simple inheritance. In **simple inheritance** each derived type has only one immediate base type. The complement to simple inheritance is multiple inheritance. In **multiple inheritance** a derived type has two or more base types. Figure 9.2 illustrates an example of multiple inheritance. In this text we consider only simple inheritance.

The class derivations illustrated in both Figures 9.1 and 9.2 are formally referred to as **class hierarchies,** because they illustrate the hierarchy, or order, in which one class is derived from another. Now we look at how to derive one class from another.

---

[1] By convention, arrows always point from the derived class to the base class.

FIGURE 9.1 Relating Object Types

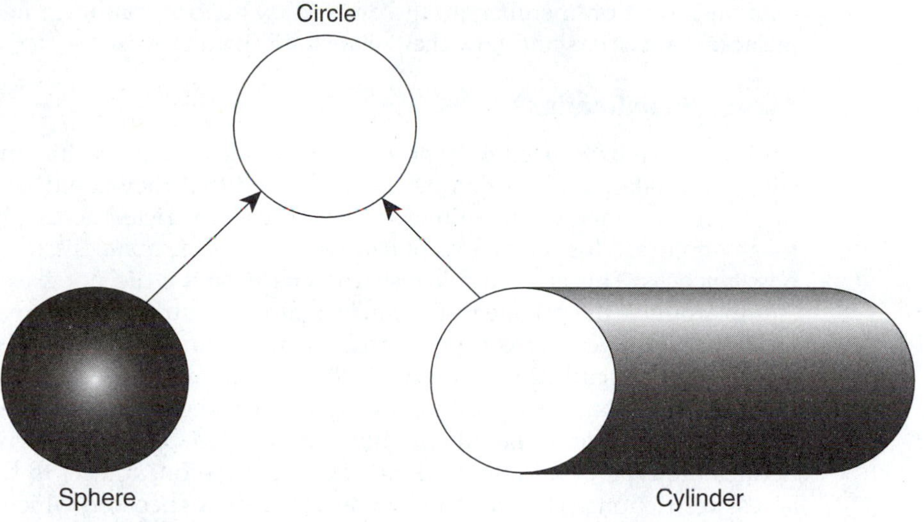

A derived class has the same form as any other class in that it consists of both a declaration and an implementation. The only difference is in the first line of the declaration section. For a derived class this line is extended to include an access specification and a base class name using the syntax:

```
class  derived-class-name : class-access  base-class-name
```

For example, if `Circle` is the name of an existing class, a new class named `Cylinder` can be derived as follows:

```
class Cylinder : public Circle
{
    // add any additional data and
    // function members in here
};  // end of Cylinder class declaration
```

FIGURE 9.2 An Example of Multiple Inheritance

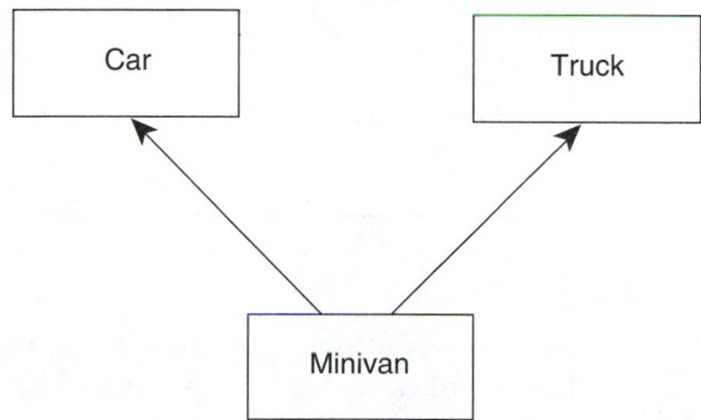

Except for the class-access specifier after the colon and the base class name, there is nothing inherently new or complicated about the construction of the `Cylinder` class. Before providing a description of the `Circle` class and adding data and function members to the derived `Cylinder` class, we need to reexamine access specifiers and how they relate to derived classes.

Access Specifications

Until now we have used only private and public access specifiers within a class. Giving all data members private status ensured that they could only be accessed by either class member functions or friends. This restricted access prevents access by any nonclass functions (except friends), *which also precludes access by any derived class functions.* This is a sensible restriction because if it did not exist anyone could "jump around" the private restriction by simply constructing a derived class.

To retain a restricted type of access across derived classes, C++ provides a third access specification, protected. Protected access behaves identically to private access in that it only permits member or friend function access, but it permits this restriction to be inherited by any derived class. The derived class then defines the type of inheritance it is willing to take on, subject to the base class's access restrictions. This is done by the class-access specifier, which is listed after the colon at the start of its declaration section. Table 9.1 lists the resulting derived class member access based on the base class member specifications and the derived class-access specifier. In Table 9.1 we can see in the shaded region that if the base class member has a protected access and the derived class specifier is public, then the derived class member will be protected to its class. Similarly, if the base class has a public access and the derived class specifier is public, the derived class member will be public. This is the most commonly used type of specification for base class data and function members, respectively, and is the one we will use. This means that for all classes intended for use as a base class, we will use a protected data member access in place of a private designation.

Table 9.1 Inherited Access Restrictions

Base Class Member	Derived Class Access	Derived Class Member
private ------------>	: private --------------->	inaccessible
protected ---------->	: private --------------->	private
public ------------->	: private --------------->	private
private ------------>	: public ---------------->	inaccessible
protected ---------->	: public ---------------->	protected
public ------------->	: public ---------------->	public
private ------------>	: protected ------------->	inaccessible
protected ---------->	: protected ------------->	protected
public ------------->	: protected ------------->	protected

An Example

To illustrate the process of deriving one class from another, we will derive a `Cylinder` class from a base `Circle` class. The definition of the `Circle` class is:

```
// class declaration

class Circle
{
  protected:
    double radius;
  public:
    Circle(double = 1.0);  // constructor
    double calcval();
};

// class implementation

// constructor
Circle::Circle(double r)  // constructor
{
  radius = r;
}

// calculate the area of a circle
double Circle::calcval(void)
{
  return(PI * radius * radius);
}
```

Except for the substitution of the access specifier protected in place of the usual private specifier for the data member, this is a standard class definition. The only variable not defined is `PI`, which is used in the `calcval()` function. We will define this as:

```
const double PI = 2.0 * asin(1.0);
```

This is simply a "trick" that forces the computer to return the value of `PI` accurate to as many decimal places as allowed by your computer. This value is obtained by taking the arcsin of 1.0, which is $\pi/2$, and multiplying the result by 2.

Having defined our base class, we can now extend it to a derived class. The definition of the derived class is:

```
// class declaration where
// Cylinder is derived from Circle

class Cylinder : public Circle
{
  protected:
    double length;  // add one additional data member and
  public:           // two additional function members
    Cylinder(double r = 1.0, double l = 1.0) : Circle(r), length(l) {}
    double calcval();
};

// class implementation

double Cylinder::calcval(void)    // this calculates a volume
{
  return (length * Circle::calcval()); // note the base function call
}
```

FIGURE 9.3 Relationship Between Circle and Cylinder Data Members

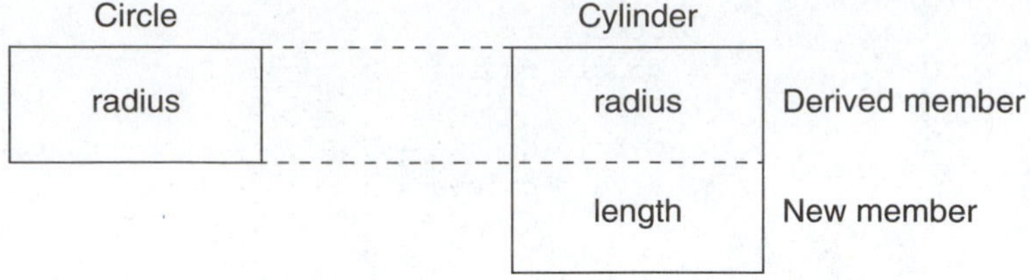

This definition encompasses several important concepts relating to derived classes. First, as a derived class, `Cylinder` contains all of the data and function members of its base class, `Circle`, plus any additional members that may be added. In this particular case, the `Cylinder` class consists of a radius data member, inherited from the `Circle` class, plus an additional length member. Thus, each `Cylinder` object contains *two* data members, as is illustrated in Figure 9.3.

In addition to having two data members, the `Cylinder` class also inherits `Circle`'s function members. This is illustrated in the `Cylinder` constructor, which uses a base member initialization list (see Section 8.1) that specifically calls the `Circle` constructor. It is also illustrated in `Cylinder`'s `calcval()` function, which makes a call to `Circle::calcval()`.

In both classes the same function name, `calcval()`, has been specifically used to illustrate the overriding of a base function by a derived function. When a `Cylinder` object calls `calcval()` it is a request to use the `Cylinder` version of the function, whereas a `Circle` object call to `calcval()` is a request to use the `Circle` version. In this case the `Cylinder` class can only access the class version of `calcval()` using the scope resolution operator, as is done in the call `Circle::calcval()`. Program 9.1 uses these two classes within the context of a complete program.

PROGRAM 9.1

```
#include <iostream.h>
#include <math.h>

const double PI = 2.0 * asin(1.0);
// class declaration

class Circle
{
  protected:
    double radius;
  public:
    Circle(double = 1.0);  // constructor
    double calcval();
};
```

(continued on next page)

(continued from previous page)

```
// implementation section for Circle
Circle::Circle(double r)  // constructor
{
  radius = r;
}

// calculate the area of a circle
double Circle::calcval(void)
{
  return(PI * radius * radius);
}

// class declaration for the derived class
// Cylinder which is derived from Circle
class Cylinder : public Circle
{
  protected:
    double length;  // add one additional data member and
  public:           // two additional function members
    Cylinder(double r = 1.0, double l = 1.0) : Circle(r), length(l) {}
    double calcval();
};

// implementation for Cylinder

double Cylinder::calcval(void)   // this calculates a volume
{
  return (length * Circle::calcval()); // note the base function call
}
```

```
int main()
{
  Circle circle_1, circle_2(2);  // create two Circle objects
  Cylinder cylinder_1(3,4);      // create one Cylinder object

  cout << "The area of circle_1 is " << circle_1.calcval() << endl;
  cout << "The area of circle_2 is " << circle_2.calcval() << endl;
  cout << "The volume of cylinder_1 is " << cylinder_1.calcval() << endl;

  circle_1 = cylinder_1;  // assign a cylinder to a Circle

  cout << "\nThe area of circle_1 is now " << circle_1.calcval() << endl;

  return 0;
}
```

The output produced by Program 9.1 is:

```
The area of circle_1 is 3.141593
The area of circle_2 is 12.566371
The volume of cylinder_1 is 113.097336

The area of circle_1 is now 28.274334
```

The first three output lines are all straightforward and are produced by the first three `cout` calls in the program. As the output shows, a call to `calcval()` using a `Circle` object activates the `Circle` version of this function, whereas a call to `calcval()` using a `Cylinder` object activates the `Cylinder` version.

The assignment statement `circle_1 = cylinder_1;` introduces another important relationship between a base and derived class: *A derived class object can be assigned to a base class object.* This should not be surprising because both base and derived classes share a common set of data member types. In this type of assignment, it is only this set of data members, which consist of all the base class data members, that is assigned. Thus, as illustrated in Figure 9.4, our `Cylinder` to `Circle` assignment results in the following memberwise assignment:

```
circle_1.radius = cylinder_1.radius;
```

The length member of the `Cylinder` object is not used in the assignment because it has no equivalent variable in the `Circle` class. The reverse cast, from base to derived class, is not as simple and requires a constructor to correctly initialize the additional derived class members not in the base class.

Before leaving Program 9.1 one additional point should be made. Although the `Circle` constructor was explicitly called using a base/member initialization list for the `Cylinder` constructor, an implicit call could also have been made. In the absence of an explicit derived class constructor, the compiler will automatically call the default base class constructor first, before the derived class constructor is called. This works because the derived class contains all of the base class data members. In a similar fashion the destructor functions are called in the reverse order—first derived class and then base class.

FIGURE 9.4 Assignment from Derived to Base Class

Circle = Cylinder

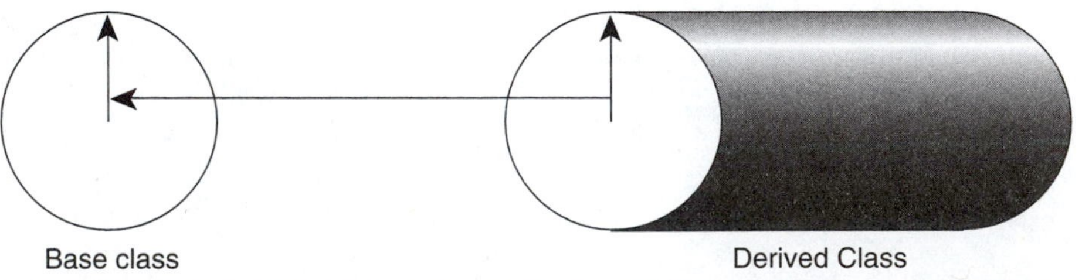

Exercises 9.1

1. Define the following terms:
   a. inheritance
   b. base class
   c. derived class
   d. simple inheritance
   e. multiple inheritance
   f. class hierarchy
2. Describe the difference between a private and a protected class member.
3. What three features must a programming language provide for it to be classified as an object-oriented language?
4. a. Modify Program 9.1 to include a derived class named `Sphere` from the base `Circle` class. The only additional class members of `Sphere` should be a constructor and a `calcval()` function that returns the volume of the sphere. (*Note:* Volume = $4/3\ \pi$ radius^3.)
   b. Include the class constructed for Exercise 4a in a working C++ program. Have your program call all of the member functions in the `Sphere` class.

9.2 POLYMORPHISM

The overriding of a base member function using an overloaded derived member function, as illustrated by the `calcval()` function in Program 9.1, is an example of polymorphism. **Polymorphism** permits the same function name to invoke one response in objects of a base class and another response in objects of a derived class. In some cases, however, this method of overriding may not work as desired. To understand why this is so, consider Program 9.2.

PROGRAM 9.2

```
#include <iostream.h>
#include <math.h>

// class declaration for the base class

class One
{
  protected:
    float a;
  public:
    One(float = 2.0);   // constructor
    float f1(float);    // a member function
    float f2(float);    // another member function
};
```

(continued on next page)

(continued from previous page)

```
// class implementation for One

One::One(float val)    // constructor
{
  a = val;
}

float One::f1(float num)   // a member function
{
  return(num/2);
}
float One::f2(float num)   // another member function
{
  return( pow(f1(num),2) );  // square the result of f1()
}

// class declaration for the derived class

class Two : public One
{
  public:
    float f1(float);     // this overrides class One's f1()
};

// class implementation for Two

float Two::f1(float num)
{
  return(num/3);
}
```

```
int main()
{
  One object_1;  // object_1 is an object of the base class
  Two object_2;  // object_2 is an object of the derived class

      // call f2() using a base class object call
  cout << "The computed value using a base class object call is "
       << object_1.f2(12) << endl;

     // call f2() using a derived class object call
  cout << "The computed value using a derived class object call is "
       << object_2.f2(12) << endl;

  return 0;
}
```

The output produced by this program is:

```
The computed value using a base class object call is 36
The computed value using a derived class object call is 36
```

As this output shows, the same result is obtained no matter which object type calls the `f2()` function. This result is produced because the derived class does not have an override to the base class `f2()` function. Thus, both calls to `f2()` result in the base class `f2()` function being called.

Once invoked, the base class `f2()` function will always call the base class version of `f1()` rather than the derived class override version. This behavior is due to a process referred to as *function binding.* In normal function calls static binding is used. In **static binding** the determination of which function is called is made at compile time. Thus, when the compiler first encounters the `f1()` function in the base class it makes the determination that whenever `f2()` is called, either from a base or derived class object, it will subsequently call the base class `f1()` function.

In place of static binding, we would like a binding method that is capable of determining which function should be invoked at run time, based on the object type making the call. This type of binding is referred to as **dynamic binding.** To achieve dynamic binding, C++ provides virtual functions.

A **virtual function** specification tells the compiler to create a pointer to a function, but not fill in the value of the pointer until the function is actually called. Then, at run time, *and based on the object making the call,* the appropriate function address is used. Creating a virtual function is extremely easy; all that is required is that the keyword `virtual` be placed before the function's return type in the declaration section. For example, consider Program 9.3, which is identical to Program 9.2 except for the virtual declaration of the `f1()` function.

PROGRAM 9.3

```
#include <iostream.h>
#include <math.h>

// class declaration for the base class

class One
{
  protected:
    float a;
  public:
    One(float = 2.0);    // constructor
    virtual float f1(float);    // a member function
    float f2(float);    // another member function
};
```

(continued on next page)

(continued from previous page)

```
// class implementation for One

One::One(float val)   // constructor
{
  a = val;
}

float One::f1(float num)  // a member function
{
  return(num/2);
}

float One::f2(float num)  // another member function
{
  return( pow(f1(num),2) );  // square the result of f1()
}


// class declaration for the derived class

class Two : public One
{
  public:
    virtual float f1(float);    // this overrides class One's f1()
};

// class implementation for Two

float Two::f1(float num)
{
  return (num/3);
}
```

```
int main()
{
  One object_1;  // object_1 is an object of the base class
  Two object_2;  // object_2 is an object of the derived class

    // call f2() using a base class object call
  cout << "The computed value using a base class object call is "
       << object_1.f2(12) << endl;

   // call f2() using a derived class object call
  cout << "The computed value using a derived class object call is "
       << object_2.f2(12) << endl;

  return 0;
}
```

The output produced by Program 9.3 is:

```
The computed value using a base class object call is 36
The computed value using a derived class object call is 16
```

As illustrated by this output, the `f2()` function now calls different versions of the overloaded `f1()` function based on the object type making the call. This selection, based on the object making the call, is the classic definition of polymorphic function behavior and is caused by the dynamic binding imposed on `f1()` by virtue of its being a virtual function.

Once a function is declared as virtual, *it remains virtual for the next derived class with or without a virtual declaration in the derived class*. Thus, the second virtual declaration in the derived class is not strictly needed, but should be included both for clarity and to ensure that any subsequently derived classes correctly inherit the function. To understand why, consider the inheritance diagram illustrated in Figure 9.5, where class C is derived from class B and class B is derived from class A. In this situation, if function `f1()` is virtual in class A, but is not declared in class B, it will not be virtual in class C. The only other requirement is that once a function has been declared as virtual the return type and parameter list of all subsequent derived class override versions *must* be the same.

FIGURE 9.5 Inheritance Diagram

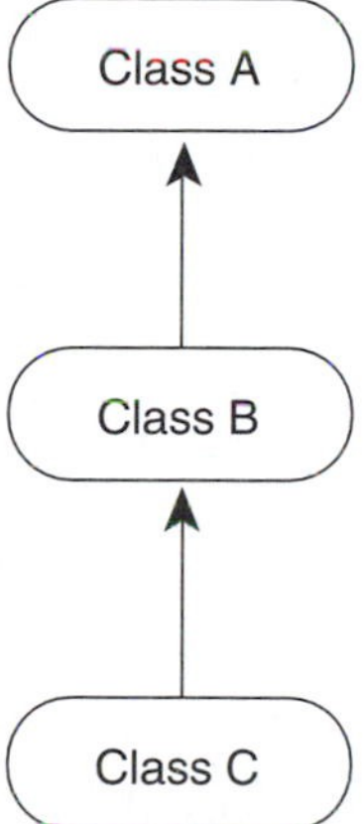

Exercises 9.2

1. Enter and execute Programs 9.2 and 9.3 on your computer so that you understand the relationship between function calls in each program.
2. Describe the two methods C++ provides for implementing polymorphism.
3. Describe the difference between static binding and dynamic binding.
4. Describe the difference between a virtual function and a nonvirtual function.
5. Describe what polymorphism is and provide an example of polymorphic behavior.

9.3 THE this POINTER

Except for static data members, which are shared by all class objects, each object maintains its own set of member variables. This permits each object to have its own clearly defined state as determined by the values stored in its member variables.

For example, consider the Date class previously defined in Program 8.1 and repeated here for convenience:

```
#include <iostream.h>

// class declaration

class Date
{
  private:
    int month;
    int day;
    int year;
  public:
    Date(int = 7, int = 4, int = 96);     // constructor
    void showdate(void);     // member function to display a Date
};

// implementation section

Date::Date(int mm, int dd, int yy)
{
  month = mm;
  day = dd;
  year = yy;
}

void Date::showdate(void)
{
  cout << month << '/' << day << '/' << year << endl;

  return;
}
```

Each time an object is created from this class, a distinct area of memory is set aside for its data members. For example, if two objects named a and b are created from this class, the memory storage for these objects would be as illustrated in Figure 9.6. Notice that each set of data members has its own starting address in memory, which corresponds to the address of the first data member for the object.

This replication of data storage is not implemented for member functions. In fact, for each class *only one copy of the member functions is retained in memory,* and each object uses these same functions.

Sharing member functions requires providing a means of identifying on which specific object data a member function should be operating. This is accomplished by providing address information to the function indicating where in memory the particular data, corresponding to a specific object, is located. This address is provided by the name of the object, which is, in fact, a reference name. For example,

FIGURE 9.6 The Storage of Two Date Objects in Memory

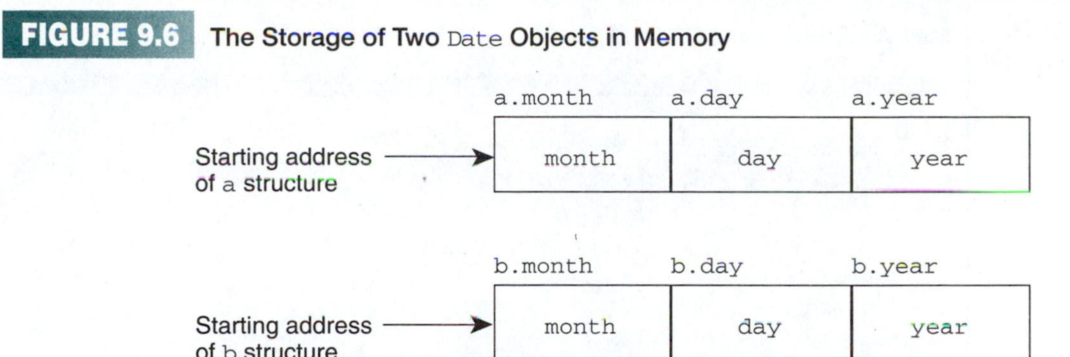

again using our Date class and assuming a is an object of this class, the statement a.showdate() passes the address of the a object into the showdate() member function. (Review Section 2.4 for information on memory addresses.)

An obvious question at this point is how this address is passed to showdate() and where it is stored. The answer is that the address is stored in a special parameter named **this**, which is automatically supplied as a hidden parameter to each nonstatic member function when the function is called.

Unlike a reference parameter, which is effectively a named constant for an address, the this argument is a pointer parameter. Although pointer parameters provide much more flexibility in using addresses than reference parameters and are explained in detail in Section 13.1, for our current purposes all that we need to know is that to gain access to the object whose address is provided by the this pointer we must apply C++'s dereference operator, *, to this.

Before proceeding to use the this pointer in a "cookbook" manner, let's take a moment to compare the differences between a pointer's address and a reference address. Recall from Section 6.5 that whenever a reference parameter is encountered it is always *the contents of the reference address* that is accessed. This type of access is referred to as automatic or implicit dereferencing of the address and effectively hides the fact that a reference parameter is fundamentally a named constant for an address. When using a pointer parameter, dereferencing is not automatic. To access the contents of the address provided by the this pointer, the notation *this or its equivalent this-> must be used, which formally provides what is known as explicit dereferencing.

Returning now to our Date class, which has three member functions, the complete parameter list of the constructor Date() function is equivalent to

```
Date(Date *this, int mm, int dd, int yy)
```

where the declaration Date *this means that the this pointer contains the address of a specific Date object in a similar manner as the declaration Date& refarg means that the refarg reference argument is the address of a Date object.[2] Similarly, the complete parameter list of showdate() is equivalent to

```
showdate(Date *this)
```

[2] Placing a space before the *, while a space is placed after the &, is by convention. Thus, Date& refarg could be written as Date &refarg and Date *this can be written as Date* this.

PROGRAM 9.4

```
#include <iostream.h>

// class declaration

class Date
{
  private:
    int month;
    int day;
    int year;
  public:
    Date(int = 7, int = 4, int = 96);      // constructor
    void showdate(void);      // member function to display a Date
};

// implementation section

Date::Date(int mm, int dd, int yy)
{
  (*this).month = mm;
  (*this).day = dd;
  (*this).year = yy;
}

void Date::showdate(void)
{
  cout << (*this).month << '/' << (*this).day << '/' << (*this).year << endl;

  return;
}

int main()
{
  Date a(4,1,97), b(12,18,98); // declare two objects

  cout << "The date stored in a is originally ";
  a.showdate();  // display the original date
  a = b;         // assign b's value to a
  cout << "After assignment the date stored in a is ";
  a.showdate();  // display a's values

  return 0;
}
```

The important point here is to understand that when a member function is called it actually receives an extra, hidden argument that is the address of a Date object. Although it is usually not necessary to do so, this pointer data member can be explicitly used within all member functions. For example, consider Program 9.4 on p. 496, which uses the hidden argument this within the body of each member function to access the appropriate data member variables.

The output produced by Program 9.4 is:

```
The date stored in a is originally 4/1/97
After assignment the date stored in a is 12/18/98
```

This is the same output produced by Program 8.1, which does not use the this pointer to access the data members. Clearly, using the this pointer in Program 9.4 is unnecessary and simply clutters the member function code. There are times, however, when an object must pass its address to other functions. In these situations, one of which we now consider, the address stored in the this pointer must explicitly be used.

The Assignment Operator Revisited

A simple assignment operator function was defined in Program 8.2 and is repeated below for convenience:

```
void Date::operator=(Date& newdate)
{
  day = newdate.day;       // assign the day
  month = newdate.month;   // assign the month
  year = newdate.year;     // assign the year
}
```

The drawback of this function is that it returns no value, making multiple assignments such as a = b = c impossible. Now that we have the this pointer at our disposal, we can fix our simple assignment operator function to provide an appropriate return type. In this case the return value should be a Date rather than a void. Making this change in the function's prototype for our assignment operator yields:

```
Date operator=(const Date&);
```

Notice also that we have declared the function's argument to be a const, which ensures that this operand cannot be altered by the function. A suitable function definition for this prototype is:

```
Date Date::operator=(const Date& newdate)
{

  day = newdate.day;       // assign the day
  month = newdate.month;   // assign the month
  year = newdate.year;     // assign the year

  return *this;
}
```

In the case of an assignment such as b = c, or its equivalent form, b.operator=(c), the function first alters b's member values from within the function and then returns the value of this object, which may be used in a subsequent assignment. Thus, a multiple assignment expression such as a = b = c is possible and is illustrated in Program 9.5.

PROGRAM 9.5

```
#include <iostream.h>

// class declaration

class Date
{
  private:
    int month;
    int day;
    int year;
  public:
    Date(int = 7, int = 4, int = 96);      // constructor
    Date operator=(const Date&);  // define assignment of a date
    void showdate(void);      // member function to display a date
};

// implementation section

Date::Date(int mm, int dd, int yy)
{
  month = mm;
  day = dd;
  year = yy;
}

Date Date::operator=(const Date& newdate)
{
  day = newdate.day;         // assign the day
  month = newdate.month;    // assign the month
  year = newdate.year;      // assign the year

  return *this;
}

void Date::showdate(void)
{
  cout << month << '/' << day << '/' << year << endl;

  return;
}

int main()
{
  Date a(4,1,97), b(12,18,98), c(1,1,99); // declare three objects

  cout << "Before assignment a's date value is ";
  a.showdate();
```

(continued on next page)

(continued from previous page)

```
  cout << "Before assignment b's date value is ";
  b.showdate();
  cout << "Before assignment c's date value is ";
  c.showdate();

  a = b = c;  // multiple assignment

  cout << "\nAfter assignment a's date value is ";
  a.showdate();
  cout << "After assignment b's date value is ";
  b.showdate();
  cout << "After assignment c's date value is ";
  c.showdate();

  return 0;
}
```

The output produced by Program 9.5 is:

```
Before assignment a's date value is 4/1/97
Before assignment b's date value is 12/18/98
Before assignment c's date value is 1/1/99

After assignment a's date value is 1/1/99
After assignment b's date value is 1/1/99
After assignment c's date value is 1/1/99
```

As noted previously in Section 8.3, the only restriction on the assignment operator function is that it can only be overloaded as a member function. It cannot be overloaded as a friend function.

Exercises 9.3

1. Discuss the difference between the automatic dereferencing that occurs when a reference argument is used and the explicit dereferencing required by the `this` argument.
2. Modify Program 9.4 so that the notation `this->` is used in place of the notation `(*this).` within the body of both the constructor and `showdate()` functions. In doing so notice that the `->` symbol is constructed using a hyphen, -, followed by a right facing arrow head, >.
3. Rewrite the `Date()`, `operator=()`, and `showdate()` member functions in Program 8.2 to explicitly use the `this` pointer when referencing all data members. Run your program and verify that the same output as produced by Program 8.2 is achieved.
4. A problem with the assignment operator defined in this section is that it does not return a suitable l-value. (Recall from Section 3.1 that an l-value is a value that can be used on the left side of an assignment statement.) Although Program 9.5 defines a return type for the `Date` assignment operator, the return type is not used as an l-value because the expression `a = b = c` is evaluated as `a = (b = c)`. Thus, in both the initial assignment `b = c` and the subsequent assignment `a = b`, the return value of the assignment operator is used as an r-value (i.e., it is used on the right-hand side of an assignment). Modify the assignment operator so that the expression returns a correct l-value. This means that in the evaluation of the expression `(a = b) = c`, the initial l-value returned should be `a`.

9.4 FOCUS ON PROBLEM SOLVING

This application presents a first look at the dynamic allocation of memory storage. This topic is presented a second time when arrays are considered in Chapter 11 and is used once again when we look at linked lists, including stacks and queues, in Chapter 15. Each presentation can be read independently.

Application 1: Dynamic Object Creation and Deletion

As each variable or object is defined in a program, sufficient storage for it is designated by the compiler and assigned from a pool of computer memory locations before the program is executed. Once specific memory locations have been assigned, they remain fixed for the lifetime of the variable and object or until the program has finished executing. For example, if a function requests storage for three nonstatic integers and five objects of a user-defined class, the storage for these integers and objects remains fixed from the point of their definition until the function finishes executing.

An alternative to this fixed allocation of memory is a dynamic allocation. Under dynamic allocation, the amount of allocated storage is determined and assigned as the function is executing, rather than being fixed prior to execution.

Although dynamic allocation of memory is most useful when dealing with lists where it allows the list to expand as new items are added and contracted as items are deleted, it can also be useful in simulation programs. For example, in simulating the arrival and departure of customers, it is helpful to have a mechanism whereby a new customer can be randomly created and then removed after being serviced. Two C++ operators, `new` and `delete`, provide this capability as described in Table 9.2.

Table 9.2

Operator Name	Description
`new`	Reserves the correct number of bytes for the variable or object type requested by the declaration. Returns the address of the first reserved location or a `NULL` address if sufficient memory is not available.
`delete`	Releases previously reserved memory.

From an operational viewpoint, dynamically allocated variables and objects created using the new operator are only accessible using the address returned by new. This means that, like the `this` pointer, the address of the newly created variable or object must be stored in a pointer variable. The mechanism for doing this is rather simple. For example, the statement `int *num = new int;` both reserves a memory area sufficient to hold one integer and places the address of this storage area into a pointer variable named `num`. This same dynamic allocation can also be made in two steps; the first step is to declare a pointer variable using a declaration statement followed by a subsequent statement requesting dynamic allocation. Using this two-step process, the single statement `int *num = new int;` can be replaced by the sequence of statements

PROGRAMMING NOTE

Using a typedef Statement

Among other uses, a `typedef` statement can be used to create a new and shorter name for pointer definitions. The syntax for a typedef statement is:

```
typedef data-type new-type-name;
```

For example, to make the name `PtrToInt` a synonym for the terms `int *` the following statement can be used:

```
typedef int * PtrToInt;
```

Such a statement would normally be placed at the top of a program file immediately after all `#includes`. Now, whenever a variable is to be declared as a pointer to an `int`, the term `PtrToInt` can be used in place of the `int *`. Thus, for example, the declaration

```
int *pointer1;
```

can be replaced by the statement

```
PtrToInt pointer1;
```

By convention all `typedef` names are written in either initial or all uppercase letters, but this is not mandatory. The names used in a `typedef` statement can be any name that conforms to C++'s identifier naming rules.

```
int *num;         // this declares a pointer variable that can
                  // store the address of an integer
num = new int;    // this reserves memory for an integer and
                  // puts the address of the memory area into num
```

In either case the allocated storage area comes from the computer's free storage area.[3] In a similar manner and of more usefulness is the dynamic allocation of a user-defined object.
For example, the declaration

```
Customer *anotherCust;
```

declares `anotherCust` as a pointer variable that can be used to store the address of a `Customer` object. The actual creation of a new `Customer` object is completed by the statement

```
anotherCust = new Customer;
```

This statement both creates a new `Customer` object and stores the address of the first reserved memory location into the pointer variable `anotherCust`. Program 9.6 on p. 503 illustrates this sequence of code within the context of a complete program.

[3] The free storage area of a computer is formally referred to as the *heap*. The heap consists of unallocated memory that can be allocated to a program, as requested, while the program is running.

POINT OF INFORMATION

Pointers versus References

The distinguishing characteristic of a pointer, either as a formal parameter or variable, is that *every pointer contains a value that is an address.* Thus, while a pointer is a variable or argument *whose contents is an address,* a reference *is an address.* As such, a reference can be thought of as a named constant, where the constant is a value that happens to be a valid memory address.

From an operational viewpoint, pointers are much more flexible than references. This is because a pointer's contents can be manipulated in much the same manner as any other variable's value. For example, if `foo` is a pointer variable, the statement `cout << foo;` displays the value stored in the pointer variable. This is identical to the operation of displaying the value of an integer or floating-point variable. That the value stored in a pointer happens to be an address is irrelevant as far as `cout` is concerned.

The disadvantage of pointers is that their very flexibility makes them more complicated to understand and use than reference arguments or variables. Since references can only be used as a named address, they are easier to use. Thus, when the compiler encounters a reference it automatically dereferences the address to obtain the contents of the address. This is not the case with pointers. If you use a pointer's name, as we have noted, you access the pointer's contents. To correctly dereference the address stored in a pointer, you must explicitly use C++'s dereference operator, `*`, in front of the pointer name. This informs the compiler that what you want is the item *whose address is in the pointer variable*.

Before looking at a sample output produced by Program 9.6 and analyzing how this output was produced by the `main()` function, consider the declaration of the `Customer` class. Notice that we have included an inline constructor function to display the message

```
*** A new customer has been created ***
```

whenever an object is created and an inline destructor function to display the message

```
!!!! This customer object has been deleted !!!!
```

whenever an object is deleted. These messages are only used to help you monitor the creation and deletion of an object when the program is executed. Also notice that we have not included the `srand()` function call within the constructor as we did in our original `Customer` class implementation presented in Section 8.6. Rather, we have made the calling of `srand()` a precondition to using any member function.

The primary reason for not including an `srand()` call in the `Customer` class constructor is that inclusion of this function would mean that it is called each time an object is created, when a single initial call to `srand()` is really all that is necessary for any single program execution. For large simulation runs where hundreds or even thousands of `Customer` objects can be created and deleted, execution times can be excessive and the savings in run times by careful placement of both function calls and calculations within repetitive loops can be dramatic.

PROGRAM 9.6

```
#include <iostream.h>
#include <iomanip.h>
#include <time.h>

// Customer class declaration
// precondition: srand() must be called once before any function methods
// postcondition: arrive(void) returns a random integer between 1 and 15
//               : gallons(void) returns a random integer between 3 and 20

#include <stdlib.h>
class Customer
{
  public:
    Customer(void) {cout << "\n**** A new customer has been created ****" << endl;};
    ~Customer(void) {cout << "!!!! This customer object has been deleted !!!!" << endl;};
    int arrive(void) {return(1 + rand() % 16);};
    int gallons(void) {return(3 + rand() % 21);};
};

int main()
{
   Customer *anotherCust;   // declare 1 pointer to an object of type Customer
   int i, howMany;
   int interval, request;

   cout << "Enter the number of customers to be created: ";
   cin >> howMany;
   srand(time(NULL));
   for(i = 1; i <= howMany; i++)
   {
     // create a new object of type Customer
     anotherCust = new Customer;

     // use the pointer to access the member functions
     interval = anotherCust->arrive();
     request = anotherCust->gallons();
     cout << "The arrival interval is " << interval << " minutes" << endl;
     cout << "The new customer requests " << request << " gallons" << endl;
     cout << "The memory address of this object is: "<< anotherCust << endl;

     // delete the created object
     // delete anotherCust;
   }

  return 0;
}
```

Sample output produced by Program 9.6 follows:

```
Enter the number of customers to be created: 4

*** A new customer has been created ***
The arrival interval is 6 minutes
The new customer requests 12 gallons
The memory address of this object is: 0x24df1216

*** A new customer has been created ***
The arrival interval is 13 minutes
The new customer requests 3 gallons
The memory address of this object is: 0x24df121e

*** A new customer has been created ***
The arrival interval is 8 minutes
The new customer requests 3 gallons
The memory address of this object is: 0x24df1226

*** A new customer has been created ***
The arrival interval is 2 minutes
The new customer requests 17 gallons
The memory address of this object is: 0x24df122e
```

As illustrated by this output, we can make the decision as to how many objects are to be created by Program 9.6 while the program is executing. Figure 9.7 illustrates the allocation of memory space corresponding to this sample output just before the program completes execution.

Now look at the `main()` function in Program 9.6 to see how this output was produced. First notice that new `Customer` objects are created using these statements:

```
Customer *anotherCust;
anotherCust = new Customer;
```

FIGURE 9.7 The Memory Allocation Produced by the Sample Execution of Program 9.6

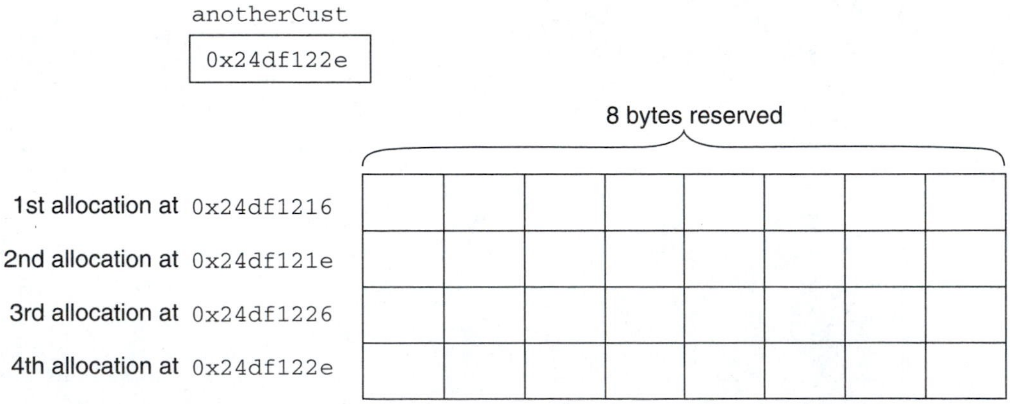

The first statement defines a single pointer variable named `anotherCust`. Each time the second statement is executed, a new object is created and its address is stored in the `anotherCust` variable (the old address is lost).[4] Notice also that this stored address can be displayed by inserting the pointer variable name in the `cout` stream as we have done in the last executable statement contained within `main()`'s body. Since the contents of a pointer variable is a value, this value, even though it happens to be an address, can be displayed using the `cout` stream. Each time the value is displayed, it simply represents the current address stored in the variable.

Notice also that the last line in `main()`'s body comments out the statement `delete anotherCust;`. This was done intentionally to force each newly created object into a new memory area. If a `delete` had been used to release the previously allocated block of storage, the operating system would typically provide the same locations right back for the next allocation. In this case you would not see the assigned address change while the programming is executing.[5] In practice, however, it is very important to delete dynamically created objects when their usefulness ends. As you can see by the sample output, if you don't, the computer system starts to effectively "eat up" available memory space.

Finally, notice the notation used to access the member functions of each dynamically created object. For example, the notation `anotherCust->arrival()` calls the `arrival()` function of the object whose address resides in the pointer variable `anotherCust`. Since dynamically created objects do not have symbolic names, they can only be accessed using the address information contained within the pointer variable. This can be done either using the notation, shown in Program 9.6, `pointerName->functionName()` or by using the equivalent notation `(*pointerName).functionName()`.

Problem 1: A Dynamic Gas Pump Simulation

In the multi-object simulation presented in Section 8.6, the same customer object was used repeatedly to simulate multiple customer arrivals. The current problem is to write a simulation that dynamically creates new and different customer objects as they are needed and then deletes each object once its task is completed. To accomplish this, you will need the information presented on dynamic memory allocation in the previous application.

Analyze the Problem All dynamic allocations require that at least one pointer variable be made available to store the starting address of the newly allocated object. The `new` operator is used to reserve the memory space, and then it returns the starting address, which should be assigned to the pointer variable. For example, the declaration

```
Customer *anotherCust;
```

---

[4] In practice the object whose address is currently in the pointer variable would have been deleted prior to reusing the pointer variable, so that the address being overwritten would be of no use anyway.

[5] The allocated storage would automatically be returned to the heap when the program has completed execution. It is, however, good practice to restore the allocated storage formally to the heap using `delete` when the memory is no longer needed. This is especially true for larger programs that make numerous requests for additional storage areas.

declares a pointer variable named `anotherCust` that can be used to store an address of a `Customer` object.[6] Once a pointer has been defined, the pointer name can be used in an assignment statement such as `anotherCust = new Customer;` that allocates new storage and also stores the starting address of the allocated area into the pointer variable.

For our simulation we will require both a `Pump` class and a `Customer` class. The `Customer` class, which is identical to that used in Program 9.6 except for the messages displayed by the constructor and destructor, is:

```
#include <stdlib.h>

// Customer class declaration
// precondition: srand() must be called once before any function methods
// postcondition: arrive(void) returns a random integer between 1 and 15
//              : gallons(void) returns a random integer between 3 and 20

class Customer
{
  public:
     Customer(void) {cout << "\n**** A new customer has arrived ****" << endl;};
    ~Customer(void) {cout << "!!!! The customer has departed !!!!" << endl;};
    int arrive(void) {return(1 + rand() % 16);};
    int gallons(void) {return(3 + rand() % 21);};
};
```

For convenience we assume that this class declaration is stored as `CUSTOM_1.H` in the `CLASSES` directory of a `C` drive.

The `Pump` class is exactly the same as that used in Program 8.13 and is repeated here for convenience:

```
// class declaration

class Pump
{
  private:
    float amtInTank;
    float price;
  public:
    Pump(float = 500.0, float = 1.00);       // constructor
    void values(void);
    void request(float);
};

// class implementation
Pump::Pump(float start, float todaysPrice)
{
  amtInTank = start;
  price = todaysPrice;
}
```

[6] Note that the width of all addresses is the same, whether they are addresses of `Customer` objects, `Pump` objects, or integer variables. Typically an address is either 16 or 32 bits wide. The reason for specifying the type of object is to inform the compiler of how many bytes must be accessed when the address is dereferenced. The allocation of memory for the object depends on how many data members it has, plus a fixed minimum size, which is typically 8 or 16 bytes.

```
void Pump::values(void)
{
  cout << "The gas tank has " << amtInTank << " gallons of gas." << endl;
  cout << "The price per gallon of gas is $" << setiosflags(ios::showpoint)
       << setprecision(2) << price << endl;

  return;
}

void Pump::request(float pumpAmt)
{
  float pumped;

  if (amtInTank >= pumpAmt)
     pumped = pumpAmt;
  else
     pumped = amtInTank;

  amtInTank -= pumped;
  cout << pumpAmt << " gallons were requested " << endl;
  cout << pumped << " gallons were pumped" << endl;
  cout << amtInTank << " gallons remain in the tank" << endl;
  cout << "The total price is $" << setiosflags(ios::showpoint)
       << setprecision(2) << (pumped * price) << endl;

  return;
}
```

We assume that this class has been thoroughly tested and has been stored on a `C:` drive in the `CLASSES` directory as `PUMP.H`.

Develop a Solution By using the preexisting classes `Pump` and `Customer`, all that remains to be developed is the control logic within the `main()` function for correctly creating `Pump` and `Customer` objects, and controlling the interaction between objects by appropriately activating class methods. A suitable control structure for `main()` is described by the algorithm

Create a Pump object with the required initial gallons of gas and price-per-gallon.
Display the values in the initialized Pump.
Set the total time to 0.

Create the first Customer object.
Obtain the Customer's interval arrival time.
Add the arrival time to the total time.

While the total time does not exceed the simulation time
    Display the total time.
    Obtain a Customer request for gas.
    Activate the Pump with the request.
    Delete this Customer object.
    Create a new Customer // next arrival.
    Obtain the Customer's interval arrival time.
    Add the arrival time to the total time.
EndWhile.

Display a message that the simulation is over.

Code the Solution The C++ code corresponding to our design is illustrated in Program 9.7.

PROGRAM 9.7

```
#include <iostream.h>
#include <iomanip.h>
#include <time.h>

// precondition: srand() must be called once before any CUSTOMER methods are used
// postcondition: arrive(void) returns a random integer between 1 and 15
//              : gallons(void) returns a random integer between 3 and 20
#include <C:\CLASSES\PUMP.H>       // note use of full path name here
#include <C:\CLASSES\CUSTOM_1.H>   // again - a full path name is used

const float SIMTIME = .5;          // simulation time in hours
const int MINUTES = 60;            // number of minutes in an hour
const float AMT_IN_TANK = 300;     // initial gallons in the tank
const float TODAYS_PRICE = 1.25;   // price-per-gallon

int main()
{
  Pump a(AMT_IN_TANK, TODAYS_PRICE);    // declare 1 object of type Pump
  Customer *anotherCust;  // declare 1 pointer to an object of type Customer
  int totalTime = 0;
  int idleTime;
  int amtRequest;
  int SimMinutes;  // simulation time in minutes

  SimMinutes = SIMTIME * MINUTES;
  cout << "\nStarting a new simulation - simulation time is "
       << SimMinutes << " minutes" << endl;
  a.values();

  srand(time(NULL));

  // create a new object of type Customer
  anotherCust = new Customer;

  // get the customer's arrival time
  idleTime = anotherCust->arrive();
  totalTime += idleTime;

  while (totalTime <= SimMinutes)
  {
```

(continued on next page)

(continued from previous page)

```
    cout << "The idle time is " << idleTime << " minutes" << endl
         << "   and we are " << totalTime
         << " minutes into the simulation." << endl;
    amtRequest = anotherCust->gallons();
    a.request(float(amtRequest));

    // delete this Customer
    delete anotherCust;

    // create the next Customer
    anotherCust = new Customer;
    // get the next arrival
    idleTime = anotherCust->arrive();
    totalTime += idleTime;
  }
  cout << "The idle time is " << idleTime << " minutes." << endl
       << "\nAs the total time now exceeds the simulation time, "  << endl
       << "   this simulation run is over." << endl;

  return 0;
}
```

Test and Correct the Program Since the `Pump` and `Customer` classes are known to correctly meet their respective specifications, testing and debugging of Program 9.7 can be restricted to testing and debugging of the `main()` function. By itself, the `main()` function in Program 9.7 uses a straightforward `while` loop that creates and deletes `Customer` objects within a simulated time span of `SIMTIME` hours. Within the program the `Pump` idle time corresponds to the time between customer arrivals. Notice that the notation used to dereference the address in the pointer variable `anotherCust` and activate the `arrival()` method is `anotherCust->arrival()`. As an alternative to this notation the notation `(*anotherCust).arrival()` could have been used. The output of a sample run verifies that the loop is operating correctly:

```
Starting a new simulation - simulation time is 30 minutes
The gas tank has 300 gallons of gas.
The price per gallon of gas is $1.25

**** A new customer has arrived ****
The idle time is 4 minutes
   and we are 4 minutes into the simulation.
14.00 gallons were requested
14.00 gallons were pumped
286.00 gallons remain in the tank
The total price is $17.50
!!!! The customer has departed !!!!
```

```
**** A new customer has arrived ****
The idle time is 16 minutes
   and we are 20 minutes into the simulation.
6.00 gallons were requested
6.00 gallons were pumped
280.00 gallons remain in the tank
The total price is $7.50
!!!! The customer has departed !!!!

**** A new customer has arrived ****
The idle time is 15 minutes.

As the total time now exceeds the simulation time,
   this simulation run is over.
```

Exercises 9.4

1. a. Describe what a pointer is.

   b. For each of the following pointer declarations, identify the name of the pointer variable and the type of object that will be accessed when the address in the pointer variable is dereferenced:

   ```
   float *b;
   int *addr_of_int;
   Customer *a;
   Pump *pointer1;
   Pump *addr_of_a_pump;
   ```

   c. If the asterisks, `*`, were removed from the declarations in Exercise 1b, what would the names immediately preceding the semicolon represent?

2. a. Describe dynamic allocation of memory.

   b. Describe the process of creating a dynamically allocated object. Specifically, discuss the roles of a pointer variable and the `new` operator in creating a dynamically allocated object.

   c. Discuss the importance of deleting dynamically allocated objects and what can happen if deletion is not used.

3. Programs 8.13 and 9.7 both produce a valid simulation. Since the type of simulation produced by each program is essentially the same, discuss the advantages and disadvantages of using multiple `Customer` objects in Program 9.7 as opposed to using a single `Customer` object in Program 8.13.

4. a. Modify Program 9.7 to use the `Customer` class defined in Program 8.13 [i.e., put the `srand()` function call back into the constructor function]. Now run the program and notice that the same arrival times are obtained for each newly created customer object. What do you think is occurring to produce this effect?

   b. To correct for the problem noticed in Exercise 3a, place the following loop in the constructor function. (Note, due to the loop the constructor can no longer be written as an inline function.)

   ```
   for(int i = 0; i < 500000; i++);
   ```

   What does this loop accomplish? Run the program and notice that the randomness of customer arrivals has been restored. What do you notice about the time it takes to execute a complete simulation? Comment about the efficiency of your modified program as compared to Program 9.7.

9.5 POINTERS AS CLASS MEMBERS[7]

As we saw in Section 7.2, a class can contain any C++ data type. Thus, the inclusion of a pointer variable in a class should not seem surprising. For example, the class declaration:

```
class Test
{
  private:
    int id_num;
    double *pt_pay;
  public:
    Test(int = 0, double * = NULL); //constructor
    void setvals(int a, double *b);
    void display();
};
```

declares a class consisting of two instance variables and three member functions. The first instance variable is an integer variable named `id_num`, and the second instance variable is a pointer named `pt_pay`, which is a pointer variable to a double-precision number. We will use the `setvals()` member function to store values into the private member variables and the `display()` function for output purposes. The implementation of these two functions along with the constructor function `Test()` is contained in the class implementation section:

```
// class implementation

Test::Test(int id, double *pt)
{
  id_num = id;
  pt_pay = pt;

   return;
}

void Test::setvals(int a, double *b)
{
  id_num = a;
  pt_pay = b;

  return;
}

void Test::display()
{
  cout << "\nEmployee number " << id_num << " was paid $"
       << setiosflags(ios::showpoint)
       << setw(6) << setprecision(2)
       << *pt_pay << endl;

  return;
}
```

[7] The material in this section requires a good grounding in pointer fundamentals. As such, it should be read after the material in Section 13.1 is covered.

In this implementation the `Test()` constructor initializes its `id_num` data member to its first argument and its pointer member to its second argument; if no arguments are given, these variables are initialized to a `0` and `NULL`, respectively. The display function simply outputs the value pointed to by its pointer member. As defined in this implementation, the `setvals()` function is very similar to the constructor and is used to alter member values after the object has been declared: The function's first argument (an integer) is assigned to `id_num` and its second argument (an address) is assigned to `pt_pay`.

The `main()` function in Program 9.8 illustrates the use of the `Test` class by first creating one object, named `emp`, which is initialized using the constructor's default arguments. The `setvals()` function is then used to assign the value 12345 and the address of the variable `pay` to the data members of this `emp` object. Finally, the `display()` function is used to display the value whose address is stored in `emp.pt_pay`. As illustrated by the program, the pointer member of an object is used like any other pointer variable.

PROGRAM 9.8

```
#include <iostream.h>
#include <iomanip.h>

// class declaration

class Test
{
  private:
    int id_num;
    double *pt_pay;
  public:
    Test(int = 0, double * = NULL);     // constructor
    void setvals(int, double *);    // access function
    void display();                 // access function
};

// implementation section

Test::Test(int id, double *pt)
{
  id_num = id;
  pt_pay = pt;
}

void Test::setvals(int a, double *b)
{
  id_num = a;
  pt_pay = b;

  return;
}
```

(continued on next page)

(continued from previous page)

```
void Test::display()
{
  cout << "\nEmployee number " << id_num << " was paid $"
       << setiosflags(ios::showpoint)
       << setw(6) << setprecision(2)
       << *pt_pay << endl;

  return;
}

int main()
{
  Test emp;
  double pay = 456.20;

  emp.setvals(12345, &pay);
  emp.display();

  return 0;
}
```

The output produced by executing Program 9.8 is:

```
Employee number 12345 was paid $456.20
```

Figure 9.8 illustrates the relationship between the data members of the `emp` object defined in Program 9.8 and the variable named `pay`. The value assigned to `emp.id_num` is the number 12345 and the value assigned to `pay` is 456.20. The address of the `pay` variable is assigned to the object member `emp.pt_pay`. Since this member has been defined as a pointer to a double-precision number, placing the address of the double-precision variable `pay` in it is a correct use of this data member.

Although the pointer defined in Program 9.8 has been used in a rather trivial fashion, the program does illustrate the concept of including a pointer in a class.

Clearly it would be more efficient to include the `pay` variable directly as a data member of the `Test` class rather than using a pointer to it. In some cases, however, pointers are advantageous. For example, assume we need to store a list of book titles. Rather than use a fixed length character array as a data member to

FIGURE 9.8 Storing an Address in a Data Member

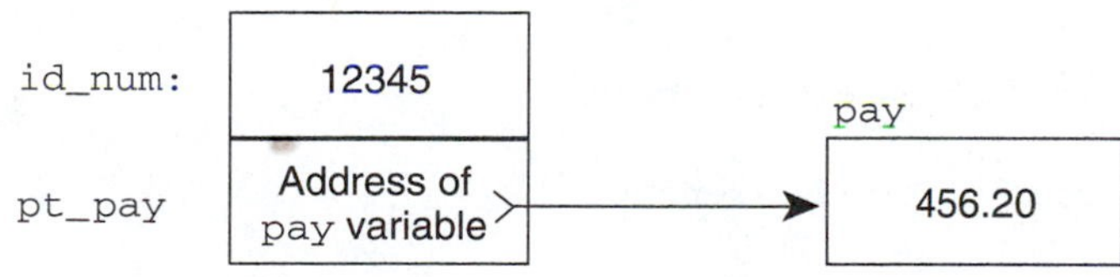

hold each title, we could include a pointer member to a character array, and then allocate the correct size array for each book title as it is needed. This arrangement is illustrated in Figure 9.9, which shows two objects, a and b, each of which consists of a single pointer data member. As depicted, object a's pointer contains the address of ("points to") a character array containing the characters DOS Primer, while object b's pointer contains the address of a character array containing the characters A Brief History of Western Civilization.

FIGURE 9.9 Two Objects Containing Pointer Data Members

Object a's data member:

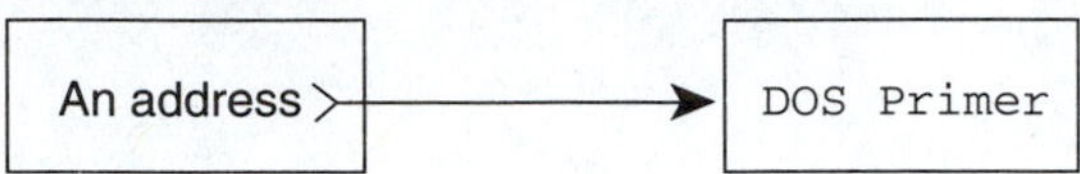

Object b's data member:

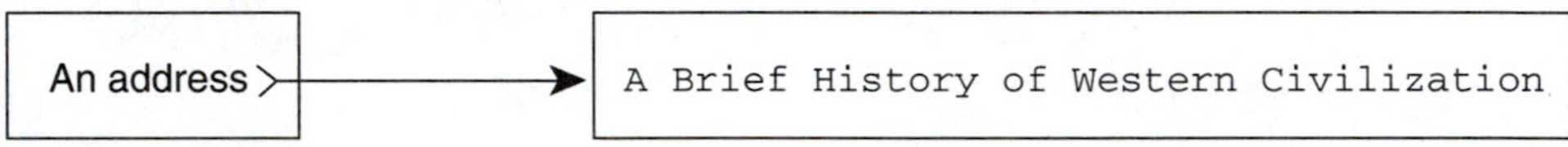

A suitable class declaration section for a list of book titles that are to be accessed as illustrated in Figure 9.9 is:

```
// class declaration
class Book
{
  private:
    char *title;    // a pointer to a book title
  public:
    Book(char * '\0');  // constructor
    void showtitle(void);   // display the title
};
```

The definition of the constructor function, Book(), and the display function, showtitle(), are defined in the implementation section as:

```
// class implementation

Book::Book(char *name)
{
  title = new char[strlen(name)+1];  // allocate memory
  strcpy(title,name);                // store the string
}

void Book::showtitle(void)
{
  cout << title << endl;
}
```

FIGURE 9.10 Allocating Memory for `title = newchar[strlen(name)+1]`

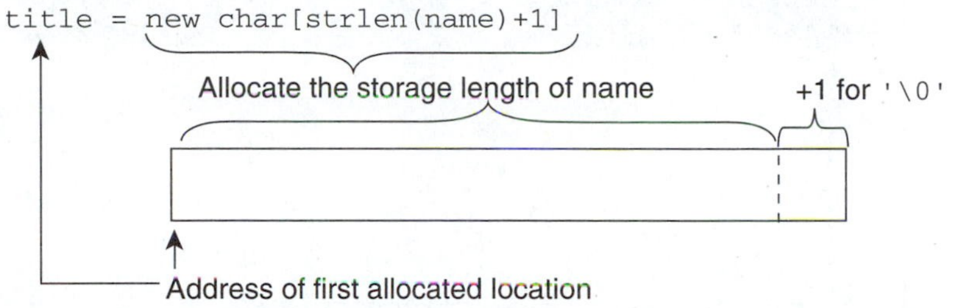

The body of the `Book()` constructor contains two statements. The first statement, `title = new char[strlen(name)+1];` performs two tasks: First, the right-hand side of the statement allocates enough storage for the length of the name argument plus one, to accommodate the end-of-string null character, `'\0'`. Next, the address of the first allocated character position is assigned to the pointer variable title. These operations are illustrated in Figure 9.10. The second statement in the constructor copies the characters in the name argument to the newly created memory allocation. If no argument is passed to the constructor, then title is the empty string; that is, title is set to `NULL`. Program 9.9 on p. 516 uses this class definition within the context of a complete program.

The output produced by Program 9.9 is:

```
DOS Primer
A Brief History of Western Civilization
```

Assignment Operators and Copy Constructors Reconsidered[8]

When a class contains no pointer data members, the compiler-provided defaults for the assignment operator and copy constructor adequately perform their intended tasks. Both of these defaults provide a member-by-member operation that produces no adverse side effects. This is not the case when a pointer member is included in the class declaration. Let's see why this is so.

Figure 9.11a on p. 517 illustrates the arrangement of pointers and allocated memory produced by Program 9.9 just before it completes execution. Let's assume that we insert the assignment statement `book2 = book1;` before the closing brace of the `main()` function. Since we have not defined an assignment operation, the compiler's default assignment is used. As we know, this assignment produces a memberwise copy (that is, `book2.title = book1.title`) and means that the address in `book1`'s pointer is copied into `book2`'s pointer. Thus, both pointers now "point to" the character array containing the characters `DOS Primer`, and the address of `A Brief History of Western Civilization` has been lost. This situation is illustrated in Figure 9.11b on p. 517.

---

[8] The material in this section pertains to the problems that occur when using the default assignment, copy constructor, and destructor functions with classes containing pointer members, and how to overcome these problems. On first reading, this section can be omitted without loss of subject continuity.

PROGRAM 9.9

```
#include <iostream.h>
#include <string.h>

// class declaration

class Book
{
  private:
    char *title;    // a pointer to a book title
  public:
    Book(char * = NULL);  // constructor
    void showtitle(void);   // display the title
};

// class implementation

Book::Book(char *strng)
{
  title = new char[strlen(strng)+1];  // allocate memory
  strcpy(title,strng);                // store the string
}

void Book::showtitle(void)
{
  cout << title << endl;

  return;
}

int main()
{
  Book  book1("DOS Primer");   // create 1st title
  Book  book2("A Brief History of Western Civilization");  // 2nd title

  book1.showtitle();   // display book1's title
  book2.showtitle();   // display book2's title

  return 0;
}
```

Since the memberwise assignment illustrated in Figure 9.11b results in the loss of the address of `A Brief History of Western Civilization`, there is no way for the program to release this memory storage (it will be cleaned up by the operating system when the program terminates). Worse, however, is the case where a destructor attempts to release the memory. Once the memory pointed to by `book2` is released (again, referring to Figure 9.11b), `book1` points

FIGURE 9.11a Before the Assignment `book2 = book1;`

book1's Pointer

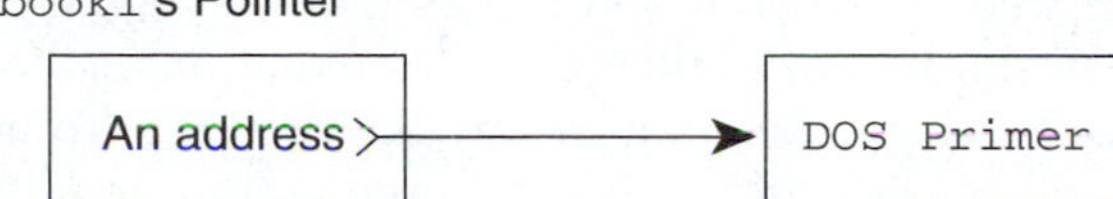

book2's Pointer

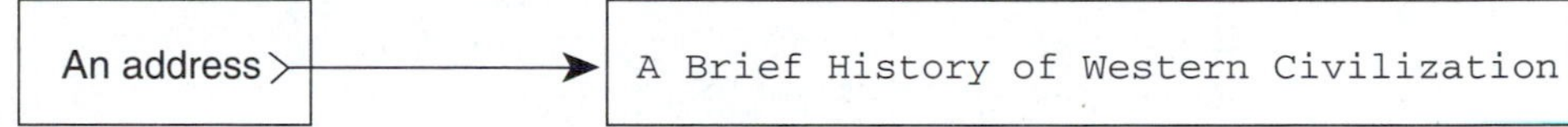

FIGURE 9.11b The Effect Produced by Default Assignment

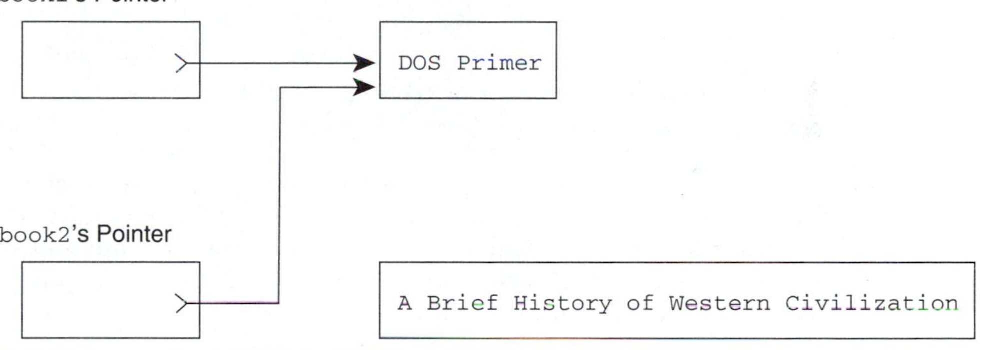

FIGURE 9.11c The Desired Effect

book1's Pointer

book2's Pointer

to an undefined memory location. If this memory area is subsequently reallocated before book1 is deleted, the deletion will release memory that another object is using. The results of this can create havoc.

What is typically desired is that the book titles themselves be copied and their pointers left alone as shown in Figure 9.11c. This situation also removes all of the side effects of a subsequent deletion of any book object. To achieve the desired assignment, we must explicitly write our own assignment operator. A suitable definition for this operator is:

```
void Book::operator=(Book& oldbook)
{
  if(oldbook.title != NULL)   // check that it exists
    delete(title);            // release existing memory
  title = new char[strlen(oldbook.title) + 1];  // allocate new memory
  strcpy(title, oldbook.title);  // copy the title
}
```

This definition cleanly releases the memory previously allocated for the object and then allocates sufficient memory to store the copied title.

The problems associated with the default assignment operator also exist with the default copy constructor, because it also performs a memberwise copy. As with assignment, these problems are avoided by writing our own copy constructor. For our Book class such a constructor is:

```
Book::Book(Book& oldbook)
{
  title = new char[strlen(oldbook.title) + 1];  // allocate new memory
  strcpy(title, oldbook.title);  // copy the title
}
```

Comparing the body of this copy constructor to the assignment operator's function body reveals that they are identical except for the deallocation of memory performed by the assignment operator. This is because the copy constructor does not have to release the existing array prior to allocating a new one, since none exists when the constructor is called.

Exercises 9.5

1. Include the copy constructor and assignment operator presented in this section in Program 9.9 and run the program to verify their operation.
2. Write a suitable destructor function for Program 9.9.
3. a. Construct a class named Car that contains the following four data members: a floating-point variable named engine_size, a character variable named body_style, an integer variable named color_code, and a character pointer named vin_ptr to a vehicle identification code. The function members should include a constructor that provides default values of 0 for each numeric data member, an 'X' for each character variable, and a NULL for each pointer; a display function that prints the engine size, body style, color code, and vehicle identification number; and an assignment operator that performs a memberwise assignment between two car objects that correctly handles the pointer member.

   b. Include the program written for Exercise 3a in a working C++ program that creates two car objects, the second of which is assigned the values of the first object.

4. Modify Program 9.9 to include the assignment statement `b = a`, then run the modified program to assess the error messages, if any, that occur.
5. Using Program 9.9 as a start, write a program that creates five `Book` objects. The program should allow the user to enter five book titles interactively and then display the entered titles.
6. Modify the program written in Exercise 5 so that the program sorts the entered book titles in alphabetical order before it displays them. (*Hint:* You will have to define a sort routine for the titles.)

9.6 COMMON PROGRAMMING ERRORS

The common programming errors associated with inheritance, polymorphism, pointers, and dynamic memory allocation are as follows:

1. Attempting to override a virtual function without using the same type and number of arguments as the original function.
2. Using the keyword `virtual` in the class implementation section. Functions are only declared as `virtual` in the class declaration section.
3. Using the default copy constructor and default assignment operators with classes containing pointer members. Since these default functions do a memberwise copy, the address in the source pointer is copied to the destination pointer. Typically this is not what is wanted since both pointers end up pointing to the same memory area.
4. Forgetting that `this` is a pointer that must be dereferenced using either `(*this)` or `this->`.

9.7 CHAPTER REVIEW

Key Terms

base class
class hierarchy
derived class
dynamic binding
inheritance
multiple inheritance
polymorphism
simple inheritance
static binding
`this` pointer
virtual function

Summary

1. *Inheritance* is the capability of deriving one class from another class. The initial class used as the basis for the derived class is referred to as the base, parent, or superclass. The derived class is referred to as either the derived, child, or subclass.
2. Base member functions can be overridden by derived member functions with the same name. The override function is simply an overloaded version of the base member function defined in the derived class.

3. *Polymorphism* is the ability for the same function name to invoke different responses based on the object making the function call. It can be accomplished using either override functions or virtual functions.
4. In *static binding* the determination of which function actually is invoked is made at compile time. In *dynamic binding* the determination is made at run time.
5. A *virtual function* specification designates that dynamic binding should take place. The specification is made in the function's prototype by placing the keyword `virtual` before the function's return type. Once a function has been declared as virtual it remains so for all derived classes as long as there is a continuous trail of function declarations through the derived chain of classes.
6. For each class only one copy of each member function is retained in memory. The address of an object's data members is provided to a member function by passing a hidden argument reference, corresponding to the memory address of the selected object, to the member function. The address is passed in a special pointer argument named `this`. The `this` pointer may be used explicitly by a member function to access a data member.
7. Pointers may be included as class data members. A pointer member adheres to the same rules as a pointer variable.
8. The default copy constructor and default assignment operators are typically not useful with classes containing pointer members. This is because these default functions do a memberwise copy in which the address in the source pointer is copied to the destination pointer, resulting in both pointers "pointing to" the same memory area. For these situations you must define your own copy constructor and assignment operator.

Exercises

1. Describe the difference between static and dynamic binding.
2. a. Create a base class named `Point` that consists of an x and y coordinate. From this class derive a class named `Circle` that has an additional data member named `radius`. For this derived class the `x` and `y` data members represent the center coordinates of a circle. The function members of the first class should consist of a constructor and a `distance` function that returns the distance between two points, where

$$\text{distance} = \sqrt{(x2 - x1)^2 + (y2 - y1)^2}$$

   Additionally, the derived class should have a constructor, an override `distance()` function that calculates the distance between circle centers, and a named `area` that returns the area of a circle.

   b. Include the classes constructed for Exercise 2a in a working C++ program. Have your program call all of the member functions in each class. In addition call the base class distance function with two `Circle` objects and explain the result returned by the function.
3. a. Using the classes constructed for Exercise 2a, derive a class named `Cylinder` from the derived `Circle` class. The `Cylinder` class should have a constructor and a member function named `area` that determines the

surface area of the cylinder. For this function use the algorithm *surface area* $= 2\pi r\,(l + r)$, where r is the radius of the cylinder and l is the length.

b. Include the classes constructed for Exercise 3a in a working C++ program. Have your program call all of the member functions in the `Cylinder` class.

c. What do you think the result might be if the base class distance function were called with two `Cylinder` objects?

4. a. Create a base class named `Rectangle` that contains `length` and `width` data members. From this class derive a class named `Box` having an additional data member named `depth`. The function members of the base `Rectangle` class should consist of a constructor and an area function. The derived `Box` class should have a constructor and an override function named `area` that returns the surface area of the box and a volume function.

   b. Include the classes constructed for Exercise 4a in a working C++ program. Have your program call all of the member functions in each class and explain the result when the `distance` function is called using two `Circle` objects.

5. a. Construct a class named `TelBook` that contains data members capable of holding a last name, first name, and telephone number. The constructor should set each of these members to an `"x"`. Additionally, create member functions to input data values, to display data values, and to assign one object's data values to another object.

   b. Include the class written for Exercise 5a in a working C++ program that tests each member function.

CHAPTER

10 I/O File Streams and Data Files

The data for the programs we have seen so far has either been assigned internally within the programs or entered interactively during program execution. This type of data entry is fine for small amounts of data. Imagine, however, a company having to type in the names and addresses of hundreds or thousands of customers every month each time bills are prepared and sent.

In this chapter we learn how to store such data outside of a program. This external data storage permits a program to use the data without the user having to recreate it each time the program is executed. Additionally, it provides the basis for sharing data between programs, so that the data output by one program can be input directly to another program.

Any collection of data that is stored together under a common name on a storage medium other than the computer's main memory is called a **data file.** Typically data files are stored on floppy diskettes, hard disks, magnetic tapes, and CD-ROMs. This chapter presents the fundamental of data files and describes how they are created and maintained in C++.

10.1 I/O FILE STREAM OBJECTS AND METHODS

To store and retrieve data on a file in C++ three items are required:

- a file
- a file stream object
- a mode.

A BIT OF BACKGROUND

Privacy, Security, and Files

Data files have been around a long time, mainly on paper stored in filing cabinets. Terms such as *open, close, records,* and *lookup* that we use in handling computer files are reminders of older techniques for accessing paper files stored in drawers.

Today most files are stored electronically, and the amount of information that is collected and stored has proliferated wildly. Because it is easier to transit bits and bytes than to ship paper folders, increasingly serious problems of security have arisen with concerns over people's privacy.

Whenever an individual fills out a government form or a credit application, submits a mail order, applies for a job, writes a check, or uses a creditcard, an electronic data trail is created. Each time those files are shared among government agencies or private enterprises, the individual loses more of his or her privacy.

To help protect U.S. citizens' constitutional rights, the Fair Credit Reporting Act was passed in 1970, followed by the Federal Privacy Act in 1974. These acts specify that it is illegal for a business to keep secret files, that you are entitled to examine and correct any data collected about you, and that government agencies and contractors must show justification for accessing your records. Efforts continue to create mechanisms that will serve to preserve an individual's security and privacy.

Files

A *file* is a collection of data that is stored under a common name, usually on a disk, magnetic tape, or CD-ROM. For example, the C++ programs that you store on disk are examples of files. The stored data in a program file is the program code that becomes input data to the C++ compiler.

A file is physically stored on an external medium such as a disk, using a unique file name referred to as the **external file name.** The external name is the name of the file as it is known by the operating system. It is the external name that is displayed when you use an operating command such as `dir` or `ls`.

Each computer operating system has its own specification as to the maximum number of characters permitted for an external file name. Table 10.1 lists these specifications for the more commonly used operating systems. To ensure that the examples presented in this text are compatible with all of the operating systems listed in Table 10.1 we will adhere to the more restrictive DOS and VMX specifications. If you are using one of the other operating systems, however, you should take advantage of the increased length specification to create descriptive file names within the context of a manageable length (generally considered to be no more that 12 to 14 characters). Very long file names should be avoided. Although such names can be extremely descriptive they do take more time to type and are prone to typing errors.

Using the DOS convention then, the following are all valid computer data file names:

```
balances.dat  records     info.dat
report.bnd    prices.dat  math.mem
```

TABLE 10.1 Maximum Allowable File Name Characters

Operating System	Maximum Length
DOS	8 characters plus an optional period and 3-character extension
VMX	8 characters plus an optional period and 3-character extension
Windows 3.1[1]	8 characters plus an optional period and 3-character extension
Windows 95	255 characters
UNIX	
Early versions	14 characters
Current versions	255 characters

Computer file names should be chosen to indicate both the type of data in the file and the application for which it is used. Frequently, the first eight characters are used to describe the data itself and an extension (the three characters after the decimal point) is used to describe the application. For example, the Lotus 1-2-3 spreadsheet program automatically applies an extension of `wk3` to all spreadsheet files, Microsoft's Word and the WordPerfect word processing programs use the extensions `doc` and `wpx` (where *x* refers to the version number), respectively, and most C++ compilers require a program file to have the extension cpp. When creating your own file names you should adhere to this practice. For example, the name `prices.bnd` is appropriate in describing a file of prices used in a bond application.

File Stream Objects and Modes

A **file stream** is any stream that connects a file stored on a physical device, such as a disk or CD-ROM, to a program. Additionally, every file stream has a mode, which determines whether the stream will be used for reading data from a file or writing data to a file. A file stream with an input mode is referred to as an **input file stream** and is used to receive or read data from a file. A file stream with an output mode is referred to as an **output file stream** and is used to send or write data to a file. Figure 10.1 illustrates the data flow from and to a file using input and output streams.

FIGURE 10.1 Input and Output File Streams

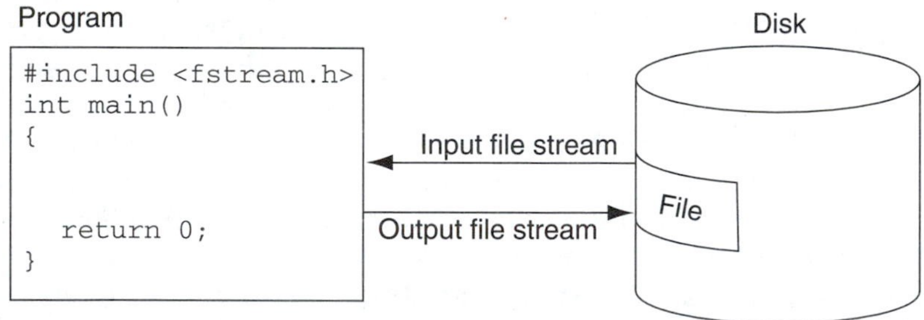

[1] Since Windows 3.1 runs under DOS, it has the same restrictions as DOS. Technically, Windows 3.1 is not an operating system at all, but an application that runs under DOS. It more properly should be referred to as a dynamic linker and file managing application.

POINT OF INFORMATION

Input and Output Streams

A *stream* is a one-way transmission path between a source and a destination. What gets sent down this transmission path is a stream of bytes. A good analogy to this "stream of bytes" is a stream of water that provides a one-way transmission path of water from a source to a destination.

Stream objects are created from stream classes. Two stream objects that we have used extensively are the input stream object named `cin` and the output stream object named cout. The `cin` object provides a transmission path from keyboard to program while the `cout` object provides a transmission path from program to terminal screen. These two objects are created from the stream classes `istream` and `ostream`, respectively, which are parent classes to the `iostream` class. When the `iostream.h` header file is included in a program using the `#include <iostream.h>` directive, the `cin` and `cout` stream objects are automatically declared and opened by the C++ compiler for the compiled program.

File streams objects provide the same capabilities as the `cin` and `cout` objects, except they connect a program to a file rather than the keyboard or terminal screen. Also file stream objects must be explicitly declared. File stream objects that will be used for input must be declared as type `ifstream`, while file stream objects that will be used for output must be declared as type `ofstream`. The classes `ifstream` and `ofstream` are made available to a program by inclusion of the `fstream.h` header file using the directive `#include <fstream.h>`.

For each file that your program uses, a distinct file stream object must be created. If you are going to both read and write to a file, both input and output file stream objects are required. Input file stream objects are declared to be of type `ifstream`, and output file streams are declared to be of type `ofstream`. For example, the declaration

```
ifstream in_stream;
```

declares an input file stream object named `in_stream` that is of type `ifstream`. Similarly, the declaration

```
ofstream out_stream;
```

declares an output file stream object named `out_stream` that is of type `ofstream`. Within a C++ program a file stream is always accessed by its appropriate stream object name, one name for reading the file and one name for writing to the file. Object names, such as `in_stream` and `out_stream`, can be any programmer-chosen names that conform to C++'s identifier rules.

File Stream Methods

Each file stream object has access to the methods defined for its respective `ifstream` or `ofstream` class. These methods include connecting a stream object name to an external file name (called *opening a file*), determining if a successful connection has been made, closing a connection (called *closing a file*), getting the next data item into the program from an input stream, putting a new data item from the program onto an output stream, and detecting when the end of a file has been reached.

Opening a file connects each file stream object to a specific external file name. This is accomplished using a file stream's open method, which is a "cookbook" procedure that accomplishes two purposes. First, opening a file establishes the physical connecting link between a program and a file. Since details of this link are handled by the computer's operating system and are transparent to the program, the programmer normally need not consider them.

From a coding perspective, the second purpose of opening a file is more relevant. Besides establishing the actual physical connection between a program and a data file, opening a file equates the file's external computer name to the stream object name used internally by the program. The method that performs this task is the `open()` method and is provided by both the `ifstream` and `ostream` classes.

In using the `open()` method to connect the file's external name to its internal object stream name, only one argument is required, which is the external file name. For example, the statement

```
in_file.open("prices.dat");
```

connects the external file named `prices.dat` to the internal program file stream object named `in_file`. This assumes, of course, that `in_file` has been declared as either an `ifstream` or `ofstream` object. If a file has been opened with the preceding statement, the program accesses the file using the internal object name `in_file`, while the computer saves the file under the external name `prices.dat`. Notice that the external file name argument passed to `open()` is a string contained between double quotes. Also notice that calling the `open()` method requires the standard object notation where the name of the desired method, in this case `open()`, is preceded by a period and an object name.

When an existing file is connected to an input file stream, the file's data is made available for input, starting at the first data item in the file. Similarly, a file connected to an output file stream creates a new file and makes the file available for output. If a file exists with the same name as a file opened for output, the old file is erased and all of its data is lost.

When opening a file, for input or output, good programming practice requires that you check that the connection has been established before attempting to use the file in any way. The check can be made using the `fail()` method. This method will return a true value, which is a 1, if the open was successful, or a false value, which is a 0, if the open failed. Typically the `fail()` method is used in code similar to the following, which attempts to open a file named `prices.dat`, checks that a valid connection was made, and reports an error message if the file was not successfully opened for input:

```
ifstream in_file;  // any object name can be used here

in_file.open("prices.dat");  // open the file

// check that the connection was successfully opened
if (in_file.fail())
{
  cout << "\nThe file was not successfully opened"
       << "\n Please check that the file currently exists."
       << endl;
  exit(1);
}
```

If the `fail()` method returns a true, which indicates that the open failed, a message is displayed by this code and the `exit()` function, which is a request to the operating system to end program execution immediately, is called. The `exit()` function requires inclusion of the `stdlib.h` header function in any program that uses this function, and `exit()`'s single integer argument is passed directly to the operating system for possible further operating system program action or user inspection. Throughout the remainder of the text, we will include this type of error checking whenever a file is opened.

Program 10.1 illustrates the statements required to open a file in read mode and includes an error-checking routine to ensure that a successful open was obtained.

PROGRAM 10.1

```
#include <fstream.h>
#include <stdlib.h>    // needed for exit()

int main()
{
  ifstream in_file;

  in_file.open("prices.dat");  // open the file with the
                               // external name prices.dat
  if (in_file.fail())  // check for a successful open
  {
    cout << "\nThe file was not successfully opened"
         << "\n Please check that the file currently exists."
         << endl;
    exit(1);
  }

  cout << "\nThe file has been successfully opened for reading."
       << endl;

  return 0;
}
```

A sample run using Program 10.1 produced the output:

```
The file has been successfully opened for reading.
```

Although Program 10.1 can be used to open an existing file for input, it clearly lacks statements to either read the file's data or close the file. These topics are discussed shortly. Before leaving Program 10.1, however, two items should be noted. First, the `iostream.h` header file did not have to be included in the program to use the `cout` object because its definition is incorporated within the `fstream.h`

POINT OF INFORMATION

Checking for a Successful Connection

It is important to check that the `open()` method successfully established a connection between a file stream and an external file. This is because the `open()` call is really a request to the operating system that can fail for a variety of reasons. Chief among these reasons is a request to open an existing file for reading that the operating system cannot locate. If the operating system cannot satisfy the open request, for whatever reason, you need to know about it and gracefully terminate your program. Failure to do so almost always results in some abnormal program behavior or a subsequent program crash.

The most common method for checking that a fail did not occur is the one coded in Program 10.1, and is repeated below for convenience:

```
in_file.open("prices.dat");  // request to open the file

if (in_file.fail())    // check for a failed connection
{
  cout << "\nThe file was not successfully opened"
          << "\n Please check that the file currently exists."
       << endl;
  exit(1);
}
```

Alternatively, you may encounter programs that use `fstream` objects in place of both `ifstream` and `ofstream` objects. When using `fstream`'s `open()` method two arguments are required; a file's external name and an explicit mode indication. If the `open()` function is not successful, the `fstream` stream object is assigned the named constant `NULL`. Using this named constant, the open request and check typically appear as follows:

```
fstream in_file;

infile.open("external file name", ios::in);
if (in_file == NULL)
{
 cout << "\nThe file was not successfully opened"
         << "\n Please check that the file currently exists."
      << endl;
 exit(1);
}
```

Many times the conditional expression `in_file == NULL` is replaced by the equivalent expression `!in_file`. Although we will always use `ifstream` and `ofstream` objects, be prepared to encounter the style that uses `fstream` objects.

header file. Next, it is possible to combine the declaration of an `fstream` object and its associated open statement into one statement. For example, the following two statements in Program 10.1

```
ifstream in_file;
in_file.open("prices.dat"); // open the file
```

can be combined into this single statement:

```
ifstream in_file("prices.dat);
```

In this text we will continue to declare all `ifstream` and `ofstream` objects at the top of the program and explicitly call the `open()` method in a separate statement. You may, however, choose to use the alternative single statement form.

Embedded and Interactive File Names

Program 10.1 has two practical problems:

1. The external file name is embedded within the program code.
2. There is no provision for a user to enter the desired file name while the program is executing.

Thus, as Program 10.1 is written, if the file name is to change a programmer must modify the external file name in the call to `open()` and recompile the program. Both of these problems can be alleviated by assigning the file name to a string variable.

A **string variable** is a variable that can hold a string value, which is any sequence of zero or more characters enclosed within double quotes. For example, `"Hello World"`, `"prices.dat"`, and `""` are all strings. Notice that strings are always written with double quotes that delimit the beginning and end of a string but are not stored as part of the string.

Although the concepts, storage, and manipulation of strings and string variables are discussed in detail in Chapter 12, the declaration of a string variable is extremely simple. For example, while the declaration

```
char filename = 'a';
```

declares a character variable named `filename` and initializes this character variable to the single letter `a`, the declaration

```
char filename[21] = "prices.dat";
```

declares a string variable capable of holding 21 characters in total and initializes the string variable with the string value `"prices.dat"`.

In declaring and initializing a string variable three items must be considered. First, the maximum length of the string must be specified within brackets immediately after the variable's name. This is the purpose of the `[21]` in the preceding declaration. Secondly, *the number in brackets always represents one less than the maximum number of characters that you can assign to the variable.* This is because the compiler always adds a final end-of-string character to terminate the string. Thus the string value `"prices.dat"`, which consists of 10 characters, is actually stored as 11 characters. The extra character is an end-of-string marker supplied by the compiler. Finally, each initializing string value can be any sequence of characters from zero to one less than the maximum length specifier in brackets. Thus the maximum string value assignable to the string variable filename is a string value consisting of 20 characters.

Once a string variable is declared to store a file name it can be used in one of two ways. First, as shown in Program 10.1a, it can be placed at the top of a program to clearly identify a file's external name, rather than embed it within an `open()` method call.

POINT OF INFORMATION

Character and String Variables

The primary difference between character and string variables is that a character variable can only store a single character value, while a string variable can store a string value of zero or more characters. The stored value, however, always contains an additional end-of-string symbolic constant named `NULL`. For example, consider the declarations

```
char nameOne = 'x';
char nameTwo[2] = "x";
```

First notice that the initializing character value is enclosed within single quotes, while the initializing string value is enclosed in double quotes. In the first case only one character, an `x`, is stored in the character variable `nameOne`. In the second case two characters are stored. These consist of the `x` character plus an end-of-string termination character supplied by the compiler. For all string variables, this character is the named constant `NULL`, which has the value `'\0'`. As we will see in Chapter 12, this end-of-string `NULL` constant is extremely useful in processing strings. This is because it provides a relatively easy method of always determining where a string ends without knowing, before hand, the actual string length. Because of this terminating `NULL`, a string value such as `""` is not stored as an empty string, but consists of the single `NULL` terminating character.

One other very important difference between character and string variables is that *assignment to a string variable is always invalid except within a declaration statement.* Assignment in nondeclarative statements is accomplished using the `strcopy()` function, which is described in Chapter 12.

PROGRAM 10.1a

```
#include <fstream.h>
#include <stdlib.h>

const int MAXLENGTH = 21;  // maximum file name length

char file1[MAXLENGTH] = "prices.dat";    // place the file name up front

int main()
{
  ifstream in_file;

  in_file.open(file1);  // open the file

  if (in_file.fail())  // check for successful open
  {
    cout << "\nThe file named " << file1 << " was not successfully opened"
      << "\n Please check that the file currently exists." << endl;
    exit(1);
  }

  cout << "\nThe file has been successfully opened for reading.\n";

  return 0;
}
```

In reviewing Program 10.1a notice that we have used the named constant `MAXLENGTH` to define the length of the string variable `file1` and that we have declared and initialized this string variable at the top of the program for easy file identification. Next notice that when a string variable is used, as opposed to a string value, the variable name is *not* enclosed within double quotes, as in the `open()` method call. Finally, notice that in the `fail()` method code we can display the file's external name by inserting the string variable's name in the `cout` standard output stream. For all of these reasons, we will continue to identify the external names of files in this manner.

Another extremely useful role played by string variables is to permit the user to enter the file name while the program is executing. For example, the code

```
const int MAXLENGTH = 21;
char file1[MAXLENGTH];

cout << "Please enter the name of the file you wish to open: ";
cin  >> file1;
```

allows a user to enter a file's external name at run time. The only restriction in this code is that the user *must not* enclose the entered string value in double quotes, which is a plus, and that the entered string value cannot contain any blanks. The reason for this is that the program will terminate string entry when it encounters a blank.

Program 10.1b uses this code in the context of a complete program.

PROGRAM 10.1b

```
#include <fstream.h>
#include <stdlib.h>

const int MAXLENGTH = 21;   // maximum file name length

char file1[MAXLENGTH];

int main()
{
  ifstream in_file;

  cout << "Please enter the name of the file you wish to open: ";
  cin  >> file1;

  in_file.open(file1);  // open the file

  if (in_file.fail())  // check for successful open
  {
    cout << "\nThe file named " << file1 << " was not successfully opened"
      << "\n Please check that the file currently exists." << endl;
    exit(1);
  }

  cout << "\nThe file has been successfully opened for reading.\n";

  return 0;
}
```

POINT OF INFORMATION

Using `fstream` Objects

In using both `ifstream` and `ofstream` objects the mode, input or output, is implied by the object. Thus, `ifstream` objects can only be used for input while `ofstream` objects can only be used for output.

Another means of creating file streams is to use `fstream` objects which can be used for input or output but require an explicit mode specification. An `fstream` object is declared using the syntax

```
fstream object-name;
```

When using the `fstream` class's `open()` member function, two arguments are required: a file's external name and a mode indicator. Permissible mode indicators are as follows:

Indicator	Description
`ios::in`	Open in input mode.
`ios::out`	Open in output mode.
`ios::app`	Open in append mode.
`ios::ate`	Go to the end of the opened file.
`ios::binary`	Open in binary mode (default is text).
`ios::trunc`	Delete file contents if it exists.
`ios::nocreate`	If file does not exist, open fails.
`ios::noreplace`	If file exists, open for output fails.

As with `ofstream` objects, an `fstream` object in output mode creates a new file and makes the file available for writing. If a file exists with the same name as a file opened for output, the old file is erased. For example, assuming that `file1` has been declared as an object of type `fstream` using the statement

```
fstream file1;
```

then the statement

```
file1.open("prices.dat",ios::out);
```

attempts to open the file named `prices.dat` for output. Once this file has been opened the program accesses the file using the internal object name `file1`, while the computer saves the file under the external name `prices.dat`.

An `fstream` file object opened in append mode means that an existing file is available for data to be added to the end of the file. If the file opened for appending does not exist, a new file with the designated name is created and made available to receive output from the program. For example, again assuming that `file1` has been declared to be of type `fstream`, the statement

```
file1.open("prices.dat",ios::app);
```

attempts to open the file named `prices.dat` and makes it available for data to be appended to the end of the file.

Finally, an `fstream` object successfully opened in input mode means that an existing external file has been opened and its data is available as input. For example, assuming that `file1` has been declared to be of type `fstream`, the statement

```
file1.open("prices.dat",ios::in);
```

attempts to open a file named `prices.dat` for input.

A sample run using Program 10.1b produced the output:

```
Please enter the name of the file you wish to open: foobar
The file named foobar was not successfully opened
 Please check that the file currently exists.
```

Closing a File

A file is closed using the `close()` method. This method breaks the connection between the file's external name and the file stream object, which can then be used for another file. For example, the statement

```
in_file.close();
```

closes the `in_file` stream's connection to its current file. As indicated, the `close()` method takes no argument.

Since all computers have a limit on the maximum number of files that can be open at one time, closing files that are no longer needed makes good sense. Any open files existing at the end of normal program execution will be automatically closed by the operating system.

Exercises 10.1

1. a. Enter and execute Program 10.1 on your computer.
   b. Add a `close()` method to Program 10.1 and then execute the program.
2. a. Enter and execute Program 10.1a on your computer.
   b. Add a `close()` method to Program 10.1a and then execute the program.
3. a. Enter and execute Program 10.1b on your computer.
   b. Add a `close()` method to Program 10.1b and then execute the program.
4. Using the reference manuals provided with your computer's operating system, determine:
   a. the maximum number of characters that can be used to name a file for storage by the computer system
   b. the maximum number of data files that can be open at the same time
5. Would it be appropriate to call a saved C++ program a file? Why or why not?
6. a. Write a suitable declaration statement for each of the following `ifstream` objects: `in_data`, `prices`, `coupons`, and `file1`.
   b. Write a suitable declaration statement for each of the following `ofstream` objects: `out_date`, `rates`, `distance`, and `file2`.
7. Write individual declaration and open statements to link the following external data file names to their corresponding internal object names:

External Name	Object Name	Mode
`coba.mem`	`memo`	Output
`book.let`	`letter`	Output
`coupons.bnd`	`coups`	Output
`yield.bnd`	`pt_yield`	Input
`prices.dat`	`pri_file`	Input
`rates.dat`	`rates`	Input

8. Write close statements for each of the files opened in Exercise 7.

10.2 READING AND WRITING FILES

Reading or writing to a file involves almost identical operations for reading input from a terminal and writing data to a display screen. For writing to a file, the `cout` object is replaced by the `ofstream` object declared in the program. For example, if `out_file` is declared as an object of type `ofstream` the following output statements are valid.

```
out_file << 'a';
out_file << "Hello World!";
out_file << descrip << ' ' << price;
```

The file name in each of these statements, in place of `cout`, simply directs the output stream to a specific file instead of to the standard display device. Program 10.2 illustrates the use of an output file stream to write a list of descriptions and prices to a file.

PROGRAM 10.2

```
#include <fstream.h>
#include <stdlib.h>
#include <iomanip.h>

const int MAXLENGTH = 21;  // maximum file name length

char filename[MAXLENGTH] = "prices.dat";  // put the file name up front

int main()
{
  ofstream out_file;

  out_file.open(filename);

  if (out_file.fail())
  {
    cout << "The file was not successfully opened" << endl;
    exit(1);
  }

     // set the output file stream formats
   out_file << setiosflags(ios::fixed)
            << setiosflags(ios::showpoint)
            << setprecision(2);

     // send data to the file
   out_file << "Batteries " << 39.95 << endl
            << "Bulbs "  << 3.22 << endl
            << "Fuses " << 1.00;

   out_file.close();

   return 0;
}
```

POINT OF INFORMATION

Formatting File Stream Data

Output file streams can be formatted in the same manner as the `cout` standard output stream. For example, if an output stream named `file_out` has been declared, the statement

```
file_out << setiosflags(ios::fixed)
         << setiosflags(ios::showpoint)
         << setprecision(2);
```

formats all data inserted in the `file_out` stream in the same way that these parameterized manipulators work for the `cout` stream. The first manipulator parameter, `ios::fixed`, causes the stream to output all numbers as if they were floating-point or double-precision values. The next parameter, `ios::showpoint`, tells the stream to always provide a decimal point. Thus, a value such as 1.0 will appear as 1.0, and not 1. Finally, the setprecision manipulator tells the stream to always display 2 decimal values after the decimal point. Thus, the number 1.0 for example, will appear as 1.00.

Instead of using manipulators, you can also use the stream methods `setf()` and `precision()`. For example, the previous formatting can also be accomplished using the code:

```
file_out.setf(ios::fixed);
file_out.setf(ios::showpoint);
file.out.precision(2);
```

Which style you select is a matter of preference. In both cases the formats need only be specified once and remain in effect for every number subsequently inserted into the file stream.

When Program 10.2 is executed, a file named `prices.dat` is created and saved by the computer. The file is a sequential file consisting of the following data:

```
Batteries 39.95
Bulbs 3.22
Fuses 1.00
```

The actual storage of characters in the file depends on the character codes used by the computer. Although only 35 characters appear to be stored in the file, corresponding to the descriptions, blanks, and prices written to the file, the file actually contains 38 characters. The extra characters consist of the newline escape sequence at the end of the first two lines and the special end-of-file marker placed as the last item in the file when the file is closed. Assuming characters are stored using the ASCII code, the `prices.dat` file is physically stored as illustrated in Figure 10.2. For convenience, the character corresponding to each hexadecimal code is listed below the code. A code of 20 represents the blank character. Although the actual code used for the end-of-file marker depends on the system you are using, the hexadecimal code 26, corresponding to Control-Z, is common for the DOS operating system.

Reading data from a file is almost identical to reading data from a standard keyboard, except that the `cin` object is replaced by the `fstream` object declared in the program. For example, if `in_file` is declared as an object of type `fstream` that is opened for input, the input statement

```
in_file >> descrip >> price;
```

FIGURE 10.2 The `prices.dat` File as Stored by the Computer

```
42 61 74 74 65 72 69 65 73 20 33 39 2e 32 35 0A 42 75 6c 62 73
 B  a  t  t  e  r  i  e  s     3  9  .  2  5 \n  B  u  l  b  s
20 33 2e 32 32 0A 46 75 73 65 73 20 31 2e 30 32 26
    3  .  2  2 \n  F  u  s  e  s     1  .  0  0 ^Z
```

will read the next two items in the file and store them in the variables `descrip` and `price`.

The file stream name in this statement, in place of `cin`, simply directs the input to come from the file stream rather than the standard input device stream, `cin`. Other methods that can be used for file manipulation are listed in Table 10.2. Each of these methods must, of course, be preceded by a file stream object name.

TABLE 10.2 Stream Methods

Method Name	Description
`get(character-variable)`	Extract the next character from the input stream.
`getline(string var,int n,'\n')`	Extract characters from the input stream until either $n - 1$ characters are read or a newline is encountered (terminates the input with a `'\0'`).
`peek(character-variable)`	Return the next character in the input stream without extracting it from the stream.
`put(character-expression)`	Put the character on the output stream.
`putback(character-expression)`	Push a character back onto the input stream. Does not alter the data in the file.
`eof(void)`	Returns a `True` if a read has been attempted past the EOF (end-of-file).
`ignore(int n)`	Skip over the next `n` characters; If `n` is omitted, the default is to skip over the next single character.

Reading data from a file requires the programmer to know how the data appears in the file. This is necessary for correct "stripping" of the data from the file into appropriate variables for storage. All files are read sequentially, so that once an item is read the next item in the file becomes available for reading.

Program 10.3 illustrates how the `prices.dat` file that was created in Program 10.2 can be read. The program also illustrates how the end-of-file (EOF) marker, can be detected by the `peek()` function. As long as the EOF has not been detected, the program will continue to read characters from the file.

PROGRAM 10.3

```
#include <fstream.h>
#include <stdlib.h>
#include <iomanip.h>

const int MAXLENGTH = 21;   // maximum file name length
const int MAXCHARS = 31;    // maximum description length

char filename[MAXLENGTH] = "prices.dat";

int main()
{
  int ch;
  char descrip[MAXCHARS];
  float price;
  ifstream in_file;

  in_file.open(filename);

  if (in_file.fail())  // check for successful open
  {
    cout << "\nThe file was not successfully opened"
      << "\n Please check that the file currently exists."
      << endl;
    exit(1);
  }

    // set the format for the standard output stream
  cout << setiosflags(ios::fixed)
       << setiosflags(ios::showpoint)
       << setprecision(2);

  cout << endl;  // start on a new line

    // read and display the file's contents
  while ( (ch = in_file.peek()) != EOF ) // check next character
  {
    in_file >> descrip >> price;  // input the data
    cout << descrip << ' ' << price << endl;
  }

  in_file.close();

  return 0;
}
```

PROGRAMMING NOTE

The `ostream put()` Method

All output streams have a `put()` method that permits character-by-character output to a stream. This method works in the same manner as the character insertion operator, <<. The syntax of this method call is:

```
ostream-name.put(character-expression);
```

where the character expression can be either a character variable or character value.

For example, the following code can be used to output an `'a'` to the standard output stream:

```
cin.put('a');
```

In a similar manner, if `out_file` is an `ostream` object that has been opened to a file, the following code outputs the character value in the character variable named `keycode` to this output:

```
char keycode;
   .
   .
out_file.put(keycode);
```

Program 10.3 continues to read the file until the EOF marker has been detected. Each time the file is read, a string and a floating-point number are input to the program. The display produced by Program 10.3 is:

```
Batteries 39.95
Bulbs 3.22
Fuses 1.00
```

In place of the `in_file` extraction operator, >>, used in Program 10.3, a `getline()` method call could have been used. The `getline()` method requires three arguments: a string variable where the characters read from the file will be stored, the maximum number of characters to be input in a single read, and a terminating character. For example, the function call

```
in_file.getline(line,80,'\n');
```

causes a maximum of 79 characters (one less than the specified number) to be read from the file named `in_file` and stored starting in the string variable named `line`. The `getline()` method continues reading characters until 79 characters have been read or a newline character has been encountered. If a newline character is encountered, it is included with the other entered characters before the string is terminated with the end-of-string `NULL` marker, `\0`. Program 10.4 illustrates the use of `getline()` in a working program.

Program 10.4 is really a line-by-line text-copying program, reading a line of text from the file and then displaying it on the terminal. The output of Program 10.4 is:

```
Batteries 39.95
Bulbs 3.22
Fuses 1.00
```

PROGRAM 10.4

```
#include <fstream.h>
#include <stdlib.h>
#include <iomanip.h>

const int MAXLENGTH = 21;  // maximum file name length
const int MAXCHARS = 80;   // maximum line length

char file1[MAXLENGTH] = "prices.dat";

int main()
{
  int ch;
  char line[MAXCHARS];
  ifstream in_file;

  in_file.open(file1);

  if (in_file.fail())   // check for successful open
  {
    cout << "\nThe file was not successfully opened"
      << "\n Please check that the file currently exists."
      << endl;
    exit(1);
  }

  cout << endl;   // start on a new line

    // now read the file
  while( (ch = in_file.peek()) != EOF )
  {
    in_file.getline(line,MAXCHARS,'\n');
    cout << line << endl;
  }

  in_file.close();

  return 0;
}
```

If it were necessary to obtain the description and price as individual variables, either Program 10.3 should be used or the string returned by `getline()` in Program 10.4 must be processed further to extract the individual data items.

Standard Device Files

The file stream objects we have used have all been logical file objects. A **logical file object** is a stream that connects a file of logically related data such as a data

PROGRAMMING NOTE

The `istream get()` and `putback()` Methods

All input streams have a `get()` method that permits character-by-character input from the stream. This method works in a manner similar to character extraction using the >> operator with two important differences; if a newline character, `'\n'`, or a blank character, `' '`, is encountered, these characters are read in the same manner as any other alphanumeric character. The syntax of this method call is:

```
istream-name.get(character-variable);
```

For example, the following code can be used to read the next character from the standard input stream and store the character into the variable `ch`:

```
char ch;
cin.get(ch);
```

In a similar manner, if `in_file` is an `istream` object that has been opened to a file, the following code reads the next character in the stream and assigns it to the character `keycode`:

```
char keycode;
in_file.get(keycode);
```

In addition to the `get()` method, all input streams have a `putback()` method that can be used to put the last character read from an input stream back on the stream. This method has the syntax

```
istream-name.putback(character-expression);
```

where `character-expression` can be any character variable or character value.

The `putback()` method provides an output capability to an input stream. Note that the putback character need not be the last character read; rather, it can be any character. All putback characters, however, have no effect on the data file but only on the open input stream. Thus, the data file characters remain unchanged, although the characters subsequently read from the input stream can change. `putback()` is typically used to permit prescanning of a character from an input stream by first using a `get()` followed by an immediate return of the same character to the stream.

file to a program. In addition to logical file objects, C++ also supports physical file objects. A **physical file object** is a stream that connects to a hardware device, such as a keyboard, screen, or printer.

The actual physical device assigned to your program for data entry is formally called the standard input file. Usually this is the keyboard. When a `cin` object method call is encountered in a C++ program, a request goes to the operating system to this standard input file for the expected input. Similarly, when a `cout` object method call is encountered, the output is automatically displayed or "written to" a device that has been assigned as the standard output file. For most systems this is a terminal screen, although it can be a printer.

When a program is executed, the standard input stream `cin` is automatically connected to the standard input device. Similarly, the standard output stream `cout` is automatically connected to the standard output device. These two object streams are always available for programmer use.

Other Devices

The keyboard, display, and error-reporting devices are automatically connected to the internal stream objects named `cin`, `cout`, and `cerr`, respectively, by a C++ program using either the `iostream.h` or fstream.h header files. Additionally, other devices can be used for input or output if the name assigned by the system is known. For example, most IBM or IBM-compatible personal computers assign the name `prn` to the printer connected to the computer. For these computers a statement such as `out_file.open("prn")` connects the printer to the `ofstream` object named `out_file`. A subsequent statement, such as `out_file << "Hello World!";` would then cause the string `Hello World!` to be printed directly on the printer. Notice that as the name of an actual file, `prn` must be enclosed in double quotes in the `open()` function call.

Exercises 10.2

1. a. Write a C++ program that accepts three lines of text from the keyboard and writes each line to a file named `text.dat`.

   b. Modify Program 10.4 to read and display the data stored in the `text.dat` file created in Exercise 1a.

2. Determine the operating system command provided by your computer to display the contents of a saved file. Compare its operation with the program developed for Exercise 1b. (*Hint:* Typically the operating system command is called `LIST`, `TYPE`, or `CAT`.)

3. a. Create a file named `employ.dat` containing the following data:

```
Anthony   A   10031    7.82   12/18/62
Burrows   W   10067    9.14    6/09/63
Fain      B   10083    8.79    5/18/59
Janney    P   10095   10.57    9/28/62
Smith     G   10105    8.50   12/20/61
```

   b. Write a C++ program called `fcopy.c` to read the `employ.dat` file created in Exercise 3a and produce a duplicate copy of the file named `employ.bak`.

   c. Modify the program written in Exercise 3b to accept the names of the original and duplicate files as user input.

   d. Since the program written for Exercise 3b always copies data from an original file to a duplicate file, can you think of a better method of accepting the original and duplicate file names than prompting the user for them each time the program is executed?

4. a. Write a C++ program that opens a file and displays the contents of the file with associated line numbers. That is, the program should print `1` before displaying the first line, `2` before displaying the second line, and so on for each line in the file.

   b. Modify the program written in Exercise 4a to list the contents of the file on the printer assigned to your computer.

5. a. Create a file containing the following names, Social Security numbers, hourly rate, and hours worked:

```
Caldwell   163-98-4182   7.32   37
Memcheck   189-53-2147   8.32   40
Potter     145-32-9826   6.54   40
Rosen      163-09-4263   9.80   35
```

b. Write a C++ program that reads the data file created in Exercise 5a and computes and displays a payroll schedule. The output should list the Social Security number, name, and gross pay for each individual.

6. a. Create a file containing the following car numbers, number of miles driven, and number of gallons of gas used by each car:

Car No.	Miles Driven	Gallons Used
54	250	19
62	525	38
71	123	6
85	1,322	86
97	235	14

b. Write a C++ program that reads the data in the file created in Exercise 6a and displays the car number, miles driven, gallons used, and the miles per gallon for each car. The output should additionally contain the total miles driven, total gallons used, and average miles per gallon for all the cars. These totals should be displayed at the end of the output report.

7. a. Create a file with the following data containing the part number, opening balance, number of items sold, and minimum stock required:

Part Number	Initial Amount	Quantity Sold	Minimum Amount
QA310	95	47	50
CM145	320	162	200
MS514	34	20	25
EN212	163	150	160

b. Write a C++ program to create an inventory report based on the data in the file created in Exercise 7a. The display should consist of the part number, current balance, and the amount that is necessary to bring the inventory to the minimum level.

8. a. Create a file containing the following data:

Name	Rate	Hours
Callaway, G.	6.00	40
Hanson, P.	5.00	48
Lasard, D.	6.50	35
Stillman, W.	8.00	50

b. Write a C++ program that uses the information contained in the file created in Exercise 8a to produce the following pay report for each employee:

```
Name    Rate    Hours    Regular Pay    Overtime Pay    Gross Pay
```

Any hours worked above 40 hours are paid at time and a half. At the end of the individual output for each employee, the program should display the totals of the regular, overtime, and gross pay columns.

9. a. Store the following data in a file:

```
5 96 87 78 93 21 4 92 82 85 87 6 72 69 85 75 81 73
```

b. Write a C++ program to calculate and display the average of each group of numbers in the file created in Exercise 9a. The data is arranged in the file so that each group of numbers is preceded by the number of data items in the group. Thus, the first number in the file, 5, indicates that the next five numbers should be grouped together. The number 4 indicates that the following four numbers are a group, and the 6 indicates that the last six numbers are a group. (*Hint:* Use a nested loop. The outer loop should terminate when the EOF marker is encountered.)

10.3 RANDOM FILE ACCESS

File organization refers to the way data is stored in a file. All the files we have used have **sequential organization.** This means that the characters in the file are stored in a sequential manner, one after another. Additionally, we have read the files in a sequential manner. The way data is retrieved from the file is called **file access.** The fact that the characters in the file are stored sequentially, however, does not force us to access the file sequentially.

In **random access** any character in the file can be read directly, without first having to read all the characters stored ahead of it. To provide random access to files, each `ifstream` object establishes a file position marker. This marker is a long integer that represents an offset from the beginning of each file and keeps track of where the next character is to be read from or written to. Member functions that can be used to access and change the file position marker are listed in Table 10.3.

TABLE 10.3 File Position Marker Functions

Name[2]	Description
`seekg(offset, mode)`	For input files, move to the offset position as indicated by the mode.
`seekp(offset, mode)`	For output files, move to the offset position as indicated by the mode.
`tellg(void)`	For input files, return the current value of the file position marker.
`tellp(void)`	For output files, return the current value of the file position marker.

The seek functions allow the programmer to move to any position in the file. To understand this function, you must first clearly understand how data is referenced in the file using the file position marker.

Each character in a data file is located by its position in the file. The first character in the file is located at position 0, the next character at position 1, and so on. A character's position is also referred to as its offset from the start of the file. Thus, the first character has a 0 offset, the second character has an offset of 1, and so on, for each character in the file.

The seek functions require two arguments: the offset, as a long integer, into the file; and where the offset is to be calculated from, as determined by the mode. The three possible alternatives for the mode are `ios::beg`, `ios::cur`, and `ios::end`, which denote the beginning, current position, and the end of the file, respectively. Thus, a mode of `ios::beg` means the offset is the true offset from the start of the file. A mode of `ios::cur` means that the offset is relative to the current position in the file, and an `ios::end` mode means the offset is relative to the end of the file. A positive offset means that we are to move forward in the file

[2] The suffixes `g` and `p` in Table 10.3 denote `get` and `put`, respectively, where `get` refers to an input (get from) file and `put` refers to an output (put to) file.

PROGRAMMING NOTE

A Way to Clearly Identify a File's Name and Location

During program development test files are usually placed in the same directory as the program. Therefore, a method call such as `in_file.open("exper.dat")` causes no problems to the operating system. In production systems, however, it is not uncommon for data files to reside in one directory while program files reside in another. For this reason it is always a good idea to include the full path name of any file opened.

For example, if the `exper.dat` file resides in the directory `/test/files`, the `open()` call should include the full path name, namely, `in_file.open("/test/files/exper.dat")`. Then, no matter where the program is run from, the operating system will know where to locate the file.

Another important convention is to list all file names at the top of a program instead of embedding the names deep within the code. This can easily be accomplished by string variables to store each file name. For example, if the statements:

```
const int MAXLENGTH = 31;
char file1[MAXLENGTH] = "\test\files\exper.dat";
```

are placed at the top of a program file, the declaration statement clearly lists both the name of the desired file and its location. Then, if some other file is to be tested, all that is required is a simple one-line change at the top of the program.

Using a string variable for the file's name is also useful for the `fail()` method check. For example, consider the following code:

```
ifstream infile;

in_file.open(file1);

if (in_file.fail())
{
  cout << "\n The file named " << file1 << was not successfully opened"
       <<\n Please check that this file currently exists.";
  exit(1);
}
```

In this code the name of the file that failed to open is directly displayed within the error message without the name being embedded as a string value.

and a negative offset means we will move backward. Examples of seek function calls are shown in the following list. In these examples, assume that `in_file` has been opened as an input file and `out_file` as an output file:

```
in_file.seekg(4L,ios::beg);     // go to the fifth character in the input file
out_file.seekp(4L,ios::beg);    // go to the fifth character in the output file
in_file.seekg(4L,ios::cur);     // move ahead five characters in the input file
out_file.seekp(4L,ios::cur);    // move ahead five characters in the output file
in_file.seekg(-4L,ios::cur);    // move back five characters in the input file
out_file.seekp(-4L,ios::cur);   // move back five characters in the output file
in_file.seekg(0L,ios::beg);     // go to start of the input file
out_file.seekp(0L,ios::beg);    // go to start of the output file
in_file.seekg(0L,ios::end);     // go to end of the input file
out_file.seekp(0L,ios::end);    // go to end of the output file
in_file.seekg(-10L,ios::end);   // go to 10 characters before the input file's end
out_file.seekp(-10L,ios::end);  // go to 10 characters before the output file's end
```

Notice in these examples that the offset passed to `seekg()` and `seekp()` must be a long integer.

As opposed to the seek functions that move the file position marker, the tell functions simply return the offset value of the file position marker. For example, if 10 characters have already been read from an input file named `in_file`, the function call

```
in_file.tellg();
```

returns the long integer `10`. This means that the next character to be read is offset 10 byte positions from the start of the file, and is the eleventh character in the file.

Program 10.5 illustrates the use of `seekg()` and `tellg()` to read a file in reverse order, from last character to first. As each character is read, it is also displayed.

PROGRAM 10.5

```
#include <fstream.h>
#include <stdlib.h>

const int MAXLENGTH = 31;

char filename[MAXLENGTH] = "test.dat";

int main()
{
  char ch;
  long offset, last;

  ifstream in_file(filename);

  if (in_file.fail())    // check for successful open
  {
    cout << "\nThe file was not successfully opened"
      << "\n Please check that the file currently exists"
      << endl;
    exit(1);
  }

  in_file.seekg(0L,ios::end);    // move to the end of the file
  last = in_file.tellg();        // save the offset of the last character

  for(offset = 1L; offset <= last; offset++)
  {
    in_file.seekg(-offset, ios::end);
    ch = in_file.get();
    cout << ch << " : ";
  }

  in_file.close();

  return 0;
}
```

Assuming the file `test.dat` contains the following data,

```
The grade was 92.5
```

the output of Program 10.5 is:

```
5 : . : 2 : 9 : : s : a : w : : e : d : a : r : g : : e : h : T :
```

Program 10.5 initially goes to the last character in the file. The offset of this character, which is the end-of-file character, is saved in the variable `last`. Since `tellg()` returns a long integer, `last` has been declared as long integer.

Starting from the end of the file, `seekg()` is used to position the next character to be read, referenced from the end of the file. As each character is read, the character is displayed and the offset adjusted in order to access the next character. Note that the first offset used is -1, which represents the character immediately preceding the EOF marker.

Exercises 10.3

1. a. Either using a text editor or copying the file `test.dat` on the program source disk provided with this book, create a file named `test.dat` on the directory that contains your program files.

   b. Enter and execute Program 10.5 on your computer.

2. Rewrite Program 10.5 so that the origin for the `seekg()` function used in the `for` loop is the start of the file rather than the end.

3. The `seek()` functions return 0 if the position specified has been reached, or 1 if the position specified was beyond the file's boundaries. Modify Program 10.5 to display an error message if `seekg()` returns 1.

4. Write a program that will read and display every second character in a file named `test.dat`.

5. Using the `seek()` and `tell()` functions, write a function named `f_chars()` that returns the total number of characters in a file.

6. Write a function named `r_bytes()` that reads and displays n characters starting from any position in a file. The function should accept three arguments: a file object name, the offset of the first character to be read, and the number of characters to be read. [*Note:* The prototype for `r_bytes` should be `void r_bytes(fstream&, long, long).`]

10.4 FILE STREAMS AS FUNCTION ARGUMENTS

A file stream object can be a function argument. The only requirement is that the function's formal parameter be a reference to the appropriate stream, either as `ifstream&` or `ofstream&`. For example, in Program 10.6 an `ofstream` object named `out_file` is opened in `main()` and this stream object is passed to the function `in_out()`. Notice that the function prototype and header line for `in_out()` both declare the formal parameter as a reference to an ostream object type. The `in_out()` function is then used to write five lines of user-entered text to the file.

PROGRAM 10.6

```
#include <fstream.h>
#include <stdlib.h>

const int MAXCHARS = 21;
char fname[MAXCHARS] = "list.dat";  // here is the file we are working with

void in_out(ofstream&);     // function prototype

int main()
{

  ofstream out_file;

  out_file.open(fname);
  if (out_file.fail())    // check for a successful open
  {
    cout << "\nThe output file " << fname << " was not successfully opened"
      << endl;
    exit(1);
   }

  in_out(out_file);  // call the function

  return 0;
}
const int LINELEN = 80;  // longest length of a line of text
const int NUMLINES = 5;  // number of lines of text

void in_out(ofstream& file_out)
{
  int count;
  char line[LINELEN];  // enough storage for one line of text

  cout << "Please enter five lines of text:" << endl;
  for (count = 0; count < NUMLINES; count++)
  {
    cin.getline(line,LINELEN,'\n');
    file_out << line << endl;
  }

  return;
}
```

Within `main()` the `ofstream` object is named `out_file`. This object is passed to the `in_out()` function and is accepted as the formal parameter named `file_out`, which is declared to be a reference to an `ofstream` object type. The function `in_out()` then uses its reference parameter, `out_file`, as an output

PROGRAM 10.7

```
#include <fstream.h>
#include <stdlib.h>

int get_open(ofstream&);  // pass a reference to an ofstream
void in_out(ofstream&);   // pass a reference to an ofstream

int main()
{

  ofstream out_file;     // file1 is an fstream object

  get_open(out_file);    // open the file
  in_out(out_file);      // write to it
}
const int MAXCHARS = 21;

int get_open(ofstream& file_out)
{
  char name[MAXCHARS];

  cout << "\nEnter a file name: " << endl;
  cin.getline(name,MAXCHARS,'\n');

  file_out.open(name);        // open the file

  if (file_out.fail())        // check for successful open
  {
    cout << "Cannot open the file" << endl;
    exit(1);
  }
  else
    return 0;
}
const int NUMLINES = 5;  // number of lines
const int LINELEN = 80;  // maximum line length

void in_out(ofstream& file_out)
{
  int count;
  char line[LINELEN];    // enough storage for one line of text

  cout << "Please enter five lines of text:" << endl;
  for (count = 0; count < NUMLINES; ++count)
  {
    cin.getline(line,LINELEN,'\n');
    file_out << line << endl;
  }

  return;
}
```

file stream object in an identical manner as main() would use the file_out stream object. Notice also that Program 10.6 uses the getline() method introduced in Section 10.2. Although we have explicitly included the newline character as the third argument passed to getline(), this argument can be omitted. This is because the '\n' is a default value for the third formal parameter.

In Program 10.7 we have expanded on Program 10.6 by adding a get_open() function to perform the open. Notice that get_open(), like in_out(), accepts a reference argument to an ofstream object. After the get_open() function completes execution, this reference is passed to in_out(), as it was in Program 10.6. Although you might be tempted to write get_open() to return a reference to an ofstream, this will not work because it ultimately results in an attempt to assign a returned reference to an existing one.

Program 10.7 is simply a modified version of Program 10.6 that now allows the user to enter a file name from the standard input device and then opens the ofstream connection to the external file. If the name of an existing data file is entered, the file will be destroyed when it is opened for output. A useful "trick" that you may encounter to prevent this type of mishap is to open the entered file using an input file stream. Then, if the file exists, the fail() method will indicate a successful open (i.e., the open does not fail), which indicates that the file is available for input. This can be used to alert the user that a file with the entered name currently exists in the system and to request confirmation that the data in the file can be destroyed and the file opened for output. Before the file is reopened for output, the input file stream should be closed. The implementation of this algorithm is left as an exercise.

Exercises 10.4

1. A function named p_file() is to receive a file name as a reference to an ifstream object. What parameters are required to pass a file name to p_file()?
2. Write a function named fcheck() that checks whether a file exists. The function should return an ifstream object as a formal reference parameter. If the file exists, the function should return a value of 1, otherwise the function should return a value of zero.
3. Rewrite the get_open() function used in Program 10.7 to incorporate the file-checking procedures described in this section. Specifically, if the entered file name exists, an appropriate message should be displayed. The user should then be presented with the option of entering a new file name or allowing the program to overwrite the existing file.
4. Assume that a data file consisting of a group of individual lines has been created. Write a function named print_line() that will read and display any desired line of the file. For example, the function call print_line(ifstream& f_name,5); should display the fifth line of the passed object stream.

10.5 FOCUS ON PROBLEM SOLVING

Once a data file has been created, application programs are typically written to read and update the file with current data. In this section two such program requirements are presented. The first problem uses a file as a database for storing the 10 most recent pollen counts, which are used in the summer as allergy "irritability" measures. As a new reading is obtained it is added to the file and the oldest stored reading is deleted.

The second program requirement concerns an expanded file update procedure. In this application a file containing inventory data, consisting of book identification numbers and quantities in stock, is updated by information contained in a second file. This application requires that identification numbers in the two files be matched before a record is updated.

Problem 1: Single File Update of Pollen Counts

Pollen count readings, which are taken from August through September in the northeastern region of the United States, measure the number of ragweed pollen grains in the air. Pollen counts in the range of 10 to 200 grains per cubic meter of air are typical during this time of year. Typically, pollen counts above 10 begin to affect a small percentage of hay fever sufferers, counts in the range of 30 to 40 will noticeably bother approximately 30% of hay fever sufferers, while counts between 40 and 50 adversely affect over 60% of all hay fever sufferers.

Program Requirement A program is to be written that updates a file containing the 10 most recent pollen counts. As a new count is obtained it is to be added to the end of the file and the oldest count deleted from the file.[3] Additionally, the average of the new file's data is to be calculated and displayed. The existing file is named `pollen.in` and contains the data shown in Figure 10.3.

Analyze the Problem The input data for this problem consists of a file of 10 integer numbers and a user input value of the most recent integer value pollen count. There are two required outputs:

1. a file of the 10 most recent integer values
2. the average of the data in the updated file.

FIGURE 10.3 Data Currently in the Pollen File

```
 30 <---- Oldest pollen count
            (to be deleted)
 60
 40
 80
 90
120
150
130
160
170 <---- Last pollen count
```

[3] This type of data storage is formally referred to as a first-in/first-out (FIFO) list, which is also called a *queue*. If the list is maintained in last-in/first-out order (LIFO) it is called a *stack*.

Develop a Solution The algorithm for solving this problem is straightforward and is described by the following pseudocode:

```
main( ) function
   Display a message indicating what the program does.
   Call the Input stream function.
   Call the Output stream function.
   Call the Update function.
   Display the new 10-week average.

Input stream function
   Request the name of the input data file.
   Open an input file stream and validate a successful connection.

Output stream function
   Request the name of the output data file.
   Open an output file stream and validate a successful connection.

Update function
   Request a new pollen count reading.
   Read the oldest pollen count from the input data file.
   For the remaining input file pollen counts
      Read an input value.
      Add the value to a total.
      Write the input value to the output file stream.
   Endfor.
   Write the new pollen count to the output file stream.
   Add the new pollen count to the total.
   Calculate the average as total ÷ number of pollen counts.
   Return the new 10 week average.
   Close all files.
```

In reviewing this algorithm, notice that the oldest pollen count is read but never used in any computation. The remaining pollen counts are read, "captured" in a total, and individually written to the output data file. The last pollen count is then added to the total and also written to the output data file. Finally, the average of the most recent pollen counts is computed and displayed, and all file streams are closed.

Code the Solution Program 10.8 presents a C++ representation of the selected design where the selected algorithm has been coded as the function `pollen_update`.

PROGRAM 10.8

```
#include <fstream.h>
#include <stdlib.h>

const int MAXLENGTH = 21;  // maximum file name length

void openInput(ifstream&);    // pass a reference to an ifstream
void openOutput(ofstream&);  // pass a reference to an ofstream
float pollen_update(ifstream&, ofstream&);  // pass two references

int main()
{
  ifstream in_file;   // in_file is an istream object
  ofstream out_file;  // out_file is an ofstream object
  float average;

    // display a user message
  cout << "\n\nThis program reads the old pollen count file, "
       << "creates a current pollen"
       << "\n    count file and calculates and displays "
       << "the latest 10-week average.";

  openInput(in_file);
  openOutput(out_file);

  average = pollen_update(in_file, out_file);

  cout << "\nThe new ten week average is: " << average << endl;

  return 0;
}

// this function gets an external file name and opens the file for input
void openInput(ifstream& fname)
{
  char filename[MAXLENGTH];

  cout << "\n\nEnter the input pollen count file name: ";
  cin  >> filename;

  fname.open(filename);

  if (fname.fail())    // check for a successful open
  {
    cout << "\nFailed to open the file named " << fname << "for input"
         << "\n Please check that this file exits"
         << endl;
    exit(1);
  }
```

(continued on next page)

(continued from previous page)

```
  return;
}

// this function gets an external file name and opens the file for output
void openOutput(ofstream& fname)
{
  char filename[MAXLENGTH];

  cout << "Enter the output pollen count file name: ";
  cin  >> filename;

  fname.open(filename);

  if (fname.fail())    // check for a successful open
  {
    cout << "\nFailed to open the file named " << fname << "for output"
         << endl;
    exit(1);
  }

  return;
}
const int POLNUMS = 10; // maximum number of pollen counts

// the following function reads the pollen file
// writes a new file
// and returns the new weekly average
float pollen_update(ifstream& infile, ofstream& outfile)
{

  int i, polreading;
  int oldreading, newcount;
  float sum = 0;
  float average;

    // get the latest pollen count
  cout << "Enter the latest pollen count reading: ";
  cin  >> newcount;


    // read the oldest pollen count
  infile >> oldreading;

  // read, sum and write out the rest of the pollen counts
  for(i = 0; i < POLNUMS - 1; i++)
  {
    infile >> polreading;
    sum += polreading;
    outfile << polreading << endl;
```

(continued on next page)

(continued from previous page)

```
  }
    // write out the latest reading
  outfile << newcount << endl;

    // compute the new average
  average = (sum + newcount) / (float) POLNUMS;

  infile.close();
  outfile.close();

  cout << "\nThe output file has been written.\n";

  return average;
}
```

Test and Correct the Program Testing Program 10.8 requires that we provide both valid and invalid input data for the program. Invalid data would consist of both a nonexistent input data file name and a data file that contains fewer than 10 items. Valid data consists of a file containing 10 integers. A sample run of Program 10.8 follows with a valid input file:

```
This program reads the old pollen count file, creates a current pollen
    count file and calculates and displays the latest ten week average.

Enter the input pollen count file name: pollen.in
Enter the output pollen count file name: pollen.out
Enter the latest pollen count reading: 200

The output file has been written.

The new ten week average is: 120
```

FIGURE 10.4 The Updated Pollen File

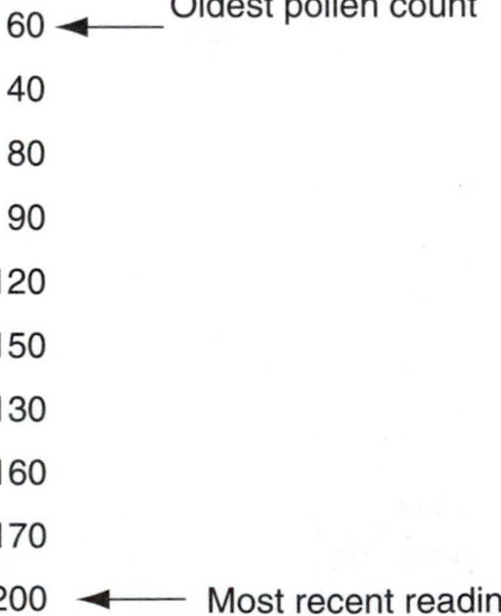

TABLE 10.4 Master File Data

Book ID No.	Quantity in Stock
125	98
289	222
341	675
467	152
589	34
622	125

TABLE 10.5 Transaction File Data

ID No.	Date	Sold	Returned	Bought
289	1/10/97	125	34	50
341	1/10/97	300	52	0
467	1/15/97	50	20	200
467	1/20/97	225	0	160
589	1/31/97	75	10	55

The updated file created by Program 10.8 is illustrated in Figure 10.4. In reviewing the contents of this file notice that the most current reading has been added to the end of the file and that the other pollen readings obtained from the original file shown in Figure 10.3, have been moved up one position in the new file. Also notice that the output of our sample run correctly calculates the new 10-week average.

Problem 2: Master/Transaction File Update

A common form of file update occurs when the current data is itself contained in a file. Here, the file to be updated is referred to as a *master file,* and the file containing the current data is referred to as a *transactions file.* As a specific example of this type of update consider the following.

Program Requirement Assume that a current master file, named `oldbook.mas`, consists of book identification numbers and quantities in stock as illustrated in Table 10.4. A transactions file, named `book.trn`, contains the quantities of each book bought, sold, or returned to stock each day. This file is sorted by ID number at the end of each month and contains the data illustrated in Table 10.5.

Write a program that uses the data in the transaction file to update the data in the master file so that at the end of the update, the master file contains a correct count of books for each identification number.

Analyze the Problem Since this application requires more than a simple modification of existing techniques, we present additional background information and perform an exploratory analysis to ensure that we understand the problem.

A standard solution when updating a master file with the data in a transactions file is to first have all the transactions in the same identification (ID) number order as the records in the master file. In this case, since the records in the master file, as illustrated in Table 10.4, are in increasing (ascending) identification number order, the transactions must also be kept in ascending order. As illustrated in Table 10.5, this is the case for the `book.trn` file.

Once the two files are in the same ID number order the standard procedure for creating an updated master file consists of reading a master record from the existing master file and one record from the transaction file. If the ID numbers of the two records match, the transaction record's information is applied to the data in the master record and another transaction record is read. As long as the transaction record's ID number matches the master record's ID number, the update of the master record continues. When the transaction record's ID number does not match the master record's ID number, which indicates that there is no further update data to be applied to the master record, an updated record is written to the new master file. Let's see how this procedure works by doing a hand calculation with the data shown in Tables 10.4 and 10.5.

The first record read from the master file has ID number 125, while the first transaction record has ID number 289. Since the ID numbers do not match, the update of this first master record is complete (in this case there is no update information) and the existing master record is written, without modification, to the new master file. Then the next master record is read, which has an ID number of 289. Since this ID number matches the transaction ID number, the inventory balance for book number 289 is updated, yielding a new balance of 181 books. Because the transaction file can contain multiple update records for the same ID number (notice the two records for ID number 467), the next transaction record is read and checked before writing an updated record to the new master file. Since the ID number of the next transaction record is not 289, the update of this book number is complete and an updated master record is written to the new master file.

This procedure continues, record by record, until the last master record has been updated. Should the end of the transaction file be encountered before the last master record is read from the existing master file, the remaining records in the existing master file are written directly to the new master file with no need to check for update information. The new master file can either be a completely new file, or each updated record can be written back to the old master file. In our update procedure we will create a new master file so that the original data in the old master file will be left intact. Now let's formalize this algorithm using a pseudocode description.

Step 2: Develop a Solution Since we will be using two master files, the old and new masters, a notation must be established to clearly distinguish between them. By convention, the existing master file is always referred to as the old master file, and the updated master file is called the new master file. Using these terms, the pseudocode description of the update procedure found in the analysis step is:

```
Open the old master file.
Open the transaction file.
Open the new master file (initially blank).
Read the first old master record.
While not at the end of the transaction file
   Read a transaction record.
   While the transaction ID does not match the old master ID
      Write an updated master record to the new master file.
      Read the next transaction record.
```

Endwhile.
If the ID numbers do match
Calculate a new balance.
Endwhile.
*** *To get here the last transaction record has just been read.*
Write the last updated master to the new master file.
While there are any remaining records in the old master file.
Read an old master record.
Write a new master record.
Endwhile.
Close all files.

Code the Solution In C++, the selected design is implemented by Program 10.9.

PROGRAM 10.9

```
#include <fstream.h>
#include <iomanip.h>
#include <stdlib.h>

const int MAXCHARS = 21;
char old_master[MAXCHARS] = "oldbook.mas";  // here are the files we will be
char new_master[MAXCHARS] = "newbook.mas";  // working with
char transactions[MAXCHARS] = "book.trn";

void do_update(void);

int main()
{
  do_update();

  return 0;
}

// update function
// precondition: both a master file named oldbook.mas and
//             : a transaction file named book.trn exist on
//             : the current directory
//             : and both files are in date order
// postcondition: a new master file named newbook.mas is created

const int MAXDATE = 8;
void do_update(void)
{
  int idmast, idtrans, balance, sold, returned, bought;
  int ch;
  char date[MAXDATE];
  ifstream oldmast, trans;
```

(continued on next page)

(continued from previous page)

```
ofstream newmast;

   // open and check the old_master file
oldmast.open(old_master);
if (oldmast.fail())
{
  cout << "\nThe input file " << old_master <<  "was not successfully opened"
       << "\n Please check that the file currently exists." << endl;
  exit(1);
}
   // open and check the new_master file
newmast.open(new_master);
if (newmast.fail())
{
  cout << "\nFailed to open the new master file " << new_master
       << " for output." << endl;
  exit(1);
}
   // open and check the transactions file
trans.open(transactions);
if (trans.fail())
{
  cout << "\nThe input file " << trans << " was not successfully opened"
       << "\n Please check that the file currently exits." << endl;
  exit(1);
}
     // read the first old master file record
oldmast >> idmast >> balance;
while( (ch = trans.peek()) != EOF)
{
     // read one transaction record
   trans >> idtrans >> date >> sold >> returned >> bought;
     // if no match keep writing and reading the master file
  while (idtrans > idmast)
  {
    newmast << '\n' << idmast << setw(6) << balance;
    oldmast >> idmast >> balance;
  }
  balance = balance + bought - sold + returned;
}
   // write the last updated new master file
newmast << '\n' << idmast << setw(6) << balance;
   // write any remaining old master records to the new master
while ( (ch = oldmast.peek()) != EOF)
{

  oldmast >> idmast >> balance;
  newmast << '\n' << idmast << setw(6) << balance;
}
```

(continued on next page)

(continued from previous page)

```
    oldmast.close();
    newmast.close();
    trans.close();
    cout << "\n....File update complete...\n";

    return;
}
```

Test and Correct the Program A sample run using Program 10.9 with an old master file containing the data illustrated in Table 10.4 and a transactions data file containing the data illustrated in Table 10.5 yielded the following data in the file `newbook.mas`:

```
125    98
289   181
341   427
467   257
589    24
622   125
```

A hand calculation using the data in Tables 10.4 and 10.5 verifies that the data in the second column reflects the correct new balance for the book identification numbers in the first column. Additional runs should now be made with the transactions file containing data for only the first book in the master file and then with data for only the last book in the master file. These two runs would successfully test the extreme values of the while loops.

Exercises 10.5

1. Write a C++ program to create the pollen file illustrated in Figure 10.3.
2. Either using the file created in Exercise 1, or using the `pollen.in` file provided on the source code disk supplied with this text, enter and run Program 10.8 on your computer.
3. a. A file named `polar.dat` contains the polar coordinates needed in a graphics program. Currently this file contains the following data:

Distance (inches)	Angle (degrees)
2.0	45.0
6.0	30.0
10.0	45.0
4.0	60.0
12.0	55.0
8.0	15.0

Write a C++ program to create this file on your computer system.

b. Using the `polar.dat` file created in Exercise 3a, write a C++ program that accepts distance and angle data from the user and adds the data to the end of the file.

c. Using the `polar.dat` file created in Exercise 3a, write a C++ program that reads this file and creates a second file named `xycord.dat`. The entries in the new file should contain the rectangular coordinates corresponding to the polar coordinates in the `polar.dat` file. Polar coordinates are converted to rectangular coordinates using the equations

$$x = r \cos \theta$$

$$y = r \sin \theta$$

where r is the distance coordinate and θ is the radian equivalent of the angle coordinate in the `polar.dat` file.

4. a. Write a C++ program to create both the `oldbook.mas` file, illustrated in Table 10.4, and the `book.trn` file, illustrated in Table 10.5. (*Note:* Do not include the column headings in the file.)

   b. Using the files created in Exercise 4a, enter and run Program 10.9 to verify its operation.

   c. Modify Program 10.9 to prompt the user for the names of the old master file, the new master file, and the transactions file. The modified program should accept these file names as input while the program is executing.

   d. Using the `book.trn` file created in Exercise 4a, write a C++ program that reads this file and displays the transaction data in it, including the heading lines shown in Table 10.5.

5. a. Write a C++ program to create a data file containing the following information:

Student ID Number	Student Name	Course Code	Course Credits	Course Grade
2333021	BOKOW, R.	NS201	3	A
2333021	BOKOW, R.	MG342	3	A
2333021	BOKOW, R.	FA302	1	A
2574063	FALLIN, D.	MK106	3	C
2574063	FALLIN, D.	MA208	3	B
2574063	FALLIN, D.	CM201	3	C
2574063	FALLIN, D.	CP101	2	B
2663628	KINGSLEY, M.	QA140	3	A
2663628	KINGSLEY, M.	CM245	3	B
2663628	KINGSLEY, M.	EQ521	3	A
2663628	KINGSLEY, M.	MK341	3	A
2663628	KINGSLEY, M.	CP101	2	B

   b. Using the file created in Exercise 5a, write a C++ program that creates student grade reports. The grade report for each student should contain the student's name and identification number, a list of courses taken, the credits and grade for each course, and a semester grade-point average. For example, the grade report for the first student is:

```
Student name: BOKOW, R.
Student ID Number: 2333021

Course Name    Course Credits    Course Grade
---------------------------------------------
 NS201               3                A
 MG342               3                A
 FA302               1                A

Total Semester Course Credits Completed: 7
Semester Grade Point Average: 4.0
```

   The semester grade-point average is computed in two steps. First, each course grade is assigned a numerical value (A = 4, B = 3, C = 2, D = 1, F = 0) and the sum of each course's grade value times the credits for each course is computed. This sum is then divided by the total number of credits taken during the semester.

6. a. Write a C++ program to create a data file containing the following information:

Student ID Number	Student Name	Course Credits	Grade-Point Average (GPA)
2333021	BOKOW, R.	48	4.0
2574063	FALLIN, D.	12	1.8
2663628	KINGSLEY, M.	36	3.5

b. Using the file created in Exercise 6a as a master file and the file created in Exercise 5a as a transactions file, write a file update program to create an updated master file.

10.6 A CLOSER LOOK AT THE iostream CLASS LIBRARY

The iostream class library provided as part of each C++ compiler is not part of the C++ language. By convention each C++ compiler provides an input/output library, named iostream, that contains a number of classes that adhere to a common specification originally defined and adopted by AT&T.

As we have already seen, the classes contained within the iostream class library access files using entities called streams. For most systems the data bytes transferred on a stream represent either ASCII characters or binary numbers.

When the data transfer between a computer and an external data file modifies the data, so that the data stored in the file is *not* an exact representation of the data as it is stored internally within the computer, the file is referred to as a **formatted file.** Examples of this are files that store their data using ASCII codes. Such files are also referred to as **text files,** and the terms *text* and *formatted* are sometimes used interchangeably.

When the data transfer between a computer and an external data file is done without modification, so that the data stored in the file *is* an exact representation of the data as it is stored internally within the computer, the file is referred to as a **binary file** or **unformatted file.**

The mechanism for reading a byte stream from a file or writing a byte stream to a file, with or without formatting, is always hidden when using a high-level language such as C++. Nevertheless, it is useful to understand this mechanism so that we can place the services provided by the iostream class library in their appropriate context.

File Stream Transfer Mechanism

The mechanism for transferring data between a program and a data file is illustrated in Figure 10.5. As shown, transferring data between a program and a file involves an intermediate file buffer contained in the computer's memory. Each opened file is assigned its own file buffer, which is simply a storage area that is used to hold the data transferred between the program and the file.

From its side, the program either writes a set of data bytes to the file buffer or reads a set of data bytes from the file buffer using a stream object.

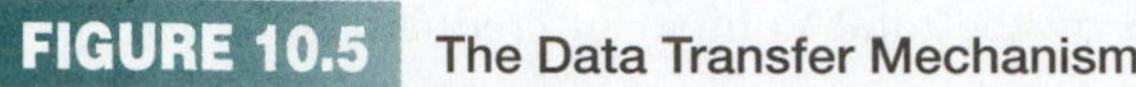

FIGURE 10.5 The Data Transfer Mechanism

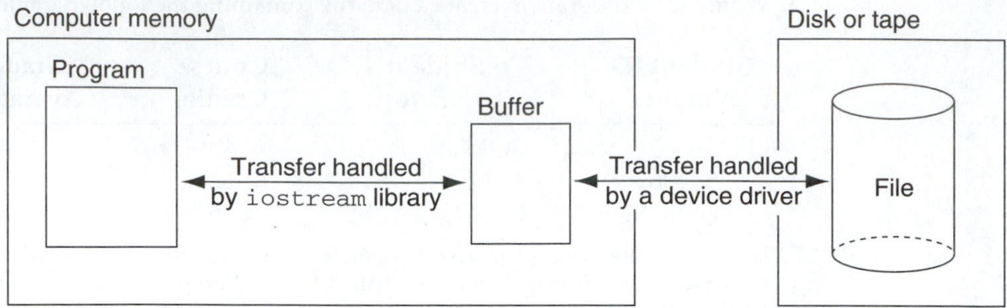

On the other side of the buffer the transfer of data between the device storing the actual data file (usually a tape, disk, or CD-ROM drive) and the file buffer is handled by special operating system programs that are referred to as **device drivers.**[4] Typically a disk device driver will only transfer data between the disk and file buffer in fixed sizes, such as 1024 bytes at a time. Thus, the file buffer provides a convenient means of permitting a device driver to transfer data in blocks of one size while the program can access them using a different size (typically as individual characters or as a fixed number of characters per line).

Components of the `iostream` Class Library

The `iostream` class library consists of two primary base classes, the `streambuf` class and the `ios` class. The `streambuf` class provides the file buffer illustrated in Figure 10.5 and a number of general routines for transferring data when little or no formatting is required. The `ios` class contains a pointer to the file buffers provided by the `streambuf` class and a number of general routines for transferring data with formatting. From these two base classes a number of other classes are derived and included in the `iostream` class library.

Figure 10.6 illustrates an inheritance diagram for the `ios` family of classes as it relates to the `ifstream`, `ofstream`, and `fstream` classes. The inheritance diagram for the `streambuf` family of classes is shown in Figure 10.7. As described in the previous chapter, the convention adopted for inheritance diagrams is that the arrows point from a derived class to a base class.

The correspondence between the classes illustrated in Figures 10.6 and 10.7, including the header files that define these classes, is listed in Table 10.6.

Thus, the `ifstream`, `ofstream`, and `fstream` classes that we have used for file access all use a buffer provided by the `filebuf` class that is defined in the `fstream.h` header file. Similarly, the `cin`, `cout`, and `cerr` `iostream` objects that

---

[4] Device drivers are not stand-alone programs but are an integral part of the operating system. Essentially the device driver is a section of operationg system code that accesses a hardware device, such as a disk unit, and handles the data transfer between the device and the computer's memory. As such it must correctly synchronize the speed of the data transferred between the computer and the device sending or receiving the data. This is because the computer's internal data transfer rate is generally much faster than any device connected to it.

FIGURE 10.6 The Base Class ios and Its Derived Classes (not all derived classes are shown)

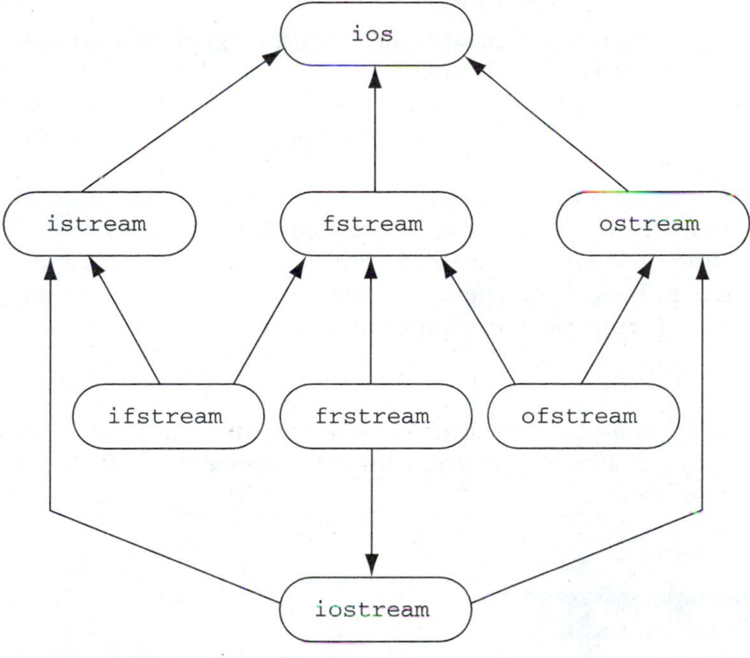

TABLE 10.6 Correspondence Between Classes

ios Class	streambuf Class	Header File
istream ostream iostream	streambuf	iostream.h or fstream.h
ifstream ofstream fstream	filebuf	fstream.h

FIGURE 10.7 The Base Class streambuf and Its Derived Classes (not all derived classes are shown)

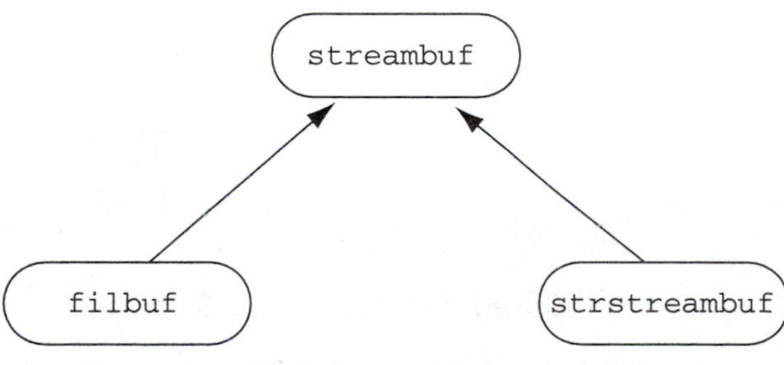

we have been using throughout the text use a buffer provided by the streambuf class and defined in both the iostream.h and fstream header files.

In-Memory Formatting

In addition to the classes illustrated in Figure 10.6, a class named strstream is also derived from the ios class. This class uses the strstreambuf class illustrated in Figure 10.6, requires the strstream.h header file, and provides capabilities for writing and reading strings to and from in-memory defined streams.

As an output stream, such streams are typically used to "assemble" a string from smaller pieces until a complete line of characters is ready to be inserted, either to cout or to a file stream. Attaching a strstream object to a buffer for this purpose is done in a manner similar to that of attaching an fstream object to an output file. For example, the statement

```
strstream inmem(buf, 72, ios::out);
```

attaches a strstream object to an existing buffer of 72 bytes in output mode. Program 10.10 illustrates using this statement within the context of a complete program.

PROGRAM 10.10

```
#include <strstream.h>
#include <iomanip.h>

int main()
{
  const int MAXCHARS = 81;  // one more than the maximum characters in a line
  int units = 10;
  float price = 36.85;
  char buf[MAXCHARS];

  strstream inmem(buf, MAXCHARS, ios::out);  // open an in-memory stream

    // write to the buffer through the stream
  inmem << "No. of units = "
     << setw(3) << units
     << "  Price per unit = $"
     << setw(8) << setprecision(2) << price << '\0';

  cout << '|' << buf << '|';

  return 0;
}
```

The output produced by Program 10.10 is:

```
|No. of units = 10 Price per unit = $ 36.85|
```

As illustrated by this output, the character buffer has been correctly filled in by insertions to the `inmem` stream (note that the end-of-string `NULL`, `\0`, which is the last insertion to the stream, is required to correctly close off the string). Once the desired character array has been filled, it would typically be written out to a file as a single string.

In a similar manner a `strstream` object can be opened in input mode. Typically such a stream would be used as a working storage area, or buffer, for storing a complete line of text from either a file or standard input. Once the buffer has been filled, the extraction operator would be used to "disassemble" the string into component parts and convert each data item into its designated data type. Doing this permits the input of data from a file on a line-by-line basis prior to assigning individual data items to their respective variables.

10.7 COMMON PROGRAMMING ERRORS

Three programming errors are common when using files. The most common error is to use the file's external name in place of the internal file stream object name when accessing the file. The only stream method that uses the data file's external name is the `open()` method. As always, all stream methods presented in this chapter must be preceded by a stream object name and the dot operator.

A second error occurs when using the EOF marker to detect the end of a file. Any variable used to accept the EOF must be declared as an integer variable. For example, if `ch` is declared as a character variable the expression

```
while ( (ch = in.file.peek()) != EOF )
```

produces an infinite loop.[5] This occurs because a character variable can never take on an EOF code. EOF is an integer value (usually −1) that has no character representation. This ensures that the EOF code can never be confused with any legitimate character encountered as normal data in the file. To terminate the loop created by the preceding expression, the variable `ch` must be declared as an integer variable.

The last error concerns the offset argument sent to the `seekg()` and `seekp()` functions. This offset must be a long integer constant or variable. Any other value passed to these functions can result in an unpredictable effect.

10.8 CHAPTER REVIEW

Key Terms

binary file	output file stream
`close()` method	random access
data file	`seekg()` method
external file name	`seekp()` method
file access	sequential organization
file organization	string variable
file stream	`tellg()` method
input file stream	`tellp()` method
`open()` method	text file

---

[5] This will not occur on UNIX systems where characters are stored as signed integers.

Summary

1. A *data file* is any collection of data stored in an external storage medium under a common name.
2. A *data file* is connected to a file stream using an `open()` method. This method connects a file's external name with an internal object name. After the file is opened, all subsequent accesses to the file require the internal object name.
3. A file can be opened and connected to either an input or output file stream. An opened output file stream either creates a new data file or erases the data in an existing opened file. An opened input file stream makes an existing file's data available for input. An error condition results if the file does not exist and can be detected using the file stream's `fail()` method.
4. All file streams must be declared as objects of either the `ifstream` or `ofstream` classes. This means that a declaration similar to either of these statements

   ```
   ifstream in_file;
   ofstream out_file;
   ```

   must be included with the declarations in which the file is opened. The stream object names `in_file` and `out_file` can be replaced with any user-selected object name.
5. In addition to any files opened within a function, the standard stream objects `cin`, `cout`, and `cerr` are automatically declared and opened when a program is run. `cin` is the object name of an input file stream used for data entry (usually from the keyboard), `cout` is the object name of an output file stream used for default data display (usually the terminal screen), and `cerr` is the object name of an output file stream used for displaying system error messages (usually the terminal screen).
6. Data files can be accessed randomly using the `seekg()`, `seekp()`, `tellg()`, and `tellp()` methods. The `g` versions of these functions are used to alter and query the file position marker for input file streams, while the `p` versions do the same for output file streams.
7. Table 10.2 in Section 10.2 lists the stream methods supplied for file manipulation.

Exercises

1. You are to write a C++ program that allows the user to enter the following information from the keyboard for each of up to 20 students in a class:

   ```
   Name    Exam 1 Grade    Exam 2 Grade    Homework Grade    Final Exam Grade
   ```

   For each student your program should first calculate a final grade, using the formula:

   ```
   Final Grade = 0.20 * Exam 1 + 0.20 * Exam 2 + 0.35 * Homework
                     + 0.25 * Final Exam
   ```

   and then assign a letter grade on the basis of 90 – 100 = A, 80 – 89 = B, 70 – 79 = C, 60 – 69 = D, less than 60 = F. All of the information, including the final grade and the letter grade, should then be displayed and written to a file.
2. Write a C++ program that permits a user to enter the following information about your small company's 10 employees and writes the sorted information to a file.

   ```
   ID No.    Sex (M/F)    Hourly Wage    Years with the Company
   ```

3. Write a C++ program that allows you to read the file created in Exercise 2, change the hourly wage or years for each employee, and create a new, updated file.
4. Write a C++ program that reads the file created in Exercise 2, one record at a time, asks for the number of hours worked by that employee each month, and calculates and displays each employee's total pay for the month.
5. a. You have collected information about cities in your state. You decide to store each city's name, population, and the name of its mayor in a file. Write a C++ program to accept the data for a number of cities from the keyboard and store the data in a file in the order in which they are entered.
   b. Read the file created in Exercise 5a, sort the data alphabetically by city name, and display the data.
6. A bank's customer records are to be stored in a file and read into a set of arrays so that an individual's record can be accessed randomly by account number. Create the file by entering five customer records, with each record consisting of an integer account number (starting with account number 1000), a first name having a maximum of 10 characters, a last name having a maximum of 15 characters, and a floating-point balance.

   Once the file is created, write a C++ program that requests a user input account number and displays the corresponding name and account balance from the file.
7. Create an ASCII file with the following data or use the file named `shipped.txt` on the diskette provided with this text. The headings are not part of the file but indicate what the data represents.

Shipped Date	Tracking Number	Part Number	First Name	Last Name	Company
04/12/97	D50625	74444	James	Lehoff	Rotech
04/12/97	D60752	75255	Janet	Lezar	Rotech
04/12/97	D40295	74477	Bill	McHenry	Rotech
04/12/97	D23745	74470	Diane	Kaiser	Rotech
04/12/97	D50892	75155	Helen	Richardson	NipNap

The format of each line in the file is identical with fixed length fields defined as follows:

Field Position	Field Name	Starting Col. No.	Ending Col. No.	Field Length
1	Shipped Date	1	8	8
2	Tracking Number	12	17	6
3	Part Number	22	26	5
4	First Name	31	35	5
5	Last Name	39	48	10
6	Company	51	64	14

Using this data file you are to write a C++ program that reads the file, and produces a report listing the date, part number, first name, last name, and company name.

Data Structures

The variables that we have used so far have all had a common characteristic: Each variable can only be used to store a single value at a time. For example, although the variables `key`, `count`, and `grade` declared in the statements

```
char key;
int count;
float grade;
```

are of different data types, each variable can only store one value of the declared data type. These types of variables are called atomic variables. An *atomic variable,* which is also referred to as a *scalar variable,* is a variable whose value cannot be further subdivided or separated into a legitimate data type.

Another method of storing and retrieving data is to use a data structure. A *data structure* is a data type whose values can be decomposed into individual data elements, each of which is either atomic or another data structure *and* it provides an access scheme for locating individual data elements within the structure. One such data structure is a class, which is presented in Part II.

In Chapter 11 we look at a data structure referred to as an *array,* which uses built-in procedural operations for both access and individual element manipulation. An array whose individual elements are characters is the method C++ uses to store strings. These array types are presented in Chapter 12. Additionally, in Chapter 13 a complete description of pointers is presented. In addition to other very useful tasks, pointers provide a very powerful access method for array processing in general and strings in particular.

In Chapter 14 we present record structures. Although record structures can be defined as classes having no member functions and all of whose data members are public, C++ provides a nonclass, procedural method of defining record structures. It is this method that is described.

Finally, in Chapter 15 we present two advanced data structures named *stacks* and *queues.* Although these two structures can also be defined as special cases of record structures, we show how to construct and use these structures as classes.

CHAPTER

11 Arrays

Frequently we may have a set of values, all of the same data type, that forms a logical group. For example, Figure 11.1 illustrates three groups of items. The first group is a list of five floating-point temperatures, the second group is a list of four character codes, and the last group is a list of six integer grades.

A simple list containing individual items of the same data type is called a *one-dimensional array*. In this chapter we describe how one-dimensional arrays are declared, initialized, stored inside a computer, and used. Additionally, we explore the use of one-dimensional arrays with example programs and present the procedures for declaring and using multidimensional arrays.

FIGURE 11.1 Three Lists of Items

Temperatures	Codes	Grades
95.75	Z	98
83.0	C	87
97.625	K	92
72.5	L	79
86.25		85
		72

11.1 ONE-DIMENSIONAL ARRAYS

A **one-dimensional array,** which is also referred to as either a **single-dimensional array** or a vector, is a list of related values with the same data type that is stored using a single group name.[1] In C++, as in other computer languages, the group name is referred to as the array name. For example, consider the list of temperatures illustrated in Figure 11.2. All the temperatures in the list are floating-point numbers and must be declared as such. However, the individual items in the list do not have to be declared separately. The items in the list can be declared as a single unit and stored under a common variable name called the *array name.* For convenience, we will choose `temp` as the name for the list shown in Figure 11.2.

To specify that `temp` is to store five individual floating-point values, we must use the declaration statement `float temp[5]`. Notice that this declaration statement gives the array (or list) name, the data type of the items in the array, and the number of items in the array. Good programming practice requires the number of array items be defined as a constant before declaring the array. Thus, the previous array declaration would, in practice, be declared using two statements, such as:

```
const int NUMELS = 5;
float temp[NUMELS];
```

Further examples of array declarations are:

```
const int NUMELS = 5;
int grade[NUMELS];

const int ARRAYSIZE = 4;
char code[ARRAYSIZE];

const int SIZE = 100;
float amount[SIZE];
```

In these declaration statements, each array is allocated sufficient memory to hold the number of data items given in the declaration statement. Thus, the array

FIGURE 11.2 A List of Temperatures

Temperatures
95.75
83.0
97.625
72.5
86.25

[1] Note that lists can be implemented in a variety of ways, some of which are further described in Chapter 14. An array is simply one implementation of a list in which all of the list elements are of the same type and each element is stored consecutively in a set of contiguous memory locations.

named `grade` has storage reserved for five integers, the array named `code` has storage reserved for four characters, and the array named `amount` has storage reserved for 100 floating-point numbers. The symbolic constants, `NUMELS`, `ARRAYSIZE`, and `SIZE` are programmer-selected names.

Figure 11.3 illustrates the storage reserved for the `code` and `grade` arrays. Each item in an array is called an *element* or *component* of the array. The individual elements stored in the arrays illustrated in Figure 11.3 are stored sequentially, with the first array element stored in the first reserved location, the second element stored in the second reserved location, and so on until the last element is stored in the last reserved location. This contiguous storage allocation for the list is a key feature of arrays because it provides a simple mechanism for easily locating any single element in the list.

FIGURE 11.3 The `code` and `grade` Arrays in Memory

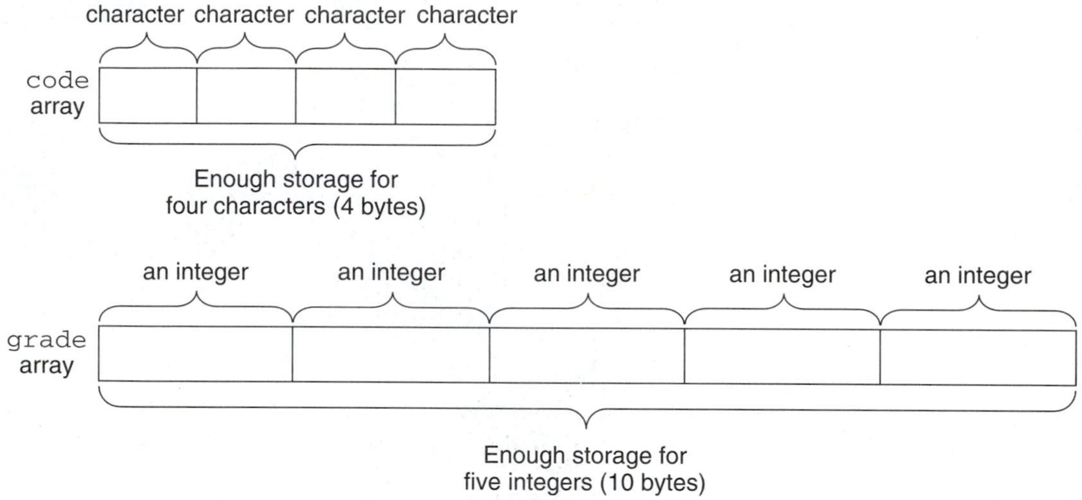

Since elements in the array are stored sequentially, any individual element can be accessed by giving the name of the array and the element's position. This position is called the element's **index** or **subscript** value (the two terms are synonymous). For a single-dimensional array, the first element has an index of 0, the second element has an index of 1, and so on. In C++, the array name and index of the desired element are combined by listing the index in braces after the array name. For example, given the declaration `float temp[5]`,

`temp[0]` refers to the first temperature stored in the `temp` array.

`temp[1]` refers to the second temperature stored in the `temp` array.

`temp[2]` refers to the third temperature stored in the `temp` array.

`temp[3]` refers to the fourth temperature stored in the `temp` array.

`temp[4]` refers to the fifth temperature stored in the `temp` array.

Figure 11.4 illustrates the `temp` array in memory with the correct designation for each array element. Each individual element is referred to as an **indexed variable**

FIGURE 11.4 Identifying Individual Array Elements

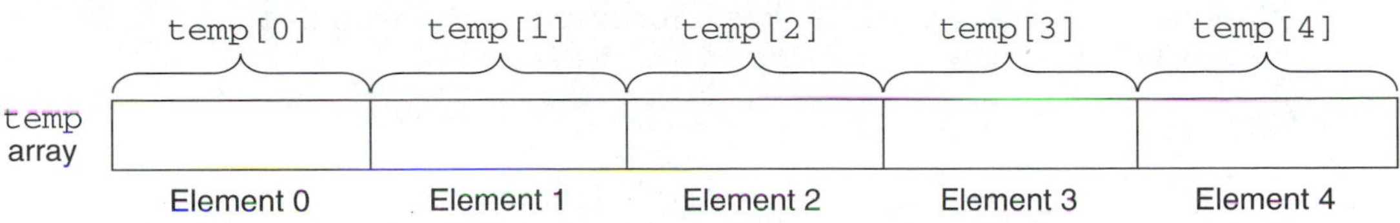

or a **subscripted variable,** because both a variable name and an index or subscript value must be used to reference the element. Remember that the index or subscript value gives the *position* of the element in the array.

The subscripted variable `temp[0]` is read as "temp sub zero." This is a shortened way of saying "the temp array subscripted by zero," and distinguishes the first element in an array from an atomic variable that could be declared as `temp0`. Similarly, `temp[1]` is read as "temp sub one," `temp[2]` as "temp sub two," and so on.

Although it may seem unusual to reference the first element with an index of zero, doing so increases the computer's speed when it accesses array elements. Internally, unseen by the programmer, the computer uses the index as an offset from the array's starting position. As illustrated in Figure 11.5, the index tells the computer how many elements to skip, starting from the beginning of the array, to get to the desired element.

FIGURE 11.5 Accessing an Individual Array Element—Element 3

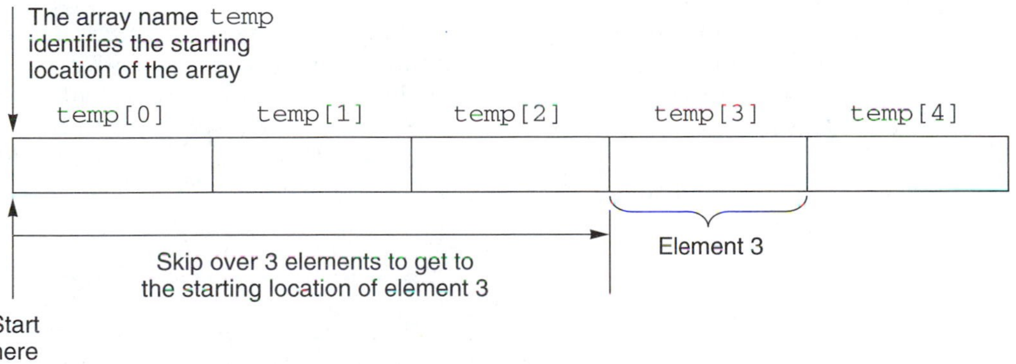

Subscripted variables can be used anywhere scalar variables are valid. Examples using the elements of the `temp` array are:

```
temp[0] = 95.75;
temp[1] = temp[0] - 11.0;
temp[2] = 5.0 * temp[0];
temp[3] = 79.0;
temp[4] = (temp[1] + temp[2] - 3.1) / 2.2;
sum = temp[0] + temp[1] + temp[2] + temp[3] + temp[4];
```

The subscript contained within brackets need not be an integer constant; any expression that evaluates to an integer may be used as a subscript.[2] In each case, of course, the value of the expression must be within the valid subscript range defined when the array is declared. For example, assuming that `i` and `j` are `int` variables, the following subscripted variables are valid:

```
temp[i]
temp[2*i]
temp[j-i]
```

One extremely important advantage of using integer expressions as subscripts is that it allows sequencing through an array by using a loop. This makes statements like

```
sum = temp[0] + temp[1] + temp[2] + temp[3] + temp[4];
```

unnecessary. The subscript values in this statement can be replaced by a `for` loop counter to access each element in the array sequentially. For example, the code

```
sum = 0;                      // initialize the sum to zero
for (i = 0; i < 5; i++)
  sum = sum + temp[i];        // add in a temperature
```

sequentially retrieves each array element and adds the element to `sum`. Here the variable `i` is used both as the counter in the `for` loop and as a subscript. As `i` increases by one each time through the loop, the next element in the array is referenced. The procedure for adding the array elements within the `for` loop is similar to the accumulation procedure we have used many times before.

The advantage of using a `for` loop to sequence through an array becomes apparent when working with larger arrays. For example, if the `temp` array contained 100 values rather than just 5, simply changing the number 5 to 100 in the `for` statement is sufficient to sequence through the 100 elements and add each temperature to the sum.

As another example of using a `for` loop to sequence through an array, assume that we want to locate the maximum value in an array of 1000 elements named `grade`. To locate the maximum value, we assume initially that the first element in the array is the largest number. Then, as we sequence through the array, the maximum is compared to each element. When an element with a higher value is located, that element becomes the new maximum. The following code does the job:

```
const int NUMELS = 1000;

maximum = grade[0];            // set the maximum to element zero
for (i = 1; i < NUMELS; i++)   // cycle through the rest of the array
  if (grade[i] > maximum)      // compare each element to the maximum
    maximum = grade[i];        // capture the new high value
```

In this code, the `for` statement consists of one `if` statement. The search for a new maximum value starts with element 1 of the array and continues through the last element. Each element is compared to the current maximum, and when a higher value is encountered it becomes the new maximum.

---

[2] Some compilers permit floating-point variables as subscripts; in these cases the floating-point value is truncated to an integer value.

POINT OF INFORMATION

Structured Data Types

In contrast to atomic types, such as integer and floating-point data, there are structured types. A *structured type,* which is sometimes referred to as a *data structure,* is any type whose values can be decomposed and are related by some defined structure. Additionally, operations must be available for retrieving and updating individual values in the data structure.

Single-dimensional arrays are examples of a structured type. In a single-dimensional array, such as an array of integers, the array is composed of individual integer values where integers are related by their position in the list. Indexed variables provide the means of accessing and modifying values in the array.

Input and Output of Array Values

Individual array elements can be assigned values interactively using the `cin` object. Examples of individual data entry statements are:

```
cin >> temp[0];
cin >> temp[1] >> temp[2] >> temp[3];
cin >> temp[4] >> grade[6];
```

In the first statement a single value will be read and stored in the variable named `temp[0]`. The second statement will cause three values to be read and stored in the variables `temp[1]`, `temp[2]`, and `temp[3]`, respectively. Finally, the last `cin` statement can be used to read values into the variables `temp[4]` and `grade[6]`.

Alternatively, a `for` loop can be used to cycle through the array for interactive data input. For example, the code

```
const int NUMELS = 5;

for (i = 0; i < NUMELS; i++)
{
  cout << "Enter a temperature: ";
  cin  >> temp[i];
}
```

prompts the user for five temperatures. The first temperature entered is stored in `temp[0]`, the second temperature entered in `temp[1]`, and so on until five temperatures have been input.

One caution should be mentioned about storing data in an array. C++ does not check the value of the index being used (called a *bounds check*). If an array has been declared as consisting of 10 elements, for example, and you use an index of 12, which is outside the bounds of the array, C++ will not notify you of the error when the program is compiled. The program will attempt to access element 12 by skipping over the appropriate number of bytes from the start of the array. Usually this results in a program crash—but not always. If the referenced location itself contains a value of the correct data type, the new value will simply overwrite the value in the referenced memory locations. This leads to more errors, which are particularly troublesome to locate when the variable legitimately assigned to the storage location is used at a different point in the program.

During output, individual array elements can be displayed using the `cout` object, or complete sections of the array can be displayed by including a `cout` statement within a `for` loop. Examples of this are:

```
cout << grade[6];
```

and

```
cout << "The value of element " << i << " is " << temp[i];
```

and

```
const int NUMELS = 20;
for (k = 5; k < = NUMELS; k++)
  cout <<  k << "    " << amount[k] << endl;
```

The first statement displays the value of the subscripted variable `grade[6]`. The second statement displays the value of the subscript `i` and the value of `temp[i]`. Before this statement can be executed, `i` would have to have an assigned value. Finally, the last example includes a `cout` object within a `for` loop. Both the value of the index and the value of the elements from 5 to 20 are displayed.

Program 11.1 illustrates these input and output techniques using an array named `grade` that is defined to store five integer numbers. Included in the program are two `for` loops. The first `for` loop is used to cycle through each array element and allows the user to input individual array values. After five values have been entered, the second `for` loop is used to display the stored values.

PROGRAM 11.1

```
#include <iostream.h>
const int MAXGRADES = 5;

int main()
{
  int i, grade[MAXGRADES];

  for (i = 0; i < MAXGRADES; i++)     // Enter the grades
  {
    cout << "Enter a grade: ";
    cin  >> grade[i];
  }

  cout << '\n';

  for (i = 0; i < MAXGRADES; i++)     // Print the grades
    cout << "grade " << i << " is " << grade[i] << endl;

  return 0;
}
```

A sample run of Program 11.1 follows:

```
Enter a grade: 85
Enter a grade: 90
Enter a grade: 78
Enter a grade: 75
Enter a grade: 92

grade 0 is 85
grade 1 is 90
grade 2 is 78
grade 3 is 75
grade 4 is 92
```

In reviewing the output produced by Program 11.1, pay particular attention to the difference between the displayed index value and the numerical value stored at that index position. The index value refers to the location of the element in the array, while the subscripted variable refers to the value stored in the designated location.

In addition to simply displaying the values stored in each array element, the elements can also be processed by appropriately referencing the desired element. For example, in Program 11.2, the value of each element is accumulated in a total, which is displayed upon completion of the individual display of each array element.

PROGRAM 11.2

```
#include <iostream.h>
const int MAXGRADES = 5;

int main()
{
  int i, grade[MAXGRADES], total = 0;

  for (i = 0; i < MAXGRADES; i++)      // Enter the grades
  {
    cout << "Enter a grade: ";
    cin  >> grade[i];
  }

  cout << "\nThe total of the grades";

  for (i = 0; i < MAXGRADES; i++)      // Display and total the grades
  {
     cout << "  " << grade[i];
     total =  total + grade[i];
  }

  cout << " is " << total << endl;

  return 0;
}
```

A BIT OF BACKGROUND

Handling Lists with LISP

Methods of handling lists have been especially important in the development of computer science and applications. In fact, in 1958 John McCarthy developed a language at the Massachusetts Institute of Technology specifically for manipulating lists. This language was named *LISP*, the acronym for *LISt* Processing. It has proved valuable for handling problems based on mathematical logic and is used extensively in artificial intelligence and pattern recognition projects.

One simple language related to LISP is named *Logo*, and has been made particularly user friendly. It incorporates a technique called "turtle graphics," by which a pointer is moved around the screen to plot geometric figures. Logo has been used widely to teach programming fundamentals to children.

LISP was one of, if not the first, OOP languages. One of the newest languages used on the Internet, which is named Java, has elements of LISP in it.

A sample run of Program 11.2 follows:

```
Enter a grade: 85
Enter a grade: 90
Enter a grade: 78
Enter a grade: 75
Enter a grade: 92

The total of the grades  85   90   78   75   92 is 420
```

Notice that in Program 11.2, unlike Program 11.1, only the values stored in each array element are displayed. Although the second `for` loop was used to accumulate the total of each element, the accumulation could also have been accomplished in the first loop by placing the statement `total = total + grade[i];` after the `cin` statement used to enter a value. Also notice that the `cout` statement used to display the total is made outside of the second `for` loop, so that the total is displayed only once, after all values have been added to the total. If this `cout` statement were placed inside of the `for` loop, five totals would be displayed, with only the last displayed total containing the sum of all of the array values.

Exercises 11.1

1. Write array declarations for the following:
   a. a list of 100 float grades
   b. a list of 50 floating-point temperatures
   c. a list of 30 characters, each representing a code
   d. a list of 100 integer years
   e. a list of 32 floating-point velocities
   f. a list of 1000 floating-point distances
   g. a list of 6 integer code numbers

2. Write appropriate notation for the first, third, and seventh elements of the following arrays:

   a. `int grade[20]`

   b. `float prices[10]`

   c. `float amps[16]`

   d. `int dist[15]`

   e. `float velocity[25]`

   f. `float time[100]`

3. a. Write individual `cin` statements that can be used to enter values into the first, third, and seventh elements of each of the arrays declared in Exercises 2a through 2f.

   b. Write a `for` loop that can be used to enter values for the complete array declared in Exercise 2a.

4. a. Write individual `cout` statements that can be used to print the values from the first, third, and seventh elements of each of the arrays declared in Exercises 2a through 2f.

   b. Write a `for` loop that can be used to display values for the complete array declared in Exercise 2a.

5. List the elements that will be displayed by the following sections of code:

   a.
   ```
   for (m = 1; m <= 5; m++)
     cout << a[m] << " ";
   ```

   b.
   ```
   for (k = 1; k <= 5; k = k + 2)
     cout <<  a[k] << " ";
   ```

   c.
   ```
   for (j = 3; j <= 10; j++)
     cout << b[j] << " ";
   ```

   d.
   ```
   for (k = 3; k <= 12; k = k + 3)
     cout << b[k] << " ";
   ```

   e.
   ```
   for (i = 2; i < 11; i = i + 2)
     cout << c[i] << " ";
   ```

6. a. Write a program to input the following values into an array named `prices`: 10.95, 16.32, 12.15, 8.22, 15.98, 26.22, 13.54, 6.45, 17.59. After the data has been entered, have your program output the values.

   b. Repeat Exercise 6a, but after the data has been entered, have your program display it in the following form:

   ```
   10.95      16.32      12.15
    8.22      15.98      26.22
   13.54       6.45      17.59
   ```

7. Write a program to input eight integer numbers into an array named `temp`. As each number is input, add the numbers into a total. After all numbers are input, display the numbers and their average.

8. a. Write a program to input 10 integer numbers into an array named `fmax` and determine the maximum value entered. Your program should contain only one loop and the maximum should be determined as array element values are being input. (*Hint:* Set the maximum equal to the first array element, which should be input before the loop used to input the remaining array values.)

   b. Repeat Exercise 8a, keeping track of both the maximum element in the array and the index number for the maximum. After displaying the numbers, print these two messages

```
The maximum value is:___
This is element number ___ in the list of numbers
```

Have your program display the correct values in place of the underlines in the messages.

c. Repeat Exercise 8b, but have your program locate the minimum of the data entered.

9. a. Write a program to input the following integer numbers into an array named `grade`: 89, 95, 72, 83, 99, 54, 86, 75, 92, 73, 79, 75, 82, 73. As each number is input, add the numbers to a total. After all numbers are input and the total is obtained, calculate the average of the numbers and use the average to determine the deviation of each value from the average. Store each deviation in an array named `deviation`. Each deviation is obtained as the element value less the average of all the data. Have your program display each deviation alongside its corresponding element from the `grade` array.

   b. Calculate the variance of the data used in Exercise 9a. The variance is obtained by squaring each individual deviation and dividing the sum of the squared deviations by the number of deviations.

10. Write a program that specifies three one-dimensional arrays named `prices`, `quantity`, and `amount`. Each array should be capable of holding 10 elements. Using a `for` loop, input values for the `prices` and `quantity` arrays. The entries in the `amount` array should be the product of the corresponding values in the `prices` and `quantity` arrays (thus, `amount[i] = price[i] * quantity[I])`. After all of the data has been entered, display the following output:

```
Price          Quantity          Amount
-----          --------          ------
```

Under each column heading display the appropriate value.

11. a. Write a program that inputs 10 float numbers into an array named `raw`. After 10 user-input numbers are entered into the array, your program should cycle through `raw` 10 times. During each pass through the array, your program should select the lowest value in `raw` and place the selected value in the next available slot in an array named `sorted`. Thus, when your program is complete, the sorted array should contain the numbers in `raw` in sorted order from lowest to highest. (*Hint:* Make sure to reset the lowest value selected during each pass to a very high number so that it is not selected again. You will need a second `for` loop within the first `for` loop to locate the minimum value for each pass.)

   b. The method used in Exercise 11a to sort the values in the array is very inefficient. Can you determine why? What might be a better method of sorting the numbers in an array?

11.2 ARRAY INITIALIZATION

Array elements can be initialized within their declaration statements in the same manner as scalar variables, except that the initializing elements must be included in braces. Examples of such initializations are:

```
int grade[5] = {98, 87, 92, 79, 85};
char codes[6] = {'s', 'a', 'm', 'p', 'l', 'e'};
double width[7] = {10.96, 6.43, 2.58, .86, 5.89, 7.56, 8.22};
```

Initializers are applied in the order in which they are written, with the first value used to initialize element 0, the second value used to initialize element 1, and so on, until all values have been used. Thus, in the declaration

```
int grade[5] = {98, 87, 92, 79, 85};
```

grade[0] is initialized to 98, grade[1] is initialized to 87, grade[2] is initialized to 92, grade[3] is initialized to 79, and grade[4] is initialized to 85.

Because white space is ignored in C++, initializations may be continued across multiple lines. For example, the declaration

```
int gallons[20] = {19, 16, 14, 19, 20, 18,   // initializing values
                   12, 10, 22, 15, 18, 17,   // may extend across
                   16, 14, 23, 19, 15, 18,   // multiple lines
                   21, 5};
```

uses four lines to initialize all of the array elements.

If the number of initializers is less than the declared number of elements listed in square brackets, the initializers are applied starting with array element 0. Thus, in the declaration

```
float length[7] = {7.8, 6.4, 4.9, 11.2};
```

only length[0], length[1], length[2], and length[3] are initialized with the listed values. The other array elements will be initialized to zero.

Unfortunately, there is no method of either indicating repetition of an initialization value or initializing later array elements without first specifying values for earlier elements.

A unique feature of initializers is that the size of an array may be omitted when initializing values are included in the declaration statement. For example, the declaration

```
int gallons[] = {16, 12, 10, 14, 11};
```

reserves enough storage room for five elements. Similarly, the following two declarations are equivalent:

```
char codes[6] = {'s', 'a', 'm', 'p', 'l', 'e'};
char codes[] = {'s', 'a', 'm', 'p', 'l', 'e'};
```

Both of these declarations set aside six character locations for an array named codes. An interesting and useful simplification can also be used when initializing character arrays. For example, the declaration

```
char codes[] = "sample";    // no braces or commas
```

uses the string "sample" to initialize the codes array. Recall that a string is any sequence of characters enclosed in double quotes. This last declaration creates an array named codes having seven elements and fills the array with the seven characters illustrated in Figure 11.6. The first six characters, as expected, consist of the letters s, a, m, p, l, and e. The last character, which is the escape sequence \0, is called the **null character.** The null character is automatically appended to all strings by the C++ compiler. This character has an internal storage code that is numerically equal to zero (the storage code for the zero character

FIGURE 11.6 A String Is Terminated with a Special Sentinel

codes[0]	codes[1]	codes[2]	codes[3]	codes[4]	codes[5]	codes[6]
s	a	m	p	l	e	\0

has a numerical value of decimal 48, so the two cannot be confused by the computer), and is used as a marker, or sentinel, to mark the end of a string. As we shall see in Chapter 12, this marker is invaluable when manipulating arrays of characters, which is how strings are stored in C++.

Once values have been assigned to array elements, either through initialization within the declaration statement or by using interactive input, the array elements can be processed as described in the previous section. For example, Program 11.3 illustrates the initialization of array elements within the declaration of the array and then uses a `for` loop to locate the maximum value stored in the array.

PROGRAM 11.3

```
#include <iostream.h>

const int MAXELS = 5;

int main()
{
  int i, max, nums[MAXELS] = {2, 18, 1, 27, 16};

  max = nums[0];

  for (i = 1; i < MAXELS; i++)
    if (max < nums[i])
      max = nums[i];

  cout << "The maximum value is " << max << endl;

  return 0;
}
```

The output produced by Program 11.3 is:

```
The maximum value is 27
```

Exercises 11.2

1. Write array declarations, including initializers, for the following:
   a. a list of 10 integer grades: 89, 75, 82, 93, 78, 95, 81, 88, 77, 82
   b. a list of five double-precision amounts: 10.62, 13.98, 18.45, 12.68, 14.76
   c. a list of 100 double-precision interest rates; the first six rates are 6.29, 6.95, 7.25, 7.35, 7.40, 7.42
   d. a list of 64 floating-point temperatures; the first 10 temperatures are 78.2, 69.6, 68.5, 83.9, 55.4, 67.0, 49.8, 58.3, 62.5, 71.6
   e. a list of 15 character codes; the first seven codes are f, j, m, q, t, w, z

2. Write an array declaration statement that stores the following values in an array named `prices`: 16.24, 18.98, 23.75, 16.29, 19.54, 14.22, 11.13, 15.39. Include these statements in a program that displays the values in the array.
3. Write a program that uses an array declaration statement to initialize the following numbers in an array named `slopes`: 17.24, 25.63, 5.94, 33.92, 3.71, 32.84, 35.93, 18.24, 6.92. Your program should locate and display both the maximum and minimum values in the array.
4. Write a program that stores the following prices in an array named `prices`: 9.92, 6.32, 12.63, 5.95, 10.29. Your program should also create two arrays named `units` and `amounts`, each capable of storing five double-precision numbers. Using a `for` loop and a `cin` statement, have your program accept five user-input numbers into the units array when the program is run. Your program should store the product of the corresponding values in the `prices` and `units` arrays in the `amounts` array (for example, `amounts[1] = prices[1] * units[1]`) and display the following output (fill in the table appropriately):

```
Price     Units     Amount
-----     -----     ------
 9.92       .          .
 6.32       .          .
12.63       .          .
 5.95       .          .
10.29       .          .
                    ------
Total:                 .
```

5. The string of characters `"Good Morning"` is to be stored in a character array named `goodstr1`. Write the declaration for this array in three different ways.
6. a. Write declaration statements to store the string of characters `"Input the Following Data"` in a character array named `messag1`, the string `"------------"` in an array named `messag2`, the string `"Enter the Date: "` in an array named `messag3`, and the string `"Enter the Account Number: "` in the array named `messag4`.

   b. Include the array declarations written in Exercise 6a in a program that uses the `cout` object to display the messages. For example, the statement

   ```
   cout << messag1;
   ```

   causes the string stored in the `messag1` array to be displayed. Your program will require four such statements to display the four individual messages. Using the `cout` object to display a string requires that the last character in the string be the end-of-string marker `\0`.
7. a. Write a declaration to store the string `"This is a test"` into an array named `strtest`. Include the declaration in a program to display the message using the following loop:

   ```
   for (i = 0; i < NUMDISPLAY; i++)
     cout << strtest[i];
   ```

   where `NUMDISPLAY` is a named constant for the number 14.

   b. Modify the `for` statement in Exercise 7a to display only the array characters `t`, `e`, `s`, and `t`.

   c. Include the array declaration written in Exercise 7a in a program that uses the `cout` object to display characters in the array. For example, the statement `cout << strtest;` will cause the string stored in the `strtest` array to be displayed. Using this statement requires that the last character in the array be the end-of-string marker `\0`.

   d. Repeat Exercise 7a using a `while` loop. [*Hint:* Stop the loop when the `\0` escape sequence is detected. The expression `while(strtest[i] != '\0')` can be used.]

11.3 ARRAYS AS FUNCTION ARGUMENTS

Individual array elements are passed to a called function in the same manner as individual scalar variables; they are simply included as subscripted variables when the function call is made. For example, the function call

```
find_min(grade[2], grade[6]);
```

passes the values of the elements `grade[2]` and `grade[6]` to the function `find_min()`.

Passing a complete array of values to a function is in many respects an easier operation than passing individual elements. The called function receives access to the actual array, rather than a copy of the values in the array. For example, if `grade` is an array, the function call `find_max(grade);` makes the complete `grade` array available to the `find_max()` function. This is different from passing a single variable to a function.

Recall that when a single scalar argument is passed to a function, the called function only receives *a copy* of the passed value, which is stored in one of the function's parameters. If arrays were passed in this manner, a copy of the complete array would have to be created. For large arrays, making duplicate copies of the array for each function call would waste computer storage and would frustrate the effort to return multiple element changes made by the called program (recall that a function directly returns at most one value). To avoid these problems, the called function is given direct access to the original array.[3] Thus, any changes made by the called function are made directly to the array itself. For the following specific examples of function calls, assume that the arrays `nums`, `keys`, `units`, and `prices` are declared as:

```
int nums[5];                      // an array of five integers
char keys[256];                   // an array of 256 characters
double units[500], prices[500]; // two arrays of 500 doubles
```

For these arrays, the following function calls can be made:

```
find_max(nums);
find_ch(keys);
calc_tot(nums, units, prices);
```

In each case, the called function receives direct access to the named array.

On the receiving side, the called function must be alerted that an array is being made available. For example, suitable function header lines for the previous functions are:

```
int find_max(int vals[5])
char find_ch(char in_keys[256])
void calc_tot(int arr1[5], double arr2[500], double arr3[500])
```

In each of these function header lines, the names in the parameter list are chosen by the programmer. However, the parameter names used by the functions still refer to the original array created outside the function. This is made clear in Program 11.4.

---

[3] This is accomplished because the starting address of the array is actually passed as an argument. The formal parameter receiving this address argument is a pointer. The intimate relationship between array names and pointers is presented in Chapter 13.

PROGRAM 11.4

```
#include <iostream.h>

const int MAXELS = 5;

int find_max(int [MAXELS]);        // function prototype

int main()
{
  int nums[MAXELS] = {2, 18, 1, 27, 16};

  cout << "The maximum value is " << find_max(nums) << endl;

  return 0;
}

// find the maximum value
int find_max(int vals[MAXELS])
{
  int i, max = vals[0];

  for (i = 1; i < MAXELS; i++)
    if (max < vals[i]) max = vals[i];

  return max;
}
```

Notice that the function prototype for `find_max()` within `main()` declares that `find_max` will return an integer and expects an array of five integers as an actual argument. It is also important to know that only one array is created in Program 11.4. In `main()` this array is known as `nums`, and in `find_max()` the array is known as `vals`. As illustrated in Figure 11.7, both names refer to the same array. Thus, in Figure 11.7 `vals[3]` is the same element as `nums[3]`.

The parameter declaration in the `find_max()` header line actually contains extra information that is not required by the function. All that `find_max()` must know is that the argument `vals` references an array of integers. Since the array has been created in `main()` and no additional storage space is needed in `find_max()`, the declaration for `vals` can omit the size of the array. Thus, an alternative function header line is:

```
int find_max(int vals[])
```

This form of the function header makes more sense when you realize that only one item is actually passed to `find_max` when the function is called, which is the starting address of the `nums` array. This is illustrated in Figure 11.8.

Since only the starting address of `the nums array` is passed to `find_max`, the number of elements in the array need not be included in the declaration for vals.[4] In fact, it is generally advisable to omit the size of the array in the function header line. For example, consider the more general form of find_max(), which can be used to find the maximum value of an integer array of arbitrary size:

FIGURE 11.7 Only One Array Is Created

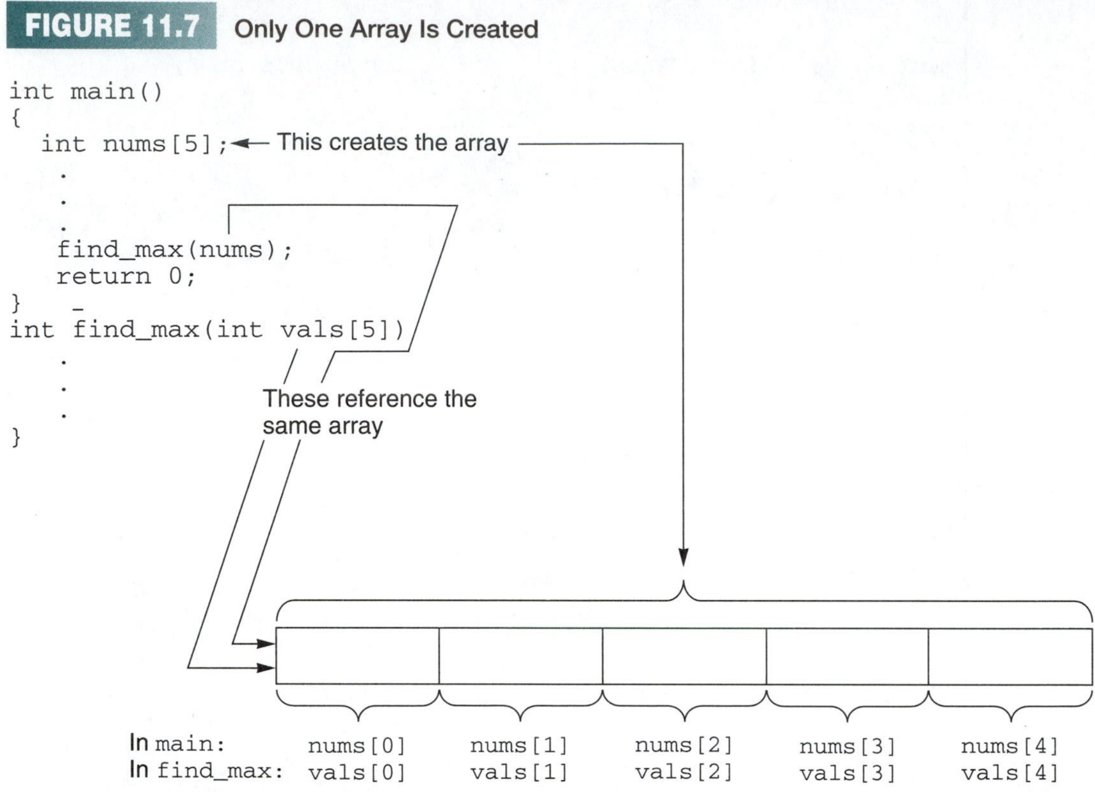

FIGURE 11.8 The Starting Address of the Array Is Passed

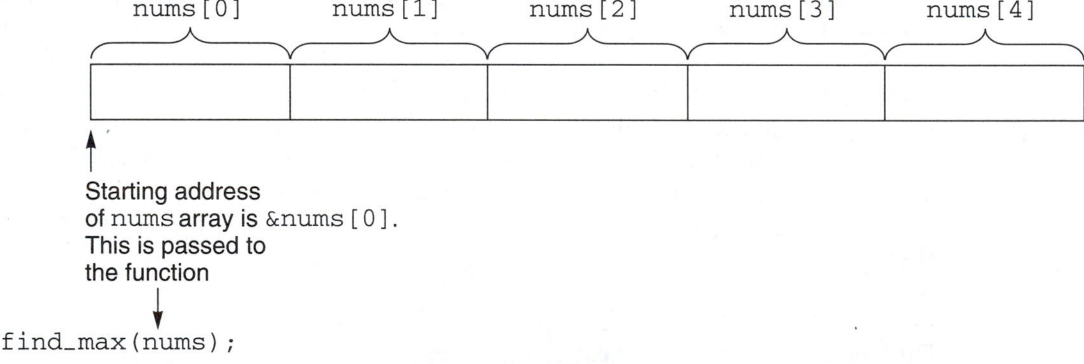

[4] An important consequence of this is that find_max() has direct access to the passed array. This means that any change to an element of the vals array actually is a change to the nums array. This is significantly different than the situation with scalar variables, where the called function does not receive direct access to the passed variable.

```
int find_max(int vals[], int num_els)    // find the maximum value
{
  int i, max = vals[0];

  for (i = 1; i < num_els; i++)
   if (max < vals[i])
     max = vals[i];

  return max;
}
```

The more general form of `find_max()` declares that the function returns an integer value. The function expects the starting address of an integer array and the number of elements in the array as arguments. Then, using the number of elements as the boundary for its search, the function's `for` loop causes each array element to be examined in sequential order to locate the maximum value. Program 11.5 illustrates the use of `find_max()` in a complete program.

PROGRAM 11.5

```
#include <iostream.h>
const int MAXELS = 5;

int find_max(int [], int);    // function prototype

int main()
{
  int nums[MAXELS] = {2, 18, 1, 27, 16};


  cout << "The maximum value is "
       << find_max(nums, MAXELS) << endl;

  return 0;
}

// find the maximum value
int find_max(int vals[], int num_els)
{
  int i, max = vals[0];

  for (i = 1; i < num_els; i++)
    if (max < vals[i]) max = vals[i];

 return max;
}
```

The output displayed by both Programs 11.4 and 11.5 is:

```
The maximum value is 27
```

Exercises 11.3

1. The following declaration was used to create the `prices` array:

   `double prices[500];`

   Write two different function header lines for a function named `sort_arr()` that accepts the `prices` array as a parameter named `in_array` and returns no value.

2. The following declaration was used to create the `keys` array:

   `char keys[256];`

   Write two different function header lines for a function named `find_key()` that accepts the `keys` array as a parameter named `select` and returns no value.

3. The following declaration was used to create the `rates` array:

   `float rates[256];`

   Write two different function header lines for a function named `prime()` that accepts the `rates` array as a parameter named `rates` and returns a floating point value.

4. a. Modify the `find_max()` function in Program 11.4 to locate the minimum value of the passed array.

   b. Include the function written in Exercise 4a in a complete program and run the program on a computer.

5. Write a program that has a declaration in `main()` to store the following numbers into an array named `rates`: 6.5, 7.2, 7.5, 8.3, 8.6, 9.4, 9.6, 9.8, 10.0. There should be a function call to `show()` that accepts the `rates` array as an argument named `rates` and then displays the numbers in the array.

6. a. Write a program that has a declaration in `main()` to store the string `"Vacation is near"` into an array named `message`. There should be a function call to `display()` that accepts `message` in an argument named `strng` and then displays the message.

   b. Modify the `display()` function written in Exercise 6a to display the first eight elements of the `message` array.

7. Write a program that declares three single-dimensional arrays named `price`, `quantity`, and `amount`. Each array should be declared in `main()` and should be capable of holding 10 double-precision numbers. The numbers that should be stored in `price` are 10.62, 14.89, 13.21, 16.55, 18.62, 9.47, 6.58, 18.32, 12.15, 3.98. The numbers that should be stored in `quantity` are 4, 8.5, 6, 7.35, 9, 15.3, 3, 5.4, 2.9, 4.8. Your program should pass these three arrays to a function called `extend()`, which should calculate the elements in the `amount` array as the product of the corresponding elements in the `price` and `quantity` arrays (for example, `amount[1] = price[1] * quantity[1]`). After `extend()` has put values into the `amount` array, the values in the array should be displayed from within `main()`.

8. Write a program that includes two functions named `calc_avg()` and `variance()`. The `calc_avg()` function should calculate and return the average of the values stored in an array named `testvals`. The array should be declared in `main()` and include the values 89, 95, 72, 83, 99, 54, 86, 75, 92, 73, 79, 75, 82, 73. The `variance()` function should calculate and return the variance of the data. The variance is obtained by subtracting the average from each value in `testvals`, squaring the values obtained, adding them, and dividing by the number of elements in `testvals`. The values returned from `calc_avg()` and `variance()` should be displayed using `cout` statements in `main()`.

11.4 DECLARING AND PROCESSING TWO-DIMENSIONAL ARRAYS

A **two-dimensional array,** which is sometimes referred to as a *table,* consists of both rows and columns of elements. For example, the following array of numbers

```
 8   16    9   52
 3   15   27    6
14   25    2   10
```

is called a two-dimensional array of integers. This array consists of three rows and four columns. To reserve storage for this array, both the number of rows and the number of columns must be included in the array's declaration. Calling the array `val`, the correct specification for this two-dimensional array is

```
int val[3][4];
```

Similarly, the declarations

```
float prices[10][5];
char code[6][26];
```

declare that the array `prices` consists of 10 rows and 5 columns of floating-point numbers and that the array `code` consists of 6 rows and 26 columns, with each element capable of holding one character.

To locate each element in a two-dimensional array, an element is identified by its position in the array. As illustrated in Figure 11.9, the term `val[1][3]` uniquely identifies the element in row 1, column 3. As with single-dimensional array variables, double-dimensional array variables can be used anywhere scalar variables are valid. Examples using elements of the `val` array are:

```
amount = val[2][3];
val[0][0] = 62;
newnum = 4 * (val[1][0] - 5);
sum_row = val[0][0] + val[0][1] + val[0][2] + val[0][3];
```

The last statement causes the values of the four elements in row 0 to be added and the sum to be stored in the scalar variable `sum_row`.

FIGURE 11.9 Each Array Element Is Identified by Its Row and Column Position

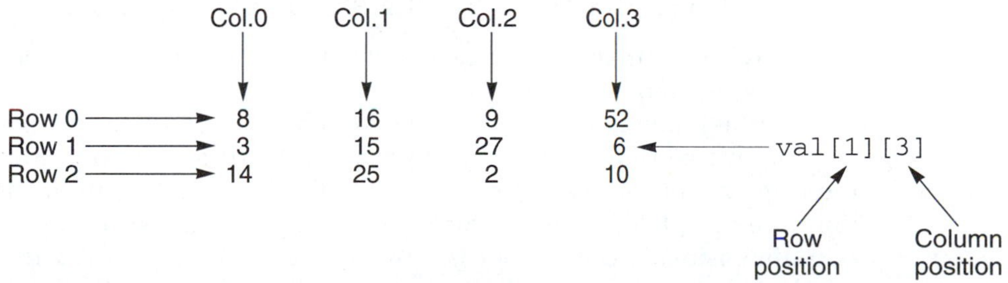

FIGURE 11.10 Storage and Initialization of the `val[]` Array

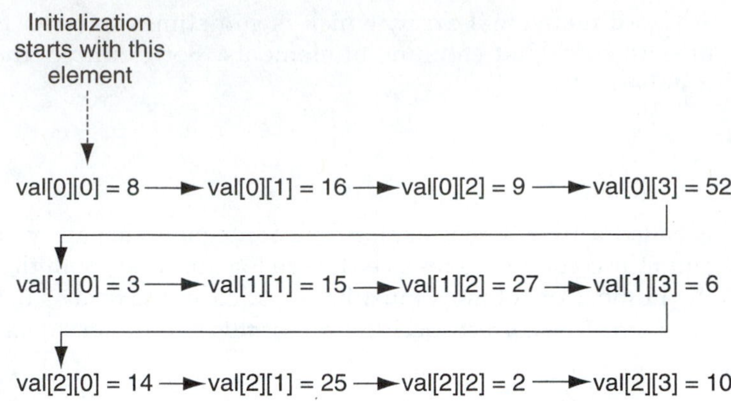

As with single-dimensional arrays, two-dimensional arrays can be initialized from within their declaration statements. This is done by listing the initial values within braces and separating them by commas. Additionally, braces can be used to separate individual rows. For example, the declaration

```
int val[3][4] = { {8,16,9,52},
                  {3,15,27,6},
                  {14,25,2,10} };
```

declares `val` to be an array of integers with three rows and four columns, with the initial values given in the declaration. The first set of internal braces contains the values for row 0 of the array, the second set of internal braces contains the values for row 1, and the third set of braces the values for row 2.

Although the commas in the initialization braces are always required, the inner braces can be omitted. Thus, the initialization for val may be written as

```
int val[3][4] = {8,16,9,52,
                  3,15,27,6,
                 14,25,2,10};
```

The separation of initial values into rows in the declaration statement is not necessary since the compiler assigns values beginning with the [0][0] element and proceeds row by row to fill in the remaining values. Thus, the initialization

```
int val[3][4] = {8,16,9,52,3,15,27,6,14,25,2,10};
```

is equally valid but does not clearly illustrate to another programmer where one row ends and another begins.

As illustrated in Figure 11.10, the initialization of a two-dimensional array is done in row order. First, the elements of the first row are initialized, then the elements of the second row are initialized, and so on, until the initializations are completed. This row ordering is also the same ordering used to store two-dimensional arrays. That is, array element [0][0] is stored first, followed by element [0][1], followed by element [0][2], and so on. Following the first row's elements are the second row's elements, and so on for all the rows in the array.

As with single-dimensional arrays, two-dimensional arrays may be displayed by individual element notation or by using loops (either `while` or `for` loops). This is illustrated by Program 11.6, which displays all of the elements of a 3 by 4 two-dimensional array using two different techniques. Notice in Program 11.6 that we have used named constants to define the array's rows and columns.

PROGRAM 11.6

```
#include <iostream.h>
#include <iomanip.h>

const int NUMROWS = 3;
const int NUMCOLS = 4;

int main()
{
  int i, j;
  int val[NUMROWS][NUMCOLS] = {8,16,9,52,3,15,27,6,14,25,2,10};

  cout << "\nDisplay of val array by explicit element"
       << '\n' << setw(4) << val[0][0] << setw(4) << val[0][1]
       << setw(4) << val[0][2] << setw(4) << val[0][3]
       << '\n' << setw(4) << val[1][0] << setw(4) << val[1][1]
       << setw(4) << val[1][2] << setw(4) << val[1][3]
       << '\n' << setw(4) << val[2][0] << setw(4) << val[2][1]
       << setw(4) << val[2][2] << setw(4) << val[2][3];

  cout << "\n\nDisplay of val array using a nested for loop";

  for (i = 0; i < NUMROWS; i++)
  {
    cout << '\n';       // print a new line for each row
    for (j = 0; j < NUMCOLS; j++)
      cout << setw(4) <<  val[i][j];
  }

  cout << endl;

  return 0;
}
```

The display produced by Program 11.6 follows:

```
Display of val array by explicit element
   8  16   9  52
   3  15  27   6
  14  25   2  10
Display of val array using a nested for loop
   8  16   9  52
   3  15  27   6
  14  25   2  10
```

The first display of the `val` array produced by Program 11.6 is constructed by explicitly designating each array element. The second display of array element values, which is identical to the first, is produced using a nested `for` loop. Nested loops are especially useful when dealing with two-dimensional arrays because they allow the programmer to designate and cycle through each element easily. In Program 11.6, the variable `i` controls the outer loop and the variable `j` controls the inner loop. Each pass through the outer loop corresponds to a single row, with the inner loop supplying the appropriate column elements. After a complete row is printed, a new line is started for the next row. The effect is a display of the array in a row-by-row fashion.

Once two-dimensional array elements have been assigned, array processing can begin. Typically, `for` loops are used to process two-dimensional arrays because, as was previously noted, they allow the programmer to designate and cycle through each array element easily. For example, the nested `for` loop illustrated in Program 11.7 is used to multiply each element in the `val` array by the scalar number 10 and display the resulting value.

PROGRAM 11.7

```
#include <iostream.h>
#include <iomanip.h>

const int NUMROWS = 3;
const int NUMCOLS = 4;

int main()
{
  int i, j;
  int val[NUMROWS][NUMCOLS] = {8,16,9,52,
                              3,15,27,6,
                             14,25,2,10};

// multiply each element by 10 and display it
  cout << "\nDisplay of multiplied elements";
  for (i = 0; i < NUMROWS; i++)
  {
    cout << '\n';    // start each row on a new line
    for (j = 0; j < NUMCOLS; j++)
    {
      val[i][j] = val[i][j] * 10;
      cout << setw(5) << val[i][j];
    }  // end of inner loop
  }    // end of outer loop
  cout << endl;

  return 0;
}
```

The output produced by Program 11.7 follows:

```
Display of multiplied elements
  80 160  90 520
  30 150 270  60
 140 250  20 100
```

Passing two-dimensional arrays into a function is a process identical to passing single-dimensional arrays. The called function receives access to the entire array. For example, the function call `display(val);` makes the complete `val` array available to the function named `display()`. Thus, any changes made by `display()` will be made directly to the `val` array. Assuming that the following two-dimensional arrays named `test`, `code`, and `stocks` are declared as:

```
int test[7][9];
char code[26][10];
float stocks[256][52];
```

the following function calls are valid:

```
find_max(test);
obtain(code);
price(stocks);
```

On the receiving side, the called function must be alerted that a two-dimensional array is being made available. For example, assuming that each of the previous functions returns an integer, suitable function header lines for the functions are:

```
int find_max(int nums[7][9])
int obtain(char key[26][10])
int price(float names[256][52])
```

In each of these function header lines, the parameter names chosen are local to the function. However, the internal local names used by the function still refer to the original array created outside the function. Program 11.8 illustrates passing of a local, two-dimensional array into a function that displays the array's values.

Only one array is created in Program 11.8. This array is known as `val` in `main()` and as `nums` in `display()`. Thus, `val[0][2]` refers to the same element as `nums[0][2]`.

Notice the use of the nested `for` loop in Program 11.8 for cycling through each array element. In Program 11.8, the variable `row_num` controls the outer loop and the variable `col_num` controls the inner loop. For each pass through the outer loop, which corresponds to a row, the inner loop makes one pass through the column elements. After a complete row is printed, the `\n` escape sequence causes a new line to be started for the next row. The effect is a display of the array in a row-by-row fashion:

```
 8 16  9 52
 3 15 27  6
14 25  2 10
```

The argument declaration for `nums` in `display()` contains extra information that is not required by the function. The declaration for `nums` can omit the row size of the array. Thus, an alternative function prototype is:

```
display(int nums[][4]);
```

PROGRAM 11.8

```
#include <iostream.h>
#include <iomanip.h>

const int ROWS = 3;
const int COLS = 4;

void display(int [ROWS][COLS]);     // function prototype

int main()
{
  int val[ROWS][COLS] = {8,16,9,52,
                         3,15,27,6,
                        14,25,2,10};

  display(val);

  return 0;
}

void display(int nums[ROWS][COLS])
{
  int row_num, col_num;

  for (row_num = 0; row_num < ROWS; row_num++)
  {
    for(col_num = 0; col_num < COLS; col_num++)
      cout << setw(4) <<nums[row_num][col_num];
    cout << endl;
  }

  return;
}
```

The reason why the column size must be included while the row size is optional becomes obvious when you consider how the array elements are stored in memory. Starting with element `val[0][0]`, each succeeding element is stored consecutively, row by row, as `val[0][0]`, `val[0][1]`, `val[0][2]`, `val[0][3]`, `val[1][0]`, `val[1][1]`, etc., as illustrated in Figure 11.11.

FIGURE 11.11 Storage of the `val` Array

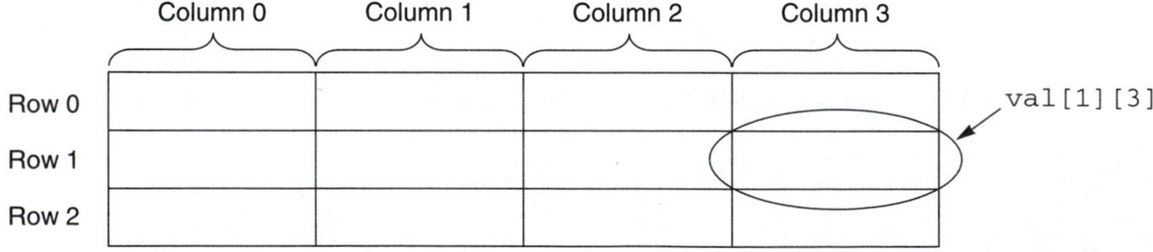

As with all array accesses, an individual element of the `val` array is obtained by adding an offset to the starting location of the array. For example, element `val[1][3]` of the `val` array illustrated in Figure 11.11 is located at an offset of 14 bytes from the start of the array. Internally, the compiler determines this offset using the following calculation:

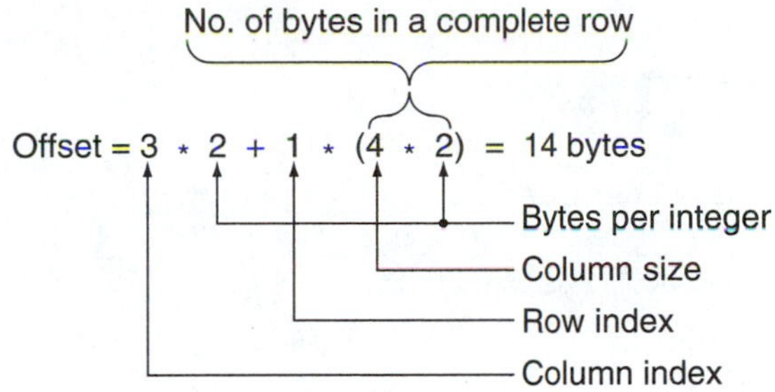

The column size is necessary in the offset calculation so that the compiler can determine the number of positions to skip over in order to get to the desired row.

Internal Array Element Location Algorithm

Internally, each individual element in an array is obtained by adding an offset to the starting address of the array. Thus, the memory address of each array element is internally calculated as

Address of element i = starting array address + the offset

For single-dimensional arrays the offset to the element with index `i` is calculated as:

*Offset = i * the size of an individual element*

For two-dimensional arrays, the same address calculation is made, except that the offset is determined as follows:

*Offset = column index value * the size of an individual*
*+ row index value * number of bytes in a complete row*

where the number of bytes in a complete row is calculated as:

number of bytes in a complete row =
*maximum column specification * the size of an individual element*

FIGURE 11.12 The Offset to the Element with an Index Value of 5

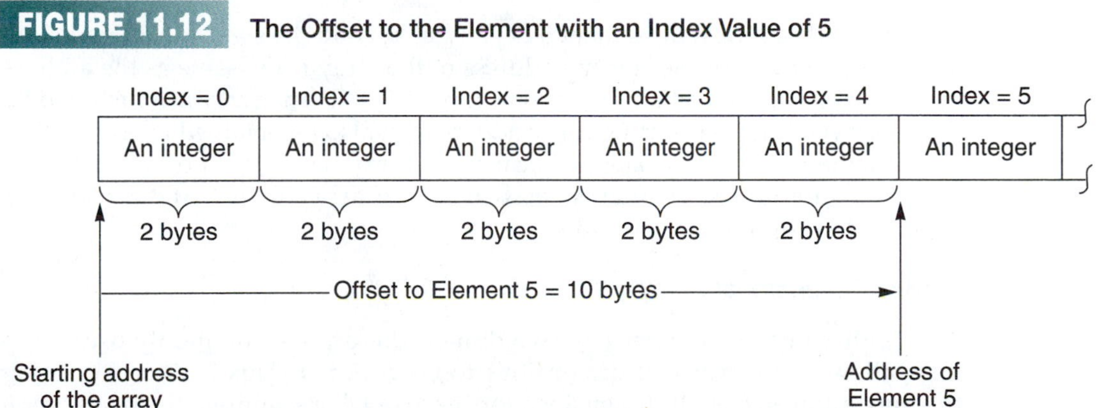

For example, as illustrated in Figure 11.12, for an array of integers where each integer is stored using 2 bytes, the offset to the element whose index value is 5 would be 5 * 2 = 10.

Using the address operator, &, we can check this address algorithm. For example, consider Program 11.9.

PROGRAM 11.9

```
#include <iostream.h>

const int NUMELS = 20;

int main()
{
  int arr[NUMELS];

  cout << "The starting address of the arr array is: "
       << &arr[0] << endl;
  cout << "The storage size of each array element is: "
       << sizeof(int) << endl;
  cout << "The address of element number 5 is: "
       << &arr[5] << endl;
  cout << "The starting address of the array, "
       << "\ndisplayed using the notation arr, is: "
       << arr << endl;

  return 0;
}
```

The output produced by executing Program 11.9 is:

```
The starting address of the arr array is: 0x2401ffce
The storage size of each array element is: 2
The address of element number 5 is: 0x2401ffd8
The starting address of the array,
displayed using the notation arr, is: 0x2401ffce
```

Notice that the address of element 5 is 10 bytes beyond the starting address of the array. Also notice that the starting address of the array is the same as the address of the zeroth element, which is coded as `&arr[0]`. Alternatively, as illustrated by the displayed line, the starting array address can also be obtained as `arr`, which is the name of the array. This is because an array name is a pointer constant, which is an address. (The close association of array names and pointers is explained in depth in Chapter 13.)

Larger Dimensional Arrays

Although arrays with more than two dimensions are not commonly used, C++ does allow any number of dimensions to be declared. This is done by listing the maximum size of all dimensions for the array. For example, the declaration

FIGURE 11.13 Representation of a Three-Dimensional Array

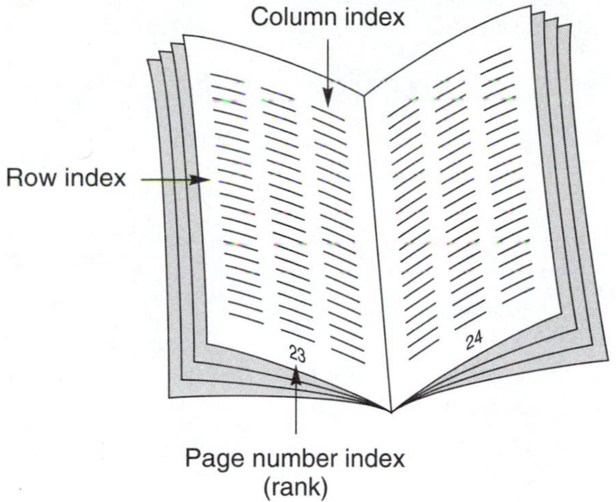

`int response[4][10][6];` declares a three-dimensional array. The first element in the array is designated as `response[0][0][0]` and the last element as `response[3][9][5]`.

Conceptually, as illustrated in Figure 11.13, a three-dimensional array can be viewed as a book of data tables. Using this visualization, the first index can be thought of as the location of the desired row in a table, the second index value as the desired column, and the third index value, which is often called the *rank*, as the page number of the selected table. Similarly, arrays of any dimension can be declared. Conceptually, a four-dimensional array can be represented as a shelf of books, where the fourth dimension is used to declare a desired book on the shelf, and a five-dimensional array can be viewed as a bookcase filled with books where the fifth dimension refers to a selected shelf in the bookcase. Using the same analogy, a six-dimensional array can be considered as a single row of bookcases where the sixth dimension references to the desired bookcase in the row; a seven-dimensional array can be considered as multiple rows of bookcases where the seventh dimension references the desired row, and so on. Alternatively, arrays of three, four, five, six, etc., dimensional arrays can be viewed as mathematical n-tuples of order three, four, five, six, etc., respectively.

Exercises 11.4

1. Write appropriate specification statements for:
   a. an array of integers with 6 rows and 10 columns
   b. an array of integers with 2 rows and 5 columns
   c. an array of characters with 7 rows and 12 columns
   d. an array of characters with 15 rows and 7 columns
   e. an array of floating-point numbers with 10 rows and 25 columns
   f. an array of floating-point numbers with 16 rows and 8 columns

2. Determine the output produced by the following program:

```
#include <iostream.h>
const int ROWS = 3;
const int COLS = 4;
int main()
{
  int i, j, val[3][4] = {8,16,9,52,3,15,27,6,14,25,2,10};

  for (i = 0; i < ROWS; i++)
  {
    for (j = 0; j < COLS; j++)
      cout << val[i][j] << " ";
    cout << endl;
  }
  return 0;
}
```

3. a. Write a C++ program that adds the values of all elements in the `val` array used in Exercise 2 and displays the total.

   b. Modify the program written for Exercise 3a to display the total of each row separately.

4. Write a C++ program that adds equivalent elements of the two-dimensional arrays named `first` and `second`. Both arrays should have two rows and three columns. For example, `element [1][2]` of the resulting array should be the sum of `first[1][2]` and `second[1][2]`. The first and second arrays should be initialized as follows:

First			Second		
16	18	23	24	52	77
54	91	11	16	19	59

5. a. Write a C++ program that finds and displays the maximum value in a two-dimensional array of integers. The array should be declared as a 4 × 5 array of integers and initialized with this data: 16, 22, 99, 4, 18, −258, 4, 101, 5, 98, 105, 6, 15, 2, 45, 33, 88, 72, 16, 3.

   b. Modify the program written in Exercise 5a so that it also displays the maximum value's row and column subscript numbers.

6. Write a C++ program to select the values in a 4 × 5 array of integers in increasing order and store the selected values in the single-dimensional array named `sort`. Use the data statement given in Exercise 5a to initialize the two-dimensional array.

7. a. A professor has constructed a two-dimensional array of float numbers having three rows and five columns. This array currently contains the test grades of the students in the professor's advanced compiler design class. Write a C++ program that reads 15 array values and then determine the total number of grades in these ranges: less than 60, greater than or equal to 60 and less than 70, greater than or equal to 70 and less than 80, greater than or equal to 80 and less than 90, and greater or equal to 90.

   b. Entering 15 grades each time the program written for Exercise 7a is run is cumbersome. What method, therefore, is appropriate for initializing the array during the testing phase?

   c. How might the program you wrote for Exercise 7a be modified to include the case of no grade being present? That is, what grade could be used to indicate an invalid grade and how would your program have to be modified to exclude counting such a grade?

8. a. Write a function that finds and displays the maximum value in a two-dimensional array of integers. The array should be declared as a 10-row × 20-column array of integers in `main()` and the starting address of the array should be passed to the function.

b. Modify the function written in Exercise 8a so that it also displays the row and column number of the element with the maximum value.

c. Can the function you wrote for Exercise 8a be generalized to handle any size two-dimensional array?

11.5 FOCUS ON PROBLEM SOLVING

The next two applications are presented to illustrate single-dimensional array processing and further our understanding of using arrays as function arguments. In the first application, two statistical functions are created to determine the average and standard deviation of an array of numbers. In the second application, a function is used to insert an identification number into an existing array that is maintained in a sorted order.

Application 1: Statistical Analysis

Two functions are to be developed to determine the average and standard deviation of a list of integer numbers. Each function must be capable of accepting the numbers as an array and returning their calculated values to the calling function. We now apply the top-down development procedure to develop the required functions.

Analyze the Problem The statement of the problem indicates that two output values are required: an average and a standard deviation.

The input item defined in the problem statement is a list of integer numbers. Because the size of the list is not specified in the problem statement and to make our functions as general as possible, both functions will be designed to handle any size list passed to it. This requires that the exact number of elements in the array must also be passed to each function at the time of the function call. From each function's viewpoint this means that it must be capable of receiving at least two input items as arguments: an array of arbitrary size and an integer number corresponding to the number of elements in the passed array.

Develop a Solution The I/O specifications determined when we analyzed the problem imply that the argument list of each function must be capable of receiving at least two items: one argument to accommodate the integer array and the second argument to accept an integer. The first function is to return the average of the numbers in the passed array and the second function the standard deviation. These items are determined as follows:

Calculate the average by adding the grades and dividing by the number of grades that was added.
Determine the standard deviation by:

1. *Subtracting the average from each individual grade.*
   This results in a set of new numbers, each of which is called a deviation.
2. *Square each deviation found in the previous step.*
3. *Add the squared deviations and divide the sum by the number of deviations.*
4. *The square root of the number found in the previous step is the standard deviation.*

A BIT OF BACKGROUND

Statistics

The sum, sum of squares, and average of a list of numbers are commonly used quantities in statistics.

By all means take a course in statistics! Some of the most important applications of mathematics and computing to the real world are in the area of statistics. Whether you are in business, engineering, politics, government, weather forecasting, sports, education, or virtually any other field you can name, being able to handle statistics will give you a decided advantage. It has been claimed that "statistics don't lie, but some statisticians do," and this is true. Statistical methods and data are sometimes misused by people to convince others—people who do not understand statistics—of something the statistics really do not support.

Notice that the calculation of the standard deviation requires the average, which means that the standard deviation can be calculated only after the average has been computed. Thus, in addition to requiring the array of integers and the number of values in the array, the standard deviation function also requires that the average be passed to it. This is the advantage of specifying the algorithm, in detail, before any coding is done; it ensures that all necessary inputs and requirements are discovered early in the programming process.

To ensure that we understand the required processing, we will do a hand calculation. For this calculation we will arbitrarily assume that the average and standard deviation of the following 10 grades are to be determined: 98, 82, 67, 54, 78, 83, 95, 76, 68, and 63. The average of this data is determined to be

$$\begin{aligned}\text{Average} &= (98 + 82 + 67 + 54 + 78 + 83 + 95 + 76 + 68 + 63)/10 \\ &= 76.4\end{aligned}$$

The standard deviation is calculated by first determining the sum of the squared deviations. The standard deviation is then obtained by dividing the resulting sum by 10 and taking its square root.

$$\begin{aligned}\text{sum of squared deviations} &= (98 - 76.4)^2 + (82 - 76.4)^2 \\ &+ (67 - 76.4)^2 + (54 - 76.4)^2 \\ &+ (78 - 76.4)^2 + (83 - 76.4)^2 \\ &+ (95 - 76.4)^2 + (76 - 76.4)^2 \\ &+ (68 - 76.4)^2 + (63 - 76.4)^2 \\ &= 1730.400700\end{aligned}$$

$$\text{standard deviation} = \sqrt{1730.4007/10} = \sqrt{173.04007} = 13.154470$$

Having specified the algorithm required of each function, we are now in a position to code them.

Code the Solution In writing functions it is convenient to concentrate initially on the header line. The body of the function can then be written to process the input arguments correctly to produce the desired results.

Naming our averaging function `find_avg()`, and arbitrarily selecting the parameter names `nums` and `numel` for the passed array and the number of elements, respectively, the function header becomes

```
float find_avg(int nums[], int numel)
```

This begins the definition of the averaging function and it allows the function to accept an array of integer values and an integer number. As illustrated by the hand calculation, the average of a set of integer numbers can be a floating-point number; therefore, the function is defined as returning a floating-point value. The body of the function calculates the average as described by the algorithm developed earlier. Thus, the completed `find_avg()` function becomes:

```
float find_avg(int nums[], int numel)
{
  int i;
  float sumnums = 0.0;

  for (i = 0; i < numel; i++)  // calculate the sum of the grades
    sumnums = sumnums + nums[i];

  return (sumnums / numel);    // calculate and return the average
}
```

In the body of the function is a `for` loop to sum the individual numbers. Notice also that the termination value of the loop counter in the `for` loop is `numel`, the number of integers in the array that is passed to the function through the parameter list. The use of this parameter gives the function its generality and allows it to be used for input arrays of any size. For example, calling the function with the statement

```
find_avg(values,10)
```

tells the function that `numel` is 10 and the `values` array consists of 10 values, while the statement

```
find_avg(values,1000)
```

tells `find_avg()` that `numel` is 1000 and that the `values` array consists of 1000 numbers. In both calls the actual argument named `values` corresponds to the parameter named `nums` within the `find_avg()` function.

Using similar reasoning as that for the averaging function, the function header for the standard deviation routine, which we will name `std_dev()`, becomes:

```
float std_dev(int nums[], int numel, float av)
```

This header begins the definition of the `std_dev()` function. It defines the function as returning a floating-point value and accepting an array of integers, an integer value, and a floating-point value as inputs to the function. The body of the `std_dev()` function must calculate the standard deviation as described in the development step. The complete standard deviation function becomes:

```
float std_dev(int nums[], int numel, float av)
{
  int i;
  float sumdevs = 0.0;

  for (i = 0; i < numel; i++)
    sumdevs = sumdevs + pow((nums[i] - av),2.0);

  return(sqrt(sumdevs/numel));
}
```

PROGRAM 11.10

```
#include <iostream.h>
#include <iomanip.h>
#include <math.h>

const int NUM_ELS = 10;

float find_avg(int [], int);            // function prototype
float std_dev(int [], int, float);      // function prototype

int main()
{
  int values[NUM_ELS] = {98, 82, 67, 54, 78, 83, 95, 76, 68, 63};
  float average, stddev;

  average = find_avg(values, NUM_ELS); // call the function
  stddev = std_dev(values, NUM_ELS, average); // call the function

  cout << "The average of the numbers is "
       << setw(5) << setiosflags(ios::showpoint)
       << setprecision(2) << average << endl;

  cout << "The standard deviation of the numbers is "
       << setw(5) << setiosflags(ios::showpoint)
       << setprecision(2) << stddev << endl;

  return 0;
}

float find_avg(int nums[], int numel)
{
  int i;
  float sumnums = 0.0;

  for (i = 0; i < numel; i++)  // calculate the sum of the grades
    sumnums = sumnums + nums[i];

  return (sumnums / numel);     // calculate and return the average
}

float std_dev(int nums[], int numel, float av)
{
  int i;
  float sumdevs = 0.0;

  for (i = 0; i < numel; i++)
    sumdevs = sumdevs + pow((nums[i] - av),2);

  return(sqrt(sumdevs/numel));
}
```

Test and Correct the Program Testing a program's function requires writing a main program unit to call the function and display the returned results. Program 11.10 uses such a main unit to set up a `grade` array with the data previously used in our hand calculation and to call the `find_avg` function.

A test run using Program 11.10 produced the following display:

```
The average of the numbers is 76.40
The standard deviation of the numbers is 13.15
```

Although this result agrees with our previous hand calculation, testing is really not complete without verifying the calculation at the boundary points. In this case such a test consists of checking the calculation with all of the same values, such as all 0's and all 100's. Another simple test would be to use five 0's and five 100's. We leave these tests as an exercise.

Application 2: List Maintenance

A common programming problem is to maintain a list in either numerical or alphabetical order. For example, telephone lists are traditionally kept in alphabetical order, whereas lists of part numbers are kept in numerical order.

As part of an overall maintenance program, a function is to be written that correctly inserts a three-digit identification code within a list of numbers. The list is maintained in increasing number order and duplicate identification codes are not allowed. In this application such a function will be written. A maximum list size of 100 values will be allowed and a sentinel value of 9999 will be used to indicate the end of the list. Thus, for example, if the current list contains nine identification codes, the tenth position in the list will contain the sentinel value.

We again use the top-down function development approach.

Analyze the Problem The required output is an updated list of three-digit codes in which the new code has been inserted correctly into the existing list.

The input items for this function are the existing array of identification codes and the new code that is to be inserted into the list.

Develop a Solution Insertion of an identification code into the existing list requires the following processing:

Determine where in the list the new code should be placed.
    This is done by comparing the new code to each value in the current list until either a match is found, an identification code larger than the new code is located, or the end of the list is encountered.
If the new code matches an existing code
   display a message that the code already exists.
Else
   to make room for the new element in the array move
      each element down one position. This is done by
      starting from the sentinel value and moving each
      item down one position until the desired position
      in the list is vacated.
   Insert the new code in the vacated position.
Endif.

For our hand calculation assume that the list of identification codes consists of the numbers illustrated in Figure 11.14a. If the number code 142 is to be inserted into this list, it must be placed in the fourth position in the list, after the number 136.

FIGURE 11.14 Updating an Ordered List of Identification Numbers

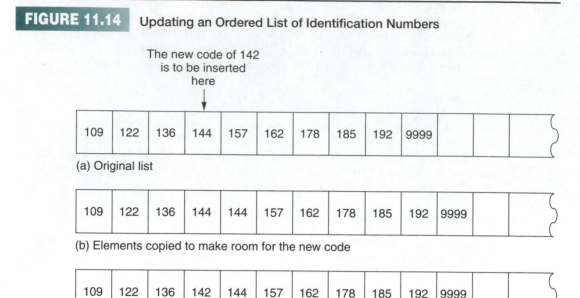

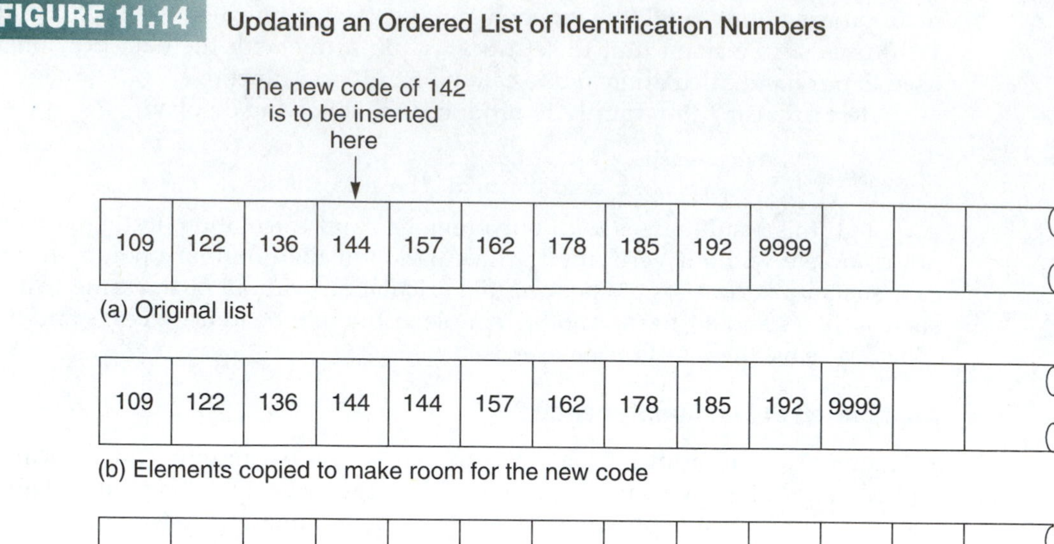

To make room for the new code, all of the codes from the fourth position to the end of the list must be moved one position down, as illustrated in Figure 11.14b. The move is always started from the end of the list and proceeds from the sentinel value back until the desired position in the list is reached. (You can convince yourself that if the copy proceeded forward from the fourth element the number 144 would be reproduced in all subsequent locations until the sentinel value was reached.) After the movement of the necessary elements, the new code is inserted in the correct position. This creates the updated list shown in Figure 11.14c.

Code the Solution For this problem we will use the parameter name `idcode` for the passed array of identification numbers and the parameter name `newcode` for the new code number to be inserted into the array. Here, the passed array is used for both receiving the original array of numbers and as the final, updated array. Internal to the function we will use a variable named `newpos` to hold the position in the list where the new code is to be inserted and the variable named `trlpos` to hold the position value of the sentinel. The variable `i` will be used as a running index value.

Using these argument and variable names, the function named `insert()` performs the required processing. After accepting the array and the new code value as arguments, insert performs the four major tasks described by the pseudocode selected in the design step.

```
void insert(int idcode[], int newcode)
{
  int i, newpos, trlpos;

  // find correct position to insert the new code
  i = 0;
```

```
    while (idcode[i] < newcode)
      i++;
    if (idcode[i] == newcode)
      cout << "\nThis identification code is already in the list";
    else
    {
      newpos = i;     // found the position for the new code

      // find the end of the list
      while (idcode[i] != 9999)
        i++;
      trlpos = i;

      // move idcodes over one position
      for (i = trlpos; i >= newpos; --i)
        idcode[i+1] = idcode[i];

      // insert the new code
      idcode[newpos] = newcode;
    }
  }
```

The first task accomplished by the function is to determine the correct position for the new code. This is done by cycling through the list as long as each value encountered is less than the new code. Since the sentinel value of 9999 is larger than any new code, the looping must stop when the sentinel value is reached.

After the correct position is determined, the position of the sentinel value, which is the last element in the list, is found. Starting from this last position, each element in the list is moved down by one position, until the value in the required new position is reached. Finally, the new identification code is inserted in the correct position.

Test and Correct the Problem Program 11.11 incorporates the `insert()` function within a complete program. This allows us to test the function with the same data used in our hand calculation.

PROGRAM 11.11

```
#include <iostream.h>

const int MAXNUM = 100;

void insert(int [], int);       // function prototype

int main()
{
  int newcode, i;
  int id[MAXNUM] = {109, 122, 136, 144, 157, 162, 178, 185, 192, 9999};

  cout << "\nEnter the new identification code: ";
  cin  >> newcode;
```

(continued on next page)

(continued from previous page)

```
  insert(id, newcode);

  cout << "\nThe updated list is:";
  i = 0;
  while(id[i] != 9999)
  {
    cout << " " << id[i];
    i++;
  }
  cout << endl;

  return 0;
}

void insert(int idcode[], int newcode)
{
  int i, newpos, trlpos;

  // find correct position to insert the new code
  i = 0;
  while (idcode[i] < newcode)
    i++;
  if (idcode[i] == newcode)
    cout << "\nThis identification code is already in the list";
  else
  {
    newpos = i;    // found the position for the new code

    // find the end of the list
    while (idcode[i] != 9999)
      i++;
    trlpos = i;

    // move idcodes over one position
    for (i = trlpos; i >= newpos; --i)
      idcode[i+1] = idcode[i];

    // insert the new code
    idcode[newpos] = newcode;
  }

  return;
}
```

A sample run of Program 11.11 follows:

```
Enter the new identification code: 142
The updated list is: 109 122 136 142 144 157 162 178 185 192
```

Although this result agrees with our previous hand calculation, it does not constitute full testing of the program. To be sure that the program works for all cases, test runs should be made that:

1. Duplicate an existing code.
2. Place a new identification code at the beginning of the list.
3. Place a new identification code at the end of the list.

Exercises 11.5

1. Modify Program 11.10 so that the grades are entered into the `values` array using a function named `entvals`.
2. Rewrite Program 11.10 to determine the average and standard deviation of the following list of 15 grades: 68, 72, 78, 69, 85, 98, 95, 75, 77, 82, 84, 91, 89, 65, 74.
3. Modify Program 11.10 so that a `high` function is called that determines the highest value in the passed array and returns this value to the main program unit for display.
4. Modify Program 11.10 so that a function named `sort` is called after the call to the `std_dev` function. The `sort` function should sort the grades into increasing order for display by `main()`.
5. a. Test Program 11.11 using an identification code of 86, which should place this new code at the beginning of the existing list.

   b. Test Program 11.11 using an identification code of 200, which should place this new code at the end of the existing list.
6. a. Determine an algorithm for deleting an entry from an ordered list of numbers.

   b. Write a function named `delete()`, which uses the algorithm selected in Exercise 6a, to delete an identification code from the list of numbers illustrated in Figure 11.14a.
7. Assume the following letters are stored in an array named `alphabet`: B, J, K, M, S, Z. Write and test a function named `adlet()`, which accepts both the alphabet array and a new letter as arguments, and inserts the new letter in the correct alphabetical order in the alphabet array.

11.6 SEARCHING AND SORTING

Most programmers encounter the need to both sort and search a list of data items at some time in their programming careers. For example, experimental results might have to be arranged in either increasing (ascending) or decreasing (descending) order for statistical analysis, lists of names may have to be sorted in alphabetical order, or a list of dates may have to be rearranged in ascending date order. Similarly, a list of names may have to be searched to find a particular name in the list, or a list of dates may have to be searched to locate a particular date. In this section we introduce the fundamentals of both sorting and searching lists. Note that it is not necessary to sort a list before searching it, although, as we shall see, much faster searches are possible if the list is in sorted order.

Search Algorithms

A common requirement of many programs is to search a list for a given element. For example, in a list of names and telephone numbers, we might search for a specific name so that the corresponding telephone number can be printed, or we might wish to search the list simply to determine if a name is there. The two most common methods of performing such searches are the linear and binary search algorithms.

Linear Search

In a **linear search,** which is also known as a **sequential search,** each item in the list is examined in the order in which it occurs in the list until the desired item is found or the end of the list is reached. This is analogous to looking at every name in the phone directory, beginning with Aardvark, Aaron, until you find the one you want or until you reach Zzxgy, Zora. Obviously, this is not an efficient way to search a long alphabetized list. However, a linear search has two advantages:

1. The algorithm is simple.
2. The list need not be in any particular order.

In a linear search the search begins at the first item in the list and continues sequentially, item by item, through the list. The pseudocode for a function performing a linear search is:

For all the items in the list
  Compare the item with the desired item.
  If the item was found
    Return the index value of the current item.
  EndIf.
EndFor.
Return − 1 because the item was not found.

Notice that the function's return value indicates whether the item was found or not. If the return value is −1, the item was not in the list; otherwise, the return value within the `for` loop provides the index of where the item is located within the list.

The function `linearSearch()` illustrates this procedure as a C++ function:

```
// this function returns the location of key in the list
// a -1 is returned if the value is not found
int linearSearch(int list[], int size, int key)
{
  int i;

  for (i = 0; i < size; i++)
  {
    if (list[i] == key)
      return i;
  }

  return -1;
}
```

In reviewing `linearSearch()` notice that the `for` loop is simply used to access each element in the list, from first element to last, until a match is found with the desired item. If the desired item is located the index value of the current item is returned, which causes the loop to terminate; otherwise, the search continues until the end of the list is encountered.

To test this function we have written a `main()` driver function to call it and display the results returned by `linearSearch()`. The complete test program is illustrated in Program 11.12.

PROGRAM 11.12

```
#include <iostream.h>

const int NUMEL = 10;

int linearSearch(int [], int, int);  // function prototype

int main()
{
  int nums[NUMEL] = {5,10,22,32,45,67,73,98,99,101};
  int item, location;


  cout << "Enter the item you are searching for: ";
  cin  >> item;

  location = linearSearch(nums, NUMEL, item);

  if (location > -1)
    cout << "The item was found at index location " << location
      << endl;
  else
    cout << "The item was not found in the list\n";

  return 0;
}

// this function returns the location of key in the list
// a -1 is returned if the value is not found
int linearSearch(int list[], int size, int key)
{
  int i;

  for (i = 0; i < size; i++)
  {
    if (list[i] == key)
      return i;
 }

  return -1;
}
```

Sample runs of Program 11.12 follow:

```
Enter the item you are searching for: 101
The item was found at index location 9
```

and

```
Enter the item you are searching for: 65
The item was not found in the list
```

As has already been pointed out, an advantage of linear searches is that the list does not have to be in sorted order to perform the search. Another advantage is that if the desired item is toward the front of the list, only a small number of comparisons will be done. The worst case, of course, occurs when the desired item is at the end of the list. On average, however, and assuming that the desired item is equally likely to be anywhere within the list, the number of required comparisons will be $N/2$, where N is the list's size. Thus, for a 10-element list, the average number of comparisons needed for a linear search is 5, and for a 10,000-element list, the average number of comparisons needed is 5000. As we show next, this average can be significantly reduced using a binary search algorithm.

Binary Search

In a **binary search** the list must be in sorted order. Starting with an ordered list, the desired item is first compared to the element in the middle of the list (for lists with an even number of elements, either of the two middle elements can be used). Three possibilities present themselves once the comparison is made: The desired item may be equal to the middle element, it may be greater than the middle element, or it may be less than the middle element.

In the first case the search has been successful, and no further searches are required. In the second case, since the desired item is greater than the middle element, if it is found at all it must be in the upper part of the list. This means that the lower part of the list consisting of all elements from the first to the midpoint element can be discarded from any further search. In the third case, since the desired item is less than the middle element, if it is found at all it must be found in the lower part of the list. For this case the upper part of the list containing all elements from the midpoint element to the last element can be discarded from any further search.

The complete algorithm for implementing this search strategy is illustrated in Figure 11.15 and defined by the following pseudocode:

Set the lower index to 0.
Set the upper index to one less than the size of the list.
Begin with the first item in the list.
While the lower index is less than or equal to the upper index
    Set the midpoint index to the integer average of the lower and upper index values.
    Compare the desired item to the midpoint element.
        If the desired element equals the midpoint element
            Return the index value of the current item.
        Else if the desired element is greater than the midpoint element
            Set the lower index value to the midpoint value plus 1.
        Else if the desired element is less than the midpoint element
            Set the upper index value to the midpoint value less 1.
        EndIf.
EndWhile.
Return -1 because the item was not found.

FIGURE 11.15 The Binary Search Algorithm

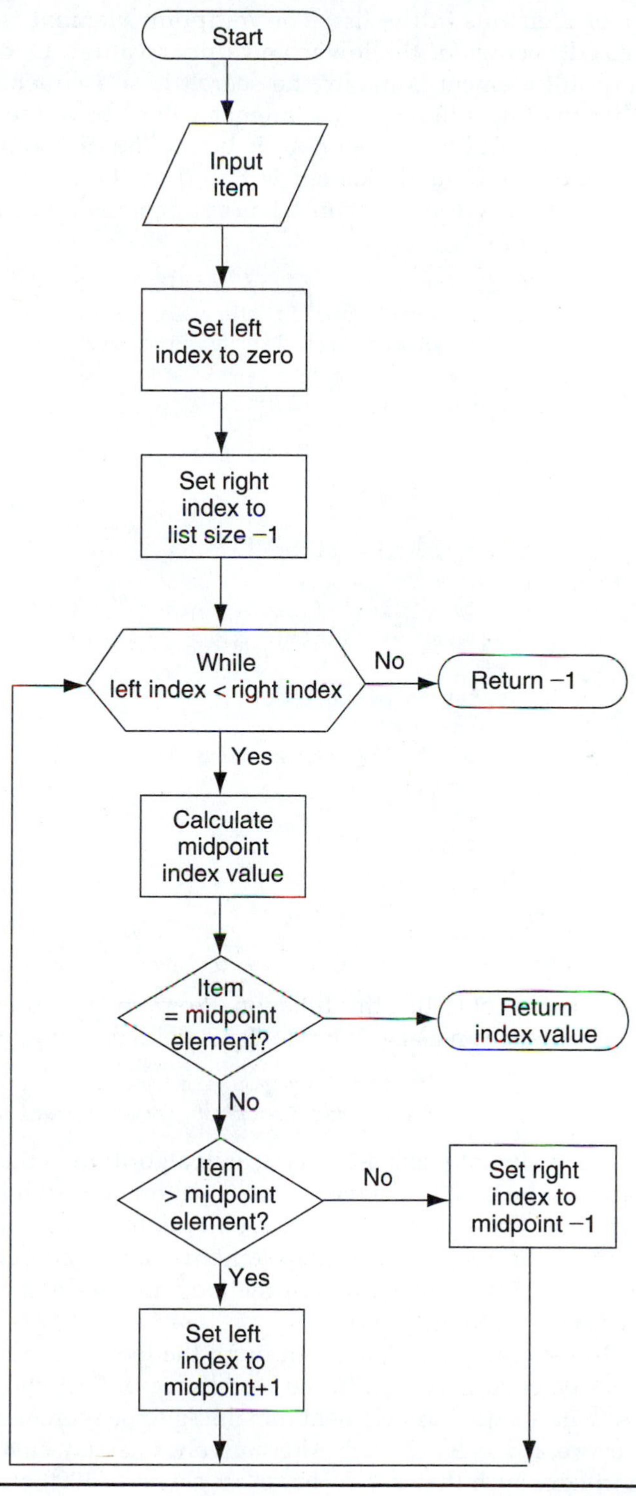

As illustrated by both the pseudocode and the flowchart of Figure 11.15, a `while` loop is used to control the search. The initial list is defined by setting the lower index value to 0 and the upper index value to one less than the number of elements in the list. The midpoint element is then taken as the integerized average of the lower and upper values. Once the comparison to the midpoint element is made, the search is subsequently restricted by moving either the lower index to one integer value above the midpoint, or by moving the upper index one integer value below the midpoint. This process is continued until the desired element is found or the lower and upper index values become equal. The function `binarySearch()` presents the C++ version of this algorithm.

```
// this function returns the location of key in the list
// a -1 is returned if the value is not found
int binarySearch(int list[], int size, int key)
{
  int left, right, midpt;

  left = 0;
  right = size - 1;

  while (left <= right)
  {
    midpt = (int) ((left + right) / 2);
    if (key == list[midpt])
    {
      return midpt;
    }
    else if (key > list[midpt])
      left = midpt + 1;
    else
      right = midpt - 1;
  }

  return -1;
}
```

For purposes of testing this function, Program 11.13 is used.

A sample run using Program 11.13 yielded the following:

```
Enter the item you are searching for: 101
The item was found at index location 9
```

The value of using a binary search algorithm is that the number of elements that must be searched is cut in half each time through the `while` loop. Thus, the first time through the loop N elements must be searched; the second time through the loop $N/2$ of the elements have been eliminated and only $N/2$ remain. The third time through the loop another half of the remaining elements have been eliminated, and so on.

In general, after p passes through the loop, the number of values remaining to be searched is $N/(2^p)$. In the worst case the search can continue until there is less than or equal to 1 element remaining to be searched. Mathematically, this can be expressed as $N/(2^p) \leq 1$. Alternatively, this may be rephrased as p is the smallest integer such that $2^p \geq N$. For example, for a 1000-element array, N is 1000 and

PROGRAM 11.13

```
#include <iostream.h>

const int NUMEL = 10;

int binarySearch(int [], int, int);  // function prototype

int main()
{
  int nums[NUMEL] = {5,10,22,32,45,67,73,98,99,101};
  int item, location;

  cout << "Enter the item you are searching for: ";
  cin  >> item;
  location = binarySearch(nums, NUMEL, item);
  if (location > -1)
    cout << "The item was found at index location "
      << location << endl;
  else
    cout << "The item was not found in the array\n";

  return 0;
}

// this function returns the location of key in the list
// a -1 is returned if the value is not found
int binarySearch(int list[], int size, int key)
{
  int left, right, midpt;

  left = 0;
  right = size - 1;

  while (left <= right)
  {
    midpt = (int) ((left + right) / 2);
    if (key == list[midpt])
    {
      return midpt;
    }
    else if (key > list[midpt])
      left = midpt + 1;
    else
      right = midpt - 1;
  }

  return -1;
}
```

TABLE 11.1 A Comparison of `while` Loop Passes for Linear and Binary Searches

Array Size	10	50	500	5,000	50,000	500,000	5,000,000	50,000,000
Average linear search passes	5	25	250	2,500	25,000	250,000	2,500,000	25,000,000
Maximum linear search passes	10	50	500	5,000	50,000	500,000	5,000,000	50,000,000
Maximum binary search passes	4	6	9	13	16	19	23	26

the maximum number of passes, *p*, required for a binary search is 10. Table 11.1 compares the number of loop passes needed for a linear and binary search for various list sizes. As illustrated, the maximum number of loop passes for a 50-item list is almost 10 times more for a linear search than for binary search, and the difference is even more spectacular for larger lists. As a rule of thumb, 50 elements are usually taken as the switchover point: For lists smaller than 50 elements linear searches are acceptable; for larger lists a binary search algorithm should be used.

Big O Notation

On average, over a large number of linear searches with *N* items in a list, we would expect to examine half ($N/2$) of the items before locating the desired item. In a binary search the maximum number of passes, *p*, occurs when $(N/2)^p = 1$. This relationship can be algebraically manipulated to $2p = N$, which yields $p = \log_2 N$, which approximately equals $3.33 \log_{10} N$.

For example, finding a particular name in an alphabetical directory with $N =$ 1000 names would require an average of 500 ($N/2$) comparisons using a linear search. With a binary search, only about 10 ($\approx 3.3 \times \log^{10} 1000$) comparisons would be required.

A common way to express the number of comparisons required in any search algorithm using a list of *N* items is to give the order of magnitude of the number of comparisons required, on average, to locate a desired item. Thus, the linear search is said to be of order *N* and the binary search of order $\log_2 N$. Notationally, this is expressed as $O(N)$ and $O(\log_2 N)$, where the O is read as "the order of" and the notation is called **Big O notation.**

Sort Algorithms

For sorting data, two major categories of sorting techniques exist, called internal and external sorts, respectively. **Internal sorts** are used when the data list is not too large and the complete list can be stored within the computer's memory, usually in an array. **External sorts** are used for much larger data sets that are stored in large external disk or tape files and cannot be accommodated within the computer's memory as a complete unit. Here we present four internal sort algorithms that range from the simple and slow to the complex and fast. The first three algorithms presented are all quite commonly used when sorting lists with less than approximately 50 elements. For larger lists more sophisticated sorting algorithms, such as the quicksort algorithm, are typically employed.

Selection Sort

One of the simplest sorting techniques is the selection sort. In a **selection sort** the smallest value is initially selected from the complete list of data and exchanged with the first element in the list. After this first selection and exchange, the next smallest element in the revised list is selected and exchanged with the second element in the list. Since the smallest element is already in the first position in the list, this second pass need only consider the second through the last elements. For a list consisting of N elements, this process is repeated $N - 1$ times, with each pass through the list requiring one less comparison than the previous pass.

For example, consider the list of numbers illustrated in Figure 11.16. The first pass through the initial list results in the number 32 being selected and exchanged with the first element in the list. The second pass, made on the reordered list, results in the number 155 being selected from the second through fifth elements. This value is then exchanged with the second element in the list. The third pass selects the number 307 from the third through fifth elements in the list and exchanges this value with the third element. Finally, the fourth and last pass through the list selects the remaining minimum value and exchanges it with the fourth list element. Although each pass in this example resulted in an exchange, no exchange would have been made in a pass if the smallest value were already in the correct location.

In pseudocode, the selection sort is described as:

Set interchange count to zero (not required, but done just to keep track of the interchanges).
For each element in the list from first to next-to-last
Find the smallest element from the current element being referenced to the last element by:
Setting the minimum value equal to the current element.
Saving (storing) the index of the current element.
For each element in the list from the current element + 1 to the last element in the list
If element [inner loop index] < minimum value
Set the minimum value = element [inner loop index].
Save the index the new found minimum value.
EndIf.
EndFor
Swap the current value with the new minimum value.
Increment the interchange count.
EndFor.
Return the interchange count.

FIGURE 11.16 A Sample Selection Sort

Initial List	Pass 1	Pass 2	Pass 3	Pass 4
690	32	32	32	32
307	307	155	144	144
32	690	690	307	307
155	155	307	690	426
426	426	426	426	690

The function selection_sort incorporates this procedure into a C++ function:

```
int selection_sort(int num[], int numel)
{
  int i, j, min, minidx, temp, moves = 0;

  for ( i = 0; i < (numel - 1); i++)
  {
    min = num[i];     // assume minimum is the first array element
    minidx = i;       // index of minimum element
    for(j = i + 1; j < numel; j++)
    {
      if (num[j] < min)     // if we've located a lower value
      {                     // capture it
        min = num[j];
        minidx = j;
      }
    }
    if (min < num[i])    // check if we have a new minimum
    {                    // and if we do, swap values
      temp = num[i];
      num[i] = min;
      num[minidx] = temp;
      moves++;
    }
  }

  return moves;
}
```

The selection_sort function expects two arguments: the list to be sorted and the number of elements in the list. As specified by the pseudocode, a nested set of for loops performs the sort. The outer for loop causes one less pass through the list than the total number of data items in the list. For each pass, the variable min is initially assigned the value num[i], where i is the outer for loop's counter variable. Since i begins at 0 and ends at one less than numel, each element in the list, except the last, is successively designated as the current element.

The inner loop is used in the function cycles through the elements below the current element to select the next smallest value. Thus, this loop begins at the index value i+1 and continues through the end of the list. When a new minimum is found, its value and position in the list are stored in the variables named min and minidx, respectively. Upon completion of the inner loop, an exchange is made only if a value less than that in the current position was found.

For purposes of testing selection_sort, Program 11.14 was constructed. This program implements a selection sort for the same list of 10 numbers that was previously used to test our search algorithms. For later comparison to the other sorting algorithms that will be presented, the number of actual moves made by the program to get the data into sorted order is counted and displayed.

The output produced by Program 11.14 is as follows:

```
The sorted list, in ascending order, is:
  5 10 22 32 45 67 73 98 99 101
8 moves were made to sort this list
```

PROGRAM 11.14

```
#include <iostream.h>

const int NUMEL = 10;

int selection_sort(int [], int);

int main()
{
  int nums[NUMEL] = {22,5,67,98,45,32,101,99,73,10};
  int i, moves;

  moves = selection_sort(nums, NUMEL);

  cout << "The sorted list, in ascending order, is:\n";
  for (i = 0; i < NUMEL; i++)
    cout << "  " <<nums[i];

  cout << '\n' << moves << " moves were made to sort this list\n";

  return 0;
}

int selection_sort(int num[], int numel)
{
  int i, j, min, minidx, temp, moves = 0;

  for ( i = 0; i < (numel - 1); i++)
  {
    min = num[i];    // assume minimum is the first array element
    minidx = i;      // index of minimum element
    for(j = i + 1; j < numel; j++)
    {
      if (num[j] < min)     // if we've located a lower value
        {                      // capture it
        min = num[j];
        minidx = j;
      }
    }
    if (min < num[i])   // check if we have a new minimum
    {                   // and if we do, swap values
      temp = num[i];
      num[i] = min;
      num[minidx] = temp;
      moves++;
    }
  }

  return moves;
}
```

Clearly, the number of moves displayed depends on the initial order of the values in the list. An advantage of the selection sort is that the maximum number of moves that must be made is $N - 1$, where N is the number of items in the list. Further, each move is a final move that results in an element residing in its final location in the sorted list.

A disadvantage of the selection sort is that $N(N - 1)/2$ comparisons are always required, regardless of the initial arrangement of the data. This number of comparisons is obtained as follows: The last pass always requires one comparison, the next-to-last pass requires two comparisons, and so on, to the first pass, which requires $N - 1$ comparisons. Thus, the total number of comparisons is:

$$1 + 2 + 3 + \ldots + (N - 1) = N(N - 1)/2 = N^2/2 - N/2.$$

For large values of N the N^2 dominates, and the order of the selection sort is $O(N^2)$.

Exchange (Bubble) Sort

In an **exchange** or **bubble sort** elements of the list are exchanged with one another in such a manner that the list becomes sorted. If the list is to be sorted in ascending (from smallest to largest) order, the smaller value of the two being compared is always placed before the larger value. For lists sorted in descending (from largest to smallest) order, the smaller of the two values being compared is always placed after the larger value.

For example, assume that a list of values is to be sorted in ascending order. If the first element in the list is larger than the second, the two elements are interchanged. Then the second and third elements are compared. Again, if the second element is larger than the third, these two elements are interchanged. This process continues until the last two elements have been compared and exchanged, if necessary. If no exchanges were made during this initial pass through the data, the data is in the correct order and the process is finished; otherwise, a second pass is made through the data, starting from the first element and stopping at the next-to-last element. The reason for stopping at the next-to-last element on the second pass is that the first pass always results in the most positive value "sinking" to the bottom of the list.

As a specific example of this process, consider the list of numbers illustrated in Figure 11.17. The first comparison results in the interchange of the first two element values, 690 and 307. The next comparison, between elements 2 and 3 in the revised list, results in the interchange of values between the second and third elements, 690 and 32. This comparison and possible switching of adjacent values is continued until the last two elements have been compared and possibly switched. This process completes the first pass through the data and results in

FIGURE 11.17 The First Pass of an Exchange "Bubble" Sort

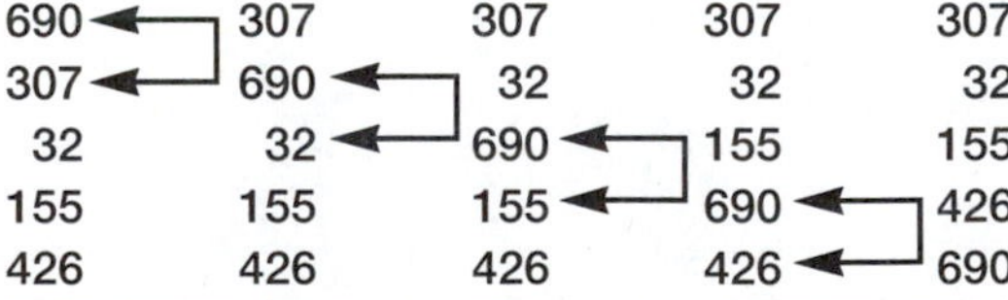

the largest number moving to the bottom of the list. As the largest value sinks to its resting place at the bottom of the list, the smaller elements slowly rise, or "bubble," to the top of the list. This bubbling effect of the smaller elements is what gave rise to the name "bubble" sort for this sorting algorithm.

Because the first pass through the list ensures that the largest value always moves to the bottom of the list, the second pass stops at the next-to-last element. This process continues with each pass stopping at one higher element than the previous pass, until either $N - 1$ passes through the list have been completed or no exchanges are necessary in any single pass. In both cases the resulting list is in sorted order. The pseudocode describing this sort follows:

```
Set interchange count to zero (not required, but done just to
   keep track of the interchanges).
For the first element in the list to one less than the last element (i index)
  For the second element in the list to the last element (j index)
    If num[j] < num[j – 1]
    {
      swap num[j] with num[j – 1]
      increment interchange count
    }
  EndFor.
EndFor.
Return interchange count.
```

This sort algorithm is coded in C++ as the function `bubble_sort`, which is included within Program 11.15 for testing purposes. This program tests `bubble_sort` with the same list of 10 numbers used in Program 11.14 to test `selection_sort`. For comparison to the earlier selection sort, the number of adjacent moves (exchanges) made by `bubble_sort` is also counted and displayed.

Here is the output produced by Program 11.15.

```
The sorted list, in ascending order, is:
  5 10 22 32 45 67 73 98 99 101
18 moves were made to sort this list
```

As with the selection sort, the number of comparisons using a bubble sort is $O(N^2)$ and the number of required moves depends on the initial order of the values in the list. In the worst case, when the data is in reverse sorted order, the selection sort performs better than the bubble sort. Here both sorts require $N(N - 1)/2$ comparisons, but the selection sort needs only $N - 1$ moves, whereas the bubble sort needs $N(N - 1)/2$ moves. The additional moves required by the bubble sort result from the intermediate exchanges between adjacent elements to "settle" each element into its final position. In this regard the selection sort is superior, because no intermediate moves are necessary. For random data, such as that used in Programs 11.14 and 11.15, the selection sort generally performs equal to or better than the bubble sort.

A modification to the bubble sort (see Exercise 4), which causes the sort to terminate when the list is in order regardless of the number of passes made, can make the bubble sort operate as an $O(N)$ sort in specialized cases.

Quicksort

The selection and exchange sorts both require $O(N^2)$ comparisons, which make them very slow for long lists. The **quicksort** algorithm, which is also called a

PROGRAM 11.15

```
#include <iostream.h>

const int NUMEL = 10;

int bubble_sort(int [], int);

int main()
{
  int nums[NUMEL] = {22,5,67,98,45,32,101,99,73,10};
  int i, moves;

  moves = bubble_sort(nums, NUMEL);

  cout << "The sorted list, in ascending order, is:\n";
  for (i = 0; i < NUMEL; i++)
    cout << "  " <<nums[i];

  cout << '\n' << moves << " were made to sort this list\n";

  return 0;
}

int bubble_sort(int num[], int numel)
{
  int i, j, temp, moves = 0;

  for ( i = 0; i < (numel - 1); i++)
  {
    for(j = 1; j < numel; j++)
    {
      if (num[j] < num[j-1])
      {
     temp = num[j];
     num[j] = num[j-1];
     num[j-1] = temp;
     moves++;
      }
    }
  }

  return moves;
}
```

FIGURE 11.18 A First Quicksort Partition

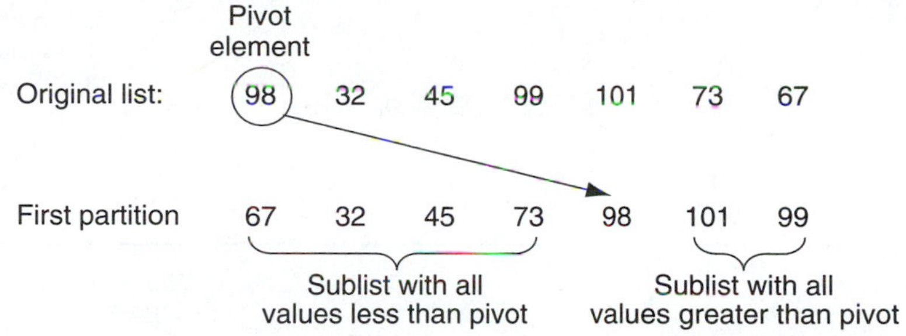

partition sort, divides a list into two smaller sublists and sorts each sublist by partioning into smaller sublists, and so on.[5] The order of a quicksort is $N \log_2 N$. Thus, for a 1,000-item list, the total number of comparisons for a quicksort is of the order of $1000(3.3 \log_{10}1000) \approx 1000(10) = 10{,}000$ compared to $1000(1000) = 1{,}000{,}000$ for a selection or exchange sort.

The quicksort puts a list into sorted order by a partitioning process. At each stage the list is partitioned into sublists so that a selected element, called the pivot, is placed in its correct position in the final sorted list. To understand the process, consider the list illustrated in Figure 11.18. The original list shown consists of seven numbers. Designating the first element in the list, 98, as the pivot element, the list is rearranged as shown in the first partition. Notice that this partition results in all values less than 98 residing to its left and all values greater than 98 to its right. For now, disregard the exact order of the elements to the left and right of the 98 (in a moment we will see how the arrangement of the numbers came about).

The numbers to the left of the pivot constitute one sublist and the numbers to the right another sublist, which individually must be reordered by a partitioning process. The pivot for the first sublist is 67 and the pivot for the second sublist is 101. Figure 11.19 shows how each of these sublists is partitioned using their

FIGURE 11.19 Completing the Quicksort

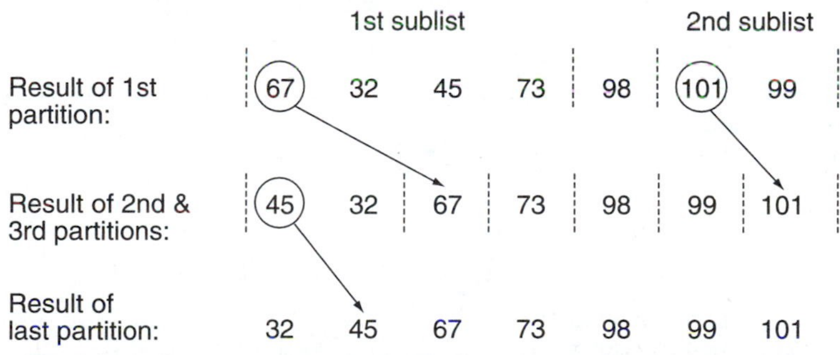

[5] This algorithm was developed by C. A. R. Hoare and first described by him in an article entitled "QuickSort" in *Computer Journal* (Vol. 5, pp. 10–15) in 1962. This sorting algorithm was so much faster than previous algorithms that it became known as the quicksort.

FIGURE 11.20 Start of the Scanning Process

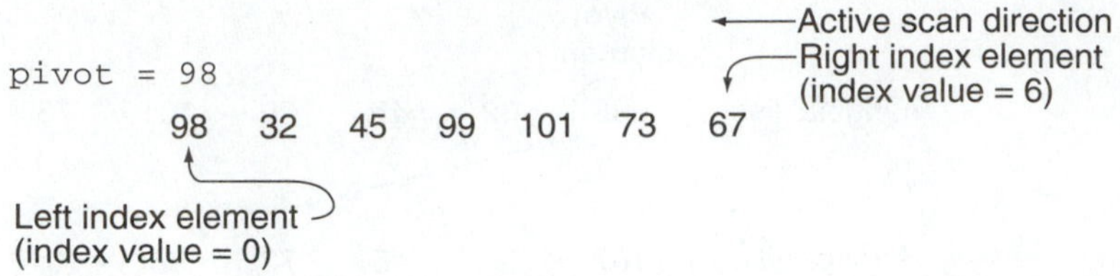

respective pivot elements. The partitioning process stops when a sublist has only one element. In the case illustrated in Figure 11.19, a fourth partition is required for the sublist containing the values 45 and 32, since all other sublists have only one element. Once this last sublist is partitioned, the quicksort is completed and the original list is in sorted order.

As we have illustrated, the key to the quicksort is its partitioning process. An essential part of this process is that each sublist is rearranged in place; that is, elements are rearranged within the existing list. This rearrangement is facilitated by first saving the value of the pivot, which frees its slot to be used by another element. The list is then examined from the right, starting with the last element in the list, for a value less than the pivot; when one is found it is copied to the pivot slot. This copy frees a slot at the right of the list for use by another element. The list is now examined from the left for any value greater than the pivot; when one is found it is copied to the last freed slot. This right-to-left and left-to-right scan is continued until the right and left index values meet. The saved pivot element is then copied into this slot. At that point all values to the left of the index are smaller than the pivot value and all values to the right are greater. Before providing the pseudocode for this process, we will show all of the steps required to complete one partition using our previous list of numbers.

Consider Figure 11.20, which shows our original list of Figure 11.18 and the positions of the initial left and right indexes. As shown in the figure, the pivot value has been saved into a variable named `pivot`; the right index points to the last list element and is the active index. Using this index the scan for elements less than the pivot value of 98 begins.

FIGURE 11.21 List After the First Copy

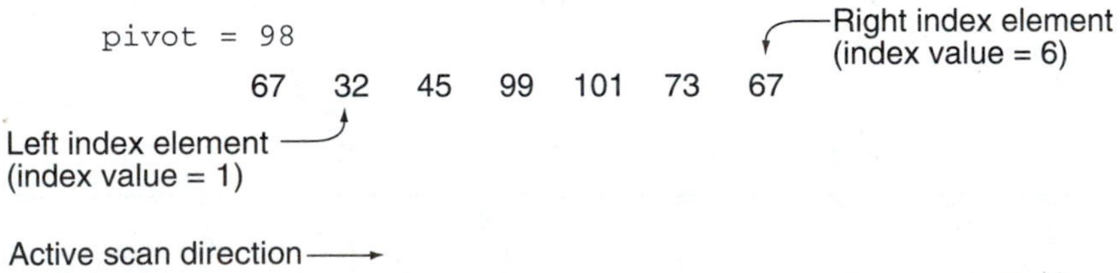

FIGURE 11.22 Start of Second Right-Side Scan

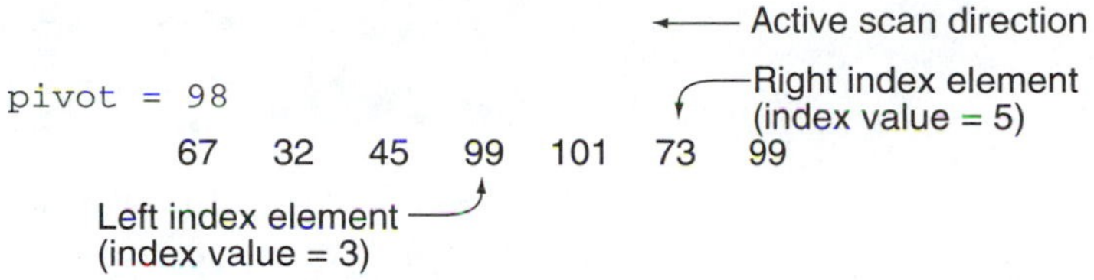

Since 67 is less than the pivot value of 98, the 67 is moved into the pivot slot (the pivot value is not lost because it has been assigned to the variable `pivot`) and the left index is incremented. This results in the arrangement shown in Figure 11.21. Notice that the element pointed to by the right index is now available for the next copy, since its value, 67, has been reproduced as the first element. (This will always be the case; when a scan stops its index will indicate the position available for the next move.)

Scanning of the list shown in Figure 11.21 continues from the left for a search of all values greater than 98. This occurs when the 99 is reached. Since 99 is greater than the pivot value of 98, the scan stops and the 99 is copied into the position indicated by the right index. The right index is then decremented, which produces the situation illustrated in Figure 11.22.

Scanning of the list shown in Figure 11.22 now continues from the right in a search for values less than the pivot. Since 73 qualifies, the right scan stops, the 73 is moved into the position indicated by the left index, and the left index is incremented. This results in the list shown in Figure 11.23.

Scanning of the list shown in Figure 11.23 now resumes from the left in a search for values greater than 98. Since 101 qualifies, this scan stops and the 101 is moved into the slot indicated by the right index, and the right index is incremented. This results in the list illustrated in Figure 11.24. Notice in this figure that left and right indices are equal. This is the condition that stops all scanning and indicates the position where the pivot should be placed. Doing so results in completion of this partition with the list in the following order:

```
67 32 45 73 98 101 99
```

FIGURE 11.23 Start of Second Left-Side Scan

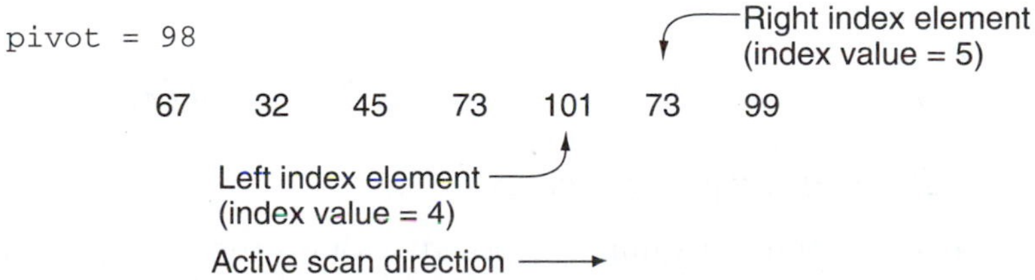

FIGURE 11.24 Position of List Elements After the 101 Is Moved

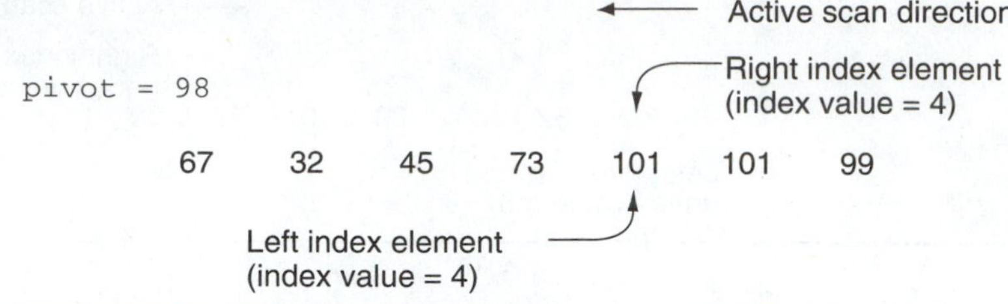

Compare this list with the one previously shown for the first partition in Figure 11.18. As is seen, they are the same. Here the pivot has been placed so that all elements less than it are to its left and all values greater than it are to its right. The same partitioning process would now be applied to the sublists on either side of the partition.

The pseudocode describing this partitioning process follows:

Set the pivot to the value of the first list element.
Initialize the left index to the index of the first list element.
Initialize the right index to the index of the last list element.
While (left index ≠ right index)
   // scan from the right, skipping over larger values.
   While (right index element ⩽ pivot) // skip over larger values.
      Decrement right index.
   EndWhile.
   If (right index ≠ left index)
      Move the lower value into the slot indicated by the left index.
      Increment the left index.
   EndIf.
   // scan from the left, skipping over smaller values
   While (left index element ≤ pivot) // skip over smaller values.
      Increment left index.
   EndWhile.
   If (left index ≠ right index)
      Move the higher value into the slot indicated by the right index.
      Decrement the right index.
   EndIf.
EndWhile.
Move the pivot into the slot indicated by the left or right index (they are equal here).
Return the left (or right) index.

The function partition, contained within Program 11.16, codes this algorithm in C++.

PROGRAM 11.16

```
#include <iostream.h>

const int NUMEL = 7;

int partition(int [], int, int);  // function prototype

int main()
{
  int nums[NUMEL] = {98,32,45,99,101,73,67};
  int i, pivot;

  pivot = partition(nums, 0, NUMEL-1);

  cout << "\nThe returned pivot index is " << pivot;
  cout << "\nThe list is now in the order:\n";
  for (i = 0; i < NUMEL; i++)
    cout << "  " <<nums[i];
  cout << endl;

  return 0;
}

int partition(int num[], int left, int right)
{
  int pivot, temp;

  pivot = num[left];  // "capture" the pivot value, which frees up one slot
  while (left < right)
  {
      // scan from right to left
    while(num[right] >= pivot && left < right)  // skip over larger or equal values
      right--;
    if (right != left)
    {
      num[left] = num[right];   // move the higher value into the available slot
      left++;
    }
      // scan from left to right
    while (num[left] <= pivot && left < right) // skip over smaller or equal values
      left++;
    if (right != left)
    {
      num[right] = num[left];  // move lower value into the available slot
      right--;
    }
  }
  num[left] = pivot;  // move pivot into correct position

  return left;        // return the pivot index
}
```

Program 11.16 is simply used to test the function. Notice that it contains the same list that we used in our hand calculation. A sample run using Program 11.16 produced this output:

```
The returned pivot index is 4
The list is now in the order:
  67 32 45 73 98 101 99
```

Notice that this output produces the result previously obtained by our hand calculation. The importance of the returned pivot index is that it defines the sublists that will be subsequently partitioned. The first sublist consists of all elements from the first list element to the element whose index is 3 (one less than the returned pivot index) and the second sublist consists of all elements starting at index value 5 (one more than the returned pivot index) and ending at the last list element.

The quicksort uses the returned pivot value in determining whether additional calls to partition are required for each sublist defined by the list segments to the left and right of the pivot index. This is done using the following recursive logic:

Quicksort(list, lower index, upper index)
  Calculate a pivot index calling partition(list, lower index, upper index).
  If (lower index < pivot index)
      quicksort(list, lower, pivot index − 1).
  If (upper index > pivot index)
      quicksort(list, upper, pivot index + 1).

The C++ code for this logic is described by the quicksort function contained within Program 11.17. As indicated, quicksort requires a partition to both rearrange lists and return its pivot value.

PROGRAM 11.17

```
#include <iostream.h>

const int NUMEL = 7;

void quicksort(int [], int, int);  // function prototypes
int partition(int [], int, int);

int main()
{
 int nums[NUMEL] = {67,32,45,73,98,101,99};
 int i;

 quicksort(nums, 0, NUMEL-1);

 cout << "\nThe sorted list, in ascending order, is:\n";
 for (i = 0; i < NUMEL; i++)
   cout << "  " <<nums[i];
 cout << endl;
```

(continued on next page)

```
  return 0;
}

void quicksort(int num[], int lower, int upper)
{
  int i, j, pivot;

  pivot = partition(num,lower, upper);

  if (lower < pivot)
     quicksort(num, lower, pivot - 1);
  if (upper > pivot)
     quicksort(num, pivot + 1, upper);

  return;
}


int partition(int num[], int left, int right)
{
  int pivot, temp;

  pivot = num[left];  // "capture" the pivot value, which frees up one slot
  while (left < right)
  {
      // scan from right to left
    while(num[right] >= pivot && left < right)  // skip over larger or equal values
      right--;
    if (right != left)
    {
      num[left] = num[right];    // move the higher value into the available slot
      left++;
    }
      // scan from left to right
    while (num[left] <= pivot && left < right) // skip over smaller or equal values
      left++;
    if (right != left)
    {
      num[right] = num[left];  // move lower value into the available slot
      right--;
    }
  }
  num[left] = pivot;  // move pivot into correct position

  return left;       // return the pivot index
}
```

Here is the output produced by Program 11.17.

```
The sorted list, in ascending order, is:
32 45 67 73 98 99 101
```

As indicated by this output, quicksort correctly sorts the test list of numbers. Figure 11.25 shows the sequence of calls made to quicksort by Program 11.17. In this figure left-pointing arrows indicate calls made because the first `if` condition (`lower < pivot`) was true, and right-pointing arrows indicate calls made because the second `if` condition (`upper > pivot`) was true.

FIGURE 11.25 The Sequence of Calls Made by Program 11.17

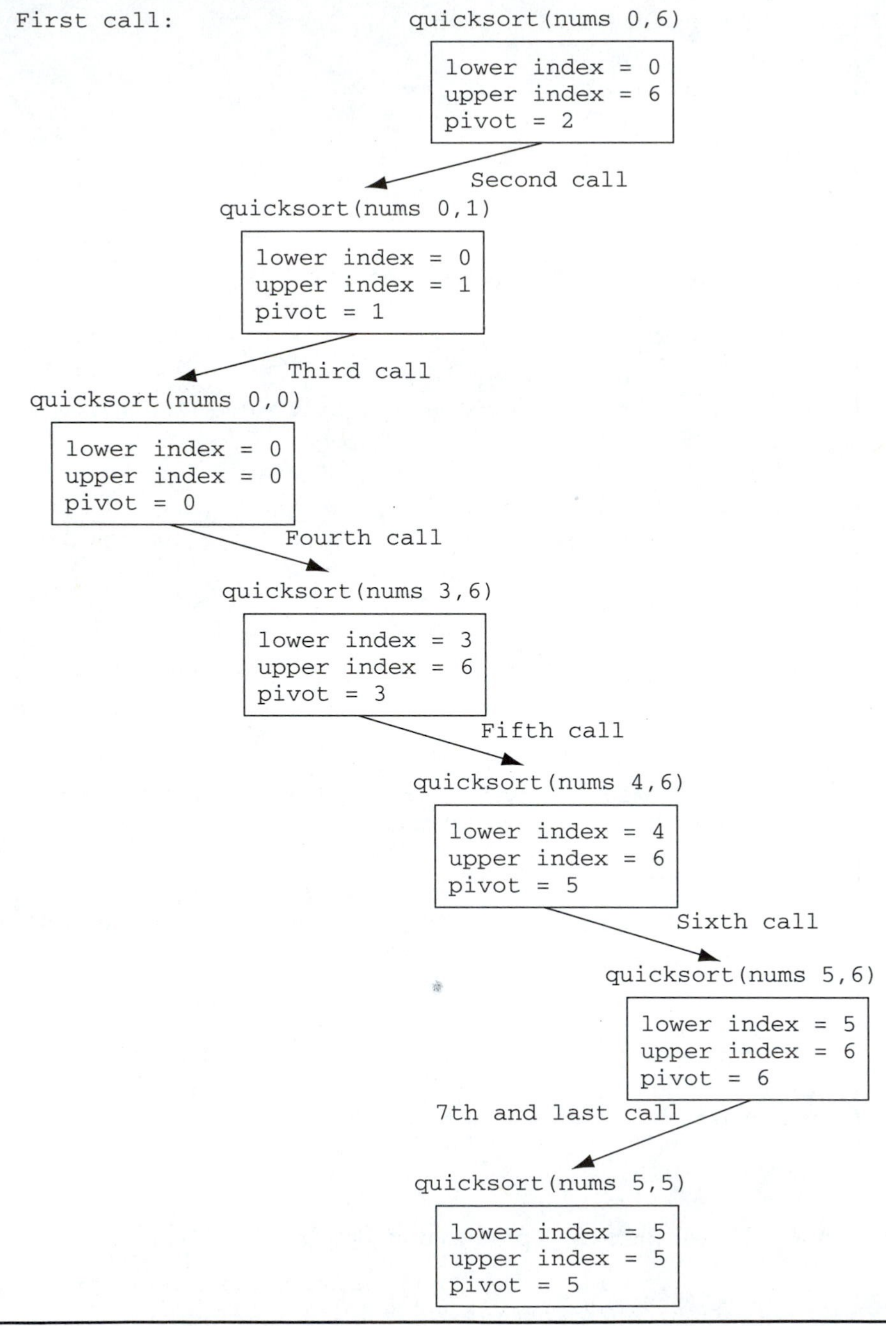

Exercise 11.6

1. a. Modify Program 11.14 to use a list of 10 randomly generated numbers and determine the number of moves required to put the list in order using a selection sort. Display both the initial list and the reordered list.

   b. Redo Exercise 1a using a bubble sort.

2. For the functions `selection_sort`, `bubble_sort`, and `quicksort`, the sorting can be done in decreasing order by a simple modification. In each case identify the required changes and then rewrite each function to accept a flag indicating whether the sort should be in increasing or decreasing order. Modify each routine to correctly receive and use this flag argument.

3. a. The selection and bubble sort both use the same technique for swapping list elements. Replace the code in these two functions that performs the swap by a call to a function named `swap`. The prototype for swap should be

   ```
   void swap(int&, int&)
   swap()
   ```

   `swap()` itself should be constructed using the algorithm presented in Section 6.5.

   b. Describe why the quicksort function does not require the swapping algorithm used by the selection and bubble sorts.

4. An alternate form of the bubble sort is presented in the following program:

```
#include <iostream.h>
const int TRUE = 1;
const int FALSE = 0;
void main(void)
{
  int nums[10] = {22,5,67,98,45,32,101,99,73,10};
  int i, temp, moves, npts, outord;

  moves = 0;
  npts = 10;
  outord = TRUE;
  while (outord && npts > 0)
  {
    outord = FALSE;
    for ( i = 0; i < npts - 1; i++)
      if (nums[i] > nums[i+1])
      {
        temp = nums[i+1];
        nums[i+1] = nums[i];
        nums[i] = temp;
        outord = TRUE;
        moves++;
      }
    npts--;
    }
  cout << "The sorted list, in ascending order, is:\n";
  for (i = 0; i < 10; i++)
    cout << "  " << nums[i];
  cout << '\n' << moves
       << " moves were made to sort this list\n";
}
```

An advantage of this version of the bubble sort is that processing is terminated whenever a sorted list is encountered. In the best case, when the data is in sorted order to begin with, an exchange sort requires no moves (the same for the selection sort) and only $N - 1$ comparisons. [The selection sort always requires $N(N - 1)/2$ comparisons.]

After you have run this program to convince yourself that it correctly sorts a list of integers, rewrite the sort algorithm it contains as a function named `newbubbl`, and test your function using the driver function contained in Program 11.15.

5. a. Modify Program 11.17 to use a larger test list consisting of 20 numbers.

   b. Modify Program 11.17 to use a list of 100 randomly selected numbers.

6. A company currently maintains two lists of part numbers, where each part number is an integer. Write a C++ program that compares these lists of numbers and displays the numbers, if any, that are common to both. (*Hint:* Sort each list prior to making the comparison.)

7. Redo Exercise 6, but display a list of part numbers that appear only on one list, but not both.

8. Rewrite the binary search algorithm to use recursion rather than iteration.

11.7 COMMON PROGRAMMING ERRORS

Four common errors are associated with using arrays:

1. Forgetting to declare the array. This error results in a compiler error message equivalent to "Invalid indirection" each time a subscripted variable is encountered within a program. The exact meaning of this error message will become clear in Chapter 13 when the correspondence between arrays and pointers is established.

2. Using a subscript that references a nonexistent array element. For example, declaring the array to be of size 20 and using a subscript value of 25. This error is not detected by most C++ compilers. It will, however, result in a run-time error that results either in a program crash or a value that has no relation to the intended element being accessed from memory. In either case it is usually an extremely troublesome error to locate. The only solution to this problem is to make sure, either by specific programming statements or by careful coding, that each subscript references a valid array element.

3. Not using a large enough conditional value in a `for` loop counter to cycle through all the array elements. This error usually occurs when an array is initially specified to be of size `n` and there is a `for` loop within the program of the form `for (i = 0; i < n; i++)`. The array size is then expanded but the programmer forgets to change the interior `for` loop parameters. Declaring an array's size using a named constant and consistently using the named constant throughout the function in place of the variable `n` eliminates this problem.

4. Forgetting to initialize the array. Although many compilers automatically set all elements of integer and real valued arrays to zero, and all elements of character arrays to blanks, it is up to the programmer to ensure that each array is correctly initialized before processing of array elements begins.

11.8 CHAPTER REVIEW

Key Terms

Big O notation	one-dimensional array
binary search	quicksort
exchange sort	selection sort
index	single-dimensional array
indexed variable	subscript
linear (sequential) search	subscripted variable
null character ('\0')	two-dimensional array

Summary

1. A single-dimensional array is a data structure that can be used to store a list of values of the same data type. Such arrays must be declared by giving the data type of the values that are stored in the array and the array size. For example, the declaration:

```
int num[100];
```

creates an array of 100 integers. A preferable approach is to first use a named constant for the array size, and then use this constant in the definition of the array. For example:

```
const int MAXSIZE = 100;
```

and

```
int num[MAXSIZE];
```

2. Array elements are stored in contiguous locations in memory and referenced using the array name and a subscript, for example, `num[22]`. Any non-negative integer value expression can be used as a subscript and the subscript 0 always refers to the first element in an array.

3. A two-dimensional array is declared by listing both a row and a column size with the data type and name of the array. For example, the declaration:

```
int mat[5][7];
```

creates a two-dimensional array consisting of five rows and seven columns of integer values.

4. Two-dimensional arrays may be initialized when they are declared. This is accomplished by listing the initial values, in a row-by-row manner, within braces and separating them with commas. For example, the declaration:

```
int vals[3][2] = { {1, 2},
                   {3, 4},
                   {5, 6} };
```

produces the following 3-row by 2-column array:

```
1 2
3 4
5 6
```

As C++ uses the convention that initialization proceeds in row-wise order, the inner braces can be omitted. Thus, an equivalent initialization is provided by the statement:

```
int vals[3][2] = { 1, 2, 3, 4, 5, 6};
```

5. Arrays are passed to a function by passing the name of the array as a parameter. The value actually passed is the address of the first array storage location. Thus, the called function receives direct access to the original array and not a copy of the array elements. Within the called function a formal parameter must be declared to receive the passed array name. The declaration of the formal parameter can omit the row size of the array.
6. The linear search is an O(*N*) search. It examines each item in a list until the searched item is found or until it is determined that the item is not in the list.
7. The binary search is an $O(\log_2 N)$ search. It requires that a list be in sorted order before it can be applied.
8. The selection and exchange sort algorithms require an order of magnitude of N^2 comparisons for sorting a list of *N* items.
9. The quicksort algorithm requires an order of magnitude of $N \log_2 N$ comparisons to sort a list of *N* items.

Exercises

1. a. Write a C++ program that reads a list of floating-point grades from the keyboard into an array named `grade`. The grades are to be counted as they are read, and entry is to be terminated when a negative value has been entered. Once all of the grades have been input, your program should find and display the sum and average of the grades. The grades should then be listed with an asterisk (*) placed in front of each grade that is below the average.

   b. Extend the program written for Exercise 1a to display each grade and its letter equivalent. Assume the following scale:

      A grade between 90 and 100 is an A.
      A grade greater than or equal to 80 and less than 90 is a B.
      A grade greater than or equal to 70 and less than 80 is a C.
      A grade greater than or equal to 60 and less than 70 is a D.
      A grade less than 60 is an F.

2. Define an array named `PeopleTypes` that can store a maximum of 50 integer values that will be entered at the keyboard. Enter a series of 1's, 2's, 3's, and 4's into the array, where a 1 represents an infant, a 2 represents a child, a 3 represents a teenager, and a 4 represents an adult that was present at a local school function. Any other integer value should not be accepted as valid input, and data entry should stop when a negative value has been entered.

   Your program should count the number of each 1, 2, 3, and 4 in the array and output a list of how many infants, children, teenagers, and adults were at the school function.

3. Given a one-dimensional array of integer numbers, write and test a function that prints the elements in reverse order.
4. Write and test a function that returns *the position* of the largest and smallest values in an array of floating-point numbers.
5. Read a set of numerical grades from the keyboard into an array. The maximum number of grades is 50, and data entry should be terminated when a negative number has been entered. Have your program sort and print the grades in *descending* order.

6. a. Define an array with a maximum of 20 integer values and either fill the array with numbers input from the keyboard or assigned by the program. Then write a function named `split()` that reads the array and places all zero or positive numbers into an array named `positive` and all negative numbers into an array named `negative`. Finally have your program call a function that displays the values in both the `positive` and `negative` arrays.

   b. Extend the program written for Exercise 6a to sort the `positive` and `negative` arrays into ascending order before they are displayed.

7. Using the `srand()` and `rand()` C++ library functions fill an array of 1000 floating-point numbers with random numbers that have been scaled to the range 1 to 100. Then determine and display the number of random numbers having values between 1 and 50 and the number having values greater than 50. What do you expect the output counts to be?

8. In many statistical analysis programs, data values that are considerably outside the range of the majority of values are simply dropped from consideration. Using this information, write a C++ program that accepts up to 10 floating-point values from a user and determines and displays the average and standard deviation of the input values. All values that are more than four standard deviations away from the computed average are to be displayed and dropped from any further calculation, and a new average and standard deviation should be computed and displayed.

9. Given a one-dimensional array of floating-point numbers named `num`, write a function that determines the sum of the numbers

   a. using repetition

   b. using recursion (*Hint:* If $n = 1$, then the sum is `num[0]`; otherwise, the sum is `num[n]` plus the sum of the first $n - 1$ elements.)

10. Your professor has asked you to write a C++ program that can be used to determine grades at the end of the semester. For each student, who is identified by an integer number between 1 and 60, four examination grades must be kept. Additionally, two final grade averages must be computed. The first grade average is simply the average of all four grades. The second grade average is computed by weighting the four grades as follows: the first grade gets a weight of 0.2, the second grade gets a weight of 0.3, the third grade a weight of 0.3, and the fourth grade a weight of 0.2; that is, the final grade is computed as

    ```
    0.2 * grade-1 + 0.3 * grade-2 + 0.3 * grade-3 + 0.2 * grade-4.
    ```

    Using this information you are to construct a 60×6 two-dimensional array, in which the first column is used for the student number, the next four columns for the grades, and the last two columns for the computed final grades. The output of the program should be a display of the data in the completed array.

    For test purposes the professor has provided the following data:

Student	Grade 1	Grade 2	Grade 3	Grade 4
1	100	100	100	100
2	100	0	100	0
3	82	94	73	86
4	64	74	84	94
5	94	84	74	64

11. Modify the program written for Exercise 10 by adding an eighth column to the array. The grade in the eighth column should be calculated by computing the average of the top three grades only.

12. a. You are to create a two-dimensional list of integer part numbers and quantities of each part in stock and write a function that displays the data in the array in *decreasing* quantity order. Assume that no more than 100 different parts are being kept track of, and test your program with the following data:

Part No.	Quantity
1001	62
949	85
1050	33
867	125
346	59
1025	105

b. Modify the function written in Exercise 12a to display the data in part number order.

13. Assume that the answers to a true–false test are as follows:

T T F F T. Given a two-dimensional answer array where each row corresponds to the answers provided on one test, write a function that accepts the two-dimensional array and the number of tests as arguments, and returns a one-dimensional array containing the grades for each test. (Assume each question is worth 5 points, so that the maximum possible grade is 25.) Test your function using the following data:

Test 1:	T	F	T	T	T
Test 2:	T	T	T	T	T
Test 3:	T	T	F	F	T
Test 4:	F	T	F	F	F
Test 5:	F	F	F	F	F
Test 6:	T	T	F	T	F

14. Modify the function that you wrote for Exercise 13 so that each test is stored in column order rather than row order.

15. Write a function that can be used to sort the elements of a 3 × 4 two-dimensional array of integers so that the lowest value is in element position [0][0], the next highest value in element position [0][1], and the highest value in element position [2][3].

16. A magic square is a square of numbers with N rows and N columns in which each of the integer values from 1 to ($N * N$) appears exactly once, and in which the sum of each column, each row, and each diagonal is the same value. For example, Figure 11.26 shows a magic square in which $N = 3$ and the sum of the rows, columns, and diagonal is 15. Write a program that constructs and displays a magic square for any give odd number N. The algorithm is:

Insert the value 1 in the middle of the first row (element [0][N%2]).
After a value, x, has been placed, move up one row and to the right one column. Place the next number, x + 1, there, unless:
(1) You move off the top (row = – 1) in any column. Then move to the bottom row and place the next number, x + 1, in the bottom row of that column.

FIGURE 11.26 A Magic Square

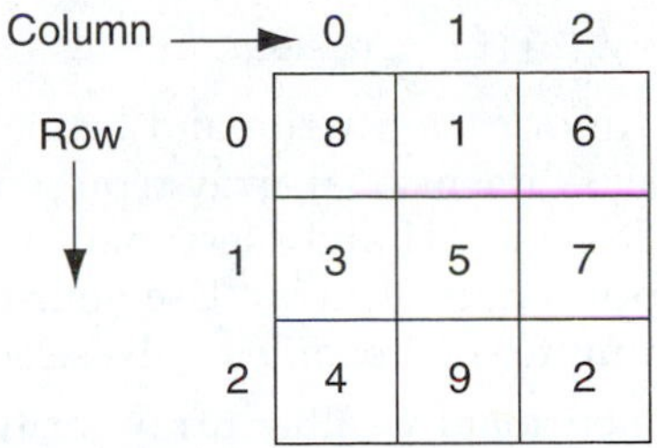

(2) You move off the right end (column = N) of a row. Then place the next number, x + 1, in the first column of that row.

(3) You move to a position that is already filled or out of the upper-right corner. Then place the next number, x + 1, immediately below x.

Stop when you have placed as many elements as there are in the array.

17. Among other applications Pascal's triangle (see Figure 11.27) provides a means of determining the number of possible combinations of n things taken r at a time. For example, the number of possible combinations of five people ($n = 5$) taken two at a time ($r = 2$) is 10.

FIGURE 11.27 Pascal's Triangle

	r						
n	**0**	**1**	**2**	**3**	**4**	**5**	**•••**
0	1						
1	1	1					
2	1	2	1				
3	1	3	3	1			
4	1	4	6	4	1		
5	1	5	10	10	5	1	
• • •							

Each row of the triangle begins and ends with 1. Every other in a row is the sum of the element directly above it with the element to the left of the one above it. That is,

```
element[n][r] = element[n - 1][r] + element[n - 1][r - 1]
```

Using this information write and test a C++ program to create the first 11 rows of a two-dimensional array representing Pascal's triangle. For any given value of *n* less than 11 and *r* less than or equal to *n*, the program should display the appropriate element. Use your program to determine in how many ways a committee of 8 people can be selected from a group of 10 people.

18. A three-dimensional weather array for the months of July and August 1995 has planes labeled by the month numbers 7 and 8. In each plane there are rows, numbered 1 though 31, representing the days, and two columns labeled H and L that represent the day's high and low temperatures, respectively.

    Use this information to write a C++ program that either prompts for or assigns the high and low temperatures for each element of the arrays. Then allow the user to request

    - any day's high and low temperature
    - average high and low temperatures for a given month
    - month and day with the highest temperature
    - month and day with the lowest temperature

CHAPTER

12 Strings

Each computer language has its own method of handling strings of characters. Some languages, such as C++, have an extremely rich set of string manipulation functions and capabilities. Other languages, such as FORTRAN, which is predominantly used for numerical calculations, added string handling capabilities with later versions of the compiler. Languages such as LISP, which are targeted for list handling applications, provide an exceptional string manipulation capability.

On a fundamental level, strings in C++ are simply arrays of characters that can be manipulated using standard element-by-element array-processing techniques. On a higher level, string library functions are available for treating strings as complete entities. This chapter explores the input, manipulation, and output of strings using both approaches. In the next chapter we present C++'s most powerful string manipulation techniques, which rely on pointers.

12.1 STRING FUNDAMENTALS

A **string literal** is any sequence of characters enclosed in double quotes. A string literal is also referred to as a string value and more conventionally as a **string.** Examples of strings are `"This is a string"`, `"Hello World!"`, and `"xyz 123 *!#@&"`.

A string is stored as an array of characters terminated by a special end-of-string symbolic constant named **`NULL`**. The value assigned to the NULL constant is the escape sequence `\0` and is the sentinel that marks the end of every string. For example, Figure 12.1 illustrates how the string `"Good Morning!"` is stored

FIGURE 12.1 Storing a String in Memory

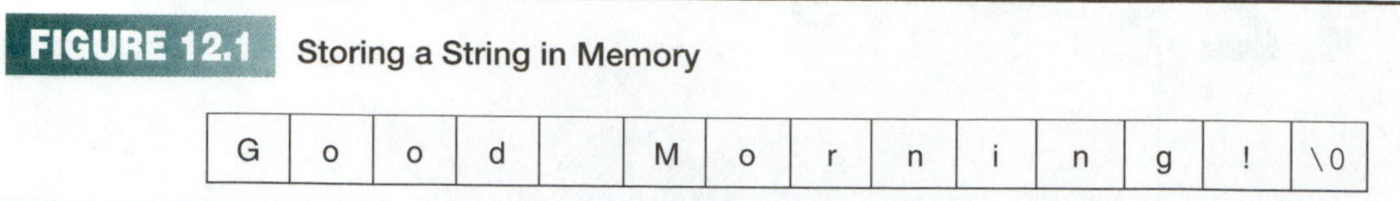

in memory. The string uses 14 storage locations, with the last character in the string being the end-of-string marker `\0`. The double quotes are not stored as part of the string.

Since a string is stored as an array of characters, the individual characters in the array can be input, manipulated, or output using standard array-handling techniques. The end-of-string null character is useful for detecting the end of the string when handling strings in this fashion.

String Input and Output

Although you have a choice of using either library or user-written functions for processing a string already in memory, inputting a string from a keyboard or displaying a string usually requires some reliance on standard library routines or class methods. Table 12.1 lists the commonly available objects, methods, and library routines for both character-by-character and complete string input/output.

TABLE 12.1 String and Character Library Routines[1]

C++ Routine	Description	C Routine
`cout`	General-purpose screen output	`printf()`
`cout`	String output to screen	`puts()`
`cout`	Character output to screen	`putchar()`
`cin`	General-purpose screen input	`scanf()`
`cin.getline()`	String input from terminal	`gets()`
`cin.get()`	Character input from terminal	`getchar()`

As listed in Table 12.1, in addition to the `cout` and `cin` streams, C++ provides two routines, `cin.getline()` and `cin.get()`, that were especially designed for string and character input. Earlier C functions that provide similar features to these C++ routines, and are still available in C++, are `gets()` and `getchar()`. For output C provided the `puts()` and `putchar()` functions; the features of these two functions are essentially provided in C++ by `cout`. Programs that use the newer C++ stream I/O must include the `iostream.h` header, while the older C functions require the `stdio.h` header.

Program 12.1 illustrates the use of the `cin.getline()` and `cout` routines to input and output a string entered at the user's terminal.

[1] Additionally, the functions `getche()` and `putch()` are available in C++. These are character input and output functions that provide features identical to `getchar()` and `putchar()`, but are specifically written for IBM-compatible PCs.

PROGRAM 12.1 Input and Output of a String

```
#include <iostream.h>

const int MAXCHARS = 81;

int main()
{
  char message[MAXCHARS];    // enough storage for a complete line

  cout << "Enter a string:\n";

  cin.getline(message,MAXCHARS,'\n');

  cout << "The string just entered is:\n"
       << message << endl;

  return 0;
}
```

The following is a sample run of Program 12.1:

```
Enter a string:
This is a test input of a string of characters.
The string just entered is:
This is a test input of a string of characters.
```

The `cin.getline()` method used in Program 12.1 continuously accepts and stores characters typed at the terminal into the character array named `message` until either 80 characters are entered (the 81st character is then used to store the end-of-string `NULL` character, `\0`), or the enter key is detected. Pressing the enter key at the terminal generates a newline character, `\n`, which is interpreted by `cin.getline()` as the end-of-line entry. All the characters encountered by `cin.getline()`, except the newline character, are stored in the `message` array. Before returning, the `cin.getline()` function appends a `NULL` character, `'\0'`, to the stored set of characters, as illustrated in Figure 12.2. The `cout` object is then used to display the string.

Although the `cout` object is used in Program 12.1 for string output, `cin` could not be used in place of `cin.getline()` for string input. This is because the `cin` object reads a set of characters up to either a blank space or a newline

FIGURE 12.2 Inputting a String with `cin.getline()`

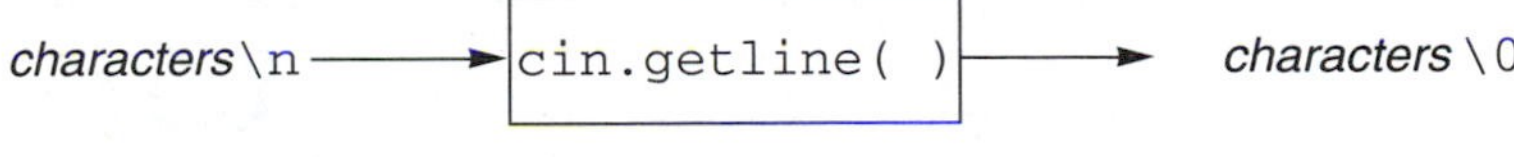

`cin.getline( )` substitutes `\0` for the entered `\n`

character. Thus, attempting to enter the characters `This is a string` using the statement `cin >> message;` only results in the word `This` being assigned to the `message` array. Entering the complete line using a `cin` object requires a statement such as

```
cin >> message1 >> message2 >> message3 >> message4;
```

Here, the word `This` is assigned to the string `message1`, the word `is` is assigned to the string `message2`, and so on. The fact that a blank terminates a `cin` extraction operation restricts `cin`'s usefulness for entering string data and is the reason for using `cin.getline()`.

In its most general form, the `cin.getline()` function has the syntax

```
cin.getline(str, terminating-length, terminating-char)
```

where `str` is a string or character pointer variable, *terminating-length* is an integer constant or variable indicating the maximum number of input characters that can be input, and *terminating-char* is an optional character constant or variable specifying the terminating character. If this optional third argument is omitted, the default terminating character is the newline (`'\n'`) character. Thus, the statement `cin.getline(message,MAXCHARS,'\n');` can be used in place of the statement `cin.getline(message,MAXCHARS);`. Both of these functions stop reading characters when the return key is pressed or until `MAXCHARS-1` characters have been read, whichever comes first. Since `cin.getline()` permits specification of any terminating character for the input stream, a statement such as `cin.getline(message,MAXCHARS,'x');` is also valid. This particular statement will stop accepting characters whenever the `x` key is pressed. In all future programs we will assume that input is terminated by the enter key, which generates a newline character. As such the optional third argument passed to `getline()`, which is the terminating character, will be omitted.

String Processing

Strings can be manipulated using either standard library functions or standard array-processing techniques. The library functions typically available for use are presented in the next section. For now we will concentrate on processing a string in a character-by-character fashion. This will allow us to understand how the standard library functions are constructed and to create our own library functions. For a specific example, consider the function **`strcopy()`**, which copies the contents of `string2` to `string1`.

```
// copy string2 to string 1
void strcopy(char string1[], char string2[])
{
  int i = 0;                    // i will be used as a subscript

  while (string2[i] != '\0')    // check for the end-of-string
  {
    string1[i] = string2[i];    // copy the element to string1
    i++;
  }
  string1[i] = '\0';            // terminate the first string

  return;
}
```

Although this string copy function can be shortened considerably and written more compactly, which is done later in this section, the function illustrates the main features of string manipulation. The two strings are passed to `strcopy()` as arrays. Each element of `string2` is then assigned to the equivalent element of `string1` until the end-of-string marker is encountered. The detection of the null character forces the termination of the `while` loop controlling the copying of elements. Since the null character is not copied from `string2` to `string1`, the last statement in `strcopy()` appends an end-of-string character to `string1`. Prior to calling `strcopy()`, the programmer must ensure that sufficient space has been allocated for the `string1` array to be able to store the elements of the `string2` array. Program 12.2 includes the `strcopy()` function in a complete program. Notice that the function prototype for `strcopy()` declares that the function expects to receive two character arrays.

PROGRAM 12.2

```
#include <iostream.h>

const int MAXCHARS = 81;

void strcopy(char [], char []); // function prototype

int main()
{
  char message[MAXCHARS];       // enough storage for a complete line
  char new_message[MAXCHARS];   // enough storage for a copy of message
  int i;

  cout << "Enter a sentence: ";
  cin.getline(message,MAXCHARS);         // get the string
  strcopy(new_message,message);    // pass two array addresses
  cout << "The copied string is:\n"
       << new_message << endl;

  return 0;
}

void strcopy(char string1[], char string2[])   // copy string2 to string1
{
  int i = 0;                      // i will be used as a subscript

  while (string2[i] != '\0')      // check for the end-of-string
  {
    string1[i] = string2[i];      // copy the element to string1
    i++;
  }
  string1[i] = '\0';              // terminate the first string

  return;
}
```

The following is a sample run of Program 12.2:

```
Enter a sentence: How much wood could a woodchuck chuck.
The copied string is:
How much wood could a woodchuck chuck.
```

Detecting the End-of-String `NULL` Character The NULL character that marks the end of each string is extremely important in user-created string processing functions. Frequently, however, it is effectively disguised by C++ programmers. This is because the numerical value of the NULL character is zero, which is considered false in relational expressions.

To understand how the NULL is typically used by C++ programmers, reconsider the `strcopy()` function used in Program 12.2. This function, which is repeated below for convenience, is used to copy the characters from one array to another array, one character at a time until the end-of-string NULL is detected.

```
void strcopy(char string1[], char string2[])   // copy string2 to string1
{
  int i = 0;

  while (string2[i] != '\0')     // check for the end-of-string
  {
    string1[i] = string2[i];     // copy the element to string1
    i++;
  }
  string1[i] = '\0';             // terminate the first string

  return;
}
```

As currently written, the subscript `i` in the `strcopy()` function is used successively to reference each character in the array named `string1` by "marching along" the string one character at a time. The `while` statement in `strcopy()` tests each character to ensure that the end of the string has not been reached. As with all relational expressions, the tested expression, `string2[i] != '\0'`, is either true or false. Using the string `this is a string` illustrated in Figure 12.3 as an example, as long as `string2[i]` does not reference the end-of-string character the value of the expression is nonzero and is considered to be true. The expression is only false when the value of the expression is zero. This occurs when the last element in the string is accessed.

Recall that C++ defines false as zero and true as anything else. Thus, the expression `string2[i] != '\0'` becomes zero, or false, when the end of the string is reached. It is nonzero, or true, everywhere else. Since the NULL character has an internal value of zero by itself, the comparison to `'\0'` is not necessary. When `string2[i]` references the end-of-string character, the value of `string2[i]` is zero. When `string2[i]` references any other character, the value of `string2[i]` is the value of the code used to store the character and is nonzero. Figure 12.4 on p. 644 lists the ASCII codes for the string `this is a string`. As seen in the figure, each element has a nonzero value except for the NULL character.

FIGURE 12.3 The `while` Test Becomes False at the End of the String

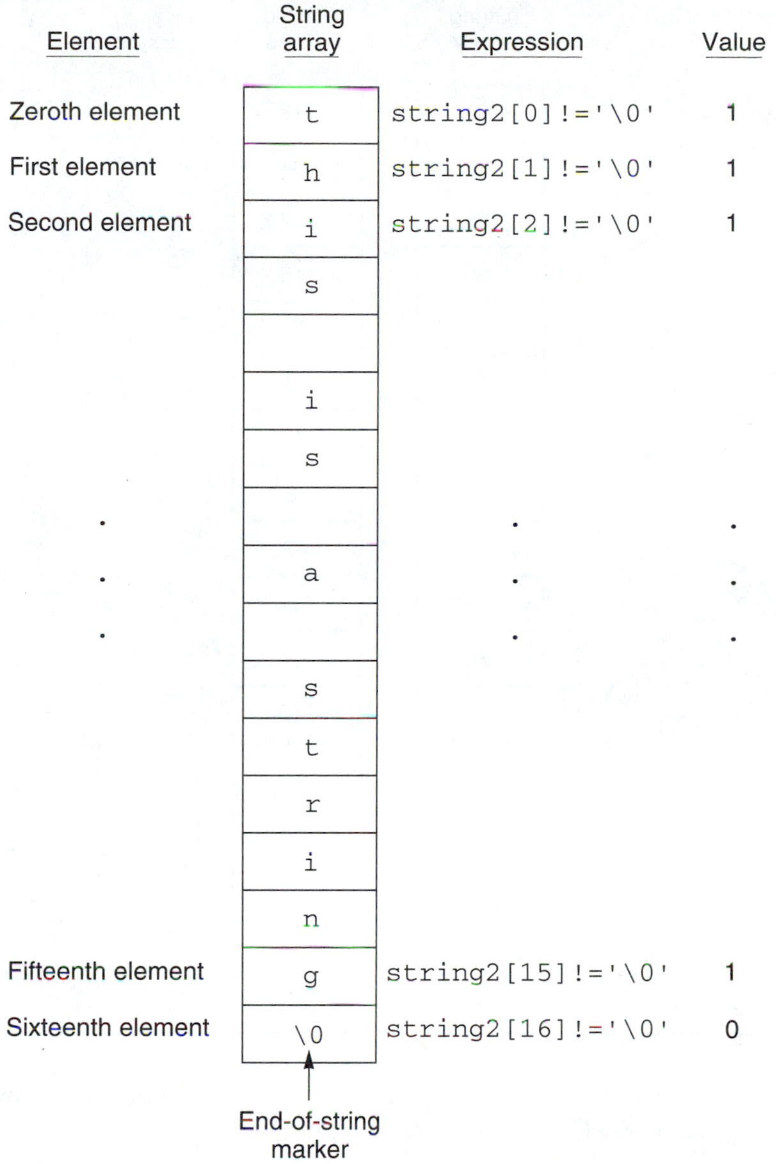

Element	String array	Expression	Value
Zeroth element	t	`string2[0]!='\0'`	1
First element	h	`string2[1]!='\0'`	1
Second element	i	`string2[2]!='\0'`	1
	s		
	i		
	s		
.		.	.
.	a	.	.
.		.	.
	s		
	t		
	r		
	i		
	n		
Fifteenth element	g	`string2[15]!='\0'`	1
Sixteenth element	\0	`string2[16]!='\0'`	0

End-of-string marker

Since the expression `string2[i]` is only zero at the end of a string and nonzero for every other character, the expression `while (string2[i] != '\0')` can be replaced by the simpler expression `while (string2[i])`. Although this may appear confusing at first, the revised test expression is certainly more compact than the longer version. Since end-of-string tests are frequently written by professional C++ programmers in this shorter form, it is

FIGURE 12.4 The ASCII Codes Used to Store `this is a string`

String array	Stored codes	Expression	Value
t	116	string2[0]	116
h	104	string2[1]	104
i	105	string2[2]	105
s	115		
	32		
i	105		
s	115		
	32	.	.
a	97	.	.
	32	.	.
s	115		
t	116		
r	114		
i	105		
n	110		
g	103	string2[15]	103
\0	0	string2[16]	0

worthwhile to be familiar with this expression. Including this expression in `strcopy()` results in the following version:

```
void strcopy(char string1[], char string2[])   // copy string2 to string1
{
  int i = 0;

  while (string2[i])
  {
    string1[i] = string2[i];    // copy the element to string1
    i++;
  }
  string1[i] = '\0';            // terminate the first string

  return;
}
```

The second modification that would be made to this string copy function by a C++ programmer is to include the assignment inside the test portion of the `while` statement. Our new version of the string copy function is:

```
void strcopy(char string1[], char string2[])   // copy string2 to string1
{
  int i = 0;

  while (string1[i] = string2[i])
    i++;

  return;
}
```

Notice that including the assignment statement within the test part of the while statement eliminates the necessity of separately terminating the copied string with the null character. The assignment within the parentheses ensures that the null character is copied from `string2` to `string1`. The value of the assignment expression only becomes zero after the null character is assigned to `string1`, at which point the `while` loop is terminated.

Character-by-Character Input

Just as strings can be processed using character-by-character techniques, they can also be entered and displayed in this manner. For example, consider Program 12.3, which uses the character-input function `cin.get()` to accept a string one character at a time. The shaded portion of Program 12.3 essentially replaces the `cin.getline()` function previously used in Program 12.2.

PROGRAM 12.3

```
#include <iostream.h>

const int MAXCHARS = 81;

int main()
{
  char message[MAXCHARS], c;

  cout << "Enter a sentence:\n";

  int i = 0;
  while(i < MAXCHARS && (c = cin.get()) != '\n')
  {
    message[i] = c;    // store the character
    i++;
  }
  message[i] = '\0';  // terminate the string

  cout << "\nThe sentence just entered is: "
       << message << endl;

  return 0;
}
```

A BIT OF BACKGROUND

Anagrams and Palindromes

Some of the most challenging and fascinating word games are played with anagrams and palindromes.

An *anagram* is a rearrangement of the letters in a word or phrase that makes another word or phrase. Although the letters of the word *door* can be rearranged to spell *orod* and *doro,* it is more exciting to discover the words *odor* and *rood.* A word, phrase, or sentence that reads the same forward and backward, such as *top spot* is a *palindrome.*

The origins of most known anagrams and palindromes are lost to anonymity. Here are some collected by Richard Manchester in *The Mammoth Book of Fun and Games* (Hart Publishing Co. Inc., New York City, 1977; pp. 229–231);

Apt anagrams:

- The Mona Lisa -> No hat, a smile
- The United States of America -> Attaineth its cause: freedom!

Interesting palindromes:

- Live not on evil!
- 'Tis Ivan on a visit.
- Yreka Bakery (This is a real place in Yreka, California.)
- Able was I ere I saw Elba. (Might Napoleon have coined this one?)
- Madam, I'm Adam.
- A man, a plan, a canal: Panama!

Computers can be programmed to detect palindromes and find anagrams, but the human brain may be more efficient for doing this.

The following is a sample run of Program 12.3:

```
Enter a sentence:
This is a test input of a string of characters.
The sentence just entered is:
This is a test input of a string of characters.
```

The `while` statement in Program 12.3 causes characters to be read providing the number of characters entered is less than `MAXCHARS` and the character returned by `cin.get()` is not the newline character. The parentheses surrounding the expression `c = cin.get()` are necessary to assign the character returned by `cin.get()` to the variable `c` prior to comparing it to the newline escape sequence. Without the surrounding parentheses, the comparison operator, `!=`, which takes precedence over the assignment operator, causes the entire expression to be equivalent to

```
c = (cin.get() != '\n')
```

which is an invalid application of `cin.get()`.[2]

Program 12.3 also illustrates a very useful technique for developing functions. The shaded statements constitute a self-contained unit for entering a complete line of characters from a terminal. As such, these statements can be removed from `main()` and placed together as a new function. Program 12.4 illustrates placement of these statements in a separate function named `getaline()`.

---

[2] The equivalent statement in C is `c = (getchar() != '\n')`, which is a valid expression that produces an unexpected result for most beginning programmers. Here the character returned by `getchar()` is compared to `'\n'`, and the value of the comparison is either 0 or 1, depending on whether or not `getchar()` received the newline character. This value, either 0 or 1, is then assigned to `c`.

PROGRAM 12.4

```
#include <iostream.h>

const int MAXCHARS = 81;

void getaline(char []);  // function prototype

int main()
{
  char message[MAXCHARS];   // enough storage for a complete line
  int i;

  cout << "Enter a sentence: ";
  getaline(message);
  cout << "\nThe sentence just entered is: "
       << message << endl;

  return 0;
}

void getaline(char strng[])
{
  int i = 0;
  char c;

  while(i < MAXCHARS && (c = cin.get()) != '\n')
  {
    strng[i] = c;       // store the character entered
    i++;
  }
  strng[i] = '\0';      // terminate the string

  return;
}
```

Exercises 12.1

1. a. The following function can be used to select and display all vowels contained within a user-input string:

```
void vowels(char strng[])
{
  int i = 0;
  char c;
  while ((c = strng[i++]) != '\0')
    switch(c)
    {
       case 'a':
       case 'e':
       case 'i':
```

```
        case 'o':
        case 'u':
          cout << c;
      } // end of switch
      cout << endl;

    return;
  }
```

Notice that the switch statement in `vowels()` uses the fact that selected cases "drop through" in the absence of `break` statements. Thus, all selected cases result in a `cout` object call. Include `vowels()` in a working program that accepts a user-input string and then displays all vowels in the string. In response to the input `How much is the little worth worth?`, your program should display `ouieieoo`.

b. Modify `vowels()` to count and display the total number of vowels contained in the string passed to it.

2. Modify the `vowels()` function of Exercise 1 to count and display the individual numbers of each vowel contained in the string.

3. a. Write a C++ function to count the total number of characters, including blanks, contained in a string. Do not include the end-of-string marker in the count.

   b. Include the function written for Exercise 3a in a complete working program.

4. Write a program that accepts a string of characters from a terminal and displays the hexadecimal equivalent of each character.

5. Write a C++ program that accepts a string of characters from a terminal and displays the string one word per line.

6. Write a function that reverses the characters in a string. (*Hint:* This can be considered as a string copy starting from the back end of the first string.)

7. Write a function called `del_char()` that can be used to delete characters from a string. The function should take three arguments: the string name, the number of characters to delete, and the starting position in the string where characters should be deleted. For example, the function call `del_char(strng,13,5)`, when applied to the string `all enthusiastic people`, should result in the string `all people`.

8. Write a function called `add_char()` to insert one string of characters into another string. The function should take three arguments: the string to be inserted, the original string, and the position in the original string where the insertion should begin. For example, the call `add_char(" for all",message,6)` should insert the characters `for all` in `message` starting at `message[5]`.

9. a. Write a C++ function named `to_upper()` that converts lowercase letters into uppercase letters. The expression `c - 'a' + 'A'` can be used to make the conversion for any lowercase character stored in c.

   b. Add a data input check to the function written in Exercise 9a to verify that a valid lowercase letter is passed to the function. A character, in ASCII, is lowercase if it is greater than or equal to `a` and less than or equal to `z`. If the character is not a valid lowercase letter, have the function `to_upper()` return the passed character unaltered.

   c. Write a C++ program that accepts a string from a terminal and converts all lowercase letters in the string to uppercase letters.

10. Write a C++ program that accepts a string from a terminal and converts all uppercase letters in the string to lowercase letters.

11. Write a C++ program that counts the number of words in a string. A word is encountered whenever a transition from a blank space to a nonblank character is encountered. Assume the string contains only words separated by blank spaces.

12.2 LIBRARY FUNCTIONS

C++ does not provide built-in operations for complete arrays, such as array assignment or array comparisons. Since a string is just an array of characters terminated with a '\0' character, this means that assignment and relational operations are *not* provided for strings. Extensive collections of string handling functions and routines, however, that effectively supply string assignment, comparison, and other very useful string operations are included with all C++ compilers. The more commonly used routines are listed in Table 12.2.

TABLE 12.2 String Library Routines (Required Header File is `string.h`)

Name	Description	Example
`strcpy(string_var, string_exp)`	Copies `string_exp` to `string_var`, including the `'\0'`.	`strcpy(test, "efgh")`
`strcat(string_var, string_exp)`	Appends `str_exp` to the end of the string value contained in `string_var`.	`strcat(test, "there")`
`strlen(string_exp)`	Returns the length of the string. Does not include the `'\0'` in the length count.	`strlen("Hello World!")`
`strcmp(string_exp1, string_exp2)`	Compares `string_exp1` to `string_exp2`. Returns a negative integer if `string_exp1 < string_exp2`, `0` if `string_exp1 == string_exp2`, and a positive integer if `string_exp1 > string_exp2`.	`strcmp("Bebop", "Beehive")`
`strncpy(string_var, string_exp, n)`	Copies at most `n` characters of `string_exp` to `string_var`. If `string_exp` has fewer than `n` characters it will pad `string_var` with `'\0's`.	`strncpy(str1, str2, 5)`
`strncmp(string_exp1, string_exp2, n)`	Compare at most `n` characters of `string_exp1` to `string_exp2`. Returns the same values as `strcmp()` based on the number of characters compared.	`strncmp("Bebop", "Beehive", 2)`
`strchr(string_exp, character)`	Locates the position of the first occurrence of the character within the string. Returns the address of the character.	`strchr("Hello", 'l')`
`strtok(string_exp, character)`	Parses `string1` into tokens. Returns the next sequence of characters contained in `string1` up to but not including the delimiter character `ch`.	`strtok("Hello there World!, ' ')`

String library functions are called in the same manner as all C++ functions. This means that the appropriate declarations for these functions, which are contained in the standard header files `<string.h>` must be included in your program before the function is called.

PROGRAMMING NOTE

Initializing and Processing Strings

Each of the following declarations produces the same result:

```
char test[5] = "abcd";
char test[] = "abcd";
char test[5] = {'a', 'b', 'c', 'd', '\0'};
char test[] = {'a', 'b', 'c', 'd', '\0'};
```

Each declaration creates storage for exactly five characters and initializes this storage with the characters `'a'`, `'b'`, `'c'`, `'d'`, and `'\0'`. Since a string literal is used for initialization in the first two declarations, the compiler automatically supplies the end-of-string NULL character.

String variables declared in either of these ways shown preclude the use of any subsequent assignments, such as `test = "efgh";`, to the character array. In place of an assignment you can use the `strcpy()` function, such as `strcpy(test, "efgh")`. The only restriction on using `strcpy()` is the size of the declared array, which in this case is 5 elements. Attempting to copy a larger string value into `test` causes the copy to overflow the destination array beginning with the memory area immediately following the last array element. This overwrites whatever was in these memory locations and typically cause a run-time crash when the overwritten areas are accessed via their legitimate identifier name(s).

The same problem can arise when using the `strcat()` function. It is your responsibility to ensure that the concatenated string will fit into the original string.

An interesting situation arises when string variables are defined using pointers (see Section 13.6). In these situations assignments can be made after the declaration statement.

Finally, a string class can be defined (see Section 12.4) in such a way that permits assignment, copy, and concatenation in a manner that checks for sufficient memory space before these operations are performed.

The most commonly used functions listed in Table 12.2 are the first four. The `strcpy()` function copies a source string expression, which consists of either a string literal or the contents of a string variable, into a destination string variable. For example, in the function call `strcpy(string1, "Hello World!")` the source string literal `"Hello World!"` is copied into the destination string variable `string1`. Similarly, if the source string is a string variable named `src_string`, the function call `strcpy(string1, src_string)` copies the contents of `src_string`, into `string1`. In both cases it is the programmer's responsibility to ensure that `string1` is large enough to contain the source string (see accompanying Programming Note).

The `strcat()` function appends a string expression onto the end of a string variable. For example, if the contents of a string variable named `dest_string` is `"Hello"`, then the function call `strcat(dest_string, " there World!")` results in the string value `"Hello there World!"` being assigned to `dest_string`. As with the `strcpy()` function, it is the programmer's responsibility to ensure that the destination string has been defined to be large enough to hold the additional concatenated characters.

The `strlen()` function returns the number of characters in its string argument but does not include the terminating NULL character in the count. For example, the value returned by the function call `strlen("Hello World!")` is 12.

Finally two string expressions may be compared for equality using the `strcmp()` function. Each character in a string is stored in binary using either the ASCII or EBCDIC code. Although these codes are different, they have some characteristics in common: In each of them, a blank precedes (is less than) all letters and numbers; the letters of the alphabet are stored in order from A to Z; and the digits are stored in order from 0 to 9. (It is important to note that in ASCII the letters come before, or are less than, the digits, whereas in EBCDIC the letters follow, or are greater than, the digits.)

When two strings are compared, their individual characters are compared a pair at a time (both first characters, then both second characters, and so on). If no differences are found, the strings are equal; if a difference is found, the string with the first lower character is considered the smaller string. Thus,

`"Hello"` is less than `"Good Bye"` because the first `'H'` in `Hello` is less than the first `'G'` in `Good Bye`.

`"Hello"` is less than `"hello"` because the first `'H'` in `Hello` is less than the first `'h'` in `hello`.

`"Hello"` is less than `"Hello "` because the `'\0'` terminating the first string is less than the `' '` in the second string.

`"SMITH"` is greater than `"JONES"` because the first `'S'` in `SMITH` is greater than the first `'J'` in `JONES`.

`"123"` is greater than `"1227"` because the third character, the `'3'` in `123` is greater than the third character, the `'2'` in `1227`.

`"1237"` is greater than `"123"` because the fourth character, the `'7'`, in `1237` is greater than the fourth character, the `'\0'` in `123`.

`"Behop"` is greater than `"Beehive"` because the third character, the `'h'`, in `Behop` is greater than the third character, the `'e'`, in `Beehive`.

Program 12.5 uses the string functions we have discussed within the context of a complete program.

Sample output produced by Program 12.5 follows:

```
Hello is less than Hello there

The length of string1 is 5 characters
The length of string2 is 11 characters

After concatenation, string1 contains the string value
Hello there World!
The length of this string is 18 characters

Type in a sequence of characters for string2: It's a wonderful day
After copying string2 to string1, the string value in string1 is:
It's a wonderful day
The length of this string is 20 characters

The starting address of the string1 string is: 0x8f3bffc4
```

Except for the last displayed line, the output of Program 12.5 follows the discussion presented for the string library functions. As demonstrated by this output, the extraction operator << automatically dereferences a string variable and displays the contents contained in the variable. Sometimes, however, we really want to see the address of the string. As shown in Program 12.5, this can be done by casting the string variable name using the expression `(void *)`. Another

PROGRAM 12.5

```
#include <iostream.h>
#include <string.h>   // required for the string function library

const int MAXELS = 50;

int main()
{
  char string1[MAXELS] = "Hello";
  char string2[MAXELS] = "Hello there";
  int n;

  n = strcmp(string1, string2);

  if (n < 0)
    cout << string1 << " is less than " << string2 << endl;
  else if (n == 0)
    cout << string1 << " is equal to " << string2 << endl;
  else
    cout << string1 << " is greater than " << string2 << endl;

  cout << "\nThe length of string1 is " << strlen(string1)
       << " characters" << endl;
  cout << "The length of string2 is " << strlen(string2)
       << " characters" << endl;

  strcat(string1," there World!");

  cout << "\nAfter concatenation, string1 contains "
       << "the string value\n" << string1
       << "\nThe length of this string is "
       << strlen(string1) << " characters" << endl;

  cout << "\nType in a sequence of characters for string2: ";
  cin.getline(string2, MAXELS);

  strcpy(string1, string2);

  cout << "After copying string2 to string1, "
       << "the string value in string1 is:\n" << string2
       << "\nThe length of this string is "
       << strlen(string1) << " characters" << endl;

  cout << "\nThe starting address of the string1 string is: "
       << (void *) string1 << endl;

  return 0;
}
```

TABLE 12.3 Character Library Routines (Required Header File is `ctype.h`)

Required Prototype	Description	Example
`int isalpha(char)`	Returns a nonzero number if the character is a letter; otherwise it returns a zero.	`isalpha('a')`
`int isupper(char)`	Returns a nonzero number if the character is uppercase; otherwise it returns a zero.	`isupper('a')`
`int islower(char)`	Returns a nonzero number if the character is lowercase; otherwise it returns a zero.	`islower('a')`
`int isdigit(character)`	Returns a nonzero number if the character is a digit (0 through 9); otherwise it returns a zero.	`isdigit('a')`
`int isascii(character)`	Returns a nonzero number if the character is an ASCII character; otherwise it returns a zero.	`isascii('a')`
`int isspace(character)`	Returns a nonzero number if the character is a space; otherwise it returns a zero.	`isspace(' ')`
`int isprint(character)`	Returns a nonzero number if the character is a printable character; otherwise it returns a zero.	`isprint('a')`
`int iscntrl(character)`	Returns a nonzero number if the character is a control character; otherwise it returns a zero.	`iscntrl('a')`
`int ispucnt(character)`	Returns a nonzero number if the character is a punctuation character; otherwise it returns a zero.	`ispucnt('!')`
`int toupper(char)`	Returns the uppercase equivalent if the character is lowercase; otherwise it returns the character unchanged.	`toupper('a')`
`int tolower(char)`	Returns the lowercase equivalent if the character is uppercase; otherwise it returns the character unchanged.	`tolower('A')`

method would be to send the expression `&string1[0]` to the `cout` object. This expression is read as "the *address* of the `string[0]` element," which is also the starting address of the complete character array.

Character Routines

In addition to string manipulation functions, all C++ compilers also include the character handling routines listed in Table 12.3. The prototypes for each of these routines are contained in the header file `ctype.h`, which should be included in any program that uses these routines.

Since all of the routines listed in Table 12.3 return a nonzero integer (i.e, a true value) if the character meets the desired condition and a zero integer (i.e., a false value) if the condition is not met, these functions can be used directly within an `if` statement. For example, consider the following code segment:

```
char ch;

ch = cin.get();   // get a character from the keyboard

if(isdigit(ch))
  cout < "The character just entered is a digit" << endl;
else if(ispunct(ch))
  cout << "The character just entered is a punctuation mark" << endl;
```

Notice that the character routine is included as a condition within the `if` statement because the function effectively returns either a true (nonzero) or false (zero) value.

Program 12.6 illustrates the use of the `toupper()` routine within the function `ConvertToUpper()`, which is used to convert all lowercase string characters into their uppercase form.

PROGRAM 12.6

```
#include <iostream.h>
#include <ctype.h>      // required for the character function library

const int MAXCHARS = 100;

void ConvertToUpper(char []);

int main()
{
  char message[MAXCHARS];

  cout << "\nType in any sequence of characters: ";

  cin.getline(message,MAXCHARS);

  ConvertToUpper(message);

  cout << "The characters just entered, in uppercase are: "
       << message << endl;

  return 0;
}

// this function converts all lowercase characters to uppercase
void ConvertToUpper(char message[])
{
  for(int i = 0; message[i] != '\0'; i++)
    message[i] = toupper(message[i]);

  return;
}
```

The output produced when Program 12.6 is executed is:

```
Type in any sequence of characters: this is a test OF 12345.
The characters just entered, in uppercase are: THIS IS A TEST OF 12345.
```

Notice that the `toupper()` library function only converts lowercase letters and that all other characters are unaffected.

TABLE 12.4 String Conversion Routines (Required Header File is `stdlib.h`)

Prototype	Description	Example
`int atoi(string_exp)`	Converts an ASCII string to an integer. Conversion stops at the first non-integer character.	`atoi("1234")`
`double atof(string_exp)`	Converts an ASCII string to a double-precision number. Conversion stops at the first character that cannot be interpreted as a double.	`atof("12.34")`
`char[] itoa(string_esp)`	Converts an integer to an ASCII string. The space allocated for the returned string must be large enough for the converted value.	`itoa(1234)`

Conversion Routines

The last group of standard string library routines, listed in Table 12.4, is used to convert strings to and from integer and double-precision data types. The prototypes for each of these routines are contained in the header file `stdlib.h`, which should be included in any program that uses these routines.

Program 12.7 illustrates the use of the `atoi()` and `atof()` functions.

PROGRAM 12.7

```
#include <iostream.h>
#include <string.h>
#include <stdlib.h>     // required for string conversion function library

const int MAXELS = 20;

int main()
{
  char string[MAXELS] = "12345";
  int num;
  double dnum;

  num = atoi(string);

  cout << "The string \"" << string << "\" as an integer number is: "
       << num;
  cout << "\nThis number divided by 3 is: " << num / 3 << endl;

  strcat(string, ".96");

  dnum = atof(string);

  cout << "The string \"" << string << "\" as a double number is: "
       << dnum;
  cout << "\nThis number divided by 3 is: " << dnum / 3 << endl;

  return 0;
}
```

The output produced when Program 12.7 is executed is:

```
The string "12345" as an integer number is: 12345
This number divided by 3 is: 4115
The string "12345.96" as a double number is: 12345.96
This number divided by 3 is: 4115.32
```

As this output illustrates, once a string has been converted to either an integer or double precision value, mathematical operations on the numerical value are valid.

Exercises 12.2

1. Enter and execute Program 12.5 on your computer.
2. Enter and execute Program 12.6 on your computer.
3. Enter and execute Program 12.7 on your computer.
4. Write the following declaration statement in three additional ways:

   ```
   char string[] = "Hello World";
   ```

5. a. Write a function named `length()` that returns the length of a string, without using any standard library functions.

   b. Write a simple `main()` function to test the `length()` function written for Exercise 5a.

6. a. Write a function named `compare()` that compares two strings and returns an integer value of:

   –1 if the first string is less than the second string.
   0 if the two strings are equal.
   1 if the first string is greater than the second string.
   Do not use any standard library functions in the `compare()` function.

   b. Write a simple `main()` function to test the `compare()` function written for Exercise 6a.

7. a. Write a C++ function named `ctype()` that determines the ASCII type of any integer in the range 0 to 127. If the number represents a printable ASCII character, print the character with one of the following appropriate messages:

   ```
   The ASCII character is a lowercase letter.
   The ASCII character is an uppercase letter.
   The ASCII character is a digit.
   The ASCII character is a punctuation mark.
   The ASCII character is a space.
   ```

   If the ASCII character is a nonprintable character, display its ASCII code in decimal format and the message `The ASCII character is a nonprintable character.`

   b. Write a simple `main()` function to test the function written for Exercise 7a. The `main()` function should generate 20 random numbers in the range 0 to 127 and call `ctype()` for each generated number.

8. a. Include the string library functions `strlen()`, `strcat()`, and `strncat()` within a function having the prototype `int concat(char string1[], char string2[], int maxlength)`. The `concat()` function should perform a complete concatenation of `string2` to `string1` only if the length of the concatenated string does not exceed `maxlength`, which is the maximum length defined for `string1`. If the concatenated string will exceed `maxlength`, concatenate only the characters in `string2` so the maximum combined string length is equal to `maxlength - 1`, which provides enough room for the end-of-string `NULL` character.

b. Write a simple `main()` function to test the `concat()` function written for Exercise 8a.

9. a. Write a function named `countlets()` that returns the number of letters in an entered string. Digits, spaces, punctuation, tabs, and newline characters should not be included in the returned count.

b. Write a simple `main()` function to test the `countlets()` function written for Exercise 9a.

12.3 FOCUS ON PROBLEM SOLVING

In this section we focus on constructing two string processing functions. The first function will be used to count the number of characters in a string. The purpose of this problem is to reinforce our concept of a C++ string and how characters can be accessed one at a time. The second function will be used to count words. Although this seems a simple problem at first glance, it is more typical in that it brings up a set of issues that must be addressed before a final algorithm can be selected. Chief among these issues is coming up with a suitable criteria for what constitutes a word. This is necessary so that the function can correctly identify and count a word when it encounters one.

Problem 1: Character Counting

In this problem we want to pass a string to a function and have the function return the number of characters in the string. For our current purposes any character in the string, whether it is a blank, printable, or nonprintable character, is to be counted. The end-of-string null is not to be included in the final count. Although this problem can be solved using the `strlen()` function, we want a userwritten version both to illustrate how such functions are constructed and for further modification in Problem 2.

Analyze the Problem This problem is rather straightforward in its I/O requirements: The input to the function is a string and the output returned by the function is the number of characters in the string. Since a string in C++ is simply an array of characters, we can pass the string to our function simply by passing the character array. Because the function is to return an integer value, the number of characters in the string, we define it as returning an `int`.

Develop a Solution Once the function receives the string, it must start at the beginning of the string and count each character it encounters as it "marches along" to the end of the string. Because each C++ string is terminated by a `\0` character, we can use this as a sentinel to tell us when the count should stop. As illustrated in Figure 12.5, we examine each character by indexing through the array until the sentinel is reached.

The pseudocode describing our character counting algorithm follows:

Accept the string as an array argument.
Initialize a count to 0.
For all the characters in the array
   Increment the count.
EndFor.
Return the count.

FIGURE 12.5 Counting Characters in a String

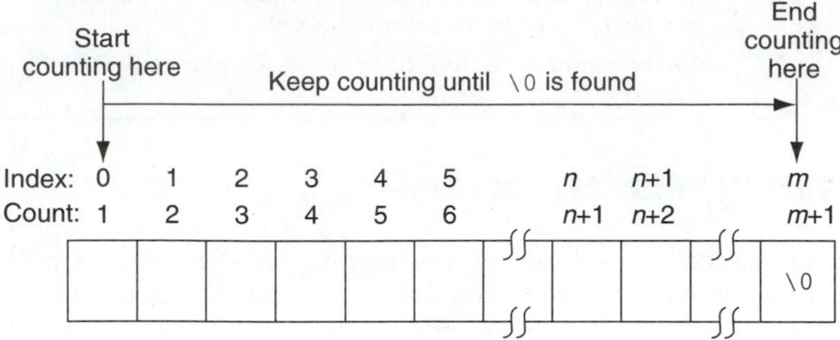

Code the Solution The C++ code corresponding to our pseudocode solution is:

```
int countchar(char list[])
{
  int i, count = 0;

  for(i = 0; list[i] != '\0'; i++)
    count++;

  return(count);
}
```

Notice that we have used a `for` loop within `countchar`. We could just as easily replace this with a `while` loop.

Test and Correct the Program To test the function, we create a main driver function whose sole purpose is to exercise `countchar`. Program 12.8 includes both the `main()` driver and `countchar()`.

A sample run using Program 12.8 follows:

```
Type in any number of characters: This is a test of character counts
The number of characters just entered is 34
```

Problem 2: Word Counting

This problem is more complicated than the previous problem, because we must first determine the criteria for identifying a word. At first glance, since each word is followed by a blank space, we might be tempted to simply count spaces. For example, consider the situation pictured in Figure 12.6. The problem with this approach is that the last word will not have a trailing blank. Even more troublesome are the cases where more than one blank is used between words and leading blanks are used before the first word. We will have to keep these situations in mind when we develop a solution for counting words.

Analyze the Problem From an I/O standpoint this problem is straightforward: The input to the function is a string and the output returned by the function is the number of words in the string. Since a string in C++ is simply an array of characters, we can pass the string to our function simply by passing the character

PROGRAM 12.8

```
#include <iostream.h>

const int MAXNUM = 1000;

int countchar(char []);   // function prototype

int main()
{
  char message[MAXNUM];
  int numchar;

  cout << "\nType in any number of characters: ";

  cin.getline(message,MAXNUM);
  numchar = countchar(message);
  cout << "The number of characters just entered is "
       << numchar << endl;

  return 0;
}

int countchar(char list[])
{
  int i, count = 0;

  for(i = 0; list[i] != '\0'; i++)
    count++;

  return count;
}
```

array. Because the function is to return an integer value, the number of words in the string, we define it as returning an `int`.

Develop a Solution As we have seen in Figure 12.6, we must come up with an algorithm for determining when to increment our word counter; that is, we must algorithmically define what constitutes a word. Counting spaces will not work without a modification that accounts for extra blanks. An alternative is to increment a counter only when the first character of a word is detected. This approach has the advantages of a positive test for a word and is the approach we will take.

FIGURE 12.6 A Sample Line of Words

t	h	i	s		i	s		t	h	e		t	y	p	i	c	a	l		c	a	s	e

Once this character is found, we can set a flag indicating that we are in a word. This flag can stay on until we come out of a word, which is signified by detecting a blank space. At this point we set the flag to not-in-a-word. The not-in-a-word condition will remain true until a nonblank character is again detected. A pseudocode description of this algorithm is:

Set an inword flag to NO.
Set the word count to 0.
For all the characters in the array
    If the current character is a blank
      Set inword to NO.
    Else if (inword equals NO)
      Set inword to YES.
      Increment the word count.
    EndIf.
EndFor.
Return the count.

The key to this algorithm is the `if-else` condition. If the current character is a blank, the inword flag is set to NO, *regardless* of what it was on the previous character. The else condition is only executed if the current character is not a blank and checks if we were not in a word. In this case (current character not a blank and we are not in a word) we must be making the transition from a blank to a nonblank character. Since this is the criterion for determining that we are in a word, the inword flag is set to YES and the word count is incremented.

Code the Solution The C++ code corresponding to our solution is:

```
int countword(char list[])
{
  const int YES = 1;
  const int NO = 0;
  int i, inaword, count = 0;

  inaword = NO;
  for(i = 0; list[i] != '\0'; i++)
  {
    if (list[i] == ' ')
      inaword = NO;
    else if (inaword == NO)
    {
      inaword = YES;
      count++;
    }
  }
  return(count);
}
```

Test and Correct the Problem To test the function, we create a `main()` driver function whose sole purpose is to exercise `countword()`. Program 12.9 includes both the `main()` driver and `countword()`.

PROGRAM 12.9

```
#include <iostream.h>

const int MAXNUM = 1000;
const int YES = 1;
const int NO = 0;

int countword(char []);  // function prototype

int main()
{
  char message[MAXNUM];
  int numword;

  cout << "\nType in any number of words: ";

  cin.getline(message,MAXNUM);

  numword = countword(message);

  cout << "The number of words just entered is "
       << numword << endl;

  return 0;
}

int countword(char list[])
{
  int i, inaword, count = 0;

  inaword = NO;
  for(i = 0; list[i] != '\0'; i++)
  {
    if (list[i] == ' ')
      inaword = NO;
    else if (inaword == NO)
    {
      inaword = YES;
      count++;
    }
  }

  return count;
}
```

A sample run using Program 12.9 follows:

```
Type in any number of words: This is a test line with a bunch of words
The number of words just entered is 10
```

Further tests that should be performed using Program 12.9 are as follows:

- Enter words with multiple spaces between them.
- Enter words with leading spaces before the first word.
- Enter words with trailing spaces after the last word.
- Enter a sentence that ends in a period or question mark.

Exercises 12.3

1. Modify the `countchar()` function in Program 12.8 to omit blank spaces from the count.
2. Create a function named `cvowels()` that counts and returns the number of vowels in a passed string.
3. Modify the `countword()` function in Program 12.9 so that it counts both characters and words. (*Hint:* Refer to Section 6.5 on how to return multiple values.)
4. Modify the `countword()` function in Program 12.9 to indirectly return the number of words and characters entered, excluding blank spaces, and to directly return the average number of characters per word.
5. Write a function to count the number of lines entered.
6. Write a function to count the number of sentences entered; assume a sentence ends in either a period, question mark, or exclamation point.
7. Modify the function written for Exercise 6 to count the number of words as well as the number of sentences. The function should return the average words per sentence.
8. The Fog index is an index used by editors to grade the reading level difficulty of an article, and is described in detail in the boxed article.[3]

   For this exercise obtain samples of at least 10 sentences from any four textbooks you are currently using. For each of these samples manually determine the number of words and big words (these are defined in the accompanying boxed article) contained in the sample. Then write a C++ function to accept the sentences, calculate a Fog index, and return it. Check the value returned by your function against your hand calculations.

Editors worry about the reading level of their publications. For example, the *Wall Street Journal* aims for a Fog index of 11, the *New York Times* about 15, and the *New York Daily News* 9. The Fog index is a formula generally used to find an approximate reading grade level by measuring the sentence length and the fraction of words with three or more syllables. While reading difficulty is critically dependent on concepts and the presentation, neither factor enters the Fog index.

(continued on next page)

[3] The *NLA News*, Vol. 7, No. 9, May 1991. Permission to reproduce this article was kindly granted by Dr. John Truxal, codirector of the New Liberal Arts Program of the Alfred P. Sloan Foundation.

(continued from previous page)

We looked at one recent issue of *NLA News* and worked out the Fog index for several articles:

Quantitative methods:	10
Museum staff member:	12
Political scientist:	18
Sociologist:	19

In other words, the last sample is read easily by someone reading at grade 19 level (roughly the doctorate).

To find the Fog index, pick a sample of at least 100 words. Omit all proper names, and then:

1. Count the number of sentences. Clauses separated by colons or semicolons are treated as separate sentences.
2. Count the number of "Big Words"—words of three or more syllables. Do not include words that reach three syllables because of "es" or "ed" endings, or because they are compounds of simple words, such as everything or seventeen).
3. Substitute into this formula:

$$\text{Fog index} = 0.4 \; \frac{\text{number of words}}{\text{number of sentences}} + 100 \; \frac{\text{number of big words}}{\text{number of words}}$$

As an example, we look at the first three paragraphs of this article. After we leave out numbers and proper names, we have the sample shown in the following box. There are 102 words, 6 sentences, and 19 big words (italicized in the following box).

Editors worry about the reading level of their *publications*. For example, the Wall Street Journal aims for a Fog index of 1, the New York Times about 15, and the New York Daily News 9. The Fog index is a *formula generally* used to find an *approximate* reading grade level by measuring the sentence length and the fraction of words with three or more *syllables*. While reading *difficulty* is *critically dependent* on concepts and the *presentation*, neither factor enters the Fog index.

We looked at one recent issue of NLA News and worked out the Fog index for *several articles*:

Quantitative methods:	10
Museum staff member:	12
Political scientist:	18
Sociologist:	19

In other words, the last sample is read *easily* by someone reading at grade level (roughly the *doctorate*).

For this case the formula gives

$$0.4 * (102/6 + 100 * 19/102) = 14$$

The reading level is grade 14 (college sophomore).

In applying the Fog index to an "I Can Read It All By Myself" book, we find an index of 2—second grade reading level.

12.4 IMPLEMENTATION OF A CLASS STRING[4]

Although strings can be manipulated using both standard element-by-element array operations and string library functions, these techniques do have disadvantages. For example, there are no string assignment operators and the defined array size can be exceeded using both the `strcpy()` and `strcat()` functions. Additionally, since input of a string value using `cin` is terminated at the first blank character, any string with an embedded space must be input using the `cin.getline()` method.

The underlying cause of all these problems is that strings are not a unique data type. Rather they are implemented as character arrays whose last value is the `NULL`, `'\0'`, character. Since C++ provides for user-defined data types, however, we can remove the disadvantages of processing strings as character arrays by defining a `String` class. In this section we both specify the interface to such a class and then develop the implementation.

From a user interface viewpoint, we would want our string class to provide all of the processing currently available using both array element processing techniques and standard library functions, without the disadvantages. Thus, at a minimum our string class should provide for the following:

1. creation of a string object
2. initialization of a string object using another string object
3. initialization of a string object using a string literal
4. string length determination
5. an assignment operator, =, for assignment from a string object to a string object
6. an assignment operator, =, for assignment from a string literal to a string object
7. a concatenation operator, +, for concatenation from a string object to a string object
8. a concatenation operator, +, for concatenation from a string literal to a string object
9. an equality operator, ==, for comparing two string objects to a string object
10. an equality operator, ==, for comparing a string literal to a string object
11. an extraction operator, >>, for extracting strings having embedded blank spaces from the `cin` standard input stream
12. an insertion operator, <<, for inserting strings onto the `cout` standard output stream.

A `String` class definition that incorporates all of these operations except the 10th, which is left as an exercise, is shown in Figure 12.7. The conditional preprocessor directive `#ifndef` at the top of this class definition is explained in detail in the Programming Note box on page 668. Briefly, this directive checks to see if the `iostream.h` header file has been included; if it has not been previously defined, the `#include` directive is then issued. The reason for these statements is to ensure that both the `iostream.h` and `string.h` files are always included, but only once, because the class methods use functions declared in these two header files.

---

[4] This section requires an understanding of the class material presented in Chapters 7 and 8.

FIGURE 12.7 The String Class Definition (Stored as the Header File STCLASS.H)

```
#ifndef iostream.h
  #include <iostream.h>
#endif

#ifndef string.h
  #include <string.h>
#endif

// precondition: requires that the named MAXCHARS be defined before this
// class definition is included in a program

// declaration section

class String
{
  private:
    char string[MAXCHARS];
    int stringLength;
  public:

      // constructors
    String();
      // copy constructor for initialization with a string object
    String(const String&);
      // constructor for initialization with a string literal
    String(const char initLiteral[]);

      // additional methods
      // access method to examine stringLength attribute
    int length();
      // assignment of a string object to a string object
    String& operator =(const String&);
      // assignment of a string literal to a string object
    String& operator =(const char strLiteral[]);
      // concatenation of string object to a string object
    String& operator +(const String&);
      // concatenation of a string literal to a string object
    String& operator +(const char strLiteral[]);
      // equality operator for comparison to a string object
    int operator ==(const String&);
      // overloaded extraction operator
    friend istream& operator >>(istream&, String&);
      // overloaded insertion operator
    friend ostream& operator <<(ostream&, const String&);
};

// implementation section

String::String()
{
```

(continued on next page)

(continued from previous page)

```
  string[0] = '\0';  // terminate the string
  stringLength = 0; // set its length attribute
}

  // requires string.h
  // copy constructor for initializing with a string object
String::String(const String& initstring)
{
  strncpy(string, initstring.string, MAXCHARS);
  stringLength = initstring.stringLength;
}

  // requires string.h
  // constructor for initializing with a string literal
String::String(const char initLiteral[]) // literal initially could be more than MAXCHARS characters
{
  strncpy(string, initLiteral, MAXCHARS); // only copy up to MAXCHARS characters
  stringLength = strlen(initLiteral);
}

int String::length()
{
  return stringLength;
}

  // requires string.h
  // assignment operator for a string variable to a string variable
String& String::operator =(const String& newstring)
{

  strcpy(string, newstring.string);
  stringLength = newstring.stringLength;

  return *this;
}

  // requires string.h
  // assignment operator for a string literal to a string variable
String& String::operator =(const char strLiteral[])
{
  strncpy(string, strLiteral, MAXCHARS);
  stringLength = strlen(strLiteral);
  string[stringLength] = '\0';

  return *this;
}

  // requires string.h
  // concatenation operator for a string object to a string object
String& String::operator +(const String& newstring)
{
  int newlength;
```

(continued on next page)

(continued from previous page)

```
  newlength = stringLength + newstring.stringLength;
  if(newlength > MAXCHARS)
    newlength = MAXCHARS;

  strncat(string, newstring.string, newlength - stringLength);
  stringLength = newlength;

  return *this;
}

  // requires string.h
  // concatenation operator for a string literal to a string object
String& String::operator +(const char strLiteral[MAXCHARS])
{
  int newlength;

  newlength = stringLength + strlen(strLiteral);
  if(newlength > MAXCHARS)
    newlength = MAXCHARS;

  strncat(string, strLiteral, newlength - stringLength);
  stringLength = newlength;

  return *this;
}

  // requires string.h
  // equality operator for comparison to a string object
int String::operator ==(const String& compString)
{
  return !strcmp(string, compString.string);
}

  // requires iostream.h
  // overloaded insertion operator for string input
istream& operator >>(istream& in, String& newstring)
{
  char ch;
  int i = 0;

  in.get(ch);
  while(ch != '\n' && i < MAXCHARS - 1)
  {
    newstring.string[i] = ch;
    in.get(ch);
    i++;
  }
  newstring.stringLength = i;
  newstring.string[i] = '\0';  // terminate the string

  return in;
}
```

(continued on next page)

PROGRAMMING NOTE

Conditional Preprocessor Directives

In addition to the `#include` directive, the preprocessor provides a number of other useful directives. Two of the more useful of these are the conditional directives, `#ifndef`, which means "if not defined," and `#ifdef`, which means "if defined." These directives work in almost the same manner as the `if` and `else` statements. For example, the syntax of the `#ifndef` statement is:

```
#ifndef condition
  process the statements placed here
#else
  process the statements placed here
#endif
```

As with the `if-else` statement, the `#else` directive is optional.

Both the `#ifndef` and `#ifdef` directives permit *conditional compilation*, in that the statements immediately following these directives, up to either the `#else` or `#endif` directives, are processed only if the condition is true, while the statements following the `#else` are processed only if the condition is false.

By far, the `#ifndef` directive is the most frequently used conditional preprocessor directive. The most common usage of this directive is in the form:

```
#ifndef header-file
  #include <header-file>
#endif
```

For example,

```
#ifndef iostream.h
  #include <iostream.h>
#endif
```

This statement checks whether the `iostream.h` header file has already been included. Only if it *has not* been previously defined is the `#include` directive executed. This prevents multiple inclusions of the `iostream.h` header file.

`#ifdef` works in a similar manner as `#ifndef`, except that the statements immediately following the `#ifdef` up to either the `#else` or `#endif` directives, are only executed if the tested condition *has been* defined.

The relationship between the `#ifdef` and `#ifndef` directives is that `#ifndef` condition performs the same task as the `#ifdef!` condition, and these two statements can be used interchangeably.

(continued from previous page)

```
  // requires iostream.h
  // overload insertion operator for string output
ostream& operator <<(ostream& out, const String& outstring)
{
  int i;

  for( i = 0; i < outstring.stringLength; i++)
   out << outstring.string[i];

  return out;
}
```

Notice in the String class declaration section of Figure 12.7 that a `String` data type consists of both character array and string length attributes. Because these attributes are private, a user of the class need never know of their existence. All that is required is that the public portions of the class declaration section be made available to potential String class users.

The means of providing the available class methods to programmers is to include the function prototypes and any additional pre- or postcondition information within an interface header file that is open to public inspection. Figure 12.8 illustrates a header file named `STRCLASS.H` that should be placed in the directory containing the standard library header files and included in any program that uses the `String` class.[5] The `STRCLASS.H` interface header file assumes that the actual `String` class definition, previously shown in Figure 12.7, has been stored as a file named `STCLASS.H` in the standard header file directory. Normally only the compiled version of this class definition would be available to users, which prevents any tampering or changing of the class definition by unauthorized personnel.

Notice that the `STRCLASS.H` header file permits a class user to set the value of the named constant MAXCHARS, which is used to define the maximum allowable string length. It is currently set for 200 characters, which is large enough for most strings.

Assuming that the two header files `STCLASS.H` and `STRCLASS.H` as shown in Figures 12.7 and 12.8, respectively, have been created, Program 12.10 illustrates how the `String` class can be incorporated within a working program.

In reviewing Program 12.10 notice that the only requirement in using the `String` class is the inclusion of the interface header file `STRCLASS.H`. This file subsequently includes the actual `String` class definition stored in `STCLASS.H`.

The purpose of Program 12.10 is to test all of the `String` class methods. Sample output of this program is:

```
---- Test of object initializations ----
  string1, which was initialized by a string literal,
     has the value: Hello World!
  string2, which was initialized by a string object,
     has the value: Hello World!
  The string lengths of string1 through string4 are: 12, 12, 0, and 0

---- Test of string input and output ----
  Enter a string to be assigned to string4: This is a test of
  string4 is now: This is a test of
  The length of this string is 17

---- Test of string assignment ----
  After assigning string4 to string3, string3 is now:
     This is a test of
  After assigning a string literal to string4, string4 is now:
     test of a string literal
  The length of this string is: 24
```

(continued on p. 672)

[5] If you place this header file, which is on the source diskette provided with this text, in your program directory, you would include it in your program using the preprocessor directive `#include "STRCLASS.H"`. The double quotes tells the preprocessor to look in the current directory, while the angle bracket pair, < >, tells the preprocessor to look in the default standard library header directory.

FIGURE 12.8 The String Class Interface (Stored as the STRCLASS.H Header File)

```
// This is the header file named STRCLASS.H, which contains
//   the interface for the String class
// This header file, which provides descriptions of the String
//   class methods should be made available for inspection by
//   any programmer wishing to use the String Class
// This header file also includes the constant MAXCHARS,
//   which sets the maximum number of characters allowed in a
//   string and can be changed by the programmer
// It also includes the String class definition, which is
//   contained in the header file STCLASS.H

// The next statement defines the maximum number of characters
//   allowed in a string and can be changed to meet your
//   particular needs for a maximum string length

const int MAXCHARS = 200;

// The next statement includes the String class definition

#include <STCLASS.H>

// The public methods in the String class are:

// constructors:
//      constructor that initializes a zero length string
//   String();
//      copy constructor for initialization with a string object
//   String(const String&);
//      constructor for initialization with a string literal
//   String(const char initLiteral[]);

// other class methods:
//      access method to examine a string's length
//   int length();
//      assignment of a string object to a string object
//   String& operator =(const String&);
//      assignment of a string literal to a string object
//   String& operator =(const char strLiteral[]);
//      concatenation of string object to a string object
//   String& operator +(const String&);
//      concatenation of a string literal to a string object
//   String& operator +(const char strLiteral[]);
//      equality operator for comparison to a string object
//   int operator ==(const String&);
//      extraction operator for string input
//   friend istream& operator >>(istream&, String&);
//      insertion operator for string output
//   friend ostream& operator <<(ostream&, const String&);
```

PROGRAM 12.10

```
#include <iostream.h>
#include <STRCLASS.H>

int main()
{
  String string1 = "Hello World!";  // initialize with a string literal
  String string2 = string1;         // initialize with a string object
  String string3, string4;

  cout << "\n---- Test of object initializations ----" << endl;
  cout << "  string1, which was initialized by a string literal,\n"
       << "     has the value: " << string1 << endl;
  cout << "  string2, which was initialized by a string object,\n"
       << "     has the value: " << string2 << endl;
  cout << "  The string lengths of string1 through string4 are: "
       << string1.length() << ", " << string2.length() << ", "
       << string3.length() << ", and " << string4.length() << endl;

  cout << "\n---- Test of string input and output ----" << endl;
  cout << "  Enter a string to be assigned to string4: ";
  cin  >> string4;
  cout << "  string4 is now: " << string4;
  cout << "\n  The length of this string is " << string4.length() << endl;

  cout << "\n---- Test of string assignment ----" << endl;
  string3 = string4;
  cout << "  After assigning string4 to string3, string3 is now:\n     "
       << string3 << endl;
  string4 = "test of a string literal";
  cout << "  After assigning a string literal to string4, string4 is now:\n     "
       << string4 << endl;
  cout << "  The length of this string is: " << string4.length() << endl;

  cout << "\n---- Test of string concatenation ----" << endl;
  string3 = string3 + " " + string4;
  cout << "After concatenation, string3 is now: " << string3 << endl;

  cout << "\n---- Test of string comparison ----" << endl;
  if (string1 == string2)
    cout << "  string1 and string2 are equal" << endl;
  else
    cout << "  string1 and string2 are not equal" << endl;
  if (string3 == string4)
    cout << "  string3 and string4 are equal" << endl;
  else
    cout << "  string3 and string4 are not equal" << endl;

  return 0;
}
```

```
---- Test of string concatenation ----
After concatenation, string3 is now: This is a test of test of a
string literal

---- Test of string comparison ----
  string1 and string2 are equal
  string3 and string4 are not equal
```

As seen by this output, the defined class methods work as expected.

Exercises 12.4

1. Enter and run Program 12.10 on your computer. (*Hint:* Make sure that the header files `STRCLASS.H` and `STCLASS.H` are available. You may copy these files from the source code diskette provided with the text.)
2. a. Add a member function to the `String` class that appends a single character to the end of a `String` object. For example, if a `String` object named `test` has been declared, the method call `test.append('s');` should append the letter `s` to the string value in the attribute `test.string`. Make sure that your method correctly updates the length attribute of the `test String` object.

   b. Write a simple `main()` function to test the method written for Exercise 2a.
3. a. Add a member function to the `String` class that overloads the == relational operator so that it may be used to compare a `String` variable to a `String` literal.

   b. Write a simple `main()` function to test the method written for Exercise 3a.
4. a. Add a member function to the `String` class that overloads the <= relational operator so that it may be used to compare `String` variables to `String` variables.

   b. Write a simple `main()` function to test the method written for Exercise 4a.
5. a. Add a member function to the `String` class that overloads the <= relational operator so that it may be used to compare `String` variables to `String` literals.

   b. Write a simple `main()` function to test the method written for Exercise 5a.
6. a. Add a member function to the `String` class that overloads the >= relational operator so that it may be used to compare `String` variables to `String` variables.

   b. Write a simple `main()` function to test the method written for Exercise 6a.
7. a. Add a member function to the `String` class that overloads the >= relational operator so that it may be used to compare `String` variables to `String` literals.

   b. Write a simple `main()` function to test the method written for Exercise 7a.
8. a. Add a member function to the `String` class that converts all lowercase characters to uppercase.

   b. Write a simple `main()` function to test the method written for Exercise 8a.
9. a. Add a member function to the `String` class that converts all uppercase characters to lowercase.

   b. Write a simple `main()` function to test the method written for Exercise 9a.
10. a. Add a member function named `extract` to the `String` class that extracts `n` characters from a `String` argument starting at position `m`. For example, if the value `"Hello there World!"` is stored in the `String` object named `test`, then the function call `test.extract(newtest, 7,5);` should extract the characters there and place them in the string attribute of the `String` object named `newtest`. Be sure to also correctly set the length attribute of the new string.

    b. Write a simple `main()` function to test the method written for Exercise 10a.

12.5 COMMON PROGRAMMING ERRORS

The common errors associated with defining and processing strings are:

1. Not providing sufficient space for the string to be stored. A simple variation of this is not providing space for the end-of-string null character when a string is defined as an array of characters.
2. Not including the `'\0'` terminating character when the array is initialized character by character. For example, the definition

   ```
   char string[] = {'H', 'e', 'l', 'l', 'o'};
   ```

   does not create a valid string because a terminating `NULL` character, `'\0'`, is not included in the initialization.
3. Not realizing that the `strcmp()` function returns a value of 0, which is equivalent to false, when the strings being compared are equal. Thus, the condition `!stcmp(string1, string2)` should be used to determine if the strings are equal.

12.6 CHAPTER REVIEW

Key Terms

`cin.get()`	`strcpy()`
`cin.getline()`	string
`isalpha()`	`strlen()`
`isdigit()`	`tolower()`
`NULL`	`toupper()`
`strcat()`	

Summary

1. A string is an array of characters that is terminated by the null character.
2. Strings can always be processed using standard array-processing techniques. The input and display of a string, however, always require reliance on a standard library function.
3. The `cin` object and the `cin.get()` and `cin.getline()` methods can be used to input a string. The `cin` object tends to be of limited usefulness for string input because it terminates input when a blank is encountered.
4. The `cout` object can be used to display strings.
5. Many standard library functions exist for processing strings as a complete unit. Internally, these functions manipulate strings in a character-by-character manner.
6. Character arrays can be initialized using a string assignment of the form

   ```
   char arr_name[ ] = "text";
   ```

   This initialization is equivalent to

   ```
   char arr_name[ ] = {'t','e','x','t','\0'};
   ```

Exercises

1. Determine the value of `text[0]`, `text[3]`, and `text[10]`, assuming that `text` is an array of characters and the following has been stored in the array:
   a. now is the time
   b. rocky raccoon welcomes you
   c. Happy Holidays
   d. The good ship
2. Write a function named `remove()` that returns nothing and deletes all occurrences of its character argument from a string. The function should take two arguments: the string name and the character to be removed. For example, if message contains the string `Happy Holidays`, the function call `remove(message,'H')` should place the string `appy olidays` into `message`.
3. Write a function that adds a single character at the end of an existing string. The function should replace the existing `\0` character with the new character and append a new `\0` at the end of the string. The function returns nothing.
4. Write a function that deletes a single character from the end of a string. This is effectively achieved by moving the `\0` character one position closer to the start of the string. The function returns nothing.
5. Write a function named `trimfrnt()` that deletes all leading blanks from a string.
6. Write a function named `trimrear()` that deletes all trailing blanks from a string.
7. Write a function named `addchars()` that adds `n` occurrences of a character to a string. For example, the call `addchars(message, 4, '!")` should add four exclamation marks at the end of message.
8. Write a function named `extract()` that accepts two strings, `s1` and `s2`, and two integer numbers, `n1` and `n2`, as arguments. The function should extract `n2` characters from `s2`, starting at position `n1`, and place the extracted characters into `s1`. For example, if string `s1` contains the characters `05/18/95 D169254 Rotech Systems`, the function call `extract(s1, s2, 18, 6)` should create the string `Rotech` in `s2`. Note that the starting position for counting purposes is in position one. Be sure to close off the returned string with a `'\0'` and make sure that string `s1` is defined in the calling function to be large enough to accept the extracted values.
9. Given a one-dimensional array of characters, write and test a function that prints the elements in reverse order.
10. Write and test a function that uses an array of characters and returns the position of the first occurrence of a user-specified letter in the array or a −1 if the letter does not occur.
11. A word or phrase that reads the same forwards and backwards is a palindrome (see box on p. 646). Write a C++ program that accepts a line of text as input and examines the entered text to determine if it is a palindrome. If the entered text is a palindrome, display the message `This is a palindrome`. If a palindrome was not entered, the message `This is not a palindrome` should be displayed.
12. Write a C++ program that first initializes a two-dimensional array defined as `list[5][30]` with the following five strings:

```
"04/12/72 74444 Bill Barnes"
"12/28/65 75255 Harriet Smith"
"10/17/54 74477 Joan Casey"
"02/18/48 74470 Deane Fraser"
"06/15/56 75155 Jan Smiley"
```

Your program should include a function named `printit()` that displays each string in the array. (*Hint:* `&list[i][0]` is the address of the *i*th string in the array.)

13. Write a C++ program that first initializes a two-dimensional array defined as `list[5][51]` with the following five strings (do not include headings—they are here merely to indicate what the data represents):

Shipped Date	Track No.	Part No.	First Name	Last Name	Company
04/12/96	D50625	74444	James	Lehoff	Rotech Sys.
04/12/96	D60752	75255	Janet	Lezar	Rotech Sys.
04/12/96	D40295	74477	Bill	McHenry	Rotech Sys.
04/12/96	D23745	74470	Diane	Kaiser	Rotech Sys.
04/12/96	D50892	75155	Helen	Richardson	NipNap Inc.

The format of each line in the array is identical with fixed length fields defined as follows:

Field Position	Field Name	Starting Col. No.	Ending Col. No.	Field Length
1	Shipped Date	1	8	8
2	Tracking Number	10	15	6
3	Part Number	17	21	5
4	First Name	23	27	5
5	Last Name	29	38	10
6	Company	40	50	11

Using this data your C++ program should extract the date, part number, first initial, last name, and company name and produce a report listing the extracted data. (*Hint:* Use the `extract()` function created in Exercise 8.)

14. Write a C++ program that displays the data given in Exercise 13 so that the displayed lines are in increasing employee number order, where the second field is the employee number. (*Hint:* Use the `extract()` function developed for Exercise 8 and the selection sort described in Section 11.6.)

15. Some prisoners of war devised a system of communicating with each other through the walls of solitary confinement cells. This system is based on arranging the letters of the alphabet in 5 rows as follows:

```
a  b  c  d  e
f  g  h  i  j
l  m  n  o  p
q  r  s  t  u
v  w  x  y  z
```

The prisoners spelled messages to each other by tapping the row and column number of the letters on the wall, substituting *c* for the omitted *k*. For example, *h* would be 2 taps (row 2), a short pause, and then 3 taps (column 3); and *help* would be "2,3 1,5 3,1 3,5" the digit pairs representing the number of taps for row and column.

Write a program that loads a two-dimensional array with the letters shown in the table. Then write a function to search the array for the letters in a given string and to convert the string to taps, representing the row, column number pairs.

CHAPTER

13 Addresses, Pointers, and Arrays

Languages such as C, C++, Pascal, Modula-2, and FORTRAN 90 all provide a feature called *pointers,* which permit the construction of dynamically linked lists (see Sections 14.4, 15.2, and 15.4). One of C++'s advantages is that it also allows the programmer to directly access the addresses of variables and manipulate them using pointer arithmetic; that is, addresses can be added, subtracted, and compared. This is a feature that is not provided in either Pascal, Modula-2, or FORTRAN 90.

This chapter presents the basics of declaring pointer variables to store addresses. Additionally, methods of using pointer variables to access and use their stored addresses in meaningful ways are presented.

13.1 ADDRESSES AND POINTERS

As we saw in Section 2.4, to display the address of a variable we can use C++'s address operator, `&`, which means "the address of." When used in a nondeclarative statement, the address operator placed in front of a variable's name refers to the address of the variable.[1] For example, in a nondeclarative statement, `&num` means *the address of* `num`, `&miles` means *the address of* miles, and `&foo` means *the address of* foo. Program 13.1, which is a copy of Program 2.9, uses the address operator to display the address of the variable `num`.

---

[1]As we saw in Chapter 6, when used in declaring reference arguments the ampersand refers to the data type *preceding* it. Thus, both the declarations `float& num` and `float #` are read as "`num` is the address of a `float`," or more commonly as "`num` is a reference to a `float`."

PROGRAM 13.1

```
#include <iostream.h>

int main()
{
  int num;

  num = 22;
  cout << "num = " << num << endl;
  cout << "The address of num = " << &num << endl;

  return 0;
}
```

The output of Program 13.1 is

```
num = 22
The address of num = 0x8f5afff4
```

Figure 13.1 illustrates both the contents and address of the num variable provided by the output of Program 13.1.

As was mentioned in Section 2.4, address information will change depending on what computer is executing the program and how many other programs are currently loaded into memory.

Storing Addresses

Besides displaying the address of a variable, as was done in Program 13.1, we can also store addresses in suitably declared variables. For example, the statement

```
num_addr = &num;
```

stores the address corresponding to the variable num in the variable num_addr, as illustrated in Figure 13.2. Similarly, the statements

```
d = &m;
tab_point = &list;
chr_point = &ch;
```

FIGURE 13.1 A More Complete Picture of the Variable num

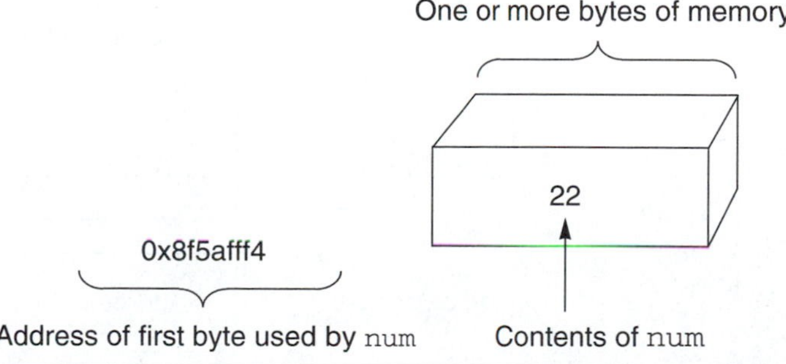

FIGURE 13.2 Storing num's Address into num_addr

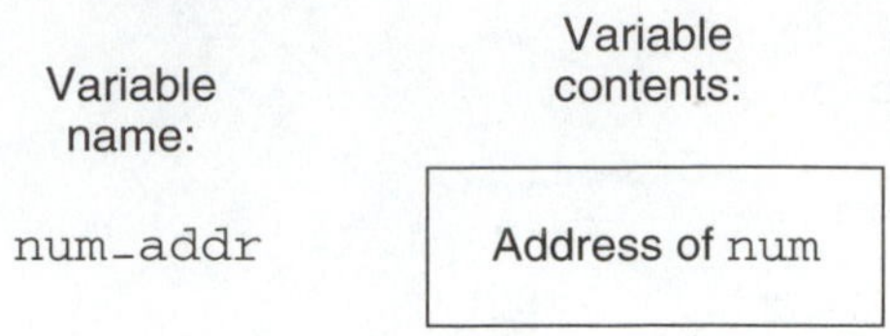

Variable name:	Variable contents:
num_addr	Address of num

store the addresses of the variables m, list, and ch in the variables d, tab_point, and chr_point, respectively, as illustrated in Figure 13.3. The variables num_addr, d, tab_point, and chr_point are formally called **pointer variables,** or *pointers* for short. **Pointers** are simply variables that are used to store the addresses of other variables.

Using Addresses

To use a stored address, C++ provides us with an **indirection operator,** *. The * symbol, when followed by a pointer (with a space permitted both before and after the *), means *the variable whose address is stored in.* Thus, if num_addr is a pointer (remember that a pointer is a variable that stores an address), *num_addr means *the variable whose address is stored in* num_addr. Similarly, *tab_point means *the variable whose address is stored in* tab_point, and *chr_point means *the variable whose address is stored in* chr_point. Figure 13.4 shows the relationship between the address contained in a pointer variable and the variable ultimately addressed.

Although *d literally means *the variable whose address is stored in* d, this is commonly shortened to the statement *the variable pointed to by* d. Similarly, referring to Figure 13.4, *y can be read as *the variable pointed to by* y. The value ultimately obtained, as shown in Figure 13.4, is qqqq.

When using a pointer variable, the value that is finally obtained is always found by first going to the pointer variable (or pointer, for short) for an address. The address contained in the pointer is then used to get the desired contents.

FIGURE 13.3 Storing More Addresses

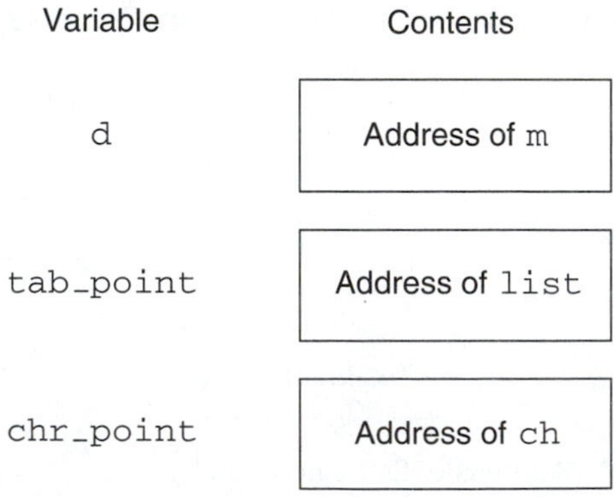

Variable	Contents
d	Address of m
tab_point	Address of list
chr_point	Address of ch

FIGURE 13.4 Using a Pointer Variable

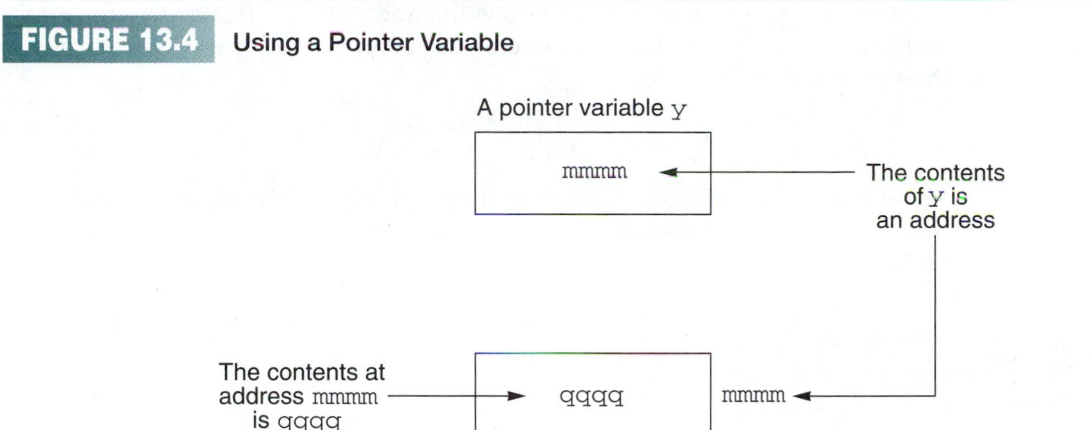

Certainly, this is a rather indirect way of getting to the final value and, not unexpectedly, the term **indirect addressing** is used to describe this procedure.

Because use of a pointer requires the computer to do a double lookup (first the address is retrieved, then the address is used to retrieve the actual data), a worthwhile question is, why would you want to store an address in the first place? The answer to this question rests on the intimate relationship between pointers and arrays and the ability of pointers to create and delete new variable storage locations dynamically, as a program is running. Both of these topics are presented later in this chapter. For now, however, given that each variable has a memory address associated with it, the idea of actually storing an address should not seem overly strange.

Declaring Pointers

Like all variables, pointers must be declared before they can be used to store an address. When we declare a pointer variable, C++ requires that we also specify the type of variable that is pointed to. For example, if the address in the pointer `num_addr` is the address of an integer, the correct declaration for the pointer is:

```
int *num_addr;
```

This declaration is read as *the variable pointed to by* `num_addr` (from the `*num_addr` in the declaration) *is an integer.*[2]

Notice that the declaration `int *num_addr;` specifies two things: First, that the variable pointed to by `num_addr` is an integer; second, that `num_addr` must be a pointer (because it is used with the indirection operator `*`). Similarly, if the

[2] Pointer declarations may also be written in the form `data-type* pointer-name;` where a space is placed between the indirection operator symbol and the pointer variable name. This form, however, becomes error prone when multiple pointer variables are declared in the same declaration statement and the asterisk symbol is inadvertently omitted after the first pointer name is declared. For example, the declaration `int* num1, num2;` declares `num1` as a pointer variable and `num2` as an integer variable. To more easily accommodate multiple pointers in the same declaration and clearly mark a variable as a pointer, we will adhere to the convention that places an asterisk directly in front of each pointer variable name. This type of error rarely occurs with reference declarations because references are almost exclusively used as formal parameters and single declarations of parameters are mandatory.

pointer tab_point points to (contains the address of) a floating-point number and chr_point points to a character variable, the required declarations for these pointers are:

```
float *tab_point;
char *chr_point;
```

These two declarations can be read, respectively, as *the variable pointed to by* tab_point *is a float* and *the variable pointed to by* chr_point *is a char.* Consider Program 13.2.

PROGRAM 13.2

```
#include <iostream.h>

int main()
{
  int *num_addr;       // declare a pointer to an int
  int miles, dist;     // declare two integer variables

  dist = 158;          // store the number 158 into dist
  miles = 22;          // store the number 22 into miles
  num_addr = &miles;   // store the 'address of miles' in num_addr

  cout << "The address stored in num_addr is " << num_addr << endl;
  cout << "The value pointed to by num_addr is " << *num_addr << "\n\n";

  num_addr = &dist;  // now store the address of dist in num_addr
  cout << "The address now stored in num_addr is " << num_addr << endl;
  cout << "The value now pointed to by num_addr is " << *num_addr << endl;

  return 0;
}
```

The output of Program 13.2 is:

```
The address stored in num_addr is 0x8f5ffff4
The value pointed to by num_addr is 22

The address now stored in num_addr is 0x8f5ffff2
The value now pointed to by num_addr is 158
```

The only use for Program 13.2 is to help us understand "what gets stored where." Let's review the program to see how the output was produced.

The declaration statement int *num_addr; declares num_addr to be a pointer variable used to store the address of an integer variable. The statement num_addr = &miles; stores the address of the variable miles into the pointer num_addr. The first activation of cout causes this address to be displayed. The second activation of cout in Program 13.2 uses the indirection operator to retrieve and print out *the value pointed to by* num_addr, which is, of course, the value stored in miles.

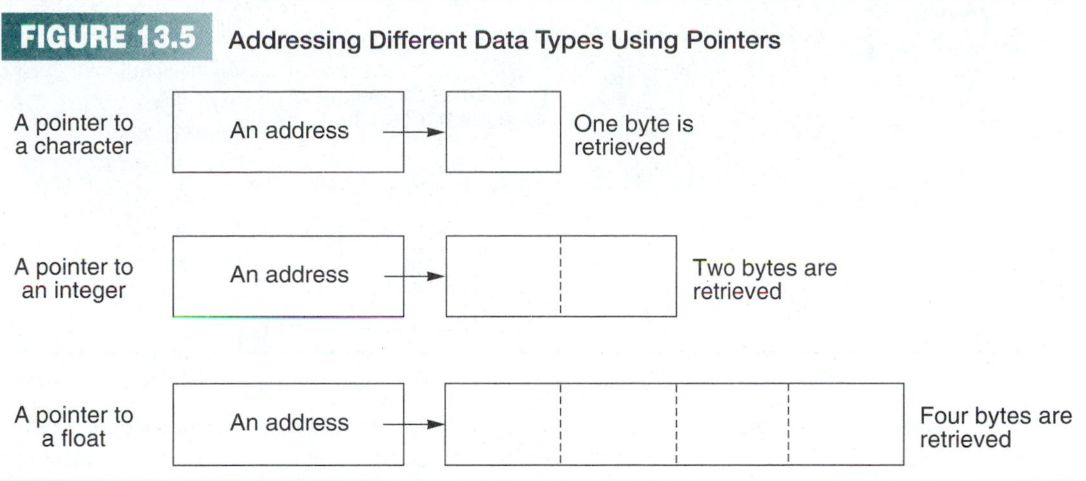

FIGURE 13.5 Addressing Different Data Types Using Pointers

Because `num_addr` has been declared as a pointer to an integer variable, we can use this pointer to store the address of any integer variable. The statement `num_addr = &dist` illustrates this by storing the address of the variable `dist` in `num_addr`. The last two `cout` activations verify the change in `num_addr`'s value and that the new stored address does point to the variable `dist`. As illustrated in Program 13.2, only addresses should be stored in pointers.

It certainly would have been much simpler if the pointer used in Program 13.2 could have been declared as pointer `num_addr;`. Such a declaration, however, conveys no information as to the storage used by the variable whose address is stored in `num_addr`. This information is essential when the pointer is used with the indirection operator, as it is in the second `cout` activation in Program 13.2. For example, if the address of an integer is stored in `num_addr`, then only 2 bytes of storage are typically retrieved when the address is used. If the address of a character is stored in `num_addr`, only 1 byte of storage would be retrieved, and a float typically requires the retrieval of 4 bytes of storage. The declaration of a pointer must, therefore, include the type of variable being pointed to. Figure 13.5 illustrates this concept.

References and Pointers

At this point you might be asking what the difference is between a pointer and a reference. Essentially, a reference is a named constant for an address; as such, the address named as a reference cannot be altered. Since a pointer is a variable, the address in the pointer can be changed. For simple applications, the use of references over pointers is easier and clearly preferred. This is due to the automatic dereferencing of a reference.

For example, in passing a scalar variable's address as a function argument, references provide a simpler notational interface and are usually preferred. The same is true when we consider references to structures, which is the topic of the next chapter. For other situations, such as dynamically allocating new sections of memory for additional variables as a program is running or using alternatives to array notation (both topics are presented in this chapter), pointers are required.

FIGURE 13.6 sum Is an Alternative Name for total

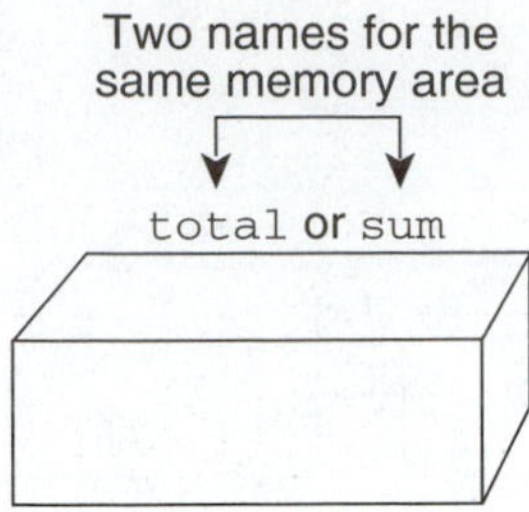

Reference Variables3 References are used almost exclusively as formal function parameters and return types. Nevertheless, reference variables are also available in C++. For completeness we now show how such variables can be declared and used.

Once a variable has been declared it may be given additional names. This is accomplished using a reference declaration, which has the form:

data-type& new_name = existing_name;

For example, the reference declaration

```
float& sum = total;
```

equates the name sum to the name total—both now refer to the same variable, as illustrated in Figure 13.6.

Once another name has been established for a variable using a reference declaration, the new name, which is referred to as an *alias,* can be used in place of the original name. For example, consider Program 13.3:

PROGRAM 13.3

```
#include <iostream.h>

int main()
{
  float total = 20.5;     // declare and initialize total
  float& sum = total;     // declare another name for total

  cout << "sum = " << sum << endl;
  sum = 18.6;             // this changes the value in total
  cout << "total = " << total << endl;

  return 0;
}
```

[3] This section may be omitted with no loss of subject continuity.

The following output is produced by Program 13.3:

```
sum = 20.5
total = 18.6
```

Since the variable `sum` is simply another reference to the variable `total`, it is the value stored in `total` that is obtained by the first `cout` object in Program 13.3. Changing the value in `sum` then changes the value in `total`, which is displayed by the second `cout` object in Program 13.3.

In constructing references, two considerations must be kept in mind. First, the reference should be of the same data type as the variable it refers to. For example, the sequence of declarations

```
int num = 5;
double& numref = num;
```

does not equate `numref` to `num`, since they are not of the same data type. Rather, since the compiler cannot correctly associate the reference with a variable, it creates an unnamed variable of the reference type first, and then references this unnamed variable with the reference variable. Such unnamed variables are called **anonymous variables.** For example, consider Program 13.4, which illustrates the effect of creating an anonymous variable.

PROGRAM 13.4

```
#include <iostream.h>

int main()
{
  int num = 10;
  float& numref = num;    // this does not equate numref to num
                          // instead, it equates numref to an
                          // anonymous floating-point variable
  numref = 20.5;
  cout << "The value of num is " << num << endl;
  cout << "The value of numref is " << numref << endl;

  return 0;
}
```

The output produced by Program 13.4 is:

```
The value of num is 10
The value of numref is 20.5
```

Notice that the value of `num` is not affected by the value stored in `numref`. This is because `numref` could not be created as a reference for `num`; rather, it is another name for an unnamed (anonymous) floating-point variable that can only be reached using the reference name `numref`.

Just as declaring a reference to an incorrect data type produces an anonymous variable, so does equating a reference to a constant. For example, the declaration

```
int& val = 5;  // an anonymous variable is created
```

creates an anonymous variable with the number 5 stored in it. The only way to access this variable is by the reference name. Clearly, creating references to anonymous variables should be avoided. Once a reference name has been equated to either a legal variable or an anonymous one, the reference cannot be changed to refer to another variable.

As with all declaration statements, multiple references may be declared in a single statement as long as each reference name is preceded by the ampersand symbol. Thus, the declaration

```
float& sum = total, &  average;
```

creates two reference variables named sum and average.[4]

Another way of looking at references is to consider them as pointers with restricted capabilities that implicitly hide a lot of referencing that is explicitly required with pointers.

For example, consider the statements

```
int b;       // b is an integer variable
int& a = b; // a is a reference variable that stores b's address
a = 10;      // this changes b's value to 10
```

Here, a is declared as a reference variable that is effectively a named constant for the address of the b variable. Since the compiler knows from the declaration that a is a reference variable, it automatically assigns the address of b (rather than the contents of b) to a in the declaration statement. Finally, in the statement a = 10; the compiler uses the address stored in a to change the value stored in b to 10. The advantage of using the reference is that it automatically performs an indirect access of b's value without the need for explicitly using the indirection symbol, *. As noted previously, this type of access is referred to as an *automatic dereference.*

Implementing this same correspondence between a and b using pointers is done by the following sequence of instructions:

```
int b;        // b is an integer variable
int *a = &b; // a is a pointer - store b's address in a
*a = 10;      // this changes b's value to 10 by explicit
              // dereference of the address in a
```

Here, a is defined as a pointer that is initialized to store the address of b. Thus, *a, which can be read as either "the variable whose address is in a" or "the variable pointed to by a" is b, and the expression *a = 10 changes b's value to 10. Notice in the pointer case that the stored address can be altered to point to another variable; in the reference case the reference variable cannot be altered to refer to any variable except the one to which it is initialized. Also notice that to dereference a, we must explicitly use the indirection operator, *. As you might expect, the * is also referred to as the dereferencing operator.

---

[4] Reference declarations may also be written in the form data-type &new_name = existing name; where a space is placed before the ampersand symbol and the reference variable name. This form is not used much, however, probably to distinguish reference variable address notation from that used in assigning addresses to pointer variables.

A BIT OF BACKGROUND

Admiral Grace Hopper, USN

Grace Hopper received a Ph.D. from Yale University and joined the Naval Reserve in 1943. In her assignment to the Bureau of Ordinance Computation Project at Harvard University she programmed the Mark I, the first large-scale, electromechanical, digital computer. Later she applied her outstanding talents in mathematics as senior programmer of the UNIVAC I.

Commodore Hopper became a pioneer in the development of computer languages and served on the Conference of Data Systems Languages (CODASYL) committee. She helped develop COBOL and is credited with producing the first practical program in that language. In 1959 she developed a COBOL compiler, which allowed programs written in a standardized language to be transported between different computers for the first time.

An interesting sidelight to her career was that her entry into her log book, dated September 19, 1945, at 15:45 hours recorded "First actual case of bug being found." It was an actual insect that had shorted a relay in the Mark I.

Admiral Hopper remained a colorful figure in the computing community after her retirement from active duty in the U.S. Navy in August 1986 at the age of 79.

Exercises 13.1

1. If average is a variable, what does &average mean?
2. For the variables and addresses illustrated in Figure 13.7, determine &temp, &dist, &date, and &miles.
3. a. Write a C++ program that includes the following declaration statements. Have the program use the address operator and the cout object to display the addresses corresponding to each variable.

```
int num, count;
long date;
float yield;
double price;
```

   b. After running the program written for Exercise 3a, draw a diagram of how your computer has set aside storage for the variables in the program. On your diagram, fill in the addresses displayed by the program.

   c. Modify the program written in Exercise 3a to display the amount of storage your computer reserves for each data type [use the sizeof() operator]. With this information and the address information provided in Exercise 3b, determine if your computer set aside storage for the variables in the order in which they were declared.
4. If a variable is declared as a pointer, what must be stored in the variable?
5. Using the indirection operator, write expressions for the following:
   a. the variable pointed to by x_addr
   b. the variable whose address is in y_addr
   c. the variable pointed to by pt_yld
   d. the variable pointed to by pt_miles

e. the variable pointed to by `mptr`
f. the variable whose address is in `pdate`
g. the variable pointed to by `dist_ptr`
h. the variable pointed to by `tab_pt`
i. the variable whose address is in `hours_pt`

6. Write declaration statements for the following:
   a. The variable pointed to by `y_addr` is an integer.
   b. The variable pointed to by `ch_addr` is a character.
   c. The variable pointed to by `pt_yr` is a long integer.
   d. The variable pointed to by `amt` is a double precision variable.
   e. The variable pointed to by `z` is an integer.
   f. The variable pointed to by `qp` is a floating-point variable.
   g. `date_pt` is a pointer to an integer.
   h. `yld_addr` is a pointer to a double-precision variable.
   i. `amt_pt` is a pointer to a floating-point variable.
   j. `pt_chr` is a pointer to a character.
7. a. What are the variables `y_addr`, `ch_addr`, `pt_yr`, `amt`, `z`, `qp`, `date_ptr`, `yld_addr`, `amt_pt`, and `pt_chr` used in Exercise 6 called?
   b. Why are the variable names `amt`, `z`, and `qp` used in Exercise 6 not good choices for pointer variable names?

FIGURE 13.7 Memory Bytes for Exercise 2

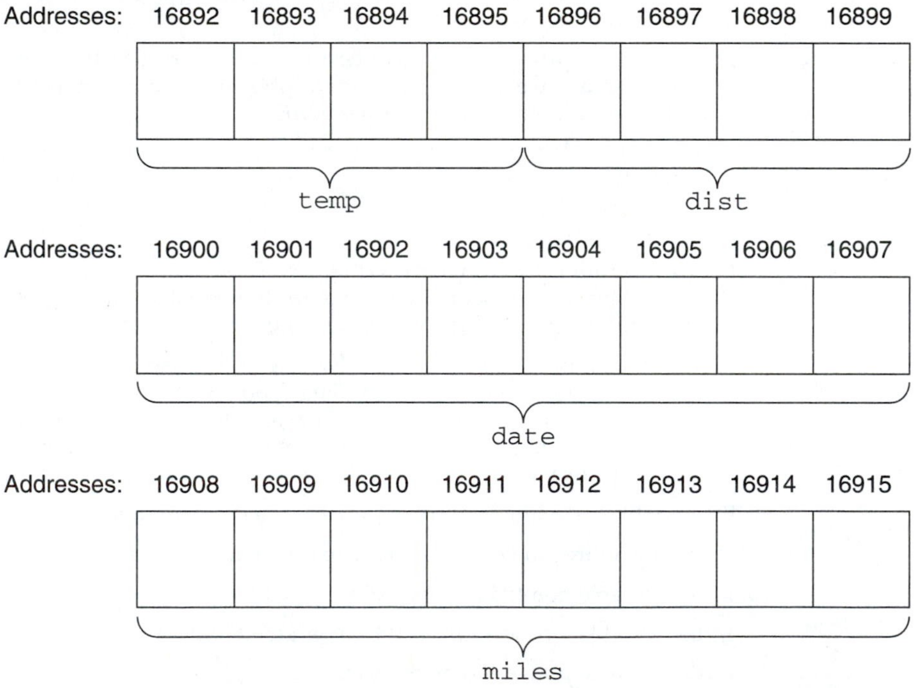

Addresses:	16892	16893	16894	16895	16896	16897	16898	16899
	`temp`				`dist`			

Addresses:	16900	16901	16902	16903	16904	16905	16906	16907
	`date`							

Addresses:	16908	16909	16910	16911	16912	16913	16914	16915
	`miles`							

8. Write English sentences that describe what is contained in the following declared variables:

   a. `char *key_addr;`

   b. `int *m;`

   c. `double *yld_addr;`

   d. `long *y_ptr;`

   e. `float *p_cou;`

   f. `int *pt_date;`

9. Which of the following are declarations for pointers?:

   a. `long a;`

   b. `char b;`

   c. `char *c;`

   d. `int x;`

   e. `int *p;`

   f. `double w;`

   g. `float *k;`

   h. `float l;`

   i. `double *z;`

10. For the following declarations,

```
int *x_pt, *y_addr;
long *dt_addr, *pt_addr;
double *pt_z;
int a;
long b;
double c;
```

   determine which of the following statements are valid:

   a. `y_addr = &a;`

   b. `y_addr = &b;`

   c. `y_addr = &c;`

   d. `y_addr = a;`

   e. `y_addr = b;`

   f. `y_addr = c;`

   g. `dt_addr = &a;`

   h. `dt_addr = &b;`

   i. `dt_addr = &c;`

   j. `dt_addr = a;`

   k. `dt_addr = b;`

   l. `dt_addr = c;`

   m. `pt_z = &a;`

   n. `pt_addr = &b;`

   o. `pt_addr = &c;`

   p. `pt_addr = a;`

q. `pt_addr = b;`

r. `pt_addr = c;`

s. `y_addr = x_ pt;`

t. `y_addr = dt_addr;`

u. `y_addr = pt_addr;`

11. For the variables and addresses illustrated in Figure 13.8, fill in the appropriate data as determined by the following statements:

a. `pt_num = &m;`

b. `amt_addr = &amt;`

c. `*z_addr = 25;`

d. `k = *num_addr;`

e. `pt_day = z_addr;`

f. `*pt_yr = 1987;`

g. `*amt_addr = *num_addr;`

FIGURE 13.8 Memory Locations for Exercise 11

Variable	Address	Contents	Variable	Address	Contents
pt_num	500		amt_addr	564	
z_addr	8024	20492	num_addr	10132	18938
pt_day	14862		pt_yr	15010	694
years	694		m	8096	
amt	16256		firstnum	18938	154
balz	20492		k	24608	

12. Using the `sizeof()` operator, determine the number of bytes used by your computer to store the address of an integer, character, and double-precision number. [*Hint:* `sizeof(*int)` can be used to determine the number of memory bytes used for a pointer to an integer.] Would you expect the size of each address to be the same? Why or why not?

FIGURE 13.9 The `grade` Array in Storage

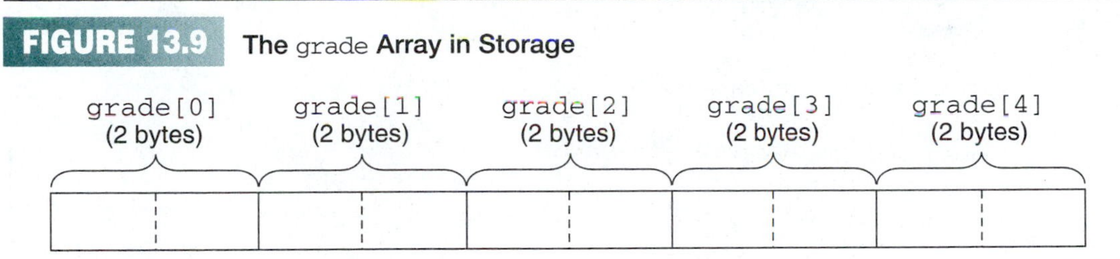

13.2 ARRAY NAMES AS POINTERS

Although pointers are simply, by definition, variables used to store addresses, there is also a direct and intimate relationship between array names and pointers. In this section we describe this relationship in detail.

Figure 13.9 illustrates the storage of a single-dimensional array named `grade`, which contains five integers. Assume that each integer requires 2 bytes of storage.

Using subscripts, the third element in the `grade` array is referred to as `grade[3]`. The use of a subscript, however, conceals the extensive use of addresses by the computer. Internally, the computer immediately uses the subscript to calculate the address of the desired element based on both the starting address of the array and the amount of storage used by each element. Accesssing the element `grade[3]` forces the compiler, internally, to make the address computation

```
&grade[3] = &grade[0] + (3 * sizeof(int))
```

Remembering that the address operator, `&`, means "the address of," this last statement is read "the address of `grade[3]` equals the address of `grade[0]` plus 6." Figure 13.10 illustrates the address computation used to locate `grade[3]`.

FIGURE 13.10 Using a Subscript to Obtain an Address

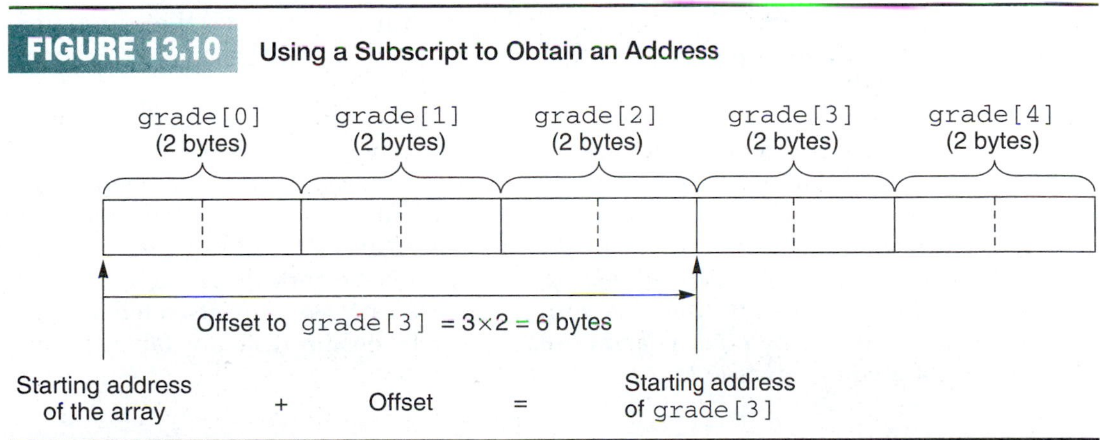

Recall that a pointer is a variable used to store an address. If we create a pointer to store the address of the first element in the grade array, we can mimic the operation used by the computer to access the array elements. Before we do this, let us first consider Program 13.5.

PROGRAM 13.5

```
#include <iostream.h>

const int ARRAYSIZE = 5;

int main()
{
  int i, grade[ARRAYSIZE] = {98, 87, 92, 79, 85};

  for (i = 0; i < ARRAYSIZE; i++)
    cout << "\nElement " << i << " is " << grade[i];
  cout << endl;

  return 0;
}
```

When Program 13.5 is run, the following display is obtained:

```
Element 0 is 98
Element 1 is 87
Element 2 is 92
Element 3 is 79
Element 4 is 85
```

Program 13.5 displays the values of the array grade using standard subscript notation. Now, let us store the address of array element 0 in a pointer. Then, using the indirection operator, *, we can use the address in the pointer to access each array element. For example, if we store the address of grade[0] into a pointer named g_ptr (using the assignment statement g_ptr = &grade[0];), then, as illustrated in Figure 13.11, the expression *g_ptr, which means "the variable pointed to by g_ptr," references grade[0].

One unique feature of pointers is that offsets may be included in expressions using pointers. For example, the 1 in the expression *(g_ptr + 1) is an *offset*. The complete expression references the integer that is one beyond the variable pointed to by g_ptr. Similarly, as illustrated in Figure 13.12, the expression *(g_ptr + 3) references the variable that is three integers beyond the variable pointed to by g_ptr. This is the variable grade[3].

Table 13.1 lists the complete correspondence between elements referenced by subscripts and by pointers and offsets. The relationships listed in Table 13.1 are illustrated in Figure 13.13.

FIGURE 13.11 The Variable Pointed to by `*g_ptr` Is `grade[0]`

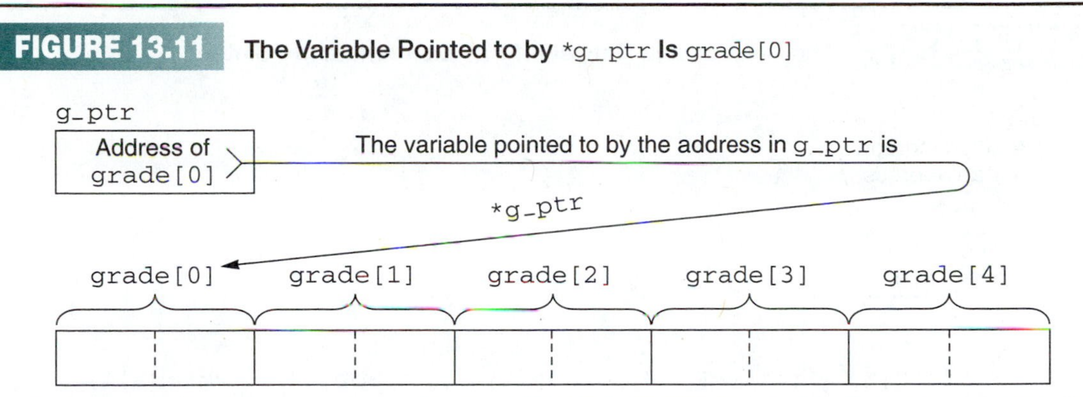

FIGURE 13.12 An Offset of 3 from the Address in `g_ptr`

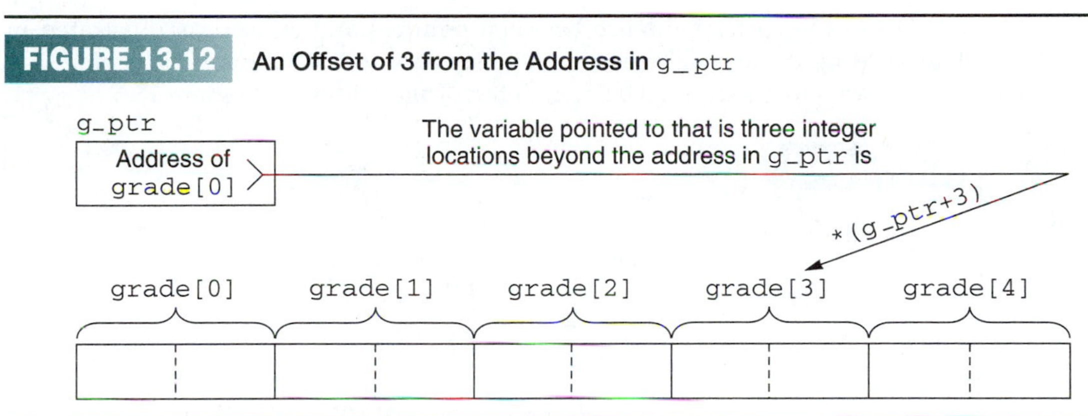

TABLE 13.1 Array Elements May Be Referenced in Two Ways

Array Element	Subscript Notation	Pointer Notation
Element 0	`grade[0]`	`*g_ptr`
Element 1	`grade[1]`	`*(g_ptr + 1)`
Element 2	`grade[2]`	`*(g_ptr + 2)`
Element 3	`grade[3]`	`*(g_ptr + 3)`
Element 4	`grade[4]`	`*(g_ptr + 4)`

FIGURE 13.13 The Relationship Between Array Elements and Pointers

g_ptr
(enough storage for an address)

Address of grade[0]

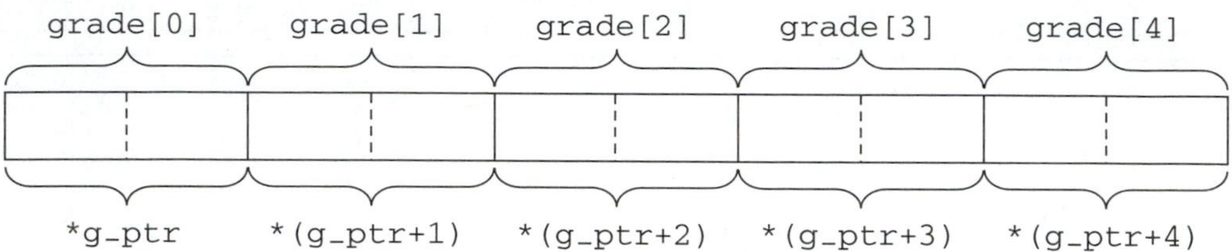

Using the correspondence between pointers and subscripts illustrated in Figure 13.13, the array elements previously accessed in Program 13.5 using subscripts can now be accessed using pointers. This is done in Program 13.6.

PROGRAM 13.6

```
#include <iostream.h>

const int ARRAYSIZE = 5;

int main()
{
  int *g_ptr;               // declare a pointer to an int

  int i, grade[ARRAYSIZE] = {98, 87, 92, 79, 85};

  g_ptr = &grade[0];        // store the starting array address
  for (i = 0; i < ARRAYSIZE; i++)
    cout << "\nElement " << i << " is " << *(g_ptr + i);
  cout << endl;

  return 0;
}
```

The following display is obtained when Program 13.6 is run:

```
Element 0 is 98
Element 1 is 87
Element 2 is 92
Element 3 is 79
Element 4 is 85
```

Notice that this is the same display produced by Program 13.5.

The method used in Program 13.6 to access individual array elements simulates how the compiler internally references all array elements. Any subscript used by a programmer is automatically converted to an equivalent pointer expression by the compiler. In our case, since the declaration of `g_ptr` included the information that integers are pointed to, any offset added to the address in `g_ptr` is automatically scaled by the size of an integer. Thus, `*(g_ptr + 3)`, for example, refers to the address of `grade[0]` plus an offset of 6 bytes (3 * 2), where we have assumed `sizeof(int) = 2`. This is the address of `grade[3]`, as illustrated in Figure 13.10.

The parentheses in the expression `*(g_ptr + 3)` are necessary to correctly reference the desired array element. Omitting the parentheses results in the expression `*g_ptr + 3`. Due to the precedence of the operators, this expression adds 3 to "the variable pointed to by `g_ptr`." Since `g_ptr` points to `grade[0]`, this expression adds the value of `grade[0]` and 3 together. Note also that the expression `*(g_ptr + 3)` does not change the address stored in `g_ptr`. Once the computer uses the offset to locate the correct variable from the starting address in `g_ptr`, the offset is discarded and the address in `g_ptr` remains unchanged.

Although the pointer `g_ptr` used in Program 13.5 was specifically created to store the starting address of the grade array, this was, in fact, unnecessary. When an array is created, the compiler automatically creates an internal pointer constant for it and stores the starting address of the array in this pointer. In almost all respects, a pointer constant is identical to a pointer variable created by a programmer; but, as we shall see, there are some differences.

For each array created, the name of the array becomes the name of the pointer constant created by the compiler for the array, and the starting address of the first location reserved for the array is stored in this pointer. Thus, declaring the grade array in both Programs 13.5 and 13.6 actually reserved enough storage for five integers, created an internal pointer named `grade`, and stored the address of `grade[0]` in the pointer. This is illustrated in Figure 13.14.

The implication is that every reference to `grade` using a subscript can be replaced by an equivalent reference using `grade` as a pointer. Thus, wherever the expression `grade[i]` is used, the expression `*(grade + i)` can also be used.

FIGURE 13.14 Creating an Array Also Creates a Pointer

grade

&grade[0]

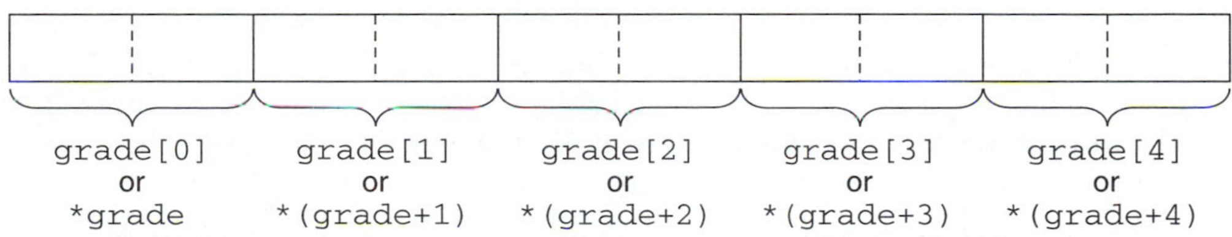

This is illustrated in Program 13.7, where grade is used as a pointer to reference all of its elements.

PROGRAM 13.7

```
#include <iostream.h>

const int ARRAYSIZE = 5;

int main()
{
  int i, grade[ARRAYSIZE] = {98, 87, 92, 79, 85};

  for (i = 0; i < ARRAYSIZE; i++)
    cout << "\nElement " << i << " is " << *(grade + i);
  cout << endl;

  return 0;
}
```

Executing Program 13.7 produces the same output previously produced by Programs 13.5 and 13.6. However, using grade as a pointer made it unnecessary to declare and initialize the pointer g_ptr used in Program 13.6.

In most respects an array name and pointer can be used interchangeably. *A true pointer, however, is a variable and the address stored in it can be changed. An array name is a pointer constant and the address stored in the pointer cannot be changed by an assignment statement.* Thus, a statement such as `grade = &grade[2];` is invalid. This should come as no surprise. Since the whole purpose of an array name is to correctly locate the beginning of the array, allowing a programmer to change the address stored in the array name would defeat this purpose and lead to havoc whenever array elements were referenced. Also, expressions taking the address of an array name are invalid because the pointer created by the compiler is internal to the computer, not stored in memory as are pointer variables. Thus, trying to store the address of grade using the expression &grade results in a compiler error.

An interesting sidelight to the observation that elements of an array can be referenced using pointers is that a pointer reference can always be replaced with a subscript reference. For example, if num_ptr is declared as a pointer variable, the expression `*(num_ptr + i)` can also be written as `num_ptr[i]`. This is true even though num_ptr is not created as an array. As before, when the compiler encounters the subscript notation, it replaces it internally with the pointer notation.

Dynamic Array Allocation[5]

As each variable is defined in a program, sufficient storage for it is assigned from a pool of computer memory locations made available to the compiler. Once specific memory locations have been reserved for a variable, these locations are fixed for the life of that variable, whether they are used or not. For example, if a function requests storage for an array of 500 integers, the storage for the array is allo-

[5] This topic may be omitted on first reading with no loss of subject continuity.

cated and fixed from the point of the array's definition. If the application requires fewer than 500 integers, the unused allocated storage is not released back to the system until the array goes out of existence. If, on the other hand, the application requires more than 500 integers, the size of the integer array must be increased and the function defining the array recompiled.

An alternative to this fixed or static allocation of memory storage locations is the dynamic allocation of memory. Under a dynamic allocation scheme, the amount of storage to be allocated is determined and adjusted as the program is run, rather than being fixed at compile time.

The dynamic allocation of memory is extremely useful when dealing with lists, because it allows the list to expand as new items are added and contract as items are deleted. For example, in constructing a list of grades, the exact number of grades ultimately needed may not be known. Rather than creating a fixed array to store the grades, it is extremely useful to have a mechanism whereby the array can be enlarged and shrunk as necessary. Two C++ operators, `new` and `delete`, that provide this capability are described in Table 13.2. (These operators require the `stdlib.h` header file.)

Explicit dynamic storage requests for scalar variables or arrays are made either as part of a declaration or assignment statement.[6] For example, the declaration statement `int *num = new int;` reserves an area sufficient to hold one integer and places the address of this storage area into the pointer `num`. This same dynamic allocation can be made by first declaring the pointer using the declaration statement `int *num;` and then subsequently assigning the pointer an address with the assignment statement `num = new int;`. In either case the allocated storage area comes from the computer's free storage area.[7]

In a similar manner and of more usefulness is the dynamic allocation of arrays. For example, the declaration

```
int *grades = new int[200];
```

reserves an area sufficient to store 200 integers and places the address of the first integer into the pointer `grades`. Although we have used the constant 200 in this example declaration, a variable dimension can be used. For example, consider the following sequence of instructions:

```
cout << "Enter the number of grades to be processed: ";
cin  >> numgrades;
int *grades = new int[numgrades];
```

TABLE 13.2 Dynamic Allocation Operators

Operator Name	Description
new	Reserves the number of bytes requested by the declaration. Returns the address of the first reserved location or NULL if sufficient memory is not available.
delete	Releases a block of bytes previously reserved. The address of the first reserved location is passed as an argument to the function.

[6] Note that the compiler automatically provides this dynamic allocation and deallocation from the stack for all auto variables.

[7] The free storage area of a computer is formally referred to as the *heap*. The heap consists of unallocated memory that can be allocated to a program, as requested, while the program is running.

In this sequence the actual size of the array that is created depends on the number input by the user. Since pointer and array names are related, each value in the newly created storage area can be accessed using standard array notation, such as `grades[i]`, rather than the equivalent pointer notation `*(grades + i)`. Program 13.8 illustrates this sequence of code in the context of a complete program.

PROGRAM 13.8

```
#include <iostream.h>
#include <stdlib.h>

int main()
{
  int numgrades, i;

  cout << "Enter the number of grades to be processed: ";
  cin  >> numgrades;

  int *grades = new int[numgrades];  // create the array

  for(i = 0; i < numgrades; i++)
  {
    cout << "  Enter a grade: ";
    cin  >> grades[i];
  }
  cout << "\nAn array was created for " << numgrades << "integers\n";
  cout << " The values stored in the array are:";
  for (i = 0; i < numgrades; i++)
    cout << "\n   " << grades[i];
  cout << endl;

  delete grades;   // return the storage to the heap

  return 0;
}
```

Notice in Program 13.8 that the `delete` operator has been used to restore the allocated block of storage to the operating system while the programming is executing.[8] The only address required by `delete` is the starting address of the block of storage that was dynamically allocated. Thus, any address returned by

[8] The allocated storage should automatically be returned to the heap, by the operating system, when the program has completed execution. Since this is not always the case, however, it is extremely important to formally restore dynamically allocated memory to the heap when the storage is no longer needed. The term memory leak is used to describe the condition that occurs when dynamically allocated memory is not formally returned using the `delete` operator and the operating system does not reclaim the allocated memory area.

A BIT OF BACKGROUND

Numerosophy

The ancient Greeks attached great philosophical and religious significance to numbers. They considered the natural (counting) numbers, 1, 2, 3, . . . , to be examples of perfection, and ratios of whole numbers (fractions) as somewhat suspect. Diophantus (third century B.C.) called negative numbers "absurd."

According to tradition, Hipparchus (second century B.C.) was drowned when he discussed the scandalous irrational nature of the square root of 2 outside of the Pythagorean Society. The first mention of the square root of a negative number was by Heron of Alexandria (third century A.D.). Such concepts were treated with disbelief and even considered wicked. Today, of course, it is not unusual to use negative, irrational, "artificial," and complex numbers all at once to represent such concepts as vectors and points in a plane. The Greeks of that Golden Age would probably regard our modern mathematics as truly degenerate.

`new` can subsequently be used by `delete` to restore the reserved memory to the computer. The `delete` operator does not alter the address passed to it, but simply removes the storage that the address references. Following is a sample run using Program 13.8:

```
Enter the number of grades to be processed: 4
  Enter a grade: 85
  Enter a grade: 96
  Enter a grade: 77
  Enter a grade: 92

An array was created for 4 integers
 The values stored in the array are:
   85
   96
   77
   92
```

Exercises 13.2

1. Replace each of the following references to a subscripted variable with a pointer reference:

   a. `prices[5]`
   b. `grades[2]`
   c. `yield[10]`
   d. `dist[9]`
   e. `mile[0]`
   f. `temp[20]`
   g. `celsius[16]`
   h. `num[50]`
   i. `time[12]`

2. Replace each of the following references using a pointer with a subscript reference:
   a. `*(message + 6)`
   b. `*amount`
   c. `*(yrs + 10)`
   d. `*(stocks + 2)`
   e. `*(rates + 15)`
   f. `*(codes + 19)`
3. a. List the three things that the declaration statement `double prices[5];` causes the compiler to do.
   b. If each double-precision number uses 8 bytes of storage, how much storage is set aside for the prices array?
   c. Draw a diagram similar to Figure 13.14 for the prices array.
   d. Determine the byte offset relative to the start of the `prices` array, corresponding to the offset in the expression `*(prices + 3)`.
4. a. Write a declaration to store the string `"This is a sample"` into an array named `samtest`. Include the declaration in a program that displays the values in `samtest` using a `for` loop and pointer references to each element in the array.
   b. Modify the program written in Exercise 4a to display only array elements 10 through 15 (these are the letters s, a, m, p, l, and e).
5. Write a declaration to store the following values into an array named `rates`: 12.9, 18.6, 11.4, 13.7, 9.5, 15.2, 17.6. Include the declaration in a program that displays the values in the array using pointer notation.

13.3 POINTER ARITHMETIC

Pointer variables, like all variables, contain values. The value stored in a pointer is, of course, an address. Thus, by adding and subtracting numbers to pointers we can obtain different addresses. Additionally, the addresses in pointers can be compared using any of the relational operators (`==`, `!=`, `<`, `>`, etc.) that are valid for comparing other variables. In performing arithmetic on pointers, we must be careful to produce addresses that point to something meaningful. In comparing pointers we must also make comparisons that make sense. Consider these declarations:

```
int nums[100];
int *n_pt;
```

To set the address of `nums[0]` into `n_pt`, either of the following two assignment statements can be used:

```
n_pt = &nums[0];
n_pt = nums;
```

The two assignment statements produce the same result because `nums` is a pointer constant that itself contains the address of the first location in the array. This is, of course, the address of `nums[0]`. Figure 13.15 illustrates the allocation of memory resulting from the previous declaration and assignment statements, assuming that each integer requires 2 bytes of memory and that the location of the beginning of the `nums` array is at address 18934.

FIGURE 13.15 The nums Array in Memory

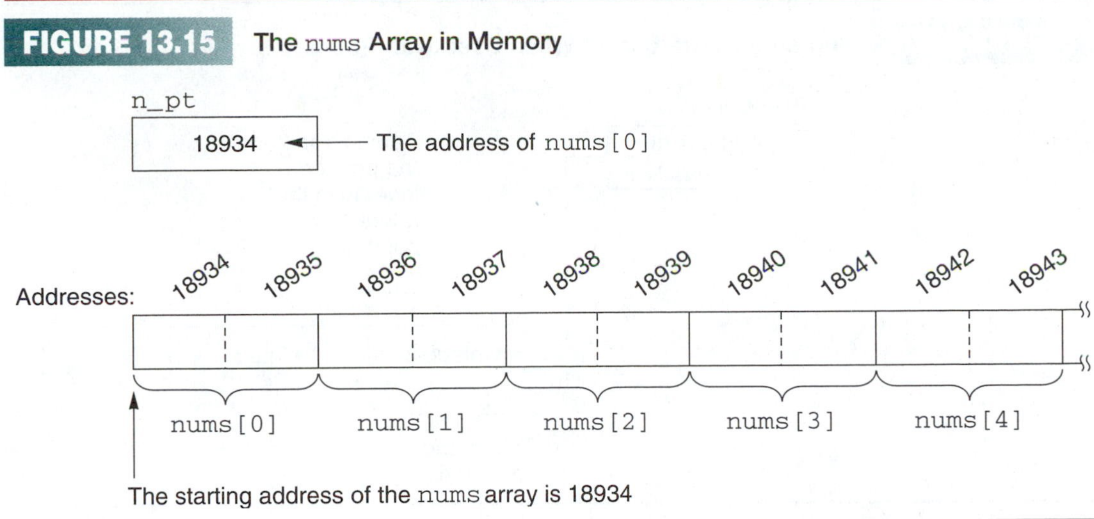

Once n_pt contains a valid address, values can be added and subtracted from the address to produce new addresses. When adding or subtracting numbers to pointers, the computer automatically adjusts the number to ensure that the result still "points to" a value of the correct type. For example, the statement `n_pt = n_pt + 4;` forces the computer to scale the 4 by the correct number to ensure that the resulting address is the address of an integer. Assuming that each integer requires 2 bytes of storage, as illustrated in Figure 13.15, the computer multiplies the 4 by 2 and adds the result, 8, to the address in n_pt. The resulting address is 18942, which is the correct address of nums[4].

This automatic scaling by the computer ensures that the expression `n_pt + i`, where i is any positive integer, correctly points to the *i*th element beyond the one currently being pointed to by n_pt. Thus, if n_pt initially contains the address of nums[0], `n_pt + 4` is the address of nums[4], `n_pt + 50` is the address of nums[50], and `n_pt + i` is the address of nums[i]. Although we have used actual addresses in Figure 13.15 to illustrate the scaling process, the programmer need never know or care about the actual addresses used by the computer. The manipulation of addresses using pointers generally does not require knowledge of the actual address.

Addresses can also be incremented or decremented using both prefix and postfix increment and decrement operators. Adding one to a pointer causes the pointer to point to the next element of the type being pointed to. Decrementing a pointer causes the pointer to point to the previous element. For example, if the pointer variable p is a pointer to an integer, the expression p++ causes the address in the pointer to be incremented to point to the next integer. This is illustrated in Figure 13.16. In reviewing this figure, notice that the increment added to the pointer is correctly scaled to account for the fact that the pointer is used to point to integers. It is, of course, up to the programmer to ensure that the correct type of data is stored in the new address contained in the pointer.

FIGURE 13.16 Increments Are Scaled When Used with Pointers

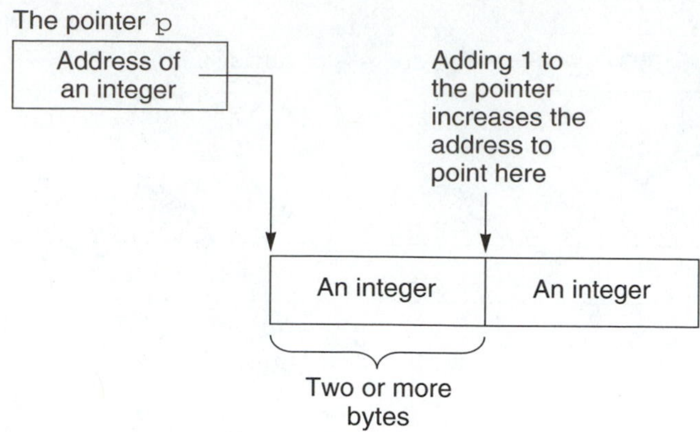

The increment and decrement operators can be applied as both prefix and postfix pointer operators. All of the following combinations using pointers are valid:

```
*pt_num++      // use the pointer and then increment it
*++pt_num      // increment the pointer before using it
*pt_num--      // use the pointer and then decrement it
*--pt_num      // decrement the pointer before using it
```

Of the four possible forms, the most commonly used is the form `*pt_num++`. This is because such an expression allows each element in an array to be accessed as the address is "marched along" from the starting address of the array to the address of the last array element. The use of the increment operator is shown in Program 13.9. In this program each element in the `nums` array is retrieved by successively incrementing the address in `n_pt`.

PROGRAM 13.9

```
#include <iostream.h>

const int NUMS = 5;

int main()
{
  int nums[NUMS] = {16, 54, 7, 43, -5};
  int i, total = 0, *n_pt;

  n_pt = nums;     // store address of nums[0] in n_pt
  for (i = 0; i < NUMS; i++)
    total = total + *n_pt++;
  cout << "The total of the array elements is " << total << endl;

  return 0;
}
```

The output produced by Program 13.9 is:

```
The total of the array elements is 115
```

The expression `total = total + *n_pt++` used in Program 13.9 accumulates the values "pointed to" by the `n_pt` pointer variable. Within this expression, the term `*n_pt++` first causes the computer to retrieve the integer pointed to by `n_pt`. This is done by the `*n_pt` part of the term. The postfix increment, `++`, then adds one to the address in `n_pt` so that `n_pt` now contains the address of the next array element. The increment is, of course, scaled by the computer so that the actual address in `n_pt` is the correct address of the next array element.

Pointers may also be compared. This is particularly useful when dealing with pointers that point to elements in the same array. For example, rather than using a counter in a `for` loop to access each element in an array correctly, the address in a pointer can be compared to the starting and ending address of the array itself. The expression

```
n_pt <= &nums[4]
```

is true (nonzero) as long as the address in `n_pt` is less than or equal to the address of `nums[4]`. Since `nums` is a pointer constant that contains the address of `nums[0]`, the term `&nums[4]` can be replaced by the equivalent term `nums + 4`. Using either of these forms, Program 13.9 can be rewritten as Program 13.10 to continue adding array elements while the address in `n_pt` is less than or equal to the address of the last array element.

PROGRAM 13.10

```
#include <iostream.h>

const int NUMS = 5;

int main()
{
  int nums[NUMS] = {16, 54, 7, 43, -5};
  int total = 0, *n_pt;

  n_pt = nums;     // store address of nums[0] in n_pt
  while (n_pt < nums + NUMS)
    total += *n_pt++;
  cout << "The total of the array elements is " << total << endl;

  return 0;
}
```

Notice that in Program 13.10 the compact form of the accumulating expression, `total += *n_pt++`, was used in place of the longer form, `total = total + *n_pt++`. Also, the expression `nums + NUMS` does not change the address in `nums`. This expression first retrieves the address in `nums`, adds 5 to this address (appropriately scaled) and uses the result for comparison purposes. Expressions such as `*nums++` that attempt to change the address are invalid.

Expressions such as `*nums` or `*(nums + i)`, which use the address without attempting to alter it, are valid.

Pointer Initialization

Like all variables, pointers can be initialized when they are declared. When initializing pointers, however, you must be careful to set an address in the pointer. For example, an initialization such as

```
int *pt_num = &miles;
```

is only valid if `miles` is declared as an integer variable prior to `pt_num`. Here we are creating a pointer to an integer and setting the address in the pointer to the address of an integer variable. Notice that if the variable `miles` is declared subsequently to `pt_num`, as follows,

```
int *pt_num = &miles;
int miles;
```

an error occurs. This is because the address of `miles` is used before `miles` has even been defined. Since the storage area reserved for `miles` has not been allocated when `pt_num` is declared, the address of `miles` does not yet exist.

Pointers to arrays can be initialized within their declaration statements. For example, if `prices` has been declared an array of floating-point numbers, either of the following two declarations can be used to initialize the pointer named `zing` to the address of the first element in prices:

```
float *zing = &prices[0];
float *zing = prices;
```

The last initialization is correct because `prices` is itself a pointer constant containing an address of the proper type. (The variable name `zing` was selected in this example to reinforce the idea that any variable name can be selected for a pointer.)

Exercises 13.3

1. Replace the `while` statement in Program 13.10 with a `for` statement.
2. a. Write a program that stores the following numbers in an array named `rates`: 6.25, 6.50, 6.8, 7.2, 7.35, 7.5, 7.65, 7.8, 8.2, 8.4, 8.6, 8.8, 9.0. Display the values in the array by changing the address in a pointer called `disp_pt`. Use a `for` statement in your program.

   b. Modify the program written in Exercise 2a to use a `while` statement.
3. a. Write a program that stores the string `Hooray for All of Us` into an array named `strng`. Use the declaration `strng[] = "Hooray for All of Us";`, which ensures that the end-of-string escape sequence `\0` is included in the array. Display the characters in the array by changing the address in a pointer called `mess_pt`. Use a `for` statement in your program.

   b. Modify the program written in Exercise 3a to use the `while` statement: `while (*mess_pt++ != '\0')`.

   c. Modify the program written in Exercise 3a to start the display with the word `All`.
4. Write a program that stores the following numbers in an array named `miles`: 15, 22, 16, 18, 27, 23, 20. Have your program copy the data stored in `miles` to another array named `dist` and then display the values in the `dist` array.

5. Write a program that stores the following letters in an array named `message`:

```
This is a test.
```

Have your program copy the data stored in `message` to another array named `mess2` and then display the letters in the `mess2` array.

13.4 PASSING ADDRESSES

We have already seen one method of passing addresses to a function. This was accomplished using reference variables, as was described in Section 6.5. Although passing reference variables to a function provides the function with the address of the passed variables, it is an implied use of addresses because the function call does not reveal the fact that reference variables are being used. For example, the function call `swap(num1, num2);` does not reveal whether `num1` or `num2` is a reference variable. Only by looking at the declaration for these variables or by examining the function header line for `swap()` are the data types of `firstnum` and `secnum` revealed.

In contrast to implicitly passing addresses using reference variables, addresses can be explicitly passed using pointer variables. Let us see how this is accomplished.

To explicitly pass an address to a function, we place the address of operator, `&`, in front of the variable being passed. For example, the function call

```
swap(&firstnum, &secnum);
```

passes the addresses of the variables `firstnum` and `secnum` to `swap()`, as illustrated in Figure 13.17. Explicitly passing addresses using the address operator effectively is a *call by reference* because the called function can reference, or access, variables in the calling function using the passed addresses. As we saw in Section 6.5 calls by reference are also accomplished using reference variables. Here we will use the passed addresses and pointers to directly access the variables `first-num` and `secnum` from within `swap()` and exchange their values—a procedure that was previously accomplished in Program 6.12 using reference variables.

FIGURE 13.17 Explicitly Passing Addresses to `swap()`

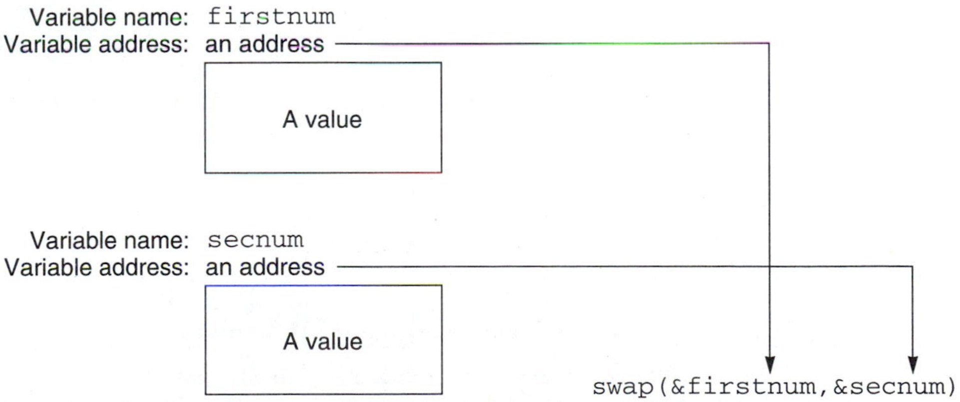

One of the first requirements in writing swap() is to construct a function header line that correctly receives and stores the passed values, which in this case are two addresses. As we saw in Section 13.1, addresses are stored in pointers, which means that the arguments of swap() must be declared as pointers.

Assuming that firstnum and secnum are double-precision variables, and that swap() returns no value, a suitable function header line for swap() is

```
void swap(double *nm1_addr, double *nm2_addr)
```

The choice of the parameter names nm1_addr and nm2_addr is, as with all parameter names, up to the programmer. The declaration double *nm1_addr, however, declares that the parameter named nm1_addr will be used to store the address of a double-precision value. Similarly, the declaration double *nm2_addr declares that nm2_addr will also store the address of a double-precision value.

Before writing the body of swap() to exchange the values in firstnum and secnum, let's first check that the values accessed using the addresses in nm1_addr and nm2_addr are correct. This is done in Program 13.11.

PROGRAM 13.11

```
#include <iostream.h>

void swap(double *, double *);      // function prototype

int main()
{
  double firstnum = 20.5, secnum = 6.25;

  swap(&firstnum, &secnum);           // call swap

  return 0;
}

// this function illustrates passing pointer arguments
void swap(double *nm1_addr, double *nm2_addr)
{

  cout << "The number whose address is in nm1_addr is "
       << *nm1_addr << endl;
  cout << "The number whose address is in nm2_addr is "
       << *nm2_addr << endl;

  return;
}
```

The output displayed when Program 13.11 is run is:

```
The number whose address is in nm1_addr is 20.5
The number whose address is in nm2_addr is 6.25
```

FIGURE 13.18 Storing Addresses in Parameters

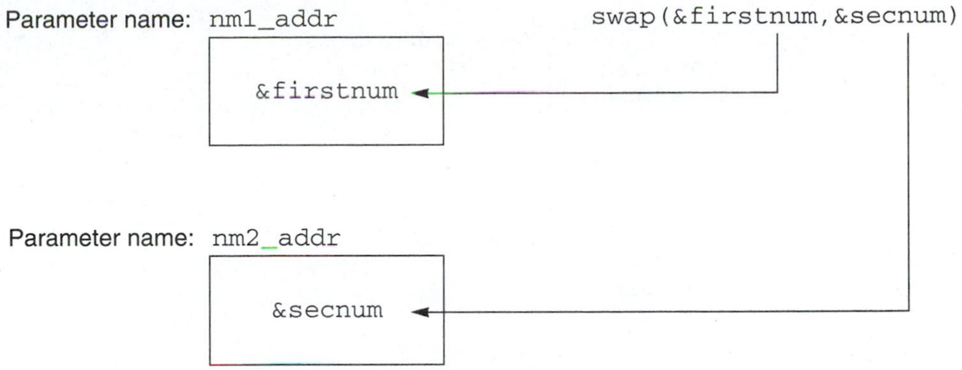

In reviewing Program 13.11, note two things. First, the function prototype for `swap()`

```
void swap(double *, double *);
```

declares that `swap()` returns no value directly and that its parameters are two pointers that "point to" double-precision values. As such, when the function is called it will require that two addresses be passed, and that each address be the address of a double-precision value.

The second item to notice is that within `swap()` the indirection operator is used to access the values stored in `firstnum` and `secnum`. `swap()` itself has no knowledge of these variable names, but it does have the address of `firstnum` stored in `nm1_addr` and the address of `secnum` stored in `nm2_addr`. The expression `*nm1_addr` used in the first `cout` stream means "the variable whose address is in `nm1_addr`." This is, of course, the variable `firstnum`. Similarly, the second `cout` stream obtains the value stored in `secnum` as "the variable whose address is in `nm2_addr`." Thus, we have successfully used pointers to allow `swap()` to access variables in `main()`. Figure 13.18 illustrates the concept of storing addresses in arguments.

Having verified that `swap()` can access `main()`'s local variables `firstnum` and `secnum`, we can now expand `swap()` to exchange the values in these variables. The values in `main()`'s variables `firstnum` and `secnum` can be interchanged from within `swap()` using the three-step interchange algorithm previously described in Section 6.5, which for convenience is relisted here:

1. Store `firstnum`'s value in a temporary location.
2. Store `secnum`'s value in `firstnum`.
3. Store the temporary value in `secnum`.

Using pointers from within `swap()`, this takes the form:

1. Store the value of the variable pointed to by `nm1_addr` in a temporary location. The statement `temp = *nm1_addr;` does this (see Figure 13.19).
2. Store the value of the variable whose address is in `nm2_addr` in the variable whose address is in `nm1_addr`. The statement `*nm1_addr = *nm2_addr;` does this (see Figure 13.20).
3. Move the value in the temporary location into the variable whose address is in `nm2_addr`. The statement `*nm2_addr = temp;` does this (see Figure 13.21).

FIGURE 13.19 Indirectly Storing `firstnum`'s Value

nm1_addr
Address of firstnum
(a) Go to the address for a value
firstnum
A value
(b) Store the value found
temp
firstnum's value

FIGURE 13.20 Indirectly Changing `firstnum`'s Value

nm1_addr
Address of firstnum
This address points here
firstnum
Goes here
*nm1_addr=*nm2_addr
nm2_addr
Address of secnum
This address points here
secnum
This value

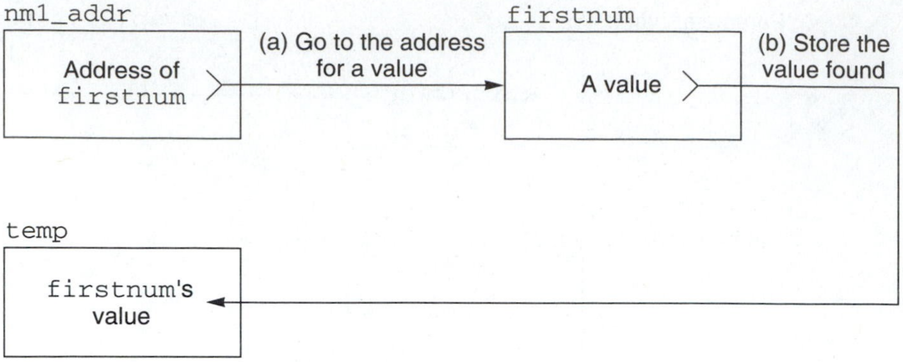

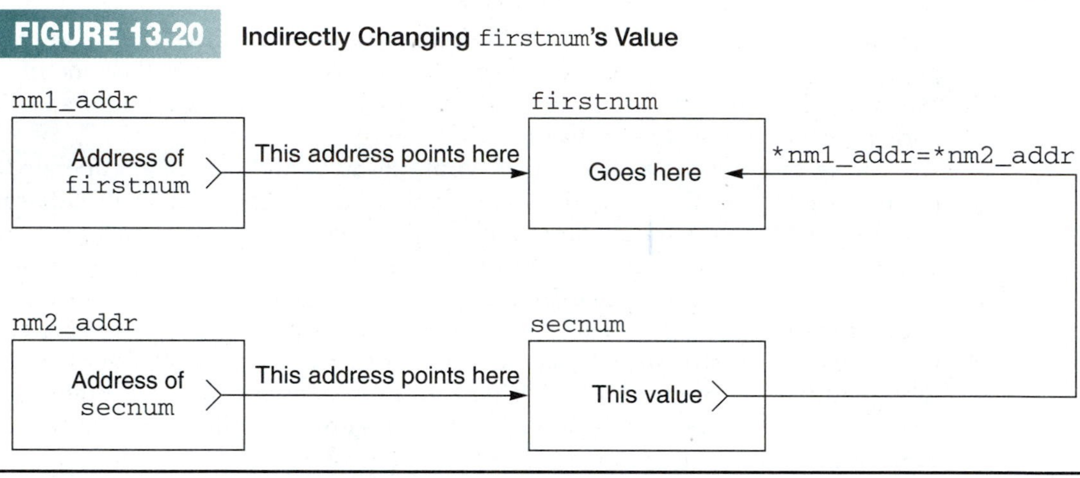

FIGURE 13.21 Indirectly Changing `secnum`'s Value

nm2_addr
Address of secnum
Locate the address
secnum
firstnum's value
temp
firstnum's value
Store the value

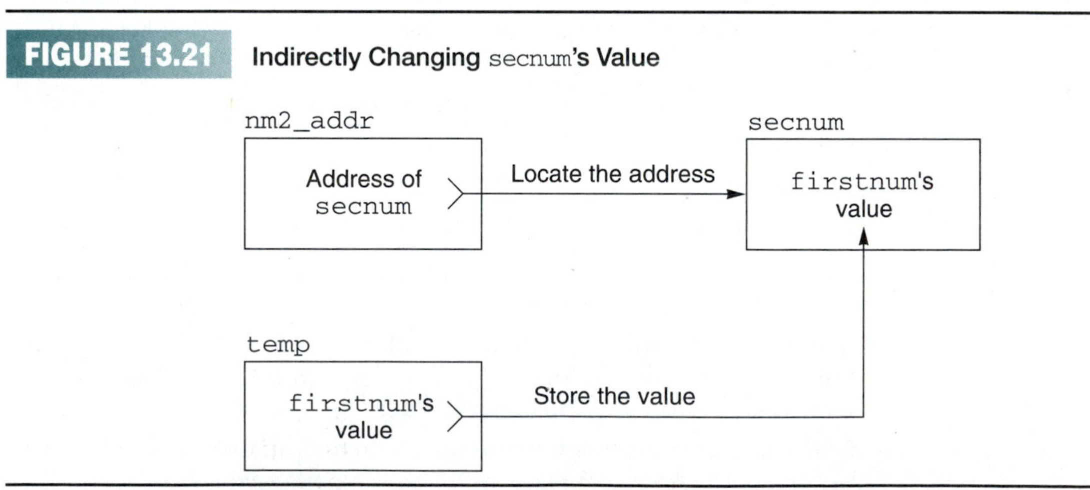

Program 13.12 contains the final form of swap(), written according to our description.

PROGRAM 13.12

```
#include <iostream.h>

void swap(double *, double *);      // function prototype

int main()
{
  double firstnum = 20.5, secnum = 6.25;


  cout << "The value stored in firstnum is: " << firstnum << endl;
  cout << "The value stored in secnum is: " << secnum << "\n\n";
  swap(&firstnum, &secnum);           // call swap

  cout << "The value stored in firstnum is now: "
       << firstnum <<  endl;
  cout << "The value stored in secnum is now: "
       << secnum << endl;

  return 0;
}

// this function swaps the values in its two arguments
void swap(double *nm1_addr, double *nm2_addr)
{
  double temp;

  temp = *nm1_addr;               // save firstnum's value
  *nm1_addr = *nm2_addr;          // move secnum's value into firstnum
  *nm2_addr = temp;               // change secnum's value

  return;
}
```

The following sample run was obtained using Program 13.12:

```
The value stored in firstnum is: 20.5
The value stored in secnum is: 6.25

The value stored in firstnum is now: 6.25
The value stored in secnum is now: 20.5
```

As illustrated in this output, the values stored in main()'s variables have been modified from within swap(), which was made possible by the use of pointers. The interested reader should compare this version of swap() with the version using references that was presented in Program 6.12. The advantage of using pointers in preference to references is that the function call itself explicitly designates that addresses are being used, which is a direct alert that the function will most likely alter variables of the calling function. The advantages of using references is that the notation is much simpler.

Generally, for functions such as `swap()`, the notational convenience wins out, and references are used. In passing arrays to functions, however, which is our next topic, the compiler automatically passes an address. This dictates that pointer variables will be used to store the address.

Passing Arrays

When an array is passed to a function, its address is the only item actually passed. By this we mean the address of the first location used to store the array, as illustrated in Figure 13.22. Since the first location reserved for an array corresponds to element 0 of the array, the "address of the array" is also the address of element 0.

For a specific example in which an array is passed to a function, consider Program 13.13. In this program, the nums array is passed to the `find_max()` function using conventional array notation.

PROGRAM 13.13

```
#include <iostream.h>

const int NUMPTS = 5;

int find_max(int [], int);     // function prototype

int main()
{
  int nums[NUMPTS] = {2, 18, 1, 27, 16};

  cout << "\nThe maximum value is "
       << find_max(nums,NUMPTS) << endl;
}

// this function returns the maximum value in an array of ints
int find_max(int vals[], int num_els)
{
  int i, max = vals[0];

  for (i = 1; i < num_els; i++)
   if (max < vals[i])
     max = vals[i];

  return max;
}
```

The output displayed when Program 13.13 is executed is:

```
The maximum value is 27
```

FIGURE 13.22 The Address of an Array, which Is the Address of the First Location Reserved for the Array, Becomes a Function's Parameter

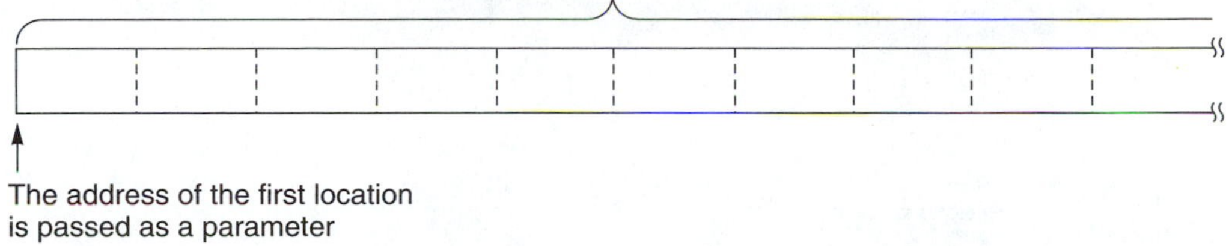
An array is a series of memory locations
The address of the first location
is passed as a parameter

The parameter named `vals` in the header line declaration for `find_max()` actually receives the address of the array `nums`. As such, `vals` is really a pointer, since pointers are variables (or arguments) used to store addresses. Since the address passed into `find_max()` is the address of an integer, another suitable header line for `find_max()` is:

```
int find_max(int *vals, int num_els) // here vals is declared as
                                     // a pointer to an integer
```

The declaration `int *vals` in the header line declares that `vals` is used to store an address of an integer. The address stored is, of course, the location of the beginning of an array. The following is a rewritten version of the `find_max()` function that uses the new pointer declaration for `vals`, but retains the use of subscripts to refer to individual array elements:

```
int find_max(int *vals, int num_els)    // find the maximum value
{
  int i, max = vals[0];

  for (i = 1; i < num_els; i++)
   if (max < vals[i])
     max = vals[i];

  return max;
}
```

Regardless of how `vals` is declared in the function header or how it is used within the function body, it is truly a pointer variable. Thus, the address in `vals` may be modified. This is not true for the name `nums`. Because `nums` is the name of the originally created array, it is a pointer constant. As described in Section 13.2, this means that the address in `nums` cannot be changed and that the address of `nums` itself cannot be taken. No such restrictions, however, apply to the pointer variable named `vals`. All the address arithmetic that we learned in the previous section can be legitimately applied to `vals`.

We shall write two additional versions of `find_max()`, both using pointers instead of subscripts. In the first version we simply substitute pointer notation for subscript notation. In the second version we use address arithmetic to change the address in the pointer.

As previously stated, access to an array element using the subscript notation `array_name[i]` can always be replaced by the pointer notation `*(array_name + i)`. In our first modification to `find_max()`, we make use of this correspondence by simply replacing all references to `vals[i]` with the equivalent expression `*(vals + i)`.

```
int find_max(int *vals, int num_els)   // find the maximum value
{
  int i, max = *vals;

  for (i = 1; i < num_els; i++)
   if (max < *(vals + i) )
     max = *(vals + i);

  return max;
}
```

Our next version of `find_max()` makes use of the fact that the address stored in `vals` can be changed. After each array element is retrieved using the address in `vals`, the address itself is incremented by one in the altering list of the `for` statement. The expression `max = *vals` previously used to set `max` to the value of `vals[0]` is replaced by the expression `max = *vals++`, which adjusts the address in `vals` to point to the second element in the array. The element assigned to `max` by this expression is the array element pointed to by `vals` before `vals` is incremented. The postfix increment, `++`, does not change the address in `vals` until after the address has been used to retrieve the array element.

```
int find_max(int *vals, int num_els)   // find the maximum value
{
  int i, max = *vals++;   // get the first element and increment
  for (i = 1; i < num_els; i++, vals++)
  {
    if (max < *vals)
      max = *vals;
  }
  return max;
}
```

Let us review this version of `find_max()`. Initially the maximum value is set to "the thing pointed to by vals." Since `vals` initially contains the address of the first element in the array passed to `find_max()`, the value of this first element is stored in `max`. The address in `vals` is then incremented by one. The one that is added to `vals` is automatically scaled by the number of bytes used to store integers. Thus, after the increment, the address stored in `vals` is the address of the next array element. This is illustrated in Figure 13.23. The value of this next element is compared to the maximum and the address is again incremented, this time from within the altering list of the `for` statement. This process continues until all the array elements have been examined.

The version of `find_max()` that you should choose is a matter of personal style and taste. Generally, beginning programmers feel more at ease using subscripts rather than pointers. Also, if the program uses an array as the natural storage structure for the application and data at hand, an array reference using subscripts is more appropriate to clearly indicate the intent of the program. For example, when applied to character arrays, which is the topic of the next section, the use of pointers becomes an increasingly useful and powerful tool in its own right. In these instances there is no simple or easy equivalence to the use of subscripts.

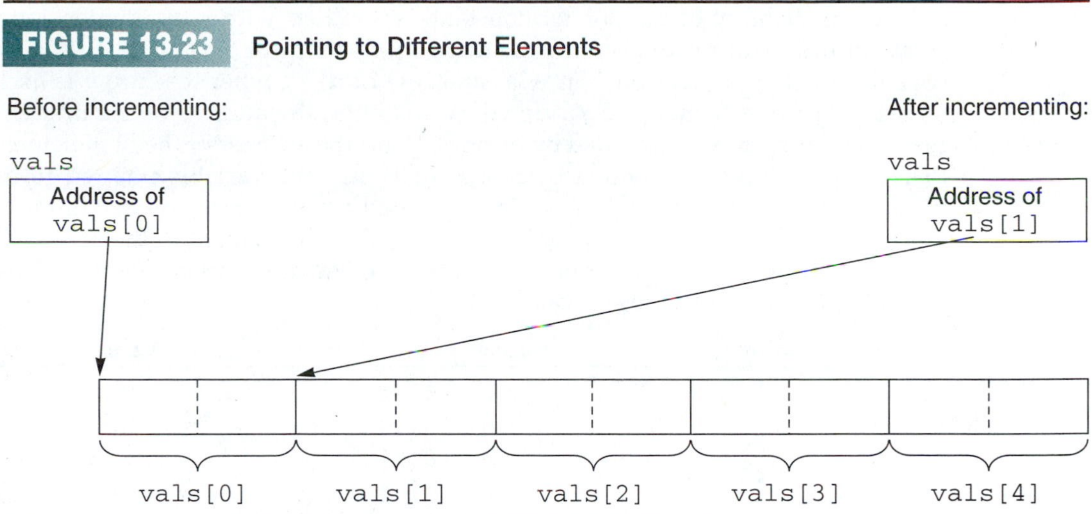

FIGURE 13.23 Pointing to Different Elements

One further "neat trick" can be gleaned from our discussion. Since passing an array to a function really involves passing an address, we can just as well pass any valid address. For example, the function call `find_max(&nums[2],3)` passes the address of `nums[2]` to `find_max()`. Within `find_max()` the pointer `vals` stores the address and the function starts the search for a maximum at the element corresponding to this address. Thus, from `find_max()`'s perspective, it has received an address and proceeds appropriately.

Advanced Pointer Notation[9]

Access to multidimensional arrays can also be made using pointer notation, although the notation becomes more and more cryptic as the array dimensions increase. An extremely useful application of this notation occurs with two-dimensional character arrays, one of the topics in Section 13.6. Here we consider pointer notation for two-dimensional numeric arrays. For example, consider the declaration

```
int nums[2][3] = { {16,18,20},
                   {25,26,27} };
```

This declaration creates an array of elements and a set of pointer constants named `nums`, `nums[0]`, and `nums[1]`. The relationship between these pointer constants and the elements of the `nums` array is illustrated in Figure 13.24.

FIGURE 13.24 Storage of the `nums` Array and Associated Pointer Constants

nums: Address of nums[0] → nums[0]: Address of nums[0][0] → 16, 18, 20 (nums[0][0] nums[0][1] nums[0][2])

nums[1]: Address of nums[1][0] → 25, 26, 27 (nums[1][0] nums[1][1] nums[1][2])

[9] This topic may be omitted with no loss of subject continuity.

The availability of the pointer constants associated with a two-dimensional array allows us to reference array elements in a variety of ways. One way is to consider the two-dimensional array as an array of rows, where each row is itself an array of three elements. Considered in this light, the address of the first element in the first row is provided by `nums[0]` and the address of the first element in the second row is provided by `nums[1]`. Thus, the variable pointed to by `nums[0]` is `num[0][0]` and the variable pointed to by `nums[1]` is `num[1][0]`. Once the nature of these constants is understood, each element in the array can be accessed by applying an appropriate **offset** to the appropriate pointer. Thus, the following notations are equivalent:

Pointer Notation	Subscript Notation	Value
`*nums[0]`	`nums[0][0]`	16
`*(nums[0] + 1)`	`nums[0][1]`	18
`*(nums[0] + 2)`	`nums[0][2]`	20
`*nums[1]`	`nums[1][0]`	25
`*(nums[1] + 1)`	`nums[1][1]`	26
`*(nums[1] + 2)`	`nums[1][2]`	27

We can now go even further and replace `nums[0]` and `nums[1]` with their respective pointer notations, using the address of `nums`. As illustrated in Figure 13.24, the variable pointed to by `nums` is `nums[0]`. That is, `*nums` is `nums[0]`. Similarly, `*(nums + 1)` is `nums[1]`. Using these relationships leads to the following equivalences:

Pointer Notation	Subscript Notation	Value
`*(*nums)`	`nums[0][0]`	16
`*(*nums + 1)`	`nums[0][1]`	18
`*(*nums + 2)`	`nums[0][2]`	20
`*(*(nums + 1))`	`nums[1][0]`	25
`*(*(nums + 1) + 1)`	`nums[1][1]`	26
`*(*(nums + 1) + 2)`	`nums[1][2]`	27

The same notation applies when a two-dimensional array is passed to a function. For example, assume that the two-dimensional array `nums` is passed to the function `calc()` using the call `calc(nums);`. Here, as with all array passes, an address is passed. A suitable function header line for the function `calc()` is

```
calc(int pt[2][3])
```

As we have already seen, the argument declaration for `pt` can also be

```
calc(int pt[][3])
```

Using pointer notation, another suitable declaration is:

```
calc(int (*pt)[3])
```

In this last declaration the inner parentheses are required to create a single pointer to objects of three integers. Each object is, of course, equivalent to a single row of the `nums` array. By suitably offsetting the pointer, each element in the array can be accessed. Notice that without the parentheses the declaration becomes

```
int *pt[3]
```

which creates an array of three pointers, each one pointing to a single integer.

Once the correct declaration for `pt` is made (any of the three valid declarations can be used), the following notations within the function `calc()` are all equivalent:

Pointer Notation	Subscript Notation	Value
`*(*pt)`	`pt[0][0]`	16
`*(*pt+1)`	`pt[0][1]`	18
`*(*pt+2)`	`pt[0][2]`	20
`*(*(pt+1))`	`pt[1][0]`	25
`*(*(pt+1)+1)`	`pt[1][1]`	26
`*(*(pt+1)+2)`	`pt[1][2]`	27

The last two notations using pointers are encountered in more advanced C++ programs. The first of these occurs because functions can return any valid C++ scalar data type, including pointers to any of these data types. If a function returns a pointer, the data type being pointed to must be declared in the function's declaration. For example, the declaration

```
int *calc()
```

declares that `calc()` returns a pointer to an integer value. This means that an address of an integer variable is returned. Similarly, the declaration

```
float *taxes()
```

declares that `taxes()` returns a pointer to a floating-point value. This means that an address of a floating-point variable is returned.

In addition to declaring pointers to integers, floating-point numbers, and C++'s other data types, pointers can also be declared that point to (contain the address of) a function. Pointers to functions are possible because function names, like array names, are themselves pointer constants. For example, the declaration

```
int (*calc)()
```

declares `calc()` to be a pointer to a function that returns an integer. This means that `calc` will contain the address of a function, and the function whose address is in the variable `calc` returns an integer value. If, for example, the function `sum()` returns an integer, the assignment `calc = sum;` is valid.

Exercises 13.4

1. The following declaration was used to create the `prices` array:

   ```
   double prices[500];
   ```

   Write three different header lines for a function named `sort_arr` that accepts the `prices` array as a parameter named `in_array`.

2. The following declaration was used to create the `keys` array:

   ```
   char keys[256];
   ```

   Write three different header lines for a function named `find_key` that accepts the `keys` array as a parameter named `select`.

3. The following header lines was used to create the `rates` array:

   ```
   float rates[256];
   ```

Write three different header lines for a function named `prime` that accepts the `rates` array as a parameter named `rates`.

4. Modify the `find_max()` function to locate the minimum value of the passed array. Write the function using only pointers.
5. In the last version of `find_max()` presented, `vals` was incremented inside the altering list of the `for` statement. Instead, suppose that we do the incrementing within the condition expression of the `if` statement, as follows:

```
int find_max(int *vals, int num_els)     // incorrect version
{
  int i, max = *vals++;     // get the first element and increment

  for (i = 1; i < num_els; i++)
    if (max < *vals++)
      max = *vals;
  return (max);
}
```

This version produces an incorrect result. Determine why.

6. a. Write a program that has a declaration in `main()` to store the following numbers into an array named `rates`: 6.5, 7.2, 7.5, 8.3, 8.6, 9.4, 9.6, 9.8, 10.0. There should be a function call to `show()` that accepts `rates` as an argument named `rates` and then displays the numbers using the pointer notation `*(rates + i)`.

   b. Modify the `show` function written in Exercise 6a to alter the address in `rates`. Always use the expression `*rates` rather than `*(rates + i)` to retrieve the correct element.

13.5 POINTERS AND STRING LIBRARY FUNCTIONS

Pointers are exceptionally useful in constructing string handling functions. When pointer notation is used in place of subscripts to access individual characters in a string, the resulting statements are both more compact and more efficient. In this section we describe the equivalence between subscripts and pointers when accessing individual characters in a string.

Consider the `strcopy()` function introduced in Section 12.1. This function was used to copy the characters of one string to a second string. For convenience, this function is repeated below:

```
void strcopy(char string1[], char string2[])    // copy string2 to string1
{
  int i = 0;

  while (string1[i] = string2[i])
    i++;
  return;
}
```

The conversion of `strcopy()` from subscript notation to pointer notation is now straightforward. Although each subscript version of `strcopy()` can be rewritten using pointer notation, the following is the equivalent of our last subscript version:

```
void strcopy(char *string1, char *string2)    // copy string2 to string1
{
  while (*string1 = *string2)
  {
    string1++;
    string2++;
  }
  return;
}
```

In both subscript and pointer versions of `strcopy()`, the function receives the name of the array being passed. Recall that passing an array name to a function actually passes the address of the first location of the array. In our pointer version of `strcopy()`, the two passed addresses are stored in the pointer arguments `string1` and `string2`, respectively.

The declarations `char *string1;` and `char *string2;` used in the pointer version of `strcopy()` indicate that `string1` and `string2` are both pointers containing the address of a character, and stress the treatment of the passed addresses as pointer values rather than array names. These declarations are equivalent to the declarations `char string1[]` and `char string2[]`, respectively.

Internal to `strcopy()`, the pointer expression `*string1`, which refers to "the element whose address is in `string1`," replaces the equivalent subscript expression `string1[i]`. Similarly, the pointer expression `*string2` replaces the equivalent subscript expression `string2[i]`. The expression `*string1 = *string2` causes the element pointed to by `string2` to be assigned to the element pointed to by `string1`. Since the starting addresses of both strings are passed to `strcopy()` and stored in `string1` and `string2`, respectively, the expression `*string1` initially refers to `string1[0]` and the expression `*string2` initially refers to `string2[0]`.

Consecutively incrementing both pointers in `strcopy()` with the expressions `string1++` and `string2++` simply causes each pointer to "point to" the next consecutive character in the respective string. As with the subscript version, the pointer version of `strcopy()` steps along, copying element by element, until the end of the string is copied. One final change to the string copy function can be made by including the pointer increments as postfix operators within the test part of the `while` statement. The final form of the string copy function is:

```
void strcopy(char *string1, char *string2)    // copy string2 to string1
{
  while (*string1++ = *string2++)
    ;
  return;
}
```

There is no ambiguity in the expression `*string1++ = *string2++` even though the indirection operator, `*`, and the increment operator, `++`, have the same precedence. Here the character pointed to is accessed before the pointer is incremented. Only after completion of the assignment `*string1 = *string2` are the pointers incremented to correctly point to the next characters in the respective strings.

The string copy function included in the standard library supplied with C++ compilers is typically written exactly like our pointer version of `strcopy()`.

Exercises 13.5

1. Determine the value of `*text`, `*(text + 3)`, and `*(text + 10)`, assuming that `text` is an array of characters and the following has been stored in the array:

   a. now is the time

   b. rocky raccoon welcomes you

   c. Happy Holidays

   d. The good ship

2. a. The following function, `convert()`, "marches along" the string passed to it and sends each character in the string one at a time to the `to_upper()` function until the null character is encountered.

```
void convert(char strng[])    // convert a string to uppercase letters
{
  int i = 0;
  while (strng[i] != '\0')
  {
    strng[i] = to_upper(strng[i]);
    i++;
  }
  return;
}

char to_upper(char letter)   // convert a character to uppercase
char letter;
{
  if( (letter >= 'a') && (letter <= 'z') )
    return (letter - 'a' + 'A');
  else
    return (letter);
}
```

   The `to_upper()` function takes each character passed to it and examines it to determine if the character is a lowercase letter (a lowercase letter is any character between *a* and *z*, inclusive). Assuming that characters are stored using the standard ASCII character codes, the expression `letter - 'a' + 'A'` converts a lowercase letter to its uppercase equivalent. Rewrite the `convert()` function using pointers.

   b. Include the `convert()` and `to_upper()` functions in a working program. The program should prompt the user for a string and echo the string back to the user in uppercase letters.

3. Using pointers, repeat Exercise 1b from Section 12.1.

4. Using pointers, repeat Exercise 2 from Section 12.1.

5. Using pointers, repeat Exercise 3 from Section 12.1.

6. Write a function named `remove()` that returns nothing and deletes all occurrences of a character from a string. The function should take two arguments: the string name and the character to be removed. For example, if message contains the string `Happy Holidays`, the function call `remove(message,'H')` should place the string `appy  olidays` into message. Use pointer notation in your function.

7. Using pointers, repeat Exercise 6 from Section 12.1.

8. Write a function that uses pointers to add a single character at the end of an existing string. The function should replace the existing `\0` character with the new character and append a new `\0` at the end of the string. The function returns nothing.

9. Write a function that uses pointers to delete a single character from the end of a string. This is effectively achieved by moving the \0 character one position closer to the start of the string. The function returns nothing.

10. Determine the string handling functions that are available with your C++ compiler. For each available function, list the data types of the arguments expected by the function and the data type of any returned value.

13.6 STRING DEFINITIONS AND POINTER ARRAYS

The definition of a string automatically involves a pointer. For example, the definition `char message1[80];` both reserves storage for 80 characters and automatically creates a pointer constant, `message1`, which contains the address of `message1[0]`. As a pointer constant, the address associated with the pointer cannot be changed—it must always "point to" the beginning of the created array.

Instead of creating a string as an array, however, it is also possible to create a string using a pointer. For example, the definition `char *message2;` creates a pointer to a character. In this case, `message2` is a true pointer variable. Once a pointer to a character is defined, assignment statements, such as `message2 = "this is a string";`, can be made. In this assignment, `message2`, which is a pointer, receives the address of the first character in the string.

The main difference in the definitions of `message1` as an array and `message2` as a pointer is in the way the pointer is created. Defining `message1` using the declaration `char message1[80]` explicitly calls for a fixed amount of storage for the array. This causes the compiler to create a pointer constant. Defining `message2` using the declaration `char *message2` explicitly creates a pointer variable first. This pointer is then used to hold the address of a string when the string is actually specified. This difference in definitions has both storage and programming consequences.

From a programming perspective, defining `message2` as a pointer to a character allows string assignments, such as `message2 = "this is a string";`, to be made within a program. Similar assignments are not allowed for strings defined as arrays. Thus, the statement `message1 = "this is a string";` is not valid. Both definitions, however, allow initializations to be made using a string assignment. For example, both of the following initializations are valid:

```
char message1[81] = "this is a string";
char *message2 = "this is a string";
```

From a storage perspective, the allocation of space for `message1` and `message2` is quite different. As illustrated in Figure 13.25, both initializations cause the computer to store the same string internally. In the case of `message1`, a specific set of 81 storage locations is reserved and the first 17 locations are initialized. For `message1`, different strings can be stored, but each string will overwrite the previously stored characters. The same is not true for `message2`.

The definition of `message2` reserves enough storage for one pointer. The initialization then causes the string to be stored in memory and the address of the string's first character, in this case the address of the `t`, to be loaded into the pointer. If a later assignment is made to `message2`, the initial string remains in memory and new storage locations are allocated to the new string. For example, consider the following sequence of instructions:

```
char *message2 = "this is a string";
message2 = "A new message";
```

FIGURE 13.25 String Storage Allocation

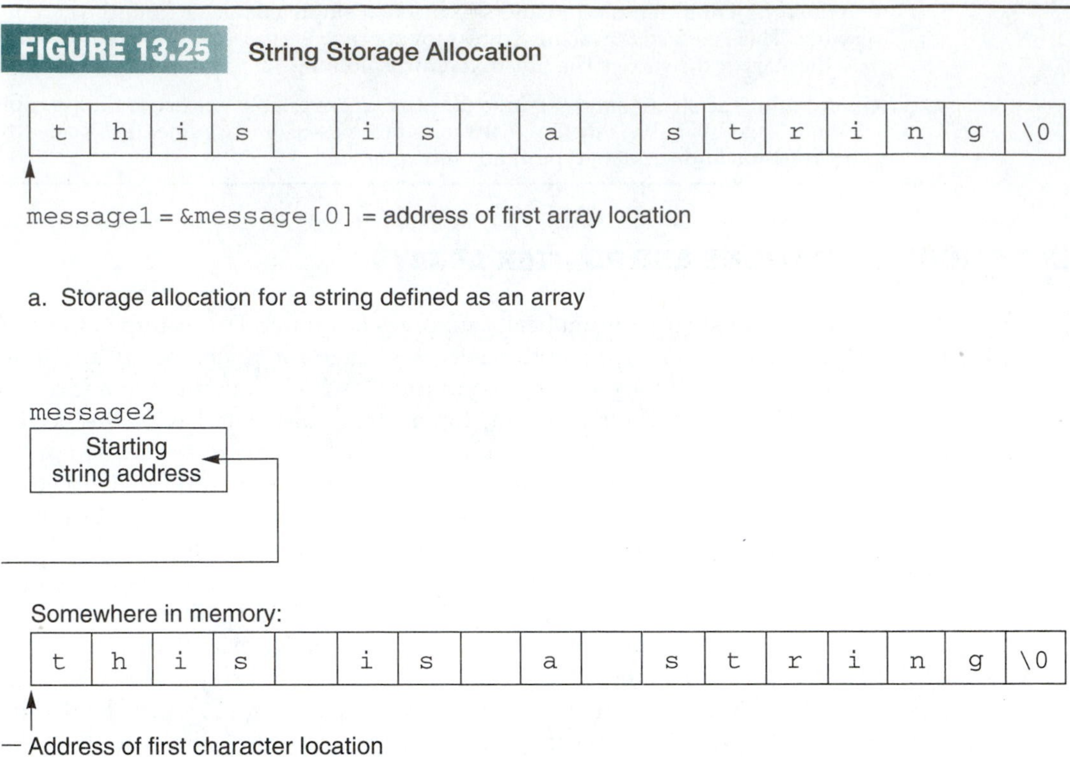

The first statement defines `message2` as a pointer variable, stores the initialization string in memory, and loads the starting address of the string (the address of the `t` in this case) into `message2`. The next assignment statement causes the computer to store the second string and change the address in `message2` to point to the starting location of this new string.

It is important to realize that the second string assigned to `message2` does not overwrite the first string, but simply changes the address in `message2` to point to the new string. As illustrated in Figure 13.26, both strings are stored inside the computer. Any additional string assignment to `message2` would result in the additional storage of the new string and a corresponding change in the address stored in `message2`. Doing so also means that we no longer have access to the original memory location.

Pointer Arrays

The declaration of an array of character pointers is an extremely useful extension to single string pointer declarations. For example, the declaration

```
char *seasons[4];
```

creates an array of four elements, where each element is a pointer to a character. As individual pointers, each pointer can be assigned to point to a string using string assignment statements. Thus, the statements

FIGURE 13.26 Storage Allocation Using a Pointer Variable

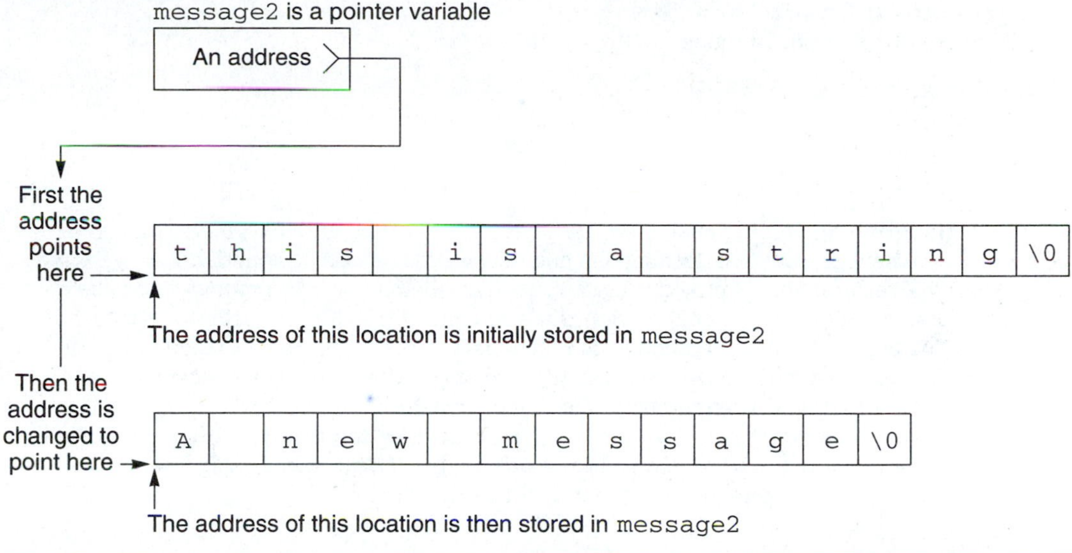


```
seasons[0] = "Winter";
seasons[1] = "Spring";
seasons[2] = "Summer";
seasons[3] = "Fall";    // note: string lengths may differ
```

set appropriate addresses into the respective pointers. Figure 13.27 illustrates the addresses loaded into the pointers for these assignments. As illustrated, the `seasons` array does not contain the actual strings assigned to the pointers. These strings are stored elsewhere in the computer, in the normal data area allocated to the program. The array of pointers contains only the addresses of the starting location for each string.

FIGURE 13.27 The Addresses Contained in the `seasons[]` Pointers

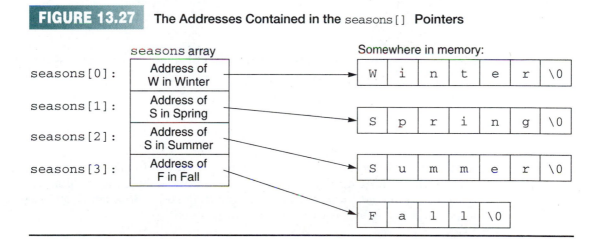

	seasons array	Somewhere in memory:
seasons[0]:	Address of W in Winter	W i n t e r \0
seasons[1]:	Address of S in Spring	S p r i n g \0
seasons[2]:	Address of S in Summer	S u m m e r \0
seasons[3]:	Address of F in Fall	F a l l \0

PROGRAMMING NOTE

Allocating Space for a String

Although the two declarations

```
char test[5] = "abcd";
```

and

```
char *test = "abcd";
```

both create storage for the characters `'a'`, `'b'`, `'c'`, `'d'`, and `'\0'`, there is a subtle difference between the two declarations and how values can be assigned to `test`. Except within the declaration, an array declaration, such as `char test[5];` precludes the use of any subsequent assignment expression, such as `test = "efgh"`, to assign values to the array. The use of a `strcpy()`, such as `strcpy(test,"efgh")`, however, is subsequently valid. The only restriction on `strcpy()` is the size of the array, which in this case is 5 elements. This situation is reversed when a pointer is created.

A pointer declaration, such as `char *test;`, precludes the use of `strcpy()` to initialize the memory locations pointed to by the pointer, but it does allow assignments. For example, the following sequence of statements is valid:

```
char *test;
test = "abcd";
test = "here is a longer string";
```

Once a string of characters has been assigned to test, `strcpy()` can be used provided the copy uses no more elements than are currently contained in the string.

The difference in usage is explained by the fact that the compiler automatically allocates sufficient new memory space for any string pointed to by a pointer variable, but does not do so for an array of characters. The array size is fixed by the definition statement.

Formally, any expression that yields a value that can be used on the left side of an assignment expression is said to be an l-value. (Similarly, any expression that yields a value that can be used on the right side of an assignment statement is said to be an r-value.) Thus, a pointer variable can be an l-value but an array name cannot.

The initializations of the `seasons` array can also be incorporated directly within the definition of the array, as follows:

```
char *seasons[4] = {"Winter",
                    "Spring",
                    "Summer",
                    "Fall"};
```

This declaration both creates an array of pointers and initializes the pointers with appropriate addresses. Once addresses have been assigned to the pointers, each pointer can be used to access its corresponding string. Program 13.14 uses the `seasons` array to display each season using a `for` loop.

PROGRAM 13.14

```
#include <iostream.h>

const int NUMSEASONS = 4;

int main()
{
  int n;
  char *seasons[] = {"Winter",
                     "Spring",
                     "Summer",
                     "Fall"};

  for(n = 0; n < NUMSEASONS; n++)
    cout << "\nThe season is " << seasons[n];
  cout << endl;

  return 0;
}
```

The output obtained for Program 13.14 is:

```
The season is Winter
The season is Spring
The season is Summer
The season is Fall
```

The advantage of using a list of pointers is that logical groups of data headings can be collected and accessed with one array name. For example, the months in a year can be collectively grouped in one array called `months`, and the days in a week collectively grouped in an array called `days`. The grouping of like headings allows the programmer to access and print an appropriate heading by simply specifying the correct position of the heading in the array. Program 13.15 uses the seasons array to correctly identify and display the season corresponding to a user-input month.

Except for the expression `n = (n % 12) / 3`, Program 13.15 is rather straightforward. The program requests the user to input a month and accepts the number corresponding to the month using a `cin` object call. The expression `n = (n % 12) / 3`, then uses a common program "trick" to scale one set of numbers into a second more useful set. In this case the first set is the numbers 1 through 12 and the second set the numbers 0 through 3. Thus, the months of the year, which correspond to the numbers 1 through 12, are adjusted to the correct season subscript. The expression `n % 12` adjusts the month entered so that it lies within the range 0 through 11, with 0 corresponding to December, 1 for January, and so on. Dividing by 3 causes the resulting number to range between 0 and 3, corresponding to the possible seasons elements. The result of the division by 3 is assigned to the integer variable `n`. The months 0, 1, and 2, when divided by 3, are set to 0; the months 3, 4, and 5 are set to 1; the months 6,

PROGRAM 13.15

```
#include <iostream.h>

int main()
{
  int n;
  char *seasons[] = {"Winter",
                     "Spring",
                     "Summer",
                     "Fall"};

  cout << "\nEnter a month (use 1 for Jan., 2 for Feb., etc.): ";
  cin  >> n;
  n = (n % 12) / 3;     // create the correct subscript
  cout << "The month entered is a "<< seasons[n]
       << " month." << endl;

  return 0;
}
```

7, and 8 are set to 2; and the months 9, 10, and 11 are set to 3. This is equivalent to the following assignments:

Months	Season
December, January, February	Winter
March, April, May	Spring
June, July, August	Summer
September, October, November	Fall

The following is a sample of output obtained for Program 13.15:

```
Enter a month (use 1 for Jan., 2 for Feb., etc.): 12
The month entered is a Winter month.
```

Exercises 13.6

1. Write two declaration statements that can be used in place of the declaration `char text[] = "Hooray!";`.

2. Determine the value of `*text`, `*(text + 3)`, and `*(text + 7)` for each of the following sections of code:

   a.
   ```
   char *text;
   char message[] = "the check is in the mail";
   text = message;
   ```

   b.
   ```
   char *text;
   char formal[] = {'t','h','i','s',' ','i','s',' ','a','n',' ',
                    'i','n','v','i','t','a','t','i','o','n','\0'};
   text = &formal[0];
   ```

   c.
   ```
   char *test;
   char more[] = "Happy Holidays";
   text = &more[4];
   ```

d.
```
char *text, *second;
char blip[] = "The good ship";
second = blip;
text = ++second;
```

3. Determine the error in the following program:

```
#include <iostream.h>

int main()
{
  int i = 0;
  char message[] = {'H','e','l','l','o','\0'};

  for( ; i < 5; i++)
  {
    cout << *message;
    ++message;
  }

  return 0;
}
```

4. a. Write a C++ function that displays the day of the week corresponding to a user-entered input number between 1 and 7. That is, in response to an input of 2, the program displays the name Monday. Use an array of pointers in the function.

   b. Include the function written for Exercise 4a in a complete working program.

   c. Modify the function written in Exercise 4a so that the function returns the address of the character string containing the proper day to be displayed.

5. Write a function that will accept 10 lines of user-input text and store the entered lines as 10 individual strings. Use a pointer array in your function.

13.7 COMMON PROGRAMMING ERRORS

In using the material presented in this chapter, be aware of the following possible errors:

1. Attempting to store an address in a variable that has not been declared as a pointer.
2. Using a pointer to access nonexistent array elements. For example, if `nums` is an array of 10 integers, the expression `*(nums + 15)` points six integer locations beyond the last element of the array. Because C++ does not do any bounds checking on array accesses, this type of error is not caught by the compiler. This is the same error, disguised in pointer notation form, that occurs when using a subscript to access an out-of-bounds array element.
3. Incorrectly applying the address and indirection operators. For example, if `pt` is a pointer variable, the expressions

```
pt = &45              // INVALID
pt = &(miles + 10)    // INVALID
```

   are both invalid because they attempt to take the address of a value.

   Notice that the expression `pt = &miles + 10`, however, is valid. Here, 10 is added to the address of `miles`. Again, it is the programmer's responsibility to ensure that the final address "points to" a valid data element.

4. Taking addresses of pointer constants. For example, given the declarations

```
int nums[25];
int *pt;
```

the assignment

```
pt = &nums;    // INVALID
```

is invalid. `nums` is a pointer constant that is itself equivalent to an address. The correct assignment is `pt = nums`.

5. Taking addresses of a reference argument, reference variable, or register variable. The reason for this is that reference arguments and variables are essentially the same as pointer constants, in that they are named address values. Similarly, the address of a register variable cannot be taken. Thus, for the declarations

```
register total;
int *pt_tot;
```

the assignment

```
pt_tot = &total;   // INVALID
```

is invalid. The reason for this is that register variables are stored in a computer's internal registers, and these storage areas do not have standard memory addresses.

6. Initializing pointer variables incorrectly. For example, the initialization

```
int *pt = 5;    // INVALID
```

is invalid. Since `pt` is a pointer to an integer, it must be initialized with a valid address.

7. Becoming confused about whether a variable *contains* an address or *is* an address. Pointer variables and pointer arguments contain addresses. Although a pointer constant is synonymous with an address, it is useful to treat pointer constants as pointer variables with two restrictions:

   - The address of a pointer constant cannot be taken.
   - The address "contained in" the pointer constant cannot be altered.

   Except for these two restrictions, pointer constants and variables can be used almost interchangeably. Therefore, when an address is required any of the following can be used:

   - a pointer variable name
   - a pointer argument name
   - a pointer constant name
   - a nonpointer variable name preceded by the address operator (e.g., `&variable`)
   - a nonpointer argument name preceded by the address operator (e.g., `&argument`).

   Some of the confusion surrounding pointers is caused by the cavalier use of the word *pointer*. For example, the phrase "a function requires a pointer argument" is more clearly understood when it is realized that the phrase really means "a function requires an address as an argument." Similarly, the phrase "a function returns a pointer" really means "a function returns an address."

If you are ever in doubt as to what is really contained in a variable or how it should be treated, use the cout object to display the contents of the variable, the "thing pointed to," or "the address of the variable." Seeing what is displayed frequently helps sort out what is really in the variable.

8. Misunderstanding the terminology. For example, if text is defined as

```
char *text;
```

the variable text is sometimes referred to as a string. Thus, the terminology "store the characters Hooray for the Hoosiers into the text string" may be encountered. Strictly speaking, calling text a string or a string variable is incorrect. The variable text is a pointer that contains the address of the first character in the string. Nevertheless, referring to a character pointer as a string occurs frequently enough that you should be aware of it.

9. Using the default copy constructor and default assignment operators with classes containing pointer members. Since these default functions do a memberwise copy, the address in the source pointer is copied to the destination pointer. Typically this is not desirable because both pointers end up pointing to the same memory area.

13.8 CHAPTER REVIEW

Key Terms

address operator
indirect addressing
indirection operator
offset
pointer
pointer variable

Summary

1. Every variable has a data type, an address, and a value. In C++ the address of a variable can be obtained by using the address operator &.
2. A pointer is a variable that is used to store the address of another variable. Pointers, like all C++ variables, must be declared. The indirection operator, *, is used both to declare a pointer variable and to access the variable whose address is stored in a pointer.
3. An array name is a pointer constant. The value of the pointer constant is the address of the first element in the array. Thus, if val is the name of an array, val and &val[0] can be used interchangeably.
4. Any access to an array element using subscript notation can always be replaced using pointer notation. That is, the notation a[i] can always be replaced by the notation *(a + i). This is true whether a was initially declared explicitly as an array or as a pointer.

5. Arrays can be dynamically created as a program is executing. For example, the sequence of statements:

```
cout << "Enter the array size: ";
cin  >> num;
int *grades = new int[num];
```

creates an array named `grades` of size `num`. The area allocated for the array can be dynamically destroyed using the delete operator. For example, the statement `delete grades;` will release the allocated area for the `grades` array.

6. Arrays are passed to functions as addresses. The called function always receives direct access to the originally declared array elements.

7. When a single-dimensional array is passed to a function, the argument declaration for the function can be either an array declaration or a pointer declaration. Thus, the following parameter declarations are equivalent:

```
float a[];
float *a;
```

8. Pointers can be incremented, decremented, compared, and assigned. Numbers added to or subtracted from a pointer are automatically scaled. The scale factor used is the number of bytes required to store the data type originally pointed to.

Exercises

1. Write a function named `trimfrnt()` that deletes all leading blanks from a string. Write the function using pointers with a return type of `void`.
2. Write a function named `trimrear()` that deletes all trailing blanks from a string. Write the function using pointers and with a return type of `void`.
3. Write a C++ program that asks for two lowercase characters. Pass the two entered characters using pointers to a function named `capit()`. The `capit()` function should capitalize the two letters and return the capitalized values to the calling function through its pointer arguments. The calling function should then display all four letters.
4. Write a program that declares three single-dimensional arrays named `miles`, `gallons`, and `mpg`. Each array should be capable of holding 10 elements. In the `miles` array store the numbers 240.5, 300.0, 189.6, 310.6, 280.7, 216.9, 199.4, 160.3, 177.4, 192.3. In the `gallons` array store the numbers 10.3, 15.6, 8.7, 14, 16.3, 15.7, 14.9, 10.7, 8.3, 8.4. Each element of the `mpg` array should be calculated as the corresponding element of the `miles` array divided by the equivalent element of the `gallons` array. For example, `mpg[0] = miles[0] / gallons[0]`. Use pointers when calculating and displaying the elements of the `mpg` array.
5. a. Write a program that has a declaration in `main` to store the string `Vacation is near` into an array named `message`. There should be a function call to display that accepts `message` in an argument named `strng` and then displays the message using the pointer notation `*(strng + i)`.

   b. Modify the display function written in Exercise 5a to alter the address in `message`. Also use the expression `*strng` rather than `*(strng + i)` to retrieve the correct element.

6. Write a program that declares three single-dimensional arrays named `price`, `quantity`, and `amount`. Each array should be declared in `main` and be capable of holding 10 double-precision numbers. The numbers to be stored in `price` are 10.62, 14.89, 13.21, 16.55, 18.62, 9.47, 6.58, 18.32, 12.15, 3.98. The numbers to be stored in `quantity` are 4, 8.5, 6, 7.35, 9, 15.3, 3, 5.4, 2.9, 4.8. Have your program pass these three arrays to a function called `extend()`, which calculates the elements in the amount `array` as the product of the equivalent elements in the `price` and `quantity` arrays. For example, `amount[1] = price[1] * quantity[1]`.

   After `extend()` has put values into the `amount` array, display the values in the array from within `main()`. Write the `extend` function using pointers.

7. a. Determine the output of the following program:

```
#include <iostream.h>

const int ROWS = 2;
const int COLS = 3;

void arr(int [] []); // equivalent to void arr(int (*) []);

int main()
{
  int nums[ROWS][COLS] = { {33,16,29},
                           {54,67,99}};
  arr(nums);

  return 0;
}
void arr(int (*val) [3])
{
  cout << '\n' << *(*val);
  cout << '\n' << *(*val + 1);
  cout << '\n' << *(*(val + 1) + 2);
  cout << '\n' << *(*val) + 1;

  return;
}
```

   b. Given the declaration for `val` in the `arr` function, would the reference `val[1][2]` be valid within the function?

8. Define an array of 10 pointers to floating-point numbers. Then read 10 numbers into the individual locations referenced by the pointers. Now add all of the numbers and store the result in a pointer-referenced location. Display the contents of all of the locations.

CHAPTER

14 Records as Data Structures

An array allows access to a list or table of data of the same data type using a single variable name. At times, however, we may want to store information of varying types—such as a string name, an integer part number, and a double precision price—together in one structure. A data structure that stores different types of data under a single variable name is called a *record*.

To make the discussion more tangible, consider data items that might be stored for a video game character, as illustrated in Figure 14.1. Each of the individual data items listed in Figure 14.1 is an entity by itself that is referred to as a **data field.** Taken together, all the data fields form a single unit that is referred to as a **record.** In C++, a record is referred to as a **structure** and we will use these two terms interchangeably.

Although there could be hundreds of characters in a video game, the form of each character's record is identical. In dealing with records it is important to distinguish between a record's form and its contents.

FIGURE 14.1 Typical Components of a Video Game Character

```
Name:
Type:
Location in Dungeon:
Strength Factor:
Intelligence Factor:
Type of Armor:
```

FIGURE 14.2 The Form and Contents of a Record

```
Name: Golgar
Type: Monster
Location in Dungeon: G7
Strength Factor: 78
Intelligence Factor: 15
Type of Armor: Chain Mail
```

A record's form consists of the symbolic names, data types, and arrangement of individual data fields in the record. The record's contents refers to the actual data stored in the symbolic names. Figure 14.2 shows acceptable contents for the record form illustrated in Figure 14.1.

In this chapter, we describe the C++ statements required to create, fill, use, and pass records between functions.

14.1 SINGLE RECORDS

To use a record, we need to carry out the same two steps needed for using any variable. First, the record must be declared. Then specific values can be assigned to the individual record elements. To declare a record, we must list the data types, data names, and arrangement of data items. For example, the definition

```
struct
{
  int month;
  int day;
  int year;
} birth;
```

gives the form of a record structure called `birth` and reserves storage for the individual data items listed in the structure. The `birth` structure consists of three data items or fields, which are called **structure members.**

Assigning actual data values to the data items of a structure is called *populating* the structure, and is a relatively straightforward procedure. Each member of a structure is accessed by giving both the structure name and individual data item name, separated by a period. Thus, `birth.month` refers to the `month` member of the `birth` structure, `birth.day` refers to the `day` member of the structure, and `birth.year` refers to the `year` member. Program 14.1 illustrates how values are assigned to the individual members of the birth structure.

The output produced by Program 14.1 is:

```
My birth date is 12/28/82
```

As in most C++ statements, the spacing of a structure definition is not rigid. For example, the `birth` structure could just as well have been defined

```
struct {int month; int day; int year;} birth;
```

PROGRAM 14.1

```
// a program that defines and populates a record
#include <iostream.h>
int main()
{
  struct
  {
    int month;
    int day;
    int year;
  } birth;
  birth.month = 12;
  birth.day = 28;
  birth.year = 82;

  cout << "My birth date is "
       << birth.month << '/'
       << birth.day   << '/'
       << birth.year  << endl;
  return 0;
}
```

Also, as with all C++ definition statements, multiple variables can be defined in the same statement. For example, the definition statement

```
struct
{
  int month;
  int day;
  int year;
} birth, current;
```

creates two structure variables having the same form. The members of the first structure are referenced by the individual names `birth.month`, `birth.day`, and `birth.year`, while the members of the second structure are referenced by the names `current.month`, `current.day`, and `current.year`. Notice that the form of this particular structure definition statement is identical to the form used in defining any program variable: The data type is followed by a list of variable names.

The most commonly used modification for defining structure types is listing the form of the structure with no following variable names. In this case, however, the list of structure members must be preceded by a user-selected data type name. For example, in the declaration

```
struct Date
{
  int month;
  int day;
  int year;
};
```

the term Date is a structure type name: It defines a new data type that is a data structure of the declared form.[1] By convention the first letter of a user-selected data type name is uppercase, as in the name Date, which helps to identify them when they are used in subsequent definition statements. Here, the declaration for the Date structure creates a new data type without actually reserving any storage locations. As such it is not a definition statement. It simply declares a Date structure type and describes how individual data items are arranged within the structure. Actual storage for the members of the structure is reserved only when specific variable names are assigned. For example, the definition statement

```
Date birth, current;
```

reserves storage for two date structure variables named birth and current, respectively. Each of these individual structures has the form previously declared for the Date structure.[2]

The declaration of a structure data type, like all declarations, can be global or local. Program 14.2 illustrates the global declaration of a Date data type. Internal to main(), the variable birth is defined as a local variable of Date type.

PROGRAM 14.2

```
#include <iostream.h>
struct Date // this is a global declaration
{
  int month;
  int day;
  int year;
};

int main()
{
  Date birth;

  birth.month = 12;
  birth.day = 28;
  birth.year = 82;

  cout << "My birth date is " << birth.month << '/'
                   << birth.day   << '/'
                   << birth.year  << endl;

  return 0;
}
```

---

[1] For completeness we should mention that a C++ structure can also be declared as a class with no member functions and all public data members. Similarly, a C++ class can be declared as a struct having all private data members and all public member functions. Thus, C++ provides two syntaxes for both structs and classes. The conventin, however, is not to mix notations and to use structures for creating record types and classes for providing true information and implementation hiding.

[2] The type name in C++ for this declaration is Date. In C the type name would be struct Date and defining variables, such as birth and current, would be defined as struct Date birth, current;.

The output produced by Program 14.2 is identical to the output produced by Program 14.1.

The initialization of structures follows the same rules as those used for the initialization of arrays: Global and local structures may be initialized by following the definition with a list of initializers. For example, the definition statement

```
Date birth = {12, 28, 72};
```

can be used to replace the first four statements internal to `main()` in Program 14.2. Notice that the initializers are separated by commas, not semicolons.

The individual members of a structure are not restricted to integer data types, as illustrated by the `Date` structure. Any valid C++ data type can be used. For example, consider an employee record consisting of the following data items:

```
Name:
Identification Number:
Regular Pay Rate:
Overtime Pay Rate:
```

A suitable declaration for these data items is:

```
struct Pay_rec
{
  char name[20];
  int id_num;
  float reg_rate;
  float ot_rate;
};
```

Once the `Pay_rec` data type is declared, a specific structure variable using this type can be defined and initialized. For example, the definition

```
Pay_rec employee = {"H. Price",12387,15.89,25.50};
```

creates a structure named `employee` of the `Pay_rec` data type. The individual members of `employee` are initialized with the respective data listed between braces in the definition statement.

Notice that a single structure is simply a convenient method for combining and storing related items under a common name. Although a single structure is useful in explicitly identifying the relationship among its members, the individual members could be defined as separate variables. One of the real advantages to using structures is only realized when the same data type is used in a list many times over. Creating lists with the same data type is the topic of the next section.

Before leaving single structures, it is worth noting that the individual members of a structure can be any valid C++ data type, including both arrays and structures. An array of characters was used as a member of the employee structure defined previously. Accessing an element of a member array requires giving the structure's name, followed by a period, followed by the array designation. For example, `employee.name[4]` refers to the fifth character in the `employee.name` array.

Including a structure within a structure follows the same rules for including any data type in a structure. For example, assume that a structure is to consist of a name and a date of birth, where a `Date` structure has been declared as:

```
struct Date
{
  int month;
  int date;
  int year;
};
```

POINT OF INFORMATION

Homogeneous and Heterogeneous Data Structures

Both arrays and records are structured data types. The difference between these two data structures is the types of elements they contain. An array is a *homogeneous* data structure, which means that each of its components must be of the same type. A record is a *heterogeneous* data structure, which means that each of its components can be of different data types. Thus, an array of records would be a homogeneous data structure whose elements are of the same heterogeneous type.

A suitable definition of a structure that includes a name and a `Date` structure is:

```
struct
{
  char name[20];
  Date birth;
} person;
```

Notice that in declaring the `Date` structure, the term `Date` is a data type name; thus it appears before the braces in the declaration statement. In defining the `person` structure variable, `person` is a variable name; thus it is the name of a specific structure. The same is true of the variable named `birth`. This is the name of a specific `Date` structure. Individual members in the `person` structure are accessed by preceding the desired member with the structure name followed by a period. For example, `person.birth.month` refers to the `month` variable in the `birth` structure contained in the `person` structure.

Exercises 14.1

1. Declare a structure data type named `S_temp` for each of the following records:
   a. a student record consisting of a student identification number, number of credits completed, and cumulative grade-point average
   b. a student record consisting of a student's name, date of birth, number of credits completed, and cumulative grade-point average
   c. a mailing list consisting of the items previously illustrated in Figure 14.1
   d. a stock record consisting of the stock's name, the price of the stock, and the date of purchase
   e. an inventory record consisting of an integer part number, part description, number of parts in inventory, and an integer reorder number
2. For the individual data types declared in Exercise 1, define a suitable structure variable name, and initialize each structure with the appropriate following data:
   a.
   ```
   Identification Number: 4672
   Number of Credits Completed: 68
   Grade-Point Average: 3.01
   ```
   b.
   ```
   Name: Rhona Karp
   Date of Birth: 8/4/60
   Number of Credits Completed: 96
   Grade-Point Average: 3.89
   ```

c. ```
Name: Kay Kingsley
Street Address: 614 Freeman Street
City: Indianapolis
State: IN
Zip Code: 07030
```

d. ```
Stock: IBM
Price Purchased: 134.5
Date Purchased: 10/1/86
```

e. ```
Part Number: 16879
Description: Battery
Number in Stock: 10
Reorder Number: 3
```

3. a. Write a C++ program that prompts a user to input the current month, day, and year. Store the data entered in a suitably defined record and display the date in an appropriate manner.

   b. Modify the program written in Exercise 3a to use a record that accepts the current time in hours, minutes, and seconds.

4. Write a C++ program that uses a structure for storing the name of a stock, its estimated earnings per share, and its estimated price-to-earnings ratio. Have the program prompt the user to enter these items for five different stocks, each time using the same structure to store the entered data. When the data has been entered for a particular stock, have the program compute and display the anticipated stock price based on the entered earnings and price-per-earnings values. For example, if a user entered the data `XYZ 1.56 12`, the anticipated price for a share of XYZ stock is (1.56)*(12) = $18.72.

5. Write a C++ program that accepts a user-entered time in hours and minutes. Have the program calculate and display the time one minute later.

6. a. Write a C++ program that accepts a user-entered date. Have the program calculate and display the date of the next day. For purposes of this exercise, assume that all months consist of 30 days.

   b. Modify the program written in Exercise 6a to account for the actual number of days in each month.

## 14.2 ARRAYS OF STRUCTURES

The real power of structures is realized when the same structure is used for lists of data. For example, assume that the data shown in Figure 14.3 must be processed. Clearly, the employee numbers can be stored together in an array of integers, the names in an array of pointers, and the pay rates in an array of either floating-point or double-precision numbers. In organizing the data in this fashion, each column in Figure 14.3 is considered to be a separate list, which is stored in its own array. The correspondence between items for each individual employee is maintained by storing an employee's data in the same array position in each array.

The separation of the complete list into three individual arrays is unfortunate, since all of the items relating to a single employee constitute a natural organization of data into records, as illustrated in Figure 14.4 on p. 746. Using a structure, the integrity of the data organization as a record can be maintained and reflected by the program. Under this approach, the list illustrated in Figure 14.4 can be processed as a single array of 10 structures.
```

FIGURE 14.3 A List of Employee Data

Employee Number	Employee Name	Employee Pay Rate
32479	Abrams, B.	6.72
33623	Bohm, P.	7.54
34145	Donaldson, S.	5.56
35987	Ernst, T.	5.43
36203	Gwodz, K.	8.72
36417	Hanson, H.	7.64
37634	Monroe, G.	5.29
38321	Price, S.	9.67
39435	Robbins, L.	8.50
39567	Williams, B.	7.20

Declaring an array of structures is the same as declaring an array of any other variable type. For example, if the data type `Pay_rec` is declared as

```
struct Pay_rec
{
  int id_num;
  char name[20];
  float rate;
};
```

then an array of 10 such structures can be defined as

```
Pay_rec employee[10];
```

This definition statement constructs an array of 10 elements, each of which is a structure of the data type `Pay_rec`. Notice that the creation of an array of 10 structures has the same form as the creation of any other array. For example, creating an array of 10 integers named `employee` requires the declaration

```
int employee[10];
```

In this declaration the data type is integer, whereas in the earlier declaration for `employee` the data type is `Pay_rec`.

Once an array of structures is declared, a particular data item is referenced by giving the position of the desired structure in the array followed by a period and the appropriate structure member. The variable `employee[0].rate`, for example, references the `rate` member of the first `employee` structure in the `employee` array. Including structures as elements of an array permits a list of records to be processed using standard array programming techniques. Program 14.3 displays the first five employee records illustrated in Figure 14.4.

PROGRAM 14.3

```
#include <iostream.h>
#include <iomanip.h>

const int MAXNAME = 20;  // maximum characters in a name
const int NUMRECS = 5;   // maximum number of records

struct Pay_rec    // this is a global declaration
{
  long id;
  char name[MAXNAME];
  float rate;
};
int main()
{
  int i;
  Pay_rec employee[NUMRECS] = {
                              { 32479, "Abrams, B.", 6.72 },
                              { 33623, "Bohm, P.", 7.54},
                              { 34145, "Donaldson, S.",  5.56},
                              { 35987, "Ernst, T.", 5.43 },
                              { 36203, "Gwodz, K.", 8.72 }
                              };

  cout << '\n';   // start on a new line
  cout << setiosflags(ios::left);  // left justify the output
  for ( i = 0; i < NUMRECS; i++)
    cout << setw(7)  << employee[i].id
         << setw(15) << employee[i].name
         << setw(6)  << employee[i].rate << endl;

  return 0;
}
```

The output displayed by Program 14.3 is:

```
32479    Abrams, B.       6.72
33623    Bohm, P.         7.54
34145    Donaldson, S.    5.56
35987    Ernst, T.        5.43
36203    Gwodz, K.        8.72
```

In reviewing Program 14.3, notice the initialization of the array of structures. Although the initializers for each structure have been enclosed in inner braces,

FIGURE 14.4 A List of Records

	Employee Number	Employee Name	Employee Pay Rate
1st record →	32479	Abrams, B.	6.72
2nd record →	33623	Bohm, P.	7.54
3rd record →	34145	Donaldson, S.	5.56
4th record →	35987	Ernst, T.	5.43
5th record →	36203	Gwodz, K.	8.72
6th record →	36417	Hanson, H.	7.64
7th record →	37634	Monroe, G.	5.29
8th record →	38321	Price, S.	9.67
9th record →	39435	Robbins, L.	8.50
10th record →	39567	Williams, B.	7.20

these are not strictly necessary because all members have been initialized. As with all external and static variables, in the absence of explicit initializers, the numeric elements of both static and external arrays or structures are initialized to zero and their character elements are initialized to `NULL`s. The `setiosflags(ios::left)` manipulator included in the `cout` object stream forces each name to be displayed left-justified in its designated field width.

Exercises 14.2

1. Define arrays of 100 structures for each of the data types described in Exercise 1 of the previous section.
2. a. Using the data type

```
struct Mon_days
{
  char name[10];
  int days;
};
```

   define an array of 12 structures of type `Mon_days`. Name the array `convert[]`, and initialize the array with the names of the 12 months in a year and the number of days in each month.

   b. Include the array created in Exercise 2a in a program that displays the names and number of days in each month.
3. Using the data type declared in Exercise 2a, write a C++ program that accepts a month from a user in numerical form and displays the name of the month and the number of days in the month. Thus, in response to an input of 3, the program would display `March has 31 days`.

4. a. Declare a single structure data type suitable for an `Employee` record of the following type:

Number	Name	Rate	Hours
3462	Jones	4.62	40
6793	Robbins	5.83	38
6985	Smith	5.22	45
7834	Swain	6.89	40
8867	Timmins	6.43	35
9002	Williams	4.75	42

   b. Using the data type declared in Exercise 4a, write a C++ program that interactively accepts the Exercise 4a data into an array of six structures. Once the data has been entered, the program should create a payroll report listing each employee's name, number, and gross pay. Include the total gross pay of all employees at the end of the report.

5. a. Declare a single structure data type suitable for a `Car` record of the following type:

Car Number	Miles Driven	Gallons Used
25	1,450	62
36	3,240	136
44	1,792	76
52	2,360	105
68	2,114	67

   b. Using the data type declared for Exercise 5a, write a C++ program that interactively accepts the above data into an array of five structures. Once the data has been entered, the program should create a report listing each car number and the miles per gallon achieved by the car. At the end of the report include the average miles per gallon achieved by the complete fleet of cars.

14.3 RECORD STRUCTURES AS FUNCTION ARGUMENTS

Individual structure members may be passed to a function in the same manner as any scalar variable. For example, given the structure definition

```
struct
{
  int id_num;
  double pay_rate;
  double hours;
} emp;
```

the statement

```
display(emp.id_num);
```

passes a copy of the structure member `emp.id_num` to a function named `display()`. Similarly, the statement

```
calc_pay(emp.pay_rate,emp.hours);
```

passes copies of the values stored in structure members `emp.pay_rate` and `emp.hours` to the function `calc_pay()`. Both functions, `display()` and `calc_pay`, must declare the correct data types of their respective arguments.

Complete copies of all members of a structure can also be passed to a function by including the name of the structure as an argument to the called function. For example, the function call

```
calc_net(emp);
```

passes a copy of the complete `emp` structure to `calc_net()`. Internal to `calc_net()`, an appropriate declaration must be made to receive the structure. Program 14.4 declares a global data type for an employee record. This type is then used by both the `main()` and `calc_net()` functions to define specific structures with the names `emp` and `temp`, respectively.

PROGRAM 14.4

```
#include <iostream.h>
#include <iomanip.h>

struct Employee         // declare a global type
{
  int id_num;
  double pay_rate;
  double hours;
};

double calc_net(Employee);  // function prototype

int main()
{
  Employee emp = {6782, 8.93, 40.5};
  double net_pay;

  net_pay = calc_net(emp);       // pass copies of the values in emp

    // set output formats
  cout << setw(10)
       << setiosflags(ios::fixed)
       << setiosflags(ios::showpoint)
       << setprecision(2);

  cout << "The net pay for employee " << emp.id_num
       << " is $" << net_pay << endl;;

  return 0;
}

double calc_net(Employee temp)  // temp is of data type Employee
{
  return (temp.pay_rate * temp.hours);
}
```

The output produced by Program 14.4 is:

```
The net pay for employee 6782 is $361.66
```

In reviewing Program 14.4, observe that both `main()` and `calc_net()` use the same data type to define their individual structure variables. The structure variable defined in `main()` and the structure variable defined in `calc_net()` are two completely different structures. Any changes made to the local `temp` variable in `calc_net()` are not reflected in the `emp` variable of `main()`. In fact, since both structure variables are local to their respective functions, the same structure variable name could have been used in both functions with no ambiguity.

When `calc_net()` is called by `main()`, copies of `emp`'s structure values are passed to the `temp` structure. `calc_net()` then uses two of the passed member values to calculate a number, which is returned to `main()`.

An alternative to the pass-by-value function call illustrated in Program 14.4, in which the called function receives a copy of a structure, is a pass-by-reference that passes a reference to a structure. Doing so permits the called function to access directly and alter values in the calling function's structure variable. For example, referring to Program 14.4, the prototype of `calc_net()` can be modified to

```
double calc_net(Employee&);
```

If this function prototype is used and the `calc_net()` function is rewritten to conform to it, the `main()` function in Program 14.4 may be used as is. Program 14.4a illustrates these changes within the context of a complete program.

Program 14.4a produces the same output as Program 14.4, except that the `calc_net()` function in Program 14.4a receives direct access to the `emp` structure rather than a copy of it. This means that the variable name `temp` within `calc_net` is an alternate name for the variable `emp` in `main()`, and any changes to `temp` are direct changes to `emp`. Although the same function call, `calc_net(emp)`, is made in both programs, the call in Program 14.4a passes a reference, whereas the call in Program 14.4 passes values.

Passing a Pointer

In place of passing a reference, a pointer can be used. To use a pointer, we must, in addition to modifying the function's prototype and header line, modify the call to `calc_net()` in Program 14.4 to

```
calc_net(&emp);
```

Here the function call clearly indicates that an address is being passed (which is not the case in Program 14.4a). The disadvantage, however, is in the dereferencing notation required internal to the function. However, because pointers are widely used in practice, it is worthwhile to become familiar with the notation used.

To store the passed address correctly, `calc_net()` must declare its argument as a pointer. A suitable function definition for `calc_net()` is

```
calc_net(Employee *pt)
```

Here, the declaration for `pt` declares this argument as a pointer to a structure of type `Employee`. The pointer variable, `pt`, receives the starting address of a structure whenever `calc_net()` is called. Within `calc_net()`, this pointer is used to directly reference any member in the structure. For example, `(*pt).id_num`

PROGRAM 14.4A

```
#include <iostream.h>
#include <iomanip.h>

struct Employee       // declare a global type
{
  int id_num;
  double pay_rate;
  double hours;
};

double calc_net(Employee&);    // function prototype

int main()
{
  Employee emp = {6782, 8.93, 40.5};
  double net_pay;

  net_pay = calc_net(emp);       // pass a reference

    // set output formats
  cout << setw(10)
       << setiosflags(ios::fixed)
       << setiosflags(ios::showpoint)
       << setprecision(2);

  cout << "The net pay for employee " << emp.id_num
       << " is $" <<  net_pay << endl;

  return 0;
}
double calc_net(Employee& temp)   // temp is a reference variable
{
  return (temp.pay_rate * temp.hours);
}
```

refers to the `id_num` member of the structure, `(*pt).pay_rate` refers to the `pay_rate` member of the structure, and `(*pt).hours` refers to the `hours` member of the structure. These relationships are illustrated in Figure 14.5. The parentheses around the expression `*pt` in this figure are necessary to initially access "the structure whose address is in `pt`." This is followed by a reference to access the desired member within the structure. In the absence of the parentheses, the structure member operator `.` takes precedence over the indirection operator. Thus, the expression `*pt.hours` is another way of writing `*(pt.hours)`, which would refer to "the variable whose address is in the `pt.hours` variable." This last expression clearly makes no sense because there is no structure named `pt` and `hours` does not contain an address.

FIGURE 14.5 A Pointer Can Be Used to Access Structure Members

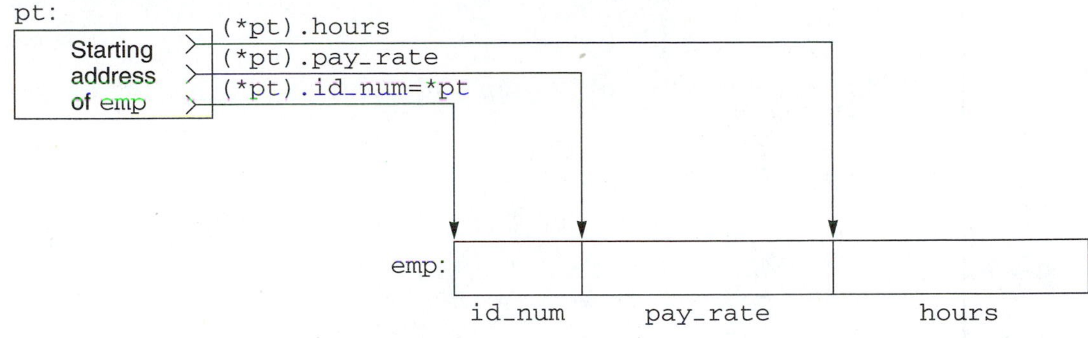

As illustrated in Figure 14.5, the starting address of the emp structure is also the address of the first member of the structure.

The use of pointers in this manner is so common that a special notation exists for it. The general expression *(*pointer).member* can always be replaced with the notation pointer->member, where the -> operator is constructed using a minus sign followed by a right-facing arrow (greater than symbol). Either expression can be used to locate the desired member. For example, the following expressions are equivalent:

```
(*pt).id_num      can be replaced by    pt->id_num
(*pt).pay_rate    can be replaced by    pt->pay_rate
(*pt).hours       can be replaced by    pt->hours
```

Program 14.5 illustrates how to pass a structure's address and use a pointer with the new notation to directly reference the structure.

The name of the pointer argument declared in Program 14.5 is, of course, selected by the programmer. When calc_net() is called, emp's starting address is passed to the function. Using this address as a starting point, individual members of the structure are accessed by including their names with the pointer.

As with all C++ expressions that access a variable, the increment and decrement operators can also be applied to them. For example, the expression

```
++pt->hours
```

adds one to the hours member of the emp structure. Since the -> operator has a higher priority than the increment operator, the hours member is accessed first and then the increment is applied.

Alternatively, the expression (++pt)->hours uses the prefix increment operator to increment the address in pt before the hours member is accessed. Similarly, the expression (pt++)->hours uses the postfix increment operator to increment the address in pt after the hours member is accessed. In both of these cases, however, a sufficient number of defined structures must exist to ensure that the incremented pointers actually point to legitimate structures.

As an example, Figure 14.6 illustrates an array of three structures of type employee. Assuming that the address of emp[1] is stored in the pointer variable pt, the expression ++pt changes the address in pt to the starting address of emp[2], while the expression --pt changes the address to point to emp[0].

PROGRAM 14.5

```
#include <iostream.h>
#include <iomanip.h>

struct Employee   // declare a global type
{
  int id_num;
  double pay_rate;
  double hours;
};
double calc_net(Employee *);   //function prototype

int main()
{
  Employee emp = {6782, 8.93, 40.5};
  double net_pay;

  net_pay = calc_net(&emp);      // pass an address

    // set output formats
  cout << setw(10)
       << setiosflags(ios::fixed)
       << setiosflags(ios::showpoint)
       << setprecision(2);

  cout << "The net pay for employee " << emp.id_num
       << " is $" << net_pay << endl;

  return 0;
}

double calc_net(Employee *pt) // pt is a pointer to a
{                             // structure of Employee type
  return (pt->pay_rate * pt->hours);
}
```

FIGURE 14.6 Changing Pointer Addresses

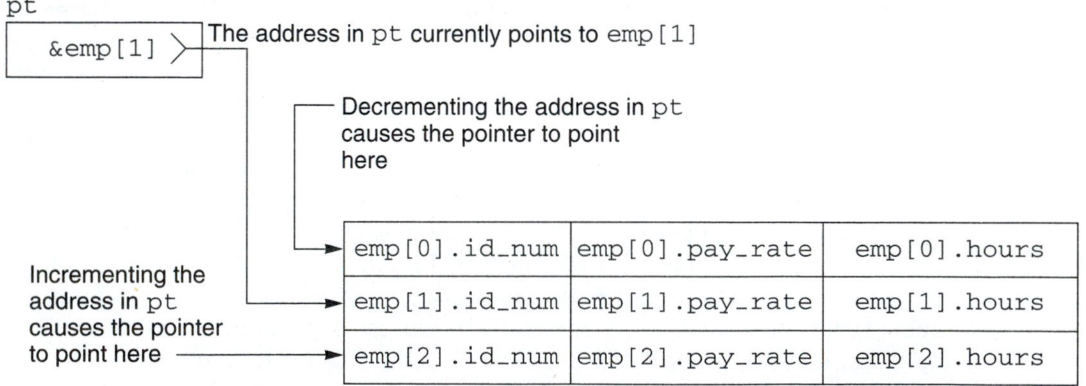

Returning Structures

In practice, most structure handling functions receive direct access to a structure by receiving a structure's address. Then any changes to the structure can be made directly from within the function. If you want to have a function return a separate structure, however, you must follow the same procedures for returning complete data structures as for returning scalar values. These procedures include declaring the function appropriately and alerting any calling function to the type of data structure being returned. For example, the function `get_vals()` in Program 14.6 returns a complete structure to `main()`.

PROGRAM 14.6

```
#include <iostream.h>
#include <iomanip.h>

struct Employee    // declare a global type
{
  int id_num;
  double pay_rate;
  double hours;
};

struct Employee get_vals(void);    // function prototype

int main()
{
  Employee emp;

  emp = get_vals();
  cout << "\nThe employee id number is " << emp.id_num
       << "\nThe employee pay rate is $" << emp.pay_rate
       << "\nThe employee hours are " << emp.hours << endl;

  return 0;
}

struct Employee get_vals(void) // return an employee structure
{
  Employee next;

  next.id_num = 6789;
  next.pay_rate = 16.25;
  next.hours = 38.0;

  return next;
}
```

The following output is displayed when Program 14.6 is run:

```
The employee id number is 6789
The employee pay rate is $16.25
The employee hours are 38
```

Since the `get_vals()` function returns a structure, the function header for `get_vals()` must specify the type of structure being returned. Because `get_vals()` does not receive any arguments, the function header has no argument declarations and consists of the line

```
Employee get_vals(void);
```

Within `get_vals()`, the variable next is defined as a structure of the type to be returned. After values have been assigned to the next structure, the structure values are returned by including the structure name within the parentheses of the return statement.

On the receiving side, `main()` must be alerted that the function `get_vals()` will be returning a structure. This is handled by the function prototype for `get_vals()`. Notice that these steps for returning a structure from a function are identical to the normal procedures for returning scalar data types previously described in Chapter 6.

Exercises 14.3

1. Write a C++ function named `days()` that determines the number of days from the turn of the century for any date passed as a structure. Use the `Date` structure:

```
struct Date
{
  int month;
  int day;
  int year;
};
```

In writing the `days()` function, use the convention that all years have 360 days and each month consists of 30 days. The function should return the number of days for any `Date` structure passed to it. Make sure you declare the returned variable a long integer to reserve sufficient room for converting dates such as 12/19/89.

2. Write a C++ function named `dif_days()` that calculates and returns the difference between two dates. Each date is passed to the function as a structure using the following global type:

```
struct Date
{
  int month;
  int day;
  int year;
};
```

The `dif_days()` function should make two calls to the `days()` function written for Exercise 1.

3. a. Rewrite the `days()` function written for Exercise 1 to receive a reference to a `Date` structure, rather than a copy of the complete structure.

   b. Redo Exercise 3a using a pointer rather than a reference.

4. a. Write a C++ function named `larger()` that returns the later date of any two dates passed to it. For example, if the dates 10/9/62 and 11/3/62 are passed to `larger()`, the second date would be returned.

   b. Include the `larger()` function written for Exercise 4a in a complete program. Store the `Date` structure returned by `larger()` in a separate `Date` structure and display the member values of the returned `Date`.

5. a. Modify the function `days()` written for Exercise 1 to account for the actual number of days in each month. Assume, however, that each year contains 365 days (that is, do not account for leap years).

   b. Modify the function written for Exercise 5a to account for leap years.

14.4 LINKED LISTS

A classic data handling problem arises when we need to make additions or deletions to existing records that are maintained in a specific order. This is best illustrated by considering the alphabetical telephone list shown in Figure 14.7. Starting with this initial set of names and telephone numbers, we desire to add new records to the list in the proper alphabetical sequence, and to delete existing records in such a way that the storage for deleted records is eliminated.

Although the insertion or deletion of ordered records can be accomplished using an array of structures, these arrays are not efficient representations for adding or deleting records internal to the array. Arrays are fixed and prespecified in size. Deleting a record from an array creates an empty slot that requires either special marking or a shifting up of all elements below the deleted record to close the empty slot. Similarly, adding a record to the body of an array of structures requires that all elements below the addition be shifted down to make room for the new entry; or the new element could be added to the bottom of the existing array and the array then resorted to restore the proper order of the records. Thus, either adding or deleting records to such a list generally requires that we restructure and rewrite the list—a cumbersome, time-consuming, and inefficient practice.

A linked list provides a convenient method for maintaining a constantly changing list, without the need to continually reorder and restructure the complete list. A **linked list** is simply a set of structures in which each structure contains at least one member whose value is the address of the next logically ordered structure in the list. Rather than requiring each record to be physically stored in

FIGURE 14.7 A Telephone List in Alphabetical Order

Acme, Sam
(201) 898-2392
Dolan, Edith
(213) 682-3104
Lanfrank, John
(415) 718-4581
Mening, Stephen
(914) 382-7070
Zemann, Harold
(718) 219-9912

FIGURE 14.8 Using Pointers to Link Structures

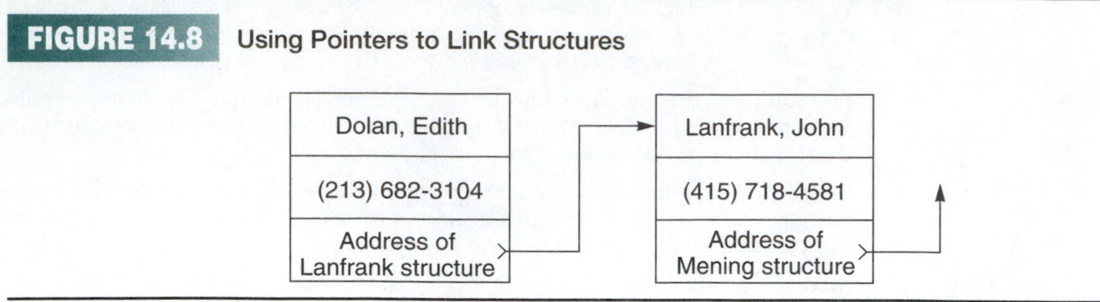

the proper order, each new record is physically added wherever the computer has free space in its storage area. The records are "linked" by including the address of the next record in the record immediately preceding it. From a programming standpoint, the current record being processed contains the address of the next record, no matter where the next record is actually stored.

The concept of a linked list is illustrated in Figure 14.8. Although the actual data for the Lanfrank structure illustrated in the figure may be physically stored anywhere in the computer, the additional member included at the end of the Dolan structure maintains the proper alphabetical order. This member provides the starting address of the location where the Lanfrank record is stored. As you might expect, this member is a pointer.

To see the usefulness of the pointer in the Dolan record of Figure 14.8, let us add a telephone number for June Hagar into the alphabetical list shown in Figure 14.7. The data for June Hagar is stored in a data structure using the same type as that used for the existing records. To ensure that the telephone number for Hagar is correctly displayed after the Dolan telephone number, the address in the Dolan record must be altered to point to the Hagar record, and the address in the Hagar record must be set to point to the Lanfrank record. This is illustrated in Figure 14.9. Notice that the pointer in each structure simply points to the location of the next ordered structure, even if that structure is not physically located in the correct order.

FIGURE 14.9 Adjusting Addresses to Point to Appropriate Records

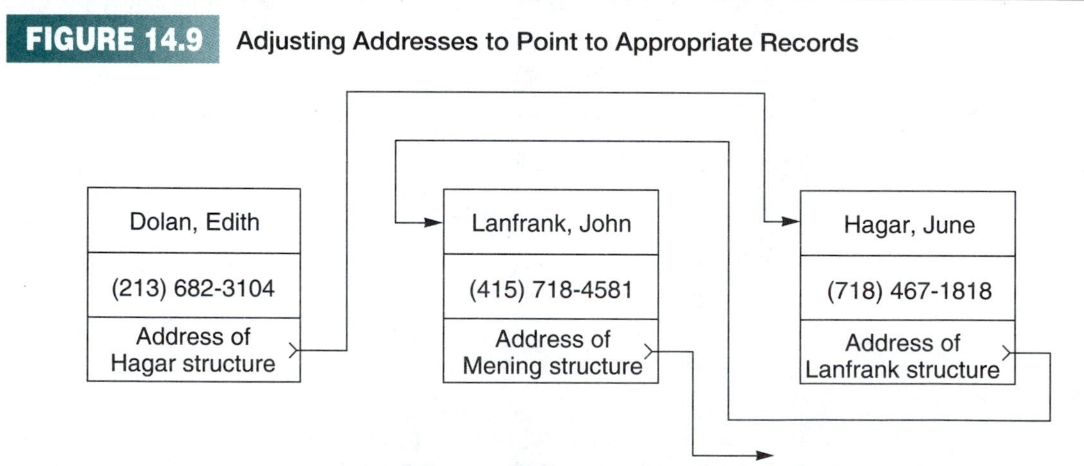

FIGURE 14.10 Use of the Initial and Final Pointer Values

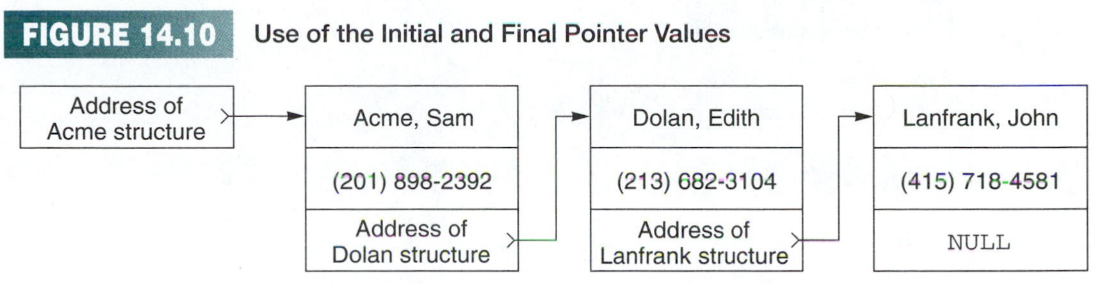

Removal of a structure from the ordered list is the reverse process of adding a record. The actual record is logically removed from the list by simply changing the address in the structure preceding it to point to the structure immediately following the deleted record.

Each structure in a linked list has the same format; however, it is clear that the last record cannot have a valid pointer value that points to another record, because there isn't another record. C++ provides a special pointer value called `NULL` that acts as a sentinel or flag to indicate when the last record has been processed. The `NULL` pointer value, like its end-of-string counterpart, has a numerical value of zero.

Besides an end-of-list sentinel value, a special pointer must also be provided for storing the address of the first structure in the list. Figure 14.10 illustrates the complete set of pointers and structures for a list consisting of three names.

The inclusion of a pointer in a structure should not seem surprising. As we discovered in Section 14.1, a structure can contain any C++ data type. For example, the structure declaration

```
struct Test
{
  int id_num;
  double *pt_pay
};
```

declares a structure type consisting of two members. The first member is an integer variable named `id_num`, and the second variable is a pointer named `pt_pay`, which is a pointer to a double-precision number. Program 14.7 illustrates that the pointer member of a structure is used like any other pointer variable.

FIGURE 14.11 Storing an Address in a Structure Member

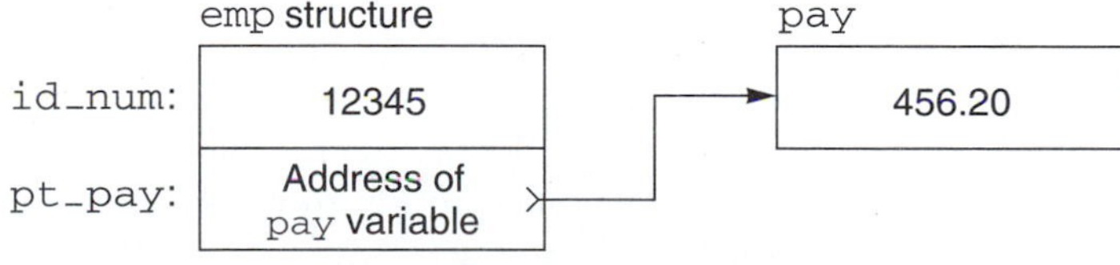

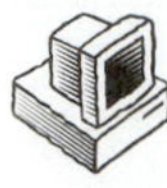

PROGRAM 14.7

```
#include <iostream.h>
#include <iomanip.h>

struct Test
{
  int id_num;
  double *pt_pay;
};

int main()
{
  Test emp;
  double pay = 456.20;

  emp.id_num = 12345;
  emp.pt_pay = &pay;

    // set output formats
  cout << setw(6)
       << setiosflags(ios::fixed)
       << setiosflags(ios::showpoint)
       << setprecision(2);

  cout << "\nEmployee number " << emp.id_num << " was paid $"
       << *emp.pt_pay << endl;

  return 0;
}
```

The output produced by executing Program 14.7 is:

```
Employee number 12345 was paid $456.20
```

Figure 14.11 illustrates the relationship between the members of the `emp` structure defined in Program 14.7 and the variable named `pay`. The value assigned to `emp.id_num` is the number `12345` and the value assigned to `pay` is `456.20`. The address of the `pay` variable is assigned to the structure member `emp.pt_pay`. Because this member has been defined as a pointer to a double-precision number, placing the address of the double-precision variable `pay` in it is a correct use of this member. Finally, because the member operator `.` has a higher precedence than the indirection operator `*`, the expression used in the `cout` stream in Program 14.7 is correct. The expression `*emp.pt_pay` is equivalent to the expression `*(emp.pt_pay)`, which is translated as "the variable whose address is contained in the member `emp.pt_pay`."

Although the pointer defined in Program 14.7 has been used in a rather trivial fashion, the program does illustrate the concept of including a pointer in a structure. This concept can be easily extended to create a linked list of structures suitable for storing the names and telephone numbers listed in Figure 14.7. The following declaration creates a type for such a structure:

```
struct Tele_typ
{
  char name[30];
  char phone_no[15];
  Tele_typ *nextaddr;
};
```

The `Tele_typ` type consists of three members. The first member is an array of 30 characters, suitable for storing names with a maximum of 29 letters and an end-of-string `NULL` marker. The next member is an array of 15 characters, suitable for

PROGRAM 14.8

```
#include <iostream.h>

const int MAXNAME = 30;  // maximum no. of characters in a name
const int MAXTEL = 15;   // maximum no. of characters in a telephone number

struct Tele_typ
{
  char name[MAXNAME];
  char phone_no[MAXTEL];
  Tele_typ *nextaddr;
};

int main()
{
  Tele_typ t1 = {"Acme, Sam","(201) 898-2392"};
  Tele_typ t2 = {"Dolan, Edith","(213) 682-3104"};
  Tele_typ t3 = {"Lanfrank, John","(415) 718-4581"};
  Tele_typ *first;     // create a pointer to a structure

  first = &t1;         // store t1's address in first
  t1.nextaddr = &t2;   // store t2's address in t1.nextaddr
  t2.nextaddr = &t3;   // store t3's address in t2.nextaddr
  t3.nextaddr = NULL;  // store a NULL address in t3.nextaddr

  cout << '\n' << first->name
       << '\n' << t1.nextaddr->name
       << '\n' << t2.nextaddr->name
       << endl;

  return 0;
}
```

storing telephone numbers with their respective area codes. The last member is a pointer suitable for storing the address of a structure of the `Tele_typ` type.

Program 14.8 illustrates the use of the `Tele_typ` type by specifically defining three structures having this form. The three structures are named `t1`, `t2`, and `t3`, respectively, and the name and telephone members of each of these structures are initialized when the structures are defined, using the data listed in Figure 14.7.

The output produced by executing Program 14.8 is:

```
Acme, Sam
Dolan, Edith
Lanfrank, John
```

Program 14.8 demonstrates the use of pointers to access successive structure members. As illustrated in Figure 14.12, each structure contains the address of the next structure in the list.

FIGURE 14.12 The Relationship Between Structures in Program 14.8

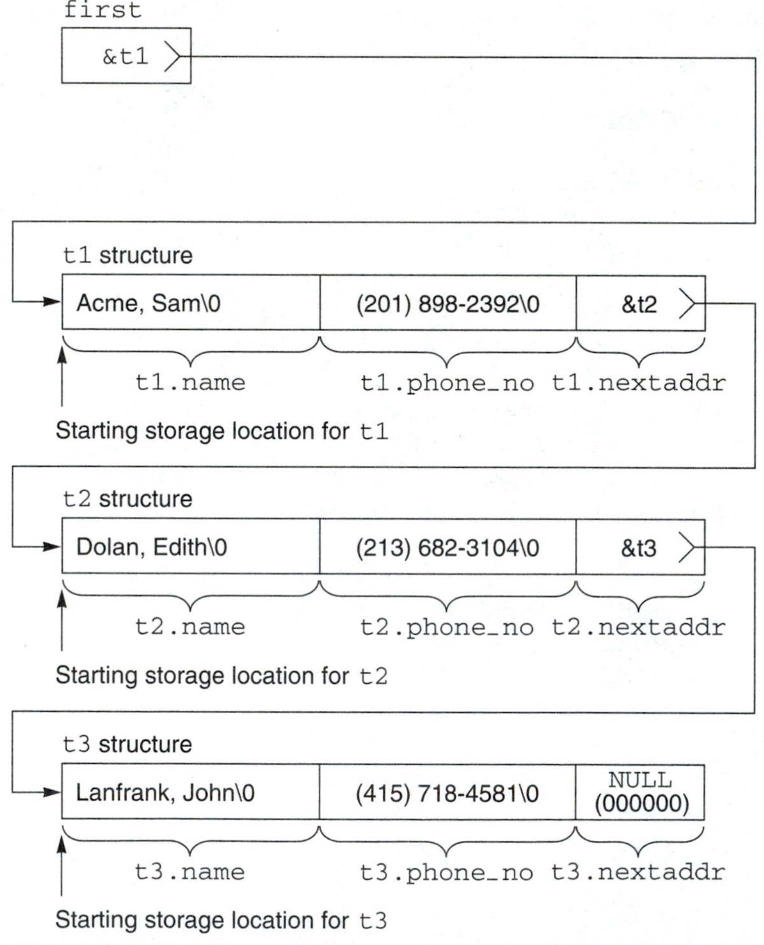

The initialization of the names and telephone numbers for each of the structures defined in Program 14.8 is straightforward. Although each structure consists of three members, only the first two members of each structure are initialized. Because both of these members are arrays of characters, they can be initialized with strings. The remaining member of each structure is a pointer. To create a linked list, each structure pointer must be assigned the address of the next structure in the list.

The four assignment statements in Program 14.8 perform the correct assignments. The expression `first = &t1` stores the address of the first structure in the list in the pointer variable named `first`. The expression `t1.nextaddr = &t2` stores the starting address of the `t2` structure into the pointer member of the `t1` structure. Similarly, the expression `t2.nextaddr = &t3` stores the starting address of the `t3` structure into the pointer member of the `t2` structure. To end the list, the value of the `NULL` pointer, which is zero, is stored into the pointer member of the `t3` structure.

Once values have been assigned to each structure member and correct addresses have been stored in the appropriate pointers, the addresses in the pointers are used to access each structure's name member. For example, the expression `t1.nextaddr->name` refers to the `name` member of the structure whose address is in the `nextaddr` member of the `t1` structure. The member operator `.` and the structure pointer operator `->` have equal precedence, and are evaluated from left to right. Thus, the expression `t1.nextaddr->name` is evaluated as `(t1.nextaddr)->name`. Since `t1.nextaddr` contains the address of the `t2` structure, the proper name is accessed.

The expression `t1.nextaddr->name` can, of course, be replaced by the equivalent expression `(*t1.nextaddr).name`, which uses the more conventional indirection operator. This expression also refers to "the name member of the variable whose address is in `t1.nextaddr`."

The addresses in a linked list of structures can be used to loop through the complete list. As each structure is accessed, it can be either examined to select a specific value or used to print a complete list. For example, the `display()` function in Program 14.9 illustrates the use of a `while` loop, which uses the address in each structure's pointer member to cycle through the list and successively display data stored in each structure.

The output produced by Program 14.9 is:

```
Acme, Sam       (201) 898-2392
Dolan, Edith    (213) 682-3104
Lanfrank, John  (415) 718-4581
```

The important concept illustrated by Program 14.9 is the use of the address in one structure to access members of the next structure in the list. When the `display()` function is called, it is passed the value stored in the variable named `first`. Since `first` is a pointer variable, the actual value passed is an address (the address of the `t1` structure). The `display()` function accepts the passed value in the parameter named `contents`. To store the passed address correctly, `contents` is declared as a pointer to a structure of the `Tele_typ` type. Within `display()`, a `while` loop is used to cycle through the linked structures, starting with the structure whose address is in `contents`. The condition tested in the `while` statement compares the value in `contents`, which is an address, to the `NULL` value. For each valid address the name and phone number members of the

PROGRAM 14.9

```
#include <iostream.h>
#include <iomanip.h>

const int MAXNAME = 20; // maximum no. of characters in a name
const int MAXTEL = 15;  // maximum no. of characters in a telephone number

struct Tele_typ
{
  char name[MAXNAME];
  char phone_no[MAXTEL];
  Tele_typ *nextaddr;
};

void display(Tele_typ *);        // function prototype

int main()
{
  Tele_typ t1 = {"Acme, Sam","(201) 898-2392"};
  Tele_typ t2 = {"Dolan, Edith","(213) 682-3104"};
  Tele_typ t3 = {"Lanfrank, John","(415) 718-4581"};
  Tele_typ *first;    // create a pointer to a structure

  first = &t1;         // store t1's address in first
  t1.nextaddr = &t2;  // store t2's address in t1.nextaddr
  t2.nextaddr = &t3;  // store t3's address in t2.nextaddr
  t3.nextaddr = NULL; // store the NULL address in t3.nextaddr

  display(first);     // send the address of the first structure

  return 0;
}

void display(Tele_typ *contents) // contents is a pointer to a structure
{                                // of type Tele_typ
  while (contents != NULL)    // display until end of linked list
  {
    cout << '\n' << setiosflags(ios::left)
         << setw(30) << contents->name
         << setw(20) << contents->phone_no ;
    contents = contents->nextaddr;     // get next address
  }
  cout << endl;

  return;
}
```

addressed structure are displayed. The address in `contents` is then updated with the address in the pointer member of the current structure. The address in `contents` is then retested, and the process continues while the address in `contents` is not equal to the `NULL` value. `display()` "knows" nothing about the names of the structures declared in `main()` or even how many structures exist. It simply cycles through the linked list, structure by structure, until it encounters the end-of-list `NULL` address. Since the value of `NULL` is zero, the tested condition `contents!= NULL` can be replaced by the equivalent expression `contents`.

A disadvantage of Program 14.9 is that exactly three structures are defined in `main()` by name and storage for them is reserved at compile time. Should a fourth structure be required, the additional structure would have to be declared and the program recompiled. In the next section we show how to have the computer dynamically allocate and release storage for structures at run time, as storage is required. Only when a new structure is to be added to the list, and while the program is running, is storage for the new structure created. Similarly, when a structure is no longer needed and can be deleted from the list, the storage for the deleted record is relinquished and returned to the computer.

Exercises 14.4

1. Modify Program 14.9 to prompt the user for a name. Have the program search the existing list for the entered name. If the name is in the list, display the corresponding phone number; otherwise display this message: `The name is not in the current phone directory.`
2. Write a C++ program containing a linked list of 5 integer numbers. Have the program display the numbers in the list.
3. Using the linked list of structures illustrated in Figure 14.12, write the sequence of steps necessary to delete the record for Edith Dolan from the list.
4. Generalize the description obtained in Exercise 3 to describe the sequence of steps necessary to remove the nth structure from a list of linked structures. The nth structure is preceded by the $(n-1)$st structure and followed by the $(n + 1)$st structure. Make sure to store all pointer values correctly.
5. a. A doubly linked list is a list in which each structure contains a pointer to both the following and previous structures in the list. Define an appropriate type for a doubly linked list of names and telephone numbers.

   b. Using the type defined in Exercise 5a, modify Program 14.9 to list the names and phone numbers in reverse order.

14.5 DYNAMIC DATA STRUCTURE ALLOCATION

We have already encountered the concept of explicitly allocating and deallocating memory space using the new and delete operators (see Section 13.2). For convenience the description of these operators is repeated in Table 14.1. This ability to dynamically allocate memory is especially useful when dealing with a list of structures, because it permits the list to expand as new records are added and contract as records are deleted.

TABLE 14.1

Operator Name	Description
new	Reserves the number of bytes required by the requested data type. Returns the address of the first reserved location or NULL if sufficient memory is not available.
delete	Releases a block of bytes previously reserved. The address of the first reserved location is passed as an argument to the function.

In requesting additional storage space, the user must provide the `new` function with an indication of the amount of storage needed. This is done by requesting enough space for a particular type of data. For example, either of the two expressions `new(int)` or `new int` (the two forms may be used interchangeably) requests enough storage to store an integer number. A request for enough storage for a data structure is made in the same fashion. For example, using the declaration

```
struct Tel_typ
{
  char name[25];
  char phone_no[15];
};
```

the expressions `new Tel_typ` and `new(Tel_typ)` both reserve enough storage for one `Tel_typ` data structure.

In allocating storage dynamically, we have no advance indication as to where the computer system will physically reserve the requested number of bytes, and we have no explicit name to access the newly created storage locations. To provide access to these locations, `new` returns the address of the first location that has been reserved. This address must be assigned to a pointer. The return of an address by `new` is especially useful for creating a linked list of data structures. As each `new` structure is created, the address returned by `new` to the structure can be assigned to a pointer member of the previous structure in the list. Program 14.10 illustrates the use of `new` to create a structure dynamically in response to a user-input request.

A sample session produced by Program 14.10 is:

```
Do you wish to create a new record (respond with y or n): y
Enter a name: Monroe, James
Enter the phone number: (617) 555-1817
The contents of the record just created is:
Name: Monroe, James
Phone Number: (617) 555-1817
```

In reviewing Program 14.10, notice that only two variable declarations are made in `main()`. The variable `key` is declared as a character variable and the variable `rec_point` is declared as being a pointer to a structure of the `Tel_typ` type. Since the declaration for the type `tel_typ` is global, `Tel_typ` can be used within `main()` to define `rec_point` as a pointer to a structure of the `Tel_typ` type.

If a user enters `y` in response to the first prompt in `main()`, a call to `new` is made for the required memory to store the designated structure. Once `rec_point` has been loaded with the proper address, this address can be used to access the newly created structure. The function `populate()` is used to

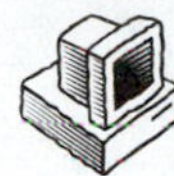

PROGRAM 14.10

```
// a program illustrating dynamic structure allocation
#include <iostream.h>
#include <string.h>

const int MAXNAME = 30; // maximum no. of characters in a name
const int MAXTEL = 15;  // maximum no. of characters in a telephone number

struct Tel_typ
{
  char name[MAXNAME];
  char phone_no[MAXTEL];
};

void populate(Tel_typ *); // function prototype needed by main()
void disp_one(Tel_typ *); // function prototype needed by main()

int main()
{
  char key;
  Tel_typ *rec_point;     // rec_point is a pointer to a
                          // structure of type Tel_typ

  cout << "Do you wish to create a new record (respond with y or n): ";
  key = cin.get();
  if (key == 'y')
  {
    key = cin.get();       // get the Enter key in buffered input
    rec_point = new Tel_typ;
    populate(rec_point);
    disp_one(rec_point);
  }
  else
    cout << "\nNo record has been created.";

  return 0;
}

  // input a name and phone number
void populate(Tel_typ *record) // record is a pointer to a
  {                            // structure of type Tel_typ
    cout << "Enter a name: ";
    cin.getline(record->name,MAXNAME);
    cout << "Enter the phone number: ";
    cin.getline(record->phone_no,MAXTEL);

    return;
  }
  // display the contents of one record
void disp_one(Tel_typ *contents)  // contents is a pointer to a
{                                 // structure of type Tel_typ
  cout << "\nThe contents of the record just created is:"
       << "\nName: " << contents->name
       << "\nPhone Number: " << contents->phone_no << endl;

  return;
}
```

prompt the user for data needed in filling the structure and to store the user-entered data in the correct members of the structure. The argument passed to populate() in main() is the pointer rec_point. Like all passed arguments, the value contained in rec_point is passed to the function. Since the value in rec_point is an address, populate() receives the address of the newly created structure and can directly access the structure members.

Within populate(), the value received by it is stored in the parameter named record. Since the value to be stored in record is the address of a structure, record must be declared as a pointer to a structure. This declaration is provided by the statement Tel_typ *record;. The statements within populate() use the address in record to locate the respective members of the structure.

The disp_one() function in Program 14.10 is used to display the contents of the newly created and populated structure. The address passed to disp_one() is the same address that was passed to populate(). Since this passed value is the address of a structure, the parameter name used to store the address is declared as a pointer to the correct structure type.

Once you understand the mechanism of calling new, you can use this function to construct a linked list of structures. As described in the previous section, the structures used in a linked list must contain at least one pointer member. The address in the pointer member is the starting address of the next structure in the list. Additionally, a pointer must be reserved for the address of the first structure, and the pointer member of the last structure in the list is given a NULL address to indicate that no more members are being pointed to. Program 14.11 illustrates the use of new to construct a linked list of names and phone numbers. The populate() function used in Program 14.11 is the same function used in Program 14.10, and the display() function is the same function used in Program 14.9.

PROGRAM 14.11

```
#include <iostream.h>
#include <iomanip.h>

const int MAXNAME = 30; // maximum no. of characters in a name
const int MAXTEL = 15;  // maximum no. of characters in a telephone number
const int MAXRECS = 3;  // maximum no. of records

struct Tel_typ
{
  char name[MAXNAME];
  char phone_no[MAXTEL];
  Tel_typ *nextaddr;
};

void populate(Tel_typ *); // function prototype needed by main()
void display(Tel_typ *);  // function prototype needed by main()
```

(continued on next page)

(continued from previous page)

```
int main()
{
  int i;
  Tel_typ *list, *current; // two pointers to structures of type Tel_typ

   // get a pointer to the first structure in the list
  list = new Tel_typ;
  current = list;

   // populate the current structure and create the remaining structures
  for(i = 0; i < MAXRECS - 1; i++)
  {
    populate(current);
    current->nextaddr = new Tel_typ;
    current = current->nextaddr;
  }

  populate(current); // populate the last structure
  current->nextaddr = NULL; // set the last address to a NULL address
  cout << "\nThe list consists of the following records:\n";
  display(list); // display the structures

  return 0;
}
  // input a name and phone number
void populate(Tel_typ *record) // record is a pointer to a
{                              // structure of type Tel_typ
  cout << "Enter a name: ";
  cin.getline(record->name,MAXNAME);
  cout << "Enter the phone number: ";
  cin.getline(record->phone_no,MAXTEL);

  return;
}

void display(struct Tel_typ *contents) // contents is a pointer to a
{                                      // structure of type Tel_typ
  while (contents != NULL)  // display till end of linked list
  {
    cout << '\n' << setiosflags(ios::left)
         << setw(30) << contents->name
         << setw(20) << contents->phone_no;
    contents = contents->nextaddr;
  }
  cout << endl;

  return;
}
```

The first time new is called in Program 14.11 it is used to create the first structure in the linked list. As such, the address returned by new is stored in the pointer variable named list. The address in list is then assigned to the pointer named current. This pointer variable is always used by the program to point to the current structure. Since the current structure is the first structure created, the address in the pointer named list is assigned to the pointer named current.

Within main()'s for loop, the name and phone number members of the newly created structure are populated by calling populate() and passing the address of the current structure to the function. Upon return from populate(), the pointer member of the current structure is assigned an address. This address is the address of the next structure in the list, which is obtained from new. The call to new creates the next structure and returns its address into the pointer member of the current structure. This completes the population of the current member. The final statement in the for loop resets the address in the current pointer to the address of the next structure in the list.

After the last structure has been created, the final statements in main() populate this structure, assign a NULL address to the pointer member, and call the display() function to display all the structures in the list. A sample run of Program 14.11 follows:

```
   Enter a name: Acme, Sam
   Enter the phone number: (201) 898-2392
   Enter a name: Dolan, Edith
   Enter the phone number: (213) 682-3104
   Enter a name: Lanfrank, John
   Enter the phone number: (415) 718-4581
The list consists of the following records:

Acme, Sam                      (201) 898-2392
Dolan, Edith                   (213) 682-3104
Lanfrank, John                 (415) 718-4581
```

Just as new dynamically creates storage while a program is executing, the delete function restores a block of storage to the computer while the programming is executing. The only argument required by delete is the starting address of a block of storage that was dynamically allocated. Thus, any address returned by new can subsequently be passed to delete to restore the reserved memory to the computer. delete does not alter the address passed to it, but simply removes the storage referenced by the address.

Exercises 14.5

1. As described in Table 14.1, the new operator returns either the address of the first new storage area allocated or NULL if insufficient storage is available. Modify Program 14.11 to check that a valid address has been returned before a call to populate() is made. Display an appropriate message if sufficient storage is not available.

2. Write a C++ function named remove() that removes an existing structure from the linked list of structures created by Program 14.11. The algorithm for removing a linked structure should follow the sequence developed for removing a structure in Exercise 4 in Section 14.4. The argument passed to remove() should be the address of the structure preceding the record to be removed. In the removal function, make sure that the value of the pointer in the removed structure replaces the value of the pointer member of the preceding structure before the structure is removed.

3. Write a function named `insert()` that inserts a structure into the linked list of structures created in Program 14.11. The algorithm for inserting a structure in a linked list should follow the sequence for inserting a record illustrated in Figure 14.9. The argument passed to `insert()` should be the address of the structure preceding the structure to be inserted. The inserted structure should follow this current structure. The `insert()` function should create a new structure dynamically, call the `populate()` function used in Program 14.11, and adjust all pointer values appropriately.

4. We desire to insert a new structure into the linked list of structures created by Program 14.11. The function developed to do this in Exercise 3 assumed that the address of the preceding structure is known. Write a function called `find_rec()` that returns the address of the structure immediately preceding the point at which the new structure is to be inserted. [*Hint:* `find_rec()` must request the new name as input and compare the entered name to existing names to determine where to place the new name.]

5. Write a C++ function named `modify()` that can be used to modify the name and phone number members of a structure of the type created in Program 14.11. The argument passed to `modify()` should be the address of the structure to be modified. The `modify()` function should first display the existing name and phone number in the selected structure and then request new data for these members.

6. a. Write a C++ program that initially presents a menu of choices for the user. The menu should consist of the following choices:

```
A. Create an initial linked list of names and phone numbers.
B. Insert a new structure into the linked list.
C. Modify an existing structure in the linked list.
D. Delete an existing structure from the list.
E. Exit from the program.
```

Upon the user's selection, the program should execute the appropriate functions to satisfy the request.

b. Why is the original creation of a linked list usually done by one program, and the options to add, modify, or delete a structure in the list provided by a different program?

14.6 FOCUS ON PROBLEM SOLVING

In this section we focus on two problems that use and manipulate data structures. The first problem is concerned with obtaining data for a single record that is to be used in preparing a set of shipping instructions. The second problem addresses the processing of an array of records.

Problem 1: Populating and Processing a Record

In this problem a customer will call in an order for bicycles, giving his or her name, address, number of bicycles desired, and the kind of bicycle. For now, all bicycles on one order must be the same kind (a restriction removed in Exercise 3 at the end of this section). Mountain bikes cost $269.95 each and street bikes $149.50. The total bill is to be calculated for the order. Additionally, based on the user's knowledge of the customer, the customer will be classified as either a good or bad credit risk. Based on the input data, the computer is to prepare shipping instructions listing the customer's name, address, number and type of bikes, and the total amount due. Based on the creditworthiness of the customer, the computer must indicate on the shipping instructions if this is a C.O.D. (cash on delivery) shipment or whether the customer will be billed separately.

FIGURE 14.13 Customer Record Layout

Field No.	Field Contents	Field Type
1	Customer name	Character[50]
2	Customer address	Character[50]
3	Bicycles ordered	Integer
4	Bicycle type	Character—M or S
5	creditworthiness	Character—Y or N
6	Dollar value of order	Float

Analyze the Problem The input and output requirements of this problem are relatively simple. On the input side the items that must be obtained are:

1. customer's name
2. customer's address
3. number of bicycles ordered
4. type of bicycle (mountain or street)
5. creditworthiness of the customer (good or bad).

For output, a set of shipping instructions is to be generated. The instructions must contain the first four input items, the total cost of the order, and the type of billing. The total cost is obtained as the number of bicycles ordered (input item number 2) times the appropriate cost per bicycle, while the type of billing is determined by the creditworthiness of the customer (input item number 5). If the customer is creditworthy, a bill will be sent; otherwise, the order requires cash payment on delivery.

Develop a Solution The input data can be considered to be a record, with the five input items as fields within the record. Additionally, we will add a sixth field to contain the total dollar value of the order. Figure 14.13 illustrates the data types that we will use for this customer record.

A suitable data structure for the record layout of Figure 14.13 is:

```
#define MAXSTRLEN 50
struct Customer
{
  char name[MAXSTRLEN];
  char address[MAXSTRLEN];
  int numbikes;
  char biketype;
  char goodrisk;
  float amount;
};
```

Having developed a suitable layout for the data, the design of the program is rather straightforward. The program will have to request the input data, determine the total dollar value of the order, and then print the shipping instructions. For this problem we will use one function to populate the

FIGURE 14.14 Structure Chart

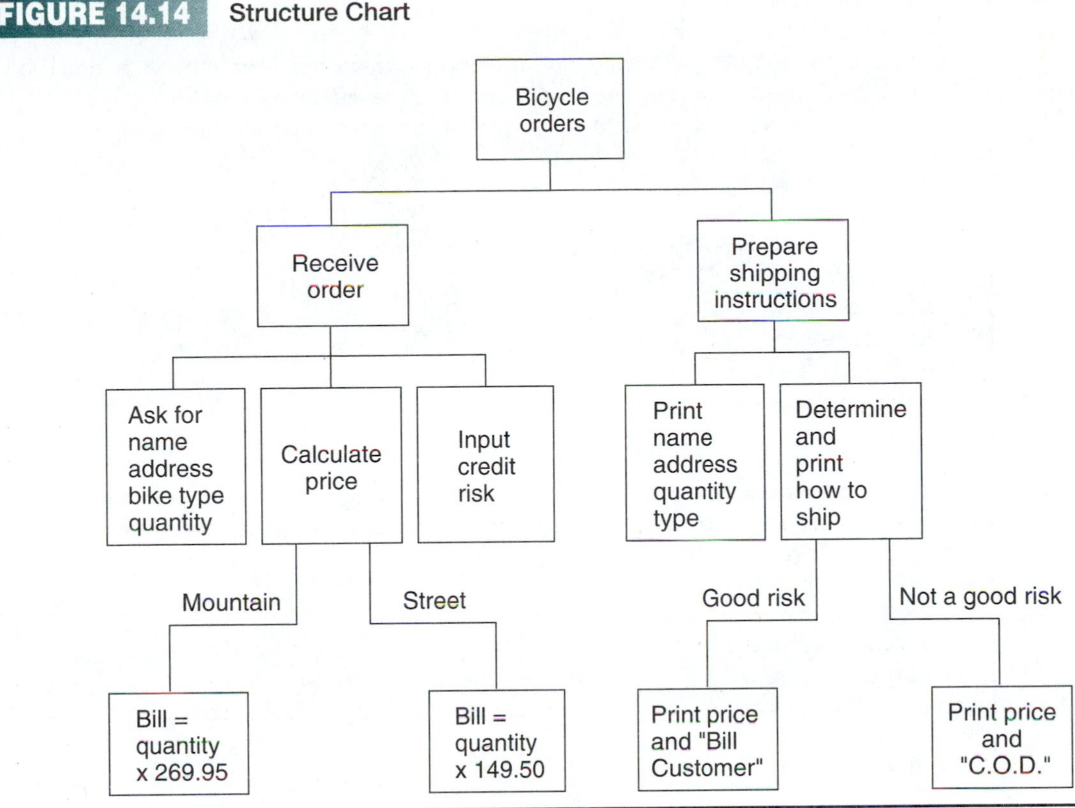

structure and a second function to print the shipping instructions. Figure 14.14 presents a structure chart for this solution. In pseudocode the solution is:

Define the record

Function main
Populate the data using the function recvorder.
Print the shipping instructions using the function shipslip.

Function recvorder
Input data for name, address, number of bicycles, type of bicycle, and credit type.
Calculate dollar value of order.

Function shipslip
Print name, address, number of bicycles, and type of bicycle.
Determine if this is a C.O.D. or separate billable order.
Print the order type and the dollar value of the order.

Code the Solution The C++ code corresponding to our solution is contained in Program 14.12. Notice that the code uses named constants for the maximum string length and the prices of the bicycles. This is in keeping with good programming practice that "magic" numbers are not buried deep within the code where they will be hard to locate. Also notice that the function `recvorder` validates the data entered for bike and credit risk type before storing values in the appropriate data fields.

PROGRAM 14.12

```
#include <iostream.h>
#include <iomanip.h>
#include <ctype.h>

const int MAXSTRLEN = 50;     // maximum character length of a string
const float MPRICE = 269.95;  // price of a mountain bike
const float SPRICE = 149.50;  // price of a street bike

struct Customer
{
  char name[MAXSTRLEN];
  char address[MAXSTRLEN];
  int numbikes;
  char biketype;
  char goodrisk;
  float amount;
};

Customer recvorder(void);  // function prototype needed for main()
void shipslip(Customer);   // function prototype needed for main()

int main()
{
  Customer client;
  client = recvorder();  // enter the order
  shipslip(client);      // prepare shipping instructions

  return 0;
}

 // enter an order
 // precondition: requires MPRICE, which is the price of a mountain bike
 //             : and SPRICE, which is the price of a street bike

Customer recvorder(void) // return a structure of type Customer
{
  Customer record;  // record is local to this function
  char btype = 'N';
  char risk = 'U';
  float price;

  cout << "\nEnter customer information: ";
  cout << "\n Name: ";
  cin.getline(record.name, MAXSTRLEN);
  cout << " Address: ";
  cin.getline(record.address, MAXSTRLEN);
  cout << "\nHow many Bicycles are ordered: ";
  cin >> record.numbikes;
  cout << "Type of Bicycle ordered:";
  while( !(btype == 'M' || btype == 'S') )
  {
```

(continued on next page)

(continued from previous page)

```
    cout << "\n M Mountain";
    cout << "\n S Street";
    cout << "\nChoose one (M or S): ";
    cin >> btype;
    btype = toupper(btype);    // make sure it's in uppercase
  }
      // determine the price of the bike
  if (btype == 'M')
    price = MPRICE;
  else if (btype == 'S')
    price = SPRICE;

  record.amount = record.numbikes * price;
  record.biketype = btype;

  while( !(risk == 'Y' ||  risk == 'N') )
  {
    cout << "\nIs this customer a good risk (Y or N): ";
    cin >> risk;
    risk = toupper(risk);
  }
  record.goodrisk = risk;

  return record;
}
 // prepare a shipping list
void shipslip(Customer record)
{
  cout << "\n        Shipping Instructions:";
  cout << "\nTo: " << record.name;
  cout << "\n    " << record.address;
  cout << "\nShip: " << record.numbikes;
  if (record.biketype == 'M')
    cout << " Mountain Bikes";
  else if (record.biketype == 'S')
    cout << " Street Bikes";

    // set output formats
  cout << setw(6)
       << setiosflags(ios::fixed)
       << setiosflags(ios::showpoint)
       << setprecision(2);

  if (record.goodrisk == 'Y')
    cout << "\nby freight, and bill the customer $"
      << record.amount << endl;
  else
    cout << "\nC.O.D.   Amount due on delivery = $"
      << record.amount << endl;

  return;
}
```

Notice in Program 14.12 that the function `recvorder()` returns a single data structure to `main()`, while `shipslip()` receives a single data structure as its argument. Also notice that within each function, assignments and displayed values are performed for *individual* values in the fields, not for the entire record.

Test and Correct the Program The errors most likely to be encountered in a program that uses records are those related to undefined or incompatible variables. Such errors occur when the user attempts to use a field name alone (such as `numbikes`), without specifying the record to which it belongs (`record.numbikes`). Another common mistake is to attempt to use a record name without specifying the field (such as writing `record` instead of `record.name`).

Testing should include valid data as well as illegal values for `record.biketype` and `record.goodrisk`, and perhaps addresses that exceed 50 characters. Check some results to make sure that the final dollar amount of the bill is calculated correctly. Here is a sample run:

```
 Enter customer information:
 Name:    Jim Watson
 Address: 2 Hopper Lane, Rye NH 86662

How many Bicycles are ordered: 6
Type of Bicycle ordered:
   M Mountain
   S Street
Choose one (M or S): S

Is this customer a good risk (Y or N): Y

        Shipping Instructions:
To: Jim Watson
    2 Hopper Lane, Rye NH 86662
Ship: 6 Street Bikes
by freight, and bill the customer $897.00
```

Problem 2: Sorting and Searching an Array of Records

Arrays of records can be sorted and searched just like an array of any other type of data. An entire record can be assigned, as a single unit, to another record variable of the same type, and when that is done all of the fields within it are moved. This is a distinct advantage of records over parallel arrays, where each field must be moved individually.

Usually, when sorting or searching a database consisting of an array of records, you are interested in a particular field in each record. For example, you may want to sort in order of increasing age or alphabetically by last name. The field sorted on is referred to as the **key field**, and sorting and searching are said to be performed "by record key."

Different fields can be designated as keys at different times for different purposes. Searching is facilitated when the key is unique in each record; that is, when no two records have the same key value. Therefore, it is common for unique values, such as social security number, employee number, or account number, to be designated as the primary key of a record. If a primary key (such as a last name) is not unique, then another field is often designated as a secondary key, and the sorting and searching occur first in order by the primary key, and then by the secondary key.

In this problem we are going to sort an array of employee records by name, and then search for all employees making less than a user-entered hourly rate. For this problem assume that our database consists of the records shown in Figure 14.15.

Analyze the Problem The inputs to this problem consist of the records contained within the database, which are listed in Figure 14.15, and a user-input hourly rate.

The required outputs are the list of employee records, sorted by name, and a listing of all employees having an hourly rate less than the input value.

Develop a Solution The data shown in Figure 14.15 will be stored in an array of data structures. We will use a selection sort (see Section 11.6) to sort the array into alphabetical order by name; thus the name field is our primary key field. The sorted array will then be displayed to the screen.

A linear search through the sorted array of records is then performed, using the rate field as the key field, to find and display all employees having a lower hourly rate than a user-input value. Thus, our program will do the following:

- Define the array of employee records.
- Sort the array by the name field and display the sorted array.
- Prompt the user for an hourly rate and accept the input data.
- Search the sorted array and display all employees making less than the input hourly rate.

Refining this initial algorithm, the following pseudocode expands on how the program will input and process the data.

Function main
Define an array of data structures and populate it.
Sort the array of data structures using the function selsort.
Display the sorted array using the function display.
Prompt the user for an hourly rate and accept the data.
Perform a linear search for records having a lower hourly rate and display the employee number and name for all records found.
Function selsort
Perform a selection sort on the array based on the name field.
Function display
For each record in the array
Display the record's contents.
EndFor
Function linsearch
Search each record and examine its rate field.
If the rate value is less than the input value
Display the record's number and name fields.
EndIf

Code the Solution Program 14.13 illustrates C++ code that performs the steps indicated by our program solution. In examining the code, notice that we have used a named constant for the array size and that we have made all functions

FIGURE 14.15 An Unsorted Array of Employee Records

Employee Number	Employee Name	Hourly Rate
34145	Donaldson, S.	5.56
33623	Bohm, P.	7.54
36203	Gwodz, K.	8.72
32479	Abrams, B.	6.72
35987	Ernst, T.	5.43

general purpose in that they are not restricted for sorting and searching only five records; they can be used for any array size. If you are unfamiliar with the code used in the `selsort()` function, you should review Section 11.6.

PROGRAM 14.13

```
#include <iostream.h>
#include <iomanip.h>
#include <string.h>

const int MAXNAME = 30;    // maximum no. of characters in a name
const int ARRAYSIZE = 5;  // maximum no. of records in the array

struct Pay_rec // construct a global template

{
  long id;
  char name[MAXNAME];
  float rate;
};

  // function prototypes needed by main()
void selsort(Pay_rec [], int); // 1st parameter is an array of records
void display( Pay_rec [], int);
void linsearch(Pay_rec [], int, float);

int main()
{
  Pay_rec employee[ARRAYSIZE] = { { 34145, "Donaldson, S.",  5.56},
                                  { 33623, "Bohm, P.", 7.54},
                                  { 36203, "Gwodz, K.", 8.72 },
                                  { 32479, "Abrams, B.", 6.72 },
                                  { 35987, "Ernst, T.", 5.43 } };
  float cutrate;
```

(continued on next page)

(continued from previous page)

```
  selsort(employee, ARRAYSIZE);
  display(employee, ARRAYSIZE);
  cout << "\nEnter the cutoff pay rate: ";
  cin  >> cutrate;
  linsearch(employee, ARRAYSIZE, cutrate);

  return 0;
}

void selsort(Pay_rec array[], int numel)
{
  int i, j, minidx;
  char minstrng[MAXNAME];
  Pay_rec temp;

  for(i = 0; i < (numel - 1); i++)
  {
    strcpy(minstrng, array[i].name); //assume minimum is first name in list
    minidx = i;
    for(j = i + 1; j < numel; j++)
    {
      if ( strcmp(array[j].name, minstrng) < 0 ) // if we've located a
      {                                         // lower name, capture it
     strcpy(minstrng, array[j].name);
     minidx = j;
      }
    }
    if ( strcmp(minstrng, array[i].name) < 0 ) // check for a new minimum
    {
      temp = array[i];
      array[i] = array[minidx];
      array[minidx] = temp;
    }
  }
}
void linsearch(Pay_rec array[], int numel, float minrate)
{
  int i;
  cout << "\nThe employees making less than this rate are:";
  for (i = 0; i < numel; i++)
    if (array[i].rate < minrate)
      cout << "\n " << array[i].id << "  "
           << setw(20) << setiosflags(ios::left) << array[i].name;
  cout << endl;

  return;
}
```

(continued on next page)

(continued from previous page)

```
void display(struct Pay_rec array[], int numel)
{
  int i;

  cout << "\nThe sorted array of structures is:";
  for (i = 0; i < numel; i++)
    cout << "\n   " << array[i].id << "  "
         << setw(20) << setiosflags(ios::left) << array[i].name
         << setw(8) << setprecision(2) << array[i].rate;
    cout << endl;

  return;
}
```

Test and Correct the Program The sort and search procedures are modifications of those in Section 11.6. Compare these to see what changes have been made to accommodate record arrays.

This is clearly a lengthy program, but debugging can be straightforward if you begin with the main function and then follow through each called function. Substituting stub functions (or just inserting `cout` object streams to indicate when you enter and exit each function) will help you trace the program's flow and locate errors. Here is a sample run:

```
The sorted array of structures is:
  32479    Abrams, B.        6.72
  33623    Bohm, P.          7.54
  34145    Donaldson, S.     5.56
  35987    Ernst, T.         5.43
  36203    Gwodz, K.         8.72

Enter the cutoff pay rate: 7.00

The employees making less than this rate are:
  32479    Abrams, B.
  34145    Donaldson, S.
  35987    Ernst, T.
```

Exercises 14.6

1. Write a C++ program that defines a record for a single item inventory in a store. The record should contain fields for the description, inventory number, storage bin location, quantity on hand, and wholesale cost of the item. A function should allow you to request a new wholesale cost and quantity on hand. If the quantity drops below 10, display a warning message that the stock is low.

2. Develop a program that handles a single record describing the produce in your store. The record should have fields for the produce name (such as apples, oranges, and bananas), quantity on hand, and retail price. As you order or sell each type, the quantity on hand will change. If the amount on hand of any type falls below 30, print a message suggesting that more be ordered. If the amount on hand increases to more than 200, print a message that advertises them for sale at 25% off the regular retail price.

3. Modify Program 14.12 so that a customer may order a variety of kinds of bicycles. (*Hint:* Change the record so that there is a number field for each bicycle type containing how many of that type were ordered. Name these fields `nummtnbikes`, `numstbikes`, and eliminate the `biketype` field.)

4. Construct a data structure that contains all of the short biographical information about yourself that you might think is important, such as name, age, height, hair color, eye color, monthly salary, address, and so on. Write a C program that will allow you to enter data into the record and to change the contents of the fields when necessary.

5. Expand the inventory problem of Exercise 1 to handle an array of up to five item records. Load the inventory array with five records. Have the program give you a report of all of the inventory items and make up order forms for those whose quantity is less than 10 items on hand.

6. Modify Program 14.12 to handle an array of records so that you can take five orders for bicycles during the day and prepare shipping orders for all of them at once at the end of the day.

7. a. Representative information about a group of medical patients is shown in Figure 14.16. Define a data structure that will record this information for five patients.

   b. Using the data structure defined in Exercise 7a, write a C++ program that displays the patient's name, address, total days of care (`Inpatient + Outpatient`), and total charges (`Hospital + Doctor + Pharmacy`). Print bills for all patients 65 or older, with their name, address, and a listing of their hospital, doctor, and pharmacy charges. Then calculate and print on the bill a display of the total charges less a 20% senior-citizen discount.

   Test your program using the following data:

```
Robert Sorensen
1182 25th Street
Remington OR 98762
61        217.90        84.25      63.44        2      6
Rita Martinez
815 Buchanan Ave
Williams AZ 82173
27        582.96       479.63      84.90       29      0
Francine Appleton
513 Perington Blvd
St. Francis MN 21394-3005
68       2123.23       654.00     228.21       32      5
George Thomas
10865 Doughboy St
Los Angeles CA 90413-8273
53        105.49       486.88     241.56        2     45
Gary Allred
226 Mountain Road
Hoover NB 70014-1275
78        409.54       441.32     142.09       31      0
```

FIGURE 14.16 Patient Information for Exercise 6

Name	Address	Age	Amount owed	Days of care
First Last	Street City State Zip code		Hospital Doctor Pharmacy	Inpatient Outpatient
Robert Sorenson	1182 25th Street Remington OR 98762	61	$217.90 84.25 63.44	2 6

14.7 UNIONS[3]

A **union** is a data type that reserves the same area in memory for two or more variables, each of which can be a different data type. A variable that is declared as a union data type can be used to hold a character variable, an integer variable, a double-precision variable, or any other valid C++ data type. Each of these types—but only one at a time—can actually be assigned to the union variable.

The definition of a union has the same form as a structure definition, with the keyword union used in place of the keyword structure. For example, the declaration

```
union
{
  char key;
  int num;
  double price;
} val;
```

creates a union variable named val. If val were a structure it would consist of three individual members. As a union, however, val contains a single member that can be either a character variable named key, an integer variable named num, or a double-precision variable named price. In effect, a union reserves sufficient memory locations to accommodate its largest member's data type. This same set of locations is then referenced by different variable names depending on the data type of the value currently residing in the reserved locations. Each value stored overwrites the previous value, using as many bytes of the reserved memory area as necessary.

Individual union members are referenced using the same notation as structure members. For example, if the val union is currently being used to store a character, the correct variable name to access the stored character is val.key. Similarly, if the union is used to store an integer, the value is accessed by the name val.num, and a double-precision value is accessed by the name val.price. In using union members, it is the programmer's responsibility to ensure that the correct member name is used for the data type currently residing in the union.

Typically a second variable is used to keep track of the current data type stored in the union. For example, the following code could be used to select the appropriate member of val for display. Here the value in the variable u_type determines the currently stored data type in the val union:

```
switch(u_type)
{
  case 'c': cout << val.key;
            break;
  case 'i': cout << val.num;
            break;
  case 'd': cout << val.price;
            break;
  default : cout << "Invalid type in u_type : " << u_type;
}
```

[3] This topic may be omitted on first reading with no loss of subject continuity.

As they are in structures, a data type can be associated with a union. For example, the declaration

```
union Date_time
{
  long int days;
  double time;
};
```

provides a union data type without actually reserving any storage locations. This data type can then be used to define any number of variables. For example, the definition

```
Date_time first, second, *pt;
```

creates a union variable named `first`, a union variable named `second`, and a pointer that can be used to store the address of any union having the form of `Date_time`. Once a pointer to a union has been declared, the same notation used to access structure members can be used to access union members. For example, if the assignment `pt = &first;` is made, then `pt->date` references the date member of the union named `first`.

Unions may themselves be members of structures or arrays, or structures, arrays, and pointers may be members of unions. In each case, the notation used to access a member must be consistent with the nesting employed. For example, in the structure defined by

```
struct
{
  char u_type;
  union
  {
    char *text;
    float rate;
  } u_tax;
} flag;
```

the variable rate is referenced as

```
flag.u_tax.rate
```

Similarly, the first character of the string whose address is stored in the pointer text is referenced as

```
*flag.u_tax.text
```

Exercises 14.7

1. Assume the following definition has been made:

   ```
   union
   {
     float rate;
     double taxes;
     int num;
   } flag;
   ```

   For this union write appropriate `cout` streams to display the various members of the union.

2. Define a union variable named `car` that contains an integer named `year`, an array of 10 characters named `name`, and an array of 10 characters named `model`.

3. Define a union variable named `lang` that would allow a floating-point number to be referenced by both the variable names `interest` and `rate`.
4. Declare a union data type named `Amt` that contains an integer variable named `int_amt`, a double-precision variable named `dbl_amt`, and a pointer to a character named `pt_key`.
5. a. What do you think will be displayed by the following section of code?:

```
union
{
  char ch;
  float btype;
} alt;
alt.ch = 'y';
cout << alt.btype;
```

   b. Include the code presented in Exercise 5a in a program and run the program to verify your answer to Exercise 5a.

14.8 COMMON PROGRAMMING ERRORS

Three common errors are often made when using structures or unions. The first error occurs because structures and unions, as complete entities, cannot be used in relational expressions. For example, even if `Tel_typ` and `Phon_type` are two structures of the same type, the expression `Tel_typ == Phon_typ` is invalid. Individual members of a structure or union can, of course, be compared, if they are of the same data type, using any of C++'s relational operators.

The second common error is really an extension of a pointer error as it relates to structures and unions. Whenever a pointer is used to "point to" either of these data types, or whenever a pointer is itself a member of a structure or a union, take care to use the address in the pointer to access the appropriate data type. Should you be confused about just what is being pointed to, remember: "If in doubt, print it out."

The final error relates specifically to unions. Since a union can store only one of its members at a time, you must be careful to keep track of the currently stored variable. Storing one data type in a union and accessing it by the wrong variable name can result in an error that is particularly troublesome to locate.

14.9 CHAPTER REVIEW

Key Terms

data field
key field
linked list
record
structure
structure member
union

Summary

1. A *structure* allows individual variables to be grouped under a common variable name. Each variable in a structure is accessed by its structure variable name, followed by a period, followed by its individual variable name. Another term for a data structure is a *record*. One form for declaring a structure is:

```
struct
{
  individual member declarations;
} structure_name;
```

2. A data type can be created from a structure using the declaration form

```
struct Data-type
{
  individual member declarations;
};
```

Individual structure variables may then be defined as this Data-type. By convention, the first letter of the Data-type name is always capitalized.

3. Structures are particularly useful as elements of arrays. Used in this manner, each structure becomes one record in a list of records.
4. Complete structures can be used as function arguments, in which case the called function receives a copy of each element in the structure. The address of a structure may also be passed, either as a reference or a pointer, which provides the called function with direct access to the structure.
5. Structure members can be any valid C++ data type, including other structures, unions, arrays, and pointers. When a pointer is included as a structure member a linked list can be created. Such a list uses the pointer in one structure to "point to" (contain the address of) the next logical structure in the list.
6. Unions are declared in the same manner as structures. The definition of a union creates a memory overlay area, with each union member using the same memory storage locations. Thus, only one member of a union can be active at a time.

Exercises

1. Define a record data type and member variables for a business, including fields for the business name, description of the product or services, address, number of employees, and annual revenue.
2. Define a record data type and member variables for a single kind of screw in your parts inventory, with fields for inventory number, screw length, diameter, kind of head (Phillips or standard slot), material (steel, brass, other), and cost.
3. A record type is defined as:

```
struct Inventory
{
  char description[50];
  int prodnum;
  int quantity;
  float price;
};
```

Write the following:

   a. a declaration for an array of 100 records of type Inventory
   b. an assignment of inventory number 4355 to the 83rd Inventory item
   c. a statement that displays the price of the 15th Inventory item.

4. Define an array of records for up to 50 factory employees, in which each record contains fields for name, age, social security number, hourly wage, and years with the company. Write the following:
   a. statements that display the name and number of years with the company for the 25th employee in the array
   b. a loop that, for every employee, adds 1 to the number of years with the company and that adds 50 cents to the hourly wage.
5. a. In two dimensions, a vector is a pair of numbers that represents directed arrows in a plane, as shown by the vectors V1 and V2 in Figure 14.17.

FIGURE 14.17 Graph for Exercise 5

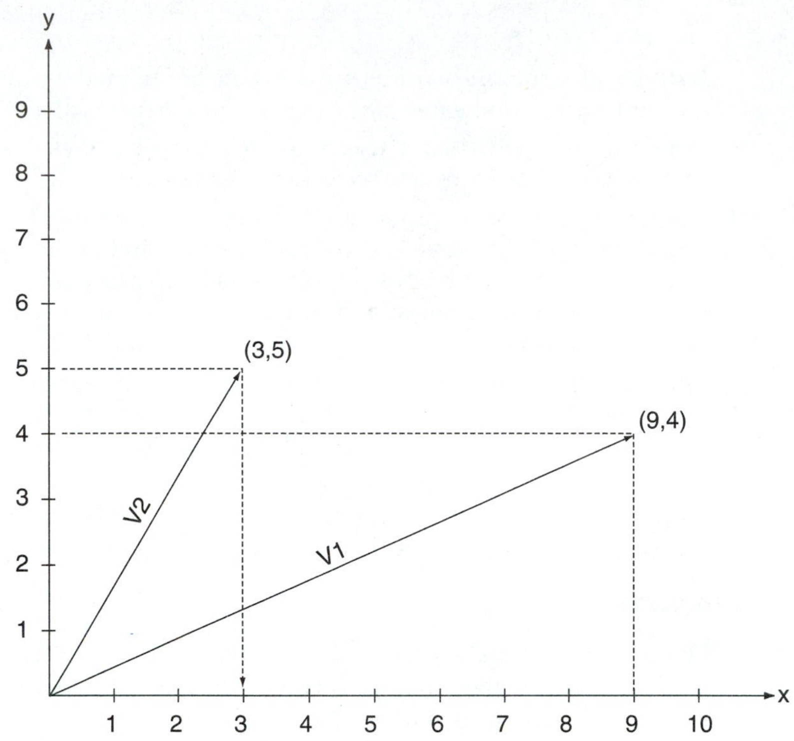

Two-dimensional vectors can be written in the form (*a*,*b*), where *a* and *b* are called the *x* and *y* components of the vector. For example, for the vectors illustrated in Figure 14.17, V1 = (9, 4) and V2 = (3, 5). For vectors, the following operations apply:

If V1 = (a,b) and V2 = (c,d)

V1 + V2 = $(a,b) + (c,d) = (a + c, b + d)$

V1 − V2 = $(a,b) - (c,d) = (a - c, b - d)$

Using this information write a C++ program that defines an array of two vector records, where each record consists of two floating-point components *a* and *b*. Your program should permit a user to enter two vectors, call two functions that return the sum and difference of the entered vectors, and display the results calculated by these functions.

b. In addition to the operations defined in Exercise 5a, two additional vector operations are negation and absolute value. For a vector V1 with components (*a*,*b*) these operations are defined as follows:

```
negation: -V1 = -(a,b) = (-a,-b)
absolute value: |V1| = sqrt(a * a + b * b)
```

Using this information modify the program that you wrote for Exercise 5a to display the negation and absolute values of both vectors input by a user as well as the negation and absolute value of the sum of the two input vectors.

CHAPTER

15 Object-Oriented Stacks and Queues

As we have seen in Sections 13.2 and 14.5, C++ provides a mechanism for dynamically allocating memory that permits memory space to grow or diminish under run-time program control. **Dynamic memory allocation** makes it unnecessary to reserve a fixed amount of memory for a scalar variable, array, or structure in advance. Rather, requests are made for allocating and releasing memory space while the program is running. In this chapter we present two types of data structures that commonly use dynamic memory allocation in their construction: stacks and queues. Additionally, stacks and queues can also be represented using arrays, which do not use dynamic allocation. As an introduction to stacks and queues, their implementation as objects using fixed array sizes are presented first.

15.1 INTRODUCTION TO STACKS

A **stack** is a special type of list in which records can only be added and removed from the top of the list. As such it is a last-in/first-out (**LIFO**) data structure—a structure in which the last item added to the list is the first item that can be removed. An example of this type of operation is a stack of dishes in a cafeteria, where the last dish placed on top of the stack is the first dish removed. Another example is an "in basket" on a desk, where the last paper placed in the basket is typically the first one removed. Stacks provide this simple reversal capability.

Consider Figure 15.1, which illustrates an existing list of three last names. As shown, the top name on this list is Barney. If we now restrict access to the list so that names can only be added and removed from the top of the list, then the list becomes a stack. This requires that we clearly designate which end of the list is the top and

A BIT OF BACKGROUND

Dr. Lukasiewicz and RPN

Dr. Jan Lukasiewicz, born in 1878, studied and taught mathematics at the University of Lvov, in Poland, before becoming a respected professor at the University of Warsaw. He received an appointment in 1919 to the post of Minister of Education in Poland and, with Stanislaw Lesniewski, founded the Warsaw School of Logic.

After World War II, Dr. Lukasiewicz and his wife, Regina, found themselves exiled in Belgium. When he was offered a professorship at the Royal Academy in Dublin, they moved to Ireland, where they remained until his death in 1956.

In 1951 Dr. Lukasiewicz developed a new set of postfix algebraic notation, which was critical in the design of early microprocessors in the 1960s and 1970s.

The actual implementation of postfix algebra was done using stack arithmetic, in which data were pushed on a stack and popped off when an operation needed to be performed. Such stack handling instructions require no address operands and made it possible for very small computers to handle large tasks effectively.

Stack arithmetic, which is based on Dr. Lukasiewicz's work, reverses the more commonly known prefix algebra, and it became known as Reverse Polish Notation (RPN). Pocket calculators developed by the Hewlett-Packard Corporation are especially notable for their use of RPN and have made stack arithmetic the favorite of many scientists and engineers.

which the bottom. Since the name Barney is physically placed above the other names in Figure 15.1, by implication, this is considered the top of the list. To signify this explicitly, however, we have used an arrow to clearly point to the list's top.

Figure 15.2 illustrates how the stack expands and contracts as names are added and deleted. For example, in Figure 15.2b the name Ventura has been added to the top of the initial list shown in Figure 15.2a. By Figure 15.2c a total of two new names have been added and the top of the list has changed accordingly. By now removing the top name, Lanfrank, from the list shown in Figure 15.2c, the stack shrinks to that shown in Figure 15.2d, where Ventura now resides at the top of the stack. As names continue to be removed from the list, as shown in Figures 15.2e and 15.2f, the stack continues to contract.

Although Figure 15.2 is an accurate representation of a list of names, it actually contains additional information that is not provided by a true stack structure. When adding names to a stack or removing them, no record is kept of how many names have been added or deleted or of how many items the stack actually contains at any one time.

FIGURE 15.1 A List of Last Names

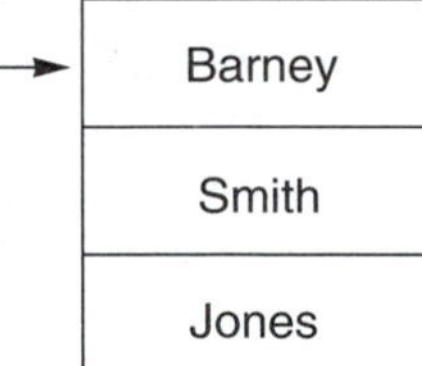

FIGURE 15.2 An Expanding and Contracting Stack of Names

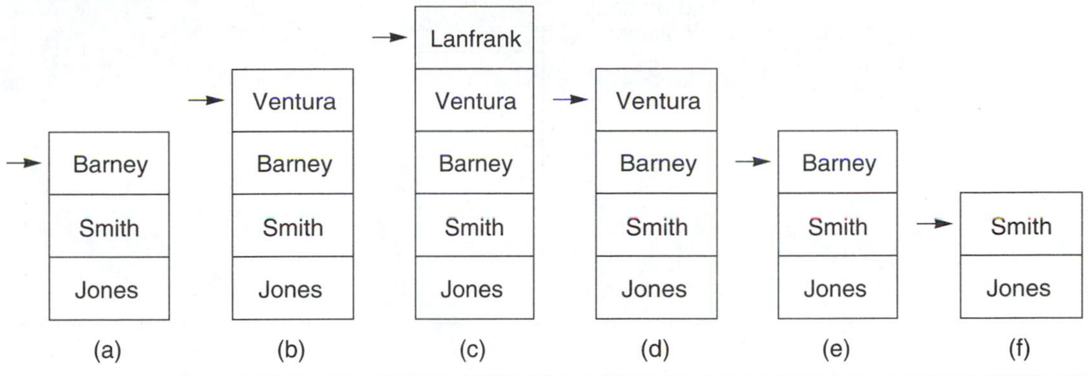

For example, in examining each of the illustrations in Figure 15.2 you can determine how many names are on the list. In a true stack the only item that can be seen and accessed is the top item on the list. To find out how many items the list contains would require continual removal of the top item until no more items exist.

Creating a Stack

Creating a stack requires that the following four components be present:

- a structure for holding items in the list
- a method of designating the current top stack item
- an operation for placing a new item on the stack
- an operation for removing an item from the stack.

By convention, the operation of placing a new item on the top of a stack is called a **push** and the operation of removing an item from a stack is called a **pop.** How each of these operations is actually implemented depends on the structure used to represent a stack. In practice, two data structures are typically used: arrays and dynamically linked lists. In this section, we present an array implementation. The dynamically linked list representation of a stack is presented in Section 15.2.

Array Implementation

Implementing a stack as an array is convenient for simple lists consisting of built-in data types such as `int`s and `char`s. In such an implementation the stack elements are stored as individual array elements and the top of the stack is maintained by an integer variable containing the index value of the currently topmost stack item. For example, consider the list of integers illustrated in Figure 15.3. The top element on the list is the integer 84 and the index value designating this top-of-list element is 5.

The push operation for a stack implemented as an array consists of the following steps:

Increment the index value in the top-of-stack designator.
Place the new element at the index value contained in the top-of-stack designator.

FIGURE 15.3 A Stack of Integers

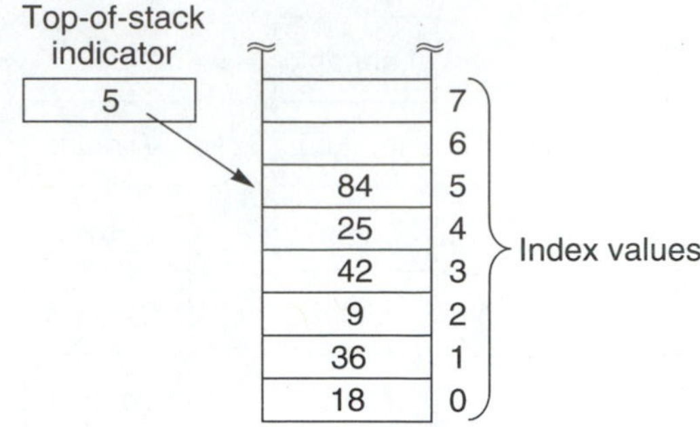

For example, if we push the integer 76 onto the stack illustrated in Figure 15.3, we get the stack shown in Figure 15.4.

Attempting to push an element that results in exceeding the array's size produces an error called **overflow.** To avoid an overflow error, the stack's size should always be checked before a push is attempted. In practice a function with a name such as `isfull()` is used to determine if the stack has reached its maximum defined size using the following logic:

If the stack is full
  Return a value indicating the stack is full.
Else
  Return a value indicating the stack is not full.

For removing an item from a stack the pop operation is implemented as a function that performs the following steps:

Return the top-of-stack element.
Decrement the index value in the top-of-stack designator.

For example, Popping the top element from the stack shown in Figure 15.4 results in the stack shown in Figure 15.3.

FIGURE 15.4 The Stack After a Push

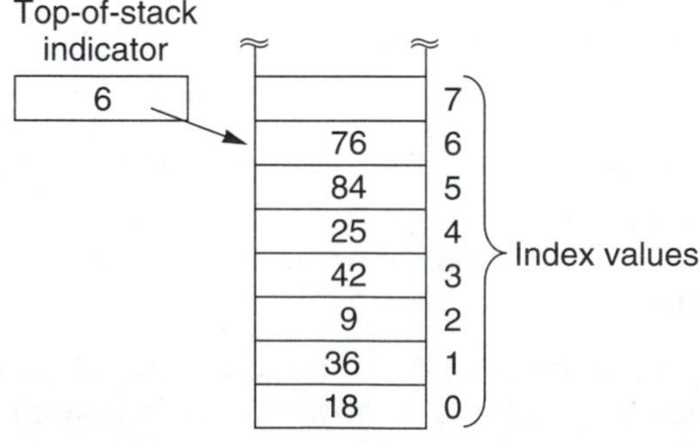

Attempting to pop an element from an empty stack results in an error called **underflow.** To avoid this error, a check should be made that the stack is not empty before a pop operation is performed. In practice a function with a name such as `isempty()` is used to determine whether the stack is empty or not.

As a class each stack can be described as consisting of a top-of-stack position indicator and an array, with member functions to initialize the stack, push, and pop functions, and functions to determine whether the stack is full or empty. As such, a suitable integer stack class declaration is:

```
const int MAXSTACK = 100;
const int TRUE = 1;
const int FALSE = 0;

// class declaration
class Stack
{
  private:
    int top;    // top-of-stack position
    int num[MAXSTACK];
  public:
    Stack(void);    // constructor
    void push(int);
    int pop(void);
    int isempty(void);
    int isfull(void);

};
```

Notice that in this declaration any stack object that is defined to be of type `Stack` will consist of both a top-of-stack position variable, `top`, and an array of 100 integers named `num`.

Let's now consider the specific implementation of each member function, starting with the constructor.

Because the stack is being implemented as an array, it is appropriate to have the constructor initialize the top-of-stack position indicator to an index value of –1. Besides representing an empty array condition, incrementing this value the first time will ensure that the first array position is used for the first stack integer. Thus, the code for the constructor is:

```
Stack()   // constructor
{
  top = -1;  // initialize the top-of-stack position
}
```

The `push()` function implements the pseudocode for a push previously given; that is, when a value is to be pushed onto the stack the index value in the top-of-stack designator is first incremented and this new index value is used to place the element at the top of the stack. The code for this function is:

```
void push(int value)
{
  top++;    // increment the index stored in top
  num[top] = value;  // store the value
}
```

The pop() function must first access the top-of-stack element, decrement the top-of-stack index value, and then return the popped value. Its code is:

```
int pop(void)
{
  int topval;

  topval = num[top];  // retrieve the top element
  top--;              // decrement the index stored in top
  return(topval);
}
```

The isempty() and isfull() functions are also straightforward. The isempty() function simply determines if the array has no stored values, which occurs when the index value equals –1. Similarly, the isfull() function determines if the stack is full, which occurs when the index value equals (MAXSTACK - 1). The code for these two functions is:

```
int isempty(void)
{
  if (top == -1)
    return TRUE;
  else
    return FALSE;
}

int isfull(void)
{
  if (top == MAXSTACK - 1)
    return TRUE;
  else
    return FALSE;
}
```

We will soon see how to write both the isempty() and isfull() functions using a single line of code and implement them as inline functions, but for now we will use the longer but clearer versions listed here.

Program 15.1 incorporates our Stack class within a program. The main() function defines a single stack object named digits and restricts input values to single-digit integers.

Following is a sample run using Program 15.1:

```
Enter as many digits as you wish, one per line
To stop entering digits, enter a number greater than 9
Enter a digit: 1
Enter a digit: 2
Enter a digit: 3
Enter a digit: 4
Enter a digit: 10

The values popped from the stack are:
4
3
2
1
```

PROGRAM 15.1

```
#include <iostream.h>

const int MAXSTACK = 100;
const int TRUE = 1;
const int FALSE = 0;

// class declaration

// preconditions: requires that MAXSTACK, the maximum size of the stack, be defined
//              : requires that TRUE be defined as a nonzero integer
//              : requires that FALSE be defined as 0

class Stack
{
  private:
    int top;    // top-of-stack position
    int num[MAXSTACK];

  public:
    Stack(void);    // constructor
    void push(int);
    int pop(void);
    int isempty(void);
    int isfull(void);

};

// implementation section

Stack::Stack()  // constructor
{
  top = -1;  // initialize the top-of-stack position
}

void Stack::push(int value)
{
  top++;    // increment the index stored in top
  num[top] = value;  // store the value
}

int Stack::pop(void)
{
  int topval;

  topval = num[top];  // retrieve the top element
  top--;              // decrement the index stored in top
  return(topval);
}
```

(continued on next page)

(continued from previous page)

```
int Stack::isempty(void)
{
  if (top == -1)
    return TRUE;
  else
    return FALSE;
}

int Stack::isfull(void)
{
  if (top == MAXSTACK - 1)
    return TRUE;
  else
    return FALSE;
}
```

```
int main()
{
  Stack digits;     // define a Stack named digits
  int newnum;

  cout << "Enter as many digits as you wish, one per line"
       << "\nTo stop entering digits, enter a number greater than 9\n";
  while (1)
  {
    cout << "Enter a digit: ";
    cin >> newnum;
    if (newnum > 9)
      break;
    if (digits.isfull()) // check for overflow
    {
      cout << "\nNo more storage allocation space"
           << "\nThe last digit has not been entered on the stack" << endl;
      break;
    }
    else
      digits.push(newnum); // push value onto the stack
  }

  // pop and display digits from the stack

 cout << "\nThe values popped from the stack are:\n";
 while(!digits.isempty())   // check for underflow
 {
   cout << digits.pop() << endl;
 }

 return 0;
}
```

In reviewing this run notice that the elements have been correctly popped from the stack in the reverse order from which they were pushed.

Before leaving Program 15.1 it is worthwhile to comment on programming style. In each `Stack` member function we have emphasized code clarity over code economy. For example, notice that the two statements used in the `push()` function, namely,

```
top++;    // increment the index stored in top
num[top] = value;   // store the value
```

can be replaced by the single statement

```
num[++top] = value;
```

Although both of these implementations correctly implement the pseudocode description required of the function, the single-line implementation is more compact and terse than the two-line version.

In a similar manner, the `pop()` function can be replaced by the following implementation:

```
int pop(void)
{
  return (num[top--]);
}
```

Again, the coding here, although correct, is much more terse and compact than the implementation used in Program 15.1. Similarly, the four statements defining the body of the `isempty()` function:

```
if (top == -1)
  return TRUE;
else
  return FALSE;
```

can be replaced by the more compact but cryptic statement

```
return (top == -1);
```

Here the value contained within the variable `top` is compared to the value –1. If the comparison is true, the expression itself will have a value of 1, else the expression will be 0. Thus, either a 1 or 0 will be returned by the statement, indicating that the array is empty (return value equals 1, i.e., true) or that the array is not empty (return value is 0, i.e., false). In a similar manner, the `isfull()` function can also be reduced to a one-statement function. Using this more compact coding style and incorporating it within inline functions, a more code-efficient declaration for the `Stack` class presented in Program 15.1 is as follows:

```
const int MAXSTACK = 100;
const int TRUE = 1;
const int FALSE = 0;

// class declaration

// preconditions: requires that MAXSTACK, the maximum size of the
//               : stack, be defined
//               : requires that TRUE be defined as a nonzero integer
//               : requires that FALSE be defined as 0
```

```
class Stack
{
  private:
    int top;    // top-of-stack position
    int num[MAXSTACK];

  public:
    Stack(void)  { top = -1; }    // constructor
    void push(int value) { num[++top] = value; }
    int pop(void) { return (num[top--]); }
    int isempty(void) { return (top == -1); }
    int isfull(void)  { return (top == MAXSTACK - 1); }
};
```

Note that neither class implementation is inherently better. The balance between code clarity and code compactness is always an issue in programming and you will encounter both styles in your programming career. In general, however, if there is any doubt as to the purpose of your code, clarity should always take precedence over compactness. We should also emphasize that cryptic programming simply done for show is always a sign of bad form that marks one as an inexperienced programmer.

Exercises 15.1

1. Modify the class `Stack` to include a stack of characters rather than a stack of integers.
2. Modify Program 15.1 to instantiate three stacks of digits named `digits1`, `digits2`, and `digits3`, respectively. Initialize `digits1` to contain the digits 9, 8, 5, and 2, which is the number 2589 in reverse digit order. Similarly, the `digits2` stack should be initialized to contain the digits 3, 1, 4, and 7, which is the number 7413 in reverse digits order. Calculate and place the sum of these two numbers in `digits3`. This sum should be obtained by popping the respective elements from `digits1` and `digits2` and adding them together with a variable named `carry`, which is initialized to 0. If the sum of the two popped elements and `carry` does not exceed 10 the sum should be pushed onto `digits3` and the carry set to 0; otherwise, the carry should be set to 1 and the units digit of the sum pushed onto the `digits3` stack.
3. Write a C++ program that permits a user to enter a maximum of 100 integers into a stack object. Then have your program do the following:
   a. Reverse the stack contents into a second stack of integers.
   b. Using two additional stacks, reverse the contents in the original stack. Thus, if the stack originally contains the integers 1, 2, 3, and 4, at the end of your program it should contain the integers 4, 3, 2, and 1.
4. Write a C++ program that permits a user to enter a maximum of 50 characters into a stack object. Then have your program sort the stack contents into increasing order. Thus, if the contents of the stack are initially D, E, A, and B, the final contents of the stack will be A, B, D, and E.
5. Stacks can be used efficiently to determine whether the parentheses in an expression are correctly balanced. This means that each left-facing parenthesis is matched by a right-facing parenthesis. For example, consider the string

   ```
   (a + b) / ((x + y) * z)
   ```

   Using a stack, each character in this string, starting from the left, is examined. If the character is a left-facing parenthesis, it is pushed onto the stack. Whenever a right-facing parenthesis is encountered, the top stack element is popped. An unbalanced expression results if a right-facing parenthesis is encountered and the stack is empty or if the stack is not empty when the end of the string is encountered. Using this information write a C++ program that permits the user to type in a string and determines if the string contains a balanced set of parentheses.

6. The program written for Exercise 5 can be expanded to include braces, { }, and brackets, [ ], as well as parentheses delimiters. For example, consider the string

```
{ (a + b) / [(x + y) * z] }
```

To determine if such strings contain balanced pairs of braces, brackets, and parentheses using a stack, each left-facing delimiter is pushed onto a stack of characters starting from the leftmost character. Whenever a right-facing delimiter is encountered the top stack element is popped. An unbalanced expression results if a right-facing delimiter is encountered and the popped element is not its matching left-facing delimiter or if the stack is not empty when the end of the string is encountered. Using this information write a C++ program that permits the user to type in a string and determines if the string contains a balanced set of braces, brackets, or parentheses.

15.2 DYNAMICALLY LINKED STACK IMPLEMENTATION

Although an array implementation for stacks can be used for simple stacks consisting of built-in data types, due to the preallocated array size, there is always one disadvantage in doing so. This is because, for small stacks that underutilize the array, the space is unavailable for any other use, and for large stacks the fixed array size can lead to stack overflow. An alternative to using an array is to construct a stack from a dynamically linked list of records that expands and contracts as required.

Recall from Section 14.4 that each record in a linked list must contain at least one pointer member. As a specific example of such a list, consider Figure 15.5, which illustrates a stack consisting of three linked records. As shown, each record consists of a name member and a pointer member containing the address of the

FIGURE 15.5 A Stack Consisting of Three Records

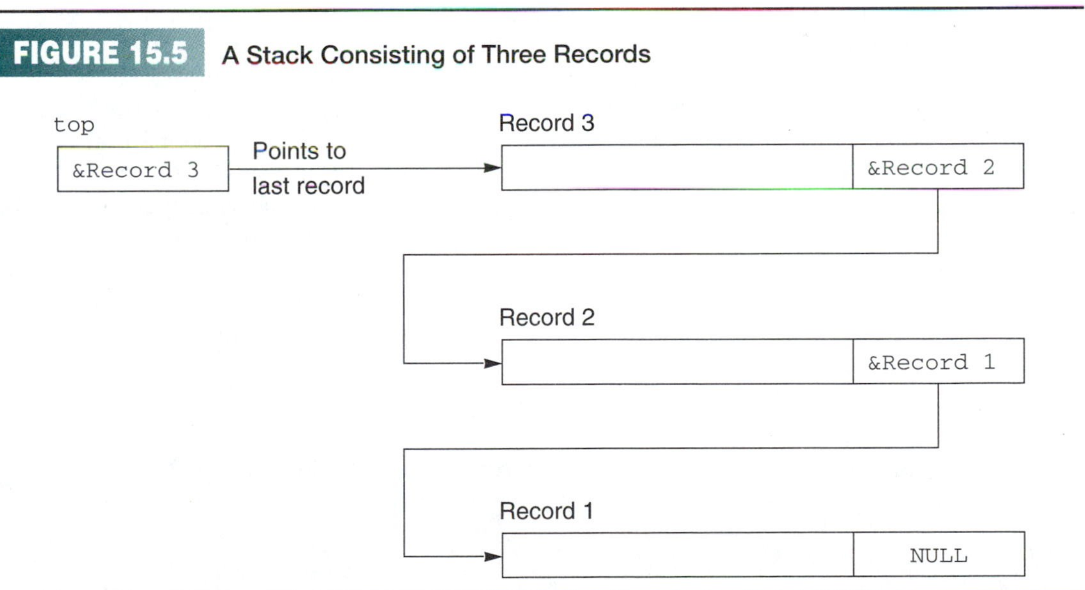

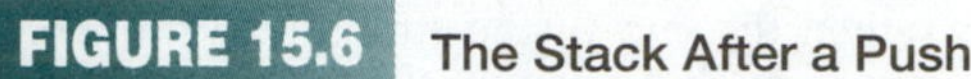

FIGURE 15.6 The Stack After a Push

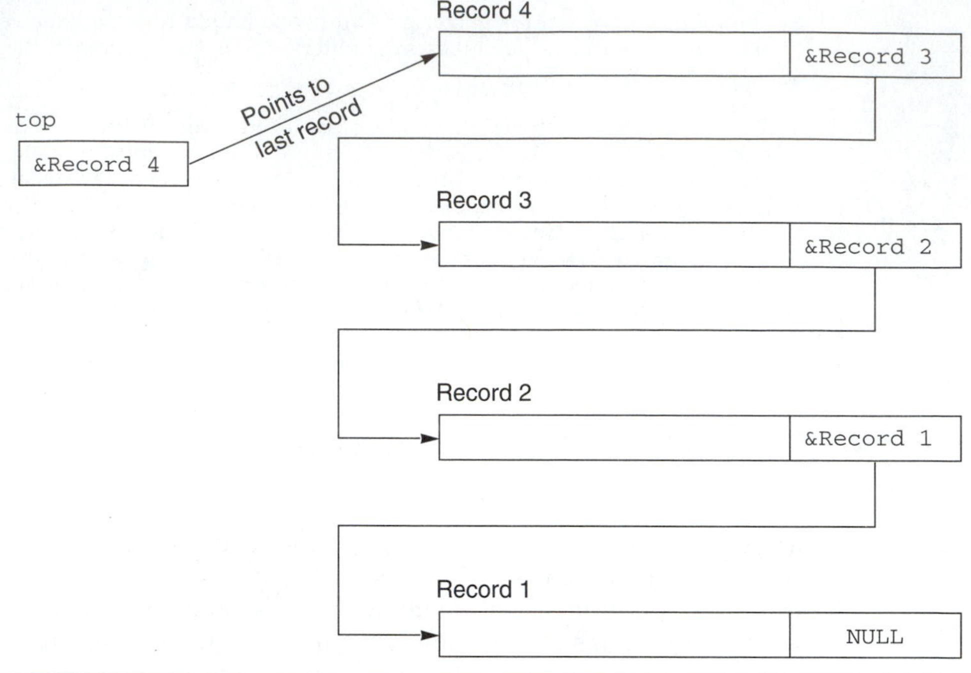

previous record stored on the stack. In addition, there is a separate stack pointer, which we will call the top-of-stack pointer (top), that contains the address of the last record added to the stack.

To use dynamic memory allocation, we create a new record with the `new` operator when information is to be pushed onto the stack and free a record's space using the `delete` operator after a pop operation. For example, if we were to push a new record onto the stack illustrated in Figure 15.5, the resulting stack would contain an additional record and appear as shown in Figure 15.6.

The only record that can be removed from a stack is always the topmost record. Thus, for the stack shown in Figure 15.6, the next record that can be removed is record 4. After this record is removed ("popped"), record 3 can be removed, and so on. Thus, for example, if a pop operation is carried out on the stack illustrated in Figure 15.6, the stack would revert to that shown in Figure 15.5.

As a specific demonstration of a dynamically allocated stack, assume the following class declaration, which can be used for the stack illustrated in Figures 15.5 and 15.6:

```
// class declaration

// precondition: requires that MAXCHARS, the maximum size of the
//             : name attribute, be defined

class Stack
{
```

```
  private:
    struct NameRec
    {
      char name[MAXCHARS];
      NameRec *prioraddr;
    };
    NameRec *top;      // top-of-stack pointer

  public:
    Stack(void);  // constructor
    void push(char *);
    char *pop(void);
    int isempty(void);
};
```

First consider this class's private data members. The first data element is a structure that consists of two fields, a name field consisting of an array of characters and a pointer field. This structure is consistent with all linked lists in that each record has at least one information field, which in this case is a name, and a pointer field to hold the address of the previous stack record. Finally, the last data element is a top-of-stack pointer that will be used to hold the address of the topmost stack record.

Now consider the class's public functions. As listed there is a constructor, which will be used to initialize the top-of-stack pointer. Next there is a `push()` and `pop()` function. The `push()` function will be used to place a string of characters (an array) on the stack, while the `pop()` will effectively return an array of characters. Since passing an array of characters is equivalent to passing the address of the first array character, we have used the declaration `char *` in preference to `char []`. Finally there is an `isempty()` function that will be used to test for an empty stack. Notice that there is no `isfull()` function to test for a full stack. Such a function is not required because we are not constrained to a fixed stack size. As we shall shortly see, the `isfull()` function is effectively replaced by a check that the operating system has sufficient memory for each new record request.

We now present the implementation of each of these member functions. The constructor function is only used to initialize the top to a `NULL`, and is defined simply as

```
Stack(void)  // constructor
{
  top = NULL;
}
```

Dynamically pushing a new name on the stack requires the following algorithm:

PUSH(a name)
  Dynamically create a new record
  If the record was not created
    Print an error message
  Else
    Put the address in the top-of-stack pointer into
      the address field of the new record
    Fill in the name field of the new record
    Put the address of the new record into the top-of-stack
      pointer
  EndIf

The following function performs this operation:

```
void push(char *newname)
{
  NameRec *new_addr;  // a pointer to a NameRec

  new_addr = new (NameRec);
  if (new_addr == NULL)
   {
     cout <<"\n No more storage allocation space"
       << "\n The last name has not been entered on the stack"
       << endl;
   }
   else
   {
     strcpy(new_addr->name, newname);  // store the name
     new_addr->prioraddr = top;        // store the address
     top = new_addr;                   // update top
   }

  return;
}
```

The operation of popping a record off the stack is defined by the algorithm:

pop( )
Store the name field pointed to by the top-of-stack pointer into a name array.
Free the record pointed to by the top-of-stack pointer.
Move the address in the work area address field into the top-of-stack pointer.
Return the name array to the calling function.

The following function definition performs these tasks:

```
char *pop(void) // return a pointer to a name
{
  NameRec *temp_addr;
  char name[MAXCHARS];

  strcpy(name,top->name);  // retrieve the name from top-of-stack
  temp_addr = top->prioraddr;  // retrieve prior address
  delete(top);                 // free record's memory space
  top = temp_addr;         // update the top-of-stack pointer
  return name;
}
```

Finally, the `isempty()` function simply examines the address in the top-of-stack pointer. If this address is a `NULL`, the stack is empty; otherwise, the stack is nonempty. Here is the definition for `isempty()`:

```
int isempty(void)
{
  if (top == NULL)
    return TRUE;
  else
    return FALSE;
}
```

PROGRAM 15.2

```
#include <iostream.h>
#include <string.h>

const int MAXCHARS = 30;
const int TRUE = 1;
const int FALSE = 0;

// class declaration
// preconditions: requires that MAXCHARS, the maximum size of a name, be defined
//              : requires that TRUE be defined as a nonzero integer
//              : requires that FALSE be defined as 0

class Stack
{
  private:
    struct NameRec
    {
      char name[MAXCHARS];
      NameRec *prioraddr;
    };
    NameRec *top;      // top-of-stack pointer
  public:
    Stack(void);  // constructor
    void push(char *);
    char *pop(void);
    int isempty(void);
};

// implementation section
Stack::Stack(void)  // constructor
{
  top = NULL;
}

void Stack::push(char *newname)
{
  NameRec *new_addr;  // a pointer to a NameRec

  new_addr = new (NameRec);
  if (new_addr == NULL)
   {
     cout << "\n No more storage allocation space"
          << "\n The last name has not been entered on the stack"
          << endl;
   }
   else
   {
```

(continued on next page)

(continued from previous page)

```
    strcpy(new_addr->name, newname);  // store the name
    new_addr->prioraddr = top;        // store the address
    top = new_addr;                   // update top
  }

  return;
}

char *Stack::pop(void) // return a pointer to a name
{
  NameRec *temp_addr;
  char name[MAXCHARS];

  strcpy(name,top->name);  // retrieve the name from top-of-stack
  temp_addr = top->prioraddr;  // retrieve prior address
  delete(top);                 // free record's memory space
  top = temp_addr;         // update the top-of-stack pointer
  return name;
}

int Stack::isempty(void)
{
  if (top == NULL)
    return TRUE;
  else
    return FALSE;
}
```

```
int main()
{
 char newname[MAXCHARS];
 Stack namestack;   // define a Stack object

 cout << "Enter as many names as you wish, one per line"
      << "\nTo stop entering names, enter a single x\n";
 while (1)
 {
   cout << "Enter a name: ";
   cin.getline(newname,MAXCHARS);
   if (strcmp(newname,"x") == 0)
     break;
   else
     namestack.push(newname);
 }
```

(continued on next page)

(continued from previous page)

```
  // pop and display names from the stack
  cout << "\nThe names popped from the stack are:\n";
  while (!namestack.isempty())
  {
    strcpy(newname,namestack.pop());
    cout << newname << endl;
  }

  return 0;
}
```

Program 15.2 on p. 799 illustrates use of the `Stack` class within the context of a complete program. In general, this program is straightforward in that only one object of type `Stack` is defined, which initially consists of the top-of-stack pointer and a single record. It is worth noting that this initially created record is never used in the dynamically allocated stack. The first record containing useful data is created by the `push()` function, which first allocates memory for a new record structure, fills in the fields of the newly created record, and then adjusts the address in the top-of-stack pointer. Similarly, each additional record is created, populated, and linked into the `namestack` object. In a similar manner, the `pop()` function removes records from the linked stack and passes the popped name to its calling function. A sample run using Program 15.2 produced the following:

```
Enter as many names as you wish, one per line
To stop entering names, enter a single x
Enter a name: Jane Jones
Enter a name: Bill Smith
Enter a name: Jim Robinson
Enter a name: x

The names popped from the stack are:
Jim Robinson
Bill Smith
Jane Jones
```

Exercises 15.2

1. a. Describe the steps necessary to perform a push operation on a stack.
   b. Describe the steps necessary to perform a pop operation on a stack.
   c. What value should the top-of-stack pointer contain when the stack is empty?
2. Assume that the first record allocated by Program 15.2 is allocated at memory location 100, the second at memory location 150, and the third at memory location 200. Using this information, construct a figure similar to Figure 15.5 showing the values in the `top` and each record after the third name has been pushed onto the stack.
3. State whether a stack structure would be appropriate for each of the following tasks. Indicate why or why not.

A BIT OF BACKGROUND

Stacking the Deque

Stacks and *queues* (pronounced "cues") are two special forms of a more general data structure called a *dequeue (pronounced "decue")* or *deque* (pronounced "deck"). Dequeue stands for *double-ended queue.*

In a deque structure, data can be handled in one of four ways:

1. Insert at the end and remove from the end. This is the last-in/first-out (LIFO) stack structure.
2. Insert at the end and remove from the beginning. This is the first-in/first-out (FIFO) queue structure.
3. Insert at the beginning and remove from the end, which represents a type of inverted FIFO queue.
4. Insert at the beginning and remove from the beginning, which also is a LIFO technique.

Implementation 1 (stack structure) was presented in Section 15.1 and implementation 2 (queue structure) is presented in Section 15.4. Implementations 3 and 4 are sometimes used for keeping track of memory addresses—such as when programming is done in machine language or when records are handled in a file. When a high-level language, such as C, manages the data area automatically, users may not be aware of where the data are being stored or of which type of deque is being applied.

a. A word processor must remember a line of up to 80 characters. Pressing the backspace key deletes the previous character, and pressing CTRL/backspace deletes the entire line. Users must be able to undo deletion operations.

b. Customers must wait one to three months for delivery of their new automobiles. The dealer creates a list that will determine the "fair" order in which customers should get their cars; the list is to be prepared in the order in which customers placed their requests for a new car.

c. You are required to search downward in a pile of magazines to locate the issue for last January. Each magazine was placed on the pile as soon as it was received.

d. A programming team accepts jobs and prioritizes them on the basis of urgency.

e. A line is formed at a bus stop.

4. Modify the class declaration for `Stack` so that both the constructor and `isempty()` functions are written as single-statement inline functions.
5. Write a destructor function for the `Stack` class that traverses each record in the stack and frees them one by one.
6. Write a stack program that accepts a record consisting of an integer identification number and a floating-point hourly pay rate.
7. Add a menu function to Program 15.2 that gives the user a choice of adding a name to the stack, removing a name from the stack, or listing the contents of the stack without removing any records from it.

15.3 INTRODUCTION TO QUEUES

A **queue** (pronounced "cue") is a list in which items are added to one end of the list, called the top, and removed from the other end of the list, called the bottom. The effect of this arrangement is to ensure that items are removed from the list in

FIGURE 15.7 A Queue with Its Pointers

Harriet Wright ← Last name on the queue (`queue_in`)
Jim Robinson
Bill Smith
Jane Jones ← First name on the queue (`queue_out`)

the exact order in which they were entered. This means that the first item placed on the list is the first item to be removed, the second item placed on the list is the second item to be removed, and so on. As such, a queue is a first-in/first-out **(FIFO)** data structure—a structure in which the first item added to the list is the first item that can be removed.

As an example of a queue, consider a waiting list of people who want to purchase season tickets to a professional football team. The first person on the list is to be called for the first set of tickets that becomes available, the second person is to be called for the second available set, and so on. For purposes of illustration assume that the names of the people currently on the list are shown in Figure 15.7. As illustrated, the names have been added in the same fashion as on a stack; that is, as new names are added to the list they have been stacked on top of the existing names. The difference in a queue is in how the names are popped off the list. Clearly the people on this list expect to be serviced in the order in which they were placed on the list—that is, first-in/first-out. Thus, unlike a stack, the most recently added name to the list *is not* the first name removed. Rather, the oldest name still on the list is always the next name removed.

To keep the list in proper order, where new names are added to one end of the list and old names are removed from the other end, it is convenient to use two pointers: one that points to the front of the list for the next person to be serviced, and one that points to the end of the list where new people will be added. The pointer that points to the front of the list where the next name is to be removed will be referred to as the `queue_out` pointer. The second pointer, which points to the last person in the list and indicates where the next person entering the list is to be placed, will be called the `queue_in` pointer. Thus, for the list shown in Figure 15.7, `queue_out` points to Jane Jones and `queue_in` to Harriet Wright. If Jane Jones were now removed from the list and Lou Hazlet and Teresa Filer were added, the queue and its associated position indicators would appear as in Figure 15.8.

FIGURE 15.8 The Updated Queue Pointers

Teresa Filer ← `queue_in`
Lou Hazlet
Harriet Wright
Jim Robinson
Bill Smith ← `queue_out`

Creating a Queue

To create a queue, the following five components must be present:

- a structure for holding items in the list
- a method of designating the current top queue item
- a method of designating the current bottom queue item
- an operation for placing a new item on the queue
- an operation for removing an item from the queue.

The operation of placing a new item on top of the queue is formally referred to as **enqueueing** and the operation of removing an item from a queue is formally referred to as **serving.** As you might expect, enqueueing on a queue is an operation similar to that of pushing on one end of a stack, and serving from a queue is an operation similar to that of popping from the other end of a stack. How each of these operations is actually implemented depends on the structure used to represent a queue. In practice, as with stacks, two data structures can be used: arrays and dynamically linked lists. In this section, we present an array implementation. The dynamically linked list representation of a queue is presented in Section 15.4.

Array Implementation

As we shall see, implementing a queue using an array has certain drawbacks that are removed when a dynamic list approach is taken. Nevertheless, for understanding what a queue is and for simple lists consisting of built-in data types such as `ints` and `chars`, an array implementation is useful. In such an implementation the queue elements are stored as individual array elements, an integer variable is used to designate the currently topmost queue item, and another integer variable is used to designate the bottommost queue item. For example, consider the list of integers illustrated in Figure 15.9. The top element on the list is the integer 84 and the index value designating this top-of-queue element is 5, which we have stored in a variable named `queue_in`.

The enqueue operation for a queue implemented as an array consists of the following steps:

Increment the index value in the top-of-queue designator.
Place the new element at the index value contained in the top-of-queue designator.

FIGURE 15.9 A Queue of Integers

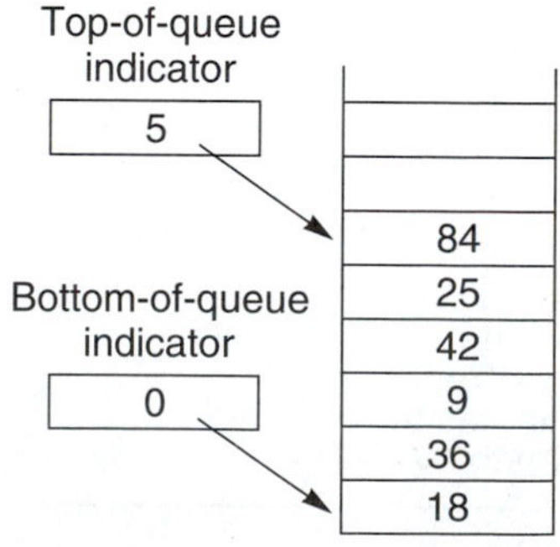

FIGURE 15.10 The Queue After an Enqueue

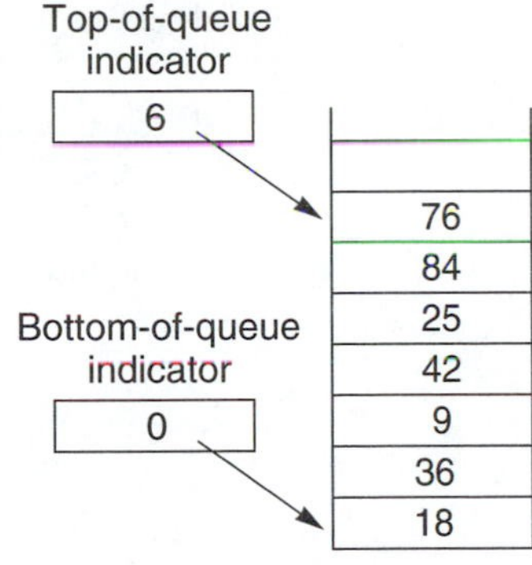

For example, placing the integer 76 onto the queue illustrated in Figure 15.9 results in the queue shown in Figure 15.10.

Attempting to add an element into a full queue produces an error called **overflow.** To avoid an overflow error the queue's size should always be checked before an enqueue is attempted. In practice, a function with a name such as `isfull()` is used to determine if the queue has reached its maximum defined size. As we will see shortly, determining when a queue is full is not as easy as simply seeing if the last array element has been used; it also has an effect on the final serve algorithm. Nevertheless, a simple check would use the following basic logic:

If the queue is full
    Return a value indicating the queue is full
Else
    Return a value indicating the queue is not full.

For removing an item from a queue the serve operation is implemented as a function that performs the following steps:

Increment the index value in the bottom-of-queue designator.
Return the bottom-of-queue element.

For example, using this algorithm for serving the bottom element from the queue shown in Figure 15.10 results in the queue shown in Figure 15.11.

Attempting to serve an element from an empty queue results in an error called **underflow.** To avoid this error, a check should be made that the queue is not empty before a serve is performed. In practice, a function with a name such as `isempty()` is used to determine whether the queue is empty or not.

The `isempty()` function is rather easy to construct once we understand what constitutes an empty queue. Clearly, when the queue is created, both `queue_in` and `queue_out` positions can be set to –1 to indicate an empty queue. As items are placed on the queue the `queue_in` indicator is incremented, and as items are removed the `queue_out` indicator is incremented. For example, consider Figure 15.12, where three integers have been placed on the queue and three integers have been served. As shown, `queue_in` and `queue_out` point to

FIGURE 15.11 The Queue After a Serve

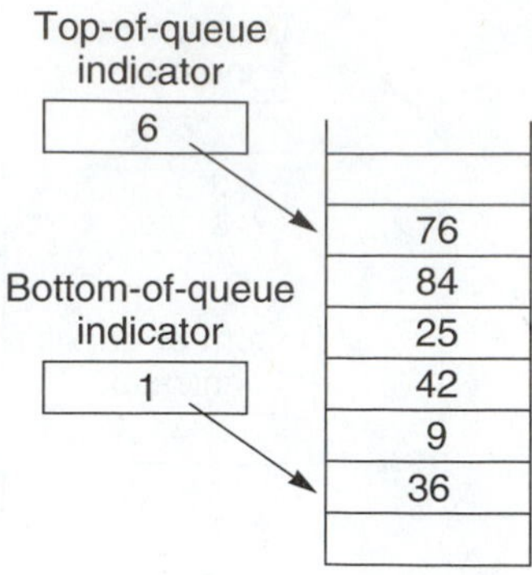

the same element, indicating that the last element enqueued has also been served. Thus, the condition indicating an empty queue is that `queue_out == queue_in`. When this situation has been reached, `queue_in` and `queue_out`, if they are not already equal to –1, should be set to –1 to ensure that the next enqueue operation uses the first array element's position.

It is not as simple to determine when a queue is full. At first glance we might be tempted to say that the queue is full when the topmost array position has been used. This, however, is not correct. As an example, consider the case shown in Figure 15.13, where an array of six integers has been used. As shown, although six integers have been enqueued, which fills the array, three integers have also been served. Thus, although the topmost array element has been filled, two slots are available at the bottom of the array.

The case illustrated in Figure 15.13 can be handled by a variety of methods. Three commonly used solutions are as follows:

1. Shift the entire queue down by one element each time a serve operation is performed.
2. Shift the entire queue down to the bottom of the queue only when the topmost element has been used and there are available bottom slots in the array.
3. Use a circular queue, in which the top of the queue starts refilling from the bottom of the array.

FIGURE 15.12 An Empty Queue (`queue_in == queue_out`)

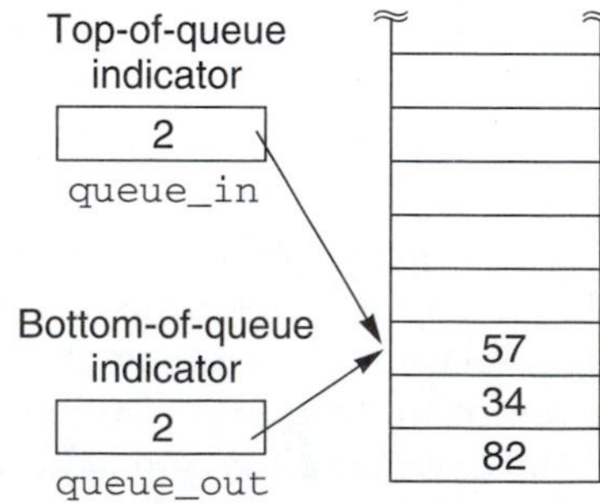

FIGURE 15.13 A Nonfull Queue

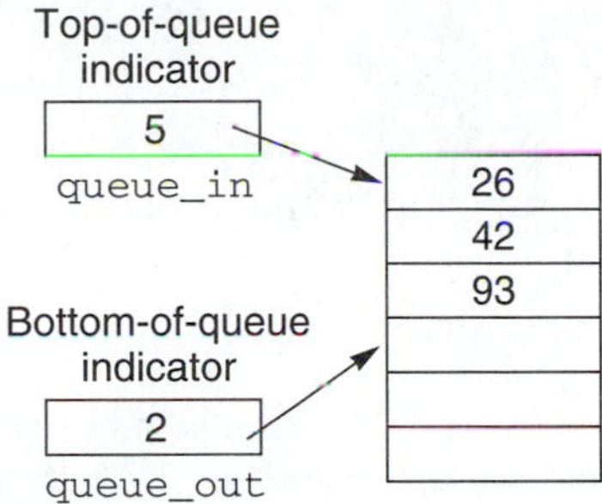

For simplicity, we will adopt the first solution, although it does add the extra processing burden of shifting array elements each time a serve is performed. Additionally, it modifies our serve algorithm by ensuring that the bottommost element in a nonempty queue always resides in array position 0. This eliminates the need for a specific `queue_out` position indicator.

Using this implementation, a `Queue` class can be described as consisting of a `queue_in` position indicator and an array, with member functions to initialize the queue, enqueue, and serve functions, and functions to determine whether the queue is full or empty. As such, a suitable integer queue class declaration is:

```
const int MAXQUEUE = 100;
const int TRUE = 1;
const int FALSE = 0;

// class declaration

// preconditions: requires that MAXQUEUE, the maximum size of
//              : the queue, be defined
//              : requires that TRUE be defined as a nonzero integer
//              : requires that FALSE be defined as 0

class Queue
{
  private:
    int queue_in;    // top-of-queue position
    int num[MAXQUEUE];

  public:
    Queue(void);    // constructor
    void enqueue(int);
    int serve(void);
    int isempty(void);
    int isfull(void);
};
```

In this declaration each defined queue object will consist of two data members: an integer variable named `queue_in` and one integer array to hold the queue.

We now describe the implementation of each member function. The constructor simply consists of initializing the queue_in pointer to –1 and can be coded as:

```
Queue()   // constructor
{
  queue_in = -1;    // initialize the top-of-queue position
}
```

The enqueue() function is coded using the algorithm previously listed and is coded as:

```
void enqueue(int value)
{
  queue_in++;    // increment the index stored in queue_in
  num[queue_in] = value;  // store the value

  return;
}
```

The serve algorithm is slightly more processing intensive because of the need to shift array elements down one position after the position 0 element has been accessed. The code for this function is:

```
int serve(void)
{
  int i, botval;

  botval = num[0];        // retrieve the first array element
  for(i = 0; i < queue_in; ++i)  // shift all elements down
    num[i] = num[i+1];
  queue_in--;             // adjust the queue_in position

  return botval;
}
```

Because our serve algorithm always accesses array element 0, the list is empty whenever queue_in equals –1. Thus, the code for isempty() is:

```
int isempty(void)
{
  if (queue_in == -1)
  {
    return TRUE;
  }
  else
    return FALSE;
}
```

Finally, the code for isfull() must now only check that the upper limits of the array have not been reached. The code for this function is:

```
int isfull(void)
{
  if (queue_in == MAXQUEUE - 1)
    return TRUE;
  else
    return FALSE;
}
```

Program 15.3 incorporates our Queue class within a program that defines a single queue object named digits that is used to store single-digit integers only.

PROGRAM 15.3

```
#include <iostream.h>

const int MAXQUEUE = 100;
const int TRUE = 1;
const int FALSE = 0;

// class declaration

// preconditions: requires that MAXQUEUE, the maximum size of the queue, be defined
//              : requires that TRUE be defined as a nonzero integer
//              : requires that FALSE be defined as 0


class Queue
{
  private:
    int queue_in;    // top-of-queue position
    int num[MAXQUEUE];

  public:
    Queue(void);    // constructor
    void enqueue(int);
    int serve(void);
    int isempty(void);
    int isfull(void);

};

// implementation section

Queue::Queue()  // constructor
{
  queue_in = -1;    // initialize the top-of-queue position
}

void Queue::enqueue(int value)
{
  queue_in++;   // increment the index stored in queue_in
  num[queue_in] = value;  // store the value

  return;
}

int Queue::serve(void)
{
```

(continued on next page)

(continued from previous page)

```
  int i, botval;

  botval = num[0];         // retrieve the first array element
  for(i = 0; i < queue_in; i++)  // shift all elements down
    num[i] = num[i+1];
  queue_in--;

  return botval;
}

int Queue::isempty(void)
{
  if (queue_in == -1)
    return TRUE;
  else
    return FALSE;
}

int Queue::isfull(void)
{
  if (queue_in == MAXQUEUE - 1)
    return TRUE;
  else
    return FALSE;
}
```

```
int main()
{
  Queue digits;     // define a Queue named digits
  int newnum;

  cout << "Enter as many digits as you wish, one per line"
       << "\nTo stop entering digits, enter a number greater than 9\n";
  while (1)
  {
    cout << "Enter a digit: ";
    cin >> newnum;
    if (newnum > 9)
      break;
    if (digits.isfull()) // check for overflow
    {
      cout << "\nNo more storage allocation space"
           << "\nThe last digit has not been entered on the queue"
           << endl;
      break;
    }
    else
      digits.enqueue(newnum); // enqueue value onto the queue
  }
```

(continued on next page)

(continued from previous page)

```
    // serve and display digits from the queue

  cout << "\nThe values served from the queue are:\n";
  while(!digits.isempty())    // check for underflow
  {
    cout << digits.serve() << endl;
  }

  return 0;
}
```

A sample run of Program 15.3 follows:

```
Enter as many digits as you wish, one per line
To stop entering digits, enter a number greater than 9
Enter a digit: 1
Enter a digit: 2
Enter a digit: 3
Enter a digit: 4
Enter a digit: 10

The values served from the queue are:
1
2
3
4
```

In reviewing this run, notice that the elements have been correctly served from the queue in the same order in which they were enqueued.

Exercises 15.3

1. Rewrite the class declaration for `Queue` given in Program 15.3 so that the constructor, `isempty()`, and `isfull()` functions are implemented as single-statement inline functions within the declaration section.
2. Modify the `Queue` class given in Program 15.3 to include a list of characters rather than a stack of integers.
3. Write a C++ program that permits a user to enter a maximum of 50 characters into a queue object. Then have your program sort the queue contents into increasing order. Thus, if the contents of the queue are initially D, E, A, and B, the final contents of the queue will be A, B, D, and E.
4. Rewrite the class declaration for `Queue` given in Program 15.3 so that it contains a `queue_out` integer member. The `serve()` function should not shift any array elements, as is done in Program 15.3, and should only implement the following algorithm:

   Increment the index value in queue_out.
   Return the bottom-of-queue element.

   Additionally, the `isempty()` function should be modified so that when the `queue_in` value equals the `queue_out` value, both values are reset to –1. Finally, modify the `isfull()` function to shift all array elements down to the beginning of the array only when the topmost array position has been used and there are empty positions at the bottom of the array. The `isfull()` function should only report a full queue when `queue_out == (MAXQUEUE - 1)` and `(queue_in == -1)`.

5. What is the advantage of the `isfull()` algorithm described in Exercise 4 over implementing an array shift within `serve()`, as is done in Program 15.3?

15.4 DYNAMICALLY LINKED QUEUE IMPLEMENTATION

As a specific example of a dynamically linked queue, consider Figure 15.14, which illustrates a queue consisting of three linked records. As shown, each record consists of a name member and a pointer member. Unlike a linked stack, where the pointer member points to the previous record in the list, in a linked queue each pointer member points to the next list record. In addition, there are two separate queue pointers, the `queue_in` pointer that contains the address of the last record added to the queue, and the `queue_out` pointer that contains the address of the first record stored on the queue.

To use dynamic memory allocation, we create a new record with the `new` operator when information is to be placed onto the queue and free a record's space using the `delete` operator after a pop operation. For example, if we were to add a new record onto the queue illustrated in Figure 15.14, the resulting queue would appear as shown in Figure 15.15.

The only record that can be removed from a queue is always the earliest record put on the queue. Thus, for the queue shown in Figure 15.15, the next record that can be removed is record 1. After this record is removed ("served"), record 2 can be removed, and so on. If a serve operation is carried out on the queue illustrated in Figure 15.15, the queue would consist of the records and pointers shown in Figure 15.16.

FIGURE 15.14 An Existing Queue

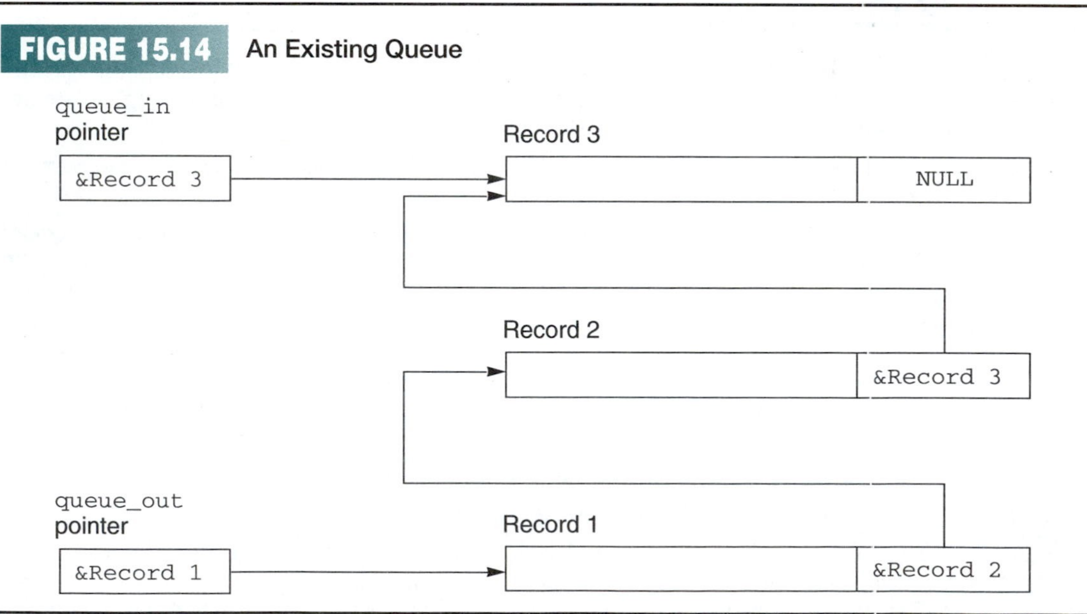

FIGURE 15.15 The Queue After an Enqueue

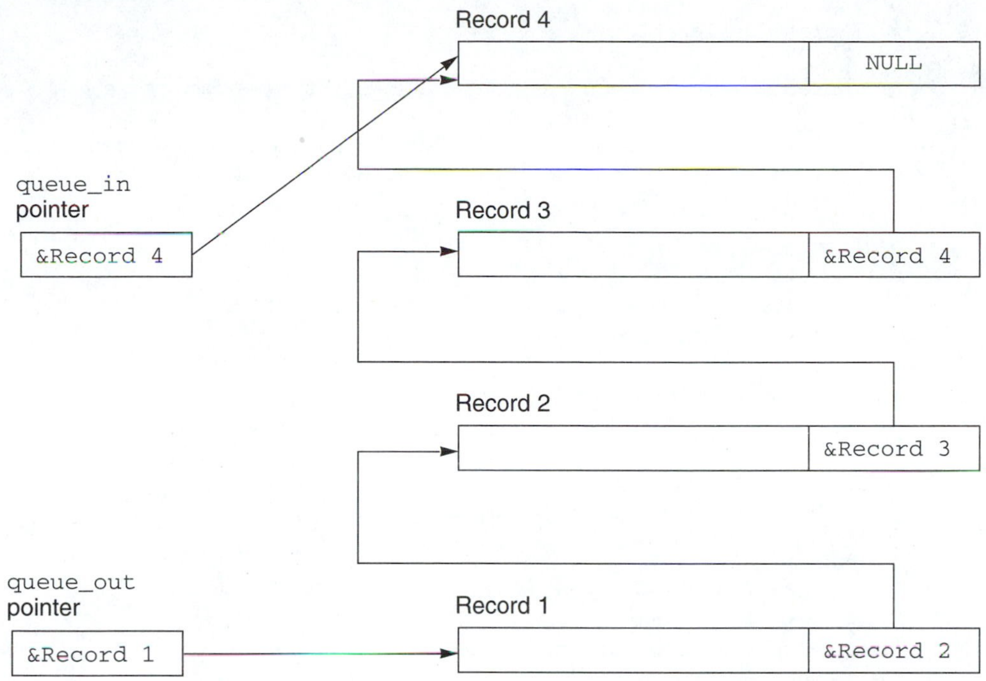

Record 4
NULL
queue_in
pointer
&Record 4
Record 3
&Record 4
Record 2
&Record 3
queue_out
pointer
&Record 1
Record 1
&Record 2

FIGURE 15.16 The Queue After a Serve

Record 4
NULL
queue_in
pointer
&Record 4
Record 3
&Record 4
queue_out
pointer
&Record 2
Record 2
&Record 3

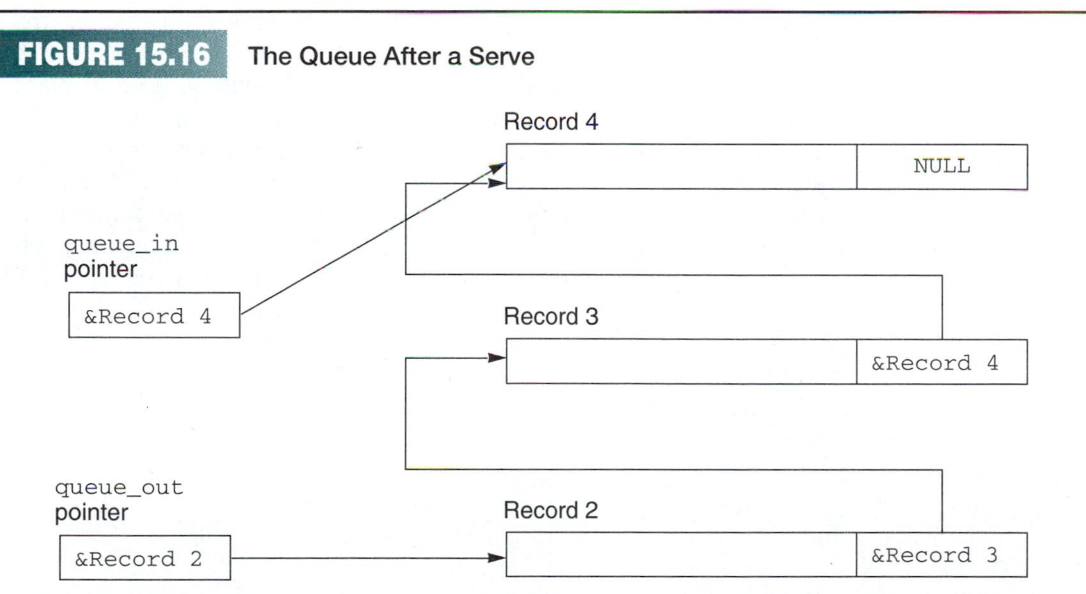

As a specific demonstration of a dynamically allocated queue, assume the following class declaration, which can be used for the queue illustrated in Figures 15.14 to 15.16:

```
// class declaration

// preconditions: requires that MAXCHARS, the maximum size of
//              : a name, be defined
//              : requires that TRUE be defined as a nonzero integer
//              : requires that FALSE be defined as 0

class Queue
{
  private:
    struct NameRec
    {
     char name[MAXCHARS];
     NameRec *nextaddr;
    };
    NameRec *queue_in;  // top-of-queue pointer
    NameRec *queue_out; // bottom-of-queue pointer

  public:
    Queue(void);    // constructor
    void enque(char *);
    char *serve(void);
    int isempty(void);
};
```

First consider this class's private data members. The first data element is a structure that consists of two fields, a name field consisting of an array of characters and a pointer field. This structure is consistent with all linked lists in that each record has at least one information field, which in this case is a name, and a pointer field to hold the address of the next queue record. Finally, the last two data elements are the queue_in and queue_out pointers.

Now consider the class's public functions. As listed there is a constructor, which will be used to initialize the queue_in and queue_out pointers. Next there are the enque() and serve() functions. The enque() function will be used to place a string of characters (an array) on the queue, whereas the serve() will effectively return an array of characters. Since passing an array is equivalent to passing the address of the first array character, we have used the declaration char * in preference to char []. Finally we will use an isempty() function to test for an empty queue. Notice that there is no isfull() function to test for a full queue. Such a function is not required because we are not constrained to a fixed queue size. As we shall see shortly, the isfull() function is effectively replaced by a check that the operating system has sufficient memory for each new record request.

We now present the actual implementation of each of these member functions. The constructor function is only used to initialize the queue_in and queue_out pointers to a NULL, and is defined simply as

```
Queue(void)    // constructor
{
  queue_in = NULL;
  queue_out = NULL;
}
```

Dynamically adding a new record onto an existing queue requires the following algorithm:

Enqueue (add a new name to an existing queue).
  Dynamically create a new record.
  If the record was not created
    Print an error message.
  Else
    Set the address field of the new record to a NULL.
    Fill in the name field of the new record.
    Set the address field of the prior record (which is pointed to by the queue_in pointer) to the address of the newly created record.
    Update the address in the queue_in pointer with the address of the newly created record.
EndIf.

The following function performs this operation:

```
void enque(char *newname)
{
  NameRec *new_addr;  // a pointer to a NameRec

  new_addr = new (NameRec);
  if (new_addr == NULL)
  {
    cout << "\No more storage allocation space"
      << "\nThe last name has not been entered on the queue"
      << endl;
  }
  else
  {
    strcpy(new_addr->name, newname);    // store the name
    new_addr->nextaddr = NULL;          // set the address to NULL
       // empty queue checks
    if(queue_in != NULL)     // can be replaced by if(!isempty())
      queue_in->nextaddr = new_addr;
    if(queue_out == NULL)    // can be replaced by if(isempty())
       queue_out = new_addr;
    queue_in   = new_addr;
  }

  return;
}
```

Notice the two `if` statements within the `else` block. These statements handle the case where a record is being enqueued onto a new queue that has no existing records.

The operation of serving a record from an existing queue is defined by the algorithm:

Serve (remove a record an existing queue).
  Move the name field pointed to by the queue_out pointer into a temporary name array.
  Move the address field pointed to by the queue_out pointer into a temporary pointer variable.
  Free the record pointed to by the queue_out pointer.
  Move the address in the temporary pointer variable into the queue_out pointer.
  Return the address of the temporary name array.

A function definition follows that performs these tasks:

```
char *serve(void)
{
  NameRec *temp_addr;
  char name[MAXCHARS];

  strcpy(name, queue_out->name);  // retrieve the name from queue bottom
  temp_addr = queue_out->nextaddr;  // retrieve next address
  delete(queue_out);                // free record's memory space
  queue_out = temp_addr;         // update the bottom-of-queue pointer
  return name;
}
```

Finally, the isempty() function simply examines the address in the queue_out pointer. If this address is a NULL, the stack is empty; otherwise, the stack is nonempty. Here is the definition for isempty();

```
int isempty(void)
{
  if (queue_out == NULL)
    return TRUE;
  else
    return FALSE;
}
```

PROGRAM 15.4

```
#include <iostream.h>
#include <string.h>

const int MAXCHARS = 30;
const int TRUE = 1;
const int FALSE = 0;

// class declaration

// preconditions: requires that MAXCHARS, the maximum size of a name, be defined
//              : requires that TRUE be defined as a nonzero integer
//              : requires that FALSE be defined as 0


class Queue
{
  private:
    struct NameRec
    {
        char name[MAXCHARS];
        NameRec *nextaddr;
    };
    NameRec *queue_in;  // top-of-queue pointer
    NameRec *queue_out; // bottom-of-queue pointer
```

(continued on next page)

(continued from previous page)

```
  public:
    Queue(void);    // constructor
    void enque(char *);
    char *serve(void);
    int isempty(void);
};

// implementation section

Queue::Queue(void)    // constructor
{
  queue_in = NULL;
  queue_out = NULL;
}

void Queue::enque(char *newname)
{
  NameRec *new_addr;  // a pointer to a NameRec

  new_addr = new (NameRec);
  if (new_addr == NULL)
  {
    cout << "\No more storage allocation space"
         << "\nThe last name has not been entered on the queue"
         << endl;
  }
  else
  {
    strcpy(new_addr->name, newname);   // store the name
    new_addr->nextaddr = NULL;         // set the address to NULL
       // empty queue checks
    if(queue_in != NULL)     // can be replaced by if(!isempty())
      queue_in->nextaddr = new_addr;
    if (queue_out == NULL)    // can be replaced by if(isempty())
       queue_out = new_addr;
    queue_in  = new_addr;
  }

  return;
}

char *Queue::serve(void)
{
  NameRec *temp_addr;
  char name[MAXCHARS];
```

(continued on next page)

(continued from previous page)

```
  strcpy(name, queue_out->name);  // retrieve the name from queue bottom
  temp_addr = queue_out->nextaddr;  // retrieve next address
  delete(queue_out);                // free record's memory space
  queue_out = temp_addr;          // update the bottom-of-queue pointer
  return name;
}

int Queue::isempty(void)
{
  if (queue_out == NULL)
    return TRUE;
  else
    return FALSE;
}
```

```
int main()
{
  char newname[MAXCHARS];
  Queue namequeue;    // define a Queue object

  cout << "Enter as many names as you wish, one per line"
       << "\nTo stop entering names, enter a single x\n";
  while (1)
  {
    cout << "Enter a name: ";
    cin.getline(newname,MAXCHARS);
    if (strcmp(newname,"x") == 0)
      break;
    else
      namequeue.enque(newname);
  }

    // serve and display names from the queue
  cout << "\nThe names served from the queue are:\n";
  while(!namequeue.isempty())   // display till end of queue
  {
    strcpy(newname, namequeue.serve());
    cout << newname << endl;
  }

  return 0;
}
```

Program 15.4 illustrates using the `Queue` class within the context of a complete program. In general, Program 15.4 is straightforward in that only one object of type `Queue` is defined, which initially consists of two pointer members and a single record. It is worth noting that this initially created record is never used in the dynamically allocated queue. The first record containing useful data is created by the `enque()` function, which first allocates memory for a new record

A BIT OF BACKGROUND

Artificial Intelligence

One of the major steps toward creating dynamic machines that "learn" as they work is the development of dynamic data structures.

In 1950, Alan Turing proposed a test in which an expert enters questions at an isolated terminal. Presumably, artificial intelligence (AI) is achieved when the expert cannot discern whether the answers returned to the screen have been produced by a human or by a machine. Although there are problems with the Turing test, its concepts have spawned numerous research efforts.

By the mid-1960s, many artificial intelligence researchers believed the efforts to create "thinking machines" were futile. Today, however, much lively research and development is focused on such topics as dynamic problem solving, computer vision, parallel processing, natural language processing, and speech and pattern recognition—all of which are encompassed within the field of artificial intelligence.

Development of techniques that allow machines to emulate humans have proliferated in recent years with the development of computers that are smaller, faster, more powerful, and less expensive. Most people agree that computers could never replace all human decision making. There is also general agreement that society must remain alert and remain in control of important decisions that require human compassion, ethics, and understanding.

structure, fills in the fields of the newly created record, and then adjusts the `queue_in` and `queue_out` pointer addresses accordingly. Similarly, each additional record is created, populated, and linked into the `namequeue` object. In a similar manner, the `serve()` function removes records from the linked queue and passes the name to its calling function. A sample run using Program 15.4 produced the following:

```
Enter as many names as you wish, one per line
To stop entering names, enter a single x
Enter a name: Jane Jones
Enter a name: Bill Smith
Enter a name: Jim Robinson
Enter a name: x

The names served from the queue are:
Jane Jones
Bill Smith
Jim Robinson
```

Exercises 15.4

1. a. Describe the steps necessary to add a record to an existing queue.
   b. Describe the steps necessary to remove a record from an existing queue.
   c. What value should the `queue_in` and `queue_out` pointers contain when a queue is empty?

2. Assume that the first record allocated by Program 15.4 is allocated at memory location 100, the second at memory location 150, and the third at memory location 200. Using this information, construct a figure similar to Figure 15.14 showing the values in the `top` and each record after the third name has been pushed onto the stack.
3. State whether a queue, a stack, or neither structure would be appropriate for each of the following tasks. Indicate why or why not.
   a. A waiting list of customers to be seated in a restaurant.
   b. A group of student tests waiting to be graded.
   c. An address book listing names and telephone numbers in alphabetical order.
   d. Patients waiting for service in a doctor's office.
4. Modify the class declaration for `Queue` given in Program 15.4 so that both the constructor and `isempty()` functions are written as single-statement inline functions.
5. Write a queue program that accepts a record consisting of an integer identification number and a floating-point hourly pay rate.
6. The two `if` statements contained within the `serve()` function of Program 15.4 contain comments that indicate they can be rewritten using the `isempty()` function. What is the advantage and disadvantage of replacing the tested expressions with the indicated calls to `isempty()`?
7. a. Reverse the placement of the two `if` statements within the `serve()` function in Program 15.4 and verify that it has no effect on the program's operation.
   b. Replace the two `if` statements, as they are placed within Program 15.4, with calls to `isempty()` as indicated in the comments contained within the program. Verify that the program executes properly.
   c. Reverse the placement of the two `if` statements using the calls to `isempty()`. Determine why the program no longer operates correctly.
8. Add a menu function to Program 15.4 that gives the user a choice of adding a name to the queue, removing a name from the queue, or listing the contents of the queue without removing any records from it.

15.5 COMMON PROGRAMMING ERRORS

The five most common programming errors in using dynamically allocated stacks and queues are:

1. Not checking the return pointer provided by `new`. If this operator returns a `NULL` pointer, the user should be notified that the allocation did not take place and the normal program operation must be altered in an appropriate way. You simply cannot assume that all calls to `new` result in the requested allocation of memory space.
2. Not correctly updating all relevant pointer addresses when adding or removing records from dynamically created stacks and queues. Unless extreme care is taken when updating addresses, each of these dynamic data structures can quickly become corrupted.
3. Forgetting to free previously allocated memory space when the space is no longer needed. This is typically only a problem in a large application program that is expected to run continuously and can make many requests for allocated space based on user demand.

4. Not preserving the integrity of the addresses contained in the top-of-stack pointer when dealing with a linked stack and the queue-in and queue-out pointers when dealing with a linked queue. Because each of these pointers locates a starting position in their respective data structures, the complete list will be lost if the starting addresses are incorrect.
5. Related to the previous error is the equally disastrous one of not correctly updating internal record pointers when inserting and removing records from a stack or queue. Once an internal pointer within these linked lists contains an incorrect address, it is almost impossible to locate and reestablish the missing set of records.

15.6 CHAPTER REVIEW

Key Terms

dynamic memory allocation	push
enqueueing	queue
FIFO	serving
LIFO	stack
overflow	underflow
pop	

Summary

1. One of the most important uses of dynamic allocation is that of creating adjustable-size data structures, such as stacks and queues. Both of these data structures, when created dynamically, require a pointer member to store the address of either the next or previous record in the list.
2. A *stack* is a list consisting of records that can only be added and removed from the top of the list. Such a structure is a last-in/first-out (LIFO) list in which the last record added to the list is the first record removed. Stacks can be implemented using arrays or linked lists. When implemented using an array, the order of stack items is maintained by the item's position in the array. However, an additional integer variable is required to indicate the array position of the topmost stack element. When implemented as a linked list, the pointer member of each record in a stack always points to the prior record in the list. Additionally, one pointer variable is always required to contain the address of the current top-of-stack record.
3. A *queue* is a list consisting of records that are added to the top of the list and removed from the bottom of the list. Such a structure is a first-in/first-out (FIFO) list in which records are removed in the order in which they were added. Queues can be implemented using arrays or linked lists. When implemented using an array, the order of queue items is maintained by the item's position in the array. When implemented as a linked list, the pointer member of each record in a queue always points to the next record in the list. Additionally, one pointer is always required to contain the address of the current top-of-queue record and one pointer to contain the current bottom-of-queue record.

Exercises

1. Implement a stack that represents an "in box" on your desk. Each record in the stack should consist of a character field of up to 50 characters and an integer field. The character field is used to describe the task to be done and the integer contains a time stamp of when the job arrived; for example, 950 and 1426 would represent 9:50 A.M. and 2:26 P.M., respectively. Your secretary fills the box with a number of tasks when the mail arrives in the morning and adds work periodically. You work continuously, all day long, to pop the tasks from the stack and take care of them. All tasks must be completed by the end of the day.

2. A group of people have arrived at a bus stop and are lined up in the order indicated:

1. Chaplin	4. Laurel	7. Oliver	10. Garland
2. West	5. Smith	8. Hardy	11. Wayne
3. Taylor	6. Grisby	9. Burton	12. Stewart

   a. Read the names from an input file into a stack and display the order in which they board the bus (*Hint:* Use two stacks.)

   b. Read the names from an input file into a queue and display the order in which they board the bus.

3. Write a single-line word processor. As characters are typed they are to be pushed onto a stack. Some characters have special meanings:

`#`	Erase the previous character (pop it from the stack).
`@`	Kill the entire line (empty the stack).
`?`, `!`, `.`, or `Enter`	Terminate line entry. Move the characters to an array and write the contents of the array to the screen.

4. In recursive functions, the parameters are usually stored on a stack. For example, when the function

```
int factorial(int n)
{
   int fact;

   if (n = 0)
     fact = 1;
   else
     fact = n * Factorial(n - 1);
   return (fact);
}
```

   is called, the successive values of the parameter `n` are stored on a stack. For example, if the initial call were value = factorial(5), then 5 would be pushed on to the stack for `n`. The next call to factorial would push 4, then 3, and so on, until the last parameter value of 0 is pushed. Then the values would be popped one at a time and multiplied by the previous product until the stack is empty.

   Using this information, write a C++ program that performs the same operation as the factorial procedure for a given value of `n`, entered by the user. After each push, the contents of the stack should be displayed. After each pop, the contents of the stack and the value of factorial should be displayed. Once the display indicates proper operation of your function, stop the display and simply have the function return the proper factorial value.

5. Write a queue-handling program that asks each customer for their names as they place orders at a fast food restaurant. Each record in the queue should consist of a name field with a maximum of 20 characters and an integer field, which keeps track of the total number of customers served. The value in the integer field should be automatically provided by the program each time a name is entered. Orders are processed in the same sequence as they are placed. The order taker examines the queue and calls the names when the order is ready. When the queue is empty, print a message telling the staff to take a break.

6. Descriptions of jobs waiting in a computer for the printer are generally kept in a queue. Write a C++ program that keeps track of printing jobs, recorded by user name and anticipated printer time (in seconds) for the job. Add jobs to the queue as printouts are requested, and remove them from the queue as they are serviced. When a user adds a job to the queue, display a message giving an estimate of how long it will be before the job is printed. The estimate is to consist of the sum of all the prior jobs in the queue (*Hint:* Store the accumulated times in a separate variable.)

7. a. On your electronic mail terminal you receive notes to call people. Each message contains the Name and Phone number of the caller as well as a date in the form `month/day/year` and a 24-hour integer clock in the form `hours:minutes` that records the time that the message was received. A `Latest Attempt` field is initially set to 0, indicating that no attempt has yet been made to return the call. For example, a particular record may appear as:

```
Jan Williamson (215)666-7777   8/14/96   17:05   0
```

Write a C++ program that stores these records in a queue as they arrive and feeds them to you, one at a time, on request. If you cannot reach a person when you try to call, place that record at the end of the queue and fill the `Latest Attempt` field with the time you tried to return the call, in the form `DaysLater/hours:min`. Thus, if your last unsuccessful attempt to return Jan Williamson's call was on 8/16/96 at 4:20, the new enqueued record would be

```
Jan Williamson (215)666-7777   8/14/96   17:05   2/16:20
```

   b. Modify the program written for Exercise 7 so that the time and date fields are automatically filled in using system calls to time and date functions provided by your compiler.

Appendixes

APPENDIX

A Operator Precedence Table

Table A.1 presents the symbols, precedence, descriptions, and associativity of C++'s operators. Operators toward the top of the table have a higher precedence than those toward the bottom. Operators within each box have the same precedence and associativity.

TABLE A.1 Summary of C++ Operators

Operator	Description	Associativity
`()`	Function call	Left to right
`[]`	Array element	
`->`	Structure member pointer reference	
`.`	Structure member reference	
`++`	Increment	Right to Left
`--`	Decrement	
`-`	Unary minus	
`!`	Logical negation	
`~`	One's complement	
`(type)`	Type conversion (cast)	
`sizeof`	Storage size	
`&`	Address of	
`*`	Indirection	
`*`	Multiplication	Left to right
`/`	Division	
`%`	Modulus (remainder)	
`+`	Addition	Left to right
`-`	Subtraction	
`<<`	Left shift	Left to right
`>>`	Right shift	
`<`	Less than	Left to right
`<=`	Less than or equal to	
`>`	Greater than	
`>=`	Greater than or equal to	
`==`	Equal to	Left to right
`!=`	Not equal to	
`&`	Bitwise AND	Left to right
`^`	Bitwise exclusive OR	Left to right
`|`	Bitwise inclusive OR	Left to right
`&&`	Logical AND	Left to right
`||`	Logical OR	Left to right
`?:`	Conditional expression	Right to left
`=`	Assignment	Right to left
`+=  -=  *=`	Assignment	
`/=  %=  &=`	Assignment	
`^=  |=`	Assignment	
`<<=  >>=`	Assignment	
`,`	Comma	Left to right

APPENDIX

B ASCII Character Codes

Key(s)	Dec	Oct	Hex	Key	Dec	Oct	Hex	Key	Dec	Oct	Hex
Ctrl 1	0	0	0	+	43	53	2B	V	86	126	56
Ctrl A	1	1	1	’	44	54	2C	W	87	127	57
Ctrl B	2	2	2	–	45	55	2D	X	88	130	58
Ctrl C	3	3	3	.	46	56	2E	Y	89	131	59
Ctrl D	4	4	4	/	47	57	2F	Z	90	132	5A
Ctrl E	5	5	5	0	48	60	30	[	91	133	5B
Ctrl F	6	6	6	1	49	61	31	\	92	134	5C
Ctrl G	7	7	7	2	50	62	32	]	93	135	5D
Ctrl H	8	10	8	3	51	63	33	^	94	136	5E
Ctrl I	9	11	9	4	52	64	34	–	95	137	5F
\n	10	12	A	5	53	65	35	'	96	140	60
Ctrl K	11	13	B	6	54	66	36	a	97	141	61
Ctrl L	12	14	C	7	55	67	37	b	98	142	62
RETURN	13	15	D	8	56	70	38	c	99	143	63
Ctrl N	14	16	E	9	57	71	39	d	100	144	64
Ctrl O	15	17	F	:	58	72	3A	e	101	145	65
Ctrl P	16	20	10	;	59	73	3B	f	102	146	66
Ctrl Q	17	21	11	<	60	74	3C	g	103	147	67
Ctrl R	18	22	12	=	61	75	3D	h	104	150	68
Ctrl S	19	23	13	>	62	76	3E	i	105	151	69
Ctrl T	20	24	14	?	63	77	3F	j	106	152	6A
Ctrl U	21	25	15	@	64	100	40	k	107	153	6B
Ctrl V	22	26	16	A	65	101	41	l	108	154	6C
Ctrl W	23	27	17	B	66	102	42	m	109	155	6D
Ctrl X	24	30	18	C	67	103	43	n	110	156	6E
Ctrl Y	25	31	19	D	68	104	44	o	111	157	6F
Ctrl Z	26	32	1A	E	69	105	45	p	112	160	70
Esc	27	33	1B	F	70	106	46	q	113	161	71
Ctrl <	28	34	1C	G	71	107	47	r	114	162	72
Ctrl /	29	35	1D	H	72	110	48	s	115	163	73
Ctrl =	30	36	1E	I	73	111	49	t	116	164	74
Ctrl –	31	37	1F	J	74	112	4A	u	117	165	75
Space	32	40	20	K	75	113	4B	v	118	166	76
!	33	41	21	L	76	114	4C	w	119	167	77
"	34	42	22	M	77	115	4D	x	120	170	78
#	35	43	23	N	78	116	4E	y	121	171	79
$	36	44	24	O	79	117	4F	z	122	172	7A
%	37	45	25	P	80	120	50	{	123	173	7B
&	38	46	26	Q	81	121	51	|	124	174	7C
'	39	47	27	R	82	122	52	}	125	175	7D
(	40	50	28	S	83	123	53	~	126	176	7E
)	41	51	29	T	84	124	54	del	127	177	7F
*	42	52	2A	U	85	125	55				

APPENDIX

Program Entry, Compilation, and Execution

In this appendix we examine the steps required to enter, compile, and execute compiled versions of C++ programs. These steps are:

1. logging into (and eventually out of) the computer
2. creating and editing the program
3. compiling and linking the program
4. loading and executing the program.

Logging Into and Out Of the Computer

As illustrated in Figure C.1, a computer can be thought of as a self-contained world that is entered by a special set of steps called a *login procedure*. For computers such as IBM personal computers (PCs), and other desk-top computers, the login procedure is as simple as turning on the computer's power switch. Larger multiuser systems,

FIGURE C.1 Viewing a Computer as a Self-Contained World

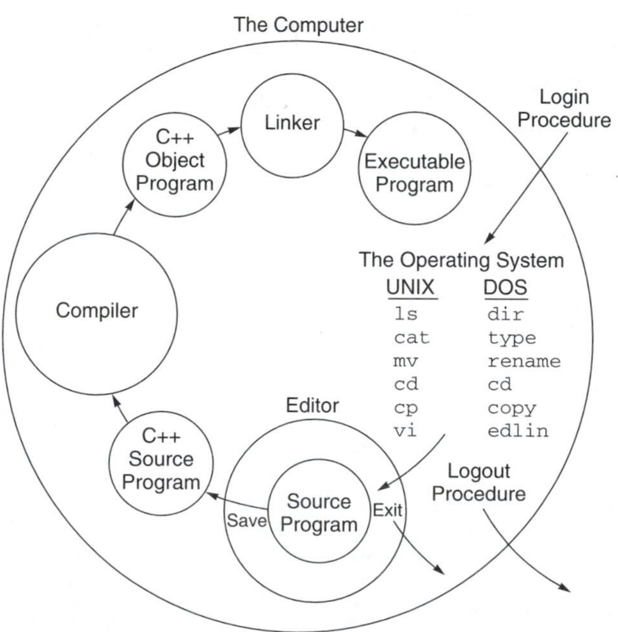

TABLE C.1 Operating System Commands (Fill in for your system)

Task	Command	Example
Log-in procedure		
Log-out procedure		
List a program		
Copy a program		
Delete a program		
Rename a program		

such as DEC VAX computers, typically require a login procedure consisting of turning a terminal on and supplying an account number and password.

Once you have successfully logged in to your computer system you are automatically under the control of a computer program called the operating system (unless the computer is programmed to switch you into a specific application program). The *operating system* is the program that effectively runs the computer. It is used to gain access to the services provided by the computer, which include the programs needed for entering, compiling, and executing a C++ program.

Communicating with the operating system is accomplished either by using a specific set of commands that are recognized by the operating system or by selecting graphical icons presented in a window. Although each computer system type (IBM, Apple, DEC, etc.) has one or more available operating systems, all operating systems provide commands that permit logging on to the system, exiting from the system, creating programs and a means of quickly listing, deleting, copying, and renaming programs.

The specific operating system commands and any additional steps used for exiting from a computer, such as turning the power off, are collectively referred to as the *logout procedure*. Make sure you know the logout procedure for your computer at the time you login to ensure that you can effectively "escape" when you are ready to leave the system. The operating system command for listing a program typically has a name such as `LIST`, `TYPE`, `cat`, or `PRINT`; the command for deleting a program typically has a name such as `DELETE`, `DEL`, `ERASE`, `UNSAVE`, `REMOVE`, or `rm`; the command for copying a program typically has a name such as `COPY`, `COP`, or `cp`; and the operating system command for renaming a program typically has a name such as `RENAME`, `REN`, `RN`, or `mv`. Use Table C.1 to list the specific operating system command names used by your system to perform these tasks.

The commands to list, copy, delete, or rename a program are all concerned with manipulating existing programs. Let us now turn our attention to creating, compiling, and executing a new C++ program. The procedures for doing these tasks are illustrated in Figure C.2. As shown in this figure, the procedure for creating an executable C++ program consists of three distinct operations: editing, compiling, and linking.

Editing

Both the creation of a new C++ program and the modification of an existing C++ program require the use of an editor program. The function of such a program is to allow a user to type statements at a keyboard and to save the typed statements together under a common name, called a *source program file name*.

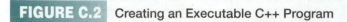

FIGURE C.2 Creating an Executable C++ Program

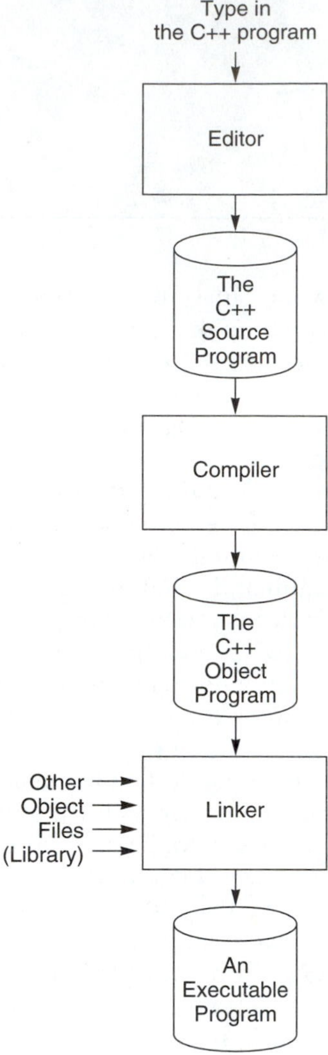

As illustrated in Figure C.1, an editor program is contained within the environment controlled by the operating system, either as a separate program or as part of the services provided with a C++ compiler. This means that the editor program can only be accessed using an operating system command, which either starts up the editor program directly or the C++ compiler that provides its own editor.

Some editors handle one line at a time; to add, change, or delete text, you refer to a specific line by number and edit that line. Line editors are sometimes inconvenient to use, but they make efficient use of memory and CPU time. Full-screen editors permit you to move the cursor to insert, delete, or change text at any point on the screen. Many C++ compilers for small computers are packaged with an editor; on larger machines you will have to use the general editor for that machine.

TABLE C.2 Editor Commands (Fill in for your system)

Task	Command(s)	Example
Save the program and exit from the editor		
Save the program without exiting from the editor		
Exit from the editor without saving the program		
Switch to text mode (if applicable)		
Switch to command mode (if applicable)		
List the complete program from within the editor		
Delete the complete program from within the editor		
Delete a set of lines from within the editor		
Delete a single line from within the editor		
Name a program from within the editor		
Search for text from within the editor		
Search and replace text from within the editor		

Once the editor program has been requested the operating system relinquishes control to this program. Again, as illustrated in Figure C.1, this means that you temporarily leave the world controlled by the operating system and its commands and enter the world controlled by the editor. The editor, like the operating system, has its own set of services and commands and you will need to become familiar with these commands to create and modify your source programs. The services provided by the editor include entering C++ statements, modifying and deleting existing C++ statements in a program, listing a program, naming a program, saving a program, and exiting from the editor back into the operating system with or without saving the program.

In using an editor you must carefully distinguish between entering a C++ statement and entering an editor command. Some editors make this distinction by using special keys to alert the editor that what is being typed is a command to the editor rather than the line of a program (for example, in older versions of BASIC the line number automatically informs the editor that the entered line is a statement and the absence of a line number informs the editor that the entered line is an editor command). Other editors contain two modes: a text mode for entering and modifying program statements and a command mode for entering editor commands. For this latter type of editor there is always a means of switching from text to command mode and back from command to text mode. In both cases the commands recognized by the editor depend on the editor being used. After filling in the operating system command needed to enter the editor, use Table C.2 to list the specific editor command names or procedures provided by your editor.

```
Operating system command
to enter the editor:__________________________
```

Compiling and Linking

The translation of a C++ source program into a form that can be executed by the computer is accomplished using a program called a *compiler*. The compiler, like the editor, is accessed using an operating system command. Each operating system uses a different command for calling the compiler into action and giving the compiler the name of the source file that is to be translated. Determine and then list the command used by your computer for performing this operation:

```
Command to compile a program:____________________
```

The output produced by the compiler is called an object program. An *object program* is simply a translated version of the source program that can be executed by the computer system with one more processing step. Let us see why this is so.

Most C++ programs contain statements that use preprogrammed routines for input and output and for finding such quantities as square roots, absolute values, and other commonly encountered mathematical calculations. Additionally, a large C++ program may be stored in two separate program files. In such a case, each file can be compiled separately. However, both files must ultimately be combined to form a single program before the program can be executed. In both of these cases it is the task of the linker to combine all of the preprogrammed routines and individual object files into a single program ready for execution. This final program is called an *executable program*. Determine and then list the command used by your compiler for performing this operation.

```
Command to compile and link a program:_______________
```

A Word of Caution

You will want to print the source code files to the screen or printer using operating system commands, such as `TYPE`, `PRINT`, or something similar—so that you can see and work with these files. This can be done because the source program is actually text consisting of a sequence of character codes. Do NOT, however, try to print the object or executable files in the same manner, because these files consist of binary numbers, not text. If you attempt to print these files, at best, you will see unrecognizable characters on the screen or printer as the binary code comprising these files is displayed as text. Even worse, you may lock up the keyboard or print a ream of paper with one character on each page when some of the binary codes perform terminal control functions.

Executing

Finally, once a C++ source program has been compiled and linked, it must be executed. To execute (or run) the program you simply type the name of the executable file in response to the operating system prompt. Determine and then list the command for performing this operation:

```
Command to execute a
compiled and linked program:___________________
```

APPENDIX

D Input, Output, and Standard Error Redirection

The display produced by the `cout` object is normally sent to the terminal where you are working. This terminal is called the standard output device because it is where the display is automatically directed, in a standard fashion, by the interface between your C++ program and your computer's operating system.

On most systems it is possible to redirect the output produced by `cout` to some other device, or to a file, using the output redirection symbol, >, at the time the program is invoked. In addition to the symbol, you must specify where you want the displayed results to be sent.

For purposes of illustration, assume that the command to execute a compiled program named `salestax`, without redirection, is:

```
salestax
```

This command is entered after your computer's system prompt is displayed on your terminal. When the `salestax` program is run, any `cout` objects activated within it automatically cause the appropriate display to be sent to your terminal. Suppose we would like to have the display produced by the program sent to a file named `results`. To do this requires the command

```
salestax > results
```

The redirection symbol, >, tells the operating system to send any display produced by `cout` directly to a file named `results` rather than to the standard output device used by the system. The display sent to `results` can then be examined by using either an editor program or issuing another operating system command. For example, under the UNIX® operating system the command

```
cat results
```

causes the contents of the file `results` to be displayed on your terminal. The equivalent command under the IBM PC disk operating system (DOS) is:

```
type results
```

In redirecting an output display to a file, the following rules apply:

1. If the file does not exist, it will be created.
2. If the file exists, it will be overwritten with the new display.

In addition to the output redirection symbol, the output append symbol, >>, can also be used. The append symbol is used in the same manner as the redirection symbol, but causes any new output to be added to the end of a file. For example, the command

```
salestax >> results
```

causes any output produced by `salestax` to be added to the end of the `results` file. If the `results` file does not exist, it will be created.

Besides having the display produced by `cout` redirected to a file, using either the > or >> symbols, the display can also be sent to a physical device connected to your computer, such as a printer. You must, however, know the name used by your computer for accessing the desired device. For example, on an IBM PC or compatible computer, the name of the printer connected to the terminal is designated as `prn` and on a UNIX system it is typically `lpr`. Thus, if you are working on an IBM or compatible machine, the command

```
salestax > prn
```

causes the display produced in the `salestax` program to be sent directly to the printer connected to the terminal.

Corresponding to output redirection, it is also possible to redesignate the standard input device for an individual program run using the input redirection symbol, <. Again, the new source for input must be specified immediately after the input redirection symbol.

Input redirection works in a similar fashion to output redirection but affects the source of input for the `cin` stream. For example, the command

```
salestax < dat_in
```

causes any input functions within `salestax` that normally receive their input from the keyboard to receive it from the `dat_in` file instead. This input redirection, like its output counterpart, is only in effect for the current execution of the program. As you might expect, the same run can have both an input and output redirection. For example, the command

```
salestax < dat_in > results
```

causes an input redirection from the file `dat_in` and an output redirection to the file `results`.

In addition to standard input and output redirection, the device to which all error messages are sent can also be redirected. On many systems this file is given an operating system designation as device file 2. Thus, the redirection

```
2> err
```

causes any error messages that would normally be displayed on the standard error device, which is usually your terminal, to be redirected to a file named `err`. As with standard input and output redirection, standard error redirection can be included on the same command line used to invoke a program. For example, the command

```
salestax < dat_in > show 2> err
```

causes the compiled program named `salestax` to receive its standard input from a file named `dat_in`, write its results to a file named `show`, and send any error messages to a file named `err`.

Because the redirection of input, output, and error messages is generally a feature of the operating system used by your computer and not typically part of your C++ compiler, you must check the manuals for your particular operating system to ensure these features are available.

APPENDIX

E Floating-Point Number Storage

The two's complement binary code used to store integer values was presented in Section 1.6. In this appendix we present the binary storage format typically used in C++ to store single-precision and double-precision numbers, which are stored as floats and doubles, respectively. Collectively, both single- and double-precision values are commonly referred to as floating-point values.

Like their decimal number counterparts that use a decimal point to separate the integer and fractional parts of a number, floating-point numbers are represented in a conventional binary format with a binary point. For example, consider the binary number 1011.11. The digits to the left of the binary point (1011) represent the integer part of the number and the digits to the right of the binary point (11) represent the fractional part.

To store a floating-point binary number a code similar to decimal scientific notation is used. To obtain this code the conventional binary number format is separated into a mantissa and an exponent. The following examples illustrate floating-point numbers expressed in this scientific notation.

Conventional Binary Notation	Binary Scientific Notation
1010.0	1.01 exp 011
−10001.0	−1.0001 exp 100
0.001101	1.101 exp −011
−0.000101	−1.01 exp −100

In binary scientific notation, the term exp stands for exponent. The binary number in front of the exp term is the mantissa and the binary number following the exp term is the exponent value. Except for the number zero, the mantissa always has a single leading 1 followed immediately by a binary point. The exponent represents a power of 2 and indicates the number of places the binary point should be moved in the mantissa to obtain the conventional binary notation. If the exponent is positive, the binary point is moved to the right. If the exponent is negative, the binary point is moved to the left. For example, the exponent 011 in the number

1.01 exp 011

means move the binary point three places to the right, so that the number becomes 1010. The -011 exponent in the number

1.101 exp –011

means move the binary point three places to the left, so that the number becomes

.001101

In storing floating-point numbers, the sign, mantissa, and exponent are stored individually within separate fields. The number of bits used for each field determines the precision of the number. Single-precision (32 bit), double-precision (64 bit), and extended-precision (80 bit) floating-point data formats are defined by the Institute of Electrical and Electronics Engineers (IEEE) Standard 754-1985 to have the characteristics given in Table E.1. The format for a single-precision floating-point number is illustrated in Figure E.1.

TABLE E.1 IEEE Standard 754-1985 Floating-Point Specification

Data Format	Sign Bits	Mantissa Bits	Exponent Bits
Single precision	1	23	8
Double precision	1	52	11
Extended precision	1	64	15

The sign bit shown in Figure E.1 refers to the sign of the mantissa. A sign bit of 1 represents a negative number and a zero sign bit represents a positive value. Since all mantissas, except for the number zero, have a leading 1 followed by their binary points, these two items are never stored explicitly. The binary point implicitly resides immediately to the left of mantissa bit 22, and a leading 1 is always assumed. The binary number zero is specified by setting all mantissa and exponent bits to 0. For this case only, the implied leading mantissa bit is also zero.

The exponent field contains an exponent that is biased by 127. For example, an exponent of 5 would be stored using the binary equivalent of the number 132 (127 + 5). Using eight exponent bits, this is coded as 100000100. The addition of 127 to each exponent allows negative exponents to be coded within the exponent field without the need for an explicit sign bit. For example, the exponent –011, which corresponds to –3, would be stored using the binary equivalent of +124 (127 – 3).

FIGURE E.1 Single-Precision Floating-Point Number Storage Format

Bit	31	30 ⟷ 23	22 ⟵⟶ 0
	Sign	Exponent	Mantissa

FIGURE E.2 The Encoding and Storage of the Decimal Number 59.75

1	10000100	11011110000000000000000

Figure E.2 illustrates the encoding and storage of the decimal number 59.75 as a 64-bit single-precision binary number. The sign, exponent, and mantissa are determined as follows. The conventional binary equivalent of

-59.75

is

-111011.11

Expressed in binary scientific notation this becomes

-1.1101111 exp 101

The minus sign is signified by setting the sign bit to 1. The mantissa's leading 1 and binary point are omitted and the 23-bit mantissa field is encoded as

11011110000000000000000

The exponent field encoding is obtained by adding the exponent value of 101 to 1111111, which is the binary equivalent of the 127_{10} bias value:

$$\begin{array}{rcr} 1\,1\,1\,1\,1\,1\,1 & = & 127_{10} \\ +\,1\,0\,1 & = & 5_{10} \\ \hline 1\,0\,0\,0\,0\,1\,0\,0 & = & 132_{10} \end{array}$$

APPENDIX

Additional Capabilities

THE typedef DECLARATION STATEMENT

The `typedef` declaration statement permits us to construct alternate names for an exiting C++ data type name. For example, the statement:

```
typedef float REAL;
```

makes the name `REAL` a synonym for `float`. The name `REAL` can now be used in place of the term `float` anywhere in the program after the synonym has been declared. For example, the definition:

```
REAL val;
```

is equivalent to the definition:

```
float val;
```

The `typedef` statement does not create a new data type; it creates a new name for an existing data type. Using uppercase names in `typedef` statements is not mandatory. It is done simply to alert the programmer to a user-specified name, similar to the way uppercase names are used in `const` statements. In fact, the equivalence produced by a `typedef` statement can frequently be produced equally well by a `const` statement. The difference between the two, however, is that `typedef` statements allow for text replacements that are not possible with a `const` statement. For example, the statement:

```
typedef float REAL;
```

actually specifies that `REAL` is a placeholder that will be replaced with another variable name. A subsequent declaration such as

```
REAL val;
```

has the effect of substituting the variable named `val` for the placeholder named `REAL` in the terms following the word `typedef`. Substituting `val` for `REAL` in the `typedef` statement and retaining all terms after the reserved word `typedef` results in the equivalent declaration `float val;`.

Once the mechanics of the replacement are understood, more useful equivalences can be constructed. Consider the following statement:

```
typedef int ARRAY[100];
```

Here, the name `ARRAY` is actually a placeholder for any subsequently defined variables. Thus, a statement such as `ARRAY first, second;` is equivalent to these two definitions:

```
int first[100];
int second[100];
```

Each of these definitions is obtained by replacing the name `ARRAY` with the variable names `first` and `second` in the terms following the reserved word `typedef`.

As another example, consider the following statement:

```
typedef struct
{
  char name[20];
  int id_num;
} EMP_REC;
```

Here `EMP_REC` is a convenient placeholder for any subsequent variable. For example, the declaration `EMP_REC employee[75];` is equivalent to the declaration

```
struct
{
  char name[20];
  int id_num;
} employee[75];
```

This last declaration is obtained by directly substituting the term `employee[75]` in place of the word `EMP_REC` in the terms following the word `typedef` in the original `typedef` statement.

THE enum SPECIFIER

The `enum` specifier creates an enumerated data type, which is simply a user-defined list of values that is given its own data type name. Such data types are identified by the reserved word `enum` followed by an optional, user-selected name for the data type and a listing of acceptable values for the data type. Consider the following user-specified data types:

```
enum flag {true, false};
enum time {am, pm};
enum day {mon, tue, wed, thr, fri, sat, sun};
enum color {red, green, yellow};
```

The first user-specified data type is a type named `flag`. Any variable subsequently declared to be of this type can take on only a value of 1 (true) or 0 (false). The second statement creates a data type named `time`. Any variable subsequently declared to be of type `time` can take on only a value of `am` or `pm`. Similarly, the third and fourth statements create the data types `day` and `color`, respectively, and list the valid values for variables of these two types. For example, the statement

```
enum day a,b,c;
```

declares the variables `a, b`, and `c` to be of type `day`, and is consistent with the declaration of variables using standard C++ data types such as `char, int,` float, or double. Once variables have been declared as enumerated types, they may be assigned values or compared to variables or values appropriate to their type. This again is consistent with standard variable operations. For example, for the variables a, b, and c declared earlier, the following statements are valid:

```
a = red;
b = a;
if (c == yellow)
  cout << "The color is yellow" << endl;
```

Internally, the acceptable values for each enumerated data type are ordered and assigned sequential integer values beginning with 0. For example, for the values of the user-defined type color, the correspondences created by the C++ compiler are that red is equivalent to 0, green is equivalent to 1, and yellow is equivalent to 2. The equivalent numbers are required when inputting values using cin or displaying values using cout. Program F.1 illustrates a user-defined data type.

PROGRAM F.1

```
#include <iostream.h>
int main()
{
  enum color {red,green,yellow};
  enum color crayon = red;     // crayon is declared to be of type
                   // color and initialized to red

  cout << "\nThe color is " << crayon << endl;
  cout << "Enter a value: ";
  cin  >> crayon;
  if (crayon == red)
    cout << "The crayon is red." << endl;
  else if (crayon == green)
    cout << "The crayon is green." << endl;
  else if (crayon == yellow)
    cout << "The crayon is yellow." << endl;
  else
    cout << "The color is not defined.\n" << endl;

  return 0;
}
```

A sample run of Program F.1 produced the following output:

```
The color is 0
Enter a value: 2
The crayon is yellow.
```

As illustrated in this program, expressions containing variables declared as user-defined data types must be consistent with the values specifically listed for the type. Although a switch statement would be more appropriate in Program F.1, the expressions in the if-else statement better highlight the use of enumerated values. Program F.1 also shows that the initialization of a user-specified data type variable is identical to the initialization of standard data type variables. For input and output purposes, however, the equivalent integer value assigned by the C++ compiler to each enumerated value must be used in place of the actual data type value. This is also seen in the program.

To assign equivalent integers to each user-specified value, the C++ compiler retains the order of the values as they are listed in the enumeration. A side effect of this ordering is that expressions can be constructed using relational and logical operators. For example, for the data type `color` created in Program F.1, expressions such as `crayon < yellow` and `red < green` are both valid.

The numerical value assigned by the compiler to enumerated values can be altered by direct assignment when a data type is created. For example, the definition

```
enum color (red,green = 7, yellow);
```

causes the compiler to associate the value `red` with the integer `0` and the value `green` with the integer `7`. Altering the integer associated with the value `green` causes all subsequent integer assignments to be altered too; thus, the value `yellow` is associated with the integer `8`. If any other values were listed after `yellow`, they would be associated with the integers `9, 10, 11`, etc., unless another alteration was made.

The name of an enumerated user-defined data type can be omitted in its definition. For example, the declaration

```
enum {red,green,yellow} crayon;
```

defines `crayon` to be a variable of an unnamed data type with the valid values of `red, green`, and `yellow`.

Scope rules applicable to the standard C++ data types also apply to enumerated data types. For example, placing the statement `enum color {red, green, yellow};` before the `main()` function in Program F.1 would make the data type named `color` global and available for any other function in the file.

Finally, because there is a one-to-one correspondence between integers and user-defined data types, the cast operator can either coerce integers into a user-specified data value or coerce a user-specified value into its equivalent integer. Assuming that `val` is an integer variable with a value of 1, and color has been declared as in Program F.1, the expression `(enum color) val` has a value of `green` and the expression `(int) yellow` has a value of 2. The compiler will not warn you, however, if a cast to a nonexistent value is attempted.

CONDITIONAL EXPRESSIONS

In addition to expressions formed with the arithmetic, relational, logical, and bit operators, C++ provides a conditional expression. A conditional expression uses the conditional operator, `?:`, and provides an alternate way of expressing a simple `if-else` statement.

The syntax of a conditional expression is:

```
expression1 ? expression2 : expression3
```

If the value of `expression1` is nonzero (true), `expression2` is evaluated; otherwise `expression3` is evaluated. The value for the complete conditional expression is the value of either `expression2` or `expression3`, depending on which expression was evaluated. As always, the value of the expression may be assigned to a variable.

Conditional expressions are most useful in replacing simple `if-else` statements. For example, the `if-else` statement:

```
if ( hours > 40)
  rate = .045;
else
  rate = .02;
```

can be replaced with the following one-line conditional statement:

```
rate = (hours > 40) ? .045 : .02;
```

Here, the complete conditional expression

```
(hours > 40) ? .045 : .02
```

is evaluated before any assignment is made to `rate`, because the conditional operator `?:` has a higher precedence than the assignment operator. Within the conditional expression, the expression `hours > 40` is evaluated first. If this expression has a nonzero value, which is equivalent to a logical true value, the value of the complete conditional expression is set to .045; otherwise the conditional expression has a value of .02. Finally, the value of the conditional expression, either .045 or .02, is assigned to the variable rate.

The conditional operator `?:` is unique in C++ in that it is a ternary operator. This means that the operator connects three operands. The first operand is always evaluated first. It is usually a conditional expression that uses the logical operators. The next two operands are any other valid expressions, which can be single constants, variables, or more general expressions. The complete conditional expression consists of all three operands connected by the condition operator symbols, `?` and `:`.

Conditional expressions are only useful in replacing `if-else` statements when the expressions in the equivalent `if-else` statement are not long or complicated. For example, the statement:

```
max_val = a > b ? a : b;
```

is a one-line statement that assigns the maximum value of the variables `a` and `b` to `max_val`. A longer, equivalent form of this statement is

```
if (a > b)
  max_val = a;
else
  max_val = b;
```

Because of the length of the expressions involved, a conditional expression would not be useful in replacing the following `if-else` statement:

```
if (amount > 20000)
  taxes = .025(amount - 20000) + 400;
else
  taxes = .02 * amount;
```

MACROS

The `const` keyword used in C++ was not available in C. Instead C used a `#define` preprocessor statement to create named constants. For example, the statement:

```
#define SALESTAX 0.05
```

equates the symbolic name SALESTAX to the number 0.05. When SALESTAX is used in any subsequent statement or expression the equivalent value of 0.05 is substituted for the symbolic name. The substitutions are made by both the C and C++ preprocessor just prior to program compilation.

Both C and C++ place no restrictions on the equivalences that can be established with the #define statement. Thus, in addition to using #define preprocessor statements for simple equivalences, these statements can also be used to equate symbolic names to text, a partial or complete expression, and may even include arguments. When the equivalence consists of more than a single value, operator, or variable, the symbolic name is referred to as a **macro,** and the substitution of the text in place of the symbolic name is called a **macro expansion** or **macro substitution.** The word *macro* refers to the direct, in-line expansion of one word into many words. For example, the equivalence established by the statement

```
#define ANSWER "The answer is "
```

enables us to write the statement:

```
cout <<  ANSWER
```

When this statement is encountered by the preprocessor, the symbolic name ANSWER is replaced by the equivalent text "The answer is ". The compiler always receives the expanded version after the text has been inserted in place of the symbolic name by the preprocessor.

In addition to using #define statements for straight text substitutions, these statements can also be used to define equivalences that use arguments. For example, in the equivalence statement:

```
#define SQUARE(x)    x * x
```

x is an argument. Here, SQUARE(x) is a true macro that is expanded into the expression x * x, where x is itself replaced by the variable or constant used when the macro is utilized. For example, the statement:

```
y = SQUARE(num);
```

is expanded into the statement:

```
y = num * num;
```

The advantage of using a macro such as SQUARE(x) is that since the data type of the argument is not specified, the macro can be used with any data type argument. If num, for example, is an integer variable, the expression num * num produces an integer value. Similarly, if num is a double-precision variable, the SQUARE(x) macro produces a double-precision value. This is a direct result of the text substitution procedure used in expanding the macro and is an advantage of making SQUARE(x) a macro rather than a function.

Care must be taken when defining macros with arguments. For example, in the definition of SQUARE(x), there must be no space between the symbolic name SQUARE and the left parenthesis used to enclose the argument. There can, however, be spaces within the parentheses if more than one argument is used.

Additionally, because the expansion of a macro involves direct text substitution, unintended results may occur if you do not use macros carefully. For example, the assignment statement:

```
val = SQUARE(num1 + num1);
```

does not assign the value of `(num1 + num2)`^{2} to `val`. Rather, the expansion of `SQUARE(num1 + num2)` results in the equivalent statement:

```
val =  num1 + num2 * num1 + num2;
```

This statement results from the direct text substitution of the term `num1 + num2` for the argument `x` in the expression `x * x` that is produced by the preprocessor.

To avoid unintended results, always place parentheses around all macro arguments wherever they appear in the macro. For example, the definition

```
#define SQUARE(x)   (x) * (x)
```

ensures that a correct result is produced whenever the macro is invoked. Now the statement

```
val = SQUARE(num1 + num2);
```

is expanded to produce the desired assignment

```
val = (num1 + num2) * (num1 + num2);
```

Macros are extremely useful when the calculations or expressions they contain are relatively simple and can be kept to one or at most two lines. Larger macro definitions tend to become cumbersome and confusing and are better written as functions. If necessary, a macro definition can be continued on a new line by typing a backslash character, \, before the return or enter key is pressed. The backslash acts as an escape character that causes the preprocessor to treat the return literally and not include it in any subsequent text substitutions.

COMMAND LINE ARGUMENTS

Arguments can be passed to any function in a program, including the `main()` function. In this section we describe the procedures for passing arguments to `main()` when a program is initially invoked and having `main()` correctly receive and store the arguments passed to it. Both the sending and receiving sides of the transaction must be considered. Fortunately, the interface for transmitting arguments to a `main()` function has been standardized in C++, so both sending and receiving arguments can be done almost mechanically.

All the programs that have been run so far have been invoked by typing the name of the executable version of the program after the operating system prompt is displayed. The command line for these programs consists of a single word, which is the name of the program. For computers that use the UNIX operating system, the prompt is usually the `$` symbol and the executable name of the program is `a.out`. For these systems, the simple command line

```
$a.out
```

begins program execution of the last compiled source program currently residing in `a.out`.

If you are using a C++ compiler on an IBM PC, the equivalent operating system prompt is either `A>` or `C>`, and the name of the executable program is typically the same name as the source program with an `.exe` extension rather than a `.c` extension. Assuming that you are using an IBM PC with the `C>` operating system prompt, the complete command line for running an executable program named `showad.exe` is `C> showad`. As illustrated in Figure F.1, this command line

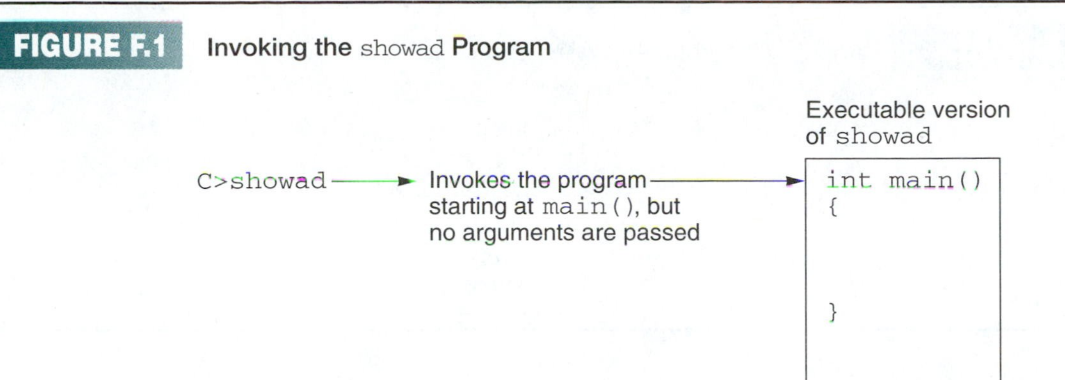

FIGURE F.1 Invoking the showad Program

causes the showad program to begin execution with its main() function, but no arguments are passed to main().

Now assume that we want to pass the three separate string arguments three blind mice directly into showad's main function. Sending arguments into a main() function is extremely easy. It is accomplished by including the arguments on the command line used to begin program execution. Because the arguments are typed on the command line, they are, naturally, called command line arguments. To pass the arguments three blind mice directly into the main() function of the showad program, we only need to add the desired words after the program name on the command line:

```
C> showad three blind mice
```

Upon encountering the command line showad three blind mice, the operating system stores it as a sequence of four strings. Figure F.2 illustrates the storage of this command line, assuming that each character uses one byte of storage. As shown in the figure, each string terminates with the standard C++ null character \0.

Sending command line arguments to main() is always this simple. The arguments are typed on the command line and the operating system nicely stores them as a sequence of separate strings. We must now handle the receiving side of the transaction and let main() know that arguments are being passed to it.

Arguments passed to main(), like all function arguments, must be declared as part of the function's definition. To standardize argument passing to a main() function, only two items are allowed: a number and an array. The number is an integer variable, which conventionally is named argc (short for argument counter), and the array is a one-dimensional list, which is conventionally named argv (short for argument values). Figure F.3 illustrates these two arguments. The integer passed to main() is the total number of items on the command line. In our example, the value of argc passed to main() is 4, which includes the name of the program plus the three command line arguments. The one-dimensional list

FIGURE F.2 The Command Line Stored in Memory

s	h	o	w	a	d	\0	t	h	r	e	e	\0	b	l	i	n	d	\0	m	i	c	e	\0

FIGURE F.3 An Integer and an Array Are Passed to `main()`

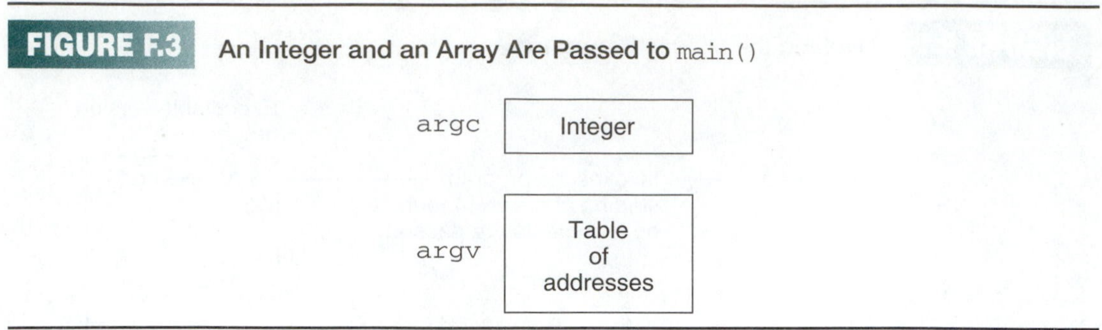

passed to `main()` is a list of pointers containing the starting storage address of each string typed on the command line, as illustrated in Figure F.4.

We can now write the complete function definition for `main()` to receive arguments by declaring their names and data types. For `main`'s two arguments the names conventionally used are `argv` and `argc`, respectively.[1] Because `argc` will store an integer value, its declaration will be `int argc`. Because `argv` is the name of an array whose elements are addresses that point to where the actual command line arguments are stored, its proper declaration is `char *argv[]`. This is nothing more than the declaration of an array of pointers. It is read "`argv` is an array whose elements are pointers to characters." Putting all this together, the full function header for a `main()` function that will receive command line arguments is:

```
int main(int argc, char *argv[])
```

No matter how many arguments are typed on the command line, `main()` only needs the two standard pieces of information provided by `argc` and `argv`: the number of items on the command line and the list of starting addresses indicating where each argument is actually stored.

FIGURE F.4 Addresses Are Stored in the `argv` Array

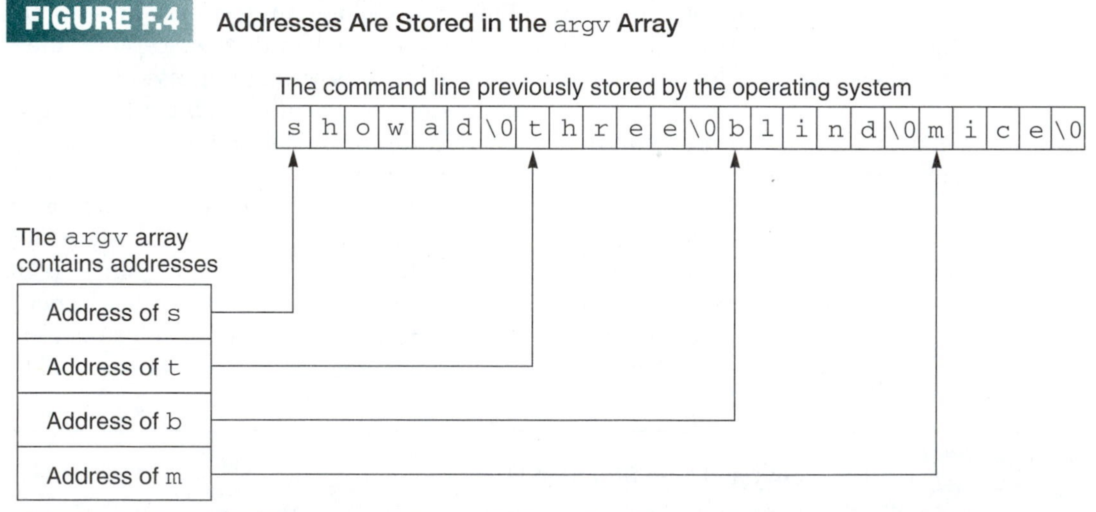

[1] These names are not required, and any valid C++ identifier can be used in their place.

Program F.2 verifies our description by printing the data actually passed to `main()`. The variable `argv[i]` used in Program F.2 contains an address. The purpose of inserting the expression `(void *)argv[i]` into the first `cout` stream is to force the address value contained in `argv[i]` to be displayed. If this cast is not used, the address in `argv[i]` is automatically dereferenced by the insertion operator, <<, because this operator has been overloaded to perform dereferences on all pointer variables. Thus, in the absence of the cast, the string value pointed to by the address in `argv[i]` would be printed. Similarly, the string notation `*argv[i]` in the second `cout` stream refers to "the character pointed to" by the address in `argv[i]`.

PROGRAM F.2

```
#include <iostream.h>
int main(int argc, char *argv[])
{
  int i;

  cout << "\nThe number of items on the command line is "
       << argc << '\n' << endl;
  for(i = 0; i < argc; i++)
  {
    cout << "The address stored in argv[" << i <<"] is "
         << (void *)argv[i] << endl;
    cout << "The character pointed to is " << *argv[i] << endl;
  }

  return 0;
}
```

Assuming that the executable version of Program F.2 is named `showad.exe`, a sample output for the command line `showad three blind mice` is[2]:

```
The number of items on the command line is 4

The address stored in argv[0] is 0x2412ffda
The character pointed to is s
The address stored in argv[1] is 0x2412ffeb
The character pointed to is t
The address stored in argv[2] is 0x2412fff1
The character pointed to is b
The address stored in argv[3] is 0x2412fff7
The character pointed to is m
```

The addresses displayed by Program F.2 clearly depend on the machine used to run the program. Figure F.5 illustrates the storage of the command line as displayed by the sample output. As anticipated, the addresses in the `argv` array "point" to the starting characters of each string typed on the command line.

---

[2] Some compilers store the full path name of the program in `argv[0]`.

FIGURE F.5 The Command Line Stored in Memory

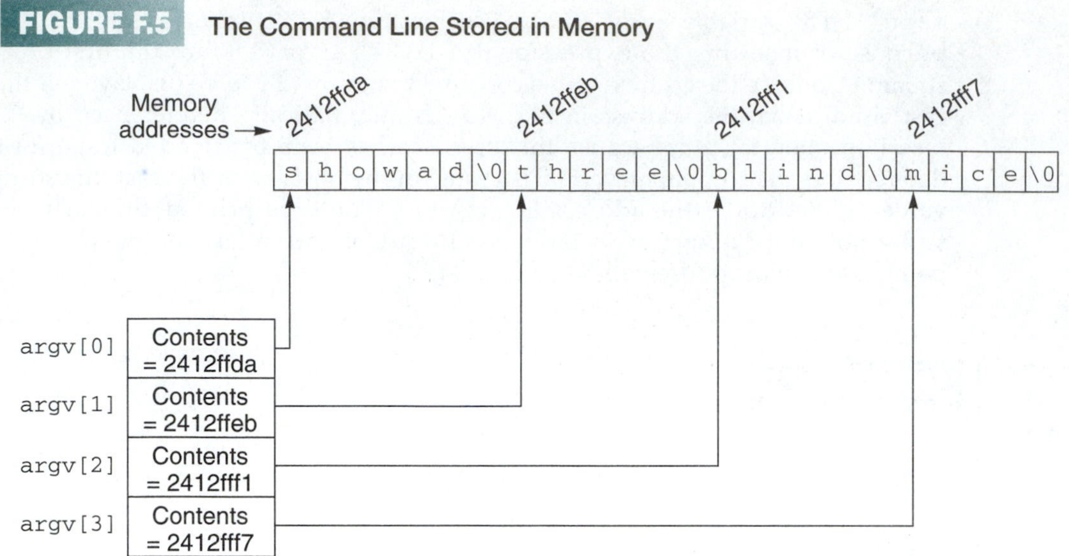

Once command line arguments are passed to a C++ program, they can be used like any other C++ strings. Program F.3 causes its command line arguments to be displayed from within `main()`.

PROGRAM F.3

```
// A program that displays its command line arguments
#include <iostream.h>
int main(int argc, char *argv[])
{
  int i;

  cout << "\nThe following arguments were passed to main(): ";
  for (i = 1; i < argc; i++)
    cout << argv[i] << " ";
  cout << endl;

  return 0;
}
```

Assuming that the name of the executable version of Program F.3 is `a.out`, the output of this program for the command line `a.out three blind mice` is:

```
The following arguments were passed to main(): three blind mice.
```

Notice that when the addresses in `argv[]` are inserted into the `cout` stream in Program F.3, the strings pointed to by these addresses are displayed. As was mentioned previously, this occurs because `cout` automatically dereferences these addresses and performs the required indirection to locate the actual string that is displayed.

One final comment about command line arguments is in order. Any argument typed on a command line is considered to be a string. If you want numerical data passed to `main()`, it is up to you to convert the passed string into its numerical counterpart. This is seldom an issue, however, since most command line arguments are used as flags to pass appropriate processing control signals to an invoked program.

APPENDIX

G Solutions to Selected Odd-Numbered Exercises

EXERCISES 1.1

1.a. A **computer program** is a structured combination of data and instructions used to operate a computer.

b. **Programming** is the process of using a programming language to produce a computer program.

c. A **programming language** is the set of instructions, data, and rules that can be used to construct a program.

d. A **high-level language** is a programming language that uses instructions that resemble a written language, such as English, and can be translated to run on a variety of computer types.

e. A **low-level language** is a programming language that uses instructions that are directly tied to one type of computer. They consist of machine level and assembly languages.

f. A **machine language** contains the binary codes that can be executed by a computer. Such languages are frequently referred to as *executables*.

g. An **assembly language** permits symbolic names to be used for mathematical operations and memory addresses. Assembly languages are low-level languages.

h. A **procedure-oriented language** has instructions that are used to create procedures, where a procedure is a logically consistent set of instructions that produce a specific result.

i. An **object-oriented language** permits the construction of objects that can be manipulated and displayed. Such languages are gaining increasing usage in graphical-oriented programs.

j. A **source program** consists of the program statements comprising a C++ or other programming language program.

k. A **compiler** is a program that is used to translate a high-level source program as a complete unit before any one statement is actually executed.

l. An **interpreter** is a program that translates individual source program statements, one at a time, into executable statements. Each statement is executed immediately after translation.

3.a. Analytical engine—England. The first recorded attempt at creating a machine that would respond to precoded and changeable instructions.

b. ABC—Iowa State University. The first successful computer to manipulate binary numbers under program control. The program consisted of external wiring.

c. ENIAC—University of Pennsylvania. The first successful large-scale computer. It used external wiring to control its operation and could perform 5000 additions or 360 multiplications per second.

d. Mark I—Harvard University. An early large-scale computer built at Harvard University that used mechanical relay switches to store numbers.

e. EDSAC—Cambridge University, England. The first successful large-scale computer that used a stored program in its memory to control its operation.

5.a. Low-level languages use instructions that are directly tied to one computer and generally execute at the fastest level possible. High-level languages are portable, but must be compiled into a low-level language before execution.

b. A procedure-oriented language uses instructions to create procedures, which are self-contained units that manipulate input values to produce resulting outputs. An object-oriented language permits the construction of objects, such as rectangles, that can be manipulated and displayed. Typically object-oriented languages are used for producing programs that have a graphical component.

7.a. Add the data in memory location 1 to the data in memory location 2. Multiply the data in memory location 3 by the data in memory location 2. Subtract the data in memory location 4 from the data in memory location 3. Divide the data in memory location 3 by the data in memory location 5.

b. $3 + 5 = 8$
$6 * 3 = 18$
$14 - 6 = 8$
$6 / 4 = 1.5$

EXERCISES 1.3

1.a. Clearly define the problem—To ensure that the problem is clearly understood, including what inputs will be given and what outputs are required.
Develop a solution—Define an appropriate set of steps, called an algorithm, to solve the problem.
Code the solution—Write the program by translating the solution into a source program.
Test and correct the program—Test the completed computer program to ensure that it does provide a solution to the problem.

b. Documentation—Provide adequate user documentation for people who will use the program and programmer documentation for people who will have to maintain the program.
Maintenance—Keep the solution up to date by making modifications required whether due to changes in requirements or because errors are found during program execution.

3. If Phase I is 40% of the total effort, then coding represents 20% of 40% = (0.2) × (0.4) = 0.08 = 8% of the total effort.

5. A fixed fee is a good choice if you have experience in exactly what is wanted, or are selling an existing program to a new client, or both you and the client are in total agreement as to what will be produced; otherwise, it is generally a bad choice for both parties. On the positive side is that you do know how much you will receive for your work and the client knows how much they will have to pay. The disadvantage is that unless you both are very clear as to what will be produced, you may end up doing double and triple the amount of work contracted for very little if any additional funding. This occurs because after the client sees the program, new features immediately present themselves. You, as a programmer, may claim these are additional features, while the client may claim them as normal features that you should have incorporated as part of a useful program. No matter how the issue is resolved, generally, one or both sides may feel they have been deceived.

EXERCISES 1.4

1.a. One possible solution:
Make sure the car is parked, the engine is off, and the key is out of the ignition switch.
Go to the trunk.
Put the correct key into the trunk.
Open the trunk.
Remove the spare tire and the jack.
Put the jack under the car . . . and so on.

b. Go to a phone.
Remove the handset from the phone.
Wait for the dial tone.
Take out the correct change for the call.
Put the correct change into the phone.
Dial the number.

c. Arrive at the store.
Walk through the door.
Go to the bread aisle.
Select the desired bread.
Go to the cashier.
Pay for the bread and leave.

d. Prepare the turkey.
Preheat the oven.
Open the oven door.

Put the turkey in the oven.
Close the oven door.
Wait the appropriate time for the turkey to cook.

2.a. Since all of these algorithms produce the same result and they all contain the same number of steps, none of them is superior to any of the others.

b. In this case the algorithm "Use Yellow first, Green second, Black last" is best because yellow is the lightest color, green will mask the yellow on the brush, and finally black with hide the green on the brush.

3.

Step 1: Pour the contents of the first cup into the third cup.
Step 2: Rinse out the first cup.
Step 3: Pour the contents of the second cup into the first cup.
Step 4: Rinse out the second cup.
Step 5: Pour the contents of the third cup into the second cup.

5.

Step 1: Compare the first number with the second number and use the smallest of these numbers for the next step.
Step 2: Compare the smallest number found in step 1 with the third number. The smallest of these two numbers is the smallest of all three numbers.

7.a.

Step 1: Compare the first name in the list with the name WESTBY. If the names match, stop the search; else go to step 2.
Step 2: Compare the next name in the list with the name WESTBY. If the names match, stop the search; else repeat this step.

EXERCISES 1.5

1.a. An **attribute** represents a characteristic of an object; specifically, it is a data member of the object.

b. The **behavior** of an object defines how the object can be activated and the response that will be produced. It is specified by the object's member and friend functions.

c. The **state** of an object defines how the object appears at the moment. It is specified by the values assigned to the object's data member variables.

d. A **model** is a representation of a real object.

e. A **class** defines the attributes and behavior of a category of set of a objects. As such it is a general representation from which specific objects can be created.

f. An **object** is a specific instance of a class. As such, values have been assigned to its data members.

g. The set of and behavior defining a class is frequently referred to as the class **interface**.

3.a.

i. the title, author, subject, publisher, and date of publication
ii. the type, size, and cost
iii. the type (ballpoint, ink cartridge, or ink refillable), the manufacturer, the color, the cost
iv. the manufacturer of the tape, its length, type, and contents
v. the manufacturer, cost, size, and capabilities (such as rewind, fast forward, record, etc.)
vi. its speed, capacity, cost of installation, cost of operation, cost of maintenance, manufacturer
vii. its manufacturer, overall size, color, cost, engine size, seating capacity, model type, estimated miles per gallon

b. These attributes model a class of objects. Only when specific values are assigned to these attributes is a specific object identified.

7. Animate objects can also be modeled and classified by classes. For example dogs and cats can be grouped together under the category pets, with an attribute of type. In general the attributes included in the class represent characteristics that are of concern for those using the class. For a veterinarian, a more useful attribute might consist of whether the animal has been inoculated or not.

9.a. The concatenation of two strings to yield a combined string.
An operation to determine the length of a string, in characters.
An operation to search a string for a particular character and report the position of the character in the string.

An operation to extract a given number of characters from a string where the starting position of the first character to be extracted is given.

b. Subtract one string from another string.
Multiply one string by another string.
Divide one string by another string.

11. The responding memo could include the following questions:
How many projects have you been involved in?
In what capacity were you involved in the projects?
When you started the project, how many of these projects were considered completely specified?
In retrospect, after the project was completed, how many of the projects that were thought to be completely specified were, in fact, completely specified?
One way of approaching the interviewees might be through a memorandum to each perspective employee requesting his/her help in the project, requesting their approval, and alerting them that they will be called on for their experience with prior projects.
Possibly another way is for the interviewees to be contacted first by telephone.
Some consideration might be given to first requesting permission to contact the interviewees by a general directive of upper management.

13.a. Generally homework problems give exactly the right amount of information to be solved. It is important to realize this, because in real-life situations there is typically both extraneous and insufficient information.

b. One possibility is to have each team member give an educated guess at the percentage of problems for which exactly the right amount of information was given, and then take an average of these guesses.

c. The purpose of this part of the exercise is to begin to become aware of how you feel and react to situations that contain ambiguity.

d. The purpose of this part of the exercise is to become aware of what you do in response to situations that are not completely specified. For example, you might report in part c that you get annoyed and angry. You might then use this to solve the problem and "show the professor" or you might use your feelings as an excuse not to complete the assignment.

e. It is generally quite enlightening to see how other people feel and react to their feelings. Some people use their feelings to behave in one way, while others may have similar feelings but behave in an entirely different manner.

EXERCISES 1.8

1. machine languages, which are low-level languages
assembly languages, which are low-level languages
procedure-oriented languages, which are high-level languages
object-oriented languages, which are high-level languages

3. An **algorithm** is a step-by-step sequence of instructions that must terminate and describe how the data are to be processed to produce the desired output.

5.a.
One input—the radius
One output—the circumference

b.
Two inputs—two real numbers
Five outputs—the sum, difference, produce, and two quotients

c.
Five inputs—the four grades plus the value for each grade, which is 3
One output—the average grade

7. Assuming that the average typist can type 50 words per minute and that the average word consists of 5 characters, the time it would take to enter all of the sales is [300 (char/sale) × (200 sales)] / [(50 words / minute) × (5 char / word)] = (60,000 char) / (250 char / min) = 240 minutes = 4 hours of nonstop typing

Note: your estimate will differ depending on the average speed you assign to the typist and your estimate of the number of characters per word. The important point is that you can tell the client that one typist should be sufficient to handle all of the input.

EXERCISES 2.1

1.

`m1234()`	Valid. Not a mnemonic.
`new_bal()`	Valid. A mnemonic.
`abcd()`	Valid. Not a mnemonic.
`A12345()`	Valid. Not a mnemonic.
`1A2345()`	Invalid. Violates Rule 1; starts with a number.
`power()`	Valid. A mnemonic.
`abs_val()`	Valid. A mnemonic.
`mass()`	Valid. A mnemonic.
`do()`	Invalid. Violates Rule 3; is a reserved word.
`while()`	Invalid. Violates Rule 3; is a reserved word.
`add_5()`	Valid. Could be a mnemonic.
`taxes()`	Valid. A mnemonic.
`net_pay()`	Valid. A mnemonic.
`12345()`	Invalid. Violates Rule 1; starts with a number.
`int()`	Invalid. Violates Rule 3; a reserved word.
`new_balance()`	Valid. A mnemonic.
`a2b3c4d5()`	Valid. Not a mnemonic.
`salestax()`	Valid. A mnemonic.
`amount()`	Valid. A mnemonic.
`$sine()`	Invalid. Violates Rule 1; starts with a special character.

3.a. These functions, as indicated by their names, most likely would be in a billing program for the following purposes:

```
input_price();      // input the price of the item
calc_salestax();    // compute required salestax
calc_total();       // determine balance owed
```

b.

They would be called in the order listed above.

5.a. `void main() or void main(void)`

b. `char main() or char main(void)`

c. `float main() or float main(void)`

d. `double main() or double main(void)`

7.a.
```
#include <iostream.h>
int main()
{
  cout << " Computers, computers everywhere\n";
  cout << "    as far as I can see\n";
  cout << " I really, really like these things,\n";
  cout << "    Oh joy, Oh joy for me!\n";

  return 0;
}
```

9. The two operations are a line feed to bring the cursor down one line, and a carriage return to bring the cursor to the first column of the current line.

Note for Exercises 11 through 15: Many solutions are possible for these exercises. The following are possible answers.

11. Determine the placement of the light fixtures.
If you are capable of doing so
  Purchase the necessary materials including the fixtures
  and wire the lights in accordance with local ordinances.
Else hire a licensed electrician.

13. Determine the courses needed for law school.
Take the right courses.
Maintain an appropriate grade average.
Prepare for the LSATs.
Contact law schools for admission interview requirements.
Determine what area of law you want to practice.
Get letters of recommendation.

15. Select and reserve a camp site.
Prepare list of items to take along.
Purchase needed supplies.
Reserve a camper at the rental agency (optional).
Arrange for someone to feed plants and watch house.
Make arrangements for care of pets (optional).
Check and service automobile.

EXERCISES 2.2

1.a. Yes.
b. It is not in standard form. To make programs more readable and easier to debug, the standard form presented in Section 2.2 of the text should be used.
3.a. Two backslashes in a row causes one backslash to be displayed.
b. cout << "\\ is a backslash.\n";

EXERCISES 2.3

1.a. float or double
b. integer
c. float or double
d. integer
e. float or double
f. character
3. 1.26e2 6.5623e2 3.42695e3 4.8932e3 3.21e-1 1.23e-2 6.789e-3
5.a. `3 + 4 * 6 = 3 + 24 = 27`
b. `3 * 4 / 6 + 6 = 12 / 6 + 6 = 2 + 6 = 8`
c. `2 * 3 / 12 * 8 / 4 = 6 / 12 * 8 / 4 = 0 * 8 / 4 = 0`
d. `10 * (1 + 7 * 3) = 10 * (1 + 21) = 10 * 22 = 220`
e. `20 - 2 / 6 + 3 = 20 - 0 + 3 = 23`
f. `20 - 2 / (6 + 3) = 20 - 2 / 9 = 20 - 0 = 20`
g. `(20 - 2) / 6 + 3 = 18 / 6 + 3 = 3 + 3 = 6`
h. `(20 - 2) / (6 + 3) = 18 / 9 = 2`
i. `50 % 20 = 10`
j. `(10 + 3) % 4 = 13 % 4 = 1`
7. Since all of the operands given are integers, the result of each expression is an integer value.
a. `10 / 5 + 3 = 2 + 3 = 5`
b. `50 / 5 + 10 - 10 * 1 = 10 + 10 - 10 = 10`
c. `50 - 3 * 10 + 4 * 1 = 50 - 30 + 4 = 24`
d. `1 / 5 = 0 (truncation)`
e. `18 / 5 = 3`
f. `-5 * 10 = -50`
g. `-50 / 20 = -2`
h. `(50 + 10) / (5 + 1) = 60 / 6 = 10`
i. `50 + 10 / 5 + 1 = 50 + 2 + 1 = 53`
9. answer1 is the integer 2
answer2 is the integer 5
11.

```
#include<iostream.h>
int main()
{
  cout << "3.0 * 5.0 = " << 3.0*5.0 << '\n';
  cout << "7.1 * 8.3 - 2.2 = " << 7.1 * 8.3-2.2 << '\n';
  cout << "3.2 / (6.1 * 5) = " << 3.2 / (6.1*5) << '\n';

  return 0;
}
```

EXERCISES 2.4

1. The following are not valid:

`12345`	Does not begin with either a letter or underscore.
`while`	Reserved word.
`$total`	Does not begin with either a letter or underscore.
`new bal`	Cannot contain a space.
`9ab6`	Does not begin with either a letter or underscore.
`sum.of`	Contains a special character.
`3sum`	Does not begin with either a letter or underscore.
`for`	Reserved word.
`tot.al`	Contains a special character.
`c$five`	Contains a special character.

The following convey no information about the variable:

`a243 r2d2 cc_a1 c3po okay a awesome goforit`

3.a. int count;
 b. float grade;
 c. double yield;
 d. char initial;

5.a. int firstnum, secnum;
 b. float price, yield, coupon;
 c. double maturity;

7.a.
```
#include <iostream.h>  // includes the iostream.h header file
int main() // function header line
{  // start of function body
  int num1, num2, total; // declare the integer variables num1, num2, and total

  num1 = 25;     // assign the integer 25 to num1
  num2 = 30;     // assign the integer 30 to num2
  total = num1 + num2;  // assign the sum of num1 and num2 to total
  cout << "The total of " << num1 << " and "
       << num2 << " is " << total; // displays: The total of 25 and 30 is 55.

  Return 0; // returns control to the operating system
} // end of function body
```
 b. `The total of 25 and 30 is 55.`

9.
```
#include <iostream.h>
int main()
{
  int length, width, perimeter;

  length = 16;
  width = 18;
  perimeter = 2 * (length + width);
  cout << "The perimeter is " << perimeter << endl;

  return 0;
}
```

11. The average is 16.5, but the program will store 16 in the variable average. To ensure that the correct answer will be displayed, the variable average must be declared as a float value.

EXERCISES 2.6

1.a. One output: the dollar amount
 b. Five Inputs: halfdollars, quarters, dimes, nickels, pennies
 c. Dollar amount = 0.50 * halfs + 0.25 * quarters + 0.10 * dimes + 0.05 * nickels + 0.01 * pennies
 d. Dollar amount = 0.50 * 0 + 0.25 * 17 + 0.10 * 24 + 0.05 * 16 + 0.01 * 12 = 7.57

3.a. One output—the amount of Ergies
 b. Two inputs—Fergies, Lergies
 c. Ergies = Fergies * sqrt(Lergies)
 d. Ergies = 14.65 * sqrt(Lergies) = 29.3

5.a. One output—distance
 b. Three inputs—s, d, and t
 c. distance = s–0.5 * d * t * t

7.a. four outputs—gross pay and net pay for both individuals
 b. six inputs—the two hourly rates, tax rate, medical benefit rate, number of hours worked for each individual
 c.
```
Gross1 = rate1 * hours1
Gross2 = rate2 * hours2
Net1 = gross1 - gross1 * taxrate - gross1 * medrate
Net2 = gross2 - gross2 * taxrate - gross2 * medrate
```
 d.
```
Gross1 = 8.43 * 40 = 337.20
Gross2 = 5.67 * 35 = 198.45
Net1 = 337.20 - 337.20 * 0.20 - 337.20 * 0.02 = 263.02
Net2 = 198.45 - 198.45 * 0.20 - 198.45 * 0.02 = 154.79
```

9.a. One output: y
 b. Two inputs: e and x
 c. `y = pow(e, x)`
 d. `y = pow(2.718, 10) = 22003.64`

EXERCISES 2.7

1.a.
```
#include <iostream.h>
int main()
{
  float time, length, pi;

  pi = 3.1416;
  time = 2.0;
  length = 12.0 * 32.2 * time / (2.0*pi) * time / (2.0*pi);
  cout << " The length is " << length << " inches\n";

  return 0;
}
```

3.a.
```
#include <iostream.h>
int main()
{
  unsigned long numin, lines;

  numin = 1000;
  lines = numin * (numin - 1) / 2;
  cout << "The number of lines needed is " << lines << ".\n";

  return 0;
}
```

5.a.
```
#include <iostream.h>
int main()
{
  float fahr, cel;
  fahr = 98.6;
  cel = (5.0 / 9.0) * (fahr - 32.0);
  cout << "For a fahrenheit temperature of " << fahr << "degrees,"
       << "the equivalent\n"
       << "celsius temperature is " << cel << " degrees" << endl;

  return 0;
}
```

7.a.

```
#include <iostream.h>
int main()
{
  float speed = 58.0, dist = 183.67, time;
  time = dist / speed;
  cout << "The elapsed time for the trip is " << time << " hours.\n";

  return 0;
}
```

9.a.

```
#include <iostream.h>
#include <math.h>
int main()
{
  int Tinit = 150, A = 60, t = 20;
  float e = 2.71828, k = 0.0367, Tfin;

  Tfin = (Tinit - A) * pow(e, -k * t) + A;
  cout << "The final temperature is " << Tfin << endl;

  return 0;
}
```

EXERCISES 2.8

1. Your response should include the following:
   Abstraction is a central concept that forms the basis of object-oriented programming. All physical objects can be considered as practical and tangible items that come from a larger group. For example, each person is a particular instance of the group human being. Similarly, each whole number is an instance of the group integer. These larger groups are called abstractions, since they refer to a general type rather than a particular object. What OOP provides is a means of allowing the programmer to construct new abstract types that have not already been defined by the programming language. This capability to define new group types, which are formally referred to as abstract data types, and in C++ are referred to as classes, is essentially what distinguishes OOP programming languages from older procedural programming languages.

EXERCISES 2.10

1.a. valid
 b. not valid since the variable distance is not declared.
 c. valid
 d. valid
 e. valid but nonsensical since average is a float that will be converted to an integer by assignment. Converting a float to a float makes no sense.
 f. valid
 g. valid
 h. not valid since the modulus operator is not defined for floats
 i. valid
 j. valid
 k. valid
 l. valid
 m. valid
 n. valid but dangerous since the result of the subtraction, which is a float, will be truncated to an integer
 o. valid

3. Since all of the operands given are floating-point numbers, the result of each valid expression is a floating-point number.
 a. 5.
 b. 10.

c. 24.
d. 0.2
e. 3.6
f. –50.
g. –2.5
h. 10.
i. 53.

5. The algorithm does not solve the problem because it fails when both numbers have the same value. According to the algorithm this case will result in an indication that the second number is larger than the first.

7.a. `'A' + 32 = 'a'`
`'Z' + 32 = 'z'`

b. `'a' - 'A' = 32`

c. `uppercase letter + 'a' - 'A' = lowercase letter`

EXERCISES 3.1

1. `c = 2 * 3.1416 * r;`
3. `celsius = 5.0 / 9.0 * (fahrenheit - 32.0);`
5. `elapsed_time = (total_dist / avg_speed) * 60.0;`
7. ```
   The first integer displayed is 4.
   The second integer displayed is 4.
   ```
9. ```
   The sum is 0.
   The sum is 26.27.
   The final sum is 28.238.
   ```

11.a.

```
#include <iostream.h>
int main()
}
    <-- missing declaration for all variables
  width = 15      <-- missing semicolon
  area = length * width; <-- no value assigned to length
  cout << "The area is " << area  <-- missing ;
       <-- missing return statement
}
```

The corrected program is:

```
#include <iostream.h>
int main()
{
  int length, width, area;
  width = 15;
  length = 20; // must be assigned some value
  area = length * width;
  cout << "The area is " << area;

  return 0;
}
```

b.

```
#include <iostream.h>
int main()
{
  int length, width, area;

  length = 20; area = length * width; <-- this should come after the assignment of values to length and width
  width = 15;
  cout << "The area is \n" << area;
        <-- missing return statement
}
```

The corrected program is:

```
#include <iostream.h>
int main()
{
  int length, width, area;

  length = 20;
  width = 15;
  area = length * width;
  cout << "The area is \n" << area;

  return 0;
}
```

c.

```
#include <iostream.h>
int main()
{
  int length = 20, width = 15, area;

  length * width = area; <-- incorrect assignment statement
  cout << "The area is " << area;
      <-- missing return statement
}
```

The corrected program is:

```
#include <iostream.h>
int main()
{
  int length = 20, width = 15, area;
  area = length * width;
  cout << "The area is \n" << area;

  return 0;
}
```

EXERCISES 3.2

1. answer1 is the integer 2.
2. answer2 is the integer 5.

5.a. The double quote after the second insertion symbol should come before the symbol and the parentheses at the end of the statement should be a semicolon.
  b. The setw(4) manipulator should not be enclosed in double quotes.
  c. The setprecision(5) manipulator should not be enclosed in double quotes.
  d. The statement should be cout << "Hello World!";
  e. The setw(6) manipulator should appear before the insertion of the number 47.
  f. The setprecision(2) manipulator should appear before the insertion of the number .768.

EXERCISES 3.3

1.a. `sqrt(6.37)`
  b. `sqrt(x - y)`
  c. `sin(30.0 * 3.1416 / 180.0)`
  d. `sin(60.0 * 3.1416 / 180.0)`
  e. `abs(pow(a,2.0) - pow(b,2.0)) or abs(a*a + b*b)`
  f. `exp(3.0)`

3.a. `b = sin(x) – cos(x);`
  b. `b = pow(sin(x),2) – pow(cos(x),2);`
  c. `area = (c * b * sin(a)) / 2;`
  d. `c = sqrt(pow(a,2) + pow(b,2));`
  e. `p = sqrt(abs(m - n));`
  f. `sum = (a * (pow(r,n) - 1)) / (r - 1);`

5.

```
#include <iostream.h>
#include <math.h>
int main()
{
  float dist, x1 = 7.0, y1 = 12.0, x2 = 3.0, y2 = 9.0;

  dist = sqrt(pow((x1-x2),2.0) + pow((y1 - y2),2.0));
  cout << "The distance is " << dist << endl;

  return 0;
}
```

7.

```
#include <iostream.h>
#include <math.h>
int main()
{
  int year = 1995;
  double population;

  population = 5.5 * pow(2.7818,(0.02 * (year - 1990));
  cout << The estimated world population in " << year
       << " is " << population << endl;

  return 0;
}
```

EXERCISE 3.4

1.a. `cin >> firstnum;`
 b. `cin >> grade;`
 c. `cin >> secnum;`
 d. `cin >> keyval;`
 e. `cin >> month >> years >> average;`
 f. `cin >> num1 >> num2 >> grade1 >> grade2;`
 g. `cin >> interest >> principal >> capital >> price >> yield;`
 h. `cin >> ch >> letter1 >> letter2 >> num1 >> num2 >> num3;`
 i. `cin >> temp1 >> temp2 >> temp3 >> volts1 >> volts2;`

3.a.

```
#include <iostream.h>
int main()
{
  float radius, area;

  cout << "Enter the radius of a circle: ";
  cin >> radius;
  area = 3.1416 * pow(radius,2);
  cout << "The area is " << area << endl;

  return 0;
}
```

5.

```
#include <iostream.h>
int main()
{
  float num, total, average;

  total = 0;
  cout << "Enter a number: ";
  cin  >> num;
  total = total + num;
  cout << "Enter a second number: ";
  cin  >> num;
  total = total + num;
  cout << "Enter a third number: ";
  cin  >> num;
  total = total + num;
  cout << "Enter a fourth number: ";
  cin  >> num;
  total = total + num;
  cout << "The average is " << total / 4.0 << endl;

  return 0;
}
```

9.

```
#include <iostream.h>
int main()
{
  float num1, num2, temp;

  cout << "Please type in a number: ";
  cin  >> num1;
  cout << "Please type in another number: ";
  cin  >> num2;
  cout << "\nBefore the swap num1 is " << num1
       << " and num2 is " << num2 << endl;
  temp = num1; // store num1 in temp
  num1 = num2; // copy num2 to num1
  num2 = temp; // copy temp to num2
  cout << "\nAfter the swap num1 is " << num1
       << " and num2 is " << num2 << endl;

  return 0;
}
```

EXERCISES 3.5

1.

```
#include <iostream.h>
const float PI = 3.1416;
int main()
{
  float radius, circum;

  cout << "\nEnter a radius: ";
  cin  >> radius;
  circum = 2.0 * PI * radius;
  cout << "\nThe circumference of the circle is " << circum << endl;

  return 0;
}
```

3.

```
#include <iostream.h>
const float CONVERT = 5.0/9.0;
const float FREEZING = 32.0;
int main()
{
  float fahren, celsius;

  cout << "Enter a temperature in degrees Fahrenheit: ";
  cin  >> fahren;
  celsius = CONVERT * (fahren - FREEZING);
  cout << "\nThe equivalent Celsius temperature is "
       << celsius << endl;

  return 0;
}
```

EXERCISES 3.6

3. The problem with the program is that the request for data comes between the heading and data lines produced by the program. For example, a typical output is:

```
e to the x        Approximation        Difference
----------        -------------        ----------
Enter a value of x: 2
 7.389056            1.000000            6.389056
 7.389056            3.000000            4.389056
 7.389056            5.000000            2.389056
 7.389056            6.333333            1.055723
```

5.a. The computed standard normal deviate for the data is 1.325.

b.

```
#include <iostream.h>
int main()
{
  float x, mu, sigma, deviate;

  cout << "Enter a value of x: ";
  cin  >> x;
  cout << "Enter the mean: ";
  cin  >> mu;
  cout << "Enter the standard deviation: ";
  cin  >> sigma;
  deviate = (x - mu) / sigma;
  cout << "The standard normal deviate is " << deviate << endl;

  return 0;
}
```

EXERCISES 3.7

1.a. Clarity means that another programmer can read and understand your code and that the program clearly identifies to a user what inputs are required and what outputs are produced.

b. Efficiency means that a program or function produces its results in the most time efficient manner.

c. Robustness means that a program or function will not fail even if it receives improper data.

d. Extensibility means that a program can easily be modified and extended to handle cases and situations that the original designers did not expect.

e. Reusability means that existing code can be easily reused within either an existing or new project.

f. Programming-in-the-large means that large, complex programs can be sub-divided and written using teams of programmers.

3. The purpose of this exercise is to make students aware of how they approach assignments and, if their past approach is not conducive to a professional approach, to make them aware that other approaches can be taken.

EXERCISES 3.10

1.a.

```
#include<iostream.h>
int main()
{
  float slope, x1, x2, y1, y2;

  x1 = 3;
  x2 = 8;
  y1 = 7;
  y2 = 12;

  slope = (y2 - y1) / (x2 - x1);
  cout << "The slope of the line is " << slope << endl;

  return 0;
}
```

b. At least one hand calculation to verify the result needs to be made.

c. The slope is 0.4.

d. This clearly is a valid case and corresponds to a boundary condition. In this case the line is parallel to the *y* axis and has an infinite slope. Some check will have to be added to the program to isolate this case so the program provides the correct result, in a way that the user understands, to the input data.

3.

```
#include<iostream.h>
#include <iomanip.h>
int main()
{
  float slope, x1, x2, y1, y2;

  x1 = 3;
  x2 = 8;
  y1 = 7;
  y2 = 12;
  slope = (y2 - y1) / (x2 - x1);

  cout << setiosflags(ios::fixed)
       << setiosflags(ios::showpoint)
       << setprecision(2);

  cout << "The slope of the line is " << setw(6) << slope << endl;

  return 0;
}
```

5.a.

```
#include<iostream.h>
int main()
{
  int change, dollars, quarters, dimes, nickels, pennies;
  float paid = 10.00, check = 6.06;

  change = (paid - check) * 100;
  dollars = change / 100;
  quarters = (change - dollars * 100) / 25;
  dimes = (change - dollars * 100 - quarters * 25) / 10;
  nickels = (change - dollars * 100 - quarters * 25 - dimes * 10) / 5;
  pennies = (change - dollars * 100 - quarters * 25 - dimes * 10 -nickels * 5);
  cout << "The change consists of:\n";
  cout << dollars << " dollars\n";
  cout << quarters << " quarters\n";
  cout << dimes << " dimes\n";
  cout << nickels << " nickels\n";
  cout << pennies << " pennies\n";

  return 0;
}
```

7.

```
#include<iostream.h>
#include<math.h>
int main()
{
  float num;

  cout << "Enter the number to find the fourth root of: ";
  cin  >> num;
  cout << "The fourth root is " << pow(num, 1.0/4.0) << endl;

  return 0;
}
```

9.

```
#include <iostream.h>
#include <iomanip.h>
#include <math.h>
int main()
{
  float a, x, r, n;
  cout << "Enter amount of the initial deposit: ";
  cin  >> x;
  cout << "Enter the interest rate as a percent (ie. 8.3): ";
  cin  >> r;
  cout << "Enter the time period in years: ";
  cin  >> n;
  a = x * pow((1.0 + r / 100), n);
  cout << setiosflags(ios::fixed)
       << setiosflags(ios::showpoint)
       << setprecision(2);
  cout << "The amount of money available would be $" << a << endl;

  return 0;
}
```

13. Your return memorandum should stress that the main advantages of OOP are code reusability. This occurs because OOP is based on creating classes of objects that can be included and used in new programs. The downside of OOP is that a new way of thinking about programming, in terms of objects and their interactions, must be learned.

17. This exercise is meant to explore the flipside of Exercise 16. Just as there are positive technical and personality traits that work to an individual's advantage, there are technical and personality traits that work to an individual's disadvantage.

EXERCISES 4.1

1.a. The relational expression is true. Therefore, its value is 1.
b. The relational expression is true. Therefore, its value is 1.
c. The final relational expression is true. Therefore, its value is 1.
d. The final relational expression is true. Therefore, its value is 1.
e. The final relational expression is true. Therefore, its value is 1.
f. The arithmetic expression has a value of 10.
g. The arithmetic expression has a value of 4.
h. The arithmetic expression has a value of 0.
i. The arithmetic expression has a value of 10.

3.a. `age == 30`
b. `temp > 98.6`
c. `ht < 6.00`
d. `month == 12`
e. `let_in == 'm'`
f. `age == 30 && ht > 6.00`
g. `day == 15 && month == 1`
h. `age > 50 || employ >= 5`
i. `id < 500 && age > 55`
j. `len > 2.00 && len < 3.00`

EXERCISES 4.2

1.a.
```
if (angle == 90)
cout << The angle is a right angle";
    else
cout << The angle is not a right angle";
```
b.
```
if (temperature > 100)
  cout << above the boiling point of water";
else
  cout << below the boiling point of water";
```
c.
```
if (number > 0)
  number = number + possum;
else
  number = number - possum;
```
d.
```
if (slope < .5)
  flag = 0;
else
  flag = 1;
```
e.
```
if ((num1 - num2) < .001)
  approx = 0;
else
  approx = (num1 - num2) / 2.0;
```
f.
```
if ((temp1 - temp2) > 2.3)
  error = (temp1 - temp2) * factor;
```
g.
```
if ((x > y) && (z < 20))
  cin >> p;
```
h.
```
if ((distance > 20) && (distance < 35))
  cin >> time;
```

3.

```
#include <iostream.h>
int main()
{
  float num1, num2;

  cout << "Enter a number: ";
  cin  >> num1;
  cout << "Enter another number: ";
  cin  >> num2;
  if (num1 > num2)
    cout << "The first number is greater.\n";
  else
    cout << "The first number is smaller.\n";

  return 0;
}
```

If the two numbers entered are equal, the else statement will be executed, which would not be a true statement.

5.a.

```
#include <iostream.h>
int main()
{
  float grade;

  cout << "Enter the grade: ";
  cin  >> grade;
  if (grade >= 70.0)
    cout << "A passing grade.\n";
  else
    cout << "A failing grade.\n";

  return 0;
}
```

b. At least three runs should be made: one input under 70.0, one at 70.0, and one over 70.0. Another run, if necessary, might be made for some unexpected input, such as "seventy."

EXERCISES 4.3

1.

```
#include<iostream.h>
main()
{
  char marcode;
  cout << " Enter a marital code: ";
  cin  >> marcode;

  if (marcode == 'M' || marcode == 'm')
    cout << "Individual is married.\n";
  else if (marcode == 'S' || marcode == 's')
    cout << "Individual is single.\n";
  else if (marcode == 'D' || marcode == 'd')
    cout << "Individual is divorced.\n";
  else if (marcode == 'W' || marcode == 'w')
    cout << "Individual is widowed.\n";
  else
    cout << "An invalid code was entered.\n";
  cout << "Thanks for participating in the survey\n";

  return 0;
}
```

3.
```
#include <iostream.h>
int main()
{
  float angle;

  cout << "Enter the angle: ";
  cin  >> angle;
  if (angle < 90.0)
    cout << "The angle is acute.\n";
  else if (angle == 90.0)
    cout << "The angle is a right angle.\n";
  else if (angle > 90.0)
    cout << "The angle is obtuse.\n";

  return 0;
}
```

5.
```
#include <iostream.h>
int main()
{
  float grade;
  char letter;

  cout << "Enter the student's numerical grade: ";
  cin  >> grade;
  if (grade >= 90.0) letter = 'A';
  else if (grade >= 80.0) letter = 'B';
  else if (grade >= 70.0) letter = 'C';
  else if (grade >= 60.0) letter = 'D';
  else letter = 'F';
  cout << "The student receives a grade of " << letter << endl;

  return 0;
}
```

Notice that an if-else chain is used. If simple if statements were used, a grade entered as 75.5, for example, would be assigned a 'C' because it was greater than 60.0. But the grade would then be reassigned to 'D' because it is also greater than 60.0.

7.
```
#include <iostream.h>
int main()
{
  float fahr, cels, in_temp;
  char letter;

  cout << "Enter a temperature followed by";
  cout << " one space and the temperature's type\n";
  cout << " (an f designates a fahrenheit temperature";
  cout << "  and a c designates a celsius temperature): ";
  cin  >> in_temp >> letter;
  if (letter == 'f' || letter == 'F')
  {
    cels = (5.0/9.0)*(in_temp-32.0);
    cout << in_temp << " degrees Fahrenheit = "
         << cels << " degrees Celsius\n";
  }
  else if (letter == 'c' || letter == 'C')
  {
    fahr = (9.0/5.0)*in_temp + 32.0;
    cout << in_temp << " degress Celsius = "
         << fahr << " degrees Fahrenheit\n";
  }
  else
    cout << "The data entered is invalid.\n";

  return 0;
}
```

9.a. This program will run. It will not, however, produce the correct result.

b. & c. This program evaluates correct incomes for mon_sales less than 20000.00 only. If 20000.00 or more were entered, the first else-if statement would be executed and all others would be ignored. That is, for 20000.00 or more, the income for >= 10000.00 would be calculated and displayed. Had if statements been used in place of the else-if statements, the program would have worked correctly, but inefficiently (see comments for Exercise 4b).

EXERCISES 4.4

1.

```
switch (let_grad)
{
  case 'A':
    cout <<  "The numerical grade is between 90 and 100\n";
    break;
  case 'B':
    cout <<  "The numerical grade is between 80 and 89.9\n";
    break;
  case 'C':
    cout <<  "The numerical grade is between 70 and 79.9\n";
    break;
  case 'D':
    cout <<  "How are you going to explain this one\n";
    break;
  default:
    cout <<  "Of course I had nothing to do with the grade.\n";
    cout <<  "It must have been the professor's fault.\n";
}
```

3.

```
switch (code)
{
  case 1:
    cout << "360 Kilobyte Drive (5 1/2 inch)\n";
    break;
  case 2:
    cout << "1.2 Megabyte Drive (5 1/2 inch)\n";
    break;
  case 3:
    cout << "722 Kilobyte Drive (3 1/4 inch)\n";
    break;
  case 4:
    cout << "1.4 Megabyte Drive (3 1/4 inch)\n";
  break;
}
```

5. The expression in the switch statement must evaluate to an integer quantity and be tested for equality. The if-else chain in Program 4.6 uses floating-point values and inequalities, violating both requirements of the switch statement's requirements.

EXERCISE 4.5

1.a.

```
#include <iostream.h>
int main()
{
  int opselect;
  double fnum, snum;

  cout << "Please type in two numbers: ";
  cin  >> fnum >> snum;
  cout << "Enter a select code: \n";
  cout << "   a 1 for addition\n";
  cout << "   a 2 for multiplication\n";
  cout << "   or a 3 for division: ";
  cin  >> opselect;
  switch (opselect)
  {
    case 1:
      cout << "The sum of the numbers entered is " << fnum + snum << endl;
      break;
    case 2:
      cout << "The product of the numbers entered is " << fnum * snum << endl;
      break;
    case 3:
      cout << "The first number divided by the second is " << fnum / snum << endl;
      break;
  }       // end of switch
  return 0;
}
```

b. Typically a message such as "Floating point error: Divide by 0" will be displayed.

c.

```
#include <iostream.h>
int main()
{
  int opselect;
  double fnum, snum;

  cout << "Please type in two numbers: ";
  cin  >> fnum >> snum;
  cout << "Enter a select code: \n";
  cout << "   a 1 for addition\n";
  cout << "   a 2 for multiplication\n";
  cout << "   or a 3 for division: ";
  cin  >> opselect;
  switch (opselect)
  {
    case 1:
      cout << "The sum of the numbers entered is " << fnum + snum << endl;
      break;
    case 2:
      cout << "The product of the numbers entered is " << fnum * snum << endl;
      break;
    case 3:
   if (snum == 0)
     cout <<  "Division by zero is not permitted!\n";
   else
        cout << "The first number divided by the second is " << fnum / snum << endl;
      break;
  }       // end of switch

  return 0;
}
```

3.a.

```
#include <iostream.h>
int main()
{
  float angle;

  cout << "Enter an angle: ";
  cin  >> angle;

  if (angle < 0 || angle > 360)
    cout << "An incorrect angle was entered.\n";
  else if (angle > 0 && angle < 90)
    cout << "The angle is in quadrant I.\n";
  else if (angle > 90 && angle < 180)
    cout << "The angle is in quadrant II.\n";
  else if (angle > 180 && angle < 270)
    cout << "The angle is in quadrant III.\n";
  else if (angle > 270 && angle < 360)
    cout << "The angle is in quadrant IV.\n";

  return 0;
}
```

b.

```
#include <iostream.h>
int main()
{
  float angle;

  cout << "Enter an angle: ";
  cin  >> angle;

  if (angle < 0 || angle > 360)
    cout << "An incorrect angle was entered.\n";
  else if (angle > 0 && angle < 90)
    cout << "The angle is in quadrant I.\n";
  else if (angle > 90 && angle < 180)
    cout << "The angle is in quadrant II.\n";
  else if (angle > 180 && angle < 270)
    cout << "The angle is in quadrant III.\n";
  else if (angle > 270 && angle < 360)
    cout << "The angle is in quadrant IV.\n";
  else if (angle == 0)
    cout << "The angle is on the positive X axis.\n";
  else if (angle == 90)
    cout << "The angle is on the positive Y axis.\n";
  else if (angle == 180)
    cout << "The angle is on the negative X axis.\n";
  else if (angle == 270)
    cout << "The angle is on the negative Y axis.\n";

  return 0;
}
```

5.a.

```
#include <iostream.h>
#include <iomanip.h>
int main()
{
  int year, weight, wclass;
  float fee;

  cout << "Enter a model year: ";
  cin  >> year;
  cout << "Enter a weight in pounds: ";
  cin  >> weight;
  if (year <= 1970)
  {
    if (weight < 2700)
    {
      wclass = 1;
      fee = 16.50;
    }
    else if (weight >= 2700 && weight <= 3800)
    {
      wclass = 2;
      fee = 25.50;
    }
     else if (weight > 3800)
    {
      wclass = 3;
      fee = 46.50;
    }
  }
  else if (year >= 1971 && year <= 1979)
  {
    if (weight < 2700)
    {
      wclass = 4;
      fee = 27.00;
    }
    else if (weight >= 2700 && weight <= 3800)
    {
      wclass = 5;
      fee = 30.50;
    }
    else if (weight > 3800)
    }
      wclass = 6;
      fee = 52.50;
    }
  }
  else if (year >= 1980)
  {
    if (weight < 3500)
    {
      wclass = 7;
      fee = 19.50;
    }
    else if (weight >= 3500)
    {
      wclass = 8;
      fee = 52.50;
    }
  }
```

(continued on next page)

(continued from previous page)

```
cout << setiosflags(ios::fixed)
     << setiosflags(ios::showpoint)
     << setprecision(2);
cout << "The weight class is " << wclass
     << " and the registration fee is $" << fee << endl;

return 0;
}
```

7.

```
#include <iostream.h>
int main()
{
  int card1, card2, card3, total;

  cout << "Enter three cards." << endl
    << "(Enter an ace as 1 and picture cards as 10): ";
  cin  >> card1 >> card2 >> card3;

  total = card1 + card2 + card3;
  if (total < 21 && (card1 == 1 || card2 == 1 || card3 == 1))
    if (total - 1 + 11 <= 21)
      total = total - 1 + 11;
  cout << "The total is " << total << endl;

  return 0;
}
```

Note: The only useful possibility of counting the ace as an 11 rather than as a 1 occurs when the total is less than 21 and one of the cards is an ace.

EXERCISES 4.6

1.a. Abstraction—the process of concentrating on the essentials of what an object is and does before making any decisions about how the object will be implemented. Concentrating on the general characteristics that define an object apart from the specific attributes of a single specific object.

b. Encapsulation—the process of combining the internal implementation of an abstract data class and hiding the details of the implementation from objects not in the class.

c. Extensibility—the ability of program code to be easily extended to handle cases not considered in the original design.

d. Implementation—the details of how an abstract data type is constructed. This includes both the data types used for the abstract data type and the functions defined for operating on the abstract data type.

e. Information hiding—keeping the implementation details of how an abstract data type is constructed private. Hiding the implementation details ensures that users cannot inadvertently modify the behavior of the class and affect its operation.

3.a. a three digit or four digit extension number

b. an area code, exchange, and extension number

c. a country code, area code, exchange, and extension number

5.a. attributes: type, color, size
behavior: response to brakes, steering, and possibly shifting

b. attributes: type, size, subject, binding, age
behavior: how the book responds when left open on a desk (i.e., does it lay flat or tend to close?)

c. attributes: type, color, size
behavior: its response to being drawn across a page

d. attributes: gender, age, height, weight, color, occupation, etc.
   behavior: how the person responds to questions, drives, walks, talks, etc.

e. attributes: type, memory size, speed
   behavior: how the printer prints a page

Note that inanimate objects, such as a pencil, book, or printer, have a much smaller set of attributes and behaviors than more complex objects, such as people. As such, inanimate objects are much easier to model.

EXERCISES 4.9

1.a.

```
cout << "Enter two temperatures: ";
cin  >> temp_one >> temp_two;
if (temp_one == temp_two)
  cout << temp_one;
```

b.

```
cout << "Enter two capital letters: ";
cin  >> letter1 >> letter2;
    // the following two statements can be used to
    //   ensure capital letters - if you use them
    //   you must #include<ctype.h>

letter1 = toupper(letter1);  // ensure a capital letter
letter2 = toupper(letter2);  // ensure a capital letter
if (letter1 <= letter2)
  cout << letter1 << letter2;
else
  cout << letter2 << letter1;
```

c.

```
cout << "Enter three integer values: ";
cin  >> num1 >> num2 >> num3;
if (num1 < num2 && num1 < num3)   // num1 is the smallest
  if (num2 < num3)
     cout <<  num1 << " "<< num2 << " "<< num3;
   else
     cout <<  num1 << " "<< num3 << " "<< num2;
else if (num2 < num1 && num2 < num3)   // num2 is the smallest
  if (num1 < num3)
    cout << num2 << " " <<  num1 << " "<< num3;
  else
    cout <<  num2 << " " <<  num3 << " "<<  num1;
else    // num3 is the smallest
  if (num1 < num2)
    cout << "    \n" << num3, num1, num2;
  else
    cout << "    \n" << num3, num2, num1;
```

3.a.

```
#include <iostream.h>
int main()
{
  char in_key;

  cout << "Type a u if you feel great today: ";
  cin  >> in_key;
  if (in_key == 'u' || in_key == 'U')
    cout << "I feel great today!\n";
  else
   cout << "I feel down today #$*!\n";

  return 0;
}
```

b. At least three runs should be made: one input alphabetically less than 'u', one with 'u', and one alphabetically greater than 'u'. Another run, if necessary, might be made for capital letters or numeric values.

5.a.

```
#include <iostream.h>
int main()
{
  char in_key;

  cout << "Enter a letter: ";
  cin  >> in_key;
  if (in_key >= 'A' && in_key <= 'Z')
    cout << "The character just entered is an uppercase letter\n";
  else
    cout << "The character just entered is not an uppercase letter\n";

  return 0;
}
```

7. The error is that the intended relational expression letter == 'm' has been written as the assignment expression letter = 'm'. When the expression is evaluated the character m is assigned to the variable letter and the value of the expression itself is the value of 'm'. Since this is a nonzero value, it is taken as true and the message is displayed. Thus, as written in the program, the if statement is equivalent to the following two statements:

```
letter = 'm';
if (letter)
  cout << "Hello there!\n";
```

A correct version of this if statement is:

```
if (letter == 'm')
  cout << "Hello there!\n";
```

11. In your return memo you should explain that encapsulation is one of the key elements of OOP. This is because OOP is ultimately concerned with creating new data types and constructing them in such a way that users can use these data types without constantly reinventing them or knowing the internal details of how they are constructed. This is accomplished by encapsulating the implementation details of how the data type is constructed within a class and keeping the implementation hidden from the user. Hiding the implementation details ensures that a user cannot inadvertently modify the behavior of the class and affect its operation.

13. Potential objects are the pump, the gun, the holster, the supply tank, pump display, and pump meter.

EXERCISES 5.2

1.

```
#include <iostream.h>
int main()
{
  int count = 2;

  while (count <= 10)
  {
    cout << count << " ";
    count = count + 2;
  }

return 0;
}
```

3.a. 21 items are displayed, which are the integers from 1 to 21.

c. 21 items are displayed, which are the integers from 0 to 20.

5.

```
#include <iostream.h>
int main()
{
  int pcount, count = 0;

  while (count <= 9)
  {
    pcount = count;
    while (pcount > 0)
    {
      cout << " ";
      pcount--;
    }
    cout << count<< endl;
    count++;
  }

  return 0;
}
```

7.

```
#include <iostream.h>
#include <iomanip.h>
int main()
{
  int feet;
  float meters;

  cout << "FEET      METERS\n";
  cout << "----      ------\n";
  feet = 3;

  while (feet <= 30)
  {
    meters = feet / 3.28;
    cout << setiosflags(ios::fixed)
         << setiosflags(ios:: showpoint);
    cout << setw(3) << feet
         << setw(11) << setprecision(2)
         << meters << endl;
    feet = feet + 3;
  }

  return 0;
}
```

9.

```
#include <iostream.h>
#include <iomanip.h>
int main()
{
  float time, miles;
  cout << "TIME     MILES\n";
  cout << "----     -----\n";
  time = .5;

  while (time <= 4)
  {
    miles = 55 * time;
    cout << setiosflags(ios::fixed)
         << setiosflags(ios::showpoint);
    cout << setw(4) << setprecision(1) << time
         << setw(10) << setprecision(2) << miles << endl;
    time = time + .5;
  }

  return 0;
}
```

EXERCISES 5.3

1. The only modification that needs to be made is to change the named constant MAXNUMS to be equal to 8 instead of 4.

3.a.

```
#include <iostream.h>
#include <iomanip.h>
int main()
{
  float cels, fahr, incr;
  int num, count = 0;

  cout << "Enter the starting temperature ";
  cout << "in degrees Celsius: ";
  cin  >> cels;
  cout << "Enter the number of conversions to be made: ";
  cin  >> num;
  cout << "Now enter the increment between conversions ";
  cout << "in degrees Celsius: ";
  cin  >> incr;
  cout << "\nCelsius     Fahrenheit\n";
  cout << "---------     ----------\n";
  while (count <= num)
  {
    fahr = (9.0/5.0)*cels + 32.0;
    cout << setiosflags(ios::fixed)
         << setiosflags(ios::showpoint)
         << setprecision(2);
    cout << setw(6) << cels
         << setw(14)<< fahr << endl;
    cels = cels + incr;
    count++;
  }

  return 0;
}
```

5. The only modification that needs to be made is to change the named constant MAXNUMS to be equal to 10 instead of 4.

7. This program still calculates the correct values, but the average is now calculated four times. Since only the final average is desired, it is better to calculate the average once outside of the while loop.

9.

```
#include <iostream.h>
#include <iomanip.h>
#include <math.h>
const int MAXTERM = 10;
int main()
{
  int a = 1, n = 1;
  float  r = 0.5, nthTerm, total = 0;

  cout << "Term No.  Term Value\n";
  cout << "--------  ----------\n";
  while (n <= MAXTERM)
  {
  nthTerm = a * pow(r, n - 1);
    total = total + nthTerm;
    cout << setw(5) << n
           << setw(16) << nthTerm << endl;
    ++n;
  }
  cout << "\nThe total of the series is " << total <<endl;

  return 0;
}
```

13.

```
 #include <iostream.h>
const int SENTVAL = 999;
int main()
{
  int id, inven, income, outgo, bal;

  cout << "Enter a book ID or 999 to exit: ";
  cin  >> id;
  while (id != SENTVAL)
  {
    cout << "Enter inventory at the beginning of the month: ";
    cin  >> inven;
    cout << "Enter the number of copies received during the month: ";
    cin  >> income;
    cout << "Now enter the number of copies sold during the month: ";
    cin  >> outgo;
    bal = inven + income - outgo;
    cout << "\nBook # " << id
         << " new balance is " << bal;
    cout << "\nEnter a book ID or 999 to exit: ";
    cin  >> id;
  }

  return 0;
}
```

Notice that the lines for entering the book ID are repeated. This is a characteristic of the while statement used in this way. If these lines were only included inside the while loop, the user would not be able to exit without creating an inventory for book number 999 and the program would calculate and print a new balance for the "phantom" book with ID number 999.

EXERCISES 5.4

1.a. `for ( i = 1; i <= 20; ++i)`
b. `for (icount = 1; icount <= 20;  icount = icount + 2)`
c. `for (j = 1; j <= 100; j = j + 5)`
d. `for (icount = 20; icount >= 1;  -icount)`
e. `for (icount = 20; icount >= 1; icount = icount - 2)`
f. `for (count = 1.0; count <= 16.2; count = count + 0.2)`
g. `for (xcnt = 20.0; xcnt >= 10.0; xcnt = xcnt - 0.5)`

3.a. 55
b. 1024
c. 75
d. -5
e. 40320
f. 0.03125

5.

```
#include <iostream.h>
#include <iomanip.h>
const int MAXNUM = 20;
int main()
{
  int num;

  cout << "NUMBER    SQUARE    CUBE\n";
  cout << "------    ------    ----\n";
  for (num = 0; num <= MAXNUM; num += 2)
    cout << setw(3) << num << "         "
   << setw(3) << num * num << "       "
   << setw(4) << num * num * num << endl;

  return 0;
}
```

7.

```
#include <iostream.h>
#include <iomanip.h>
int main()
{
  int count;
  float fahr, celsius;

  cout << "Fahrenheit      Celsius\n";
  cout << "----------      -------\n";
  cout << setiosflags(ios::fixed)
       << setiosflags(ios::showpoint);
  for (fahr = 20.0, count = 1; count <= 20; ++count)
  {
    celsius = (5.0 / 9.0) * (fahr - 32.0);
    cout << setw(6) << setprecision(1) << fahr
         << setw(16) << setprecision(2) << celsius << endl;

    fahr += 4;
  }

  return 0;
}
```

9.a.

```
#include <iostream.h>
#include <iomanip.h>
const float STARTSAL = 25000;
const float INCREMENT = 1500;
int main()
{
  long salary = STARTSAL;
  int year;

   cout << "Year      Salary\n";
   cout << "----      ------\n";
   for (year = 1; year <= 10; year++)
   }
     cout << setw(3) << year
          << setw(12) << salary << endl;
     salary += INCREMENT;
   }

  return 0;
}
```

b.

```
#include <iostream.h>
#include <iomanip.h>
const float STARTSAL = 25000;
const float INCREMENT = 0.05;
int main()
{
  long salary = STARTSAL;
  int year;

   cout << "Year      Salary\n";
   cout << "----      ------\n";
   for (year = 1; year <= 10; year++)
   {
     cout << setw(3) << year
          << setw(12) << salary << endl;
     salary = salary * (1 + INCREMENT);
   }

    return 0;
}
```

11.

```
#include <iostream.h>
#include <iomanip.h>
#include <math.h>
int main()
{
  float prob, ex;
  int lamda = 3;  // average no. of arrivals per minute
  long factorial = 1;  // denominator of the probability expression
  int customer;

  cout << " No. of\n";
  cout << "Arriving\n";
  cout << "Customers     Probability\n";
  cout << "---------     -----------\n";

  ex = exp(-lamda);   // only need to do this calculation once
  for (customer = 1; customer <= 10; customer++)
  {
     factorial = factorial * customer;
     prob = (pow(lamda,customer) * ex / factorial);
     cout << setw(5) << customer
          << setw(17) << setprecision(6) << prob << endl;
  }

  return 0;
}
```

13.

```
#include <iostream.h>
int main()
{
  int n, preceed1, preceed2, term;
  long fib;

  cout << "Enter the desired term: ";
  cin  >> n;
  if (n < 3)
    fib = n - 1;
  else
  {
    preceed2 = 0;
    preceed1 = 1;
    for (term = 3; term <= n; ++term)
    {
      fib = preceed1 + preceed2;
        // now adjust the preceding terms for the next calculation
      preceed2 = preceed1;
      preceed1 = fib;
    }
  }
  cout << "The Fibonacci number for term " << n << " is " << fib << endl;

  return 0;
}
```

EXERCISES 5.5

1.

```
#include <iostream.h>
const int MAXCOUNT = 6;
int main()
{
  int count;
  float fahren, celsius;

  for(count = 1; count <= MAXCOUNT; count++)
  {
    cout << "Enter a fahrenheit temperature: ";
    cin  >>  fahren;
    celsius = (5.0/9.0)*(fahren - 32.0);
    cout << " The corresponding celsius temperature is "
         << celsius << " degrees" <<endl;
  }

  return 0;
}
```

3.

```
#include <iostream.h>
int main()
{
  int count, reps;
  float gallons, liters;

  cout << "Please type in the total number of data values ";
  cout << "to be converted: ";
  cin >>  reps;
  for(count = 1; count <= reps; count++)
  {
    cout << "Enter the number of gallons: ";
    cin  >>  gallons;
    liters = 3.785 * gallons;
    cout << "  The corresponding number of liters is " << liters << endl;
  }

  return 0;
}
```

5.

```
#include <iostream.h>
int main()
{
  int i, reps, poscnt, negcnt;
  float usenum, postot, negtot, posavg, negavg;
  postot = 0;
  negtot = 0;
  poscnt = 0;
  negcnt = 0;

  cout << "Please type in the total number of data values ";
  cout << "to be added: ";
  cin  >>  reps;
  for(i = 1; i <= reps; i++)
  {
    cout << "Enter a number (positive or negative) : ";
    cin  >>  usenum;
    if (usenum > 0)
    {
      poscnt++;
      postot = postot + usenum;
    }
 else if (usenum < 0)
    {
      negcnt++;
      negtot = negtot + usenum;
    }
  }
  posavg = postot / poscnt;
  negavg = negtot / negcnt;
  cout << "The positive average is " << posavg << endl;
  cout << "The negative average is " << negavg << endl;

  return 0;
}
```

7.

```
#include <iostream.h>
int main()
{
  int count = 0, i = 0, num;

  cout << "The first 20 whole numbers divisible by 3 are:\n";
while (count < 20)
{
  i++;
  if(i%3 == 0)  // can be replaced by if(!(i%3))
  {
    count++;
    cout << i << "  ";
  }
}

 return 0;
}
```

9.a.

```
#include <iostream.h>
 #include <iomanip.h>
 #include <math.h>
 int main()
 {
   double x, y;
   cout << "x value      y value\n";
   cout << "-------      -------\n";
   cout << setiosflags(ios::showpoint);
   for (x = 5.0; x <= 10.0; x = x + 0.2)
   {
     y = 3 * pow(x,5) - 2 * pow(x,3) + x;
     cout << setw(8) << x
          << setw(14) << y << endl;
   }

   return 0;
 }
```

b.

```
#include <iostream.h>
 #include <iomanip.h>
 #include <math.h>
 int main()
 {
   double x, y;

   cout << "x value      y value\n";
   cout << "-------      -------\n";
   cout << setiosflags(ios::showpoint);
   for (x = 1.0; x <= 3.0; x = x + 0.1)
   {
     y = 1 + x + pow(x,2)/2.0 + pow(x,3)/6.0 + pow(x,4)/24.0;
     cout << setw(7) << x
          << setw(13) << y << endl;
   }
   return 0;
 }
```

c.

```
#include <iostream.h>
 #include <iomanip.h>
 #include <math.h>
 int main()
 {
   double t, y;

   cout << "t value      y value\n";
   cout << "-------      -------\n";
   cout << setiosflags(ios::showpoint);
   for (t = 4; t <= 10.0; t = t + 0.2)
   {
     y = 2 * exp(0.8*t);
     cout << setw(7) << t
          << setw(13) << y << endl;
   }

   return 0;
 }
```

EXERCISES 5.6

1.

```
#include <iostream.h>
const int EXPERS = 4;
const int RESULTS = 6;
int main()
{
  int i, j;
  float total, avg, data;

  for (i = 1; i <= EXPERS; i++)
  {
    cout << "Enter " << RESULTS << " results for experiment #" << i << ": ";
    for (j = 1, total = 0.0; j <= RESULTS; j++)
    {
      cin >>  data;
      total += data;
    }
    avg = total/RESULTS;
    cout << "   The average for experiment #" << i << " is " << avg << endl;
  }

  return 0;
}
```

Note: When entering data for each experiment, the six individual results may be entered on one line with a space between each entry, on six individual lines, or any combination of these.

3.a.

```
#include <iostream.h>
const int BOWLERS = 5;
const int GAMES = 3;
int main()
{
  int bowler, game;
  float score, plyr_tot, plyr_avg;

  for(bowler = 1; bowler <= BOWLERS; ++bowler)
  {
    for(game = 1, plyr_tot = 0; game <= GAMES; game++)
    {
      cout << "Enter the score for bowler " << bowler << " game "<< game <<": ";
       cin  >> score;
      plyr_tot = plyr_tot + score;
    }
    plyr_avg = plyr_tot / GAMES;
    cout << "   The average for bowler " << bowler << " is " << plyr_avg << endl;
  }

  return 0;
  }
```

b.

```
#include <iostream.h>
const int BOWLERS = 5;
const int GAMES = 3;
int main()
{
  int bowler, game;
  float score, plyr_tot, plyr_avg, team_tot, team_avg;

  for(bowler = 1, team_tot = 0; bowler <= BOWLERS; ++bowler)
  {
    for(game = 1, plyr_tot = 0; game <= GAMES; ++game)
    {
      cout << "Enter the score for bowler " << bowler << " game " << ": ";
      cin  >> score;
      plyr_tot = plyr_tot + score;
    }
    team_tot = team_tot + plyr_tot;
    plyr_avg = plyr_tot / GAMES;
    cout << "   The average for bowler " << bowler << " is " << plyr_avg << endl;
  }
  team_avg = team_tot / (BOWLERS * GAMES);
  cout << "The average for the whole team is " << team_avg << endl;

  return 0;
}
```

5.

```
#include <iostream.h>
#include <iomanip.h>
#include <math.h>
const float SMALLDIF = 0.00001;

int main()
{
  float x, y, z;
  cout << setiosflags(ios::fixed)
    << setiosflags(ios::showpoint)
    << setprecision(2);
  cout << "   x         z          y    \n";
  cout << "-------   -------   -------\n";
  for (x = 1.0; x <= 5.0; x += 1)
    for (z = 2.0; z <= 6.0; z += 1)
      if (fabs(x - z) > SMALLDIF)
      {
       y = x * z / (x - z);
       cout << setw(6) << x
            << setw(6) << z
            << setw(6) << y << endl;
      }
      else
       cout << setw(6) << x
             << setw(6) << z
             << " FUNCTION UNDEFINED" << endl;
  return 0;
}
```

7.

```
#include <iostream.h>
#include <iomanip.h>
int main()
{
  long sal;
  int dep;
  float deduct;

  cout << "            |<----------------------- Deducti";
  cout << "ons ------------------------>|\n";
  cout << " Salary     |  0          1          2       ";
  cout << "   3           4          5    |\n";
  cout << " --------       --------      --------       ";
  cout << " --------       --------      --------\n";
  for(sal = 10000L; sal <= 50000L; sal += 10000L)
  {
    cout << sal << "    ";
    for(dep = 0; dep <= 5; dep++)
    {
      deduct =  dep * 500 + 0.05 * (50000L - sal);
      cout << "      " << setw(5) << deduct;
    }
    cout << endl;
  }

  return 0;
}
```

EXERCISES 5.7

1.a.

```
#include <iostream.h>
 const int LOWGRADE = 0;
 const int HIGHGRADE = 100;
 int main()
 {
   int grade;

   do
   {
     cout << "Enter a grade: ";
     cin  >>  grade;
   } while (grade < LOWGRADE || grade > HIGHGRADE);
   cout << "\nThe grade entered is " << grade << endl;

   return 0;
 }
```

b.
```
#include <iostream.h>
const int LOWGRADE = 0;
const int HIGHGRADE = 100;
int main()
{
  int grade;

  do
  {
    cout << "Enter a grade: ";
    cin  >>  grade;
    if (grade < LOWGRADE || grade > HIGHGRADE)
     cout << "Invalid grade - please retype it.\n";
  } while (grade < LOWGRADE || grade > HIGHGRADE);
  cout << "\nThe grade entered is " << grade << endl;

  return 0;
}
```

c.
```
#include <iostream.h>
const int LOWGRADE = 0;
const int HIGHGRADE = 100;
const int SENTINEL = 999;
int main()
{
  int grade;
  do
  {
    cout << "Enter a grade: ";
    cin  >>  grade;
    if (grade == SENTINEL)
      return 0;
    else if (grade < LOWGRADE || grade > HIGHGRADE)
     cout << "Invalid grade - please retype it.\n";
  } while (grade < LOWGRADE || grade > HIGHGRADE);
  cout << "\nThe grade entered is " << grade << endl;

  return 0;
}
```

d.
```
#include <iostream.h>
const int LOWGRADE = 0;
const int HIGHGRADE = 100;
int main()
{
  int grade, badGrade = 0;

  do
  {
    cout << "Enter a grade: ";
    cin  >>  grade;
    if (grade < LOWGRADE || grade > HIGHGRADE)
    {
      badGrade++;
      if (badGrade == 5)
        return 0;
    else
      cout << "Invalid grade - please retype it.\n";
    }
  } while (grade < LOWGRADE || grade > HIGHGRADE);
  cout << "\nThe grade entered is " << grade << endl;

  return 0;
}
```

3.a.

```
#include <iostream.h>
int main()
{
  int num, digit;

  cout << "Enter an integer: ";
  cin  >>  num;
  cout << "The number reversed is: ";
  do
  {
    digit = num % 10;
    num /= 10;
    cout << digit;
  } while (num > 0);

  return 0;
}
```

5.

```
#include <iostream.h>
#include <math.h>
const float OKDIF = 0.00001;
int main()
{
  float num, root, approx;

  cout << "Enter a number for which you want the square root: ";
  cin  >>  num;
  cout << "Enter your best guess for this number's square root: ";
  cin  >>  approx;
  do
  {
    root = approx;    // save the approx
    approx = (num/root + root)/2.0;      // calculate a new approx
    cout << "new approx = " << approx << endl;
  }
  while ( fabs(approx - root) > OKDIF);
  cout << "The square root is " << approx << endl;

  return 0;
}
```

EXERCISES 5.8

1.a. An aggregation is a specific type of an association between objects where one object is composed of one or more other objects.

b. An association refers to a relationship between classes.

c. A class describes the properties and operations that each object must have to be a member of the class.

d. A dynamic model describes when things happen to objects being modeled in the system.

e. A functional model is a procedural model that defines the algorithms applicable to each object being modeled in a system.

f. A generalization is a relationship between classes in which one class is derived from another class.

g. Inheritance is a synonym for generalization and refers to the relationship between classes in which one class is derived from another class.

h. Multiplicity refers to the number of objects of one class that are associated with another class.

i. An object refers to a specific, single member of a class.

j. An object diagram graphically illustrates a system's objects, classes, and relationships between them.

k. An object model is used to describe the attributes and operations for each type of object being modeled in a system and the relationships between each object.

EXERCISES 5.10

1.a.

```
#include<iostream.h>
int main()
{
  int num;

  for(num = 33; num >= 3; num -= 3)
    cout << num << "  ";
  cout << endl;

  return 0;
}
```

b.

```
#include<iostream.h>
int main()
{
  char letter;

  for(letter = 'Z'; letter >= 'A'; letter--)
    cout << letter << "  ";
  cout << endl;

  return 0;
}
```

3.

```
#include <iostream.h>
#include <math.h>
const float OKDIF = 0.000001;

int main()
{
  double next_approx = 1.0; // first approximation
  double old_approx;
  int i = 1;
  double factor = 1;

  old_approx = 0;  // make sure the loop starts

  while(fabs(next_approx - old_approx) > OKDIF)
  {
    old_approx = next_approx;
    factor = factor * i;
    next_approx = old_approx + 1/factor;
    i++;
  }
  cout << "Euler's number, accurate to " << OKDIF
       << " is " << next_approx << endl;

  return 0;
}
```

5.

```
#include <iostream.h>
#include <iomanip.h>
int main()
{
  float balance = 5000.0;
  float rate = 0.09/12;
  float payment = 159;
  float interest, principal;

  cout << "  Beginning    Interest   Principal  Ending Loan\n";
  cout << "   Balance     Payment     Payment     Balance  \n";
  cout << "-------------------------------------------------\n";

  cout << setiosflags(ios::fixed)
       << setiosflags(ios::showpoint)
       << setprecision(2);

  while(balance > 0.05)
  {
    cout << setw(11) << balance;
    interest = rate * balance;
    principal = payment - interest;
    balance = balance - principal;
    cout << setw(10) << interest
         << setw(10) << principal
         << setw(10) << balance << endl;
  }

  return 0;
}
```

Note: The last balance will always be a penny or two off due to fractional amounts. Therefore, the while loop stops when a balance of 5 cents or less is achieved. It is instructive to run this program and alter the 0.05 in the while statement to 0.0. In practice, the last payment would be altered to achieve a zero balance.

7.

```
#include <iostream.h>
#include <iomanip.h>
#include <math.h>
const float MINRATE = 1.0;
const float MAXRATE = 20.0;

int main()
{
  float balance, rate, years;
  float payment;  // monthly payment, in dollars
  float mrate;    // monthly interest rate
  float interest, principal;
  float cumint = 0.0, cumpay = 0.0;
  int pmtnum = 0;

  cout << "What is the amount of the loan? $ ";
  cin  >> balance;
  do
  {
    cout << "What is the annual percentage rate? (ex. enter 14 for 14%): ";
    cin  >> rate;
  }
```

(continued on next page)

(continued from previous page)

```
    while (rate < MINRATE || rate > MAXRATE);
    cout << "How many years will you take to pay back the loan? ";
    cin  >> years;

    mrate = rate/(12.0 * 100.0);  // monthly rate as a decimal
    payment =  balance * mrate/(1.0 - pow((1.0+mrate),-(years*12.0)));
    payment = (int(payment * 100 + 0.5))/100.0;  // round to cents
    cout << setiosflags(ios::fixed)
         << setiosflags(ios::showpoint)
         << setprecision(2);
    cout << "Amount  Annual % Interest  Years  Monthly Payment\n"
         << balance << setw(12) << rate
         << setw(12) << years << setw(14) << payment << "\n\n";
    cout << "Payment  Interest   Principal   Cumulative"
         << "   Total Paid   New Balance\n";
    cout << "Number      Paid        Paid        Interest"
         << "       to Date       Due      \n";
    cout << "---------------------------\n";
    while(balance > 0.05)
    {
      pmtnum++;
      interest = balance * mrate;
      principal = payment - interest;
      cumint += interest;
      cumpay += payment;
      balance = balance - principal;
      cout << setw(4)  << pmtnum
           << setw(11) << interest
           << setw(12) << principal
           << setw(12) << cumint
           << setw(14) << cumpay
           << setw(14) << balance << endl;
    }
    return 0;
  }
```

Note: The rounding of the payment to a whole number of cents means that the last balance will not exactly reach zero. It is for this reason that the while statement stops the loop when the remaining balance is less than or equal to a nickel. In practice, the last payment would be altered to achieve a zero balance.

9.

```
#include <iostream.h>
#include <math.h>
const int BASE = 3;
const int MAX = 30000L;
int main()
{
  int n = 0;
  long PowerOfThree = 1L;

  while(PowerOfThree <= MAX)
  {
    PowerOfThree = 3 * PowerOfThree;
    n++;
  }
  cout << "The value of n is " << n << endl;
  cout << BASE << " raised to the power " << n << " is " << pow(3,n) << endl;

  return 0;
}
```

Note: Long integers are used here because of the possibility that the next power of three value will exceed 32,000, which it does. As a check, we have used the power function to ensure that our calculation of PowerOfThree is correct.

17. Your return memorandum should indicate that top-down analysis and design is concerned with describing the functional relationships between procedures. In an OOP environment, the basis of a program is the description of objects in terms of their attributes and behavior and how the various objects interact.

EXERCISES 6.1

1.a. factorial( ) expects to receive one integer value.
 b. price( ) expects to receive one integer and two double precision values, in that order.
 c. An int and two double-precision values, in that order, must be passed to yield( ).
 d. A character and two floating-point values, in that order, must be passed to interest( ).
 e. Two floating-point values, in that order, must be passed to total( ).
 f. Two integers, two characters, and two floating-point values, in that order, are expected by roi( ).
 g. Two integers and two character values, in that order, are expected by get_val( ).

3.a. The FindAbs( ) function is included in the program written for Exercise 3b.
 b.

```
#include <iostream.h>
void FindAbs(double);   // function prototype needed by main()
int main()
{
  double dnum;

  cout << "Enter a number: ";
  cin >> dnum;
  FindAbs(dnum);

  return 0;
}

void FindAbs(double num)
{
  double val;

  if (num < 0)
    val = -num;
  else
    val = num;
  cout << "The absolute value of " << num << " is " << val << endl;
  return;
}
```

5.a. The SqrIt( ) function is included in the program written for Exercise 5b.
 b.

```
#include <iostream.h>
void SqrIt(double);   // function prototype needed by main()
int main()
{
  double first;

  cout << "\nEnter a number: ";
  cin >> first;
  SqrIt(first);

  return 0;
}

void SqrIt(double num)
{
  cout << "The square of " << num << " is " << (num*num) << endl;

  return;
}
```

7.a. The function for producing the required table is included in the larger program written for Exercise 7b.

b.

```
#include <iostream.h>
#include <iomanip.h>
void table(void);    // function prototype needed by main()

int main()
{
  table();              // call the function

  return 0;
 }

 void table(void)
{
  int num;

 cout << "\nNUMBER    SQUARE    CUBE"
      << "\n------    ------    ----\n";
 for (num = 1; num <= 10; num++)
   cout << setw(3) << num << "         "
        << setw(3) << num * num << "       "
        << setw(4) << num * num * num << endl;

    return;
  }
```

EXERCISES 6.2

1.

```
#include <iostream.h>
float FindMax(float, float);  // the function prototype needed by main()

int main()
{
  float firstnum, secnum, max;

  cout << "\nEnter a number: ";
  cin  >> firstnum;
  cout << "Great! Please enter a second number: ";
  cin  >> secnum;

  max = FindMax(firstnum, secnum); // the function is called here

  cout << "\nThe maximum of the two numbers is " << max << endl;

  return 0;
}

float FindMax(float x, float y)
{                        // start of function body
  float maxnum;          // variable declaration

  if (x >= y)            // find the maximum number
    maxnum = x;
  else
    maxnum = y;

  return maxnum;         // return statement
}
```

3.a. void check(int num1, float num2, double num3)
b. double FindAbs(double x);
c. float Mult(float first, float second)
d. int SqrIt(int number)
e. int PowFun(int num, int exponent)
f. either void table(void) or void table( )

5.a. The Mult( ) function is included in the program written for Exercise 5b.
b.

```
#include <iostream.h>
double Mult(double, double);     // function prototype needed by main()
int main()
{
  double first, second;

  cout << "Please enter a number: ";
  cin  >> first;
  cout << "Please enter another number: ";
  cin  >>  second;
  cout << "The product of these numbers is "
       << Mult(first,second) << endl;

  return 0;
}

double Mult(double num1, double num2)
{
  return (num1*num2);
}
```

7. The polynomial function is included in the following working program:

```
#include <iostream.h>
int main()
{
  float a, b, c, x, result;
  float PolyTwo(float, float, float, float); // prototype

  cout << "Enter the coefficient for the x squared term : ";
  cin  >> a;
  cout << "Enter the coefficient for x : ";
  cin  >> b;
  cout << "Enter the constant: ";
  cin  >> c;
  cout << "Enter the value for x: ";
  cin  >> x;
  result = PolyTwo(a, b, c, x);
  cout << "\nThe result is " <<  result;

  return 0;
}

float PolyTwo(float c1, float c2, float c3, float x)
{
  return (c1*x*x + c2*x + c3);
}
```

11.a. The fracpart( ) function is included in the program written for Exercise 11b.

b.

```
#include <iostream.h>
double fracpart(double);  // function prototype needed by main()
int whole(double);       // function prototype needed by fracpart()
int main()
{
  double num;

  cout << "Enter a number: ";
  cin  >> num;
  cout << "\nThe fraction part of " << num
       << " is " << fracpart(num) << endl;

  return 0;
}

double fracpart(double x)
{
  return (x - whole(x));
}

int whole(double n)
{
  int a;

  a = n;   // a = int (n) is preferred - see Section 3.3
  return a;
}
```

EXERCISES 6.3

1.a.

Variable Name	Data Type	Scope
price	integer	global to main(), roi(), and step()
years	long integer	global to main(), roi(), and step()
yield	double-precision	global to main(), roi(), and step()
bondtype	integer	local to main() only
interest	double-precision	local to main() only
coupon	double-precision	local to main() only
count	integer	local to roi() only
eff_int	double-precision	local to roi() only
numofyrs	integer	local to step() only
fracpart	float	local to step() only

Note that although arguments of each function assume a value that is dependent on the calling function, these arguments can change values within their respective functions. This makes them behave as if they were local variables within the called function.

3. The parameter p is local to One( ).
The variables a and b are global to main( ), One( ), and Two( ).
The variables c, d, e, and f are local to main( ).
Th variables m and n are local to One( ).
The variables p, d, q, and r are local to Two.

5. The following is displayed:

```
20
10
```

Even though the global and local variables have the same name, main( ) cannot access the global variable firstnum because the declaration in main( ) has precedence over the global declaration. The global variable firstnum can, however, be accessed in main( ) by using the global scope resolution operator.

EXERCISES 6.4

1.a. Local variables may be automatic, static, or register. It is important to realize that not all variables declared inside of functions are necessarily local. An example of this is an external variable.

b. Global variables may be static or external.

3. The first function declares yrs to be a static variable and assigns a value of one to it only once when the function is compiled. Each time the function is called thereafter, the value in yrs is increased by two. The second function also declares yrs to be static, but assigns it the value one every time it is called, and the value of yrs after the function is finished will always be 3. By resetting the value of yrs to 1 each time it is called, the second function defeats the purpose of declaring the variable to be static.

5. The scope of a variable tells where the variable is recognized in the program and can be used within an expression. If, for example, the variable years is declared inside a function, it is local and its scope is inside that function only. If the variable is declared outside of any function, it is global and its scope is anywhere below the declaration but within that file, unless another file of the same program extends the scope of the variable by declaring the variable to be external.

EXERCISES 6.5

1.a. `float& amount;`

b. `double& price`

c. `int& minutes;`

d. `char& key;`

e. `double& yield;`

3.

```
#include <iostream.h>
void FindMax(int, int, int& );  // function prototype needed by main()
int main()
{
  int firstnum, secnum, max;

  cout << "Enter a number: ";
  cin  >>  firstnum;
  cout << "Great! Please enter a second number: ";
  cin  >>  secnum;

  FindMax(firstnum, secnum, max); // call the function

  cout << "\nThe maximum of the two numbers is " << max << endl;

  return 0;
}

void FindMax(int x, int y, int& maxval)
{
  if (x >= y)
   maxval = x;
  else
   maxval = y;
  return;
}
```

5.

```
void time(int tot_sec, int& hrs, int& mins, int& secs)
{
  hrs = tot_sec/3600;  // 3600 seconds = 1 hour
                       //  Integer division yields the whole
   //  number of times 3600 goes into tot_sec
  tot_sec -= hrs * 3600;
  mins = tot_sec/60;
  tot_sec -= mins * 60;
  secs = tot_sec;

  return;
}
```

EXERCISES 6.6

1.

```
#include <iostream.h>
int fibon(int);   // function prototype needed by main()
int main()
{
  int n, result;

  cout << "Enter the desired term: ";
  cin  >> n;
  result = fibon(n-1);  // the series starts with term 0, not 1
  cout << "Term " << n << " of the Fibonacci sequence is " << result << endl;

  return 0;
}

int fibon(int n)
{
  if(n < 2)
    return(n);
  else
    return(fibon(n-1) + fibon(n - 2));
}
```

3.

```
#include <iostream.h>
int XToTheN(int, int);   // function prototype needed by main()
int main()
{
  int x, n, result;

  cout << "Enter the value of x and n: ";
  cin  >> x >> n;
  result = XToTheN(x, n);
  cout << x << " raised to the power " << n << " is " << result << endl;

  return 0;
}

int XToTheN(int x, int n)
{
  if(n == 0)
    return 1;
  else
    return (x * XToTheN(x, n-1));
}
```

5.

```
#include <iostream.h>
int arithseq(int, int, int);  // function prototype needed by main()
int main()
{
  int n, a, d, result;

  cout << "Enter the desired term: ";
  cin  >> n;
  cout << "Enter the first term and common difference: ";
  cin  >> a >> d;
  result = arithseq(a, d, n);
  cout << "Term " << n << " of the sequence is " << result << endl;

  return 0;
}

int arithseq(int a, int d, int n)
{
  if(n == 1)
    return a;
  else
    return (d + arithseq(a, d, n-1));
}
```

EXERCISES 6.7

1.

```
#include <iostream.h>
#include <iomanip.h>
#include <stdlib.h>
#include <time.h>
int main()
{
  int heads = 0;  // initialize heads count;
  int tails = 0;   // initialize tails count;
  int i, tosses;
  float flip, perheads, pertails;

  cout << "Enter the number of tosses: ";
  cin  >> tosses;

  srand(time(NULL));
  for (i = 1; i <= tosses; ++i)
    {
    flip = float(rand())/RAND_MAX;  // scale the number between 0 and 1;
    if (flip > 0.5)
      heads = heads + 1;
    else
      tails = tails + 1;
  }
  perheads = (heads / (float)tosses) * 100.0;
  pertails = (tails / (float)tosses) * 100.0;
  cout << "\nHeads came up " << perheads << " percent of the time\n";
  cout << "Tails came up " << pertails << " percent of the time\n";

  return 0;
 }
```

3.

```
#include <iostream.h>
#include <stdlib.h>
#include <time.h>
const int DEBUG = 0;
int main()
{
  int guess, count, val;
  float rnum;
        char choice;

        srand(time(NULL));
  do
  {
    rnum = rand();
    val = int(rnum/RAND_MAX * 100);
    if (DEBUG)
    cout << "rnum = " << rnum << " val = " << val;
    count = 0;
    do
    {
      cout << "\nEnter your guess: ";
      cin  >> guess;
      count++;
      if (guess < val)
        cout << "\nYour guess was too low - guess again!";
      else if (guess > val)
        cout << "\nYour guess was too high - guess again!";
    }while (guess != val);

    cout << "\nCongratulations!  You did it in " << count << " guesses\n";
    cout << "WOULD YOU LIKE TO PLAY AGAIN - 'Y'/'N'?: ";
    cin  >> choice;

  }while (choice == 'Y' || choice == 'y');

  return 0;
}
```

5.

```
#include <iostream.h>
const int NUMSELS = 1000 ; // number of random no. selections
float rand(float);   // function prototype needed by main();
int main()
{
  int i;
  float seed, factor;
  int zerocount, onecount, twocount, threecount;
  int fourcount, fivecount, sixcount, sevencount;
  int eightcount, ninecount, val;

    zerocount = onecount = twocount = threecount = fourcount = 0;
    fivecount = sixcount = sevencount = eightcount = ninecount = 0;
    cout << "Enter an odd 6 digit number not ending in 5: ";
    cin >> seed;

    for (i = 1; i <= NUMSELS; i++)
    {
      seed = rand(seed);
      val = int((seed/1.e6)*10);
      switch (val)
```

(continued on next page)

(continued from previous page)

```
        {
          case 0:
           zerocount++;
           break;
          case 1:
           onecount++;
           break;
          case 2:
           twocount++;
           break;
          case 3:
           threecount++;
           break;
          case 4:
           fourcount++;
           break;
          case 5:
           fivecount++;
           break;
          case 6:
           sixcount++;
           break;
          case 7:
           sevencount++;
           break;
          case 8:
           eightcount++;
           break;
          case 9:
           ninecount++;
        }
    }
    factor = 100.0 / NUMSELS;
    cout << " Zeros: " << zerocount * factor << "%\n";
    cout << " Ones:  " << onecount * factor << "%\n";
    cout << " Twos:  " << twocount * factor << "%\n";
    cout << " Threes:" << threecount * factor << "%\n";
    cout << " Fours: " << fourcount * factor << "%\n";
    cout << " Fives: " << fivecount * factor << "%\n";
    cout << " Sixes: " << sixcount * factor << "%\n";
    cout << " Sevens:" << sevencount * factor << "%\n";
    cout << " Eights:" << eightcount * factor << "%\n";
    cout << " Nines: " << ninecount * factor << "%\n";

    return 0;
  }

  float rand(float x)
  {
    int i;
    i = int(997.0 * x / 1.e6);
    x = 997.0 * x - i * 1.e6;
    return(x);
  }
```

7.

```
int quadrant(float angle)
{
  int val;

  if (angle < 0 || angle >= 360)
    val = -1;
  else if (angle >= 0 && angle < 90)
    val = 1;
  else if (angle >= 90 && angle < 180)
    val = 2;
  else if (angle >= 180 && angle < 270)
    val = 3;
  else if (angle >= 270 && angle < 360)
    val = 4;
  else
    val = 0;
  return val;
}
```

9.

```
  float regfee(int year, int weight)
{
  float fee;

  if (year <= 1970)
  {
    if (weight < 2700)
      fee = 16.50;
    else if (weight >= 2700 && weight <= 3800)
      fee = 25.50;
    else if (weight > 3800)
      fee = 46.50;
  }
  else if (year >= 1971 && year <= 1979)
  {
    if (weight < 2700)
      fee = 27.00;
    else if (weight >= 2700 && weight <= 3800)
      fee = 30.50;
    else if (weight > 3800)
      fee = 52.50;
  }
  else if (year >= 1980)
  {
    if (weight < 3500)
      fee = 19.50;
    else if (weight >= 3500)
      fee = 52.50;
  }
  return fee;
}
```

EXERCISES 6.8

1. The object model is the most important of the three. This model describes the attributes and operations of each object. The dynamic model describes the operations that are then incorporated into the object model. Finally, the functional model describes how each operation is performed by defining the algorithms used in each operation.

EXERCISES 6.10

1.

```
#include <iostream.h>
int main()
{
  int i;
  float num, den;
  float FractionToDecimal(float, float);

  for(i = 0; i < 3; i++)
  {
    cout << "Enter a numerator and denominator: ";
    cin  >> num >> den;
    cout << "The return value is " << FractionToDecimal(num, den) << endl;
  }

  return 0;
}

float FractionToDecimal(float numerator, float denominator)
{
  return numerator/denominator;
}
```

Note: Whenever a function is created, a driver function must be constructed to test the function. In this case it is easy to let the driver function request three sets of values. In this case the first test data should be within the normal range of data for the function, while the second and third data sets test the boundary points. Thus, a useful set of test data might be 1 and 2; 0 and 1; 2 and 0.

3.a.

```
#include <iostream.h>
float addfrac(float, float, float, float);   // function prototype needed by main()
float FractionToDecimal(float, float);       // function prototype needed by main()
float multfrac(float, float, float, float); // function prototype needed by main()

int main()
{
  float n1, n2, d1, d2;
  char choice;
  float result;
  cout << "A.  Add two fractions\n";
  cout << "B. Convert a fraction to a decimal\n";
  cout << "C. Multiply two fractions\n";
  cout << "D. Quit\n";
  cout << "    Enter your choice (A, B, C, or D): ";
  cin  >> choice;
     switch(choice)
  {
    case 'a': case'A':
      cout << "Enter the numerator and denominator of the first fraction: ";
      cin  >> n1 >> d1;
      cout << "Enter the numerator and denominator of the second fraction: ";
      cin  >> n2 >> d2;
      result = addfrac(n1, d1, n2, d2);
      break;
    case 'b': case 'B':
      cout << "Enter the numerator and denominator of the fraction: ";
      cin  >> n1 >> d1;
      result = FractionToDecimal(n1, d1);
      break;
```

(continued on next page)

(continued from previous page)

```
      case 'c': case 'C':
        cout << "Enter the numerator and denominator of the first fraction: ";
        cin  >> n1 >> d1;
        cout << "Enter the numerator and denominator of the second fraction: ";
        cin  >> n2 >> d2;
        result = multfrac(n1, d1, n2, d2);
        break;
      default:
        break;
    }

    return 0;
  }

  // here are the stub functions

  float addfrac(float num1, float den1, float num2, float den2)
  {
    cout << "Into addfrac()\n";
    cout << "The passed values are: " << num1 << "  "
              << den1 << "  "
              << num2 << "  "
              << den2 << endl;
    return -1.0;
  }

  float FractionToDecimal(float num1, float den1)
  {
    cout << "Into FractionToDecimal()\n";
    cout << "The passed values are: " << num1 << "  "
                                      << den1 << endl;
    return -1.0;
  }

  float multfrac(float num1, float den1, float num2, float den2)
  {
    cout << "Into multfrac()\n";
    cout << "The passed values are: " << num1 << "  "
          << den1 << "  "
          << num2 << "  "
          << den2 << endl;
    return -1.0;
  }
```

5.

```
#include <iostream.h>
int gcd(int, int);  // function prototype needed by main()
int main()
{
  int num1, num2, result;

  cout << "Enter two integer values: ";
  cin  >> num1 >> num2;
  result = gcd(num1, num2);
  cout << "The return value from gcd() is " << result << endl;
  return 0;
}

// here is the stub
int gcd(int n1, int n2)
{
  return (n1 + n2);
}
```

Returning n1*n2 is not a good idea, because if one of the test values was 0, a zero would be returned. This gives no indication that the second value was correctly received.

7.a. The tax( ) function is included in the program written for Exercise 7b.

b.

```
#include <iostream.h>
#include <iomanip.h>
float tax(float, float);  // function prototype needed by main()
int main()
{
  float amount, rate;

  cout << "Enter the dollar amount and tax rate: ";
  cin  >> amount >> rate;
  cout << setiosflags(ios::fixed)
       << setiosflags(ios::showpoint)
       << setprecision(2);
  cout << "The tax due is $" << tax(amount, rate) << endl;

  return 0;
}

float tax(float a, float r)
{
  return (a * r);
}
```

9.a. The convertdays( ) function is included in the program written for Exercise 9b.

b.

```
#include <iostream.h>
long convertdays(int, int, int);  // function prototype needed by main()

int main()
{
  int month, day, year;

  cout << "Enter the month, day, and year: ";
  cin  >> month >> day >> year;
  cout << "The integer code is " << convertdays(month, day, year) << endl;

  return 0;
}

long convertdays(int m, int d, int y)
{
   return (y*10000L + m*100L + d);
}
```

EXERCISES 7.1

1.a. A class is a programmer-defined data type. The class specifies both the types of data and the types of operations that may be performed on the data.
b. An object is a specific instance of a class.
c. The declaration section declares both the data types and function prototypes of a class.
d. The implementation section defines the class's functions.
e. An instance variables is another name for a class data member.
f. A member function is a function declared in the class declaration section.
g. A data member is a variable declared in the class declaration section.
h. A member function that has the same name as the class and is used to initialize an object's data members.
i. Class instance is synonymous with an object.
j. Services are synonyms for the functions defined in a class implementation section.
k. Methods are synonyms for the functions defined in a class implementation section.

3.a. The class implementation section is included within the complete program written for Exercise 4a.

4.a.

```
#include <iostream.h>
#include <iomanip.h>
// declaration section
class Time
{
  private
    int hours;
    int mins;
    int secs;
  public:
    Time(int = 0, int = 0, int = 0);        // constructor
    void settime(int, int, int); // member function to assign a time
    void showdata(void);          // member function to display a time
};

// implementation section
Time::Time(int hh, int mm, int ss)
{
  hours = hh;
  mins = mm;
  secs = ss;
}
void Time::settime (int hh, int mm, int ss)
{
  hours = hh;
  mins = mm;
  secs = ss;
}
void Time::showdata(void)
{
  cout << "The time is "
       << setw(2) << setfill('0') << hours << ':'
       << setw(2) << setfill('0') << mins << ':'
       << setw(2) << setfill('0') << secs << endl;
}

int main()
{
  Time a, b, c(8,20,10);  // declare 3 objects

  b.settime(1,8,3);   // assign values to b's data members
  a.showdata();       // display object a's values
  b.showdata();       // display object b's values
  c.showdata();       // display object c's values

  return 0;
}
```

5. The class name should begin with a capital letter (i.e., Employee). The data members should be declared as private and the function members should be declared as public. Additionally, the declaration for the constructor prototype should be class(int, char *).

7.

```
#include <iostream.h>
// class declaration
class Date
{
  private:
     int month;
     int day;
     int year;
   public:
     Date(int = 7, int = 4, int = 96);         // constructor
     void setdate(int, int, int); // member function to assign a date
     void showdate(void);         // member function to display a date
     int leapyr(void);            // the additional member function

};

// implementation section
Date::Date(int mm, int dd, int yy)
{
  month = mm;
  day = dd;
  year = yy;
}
void Date::setdate(int mm, int dd, int yy)
{
  month = mm;
  day = dd;
  year = yy;
}
void Date::showdate(void)
{
  cout << "The date is " << month << '/' << day << '/' << year << endl;
}
int Date::leapyr(void)
{
  int fullyr;

  fullyr = year + 1900;
  if( (fullyr % 4 == 0 && fullyr % 100 != 0) || (fullyr % 400 == 0) )
    return 1;    // is a leap year
  else
    return 0;    // is not a leap year
}

int main()
{
  Date a, b, c(4,1,98);  // declare 3 objects

  b.setdate(12,25,97);  // assign values to b's data members
  a.showdate();
  cout << "  The leap year indicator is " << a.leapyr() << endl;
  b.showdate();
  cout << "  The leap year indicator is " << b.leapyr() << endl;
  c.showdate();
  cout << "  The leap year indicator is " << c.leapyr() << endl;
  return 0;
}
```

EXERCISES 7.2

1.a. true
b. false
c. true
d. false
e. true
f. false
g. false
h. true
i. true
j. true
k. false
l. false
m. false
n. true
o. false

3.

```
#include <iostream.h>

// class declaration
class Date
{
  private:
     long yymmdd;
  public:
     Date(int, int, int);      // constructor
     Date(long = 960704);      // default constructor
     void showdate(void);      // member function to display a Date
};

// implementation section
Date::Date(int mm, int dd, int yy)
{
  yymmdd = yy * 10000L + mm * 100L + dd;
}
Date::Date(long ymd)
{
  yymmdd = ymd;
}
void Date::showdate(void)
{
  int year, month, day;

  year = (int)(yymmdd/10000.0);     // extract the year
  month = (int)( (yymmdd - year * 10000.0)/100.00 ); // extract the month
  day = (int)(yymmdd - year * 10000.0 - month * 100.0); // extract the day
  cout << "The Date is " << month << "/" << day << "/" << year << "\n";
}

int main()
{
  Date a, b(4,1,98), c(970515); // declare three objects

  a.showdate();          // display object a's values
  b.showdate();          // display object b's values
  c.showdate();          // display object c's values

  return 0;
}
```

EXERCISES 7.3

3.

```
#include <iostream.h>
#include <stdlib.h>
#include <time.h>
const int MAXFLOOR = 15;
const int NOMOVE = 0;  // code for no elevator movement
const int MOVEDUP = 1; // code for elevator moved up
const int MOVEDDOWN = 2; // code for elevator moved down
const int MAXREQS = 5;

// class declaration

class Elevator
{
  private:
    int cur_floor;
  public:
    Elevator(int = 1);   // constructor
    int request(int);
};

// implementation section

Elevator::Elevator(int cfloor)
{
  cur_floor = cfloor;
}

int Elevator::request(int newfloor)
{
  int code;

  if (newfloor < 1 || newfloor > MAXFLOOR || newfloor == cur_floor)
    code = NOMOVE;
  else if ( newfloor > cur_floor)  // move elevator up
  {
 cout << "\nStarting at floor " << cur_floor << endl;
    while (newfloor > cur_floor)
    {
      cur_floor++;     // add one to current floor
      cout << "   Going Up - now at floor " << cur_floor << endl;
    }
    cout << "Stopping at floor " << cur_floor << endl;
    code = MOVEDUP;
  }
  else  // move elevator down
  {
 cout << "\nStarting at floor " << cur_floor << endl;
    while (newfloor < cur_floor)
    {
      cur_floor--;   // subtract one from current floor
      cout << "   Going Down - now at floor " << cur_floor << endl;
    }
    cout << "Stopping at floor " << cur_floor << endl;
    code = MOVEDDOWN;

  }

  return code;
}
```

(continued on next page)

(continued from previous page)

```
int main()
{
  Elevator a;    // declare an object of type Elevator
  int newfloor, moved, requests = 0;

  srand(time(NULL));
  while (requests < MAXREQS)
  {
    newfloor = (1 + rand() % 16);
    moved = a.request(newfloor);
    if (moved)
     ++requests;
  }

  return 0;
}
```

5.

```
// class declaration
class Person
{
  public:
    Person(void);    //constructor
    int arrive(void);
    int gallons(void);
};

// implementation section

Person::Person()
{
  srand(time(NULL));
}

int Person::arrive()
{
  return (1 + rand() % 16);
}

int Person::gallons()
{
  return (3 + rand() % 21);
}
```

EXERCISES 7.5

1.a. An attribute represents a characteristic of an object; specifically, it is a data member of the object.

b. The behavior of an object defines how the object can be activated and the response that will be produced. It is specified by the object's member and friend functions.

c. The state of an object defines how the object appears at the moment. It is specified by the values assigned to the object's data member variables.

d. A model is a representation of a real object.

e. A class defines the attributes and behavior of a category of a set of objects. As such it is a general representation from which specific objects can be created.

f. An object is a specific instance of a class. As such, values have been assigned to its data members.

g. The set of attributes and behavior defining a class is frequently referred to as the class's interface.

3.a.

i. the title, author, subject, publisher, and date of publication
ii. the type, size, and cost
iii. the type (ballpoint, ink cartridge, or ink refillable), the manufacturer, the color, the cost
iv. the manufacturer of the tape, its length, type, and contents
v. the manufacturer, cost, size, and capabilities (such as rewind, fast forward, record, etc.)
vi. its speed, capacity, cost of installation, cost of operation, cost of maintenance, manufacturer
vii. its manufacturer, overall size, color, cost, engine size, seating capacity, model type, estimated miles per gallon

b. These attributes model a class of objects. Only when specific values are assigned to these attributes is a specific object identified.

5. Animate objects can also be modeled and classified by classes. For example dogs and cats can be grouped together under the category pets, with an attribute of type. In general the attributes included in the class represent characteristics that are of concern for those using the class. For a veterinarian, a more useful attribute might consist of whether the animal has been inoculated or not.

EXERCISES 8.1

1. Assignment stores a value into an existing variable or object; that is, it occurs after the variable or object has been created by a definition statement. Initialization occurs at the time a new variable or object is created and is part of the creation process.

3.a. The required class is contained within the program solution to Exercise 3b.

b.

```
#include <iostream.h>
#include <iomanip.h>
// class declaration
class Complex
{
  private:
    float real;
    float imaginary;
  public:
    Complex(float = 0, float = 0);      // constructor
    void operator=(Complex& ); // overloaded assignment operator function
    void showdata(void);        // display member function
};
// implementation section
Complex::Complex(float re, float im)
{
  real = re;
  imaginary = im;
}
void Complex::operator=(Complex& oldnum)
{
  real = oldnum.real;
  imaginary = oldnum.imaginary;
  return;
}
void Complex::showdata(void)
{
  float c;
  char sign = '+';

  c = imaginary;
  if (c < 0)
  {
```

(continued on next page)

(continued from previous page)

```
      sign = '-';
      c = -c;
    }
    cout << "The complex number is "
         << real << ' ' << sign << ' ' << c << "i\n";
    return;
  }
  int main()
  {
    Complex a(4.2, 3.6), b;  // declare 2 objects

    a.showdata();      // display object a's values
    b.showdata();      // display object b's values
    b = a;             // assign a to b
    b.showdata();      // display object b's values

    return 0;
  }
```

EXERCISES 8.2

1.a.

```
#include <iostream.h>
// class declaration
class Employee
{
  private:
    static float tax_rate;
    static int numemps;
    int id_num;
  public:
    Employee(int = 0);     // constructor
    void display();    // access function
};

// static member definition
float Employee::tax_rate = 0.0025;
int Employee::numemps = 0;
// class implementation
Employee::Employee(int num)
{
  id_num = num;
  numemps++;
}
void Employee::display()
{
  cout << "Employee number " << id_num
       << " has a tax rate of " << tax_rate << endl;
  cout << "There are currently " << numemps
       << " Employee objects" << endl;
  return;
}

int main()
{
  Employee emp1(11122);

  emp1.display();

  Employee emp2(11133);  // create a second object

  emp2.display();

  return 0;
}
```

3. Yes, the three statements could be replaced by the single statement.

5.
```
#include <iostream.h>
#include <math.h>

// class declaration
class Complex
{
  // friends list
  friend Complex addcomplex(Complex&, Complex&);
  private:
    float real;
    float imag;
  public:
    Complex(float = 0, float = 0);  // constructor
    void display();

};

// class implementation
Complex::Complex(float rl, float im)
{
  real = rl;
  imag = im;
}
void Complex::display()
{
  char sign = '+';

  if(imag < 0) sign = '-';
  cout << real << sign << fabs(imag) << 'i';
  return;
}

// friend implementation
Complex addcomplex(Complex& a, Complex& b)
{
  Complex temp;
  temp.real = a.real + b.real;
  temp.imag = a.imag + b.imag;

  return temp;
}

int main()
{
  Complex a(3.2, 5.6), b(1.1, -8.4), c;

  cout << "\nThe first complex number is ";
  a.display();
  cout << "\nThe second complex number is ";
  b.display();

  c = addcomplex(a,b);

  cout << "\n\nThe sum of these two complex numbers is ";
  c.display();

  return 0;
}
```

EXERCISES 8.3

1.a. The required function is included within the following working program:

```
#include <iostream.h>
// class declaration
class Date
{
  private:
     int month;
     int day;
     int year;
   public:
     Date(int = 7, int = 4, int = 94);      // constructor
     int operator>(Date& );  // declare the operator > function
     void showdate(void);  // member function to display a Date
};

// implementation section
Date::Date(int mm, int dd, int yy)
{
  month = mm;
  day = dd;
  year = yy;
}
int Date::operator>(Date& date2)
{
  long dt1, dt2;

  dt1 = year*10000L + month*100 + day;
  dt2 = date2.year*10000L + date2.month*100 + date2.day;
  if (dt1 > dt2)
    return 1;
  else
    return 0;
}

int main()
{
   Date a(4,1,96), b(12,18,95), c(4,1,96); // declare 3 objects

   if (a > b)
     cout << "Date a greater than b \n";
   else
     cout << "Date a less than or equal to b \n";

   if (a > c)
     cout << "Date a greater than c \n";
   else
     cout << "Date a less than or equal to c \n";

  return 0;
}
```

3.a. This operator function provides the same result as the operator( ) function used in Program 13.2.

5.a. The required function is incorporated within the complete program written for Exercise 5b.

b.

```
#include <iostream.h>
// class declaration
class Date
{
  private:
     int month;
     int day;
     int year;
   public:
     Date(int = 0, int = 0, int = 0);     // constructor
     Date operator+(int);     // overload the + operator
     void showdate(void);     // member function to display a Date
};

// implementation section
Date::Date(int mm, int dd, int yy)
{
  month = mm;
  day = dd;
  year = yy;
}
Date Date::operator+(int days)
{
  int daysrem;   // days remaining in the month
  int ds[] = {0,31,28,31,30,31,30,31,31,30,31,30,31};
  Date temp;  // a temporary Date to store the result

  temp.day = day;
  temp.month = month;
  temp.year = year;

  daysrem = ds[month] - temp.day;
  while(daysrem < days)
  {
    temp.month++;
    if(temp.month > 12)
    {
      temp.month = 1;
      temp.year++;
    }
    temp.day = 1;
    days -= (daysrem + 1);
    daysrem = ds[month] - temp.day;
  }
  // now the days remaining is within the current month
  temp.day = temp.day + days;
  return temp;     // the values in temp are returned
}

void Date::showdate(void)
{
  cout << month << "/" << day << "/" << year;
  return;
}

int main()
{
  Date a(12,15,98), b; // declare two objects
```

(continued on next page)

(continued from previous page)

```
    cout << "The initial Date is ";
    a.showdate();
    b = a + 18;   // add in 18 days
    cout << "\nThe new Date is ";
    b.showdate();
    cout << endl;
    return 0;
  }
```

EXERCISES 8.4

1. The function's prototype is:

```
Date operator()(int);    // overload the () operator
```

The function's definition is:

```
Date Date::operator()(int days)
{
  Date temp;  // a temporary Date to store the result

  temp.day = day + days;  // add the days
  temp.month = month;
  temp.year = year;
  while (temp.day > 30)    // now adjust the months
  {
    temp.month++;
    temp.day -= 30;
  }
  while (temp.month > 12)  // adjust the years
  {
    temp.year++;
    temp.month -= 12;
  }
  return temp;     // the values in temp are returned
}
```

EXERCISES 8.5

1.a. Conversion from a built-in type to a built-in type is accomplished by C++'s implicit conversion rules or by explicit casting.

Conversion from a built-in type to a user-defined type is accomplished by a type conversion constructor.

Conversion from a user-defined type to a built-in type is accomplished by a conversion operator function.

Conversion from a user-defined type to a built-in type is accomplished by a conversion operator function.

b. A type conversion constructor is a constructor whose first parameter is not a member of its class and whose remaining parameters, if any, have default values.

A conversion operator function is a class member operator function having the name of a built-in data type or class.

3.

```
#include <iostream.h>

// class declaration for Date
class Date
{
  private:
    int month, day, year;
  public:
    Date(int = 7, int = 4, int = 94);     // constructor
    operator long();          // conversion operator function
    void showdate(void);
};
// constructor
Date::Date(int mm, int dd, int yy)
{
  month = mm;
  day = dd;
  year = yy;
}
// conversion operator function converting from Date to long
Date::operator long()    // must return a long
{
  int mp, yp, t;
  long julian;

  if (month <= 2)
  {
    mp = 0;
    yp = year - 1;
  }
  else
  {
    mp = int(0.4 * month + 2.3);
    yp = year;
  }
  t = int(yp/4) - int(yp/100) + int(yp/400);
  julian = 365L * year + 31L * (month - 1) + day + t - mp;
  return (julian);
}
// member function to display a Date
void Date::showdate(void)
{
  cout << month << "/" << day << "/" << year;
  return;
}

int main()
{
  Date a(1,31,85);  // declare and initialize one object of type Date
  long b;           // declare an object of type long
  b = a;            // a conversion takes place here

  cout << "a's value, in the form month/day/year is ";
  a.showdate();
  cout << "\nThis value, as a Julian integer, is " << b << endl;
  return 0;
}
```

5.

```
#include <iostream.h>

// forward declaration of class Julian
class Julian;

// class declaration for Date
class Date
{
  private:
    int month, day, year;
  public:
    Date(int = 7, int = 4, int = 94);     // constructor
    operator Julian();       // conversion operator to Julian
    void showdate(void);
};

// class declaration for Julian
class Julian
{
  private:
    long yymmdd;
  public:
    Julian(long = 0);     // constructor
    void showjulian(void);
};

// class implementation for Date
Date::Date(int mm, int dd, int yy)  // constructor
{
  month = mm;
  day = dd;
  year = yy;
}
// conversion operator function converting from Date to Julian class
Date::operator Julian()    // must return an Julian object
{
  int mp, yp, t;
  long temp;

  if (month <= 2)
  {
    mp = 0;
    yp = year - 1;
  }
  else
  {
    mp = int(0.4 * month + 2.3);
    yp = year;
  }
  t = int(yp/4) - int(yp/100) + int(yp/400);
  temp = 365L * year + 31L * (month - 1) + day + t - mp;
  return temp;
}

// member function to display a Date
void Date::showdate(void)
{
  cout << month << "/" << day << "/" << year;
  return;
}
```

(continued on next page)

```
// class implementation for Julian
Julian::Julian(long ymd)  // constructor
{
  yymmdd = ymd;
}

// member function to display a Julian
void Julian::showjulian(void)
{
  cout << yymmdd;
  return;
}

int main()
{
  Date a(1,31,95), b(3,16,96);  // declare two Date objects
  Julian c, d;                  // declare two Julian objects

  c = Julian(a);     // cast a into a Julian object
  d = Julian(b);     // cast b into a Julian object
  cout << " a's date is ";
  a.showdate();
  cout << "\n   as a Julian object this date is ";
  c.showjulian();

  cout << "\n b's date is ";
  b.showdate();
  cout << "\n   as a Julian object this date is ";
  d.showjulian();
  cout << endl;
  return 0;
}
```

Note: There is no conversion operator from Julian to Date. In general the Julian objects are extremely useful for determining actual day count differences between two dates, and for sorting dates. In practice, the Julian date would be incorporated as a data member of the Date class. Also note that the forward reference to the Julian class could be omitted in this program if the Julian class were declared prior to the Date class.

EXERCISES 8.6

3.

```
#include <iostream.h>
#include <stdlib.h>
#include <time.h>

#include <stdlib.h>
#include <time.h>
const int MAXFLOOR = 15;

// class declaration and implementation
class Person
{
  public:
    Person() {srand(time(NULL));};  // default constructor
    int call(){return (1 + rand() % (MAXFLOOR + 1));};
};

// class declaration
```

(continued on next page)

(continued from previous page)

```
class Elevator
{
  private:
    int cur_floor;
  public:
    Elevator(int = 1);   // default constructor
    void request(int);
};

// implementation section

Elevator::Elevator(int cfloor)
{
  cur_floor = cfloor;
}

void Elevator::request(int newfloor)
{
  if (newfloor < 1 || newfloor > MAXFLOOR || newfloor == cur_floor)
    ;  // do nothing
  else if ( newfloor > cur_floor)  // move elevator up
  {
    cout << "\nStarting at floor " << cur_floor << endl;
    while (newfloor > cur_floor)
    {
      cur_floor++;    // add one to current floor
      cout << "   Going Up - now at floor " << cur_floor << endl;
    }
    cout << "Stopping at floor " << cur_floor << endl;
  }
  else  // move elevator down
  {
    cout << "\nStarting at floor " << cur_floor << endl;
    while (newfloor < cur_floor)
    {
      cur_floor--;   // subtract one from current floor
      cout << "   Going Down - now at floor "
           << cur_floor << endl;
    }
    cout << "Stopping at floor " << cur_floor << endl;
  }

  return;
}

int main()
{
  Elevator a;   // declare one object of type Elevator
  Person one;   // declare one person type
  int i, FromFloor, ToFloor;

  for (i = 0; i < 3; i++)
  {
 FromFloor = one.call();
 cout << "Person called elevator from floor "
      << FromFloor << endl;
 a.request(FromFloor);  // move to the floor
 do
 {
```

(continued on next page)

```
    ToFloor = one.call();  // request a new floor
    } while (ToFloor == FromFloor);
  cout << "Person requested to go to floor "
           << ToFloor << endl;
  a.request(ToFloor);
  }

  return 0;
}
```

EXERCISES 8.8

1.a. The Cartesian class is presented within the program solution to Exercise 1b.

b.

```
#include <iostream.h>
#include <iomanip.h>

// class declaration
class Cartesian
{
  private:
    float x;
    float y;
  public:
    Cartesian(float = 0.0, float = 0.0); // constructor
    void input(float, float);  // input data member values
    void showdata(); // display data member values
    void operator=(Cartesian&); // overloaded assignment
};

// implementation section
Cartesian::Cartesian(float xval, float yval)
{
  x = xval;
  y = yval;
}

void Cartesian::input(float newx, float newy)
{
  x = newx;
  y = newy;
  return;
}

void Cartesian::showdata()
{
  cout << "(" << x << ", " << y << ")" << endl;
  return;
}

void Cartesian::operator=(Cartesian& oldnum)
{
  x = oldnum.x;
  y = oldnum.y;
  return;
}
int main()
{
```

(continued on next page)

(continued from previous page)

```
    Cartesian a, b(3.0, 2.0);  // declare 2 objects
    float xval, yval;

    cout << "Point a is initially located at ";
    a.showdata();        // display object a's values
    cout << "Point b is initially located at ";
    b.showdata();        // display object b's values
    cout << "Enter a new x and y value for point b: ";
    cin >> xval >> yval;
    b.input(xval, yval);
    cout << "Point b is now located at ";
    b.showdata;
    a = b;               // assign b to a
    cout << "Point a is now located at ";
    a.showdata();

    return 0;
  }
```

3.a. The Savings class is presented within the program solution to Exercise 3b.

b.

```
#include <iostream.h>
#include <iomanip.h>

// class declaration
class Savings
{
  private:
    static float rate;
 float balance;
    float interest;
  public:
    Savings(float = 0.0, float = 0.0); // constructor
    void input(float);  // input data member values
    void showdata(); // display data member values
    static void inrate(float);  // static function
};

// static member definition
float Savings::rate = 0.0;

// implementation section
Savings::Savings(float bal, float ival)
{
  balance = bal;
  interest  = ival;
}

void Savings::input(float newbalance)
{
  balance = newbalance;
  interest = balance * rate / 100.0;
  return;
}

void Savings::showdata()
{
  cout << "Balance  = " << balance
    << "\nRate = " << rate
```

(continued on next page)

```
    << "\nInterest = " << interest << endl;
  return;
}

void Savings::inrate(float rateval)
{
  rate = rateval;
  return;
}

int main()
{
  Savings a;  // declare one object
  float bval, rateval;

  cout << "The current values for object a are:\n";
  a.showdata();       // display object a's values
  cout << "Enter a new rate value: ";
  cin >> rateval;
  Savings::inrate(rateval);  // call the static function
  cout << "Enter a new balance: ";
  cin >> bval;
  a.input(bval);
  cout << "The new values for object a are:\n";
  a.showdata();

  return 0;
}
```

5.a. The Rec_coord and Pol_coord classes are presented within the program solution to Exercise 5b.

b.

```
#include <iostream.h>
#include <iomanip.h>
#include <math.h>
const float DegToRad = 3.1416/180.0; // degrees to radians
const float RadToDeg = 1.0/DegToRad; // radians to degrees
const int RecToPolar = 1;
const int PolarToRec = 2;

// forward declaration of class Pol_coord
class Pol_coord;

//Rec_coord class declaration
class Rec_coord
{
  // friends list
  friend void conv_pol(int, Rec_coord&, Pol_coord&);
  private:
    float xval;
    float yval;
  public:
    Rec_coord(float = 0.0, float = 0.0); // constructor
    void input(float, float);  // input data member values
    void showdata(); // display data member values
};

// Pol_coord class declaration
class Pol_coord
{
```

(continued on next page)

(continued from previous page)

```
    // friends list
    friend void conv_pol(int, Rec_coord&, Pol_coord&);
    private:
      float dist;
      float theta;
    public:
      Pol_coord(float = 0.0, float = 0.0); // constructor
      void input(float, float);  // input data member values
      void showdata(); // display data member values
  };

  // implementation section
  Rec_coord::Rec_coord(float x, float y)
  {
    xval = x;
    yval = y;
  }

  void Rec_coord::input(float newxval, float newyval)
  {
    xval = newxval;
    yval = newyval;
    return;
  }

  void Rec_coord::showdata()
  {
    cout << "(" << xval << ", " << yval << ")" << endl;
    return;
  }

  Pol_coord::Pol_coord(float r, float angle)
  {
    dist = r;
    theta = angle;
  }

  void Pol_coord::input(float newdist, float newtheta)
  {
    dist = newdist;
    theta = newtheta;
    return;
  }

  void Pol_coord::showdata()
  {
    cout << "r = " << dist << ", angle = " << theta << endl;
    return;
  }

  // friend implementation
  void conv_pol(int dir, Rec_coord& a, Pol_coord& b)
  {
    if (dir == RecToPolar)
    {
      b.dist = sqrt(pow(a.xval,2) + pow(a.yval,2));
  b.theta = atan(a.yval/a.xval) * RadToDeg;
```

(continued on next page)

(continued from previous page)

```
    }
    else if (dir == PolarToRec)
    {
      a.xval = b.dist * cos(b.theta * DegToRad);
      a.yval = b.dist * sin(b.theta * DegToRad);
    }
    return;
  }

  int main()
  {
    Rec_coord a;  // declare one object for each class
    Pol_coord b;
    float newx, newy, newr, newtheta;

    cout << "Rectangular point a is initially located at ";
    a.showdata();        // display object a's values
    cout << "Polar point b is initially located at ";
    b.showdata();
    cout << "Enter a new distance and angle for point b: ";
    cin >> newr >> newtheta;
    b.input(newr, newtheta);
    cout << "Polar point b is now located at ";
    b.showdata();
    conv_pol(PolarToRec, a, b);
    cout << "After conversion point a is now located at ";
    a.showdata();
    cout << "Enter a new x and y value for point a: ";
    cin >> newx >> newy;
    a.input(newx, newy);
    cout << "Rectangular point a is now located at ";
    a.showdata();
    conv_pol(RecToPolar, a, b);
    cout << "After conversion, point b is now located at ";
    b.showdata();

    return 0;
  }
```

EXERCISES 9.1

1.a. Inheritance is the capability of deriving one class from another class.
  b. A base class is the class that is used as the basis for deriving subsequent classes.
  c. A derived class is the class that inherits the characteristics of a base class.
  d. Simple inheritance is a type of inheritance in which the parent of each derived class is a single base class.
  e. Multiple inheritance is a type of inheritance where a derived class has two or more parent base classes.
  f. Class hierarchies are the order in which classes are derived.

3. The three features that must be provided for a programming language to be classified as object-oriented are classes, inheritance, and polymorphism. Object-based languages are languages that support objects but do not provide inheritance features.

EXERCISES 9.2

3. In static binding the determination of which function will be called is made at compile time, while in dynamic binding the determination of which function will be called is made at run time.

5. Polymorphism is the ability of a function or operator to have multiple forms. The particular form that will be invoked can be determined at run time depending on the object being used.

EXERCISES 9.3

1. Reference arguments are effectively named address values. When using the reference argument it is the contents of the address that is desired. The accessing of the contents referred to by the reference argument is automatically obtained when the reference argument identifier is used. Thus, when using a reference argument the access of the final data value is implicitly implied and automatically done. Then this argument, which is a pointer, also refers to the address of an actual data value. To obtain the data value whose address is contained in the `this` argument, however, requires explicitly using one of the dereferencing operators * or -> with the this identifier. As such, the access of the final data value is obtained using an explicit dereferencing operation.

3.
```
#include <iostream.h>

// class declaration

class Date
{
  private:
      int month;
      int day;
      int year;
    public:
      Date(int = 7, int = 4, int = 96); // constructor
      void operator=(Date&);  // define assignment of a date
      void showdate(void);  // member function to display a date
};

// implementation section

Date::Date(int mm, int dd, int yy)
{
  this->month = mm;
  this->day = dd;
  this->year = yy;
}

void Date::operator=(Date& newdate)
{

  this->day = newdate.day;        // assign the day
  this->month = newdate.month;    // assign the month
  this->year = newdate.year;      // assign the year

  return;
}

void Date::showdate(void)
{
  cout << this->month << '/' << this->day << '/'
       << this->year << endl;
  return;
}

int main()
{
  Date a(4,1,97), b(12,18,98); // declare two objects

  cout << "The date stored in a is originally ";
  a.showdate();  // display the original date
  a = b;         // assign b's value to a
  cout << "After assignment the date stored in a is ";
  a.showdate();  // display a's values

  return 0;
}
```

Note: The notation this-> can be replaced with the notation (*this). throughout the program.

EXERCISES 9.4

1.a. A pointer can be either a variable or a parameter whose contents is a memory address.

b. The pointer variable is named b and the address contained in b is the address of an integer.

c. The pointer variable is named addr_of_int and the address contained in this variable is the address of an integer.

d. The pointer variable is named a and the address contained in a is the address of a Customer object.

e. The pointer variable is named pointer1 and the address contained in this variable is the address of an object of type Pump.

f. The pointer variable is named addr_of_a_pump and the address contained in addr_of_a_pump is the address of Pump object.

3. By definition, a model is used to represent the important features of a system. For efficiency purposes a simpler model that adequately presents the desired features is better than a more complicated model. Thus, using dynamic memory allocation for an internal implementation when a simpler nondynamic model produces the same effect is overkill. Each request for new memory places an overhead on the system in terms of processing time, memory resources, and processing complexity. Program 9.7 is only useful in presenting the essentials of dynamic memory allocation within the context of a familiar application. From a programming viewpoint, Program 8.13 is superior.

EXERCISES 9.5

1.

```
#include <iostream.h>
#include <string.h>

// class declaration
class Book
{
  private:
    char *title;    // a pointer to a book title
  public:
    Book(char * = NULL);  // constructor
    Book(Book&);         // copy constructor
    void operator=(Book&);  // overloaded assignment operator
    void showtitle(void);   // display the title
};
// class implementation

Book::Book(char *strng)    // constructor
{
  title = new char[strlen(strng)+1];  // allocate memory
  strcpy(title,strng);                // store the string
}

Book::Book(Book& oldbook)    // copy constructor
{
  title = new char[strlen(oldbook.title) + 1];  // allocate new memory
  strcpy(title, oldbook.title);  // copy the title
}

void Book::operator=(Book& oldbook)
{
  if(title != NULL)  // check that it exists
    delete(title);   // release existing memory
```

(continued on next page)

(continued from previous page)

```
  title = new char[strlen(oldbook.title) + 1];  // allocate new memory
  strcpy(title, oldbook.title);  // copy the title
}

void Book::showtitle(void)
{
  cout << title << endl;
}

int main()
{
  Book book1("DOS Primer");  // create 1st title
  Book book2 = book1;          // create a copy
  Book book3("A Brief History of Western Civilization");  // 2nd title

  book1.showtitle();  // display book1's title
  book2.showtitle();  // check the copy worked
  book3.showtitle();  // display the third book title
  book2 = book3;      // assign book3 to book2
  book2.showtitle();  // check the assignment worked

  return 0;
}
```

3.a. The required class is contained within the program solution to Exercise 3b.

b.

```
#include <iostream.h>
#include <iomanip.h>
#include <string.h>
// declaration section
class Car
{
  private:
    float engine_size;
    char body_style;
    int color_code;
    char *vin_ptr;
  public:
    Car(float = 0.0, char =  'X', int = 0, char * = NULL);  // constructor
    void operator=(Car&);      // overloaded assignment operator
    void showdata(void);        // member function to display a time
};

// implementation section

Car::Car(float eng, char styl, int cd, char *pt)
{
  engine_size = eng;
  body_style = styl;
  color_code = cd;
  vin_ptr = new char[strlen(pt) + 1];   // allocate memory
  strcpy(vin_ptr, pt);                   // store the string
}

void Car::operator=(Car& oldcar)
{
  engine_size = oldcar.engine_size;
  body_style = oldcar.body_style;
  color_code = oldcar.color_code;
```

(continued on next page)

(continued from previous page)

```
    if(vin_ptr != NULL)    // check that it exists
      delete(vin_ptr);     // release existing memory
    vin_ptr = new char[strlen(oldcar.vin_ptr) + 1];  // allocate new memory
    strcpy(vin_ptr, oldcar.vin_ptr);  // copy the vin
  }
  void Car::showdata(void)
  {
    cout << "\nThe values for this object are \n"
         << "  Engine size: " << engine_size << endl
         << "  Body style: "  << body_style << endl
         << "  Color code: "  << color_code << endl
         << "  VIN: " << vin_ptr << endl;
  }

  int main()
  {
     Car a(250.0, 'S', 52, "ABC567YYY"), b;  // declare 2 objects

     a.showdata();   // display object a's values
     b.showdata();   // display object b's values
     b = a;          // assign a to b
     b.showdata();   // display object a's values

    return 0;
  }
```

EXERCISES 9.7

1. In static binding the determination of which function will be called is made at compile time, whereas in dynamic binding the determination of which function will be called is made at run time.

3.a. The required Cylinder class is contained within the program solution to Exercise 3b.

b.

```
#include <iostream.h>
#include <math.h>

const double PI = 2.0 * asin(1.0);

// class declaration
class Point
{
  protected:
    float x;
  float y;
  public:
    Point(float = 0.0, float = 0.0);  //constructor
  float distance(Point&);
};

// implementation section
Point::Point(float xval, float yval)
{
  x = xval;
  y = yval;
}

float Point::distance(Point& b)
```

(continued on next page)

(continued from previous page)

```
{
  return (sqrt(pow((x-b.x),2) + pow((y-b.y),2)));
}

// class declaration for the derived Circle class
class Circle : public Point
{
  protected:
    double radius; // add an additional data member
  public:
    Circle(float = 0.0, float = 0.0, float = 1.0);  // constructor
    float distance(Circle&);
  float area();
};

// implementation section for Circle
Circle::Circle(float centerx, float centery, float r)  // constructor
{
  x = centerx;
  y = centery;
  radius = r;
}

float Circle::distance(Circle& b)
{
  return (Point::distance(b)); // note the base function call
}

float Circle::area()   // this calculates an area
{
  return (PI * pow(radius,2));
}

// class declaration for the derived Cylinder class
class Cylinder : public Circle  // Cylinder is derived from Circle
{
  protected:
    float length;  // add one additional data member and
  public:           // two additional function members
    Cylinder(float = 0, float = 0, float = 1, float = 1);
    float distance(Cylinder&);
    float area();
};

// implementation section for Cylinder
Cylinder::Cylinder(float centx, float centy, float rad, float l)
{
  x = centx;
  y = centy;
  radius = rad;
  length = l;
}

float Cylinder::distance(Cylinder& b)
{
  return (Circle::distance(b)); // note the base function call
}
```

(continued on next page)

(continued from previous page)

```
float Cylinder::area()    // this calculates a surface area
{
  return (2.0 * PI * radius * (length + radius));
}

int main()
{
  Point a, b(4,4);
  Circle circ1, circ2(3,3,2);
  Cylinder cyl1, cyl2(4,4,2,5);

  cout << "The distance between points is " << a.distance(b) << endl;
  cout << "The area of circ1 is " << circ1.area() << endl;
  cout << "The area of circ2 is " << circ2.area() << endl;
  cout << "The distance between circle centers is " << circ1.distance(circ2) << endl;
  cout << "The area of cyl1 is " << cyl1.area() << endl;
  cout << "The area of cyl2 is " << cyl2.area() << endl;
  cout << "The distance function for these cylinders is " << cyl1.distance(cyl2) << endl;

  return 0;
}
```

Note: An inline base member initialization for the Cylinder class's constructor using the Circle class's constructor, as well as an inline base member initialization of the Circle class's constructor using the Point class's constructor could also have been used.

c. The distance function, when applied to the Cylinder class, provides the distance between centers of the starting ends of each cylinder.

EXERCISES 10.1

5. Yes. Anything stored on disk is referred to as a file. The two major divisions of files are data files and executable (program) files. Although source code files are sometimes called program files, strictly speaking they are data files used by a compiler program. A compiled C++ program is an example of an executable file.

7.a.
```
ofstream memo;
memo.open("coba.mem";
```

b.
```
ofstream letter;
letter.open("book.let");
```

c.
```
ofstream coups;
coups.open("coupons.bnd");
```

d.
```
ifstream pt_yield;
pt_yield.open("yield.bnd");
```

e.
```
ifstream pri_file;
pri_file.open("prices.dat");
```

f.
```
ifstream rates;
rates.open("rates.dat", ios::in);
```

EXERCISES 10.2

1.a.

```
#include <fstream.h>
  #include <stdlib.h>
  const int MAXCHARS = 80;
  int main()
  {
     int i;
     ofstream out;
     char strng[MAXCHARS];
     out.open("text.dat");
     if (out.fail())
     {
       cout << "The file was not successfully opened" << endl;
       exit(1);
     }
     cout << "Enter three lines of text to be stored in the file.\n";
  for (i = 1; i <= 3; i++)
     {
       cin.getline(strng, MAXCHARS, '\n');  // get input from cin stream
       out << strng << endl;
     }
     out.close();
     cout << "End of data input.\n";
     cout << "The file has been written.\n";

     return 0;
   }
```

b.

```
#include <fstream.h>
#include <stdlib.h>
const int MAXCHARS = 80;
int main()
{
  int ch;
  char line[MAXCHARS];
  ifstream in_file;

  in_file.open("text.dat");
  if (!in_file)   // check for successful open
  }
    cout << "\nThe file was not successfully opened"
  << "\n Please check that the file currently exists."
  << endl;
    exit(1);
  }
      // now read the file
  while( (ch = in_file.peek()) != EOF )
  {
    in_file.getline(line, MAXCHARS,'\n');
    cout << line << endl;
  }

  return 0;
}
```

3.a. The data may be entered in a variety of ways. One possibility is to enter the data, line by line, and write each line to a file. A second method is to use a text editor to write the data to a file. A third possibility is to enter the data as individual items and write the file as individual items. The program below uses this last approach.

```
#include <fstream.h>
#include <iomanip.h>
#include <stdlib.h>
const int MAX = 30;
int main()
{
  ofstream out;
  char name[MAX], date[MAX];
  int i;
  long id;
  float rate;

  out.open("employ.dat");
  if (out.fail())
  {
    cout << "The file was not successfully opened" << endl;
    exit(1);
  }
  for (i = 1; i <= 5; i++)    // get and write 5 records
  {
    cout << "\nEnter the name: ";
    cin  >> name;
    cout << "Enter the ID No: ";
    cin  >> id;
    cout << "Enter the rate: ";
    cin  >> rate;
    cout << "Enter the date (ex. 12/6/65): ";
    cin  >> date;
    out << setiosflags(ios::left) << setw(18) << name
<< setw(7) << id
<< setw(10) << setprecision(2) << rate
<< date << endl;
}
out.close();
cout << "End of data input.\n";
cout << "The file has been written.\n";

  return 0;
}
```

b.

```
#include <fstream.h>
#include <stdlib.h>
const int MAX = 80;
int main()
{
  ifstream in_file;
  ofstream out_file;
  char ch, line[MAX];

  in_file.open("employ.dat");
  if (in_file.fail())
  {
    cout << "\nThe input file was not successfully opened"
         << "\n Please check that the file currently exists."
         << endl;
    exit(1);
  }
  out_file.open("employ.bak");
  if (out_file.fail())
  {
```

(continued on next page)

(continued from previous page)

```
    cout << "The output file was not successfully opened" << endl;
    exit(2);
  }
  while( (ch = in_file.peek()) != EOF )
  {
    in_file.getline(line, MAX, '\n');
    out_file << line << endl;
  }
  cout << "\nFile copy completed.\n";
  in_file.close();
  out_file.close();

  return 0;
}
```

c.

```
#include <fstream.h>
#include <string.h>
#include <stdlib.h>
const int MAXLENGTH = 21;
const int MAXCHARS = 80;
int main()
{
  ifstream in_file;
  ofstream out_file;
  char ch, f_name[MAXLENGTH], s_name[MAXLENGTH], line[MAXCHARS];

  cout << "Enter the name of the file to be copied: ";
  cin  >> f_name;
  cout << "Enter the name of the new file: ";
  cin  >> s_name;
  if(strcmp(f_name, s_name) == NULL)
  {
    cout << "\nYou have specified the same name for both files.";
    cout << "\nPlease rerun using different names.";
    exit(1);
  }
  in_file.open(f_name);
  if (in_file.fail())
  {
    cout << "\nThe input file was not successfully opened"
         << "\n Please check that the file currently exists."
         << endl;
    exit(2);
  }
  out_file.open(s_name);
  if (out_file.fail())
  {
    cout << "The output file was not successfully opened" << endl;
    exit(2);
  }
  while( (ch = in_file.peek()) != EOF )
  {
    in_file.getline(line, MAXCHARS, '\n');
    out_file << line << endl;
  }
  cout << "\nFile copy completed.\n";
  in_file.close();
  out_file.close();

  return 0;
}
```

Note: The strcmp( ) function checks that the same file name is not used for both input and output. Use of this function requires inclusion of the string.h header file. The exit( ) function terminates program execution.

d. A better way would be to enter the source and destination file names on the line used to invoke the executable program. Data entered in this manner are called command line arguments. Command line arguments are described in Appendix F.

5.a. The data may be entered in a variety of ways. One possibility is to enter the data, line by line, and write each line to a file. A second method is to use a text editor to write the data to a file. A third possibility is to enter the data as individual items and write the file as individual items. The program below uses this last approach.

```
#include <fstream.h>
#include <iomanip.h>
#include <stdlib.h>
const int MAXNAME = 30;
const int MAXSOCSEC = 12;
int main()
{
  ofstream out;
  char name[MAXNAME], soc_no[MAXSOCSEC];
  int i;
  float rate, hours;

  out.open("personel.dat");
  if (out.fail())
  {
    cout << "The output file was not successfully opened" << endl;
    exit(1);
  }
  for (i = 1; i <= 4; i++)    // get and write 4 records
  {
    cout << "\nEnter the name: ";
    cin  >> name;
    cout << "Enter the Social Security No: ";
    cin  >> soc_no;
    cout << "Enter the rate: ";
    cin  >> rate;
    cout << "Enter the hours: ";
    cin  >> hours;

    // write the file
    out << setiosflags(ios::left | ios::showpoint | ios::fixed)
  << setw(30) << name << "  "
  << setw(11) << soc_no << "  "
  << setw(6) << setprecision(2) << rate << "  "
  << setw(4) << setprecision(2) << hours << endl;
  }
  out.close();
  cout << "\nEnd of data input.";
  cout << "\nThe file has been written.\n";

  return 0;
}
```

b.

```
#include <fstream.h>
#include <iomanip.h>
#include <stdlib.h>
const int MAXNAME = 30;
const int MAXSOCSEC = 12;
int main()
{
  ifstream in;
  char ch, name[MAXNAME], ss[MAXSOCSEC];
  float rate, hours, net;

  in.open("personel.dat", ios::in);
  if (in.fail())
  {
    cout << "\nThe input file was not successfully opened"
         << "\n Please check that the file currently exists."
         << endl;
    exit(1);
  }
  cout << "\nSoc. Sec. No.      Name          Net Pay\n";
  cout << "---------------    ----          -------\n";
  cout << setiosflags(ios::fixed)
  << setiosflags(ios::showpoint)
  << setprecision(2);
  while( (ch = in.peek()) != EOF )
  {
    in >> name >> ss >> rate >> hours;
    net = rate * hours;
    cout << ss << "        " << name
    << "        " << net << endl;
  }
  in.close();

  return 0;
}
```

7.a. It is assumed that the data has been created using any of the methods mentioned in the solutions to Exercises 3a and 5a and stored in a file named invent.dat.

b.

```
#include <fstream.h>
#include <iomanip.h>
#include <stdlib.h>
const int MAXCODE = 6;
int main()
{
  ifstream in;
  char p_code[MAXCODE];
  int i, i_amt, q_sold, m_amt, c_amt, o_amt;

  in.open("invent.dat");
  if (in.fail())
  {
    cout << "\nThe input file was not successfully opened"
         << "\n Please check that the file currently exists."
         << endl;
    exit(1);
  }
```

(continued on next page)

(continued from previous page)

```
    cout << "\n Part      Current    Order";
    cout << "\nNumber   Inventory   Amount";
    cout << "\n------   ---------   ------\n";
    for ( i = 1; i <= 4 i++)
    {
      in >> p_code >> i_amt >> q_sold >> m_amt;
      c_amt = i_amt - q_sold;
      o_amt = m_amt - c_amt;
      if(o_amt < 0)
  o_amt = 0;
      cout << p_code << "    "
    << setw(8) << c_amt
    << setw(8) << o_amt << endl;
    }
    in.close();

    return 0;
  }
```

9.a. It is assumed that the data has been created using any of the methods mentioned in the solutions to Exercises 3a and 5a and stored in a file named results.dat.

b.

```
  #include <fstream.h>
  #include <stdlib.h>
  int main()
  {
    ifstream in;
    int i, num_els, data;
    float total, avg;
    char ch;
    in.open("results.dat");
    if (in.fail())
    {
      cout << "\nThe input file was not successfully opened"
           << "\n Please check that the file currently exists."
           << endl;
      exit(1);
    }
    while( (ch = in.peek()) != EOF)
    {
       in   >> num_els;
       cout << "\nThe number of elements in this group is " << num_els;
       cout << "\nThe data in this group is: ";
       for ( total = 0, i = 1; i <= num_els; i++)
       {
  in >> data;     // read in data to be averaged
  cout << " " << data;
  total += data;           // add data to total
      }
      avg = total/num_els;       // compute average
      cout << "\nThe group average = " << avg << endl;
    }
    in.close();

    return 0;
  }
```

EXERCISES 10.3

5. The f_chars( ) function is included in the program listed below:

```
#include <fstream.h>
#include <stdlib.h>
const int MAXLENGTH = 15;
void f_chars(ifstream&);  // function prototype needed by main()
int main()
{
  ifstream in;
  char f_name[MAXLENGTH];

  cout << "\nEnter a file name: ";
  cin  >> f_name;
  in.open(f_name);
  if (in.fail())    // check for successful open
  {
    cout << "\nThe file was not successfully opened"
      << "\n Please check that the file currently exists."
      << endl;
    exit(1);
  }
  f_chars(in);
  in.close();

  return 0;
}
void f_chars(ifstream& fname)
{
  fname.seekg(0L,ios::end);  // move to the end of the file
  cout << "\nThere are " << fname.tellg()
    << " characters in the file.\n";
  return;
}
```

EXERCISES 10.4

1. The file name referred to in the exercise is a reference to an object of type ifstream. The function prototype for p_file( ) is p_file(ifstream&);.
3. The get_open( ) function is included below with a driver function used to test it.

```
#include <fstream.h>
#include <stdlib.h>
const int MAXCHARS = 15;
int get_open(ofstream&);   // function prototype
int main()    // driver function to test fcheck()
{
  ofstream out_file;

  get_open(out_file);

   return 0;
 }

 int get_open(ofstream& file_out)
 {
   char key, name[MAXCHARS];
   ifstream file_in;

   cout << "\nEnter a file name: " << endl;
   cin.getline(name, MAXCHARS, '\n');
```

(continued on next page)

(continued from previous page)

```
    file_in.open(name);
    if (file_in.fail())
     // the file doesn't exist - create it for writing
    file_out.open(name);
    else
    {
      file_in.close;
  cout << "\nThe file currently exists. Do you want to"
         << "\n overwrite it or exit?"
         << "\nEnter an o, or e: ";
      cin  >> key;
      if(key == 'o')
         file_out.open(name);  // now open it for output
      if (file_out.fail())
     {
       cout << "The output file was not successfully opened"
            << endl;
       exit(1);
     }
   }
   return 1;
  }
```

EXERCISES 10.5

1.

```
#include <fstream.h>
#include <stdlib.h>
const int NUMPOLS = 10;

int main()
{
  ofstream out_file;
  int i, data;

  out_file.open("pollen");

  if (out_file.fail())
  {
cout << "\nFailed to open the data file.\n";
exit(1);
  }
  cout << "\nEnter the last " << NUMPOLS
       << " pollen counts: ";
  for (i = 1; i <= NUMPOLS; i++)
  {
cin  >>  data;
out_file << data << endl;
  }
  out_file.close;

  return 1;
}
```

3.a.

```
#include <fstream.h>
#include <iomanip.h>
#include <stdlib.h>
const char fname[10] = "polar.dat";
const int LINES = 6;

int main()
{
  ofstream out_file;
  int i;
  float dist, angle;

  out_file.open(fname);

  if (out_file.fail())
  {
 cout << "\nFailed to open the data file.\n";
 exit(1);
  }
  out_file << setiosflags(ios::fixed)
     << setiosflags(ios::showpoint)
     << setprecision(1);
for (i = 1; i <= LINES; i++)
  {
cout << "Enter a distance and angle: ";
 cin  >>  dist >> angle;
 out_file << setw(5) << dist
    << setw(14) << angle << endl;
  }
  out_file.close;

  return 1;
}
```

b.

```
#include <fstream.h>
#include <iomanip.h>
#include <stdlib.h>
#include <math.h>
const float CONVERT = 3.1416/180.0; // angle to radian conversion factor
const int LINES = 6;
const char infile[10] = "polar.dat";
const char outfile[11] = "xycord.dat";
void calcxy(ifstream&, ofstream&);
int main()
{
  ifstream in;
  ofstream out;

  in.open(infile);
  if (in.fail())   // check for successful open
  {
    cout << "\nThe file was not successfully opened"
         << "\n Please check that the file currently exists."
      << endl;
    exit(1);
  }

  out.open(outfile);

  if (out.fail())
```

(continued on next page)

(continued from previous page)

```
  {
    cout << "\nFailed to open the data file.\n";
    exit(2);
  }

  calcxy(in, out);
  in.close();
  out.close();
  return 0;
}

void calcxy(ifstream& in_file, ofstream& out_file)
{
   int i;
   float dist, angle;
   float x, y;

   out_file << setiosflags(ios::fixed)
         << setiosflags(ios::showpoint)
         << setprecision(2);
   for(i = 1; i <= LINES; i++)
   {
     in_file >> dist >> angle;
     cout << "dist = " << dist << "  angle = " << angle << endl;
     x = dist * cos(angle * CONVERT);
     y = dist * sin(angle * CONVERT);
     out_file << setw(6) << x
              < setw(10) << y << endl;
   }

   return;
}
```

EXERCISES 10.8

1.

```
#include <fstream.h>
#include <iomanip.h>
#include <stdlib.h>
const int MAXSTUDENTS = 20;
const int MAXNAME = 20;
char fname[10] = "grade.dat";
int main()
{
  int i;
  char lname[MAXNAME], lgrade;
  float g1, g2, h1, f1, fingrade;
  ofstream out_file;

  out_file.open(fname);
  if (out_file.fail())
  {
    cout << "\nFailed to open the file named " << fname << endl;
    exit(1);
  }
  out_file << setiosflags(ios::fixed)
          << setiosflags(ios::showpoint)
          << setprecision(2);
  for (i = 1; i <= MAXSTUDENTS; i++)
```

(continued on next page)

(continued from previous page)

```
    {
      cout << "\nEnter student's last name (XX 0 0 0 0 to exit) & four scores: ";
      cin  >> lname >> g1 >> g2 >> h1 >> f1;
      fingrade = 0.20*g1 + 0.20*g2 + 0.35*h1 + 0.25*f1;
      if(fingrade >= 90) lgrade = 'A';
      else if (fingrade >= 80) lgrade = 'B';
      else if (fingrade >= 70) lgrade = 'C';
      else if (fingrade >= 60) lgrade = 'D';
      else fingrade = 'F';

      cout << "For this data the following data has been"
           << " written to the file:\n";
      cout << lname << " " << g1 << " " << g2 << " " << h1
           << " " << f1 << " " << fingrade << " " << lgrade << endl;
      out_file << lname << " " << g1 << " " << g2 << " " << h1
           << " " << f1 << " " << fingrade << " " << lgrade << endl;
    }

    return 0;
  }
```

3.

```
#include <fstream.h>
#include <stdlib.h>
const int EMPLOYEES = 2;
const int MAXNAME = 15;
int main()
{
  char in[MAXNAME], out[MAXNAME];
  int i;
  int id;
  char sex;
  float wage;
  int years;
  ifstream in_file;
  ofstream out_file;

  cout << "Enter the current employee file name: ";
  cin  >> in;
  cout << "Enter the name of the new output file: ";
  cin  >> out;
  in_file.open(in);
  if (in_file.fail())
  {
    cout << "\nThe file named " << in
         << " was not successfully opened"
         << "\n Please check that the file currently exists."
         << endl;
    exit(1);
  }
  out_file.open(out);
  if (out_file.fail())
  {
    cout << "\nFailed to open the file named " << out << endl;
    exit(2);
  }
  for(i = 0; i < EMPLOYEES; i++)
  {
```

(continued on next page)

(continued from previous page)

```
    in_file  >> id >> sex >> wage >> years;
    cout << "The data read from the file is: "
         << "ID No: " << id << "  Sex: " << sex
         << "  Wage rate: " << wage
         << "  Years: " << years << endl;
    cout << "Enter the new wage rate: ";
    cin  >> wage;
    out_file << id << "  " << sex << "  "
             << wage << "  " << years << endl;
  }
  cout << "This data has been written to the "
       << out << " file\n";

  return 0;
}
```

EXERCISES 11.1

1.a. `int grades[100];` e. `float velocity[32];`
 b. `float temp[50];` f. `float dist[1000];`
 c. `int code[30];` g. `int code_num[6];`
 d. `int year[100];`

3.a. `cin >> grades[0] >> grades[2] >> grades[6];`
 b. `cin >> prices[0] >> prices[2] >> prices[6];`
 c. `cin >> amps[0] >> amps[2] >> amps[6];`
 d. `cin >> dist[0] >> dist[2] >> dist[6];`
 e. `cin >> velocity[0] >> velocity[2] >> velocity[6];`
 f. `cin >> time[0] >> time[2] >> time[6];`

5.a. `a[1]  a[2]  a[3]  a[4]  a[5]`
 b. `a[1]  a[3]  a[5]`
 c. `b[3]  b[4]  b[5]  b[6]  b[7]  b[8]  b[9]  b[10]`
 d. `b[3]  b[6]  b[9]  b[12]`
 e. `c[2]  c[4]  c[6]  c[8]  c[10]`

7.

```
#include <iostream.h>
const int NUMELS = 8;
int main()
{
  int grade[NUMELS], sum, i;
  float average;

  sum = 0;   // initialize here or in the declaration
  for( i = 0; i < NUMELS; i++)
  {
    cout << "Enter a value for element number " << i << " : ";
    cin  >> grade[i];
    sum = sum + grade[i];
  }
  cout << "\nThe values stored in the array are:\n";
  for (i = 0; i < NUMELS; i++)
    cout << grade[i] << "  ";
  average = sum / NUMELS;

  cout << "\nThe average of these values is "
       << average << endl;

  return 0;
}
```

9.a.
```
#include <iostream.h>
#include <iomanip.h>
const int NUMELS = 14;
int main()
{
  int grades[NUMELS], total, i;
  float avg, deviation[NUMELS];

  total = 0;
  for(i = 0; i < NUMELS; i++)
  {
    cout << "Enter grade # " << (i + 1) << " : ";
    cin  >> grades[i];
    total += grades[i];
  }
  avg = total/NUMELS;
  cout << "\n The average of the grades is " << avg << '\n'
    << "Element     Element      Deviation\n"
    << "Number       Value        from Avg.\n"
    << "-------     -------      ----------\n";
  for(i = 0; i < NUMELS; i++)
  {
    deviation[i] = grades[i] - avg;
    cout << setiosflags(ios::showpoint) << setprecision(2);
    cout << setw(4) << i << "    "
  << setw(10) << grades[i] << "    "
  << setw(12) << deviation[i] << endl;
  }

  return 0;
}
```

11.a.
```
#include <iostream.h>
const int NUMELS = 10;
int main()
{
  double raw[NUMELS], sorted[NUMELS], min = 1.e5;
  int i, j, index;

  for(i = 0; i < NUMELS; i++)
  {
    cout << "Enter value # " << (i+1) << " : ";
    cin  >> raw[i];
  {
  for(i = 0; i < NUMELS; i++)
  }
    for(j = 0; j < NUMELS; j++)  // find the minimum for this pass
      {
      if(raw[j] < min) // look for next min
      {
      min = raw[j];
      index = j;
        }
    }
    sorted[i] = min;      // put min in next sorted element
    min = 1.e5;           // reset min for start of search
    raw[index] = 1.e7;    // don't select this element again
  }
  cout << "The elements in sorted order are:\n";
  for( i = 0; i < NUMELS; i++)
    cout << sorted[i] << '\n';

  return 0;
}
```

b. To locate each minimum, make a complete pass through the array and find the first minimum. Now only nine numbers need be searched since one has been used. After the second lowest element has been selected, only the remaining eight need be searched. Instead of 10 squared passes through the loop, only 10 factorial passes are needed. The number of passes can be reduced using a shell sort rather than a bubble sort.

EXERCISES 11.2

1.a. `int grades[10] = {89, 75, 82, 93, 78, 95, 81, 88, 77, 82};`

b. `double amount[5] = {10.62, 13.98, 18.45, 12.68, 14.76};`

c. `double rates[100] = {6.29, 6.95, 7.25, 7.35, 7.40, 7.42};`

d.
```
float temp[64] = {78.2, 69.6, 68.5, 83.9, 55.4, 67.0, 49.8,
                  58.3, 62.5, 71.6};
```

e. `char code[15] = {'f', 'j', 'm', 'q', 't', 'w', 'z'};`

3.

```
#include <iostream.h>
const int NUMELS = 9;
int main()
{
  float slopes[NUMELS] = {17.24, 25.63,  5.94,
                          33.92,  3.71, 32.84,
                          35.93, 18.24,  6.92};
  int i;
  float max = 0.0, min = 999.9;

  for(i = 0; i < NUMELS; i++)
  {
    if (slopes[i] < min) min = slopes[i];
    if (slopes[i] > max) max = slopes[i];
  }
  cout << "\nThe minimum array value is " <<  min;
  cout << "\nThe maximum array value is " << max << '\n';

  return 0;
}
```

5.

```
char goodstr1[13] = {'G', 'o', 'o', 'd', ' ',
                     'M', 'o', 'r', 'n', 'i', 'n', 'g'};
char goodstr1[] = {'G', 'o', 'o', 'd', ' ',
                   'M', 'o', 'r', 'n', 'i', 'n', 'g'};
char goodstr1[] = "Good Morning";
```

Note: This last declaration creates an array having one more character than the first two. The extra character is the null character.

EXERCISES 11.3

1.
```
void sort_arr(double in_array[500])
void sort_arr(double in_array[])
```

3.
```
float prime(float rates[256])
float prime(float rates[])
```

5.

```
#include <iostream.h>
#include <iomanip.h>
const int NUMS = 9;
void show(float []);  // function prototype
int main()
{
   float rates[NUMS] = {6.5, 7.2, 7.5, 8.3, 8.6,
            9.4, 9.6, 9.8, 10.0};

   show(rates);

  return 0;
}

 void show(float rates[])
 {
   int i;

   cout << "\nThe elements stored in the array are:\n";
   cout << setiosflags(ios::showpoint) << setprecision(2);
   for(i = 0; i < NUMS; i++)
     cout << rates[i] << "  " << endl;
 }
```

7.

```
#include <iostream.h>
#include <iomanip.h>
const int NUMVALS = 10;
void extend(double [], double [], double []); // function prototype
int main()
{
  double price[10] = {10.62, 14.89, 13.21, 16.55, 18.62,
               9.47, 6.58, 18.32, 12.15, 3.98};
  double quantity[10] = {4.0, 8.5, 6.0, 7.35, 9.0,
            15.3, 3.0, 5.4, 2.9, 4.8};
  double amount[10];

  int i;

  extend(price, quantity, amount);

  cout << "The elements in the amount array are:";
  cout << setiosflags(ios::showpoint)
       << setprecision(3) << endl;
  for(i = 0; i < NUMVALS; i++)
    cout << amount[i] << endl;

  return 0;
}
void extend(double prc[], double qnty[], double amt[])
{
  int i;

  for(i = 0; i < NUMVALS; i++)
    amt[i] = prc[i] * qnty[i];

  return;
}
```

EXERCISES 11.4

1.a. `int array[6][10];` d. `char letter[15][7];`
 b. `int codes[2][5];` e. `double vals[10][25];`
 c. `char keys[7][12];` f. `double test[16][8];`

3.

```
#include <iostream.h>
const int ROWS = 3;
const int COLS = 4;
int main()
{
  int i, j, total = 0;
  int val[ROWS][COLS] = {8,16,9,52,3,15,27,6,14,25,2,10};

  for (i = 0; i < ROWS; i++)
    for (j = 0; j < COLS; j++)
      total = total + val[i][j];
   cout << "\nThe total of the values is " << total << endl;

  return 0;
}
```

5a.

```
#include <iostream.h>
const int ROWS = 4;
const int COLS = 5;
int main()
{
  int i, j;
  int max = -999;
  int val[ROWS][COLS] = {16, 22, 99, 4, 18,
           -258, 4, 101, 5, 98,
            105, 6, 15, 2, 45,
             33, 88, 72, 16, 3};

  for (i = 0; i < ROWS; i++)
    for (j = 0; j < COLS; j++)
      if (val[i][j] > max)
        max = val[i][j];
  cout << "\nThe maximum array value is " << max << endl;

  return 0;
}
```

EXERCISES 11.5

1.

```
#include <iostream.h>
#include <math.h>
const int NUM_ELS = 10;
float find_avg(int[], int);         // function prototypes
float std_dev(int[], int, float);
void entvals(int []);

int main()
{
  int values[NUM_ELS];
  float average, stddev;

  entvals(values);
  average = find_avg(values, NUM_ELS);
  stddev = std_dev(values, NUM_ELS, average);
  cout << "The average of the numbers is "  << average << endl;
  cout << "The standard deviation of the numbers is "
       << stddev << endl;

  return 0;
}

float find_avg(int nums[], int numel)
{
  int i;
  float sumnums = 0.0;

  for (i = 0; i < numel; i++)
    sumnums = sumnums + nums[i];

  return (sumnums/numel);
}

float std_dev(int nums[], int numel, float av)
{
  int i;
  float sumdevs = 0.0;

  for (i = 0; i < numel; i++)
    sumdevs = sumdevs + pow((nums[i] - av),2);

  return sqrt(sumdevs/numel);
}

void entvals(int vals[])
{
  int i;

  for (i = 0; i < NUM_ELS; i++)
  {
    cout << "Enter value " << i + 1 << ": ";
    cin  >>  vals[i];
  }

  return;
}
```

3.

```
#include <iostream.h>
#include <math.h>
const int NUMELS = 10;
float find_avg(int[], int);          // function prototypes
float std_dev(int[], int, float);
int high(int[], int);

int main()
{
  int values[NUMELS] = {98, 82, 67, 54, 78, 83, 95, 76, 68, 63};
  int highest;
  float average, stddev;

  average = find_avg(values, NUMELS);
  stddev = std_dev(values, NUMELS, average);
  highest = high(values, NUMELS);

  cout << "\nThe average of the numbers is " << average << endl;;
  cout << "The standard deviation of the numbers is "
       << stddev << endl;
  cout << "The highest value of the numbers is "
       << highest << endl;

  return 0;
}

float find_avg(int nums[], int numel)
{
  int i;
  float sumnums = 0.0;
  for (i = 0; i < numel; i++)
    sumnums = sumnums + nums[i];

  return (sumnums/numel);
}

float std_dev(int nums[], int numel, float av)
{
  int i;
  float sumdevs = 0.0;

  for (i = 0; i < numel; i++)
    sumdevs = sumdevs + pow((nums[i] - av),2);

  return sqrt(sumdevs/numel);
}

int high(int nums[], int numel)
{
  int i;
  int max = nums[0];

  for (i = 0; i < numel; i++)
    if(nums[i] > max)
      max = nums[i];

  return max;
}
```

7.

```
  #include <iostream.h>
const int MAXCHARS = 30;  // maximum no. of characters in array
const int STARTCHARS = 6; // initial no. of characters in array
void adlet(char[], char);  // function prototype

int main()
{
  char alphabet[MAXCHARS] = {'B', 'J', 'K', 'M', 'S', 'Z'};
  char newlet;

  cout << "Enter a new letter to add: ";
  cin  >> newlet;
  adlet(alphabet, newlet);

  return 0;
}

void adlet(char alpharray[], char addlet)
{
  int i = 0, endpos, newpos;

  while(alpharray[i] < addlet && i < STARTCHARS)
    i++;
  newpos = i;

// move characters over
     for (i = STARTCHARS; i >= newpos; i--)
       alpharray[i+1] = alpharray[i];
     alpharray[newpos] = addlet;

// display characters
    for (i = 0; i <= STARTCHARS; i++)
      cout << alpharray[i];
    cout << endl;

  return;
}
```

EXERCISES 11.6

1.

```
#include <iostream.h>
#include <math.h>
#include <stdlib.h>
#include <time.h>
const int NUMEL = 10;
int selection_sort(int [], int);  // function prototype

int main()
{
  int nums[NUMEL];
  int i, moves;
  float seed;

  srand(time(NULL));  // seed the random number generator
  cout << "\nThe original array values are:\n";
  for(i = 0; i < NUMEL; i++)
  {
```

(continued on next page)

(continued from previous page)

```
      nums[i] = (int) (rand());
      cout << nums[i] << endl;
    }

    moves = selection_sort(nums, NUMEL);

    cout << "\nThe sorted list, in ascending order, is:\n";
    for (i = 0; i < NUMEL; i++)
      cout << nums[i] << endl;
    cout << moves << " moves were made to sort this list" << endl;

    return 0;
  }

  int selection_sort(int num[], int numel)
  {
    int i, j, min, minidx, temp, moves = 0;

  for ( i = 0; i < (numel - 1); i++)
    {
      min = num[i];  // assume minimum is the first array element
      minidx = i;      // index of minimum element
      for(j = i + 1; j < numel; j++)
      {
        if (num[j] < min)    // if we've located a lower value
        {                    // capture it
          min = num[j];
          minidx = j;
        }
      }
      if (min < num[i])  // check if we have a new minimum
      {                  // and if we do, swap values
        temp = num[i];
        num[i] = min;
        num[minidx] = temp;
        moves++;
      }
    }
    return moves;
  }
```

3. The swap( ) function, as it would be used in Program 8.10 is:

```
#include <iostream.h>
#include <math.h>
const int NUMEL = 10;
int selection_sort(int [], int);    // function prototypes
void swap(int&, int&);
int main()
{
  int nums[NUMEL] = {22,5,67,98,45,32,101,99,73,10};
  int i, moves;
  float seed;

  moves = selection_sort(nums, NUMEL);

  cout << "\nThe sorted list, in ascending order, is:\n";
  for (i = 0; i < NUMEL; i++)
    cout <<  nums[i] << "  ";
```

(continued on next page)

```
  cout << '\n' << moves
       << " moves were made to sort this list" << endl;

  return 0;
}

int selection_sort(int num[], int numel)
{
  int i, j, min, minidx, temp, moves = 0;

  for ( i = 0; i < (numel - 1); i++)
  {
    min = num[i];  // assume minimum is the first array element
    minidx = i;     // index of minimum element
    for(j = i + 1; j < numel; j++)
    {
      if (num[j] < min)    // if we've located a lower value
      {                    // capture it
       min = num[j];
       minidx = j;
      }
    }
    if (min < num[i])  // check if we have a new minimum
    {                  // and if we do, swap values
      swap(num[i], num[minidx]);
      moves++;
    }
  }
  return moves;
}

void swap(int& first, int& second)
{
  int temp;

  temp = first;
  first = second;
  second = temp;

  return;
}
```

5.a.

```
#include <iostream.h>
const int NUMEL = 20;
void quicksort(int[], int, int);  // function prototypes
int partition(int[], int, int);

int main()
{
  int nums[NUMEL] = {4, 7, 5, 9, 1, 3, 8, 34, 68, 74, 52, 63, 67,
       32, 45, 73, 98, 101, 99, 29};
  int i;

  quicksort(nums, 0, NUMEL-1);

  cout << "\nThe sorted list, in ascending order, is:\n";
  for (i = 0; i < NUMEL; i++)
  cout << nums[i] << endl;

  return 0;
}

void quicksort(int num[], int lower, int upper)
{
  int i, j, pivot;

  pivot = partition(num, lower, upper);
  if (lower < pivot)
    quicksort(num, lower, pivot-1);
  if (upper > pivot)
    quicksort(num, pivot+1, upper);

 return;
}

int partition(int num[], int left, int right)
{
  int pivot, temp;

  pivot = num[left];
  while (left < right)
  {
    while(num[right] >= pivot && left < right)
      right--;
    if (right != left)
    {
      num[left] = num[right];
      left++;
    }
    while(num[left] <= pivot && left < right)
      left++;
    if (right != left)
    {
      num[right] = num[left];
      right--;
    }
  }
  num[left] = pivot;

  return left;
}
```

EXERCISES 11.8

1.a.
```
#include <iostream.h>
#include <math.h>
const int MAXGRADES = 200;  // a suitably large number
float find_avg(float [], int);  // function prototypes
void display(float [], int, float);

int main()
{
  int i = 0;
  int numels;
  float grades[MAXGRADES];
  float average;

  cout << "\nEnter a grade or -1 to terminate data entry: ";
  cin  >> grades[i];
  while (grades[i] >= 0.0 && i < MAXGRADES)
  {
    i++;
    cout << "Enter a grade or -1 to terminate data entry: ";
    cin  >> grades[i];
  }
  numels = i;

  if (numels > 0)
  {
    average = find_avg(grades, numels);

    cout << "\nThe average of the grades is " << average << endl;
    display(grades, numels, average);
  }
  else
    cout << "No grades were entered\n";
}

float find_avg(float nums[], int numel)
{
  int i;
  float sumnums = 0.0;

  for (i = 0; i < numel; i++) // calculate the sum of the grades
    sumnums = sumnums + nums[i];

  return (sumnums / numel); // calculate and return the average
}

void display(float nums[], int numel, float av)
{
  int i = 0;

  cout << "\nThe grades are:\n";
  for (i = 0; i < numel; i++)
  {
    if(nums[i] < av)
      cout << "* ";
    else
      cout << "  ";
    cout << nums[i] << endl;
  }

  return;
}
```

3. The function is included with a driver function.

```
#include <iostream.h>
const int MAXNUMS = 10;
void printrev(int [], int);  // function prototype
int main()
{
  int vals[MAXNUMS] = {0, 1, 2, 3, 4, 5, 6, 7, 8, 9};

  printrev(vals, MAXNUMS);

  return 0;
}

void printrev(int num[], int numel)
{
  int i;

  for (i = (numel - 1); i >= 0; i--)
    cout << num[i] << "  ";
  cout << endl;

  return;
}
```

5.

```
#include <iostream.h>
#include <math.h>
const int MAXGRADES = 50;
void descend_sort(float [], int);  // function prototype
int main()
{
  int i = 0, j;
  float grades[MAXGRADES];

  cout << "Enter a grade or -1 to terminate data entry: ";
  cin  >> grades[i];
  while (grades[i] >= 0.0 && i < MAXGRADES)
  {
    i++;
    cout << "Enter a grade or -1 to terminate data entry: ";
    cin  >> grades[i];
  }

  if (i > 0)
  {
    descend_sort(grades, i); // call the function
    cout << "\nThe grades, in descending order, are:\n";
    for(j = 0; j < i; j++)
      cout <<  grades[j] << "  ";
    cout << endl;
  }
  else
    cout << "\nNo grades were entered" << endl;
}

void descend_sort(float num[], int numel)
{
  int i, j, max, maxidx;
  float temp;
```

(continued on next page)

(continued from previous page)

```
    for ( i = 0; i < (numel-1); i++)
    {
      max = num[i];  // assume maximum is the first array element
      maxidx = i;    // index of maximum element
      for(j = i + 1; j < numel; j++)
      {
        if (num[j] > max)    // if we've located a higher value
        {                    // capture it
         max = num[j];
         maxidx = j;
        }
      }
      if (max > num[i])  // check if we have a new maximum
      {                  // and if we do, swap values
        temp = num[i];
        num[i] = max;
        num[maxidx] = temp;
      }
    }

    return;
  }
```

EXERCISES 12.1

1.b.

```
#include <iostream.h>
const int MAXCHARS = 81;
void vowels(char []); // function prototype
int main()
{
   char line[MAXCHARS];

   cout << "Enter a string:\n";
   cin.getline(line,MAXCHARS);
   vowels(line);

   return 0;
 }

 void vowels(char strng[])
 {
   int i = 0, v = 0; // Array element number and vowel counter
   char c;

   while((c = strng[i++]) != '\0')
   switch(c)
{
     case 'a':
     case 'e':
     case 'i':
     case 'o':
     case 'u':
cout << c;
v++;
   }
   cout << endl;
   cout << "There were " << v << " vowels." << endl;

   return;
}
```

3.a. The function is included in the program written for Exercise 3b.

b.

```
#include <iostream.h>
const int MAXCHARS = 81;
void count_str(char []);  // function prototype
int main()
{
  char strng[MAXCHARS];

  cout << "Enter a line of text:\n";
  cin.getline(strng,MAXCHARS);
  count_str(strng);

  return 0;
}

void count_str(char message[])
{
  int i;
  for(i = 0; message[i] != '\0'; ++i);  // The semicolon at
                                        // the end of this
                                        // statement is the
                                        // null statement
  cout << "\nThe number of total characters, "
   << "including blanks,\nin the line just entered is "
   << i << "." << endl;

  return;
}
```

7.

```
#include <iostream.h>
void del_char(char [], int, int);   // function prototype
const int MAXCHARS = 81;
int main()
{
  char word[MAXCHARS];

  cout << "Enter a string\n";
  cin.getline(word,MAXCHARS);
  cout << "The word just entered is: " << word << '\n';
  del_char(word, 13, 5); // string, how many to delete, starting position
  cout << word << '\n';  // display the edited string

  return 0;
}

  void del_char(char strng[], int x, int pos)
  {
    int i, j;

    i = pos-1;    // first element to be deleted (actually, overwritten)
    j = i + x;    // first element beyond delete range
    while (strng[j] != '\0')
      strng[i++] = strng[j++];  // copy over an element
    strng[i] = '\0';    // close off the edited string

     return;
  }
```

This program assumes the number of characters to be deleted actually exists. Otherwise the while loop would not terminate (unless it just happened to encounter another null character somewhere in memory beyond the original string).

9.a. The to_upper( ) function is included in the program written for Exercise 9c.

c.

```
#include <iostream.h>
const int MAXCHARS = 81;
char to_upper(char ch);    // function prototype
int main()
{
  char strng[MAXCHARS];
  int i = 0;

  cout << "Enter a line of text\n";
  cin.getline(strng,MAXCHARS);
  while (strng[i] != '\0')  // get the character
  {
    strng[i] = to_upper(strng[i]); // send it to the function
    i++;                           // move to next character
  }
  cout << "The string, with all lowercase letters"
       << " converted is:\n";
  cout << strng << endl;

  return 0;
}

char to_upper(char ch)
{
   if ( ch >= 'a' && ch <= 'z')    // test it
     return (ch - 'a' + 'A');      // change it, if necessary
   else
     return ch;
}
```

11.

```
   #include <iostream.h>
  const int MAXCHARS = 81;
  int main()
  {
    char strng[MAXCHARS];
    int i = 0, count = 1;

     cout << "Enter a line of text\n";
     cin.getline(strng,MAXCHARS);
     if(strng[i] == ' ' || strng[i] == '\0')
       count--;
     while(strng[i] != '\0')
     {
       if(strng[i] == ' ' && (strng[i + 1] != ' ' && strng[i + 1] != '\0'))
   count++;      // encountered a new word
       i++;      // move to the next character
   }
   cout << "\nThe number of words in the line just entered is "
        << count << endl;

    return 0;
}
```

The program increases the word count whenever a transition from a blank to a nonblank character occurs. Thus, even if words are separated by more than one space, the word count will be incremented correctly. Initially the program assumes the text starts with a word (count = 1). If the first character is either a blank or an end-of-string null, this assumption is incorrect and the count is decremented to zero.

EXERCISES 12.2

5.a.

```
int length(char s1[])
{
  int count = 0;

  while(s1[count] != '\0')
    count++;

    return count;
}
```

Note: The statement while(s1[i] ! = '\0') can be replaced by while(s1[count]).

b.

```
#include <iostream.h>
int length(char []);
int main()
{
  char s1[] = "This is a test";

  int ret;

  ret = length(s1);
  cout << "\nThe length of the string "  << s1
       << " is " << ret << " characters." << endl;

  return 0;
}
```

7.a.

```
void chartype(int cval)
{

  if (islower(cval))
    cout << "  The ASCII character is a lowercase letter."
         << endl;
  else if (isupper(cval))
    cout << " The ASCII is an uppercase letter." << endl;
  else if (isdigit(cval))
    cout << "  The ASCII character is a digit." << endl;
  else if (ispunct(cval))
    cout << "The ASCII character is a punctuation mark." << endl;
  else if (isspace(cval))
    cout << "The ASCII character is a space." << endl;
  else if (!isprint(cval))
    cout << "The decimal code for this character is " << cval
         << "\n The ASCII character is a nonprintable character."
         << endl;
  return;
}
```

b.

```
#include <iostream.h>
#include <ctype.h>
#include <time.h>
#include <stdlib.h>
const int RANDNUMS = 20;
void chartype(int);   // function prototype
int main()
{
  int i;
  int cval;

  srand(time(NULL));
  for(i = 0; i < RANDNUMS; i++)
  {
     cval = 1 + rand() % 127;
     cout << "The value is " << cval << endl;
     chartype(cval);
   }

   return 0;
}
```

EXERCISES 12.3

1.

```
int countchar(char list[])
{
  int i, count = 0;

  for(i = 0; list[i] != '\0'; i++)
    if (list[i] != ' ')
      count++;

  return count;
}
```

3. The function is included within a complete program.

```
#include <iostream.h>
const int MAXNUM = 1000;
void countword(char [], int&, int&);  // function prototype

int main()
{
  char message[MAXNUM];
  int numword, numchar;

  cout << "\nType in any number of words: ";

  cin.getline(message,MAXNUM);
  countword(message, numword, numchar);
  cout << "The number of words just entered is " << numword;
  cout << "\nThe number of characters just entered is "
       << numchar << endl;

  return 0;
}

void countword(char list[], int& numwords, int& numchars)
```

(continued on next page)

```
{
  const int YES = 1;  // local to countword()
  const int NO = 0;

  int i, inaword, cword = 0;

  inaword = NO;
  for(i = 0; list[i] != '\0'; i++)
  {
    if (list[i] == ' ')
      inaword = NO;
    else if (inaword == NO)
    {
      inaword = YES;
      cword++;
    }
  }
  numwords = cword;    // pass the word count back
  numchars = i;   // pass the character count back

  return;
}
```

5. The function is included within a complete program.

```
#include <iostream.h>
const int MAXNUM = 1000;
int countlines(char [], int);  // function prototype

int main()
{
  char message[MAXNUM];
  int i, c, numlines, numchar;

  cout << "\nType in any number of lines of text: ";

  i = 0;
  while (c = cin.get())
  {
    if (c == EOF || i == MAXNUM)
      break;
    else
    {
      message[i] = c;  // store the entry
      i++;
    }
  }
  numlines = countlines(message, i);
  cout << "The number of lines just entered is "
       << numlines << endl;
}

int countlines(char list[], int numvals)
{
  int i, cline = 0;

  for(i = 0; i < numvals; i++)
  {
    if (list[i] == '\n')
       cline++;
  }
  cline++;  // last line is terminated with an EOF, not a \n

  return cline;
}
```

Note: Each character is accepted and stored in the message array. Entry of data is terminated at the terminal by either pressing the F6 function key or pressing ctrl and Z keys together, which generates an EOF.

EXERCISES 12.6

1.a.

```
text[0] = 'n'
text[3] = ' '
text[10] = ' '
```

b.

```
text[0] = 'r'
text[3] = 'k'
text[10] = 'o'
```

c.

```
text[0] = 'H'
text[3] = 'p'
text[10] = 'd'
```

d.

```
text[0] = 'T'
text[3] = ' '
text[10] = 'h'
```

5. The function, within the context of a complete program is:

```
#include <iostream.h>
#include <string.h>
int main()
{
  char message[] = "     this is the string";
  void trimfrnt(char []);

  cout << '|' << message << '|'  << endl;
  cout << "string length is " << strlen(message) << endl;

  trimfrnt(message);

  cout << '|' << message << '|' << endl;
  cout << "string length is " << strlen(message) << endl;

}

void trimfrnt(char strng[]) // trim leading blanks
{
  int i = 0, j = 0;

  while (strng[i++] == ' ')  // move along to the first nonblank
    ++j;
  i = 0;
  while (strng[i++] = strng[j++]) // copy over the rest of
    ;                            // the string including the '\0'
  return;
}
```

7. The function, within the context of a complete program is:

```
#include <iostream.h>
#include <string.h>
const int MAXCHARS = 1000;
void addchars(char [], int, char);

int main()
{
  char message[MAXCHARS] = "this is the string";

  cout << '|' << message << '|' << endl;
  cout << "string length is " << strlen(message) << endl;

  addchars(message, 5, '!');

  cout << '|' << message << '|' << endl;
  cout << "string length is " << strlen(message) << endl;

  return 0;
}

void addchars(char strng[], int n, char ch)
{
  int i = 0, j;

  if (n <= 0) return;
  while (strng[i++] != '\0')  // move one char past the '\0'
       ;
  j = i - 1;  // starting position for the fill
  while(n -- != 0)           // add n occurrences of the character
    strng[j++] = ch;
  strng[j] = '\0';           // terminate the string

  return;
}
```

Note: Since we are adding characters to the string, it is important to make sure that the character array has sufficient space beyond the original terminating `'\0'` to hold the additional characters.

EXERCISES 13.1

1. &average means "the address of the variable named average."

3.a.

```
#include <iostream.h>
   int main()
   {
     int num, count;
     long date;
     float yield;
     double price;

     cout << "The address of the variable num is "
          << &num << endl;
     cout << "The address of the variable count is "
          << &count << endl;
     cout << "The address of the variable date is "
          << &date << endl;
     cout << "The address of the variable yield is "
          << &yield << endl;
     cout << "The address of the variable price is "
          << &price << endl;
     return 0;
   }
```

5.a. `*x_addr`
b. `*y_addr`
c. `*pt_yld`
d. `*pt_miles`
e. `*mptr`
f. `*pdate`
g. `*dist_ptr`
h. `*tab_pt`
i. `*hours_pt`

7.a. Each of these variables is a pointer. This means that addresses will be stored in each of these variables.
b. They are not very descriptive names and do not give an indication that they are pointers.

9. All pointer variable declarations must have an asterisk. Therefore, c, e, g, and i are pointer declarations.

11.

Variable	Address	Contents
pt_num	500	8096
amt_addr	564	16256
z_addr	8024	20492
num_addr	10132	18938
pt_day	14862	20492
pt_yr	15010	694
years	694	1987
m	8096	
amt	16256	154
firstnum	18938	154
balz	20492	25
k	24608	154

EXERCISES 13.2

1.a. `*(prices + 5)`
b. `*(grades + 2)`
c. `*(yield +10)`
d. `*(dist + 9)`
e. `*mile`
f. `*(temp + 20)`
g. `*(celsius + 16)`
h. `*(num + 50)`
i. `*(time + 12)`

3.a. The declaration double prices [5]; causes storage space for five double-precision numbers, creates a pointer constant named prices, and equates the pointer constant to the address of the first element (&prices[0]).

b. `Each element in prices contains 8 bytes and there are five elements for a total of 40 bytes.`

c.

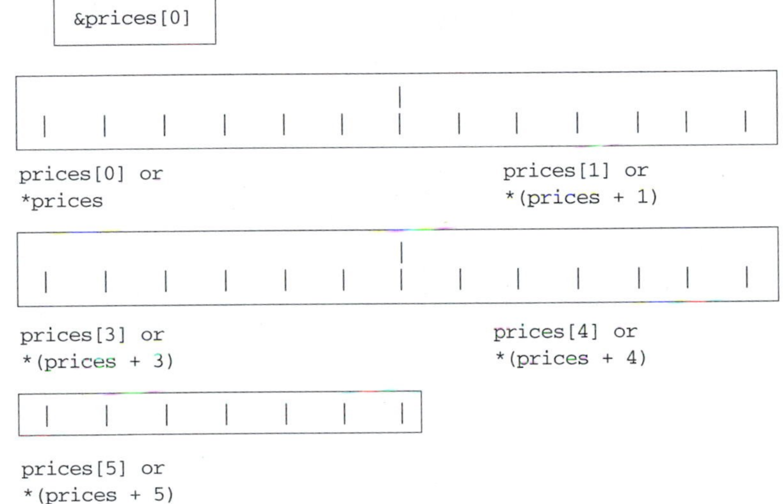

d. The byte offset for this element, from the beginning of the array, is 3 * 8 = 24 bytes.

5.

```
#include <iostream.h>
int main()
{
  float rates[] = {12.9, 18.6, 11.4, 13.7, 9.5, 15.2, 17.6};
  int i;

  cout << "The elements of the array are:\n";
  for(i = 0; i <= 6; i++)
    cout << "    " << *(rates + i);    // The variable pointed
                                        // to by rates offset by i
  return 0;
}
```

EXERCISES 13.3

3.a.

```
#include <iostream.h>
int main()
{
  char strng[] = "Hooray for all of us";
  char *mess_pt;

  mess_pt = &strng[0];    // mess_pt = strng; is equivalent
  cout << "\nThe elements in the array are: ";
  for(  ; *mess_pt != '\0'; mess_pt++)
    cout << *mess_pt;
  cout << endl;

  return 0;
}
```

Note: The expressions for(; *mess_pt != '\0'; mess_pt++) can be replaced by for(;*mess_pt; mes_pt++).

b.

```
#include <iostream.h>
int main()
{
  char strng[] = "Hooray for all of us";
  char *mess_pt;

  mess_pt = &strng[0];    // mess_pt = strng; is equivalent
  cout << "\nThe elements in the array are: ";
  while (*mess_pt != '\0')  // search for the null character
    cout <<  *mess_pt++;
  cout << endl;

  return 0;
}
```

Note: The expressions while (*mess_pt != '\0') can be replaced by while (*mess_pt).

EXERCISES 13.4

1.

```
void sort_arr(double in_array[500])
void sort_arr(double in_array[])
void sort_arr(double *in_array)
```

5. The problem to this method of finding the maximum value lies in the statement

```
if(max < *vals++)
  max = *vals;
```

This statement compares the correct value to max, but then increments the address in the pointer before any assignment is made. Thus, the element assigned to max by the expression max = *vals is one element beyond the element pointed to within the parentheses.

EXERCISES 13.5

1.a.

```
*text = 'n'
*(text + 3) = ' '
*(text + 10) = ' '
```

b.

```
*text = 'r'
*(text + 3) = 'k'
*(text + 10) = 'o'
```

c.

```
*text = 'H'
*(text + 3) = 'p'
*(text + 10) = 'd'
```

d.

```
*text = 'T'
*(text + 3) = ' '
*(text + 10) =. 'h'
```

3.

```
#include <iostream.h>
const int MAXCHARS = 80;
void vowels(char *);    // function prototype
int main()
{
  char line[MAXCHARS];

  cout << "Enter a string.\n";
  cin.getline(line, MAXCHARS);
  vowels(line);

  return 0;
}

void vowels(char *strng)  // strng treated as a pointer variable
{
  int v = 0;    // v = vowel counter
  char c;

  while((c = *strng++) != '\0')  // an address is incremented
  switch(c)
  {
    case 'a':
    case 'e':
    case 'i':
    case 'o':
    case 'u':
     cout << c;
     v++;
  }
  cout << "\nThere were " << v << " vowels.\n";
  return;
}
```

Note: The while expression can also be written as while (c = *strng++). That is, the explicit comparison != '\0' can be omitted.

5.

```
#include <iostream.h>
const int MAXCHARS = 80;
void count_str(char *);    // function prototype
int main()
{
  char strng[MAXCHARS];

  cout << "Enter a line of text\n";
  cin.getline(strng, MAXCHARS);
  count_str(strng);

  return 0;
}

void count_str(char *message)    // message as a pointer variable
{
  int count;

  for(count = 0; *message++ != '\0'; ++count) ; // The semicolon at the
                  // end of this statement is the null statement
  cout << "\nThe number of total characters, including blanks,"
       << "\nin the line just entered is " << count << ".\n";
  return;
}
```

Note: The for statement can also be written as for(count = 0; *message++; ++count) ;. That is, the explicit comparison != '\0' can be omitted.

7.

```
#include <iostream.h>
const int MAXCHARS = 80;
void reverse(char *, char *); // function prototype
int main()
{
  char forward[MAXCHARS], rever[MAXCHARS];

  cout << "\nEnter a line of text:\n";
  cin.getline(forward, MAXCHARS);
  reverse(forward,rever);
  cout << "\nThe text: " << forward;
  cout << "\nspelled backwards is: " << rever << endl;

  return 0;
}

void reverse(char *forw, char *rev)
{
  int i = 0, j = 0;

  while(*(forw + i) != '\0')         // count the elements
    ++i;                             // in the string
  for(i--; i >= 0; i--)
    *rev++ = *(forw + i);
  *rev = '\0';                    // close off reverse string
  return;
}
```

Note: The while expression can also be written as while(*(forw + i)). That is, the explicit comparison != '\0' can be omitted.

9. The function is included within a complete program.

```
#include <iostream.h>
const int MAXCHARS = 80;
void delete_c(char *strng);  // function prototype
int main()
{
  char line[MAXCHARS];

  cout << "\nEnter a line of text: ";
  cin.getline(line, MAXCHARS);
  delete_c(line);
  cout << "The new line of text, with the removed "
       << "last character is:\n";
  cout << line;

  return 0;
}

void delete_c(char *strng)
{

  while(*strng++ != '\0')     // this advances the pointer
       ;                      // one character beyond '\0 '
  strng--;                    // point to the '\0')
  --strng;                    // point to last character
  *strng = '\0';              // close the new string
  return;
}
```

Note: The while expression can also be written as while(*strng++). That is, the explicit comparison != '\0' can be omitted.

EXERCISES 13.6

1. `char *text = "Hooray!";`
   `char text[]: = {'H','o','o','r','a','y','\0'};`

3. message is a pointer constant. Therefore, the statement ++message, which attempts to alter its address, is invalid. A correct statement is cout << *(message + i);. Here the address in message is unaltered and the character pointed to is the character offset i bytes from the address corresponding to message.

5.

```
#include <iostream.h>
void get_10(void);  // function prototype
int main()  // A simple driver for the function
{
  get_10();

  return 0;
}

void get_10(void)
{
  const int MAXCHARS = 1000; // enough room for 1000 characters
  const int MAXLINES = 10;
  char message[MAXCHARS];
  char *m_ptr[MAXLINES];  // an array of 10 pointers
  char *temp_pt;          // a single pointer
  int i;

  temp_pt = message;    // point to first character
  cout << "Enter " << MAXLINES
       << " lines of text to be stored\n";
  for(i = 0; i < MAXLINES; i++)
  {
    m_ptr[i] = temp_pt;          // set address of i'th string
    cin.getline(m_ptr[i], MAXCHARS);   // get and store the string
    while (*temp_pt++ != '\0')  // move one beyond  NULL
   ;                           // and update the address
  }
  cout << endl;
  for(i = 0; i < MAXLINES; i++)          // print the strings using
    cout << m_ptr[i] << endl;   // the array of pointers
  return;
}
```

Notes:

1. The named constants, MAXCHARS and MAXLINES, which are only used within the get_10( ) function, are defined locally inside this function. Since they are integral to the function there is no reason to define them globally.
2. The message array reserves enough storage for MAXCHARS bytes. Although this is sufficient for 10 lines of text, a more judicious use of space would be to dynamically allocate space as it is needed (see Section 13.2).
3. The while expression can also be written as while(*temp_pt++). That is, the explicit comparison != '\0' can be omitted.
4. The lines of text are stored sequentially in the message array, with the m_ptr array elements containing the starting addresses of each line of text.

EXERCISES 13.7

1.

```
#include <iostream.h>
#include <string.h>

// class declaration
class Book
{
  private:
    char *title;   // a pointer to a book title
  public:
    Book(char *);  // constructor
    Book(Book &);  // copy constructor
    void operator=(Book &);  // overloaded assignment operator
    void showtitle(void);   // display the title
};
// class implementation

Book::Book(char *strng = NULL)   // constructor
{
  title = new char[strlen(strng)+1];  // allocate memory
  strcpy(title,strng);                // store the string
}

Book::Book(Book &oldbook)   // copy constructor
{
  title = new char[strlen(oldbook.title) + 1];  // allocate new memory
  strcpy(title, oldbook.title);  // copy the title
}

void Book::operator=(Book &oldbook)
{
  if(title != NULL)  // check that it exists
    delete(title);   // release existing memory
  title = new char[strlen(oldbook.title) + 1];  // allocate new memory
  strcpy(title, oldbook.title);  // copy the title
}

void Book::showtitle(void)
{
  cout << title << endl;
}

int main()
{
  Book book1("DOS Primer");   // create 1st title
  Book book2 = book1;          // create a copy
  Book book3("A Brief History of Western Civilization");  // 2nd title

  book1.showtitle();   // display book1's title
  book2.showtitle();   // check the copy worked
  book3.showtitle();   // display the third book title
  book2 = book3;       // assign book3 to book2
  book2.showtitle();   // check the assignment worked

  return 0;
}
```

3.a. The required class is contained within the program solution to Exercise 3b.

b.

```
#include <iostream.h>
#include <iomanip.h>
#include <string.h>
// declaration section
class Car
{
  private:
    float engine_size;
    char body_style;
    int color_code;
    char *vin_ptr;
  public:
    Car(float, char, int, char *);  // constructor
    void operator=(Car &); // overloaded assignment operator
    void showdata(void);    // member function to display a time
};

// implementation section

Car::Car(float eng = 0.0, char styl = 'X', int cd = 0, char *pt = NULL)
{
  engine_size = eng;
  body_style = styl;
  color_code = cd;
  vin_ptr = new char[strlen(pt) + 1];    // allocate memory
  strcpy(vin_ptr, pt);                   // store the string
}

void Car::operator=(Car &oldcar)
{
  engine_size = oldcar.engine_size;
  body_style = oldcar.body_style;
  color_code = oldcar.color_code;
  if(vin_ptr != NULL)    // check that it exists
    delete(vin_ptr);     // release existing memory
  vin_ptr = new char[strlen(oldcar.vin_ptr) + 1];  // allocate new mem-
ory
  strcpy(vin_ptr, oldcar.vin_ptr);  // copy the vin
}
void Car::showdata(void)
{
  cout << "\nThe values for this object are \n"
       << "  Engine size: " << engine_size << '\n'
       << "  Body style: " << body_style << '\n'
       << "  Color code: " << color_code << '\n'
       << "  VIN: " << vin_ptr << '\n';
}
int main()
{
   Car a(250.0, 'S', 52, "ABC567YYY"), b;  // declare 2 objects

   a.showdata();   // display object a's values
   b.showdata();   // display object b's values
   b = a;          // assign a to b
   b.showdata();   // display object a's values

  return 0;
}
```

EXERCISES 13.9

1.

```
void trimfrnt(char *strng)     // trim leading blank
{
  char *strng2;    // create a second pointer

  strng2 = strng; // both pointers point to start of string
  while (*strng2 == ' ') ++strng2;   // find first nonblank
  while (*strng++ = *strng2++)  ;    // do the copy
  return;
}
```

7.a. The following output is obtained:

```
33
16
99
34
```

This is why:

```
*(*val) = *(val[0]) = val[0][0] = 33;
*(*val + 1) = *(val[1]) = val[1][0] = 16;
*(*(val + 1) + 2) = *(*(val[1]) + 2) = *(val[1][2]) = 99;
*(*val) + 1 = *(val[0]) + 1 = val[0][0] + 1 = 33 + 1 = 34.
```

In other words, for any two-dimensional array, arr[x][y], what we really have is two levels of pointers. What is meant by *(arr + x) is that there are x number of pointers, each successively pointing to arr[1][0], arr[2][0], arr[3][0], ... , arr[x][0]. So an expression such as *(*(arr + x) + y) translates to arr[x][y].

EXERCISES 14.1

1.a.

```
struct S_temp
{
  int id_num;
  int credits;
  float avg;
};
```

b.

```
struct S_temp
{
  char name[40];
  int month;
  int day;
  int year;
  int credits;
  float avg;
};
```

c.

```
struct S_temp
{
  char name[40];
  char street[80];
  char city[40];
  char state[2];
  int zip;            // or char zip[5];
};
```

d.
```
struct S_temp
{
  char name[40];
  float price;
  char date[8];   // Assumes a date in the form XX/XX/XX
};
```

e.
```
struct S_temp
{
  int part_no;
  char desc[100];
  int quant;
  int reorder;
};
```

3.a.
```
#include <iostream.h>
int main()
{
  struct Date
  {
    int month;
    int day;
    int year;
  };     // define a structure variable named date

  Date current;  // define a structure variable named current
  cout << "\nEnter the current month: ";
  cin  >> current.month;
  cout << "Enter the current day: ";
  cin  >> current.day;
  cout << "Enter the current year: ";
  cin  >> current.year;
  cout << "\nThe date entered is : "
       << current.month << '/' << current.day
       << '/' << current.year << endl;

  return 0;
}
```

b.
```
#include <iostream.h>
#include <iomanip.h>
int main()
{
  struct Clock
  {
    int hours;
    int minutes;
    int seconds;
  };

  Clock time;    // define a structure variable named time

  cout << "\nEnter the current hour: ";
  cin  >> time.hours;
  cout << "Enter the current minute: ";
  cin  >> time.minutes;
  cout << "Enter the current second: ";
  cin  >> time.seconds;
  cout << "\nThe time entered is: "
       << setw(2) << setfill('0') << time.hours << ':'
       << setw(2) << time.minutes << ':'
       << setw(2) << time.seconds << endl;
  return 0;
}
```

Note the use of the setw and setfill manipulators. The fill character of 0 forces the field of 2 to be filled with leading zeros.

5.

```
#include <iostream.h>
#include <iomanip.h>
int main()
{
  struct Clock
  {
    int hours;
    int minutes;
  };

Clock time;

   cout << "Enter the current hour: ";
   cin  >> time.hours;
   cout << "Enter the current minute: ";
   cin  >> time.minutes;
   if(time.minutes != 59)
     time.minutes += 1;
   else
   {
     time.minutes = 0;
     if(time.hours != 12)
       time.hours += 1;
     else
       time.hours = 1;
   }
   cout << "\nThe time in one minute will be "
        << setiosflags(ios::showpoint) << setfill('0')
        << setw(2) << time.hours << ':'
        << setw(2) << time.minutes << endl;

   return 0;
  }
```

Note the use of the setw and setfill manipulators. The fill character of 0 forces the field of 2 to be filled with leading zeros.

EXERCISES 14.2

1.a. `S_temp student[100];`
b. `S_temp student[100];`
c. `S_temp address[100];`
d. `S_temp stock[100];`
e. `S_temp inventory[100];`

3.

```
#include <iostream.h>
const int MAXCHARS = 10;
const int MONTHS = 12;
struct Mon_days
{
  char name[MAXCHARS];
  int days;
};
#include <iostream.h>
int main()
{
  Mon_days convert[MONTHS] =
                {"January", 31, "February", 28, "March", 31,
      "April", 30, "May", 31, "June", 30,
      "July", 31, "August", 31, "September", 30,
      "October", 31, "November", 30, "December", 31
                };
  int i;
  cout << "\nEnter the number of a month: ";
  cin  >> i;
  cout << convert[i-1].name << " has "
   << convert[i-1].days << " days\n";

 return 0;
}
```

Note: The structure declaration for Mon_days can either be global or local to main( ).

EXERCISES 14.3

1.

```
#include <iostream.h>
struct Date
{
  int month;
  int day;
  int year;
};
long days(Date);  // function prototype

int main()
{
  Date present;
  long num;

  cout << "Enter the month: ";
  cin  >> present.month;
  cout << "Enter the day: ";
  cin  >> present.day;
  cout << "Enter the year: ";
  cin  >> present.year;
  num = days(present);
  cout << "The number of days since the turn"
       << " of the century is " << num << endl;

  return 0;
}

long days(Date temp)
{
  return (temp.day + 30*(temp.month - 1) + 360*temp.year);
}
```

Note: The reference version of the function long days( ) is written for Exercise 3a, and the pointer version for Exercise 3b.

3.a.
```
#include <iostream.h>
struct Date
{
  int month;
  int day;
  int year;
};

long days(Date& );  // function prototype

int main()
{
  Date present;
  long num;

  cout << "Enter the month: ";
  cin  >> present.month;
  cout << "Enter the day: ";
  cin  >> present.day;
  cout << "Enter the year: ";
  cin  >> present.year;
  num = days(present);
  cout << "The number of days since the turn"
       << " of the century is " << num << endl;

  return 0;
}

long days(Date& temp)
{
  return (temp.day + 30*(temp.month - 1) + 360*temp.year);
}
```

b.
```
#include <iostream.h>
struct Date
{
  int month;
  int day;
  int year;
};

long days(Date *);   // function prototype

int main()
{
  Date present;
  long num;

  cout << "Enter the month: ";
  cin  >> present.month;
  cout << "Enter the day: ";
  cin  >> present.day;
  cout << "Enter the year: ";
  cin  >> present.year;
  num = days(&present);
  cout << "The number of days since the turn"
       << " of the century is " << num << endl;

  return 0;
}


long days(Date *temp)
{
  return (temp->day + 30*(temp->month - 1) + 360*temp->year);
}
```

Note: The days( ) function can also be written as follows:

```
long days(Date *temp)
{
  return ((*temp).day + 30*((*temp).month - 1) + 360*(*temp).year);
}
```

5.

```
#include <iostream.h>
struct Date
{
  int month;
  int day;
  int year;
};

long days(Date);  // function prototype

int main()
{
  char ch;
  Date present;
  long num;

  cout << "Enter the date as mm/dd/yy: ";
  cin  >> present.month >> ch >> present.day
       >> ch >> present.year;
  num = days(present);
  cout << "The number of days since the turn of the century is "
       << num << endl;

  return 0;
}

long days(Date temp)
{
  long act_days;
  int daycount[12] = { 0, 31, 59, 90, 120, 151,
        180, 211, 241, 271, 302, 333};

  act_days = temp.day + daycount[temp.month-1] + 364*temp.year;
  return act_days;
}
```

EXERCISES 14.4

1.

```
#include <iostream.h>
#include <string.h>
const int MAXNAME = 30;
const int MAXTEL = 15;

struct Tele_typ
{
  char name[MAXNAME];
  char phone_no[MAXTEL];
   Tele_typ *nextaddr;
};
void search(Tele_typ *, char *); // function prototype
```

(continued on next page)

(continued from previous page)

```
int main()
{
  Tele_typ t1 = {"Acme, Sam", "(201) 898-2392"};
  Tele_typ t2 = {"Dolan, Edith", "(213) 682-3104"};
  Tele_typ t3 = {"Lanfrank, John", "(415) 718-4518"};
  Tele_typ *first;
  char strng[MAXNAME];

  first = &t1;
  t1.nextaddr = &t2;
  t2.nextaddr = &t3;
  t3.nextaddr = NULL;
  cout << "Enter a name: ";
  cin.getline(strng, MAXNAME);
  search(first, strng);
  cout << endl;

  return 0;
}

void search(Tele_typ *contents, char *strng)
{
  cout << strng;
  while(contents != NULL)
  {
    if(strcmp(contents->name,strng) == 0)
    {
      cout << "\nFound. The number is "
           << contents->phone_no << endl;
return;
    }
    else
    {
 contents = contents->nextaddr;
    }
  }
  cout << "\nThe name is not in the current"
       << " phone directory.\n";
  return;
}
```

3. To delete the second record, the pointer in the first record must be changed to point to the third record.

5.a.

```
const int NAMECHARS = 30;
const int PHONECHARS = 15;
struct Phone_bk
{
  char name[NAMECHARS];
  char phone_no[PHONECHARS];
   Phone_bk *previous;
   Phone_bk *next;
};
```

EXERCISES 14.5

1. The check( ) function is included below in a complete program used to verify that check( ) works correctly.

```
#include <iostream.h>
#include <iomanip.h>
#include <stdlib.h>   // need this for the exit() function

const int NAMECHARS = 30;
const int PHONECHARS = 15;

struct Tel_typ
{
  char name[NAMECHARS];
  char phone_no[PHONECHARS];
  Tel_typ *nextaddr;
};

void populate(Tel_typ *);  // function prototype
void display(Tel_typ *);   // function prototype
int check(Tel_typ *);      // function prototype

int main()
{
  int i;

  Tel_typ *list, *current;

  list =  new (Tel_typ);
  check(list);
  current = list;
  for(i = 0; i < 2; i++)
  {
    populate(current);
    current->nextaddr = new (Tel_typ);

    if (check(current->nextaddr) == 0)
    {
cout << "No available memory remains. Program terminating";
exit(0); // terminate program and return to operating system
    }
    current = current->nextaddr;
  }
  populate(current);
  current->nextaddr = NULL;
  cout << "\nThe list consists of the following records:\n";
  display(list);

  return 0;
}

int check( Tel_typ *addr)
{
  if(addr == NULL)
    return 0;
  else
    return 1;
  }
```

(continued on next page)

(continued from previous page)

```
void populate( Tel_typ *record)
{
  cout << "\nEnter a name: ";
  cin.getline(record->name, NAMECHARS);
  cout << "Enter the phone number: ";
  cin.getline(record->phone_no, PHONECHARS);
  return;
}

void display( Tel_typ *contents)
{
  while(contents != NULL)
  {
    cout << endl << setiosflags(ios::left)
         << setw(30) << contents->name
         << setw(20) << contents->phone_no;
    contents = contents->nextaddr;
  }
    return;
}
```

3. The insert( ) function in the complete program below is used to verify that insert( ) works correctly. As written, the function will insert a structure after the structure whose address is passed to it. Since the address of the first structure is passed to it, the new structure is inserted between the first and second structures.

```
#include <iostream.h>
#include <iomanip.h>

const int NAMECHARS = 30;
const int PHONECHARS = 15;
struct Tel_typ
{
  char name[NAMECHARS];
  char phone_no[PHONECHARS];
  Tel_typ *nextaddr;
};

void insert(Tel_typ *);      // function prototype
void populate(Tel_typ *);    // function prototype
void display(Tel_typ *);     // function prototype

int main()
{
  Tel_typ *list, *current;

  list = new (Tel_typ);
  populate(list); // populate the first structure
  list->nextaddr = new (Tel_typ);
  current = list->nextaddr;
  populate(current); // populate the second structure
  current->nextaddr = NULL;
  cout << "\nThe list initially consists of the following records:";
  display(list);
  insert(list);    // insert between first and second structures
  cout << "\nThe new list now consists of the following records:";
  display(list);
  cout << endl;

  return 0;
}
```

(continued on next page)

(continued from previous page)

```
void insert(Tel_typ *addr)
{
  Tel_typ *temp;
  void populate(Tel_typ *);  // function prototype

  temp = addr->nextaddr;      // save pointer to next structure
    // now change address to point to inserted structure
  addr->nextaddr = new (Tel_typ);
  populate(addr->nextaddr);  // populate the new structure
    // set address member of new structure to saved addr
  addr->nextaddr->nextaddr = temp;
  return;
}

void populate(Tel_typ *record)
{
  cout << "\nEnter a name: ";
  cin.getline(record->name, NAMECHARS);
  cout << "Enter the phone number: ";
  cin.getline(record->phone_no, PHONECHARS);
  return;
}

void display( Tel_typ *contents)
{
  while(contents != NULL)
  {
    cout << endl << setiosflags(ios::left)
         << setw(30) << contents->name
         << setw(20) << contents->phone_no;
    contents = contents->nextaddr;
  }
  return;
}
```

Notice if the populate function call is removed from the insert function, then insert( ) becomes a general insertion program that simply creates a structure and correctly adjusts the address members of each structure. Also, notice the notation used in insert( ). The expression

```
addr->nextaddr->nextaddr
```

is equivalent to

```
(addr->nextaddr)->nextaddr
```

This notation was not used in main( ) because the pointer variable current is first used to store the address in list->nextaddr using the statement:

```
current = list->nextaddr;
```

The statement:

```
current->nextaddr = NULL;
```

in int main( ) however, could have been written as:

```
list->nextaddr->nextaddr = NULL;
```

An interesting exercise is to rewrite main( ) such that the pointer variable named current is removed entirely from the function.

5. The modify( ) function in the complete program below is used to verify that modify( ) works correctly. The driver function creates a single structure, populates it, and then calls modify( ). modify( ) itself calls the function repop( ). An interesting extension is to write repop( ) such that an ENTER key response retains the original structure member value.

```
#include <iostream.h>
#include <iomanip.h>

const int NAMECHARS = 30;
const int PHONECHARS = 15;

struct Tel_typ
{
  char name[NAMECHARS];
  char phone_no[PHONECHARS];
  Tel_typ *nextaddr;
};

void populate(Tel_typ *);  // function prototype needed by main()
void modify(Tel_typ *);    // function prototype needed by main()
void display(Tel_typ *); // function prototype needed by modify()
void repop(Tel_typ *);   // function prototype needed by modify()

int main()
{

  Tel_typ *list;

  list = new (Tel_typ);
  populate(list); // populate the first structure
  list->nextaddr = NULL;
  modify(list);    // modify the structure members

  return 0;
}

void modify(Tel_typ *addr)
{
  cout << "\nThe current structure members are:";
  display(addr);
  repop(addr);
  cout << "\nThe structure members are now:";
  display(addr);
  return;
}

void populate(Tel_typ *record)
{
  cout << "\nEnter a name: ";
  cin.getline(record->name, NAMECHARS);
  cout << "Enter the phone number: ";
  cin.getline(record->phone_no, PHONECHARS);
  return;
}

void repop(Tel_typ *record)
{
  cout << "\n\nEnter a new name: ";
  cin.getline(record->name, NAMECHARS);
  cout << "Enter a new phone number: ";
  cin.getline(record->phone_no, PHONECHARS);
  return;
}
```

(continued on next page)

(continued from previous page)

```
void display(Tel_typ *contents)
{
  while(contents != NULL)
  {
    cout << endl << setiosflags(ios::left)
         << setw(30) << contents->name
         << setw(20) << contents->phone_no;
    contents = contents->nextaddr;
  }
  return;
}
```

EXERCISES 14.6

1.

```
#include <iostream.h>
#include <iomanip.h>
#include <string.h>
const int MAXDES = 40;
const int LOWQUANTITY = 10; // used in update()

struct Item
{
  char des[MAXDES];
  int number;
  int bin;
  int quantity;
  float cost;
};

void update(struct Item *);  // function prototype needed by main()

int main()
{
  struct Item inventory;

  strcpy(inventory.des, "Test Item");
  inventory.number = 22;
  inventory.bin = 56;
  inventory.quantity = 34;
  inventory.cost = 9.35;
  update(&inventory);
  cout << "\nThe data for this item is now:\n";
  cout << "Description: " <<inventory.des << endl;
  cout << "No.  Bin   Quant.  Cost\n"
       << inventory.number
       << setw(7) << inventory.bin
       << setw(7) << inventory.quantity
       << setw(9) << inventory.cost;

  return 0;
}

void update(struct Item *thisitem)
{
  cout << "\n\nThe data for this item is currently:\n";
  cout << "Description: " <<thisitem->des << endl;
  cout << "No.  Bin   Quant.  Cost\n"
       << thisitem->number
```

(continued on next page)

(continued from previous page)

```
    << setw(7) << thisitem->bin
    << setw(7) << thisitem->quantity
    << setw(9) << thisitem->cost;
  cout << "\nEnter the new quantity and cost: ";
  cin  >> thisitem->quantity >> thisitem->cost;
  if (thisitem->quantity < LOWQUANTITY)
    cout << "The stock on this item is low.\n";
  return;
}
```

3. The required structure for this program is:

```
struct Customer
{
  char name[MAXSTRLEN];
  char address[MAXSTRLEN];
  int nummtnbikes;
  int numstbikes;
  int goodrisk;
  float amount;
};
```

5.

```
#include <iostream.h>
const int MAXDES = 40;
const int MAXITEMS = 5;
const int LOWSTOCK = 10; // used by order()
struct Item
{
  char des[MAXDES];
  int number;
  int bin;
  int quantity;
  float cost;
};
void report(struct Item [], int); // function prototype needed by main()
void order(struct Item *, int);   // function prototype needed by main()

int main()
{
  struct Item inventory[MAXITEMS] = {{"Item 1", 122, 1, 55, 1.65},
                                      {"Item 2", 123, 2, 88, 2.95},
                                      {"Item 3", 124, 3,  9, 5.49},
                                      {"Item 4", 125, 4, 37, 6.53},
                                      {"Item 5", 126, 5,  7, 8.42}
                                     };

  report(inventory, MAXITEMS);
  order(inventory, MAXITEMS);

  return 0;
}

void report(struct Item inventory[], int numitems)
{
  int i;

  cout << "\n\nThe data in inventory is currently:\n";
  for (i = 0; i < numitems; i++)
```

(continued on next page)

```
    {
      cout << "  Description: " <<inventory[i].des << endl;
      cout << "    Number: "  << inventory[i].number
           << "    Bin: "     << inventory[i].bin
           << "   Quantity: " << inventory[i].quantity
           << "   Cost: "     << inventory[i].cost << endl;
    }
    return;
  }

  void order(struct Item inventory[], int numitems)
  {
    int i;

    cout << "\n\nThe following are below normal stock quantities:\n";
    for (i = 0; i < numitems; i++)
    {
      if (inventory[i].quantity < LOWSTOCK)
      {
        cout << "  Description: " <<inventory[i].des << endl;
        cout << "    Number: "  << inventory[i].number
             << "    Bin: "     << inventory[i].bin
             << "   Quantity: " << inventory[i].quantity
             << "   Cost: "     << inventory[i].cost << endl;
      }
    }
    return;
  }
```

EXERCISES 14.7

1. The cout streams are contained within the following program:

```
#include <iostream.h>
union
{
  float rate;
  double taxes;
  int num;
} flag;
int main()
{
  flag.rate = 22.5;
  cout << "\nThe rate member is " << flag.rate << endl;
  flag.taxes = 44.7;
  cout << "The taxes member is " << flag.taxes << endl;
  flag.num = 6;
  cout << "The num member is " << flag.num << endl;

  return 0;
}
```

5. Since a value has not been assigned to alt.btype, the display produced is unpredictable (the code for a `'y'` resides in the storage locations overlapped by the variables alt.ch and alt.btype). Thus, either a garbage value will be displayed or the program could even crash.

EXERCISES 14.9

1.

```
const int MAXNAME-30;
const int MAXADD1-30;
const int MAXADD2-30;
const int MAXDESC-40;
struct Business
{
  char name[MAXNAME]
  char address[MAXADD1]
  char ctystzip[MAXADD2]
  char descrip[MAXDESC]
  int employees;
  float annualrev;
};
```

3.a. `struct Inventory item[100];`

b. `inventory[83].prodnum = 4355;`

c. `cout << inventory[15].price;`

5.

```
#include <iostream.h>
const int MAXVECTS = 2;
struct VectorType
{
  int xcomp;
  int ycomp;
};

void input(struct VectorType [], int); // function prototypes needed by main()
struct VectorType sum(struct VectorType, struct VectorType);
struct VectorType diff(struct VectorType, struct VectorType);

int main()
{
  struct VectorType vector[MAXVECTS], sumvect, difvect;

  input(vector, MAXVECTS);
  sumvect = sum(vector[0], vector[1]);
  difvect = diff(vector[0], vector[1]);
  cout << "\n(" << vector[0].xcomp << "," << vector[0].ycomp << ")"
       << " + (" << vector[1].xcomp << "," << vector[1].ycomp << ")"
       << " = (" << sumvect.xcomp << "," << sumvect.ycomp << ")\n";
  cout << "\n (" << vector[0].xcomp << "," << vector[0].ycomp << ")"
       << " - (" << vector[1].xcomp << "," << vector[1].ycomp << ")"
       << " = (" << difvect.xcomp << "," << difvect.ycomp << ")\n";

  return 0;
}

void input(struct VectorType vector[], int numvects)
{
  int i;

  for (i = 0; i < numvects; i++)
  {
    cout << "Enter the x component for vector " << i + 1 << ": ";
    cin  >>  vector[i].xcomp;
```

(continued on next page)

```
    cout << "Enter the y component for vector " << i + 1 << ": ";
    cin  >>  vector[i].ycomp;
  }
  return;
}

struct VectorType sum(struct VectorType vector1, struct VectorType vector2)
{
  int i;
  struct VectorType temp;
  temp.xcomp = vector1.xcomp + vector2.xcomp;
  temp.ycomp = vector1.ycomp + vector2.ycomp;

  return temp;
}

struct VectorType diff(struct VectorType vector1, struct VectorType vector2)
{
  struct VectorType temp;

  temp.xcomp = vector1.xcomp - vector2.xcomp;
  temp.ycomp = vector1.ycomp - vector2.ycomp;
  return temp;
}
```

Notice that the input routine can be used for any number of vectors, while the sum and difference routines only work on the two specific vectors passed as arguments.

EXERCISES 15.1

1.

```
#include <iostream.h>
const int MAXSTACK = 100;
const int TRUE = 1;
const int FALSE = 0;

// class declaration

// preconditions: requires that MAXSTACK, the maximum size of the stack, be defined
//              : requires that TRUE be defined as a nonzero integer
//              : requires that FALSE be defined as 0

class Stack
{
  private:
    int top;   // top-of-stack position
    char values[MAXSTACK];

  public:
    Stack(void);   // constructor
    void push(char);
    char pop(void);
    int isempty(void);
    int isfull(void);

};

// implementation section

Stack::Stack()  // constructor
{
```

(continued on next page)

(continued from previous page)

```
    top = -1;  // initialize the top-of-stack position
  }

  void Stack::push(char value)
  {
    top++;   // increment the index stored in top
    values[top] = value;  // store the value
  }

  char Stack::pop(void)
  {
    int topval;
    topval = values[top];  // retrieve the top element
    top--;                // decrement the index stored in top
    return(topval);
  }

  int Stack::isempty(void)
  {
    if (top == -1)
      return(TRUE);
    else
      return(FALSE);
  }

  int Stack::isfull(void)
  {
    if (top == MAXSTACK - 1)
      return(TRUE);
    else
      return(FALSE);
  }

  int main()
  {
    Stack codes;    // define a Stack named codes
    char newvalues;

    cout << "Enter as many characters as you wish, one per line"
         << "\nTo stop entering digits, enter an X\n";
    while (1)
    {
      cout << "Enter a character: ";
      cin  >> newvalues;
      if (newvalues == 'X')
        break;
      if (codes.isfull()) // check for overflow
      {
        cout <<"\nNo more storage allocation space"
             << "\nThe last character has not been entered on the stack"
             << endl;
        break;
      }
      else
        codes.push(newvalues); // push value onto the stack
    }
```

(continued on next page)

(continued from previous page)

```
    // pop and display digits from the stack

  cout << "\nThe characters popped from the stack are:\n";
  while(!codes.isempty())    // check for underflow
  {
     cout << codes.pop() << endl;
  }
  return 0;
}
```

3. Using the Stack class defined in Program 15.1, the program is:

```
int main()
{
  Stack s1, s2, s3;     // define a Stack named digits
  int newnum;

  cout << "Enter as many digits as you wish, one per line"
       << "\nTo stop entering digits, enter a number greater than 9\n";
  while (1)
  {
    cout << "Enter a digit: ";
    cin >> newnum;
    if (newnum > 9)
      break;
    if (s1.isfull()) // check for overflow
    {
      cout <<"\nNo more storage allocation space"
           << "\nThe last digit has not been entered on the stack"
           << endl;
      break;
    }
    else
      s1.push(newnum); // push value onto the stack
  }

   // pop from first stack into second stack
  while(!s1.isempty())
    s2.push(s1.pop());

   // pop from second stack into third stack
  while(!s2.isempty())
    s3.push(s2.pop());

   // pop from third stack into first stack
  while(!s3.isempty())
    s1.push(s3.pop());

   // display digits from the first stack
  cout << "\nThe values popped from the stack are:\n";
  while(!s1.isempty())    // check for underflow
    cout << s1.pop() << endl;

  return 0;
}
```

EXERCISES 15.2

1.a. Dynamically create a new record.
Put the address contained in the top-of-stack pointer into the address field of the newly created record.
Populate the new record's remaining fields.
Put the address of the new record into the top-of-stack pointer.

b. Move the record contents pointed to by the top-of-stack pointer into a work area.
   Free the record pointed to by the top-of-stack pointer.
   Move the address in the work area address field into the top-of-stack pointer.

c. a NULL address

3.a. As the problem is stated this is ideal for a stack, because the last characters typed in are the first out when deletions are made. Also, the deletions can be stored in a stack for the undo operation.

b. No, because in stack order the last person on the list would be the first to receive a car.

c. Yes, because the search is from the most recent to the least recent.

d. No, in a stack the priority is last in, first out.

e. No, because the first on line is the first on the bus, which is not the last-in/first-out order used in a stack.

EXERCISES 15.3

1.

```
const int MAXQUEUE = 100;
const int TRUE = 1;
const int FALSE = 0;
// class declaration

// preconditions: requires that MAXQUEUE, the maximum size of the
//               : queue, be defined
//               : requires that TRUE be defined as a nonzero
//               : integer
//               : requires that FALSE be defined as 0

class Queue
{
  private:
    int queue_in;    // top-of-queue position
    int num[MAXQUEUE];

  public:
    Queue(void) {queue_in = -1;}    // constructor
    void enqueue(int);
    int serve(void);
    int isempty(void) {return (queue_in == -1);}
    int isfull(void) {return(queue_in == MAXQUEUE - 1);}
};

// implementation section

void Queue::enqueue(int value)
{
  queue_in++;    // increment the index stored in queue_in
  num[queue_in] = value;  // store the value

  return;
}

int Queue::serve(void)
{
  int i, botval;

  botval = num[0];          // retrieve the first array element
  for(i = 0; i < queue_in; i++)  // shift all elements down
    num[i] = num[i+1];
  queue_in--;

  return(botval);
}
```

EXERCISES 15.4

1.a. Dynamically create a new a record.
Set the address field of the new record to a NULL.
Fill in the remaining fields of the new record.
Set the address field of the prior record (which is pointed to by the queue_in pointer) to the address of the newly created record.
Update the address in the queue_in pointer with the address of the newly created record.

b. Move the contents of the record pointed to by the queue_out pointer into a work area.
Free the record pointed to by the queue_out pointer.
Move the address in the work area address field into the queue_out pointer.

c. Both pointers should contain a NULL address.

3.a. Yes, because this represents a first-in/first-out situation.

b. Yes, because this is also a first-in/first-out situation.

c. No, because the order of retrieval is not first-in/first-out.

d. Yes, because this is also a first-in/first-out situation.

Index

IMPORTANT: PLEASE READ BEFORE OPENING THIS PACKAGE
THIS PACKAGE IS NOT RETURNABLE IF SEAL IS BROKEN.

West Publishing Corporation
620 Opperman Drive
P.O. Box 64779
St. Paul, Minnesota 55164-0779

LIMITED USE LICENSE

Read the following terms and conditions carefully before opening this diskette package. Opening the diskette package indicates your agreement to the license terms. If you do not agree, promptly return the entire product and related documentation unused.

By accepting this license, you have the right to use this Software and the accompanying documentation, but you do not become the owner of these materials.

This copy of the Software is licensed to you for use only under the following conditions:

1. PERMITTED USES
You are granted a non-exclusive limited license to use the Software under the terms and conditions stated in this license. You may:

a. Use the Software on a single computer.
b. Make a single copy of the Software in machine-readable form solely for backup purposes in support of your use of the Software on a single machine. You must reproduce and include the copyright notice on any copy you make.
c. Transfer this copy of the Software and the license to another user if the other user agrees to accept the terms and conditions of this license. If you transfer this copy of the Software, you must also transfer or destroy the backup copy you made. Transfer of this copy of the Software, and the license automatically terminates this license as to you.

2. PROHIBITED USES
You may not use, copy, modify, distribute or transfer the Software or any copy, in whole or in part, except as expressly permitted in this license.

3. TERM
This license is effective when you open the diskette package and remains in effect until terminated. You may terminate this license at any time by ceasing all use of the Software and destroying this copy and any copy you have made. It will also terminate automatically if you fail to comply with the terms of this license. Upon termination, you agree to cease all use of the Software and destroy all copies.

4. DISCLAIMER OF WARRANTY
Except as stated herein, the Software is licensed "as is" without warranty of any kind, express or implied, including warranties of merchantability or fitness for a particular purpose. You assume the entire risk as to the quality and performance of the Software. You are responsible for the selection of the Software to achieve your intended results and for the installation, use and results obtained from it. West Publishing Corporation does not warrant the performance of nor results that may be obtained with the Software. West Publishing Corporation does warrant that the diskette(s) upon which the Software is provided will be free from defects in materials and workmanship under normal use for a period of 30 days from the date of delivery to you as evidenced by a receipt.

Some states do not allow the exclusion of implied warranties so the above exclusion may not apply to you. This warranty gives you specific legal rights. You may also have other rights which vary from state to state.

5. LIMITATION OF LIABILITY
Your exclusive remedy for breach by West Publishing Corporation of its limited warranty shall be replacement of any defective diskette upon its return to West at the above address, together with a copy of the receipt, within the warranty period. If West Publishing Corporation is unable to provide you with a replacement diskette which is free of defects in material and workmanship, you may terminate this license by returning the Software, and the license fee paid hereunder will be refunded to you. In no event will West be liable for any lost profits or other damages including direct, indirect, incidental, special, consequential or any other type of damages arising out of the use or inability to use the Software even if West Publishing Corporation has been advised of the possibility of such damages.

6. GOVERNING LAW
This agreement will be governed by the laws of the State of Minnesota.

You acknowledge that you have read this license and agree to its terms and conditions. You also agree that this license is the entire and exclusive agreement between you and West and supersedes any prior understanding or agreement, oral or written, relating to the subject matter of this agreement.

West Publishing Corporation